10☆CC

THE WORST BAND IN THE WORLD

LIAM NEWTON

FOREWORD BY KEVIN GODLEY

⚘88

This edition published 2020 by Rocket 88 Books
an imprint of Essential Works Limited,
29 Clerkenwell Green,
London EC1R ODU
United Kingdom
Previously published in a different edition in 2000
by Minerva Press

ISBN: 9781910978450

rocket88books.com

ACKNOWLEDGEMENTS

I'M NOT IN LOVE WITH 10CC. IT'S JUST A SILLY PHASE THAT I'VE BEEN going through for about 40 years. So, writing the first edition of this book, and then updating it all these years later, has been a real labour of love and I would like to thank all the people who helped to make it a reality. First and foremost, I would like to extend a special thank you to the people who inspired the book in the first place. Having the opportunity to meet Eric Stewart, Graham Gouldman and Kevin Godley, and to hear their thoughts and recollections first hand, was literally a dream come true. I'd particularly like to thank Kevin for writing the Foreword to this new edition. Sadly, Lol Creme was the only original member of 10cc who declined to be involved in either edition of the book. Still, to paraphrase the song, 75% of something is better than 100% of nothing.

A big thank you to all those members of the extended 10cc family who were able to fill out the story. My thanks go to drummer Paul Burgess, guitarist Rick Fenn, band manager Harvey Lisberg, tour manager Zeb White, their first label boss Jonathan King and Aubrey 'Po' Powell who, as co-founder of Hipgnosis, created so many of 10cc's iconic album covers. Special thanks to 'Po' for giving me access to previously unseen photos from the Hipgnosis archives and very kindly allowing me to reproduce them in this book.

I'd also like to thank all those people who helped and supported me in writing either the first, or updated, edition of the book, especially Gill King, Nicole Molenaar, Peter Wadsworth, Phil Loftus, Dave Jarvis and Gilly Hewer. Thank you to the wonderfully named Mal Peachey and John Conway at Rocket 88 for all their help with the publication of this updated edition and Julia Halford, my copy editor.

And, finally, thanks to Kate, Will and Billy for indulging my labour of love.

The passage of time can play havoc with the accuracy of all our memories but I've done my best to piece together the most accurate 10cc story that I can, from both my own interviews and those in the archives. Any mistakes, therefore, are mine and mine alone.

CONTENTS

In loving memory of Sheila Newton

Fresh Air For My Mama.

BY 1972 THE BIG FOUR HAD ALREADY CLAIMED ALL POINTS OF THE musical compass: ELVIS, THE BEATLES, THE STONES and DYLAN, or, culturally speaking, SEX, ART, DRUGS and BRAINS. Whatever your rebel poison it was out there somewhere and the trends set in the 60s were expanding into the 70s – quite literally. Lapels were getting wider as were trousers and ties. Hair was getting bigger along with drums, guitars and amps getting louder and wherever you looked, at least in England, people were wearing fancy dress.

Up north, however, Jumping Jack Flash was a gas, gas, gas fitter from Whalley Range and proud of it. To walk around Albert Square in loon pants, a sequinned jacket and stacked heels circa 1972 would've probably earned you a kick in the nuts and a trip to the Manchester Ship Canal *sans* 27-inch flares, because everything was a touch harder, a touch more cynical and any hint of musical pretension would've been drop-kicked down Cannon Street before it strayed a minor fifth beyond Herman's Hermits.

That said, there was a feeling that Manchester had way more to say musically, and for four young musicians, with ideas above their station, the desire to say it was keeping them awake at night. Not that they knew what IT was yet, nor did these four germs coalesce to create a full disease until combined in a petri dish called Strawberry.

The IT, as you must already know, was 10cc and this book expertly details what they did, how they did IT, undid IT and re-did IT.

P.S. Worst Band In The World, indeed?! Harrumph.

INTRODUCTION

REMINISCE AND SPECULATE

GOOD MORNING, AFTERNOON OR EVENING JUDGE! YOU STAND – OR sit – in judgement of 10cc's legacy. You have heard the case for the prosecution: the school of thought that dismisses 10cc as a 'soft rock' group from the 70s; a band who prospered at a time when pop music was languishing in the slump between the twin peaks of Beatlemania and punk rock; a group that are only remembered for a couple of records and even they are strictly 'guilty pleasures'; a band who were a little too clever for their own good, placing form before feel in the creation of their rather sterile records; a group with no discernible image beyond a vague mosaic of long hair, wide lapels and double denim. In short, a band of little importance and limited influence on the landscape of popular music; and, certainly, a group worthy of no more than a footnote in the history of the genre.

For the prosecution, 10cc are little more than a joke. They point to Ricky Gervais and Stephen Merchant who, when contemplating the kinds of records that would appeal to their fictional characters from *The Office*, figured that Dreadlock Holiday would likely be the favourite song of the show's anti-hero, Gareth Keenan. Similarly, they reference Charlie Higson, co-founder of *The Fast Show*, who pictured one of his characters, Swiss Toni, stuck in a 70s time warp, mistaken in the belief that people are "longing to hear Smokie, 10cc and Bonnie Tyler" but don't get a chance because they are "not cool anymore."

It doesn't take a rocket scientist to conclude that 10cc's reputation has not travelled well. The real 10cc has somehow got lost in translation over the intervening years. The 10cc whose early records, released on an independent record label, were championed by John Peel and banned by the BBC because they were deemed too controversial; the 10cc who became the darlings of the music press and were hailed as geniuses by critics at the time; the 10cc who used their own recording studio to experiment and innovate to their heart's content, breaking new ground in the process with cutting-edge recording techniques that were way ahead of their time. This is hardly the usual *modus operandi* of your run-of-the-mill 'soft rock' group, yet this is firmly how some remember 10cc today.

How did 10cc get categorised as the type of group that make safe, predictable 'soft rock' records, though, when their experimental approach to music-making couldn't have been more different? And how did a band that achieved such enormous critical and commercial success in their day end up being remembered for so little?

Perhaps it was because 10cc actively went out of their way to make each of their records sound different from the next rather than having a signature sound like most bands. 10cc's three UK No.1 hits could easily have been recorded by three different groups; each was even sung by a different member of the band. Having four strong songwriters, musicians and vocalists in the group, rather than a traditional frontman, made 10cc utterly unique but may have worked against them in the long run, contributing to their enduring anonymity. Yet it was this abundance of talent within the band that set 10cc apart from the rest. The fact that they also produced all their own work, and recorded in their own studio, meant that 10cc were a completely self-contained unit. And, in Eric Stewart, they even had their own in house engineer and mixer of their records, and one so skilled as to earn a Grammy nomination for his studio prowess.

Rock 'n' roll is usually all about heart and soul, with a bit of groin thrown in for good measure. 10cc dared to engage the brain and inject their music with a rare intelligence and wit. The danger with this kind of approach is that you run the risk of not connecting or engaging with an audience. Yet 10cc managed to achieve phenomenal commercial success, scoring 11 Top 10 hits in the UK, at a time when getting into the upper echelons of the charts meant selling hundreds of thousands of records. It is estimated that 10cc were one of the 10 most successful singles acts of the 70s in the UK, selling more singles in that decade than many of their more famous contemporaries, such as Queen, David Bowie, Elton John and The Sex Pistols. They were equally successful with their albums, enjoying eight Top 10 hits in the UK, and selling over 30 million albums worldwide.

Their most famous creation, I'm Not In Love, remains one of the most remarkable pop records of all time and one of the most successful – a No.1 hit that sold over 3 million copies worldwide; winner of no less than three Ivor Novello Awards; and, for many years, the nation's all-time favourite record as voted by the British public in countless polls. I'm Not In Love has now been played a remarkable 5 million times on American radio alone, which amounts to the equivalent of nearly 50 years of continuous airtime. The song has been endlessly covered (by, among others, The Pretenders, Tori Amos, Fun Lovin' Criminals, Diana Krall and Kelsey Lu), sampled (76 by Roc Marciano), mashed up (Marvin's Not In Love by Go Home Productions), used as intro music at gigs (LCD Soundsystem) and loved by generations of musicians from Elton John to Axl Rose of Guns N' Roses. If imitation is the sincerest form of flattery, then artists as diverse as Billy Joel (Just The Way You Are), R.E.M. (Star Me Kitten), U.N.K.L.E. (In A State), Ben Folds Five (Sky High) and The Ting Tings (Communication) have all paid the ultimate compliment to 10cc by trying to emulate the song's trademark choral backing on their own records. Indie supergroup, Gayngs, went one stage further by creating a whole album inspired by the song (*Relayted*). This, plus numerous other examples of the song's recent influence, led *The Guardian* to claim that I'm Not In Love was "the most influential record of 2010." Since then, the song has appeared on the *Late Night Tales* albums by the likes of The Flaming Lips and Groove Armada and featured prominently in the opening scene of the movie *Guardians of the Galaxy*, helping the accompanying soundtrack album reach No.1 in the US charts in August 2014.

Perhaps the one downside of the song's enduring popularity is that it overshadows 10cc's other musical achievements, be they other masterpieces such as I'm Mandy Fly Me, The Wall Street Shuffle and Rubber Bullets; stunning albums like *Sheet Music* and *The Original Soundtrack*; or brilliant album tracks such as Somewhere In Hollywood, Old Wild Men and Don't Hang Up. 10cc's musical palette was extraordinarily eclectic, from doo-wop pastiches (Donna) to reggae (Dreadlock Holiday) to perfectly crafted pop (The Things We Do For Love); from three-minute vignettes (Good Morning

Judge) to complex, multi-part pieces (One Night In Paris, Feel The Benefit). Few bands have ever been so skilful with song structure (The Dean and I) or as adept at using humour as successfully in their music (Silly Love). And, unlike many bands of the period, 10cc never took themselves too seriously, often having fun at their own expense (The Worst Band In The World, Art For Art's Sake).

If all of the above were not proof enough of 10cc's worth, then consider the contribution of the group's four founder members before, and after, their time with 10cc. Eric Stewart enjoyed world-wide success with The Mindbenders (A Groovy Kind of Love) before co-founding 10cc and then went on to be asked by former members of The Beatles, Abba and Pink Floyd to work on their records, either as a musician, writer or producer. But perhaps his greatest legacy is co-founding Strawberry Studios in Stockport, the first professional recording studio outside of London, and the place where the next generation of Manchester bands would make some of their most iconic recordings, including Joy Division (*Unknown Pleasures*, Love Will Tear Us Apart), New Order (*Movement*) and The Smiths (Hand In Glove, This Charming Man).

Graham Gouldman, meanwhile, penned a string of classic hits in the 1960s for the likes of The Yardbirds (For Your Love, Heart Full of Soul, Evil Hearted You), The Hollies (Look Through Any Window, Bus Stop) and Herman's Hermits (No Milk Today, Listen People) and, after 10cc, would form Wax (Bridge To Your Heart) with Andrew Gold. He has written songs with Kirsty MacColl, Gary Barlow and McFly and had his songs performed by artists as diverse as Morrissey, Led Zeppelin, Blondie, The Pixies, Fleetwood Mac and The White Stripes. In 2014, he was inducted into the Songwriters Hall of Fame in recognition of this body of work and, a year later, was named an 'Icon' by the BMI.

For their part, Kevin Godley and Lol Creme were the most successful video directors of their generation, creating iconic videos for the likes of Duran Duran (Girls On Film), The Police (Every Breath You Take) and Frankie Goes To Hollywood (Two Tribes) and achieving success with their own records (Under Your Thumb, Cry). Godley would subsequently work extensively with U2 and direct videos for bands such as Blur (Girls and Boys) and Elbow (Gentle Storm), while Creme would direct a movie (*The Lunatic*), join the

Art of Noise and play on records by Kate Bush, Pet Shop Boys and Robbie Williams.

And even that is only scratching the surface. Add the novelty hits (Neanderthal Man as Hotlegs), unexpected collaborations (producing The Ramones), musical inventions (the 'Gizmo'), film soundtracks (*Animalympics*), ear movies (*Hog Fever*), groundbreaking apps (*Youdio*), satirical books (*The Fun Starts Here*), overblown concept albums (*Consequences*), random session work (*Space Hymns*), TV shows (*One World, One Voice*), musical support (reviving Neil Sedaka's career) and numerous solo albums to the mix and you add further flavour and texture to the soup proving, as 10cc always said, that life is indeed a minestrone!

One of the main aims of the first edition of this book was to contribute in some small way to a critical re-evaluation of the band. Over the last 20 years, 10cc do, at last, seem to be getting some of the recognition that they so richly deserve. Perhaps this started with the 'Guilty Pleasures' movement, which championed 10cc and prompted some to start re-evaluating their music. The band have been cited as an influence by a plethora groups, from The Feeling to LCD Soundsystem, while their music has been regularly sampled – and not just their obvious hit records. Johnny Don't Do It and The Worst Band In The World were both sampled prominently by influential rapper J Dilla on his album *Donuts*, while Lloyd Banks sampled The Dean and I on When The Chips Are Down. Their music is regularly heard in films (*The Virgin Suicides*, *The Social Network*, *Snatch*, *Bridget Jones*), TV shows (*EastEnders*, *The X Files*, *The Office*, *Hello Ladies*) and advertising campaigns (Magic FM's TV ads).

Slowly, it has become acceptable simply to enjoy 10cc's music – and not to feel guilty about it. Critics have started to reassess 10cc's place in music history. *Uncut* described them as "the greatest British pop group of the post-Beatles era" and awarded four- or five-star ratings to each of the band's first six albums. *Mojo* called 10cc's music "virtuosic, cinematic, brilliant" and dubbed them the "cleverest pop band of its generation" before concluding, "Pop music this good is a miracle. Respect due, listen and learn, we're in the presence of greatness." Even the music industry itself has finally started to acknowledge their contribution, presenting the members of 10cc with a special Ivor Novello Award in recognition of their 'Outstanding Song Collection.'

The band's 40th anniversary, in 2012, was commemorated with the release of *Tenology*, a long overdue boxed-set anthology containing singles, album tracks, rarities and a DVD of TV appearances and videos. *Tenology* gave critics another opportunity to reassess the band's legacy and the reviews were consistently good: "After years of being dismissed as arch, pompous studioholics, it's gradually become acceptable, fashionable and perhaps obligatory to worship at the shrine of 10cc," wrote *Metro*. When BBC Four screened their documentary *I'm Not In Love – The Story of 10cc* in December 2015, it was similarly well-received. "I used to be ever so slightly embarrassed about loving 10cc," wrote *The Guardian*. "I now realise, after seeing this excellent documentary, that I was silly to feel embarrassed." At the time of writing the band have 3 million monthly listeners on Spotify.

The full case for the band's defence is laid out across the following pages. By the turn of the last page it should be abundantly clear just how significant a contribution Eric Stewart, Graham Gouldman, Kevin Godley and Lol Creme – individually and collectively – have made to pop music over the last 50 years. I hope that this second edition of their biography helps to change perceptions further and lead to more people returning a favourable verdict on the unique musical legacy of 10cc, the worst band in the world.

CHAPTER 1

FROOTY ROOTIES

ALTHOUGH IT WOULD TAKE UNTIL 1972 FOR ERIC STEWART, GRAHAM Gouldman, Kevin Godley and Lol Creme to join forces in 10cc, the paths of the group's four future members were already beginning to cross long before that. In fact, the formative years of the 10cc story follow a decidedly labyrinthine path. By the time the group released their first record, the four members of 10cc were already well-acquainted, having played together, in virtually every conceivable permutation, in a variety of Manchester bands: Creme and Godley in The Sabres; Godley and Gouldman in The Mockingbirds; Gouldman and Stewart in The Mindbenders; and Stewart, Godley and Creme in Hotlegs. The special chemistry that makes truly great bands combust eluded them, however, until all four of them came together to form 10cc.

The group's story begins in Manchester in the early 60s, in the booming music scene of the day. All across the city, thousands of teenagers, inspired by the sound of rock 'n' roll, were busy learning instruments and forming hundreds of groups, while dozens of venues were emerging for them to play in. For teenagers growing up in Britain at the time, rock 'n' roll signified escape, rebellion and excitement. It was in this heady environment that each future quarter of 10cc took their first musical steps.

The first of the four to become successful was Eric Stewart. Born in Manchester in January 1945, Stewart grew up – like all the group's members – in post-war Britain. It was a time of austerity but Stewart's upbringing with his four sisters in the family home on Prince Street in the Ardwick area of Manchester was a happy one. It was a musical household, with his mother, Connie, having a good voice and his father, Eric – an aircraft engineer by trade – an accomplished pianist and accordion player. "My father was one of those pianists who gets up at parties and plays Beethoven's Fifth or I Remember You," recalls Stewart.

However, like many boys of his age, it was the emerging sound of rock 'n' roll that really captured his imagination. Looking back, Stewart reckons that hearing Neil Sedaka's I Go Ape in 1959 on Radio Luxembourg, the only station at the time playing American rock 'n' roll, was the catalyst to pursuing a career in music.

"That song changed my life I suppose," says Stewart. "The first time I heard it on Radio Luxembourg I decided *that's* what I wanted to do. I was about fourteen. I opened the front door of my house in Manchester, turned up the volume, and shouted to my mates, 'Listen to this!' They thought I was out of my head but it really shook me up. I rushed out and bought it along with Dream Lover by Bobby Darin and Please Don't Touch by Johnny Kidd and The Pirates. I didn't even have a record player at the time!"

Despite having a piano in the house, it was the guitar that became Stewart's instrument of choice. Having eyed Fender Stratocaster and Gibson Les Paul electric guitars in the music shops on Oxford Road in Manchester, Stewart was smitten.

"I'm sure that seeing my first salmon pink Fender Stratocaster was probably my biggest influence," he acknowledges. His first experience of playing a guitar came when a friend let him borrow his white Rosetti Lucky 7 electric guitar along with an amplifier. Stewart vowed to his get his own guitar as soon as he could, which he did albeit via an unusual set of circumstances.

"I had a wonderful air rifle but while firing it I put a slug through a neighbour's window and he threatened to take my head off," recalls Stewart. "So, I went to a second-hand shop on Ashton Old Road in Manchester and swapped it for a really battered old acoustic guitar. I sat there for months and months playing along to all the records on Radio Luxembourg and found my way round most of the tunes quite easily playing by ear. We were quite a musical family, so I had some natural ability already built in to pick up tunes, lyrics and rhythms very quickly."

Inspired by the likes of Scotty Moore, James Burton and Cliff Gallup – the guitarists for Elvis Presley, Ricky Nelson and Gene Vincent respectively – Stewart developed his guitar-playing skills over the next couple of years while at school at Openshaw Technical High. Like many aspiring guitarists of the time, Stewart learned his initial craft from Bert Weedon's *Play In A Day* guitar tutor. At home after school one day there was a knock on the front door.

"There was a genial chap standing there called Charlie Barker," says Stewart. "He was lead vocalist with Jerry Lee and The Staggerlees, a Manchester band who were doing quite well in the local pubs and clubs, mostly with covers of American rock 'n' roll, and right up my street. He said, 'I hear you can play guitar.' I said, 'Yes, but I only have my acoustic.' He asked me to come for an audition, and said he'd lend me an electric guitar if I was any good. Their lead guitarist was getting married and leaving the band and I got the gig, and the free electric guitar!"

Having joined Jerry Lee and The Staggerlees, Stewart gained his first experience of playing gigs in the growing number of venues sprouting up across the city. Changing their name a year later to The Emperors of Rhythm, the group secured an audition for the BBC at the Hulme Hippodrome. "The van picked Eric Stewart and me from school and we went along," recalls the band's other guitarist, Vic Farrell. "Outside we saw two lads struggling with a big bass amp and they turned out to be John Lennon and Paul McCartney. They did two numbers, Roll Over Beethoven and Till There Was You."

Stewart recalls the experience of seeing The Beatles and the difference in the two bands' styles. "We were dressed in silver mohair suits and did rehearsed dance steps like The Shadows," recalls Stewart. "They wore leather waistcoats and jeans and had longer hair than us. I was mesmerised watching them perform. I knew they were going to be huge. There was an indefinable magic about them. They were so confident and so different from anything we had ever seen before."

Amazingly, those judging the audition didn't share Stewart's enthusiasm for The Beatles. "They failed the audition like we did but the chap holding the audition was quite impressed by us," says Farrell. "While we were packing away our gear he came over for a chat. He asked us where we were the following day, obviously expecting us to name some big club or ballroom. Without thinking

Eric very innocently said, 'Oh, we'll be at school' and the bloke's face was a picture!"

Stewart left school in 1961 and got a job working in a small drawing office producing calendars for local businesses. His real passion, though, remained music. After leaving The Emperors of Rhythm he had joined another local Manchester band called Johnny Peters and The Crestas. Then one day he had the most extraordinary stroke of good luck. Sitting in the coffee bar of a Manchester club on Lloyd Street called the Oasis on May 4, 1963, he was approached by a panic-stricken local singer he knew called Glyn Ellis, who used Wayne Fontana as a stage name (allegedly inspired in equal part by the actor John Wayne and Elvis Presley's drummer DJ Fontana). He and his band, The Jets, were active on the local music scene, had played at the Oasis several times already and had even supported The Beatles in Macclesfield earlier in the year. Now they were about to audition for Jack Baverstock of Philips Records who was up in Manchester seeking new talent. However, Fontana had a problem – only his bass player Bob Lang had turned up at the venue. The guitarist and drummer from The Jets were nowhere to be seen. Fontana approached Stewart and drummer Ric Rothwell, who was also sat in the coffee bar, and asked if they'd help out. The newly cobbled together four-piece concocted a set-list that comprised Chuck Berry's Johnny B Goode, Fats Domino's My Girl Josephine and, to demonstrate their versatility, Zip-a-Dee-Doo-Dah, which had recently been revived by Bob B Soxx and The Blue Jeans.

"We rehearsed quickly in the dressing room and we went on and did three songs," recalls Stewart. "It was no big deal, they were just the same numbers as everyone else on that circuit played. I thought nothing of it, and then went back to the coffee bar and that was it as far as I was concerned."

Jack Baverstock had other ideas. He liked what he had heard at the audition and wanted to sign Fontana but only on the proviso that his makeshift backing band became a permanent fixture.

"Wayne came in and said, 'Jack Baverstock wants to give me a recording contract – but he wants the guys who were on stage with me tonight to be in the group. Do you want to join my group?' I said, 'Yeah, I'd love to,'" recalls Stewart. "I was gobsmacked to say the least. To be offered a recording contract at eighteen years old, with the possibility of making records in London and maybe getting a hit. Wow! I was on cloud nine for days while it sank in."

Deciding to dispense with the name The Jets, they called themselves Wayne Fontana and The Mindbenders, the latter inspired by a Dirk Bogarde film of the same name, then playing at their local cinema. The newly formed four-piece signed a management deal with Ric Dixon, who had originally co-founded the Oasis club before going into management as part of Kennedy Street Enterprises. The group ventured south to London to make their first record. Like most groups of the day, Wayne Fontana and The Mindbenders didn't write their own material. Instead they were reliant on the music publishers of Denmark Street, who would invariably save the most promising new songs that came their way for established acts. Very often, new acts would have to resort to recording cover versions of songs that had already been hits in America but hadn't yet made it big in the UK. Wayne Fontana and The Mindbenders recorded two such numbers at their first recording session, Bo Diddley's Road Runner and Hello Josephine, with the latter – a slightly retitled version of the Fats Domino song they had performed at their makeshift audition – released as the band's debut single in June 1963.

"We were very, very excited about our first release," says Stewart. "We waited nervously for weeks until the record was released and held our breath each Friday when the new record charts were announced. After five weeks, we entered the charts at No.46. Sadly, we disappeared from the chart the following week, but the important thing was that we could now legitimately call ourselves a 'chart group' and our appearance fees doubled then trebled within weeks. We were being paid what seemed like huge sums of money, about £30 a night for gigs, for enjoying ourselves. We thought we'd made it!"

As the group started to play gigs, they came into contact with many other up-and-coming bands of the time. One group that they became quite friendly with was The Rolling Stones, with Keith Richards going on to describe Stewart as "a lovely guitar player". When The Stones came to Manchester, Wayne Fontana and The Mindbenders would go and see them play and the two groups would socialise together afterwards. The Stones would even borrow a few sartorial cues from the band.

"Do you remember The Mindbenders – Wayne Fontana's mob?," wrote Brian Jones in a letter to his girlfriend in October 1963. "Well, do you remember the coats they had that night they came to see us? The grey check ones with black collars, pockets etc. – I bought one today. It's real gear. I like it better than my leather one and that's good."

In April 1964, Wayne Fontana and The Mindbenders undertook a 28-date tour of the UK on a bill headlined by Roy Orbison. They enjoyed the tour and learnt a lot from him. "Roy was always wishing to help," recalls Stewart. "He would comment on our show and helped me develop my voice because his voice, Christ, he could sing like two or three octaves, and his guitar playing was wonderful, and gave me a lot of hints about guitars and tunings and string thicknesses and things like that. It was very, very useful to learn from a master. And he was such a sweet guy. He never said anything bad about anybody. He was so positive about music and was smiling all the time. A great, great man."

Unfortunately, the group's next three singles – For You, For You, Little Darlin' and The Duke of Earl – never came close to troubling the charts. So, by the time their fifth single, a cover version of Ben E King's Stop, Look and Listen only scraped into the lower reaches of the UK Top 40 in mid-1964, the group's lack of success was beginning to cause a great deal of frustration within the band, although it was clear that their fanbase were growing. In Liverpool, fans signed a nine-page petition to get the group to play again at the Cavern Club. Dated October 1964, their cover note to Bob Wooler, the compère at the venue, read: "Dear Bob, we hadn't seen The Mindbenders at the Cavern for ages and thought it about time we did; so we started a petition and found that 428 people agreed with us. As well as Cavern regulars some famous people have signed." Amongst those famous people signing the petition were The Rolling Stones, who would also talk up the band in interviews at the time.

One man who thought he could transform the fortunes of Wayne Fontana and The Mindbenders was 19-year-old former Charterhouse public schoolboy, Jonathan King. "He used to follow us around in this sort of tatty white sports car," recalls Stewart. "He'd follow us all over England and say, 'Please let me manage you. I'll make you bigger than The Beatles!' He tried to convince us that he was the next Brian Epstein. I don't know if he had worked it out mathematically or not but he seemed very sure of himself. He had seen what Epstein had done and wanted to do the same himself. He used to tell us that we needed the strength of an Epstein behind us and he thought he had that strength, though we just laughed it off at the time."

In fact, Brian Epstein had himself expressed an interest in managing the group. "When we played the Cavern in Liverpool, Brian Epstein came to watch us," recalls Stewart. "At a meeting after the show he said he loved the band and offered us a management deal that, with hindsight, could have made us much, much bigger, and much more quickly, because Brian, with The Beatles in his stable, could pull many strings. But being very young, and very green, we didn't know or realise he was gay and, at a later meeting in London, he made a pass at Wayne, who told him to 'Fuck off, Brian, I'm not a queer.' He lost interest in the group very quickly after that little episode." Former Rolling Stones manager, Andrew Loog Oldham, also saw potential in the band and invited them to record for his Immediate record label.

"Andrew had seen us on a few gigs with The Stones and we got on well, so he invited us to a studio The Stones used in Denmark Street to record a song called Um, Um, Um, Um, Um, Um that had been a big hit in America for Major Lance," says Stewart.

The band, however, were still signed to Philips Records and Oldham's attempts to extricate them from their recording contract proved unsuccessful. Jack Baverstock asked to hear their Oldham-produced recording anyway. He was unimpressed with what he heard but saw enough potential to suggest that they re-record it with him, this time for Philips. "He said that he could do a much better version than that and he threw the acetate disc across the room, breaking it," recalls Stewart. "We did re-record it but the two versions were about the same."

Released as the group's next single, the Curtis Mayfield-penned Um, Um, Um, Um, Um, Um catapulted Wayne Fontana and The

Mindbenders into the big time, reaching No.5 in the UK charts in December 1964, spending five weeks in the Top 10. Hot on its heels was the band's eponymous debut album, which had been recorded in its entirety in one day. Among its 12 tracks was one original composition, the Ellis/Stewart-penned One More Time. Although highly derivative in nature it was a gently affecting song given a nicely atmospheric production, and would rank as one of the album's highlights. Stewart enjoyed the experience of working in the studio but yearned for the opportunity to get into the control room himself and get more involved in the technical side of making records, which was frowned upon at the time.

"It was very frustrating when we were in the studio – we weren't allowed in the control room," says Stewart. "We had to stay in the studio and they would play back each take we'd done through this crappy speaker on the wall. The control room was the hallowed hall, you couldn't go in there."

The key priority for Wayne Fontana and The Mindbenders at the time was finding a follow-up single to their big hit, and Jack Baverstock had the perfect song in mind. "He played us this demo of a song by Clint Ballard Jr called The Game of Love and we thought it was fantastic," recalls Stewart.

Ever since eyeing a Gibson Les Paul guitar in the music shops of Manchester, Stewart had dreamt of playing one himself. Now, at the recording session for The Game of Love, he got the chance.

"At the session I ran into Jimmy Page, who was recording in the other studio," recalls Stewart. "I had always wanted to play a Les Paul guitar and I asked if I could try his. He said, 'Why don't you just play it on your recording?' So I did and it was great!" Stewart was so enamoured by the experience that he set out to buy his own Gibson Les Paul guitar. He would eventually buy a black 1959 model from guitarist Albert Lee, a guitar that remains in Stewart's collection to this day.

Released as their next single, The Game of Love was even more successful than its predecessor, reaching No.2 in the UK charts in March 1965 and giving the band their second Top 5 hit in the space of only three months. The group began a 21-date tour of the UK on a bill that also included Del Shannon, Herman's Hermits and The Shangri-Las. As the tour progressed, Wayne Fontana suffered from exhaustion. Rather than pull out of the shows, The Mindbenders continued without him, with Eric Stewart taking on lead vocal duties.

With Fontana back in good health, the group were invited to play at the *New Musical Express* poll-winners concert at London's Wembley Empire Pool (now Arena) on April 11, as part of a stellar line-up that included the likes of The Rolling Stones, The Kinks and The Beatles. Although their real friendship wouldn't develop until much later, Stewart immediately hit it off with Paul McCartney. "I'm backstage and Paul comes out of his dressing room, throws his arms around me and says 'Wotcher'," recalls Stewart. "Smashing bloke, very down to earth. John was a very uptight guy I didn't like too much. George and Ringo sort of grunted."

With The Game of Love selling strongly in America, the group were lined up to support another Manchester band managed by Kennedy Street Enterprises, Herman's Hermits, on a major US tour. As the tour approached, The Game of Love continued to climb the charts, eventually hitting the coveted No.1 spot that spring and selling over a million copies in America in the process. Despite their success, the group were forced to miss the opening dates of the tour because their application for a US performance visa was turned down by officials concerned with the flood of British groups 'invading' the country in the wake of The Beatles. Eventually, they were allowed into the country 'on popularity grounds', after obtaining proof from *Billboard* and *Cashbox* music magazines that their single had topped the charts.

If the group thought their troubles were behind them when they landed in New York then they were mistaken. Just as their feet touched American soil, an angry concert promoter served them with a multi-million dollar writ.

"As we stepped off the plane, this guy handed each one of us a writ for a million dollars," recalls Stewart. "He said he was suing us for not making two of our dates in New Jersey. Our manager, Ric Dixon, told him that he was essentially suing the American government, because they were the reason we couldn't make the gigs. He just walked away and we never heard from him again."

Fortunately, their American fans gave Wayne Fontana and The Mindbenders a much warmer reception.

"It was like Beatlemania," says Stewart. "The hotels we stayed in were under constant guard from security people and there were always girls waiting outside in their hundreds. When we arrived in New Orleans, we were astonished because they gave us the Freedom of the City as we stepped off the plane!"

The Game of Love also marked a financial breakthrough for some of the band's members. Publishing royalties from sales of singles were split evenly between the songs on the a-side and the b-side. With the self-penned Since You've Been Gone – written by Eric Stewart, Glyn Ellis and Bob Lang – on the b-side of The Game of Love, the band started to earn publishing royalties. In America, One More Time had been chosen as the song's b-side, which benefited Stewart and Ellis. The earnings from these songs inspired Stewart to develop his songwriting skills further.

Back at home the group were now in the position of being able to cherry pick songs for their next single. They had a choice between two Clint Ballard Jr songs for the follow-up: I'm Alive or Just a Little Bit Too Late. In hindsight, their decision to record the latter was a mistake. Despite giving the group a Top 20 hit in the UK, and a minor hit in the US, the record failed to emulate the Top 5 success of their two previous singles. To add insult to injury, The Hollies took I'm Alive, the song they had rejected, to No.1 in the UK charts, proving that the group had picked the wrong song.

Looking back, Wayne Fontana traces the group's subsequent decline to this decision. Their next single She Needs Love only reached No.32 in the UK charts, sparking off a series of rows within the band, each side blaming the other for their declining popularity. Fontana secretly dreamt of solo glory, feeling that the group were holding him back. The rest of the band were singularly unimpressed with Fontana's attitude and ego. In addition, they each had different opinions about the group's musical direction. Fontana wanted to take them in a poppier direction in the style of a PJ Proby. The group, and Stewart in particular, had other ideas.

"Eric has always been a bit aggressive with his opinions and he always had to be right," said Fontana. "He was picking the songs and I wanted to sing some others but he went, 'No, do this, do that!' So I just got sick of it and said, 'You take over. I'm off'."

Something had to give, and on October 30, 1965, halfway

through a concert at the Pavilion Gardens Ballroom in Buxton, it did. When Fontana decided to sing the ballad Save The Last Dance For Me during the show, the rest of the band did little to hide their frustration. Fontana responded by storming off stage leaving the group holding the baby.

"He just walked off stage," says Stewart. "I remember he said, 'It's all yours'."

Having successfully performed gigs already without Fontana, such as on their spring tour earlier in the year, the band decided to carry on and do the show without him.

"The audience really enjoyed it and were pleased that we didn't walk off too," says Stewart. "He had been hinting that he wanted to go out on his own for some time. I remember that the drummer had been giving him quite a hard time about it that night."

The split left Philips Records with a problem. The band's second album *Eric, Rick, Wayne and Bob – It's Wayne Fontana and The Mindbenders* had been recorded prior to the split but was now effectively redundant and would sell poorly on release in January 1966. On the positive side, Philips now had two acts, having signed both Wayne Fontana as a solo artist and The Mindbenders as a group to the label. Jack Baverstock felt he had the perfect song in mind as the debut single for The Mindbenders.

"He said, 'I've got this song that I knew wouldn't be right for Wayne's voice but I think you could sing it quite well, Eric,'" recalls Stewart. "And he played us this fantastic demo of a song called A Groovy Kind of Love."

The song had been written by a couple of 18-year-old song-writers called Carole Bayer and Toni Wine, who were working for Screen Gems in New York. With Stewart, somewhat reluctantly, taking on the role of lead vocalist, the group recorded the song as their next single. Released by Philips in December 1965, A Groovy Kind of Love climbed to No.2 in the UK, spending seven weeks in the Top 10. The group were understandably delighted. They had achieved that rare feat of surviving the departure of their lead singer, whose own debut single had barely scraped into the UK Top 40. "All we've lost is our tambourine player," said Stewart defiantly at the time.

Stewart had cause to be even more delighted than his bandmates, having written the b-side Love Is Good and thus benefitting again from the publishing royalties. With A Groovy Kind of Love still riding high in the charts, Stewart took time out from the group to marry his girlfriend, Gloria, who he'd met after one of the band's gigs at the Halifax Princess Ballroom in September 1964. With their management and record company fearing that The Mindbenders may lose some of their young female fans if any of the band's members were known to be married, the wedding at Bradford Registry Office on March 7, 1966 was a low-key affair. After a short honeymoon in London, their union nearly ended prematurely when their Jaguar E-Type caught fire on the M1 motorway on their way back up to Manchester. Luckily, the Stewarts escaped unharmed and welcomed their first child, Dieta, into the world later that year having moved into their first home together in Offerton, near Stockport.

Meanwhile, The Mindbenders had been approached to take part in the Sidney Poitier movie *To Sir, With Love*, which dealt with the social and racial issues of a black teacher coming to teach at a school in the East End of London. Appearing as themselves, filming took place in the late spring, with The Mindbenders performing the song Off and Running in the lunch break scene and It's Getting Harder All The Time at the end-of-term party. Stewart was even approached about an acting role himself around this time.

"I actually auditioned for a part in a film called *Groupie Girl*," recalls Stewart. "They said, 'You're just right for the part, you're a musician, you can identify with the character.' So they gave me the script and said, 'Learn your lines and come back and do an audition for the part with the lead girl, the groupie girl.' I went back and did the audition and they said, 'Eric, that's really good but do you mind acting in the nude? We've added some other bits to the script and we've got you running across the field with this girl in the nude.' I said, 'Forget it!' and it was just as well because when they made the film it was a disastrous flop!"

The Mindbenders released their debut album that summer, reaching the UK Top 30, before consolidating their success in America with a four-week tour, where A Groovy Kind of Love had climbed to the top of the charts, helping the record to sell over 2 million copies around the world. "I can still remember when we arrived at Kennedy Airport in New York City in mid-1966 for our first US tour," recalls Stewart. "We met Toni Wine and Carole Bayer as we came through the arrivals door and they ran up to us and hugged us shouting, 'A Groovy Kind of Love is Number One!'"

The band's agent decided to capitalise on their American success with a special gig, supporting the 'Godfather of Soul', James Brown. "Within days, with lights blazing all around me, I was in Atlanta, Georgia, running with Ric and Bob from a dressing-room tunnel to a stage in the distance that looked tiny in the middle of this vast arena that seated 28,000 people," recalls Stewart. "As I ran across that enormous playing field, I was excited and petrified at the same time."

The Mindbenders had been booked to play a short five-song set and opened with a cover of Bobby Womack's Don't Cry No More. "We finished it ... and nothing," recalls Stewart. "No applause, no cheers, no whistles. The silence was deafening. People just kept on buying soda pop, hot dogs and popcorn, and chatting to each other as if we weren't there. But being hardworking, conscientious northern lads, we carried on through another three numbers. The reaction was the same for each one of them – nix, zilch, nada! We were seriously dejected by the time we swung into A Groovy Kind of Love to finish our spot. There was a polite ripple of applause as we left the stage, numbed and bewildered, and made our way back across that vast green field."

The band sat dejected back in their dressing room, unimpressed by their agent's attempts to cheer them up by reminding them that they had just played to the biggest audience of their career and earned $64 per second in the process. Then came word that James Brown wanted to say hello. "We were ushered into his dressing room," says Stewart. "James was sat there in a green velvet dressing gown. He had a mouthful of brilliant white teeth, and the most astonishing hair, straightened, backcombed into a huge bouffant and slicked way back. He was very friendly. 'Hi guys,' he said, and shook our hands. 'You did well.' 'Did well?' I asked sheepishly. 'Yes, you went down well with the folks, boys,' he said, grinning. 'If they hadn't liked you, you wouldn't have made it back to the dressing room, ha ha.' He told us to cheer up and invited us to watch his show. That evening I saw what soul, feel and rhythm were all about, and I deliriously drank it all in."

The rest of the tour went well, with The Mindbenders proving to be a good live act. "Funnily enough, in the States, they were all amazed that a group of three people could make so much noise," said Stewart at the time. "They used to come up to us and say, 'Where's your backing group?' When we went on stage and kicked up a noise, they ate humble pie."

The group were in America when John Lennon made his infamous comment about The Beatles being 'Bigger than Jesus Christ'. The comment caused a major outcry, particularly in the Bible Belt.

"Some radio stations in the Deep South trapped us into answering questions about it," says Stewart. "They made it sound as if we agreed with them. Then they started mass burnings of our records as well!" Fortunately for Stewart, A Groovy Kind of Love had already sold over a million copies in America by then. Back at home, The Mindbenders returned to the UK Top 30 on two further occasions in 1966 with their next two singles, Can't Live With You, Can't Live Without You and Ashes to Ashes, both also written by Bayer and Wine. However, the group were starting to feel typecast as a band, particularly given that their singles were very different from the type of songs they were playing on stage, which were more rhythm and blues.

"We'd like to do a beat number for our next single," said Stewart at the time. "We don't really want to be classed as a ballad group. In our act we start off with a medley of Land of 1000 Dances, In The Midnight Hour and CC Rider. We try to integrate as many different kinds of songs as possible into the act. We've changed considerably since our break-up with Wayne."

It is ironic that Stewart was playing CC Rider live on stage long before he formed a band with a similar name. During this period, Stewart would become increasingly friendly with Justin Hayward, who had recently joined The Moody Blues. He would drop by Hayward's flat when he was in London. "Justin's wife was a friend of mine from Liverpool and I remember one night we were round there and he showed me the lyrics of this song he'd just written and I thought the words were incredible," says Stewart. "It was Nights In White Satin, though of course I never realised then that it would become one of the biggest singles of all time."

Sadly things were not looking so rosy for The Mindbenders. Their next two singles – I Want Her, She Wants Me and We'll Talk About It Tomorrow – both flopped and their album *With Woman In Mind*, released in April 1967, was largely ignored. It was hoped that their profile would be boosted by the release of *To Sir, With Love*. Released in America in June 1967, the movie was a box-office smash. Lulu's title song, with The Mindbenders' It's Getting Harder All The Time on the b-side, topped the US singles charts for five weeks, helping the accompanying soundtrack album, containing the two songs The Mindbenders perform in the film, to No.1 in the album charts. When the movie opened in Britain, in October that year, Philips released It's Getting Harder All The Time as the band's next single but it flopped. The future of The Mindbenders was starting to look bleak.

With three flops behind them, The Mindbenders took no chances with their next single. They recorded a cover of The Box Tops' No.1 US hit The Letter in the hope that it would beat the original version to chart success in the UK. The record was notable for being produced by Stewart's future partner in 10cc, Graham Gouldman. They had met at the offices of Kennedy Street Enterprises, where they both had management, and hit it off. Gouldman, who was enjoying considerable success as a songwriter at the time, enlisted the talents of John Paul Jones – the future bass guitarist in Led Zeppelin – to provide the string arrangement for the record. It nearly worked, giving The Mindbenders a minor hit, but was outsold by the original, which reached the Top 5.

"This is the first record that Graham Gouldman has produced for us and he did a great job," said Mindbender Bob Lang at the time. "Just wait until you hear the follow-up. Graham wrote and produced the record." The song in question was a re-recording of Schoolgirl, a track that had originally appeared on *With Woman In Mind*. With an updated lyric that brought the tale of teenage pregnancy to life more vividly, the new Graham Gouldman-produced version was released as a single in November 1967 but was banned by the BBC because of its subject matter and it failed to chart. Three months later when Lang left The Mindbenders, Gouldman briefly joined them as a full-time member. Gouldman wrote and produced what would turn out to be the band's final single, Uncle Joe The Ice Cream Man, which was released in August 1968. However, not even Gouldman's presence could stem the band's decline.

"We were recording the song at Olympic Studios and The Rolling Stones were next door working on their album," says Stewart. "Mick Jagger popped his head round the vocal booth door while I was singing the vocal and said, 'Why are you singing this shit?' It was the final nail in the coffin!"

Even a typically notable string arrangement from John Paul Jones couldn't prevent the record from being a flop. The pursuit of a hit single for The Mindbenders over their previous releases was at odds with the type of music that the band actually preferred to play. This was often in evidence on many of the group's b-sides, which featured Stewart originals such as My New Day and Age, The Man Who Loved Trees and the psychedelic Yellow Brick Road. These songs were full of interesting ideas, often more than the records they backed, and show Stewart's songwriting skills developing over the lifetime of the band. Yet this side of The Mindbenders was very different to the type of music that they were famous for, which lead to confusion among their fans – and promoters – at gigs.

"We got ourselves into a ballad-type rut," surmises Stewart. "People expected things like A Groovy Kind of Love to come out every three months, and we were sick of it. The band itself was quite a tight rock band, very blues-influenced. We used to love all that stuff, so we'd go to gigs and people would say, 'Well, this isn't A Groovy Kind of Love,' and we got into a terrible mix-up with our audience."

To try to challenge preconceptions, The Mindbenders embarked on a UK tour in November 1968 supporting The Who on a bill that at times also included the likes of The Small Faces and Joe Cocker. The tour included two 'all-nighters' at London's Roundhouse. By now the band's line-up featured Stewart on lead vocals and guitar, Gouldman on guitar and backing vocals, drummer Paul Hancock and bass player Jimmy O'Neil. Yet after the tour, without any hit singles or a viable audience for the music they wanted to play, there was only one option left for The Mindbenders.

"It became apparent to me that the only way we would survive would be to go into cabaret, so we did one week up in Newcastle and that was the most soul-destroying week of my life," recalls Stewart. "The compére came and gave me some jokes to tell the audience... and I died! At the end of the week we were paid off, and they paid quite nicely, but I drove the band all the way back to Manchester and disbanded the group completely. I said, 'That's it! If that's what's in store for us I don't want it!'"

Fortunately, the group's demise didn't tarnish Stewart's memories of his time with the band. "It was fantastic, young men had never been able to explore their creativity in expensive studios before that time. We mingled with great bands like The Beatles and The Stones, played at the Cavern, and toured with wonderful American artists like James Brown and Roy Orbison. It was happening so fast, like a speeded-up movie and being wired without drugs. We felt invincible. We thought it would never stop. It was great!"

CHAPTER 2

HEART FULL OF SONGS

BY THE TIME HE HAD BRIEFLY JOINED ERIC STEWART IN THE Mindbenders, Graham Gouldman was already established as one of Britain's most successful songwriters, with a string of international bestsellers to his name. The creative gene had clearly been passed down through the family. His great-grandfather had emigrated from Russia and had composed an operetta; his grandmother was very musical; and while his father, Hymie, earned his living in the 'schmutter business', his real love was writing and directing plays. His mother, Betty, also had artistic interests.

"Both my parents were involved in amateur dramatics," says Gouldman. "My dad should have been a professional writer. He was certainly good enough but he never had the opportunity, he didn't have the money. I don't know whether he really was the sort of person that would have taken the chance but he was certainly very successful in the amateur dramatics field in Manchester."

Born in May 1946, the only child of Hymie and Betty, Gouldman had a happy childhood and enjoyed growing up in an artistic household.

"It was a very happy house," recalls Gouldman. "There were always lots of people in, particularly on Friday nights. Whenever a production came into town a lot of the people would gravitate to our house and I can remember sitting at the top of the stairs looking down at all these exotic people. I loved it, it was great."

The Gouldman family home was on Kingston Close in Broughton Park, an area of North Salford. In 1951 Gouldman started at Sedgley Park Primary School in Prestwich, where he met future partner in 10cc, Kevin Godley, who was in the year above him.

"A year is a decade in school years, so you don't usually notice someone who's a year older than you but I remember Kevin very well from school," says Gouldman. "He was a wonderful artist. He used to draw pictures of knights in armour and things like that."

It was during his days at primary school that music first started to take hold of him.

"I was always interested in music, from the age of seven," says Gouldman. "My uncle bought me a radio to listen to Radio Luxembourg and I remember going to bed with it stuck in my ear. I was learning it in my sleep the way you learn a language."

Continuing his education at North Salford Secondary School, it became clear that music was his vocation.

"I never showed any sort of acumen at school," says Gouldman. "I was really terrible. I think I was just thinking about music all the time. Because my parents were artistic they encouraged me in what I was doing with music. I was lucky in that respect because a lot of my peers were being encouraged to go into business or to go to university, take up a profession if possible. But it was never in my world. My world was music, plain and simple."

Growing up in a semi-orthodox Jewish household, Gouldman followed religious traditions out of respect for his parents.

"We kept a kosher home and I'd go to the synagogue with my dad up to the age that I had my bar mitzvah at thirteen," says Gouldman. "My dad would go to the synagogue but then he'd go and watch Manchester United. He'd made some deal with God that it was okay. He used to say, 'We've all got our different levels of hypocrisy' and that was his. Football was like a religion to him."

Looking back, Gouldman feels his musical tastes were shaped in part by those early visits to the synagogue, where he first fell in love with the soulful minor chords that would later feature in his song-writing. "The melodies there were very beautiful, mournful and aching," recalls Gouldman.

Having originally wanted to play the drums – "I had lessons but I was hopeless" – Gouldman's thoughts turned to the guitar, partly inspired by one of his earliest musical influences, The Shadows. "I was drawn to the guitar because of them," recalls Gouldman. "I was one of those kids who stood in front of the mirror with a tennis racket pretending to be Hank Marvin." Gouldman swapped his tennis racket for the real thing when his cousin, Ronnie, brought him a guitar back from a holiday in Spain. "When I got the guitar I fell in love with it," recalls Gouldman. "I knew that was it. I had no second thoughts. It was obvious what was going to happen. The environment for me was amazing. A 12-year-old having a guitar in the age of skiffle, rock 'n' roll emerging out of America, Elvis, Little Richard, Buddy Holly, The Everly Brothers."

The latter's Cathy's Clown was the first record that Gouldman remembers buying, with the song spending seven weeks at the No.1 spot in May and June 1960. Cliff Richard and The Shadows were another big early influence and when they played at the Manchester Free Trade Hall on July 11, 1960, Gouldman's father pulled a few strings so that his son could attend the sold-out gig.

"My father knew the manager and they put an extra seat in and that was incredible," recalls Gouldman. "I really loved that. I was twelve or something then and that was in his early days with Move It." Gouldman's father would later immortalise the experience in a poem called *Cliff and the Boy*, demonstrating a gift with words that would later earn him the nickname 'Hyme the Rhyme': *'A friend on the staff stood in loco parentis / In case all those fans went non-compos mentis.'*

As music took a hold of the teenage Gouldman he decided it was time to form his own band and sought out kindred spirits. Hearing that one of his neighbours, Bernard Basso, had a guitar he paid him a visit, just like Charlie Barker had done to Eric Stewart. Basso was keen and they found further recruits at the youth club they both attended, the Jewish Lads' Brigade, on Middleton Road in north Manchester.

"This was in the days when people went to youth clubs," says Gouldman. "They were playing table tennis, there were social groups, there were meetings, there were discussion groups, there were bands rehearsing. It was great." At the JLB were four other teenagers equally enthralled with the music of Elvis, Cliff Richard and Lonnie Donegan, and they decided to form a group. With Gouldman on lead guitar and the newly recruited Stephen Jacobsen on rhythm guitar, Bernard Basso switched, appropriately enough, to bass. Drummer Mo Sperling, and vocalists Phil Cohen and Malcolm Wagner, completed the six-man line-up. They called themselves The Whirlwinds, inspired by groups with other elemental-sounding names at the time, such as Rory Storm and The Hurricanes. Needing somewhere to practise, Wagner's father agreed to park his Vanguard on the road so that The Whirlwinds could rehearse in his garage. Gouldman's talents stood out from the outset.

"From day one, it was evident that Graham Gouldman was awash with talent," says Wagner. "I don't think Graham could sight-read music in 1960 but he could certainly listen to any song and play it straight off. Graham took on the role of musical director from the start; he was the musical strength of our group and his quiet confidence gradually filtered through to the rest of us. It was Graham who showed Stephen what chords to play, it was Graham who showed Bernard the bass notes to play and it was Graham who organised Mo's drumming. Graham himself played terrific, f lawless lead guitar and harmonised brilliantly with Phil and myself on vocals."

Initially, The Whirlwinds had four songs in their repertoire: Lonnie Donegan's Puttin' On The Style, Cliff Richard's Travellin' Light and, to demonstrate their versatility, two older numbers Way Down Yonder In New Orleans and Alexander's Ragtime Band. However, at the end of 1960, when Wagner's parents moved house, The Whirlwinds needed to find a new rehearsal space. They struck a deal with Stan Rowe, the dynamic youth worker who ran the JLB: they could rehearse for free in the back room there provided they played at any dances organised at the club. The Whirlwinds rehearsed three nights a week at the JLB. They would mix with other groups that rehearsed there, such as The Sabres, whose line-up featured Kevin Godley, and his friend Lol Creme, thus establishing connections between three-quarters of the future line-up of 10cc.

"The JLB was very important to the three of us because we were all in different bands that rehearsed there," says Gouldman.

During the course of 1961 The Whirlwinds came to the attention of singer Frankie Vaughan, who was a patron of The National Association of Boys' Clubs. He invited them to play at the Frankie Vaughan Show for Boys' Clubs at a theatre in Wilmslow. The appearance gave the group the belief that perhaps there was a professional future for The Whirlwinds. With interest in the group building, a friend of Gouldman's parents, Victor Coss, approached them about being their manager. Coss set about getting the band some gigs. However, they had a rude awakening when auditioning for Ric Dixon, the co-owner of the Oasis club. Unimpressed with what he heard, he played the band a version of the song they had just auditioned as recorded by another local group called The Olympics. It put their version to shame and made Gouldman realise the band were not as good as he thought they were.

Undeterred, Coss suggested that The Whirlwinds incorporate some Italian and Spanish numbers into their set and soon the group had added Tu Sei Romantica and Besame Mucho into their repertoire, with Mo Sperling's operatic singing voice adding a third lead vocalist to the band. Towards the end of 1962, The Whirlwinds ventured outside of the JLB for the first time to appear at Lewis's Department Store in Manchester. By now, Gouldman had left school and got himself a job at a gentleman's outfitters called Bargains Unlimited in Salford. Then, in January 1963, he heard a record that would change everything.

"I was sitting at home in the kitchen when Please Please Me by The Beatles came on the radio and some physiological change took place in me," recalls Gouldman. "I've never had a religious experience but I guess it would be something akin to that. It knocked me out."

Later that month The Whirlwinds played their first proper gig together at The Devonshire Sporting Club in Higher Broughton, Salford. Dressed in alpaca jackets made by Bernard Basso's father, the six-piece huddled together on the stage as they made their debut performance. The group went down well but their next engagement, at Bernard Manning's Embassy Club in Harpurhey, would be a real test of their abilities. Manning, and the audience at the Embassy Club, were not backwards in coming forwards if they weren't impressed by acts performing there. The anxiety in the dressing room before the show was palpable.

"Suddenly, without warning, the dressing room door burst open and in strode the man himself, Mr Bernard Manning," recalls

Wagner. "He looked like a large unexploded bomb, smartly attired in black dinner suit, white shirt and black bow tie. Bernard had just come in to weigh us up and pile on the agony. With an accent that could make 'hello' sound threatening he boomed, 'You lads are setting me back 15 quid, so you'd better be good.' With a smile broadening into a cheeky grin, he strode past me and nonchalantly adopted a stance as he faced the corner of the dressing room wall and calmly proceeded to pee down a hole somewhere beneath him in the floorboards. We all watched on in a state of silent disbelief."

With the group's parents in the audience to watch them play, The Whirlwinds didn't know what to expect when they took to the stage but they went down very well, earning themselves a standing ovation and repeat bookings at the Embassy Club and Manning's other venue, the Palladium. During the rest of 1963 the group would be booked every Friday and Saturday night playing in clubs such as the Kingfisher in Stockport, the Twisted Wheel in Manchester and the Waterpark in Broughton Park. As their profile built, local impresario Harvey Lisberg, who also attended the JLB and regularly saw the band rehearse there, expressed an interest in managing them. Lisberg had recently graduated from the University of Manchester with a degree in commerce. He had discovered another local band, Herman's Hermits, while working as an accountant at Binder Hamlyn and had decided that a career in music management was a more interesting prospect than one in accountancy. "Sign up with me and I'll make you famous," Lisberg told The Whirlwinds. "I've got this song for you to record. You'll love it but I'm not going to let you listen to it unless you sign for me first."

The group initially rejected Lisberg's advances and the song, I'm Into Something Good, would go on to become the debut single – and UK No.1 hit – for his other charges, Herman's Hermits. By then, Lisberg had succeeded in becoming The Whirlwinds' manager and organised an audition for the band with EMI in London. The group secured a one-off record deal and were invited to record two songs at Abbey Road, where they recorded a cover version of Buddy Holly's Look At Me as their first single. Gouldman, yet to start writing his own songs at this point, turned to a future partner in 10cc to write the b-side, with Lol Creme of The Sabres coming up with Baby Not Like You. However, the single failed to chart upon release in May 1964.

By now, Gouldman had decided to have a crack at writing his own material, inspired in equal part by necessity and by The Beatles' example of writing their own songs.

"I think they really affected everybody at that time," says Gouldman. "They opened the door for songwriters, because up to that point I was with bands that used to have to go round Denmark Street in London knocking on publishers' doors. But when The Beatles came along they were an inspiration. It was like, 'If they can write songs, I'll have a go as well.' I don't think I'd have started as a songwriter in the 60s if it hadn't been for them."

The first song that Gouldman remembers writing was That's How (It's Gonna Stay). Aside from Lennon and McCartney, Gouldman would also be highly influenced by songwriters such as Burt Bacharach, Jimmy Webb and Paul Simon, and from songs he'd heard on the radio. After hearing The House Of The Rising Sun by The Animals during the summer of 1964, he 'borrowed' the same chord sequence as the start point for a new song, For Your Love. Gouldman played what he had to Harvey Lisberg, who suggested creating a new section of the song that took it to "somewhere completely different." Gouldman developed a middle eight that utilised a different tempo and shifted the tone from the minor key used in the rest of the song to a major key. Ten years later these would become trademark devices for 10cc, yet in 1964 this was quite avant-garde.

As he wrote his first songs it became increasingly apparent to Gouldman that The Whirlwinds weren't the right vehicle for his new material. He was beginning to tire of the band's cabaret shtick.

"We used to do kind of like cabaret music, we wore suits, we were a bit post-Shadows but I got fed up with that sort of music," says Gouldman. His decision to break up The Whirlwinds at the end of 1964 wasn't an easy one given that he and his friends in the group had lived and breathed making music together over the previous four years. Still, he knew it was the right thing to do and in February 1965 Gouldman formed a new group called The Mockingbirds, taking Bernard Basso and Stephen Jacobsen with him from his old band. Needing a drummer to complete their line-up, Gouldman approached Kevin Godley. "I'd heard Kevin in The Sabres and thought he was a fantastic drummer," says Gouldman. "So I spoke to him and he joined us and we became very good friends."

Gigging by night with The Mockingbirds, and still working by day as a shop assistant in Bargains Unlimited, Gouldman would use any spare time he had to work on his songs, making notes on the back of paper bags in the shop. "I used to shut up shop at lunch-time and then sit in the back writing," recalls Gouldman. "I can remember finishing off For Your Love there. It was good for business. My business."

Co-managed by Harvey Lisberg and Charlie Silverman, who were now part of the growing Kennedy Street Enterprises organisation in Manchester, The Mockingbirds secured a recording contract with Columbia. They recorded For Your Love and That's How (It's Gonna Stay) at their first recording session and Columbia chose the latter as the band's first single. Convinced that For Your Love was too good to be overlooked, Harvey Lisberg went out of his way to try and find a home for the song. He offered it to his other charges, Herman's Hermits, who recorded the song. However, their producer Mickie Most didn't think it was a single. Lisberg's next suggestion of offering the song to The Beatles was laughed off by Gouldman, who pointed out that they "seemed to be doing alright in the songwriting department". Undeterred, Lisberg set out to play the song to The Beatles who were appearing in their 1964 Christmas show at the Hammersmith Odeon in London. While he was there he met up with Ronnie Beck of Feldman's music publishers, who introduced him to Giorgio Gomelsky, the manager and producer of support band The Yardbirds. Gomelsky thought that the song had hit potential and, keen to achieve a commercial breakthrough for the group, agreed to record it as their next single.

On February 1, 1965, The Yardbirds recorded For Your Love at IBC Studios in Portland Place, London. Arranger Dave Liebman had been hired to write an organ riff for the song's introduction but when he arrived for the session no organ could be found. Instead, Liebman improvised by using a harpsichord he found in the studio, which was played at the session by Brian Auger. Convinced that there would never be a hit song featuring a harpsichord, Liebman left the session early. Yet it was this touch that Gouldman felt gave the recording something different.

"The Yardbirds' version of the song took me by surprise because I thought it was so weird," says Gouldman. "Ours used an acoustic guitar instead of a harpsichord, which was what really made their version. It was amazing."

Lisberg's faith in the song proved to be well placed. For Your Love became a huge hit, reaching No.3 in the UK in April 1965, also making No.6 in America later that summer, going on to sell over 2 million copies around the world. But while The Yardbirds achieved the commercial breakthrough they had been seeking, The Mockingbirds saw their single sink without a trace. The contrast in the two band's fortunes hit home one night during the filming of a new BBC television music show called *Top of the Pops* – then filmed in Manchester at the BBC's studio on Dickenson Road in Rusholme – where The Mockingbirds had secured the role of warm-up band.

"There was one strange moment when The Yardbirds appeared on the show performing For Your Love," says Gouldman. "Everyone clamoured round them, and there was I – just part of an anonymous group. I felt strange that night hearing them play my song."

Also feeling strange that night was The Yardbirds' guitarist, Eric Clapton. Keith Altham, then a features writer for *New Musical Express*, spotted Clapton slumped over a drink in the BBC bar after the show.

"You don't like your new single For Your Love, then?" asked Altham.

"Crap. Pop crap!" responded Clapton.

Feeling that the group had betrayed their roots as a blues band by recording the song and unhappy with the group's new direction – "a political thrust towards the top of the charts" as he called it – Clapton left the group, to be replaced by another guitar virtuoso – Jeff Beck. "I saw The Yardbirds with Jeff Beck and he just blew me away," says Gouldman. "To me he was, and still is, the ultimate player, so it was very exciting to be working with them."

It was Beck's distinctive guitar style that partly inspired Gouldman to write the riff to Heart Full of Soul, which was chosen as The Yardbirds' follow-up single. Again the song saw Gouldman deftly switching between minor and major keys and incorporating tempo changes. However, the band were underwhelmed by their first attempt at recording the song, at Advision Studios in London on April 13, largely because the sitar player, hired to play the song's riff, couldn't quite get it right.

"The sitar player couldn't get the 4/4 time signature right; it was a hopeless waste of time," says Beck. "So I said, 'Look, is this the figure?' I had the fuzz machine, a Tone Bender going. We did one take, it sounded outrageous."

Released in June 1965 it turned out to be every bit as successful as its predecessor, staying at No.2 in the UK for three weeks in July 1965, initially kept off the No.1 spot by Mr Tambourine Man by The Byrds and then Help! by The Beatles. The song was also a big hit around the world, reaching No.2 in Canada and No.9 in America, and again selling 2 million copies worldwide. Gouldman made it a hat-trick of Top 10 hits when The Yardbirds took another of his songs, Evil Hearted You, to No.3 in the UK charts in November, spending five weeks in the UK Top 10. Despite his newfound success as a songwriter, it took a while before the impact that his songs were having on the public sunk in.

"I remember once walking down Oxford Road and someone started whistling one of my songs and I thought that was pretty cool, and I suddenly realised the power of it," he recalls.

In the meantime, Gouldman's mother, Betty, had played an important role in helping to get his songs in front of one of Manchester's most successful bands, The Hollies. The group's manager, Michael Cohen, lived next door to the Gouldmans on Kingston Close and Mrs Gouldman would take every opportunity to tell Cohen about her teenage son's songwriting prowess. After asking him countless times to take a listen to her son's songs Cohen eventually phoned the band's co-founder Graham Nash asking for a favour.

"Look, I know he's probably awful and it's an imposition but I like this woman, we've been neighbours a long time," said Cohen. "Just go down there and see what this kid's about."

Nash, along with bandmates Allan Clarke and Tony Hicks, went to visit Gouldman at home.

"So we go over to the address he gave us to meet this so-called songwriter," recalls Nash in his autobiography *Wild Tales*. "Now we're The Hollies so we're not going to make it easy on him, kid or no kid. So I threw Mr Songwriter one of my best stony stares and said, 'Okay, kid – give it your best shot.'"

Gouldman and Nash have different recollections about what happened next. What seems certain though is that Gouldman played the group some of his songs, including Look Through Any Window and Going Away.

"Talk about being blown away," says Nash. "This kid wrote these amazing songs. It was incredible hearing them."

The Hollies would subsequently record both songs but first they planned to rush-release the Clint Ballard Jr song I'm Alive as their next single. Originally offered to, and rejected by, Wayne Fontana and The Mindbenders, the song had been recorded by another Manchester band managed by Kennedy Street Enterprises called The Toggery Five, whose lead singer was Paul Young of future Sad Café and Mike and The Mechanics fame. When The Hollies heard the recording – produced by their own producer, Ron Richards – they decided to record the song themselves, leading Parlophone to shelve the release of The Toggery Five's version. When The Hollies scored a No.1 hit with I'm Alive, the group offered Gouldman's Going Away to The Toggery Five by way of compensation, which they duly recorded at Abbey Road. However, it was never released, only eventually surfacing on the compilation album *Rainy City Blues* in 2012.

The Hollies recorded Look Through Any Window as their follow-up to I'm Alive. It took them all of two hours to record the song at Abbey Road on June 30, 1965. As with many of Gouldman's songs, inspiration had come from an everyday source, in this case a conversation on a train journey from London to Manchester with his co-manager, Charlie Silverman, who had come up with the title and is thus credited as the song's co-writer. Released that autumn, it went on to reach No.4 in the UK charts, and gave The Hollies their first Top 40 hit in America. It would also go on to earn Gouldman a prestigious Ivor Novello Award nomination.

Another journey, this time a ride on the No.95 bus from East Didsbury to his home in Broughton Park, would inspire Gouldman's next song, Bus Stop. But it was his father, Hymie, who helped get the song written.

"I had the title and I came home one day and he said, 'I've started something on that idea you had, and I'm going to play it for you'," says Gouldman. "He'd written *'Bus stop, wet day, she's there, I say please share my umbrella,'* and it's like when you have such a great start to a song it's kind of like the rest is easy. It's like finding your way onto a road and when you get onto the right route, you just follow it."

The middle section of the song came to Gouldman while he was travelling home on the bus.

"The whole thing came to me in my head," says Gouldman. "I didn't have a guitar but I couldn't wait to get home and put it in with the rest of the song."

Gouldman thought that Bus Stop would be perfect for The Hollies. One night, when The Mockingbirds were supporting them at Stoke Town Hall, he lured Graham Nash and Tony Hicks into the only quiet part of the building – the men's room – to play them the song. They loved it and on May 18, 1966, The Hollies recorded Bus Stop in less than two hours at Abbey Road. Released a month later, the song reached No.5 on both sides of the Atlantic, giving The Hollies their US chart breakthrough. It was a huge global hit, reaching No.1 in Canada and the Top 10 in Germany, the Netherlands and Norway, and selling 2 million copies around the world. Since its release it has been played over 4 million times on US radio alone. Arguably his finest song to date, Bus Stop remains to this day one of Gouldman's own personal favourites from his songbook, as well as Graham Nash's favourite ever Hollies song. The Hollies would go on to record another Gouldman song, Schoolgirl, at Abbey Road in the sessions for their 1967 album *Evolution*, but the recording was never completed and the song would go on to be recorded by The Mindbenders.

Still living at home with his parents, Gouldman bought a Revox tape machine on which he recorded demos of his songs. Needing to flesh out the arrangements on his demos it was at this point that Gouldman – a highly skilled guitarist – first started playing the bass guitar. "On the first track I put the guitar and vocal," recalls Gouldman. "On track two I added bass. And on the third track I added tambourine, or maybe a harmony vocal."

Like Paul McCartney and John Paul Jones, who also came to the bass guitar having mastered another instrument first, Gouldman's playing style would have a more melodic and inventive dimension to it than most. In addition to McCartney and Jones, his bass playing would be influenced over the years by the likes of Jaco Pastorious and James Jamerson.

In the meantime, with five Top 5 hits under his belt, Gouldman was on a roll. And the hits just kept on coming. The next band to strike gold with his material was Herman's Hermits, a natural progression given they were also managed by Harvey Lisberg. The band had already recorded their own versions of songs like For Your Love and Bus Stop as album tracks. Now, they too would have hit records from the Gouldman songbook.

"Graham wrote No Milk Today, Listen People, East West, Oh She's Done It Again for us," recalls the band's lead singer Peter Noone. "He was just a phenomenal songsmith. I mean, everything he played to me, I loved. And it's the construction. We turned down Carole King songs and Neil Diamond songs but we never, ever turned down a Graham Gouldman song, and I still to this day say, 'Why didn't I get him in Herman's Hermits?'"

No wonder. Listen People was a big global hit for the band, reaching No.1 in Canada, No.3 in both America and Australia, and the Top 10 in Sweden and New Zealand during the spring of 1966. Even more successful was the follow-up, No Milk Today, which reached No.1 in Australia and Norway, No.2 in New Zealand, No.3 in Sweden and No.7 in the UK that autumn. His father, Hymie, had suggested the title of the song.

"He went round to see a friend of his, who was out, but he noticed the milk bottle on the doorstep, and he came home and said, 'Why don't we write a song called No Milk Today," recalls Gouldman. "I thought it was a horrible title. I said, 'What's so interesting about milk?', and he said, 'It's nothing to do with milk! There's nobody in the house, the house is empty, the love has left the house.' He helped me see it from a whole different point of view. Thanks, Dad!"

The song was produced by Mickie Most and benefited hugely from the arranging skills of John Paul Jones. "Personally I think No Milk Today is Herman's Hermits' best recording, and perfectly captures the moment and the feel of Manchester terraced houses and what was the end of a British era," says Peter Noone. "I recall that John Paul Jones played bass guitar on the track and was also responsible for the arrangements which are brilliant and turned this perfect Graham Gouldman song into a hit."

Gouldman also wrote the band's follow-up single, East West. It was a more reflective and melancholy affair, ruminating on the loneliness of being on the road and missing home in contrast to the great life it must seem to everyone else. While not as successful as its predecessor, East West reached the Top 40 on both sides of the Atlantic. Gouldman would go on to write another song for Herman's Hermits that talked about home, even going as far as referencing specific places in and outside of Manchester. It's Nice To Be Out In The Morning managed to namecheck Ardwick, Beswick, Hulme, Harpurhey, Whalley Range, Besses o' th' Barn, Boggart Hall Clough – as well as the Manchester United holy trinity of Charlton, Best and Law – within its two and a half minutes. As the lyric points out, they may not be the sights of Rome, or the Taj Mahal, but they're home.

The Yardbirds – now with Jeff Beck replaced by guitarist Jimmy Page – returned to Gouldman to get them back on the hit trail. On December 22, 1966 they entered the studio to record You Stole My Love, a song that had been an Australian hit for Mike Furber and The Bowery Boys during the summer of 1966. Unfortunately, while The Yardbirds recorded all the backing tracks to their version it would remain unfinished without the vocals of singer Keith Relf.

Elsewhere, Cher had a minor hit with Gouldman's Behind The Door; Wayne Fontana, following his split with The Mindbenders, almost reached the UK Top 10 with Pamela, Pamela while Normie Rowe achieved the same feat with Going Home in Australia; and Jeff Beck, having left The Yardbirds, had a UK Top 30 hit in August 1967 with Tallyman. Even The Shadows, one of Gouldman's earliest musical heroes, recorded one of his songs, a rare instrumental called Naughty Nippon Nights for their 1967 album *From Hank, Bruce, Brian and John*.

For a period of about two years Gouldman was unstoppable, his songwriting talents helping to shift over 10 million records around the world. Over fifty years on, these songs continue to earn him a small fortune in songwriting royalties.

"Money was never my motivation," says Gouldman. "But actually my songs from the 60s are earning me more than ever with all the 'golden oldie' radio stations. The royalty cheque arrives with a thud!"

So, what is the secret to Gouldman's songwriting success?

"I try not to think about it too much because it's such a mysterious process that I don't really want to know how it works," says Gouldman. "I don't think there is an explanation anyway but I don't tend to dwell on it too much. I can tell you how you get to the place but I can't tell you what happens when you're at the place."

The longevity of Gouldman's songs from this period has been demonstrated time and time again since they were first written. Morrissey would record arguably the definitive version of East West in 1989, while Chris Isaak's reading of Heart Full of Soul is one of Gouldman's own personal favourite cover versions. Elsewhere, artists as diverse as Blondie (Heart Full of Soul), Led Zeppelin (For Your Love), The Pixies (Evil Hearted You), The Four Tops (For Your Love), The White Stripes (Evil Hearted You), Fleetwood Mac (For Your Love) and Rush (Heart Full of Soul) have all recorded cover versions or included Gouldman's songs in their stage set.

If there's one thread that runs through Gouldman's songs from this period it's his ability to create alchemy from everyday life: bus stop romances; the symbolism of an empty milk bottle on the doorstep; tallymen and pawnbrokers; sticky red lollies on splintery sticks; the life going on behind every door and through any window.

Yet despite his success as a songwriter, Gouldman's dream of making it with his own band continued to elude him. Having released two unsuccessful singles on Columbia, The Mockingbirds signed for the prestigious Immediate record label and released the excellent You Stole My Love, featuring Judy Driscoll on backing vocals, as their third single in October 1965. Despite its seductive guitar riff and strong hook, the single failed to chart. Gouldman even struck out alone, releasing Stop! Stop! Stop! under his own name in February 1966, but the record flopped, despite Gouldman being hailed as 'newcomer of the week' in *New Musical Express*.

"That was a terrible record – horrible," says Gouldman. "One of those things you're pressured into doing. I did that one without the Mockingbirds. I'd really rather forget it."

The Mockingbirds signed to their third record label, Decca, and released two further singles but still without success. Their final single, How To Find A Lover, was written by Peter Cowap, who Gouldman would continue to work with after The Mockingbirds split towards the end of 1966 in a couple of short-lived bands called High Society and The Manchester Mob.

At one point there was a tentative plan for Gouldman to form a new group with Hilton Valentine from The Animals and Paul Samwell-Smith from The Yardbirds, but they couldn't find a singer to complete the line-up. Instead, Harvey Lisberg suggested that Gouldman record a solo album as his next project, showcasing his own versions of songs that had been hits for other artists along with some new songs. The album was due to be produced by Peter Noone of Herman's Hermits.

"It was supposed to be something like the artist produces the writer," says Gouldman. "But he wasn't there on any of the sessions, though he is credited as a producer."

Noone was clearly preoccupied elsewhere, presumably with the opening of a new boutique in New York called The Zoo. Located at 243 East 60th Street, on Upper East Side, The Zoo was a partnership between Noone and Gouldman, designed to cater for "the male animal". As usual, Gouldman's mind was more concerned with music, as recording of his solo album got underway, without Noone, at Olympic Studios in London.

"I did the whole thing with John Paul Jones who arranged the tracks, played on it and helped to produce it," says Gouldman. "It was an important project for me at the time. I put a lot of work into it. It was also a chance to work on a big project with John Paul Jones, with whom I had worked many times before… he is a great bass and keyboard player who had an important influence on my playing."

Recorded with a nucleus of Gouldman on guitar, John Paul Jones on bass and Clem Cattini on drums, the already stellar cast was joined by engineer Eddie Kramer, who had recently completed work on Jimi Hendrix's *Electric Ladyland*.

Released by RCA in America in July 1968, entitled *The Graham Gouldman Thing*, the album benefited from some wonderful sleeve-notes: "From behind the counter of a gents' outfitters in a grimy Manchester suburb to a place in the front rank of the world's leading songwriters in three years. This is the achievement of Graham Gouldman – six feet, rangy and dreamy eyed. Citations and reviews also pay tribute to the melodic invention and distinctive style of what has become known as 'The Graham Gouldman Thing'."

A single, The Impossible Years, was released ahead of the album but failed to chart. The album was never released in the UK and, despite a heavy promotional push, it didn't sell well in America. *The Graham Gouldman Thing* finally appeared in the UK in 1992 when it was issued on CD, gaining some excellent reviews, with *Vox* magazine awarding the album an eight-out-of-ten rating.

For John Paul Jones, huge success was just around the corner, as bass guitarist in Led Zeppelin. Eddie Kramer would carry on working with Jimi Hendrix as well as working with Led Zeppelin throughout their career. Gouldman's immediate future was not so bright. When Tallyman reached the Top 30 in August 1967 it would be the last of Gouldman's songs to trouble the UK charts that decade. After his spell with Eric Stewart in The Mindbenders, he would go on to record some songs for Giorgio Gomelsky's short-lived Marmalade record label but only one song, The Late Mr Late, would see the light of day from these sessions. With the hits seemingly having dried up, the industrious Gouldman accepted an offer from the American production team of Jerry Kasenetz and Jeff Katz – instigators of 'bubblegum' music – to become a house writer for their company Kasenetz Katz.

"They wanted me to write and produce for them, so I figured, why not? Nothing else was happening for me at the time," says Gouldman. As his father Hymie used to say to him: 'Art for art's sake, money for God's sake!' So, having accepted the offer, Gouldman spent six weeks in New York at the beginning of 1969 where, in true Brill Building fashion, he would go into their offices each morning at 10am to write songs.

"After I'd finished one song towards the end of the day they'd come to me and say, 'Come on, give us one more song,' and I'd say, 'Okay' and I'd write them another song," recalls Gouldman. "I'd never worked like that before in my life, though I realise now that it was good for me. Over the period of a year I completed about 20 songs – 20 finished, recorded songs, that is – which is a very high output for me."

One of the first of these songs to see the light of day was Sausalito (Is The Place To Go). Released in August 1969 under the name of Ohio Express – one of the many band names owned by Kasenetz Katz – it went on to become a minor hit in the US, Canada and Australia. Yet it all seemed a very far cry from the success he'd experienced just a few years earlier. It hit home one day when he heard a band playing one of his songs on the street outside his hotel.

"I was staying at the Plaza Hotel in New York and outside was a band playing For Your Love," recalls Gouldman. "I knew it was just a coincidence, but I went up and said I just wanted you to know I actually wrote that song. 'Oh yeah?' Nothing. I must have been expecting him go, 'Hey man, that's fantastic! Come and meet the guys!' So I've never done that again."

Yet while the Kasenetz Katz sessions would prove to be an important stepping-stone in the development of 10cc, at the time Gouldman felt like his hitherto golden touch had deserted him. In 1969, he would record demos of new songs such as Wheel Spin, Leisurely Age and Imaginin' for Robbins Music but none of them were placed. "You're like a conduit when that magic happens," says Gouldman. "You think, how did I do that? What happened there? In 1969 I was still doing what I did, but I was out of sync with what has happening. Tastes change. The world moves on. Things alter. My principle has always been to stick to what you know best and with a bit of luck it'll come back round again. And it did."

CHAPTER 3

ART SCHOOL CANTEEN

WHILE GRAHAM GOULDMAN HAD BEEN PENNING HIT RECORDS FOR the likes of The Yardbirds and The Hollies, and Eric Stewart had been enjoying success with The Mindbenders, Kevin Godley and Lol Creme, the future other half of 10cc, had been busy pursuing artistic goals of a different kind, each studying for graphic design diplomas at art college.

Godley grew up in the Prestwich area of Manchester, the only child of Gladys and Edwin Godley, who owned four shops in Manchester, including Godleys, a four-storey emporium in Shudehill. "He sold records, tape recorders, radios, musical instruments, cameras and camping equipment," says Godley.

Having enrolled at Sedgley Park Primary School, a 20 minute walk from the family home on Sheepfoot Lane, Godley met Graham Gouldman, thus marking the first connection between the future members of 10cc. As Gouldman recalled, Godley's drawing skills were already in evidence at this early age but his interest in music would be ignited during a music lesson at school. Godley's teacher would play pieces of classical music to demonstrate what real music was all about. Then one day, to demonstrate bad music, she played the class See You Later Alligator by Bill Haley and His Comets and Hound Dog by Elvis Presley.

"As soon as that record came on I started hammering out a beat on my school desk," recalls Godley. "I was consequently thrown out of the class and put in detention. I was actually punished for enjoying Hound Dog, so that was quite significant to me. Seeing Elvis on TV was remarkable. It gave a whole new meaning to that thing dangling between my legs. We were all so affected by Elvis. We were looking for something, even though we didn't quite know it. Elvis was the start of everything."

Not being particularly academic, Godley failed his 11-plus exam. Appalled at the prospect of his son not going to a grammar school, Godley's father paid to get him into North Cestrian Grammar School. Unfortunately, the journey from Godley's home in Prestwich to his new school in Altrincham entailed making a three-hour round trip every day. "I had to walk the length of Sheepfoot Lane, jump on a bus to get into town, walk from that bus stop to the station, jump on a train to Altrincham," recalls Godley. "By the time I got to school I was fucked! And then the same coming back home and then I'd have to do my homework. Horrible, horrible, horrible."

To make matters worse, Godley was bullied at school.

"I was a weedy kid, and being Jewish and weedy wasn't a great combination as far as the bigger kids were concerned," recalls Godley. "Being bullied is so traumatic. I had to get the train home every day and they stripped me on it. They tore my clothes off and threw them down the corridor. That's a horrible thing to do to anyone. I always had the impression that other kids were laughing at me and I think I became the person I am now to counteract these feelings of inadequacy. If people are going to look at me, let it be for something good. I suppose it moulds you in some ways. I guess in my case it made me more determined to do stuff in a different way. To be seen and heard. Although it didn't feel that way at the time."

Godley's experience of being bullied would go on to become a recurring theme in his lyrics over the years and a reference to his school's motto – 'Delapsus Resurgam', from *The Pilgrim's Progress* by John Bunyan, which translated as 'When I fall I shall arise' – would even appear on a future 10cc record (I Wanna Rule The World). Unsurprisingly, Godley does not look back on his school days with a great deal of affection.

"I think of school very much like being part of *Goodbye Mr Chips*," recalls Godley. "It was like a musty old manor house, with teachers with gowns and mortar boards. I wasn't a very bright kid particularly. I was hopeless at maths; I was shit at science. The only thing I could do was art and they didn't have art on the curriculum, so I used to go to night school for that."

This would prove to be a major blessing in disguise. The arts class – which took place at the Jewish Lads' Brigade, the same youth club that Graham Gouldman also frequented – was where Godley would first meet his future creative partner, Lol Creme.

"The JLB was run by a guy called Stan Rowe, who was not Jewish at all, and he ran the whole thing and he was brilliant," says Creme. "It was his idea to have some kind of an art club and I thought that would be fun. So I went to the first meeting of the art club and that's where I met Kev and we became friends."

Born in September 1947, Laurence Creme – soon to be known by his nickname Lol – had also grown up in the Prestwich area of Manchester, living next door to Stephen Jacobson, who would become guitarist in The Whirlwinds and later The Mockingbirds. Creme's father, Harold, was a trader working on market stalls in the north of England. During his time at King David School on Eaton Road, Crumsall, Creme developed an ability to draw and harboured the ambition to one day become a cartoonist. "Even as a little kid I'd always had this big thing of wanting to work for Walt Disney when I grew up," says Creme. "I was quite certain about it. I was always drawing pictures and then later cartoons and I was very disciplined and passed my 11-plus exam because I knew that was the way to get to art college and then be a cartoonist."

Godley and Creme were both huge film buffs. From Hollywood musicals such as *An American In Paris* and *West Side Story* to more contemporary movies, they both had a love of cinema that would stay with them for the rest of their lives. So when Godley decided to borrow an 8mm cine camera from his father's shop in order to make a home movie of *Dracula*, he mentioned it to the new friend he'd met at art club. The idea of making a movie greatly appealed to Creme and he was keen to get involved.

"I was auditioned for the part of the hunchback," says Creme. "I got the part. I had my own hunch! It was my first brush with showbiz." The fact that there was no hunchback in the story of *Dracula* was immaterial. It would be the start of a personal and creative partnership that would flourish over the next three decades.

"My closest friend was Lol," says Godley. "We'd both been a bit strange as kids. We didn't have the normal interests of 12-year-old kids. We were into arty things, whereas most 12-year-olds weren't."

Deciding to create a home movie at such a young age demonstrated a remarkable ambition. Looking back, Kevin Godley believes that applied ignorance has played a key role in many of his most successful creative endeavours.

"We didn't really know anything about filmmaking but I can borrow an 8mm camera and I can try stuff," says Godley. "If I'd known what people go through to get films made, I probably would have said, 'Oh, fuck that!' But I'm deadly serious, whether it's music or videos, as soon as you know what the rules are they become barriers. If you don't know what the rules are, you just try stuff, which is exactly what we did. The problem is the more you try, the more you learn. I've always subscribed to keep a certain amount of knowledge at bay, so it's more about what you think you can do as opposed to what everyone's telling you. I think our careers, at least mine, are based on sheer ignorance at every level. I think that's what happened in 10cc."

Having progressed to Stand Grammar School in Whitefield, Lol Creme put his artistic skills to use by drawing cartoons of his teachers. He and Godley, and their arty mates, would hang out together. "There was this murky coffee bar where all the artistic types went and we'd go down there with our sunglasses on and our sketchbooks and draw," recalls Creme. "In the dark, we couldn't see a thing, but we'd draw."

Then, as he entered his teens, Creme discovered music. "I got into music as a hobby when I was about thirteen. Things took a turn for the worse educationally when I discovered the guitar."

The first records that caught his attention were Rebel Rouser and Shazam by Duane Eddy and Apache by The Shadows. As he entered his teenage years, music was also becoming an increasingly important passion for Godley. Like Creme, he too was greatly enamoured of Duane Eddy's Shazam.

"I would play it over and over," recalls Godley. "It was a meaningful moment. It was *my* moment. It was something that belonged to me. The sound this record made – the incredible noise – it was a visceral experience, just like Hound Dog, Shazam more than anything of that particular period of time, just nailed it for me. That twangy guitar sound, that roughness – I just loved it. It was simple; it wasn't hard to digest. It said everything that needed to be said without any words." For Godley, music gave him a sense of belonging that organised religion had failed to do. "That world was my parents' world and it meant nothing," says Godley. "It was hypocritical. They were probably typical Jewish parents. They made you go to the synagogue. You weren't supposed to drive on the Sabbath but, of course, they drove, they just parked around the corner. It was like, 'this is bullshit'. Meaningless. I had my own version of that and it was all music. Music said everything about who we were. It represented our very inner beings. Never with any thought of being professionals, just for the hell of it."

Godley and Gouldman would later immortalise the feeling of being teenage boys forced to go to the synagogue by their parents while sharing a rebel moment in the song Barry's Shoes. Being teenagers at the time, they were looking for something to give them a sense of identity; and rock 'n' roll provided that.

"It was all about becoming a teenager," says Godley. "Sex and smoking and the music. The whole identity, everything about it. It vaguely felt like we were part of something new. It was the opposite way to how all the straight kids were going. I knew if I became a dentist I'd lose my hair at thirty. There was a sense that something was coming. The American influence came to England very, very gradually. And it came via Elvis; it was like a visitation from an alien life form. We thought, 'Wow! This is what life is, this is what life could be'. And we all bought into it – lock, stock and Fender. And we all joined bands. Everybody joined bands."

Borrowing a Hofner 50 bass guitar from his dad's shop, Godley joined his first band, Group 17.

"I wasn't very good at it, but my next door neighbour, who was a rich boy, got a drum kit for his birthday," recalls Godley. "I visited one day when he was playing and he was dreadful. He couldn't quite get the coordination together. I sat down behind the kit and somehow it all felt natural, much more so than bass or guitar. Playing drums was the first time I really created music."

Lol Creme formed his own band, The Sabres, with his cousin, Neil Levine, on lead guitar. He asked Godley to join them on drums. They rehearsed at the Jewish Lads' Brigade and included songs such as Walk Don't Run by The Ventures and Love Potion No.9 in their repertoire. At the JLB they would run into

Graham Gouldman's group The Whirlwinds, who also rehearsed there.

"There was a rivalry between us, but The Whirlwinds were definitely the most successful," recalls Godley. "They got more bookings for weddings and bar mitzvahs, dressed in more expensive suits, had better equipment, and were allowed to rehearse in the larger room at the club, while we were cramped into a smaller room at the back."

When The Whirlwinds released their first single in May 1964, a cover of Buddy Holly's Look At Me, Graham Gouldman had yet to start writing songs himself. It was actually Lol Creme who was the first of the future members of 10cc to start writing songs, coming up with Baby Not Like You for Gouldman's group when they needed their first b-side. The song, a tale of teenage betrayal, was the first song that Creme ever had published and The Whirlwinds' recording had more energy and excitement than the a-side.

"I had just started writing a bit, about the time The Beatles were beginning to happen," recalls Creme. "Graham needed a song, so I gave him Baby Not Like You. I always loved that track because of Graham's guitar solo. I was thrilled when I heard it because Graham's an incredible guitar player."

Creme developed his own guitar playing skills and became friendly with the manager of the Oasis club, often sneaking in to see bands playing. During this time, long before they would ever meet, Creme recalls seeing Eric Stewart on stage as part of The Emperors of Rhythm. Whenever a band was playing at the club, the manager would call Creme if one of their guitarists had been taken ill.

"My big thrill was being asked to back up Bo Diddley when he appeared there," says Creme. "Another night I deputised for The Wailers, which was the group that later changed its name to Herman's Hermits. On another big night, I played a gig at the end of the pier in Blackpool backing Johnny Kidd."

At weekends, Godley would work in his father's shop. He knew instinctively that his future did not involve taking over the family business.

"I wasn't remotely interested in being in the business," says Godley. "I helped out in the shop on Saturdays but I was crap behind the till. I couldn't sell anything to save my life. I tried, though. Spent days as a teenager behind the counter demonstrating radios badly. Tape recorders, badly. Giving out the wrong change. I was hopeless. I just wanted to take everything home and play with it."

With neither of them having any intention of following in their fathers' footsteps, both Godley and Creme decided to study at art college. "Lol and I had both managed to persuade our parents that we should be at art college," recalls Godley. "It kept our parents believing that we were studying to get a degree so that we could get really good jobs in commercial art. But it was really an excuse to fuck about."

The decision to go to art college did not go down well with Godley's father. "Mum was fine, Dad wasn't," says Godley. "I was supposed to go into the family business but couldn't hack it. The only thing I could do well was draw. There really was no other choice for me. Once it became obvious that I wasn't future boss material they gave up and sent me to art school to become a qualified graphic designer."

After a time at Manchester College of Art, Godley enrolled for his pre-diploma at Ashton-under-Lyne College of Art where Lol Creme joined him. It was here that they met someone who would have a profound influence on their lives – their lecturer, Bill Clarke. He would always encourage his students to step out of their comfort zone.

"If you used a pencil he'd give you a brush; if you worked in full colour he'd say use one colour," recalls Godley. "He would say, 'Try painting with your left hand if you're right-handed', 'Try painting with your eyes closed', anything to switch off access to the obvious and force us to take a step into the unknown. He would challenge your technique to get something radically different from you that was unexpected. And I think that approach has stayed with us unconsciously throughout our creative lives. It shaped our ethos: 'If you know how it's going to turn out, do it another way.'" Having moved on to Stoke-on-Trent College of Art to study for his diploma in graphic design, Godley accepted Graham Gouldman's invitation to join him in a new group he was forming called The Mockingbirds. The group would sometimes rehearse at a warehouse that Godley's father owned on Friday Street. One warm summer's day, they found themselves jamming to Ravel's *Bolero* – not the usual material for a beat group at the time.

"We ploughed on for hours, the dynamics dipping and rising, everyone soloing and dropping back, then firing up again, the tempo holding steady and strong, regardless of how exhausted we were," recalls Godley. "It felt as if Ravel himself was conducting, pulling chords and rhythms out of us, throwing combinations of licks, runs, rolls and crashes back and forth. Don't want to get all spiritual bollocks about it but it truly was a magical session that I can still feel in my bones if I dig deep enough."

Yet, despite Gouldman's success as a songwriter for bands like The Hollies and The Yardbirds, The Mockingbirds never broke through.

"Just about all the songs we recorded were Graham's songs, but nothing happened," says Godley. "It was amazing. He was a very big writer at the time but the group chemistry didn't make it together. A lot of time and effort went into The Mockingbirds but it just didn't happen. We certainly weren't jealous of Graham's success because, if anything, it gave us a better chance of success."

All the while, The Mockingbirds were busy playing gigs, travelling to each one cramped with their equipment in the back of a Thames van. Kevin Godley has very vivid recollections of a typical gig with The Mockingbirds.

"Setting up our gear in 10 minutes flat then bashing out an hour of sophisticated soul for a crowd of pissed yobs and scrubbers speed-shagging behind the venue curtains did little to improve our confidence or status but we couldn't help ourselves," he says. "We were obsessed with music and, in that respect, were a typical band of the period playing our hearts out, night after night, in the belief that one day we'd be huge. I loved playing drums, the whole vibe, hiding at the back, being the engine of the band."

However, playing with the band, and studying for his diploma, increasingly became a challenge for Godley.

"I was still at art college and would have to get up at 6am, travel 60 miles, play a gig at night, travel back home and then get up at 6am the next morning," says Godley. "I was spending more time playing than doing graphic design and the college had a word with me about it. Eventually it just got too much so I split from the group."

Creme had enrolled at Birmingham College of Art. Despite studying at different colleges, Godley and Creme stayed in touch throughout their student days and would work together on a number of artistic projects. One involved writing a poem called Pamela and making an accompanying film for a film festival. Nothing came of it, but Graham Gouldman liked the poem and would use the lyrics for a new song Pamela, Pamela that would go on to be a big hit for Wayne Fontana. Godley and Creme earned £12 for their contribution.

By now the pair had developed a very broad and eclectic musical palette. Their love of Hollywood musicals gave them an appreciation of songwriters such as George Gershwin; but they also loved R&B and Motown. "We used to have a thing at the local pub every Friday night," recalls Godley. "People used to dance their socks off and get completely wrecked. A lot of great music was played, particularly Ain't That Peculiar by Marvin Gaye. I just loved it."

Looking back, Godley says the only thing he learned at art college was "how to dance and smoke weed." As their musical palette expanded, Godley and Creme also got into jazz. "Lol would drive down in a van from Birmingham to Stoke-on-Trent, where I was at art college, with a Hammond organ in the back," recalls Godley. "We would play loud, weird jazz all night. Annoy the neighbours."

Of course, The Beatles were also a major influence. Having given up touring, they had been liberated from writing and recording songs that had to be performed live and had therefore taken a much more experimental approach in the studio. The groundbreaking album that followed, released in June 1967, had a major impact on Godley. "I remember the day that Sgt Pepper came out," he recalls. "Everyone in college stopped working and was listening. There was a different song playing in every room. Everything changed. I didn't understand what I was listening to. Hang on, these guys have just stepped into the future and left us behind! We need to catch up real fast!" It was during this period that the two of them started writing their first songs together. "The first song we ever wrote was something called Seeing Things Green and probably the second thing we wrote was something called Cowboys and Indians," recalls Godley.

The pair recorded demos of the songs they had written on a Revox at Graham Gouldman's house and, using these demos, secured a recording contract with CBS Records. Recording sessions took place at Olympic Studios in London, where at least six Godley/Creme songs were recorded. Calling themselves The Yellow Bellow Room Boom – for reasons no one can now remember – their first single, Seeing Things Green, was released in January 1968, with Easy Life on the b-side.

"Imagine the summer of love painted by Lowry," says Godley. "We were just copying everyone else."

New Musical Express hailed it as an "impressive debut" but, unfortunately, it failed to chart and while two follow-up singles – The Best Seaside In The World coupled with Bull In A China Shop and One and One Make Love backed with Over and Above My Head – made it onto acetate they were never released. Even better was the plaintive Chaplin House, arguably Godley and Creme's best song from this period, which was also recorded but not released.

By now they were also being influenced by Bob Dylan, specifically his lyric writing. "It was saying in words what we were learning in paint and design," says Godley. "It was doing stuff with words that I'd never heard before. This new vocabulary was staggering. It was a whole new thing plugged into pop music. A whole new thing we could play with, another invention that was adding to what we now understood music to be. It was exhilarating."

Dylan's influence could be heard on a new Godley/Creme song called I'm Beside Myself. One day Godley dropped round to Graham Gouldman's house to play him the song "I'd just started listening to Bob Dylan and figured he was writing any old shit that came into his head," recalls Godley, "so I did exactly the same, and God bless him, Graham's dad dissected the meaning of this lyric and found meaning where there was none. Like a true Dylanologist."

For Kevin Godley, leaving art college was a sad moment. "I'd learned a little about graphic design but a lot about myself," says Godley. "I'd discovered sex, reefer, 22-inch flares and Motown and was just getting into my stride when my course ended."

Back in Manchester, and with no income, Graham Gouldman and his manager Harvey Lisberg offered to pay Godley and Creme a small weekly retainer. In return, they would undertake commissions, such as a mural for Lisberg's house. They would also put their art school training to use by designing and drawing the models for a series of children's books for *The Charge of the Light Brigade*, *Cromwell* and *The Railway Children*. But their passion, at the time, was elsewhere.

"By then we were getting more and more interested in music again, and the art work we were doing was just a way of earning some money," says Godley. "Graham and Harvey were interested in the songs we were writing and they were managing us just as much to get our songs published as to get our art work accepted."

Through Graham Gouldman they came to the attention of impresario Giorgio Gomelsky, who had originally managed The Rolling Stones and, four years previously, had persuaded The Yardbirds to record For Your Love.

"I was doing some work for Giorgio Gomelsky and his Marmalade label and I brought Kevin down to the session," recalls Gouldman. "I wanted Kevin to sing on one of the songs and when Giorgio heard Kev sing he couldn't believe it – he thought his voice was just fantastic. So when Giorgio was told that Kevin wrote and sang with Lol, he got them to record an album."

Christening them Frabjoy and Runcible Spoon – partly inspired by a phrase from Edward Lear's poem *The Owl and the Pussycat* – Gomelsky signed Godley and Creme to his new Marmalade Records label. "Giorgio seemed to see us as another Simon and Garfunkel," says Godley. "He was full of ideas and thought our songs were terrific."

The recording sessions at Advision Studios in London were to be produced by Reg King, lead singer with the band The Action, and arranged by Tony Meehan. Needing other musicians to help them out, Godley and Creme enlisted the talents of Graham Gouldman, who in turn asked Eric Stewart to participate too.

"Through Graham we met Eric and really liked Eric," says Creme. "That was the first time we started a relationship with Eric Stewart." With all four of them working on the songs, the sessions effectively marked the coming together of the embryonic 10cc. Yet nothing went quite to plan.

"Everything seemed to go wrong," says Godley. "We'd travel down from Manchester for the sessions, and then when we got to London there'd be no one waiting for us in the studios and then the money ran out and the LP was never released. It was all very sad because the songs were good."

Sadly, only a couple of songs from these sessions ever saw the light of day. I'm Beside Myself was released in September 1969 as a single, with Animal Song as the b-side. A third song, To Fly Away, would surface later that year on a Marmalade compilation album called *100° Proof*, although it would be credited as solely by Godley. Nonetheless, the four future members of 10cc had collectively worked together for the first time and, although it would be another three years before they came together as 10cc, the seeds of their formation had been sown.

CHAPTER 4

STRAWBERRY BUBBLEGUM

WHILE THE MINDBENDERS HAD BEEN IN THEIR DEATH THROES, ERIC Stewart had been recording demos of his songs at a local recording studio, above a Nield and Hardy hifi shop on Great Underbank in Stockport town centre. Called Inter City Studios, it was run by Peter Tattersall.

"It was a tiny studio with some stereo equipment and the walls were lined with egg boxes for sound insulation," recalls Stewart. "There was a makeshift sort of control desk tied together with sellotape and string but it was good enough for what I wanted to do, and it was the only studio near Manchester."

Stewart enjoyed working in the studio and particularly having the opportunity, for the first time, of getting inside the control room, such as it was at Inter City. When Peter Tattersall was forced to move out of the premises, he was faced with a dilemma: relocate and start up another studio or get out of the studio business altogether. He approached Eric Stewart about the prospect of joining forces with him in a new venture. Stewart grabbed the opportunity with both hands.

"At that time I was infected with the idea of becoming a recording engineer and building a studio where I could develop my own ideas as to what a studio should be like," says Stewart.

Stewart became a director of Inter City Studios on June 24, 1968. The pair searched for a suitable location for the new studio and eventually found one when the ground floor and basement of a building at 3 Waterloo Road in Stockport became available. The building had a suitably interesting and varied past: munitions factory, television shop, illegal boxing ring and, allegedly, the factory where Sir Henry Segrave's record-breaking speedboat was built between the wars.

"So we rented the building and got the bank to loan us some money to buy some more equipment," says Stewart.

The move to the new location, however, was far from smooth. Although both Stewart and Tattersall carried out much of the work themselves the equipment, once installed, refused to work properly and the soundproofing needed to be completely redesigned in order to obtain the best acoustics. Even when rectified, it was clear that it wasn't going to be up to scratch. Getting it there would require a further injection of capital, which was beyond Stewart and Tattersall's means. They turned to Graham Gouldman, who was working with Stewart in The Mindbenders at the time, and asked if he was interested in becoming a partner in the studio. Gouldman readily accepted and became a director of Inter City Studios on September 30, 1968.

"When Eric asked me if I'd like to go in with them, I jumped at the chance," says Gouldman, "because I'd always wanted to have a studio of my own, though everyone warned us at the time that we were mad to try to establish a major studio in Stockport. They all said you couldn't do it in Stockport, so far from the centre of the music business."

Undeterred, they set about turning it into a proper studio, having secured additional support from Stewart's former manager Ric Dixon and his business partner Danny Betesh, as much for their air of respectability with the banks as for their further financial input. Their connections with the local music scene, as part of Kennedy Street Enterprises, would also greatly aid the studio's chances of success. With Tattersall, Stewart, Gouldman, Dixon and Betesh all helping out, the new soundproofing was installed and the studio was ready for business, becoming the UK's first fully professional recording studio outside London. Deciding to dispense with the name Inter City Studios they resolved to come up with an alternative that would help them stand out from other studios at the time, which were mostly named after the record companies that owned them. Stewart's favourite Beatles song provided the inspiration.

"We called it Strawberry Studios after Strawberry Fields Forever," says Stewart.

The recording set-up at Strawberry involved two stereo machines slaved together. By bouncing between machines as you recorded, it was possible to add more overdubs. Stewart used the studio to record demos of songs he hoped to get placed with Feldman's music publishers. At least six demos were recorded at Strawberry: House of the Past, And My Love, Simple Man, She Cries, Mary Collinto and Ever Since I Can Remember. Elsewhere, Ric Dixon booked the studio to produce The Syd Lawrence Orchestra's first album and would go on to record a dozen albums with the band at Strawberry over the next 15 years. Lawrence's son, Martin, would even become an engineer in the studio and go on to work with the members of 10cc.

One of the first bands to record at Strawberry was Ankh, the brainchild of Dave Rohl, who would later become an engineer at the studio and, later still, a famous Egyptologist. Ankh had signed to Vertigo, and the album they recorded at Strawberry was produced by Eric Stewart, who remembers Rohl regaling everyone with tales of his trips to Egypt. The album would never be released, but Stewart was impressed by the band's drummer, Paul Burgess.

In the meantime, still working as a house writer for Kasenetz Katz, Gouldman had suggested that he record some of the songs he had written for them at Strawberry. Kasenetz Katz, seeing the cost-effectiveness of doing this, agreed to book the studio solidly for a three-month period to record Gouldman's songs.

"It was a most extraordinary stroke of good luck for us," says Stewart. "I still had some money coming in from songwriting royalties when The Mindbenders ended, because I had written the b-sides of some of their hits, but I'd run through all of that getting Strawberry started and was nearly broke when Kasenetz Katz came along."

With the sessions due to start in September 1969, Gouldman and Stewart needed other musicians to help out with the recordings. Having worked together on the recent Frabjoy and Runcible Spoon sessions, it was a natural progression to ask Kevin Godley and Lol Creme if they were interested in getting involved. Their initial reaction, however, was to reject the offer out of hand, wanting nothing to do with the kind of music for which Kasenetz Katz were renowned.

"They'd always had very high ambitions and believed in what

they were doing musically," says Gouldman. "They were absolutely appalled at recording the stuff that Kasenetz Katz wanted. I really had to persuade them to do it and in the end it was only the money that did it. We were all paid very well to churn out that stuff but it was not a time we look back on with any feeling of pride."

With Godley and Creme now on board, the embryonic 10cc spent the next three months churning out a stream of (mostly) instantly forgettable pop songs, almost as if they were working on a musical production line.

"We did a lot of tracks in a very short time," says Godley. "It was really like a machine. A lot of crap really, real shit. We used to do the voices, everything, it saved them money. We even did the female backing vocals!"

Among the Gouldman songs recorded during this period were Together, Gimme Love, When He Comes and Come On Plane. Some Godley and Creme songs would also be recorded during these sessions, such as There Ain't No Umbopo, an intriguing tale of an explorer searching for adventure in the forests of Borneo. All of these recordings, recorded at Strawberry by Gouldman, Stewart, Godley and Creme – with Godley taking the majority of the lead vocals – would be released over the next couple of years under a variety of different band names owned by Kasenetz Katz, such as Crazy Elephant, Silver Fleet and Fighter Squadron.

"Singles kept coming out under strange names that had really been recorded by us," says Creme. "I've no idea how many there were or what happened to them all."

Nor did they particularly care.

"I should think that the wax cringed when those records were pressed, they were so bad," joked Godley.

It is unlikely, then, that any of the band's members celebrated the release in 2003 of a compilation album called *Strawberry Bubblegum*, which brought together 23 songs from their pre-10cc days. While the material ranges from the sublime to the ridiculous, the package itself was put together with a great deal of care and featured detailed sleevenotes by David Wells, along with lots of archive images. In addition to some of the Kasenetz Katz recordings, it also included some of the other weird and wonderful projects that came through the doors of Strawberry Studios at the time.

With the Kasenetz Katz sessions completed, Gouldman married his wife Susan in November 1969 at the Holy Law Synagogue in Prestwich, resplendent in a black velvet suit and black silk top hat. The couple honeymooned in New York, with Gouldman staying on afterwards to continue writing for Kasenetz Katz now that their three-month booking of Strawberry had come to an end.

Back at Strawberry, the income from the sessions had been reinvested into the studio, enabling Eric Stewart and Peter Tattersall to upgrade to a new four-track Ampex tape machine. Stewart was keen to try it out as soon as it was installed and invited Godley and Creme down to the studio to put the new equipment through its paces. Stewart asked Godley to continuously play a drum pattern in the studio while he experimented with getting the best drum sound in the control room. Then they started to see what would happen if they overlaid additional drum sounds.

"We started experimenting to see how many drum tracks we could physically get on that tape by jumping stereo tracks backwards and forwards," recalls Stewart. "After about eight drum tracks, we realised there was a chant going in the background – it was Lol, about 12 feet away from the drums, just singing to keep Kevin in time on the kit."

Never intending it to be recorded, Creme had sat on the studio floor with an acoustic guitar singing a nonsense verse about a Neanderthal man just to accompany Godley while he laid down his drum tracks. The microphone on Godley's bass drum had picked up Creme singing the chant, which was something the pair had come up with while travelling in the back of a London taxi en route to a Frabjoy and Runcible recording session. It went: '*I'm a Neanderthal man / You're a Neanderthal girl / Let's make Neanderthal love / In the Neanderthal world.*'

The whole thing sounded strange and might well have remained just a musical experiment had it not been for another stroke of good luck. Dick Leahy of Philips Records, who knew Stewart from his days with The Mindbenders, and had heard of his involvement in a studio in Stockport, decided to drop in at Strawberry unannounced, while up in Manchester on business. On the basis of what he'd heard, Leahy offered, much to their amazement, a £500 advance to release the song on the Philips label.

"In all the time I'd been with The Mindbenders, no one had ever offered me money for a record," says Stewart. "It was a great confidence booster and made us realise that having made an investment Philips would work that much harder to make the record a hit, so that they would get their advance back. It couldn't have come at a better time. I'd run through all the money I'd made with The Mindbenders and was just on the point of selling my house and moving to somewhere smaller, so that I'd have a little more capital to put into the business. It was something that neither my wife nor I were very happy about, but we realised we had to do it if we were going to give Strawberry the money it needed, and then along came Dick Leahy. It was a godsend."

Unfortunately, disaster struck before the song – to be called, naturally enough, Neanderthal Man – could be released. Someone at the studio accidently erased the master tapes meaning Stewart, Godley and Creme had to try and recreate their experiment from scratch. While doing so they took the opportunity to restructure it slightly.

"Eric wrote the middle eight and we finished it off properly," says Creme. "We did it again and it was better because it had a structure."

With Neanderthal Man ready for release, the three of them now had to decide what to call themselves.

"We had no name for the group, of course," says Stewart, "but we had a secretary at the studio called Kathy Gillbourne, who had very, very nice legs and she used to wear these incredible hot pants. Green, leather hot pants. So we called the group Hotlegs!"

Fortunately the trio passed over Stewart's original suggestion of Hot Thighs. Coupled with the wonderfully titled You Didn't Like It Because You Didn't Think of It, Neanderthal Man was released in June 1970.

"It was one of those singles that you either loved or you couldn't stand," recalls Harvey Lisberg. "I'm not so certain that the group themselves were too sure about it, but after only six plays on Radio One they found themselves with a hit."

As the song entered the charts, the band got the call to appear on the influential BBC TV show *Top of the Pops*. An appearance on the show almost guaranteed further chart success and this proved to be the case.

"It was selling 3,000 a day before we did *Top of the Pops*," said Eric Stewart at the time. "Last week it sold 35,000. It looks likely to be a big seller." As the record climbed the charts, the band took time out to attend the Reading Festival in early August. "We camped there over the weekend," recalls Stewart. "We woke up one morning to the sound of Neanderthal Man playing outside our tent. When we walked outside the song was being played on thousands of radios across this huge muddy field. It was a magical moment."

Kevin Godley vividly remembers this moment too. "One minute I was just another punter lying in a rock festival tent, out in a field," says Godley. "The next I woke up to the sound of our record playing on thousands of other people's radios. That was a life-changing moment. If hearts could orgasm it would probably feel just like that."

Neanderthal Man would go on to reach No.2 in the UK charts, where it would stay for two weeks, kept off the No.1 spot by Elvis Presley's The Wonder of You. To help promote the single around the world the band made a promotional film. Nearly 50 years later, Godley came across it again online. "I've recently discovered a video we did, on YouTube, the three of us in this studio, with scantily clad girls doing Hot Gossip moves, while we just look like a bunch of knobs in a studio," said Godley.

Neanderthal Man would go on to become a huge global hit, selling over 2 million copies around the world, and reaching No.1 in Italy and France, No.3 in Switzerland, No.4 in Germany, No.7 in Austria and becoming a major hit in Canada, Australia and Japan. In America, a recording and production deal was struck with Capitol Records, which allegedly guaranteed the group a minimum income of $500,000 over a four-year period. Upon its release, Neanderthal Man clocked up sales of 250,000 in just four days, eventually reaching the US Top 30.

Yet with its repetitive lyrics and plodding, monotonous rhythm, it is hard to conceive of a song more the antithesis of everything that 10cc would become.

"We wrote it in the back of a taxi on the way to a session and it went to No.1," says Creme. "No one was more surprised than we were!"

Confusingly, just as Neanderthal Man was scaling the charts, Stewart, Godley and Creme released another single, a new slower, extended version of There Ain't No Umbopo under the band name Doctor Father. Released on the Pye record label, it wasn't commercially successful but would become an important stepping-stone in the formation of 10cc, when it came to the attention of legendary singer-songwriter Neil Sedaka. However, with Hotlegs now a chart item, it made sense to continue the group as a going concern.

"We have already started work on a first album, consisting of a conglomeration of songs which we have written ourselves, and we have a future album planned which will have a theme running through it," said Eric Stewart in an interview with *Melody Maker* in late July. "There is also a follow-up single to decide on. We have two possibilities. One is a beautiful ballad called Today with Kevin singing at his best. We haven't given a title to the other thing yet."

Yet rather than capitalise on their hit record, the band chose instead to enjoy the spoils of their success.

"I'm afraid we blew the whole thing," says Godley. "The first thing we did was take a holiday and because I'd never been able to afford a good holiday I flew off to Antigua. We also bought cars as soon as we came back and then went into the studio to make the Hotlegs album. Anyone could tell you what we did wrong. We should have stayed in England, gone on tour, made promotional appearances, given interviews to the press, TV and so on, but we just vanished to Antigua."

Living the rock star cliché, Godley bought himself a new sports car with his royalties – a white Lotus Elan with pop-up headlights.

"One time in a petrol station, feeling a tiny bit pop star pleased with myself, I was preening in a window next to the Lotus and promptly locked myself out of the car," says Godley. "No spare key. None at the gas station. Customers honking to get gas. Hours of bum-clenching embarrassment later I was released by the AA and drove home with my ego between my legs. Fame karma ... the worst kind."

Lol Creme suffered a similar kind of fame karma when he

pranged his newly purchased Aston Martin soon after in an accident. However, it turned out to be a blessing in disguise.

"I was feeling very depressed, so I went round to Eric's house," recalls Creme.

Staying with the Stewarts at the time was Gloria's sister, Angie. Creme had met her before but this time something clicked. "She cleaned up my wounds," says Creme. "And then rather than sit about feeling depressed I suggested that we go out together. So we went out for a meal and that was it!"

Meanwhile, Strawberry Studios had benefited from the success of Neanderthal Man with royalties reinvested into a further upgrade. "With the success of Neanderthal Man we bought an eight-track for the studio and got a real control desk in and we started letting the studio out to people in Manchester," says Stewart. "Before that it was basically a private studio for me and the other writers. So, now it became a successful, working studio."

With the new eight-track equipment in place, work continued on material for Hotlegs during the remainder of 1970. By October they had completed work on an ambitious 13-minute song in three parts called Suite FA, which Kevin Godley would later describe as "our version of side two of *Abbey Road*." They also had a fragment of another song, built around a melody line and the refrain *'You don't know how to ease my pain'*, but they were unable to complete it to their satisfaction. It would remain unfinished for the next 15 years. While working on the Hotlegs album, the group re-recorded some of their Frabjoy and Runcible Spoon songs, such as Fly Away. Stewart's songwriting contribution to the band could be heard on more bluesy numbers such as Run Baby Run.

"Kevin and myself write soft, melodic stuff, sort of Simon and Garfunkel things, and Eric is more into the blues and heavy music. So the album will be a combination of those two sides," said Lol Creme at the time.

The group themselves appeared to be in no hurry to issue a follow-up to Neanderthal Man.

"We're not going to rush one out just for the sake of having a follow-up," said Godley at the time. "If the record is good it'll have a better chance, so we might as well wait and get a good song."

In fact the group's profile was so low that it sparked a series of rumours in the music industry that Hotlegs had split up.

"Hotlegs are not a group in the accepted sense," said Godley at the time. "We don't play gigs, for instance. We're just three people with separate interests and one of those interests is Hotlegs. So it's always difficult with rumours because there's no group in the accepted sense that can split up."

Another of those interests was a new musical device that Godley and Creme had invented called the 'Gizmo'. It was born out of a desire to recreate the sound of strings without the expense of having to hire an orchestra.

"We were doing a session one night and we strapped Lol's Stratocaster to the wall and got an electric drill with a big rubber knob on the end and ploughed into the strings," says Godley. "From there we graduated to an electric toothbrush with a plectrum at somebody's party one night. Then it was elastic bands and electric motors until we found a way to do it."

Eric Stewart remembers the moment when Godley's experiments with an electric toothbrush gave them the breakthrough they were seeking. "We were at a party at Neil Levine's house," recalls Stewart. "Suddenly, Kevin leapt out of the bathroom with an electric toothbrush and played it against the strings of a guitar. The 'Gizmo' was born! I remember the party well. The police later raided it looking for drugs. Neil threw the grass that we had out of the window to get rid of the evidence but it bounced off the roof of the police car! Fortunately, the police didn't notice!"

In the meantime, progress on new material for Hotlegs was dissipated by their work as house band at Strawberry, where they wrote, performed or produced an extraordinarily diverse range of artists that came through the studio's doors. One project saw Stewart, Godley and Creme co-write and produce a single with northern comedian John Davidge called The Man From Nazareth. Released in November 1970 under the name John Paul Jones, it was well on its way to becoming a big Christmas hit when an injunction from the other John Paul Jones – Gouldman's former collaborator and now Led Zeppelin bass player – forced the record to be withdrawn and rereleased with the artist's name respelt John Paul Joans to avoid confusion. Despite this, it was still a Top 30 hit. Another project saw Gouldman co-write San Tokay with future Alan Parsons Project founder Eric Woolfson. The song was recorded at Strawberry with Gouldman, Stewart, Godley and Creme providing backing and with Stewart producing. It was released by Philips in January 1971, with Woolfson using the pseudonym Eric Elder, but it soon disappeared into obscurity.

By the beginning of 1971 the Hotlegs album was finally completed. Entitled *Thinks: School Stinks*, the album was released in America by Capitol in March 1971, with an ingenious album cover designed by Godley and Creme themselves. Replicating an old wooden school desk that opened to reveal its contents inside, it was an idea that would be echoed the following year for the Alice Cooper album, *School's Out*.

Thinks: School Stinks received some good reviews in America, with *Billboard* predicting that it "should prove a big item in the Top LP chart." However, neither the album nor its accompanying single, How Many Times, troubled the US charts and the album wasn't even issued by Philips in the UK.

While the music on *Thinks: School Stinks* was perfectly fine, it lacked the invention, humour and lyrical dexterity for which 10cc would go on to be renowned, not to mention the hooks. Instead it sounded very derivative, something that the group themselves weren't unduly bothered about at the time.

"The first Hotlegs album was very influenced by The Beatles and The Beach Boys and we were pleased that it sounded like a real record, i.e. it sounded like somebody else," says Godley.

Meanwhile, Graham Gouldman had come to the end of his time working for Kasenetz Katz in America; Freddie and The Dreamers had recorded a song called Susan's Tuba which lyrically marked a low point for Gouldman: '*It's Susan on the tuba / Oo be doo be doo ba / Everybody's feeling fine / Hey hey hey / Oo be doo be doo ba / Susan on the tuba / Hey hey hey hey hey.*' Amazingly, it would go on to reach No.1 in France and sell over a million copies worldwide.

Gouldman's return to the UK was hastened by the global success of Neanderthal Man. Kevin Godley immortalised the moment in a drawing. "Kevin drew this amazing cartoon of our manager, Harvey Lisberg, calling Graham in New York, with a speech caption that said, 'They're having hits, get yourself back over here!'" recalls Stewart. "The cartoon had Graham leaping across the Atlantic, with his bags in one hand and his guitar in the other. It was brilliant!"

With the future of Hotlegs uncertain, Stewart, Godley, Creme and now Gouldman continued to work as the house band at Strawberry. One project involved working on a concept album called *Space Hymns* that was the brainchild of former jazz singer, and then central heating salesman, Barrington Frost, who believed himself to be the reincarnation of the Egyptian god, Ramesses II. Along with his wife, Dorothy – who had similarly reinvented herself as the goddess of cures and protection, Selket – the pair had released a couple of singles under the name of Ramases without success and by 1970 had travelled to New York to gauge interest in their new songs. They met Harvey Lisberg there, who suggested recording them at Strawberry with Stewart, Gouldman, Godley and Creme providing musical support and production. The project would be an important one in the development of 10cc. Looking back, Godley describes it as "our creative breakthrough", the first example of the band using Strawberry as an instrument itself, pushing the boundaries and deploying the latest technology, including one of the first Moog synthesizers in the UK.

"Production-wise, *Space Hymns*, really opened the floodgates and pointed a way forwards," says Godley. "The technology caught up with the way we were thinking and therefore we finally could actually do things a lot quicker and a lot more thoroughly."

Released by Vertigo in August 1971 – wrapped in an expansive sleeve designed by Roger Dean, which allegedly showed the steeple of St George's church in Stockport blasting off into the cosmos – *Space Hymns* was not a chart success but would go on to enjoy a cult following. Among its fans was Swedish actor Peter Stormare, who would go on to release an anthology of all Ramases recordings in 2014 on his own StormVox record label. *Mojo* described *Space Hymns* as a "shimmering gem that time's tomb plunderers overlooked."

In the meantime, belated attempts were being made to try and relaunch Hotlegs. After keeping such a low profile for much of the previous year, the next few months would see the release of a new single, a repackaged version of their album and the band's first live appearances. This time they took the bold decision to distance themselves from Neanderthal Man – excluding it from their repackaged album, to be called *Song*, and their setlist when they played live. They hoped that their new single, Lady Sadie, would provide some fresh momentum upon its release in September 1971.

"It's many months since Hotlegs erupted on the pop scene with their startling Neanderthal Man and we seem to have been waiting ages for a worthy successor," said *New Musical Express*. "Well, here it is at last and in its own way it's equally as compelling and fascinating as the last one."

Its release coincided with the band's first live dates, supporting The Moody Blues on their upcoming tour of the UK. The support slot was a direct result of Eric Stewart's friendship with Justin Hayward.

"We'd wanted to play live ever since Neanderthal Man," said Stewart at the time. "The problem was purely a financial one. At that time we'd no cash. Royalties take ages to come through and as we are all well into recording techniques we were determined not to go on the road until we could afford the equipment for a perfect sound. There was no point in just going on stage with four mikes and blasting away. We'd have done ourselves no good at all. As it happens we were asked by The Moodies to join them on tour, though I had dropped a few gentle hints. I've known Justin Hayward well for a long time and some time before the tour I met him in London. He wanted to hear the album, and when he did he was so knocked out he persuaded the others to let us on the tour."

Billed as 'Hotlegs and Friends', Stewart, Godley and Creme were joined on the tour by Graham Gouldman on bass, keyboard player Mike Timoney (who had guested on *Song* and recorded his own album *The Astounding Sound of the Cordovox* at Strawberry) and second drummer Mike Gilbourne. The tour opened in London at the Royal Festival Hall on October 30, 1971, and with Stewart, Gouldman, Godley and Creme all involved, the gig effectively marked the concert debut of the embryonic 10cc.

It was Godley and Creme's first experience of playing to an audience of such a size. "I don't think I've ever been so nervous as I was that first night at the Royal Festival Hall," says Godley. "I was actually retching backstage before we went on but I was very conscious of how important it was. We played for 40 minutes and that was one of the most exciting 40 minutes of my life with 3,000 people out there in the audience. I have the clearest memories of it because of that amazingly horrible feeling I had beforehand and then this incredible feeling as we were playing. I was so high with the excitement of it all."

Despite their nervousness, the group gained good reviews in the music press but unfortunately the tour was curtailed when John Lodge of The Moody Blues was taken ill. Still, the gigs seemed to galvanise the band.

"Lol and Kevin have just started writing again after a long gap," said Stewart at the time. "I suppose the tour inspired them but we've all also been so bound up with the studios and other things that we've not really thought about Hotlegs. From now on, it's the band first though."

In December 1971, *Song* was released in the UK featuring a sleeve that was designed and drawn by Godley and Creme. The album replaced Neanderthal Man and Desperate Dan with two new songs, The Loser – the b-side to Lady Sadie – and the excellent Today, the song that Stewart had referred to as a potential follow-up to Neanderthal Man back in July 1970. It would prove to be one of the highlights of the album and was also significant in that it featured Graham Gouldman on bass and was thus one of the first recordings featuring all four future members of 10cc. However, despite this recent flurry of activity, it would prove to be too little, too late for Hotlegs. By now the band was effectively redundant.

"After we'd done the album and the tour with The Moody Blues, Hotlegs came to an abrupt end," says Stewart. "We received no offers or jobs or bookings from anyone – so we went back in the studios. I was engineering a lot of the time with other people. By now Graham had become part of it and we sat down one day and said 'Hotlegs is defunct – let's face it'."

Gouldman had one final crack at solo success, releasing the single Nowhere To Go in January 1972, produced by Eric Woolfson. He also co-wrote Because You're There with Peter Noone after the singer had left Herman's Hermits. Eric Stewart then produced two singles for The (now Herman-free) Hermits, with Peter Cowap as their new lead vocalist. The band changed their name to Sour Mash and recorded an album (*Whale of a Tale*) at Strawberry, with Stewart again in the producer's chair, although the album would not be released due to contractual problems. Another 60s veteran paying Strawberry a visit was Stewart's former bandmate, Wayne Fontana, who recorded Graham Gouldman's Together as a comeback single, with Stewart and Fontana co-producing the b-side, One Man Woman. Unfortunately the collaboration failed to get him back on the hit trail. Shirley Bassey would go on to record Together at Advision Studios, for what would become her Top 10 album *Never, Never, Never*.

Elsewhere, Eric Stewart and Graham Gouldman produced the single The Joker for Garden Odyssey – a song written by Gouldman and Barry Greenfield. In the incestuous world of Strawberry at the time, Gouldman would produce Greenfield's single Sweet America.

One bizarre chapter in the Strawberry story from around this time saw Stewart, Gouldman, Godley and Creme work on a spate of football records. Gouldman approached Everton FC about penning a single for them. He visited Goodison Park and took away a history of the club, returning 10 days later with the outline of the song For Ever Ever-ton. Even laying on a bus to bring the players from Liverpool to Stockport, Gouldman produced the song at Strawberry. Released by Philips, it sold 6,000 copies. Closer to home, the Strawberry team recorded singles for both Manchester football clubs. For United, Gouldman co-wrote Willie Morgan, which was released under the name Tristar Airbus; for City, Gouldman, Godley and Creme came up with The Boys In Blue. Quite what Gouldman's father thought of his son writing a song for his beloved Manchester United's rivals can only be imagined. While not a hit, The Boys In Blue would go on to be played at every home game ever since and in 2018 was described by City fan Noel Gallagher as "the official Manchester City theme tune". Gallagher described the b-side, Funky City, also written by Gouldman, Godley and Creme, as "even better".

The Strawberry team didn't stop there, recording singles for Leeds United and Lancashire Cricket Club, and even two songs for a local nightclub called Blinkers. It is a period that Kevin Godley looks back on like a scene from Woody Allen's *Broadway Danny Rose*.

"We paid the bills by creating audio confections for amateur ventriloquists, football teams, oddball stand-up comics, TV producers' girlfriends, a central heating salesman and his wife from Sheffield, and 'Hello' and 'Goodnight' jingles for a nightclub called Blinkers," says Godley.

A more significant visitor to the studio around this time was legendary singer-songwriter Neil Sedaka, who had sold an estimated 40 million records between 1959 and 1963 with hits such as Oh! Carol, Stairway to Heaven, Calendar Girl, Happy Birthday Sweet Sixteen and Breaking Up Is Hard To Do, but had seen his commercial success wane after 1963 as The Beatles changed the musical landscape. By 1972, Sedaka was reduced to playing on the cabaret circuit when he visited the UK. When he performed at the Golden Garter club in Manchester, Harvey Lisberg dropped by to say hello. Lisberg had met up with Sedaka – and his manager Don Kirshner – in New York the previous year seeking a song for one of his other charges, singer Tony Christie. He not only secured the song (Is This The Way To) Amarillo for Christie – a Top 20 UK hit first time around in 1971 and a No.1 in 2005 when revived by Peter Kay for *Comic Relief* – but also learned that Sedaka was a fan of the song There Ain't No Umbopo. He mentioned that the band responsible for making that record had their own studio nearby, and a few days later, Sedaka dropped into Strawberry, where Stewart, Gouldman, Godley and Creme were recording a session.

"I was extremely impressed," recalls Sedaka. "They had an extraordinary sound."

Sedaka decided to record demos of three new songs at Strawberry. While Sedaka played a residency at Batley Variety Club in West Yorkshire, Gouldman met up with him at the Queen's Hotel in Leeds to hear the songs he planned to demo and to make some chord charts so that the Strawberry team would all be prepared when he arrived. When recording started, it quickly became clear that there was a real rapport between the musicians and soon the scope of the project changed.

"He was so knocked out by the studio's atmosphere and our playing that he rang up New York, cancelled the musicians who were meant to come over and stayed and recorded the whole album with us," says Creme.

The backing tracks were laid down with Stewart in the control room engineering the sessions, while the other musicians played together at the same time in the studio: Gouldman and Creme on guitars, Godley on the drums and Sedaka at the piano. Unusually, Sedaka would record his vocal at the same time as the basic backing tracks were laid down. The rapport between the musicians meant that recording progressed quickly.

"It went like a dream," says Gouldman. "I think we finished the album in two weeks. We finished it so quickly because Neil would sing the lead vocal as we were recording. The feel of it was great. We were playing together rather than recording everything separately. Neil was a great keyboard player, he was funny and he was emotional. We really got on with him and grew very fond of him. I have a tremendous affection for both the album and working with Neil."

For all concerned, the recording of the album was a memorable experience. "It gives you such an incredible buzz to play with Neil," said Lol Creme at the time. "I mean he's our musical heritage! One night he just sat down and played a medley of his hits and it took forever. They just kept coming, one after the other. We found ourselves continually looking forward to the next day in the studio. He's such an incredible professional, he just doesn't make mistakes! When we're recording he sings and plays the piano at the same time and that vocal is the finished vocal."

The project was particularly poignant for Eric Stewart. After all, it was Sedaka's I Go Ape that had inspired him to get into music in the first place. For all of them, to be working with someone of Sedaka's standing was a dream come true, and to be doing so in their own studio in Stockport was the icing on the cake. For his part, Sedaka was equally impressed with the Strawberry team.

"Marvellous musicians, creative geniuses," says Sedaka today. "They certainly inspired me. The musicianship, the production, the playing. They bluesed it up and they pushed me in another direction. And I didn't have to look at a clock."

It had been a conscious decision, right from the early days of the studio, not to have a clock on the wall at Strawberry to constrain creativity. In its place was a sign that read: *'In the pursuit of perfection there can be no compromise.'*

Together, 11 songs were recorded, six of which Sedaka had written with his new songwriting partner, Phil Cody. Among them was the highly poignant Solitaire, its lyric using the card game as a metaphor for a man's loneliness. Feeling that the song would benefit from an orchestral arrangement, the Strawberry team drafted in Del Newman to arrange the strings. It would go on to become the title track of the new album. Elsewhere, for the first time in his career, Sedaka wrote his own lyrics for his music on tracks like That's When The Music Takes Me and Better Days Are Coming.

With recording completed, the album was mixed by Eric Stewart at Strawberry, an experience that proved eventful. "While I was mixing the album, Kevin, Lol and Graham were passing around one of these massive spliffs that Kevin used to roll," recalls Stewart. "We used to call them the 'Benson & Hedges mindfuckers', because they were so big and strong. They passed the spliff to Neil, and at that point the door to the control room in the studio opened, and in walked a policeman. Neil freaked! We all thought we were going to get busted but the policeman just said, 'Do you know that the front door of the studio is open?' I got up and accompanied the policeman off the premises, thanked him for his trouble, and walked back into the control room. I looked at Neil and he was white!"

The first single from the album, Beautiful You, gave Sedaka his first UK chart hit with new material in nearly 10 years but stalled just outside the Top 40 in November 1972. It almost reached the Top 20 in Australia too. The follow-up, That's When The Music Takes Me, was a bona fide hit single, reaching No.18 in the UK early the following year and spending 10 weeks in the Top 50. Strangely, Sedaka's version of Solitaire was never released as a single although the song would go on to become a big hit for other artists. Andy Williams' cover version would reach No.4 in the UK charts in February 1974, while The Carpenters would have a Top 20 hit in America with their version of the song. Solitaire would go on to spawn over 90 cover versions by artists as diverse as Elvis Presley, Sheryl Crow and Westlife.

The success of the *Solitaire* album gave Sedaka his critical and commercial comeback. Suitably pleased, Sedaka expressed an interest in returning to Strawberry the following spring to record his next album. Having someone of Neil Sedaka's stature record a successful album at Strawberry helped to boost the studio's credibility and enhance its reputation. As interest in the studio increased, other Manchester bands such as Barclay James Harvest chose to record there. The cynics who had said that they must be mad to open a studio in Stockport had been proven wrong.

As for Stewart, Gouldman, Godley and Creme themselves, the Sedaka sessions had not only honed their skills as musicians but also proved that they could play together as a band. Looking back, Kevin Godley sees their work with Kasenetz Katz, Ramases and Neil Sedaka as the three crucial influences in the development of 10cc. "Recording stuff with Kasenetz Katz, pretending to be various bands, was fun," recalls Godley. "Then the album we did with Ramases, *Space Hymns*, showed that, okay, we can do some really weird shit here; and then playing with Neil Sedaka as house band. Because essentially if you imagine those three things fusing together that's who we were – we were the people that could do anything, the people that could do weird shit, the people who could play together. And it was the final one, that we could play together, that led us to think maybe we can actually be a band. Those dots were joined and we went from there."

The 10cc story was about to begin.

CHAPTER 5

4% OF SOMETHING

THE SUCCESS OF NEIL SEDAKA'S SOLITAIRE ALBUM WAS THE CATALYST that prompted Eric Stewart, Graham Gouldman, Lol Creme and Kevin Godley to reassess their own future.

"There was a moment of truth," recalls Gouldman. "The four of us went out for a meal at a Chinese restaurant, and we sat down that night and just talked and talked, just realising that the time had come when we really should concentrate on doing our own work, recording our own songs and not just taking anything that came along. We knew deep down within ourselves that we were better than that, and it needed something to force us into facing that. I think it was Neil Sedaka's success that probably did it. We were a bit choked to think that we had made the whole of that first album with him, and had done it just for session fees, when we could have been recording our own material."

The Strawberry team had been recording their own songs in studio downtime. They had re-recorded the song Today, giving it a slower tempo and different arrangement. It would be released under the band name Festival by RCA later in the year, with an early Stewart/ Gouldman song, Warm Me, on the b-side. With Godley and Creme already up and running as a songwriting team, it had been a natural progression for Stewart and Gouldman to start writing together.

"Eric and I were on the same wavelength, and some of our influences crossed over with people like The Beatles and The Beach Boys, so when we first started writing together it was pretty easy. It worked straight away," recalls Gouldman. "One of the first things we ever wrote together was a song called Cry All Night. We did a demo of it at Strawberry but we never used it."

They were more enthused by their next creation, a song in the Crosby, Stills, Nash and Young vein that extolled the virtues of getting out of the city, called Waterfall. Stewart took the band's demo of it to Apple Studios in Savile Row in London, where he was overseeing the mastering of Neil Sedaka's *Solitaire* album.

"The engineer there, Georgie Peckham, suggested that I leave it with one of their executives upstairs, whose name I can't even remember. I never met him," says Stewart. "Months later he wrote back to me and said although he thought it was a very good record, he really didn't think it was commercial enough for them to release as a single. In the meantime we had recorded another track, this time one written by Kevin and Lol called Donna, which we knew had something, although we were thinking of using it as the b-side to Waterfall. It was a very silly sort of record for the time, a sort of rock 'n' roll take-off with a very high-pitched vocal and all sorts of funny sounds. We even had a telephone ringing on it."

Recorded in about eight hours, Donna had taken even less time to write. Setting out to pen a potential b-side, Godley and Creme hadn't taken the writing process entirely seriously. Deciding instead to have a bit of fun, Donna was written as an affectionate parody of the whole 50s doowop genre, with a lyric that cleverly sent up songs from that period. This not-altogether-serious approach had been carried through to the recording session. With Lol Creme adopting a Frankie Valli-esque falsetto for his lead vocal, and Godley and Gouldman weighing in with the ironic *basso profondo* backing vocals, the recording was a dead ringer for a 50s doowop track, a tribute to the group's studio skills. Donna might well have been a blatant piss-take but it occurred to them that it might have a commercial potential of its own. Unfortunately, none of the record companies they approached showed any interest in releasing the song.

Then, as luck would have it, Eric Stewart received a phone call from Jonathan King. Since meeting Stewart nine years previously, when he'd offered to manage Wayne Fontana and The Mindbenders and make them "bigger than The Beatles", King had gone on to have considerable success of his own in the music industry. Aside from his own hit records, King had discovered and named Genesis, before effectively running the Decca record label. Now he had set up his own label, UK Records. However, his first four releases on the label had all flopped.

"I was beginning to despair," says King. "I was thinking, 'I've got to find some hits', so I started phoning round a lot of friends and asking, 'Have you got anything?' One of the people I phoned was Eric Stewart and I did so for a very specific reason. Because I'd thought that Neanderthal Man by Hotlegs was a brilliant record. Brilliantly engineered, had a great, original sound to it. I was really impressed but they hadn't had anything out since. I remembered Eric from my contact in the early days of The Mindbenders so I called him up and said, 'Have you got anything?' and Eric said, 'We've got this little track but everybody's turned it down.' And I said, 'What's it called?' and he said, 'Donna'. And I said, 'Well, send it down to me.'"

Stewart sent a tape of Donna down to King's office in London's Soho Square. "I put it on and I thought, 'This is absolutely fabulous, this is an absolute smash,'" recalls King. "So immediately I wanted it and I wanted them."

King phoned Stewart straight away with an offer to release Donna. The group readily accepted but pointed out that they had no name. "Leave it with me," said King.

"I literally went to sleep with the song going through my head and during the night I had a dream that we on UK Records had a No.1 album and single on the *Billboard* chart in America and it was by 10cc," recalls King. "And I remember thinking, 'That's a really good name because it stands out, being as it's figures and letters, and it's short and it's impacty.' The reason they were called 10cc in my dream was so that I could see their name easily when I looked at the charts. Nobody else had a name starting with two numbers. So literally the next day I woke up, phoned them up and said, 'You've got your name, it's 10cc'."

Hoping that the dream would be a kind of premonition, 10cc were duly christened. It was certainly a better name than the one Kevin Godley had half-seriously suggested: Three Yids and a Yok. Members of 10cc would later embellish the story of how they got their name by claiming that King had seen a big sign with the group's name on it above Wembley Stadium in his dream; or that he saw the words '10cc: Best Band In The World' in lights outside the Hammersmith Odeon. Neither of these stories was true, however. And neither was the most apocryphal story about how 10cc got its name. "Mythology has it that the name 10cc came from the average male ejaculation being 9cc and, of course, being big butch Mancunian guys, we're gonna be, you know, 1cc more than that," says Gouldman.

The newly christened 10cc signed a one-off deal with King to release Donna on his UK Records label. Released in August 1972, with the Stewart/Gouldman-penned instrumental Hot Sun Rock on the b-side, at first it looked like it was destined to be a flop. But Jonathan King and his team at UK Records worked hard to break the record, and slowly Donna started picking up radio airplay. One of the first DJs to champion the record was John Peel on his shows *Friday Night Is Boogie Night* and *Top Gear*. Six weeks after its release, Donna finally entered the UK singles chart on September 23. 10cc had a hit on their hands.

As the single entered the Top 30 a couple of weeks later, the invitation came to appear on *Top of the Pops*. With 15 million viewers tuning into BBC1 each week to watch the programme, the appearance would be crucial to the single's success. It would also serve to introduce 10cc to the record-buying public, leaving the group with a dilemma – what image should they convey? They hadn't considered what image, if any, 10cc should have. It wasn't as if Donna had been part of some grand master plan.

"You've only got two choices," advised Jonathan King. "You either go on the show just as yourselves, wearing jeans as you usually do, or you go the whole hog, be outrageous and appear in something like polythene hot pants! There's no halfway. You've either got to play it totally straight or be outrageous."

After some discussion, the group decided to play it totally straight and go on as they normally dressed.

"We wore jeans because that's what we wear all day," explained Kevin Godley at the time. "We're just not the sort of people who can manufacture an image. Roxy Music can do it because they're all tall, snake-hipped wonders. We're short, fat creeps! These days you have to decide whether you're 'theatre' or 'music'. I think we're 'music'."

All these years later, it is interesting to speculate how the 10cc story might have panned out if they'd taken the other option and appeared on the show in polythene hot pants, landing themselves with an image that they would have had to maintain.

"You have to remember that a group only makes its break-through once and if you land yourself with an image you're stuck with it," says Stewart. "So it's got to be one that you're prepared to live with."

Ironically, when the group turned up at the studio to film their appearance on the show, presenter Tony Blackburn interpreted their resolutely non-fashionable stance as a great gimmick!

"We were amidst all that glittered fashion-wise," recalls Gouldman. "So when we walked on in our denim and jeans, Tony Blackburn walked up to us and said, 'Hey guys … great gimmick!'"

The appearance on *Top of the Pops* had the desired effect, helping to push Donna further up the charts, where it eventually reached No.2 in October, kept off the No.1 spot for two consecutive weeks by Lieutenant Pigeon's Mouldy Old Dough. Among the more than 500,000 people who bought the record was a 13-year-old boy from Basildon in Essex called Martin Gore, who "had a crush on Donna by 10cc". It was the first record he ever bought. Ten years later he would go on to enjoy his own success with Depeche Mode.

The success of Donna far and away exceeded the group's own expectations.

"I was totally unsure of what might happen," said Eric Stewart at the time. "I thought it would either be a hit or die a disastrous death. But, to be honest, I never thought it would get as high as it did."

Although clearly pleased that Donna had reached No.2, Stewart must have secretly felt he was cursed. This was the fourth time that one of his records had nearly reached the top spot in the UK only to fall at the final hurdle. For Graham Gouldman, the success was particularly sweet. He had finally achieved his ambition of having success as part of a group.

"When I was writing hits for everyone else, the one thing I wanted was to be in a band of my own," says Gouldman. "So 10cc's success was like a dream come true."

Jonathan King's prediction that Donna would be a smash hit had been proved right. It, along with Sea Side Shuffle by Terry Dactyl and The Dinosaurs and Loop Di Love by Shag, gave UK Records three much-needed Top 5 hits in the autumn of 1972. Not only did

Donna go on to become one of the year's bestselling singles in the UK it also met with some success in Europe too, reaching No.2 in both Ireland and the Netherlands, No.4 in Belgium and No.7 in France, although the song's humour seemed to get lost in translation in some quarters, leading to some interesting TV and radio promotional experiences in Europe.

"They didn't understand Donna at all," says Stewart. "They mistook Lol's voice for being female and thought we were a mad girl group! When we turned up for a TV spot in Germany they said, 'Where are the girls?'"

Outside of Europe, the record reached No.10 in New Zealand and was a minor hit in Australia. 10cc were hoping for success in America, where Donna was scheduled for release in October, distributed through London Records.

"At present our main concern is to get the record off in the States," said Stewart at the time. "If it's a success we'd like to do some concerts over there. Also, we want to have more hit singles. Just one hit doesn't mean anything these days. We found that out with Hotlegs. The whole thing was timed disastrously. We didn't follow up the hit and we released an album something like a year later, by which time we were old news. I am confident that this time we can avoid the same mistakes, but who can tell? Personally I think it's great we've been given another chance."

Sadly Donna flopped in the States, but its success elsewhere persuaded the group to continue 10cc as a going concern. King recognised that the group had huge potential and was keen to sign them to a longer-term deal. However, he also knew how expensive it would be to establish a new band through his independent record label.

"I didn't want just one hit single," says King. "I wanted a band who I could sell albums with around the world, especially in America. And I was well aware – as they were – that was going to cost. You didn't break in America without spending a fortune. Promotion, hype, all the dodgy things like paying off radio stations and DJs were all part of the business in those days. It was a very expensive thing to break records. I said to them, 'It's going to cost me a fortune to break you as I want to break you worldwide.'"

With that in mind, King outlined his five-year plan to break 10cc worldwide. "I said to them, 'I will lose a fortune in Year 1, no matter how many hits you have,'" says King. "'Year 2, with a bit of luck, I'll lose less and I'll be doing reasonably alright. My hopes are that Year 3 I'll have broken even. My hopes are that in Years 4 and 5 I'll make a fortune. At the end of Year 5, you will be completely at liberty to screw me out of an enormous amount of money to re-sign you or to go to any other record company or label in the world and, if I've broken you as big as I hope I'm going to break you at that point, you will make an absolute killing, all four of you, either from me or from someone else.' I remember saying, 'I want this to be really clear. I want you to understand absolutely and totally what's going on and stick with it.'"

The financial benefits of the deal weighed heavily in King's favour. Not only would he retain ownership of the rights to the records in perpetuity, but 10cc would only receive a royalty equating to 4% of record sales, a percentage that was quite generous by King's usual standards!

"It was actually quite a big percentage for me because 10cc produced their own stuff," says King. "Normally I produced and paid for all the records I made, which is why I gave artists a *really* low percentage. I wanted the rights in perpetuity, which I did get. And that was quite unusual since they'd paid for and made the sessions in the early days but I wanted ownership of the tracks. So as a result, I gave them a rather higher percentage than I would otherwise have given them."

The band's attempts to secure themselves a bigger cut were countered by King's standard response that "4% of something is better than 10% of nothing". The negotiation would inspire Eric Stewart and Lol Creme to write their first song together, 4% of Something, as a 'tribute' to Jonathan King's negotiating skills and the track would appear as the b-side of their next single. However, it would be misleading to think that Jonathan King received the remaining 96% of royalties.

"Don't forget that I was licensed too," says King. "Although I had my own label I was distributed by Decca, so I wasn't getting everything. A lot of it was going to Decca; a lot of it was going to retail. By the time you whittled all those things down you were dealing with a much smaller part of the cake anyway."

On top of that, King would have to invest heavily in the early years of his five-year deal to launch and establish 10cc. Bands made money in two main ways at the time: from record sales and from publishing royalties. King declined to take on the latter.

"At that point they begged me to take their publishing and I actually refused on very moral grounds," says King. "I told them, 'I'm giving you a tiny percentage royalty for your performance, you need the money from the publishing in order to keep yourselves existing. You will make money from your writing and your publishing and your touring and all the various other things that come from being a successful band, T-shirt sales and all that kind of crap'."

According to King, he also turned down the opportunity to manage the band.

"They said they'd like me to manage them as well," says King. "Because they were very keen on me, and quite rightly too. Because I was essentially the fifth member of 10cc in those early days. But I never wanted to manage anyone and said to them, 'It would be a real conflict of interest if I'm your record label and I'm your manager'."

While his contribution to 10cc's early success was considerable, his claim of being the fifth member of 10cc is a bold one, even by King's standards. The band appointed Gouldman's manager, Harvey Lisberg, and Stewart's manager, Ric Dixon, as the joint managers of 10cc and signed a five-year deal with King's UK Records. Now the question was how to follow up on the success of Donna. Mindful of their mistake as Hotlegs, the group recognised the importance of striking while the iron was still hot.

"We'd had one hit, and we kind of figured, 'Oh that did well, let's try and do something similar'," recalls Godley.

The result was another pastiche called Johnny Don't Do It, written by Godley, Creme and Gouldman, that satirised records like The Shangri-Las' tragicomic The Leader of the Pack. In 10cc's song, Johnny Kowalski and his girlfriend Francine are killed when the brakes fail on the motorbike they have stolen from Joe's Garage. Released in November 1972, the song was again championed by John Peel, an early fan of 10cc. The band was confident that the record would repeat its predecessor's success. This time, however, their instincts proved wrong; the record flopped, failing to make the UK Top 50.

"We couldn't get a booking on *Top of the Pops* to promote that single and it didn't sell very many copies at all, maybe 5,000 copies, could be 10,000, but not much more than that," says Harvey Lisberg. "We were just very unlucky because The Shangri-Las' Leader of The Pack was rereleased at the same time, and that was a record with a motorbike accident story running through it, which was a very similar idea to Johnny Don't Do It."

At the back of their minds, Stewart, Gouldman, Godley and Creme couldn't help but wonder whether 10cc would die off, just as Hotlegs had, as another of pop's one-hit wonders and another of the faceless novelty acts that had released singles on King's UK Records label. Perhaps hedging their bets they continued to work as house band and production team for projects at Strawberry. One such commission was from Carlin Music, who had formed a new company called Solid Gold Records as an outlet for the rock 'n' roll songs in their catalogue. The Strawberry team recorded covers of Da Doo Ron Ron (sung by Godley) and A Teenager In Love (sung by Stewart). In addition, Carlin commissioned an original of Creme's called Naughty Nola. That spring also saw the return of Neil Sedaka to Strawberry to record his follow-up to *Solitaire*.

Yet, in retrospect, the failure of Johnny Don't Do It was a blessing in disguise for the band. Had it been a hit, the future of 10cc might well have followed a more formulaic path based on more pastiches like Donna and Johnny Don't Do It. Instead, it gave the band the freedom to develop their own unique style. At their next writing session, Godley and Creme's approach was much more instinctive.

"Our way of writing, Lol and me, was just to accept what came out when we sat down and played and sang," recalls Godley. "So, it was like 'Okay, Johnny Don't Do It didn't work, let's not even think about what we do, let's just do.'"

With Creme playing an old Spanish guitar, and Godley sat opposite him with a notebook, what emerged was the outline of a new song called Rubber Bullets, inspired by old movies such as *Angels With Dirty Faces*.

"I think we started writing it at my parents' house, and it just came out," recalls Godley. "We knew what the feeling of this thing was, which is kind of weird because the lyric is essentially about a fictitious prison riot, taken from a fictitious black and white movie from the era of James Cagney. We were big movie buffs in those days, me and Lol, so it was one of those kinds of films … you know, with a prison riot, and there's always a padre there, and a tough cop with a megaphone. It was caricaturing those kinds of movies. But the chorus talks about rubber bullets, which weren't invented until the 70s by the British government to quell the Troubles in Northern Ireland. But it just worked."

The pair played the half-written outline of Rubber Bullets to Stewart and Gouldman knowing that it had something going for it. But Godley in particular was unsure of whether it was good enough to finish. "Kevin and Lol came into the studio with Rubber Bullets prepared to throw it away because they didn't think it was any good," says Stewart. "I thought it was a great song and Graham did too. The chorus, *'Load up with rubber bullets'*, was so grabbing. I thought it was a smash hit and said so straight away. But it wasn't finished, and it was Graham who put in the middle eight and various other bits and pieces."

Feeling that the song needed another part to it, Gouldman had volunteered to help finish the song off. "So I wrote most of the middle section," recalls Gouldman. "I also wrote the couplet, *'We've all got balls and brains / But some's got balls and chains'.* Very proud of that."

The final recording of the song was a revelation, conjuring up vivid mind pictures of Sgt Baker's heavy-handed attempts to break up the party at the local county jail, adroitly utilising humour and clever wordplay, and tempo changes that altered the mood of the song at different points. "I think one thing that we brought to the band was the idea that the motion of the song doesn't have to live in a linear place all the way through," says Godley. "It can jump around, it can change mood. It can go into a quiet room or a louder room or go up onto the roof, if you like, and change musical structure." When it came to recording Rubber Bullets, the band had a field day. 10cc would never record demos. They didn't need to, as they had Strawberry Studios at their disposal to help them shape, and experiment with, the production of their records.

"It quickly became obvious that these faders, these knobs, these little boxes, are capable of providing any noise that you can think of," says Godley. "All you have to do is think of them."

The basic backing tracks were always recorded in a similar way. "Me and Lol would play electric guitar and Kevin would play drums, and Eric would engineer in the control room," recalls Gouldman. Then the band would build up the arrangement, adding bass, lead guitar and piano and, in the case of Rubber Bullets, embellishing the song with wailing police siren sound effects and Beach Boys-style vocal harmonies. "We were influenced by them a lot," says Stewart. "Early 10cc songs like Rubber Bullets were definitely Beach Boys. The lyrical content was a bit heavier but the vocal harmonies were definitely influenced by The Beach Boys."

The group tried out a variety of ideas for different instrumentation before settling on the final arrangement. "We spent a mammoth amount of time recording Rubber Bullets," said Gouldman at the time. "It was a real epic, until we got everything absolutely right, cutting out bits here and there and adding other bits. We're all very finicky about the writing and we all want it to be absolutely perfect."

Innovative touches – like playing the bass guitar through a wah-wah pedal for the intro and recording the guitar solos at half speed so they sounded frenetic when played at the right speed – gave the record a distinctive and unique sound. "I slowed down the tape and played the guitar solo and then played it again at normal speed, so I had duelling guitars there," recalls Stewart. "One playing an octave higher and one playing the actual lead solo normal speed."

The resulting guitar effect played a key role in the overall sound of the track. "I think the guitar is actually the signature sound of the record," says Godley. It is a tribute to Stewart's studio skills that all of the vocal and instrumental overdubs on the record were achieved with only eight tracks at his disposal. "We were going on to an eight-track machine," says Stewart. "That meant a lot of track jumping to get on as many overdubs and vocals as we could, which was a bit of a risk to take because you couldn't go backwards once you'd erased a track."

Delighted with the result, Rubber Bullets was released as 10cc's next single in March 1973. There was a lot riding on it, for 10cc and for Jonathan King. After its triple whammy of Top 5 hits, King's UK Records had only landed one Top 10 hit in the 30 releases since. King and 10cc both needed another hit and Jonathan King went to extraordinary lengths to ensure they got one.

"With this record I also received a personal letter, handwritten by Jonathan King himself," wrote John Peel, reviewing the single at the time. "He writes: 'Peely, in my opinion 10cc could be a very big group indeed. Me, I was always surprised you didn't go that crazy for Johnny Don't Do It, which I liked even more than Donna, but this really is my favourite of all.' The truth of the matter is that I wrote a review of Johnny that waxed almost biblical in its unreserved praise. The record to hand is a sort of contemporary Jailhouse Rock which opens with a great deal of energy and a curious electronic percussion effect. There are some splendidly ironic lines, including a brief unloading of platitudes from the prison chaplain, and the performance and production are as witty and clean as we are growing to expect from this group. I'd love to hear a 10cc LP. There are sound effects, surfing-type harmonies and any number of greater or lesser treats. They certainly know how to make entertaining and worthwhile singles up there at Strawberry Studios. I really hope this makes up for the inexplicable failure of Johnny Don't Do It."

Unfortunately, the record's chances of success suffered a major setback when the BBC banned Rubber Bullets on the grounds of Northern Ireland sensitivity.

"We were up against some pig-headedness amongst disc jockeys who thought it was about Ireland," says Harvey Lisberg. "There was this feeling at the BBC that because rubber bullets were being used by the Army in Belfast, then our record must be connected to the IRA, with implications of political violence. It was just a coincidence. If you listen to the record you will hear that it has nothing to do with Ireland at all."

While the situation in Ireland had not been the inspiration for Rubber Bullets, the song's title and chorus meant that it had particular resonance there.

"The Irish journalist Sean O'Hagan told me an extraordinary story," recalls Godley. "When Rubber Bullets was released he lived in Armagh, and one Saturday evening, there was a crowd of kids throwing stones at an army patrol – probably a couple of Land Rovers, and the kids started singing the chorus of Rubber Bullets at them and dancing around and giving them V-signs, taunting them. Basically the soldiers responded in kind when a brick almost downed one of them. So they started firing rubber bullets at these kids. And there was a lot of scrambling after them as they were quite prized apparently. They used to sell them to journalists or put them on the mantelpiece at home."

Six weeks after its release, the song finally entered the UK singles chart. By the time the BBC lifted its ban, Rubber Bullets was already in the Top 30. With the added impetus of airplay on Radio One, and the all-important *Top of the Pops* appearance, the song climbed effortlessly into the Top 10, reaching the No.1 spot on June 23. For Eric Stewart the achievement was particularly sweet; he had finally cracked the No.1 spot after being associated with four No.2s! For Graham Gouldman, his contribution as co-writer had given him his first major success as a songwriter for over five years, helping to restore confidence in his own writing. For Kevin Godley, the timing couldn't have been better; Rubber Bullets hit the No.1 spot in the same week that he married his wife Susanne. For Lol Creme, who had married his wife Angie a month earlier, his honeymoon in the Caribbean coincided with the record reaching the top spot.

"I remember the night we got there," recalls Creme. "Our record, Rubber Bullets, had just gone to No.1 so I felt really great. I'll never forget that night. It was fantastic."

Rubber Bullets would go on to become one of the biggest-selling singles of the year in the UK, selling over 750,000 copies and enjoying a 15-week chart run. Its success prompted the release of the three songs they had recorded for Carlin Music. Over a two-week period Da Doo Ron Ron was released by RCA under the band name Grumble; A Teenager In Love was issued by EMI under the moniker Rubber Duckie (perhaps as a reference to Rubber Bullets); and Naughty Nola was released by Columbia by Lol. All featured original b-sides – Pig Bin An' Gone and Lark (both instrumentals penned by Stewart/Gouldman/Godley/Creme) and the Creme-penned Bumbler.

Rubber Bullets also reached No.1 in Ireland and Australia, where it spent 17 weeks in the charts, the Top 10 in France and the Top 20 in New Zealand, Belgium and Germany. In the US, Rubber Bullets started picking up airplay. In some parts of the country the airplay was strong – in Chicago (on WCFL, WBBM, WLS), St Louis (KXOK), Salt Lake City (KCPX) and Palm Springs (KDES) – and there were high hopes for a major hit. However, the airplay was not widespread enough to lift Rubber Bullets beyond No.73 in the US charts. Nevertheless, it had given the band a foot in the door in America.

While Rubber Bullets had been scaling the charts at home, Jonathan King had given the band an ultimatum. He wanted their debut album ready "within seven days".

"They all looked at me in horror," recalls King. "I said, 'No, I really do'. I want it in seven days, so we can get it ready and also because I want you to work under that kind of pressure."

It was a far cry from the laissez-faire attitude that Hotlegs had adopted in the 15 months it had taken them to get around to releasing their debut album. While it would take slightly longer than seven days to complete the album, King's challenge helped to focus the mind at Strawberry, where the creative juices were well and truly flowing. Such was the buzz in the studio that most of the album was in fact recorded in a very intense two-week period.

"The adrenaline was really flowing that fortnight," says Creme. "Most bands get about six hours of actual work done for every two days in the studio but we were putting in 16 solid hours a day. We worked quickly and carefully and it was very intense."

By now Strawberry had been upgraded to a 16-track facility with the installation of an iconic red, custom-made Helios recording desk, designed by Eric Stewart and Dick Swettenham. The band relished having more tracks at their disposal, particularly as their taste for songwriting and production experimentation expanded. Buoyed by the success of Donna and Rubber Bullets, Godley and Creme were on a roll and keen to develop their newfound writing style further. They found that their artistic training helped with their songwriting.

"We do write very much as we were trained to do graphic design, in that you sift through ideas," said Creme at the time. "It's very hard work for us. There's very little that comes out easily."

Among their new songs was The Dean and I, nicknamed 'the Doris Day song' in the early stages of writing because of its affinity with songs from musicals of that period.

"The inspiration for it came from sort of kitsch Hollywood musicals," says Godley. "It was Doris Day meets Frank Zappa, if you like. And the changes that track goes through, it never stops. It starts in one place and ends in another and it's full of weird dynamics, intensity and insanity and odd sounds. We all knew it was an extraordinary song but we didn't know what the hell it was. It was a very strange hybrid of a track. It was one of those things you either loved or hated."

The song certainly polarised opinion within the band. On the one hand, Graham Gouldman loved it.

"I remember listening to The Dean and I when Kevin and Lol played it for us," recalls Gouldman. "It was just such an amazing song. I could almost say if anything represented 10cc it was that song. It had everything. I mean there are so many musical changes in it. The chords are amazing. I've never heard anything like it since."

Eric Stewart was far less enthused: "I hated it," said Stewart at the time. "This is the democratic side of the group at work. We're prepared to try anything, no matter which one of the group hates the production or the song. We do try to go through and do it to its ultimate, and that particular song reminded me tremendously of Hollywood musicals like *South Pacific* and *Oklahoma*, which I abhor. I can't say I really hate them. There's not a word strong enough!"

The song was an example of the band's democratic approach in the studio.

"Whoever the writers were, we never rejected a song out of hand," says Gouldman. "If one team wrote a song, the other wouldn't say, 'That's shit!' or 'I don't wanna do it.' It was always, 'If you've gone so far as to finish a song then it's your baby and we'll adopt it, whether we like it or not, and we will try to make it a better baby.' Fortunately, as far as I was concerned, I liked pretty much everything we ever did."

The Dean and I again demonstrated that the group had a special way with words, an ever-increasing rarity in the world of pop; such a rarity, in fact, that some critics would go on to compare the band's lyrical dexterity with that of Cole Porter, in the absence of any valid comparisons among 10cc's contemporaries.

Another new song, the Godley/Creme/Gouldman collaboration Sand In My Face, was inspired by the Charles Atlas book *Dynamic Tension*, and its 'You too can have a body like mine' claims, as the song's protagonist turns to Atlas after losing his girl to Big Alex down at the beach. Having been transformed from a self-confessed nine-stone weakling into a rippling muscleman, the song has a happy resolution when he wins back his girl and kicks sand in Alex's face!

"It was sort of funny to us, because we always used to read American magazines that had adverts for Charles Atlas on the back," says Gouldman, "and, of course, we were all nine-stone weaklings!"

With the deadline looming to complete the album, the band built on and developed some song ideas that had originally started life back in the Hotlegs days.

"Speed Kills started out as a backing track that Eric did during the Hotlegs period and which he kept adding new guitar tracks to over the next 18 months," says Creme. "Eventually Kev and I did a vocal line and some lyrics to go over the top of it and it ended up on the album."

Stewart's guitar overdubs succeeded in evoking the song's subject matter: "As more and more guitars layer more and more riffs over the original figure until a wriggling, twitching high-pitched solo adds the final luxurious touch of frenetic, obsessive paranoia, Stewart evokes perfectly the unmistakable frequency of amphetamine psychosis," remarked Charles Shaar Murray in *New Musical Express* sometime later.

Another track that had its roots in the Hotlegs days was Fresh Air For My Mama. The group recycled the song's middle eight from You Didn't Like It Because You Didn't Think Of It. "Somehow it wasn't taken as far as it could have been there," says Godley. "So we decided to use that particular part in a new song."

The end result proved that 10cc weren't only capable of writing witty songs. Fresh Air For My Mama was poignant, beautifully crafted and deadly serious. The song also demonstrated 10cc's versatility as musicians, their ability to turn their hands to a variety of musical styles. Their time working as session musicians for the eclectic mix of artists that had recorded at Strawberry was now clearly paying dividends. The discipline that they had adopted for the Neil Sedaka sessions was paying off, too. In fact they asked Sedaka to guest on the album.

"We've invited him to play on a few tracks on our forthcoming album so that's something else to look forward to," said Lol Creme at the time. "A lot of the tricks we learnt from Neil we've incorporated into our own material."

Sadly, owing to other commitments, the guest appearance never came off. For his part, Sedaka tried to get Stewart, Gouldman, Godley and Creme to tour with him.

"Unfortunately, I haven't been able to get on the road with those musicians although I tried to get them for a Japanese tour, but it was at the time when Donna was a big hit for them," said Sedaka.

Because of the rush to get the album finished, 10cc's approach in the studio was to record each song as it was written. After completing a song, the writers would play the track to the rest of the band and collectively the group would work on the arrangements, including deciding who sang lead vocal. Every song was given the same amount of care and attention. "We worked on every track like a single," said Creme at the time. "All our parts are written before they are recorded. We usually lay down the music tracks and put the vocal on top as soon as possible. We used to leave the vocals to the bitter end, which didn't work because the productions were so overdone there was no room for the vocal. Now all our ideas complement the vocal, not destroy it. Almost everything, including guitar solos, is written into the songs."

As the recording sessions progressed, the group sensed 10cc's personality beginning to emerge. "An identity was beginning to form," says Creme. "It was a very exciting period and all these things were just coming together, like the ways of putting over certain emotions, and the humour."

Although the Stewart/Gouldman writing partnership only contributed two songs to the album, both are arguably among its highlights. Ships Don't Disappear In The Night (Do They?) strung together a series of Hammer Horror film references accompanied by a distinctive slide guitar riff; Boris Karloff, Bella Lugosi and Vincent Price all get a name check. The moral of the story is that we have nothing to fear from things that go bump in the night – or do we?

"There was some Vincent Price film on at the time," recalls Gouldman. "We always used to like the clichés that would go before a film, like 'Ships don't disappear in the night ... do they?'"

Better still was Headline Hustler, a song that dealt with the aspirations of a journalist on a local paper in search of scandal to progress his career. Desperate for an exposé, our hero is convinced that he is only one headline away from making a name for himself. It proved that Stewart and Gouldman were also increasingly adept at wordplay.

"We'd wanted to write something about newspaper writers," said Creme at the time. "Graham just came up with the title Headline Hustler. There's all sorts of references in there to Lord Lambton and Watergate, which I suppose, make it fairly topical. We didn't do that on purpose, it just came out that way. Basically the song is about a guy who works on a paper who everyone thinks is a nice guy. He's not though, of course, he's just a scandalmonger."

While Stewart and Gouldman were working on the song, Godley and Creme were writing The Hospital Song. "We were coming towards the end of the album and we still needed two songs," says Creme. "There was a race on, actually, who could finish first. Me and Kev were writing The Hospital Song and Graham and Eric were writing Headline Hustler and we finished first. My old man was in hospital for a long time and I had to visit him and I've always had a childhood aversion to hospitals. The Hospital Song was about a guy who had been in hospital for six months despite the fact that there was nothing wrong with him. He just lies there peeing in his bed, and really pissing off the doctors and nurses. We were almost seeing how mad we could write, see how far we could go and The Hospital Song went quite far!"

All four of the band's members look back fondly on the recording of their debut album. "We blossomed as individuals as well as a band on that first album," says Godley. "Up until that point, everyone was writing in a Beatles style or a Beach Boys style. But because the time allotted to recording that album was so short, we stopped consciously, or unconsciously, trying to copy our idols. We stopped thinking about what it should sound like, and just wrote what came off the top of our heads. The floodgates opened and, lo and behold, there was something original there. It was a great moment that was critical in each of our lives. It gave each of us, in our own individual ways, a little leg up into finding our own mode of creativity."

Crammed full of great melodies, and with the added dimension of humour and skill in the lyric department, it was smart without being too clever, ingenious without being remotely pretentious. Jonathan King's idea to put the band under time pressure to record their debut album had proven to be a smart move and forced them to follow their instincts rather than over thinking things.

The band's ingenuity only ran out when it came to thinking up an album title. Deciding to call it simply *10cc*, the album cover allowed Lol Creme to put his artistic skills to good use. His cartoon-like rendering of the band's name – each character represented by an inflatable, some with punctures repaired with bits of masking tape – reflected the band's attitude: jokey, irreverent, fun. To add an air of credibility, John Peel's "I'd love to hear a 10cc album" endorsement was added to the back cover.

Jonathan King was particularly excited about the release of the album. Up to now, UK Records had achieved hit singles but never a hit album. He sensed that was about to change.

"This is the best thing there's been since *Bridge Over Troubled Water*," he proclaimed to a room full of music journalists at an album preview at a studio just off Wardour Street in London. Released in July 1973, just three weeks after the album had been mixed, *10cc* met with universal critical acclaim.

"One of the most exciting things to hit the rather stagnant British market since The Beatles and The Stones first emerged back in the 60s," said *Record Mirror*. "Debut albums, if they are any good at all, are usually noted for their promise or freshness. Amazingly, it seems 10cc have both qualities, plus that indefinable quality that marks a very experienced and talented band. Just like all great up-and-coming bands they draw from classic rock styles and recycle it with the aid of synthesizer and brilliant studio effects into a very distinctive sound. It's tailor-made homespun British pop at its very best and an unquestionable hit. Get it."

New Musical Express was equally enthused. Ian MacDonald described it as "one of the best rock albums I've heard for several years … *10cc* is a minor masterpiece of composition, performance and production that serves the timely dual purpose of reminding us where it was once at and, if we use our loafs, where it could be at in the future."

"10cc are so damn good, it makes you wonder where they've been all this time," wrote *Let It Rock* magazine. "What 10cc have done is to combine all the elements of pop – infectious melodies, interesting lyrics, and a distinctive vocal and instrumental sound – with (studio) sophistication. That's why they're cleaning up in the singles charts and why this album, if they take any more tracks from it, could end up as *10cc's Greatest Hits*. Volume One."

Melody Maker also added its endorsement: "A unique blending of American International celluloid plots and characters and solid pop techniques in the tradition of The Beach Boys and The Beatles, using the very best modern studio facilities, new musical ability and best of all a verbal wit which is all the more refreshing for being on one immediately accessible level. There are no more hidden meanings on here than there were on Louie, Louie yet the humour is intelligent enough to stand any amount of repetition."

The paper later described the album as "*Mad* magazine set to music," an analogy which the group endorsed. "We use *Mad* magazine humour to put over a serious point, except in certain songs where we're just being frivolous for the sake of it," said Stewart at the time. "We find that if we want to say something, that's the best way for us to say it."

10cc would continue to gain critical acclaim over the coming years. "Their virtuoso fluency with all the most attractive pop music vocabulary of the last 15 years allowed them to make records that virtually consisted of nothing but hook-lines, mouth-watering musical sundaes of all your favourite pop flavours," wrote Charles Shaar Murray in *New Musical Express* sometime later. "Vocal harmonies, tricky lyrics full of claustrophobically tight punning and double-bluff put-ons, guitars a go-go, jokes and astonishingly painstaking attention to detail in all departments."

Among the album's many admirers was Paul McCartney. On July 25 he sent a postcard to 'Eric, Pete and Mob' at Strawberry Studios from his farm in Campbeltown in Scotland saying, 'Nice one, lads. Keep rockin'!'

"I've still got the postcard from Paul," says Stewart. "He'd ripped the stamp and written next to it, 'Sorry, Your Majesty'."

Another big fan was a 16-year-old from North London called John Lydon. "At the time I'd be the chap telling you that 10cc's first album was one of the greatest things I'd ever heard," says Lydon.

Three years later he would reinvent himself as Johnny Rotten in The Sex Pistols.

CHAPTER 6

FROM THE VALLEY OF THE LEPERS

DESPITE THE CRITICAL GARLANDS, AND THE NO.1 SUCCESS OF RUBBER Bullets, the band's debut album initially failed to make any impact on the UK Top 50. In hindsight, perhaps this wasn't entirely surprising. What were the public to make of 10cc? The group almost went out of their way to avoid having an image. This, plus their appearance on Jonathan King's UK label, noted for its novelty releases, were hardly the credible ingredients of a major new rock band. The latter point certainly hindered their initial progress in America. While *Rolling Stone* journalist Paul Gambaccini visited the band in Manchester and described them as the "hottest band in the UK", the senior editor of the magazine refused to run a subsequent article on 10cc because he didn't want to devote space to "one of Jonathan King's silly groups." The band's label manager at UK Records recognised the problem himself.

"I know what kind of image we've got, but that's not the way to judge this group," he said at the time. "Honestly, they're so talented. We're proud, maybe a little embarrassed ourselves, to be associated with people so good. I can't think of anyone outside of groups such as Led Zeppelin who even approach their kind of class."

Ironically, it was probably 10cc themselves who were least worried about their lack of image: "We've got enough problems making records let alone sorting out bloody images!" said Lol Creme at the time. They did concede, however, that they would need to play live if they were going to establish 10cc as a 'proper band'. "We gradually became more aware of the fact that if you want to be a successful group you've got to do live gigs," said Kevin Godley at the time. "It took us a long time to realise that."

Most groups had paid their dues on the road by the time they'd made their first record. Uniquely, 10cc, born and bred in the studio, had made a record and were now about to go out on tour to support it. No other band at the time had gone through such an unusual gestation. Going out on the road was not something that particularly appealed to them, least of all Godley and Creme.

"We liked being backroom boys at Strawberry," says Creme. "I was horrified when we had to play live."

It was with some reluctance, therefore, that the group agreed to undertake their first UK tour, to help promote their album and further establish 10cc with the record-buying public. To allow Kevin Godley greater freedom on stage, particularly on tracks where he sang lead vocal, the group decided to augment their touring line-up with another drummer. Eric Stewart had run into former Ankh drummer Paul Burgess again at a Beck, Bogert and Appice concert at the Manchester Hardrock earlier in the year, so he was front of mind when they were considering their options. Stewart recommended Burgess for the job and soon he was in.

As the band rehearsed for their upcoming tour, they decided to keep with their irreverent approach and take the cheeky step of having the voice of God introduce them on stage, played, appropriately enough, by Kevin Godley. "We just thought we'd go to the top guy to introduce the act," he joked.

The idea, according to Godley, was "ripped off from the film *The Ten Commandments*." As the house lights dimmed, the sound of wind, thunder and lightning would resound around the auditorium while the voice of God pronounced: *'Kneel, for you are on holy ground. I am the Lord thy God, the God of Abraham, Isaac and Moses. I am an omnipotent, omnipresent, inabdominal God. From the valley of the lepers… the fabulous, far out, funky, freaky, hippy, happy, zippy, zany, wicky, wacky. Ladies and gentlemen will you greet … 10cc!'*

10cc's concert debut took place on August 26, 1973 at the Douglas Palace Lido on the Isle of Man. "The group rehearsed very well before the show and then in the evening there was an audience of about 2,000, which was a fairly big crowd, and they hadn't been expecting to play to such a big audience," recalls Harvey Lisberg.

Aside from their gigs as Hotlegs supporting The Moody Blues in October 1971, this was the first time that Godley, Creme and even Gouldman had played to audiences of this size and they were concerned with how well they'd go down. The first ever song to be performed live by 10cc, and a regular opening number on their early tours, was an extended version of Speed Kills.

"Although very nervous, and worried about crowd reaction, which is something unusual for a name group, their opening number lasted for about 12 minutes, and really got the 2,000-strong audience interested in what was to come," said Danny Wilson in *Record Mirror*. "After Donna, in which the vocals sounded a bit strained, two album tracks left the crowd a bit disinterested, and the group were in danger of losing the audience for a while. Only until Rubber Bullets, however. It was just like listening to the record. From then on they could do nothing wrong. They had the fans stamping their feet, clapping their hands, and even standing on one another's shoulders. The group, and fans alike, had a ball. At one stage, Lol Creme got too close to some frantic female fans, and almost went head over heels down the five-feet drop from stage to floor. Only the timely intervention of three security men saved him from being cut off in his prime! When Kevin Godley came off the drums to end the set, with an unusually slow number, called Fresh Air For My Mama, the place was still screaming for more. It was not to be, however, 10cc had finished their first live gig. If any faults can be found, they are only in a PA which was a little too quiet, and an inexperienced mixer operator, things which will not take long to sort out."

It was a view shared by the band's co-manager Harvey Lisberg.

"Rubber Bullets went down like a storm and the only real problems they had were in reproducing the sound," says Lisberg. "They were a bit raw that night but I'd always thought they had fantastic potential as a stage act; but the next gig they did two days later at the Stoke Heavy Steam Machine was nothing like as good. In fact, it was awful. After doing so well in Douglas they were expecting to play to another audience of 2,000 but instead it was a very small crowd, probably 400, maybe 500 people. The sound was so bad and they felt the acoustics were like a glorified disco. After that they appeared at the Brunel Rooms in Swindon and then Barbarella's in Birmingham, and by the time they got to the Dunstable California Room most of the sound problems had been ironed out."

10cc's lack of experience playing live led to a problem of a different kind on the early dates of the tour – the muted response they were greeted with at the end of each song. *Melody Maker* journalist Kevin Halligan witnessed this unusual phenomenon at the band's third date in Swindon.

"You couldn't have wished a worse audience on a band than the one 10cc played to in the Brunel Rooms, Swindon, on Friday night," wrote Halligan. "This was only the third live gig the group had ever played, and most of the time they played superbly, but the audience didn't bat an eyelid. And it wasn't stoned admiration. They were just stonewalling everything the band offered. It was like a concert in a graveyard. The band didn't need any time to warm up. They were tight and rocking from the start. They broke into Speed Kills with drummers Kevin Godley and Paul Burgess backing up the energy of tight guitar duo Eric Stewart and Lol Creme. There was hardly any applause and the group went straight into Sand In My Face, a sick song about Charles Atlas freaks, but it didn't raise a laugh. When a perfect recreation of the studio sound of The Dean and I was greeted in silence the group were looking justifiably discouraged. 'More! More!' mocked Stewart and Creme."

It was only during the encores that audiences finally warmed to the band: "You're feeling all night long that you're not getting through to them, so you finish the last number and think, 'Right, let's fuck off and go home,' and the place erupts and they won't let you go home. It's mad!" said Stewart at the time.

Jonathan King and 10cc were both conscious of the need to follow up the No.1 success of Rubber Bullets with another single. The honour fell to The Dean and I, which was released in August to coincide with the tour. As with most of their previous singles, the group were very egalitarian; whoever hadn't written the a-side were always given first refusal on coming up with the b-side, with royalties thus shared equally within the band.

"It was very democratic," recalls Gouldman. "If Kev and Lol did the a-side of a single, Eric and I would do the b-side." Such was the case with The Dean and I, which featured the Stewart/Gouldman-penned Bee In My Bonnet on the flip. 10cc knew that chart success for The Dean and I would play an important role in helping to promote the album and the group themselves.

"The unfortunate truth about making singles is that you're only as good as your last one," said Stewart at the time. "With albums you get more of a chance to consolidate your success. Every time we put a single out it's like starting over again." Stewart's point was perfectly valid but, happily, the week after The Dean and I entered the UK singles chart, the band's debut album finally breached the Top 50, giving 10cc, and UK Records, their album chart debut. Having an album and a single climbing the charts provided an added impetus to the tour as it continued around the UK, stopping at such salubrious venues as the Hereford Flamingo Ballroom and Scunthorpe Baths. Perhaps not surprisingly, the band found themselves going down better at the universities than in the ballrooms. In the audience at the band's gig at Greenwich Borough Hall on October 11 was future broadcaster Danny Baker, who would go on to become a 10cc fan and describe them as "one of the greatest bands Britain has ever produced".

Yet while The Dean and I would give the band their third UK Top 10 hit – and their second No.1 in Ireland – *10cc* would only succeed in climbing to No.36 during its six-week chart run. It was disappointing given the energy that had gone into making the album and the superlative critical reviews. Riding higher in the album charts at the time was *The Tra-La Days Are Over*, the follow-up album to *Solitaire* that Neil Sedaka had recorded with 10cc at Strawberry that spring. Designed to build on the success of its predecessor, the new album sought to establish Sedaka as a contemporary hitmaker rather than a nostalgia act of the past. Sedaka clearly relished the new credibility afforded to him by the success of *Solitaire*, and moving on from his years in the wilderness, as evidenced on the new song Standing On The Inside in which he referenced 'phoney faces … backslappers' and not being on the outside anymore.

The theme of moving on from the past and embracing the future recurs on Our Last Song Together, the final song written with his old songwriting partner, Howard Greenfield, in which he declares the past is dead – hence the tra-la days are over. With strings added to the track, once again arranged by Del Newman, the song was highly poignant for Sedaka, who had written most of his classic hits with Greenfield. There was even a touching reference in the lyric to the hit they wrote back in 1962, as Sedaka sings, "*Now we know breaking up is really hard to do.*"

"Neil used to cry every time I mixed Our Last Song Together," recalls Stewart. "It was the last song he ever wrote with his friend Howie Greenfield, and it obviously meant a lot to him."

Feeling that their contribution to the album warranted more than merely session fees, they approached Sedaka seeking production royalties.

"Because they had done an excellent job I made a verbal agreement to pay them," said Sedaka.

Released in August 1973, *The Tra-La Days Are Over* would accelerate Sedaka's revival, reaching No.13 in the album charts, and going on to become his bestselling studio album to date in the UK. It also yielded two UK hit singles, with Standing On The Inside reaching No.26 in June and Our Last Song Together reaching No.31 in August. Strangely, arguably the most commercial track on the album, Love Will Keep Us Together, wasn't released as a single. The album gained positive reviews.

"This is the best music Sedaka has ever made and it's better than most of the music being made by his successors," wrote Simon Frith in *Let It Rock*.

Solitaire and *The Tra-La Days Are Over* also won acclaim among other musicians. "I wasn't aware that Neil had moved to England to try and forge a comeback until the 10cc recordings were made," says Elton John. "Those recordings relaunched Neil's career sensationally in Britain. Everybody loved those records. I was a huge fan of *The Tra-La Days Are Over*."

When Sedaka threw a party at his Mayfair flat in London, Elton John was amazed to discover that he had no record deal in America. Journalist Neil Norman remembers the party well. "It was in Neil's London flat," recalls Norman. "10cc were there as well, and Neil and Elton sat down at the piano and played Elton's song Daniel as a duet, which was wonderful, a concert-standard performance in his sitting room for about 20 very lucky people." Elton John would subsequently sign Sedaka to his new Rocket Records label and release *Sedaka's Back*, a compilation of his three most recent albums as his comeback album in the US.

In the meantime, 10cc returned to Strawberry in November 1973 to start work on their next album. 1973 had been quite a year for the band. A year that had started in uncertainty after the failure of

Johnny Don't Do It had ended in triumph with a No.1 single, plus a highly acclaimed album and their first tour of the UK successfully behind them. What was particularly gratifying for the new darlings of the music press was that success had been achieved on their own terms. They hadn't had to prostitute themselves to get there or land themselves with some false image. They had written and recorded what and how they liked and had enjoyed success with the results. One factor that the group attributed to their success was their distance from London. In interviews, the band were fiercely proud of their Manchester roots.

"Being in the north helps us to think more clearly," said Lol Creme. "In London we'd probably have all the wrong influences. We'd get seduced by ideas that wouldn't be good for us. Here we know what's right for us."

Being based so far away from the centre of the UK music scene, and having the luxury of their own studio, no one had ever told the group what they *couldn't* do.

"We've got no preconceived ideas of what we should be like," said Kevin Godley at the time. "Probably if we lived in London we'd all be stagnant and stale by now. Living where we do we've managed to develop our own style. Mind you, I don't suppose even we know what our so-called 'style' is. We just write songs with what we hope are interesting lyrics. I guess you could say we're four voyeurs from Stockport! We don't want to get in a situation where we do too many songs like The Dean and I, for instance, or too many like Donna. Ideally on our next album we'd like to record songs rather like The Beatles did in their later period. They started to write some amazing songs that other people have recorded and could record. We don't want to rely too much on clever production."

What made 10cc more remarkable than a lot of groups was the talent they had within the band. They weren't reliant on a frontman or on one songwriter. The group were self-contained. Not only could everyone sing like a bird and play with consummate skill, but they could all write, too: "Everybody contributes exactly the same amount and as everyone is aware of that we all respect each others' talents," said Gouldman at the time. "When it's time for a guitar solo, for instance, we all look to Eric."

Stewart himself, however, didn't feel that he had been pulling his weight in the band, particularly in the songwriting department. The band's debut album had essentially been Godley and Creme's baby, the duo contributing to eight of its ten songs. Stewart had only co-written four. Prior to starting work on the new album, Stewart announced to the other members of the group that he was considering leaving 10cc.

"I was feeling a bit insecure about my songwriting," says Stewart. "I hadn't contributed as much as the others to the writing on the first album. So, I sat down with the others and said, 'I'm thinking of leaving the band. I'm not as involved in the writing as you guys, I should be writing more songs,' and they all said, 'Well, write some more bloody songs then! What's stopping you? I'll write with you!' So I decided to give it another go and stay in the band."

The discussion was the catalyst to the group writing outside of their main Godley/Creme and Stewart/Gouldman writing teams, an important development for 10cc. They called their version of group therapy a 'Truth Session' and would employ it any time one or more members of the band had a group-related problem.

"If we're on the road or in the studio and there's something bugging one of us, or someone says, 'I want to leave the group,' which is something that someone says at one time or another in every group I've ever come across, then someone else will say, 'It's Truth Session time,' and we drop everything, sit down and sort it out," said Creme at the time.

Although they weren't particularly frequent, the group would have several 'Truth Sessions' over the years. "I think that Eric was the most sensitive one amongst the four of us," says Godley. "He was always sensitive to his position being undermined. Eric had a habit of disappearing behind his shades and throwing a wobbler every now and again."

With Stewart back on board, 10cc started work on their new album, interrupting recording intermittently to film an appearance of Rubber Bullets for the Christmas Day edition of *Top of the Pops* and to play various live dates in the UK up until the year end. One of the group's final engagements of 1973 was a performance at Liverpool's Top Rank Suite on December 28, where they were supported by another up-and-coming band of the time, Queen. The contrast between the two band's approaches to playing live couldn't have been more stark.

"They came along with this fantastic PA and lighting system and we, as the main band, didn't even have any lights whatsoever," said Godley at the time. "We had to rely on the roadies flashing their torches on us."

It is a gig that Eric Stewart still recalls.

"I remember rehearsing in the afternoon, we had to do a sound-check, and it was a revolving stage, and we heard this group tuning up and Brian May started to play and I thought to myself, 'Jesus Christ! This guy's better than a support band! What the hell's going on here?'" says Stewart.

Roger Taylor, of Queen, also remembers the gig and is equally complimentary about 10cc.

"They were excellent," says Taylor. "We had more of a show than they did. They had more of a session vibe, but great, inventive stuff. They weren't a stage act as such."

Queen's appearance in Liverpool was the last time that they ever supported another band in the UK. For both bands, superstardom was just around the corner.

CHAPTER 7

LOTS MORE GOODIES IN THE PIPELINE

DESPITE BEING THE MOST SUCCESSFUL ACT ON UK RECORDS, AND THE one with the most potential for the future, 10cc had yet to make much money, given their 4% royalty. 10cc's management tried to re-negotiate the terms of their contract and Jonathan King agreed to a small increased percentage for the group on the proviso that this was a one-off adjustment and that both parties would stick to the re-maining terms of their five-year deal.

As with their debut, 10cc intended to record each track of their new album as it was written. But whereas their first album had been created in a rush of adrenaline, chock-full of pastiches, highly irreverent and largely derivative in nature, the new album was intended to be more original, with a higher degree of 10cc's person-ality stamped on it. The group were keen to create a truly innovative work by breaking down any pre-existing songwriting conventions. The ethos was, 'Anything goes!'

"We know we can record good music, play good solos but what we want is *brilliant* music and *brilliant* solos, and completely scrap-ping all the preconceived ideas that people have had over the past 10 years, where everything has been based on 'This is the new *Sgt Pepper*,' 'This is the new Beatles,' 'This is the new Eric Clapton,'" said Eric Stewart at the time.

As the new darlings of the music press, 10cc now had a lot to live up to.

"When we came into the studio, everybody around us – man-agement, agency, record company – all said, 'You've got to do an incredible album now.' So, we were really worried," said Stewart.

At first, the anxiety showed. The group rejected their initial at-tempt at Baron Samedi, a new Stewart/Gouldman creation inspired by a trip to the cinema to see then current James Bond movie *Live and Let Die*. Bond villain Dr Kananga's henchman in the film is Baron Samedi, who has ties to the voodoo occult, and the pair built up a storyline, fuelled by Stewart's fondness for Dennis Wheatley novels and embellished by bizarre real-life local events. "There used to be a resident Zulu tribe at Manchester's Belle Vue Zoo," recalls Stewart. "They used to do things like walk on fire and tread on glass."

The group re-recorded Baron Samedi, this time setting it to a frantic Santana-esque samba rhythm. The result was much more evocative of the song's subject matter, showcasing Godley's percussive skills to good effect. Refreshingly, however, 10cc never resorted to mere flexing of musical muscle; the part was only there because the song needed it. Not for them, the self-indulgent guitar or drum solos so beloved of many other acts of the period. For 10cc, the song always came first. Having Baron Samedi in the can helped relieve the group's initial tension.

"At the beginning it was very, very difficult," said Gouldman at the time. "We started with the objective of not being derivative at all, which is pretty well impossible. We were very conscious that we were following a fairly successful album that had a lot of critical acclaim. We were a bit uptight but we settled down."

Adding a new dimension to the album were the songwriting collaborations outside of the two main writing teams. The first attempt to do this saw Lol Creme and Graham Gouldman collaborate while Kevin Godley teamed up with Eric Stewart.

"It was a bit scary at first; we did it to see what would happen," said Godley at the time. "Writing has a lot to do with rapport, and if you've never written with anyone before it's a weird experience, but two good songs came out of it and we continued. In the future, we might have two of us start a song and then pass it on to the others, like a chain."

Creme and Gouldman's collaboration produced The Worst Band In The World, a song that ridiculed the music business, a subject that was seen as a sacred cow in the music industry at the time. The song provided further evidence of 10cc's skill at using humour: *'Up yours / Up mine / But up everybody's that takes time.'* Even the title of the song was beautifully ironic given 10cc's elevated critical standing at the time and proved that the band could laugh at themselves. "It was tongue-in-cheek, it was meant to be fun really," says Gouldman. "Of course, we didn't think we were the worst band in the world, we thought we were the best."

Jonathan King loved the song so much that he insisted they release it immediately as their next single, even though they were only four tracks into recording their new album. Released in January 1974, the British music press loved the song too.

"Very, very funny. That's the only way to describe this record," said *Disc*. "In fact, I will award 10cc ten out of ten and a place in the Top Three."

Unfortunately, the BBC didn't get the joke and banned the record on the grounds that some of the lyrics were offensive. Or, more specifically, they found the *absence* of a certain word in the lyrics offensive! They objected to the *implication* of the word 'shit' in the song's second line. This may have been the first time that a record had been banned because a missing lyric was deemed offensive! "One guy at the Beeb told us that at a meeting on obscenity one speaker played a copy of The Worst Band In The World and said it was the filthiest record he'd ever heard!" said an astonished Eric Stewart at the time.

The BBC agreed to lift their ban on the proviso that the group re-record a radio-friendly version of the song, with the lyric changed from *'don't give a ...'* to *'don't give up'*. Knowing that BBC radio airplay and TV appearances were vital to the record's success, 10cc reluctantly agreed. The group even filmed an appearance for *Top of the Pops* but it was never shown, the single still received very little airplay, and the record flopped.

"Still to this day one of my great regrets is that we couldn't break that record," says Jonathan King. "Because it was not just a great and, I think, wildly commercial record but to me that was the peak of their art. I think that was the most artistic and the most wonderful record that they ever made. To me, it's their finest moment, my personal favourite track of all the 10cc tracks."

Of course, Rubber Bullets had demonstrated that songs could still be hits without BBC support. Jonathan King reckoned that The Worst Band In The World was simply ahead of its time. "I think Jonathan thinks, we all think, that we're not going to sell all that many records at present, but in a couple of years' time, maybe 18 months, the records we're bringing out now will be just about right for the times," said Lol Creme.

This notion of being ahead of their time didn't faze the group at all. In fact, they relished it. "We're trying not to move with the times. We're trying to move ahead of the times and it might sound a bit intricate now but we hope eventually everybody's gonna listen to it and give us our identity," said Stewart.

Back at Strawberry, 10cc were having too much fun to be overly bothered by the single's lack of success. Having quickly overcome their initial nervousness, the creative juices were well and truly flowing, with the new songs showing an incredible amount of invention. While Creme and Gouldman had been writing The Worst Band In The World, Stewart and Godley had collaborated for the first time on Oh Effendi, a song about an Englishman selling arms, and girls, to the Arabs.

"One of those unshaven guys in a white flannel suit, dabbing himself with a handkerchief," said Godley at the time. "Sidney Greenstreet, one of them." Eric Stewart's recollections of writing the song with Godley remain clear. "As soon as I started playing this riff, Kev started singing words about somebody riding across the desert on a four-wheel-drive oasis," says Stewart. "Only Kev's sense of humour could have come up with something like that. The vibe was Country and Eastern; Moroccan Roll."

The next four minutes take the listener on a vivid journey, courtesy of some typically visual, witty and articulate lyrics. 10cc's lyrical dexterity was impressive but even more remarkable for always appearing effortless and never contrived. "Humour was important," says Gouldman. "With four writers you couldn't get away with anything maudlin or sentimental or too predictable. Kev would get very angry if something wasn't original."

Not that the group's talents were restricted to writing witty songs – they could also be poignant. Old Wild Men picked up on the theme of old age, inspired by Simon and Garfunkel's Old Friends, which ruminated on what life will be like when we're older. "We thought that was such a beautiful song," says Godley. "It was our version of that, an extrapolation of that idea."

Godley and Creme's twist was to wonder what life would be like for the virile young rock stars of today when they were in their dotage. "What happens to those guys when they get old?" said Godley at the time. "We suddenly had this picture of Eric Clapton in a wheelchair. You know – what the hell is he going to be doing in 50 years' time? Then we started worrying about it ourselves."

The recording showcased 10cc's exemplary studio skills, placing the track in a beautifully fragile setting, with strong vocal performances from Stewart and Godley. The song's coda gives Old Wild Men a suitably moving conclusion with its subtle reference, and new meaning, to the old lullaby *'Twinkle twinkle little star / How I wonder what you are.'*

A lot of the credit for the song's haunting arrangement is down to the 'Gizmo', the guitar attachment that Godley and Creme had invented in their quest to recreate orchestral sounds without having to hire an orchestra. At Godley's father's suggestion, they had enlisted the services of two professors, John McConnell and Martin Jones, from the University of Manchester's Institute of Science and Technology.

"It was a bit of a patch-up of glue, cardboard, bits of metal cut out with tin snips, but an excellent kind of model to work on," said McConnell. Together they worked up a prototype that enabled them to achieve their goal of creating orchestral sounds with a guitar through infinite sustain.

"We have spent quite a lot of time and money," said Creme at the time. "We've come up with a thing that fits on to the guitar behind the bridge. When you press down it sustains the string indefinitely. You can actually play the guitar normally but as long as you hold the note with your finger it will sound. You can do a vibrato using your fingers with it. The first two strings sound like violins, the next two like violas and the bottom two like cellos. If you have two guitarists you have a 12-strong string section."

The 'Gizmo' was used to good effect on several tracks on the album and also on Gismo My Way, an instrumental that would become the b-side to their next single. The development of the instrument was typical of the extraordinary lengths that 10cc would go to for the exact sound they wanted.

"Sounds couldn't be easily accessed like they can today with samplers and synthesizers," says Godley. "If you were after a certain sound, you had to find a way of creating it. It was a very physical process but it was great fun. We were constantly pushing the process, pushing ourselves and the equipment further than it was designed to go."

There had already been a tangible sense of excitement in the air as the band broke for Christmas but, as they returned to Strawberry in the new year, further inspiration was provided by the arrival of Paul McCartney who, having been impressed by 10cc's debut album, was using the studio to produce and play on his brother's self-titled album *Mike McGear*, along with his wife Linda and his band, Wings. Stewart and Gouldman had always dreamt that one day The Beatles would record at Strawberry and now here was a former Beatle almost making the dream a reality.

One day a couple waiting at the bus stop outside Strawberry were gobsmacked when they found themselves being serenaded by McCartney playing an acoustic guitar while sitting on the studio steps. The atmosphere at Strawberry during this period was highly charged. "We would work in the studios every day until 5pm and then Paul would come in the evenings and work from 6pm until late into the night," recalls Gouldman. "So, we often overlapped. The studio was completely crammed with equipment and there was this tremendous buzz. Paul would come in and we'd play him our stuff and vice versa, and I think that kind of inspired us as well. There was just a tremendous atmosphere. There was something in the air when we did that album." Eric Stewart also looks back on the sessions fondly.

"We were so happy at the time we were doing it," he says. "We had our own studio which was booked out 24 hours a day – we were using 12 hours and Paul McCartney was using the other 12 hours, so he'd go in through the night and we'd come in in the morning. We had all this fantastic equipment lying around the studio and we were just borrowing each other's gear and playing each other what we'd just done in the studio. It was a riot; everybody was so excited about it. They'd say, 'Come and listen to what we did last night,' and we'd say, 'Oh, that's not bad, but listen to *this*!'"

McCartney was highly impressed with the music 10cc were making, and with the 'Gizmo'; on March 1, 1974, he took temporary loan of one of the early prototypes.

While at Strawberry, Mike McGear's band The Scaffold visited the studio to record the single Liverpool Lou, which was also produced by McCartney. The single would feature the 'Gizmo' prominently, played by Lol Creme, and would give the band a big hit, reaching No.7 in the UK later in the year. There was even a reference to 10cc and their studio in the title of the bizarre b-side Ten Years After On Strawberry Jam.

10cc interrupted recording later in January to make a three-day promotional visit to America. "We got off the plane in New York and went down a road called Rockaway Boulevard," said Stewart. "We thought, 'We've got to write a song about it.' Better than, say, Park Lane or The Mall. Rockaway Boulevard, it's a beautiful name. And Wall Street is a great thing to write about as well. We can't write about Scunthorpe or Barnoldswick!"

The trip would inspire Stewart and Gouldman to pen one of the new album's standout tracks. "We were crossing Wall Street and Lol came up with the title The Wall Street Shuffle," recalls Stewart. "The riff to the song's chorus came to me straight away and when we got back to England I wrote the song with Graham. At the time there was the beginning of the downfall of the pound, although it's been dropping ever since I can remember. But this time it was a very heavy run and the mark and the yen were getting stronger, and all these words you could use in other ways."

The song was a revelation, proving that Stewart and Gouldman could be just as adept at wordplay and humour as Godley and Creme. As with much of 10cc's material, the song worked on two levels. On a superficial level, it had a killer hook and a distinctive arrangement. On a deeper level, the song was crammed full of clever puns, intricate instrumentation and changes in musical direction that repaid repeated listenings. Again, underneath it all there was a serious message – that while the fat cats made another killing on Wall Street, the bums on Skid Row were living off loose change.

When recording the song, the band preferred the sound they achieved from the drum kit belonging to Gerry Conway from Wings. "Gerry had this lovely little Gretsch kit, all loose skins," recalls Stewart. "I used his drum set-up and miked it with this repeat echo, it's got this gorgeous flapping echo drum sound. Once we had that and the electric piano down, it sounded like a hit already."

The 'anything goes' ethos was vividly brought to life on Clockwork Creep, a new Godley/Creme creation, that frantically told the story of a bomb on a plane.

"You've got a very serious subject – people are hijacking planes, blowing up children – and it's in the headlines all the time," said Stewart. "It almost gets boring and that scenario should never be boring. There's an idea behind the song, and that idea is very serious, but the music is fairly humorous. It gets over the point without being boring."

Sounding almost like three or four songs crammed into one, the finished track is breathtaking, veering into the unexpected like an out-of-control rollercoaster. Tempo changes, unexpected musical and lyrical twists and turns, unusual instrumentation, witty lyrics and intricate harmonies, all fused into the space of one three-and-a-half-minute song. By the end of the track the perspectives of the bomb, plane, crew and passengers have all been aired, with each of the group's members making a cameo vocal appearance.

To help add a different tone and colour to each song the band would utilise the range of voices they had in the group. In effect, each of the band's members would audition for each vocal part until the perfect voice was found.

"If someone fancied singing something he'd record it, then we'd wave this piece of cardboard with 'Next!' written on it and someone else would pop into the booth," recalls Gouldman. "You would hang your head in shame and go back into the control room and the next person would have a go at singing the song," says Creme. "And that was the audition process for 10cc's lead vocals."

The studio walls were lined with drawings of words and phrases that the band would use. One drawing featured the word 'Next!' in an explosion of crumbling rock letters; another said 'Riiiiiiiiight!' for when the desired result was achieved. Among the other drawings on the wall was one that read, 'I'm going for a walk and/or leaving the group'.

The band would try out lots of different ideas for instrumentation and then scrap them if they weren't working.

"On a lot of tracks, we used to lay down things and then take them off afterwards, because we'd overdone it," says Gouldman.

For Godley, the excitement was again partly driven by the power of applied ignorance.

"The buzz was not knowing what you were going to get out of the session, rather than knowing," says Godley. "There was an element of everything we did had the unexpected attached to it."

The group certainly found themselves experimenting with arrangements for a new Godley and Creme collaboration. Inspired by their love of the cinema, the five-minute track, given the working title of Hollywood Song, was the band's most ambitious recording project to date.

"It's supposed to be, and hopefully will be, the definitive film song about the 20s through to the 50s – the glorious days of Hollywood," said Godley at the time.

With the title changed to Somewhere In Hollywood, the subject matter of the song was a natural choice for two men so enamoured of the world of film. "Lol and I were frustrated filmmakers," recalls Godley. "All that Americana we'd assimilated, our love of the visual image. We couldn't make a movie but we could talk about it and enjoy the whole Hollywoodness and I think I'd recently read the book about Marilyn Monroe by Norman Mailer. Hollywood and that whole world in that perfect bubble was a big part of our upbringing, we loved Hollywood musicals. So, it was part of who we were and our influence and we kind of forced it on to a record with this song. The interesting thing about Somewhere In Hollywood was that it was a futuristic song about the past. It was steeped in old Hollywood but the sound of it was quite angular and twisted in its own way."

The song would go on to become one of 10cc's best-loved album tracks and would later be described by Q magazine, incorrectly as it happens, as "the best Marilyn Monroe song ever." While Monroe had been the initial inspiration, and featured in the original lyric, it was later changed to Jean Harlow, given the number of references to Monroe in popular culture at the time, such as Elton John's Candle In The Wind.

"We're actually scrapping the Monroe out of it," explained Eric Stewart at the time. "It was written six months ago, before this big Monroe thing came up, so it's being changed to Harlow. All we're talking about is the first plastic star to be made. We thought it was Monroe but it was Harlow really. The casting couch and the whole business. And there's Lassie, of course. He was another star but he didn't get on the casting couch!"

The sound of tap dancing can be heard during one section of the song.

"Kevin created that sound by putting tap shoes on his hands and playing the rhythm on some sand that we had sprinkled on the stairs to the cellar at Strawberry," recalls Stewart.

In retrospect, the song was significant for 10cc, signalling the ambitious shape of things to come on future albums: "This was the start of something new for us," says Gouldman. "It was very involved with totally opposing sections that worked together beautifully."

For Kevin Godley, Somewhere In Hollywood was the defining song of the whole album.

"I suppose with every record there's a song that stands out as a kind of paradigm shift and that was the one for me," he says. "We were being a bit more ambitious, pushing the boundaries. For me that song got the flavour of the album – it even sounded yellow, I don't know why."

Continuing the band's penchant for bizarre subject matter, Godley and Creme's Hotel contrasted the differing aspirations of the natives on an idyllic Caribbean island dreaming of a new life on the mainland; while those on the mainland dream of escaping to an idyllic island and buying a hotel. Listening to the song today, some of the lyrics might be deemed politically incorrect to the modern listener.

The song begins with what sounds like an aviary of electronic birds, an effect that had been created on a synthesizer. "That strange sound at the beginning was done on Lol's Revox quite some time ago," said Godley at the time. "We did it on a Moog synthesizer. We just got this sound like birds and thought it would be nice to have our own particular aviary. We didn't know what to apply it to and we had Hotel partially completed as a song and we found they married together rather well."

Influential *New Musical Express* journalist Nick Kent visited Strawberry in February 1974 to interview 10cc and hear the rough tapes of the new album. The band played him early mixes of the eight new tracks they had completed so far. He was knocked out with what he heard. "10cc may very well be the most exciting band us Limeys have going for us at the moment," said Kent. "The tapes of the new album only serve to bear this out further, displaying a sound on each track that almost defies you to label it mere invigorating eclecticism, pumping away at a pace that is both frantic and meticulously crafted, and culminating in a concept which falls between something akin to musical Dada and constant rock pastiches set off by a Busby Berkeley set of dynamics." Following the visit, Kent described 10cc as "one of the most exciting British rock prospects of the 70s."

With a couple of tracks still to write and record for the new album, the band once again swapped songwriting partners. When Godley paired up with Gouldman they discussed the latter's aversion to dancing. This led them to create their own dance craze, one that anyone could do, because it involved doing absolutely nothing, and the song The Sacro Illiac was born. Stewart and Creme, meanwhile, sat down with the intention of writing 10cc's first love song. "It sounded so stupid that we had to change it to a *silly* love song," says Stewart. Silly Love gave the pair an ideal opportunity to send up the 'love song' genre and its associated clichés, and the group's 'anything goes' approach is demonstrated by the Noel Coward pastiche in the song's middle eight. Despite being the last thing one would expect in the middle of a rock song, the band pull it off with ease.

"I've got a theory that if a thing is too relaxed and too normal it becomes almost muzaky," said Creme at the time. "It has to have some tension in it somewhere, whether it's in the voices or in two rhythms vying with each other – just something that makes you sit up and gives it that brightness."

Listen carefully and you can hear a laugh at the end of the middle eight. "I recorded my vocal for the middle eight, which finishes with the lines: '*Ooh, when a romance depends on clichés and toupées and threepées,*'" recalls Stewart. "It was so silly that I laughed at the end of the line by mistake. I walked back into the control room and said, 'Shall I sing that line again?' but everyone said, 'No, leave it as it is, it's a nice spontaneous moment.' So, we left the laugh on the tape."

Continuing their love of wordplay, the group decided to call the new album *Sheet Music*. "I got a call in the studio from a fan saying, 'I love Rubber Bullets, where can I get hold of the sheet music?'"

recalls Stewart. "I'd just read a review somewhere that said we were a pile of shit and I thought, 'Well, I suppose it is *Sheet Music*, isn't it?' I liked the idea of playing on the word 'sheet', so we decided to call the album *Sheet Music*. It was very 10cc, very tongue-in-cheek."

In fact, the music emanating from Strawberry Studios at the time was anything but *sheet*. 10cc were firing on all cylinders, characterised by the fact that every possible songwriting permutation between any two band members was deployed. Each songwriting partnership had its own style. "It's amazing how your writing style changes with whoever you write with," said Gouldman at the time. "We usually start off in two pairs, Eric and myself and Kev and Lol. But later, after writing three or four songs, we feel like a change and switch around. We start talking to someone else about an idea. It's quite casual."

Gouldman acknowledged that writing with other people had changed his approach to songwriting. "It's a whole different thing," he said. "I mean the same little things are working in my brain but what comes out is different. I'm not as conservative. You know I was very much a 'two verses, middle eight, verse, middle eight, finish' type of writer but now anything goes. It's a combination of the change in me and the people I'm writing with. It's much nicer to write with somebody else because if you come out with a duff idea, someone you're working with will tell you straight away. You get something like you're tuning your guitar up and you'll play something and Eric'll say, 'Do that again.' That type of thing. It's all chemistry."

The group even tried to write one song, 18 Carat Man of Means, with all four of them present at the same time. They weren't overly pleased with the end result. "One thing that doesn't work with us is the four of us writing together," said Gouldman at the time. "Take a listen to that song as proof. It was a rush job as well, so it's not very fair. But we did get a case of 'too many cooks' because there's so many millions of ideas flying around that it's impossible to organise; and what you get also is that if one isn't contributing as much, you tend to get withdrawn which tends to create a bad feeling." The experience convinced the group that they were better off writing in pairs. For Gouldman, the new sessions marked a return to the creative peak he had experienced with his songwriting in the mid-60s. "I think I'm lucky," he says. "I had it twice – when I was writing in the 60s and when the four of us were doing *Sheet Music*. It was unbelievable. We were absolutely bursting with ideas."

This was reflected in the band's choice of subject matter on *Sheet Music*, which was diverse to say the least – voodoo, avarice, the golden days of Hollywood, cannibalism, skyjacking, the music industry, love songs, gun-running, the plight of ageing rock stars. One subject that the group avoided was the trend at the time for bands to go 'cosmic'. "We're very cynical," said Godley at the time. "If anyone came in with a very heavy song about anything, we'd crack up. We don't want to get pretentious. I think the things we're writing about now are things we know something about or things we read about in the paper. We're just not the sort of people to get into heavy, cosmic stuff. Maybe we never will be, so there's no point pretending we know about it and write about it. The one thing we're dead against is apathy. Indifferent records. We'd rather have it that people hate it or love it than say, 'Oh, it's quite nice.' A definite reaction. I mean 'quite nice' means it's a bore, doesn't it?"

Back at Strawberry, Eric Stewart's final mix of *Sheet Music* confirmed that 10cc had created something very special. To design the cover for the album, Jonathan King turned to a couple of people he'd known while living in Cambridge – Storm Thorgerson and Aubrey Powell – who had gone on to form the design team Hipgnosis in 1968. They had recently created the iconic cover for Pink Floyd's *Dark Side of the Moon* album.

"There were a lot of visual puns in our album covers, and that was what Storm was particularly famous for, thinking up ideas along those lines," recalls Powell. "And I think because 10cc's lyrics were full of puns Jonathan thought Hipgnosis might be appropriate to do album covers for them, which of course we were."

King sent the Hipgnosis team a cassette of *Sheet Music* and the band visited them at their studio at 6 Denmark Street in London to discuss the cover. King insisted that 10cc themselves had to appear on the cover, which was counter to Thorgerson and Powell's usual approach. "Hipgnosis did not normally put bands on the front and generally refused but we probably needed to pay the rent that month so we thought it was a good idea!" says Powell.

The challenge was how to feature the band on the front cover in an interesting way. Rather than use an obvious group portrait, Hipgnosis conceived a design that featured 10cc pulling a sheet from the outer edge of the sleeve into the inner part of the picture, creating an optical illusion. For the central photograph of 10cc, Powell tried out two locations. One featured the band in an outdoor setting standing in a field pulling the sheet into the frame; the other was shot in the foyer of an art deco cinema in Wood Green, North London. Built as the Gaumont Palace cinema in 1934, it was renamed the Odeon in 1962, and it was felt that this second location worked better for the cover.

"It was an interesting way of creating a piece of surrealistic art," says Powell. "So you have the band standing in the old Odeon cinema in North London with them holding a sheet which then goes out into the cover and then seems to wrap around the cover as though they are contained within a frame of the sheet. What's nice about it is that you have a sensation of being drawn into the cover. It's almost three-dimensional. And it was just a visual way of having the band on the front, which Jonathan King had wanted."

The original photograph shot by Powell was then hand-coloured by Maurice Tate to accentuate the optical illusion. The sheet was hand-tinted in a vivid yellow, while the architecture of the cinema and the band, in particular Godley's jacket and Creme's shirt, were all highlighted with bright splashes of colour. Looking back on the sleeve today, Powell regrets the hand-tinting. "I never liked the yellow," says Powell. "I remember at the time I hated the yellow colour. There's no question it stood out in the shop window but personally I didn't like it."

While illustrator George Hardie added his graphic treatment to the design, George Marino was mastering the album at Sterling Sound in New York. *Sheet Music* was previewed to the music press via a playback at Trident Studios in London, again hosted by Jonathan King. Critics responded with spontaneous applause at the end of the playback, a reaction that was subsequently reflected in almost universally glowing reviews.

"What can you say about a record that fills you with such joy you wanna cry when it ends?" wrote *Melody Maker* journalist Colin

Irwin, under the headline 10CC'S MUSIC OF GENIUS. "10cc were rightly acclaimed for their first album but this one grips the heart of rock 'n' roll like nothing I've heard before. They're The Beach Boys of Good Vibrations, they're The Beatles of Penny Lane, they're the mischievous kid next door, they're The Marx Brothers, they're Jack and Jill, they're comic cuts cartoon characters ... and they're sheer brilliance. Few records are likely to better this during the year."

The *Record Mirror* review was equally exalting: "Quite simply the best and classiest pop album since McCartney's *Band On The Run* ... An excellently played and stunningly produced delight. Great stuff."

"10cc slay the critics," said *Disc*, while *The Sunday Times* called *Sheet Music* "brilliant" and *Sounds* called it "a classic". *New Musical Express* was the only publication not universal in its praise. Ian MacDonald found that while "at least two-thirds of *Sheet Music* is, by any standard, masterly" the album was let down by "tacky non-entities like Baron Samedi, The Sacro Illiac and Oh Effendi ... The big block now must be wilful self-limitation and the root of it lies in their comfortable isolation up there in Strawberry Studios ... Don't mistake me. What's fine on *Sheet Music* is very fine indeed. But its very immaculateness begs the question: surely they want to *do* something with their thorough-going literacy, other than cracking a couple of gags and satirising the odd Third World exploiter ... It would be unfair to expect a band without their talent to tackle heavier things – but 10cc could bring off so much. Witness Speed Kills, Somewhere In Hollywood and The Worst Band In The World. Here's hoping they make the next album the uncompromising stunner this could have been."

Four decades on, *Sheet Music* continues to receive glowing reviews, featuring in the book *1001 Albums You Must Hear Before You Die* and described by *Q* magazine as "one of the great pop albums of all time". It is also the 10cc album that all four of the band's original members single out as the best they ever recorded. It remains fresh, innovative and endlessly listenable to this day. *Sheet Music* would also prove to be a hugely influential album with other musicians. Aside from Paul McCartney, other fans of the album on its release included an up-and-coming act from Sweden, who would go on to become the biggest band of the decade – Abba. 10cc would be regularly cited as an influence by the band's songwriters, Björn Ulvaeus and Benny Andersson, while singer Anni-Frid Lyngstad would go on to record a Swedish cover version of The Wall Street Shuffle on her solo album *Frida Ensam*, citing 10cc as her favourite group. Trevor Horn, Terry Hall and Martin Fry are just three of the diverse number of musicians who cite *Sheet Music* as one of their favourite albums of all time, while influential hip-hop producer J Dilla sampled The Worst Band In The World prominently on Workinonit on his 2006 album *Donuts*.

Having picked up a prestigious Ivor Novello Award at the Grosvenor House Hotel in London for Rubber Bullets earlier in the week, *Sheet Music* was released on May 24. A massive critical hit, commercially *Sheet Music* was a slow-burner, taking nearly five months to hit its No.9 peak in October 1974, as word of mouth and personal recommendation spread the word. Yet despite spending nearly six months in the album charts and earning the band a gold disc, its sales were slightly disappointing in relation to expectations. After all, this was one of the great pop albums of all time.

"We've still got to get over this problem with most people that we're not just a *Top of the Pops* band, with hit singles," said Eric Stewart at the time. "We've got an album full of good material. We're an 'in' band, but not with the public."

Overcoming this problem wouldn't be easy given the band's resolute refusal to court an image. "I think it's time that people started listening to music as opposed to watching for images," protested Creme.

The band's approach flew in the face of fashion, where image was king. "The attitude and idea of 10cc was that it was a band that produced fine music in a studio and, as far as they were concerned, that was it," says Harvey Lisberg. "They weren't going to do any gimmicks or do anything particularly gimmicky visually. So that was it – 'We're going to go on in jeans and we're gonna play it and that's it and they can like it or lump it.' And that was an attitude which I found sort of hard to cope with. But I understood what they were saying. So, you are what you are. And they wanted to do it their way. And I can't criticise them for it. They might have found it easier to be more successful by being gimmicky, but they weren't prepared to do it."

Even if the group had chosen to project an image, it was difficult to see where they would begin, given the group's 'what is typically 10cc is that nothing is typically 10cc' philosophy. Unlike a lot of bands, 10cc didn't have a frontman.

"None of us were interested in being a big star," says Gouldman. "The music was the priority for us. I think if there'd been a natural showman in the band it would have come out, but there wasn't that kind of frontman, there wasn't a kind of Freddie Mercury in the band." Looking back, Eric Stewart is glad that the band didn't adopt an image. "Maybe if we had projected ourselves more, we'd have done much better," he says. "But looking back I'm quite glad we didn't succumb to all those sartorial mistakes."

"Except for my hair," laughs Gouldman. "Big afro number. Big error!"

As 10cc prepared for their next set of gigs, the band concluded that some songs just didn't work in a live setting. "We used to get loads of requests for The Dean and I, which we tried live, but we just couldn't get it together properly on stage even though we tried," said Gouldman. "The same with Hotel, which we tried with just acoustics or just with a piano, but it didn't work. Some numbers are destined never to be done live. They're purely for records."

Other songs, such as Somewhere In Hollywood, were also hard to pull off live. "Bastard to sing," recalls Godley. "I used to come to the front to sing it but I had bits of percussion as well, like a maraca for this bit, and hit this for that, because it was all on the record. Even the first three notes were a bastard to find. But I love that song."

Meanwhile, The Wall Street Shuffle had been lined up as 10cc's next single and once again, it was critically revered: "A must for the No.1 spot," predicted *Record Mirror*; "Another gem," said *Sounds*; "A sizzler," commented *Melody Maker*. The Wall Street Shuffle returned the band to the UK Top 10 during the summer of 1974. It was 10cc's fourth Top 10 hit but was equally significant for another reason, marking Eric Stewart's first taste of success as a songwriter.

"The Wall Street Shuffle was important from my point of view, because when we did the first album, Kevin and I did a lot of the writing and Eric didn't have that much confidence in writing because he hadn't been doing much," said Creme. "The Wall Street Shuffle was important because it was one of the first tracks he'd written. He did write it with Graham but a lot of the ideas were his own. It was his first major piece of writing that was a) successful and b) very good. This gave Eric confidence as a writer and it created a whole new thing, because it took a lot of weight off our shoulders. We'd already heard the effect on the first album and *Sheet Music* saw that style come into its own. You know, the fact that we could use wit and get away with it and take things lighter than most people take them, and still make serious music – not pretentiously heavy serious music, but good music that had humour to it. And the style came into its full and the writers came to their full when they got confident. So that song was pretty important really."

The Wall Street Shuffle was also important for 10cc's development in Europe. The song was a huge hit in the Netherlands, reaching No.1 and going on to become the eighth bestselling single of the year, helping 10cc to become one of the ten bestselling acts of 1974. *Sheet Music* went on to reach the Dutch Top 20 during a four-month chart run. The single also reached No.4 in France and Belgium, No.9 in Ireland and the Top 30 in Germany. In Norway, the future members of A-ha would also be seduced by its charms and would become fans of 10cc.

"Talk about classic," says the band's lead singer Morten Harket. "It's a great pop song, and what a great band, they had so many great songs, great songwriters. Very well produced as well."

With their critical and commercial success in the UK going from strength to strength, and their popularity growing in Europe, 10cc now set their sights on replicating that success in their spiritual home – America.

CHAPTER 8

MONEY FOR GOD'S SAKE

BREAKING AMERICA IS AN ASPIRATION THAT MOST BRITISH BANDS have at some point in their careers. But for 10cc, America somehow seemed even more important given its influence on their music. Among the American icons name-checked on the band's first two albums were: Uncle Sam, Charles Atlas, Vincent Price, Howard Hughes, John Paul Getty, Bela Lugosi, Greta Garbo, Rudolph Valentino, Bing Crosby, Jean Harlow, Norman Mailer, Fred Astaire and even Lassie; while Wall Street, the Bronx, the Bowery, Hollywood, the Pentagon, Beverly Hills, the CIA, senior proms and Jack Kerouak's *The Dharma Bums* were variously name checked in their lyrics.

The group had received very favourable critical reviews in America. *Rolling Stone* described them as "one of the year's most promising new acts, and *10cc* one of its most enjoyable releases" while *Rock* magazine dubbed them "a group of amazing competence". *Circus* called their debut album "breathtaking" and went on to say: "If the Beach Boys were wired and electrified for the 70s they'd be 10cc. They have the most addicting, endearing sound to come out of England in a decade."

Elsewhere, *Billboard* called their debut album "absolutely brilliant", *Zoo World* said it was "incredible", while *Record World* described it as "a totally marvellous album that must not be missed" and *Phonograph Record* called 10cc "the most fascinating new group to emerge in ages and no true pop connoisseur can afford to miss this album". *Cashbox* even went as far as to vote 10cc 'Best New Group of 1973', called their debut album "a must" and predicted they would "break big in the US in 1974."

However, these critical raves had not translated into sales. The band's records had been released in the US via a distribution arrangement that UK Records had with London Records. Their label manager for UK Records in the US, Don Wardell, had worked tirelessly to get the band noticed in America, but only Rubber Bullets had troubled the US charts, spending eight weeks in the Top 100 but stalling at No.73. It didn't help that their records were allegedly banned in some states, such as Texas, because the name 10cc was thought to have drug connotations. Some DJs even had problems saying the band's name, thinking it was pronounced phonetically *I-ock*.

The band knew that they would need to tour there if they were to launch 10cc properly in the US. The challenge was doing this in a cost-effective way when they didn't yet have an audience. They decided to dip their toe in the water by undertaking a tour of the East Coast in mid-February 1974, kicking off with two 'residencies' – in Atlanta and in Boston. On the eve of the tour the band were asked if they were going to go off and live the rock 'n' roll lifestyle to the hilt, leaving a trail of wrecked hotel rooms in their wake?

"God, no, we're not like that," said Creme at the time. "We redecorate them. They're cleaner when we leave than when we arrive!"

Creme's quip would go on to become a recurring 10cc in-joke whenever the band hit the road. First stop on their US visit was a series of six nights at a small club called Richard's on Monroe Drive in Atlanta. It was intended to be a low-key debut, to help iron out the wrinkles of performing live without their usual PA and backline support, before moving on to higher-profile gigs later in the tour. Still, the experience wasn't quite what the group had in mind.

"When we got there the owner of the club said, 'You're playing three one-hour sets,'" recalls Stewart. "We didn't have three hours of material, so we frantically rehearsed a load of rock 'n' roll standards to supplement our set. But when we played our first gig in front of an audience we got no reaction at all, just an occasional handclap. After the gig the club owner said, 'They loved you!' We said, 'Well, they didn't show it,' but he explained that the audience were all on Quaaludes. By their standards, we had gotten a good reaction! Later in the week we were rehearsing and the janitor said, 'I play the guitar. Can I come and play with you?' We thought that things couldn't get much worse, so we invited him up on stage and he was phenomenal! This guy could have taught Eric Clapton a thing or two about blues guitar, he was incredible! But it was pretty soul-destroying being this hot little British group wanting to break America and performing in a club full of people on downers."

From Atlanta, the tour moved on to Boston for a string of dates at the Performance Center, a small two-room club on the third floor of The Garage in Harvard Square, Cambridge. By March 8, 10cc were in New York for a meet-and-greet with journalists at the Colony Club arranged by their American PR, Connie de Nave. The following night the band played the most high-profile gig of the tour at the Academy of Music on East 14th Street on a bill that also included Brian Auger and Rory Gallagher. The performance confirmed that the band still had some way to go in becoming a truly compelling live act. "Having walked off with top honors in numerous reader's and critic's polls for their vibrant debut album, 10cc's arrival in the city was greeted with great expectations," wrote *Billboard*. "It was to their credit that they were able to reproduce numbers like Donna, Sand In My Face and Headline Hustler with more of the same exquisite harmonies but strident over-blown guitar solos marred Rubber Bullets and Ships Don't Disappear In The Night, making their debut an affair met with am-bivalent reactions."

To coincide with the tour, Headline Hustler was released as the band's next single in the US, with Speed Kills on the b-side. However, it failed to build on the momentum of Rubber Bullets, again highlighting the challenge of UK Records breaking the band in America with the limited resources at their disposal. To make matters worse, Kevin Godley picked up a serious throat infection on the tour. "I contracted tracheitis of the throat," says Godley. "We had a damp, dank, dirty, sweaty dressing room. There were no fa-cilities to have a shower, so you'd go to the bar, or step outside for a breather, before going back onstage."

Godley's throat infection became so bad that the tour was cur-tailed. Godley returned to the UK to recuperate while the other members of the band took the opportunity to take a holiday: Stewart and Creme in St Lucia, Gouldman in Los Angeles. All in all it was far from the US breakthrough the band had wanted.

Back at home, the group had a few weeks off before embark-ing on their second American tour. Justin Hayward was staying up in Manchester with Eric Stewart at the time and would end up recording with 10cc over the Easter weekend following a last minute cancellation at Strawberry.

"It was right after The Moody Blues had split and I was at a bit of a loose end," says Hayward. "I was staying up with Eric for a week and he said, 'Hey, there is a day free in the studio tomorrow because someone has cancelled, has anyone got a song?' I said, 'I've got this song, originally I think I called it You Are; it was a bit naff and, of course, Lol being Lol he said so and said, 'Why don't you give it a proper noun title and call it something like Blue Guitar?' I went away and thought about it for a couple of hours and thought, yeah that works and so I rewrote the lyrics that night and we went in the studio the next day and laid down the track."

Hayward's paean to the guitar featured Godley on drums, Gouldman on bass, Stewart and Hayward on guitars and Creme on the 'Gizmo', with 10cc providing vocal backing to Hayward's lead vocal. All were pleased with the result but, as a one-off, it would remain, for now, in the can at Strawberry. Hayward would go on to become a shareholder in the studio later in the year.

Meanwhile, a second American tour was set up to coincide with the release of *Sheet Music* in May. This time around they were lined up to play in much larger venues as support act for a variety of different headliners. The outcome was very mixed, depending on the acts they were supporting.

"We supported groups like Slade," says Stewart. "It was a joke to come on to a heavy, hard rock audience and do some of the softer songs. They really didn't want to listen to what we had to say." Off stage the two bands got on well together though, and Slade guitarist Dave Hill even gave Stewart some friendly advice about moving around more on stage. "So, the next time we played I tried it," said Stewart at the time. "I wandered round the stage and to my surprise I didn't feel at all daft. And the audience seemed to appreciate it too." However, sound problems dogged the tour. As support act there wasn't always time to do a proper soundcheck before the gig, so sound problems had to be ironed out once the band were on stage. Paul Yamada experienced this when reviewing their performance at the Kiel Auditorium in St Louis.

"Much to my disappointment, and to the group's too, the beginning of the set was marred by feedback screeches and a total PA imbalance; the problems were not their own fault, since the PA was not part of their equipment, and because they were not allowed a final soundcheck," wrote Yamada in *Concert News*. "To get one, they even came on 15 minutes late, and shortened their set. It didn't work; but this is not to say that they were not enjoyable; they worked on the problems, and by their last four songs the music was well-balanced, clear and distinct. By this time, the audience also began to respond; there was even enough clapping and reaction to warrant an encore, but there just wasn't time."

Despite the sound problems, Yamada saw enough potential for the future: "Perfection is what is called for, and perfection is what 10cc seems capable of," he wrote. 10cc resolved to take their own equipment with them next time they toured America.

"Our show was often half an hour or less," recalls Gouldman. "We couldn't really do our best work because we didn't have our own sound system or lights. At times the sound and lighting were terrible. It was hard for us to adjust to being just another support group because we were well-known in England and used to starring in shows and using our own sound and lighting equipment and getting a lot of attention. On those American tours, we felt like nobodies."

Supporting Johnny Winter on a couple of dates, a bootleg of the first of these – at the Cape Cod Coliseum on May 30 – reveals the band were not averse to overstating their popularity in the UK, with Lol Creme telling the audience that their new album had gone straight into the charts at No.2 back home. The second gig supporting Winter would become the highlight of the tour, performing at New York's iconic Madison Square Garden on June 1. The concert, in front of a capacity crowd of 22,000 people, was the biggest gig the band had played up to that point. "That was a real high point in our career," says Gouldman.

Reviews of *Sheet Music* in the American music press had been glowing. "10cc continues to shine as the most creative new group in English pop," said *Trouser Press*. "There is so much under the surface here that only after 10 listenings or more does one begin to notice how brilliantly crafted the songs are. Each successive listening seems to uncover a pun, a line, or a riff that you never noticed there before." Alan Betrock in *Phonograph Record* magazine described *Sheet Music* as "one of the most convincing and valuable pop efforts of the last decade". The reviews were equally good in the national press: "A rock experience like you've never heard before," wrote Henry Edwards in *The New York Times*.

There were high hopes that The Wall Street Shuffle would finally give 10cc their American chart breakthrough, although the band had been forced to change the words *'screw me'* to *'sue me'* in order to secure radio airplay. Perhaps someone at London Records was concerned about legal action from Howard Hughes?

By now, Don Wardell had left UK Records to take up a position as Head of Promotions at London Records, where he had more control over the promotional budget for breaking records released by UK Records in the US. However, with two potential hit singles lined up by UK Records for release in America at the time Wardell knew that, even from his new position of strength within London Records, he could only break one of them. Jonathan King was forced to decide which horse to back. "Don called me up and said, 'I hate to tell you but you've got to make a choice – either Beach Baby by The First Class or The Wall Street Shuffle by 10cc. I can put one of these records in the American Top 10, which is it to be?' And I chose Beach Baby. Of course, as a businessman, I should have said 10cc, they were my band and I was trying to build this band. I knew they were a bit grumpy that things weren't going their way and I knew I'd probably end up losing them. But Beach Baby was just, to me, an even more obvious American hit. Many would say I made a mistake and I might have done."

While Beach Baby went on the reach No.4 in the US charts – and No.1 in Canada – The Wall Street Shuffle failed to even make it into the American Top 100. And, despite the critical acclaim, *Sheet Music* would only climb to No.81 in the US album charts during a 14-week chart run, ensuring 10cc never got beyond 'cult' status. Their lack of US chart success was a major bone of contention with their American record company, London Records. "We gave them two albums," said Creme at the time. "Albums that we'd really sweated on and they did fuck all with them. It was really sickening to watch that much time and effort go down the drain. Especially after the good reviews we got in the American press."

10cc's failure to break America was a big source of frustration for the band. "It's crucial we make it in America," said Godley at the time. "If you want to make it as a world group as opposed to a quite popular band in England, you have to make it in America, and I'm sure we will sooner or later. But we have a problem in that the two tours we have done, not being headliners, we had to do it in 45 minutes. Our music is so varied it's difficult to get into it in 45 minutes. So, on the gig front I don't think we've got through to people yet. We'll have to break our records first and then do a tour with the lights and everything."

10cc might not have taken America by storm, but back at home their popularity was steadily growing. *Melody Maker* published an article in July that talked of "an era of new British pop/rock" citing bands such as 10cc, Queen, Supertramp and Roxy Music as part of this new movement. "A studio band in search of an audience, 10cc are nevertheless the most thoughtful and technically talented of the British nouvelle vague," said *Melody Maker*. "They need a bit of heart and personality to increase their impact. But there's no one else in this country that's so consummately accomplished, and only America's Steely Dan can rival them in recording professionalism."

While there was a loose thread that connected these bands together, they were certainly not part of a broader cultural movement.

"I do feel that ourselves, 10cc and Roxy Music were all connected in that we were making what was sophisticated pop music," says Supertramp's John Anthony Helliwell. "But none of us were exactly friends. We didn't hang out with, say, 10cc. In fact, they rather upset our drummer Bob Siebenberg when one of those guys rudely criticised him in an interview. Bob then referred to them as '10csick'! But we appreciated their symphonic sound, the multiple vocals and their overall quality."

10cc's workload, and natural inclinations, meant that they pretty much kept themselves to themselves. "All we did during this period was play live, write and record," recalls Graham Gouldman. "We never even hung out with bands in social situations. And we never thought of bands like Roxy and Queen as rivals."

On July 7, 1974, 10cc headlined a night at the London Rock

Proms at the Olympia arena, supported by The New York Dolls. They also filmed a live performance for the BBC's *In Concert* TV series, which was broadcast on BBC2 on August 21. A couple of days later, 10cc performed their biggest UK gig to date at the Reading Festival. However, on the day of their appearance the promoters were concerned when there was no sign of the band. Ric Dixon tried to persuade festival organiser Jack Barrie that 10cc should swap places with Fumble, the band that were scheduled to follow them. However, both Barrie and Fumble were less than sold on the idea. "If they are not here in time they do not perform at all!," said Barrie. Whether or not this was just a ploy for management to bump 10cc up the running order is unclear. If it was, it didn't work; the group were fined the majority of their £750 performance fee when they did eventually turn up, taking to the stage 40 minutes after they were scheduled.

To ensure that 10cc's progression kept moving in the right direction, Silly Love was released as the band's next single in August. "Jonathan King suggested we release it, though I think the band would have preferred to hold up a little while longer until new material appeared," said Godley at the time. "But Jonathan has a very clever head on his shoulders and we take his advice on matters like these." The single gained good reviews in the music press. John Peel wrote a glowing review in *Sounds* that concluded: "Top 5? One hopes against hope that it will be so." *Record Mirror* concurred: "It would take more than galloping inflation to stop this band making it big now that they've been recognised as one of the most stylish and professional bands in the land." *Melody Maker* was equally enthusiastic: "Rapidfire renaissance of all that's ever been good and original within the much-maligned medium of rock/pop music. This bunch of musical musketeers hold out hope for coming generations."

Silly Love reached the Top 10 in the Netherlands and France, the Top 20 in Belgium and entered the UK Top 40 in mid-September.

"We wanted to keep the momentum of 10cc going," said Gouldman at the time. "Whenever we put a new single out it's like starting again, almost. Not so much now, because we're more established, but before The Wall Street Shuffle. Also we thought it would help with sales of the album which indeed it has. That's of prime importance."

As Silly Love climbed the charts it gave *Sheet Music* an added sales boost, the album finally breaching the UK Top 10 on October 5 where it stayed for the next three weeks.

A tour of the UK helped to prolong the album's chart run still further. The band's itinerary took in London's iconic Rainbow Theatre and Manchester's Free Trade Hall, a memorable moment for Gouldman given it was where he'd seen his first gig some 14 years earlier. By the time the tour wound up at Isleworth College in London on November 9, *Sheet Music* had been in the album charts for almost six months, earning the band a gold disc. There was evidence at the gig to suggest that their confidence as a live act was growing too, although it was nearly midnight before the band took to the stage after 10cc's lighting technician inadvertently blacked out half of London while setting up the gig.

"Naturally the next one and a half hours convinced us all the show had been worth waiting for," wrote Andrew Warshaw in *Melody Maker*. "Once 10cc had actually got on stage it was impossible to find a weak spot." By this point, Zeb White was in situ as part of 10cc's road crew and it would become a tradition to play a practical joke on the last night of a tour. For this gig, White had rigged up three hangman's nooses that he planned to drop just behind the heads of Creme, Stewart and Gouldman as the group played Rubber Bullets. "So, they're playing away and we dropped these three hangman's nooses," recalls White. "Of course, the crowd just fell about laughing. Lol, Eric and Graham didn't know what was happening because by the time they turned around, we'd hauled the nooses back up. And then they'd get a bit further into the song and we'd lower them down again and the crowd would start laughing again!"

Ric Dixon failed to see the funny side. Unbeknown to White, a senior record company executive was in the audience with an eye on signing 10cc to their label. By now it had become increasingly apparent that the group had outgrown UK Records. They also wanted out of their deal with London Records in America. Despite their glowing reviews in the States, the band were still without a major US hit. Worse still, King's negotiating skills, that had earlier inspired the song 4% of Something, meant that the band weren't making much money in the UK either, despite five major hit singles and now a hit album. Attempts to improve the terms of their contract with Jonathan King, however, fell on deaf ears. "I went to him and I said, 'Jonathan, we've all got families now and we've earned £19,000 between the four of us. I could go on the buses and earn more than that. Are you going to pay us any more money?'" recalls Stewart. "He said, 'I can't, guys, I've told you before – that's my deal. I have a lot of overheads with the way I publicise you guys.' I said, 'Okay, but other record companies are interested.' He said, 'Well let them make me an offer.'"

As far as King was concerned the band had signed a five-year deal with him and needed to see the remaining three years through. "He had this kind of public school attitude," says Harvey Lisberg. "You signed the contract. We're going to the letter of the contract. We're not changing it. He was just rigid."

There was certainly no shortage of record companies queuing up to sign 10cc. Among them was 24-year-old entrepreneur Richard Branson, looking to make his first major signing to his Virgin Records label. He and co-founder Simon Draper caught the train up to Manchester on January 18, 1975 to meet the band and their management. "Harvey Lisberg did most of the talking," says Branson in his autobiography *Losing My Virginity*. "He explained that 10cc was under contract to a small record firm and they would need, as Simon Draper had already guessed, a large up-front payment. They were sure that their next album would be big enough to cover this risk. Harvey Lisberg also told us that they were negotiating with Phonogram. Simon and I had a quick chat in one corner and then offered £100,000 as an up-front payment."

Phonogram had already offered a higher sum to sign 10cc and as January dragged on a bidding war ensued. "On the last day of January, Harvey Lisberg asked for £200,000," says Branson. "Simon and I agreed to go along with this. Simon was so sure about 10cc's next album that he didn't flinch when bidding reached £300,000 and then £350,000 for the down payment. We rang around the Virgin licensees in France, Germany and Holland and they agreed to support us. We also managed to get Ahmet Ertegun at Atlantic Records to pledge £200,000. This was our first big signing in the market place against the major international record companies and for the first time we were dealing with vast sums of money. Simon and I got on very well with Lol and Eric but it was clear that there was a split in the group. The day before the contract was due to be signed, Eric and Lol flew off for a holiday. The timing could have been better but they left a power of attorney with Harvey Lisberg. The day they left I wrote a letter to all the Virgin shop managers telling them about the signing and telling them to go out and buy a bottle of champagne on Virgin to celebrate."

The band's members were thrilled to be signing to Virgin and the prospect of having the muscle of Atlantic Records behind them in America. The deal also allegedly secured the band a royalty of 14%, over three times what they were receiving from Jonathan King. Spirits were high as Stewart and Creme jetted off with their families for a two-week holiday in St Lucia. However, the mood changed quickly when they arrived on the island.

"As we stepped off the plane, a guy came up to me and said, 'There's a phone call for you'," recalls Stewart. "When I picked up the phone it was Richard Branson, who was fuming. He said, 'You bastards! You've signed to Phonogram. I thought you were signing with me!' I said, 'Richard, I thought we were signing with you too, let me give Harvey a ring and find out what's happened.' So, I phoned Harvey and he said both Virgin and Phonogram had offered a million dollars for a five-album deal, but that Virgin had wanted an album every nine months, whereas Phonogram had wanted an album every 12 months. Harvey had thought that an album every nine months would be too much of a drain on us, so he'd signed with Phonogram. We'd have loved to sign with Branson, but we all agreed that an album every nine months would have been impossible."

Many years later, Simon Draper remained disappointed by the band's decision. "I was really upset about 10cc," he says. "They were just perfect for Virgin at the time, they had everything going for them." Looking back today, Lol Creme shares this disappointment and regrets that the band didn't sign with Branson.

"I can only speak for myself but I was absolutely horrified, embarrassed and disgusted, and to this day I still am," says Creme. "It's easy to have hindsight but had we been with Atlantic in America it would have been a very different story for 10cc in the States."

10cc's management had signed the band to a five-album deal

with Phonogram, for a sum believed to exceed $1m, a record transfer price for a British band at the time, and the equivalent of $4.7m today. In return, 10cc would have to deliver a new album to Phonogram every 12 months until 1979. The new record deal was announced via a press release on February 13, 1975. "This is one of the most thrilling acquisitions any record company could have made," said Tony Morris, managing director of Phonogram. "The band is already highly successful and well-established but we believe they are yet to reach their full commercial potential, either in this country or internationally. We believe that Phonogram is the best record company for the band. One of the reasons is that 10cc will be marketed and coordinated throughout the world by one company on one label – Mercury."

UK Records also issued a statement at the time. "Having discovered, launched and supported 10cc through hit singles, and eventually an album that stayed in the charts for nearly six months, we were rather disappointed when they expressed a desire to leave the label. However, a million dollars buys a lot of loyalty," said a spokesperson. Still, a million dollars reflected 10cc's standing as one of the UK's hottest properties and, besides, Jonathan King had done extremely well from the deal. He received a large payment to compensate him for the breach of 10cc's five-year contract. More significantly, he retained control of 10cc's UK Records original sound recordings in perpetuity, a lucrative seam that he would continue to mine over the coming years. It's a little-known fact that he also managed to negotiate a royalty on all *future* 10cc recordings. "When I passed them on, I received a 4% royalty on their future records, which I still get to this day," says King. "I made sure that I had 4% of something! So that's the percentage I've had ever since and still earn on a monthly basis."

Not a bad little pension from the self-proclaimed 'worst band in the world'!

CHAPTER 9

BIG BOYS DON'T CRY

THE BAND'S THIRD ALBUM WAS ALREADY IN THE CAN BY THE TIME IT was announced that they had signed with Phonogram. Recording had begun at Strawberry back in November 1974.

"I'm really looking forward to getting back into the studio," said Graham Gouldman on the eve of the new sessions. "I really miss it now. I love the whole atmosphere of the studio. I remember once we did a session at seven in the morning. Something we had to get done. When we finished we said, 'What are we doing here? Why?' We're starting recording tomorrow. As opposed to the last two albums where we've written a song and recorded it, written a song and recorded it, this time we've got a few songs to go ahead with."

Among these songs were three new Stewart/Gouldman collaborations, and the outline of a Godley and Creme 'epic' called One Night In Paris, which carried on the direction suggested by Somewhere In Hollywood on *Sheet Music*.

"What we're going to do is record the three that Eric and I have written, then we'll change partners, and then sometime later Kevin and Lol will get back together and finish their piece," said Gouldman at the time.

Of the new Stewart/Gouldman songs, one in particular marked a departure for 10cc.

"One's almost a straight love song," explained Gouldman at the time. "It's nothing like 10cc have ever done before. Millions of other people have done it but 10cc haven't done it."

The song in question was I'm Not In Love, a love song with a typical 10cc twist.

"The title was the first thing that happened," says Stewart. "My wife used to say to me, 'Why don't you say I love you more often?' I used to say to her, 'Well, if I say it too often, it'll lose its meaning.' I came up with the title I'm Not In Love – but here are all the reasons why I am very much in love. It was also quite quirky and very 10cc to turn something on its head and say, 'I'm not in love' but I am."

Stewart started the song off by himself and took what he had into the studio asking who was interested in finishing off the song with him. Graham Gouldman expressed an interest, and with Godley and Creme hard at work on One Night In Paris, the pair got down to business. "We started with the chords I had and we began bouncing ideas off each other," recalls Stewart. "Graham came up with this lovely little fill between the verses. I eventually played that on the recording with a Fender Rhodes. A beautiful progression with a beautiful sound. He also came up with the opening chords of the song, all very expectant of what is to follow."

The opening chords were somewhat reminiscent of those used by Hall and Oates on their 1974 hit She's Gone. With the shape of the song falling into place, Stewart and Gouldman wrote more lyrics for the song's other verses. "It was a conscious attempt to write a love song," says Stewart. "Lol and I had attempted to write one before but got hysterical and it ended up as Silly Love. The song is about someone who finds it hard to express his feelings in words, although it was elaborated on to make it more of a story. I mean, I never really hung a picture over a mouldy patch on the wall."

With the song's structure consisting only of verses, the pair felt that the song needed a middle section. "We got the melody for that very, very quickly," recalls Stewart. The final section of the song to be completed was the bridge. "Graham pulled that chord progression out of the bag," says Stewart. "When you've been writing with somebody for quite a long time these things just happen naturally. You find yourself searching for something that will turn you both on. That's the chemistry."

In the process of writing, a happy accident ended up improving the chord sequence of the bridge. "Eric played it on the piano, and instead of going to the top of the right chord he went to a chord a full tone below it," says Gouldman. "It was great and we kept it. It was a mistake but it actually improved the song."

After two or three days of writing, the song was finished and 10cc set to work committing it to tape. But, as with Baron Samedi at the start of the *Sheet Music* sessions, they discarded their initial attempt, which had a bossa nova feel to it in the style of The Girl From Ipanema.

"When we heard it back everyone was underwhelmed," recalls Creme. "Nobody had any real enthusiasm to carry on with it, it sounded so underwhelming." Godley felt that it was simply not up to scratch. "I hated it," he says. "I didn't get it particularly. There was something in there. We all recognised that there was something in there, but that treatment didn't really bring it to life." So the original, bossa nova version of I'm Not In Love was scrapped. "We threw it away and we even erased it, so there's no tape of that version," says Stewart. "It pissed me off no end at the time but it was also very democratic."

It was a mark of just how stringent the quality control was within 10cc that the group were prepared to throw songs away that they didn't feel were up to their standards. "If a song hasn't got it we'll do it again until it has got it or else we'll scrap it," said Lol Creme at the time. "We scrap far more stuff than we use."

But I'm Not In Love refused to die. "The bloody song stayed in my mind," says Stewart. "It had something going for it in the lyric. 'I'm not in love' was stupid, for a start. If you are madly in love with someone you don't say 'I'm not in love,' so it kept coming back to me."

When Stewart started to hear staff at Strawberry singing the song, he went back to the band to try and persuade them to give the song a second chance. Kevin Godley conceived of a completely new way to approach the track. "I think I said at the time, 'Why don't we do it with voices, not instruments just a wash of voices?'," says Godley. "Probably out of desperation to come up with something that brought this thing to life."

Godley's idea was to create a massed choir of voices that sounded like "this heroic, angelic sound of Heaven", like the one he had heard in the movie *2001: A Space Odyssey*. It was a bold idea but far easier said than done in an era before the advent of synthesizers and samplers. Eventually, Lol Creme figured out a way of making it a reality by using tape loops to create a continuous wash of sound. Tape loops would enable the vocal backing to play continuously, without the pauses for breath that would be necessary if it was a real choir.

"I'd become obsessed with tape loops after listening to the Beatles' Revolution 9," says Creme. "Our studio used to do recordings for the Mellotron, a keyboard that played pre-recorded notes. Session musicians would come in and do these painstaking recordings for every instrument of an orchestra, one note at a time, so that when they were all played together on a Mellotron it sounded like an orchestra. I was fascinated by this and wanted to try it with banks and banks of voices."

Creating this virtual choir would be a laborious task requiring them to multitrack each note of the chromatic scale, one note at a time, and then make a loop of each note before moving on to the next. So, Godley, Creme and Gouldman went into the studio and sang 'aah' in the key of A for as long as they could. Then they sang the note again and again until they had built up their choir singing the note of A. This process was then painstakingly repeated another 11 times.

A tape loop was made for each of the 12 notes. Each loop was made as long as possible to avoid the sound of where the tape had been spliced together being audible. This resulted in each tape loop being about 12 feet in physical length. Even playing back tape loops of this length in the studio presented a major technical challenge that was only solved via a Heath Robinson combination of makeshift capstans, microphone stands and vertically held screwdrivers to keep the tape tensioned as it spooled around the control room.

Stewart then recorded about seven minutes of each note of the chromatic scale onto a separate track on the 16-track machine. This meant the faders of the mixing console could now be played like a keyboard to fit with the chord changes in the song. Each fader had a specific note, so by raising three or four faders at the same time you could create a chord. With 12 of the 16 tracks taken up with vocal tracks, the group needed to bounce these down to a stereo pair so that they could free up tracks to add other sounds and instruments to the recording. Getting this right was absolutely vital because it would mean erasing the vocals to free up extra tracks.

A basic stereo backing track was put down, initially as a temporary measure just so that they could follow the basic structure of the song. To keep time, a simple bass drum rhythm was laid down. Except that using an actual bass drum didn't sound right so a bass drum sound was created on a Moog synthesizer that gave it a slightly different sound, almost like a heartbeat. It was another example of the lengths 10cc would go to get the exact sound they wanted. With Godley laying down the beat on the Moog, Stewart ran through the chords of the song on a Fender Rhodes electric piano, while Gouldman added a rhythm guitar played on a Gibson ES-335 semi-acoustic guitar directly into the desk. Then came the nerve-racking part when they mixed their virtual choir into a stereo pair.

"We had all four of us all around the mixing desk working the faders to bring the notes in as the song chords were changing," says Stewart. "That wash of sound coming in and out all the way through the song – it's the four of us on the mixing desk moving the faders. Luckily, we got it. We got it just right."

To ensure the faders never went to zero, and there was always a vocal wash in the background, a low-tech solution was employed. "I put a piece of gaffer tape across the bottom of the fader paths to stop them ever going to the bottom," says Stewart. "That meant we had a chromatic scale sizzling underneath the track all the time, a hiss just like the hum you sometimes hear at a football match when nobody's shouting. If you listen to the opening of the song, where the bass drum beats us in, you will hear a sizzling hum there that continues all the way through the track."

Even listening to it in its unfinished state, the band knew they had created something utterly unique and very special. Having bounced the massed vocals onto two tracks meant they freed up 12 tracks to add other production touches to the song. Stewart laid down a guide lead vocal for the song, while Godley and Creme added the 'It's because' refrain that comes at the end of each verse.

"They had great high voices, those two, so I multitracked them about four times on those lines," says Stewart. He then added a harmony vocal for the bridge. By now it was estimated that there were 256 vocals multitracked on the recording. At this point the only instruments were Godley's bass drum played on the Moog, Stewart's electric piano part and Gouldman's rhythm guitar. There wasn't even a bass guitar featured on the record, which was, of itself, very unusual. Equally unusually, it was then suggested that a bass guitar solo was added to the middle section.

"Graham came into the control room and played the solo," recalls Stewart. "We sat there and he played bits, and we said, 'Like that,' 'Don't like that,' 'Do that again,' and it developed."

The bass solo was another break with convention but worked perfectly in that section of the song. One section that wasn't working so well, however, was what followed in the middle eight. "There was something that stopped it working when we came to record it," says Creme. "The middle eight brought the whole thing down." The main problem with this section of the song were the lyrics. "The words just sounded naff: *'Don't feel let down / Don't get hung up / We do what we can / We do what we must.'* We looked at each other and said, 'Oh Christ, that sounds crap, doesn't it?'"

Creme suggested scrapping the vocals and simply picking out the melody on a grand piano. He also suggested having a female voice whispering 'Get it together' in this section of the song. "But the more I thought about that line, the more 'Get it together' sounded harsh," recalls Creme. "So I changed it to 'Be quiet, big boys don't cry', which felt softer and more comforting."

At that point in the proceedings Cathy Redfern, the reception-ist at Strawberry, popped her head around the door to convey a message. "She opened the studio door quietly and whispered, 'Eric, there's a phone call for you,' and left," recalls Stewart. "Lol said, 'That's it! Let's get Cathy to speak the words'."

Creme followed Cathy down the hall to the studio reception to tell her his idea. "I was twenty-one then," recalls Redfern. "I adored the boys, and they treated me like their sister. When Lol told me their idea, I thought it might be a prank. They were always kidding around. But Lol picked me up and threw me over his shoulder. In the control room, the guys were serious. They told me it was a love song and that my line should sound like I was trying to convince my boyfriend to think clearly."

Redfern went into the studio with Godley to steady her nerves, who touched her arm when it was time for her to deliver her words. After a few attempts to get the tonality right, with Redfern getting closer to the Neumann U67 microphone to softly whisper her line, one of the most evocative moments in pop was born. "She had a gorgeous voice, and there it is on the record," says Stewart.

To add a final, almost dreamlike, quality to this middle section, and the final fade-out, the band employed another unique device. "I went out and bought a child's plastic toy music box," recalls Creme. "When you pulled the box's string it played the English nursery rhyme, Boys and Girls Come Out to Play. We set up two mics in the studio about 12 feet apart, for a stereo effect. Then I swung the little box over my head between the two mics as it played the tune. We wound up with an eerie sound, shifting from one speaker to another. After Eric added stereo echo, the effect at the song's fade-out was like someone whistling in a tunnel."

As Eric Stewart mixed the track he started to get shivers up his spine. To this day, he can still recall the buzz he got when the track was finished. "I can still remember the feeling I got when I'd finished mixing it first time around," he says. "We just sat there with our mouths open, saying we've got something here that's very, very special. It made people shiver when they sat down and listened to it in the control room. We sat there, I tell you seriously, for about three days, just listening to this thing. I was looking at Kevin and the other two guys saying, 'What the fuck have we created? This is brilliant.' I'd never heard anything like it in my life. I mean, The Beach Boys were seriously good at harmonies, but they hadn't, as far as I knew, done anything this way."

So pleased were they with the end result that at the end of a session in the studio they would turn off the lights and play the song with the volume cranked up, purely for their own pleasure. One of the first people outside of the group to hear the song was DJ Andy Peebles, who worked on Piccadilly Radio in Manchester, and had become very friendly with the band.

"I became so close to Graham and Eric that they invited me to Strawberry Studios while they were mixing I'm Not In Love, which I consider to be a huge honour," says Peebles. "I remember Eric asking me, 'Do you think there are too many vocals on this?' and I gave him my opinion, whether he took any notice of what I said is another matter."

I'm Not In Love was the ultimate demonstration of 10cc's innovative use of the recording studio and their collaborative approach to making music. Each member of the band had played a critical role in attaining the end result. Their studio skills had transformed a good song into a work of art.

The band would use the massed backing vocals of I'm Not In Love on another new track, albeit in a very different way. Inspired by a sleazy newspaper story at the time, Stewart and Gouldman had penned a song with the working title Through The Keyhole, although by the time the song appeared on the album it had been retitled Blackmail.

"There was some scandal in the papers," recalls Gouldman. "There always is, but this one was particularly sleazy."

In the song, the protagonist's blackmail plot backfires when, with a typically ingenious 10cc twist at the end, the girl becomes a superstar when her husband is delighted rather than offended by the incriminating photographs and sells them on to Hugh Hefner at *Playboy* magazine. One of the production tricks that gave the song its distinctive sound involved using some of the vocal tape loops from I'm Not In Love but played at half speed to sound like cellos.

"If you slow the loop down a human voice sounds amazingly just like a cello," says Stewart. "It's got the rasp from the throat that sounds like a bow with rosin swiping across the strings. Unbelievable. Where you hear cellos chugging very, very fast in rhythm all the way through, that's the voice loops slowed down and fed through two faders, which were pushed up and down rhythmically. It was wonderful the way it worked."

The other new Stewart/Gouldman song, Flying Junk, told the tale of a drug dealer bringing in cocaine and heroin from Singapore for sale in London's King's Road. The band might have indulged in the odd Benson and Hedges 'Mindfucker', but they weren't users of Class A drugs themselves.

"We never indulged, in the studio or on the road," says Gouldman. "The music was so complicated you had to have all your wits about you. We seemed to be progressing without mind-expanding drugs anyway."

Once a new song was brought into the studio it became, as usual, group property.

"Kev and Lol would change the rhythm of one of our songs, or Eric and I would edit one of theirs," recalls Gouldman. "'Just do the best bits,' we'd say, which would bug the hell out of them sometimes.

They'd say, 'Those were the best bits!' Kev and Lol were more experimental, Eric and I more commercial. The combination was great.
Each side helped the other."

This approach was used to good effect on the wonderfully titled
The Second Sitting For The Last Supper, which took a pot shot at
that most sacred of sacred cows, religion. The song had started life
as a Stewart/Gouldman composition but ended up as collaboration
between all four members of the group.

"When Eric and I completed it we realised it was slow-moving
and we weren't happy with it even though we knew it was good,"
says Gouldman.

The pair played the song to Godley and Creme.

"Musically it was full of good ideas, but lyrically the idea didn't
quite make the point," says Creme. "So, we decided to try and make
the point a bit more strongly. On the production side we decided to
speed it up a bit, have a bit of fun with it."

The four of them spent three days rewriting the song. It was another example of how the Stewart/Gouldman and Godley/Creme
axes of the band would bring out the best in each other.

"Quite often, for example, Eric and I would write a song in
a certain way and then Kev or Lol would turn the thing round
and say, 'Why don't we do it in this tempo or this rhythm
rather than that rhythm', which would make it different and
give it a whole new angle," says Gouldman. "That happened
a lot."

The Second Sitting For The Last Supper would go on to become
one of the highlights of the new album, deftly combining a bitter
attack on the Church with a positive plea for the Second Coming.
The lyrics were as sharp as ever and, as was so often the case with
10cc songs, the group used humour to put across a very serious
point, in this case the contrast between the promised land of milk
and honey and the reality of ever-lengthening queues for the soup
kitchen and the dole in mid-70s Britain.

"I'm Jewish, three of us are Jewish, but I think the idea of Jesus
Christ is such a fabulous idea," said Creme at the time. "We're
saying that we think it'd be fantastic if a Messiah came down and
gave us some direction."

This didn't stop some critics from calling the song blasphemous.

"We called ourselves 'three Yids and a Yok' but we weren't self-conscious about whether the Messiah had come in the first place or not," says Gouldman. "There was so much bad news about, it was about time the Messiah came back!"

Such was the mutual respect within the band that seldom did anyone get overly precious about constructive criticism from another group member.

"Our ability to take criticism made by other members of the band is one of our strongest points," said Creme at the time. "Every song is the combination of two minds writing the basic bare bones of the track, and then four minds that tear the track apart, add constructive ideas lyrically or musically, so the finished product is one of four minds."

This was demonstrated well on One Night In Paris. According to Godley, the original impetus for the song came from "a desire to get away from writing about America". But while the setting of the new song was the French capital, it was still viewed through an American lens.

"In a sense it was Somewhere In Hollywood part 2," says Godley. "We were trying to re-conjure the magic of big, retro Hollywood musicals, like An American In Paris. It was like our tribute to George Gershwin in his centenary year. It was a lot of fun. Big on complexity and detail, small on groove, though."

Written almost as a mini-musical, the pair got so involved in the writing process that the multi-part piece ended up running to nearly 20 minutes. At one point there was a tentative plan for it to occupy a full side of the new album. Stewart and Gouldman, however, had other ideas.

"We criticised a large section of it, saying it wasn't needed," says Stewart. "It was just padded out to make it long. So, we started editing it down while they were actually playing it to us. Eventually we knocked it down to about eight minutes."

Having agreed the song's three-part structure, they set to work committing One Night In Paris to tape, deciding to approach the song almost like a short film.

"The lyric sheet was written as a script, with the characters at the sides of the lines, and then we had to find the people in the band whose voices would fit the characters," says Stewart. "It was a really interesting project and I think it worked fabulously."

Set deep in the heart of a Parisian red-light district, the narrative follows a night in the life of a tourist as he encounters murder, corruption and the brothel at 42 Rue de Saint Jacques, where all the girls are *'good in the sack'*.

"It was the most fun to record, trying to recreate Paris in Stockport," says Gouldman.

The group had a field day recording the song, bringing the visual subject matter to life through sound, and spent a long time in the studio experimenting with different instrumentation until they got it totally right.

"We worked on that song for about two weeks, filling it with every kind of instrument we could think of and then eventually scrapped the whole lot and went back to piano, bass and drums, which is all the song is," says Stewart.

The final recording proved that four minds were better than two.

"Musically we'd tried to stretch ourselves by setting up a new musical problem and then trying to solve it," says Creme. "It was one that took a long time to solve and it required the help of all four minds to get it to work."

Listening to the song today, Kevin Godley admires how avant-garde it is. There is just one thing he would change in retrospect.

"The thing I actually hate about it now are the French accents," says Godley. "Why did we do that? It didn't need that but by adding that layer it sort of knocked it over into comedy and pastiche, which it didn't really need to do. If it's ever performed again we'd never perform it like that because it doesn't need that. Had we written that now, with the technical know-how one has about how one can include visuals in the presentation of music, that could have been put over visually without the comedy, without the *'Allo 'Allo* accents."

Another song on the album that tipped into comedy was The Film of My Love, which, according to Gouldman, was a "massive piss-take. It was cheesy, cheese gone off, that was the idea."

The Godley/Creme song used a string of film titles and movie jargon as a corny romantic metaphor. "It was aimed at lyrics that used that sort of imagery, taking the mickey out of those cabaret-type songs," says Gouldman. "Strangely, the room emptied when it came to volunteering to do the vocals, but I had this caba-ret-type singer's voice so it didn't bother me."

While clever and witty, the problem with The Film of My Love was that it is more of a comedy record and, like most comedy records, it doesn't bear repeated listening once you've got the joke. Listening to the song today, it just sounds cheesy.

"I think by then we'd got lost in wordplay," says Godley. "It had become a crutch. It wasn't like we'd run out of things to say, it was that we ran out of things worth saying. It was kind of the beginning of 'this is who we are now'. There was no seriousness involved in what we were saying, so it gradually became a series of in-jokes and clevernesses. And we never really managed to fuse the cleverness with any true emotion, apart from I'm Not In Love."

In general, the atmosphere in the studio for the new album was more serious than it had been for *Sheet Music*, largely because of the ongoing negotiations over their new record deal that was going on in the background.

"We were right in the middle of changing record companies and there were a lot of business hassles," said Kevin Godley at the time. "One day we'd think we were doing really well and the next there'd be some Sword of Damocles hanging over our heads. It was really a bad time to do an album with all those ups and downs." The band's penchant for playing practical jokes, however, remained undimin-ished, with Peter Tattersall finding himself on the receiving end one night at Strawberry.

"10cc were recording during the day and at night I was recording this band called Oscar," recalls Tattersall. "I came in one evening with the band as 10cc were leaving. Later, the guitarist was doing a guitar solo but he kept playing this one note wrong. We would do it over and over, always with this wrong note and he'd insist he played the right note. So he did it again and this time he played it in harmony! It was brilliant, and we said, 'How did you do that solo in harmony?' and he said he hadn't. I thought, 'Oh dear, my hearing's going, I heard it harmony.' Then loads of strange things kept happening. Someone said, 'Hello there.' I turned around but there was nobody there except the roadie who was asleep behind me. Eventually the recording desk started talking to me. I called everyone into the control room and said, 'Who is it that's messing around?' They all denied it so I played back what we had just done. I went to press the button and the mixing desk said, 'Ouch!' So I started to take the panels off to see what was going on, and as I did this voice from inside the desk said, 'Don't touch that, leave me alone!'"

Unbeknown to Tattersall, the bum notes in the guitar solo and the voices he was hearing were coming from 10cc down in the Strawberry basement. "What they had done was rig one of the small talkback speakers to a microphone in the cellar with a guitar and an amp playing the solo as well and talking to me from down there," he says. "They also had a tape machine and were recording the whole thing. It went on for an hour or so. When I realised, I went down to the cellar but they had gone. I was completely wound up! The next day they were doing an interview for Radio One at Strawberry and I walked in and they just fell about laughing and they played on the radio the tape of this wind-up. And we just kept getting each other. It was such good fun."

In general, the new album saw the quartet sticking to their two main writing teams and swapping partners far less frequently than they had on *Sheet Music*, which had featured every possible writing permutation. This time around, the only track not written by the two main teams to make it onto the album was Life Is A Minestrone, a Stewart/Creme collaboration. The pair had been listening to the radio, while driving home from the studio one evening, when Creme thought he heard the disc jockey say, 'Life is a minestrone'. Stewart wasn't so sure but suggested it would make a great idea for a song, a good analogy for the diversity of experiences and emotions of life itself. The dilettante in the song tries to cram in as many of these experiences as possible. The Tower of Pisa, White House, Taj Mahal, Hanging Gardens of Babylon and even an *'eyeful of thetower in France'* are visited over the course of the song's four and a half minutes.

"The chorus was so glorious, so happy," says Gouldman. "It was written in one go even though there are three or four tempo or key changes."

Stewart and Creme had initially tried to collaborate on another new song, albeit unsuccessfully. "We thought, 'Let's do a rock 'n' roll song, it should be easy for us," said Creme at the time. "We wanted some light relief after writing difficult things, we wanted to write a Chuck Berry-type thing. We thought it'd be a cinch because it's got to be a cinch to write something as simple as that. And we sat down with really simple lyrics, 'Memphis'-type things, but I mean Chuck's done it – and he's done it better than we'll ever do it."

While Stewart and Creme were writing together, Godley and Gouldman paired up to write Channel Swimmer, an engaging song that would appear as the b-side to the band's next single.

During the recording of the album, Lol Creme became a father. He called his son Lalo.

"The name comes from the last two letters of Angela and the first two letters of mine," said Creme at the time. "We wanted an unusual name and the most unusual thing we could think of was to make up a name ourselves."

The experience inspired a new song Brand New Day.

"My wife and I just had a baby boy," said Creme at the time. "And I wanted to write them a song. It was in my head all through the pregnancy. Then I got together with Kevin and it developed strangely, but still a lullaby to my baby, Lalo, to tell him to watch his ass."

As the band's third album neared completion, thoughts turned to a title. Eric Stewart had mentioned that One Night In Paris was like the soundtrack to a film that had yet to be made. This, plus the inclusion of another song with a cinematic theme, The Film of My Love, led the group to call the album *The Original Soundtrack*. It was a nod to the visual, cinematic nature of their music. Hipgnosis, who were again drafted in to design the album cover, picked up on this theme when discussing ideas for the sleeve.

"It seemed to us that we should do something about movies, of course," recalls Aubrey Powell. "Storm and I had both been to film school and we had this old Steenbeck 16mm editing machine. So we took lots of photographs of the old Steenbeck and various bits of editing equipment. But when we looked at the photographs they somehow didn't have the romance of Hollywood. They were too cold and somehow it just didn't feel right."

Powell suggested they employ the talents of illustrator Humphrey Ocean to recreate the photographs as a pencil drawing. The photography of the Steenbeck and other film editing equipment was set up in a Soho basement and Ocean spent three weeks creating his detailed drawing, starting at the top left-hand corner and finishing it bottom right.

"There is an intensity to it," says Ocean. "If I had been a graphic designer, I think it would have been more slick, whereas I feel it's a bit clunky."

Ocean's elaborate pencil drawing is crammed full of film editing equipment. Every nook and cranny of the frame is filled to the brim with machinery, film, reels, canisters and other tiny details. Look carefully and you can even see a subtle drawing of the faces of the band hidden in the reflections. The original intention had been to have a die-cut hole in the front cover where the viewing screen appears that would reveal the photograph of 10cc from the inner spread of the gatefold sleeve. As a placeholder, Ocean left a white space in his drawing, which he later filled with an image that he had found in his collection of film annuals, of actor Anthony Perkins taken from the 1957 American western *Lonely Man*. When the die-cut idea was scrapped, the drawing of Perkins ended up making it onto the final version of the cover with the image given a spot varnish to help it stand out from the otherwise matt finish. The busy design conveyed much more than a photograph ever could.

"The sparkling wordplay of 10cc, and the richness of idea and allusion in their work, determined the 'busyness' of the design," says Thorgerson. "The quality of the sound – close, immediate and detailed – suggested that the representation should be more than ordinary photography; more real, somehow, like the hyper-real art of Humphrey Ocean."

For the band themselves, Ocean's drawing captured the spirit of 10cc and seemed intrinsically linked to the music it was conveying.

"In one rich, detailed pencil drawing he summed up the twitchy faux Gershwinisms of One Night In Paris, the panoramic end titles wash of I'm Not In Love, the Eurovision tat of The Film of My Love and the spirit of every word and note in between," says Kevin Godley. "Somehow Humphrey not only captured the sheen of the finished product but the chemical reaction that made 10cc combust."

Now it was time for 10cc to share their latest work with the world and for Phonogram to seek a return on their significant investment.

CHAPTER 10

OUR RECORDS SELL IN ZILLIONS

TO LAUNCH THE ORIGINAL SOUNDTRACK TO THE MUSIC PRESS, Phonogram threw a lavish party at a London cinema. After *Sheet Music* 10cc knew that they had a lot to live up to, and critics seemed to view the new album as more of a mixed bag.

"10cc had an awesome task when they set about recording this album," wrote Colin Irwin in *Melody Maker* under the headline 10CC LOSE THE SPARKLE. "The new darlings of rock, they had to produce something really remarkable to surpass the towering standards of their first two albums and *Sheet Music* in particular. Sadly, this one shows signs of being self-conscious of their current mighty status, as if they're trying too hard to be exceptional and original. As a result a lot of the freshness and apparent spontaneity of the music is dispersed in their striving for the ultimate record. All criticisms are, however, comparative to their other work and it still leaves most rock albums at the starting post, and without having the same impact as *Sheet Music*, it's still essential listening to any self-respecting rock fan."

Irwin's assertion that the band was 'trying too hard' rankled.

"The pressure is trying to improve on what you've done," said Lol Creme at the time. "So what happens is that you try that much harder. And when people knock that side of it, like when they say you're trying too hard. Which is you *can't* try too hard because once you stop trying you settle for what isn't good enough. I think the harder you try the better."

New Musical Express had mixed feelings about the album too: "*The Original Soundtrack* is brilliant; and I hate it," concluded Charles Shaar Murray, who was both impressed and reviled by the album. Impressed by its cleverness; repulsed by its coldness. Still, Murray conceded that "the playing is superb throughout but the production and engineering are exemplary, the melodies are exquisite, the lyrics are absolutely the sharpest, wittiest and most adroitly constructive that I've heard since ... 10cc's last album."

Other reviews, particularly those outside the music press, were far more favourable: "The sharp wit of the lyrics puts them in a class of their own. The variety of moods is similarly unequalled," said *The Sunday Times*. "Only the deaf could be disappointed," concluded *Sounds*.

Deep down, 10cc themselves knew that *The Original Soundtrack* wasn't as strong as *Sheet Music*. "There are definitely tracks on the album which I'd like to do again, notably Flying Junk, which I feel we could have done much better," said Kevin Godley at the time.

It wasn't that they felt some of the new material wasn't up to scratch, simply that they could have bettered what they'd done in their pursuit of perfection. Eric Stewart shared this view but was less happy about naming specific parts of the album that he felt were sub-optimal.

"I'd hate to name particular tracks for fear of disappointing the people who like them," said Stewart at the time. "For instance, only this morning someone came up to me and said that one track was their favourite and that's the one I'd most like to do again. Don't get me wrong, we're not ashamed of any of the tracks, and we'll stand by them all. It's just that we feel under different circumstances we could have done a better job."

Released at the beginning of March 1975, Phonogram's press ads for the album spoofed movie posters – "*The Original Soundtrack* of the book you've never read, of the film you've never seen ... in phonogramic stereo dimension." Commercially, the album was a huge and immediate success, confirming 10cc's status as one of the UK's biggest groups. The album entered the UK album charts at No.6 and would spend 19 weeks in the Top 10 alone, peaking at No.3 in mid-May as part of a 40-week chart run. *The Original Soundtrack* would go on to become the sixth bestselling new album of 1975 in the UK and the third most successful by a British group. It would also go on to become one of the UK's 100 bestselling albums of the decade.

As the band prepared to promote the album with a tour of the UK, and their first dates in Europe, the challenge in rehearsals was how to recreate their increasingly sophisticated studio recordings in a live setting. In particular, it would simply be impossible to replicate the 256 vocal overdubs of I'm Not In Love, so it was decided that the only viable solution would be to play along to a backing track of the background voices when they performed the song live. They also decided to use a backing track on One Night In Paris to play the Parisian street sounds at the start of the song. This made life more complicated for the band's front-of-house engineer Neil Levine.

"Neil is a top man but on one occasion he got his playback cues in a tangle," recalls Godley. "In the set-list of the day I'm Not In Love always followed One Night In Paris. During the show in question Neil forgot to pause the tape after the opening sound effects for One Night In Paris and the big choral wash of I'm Not In Love suddenly and embarrassingly exploded from the PA drowning out our precious Parisian operetta. Whoops! Caught red-handed."

Journalist Phil Sutcliffe witnessed this *faux pas* at the band's gig at Newcastle City Hall. In typical self-deprecating style, 10cc didn't try to bluff their way through it. They stopped playing One Night In Paris and acknowledged the mistake.

"In a gesture of splendid surrender to the gods they all laid down flat on their backs on stage and got one of those sustained laughs Jack Benny used to hold just by staring fixedly at one of his incompetent stooges," said Sutcliffe.

The band's UK tour to promote *The Original Soundtrack* was their biggest to date and the group appeared more comfortable on stage than they had on previous tours.

"The sheer ingenuity which has gone into 10cc's music before paying audiences is staggering," wrote *The Observer*. "It's very pleasant to finally have a band who can not only do it live, but do it better live."

Yet while some appreciated 10cc's ability to recreate their sophisticated studio sounds on stage, 10cc's live show continued to polarise the critics. The band's homecoming gig at Manchester's Free Trade Hall was a case in point.

"What a night it was," wrote Martin Thorpe in *Record Mirror*. "10cc back on home ground as part of their UK tour. It's obvious watching the band perform that they are very close-knit; they bounce off each other in their delivery and in their writing. And that energy on stage wanders over the audience, who on this night were a credit to the band. Three encores at the end of a set which inserted recognition in between ignorance, old tracks like Silly Love and Ships in with new tracks like Second Sitting For The Last Supper and the new single Life Is A Minestrone. The whole set proved one thing: 10cc are excellent musicians and are very soon going to be one of the biggest bands in the country."

Other critics wanted more blood, sweat and tears, more rock 'n' roll. They considered 10cc's live approach too clinical and calculated. "There's still too much of the clinical clamminess of the studio about 10cc's gigs," wrote Charles Shaar Murray in the *New Musical Express*. "Their live performances are not independent entities in themselves but attempts to reproduce in a live situation the cause-and-effect of their recordings. Some bands are fortunate enough to be able to cope equally well with the differing demands of the stage and the studio – Led Zeppelin and The Who come readily to mind – and others exist principally as performing units and produce stiff, clumsy recordings. 10cc, like it or not, function most creatively in the studio where they can polish and develop their music. Their concerts are high on music and low on visual interest."

Looking back, Kevin Godley finds it astonishing that he and Lol Creme never put their art school training to use in the band, particularly in the way they presented themselves on stage.

"It never ceases to amaze me that you had these two art school nut jobs in the band yet we never once applied our initiative, our visual initiative, to anything to do with the fucking band," says Godley. "No backdrops, no stage design, no clothes. Nothing! Except Lol did the first album cover but after that point nothing. Isn't that weird? I find that quite extraordinary. I mean, we weren't bad looking. We were presentable. We could've created a strong visual hook to hang the music on but we simply didn't bother. Presumably our minds were on higher things ... music perhaps?"

10cc's lack of visual identity was certainly a source of frustration for the band's co-manager Harvey Lisberg. "Even though 10cc's music was second to none, one of my frustrations was that they were never a really visual band," says Lisberg. When he learnt that Queen were seeking new management during the spring of 1975,

Lisberg and Led Zeppelin manager Peter Grant put together a joint proposal to manage them.

"Peter and I foresaw potential conflicts with the bands we already managed but agreed to share the load so we could quash any repercussions from our acts," says Lisberg. "So Peter Grant, Jim Beach (their lawyer), myself and all the members of Queen, had a meeting in London later that year and put it to them that we should co-manage Queen. From our point of view it felt like a *fait accompli* because Peter managed Led Zeppelin, the biggest band in the world who were outgrossing everyone in the USA while at the same time 10cc were massive in Europe and the rest of the world too. As part of the courtship, I arranged to get Roger Taylor some good tickets for Wimbledon. In the event they chose to go with John Reid."

As 10cc's tour continued around the UK, Life Is A Minestrone was lined up as the band's next single. "We saw Life Is A Minestrone as a good comeback after a long period of silence after Silly Love and we thought that would get things bubbling again," said Creme. Released on March 22, the single was very well-received by the critics. "Any top-line band who've been around a bit deserve to maybe have one classic single or maybe two if they hit it lucky," pondered Colin Irwin in *Melody Maker*. "Almost every single this Manchester quartet have made has been a classic and with consummate ease this one joins the sacred status of Rubber Bullets, The Dean and I, The Worst Band In The World, The Wall Street Shuffle et al. Inventive as always with lyrics, they manage to mention the White House, the Pope, Minnie Mouse, the Tower of Pisa and others, yet at the same time bop along with commendable bounce and zest."

The single did prove to be a good comeback record, returning 10cc to the UK Top 10 for the fifth time, peaking at No.7 in early May, helped by a couple of appearances on *Top of the Pops*. By then, 10cc's UK tour had reached London, where the group performed two sell-out nights at the Hammersmith Odeon. One of their Hammersmith shows was interrupted by John Peel who presented them with gold discs for *Sheet Music*. The gigs gained good reviews, with *Melody Maker* journalist Geoff Brown summarising what he saw under the headline SIZZLING 10CC, although as was often the case in a live situation, the group had been slow to warm up. "10cc finally took off with The Second Sitting For The Last Supper, murderously paced, neatly conceived and crisply executed. At last you surmised they'd hit a groove. One Night In Paris, the three-part *bonbon sur Soundtrack* which received a veritable clobbering from Ye Scribes is splendid. Its lyrics are monstrously clever, its jokes are genuinely witty and its construction and melody stun and attract. Hearing the track live certainly enhances the album take."

One prominent feature of 10cc's live performances was Lol Creme's sense of humour. Most gigs were peppered with wisecracks and one-liners from Creme, which served to add a good measure of fun to the proceedings. The UK tour ended on April 1, with the band back in Manchester to play an additional date at the Free Trade Hall. With the home leg of the tour over, 10cc ventured into Europe for their first gigs there, playing seven dates in Belgium, the Netherlands, Sweden and Denmark. Their path would occasionally cross over with other bands on tour at the time. The contrast between 10cc's approach to life on the road with that of the traditional rock 'n' roll group was brought into stark contrast when the tour reached Copenhagen, where the band found themselves sharing the same hotel as glam rockers Sweet.

"The hotel boasted a rather magnificent library and I was relaxing into a book one evening when Sweet came swaggering in, smoking, shouting and yelping like cartoon American Indians," recalls Godley. "I tried to hide behind the book but too late … they'd spotted me. They waved, pointed, jumped up and down then whipped their knobs out and started flapping them in people's faces. By people I mean elderly Danish people trying to get a little respite from the 20th century. I laughed unconvincingly – hypocritically – to indicate solidarity with traditional rock 'n' roll values then beat a hasty retreat as the vulgarity escalated."

The tour consolidated 10cc's European success. They had already enjoyed Top 10 hits in the Netherlands with Donna, The Wall Street Shuffle and Silly Love, and now their new single Life Is A Minestrone reached the Top 20 in the Netherlands and Belgium.

The group played another string of UK concerts, added to their schedule to keep pace with public demand, concluding at Croydon's

Fairfield Hall on May 4. "This was the last date on the tour – a tour which has asserted 10cc's position as one of the leading bands in the world of rock," wrote Les Hall in *Disc*. The group put on a good show, despite Graham Gouldman having chicken pox and a temperature of 101 degrees. Not that he received any sympathy from the band.

"Eaugh, you touched this bass – I don't want to play it. Oh gawd I feel ill already," joked Stewart. "This is an infectious little song," said Creme.

The end-of-tour party saw band and crew enjoying a custard pie fight and spraying soda syphons at each other to let off steam. With the tour over, thoughts turned to the band's next single. There was a growing belief that I'm Not In Love should be released but, at over six minutes in length, there was a concern that it was too long to receive radio airplay. However, the group had received telegrams from other record companies, not to mention some of their contemporaries, suggesting that they should release it as a single. Besides, some more enlightened DJs, such as John Peel, had already been playing the song on their radio shows as soon as it had appeared on *The Original Soundtrack*. Despite this, the group was put under pressure to edit the song down.

"The BBC asked me to edit it," recalls Stewart. "I said, 'No, I can't. What am I going to take out?' As far as I was concerned, it was like taking half of a masterpiece portrait painting out. What bit do you want to cut off? The head?"

Unfortunately, rather than stand their ground, the band acquiesced and did agree to a shortened radio edit of the song. Out went half of the intro, half of the bridge, all of the last verse and most of the outro, chopping two minutes off the song and bringing it in at a more radio-friendly 4:10. Coupled with a non-album track, Good News, I'm Not In Love was finally released on May 23. "The outstandingly beautiful track from *The Original Soundtrack* album," wrote *Melody Maker*. "A lot of people have already bought it on the album but it's such a perfectly constructed work that the song itself should quickly gain standard status in fields beyond rock. It's good to hear 10cc for once abandoning their humorously sarcastic style and concentrating purely on a reasonably unmolested ballad."

Unlike any of their previous singles, the song marked another change in direction for the band. The group felt that it would either be a big hit or an ignominious flop but no one predicted the extent to which the song would capture the public's imagination. I'm Not In Love wasn't just a hit; it became *the* hit of the summer. Within weeks of release the record had reached No.1, spending two weeks at the top and seven in the UK Top 10. Not only would I'm Not In Love go on to become one of the year's bestselling singles, it would become one of the seminal pop records of all time. And it wasn't just a hit with the public, either. Many other musicians were knocked out by it too.

"I remember Bryan Ferry saying that when he heard it on the radio in his car, he had to pull over to listen to it," says Kevin Godley.

Elton John was also a huge fan of the song, which helped him to get over a failed relationship at the time. "I played it everywhere, in the car, at home, and I'd sob like a baby," he says. "When I was making the *Blue Moves* album, a friend of mine gave me a gold disc of I'm Not In Love because the song meant so much to me."

Years before he would find fame in his own right, the song would be a big influence on Trevor Horn, who would go on to become one of the most successful producers of all time. "I thought the best-produced song ever was I'm Not In Love by 10cc, where the production really made the song," says Horn. "So I always used to say if you've got studio fever and you think your tune's really good, listen to I'm Not In Love and that'll sort you right out!"

"It's a brilliant song," says Neil Tennant of The Pet Shop Boys. "The thing to remember is that in its original context, 10cc had a very strong sense of humour and a strong sense of irony, so now I think it's regarded as a beautiful love song but at the time it had much, much more of an edge than that. And, of course, technologically at the time it was extraordinary. By the 80s you could do the backing vocals on a keyboard but in the mid-70s they had to sing it themselves and make tape loops, but it produced a better effect than it would on a keyboard."

Phonogram was thrilled. For them it was instant payback on their investment in 10cc. To cap it all, I'm Not In Love was a worldwide smash, reaching No.1 in Ireland and France – where it spent five weeks at the top – No.1 in Canada, No.3 in Australia, No.4 in New

Zealand, No.5 in Belgium and the Netherlands, No.6 in Norway, No.8 in Switzerland and Germany, and gave the band their first hit record in places such as Italy and South Africa. It would even go on to become the third bestselling single of the year in Brazil. Selling nearly 3 million copies worldwide, it easily became 10cc's biggest hit single to date.

Also benefiting from the song's success was Jonathan King with his 4% royalty. Never averse to jumping on a bandwagon, he also decided to cash in on the group's peak of success by releasing a compilation album *100cc – The Greatest Hits of 10cc*. The album brought together the group's five hits on his UK Records label, together with all their non-album b-sides, like 4% of Something and 18 Carat Man of Means. Perfectly timed for release at the end of May, the album reached No.9 in the UK charts, ensuring that 10cc had two albums in the Top 10 for much of the summer.

It marked an incredible moment in time for 10cc. The group had sold more singles than any other group in the UK during the second quarter of the year; they had two albums in the UK Top 10 with *The Original Soundtrack* and *100cc*; they were No.1 in the UK singles chart with I'm Not In Love; and the single had just broken into the Top 10 in America, finally giving them their US chart breakthrough. To cap it all, 10cc had been lined up to headline a special one-off gig at Cardiff Castle on July 12, supported by Thin Lizzy and Steeleye Span, their biggest headlining show to date. 10cc decided not to preview any new material at the gig.

"We have got five tracks written for the next album but we don't start recording for two weeks, so we will not be playing any today," said Eric Stewart before the gig.

Such was the band's popularity that demand for tickets far exceeded supply, and this despite appalling weather conditions.

"It rained and rained and rained," recalls Harvey Lisberg. "There were 15,000 people there, who had been waiting for hours to hear the group, and there'd been another 10,000 who had been turned away because they couldn't get any more people in and they were sitting there soaked through waiting for them to appear, and there was a real risk with all those volts going through the sound system that if something went wrong one of the group might get electrocuted, so we had to make especially sure that the equipment was all right."

Given the show's size, the group made more of a concession than usual to rock theatrics. "They kicked off with Silly Love, complete with a grand explosion, three arches studded with lights bursting into life on stage and a sudden dramatic illumination of the castle keep," reported Brian Harrigan in *Melody Maker*. "It was a good opening number and yet they lacked the *coup de grâce*. Take as a prime example their performance of I'm Not In Love. They utilised everything at their disposal: backing tapes, perfect harmony from Godley, Creme, Stewart and Gouldman, with extra drummer Paul Burgess doubling on keyboards and allowing the four regular members extra freedom. It was a consummate performance, but one couldn't help thinking the effect should have been the same in considerably more comfortable surroundings back at home with a stereo and a copy of *The Original Soundtrack*."

The adverse weather conditions had delayed proceedings and as the band continued their set the midnight curfew approached.

"We'd been waiting for the rain to stop and it was a Saturday night, and if we'd gone on past midnight we'd have been in trouble with the Welsh Sunday licensing laws," says Lisberg. "They were actually on stage when someone came up to me and said, 'We have been instructed by the police to pull out the electricity wires because there have been 2,500 complaints about the noise.' I had to plead with the promoter and then the chief superintendent of police, and there was a lot of signalling going on from the side of the stage to the group."

It had taken 10cc a long time to warm up but their set picked up pace and concluded strongly with Rubber Bullets, building up to "a terrific, surging climax with Creme, Stewart and Gouldman, side by side, coaxing more and more speed from their guitars," according to Harrigan.

It was clear to all that 10cc were growing in skill and confidence as a live act. *Sounds* said the band had played "one of their best sets in a long time". Charles Shaar Murray, in the *New Musical Express*, commented that the 10cc show was: "Infinitely better than it's ever been before. They seem to be rocking out a lot less self-consciously than they used to and they don't look so much as if they were back in Stockport with headphones clamped round their skulls messing with the Dolbies. From the opening Silly Love to the final boooooooogiedown Rubber Bullets, they gave a fairly convincing demonstration of their credentials as one of Britain's most consistently interesting and entertaining bands – and also proved that One Night In Paris is a far better stage number than anyone would've thought when listening to the album. Now for the bad news. Despite all the improvements to the show in terms of feel, staging, playing, quality of live sound, etc., a 10cc gig is still a case of reproducing music conceived and created for/in the studio in a live situation. It's no coincidence that they introduce numbers with 'and now we'd like to play *another track* from …' Despite their studio pre-eminence, 10cc will never be a *great* (as opposed to simply *good*) stage band until their performances take on an identity of their own and exist as something more than simply stagings of recorded performances. Groups of the standing of, say, The Who or The Stones and Led Zep develop things to the point where their records and their performances don't necessarily attempt to duplicate each other, but *complement* each other; and ultimately your memories of one experience colours the other; producing a far more three-dimensional effect. Even at their best 10cc make me feel I'm watching a videocassette."

Festivities were arranged for the bands after the show. "They laid on a medieval banquet after the gig and we got trashed," recalls Brian Robertson of Thin Lizzy. "The last thing I remember is walking through the grounds of the castle with Eric Stewart before getting arrested."

The Cardiff Castle gig marked 10cc's last UK live appearance of 1975. The next nine months were to be taken up with the recording of a new album, a major headlining tour of North America and then a tour of Europe.

As 10cc's popularity had grown, so had interest in Strawberry Studios. Even teen sensations The Bay City Rollers used Strawberry to part-record and mix their No.1 album *Once Upon a Star*. As a result 10cc themselves were finding it increasingly difficult to get studio time at Strawberry.

"We were in the ludicrous position of never being able to use our own studio because it was all booked up," said Stewart.

The group decided to build another studio to meet their own requirements. That decision prompted a discussion about where the studio, and the band themselves, should be located. They decided it was time to leave their Manchester base and move nearer to London.

"We'd reached the stage where we were thinking that we'd have to open another studio because the one that we'd got already was always fully booked, and the more we thought about it the more we realised there was just no point in having another studio up here," said Stewart at the time. "The thing was to have one in the London area, but not right in the centre of London or there'd be too many distractions there as well."

The decision to move the band's base of operations down south surprised many, given that 10cc had often cited being based in Manchester as one of the secrets of their success.

"I'd begun to find Manchester a bit stifling," said Stewart. "The reasons for us staying up here were becoming less and less important. Originally the fact that we were isolated from everything else that was going on in the business was an advantage, because we could go into the studios in Stockport and work away with no distractions, but now the studios are so successful that there's always someone else going in there to work as well. The thing we'll miss mainly now are our families who are all up here in Manchester."

Lol Creme echoed these sentiments. "It's time for a change," he said. "The centre of the music business in England is London and we've got to keep in touch with what's going on. At some point in your career you've got to do that. It would be very easy to get isolated and we don't want that."

The group started looking for a suitable location for their new studio. Eventually they found a building in the market town of Dorking in Surrey that they felt would be perfect to convert into their dream studio, to be called Strawberry Studios South. The building was located on South Street and was formerly the 800-seat Pavilion Cinema, until its closure in April 1973. The plan was to have the studio ready by the summer of 1976 in time for the recording of 10cc's fifth album.

Prior to their move south, 10cc returned to Strawberry in Stockport to start work on their fourth album. Strawberry had just benefited from another upgrade and was now a 24-track facility.

Before starting work on the album, Lol Creme reflected on *The Original Soundtrack*: "Personally I thought the album was good, but the only way I can relate it is to compare it with *Sheet Music*," he said. "I thought it had higher peaks than *Sheet Music* but lower troughs. I tend to look at it graphically. There were parts that were better and parts that were worse. *Sheet Music* was a constant album whereas *The Original Soundtrack* went higher and dipped lower in places. We took chances but you've got to do that or else you'll land yourself in a bog where everyone thinks you can only write witty songs. That wouldn't satisfy us."

So how were 10cc planning to follow up a single such as I'm Not In Love?

"To be quite honest we haven't even discussed a follow-up yet," said Creme at the time. "We don't sit down to make singles. We do tracks and then decide if one is suitable as a single. For the new album we've done four or five tracks and we haven't got one that we think is a single yet. If we don't get one we won't put a single out. We're not going to sit down and write a single specially. We daren't lower our standards. We're a fussy bunch of bastards, you know!"

CHAPTER 11

VERY 10CC, VERY WONDERFUL

"THE NEW ALBUM WILL BE AS DIFFERENT FROM *THE ORIGINAL Soundtrack* as that one was from *Sheet Music*," predicted Lol Creme halfway through the recording sessions for 10cc's fourth album. "That's the way we work. We always try to move forward but the way we work makes things hard. We have no preconceived ideas about what we're going to do, so everything is an instant surprise. It's exciting but worrying at the same time."

If the band had felt under pressure before, it was nothing compared to the pressure they were under now. Their reputation as one of the world's most innovative bands meant that expectations were always high, but now they had popularity to contend with too. Each previous album had conveniently outsold its predecessor. Repeating that trick this time around would be more difficult, particularly with *The Original Soundtrack* still riding high in the UK album charts, and with I'm Not In Love still climbing the singles charts around the world, as the new sessions began.

"The only thing to make sure of now is that we don't become complacent," said Creme at the time. "We're not an overnight sensation. We worked on getting our success, and *The Original Soundtrack* has made it mature."

Still, the band did have to contemplate following up I'm Not In Love, one of the most successful singles of all time and a landmark record in anyone's career. Aside from its global success, the song had also started to pick up awards by the truckload, walking away with the 'Best Single' award in the annual *Melody Maker* readers' poll, in which 10cc also earned top-five placings in the 'Best Album' and 'Best Band' categories. *New Musical Express* readers and critics would both vote it second in their equivalent polls.

10cc now had an identity; the public now had a preconceived notion of what 10cc represented. Perhaps with this in mind, the group approached their new album with a little more calculation than they had on previous efforts. "We actually sat down and discussed between the four of us what the content of the album might be," recalls Kevin Godley. "The discussion went something like, 'I think there should be a couple of ballads, a couple of wicky-wacky comedy songs, Kev should sing one, Lol should sing a couple, there should be a bit of rock 'n' roll ...' And I was like, 'Wait a minute! Isn't the next album about what we are next, rather than what is expected of us?' It was suddenly, 'Oh, *that's* what 10cc is about!' Suddenly we knew what we were and it took some of the pleasure out of it for me. It was not knowing what we were going to be next that was exciting; not knowing what the album was going to sound like until we'd finished it. The more calculated approach took the spark out of it for me."

The realisation of what defined 10cc went against the band's ethos, which was always opposed to formulas. It was to be the first in a number of cracks that would begin to appear within the group over the next 12 months. For their part, Godley and Creme ventured outside the studio walls for the first time to write material for the new album, renting a villa in France for a few weeks with their families. When they eventually managed to prize themselves away from the swimming pool to get down to business they had to contend with a disgruntled neighbour who objected to the sounds emanating from the piano that the pair were using for their writing session.

"We were writing for about five or ten minutes when we heard this lady's voice say, 'Enough piano! Enough piano over there!'," says Creme. "She called round to complain. My wife explained, 'They're writers, they're musicians. Anyway, we've rented this villa,' and the lady said, 'Well, we *own* this one!'"

Overall, the sojourn to France didn't prove to be particularly productive. "You really write your best stuff when you are deprived, but we were just lolling about in the swimming pool all day," recalls Godley. "We only wrote about half a song while we were in France."

While Godley and Creme had been writing their 'half a song' in France, Stewart and Gouldman had remained in England, getting together each morning at 10am. "If you only worked on blind inspiration you'd never get anything finished because every song is about 2% inspiration and 98% graft," said Stewart at the time.

Among their new creations was Art For Art's Sake, a song that had been inspired by a phrase often cited by Gouldman's father, Hymie, who would say to the group, 'Listen, boys, art for art's sake, money for God's sake!' "Eric had this riff and I just started singing *'Art for art's sake, money for God's sake'* and that was it," recalls Gouldman.

Using the phrase as the song's chorus, Stewart and Gouldman took the opportunity to take a cynical swipe at pop stars whose motivations were more financial than artistic. "We were just thinking of people who want to make money out of the business and then split, leave the country," said Stewart at the time. "Graham didn't quite like the idea because he thought we shouldn't be so controversial, but it's just another sacred cow to have a go at. You see, we're in it for the music, not the money. We haven't made any money, as Jonathan King will tell you!"

Art For Art's Sake again demonstrated that the band weren't afraid of courting controversy. Ridiculing the music business was a bit of a taboo in the industry at the time. "Sacred cows and things are lovingly demolished," said Stewart. "It's not really contempt. It's ridicule. Things like greed and money."

For 10cc, no subject was sacred. "As far as we're concerned anything and everything is there to be used," said Creme. "It's all ammunition. Why not? I think you can make something interesting out of it if you have a certain viewpoint or angle on it."

In fact, it was being suggested at the time that it would be financially advantageous for the group to spend a 'tax year' in America, also allowing them more time to break the US market, which was a high priority for them. 10cc, however, were not interested in becoming tax exiles. "There's no chance of Britain losing us to America," said Stewart at the time. "We can't become tax exiles, because we haven't any money. Anyway, I'd hate to leave Britain because it's still pretty free here."

Of the other new songs, Stewart and Gouldman's Rock 'n' Roll Lullaby had been written as a modern-day lullaby. The pair had questioned if the song was strong enough but had been persuaded to finish it by Kevin Godley.

"I was fighting against the other three in the band to have this song included on the album," said Godley at the time. "Since then we've all come to agree that it's great. It's musically and lyrically a very comfortable track to listen to. It's not like one of our strange tracks where something odd happens. It seems to work in a way that even the simplest mind could follow quite easily and most of the great songs you've ever heard in your life seem to work in that simple kind of way."

Stewart and Gouldman had written the song with Godley in mind to sing it. "Most of the time one of the writers would sing the song but there were occasions where we would write something and say, 'Maybe Kev should sing this,'" recalls Gouldman. "That's what happened with Rock 'n' Roll Lullaby because it needed his kind of voice."

Godley and Creme evolved the 'half a song' they had started in France into Don't Hang Up, a beautifully constructed song that takes place within the context of a telephone call. In between the phone ringing at the start of the song to the receiver being hung up at the end a husband pleads desperately with his wife to save their failing marriage. The more emotive subject matter marked a departure for Godley and Creme, although the song's structure was typically ingenious, filled with unexpected twists and tempo changes. The 'Gizmo' is used to good effect throughout, amid the pianos, Spanish guitars, castanets and sundry percussion. There's even a harp in there, courtesy of Mair Jones, the first guest musician ever to appear on a 10cc album. Gouldman's inventive and melodic bass work on the track also deserves special mention. There might well be a lot going on but, as always with 10cc, the production never detracted from the song's message.

"You want to cry when you hear what the guy is talking about," says Creme. "It's obviously sad and something has gone wrong with the marriage. There is nothing that detracts from Kevin singing about that subject. Even though the notes may be complicated, the actual feel, the atmosphere is direct. The heart is pouring in at the end. That's direct and it took a lot of trouble to do it."

Kevin Godley's lead vocal on the song was particularly impressive. "There's a tremendous amount of strength in the song, particularly the vocal performance, which is one of the best I've ever heard, technically and physically," says Gouldman. "And it was a very emotional thing to record, because on the one hand you're getting deeply romantic about the whole thing, the next thing you're sort of playing Spanish guitars and castanets all in one track. And it has a lovely conclusion to it which works beautifully."

Don't Hang Up would go on to become one of the highlights of the new album and rank as one of 10cc's finest creations, as would another new song inspired by an advertising campaign running at the time for the American carrier National Airlines. Their ads featured air stewardesses inviting the viewer onto their planes with slogans such as 'I'm Cheryl. Fly Me,' and 'I'm Laura. Fly me non-stop to Miami.' The ads had been highly successful but had also caused controversy because of their sexual sub-text. Having seen a tramp looking up at one of these posters, Stewart and Gouldman were inspired to write the song, I'm Mandy Fly Me. They made good progress but struggled with the lyrics.

"We all liked the song but Eric and I just couldn't nail the lyrics and that happens sometimes," says Gouldman. "So, you can say, 'Sod it, we're gonna keep this for ourselves and if some of the lyrics are a bit sub-standard, then so what?' But we never worked like that and we asked Kevin to come in and do some of the lyrics, and he did a really great job on them."

Godley helped to craft a great lyric that tells the tale of a man who dreams that the air stewardess saves his life when the plane goes down in shark-infested waters, a neat reference to the film *Jaws*, which had just come out at the time of writing. In addition to finishing off the lyrics Godley also suggested the song needed a new middle section.

"Kevin said, 'I think it just gets too bland, it just goes on, on one level, your verses and your middles. What it needs is someone to go 'Bash' on the side of your head'," recalls Stewart. "So, we changed the rhythm completely, and we put two whacking great guitar solos in there, in the middle of this quiet, soft, floaty song. Once we'd got that idea in, it just gelled into something else."

Recording of the song, however, was less straightforward, with tension building in the studio. Driving past Strawberry one night, Stewart noticed the studio light on. When he dropped in to see what was going on he discovered Lol Creme standing on a chair trying to record a guitar solo for the song. It spoke to a growing sense of disharmony in the band. Despite this, the finished recording was one of 10cc's very best. Beautifully constructed, brilliantly executed, the song starts with the sound of the onboard call button – in reality Zeb White's doorbell – that fades into the sound of a passenger listening to 10cc's Clockwork Creep on the plane.

"We tried to make it sound like the crappy headphones that are given out on a plane," says Gouldman.

All were pleased with the end result – apart from Lol Creme.

"I remember a conversation with Lol in the front office of the studio," recalls Gouldman. "We'd almost finished recording I'm Mandy Fly Me and Eric and I were really pleased with it. We thought it was just really good and Lol was sort of saying, 'Is this the direction we should be going in? Was it interesting enough? And, was it music? And was it this?' And I thought, 'What are you talking about?'"

It was another of the cracks beginning to form within the band, with the recording sessions for the new album being less harmonious than they had been before. When Godley and Gouldman collaborated on Iceberg – a song about a psychopath on the loose in New York juxtapositioned against an upbeat jazz arrangement – the pair disagreed over some of the song's lyrics. Gouldman objected, quite understandably, to a line proposed by Godley: 'Get down on all fours and shit in a handbag.'

"I was trying to loosen up Graham a bit," says Godley. "He didn't go for it, said something like, 'That's unnecessary, Godley.'"

Eric Stewart also objected to the lyric, and the tone of the song, which he found "sick and disturbing". Godley reluctantly agreed to tone the lyrics down. While Godley and Gouldman worked on Iceberg, Lol Creme and Eric Stewart wrote Lazy Ways, an atmospheric but relatively straightforward song by 10cc standards, about how we get less done but more out of our lazy days. As with *The Original Soundtrack*, the songwriting collaborations outside of the two main writing teams were once again less in evidence than they had been on *Sheet Music*, although Godley, Creme and

Gouldman collaborated on I Wanna Rule The World, which outlined the master plan of a *'specky, spotty, four-eyed, weedy little creep'* as he dreams of taking over the world. It was another example of the band's quirky and inventive writing style. Godley draws upon his own experiences in a number of places – not wanting to *'work for daddy in daddy's shop'*, the trauma of being bullied at school. He even manages to include his school's motto – 'Delapsus Resurgam' – in the lyric as the bullied protagonist dreams of getting his own back. Anyone who dismisses 10cc as 'easy listening' music should give this song a listen.

"I think that was one of our best records actually," says Gouldman today. "It's got some beautiful melodies in it even though it's like a manic song. That's why I think it works so well. You've got these opposite things happening."

Stewart was less convinced about the song or another Godley/ Creme song called Head Room, which tackled the subject of teenage sexual awakening, crammed full of puns and sexual innuendos. Still, back in the studio the songs, as usual, became group property.

"Once we actually start working in the studio the song becomes the property of all four of us and we all take a part in shaping it," said Gouldman at the time. "No one says, 'I wrote that bit,' or, 'That's how it's gonna stay.' You just can't work like that in a group like ours."

Having four such strong writers in the band was one of 10cc's real strengths, a fact that hadn't escaped their notice.

"There isn't another group in the world with four good writers," said Eric Stewart at the time. "There are groups where everyone insists on writing and what happens is you get an album with two good tracks on it," continued Creme. "But it depends on what you're in it for. If you want the standard of your album to be great then you own up and say, 'Okay, I'm not a good writer.' I mean it's happened with us. We've written songs and said, 'It's okay but I think we can do better,' and we've all worked on it rather than being possessive about it."

The band – minus Lol Creme, who was suffering with flu – took some time out from recording to see Paul McCartney's *Wings Over the World* tour when it reached Manchester's Free Trade Hall on September 12.

"The strangest thing about that Wings concert was that I bought my ticket and filed into the audience to take my seat with my wife when suddenly we were assaulted by about 20 people," said Godley at the time. "Until that had happened I hadn't realised that 10cc were that big a group ... people were coming up to me and asking me for autographs all through the show, and I'd just never realised."

After the gig, Godley, Stewart, Gouldman – and their wives – hung out with Paul and Linda McCartney, and Wings, backstage.

By now 10cc had decided to call their new album *How Dare You!*, after a book that Eric Stewart was reading at the time called *How Dare You – Positive Thinking*.

"It was one of those philosophical books that said if you are having an argument with someone and want to get your point across, you should pre-empt their criticism by saying, 'I know what you're thinking but how dare you!' before the other person has even had the chance to say anything negative," says Stewart. "I mentioned this to the others and we all thought it was funny, so we continued working on the album in that style. We used to hold up signs in the studio saying, 'How Dare You!'"

Godley and Creme also used the phrase as the title for an in-strumental track that had originally started life three or four years previously but had remained unfinished until now.

Continuing their association, the group asked Hipgnosis to start work on the album cover.

"It took a whole month before I could reduce 10cc's *How Dare You!* to some workable bottom line," says Storm Thorgerson. "In this case it was that there were a lot of connections in the lyrics involving puns and unlikely word associations. As soon as I said that to Peter Christopherson he suggested telephones, because they connect of course, and we both immediately thought of that old film thing of split-screen telephone conversations. The band rejected the filmic side of the idea but liked the telephones because unbeknown to us they already had a phone song on the record. What a connection indeed!"

Having heard some of the tracks from the new album, Hipgnosis went away to work up their idea.

"They wanted something modern and sophisticated," says

Thorgerson. "Rather than making it in the fashion of an old movie we made it in the style of middle-class naffness, epitomised at the time, by Sanderson Fabrics whose catchphrase was 'Very so and so, Very Sanderson.' So, we went around for weeks saying 'Very 10cc, Very Sanderson', which we thought was well funny, but it doesn't look so funny now in print."

The Sanderson parody would be carried through to the small print on the inner sleeve, which bore the slogan 'Very 10cc, Very Wonderful'.

"We chose characters and situations from the songs and then added a sub-plot involving the couple who appear in every shot, in the desk photo or behind the blonde lady where we see them getting out of the car," says Thorgerson. "This sad lady in the foreground is a gin-soaked housewife, wasting away in rich suburbia, while her smooth businessman husband works too hard and consequently neglects her. Hipgnosis goes socially conscious! He is furious at being interrupted at work, again. How dare she!"

Playing the gin-soaked housewife on the album cover was actress Helen Keating. "A smashing job," she recalls. "It was a lovely day, I remember. I just had to pose with lots of fake tears, like someone had just had a go at me over the phone. An 'unrequited love' job, that was the mood. It was just a job to me, totally kids' stuff, but when I told my kids they were ecstatic that I'd actually spoken to 10cc."

The back sleeve brought together a couple of characters that appeared in the songs – the air stewardess from I'm Mandy Fly Me and the heavy breather from the title track – while the inner sleeve brought together all the characters that appeared on the album cover at a party.

"We imagined a phone party, each person with their own handset talking to each other in the same room," says Aubrey Powell. "And it's a comment on how much easier it is to discuss matters on the 'blower' rather than face to face. Before the advent of the mobile phone, communication carried out largely via a device seemed improbable. Now it's totally *de rigueur*. Is this photograph now life imitating art, or was it in the stars? It was definitely on the cards. SIM cards probably. Walk into any public place now and you'll find 90% of people talking on mobile phones."

Back at Strawberry, 10cc were putting the finishing touches to the album. For a bunch of such self-confessed perfectionists, the most difficult decision facing the band was when to pronounce a song finished. "It's the hardest decision to make throughout the whole recording session," said Eric Stewart at the time. "Kevin usually says, 'No,' so we spend another day messing about. But that has to be done. You've got to try every idea that comes up just in case one of them is an absolute killer."

Godley was usually the last of the four to agree that a song was finished. "Kev always liked to push things a bit further, which was a very good thing," says Gouldman. "You'd get to a point where you'd say, 'I think this is finished now' and he would say, 'What would it be like if we did this?' or, 'What would it be like if we did that?' and we always used to try it and from what I remember it worked a lot of the time."

The group were always seeking that certain something that would give a track that extra lift. "Sometimes a track will sound good and it sounds finished but you think, 'Is there something that will take it over the edge?'," said Godley at the time.

By the time that *How Dare You!* was finished, 10cc had spent 10 weeks in the studio, a lot longer than most of the band's contemporaries, and further ammunition for their critics to crank out words like 'clinical' and 'calculated'.

"Some people say that's calculation, waiting for the right take instead of using the first," said Creme. "But the first might not have the sort of feel we have in mind. There are several ways that you could describe a feel, so we wait until whoever is singing it has exactly the right nuance and the right expression in the way they say the words. That's 'feel', and it takes a lot longer to do it our way. I think it's kidding yourself to think that you can get pissed, do the first vocal and that's really loose. Bum notes aren't 'feel'! Each track has got to completely consume you. If it's a specific atmosphere, that atmosphere has got to absorb you completely and if it doesn't then that track has failed. You're always looking for that sound that'll just lift it up and away. It's that element of magic that each track has. It can be the simplest of things. It can be obvious. It could be complicated. We don't know until we try it, something that will take a piece of music above what it was before."

Despite the differences of opinion during the recording sessions, the band were pleased with *How Dare You!*. "This album is going further than our other albums have done," said Creme at the time. "Previously we have sat down and written a fairly humorous song and it's had a bit of wit about it, some music and we were pleased. But we've done that now. In those days it was probably hard to get that to work in that way but you can't just settle for that. You've got to try something a little more. And this album's set us problems we haven't tried before, different sorts of emotions, like complete sadness or terror or using words or music in a different sort of way."

There was certainly less of their wacky humour on the new album than there had been on their previous efforts. "It's as different as any album by the same band can be," said Gouldman at the time. "I think it's a progression from the last one. I think there's been a progression on every album and I think we've done it again."

Once more the subject matter of the new songs was very diverse: from sex, greed and world domination to lullabies, fantasies and psychopaths. "We look at everything and make jokes about it and we take it all in and when we get into the studio we just spew all those sort of things out," said Creme.

Each song on a 10cc album was almost like a different article in a newspaper. "Our tracks do tend to do that sometimes, not consciously, but they do seem to be journalistic in as much as they're almost a column on a particular subject," said Creme at the time. "Musically they're journalistic in that they sum up all that we've heard. It's like on TV, you're going to get a documentary and then a film and then a discussion and that's what our albums are like, so you never get bored."

Looking back today, Kevin Godley still shares this view. "Lyrically speaking I think we were more like journalists, or novelists, or scriptwriters than we were songwriters," says Godley. "It wasn't like writing songs at all in that respect when it came to words. We wanted to say something, we were trying to capture a mood, but we were trying to tell a story. We were doing something more than a song usually does, we had an attitude which was more of an editorial or journalistic thing."

Every 10cc song had its own story to convey. "We like to write stories," said Stewart. "Most of our songs are complete stories, whereas most other people get a whole album that tells one thing. We like to tell a definite story idea in each song, or a documentary like Art For Art's Sake or The Wall Street Shuffle. It's a commentary on current affairs, if you like."

With 10cc's fourth album completed, Blue Guitar, the song that 10cc had recorded at Strawberry 18 months earlier with Justin Hayward, was about to be released as a single by Hayward and his former Moody Blues bandmate John Lodge, as a follow up to their *Blue Jays* album. "The record company didn't want to credit 10cc because they weren't on their label at the time," says Hayward.

Blue Guitar had lain dormant at Strawberry since it had been originally recorded in April 1974. "We sat on it for about 18 months and then Eric got it out again and started fiddling around with the mix," says Hayward. "John and I had made the *Blue Jays* album and we were looking for something to release to promote it and I remembered this track and I brought it out and played it to John and our producer Tony Clarke. They liked it but thought it needed something so we took it back to our studio and John added some bass onto it and Tony mixed it in a nice way and anyone who's interested will notice it's got dual production credits of 10cc and Tony Clarke. So, John Lodge is not on the first early version but was on the released single."

Feeling that Blue Guitar was missing something, they decided to add strings to it and asked Del Newman, who 10cc had worked with on the Neil Sedaka albums and who had subsequently gone on to work with the likes of Elton John and Paul Simon, to make the string arrangements. "We thought we'd go the whole way and put strings on it, so we got Del Newman in and then it was mixed by Tony Clarke at Threshold," said Stewart. "I tried to mix it but I couldn't get it anywhere near as good as that."

With *How Dare You!* completed, work started on a further upgrade at Strawberry. The décor and layout of the control room were completely overhauled by Westlake Audio, who had designed many of the world's leading studios. "We wanted to get the perfect room when we went 24-track," said Peter Tattersall at the time. "I'd seen a lot of Westlake rooms and thought they had incredible ideas. They're so advanced in studio design. The décor was pretty good as it was but it doesn't compare to the finished result now."

Westlake went to extraordinary lengths in their overhaul of the control room. The walls were decorated with a mixture of Californian pine and a certain kind of stone that had been quarried off a cliff face in Colorado, as only this type of stone absorbed sound in the most acoustically perfect way. The new control room would be opened later in the year by Westlake's Tom Hidley, who the band had chosen to help design their new Strawberry South studio.

"What we did was gather together a whole pile of albums that we really liked the sound on and we found that they were nearly all recorded in Westlake studios," said Creme at the time. "Tom Hidley, who is Westlake, came to see the old cinema we've bought. We have just used the cinema as a shell and he's designed the studio to be suspended inside the main building."

While Strawberry North was being upgraded, three-quarters of 10cc moved house as they relocated their base of operations to Surrey. Only Graham Gouldman would remain in the Manchester area, renting a flat in Mayfair in London when necessary. Lol Creme moved to Leatherhead; Eric Stewart moved into temporary accommodation at Rigden Farm in Leigh while he was having a new house designed and purpose built in Walton-on-the-Hill by architect Malcolm Lovibond, incorporating many of his own ideas into the design. Apart from a home studio, the house would also have a swimming pool and a large garage to house Stewart's growing collection of sports cars, specifically Ferraris, reflecting his passion for motor racing. The house would be called Colombe inspired by one of his favourite restaurants, La Colombe d'Or, in Saint-Paul-de-Vence in the South of France. Kevin Godley, meanwhile, bought Tara House from Keith Moon of The Who. Named by the original owner after the mansion in *Gone With The Wind*, the house on St Ann's Hill Road in Chertsey was a one-storey, four-bedroom bungalow with a roof made up of five pyramids. It was renowned for its parties such as the launch of the band's *Who's Next* album.

"The funny thing about moving in here is that everyone knows about Keith Moon," said Godley at the time. "There are little bits of Keith all over the house. There were some of his clothes hanging in the wardrobe and some very strange photographs and you've never seen so many bills in your life. There was one bill for £570 for just two weeks' supply of booze. Everyone seems to have their own stories about what Keith used to get up to. We had heard that he had driven a Rolls-Royce into the pond and just left it there, but if he did there was no trace of it when we arrived here; and then we heard that there was a wrecked Ferrari lying somewhere in the grounds, but we didn't find that either!"

As the band's thoughts turned to a tour of America to capitalise on their recent success there, each of the group's members gave interviews to author George Tremlett for a forthcoming biography on the band.

"Over the next five or ten years I think there will come a time when musically 10cc does not fulfil all our musical interests," Kevin Godley told Tremlett. "There will be things that we will all want to do outside 10cc."

Godley's words would prove to be highly prophetic.

CHAPTER 12

SOMEWHERE IN HOLLYWOOD

HAVING WANTED TO BREAK AMERICA EVER SINCE THEIR FORMATION, 10cc's US breakthrough had finally come while the band were in Stockport recording their fourth album. Entering the US Top 100 in mid-May, I'm Not In Love had climbed the American charts, entering the Top 30 during the third week of June. No.1 in the chart that week – and for the next three weeks – was Captain and Tennille's cover of Love Will Keep Us Together, one of the songs that 10cc had earlier recorded with Neil Sedaka at Strawberry. The US Top 40 also featured The Carpenters' cover of Solitaire as well as Sedaka's own That's When The Music Takes Me – recorded with 10cc for the *Solitaire* album – which would go on to give him his first Top 30 hit in the US for over ten years.

The extent of Sedaka's comeback was demonstrated by the success of *Sedaka's Back*, a compilation of his three most recent albums, featuring Stewart, Gouldman, Godley and Creme on seven of its twelve tracks, all of which were now credited as being 'produced by Neil Sedaka in association with 10cc'. Released by Elton John's Rocket Records label, the album would reach the US Top 30, spending 62 weeks on the chart and selling over 500,000 copies. The comeback was just as successful in the UK where *Laughter and Tears*, a compilation of the two albums recorded with 10cc, along with some more recent recordings, reached No.2 in the UK that summer as part of a five-month chart run, and would eventually earn a platinum disc.

Yet despite making the verbal agreement with 10cc to pay them production royalties for their work on *The Tra-La Days Are Over*, there was still no sign of any payment.

"He'll call and say, 'Hi guys, guess what I've got for you' but every time we see him he says he's forgotten his wallet," said Stewart at the time. "We haven't seen the cheque but when it comes it's gonna be such a mindfucker we're all gonna retire!"

When the payments still weren't forthcoming, 10cc initiated legal proceedings, which served to sour relations with Sedaka.

"Polydor and my accountants are now figuring out who gets what," Sedaka would subsequently say. "I have no intention of screwing them, and I'm surprised they've taken this attitude. I've spent more money on gifts than what's involved here."

By late July, I'm Not In Love had reached No.2 in the US, with only Van McCoy's The Hustle ahead of it in the chart. The following week, with I'm Not In Love outselling The Hustle, there were high hopes that 10cc were on their way to an American No.1. However, when the chart came out I'm Not In Love was still at No.2, this time behind One Of These Nights by The Eagles. The following week, with I'm Not In Love now outselling One Of These Nights, the No.1 spot seemed theirs for the taking. Unfortunately, it once again remained at No.2, this time behind Jive Talkin' by The Bee Gees. By now I'm Not In Love was beginning to run out of steam, after three consecutive weeks at No.2 behind three different No.1's, and it started to drop down the charts. By year-end, after 17 weeks in the Top 100, I'm Not In Love had sold almost a million copies in the US and become one of the 50 bestselling singles in America of 1975. Jonathan King took out full page ads in some American music papers that showed a handwritten note from him on UK Records notepaper that read: "Congratulations 10cc and Mercury for a job well done on a great record ... and thanks!" What seemed on the face of it to be a magnanimous gesture was clearly a veiled thank you for the 4% royalty he had just earned on those million sales!

Aside from being a hit with the public, I'm Not In Love also made a big impact on many American musicians.

"I love that record," says Art Garfunkel. "It's so unlike anything. It's just stream of sound."

Producer Tony Visconti would describe it as one of his favourite songs of the decade, while Billy Joel would go on to 'borrow' the song's vocal arrangement for his hit Just The Way You Are. The song would also have a profound effect on many American teenagers who were beginning to form their own bands and would go on to have success themselves in the decades to come.

"That song messes with my life, man," says Axl Rose of Guns N' Roses. "It's one of my favourite songs of all time."

Dave Grohl, of Nirvana and Foo Fighters fame, also vividly remembers the impact the song had in his youth: "I can still close my eyes and see it, in the back seat of my mom's Ford Maverick, with my arm out of the window on a summer day, and 10cc's I'm Not In Love is on the radio as we're coming back from swimming at the lake."

Wayne Coyne of The Flaming Lips and Mike Mills of R.E.M. also cite the song as a particular favourite. "It's a brilliant piece of work," says Mills. "I was around 17, an impressionable age, just trying to sort out sex and life and all that stuff, when I'm Not In Love came out. What the song told me was that no one else had sorted it out either! That here were these people who are a bit older than I am and they're having the same sort of struggles within themselves and their relationships, and that love is always going to be mysterious and painful and confusing. It's a sort of comforting song in a way."

The success of I'm Not In Love sparked interest in *The Original Soundtrack*, which had received positive reviews in the US press.

"10cc's *Original Soundtrack* is a fascinating record," wrote Ken Barnes in *Rolling Stone*. "Musically there's more going on than in 10 Yes albums, yet it's generally as accessible as a straight pop band … 10cc is among the few groups actively engaged in stretching rock's restrictive boundaries in a constructive and meaningful manner, without falling prey to pretence or excess."

Elsewhere, *L.A. Free Press* suggested that 10cc "might be the biggest thing to hit America from England since David Bowie", *Good Times* described them as "absolutely superb" and *Phonograph Record* talked of their "powerful melodies, perfect vocals and lyrics that are masterpieces in their own right". *Cashbox* felt the album would give the band their US breakthrough: "Watch out! 10cc is ready to take off with this one."

The Original Soundtrack gave 10cc their first hit album in the US, spending 25 weeks on the chart and eventually peaking at No.15 on August 2, while I'm Not In Love sat at No.2. It wasn't quite the No.1 spots in the US album and singles chart of Jonathan King's dream but it was the closest the group had come so far to making it a reality.

Wanting to capitalise on 10cc's newfound American success, King conceived a US version of the *100cc* compilation album that would contain the band's "greatest British hits" alongside other tracks that had what he described in the sleeve notes as "the essence of I'm Not In Love". The album begins with Old Wild Men, one of 10cc's finest creations but an unlikely album opener, chosen presumably because its slower tempo and Eric Stewart lead vocal provided as close a proximity to 10cc's big recent hit as King could muster. Elsewhere, King selected Somewhere In Hollywood, Fresh Air For My Mama and Waterfall alongside his favourite track, The Worst Band In The World. Released simply as *100cc* – dropping the *Greatest Hits of 10cc* given that it contained no actual US hits – the album peaked at a lowly No.161 in the US charts.

Making their first headlining tour of North America was the next phase in 10cc's plan to break the US. "The thing we want to do now is conquer the States," said Godley at the time. "We're really going to try and make it in the States and we know what we've got to do to achieve that. There's got to be 100% attention to the music, whether it's in the studio or on stage, and we're anxious to give that, though we know that we won't make money over there for a long time yet."

The tour was scheduled to run over eight weeks, taking in 31 cities across the US and Canada. The cost of headlining a tour of this scale was considerable, particularly as the band had elected to use their own PA, part of their '100% attention to the music.' They hoped it would be an investment in their future success. The original intention had been for the tour to coincide with the release of their new album. However, with *How Dare You!* not yet ready for release, the band's set drew primarily from the *10cc*, *Sheet Music* and *The Original Soundtrack* albums. The only new song to be featured in their set was Art For Art's Sake, which Phonogram in America were keen to release as the band's next single to coincide with the tour and follow up on the success of I'm Not In Love as quickly as possible. Released in a shortened and remixed form, to the irritation of 10cc themselves, Phonogram hoped that Art For Art's Sake would also pave the way for the *How Dare You!* album.

"The lovable loonies from England come up with another musically excellent song featuring strange but effective lyrics," wrote

Billboard. "Making fun of everyone with taste has always been a strong point with the foursome and their treatment of money works well here."

While in America, Godley and Creme planned to talk to a number of manufacturers about the 'Gizmo', which was felt to be so revolutionary as to have a commercial future of its own. "We have started negotiations with various people and we are going to try to get it on the market," said Creme. "The thing is all patented and everything. All that is needed now is a manufacturer. We are taking it to the States. It still needs refining for production purposes."

With the tour due to start in New York, the pair met up with Aaron Newman, founder of Musitronics, a company renowned for making high-quality effects pedals for guitarists, while they were in the Big Apple and a deal would be struck to work together on bringing the 'Gizmo' to market.

In the meantime, 10cc's North American tour opened at New York's Beacon Theater on October 25. Opening the tour with such a high-profile gig, after months off the road, was a brave move and one that didn't please everyone.

"To this taste it was a disappointing concert even if the audience did seem to like it," wrote John Rockwell in the *New York Times*. "10cc sounded neither refined enough to recreate its records nor exciting enough to appeal on a more visceral rock level." *Cashbox*, however, had a different view: "From the quality of the performance and response of the crowd, it was evident that this is a band whose time has clearly come" while observing that the band "were obviously taken aback by the tumultuous response they received from the filled house – a fitting tour opening for a group that by all rights should become a major unit here in a very short time".

The band's record company threw a party in their honour after the gig at Le Jardin, a nightclub within the Diplomat Hotel on West 43rd Street. The tour then moved on to Montreal, Quebec and Ottawa. In Canada, 10cc had enjoyed even greater chart success than in the US, with I'm Not In Love reaching No.1, becoming the sixth most successful single of the year, while *The Original Soundtrack* climbed to No.5 in the Canadian charts.

While on tour, the band learned that Blue Guitar, the song they had recorded with Justin Hayward some 18 months earlier, was climbing the charts back home, where it would eventually reach the Top 10.

"I was really knocked out to see that in the charts," said Stewart at the time. "We all got nicely drunk that night."

By mid-November the tour was working its way down the West Coast. Based in Los Angeles for a week of interviews, meetings and concerts, 10cc indulged in some rare rock star behaviour at the Beverly Hilton hotel on Wilshire Boulevard in Beverly Hills.

"We broke into the Penthouse Suite one night," recalls Zeb White. "Kev and Lol turned all the paintings round and drew all these phallic symbols and messages like 'Have a Nice Day' on the brown paper backing. On every floor outside the lifts they had these big pot plants and we filled one of the lifts with all these pot plants and we put one of the sofas in there and Lol got one of the breakfast signs, turned it round and wrote on the back, 'This lift is now closed and being used as a mobile botanical exhibition.' We then sent the lift down to reception. It was so full you could only get about two people in it, but people would get in and sit down and say, 'Oh, this is really nice!' What they didn't know was that we'd also rewired the lift, so that when they pressed the button for their floor it actually took them to a different floor!"

The hotel manager failed to see the funny side and issued them with a warning, but it failed to prevent further antics.

"We totally emptied one of the rooms," recalls White. "Everything – the TV, the minibar, the furniture, the paintings. Even the carpet! Because a lot of the stuff had gone out of the window, the hotel manager came up with the band's manager Ric Dixon, who was so red that he was nearly bursting. There was steam coming out of his ears!"

Given the cinematic nature of their music, it seemed only a matter of time before 10cc were approached to write the soundtrack to a movie.

"That's a thing that 10cc will definitely do," predicted Gouldman at the time. "When, I don't know. But I rather think we're tailor-made for it."

A potentially game-changing opportunity arose while the

band was in Los Angeles. "We've been approached to write the music for *Superman*, a new $10m movie," said Stewart at the time. "It will be great if we get it but it'll probably go to one of the big names like John Barry or Paul McCartney. It'll be nice to do because we're really into films and comics and cartoons. It comes out in most of the songs." Unfortunately, the movie was postponed and 10cc's soundtrack debut was put on hold. Still, the band's concert at the Santa Monica Civic Center on November 26 was a particularly important one, as it was to be recorded for the famed *King Biscuit Flower Hour* syndicated radio show and would be broadcast on 300 radio stations across the US later in the year. 10cc put on an excellent show and gained some rave reviews.

"Finally, that audience that hungers for melodic, inventive music, light and commercial but with remarkable substance, highly stylized but enriched by plenty of heart, sly, witty and periodically biting, was given a veritable feast," wrote Richard Cromelin in the *Los Angeles Times* under the headline DAZZLING ROCK FROM 10CC. "The basic elements with which the group so thoroughly dazzles are buoyant tunes, adventurous arrangements, four very British voices that entwine in stirring harmony, a consummate sense of musical space and movement, devilishly clever lyrics and an infectious sense of fun … the group's presentation was impeccable, the music lost nothing in translation from studio to stage and both individual personalities and c ollective identity were nicely established. The Springsteen blitz notwithstanding, the future of rock 'n' roll hasn't quite been sewn up yet."

In the audience that night was legendary producer Phil Spector, who came backstage after the show to tell the band how much he'd enjoyed the gig. Spector was a particular fan of 10cc's debut album and raved about the record. However, as he spoke, the group noticed that Spector had a firearm tucked into his belt. This, and Spector's refusal to make eye contact when he spoke, made for a flattering but disconcerting experience.

While a handful of songs from the show would appear on bootlegs such as *Going Pink On Purpose*, an edited version of the gig would eventually receive a legitimate release in 1996 as the *King*

Biscuit Flower Hour archives were issued onto CD. It succeeds in capturing the band in fine form, making a mockery of detractors' claims that the original incarnation of 10cc was unable to cut the mustard live.

"Anyone who remembers the original 10cc from the still astonishing treasure chests of crafty, inventive, smart-pop that are their 1973–1976 studio albums may be taken by surprise by the muscle of the band live," wrote Kit Aiken in *Uncut* magazine. "A fascinating, if relatively minor, document of the brightest band on the planet."

Q magazine awarded the album three stars: "This is the smart-alec Godley/Creme/Stewart/Gouldman line-up in superbly recorded and vervefully rump-kicking mode. The Sacro Illiac doing its twinkle-toed, idiosyncratically harmonised thing next door to the Kiss-meets-Sparks romp of Silly Love ... the blasting Rubber Bullets almost justifies dosh-transfer in itself."

For contractual reasons, the album excludes live versions of any post-*Sheet Music* material performed at the gig. In the early 2010s the full 1 hour 46-minute gig, complete with all the between-song banter, was posted onto the *wolfgangs.com* website. A listen is a must for any fan of the band, showing a remarkable amount of spontaneity, humour, playfulness and adventure that belies the band's reputation as a cold and clinical live act, including a great joke at Uriah Heep's expense.

10cc's US tour wound up back on the East Coast in early December. The group played two shows on the same night at the Philadelphia Tower Theater, the second one not finishing until 4am, before the tour concluded, the following night, in Boston. To celebrate the end of the tour, 10cc threw a party in an 18th-floor suite of their hotel. While their road crew dismantled the gig, the band could be found preparing plates of whipped cream for the customary end-of-tour custard pie fight. The crew's arrival triggered a 15-minute pitched battle that was only curtailed when a police officer turned up but ended up on the receiving end of a plate of whipped cream, leading to the arrest of a member of the road crew.

Overall, the band were pleased with how the tour had gone.

"We've managed to sell out most of the gigs on this tour, and although they were only in halls that hold three or four thousand, that's good for us on what is our third tour," said Gouldman at the time. "We might even break even financially on this tour, which would be a change. We've lost money on the last two. But we're not in it for the money, we're in it for the investment. It would be nice of course to be able to make money on the road somewhere along the line, but at the moment it's very expensive. But we're doing it in the hope of being able to play gigs one day in six- or eight-thousand seaters, or play a few shows in one town at a four-thousand seater, and then it becomes economically viable."

Yet, despite the success of the tour, Art For Art's Sake failed to follow up on the success of I'm Not In Love, spending five weeks in the lower reaches of the Top 100 but only managing to limp to No.83 in the charts. 10cc were disappointed but not entirely surprised. In fact, wanting to get away from being viewed as a 'singles band', the group had talked about not releasing a single from the new album at all. "Up until now we've always chosen the singles ourselves," said Gouldman. "But with this album we hadn't thought about singles at all. In fact, we were talking about not releasing a single at all. We just went along with it thinking we'd give the record company the opportunity to make that sort of decision, and in fact they were wrong in America – it didn't happen there. If it had been up to us, I doubt we'd have put it out, but you leave the business to business people. We're not ashamed of any track we've recorded, so it wouldn't be a case of, 'We don't want that out as a single.' There's no problem as far as we're concerned because we're proud of the music, every single track."

Still, the band conceded that there were things they'd do differently next time.

"We've learned a lot of lessons from this tour," said Gouldman. "One is that it is imperative to do a tour when you have an album out, which we hadn't this time. The Original Soundtrack is pretty well dead now, although it did come back on the chart somewhere near the 200 mark. It's very unlikely that we'll be over here when the next album comes out either, as we've got a British and European tour, so we'll probably plan the next American tour to coincide with when the album after that comes out. But we can see it picking up. It's amazing how we get people coming backstage who know the

One big happy family. Early press ad for Strawberry Studios, featuring Peter Tattersall, Eric Stewart, Graham Gouldman, Kevin Godley and various family members, November 15, 1969 (Thanks to Peter Wadsworth)

ONE BIG HAPPY FAMILY

People are important to us for we at Strawberry feel that the relationship we have with artistes and producers, recording with us, is as vital to producing a successful product as having good equipment; we also believe that recording is not a nine to five forget-it-and-go-home job, but one that calls for a total and complete involvement from all concerned.

Strawberry Recording Studios,
3 Waterloo Road,
Stockport, Cheshire,
England.
Tel. 061-480-9711.

"Johnny, Don't Do It!"   10c.c.   UK 22 UK RECORDS

ABOVE: Gouldman, Godley, Stewart and Creme line up for an early 10cc publicity photo in support of their debut single Donna, August 1972 (Gems/ Getty Images)

RIGHT: UK press ad for 10cc's second single Johnny Don't Do It, November 1972 (Thanks to Dave Jarvis)

Cover for 10cc's eponymous debut album released in July 1973. The 'balloons' logo was drawn by Lol Creme, reflecting the irreverent nature of the band's music

US press ad for Rubber Bullets, summer 1973 (Thanks to Dave Jarvis)

RUBBER
BULLETS
by
10c.c.

If you live in the Eastern United States you might be missing out on one of the fastest spreading singles in America. "Rubber Bullets" by 10 C.C. First it was a major hit in the U.K. And spread throughout Europe.

In America it caught on first in San Francisco and started spreading up and down the West Coast. Then, onward to the Midwest. It's just hit Chicago (WLS and WCFL) and it's now heading East.

As their song says, "There's a rumor goin' round, you know...that a fuse is gonna blow." And it's gonna blow big!

#49015

UK

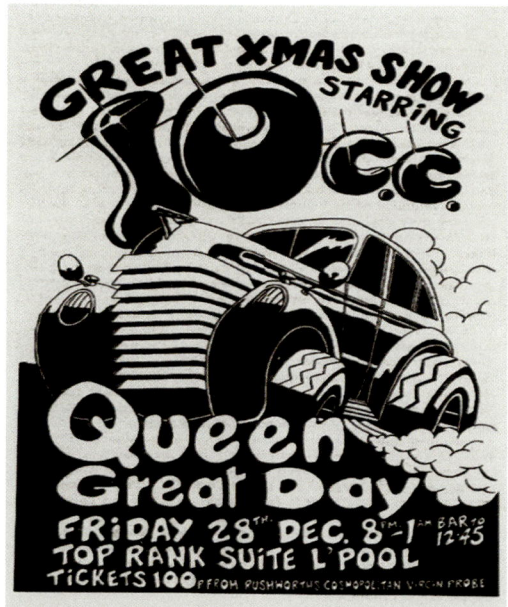

CLOCKWISE FROM TOP LEFT: Flyers from gigs in Plymouth, Hove and Liverpool on the band's first tour of the UK in 1973. The latter offered the opportunity to enjoy 10cc, Queen and a late bar for £1 (Thanks to Dave Jarvis)

ABOVE: Previously unseen out-take from the photo-shoot for 10cc's second album *Sheet Music* at the Odeon cinema, Wood Green in North London (Photo by Aubrey Powell, reproduced by kind permission)

RIGHT: Cover for 10cc's second album *Sheet Music*, released in May 1974 (Cover design by Hipgnosis, reproduced by kind permission)

ABOVE: The worst band in the world
become the darlings of the music press,
1974 (Michael Putland/Getty Images)

OPPOSITE: (top) Previously unseen
photograph for the cover of *The Original
Soundtrack*, but which Hipgnosis felt
lacked "the romance of Hollywood"
(Photo by Aubrey Powell, reproduced by
kind permission)

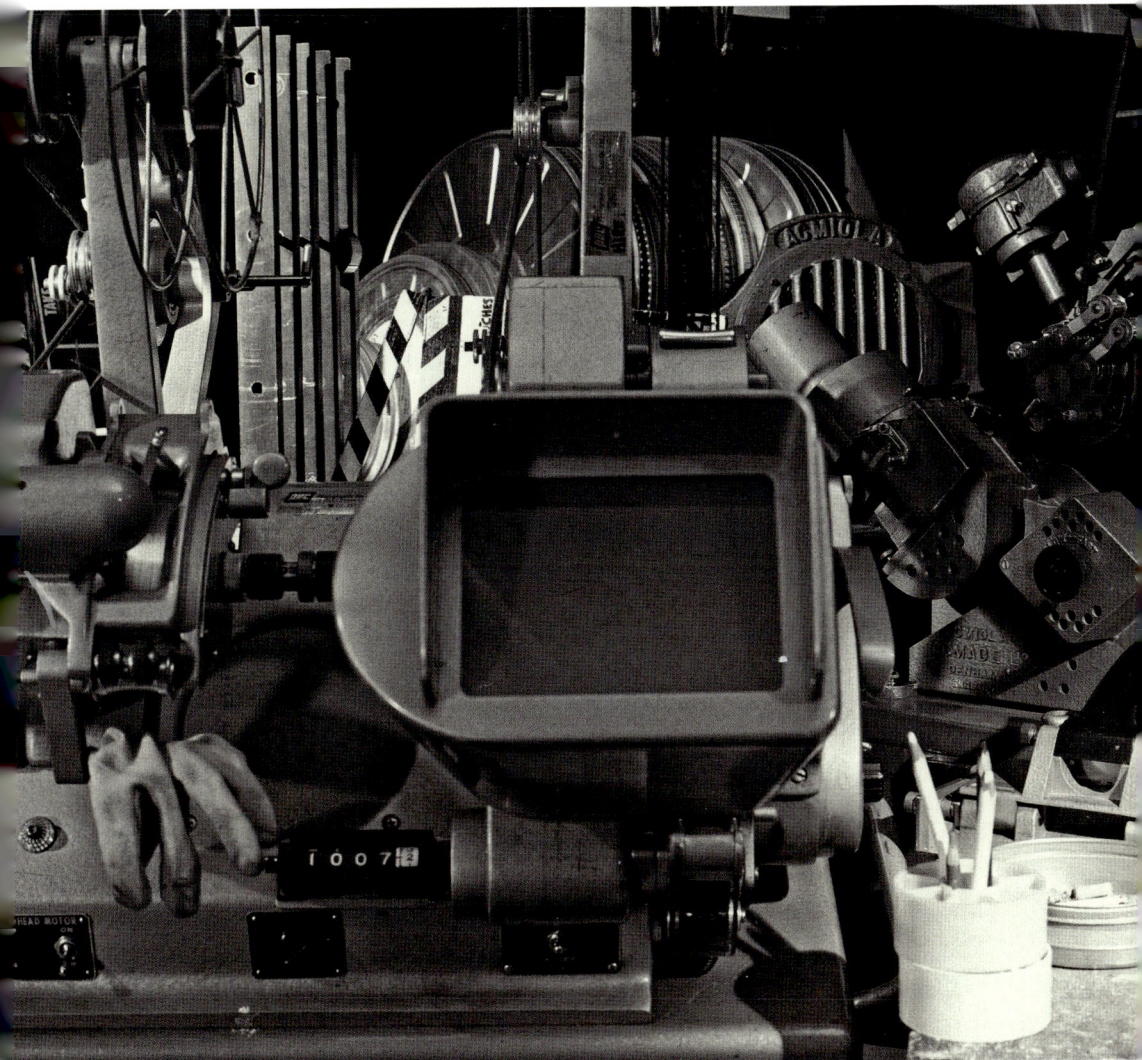

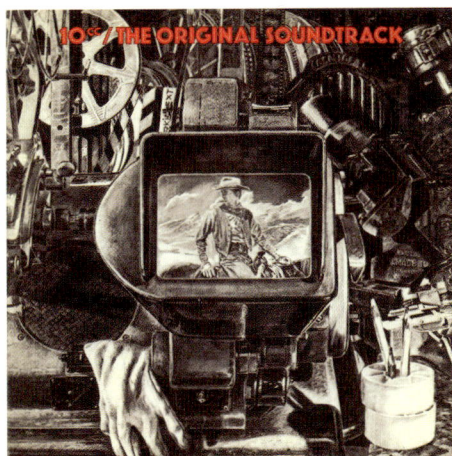

RIGHT: Final cover of 10cc's third album *The Original Soundtrack* as drawn by Humphrey Ocean which, according to Kevin Godley, "not only captured the sheen of the finished product but the chemical reaction that made 10cc combust" (Cover design by Hipgnosis, reproduced by kind permission)

ABOVE: UK press ad for 10cc's third album *The Original Soundtrack*, and eighth single Life Is A Minestrone, both released in March 1975 (Thanks to Dave Jarvis)

OPPOSITE: (top) 10cc performing at the Carré Theatre in Amsterdam on their first European tour, April 14 1975 (Gijsbert Hanekroot/Getty Images)

(bottom) poster for the band's gig at Bristol Colston Hall, April 28, 1975

(Thanks to Dave Jarvis)

COLSTON HALL • **BRISTOL**

Entertainments Manager : R. W. MUIR

Tel : 291768 and 922957 - open 10 a.m. to 8 p.m.

ONE NIGHT ONLY

MONDAY, 28th APRIL, 1975 at 7.30 p.m.

KENNEDY STREET ENTERPRISES LTD. Present

10 c.c. LIVE in CONCERT

with their special guests **FANCY**

TICKETS: £1.50, £1.25, £1.00, 80p

Printed by Electric (Modern) Printing Co. Ltd., Manchester

ABOVE: Life imitating art? Previously
unseen out-take from the photo-shoot
for the inner sleeve of *How Dare You!*
(Photo by Aubrey Powell, reproduced
by kind permission)

RIGHT: Cover for 10cc's fourth album
How Dare You!, released in January
1976 (Cover design by Hipgnosis,
reproduced by kind permission)

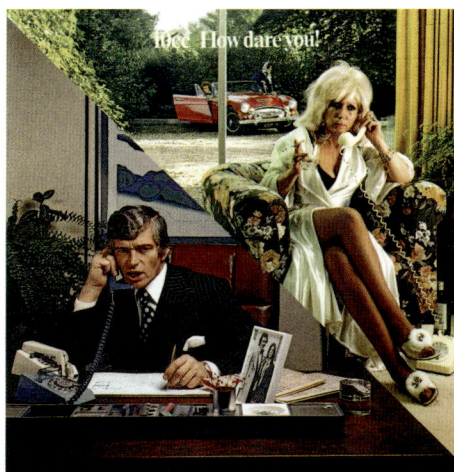

How dare you!
THE NEW ALBUM FROM
10cc

FEBRUARY
* 2nd   Sheffield, City Hall
* 3rd/4th   Manchester, Free Trade Hall
* 5th/6th   Glasgow, Apollo
* 7th/8th   Edinburgh, Usher Hall
* 9th/10th   Newcastle, City Hall
11th   –
12th/13th   Leicester, De Montfort Hall
* 14th/15th   Cardiff, Capitol
* 16th   Brighton, Dome
* 17th   London, Hammersmith Odeon
* 18th/19th   London, Hammersmith Odeon
* 20th   Portsmouth, Guildhall
* 21st/22nd   Birmingham, Odeon
* 24th/25th   Bristol, Colston Hall
26th/27th   Liverpool, Empire
* 29th   Croydon, Fairfield Hall
MARCH
1st/2nd   Oxford, New Theatre
3rd/4th   Ipswich, Gaumont

*Sold Out

GIVE IT A LISTEN

Album 9102 501
Cassette 7321 301
Cartridge 7711 501
mercury

marketed by phonogram

ABOVE: UK press ad supporting the release of *How Dare You!* (Thanks to Dave Jarvis)

LEFT: Promo badge for *How Dare You!*

ABOVE: Group portrait taken as part
of a photo session with Lord Lichfield,
January 5, 1976
(Lichfield Archive via Getty Images)

RIGHT: The original line-up played their
last gig as 'special guests' of The Rolling
Stones at Knebworth, August 21, 1976.
Just weeks later the band split
(Design by Hipgnosis, reproduced by
kind permission)

ABOVE: Eric Stewart and Graham Gouldman go it alone, December 1976 (Terry O'Neill/Getty Images)

OPPOSITE: Two previously unseen images from the photo shoot for the inner sleeve of 10cc's fifth album *Deceptive Bends* (Photos by Aubrey Powell, reproduced by kind permission)

RIGHT: Cover for *Deceptive Bends*, released in April 1977 (Cover design by Hipgnosis, reproduced by kind permission)

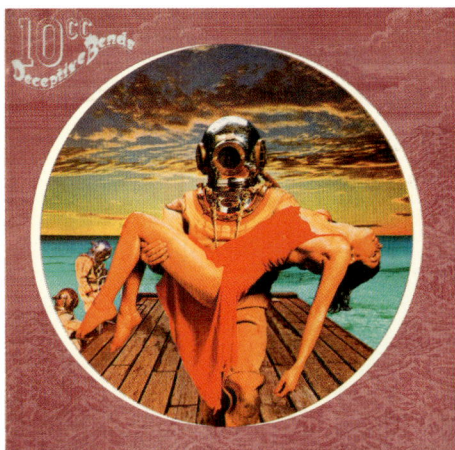

US press ad supporting the release of *Deceptive Bends* (Thanks to Dave Jarvis)

whole history of the band for the last 10 years. They're really into that kind of thing there."

The release of *How Dare You!* in January 1976 confirmed that 10cc had not yet made the commercial breakthrough in America they had hoped for, despite good reviews. "Another collection of skilled looniness from the British quartet," said *Billboard*. "10cc has developed a style and sound that most of the so-called party groups should have developed, and at this point these four are the only ones to make such a sound viable." The album entered the US charts on February 14 and six weeks later had climbed to No.47. But that was where it would stall, spending 13 weeks in the US Top 200, suggesting that many of those that had bought *The Original Soundtrack* – presumably because of I'm Not In Love – had not come back for more. TV appearances on the syndicated *Don Kirshner's Rock Concert* TV show – screening promotional films of Art For Art's Sake, Head Room and Don't Hang Up – didn't compensate for 10cc not being in America at the time to promote the album.

A second single, I'm Mandy Fly Me, stalled at a lowly No.60 in the US charts – "America thought I'm Mandy Fly Me was about taking Mandrax to calm your nerves before flying," says Kevin Godley, "when all it was really inspired by was their National Airline ads!" – while a third single, that coupled Lazy Ways with Life Is A Minestrone, failed to chart at all. Overall, their lack of American success came as a blow to the band, who had expected to build on the success they had enjoyed earlier in the year.

"We've got a lot of work to do there," conceded Lol Creme at the time. "We've been a cult band in the States for about two years, but cult bands don't sell a lot of records, and really we're in the business of communications, not art for art's sake. We don't really want to be a cult band in America, we want to break through."

CHAPTER 13

WE WANNA RULE THE WORLD

WHILE ART FOR ART'S SAKE HAD FAILED TO SET THE CHARTS ALIGHT in America, back in the UK it had been a very different story. With the non-album track Get It While You Can on the b-side, Art For Art's Sake had been released in November 1975, and entered the UK singles chart at the end of that month. 10cc made a flying visit to the UK, in a break from their North American tour, to film an all-important appearance on *Top of the Pops*, which helped lift the record further up the charts, where it eventually peaked at No.5. Their seventh Top 10 hit, Art For Art's Sake enjoyed a 10-week chart run. It was also a big hit in Ireland, reaching No.4 and spending nine weeks in the Irish Top 10. One particular fan of the song was Tony Banks of Genesis, who still cites it as one of his favourite records.

"One of the groups I really loved in the 70s was 10cc," says Banks. "Very imaginative writing; incredible number of singles, with all sorts of bits and pieces going on within them, and also some fantastic singers in the group, Eric Stewart and Kevin Godley in particular have got wonderful voices. I think Art For Art's Sake was perhaps the best of their singles. That side of 10cc I liked the best, the melodic side. But this has so many changes, a great little riff, and different ways of doing the riff each time. Very slick productions, reminiscent of Steely Dan. I just find it very appealing."

Nineteen seventy six got off to a great start for the band when I'm Not In Love was voted No.1 in Capital Radio's annual poll of their listeners' favourite songs of all time. During a seven-hour run-down on New Year's Day, DJs Kenny Everett and Roger Scott played their listeners' favourite 100 records. As the show reached its conclusion, Hey Jude by The Beatles came in at No.3; Simon and Garfunkel's Bridge Over Troubled Water was No.2; and 10cc at No.1. Later that week, 10cc's first engagement of 1976 was a date with minor royalty; a photo shoot with Lord Lichfield.

As they prepared for the release of their fourth album, the No.1 spot in the singles chart was being monopolised by Queen's Bohemian Rhapsody, a song that some critics felt had been influenced by 10cc, and particularly the band's mini-operetta One Night In Paris. "Let's just say they heard it before they did Bohemian Rhapsody – those fucking bastards!" jokes Gouldman today.

So, did Queen hear One Night In Paris before making Bohemian Rhapsody? "No," says Queen's Roger Taylor. "I remember a friend of mine playing me I'm Not In Love from their album before it was a single, and that was great. But I don't know if any of us ever heard that other one."

How Dare You! was previewed to the music press via a breakfast playback at a top London hotel and was released by Phonogram on January 9 to generally favourable reviews.

"With *How Dare You!*, their fourth album, the band has opened up a 10-point gap at the top of the rock league table," wrote Geoff Brown in *Melody Maker* under the headline STUNNING 10CC – DAREDEVILS OF ROCK. "The album is a stunner. Aside from their lyrical class, the group are brilliant producers, especially adept at mental tone and weight to colour their melodies, while their arrangements are for the most part sharply clever and their playing is energetic and exact, with Stewart's underrated lead guitar inspiring. 10cc are so intensively clever that they could afford to be smug but the superb production of their albums never masks the fact that their music is as much fun as a demonstration of intelligence and excellence."

Record Mirror was equally enthusiastic, under the headline VERY 10CC, VERY WONDERFUL: "10cc are as good as you'll get; our great white hopes indeed. They're as clinically precise and inventive with their studio work as The Beach Boys in their heyday and as sharp and personal as any of the greats."

By contrast, *New Musical Express* gave the album one of 10cc's poorest reviews to date: "On any terms this album appears to be an unloved pre-fab job, assembled by a group of musicians with little feeling for their music beyond a preoccupation with sound quality, and even that isn't fully exploited here, and even less for each other," wrote Pete Erskine. 10cc were infuriated with the review, prompting Eric Stewart to respond to the paper in writing: "Reviewers are no better equipped for sizing up the merits and demerits of a piece of music than, say, the gentlemen standing to your immediate left," wrote Stewart.

Stewart's letter sparked off an equally acidic response from *New Musical Express*, and an ongoing feud between the band and the paper would develop over the coming months. "I felt tremendously insulted that he had taken our integrity at such a low level," said Stewart later. "He talked about cash and money. And anyone who can knock our integrity as well and say that they feel we've reached a point where we feel comfortable releasing anything, to say we're at that stage, that we're just in it for the money, it really hurts. It's so stupid because the guy obviously doesn't know anything about us."

As always with 10cc, there was irony. They were being criticised for the very values they had been sending up in Art For Art's Sake. "If you just want to make money you don't have to spend three or four months in the studio pushing yourself. You'd just go in and do what the fuck you want," said Lol Creme. "To knock a thing because it appeals to a wide audience seems a horrible idea, because if you're in music, it's like communication. You should be trying to get to just about everyone you can, not trying to be like some kind of cult or have a snobbish attitude to it. That's surely the wrong approach, to my mind anyway."

10cc felt that some music critics were knocking them purely because they were no longer a 'cult' band. "Some critics change their loyalties like underwear," said Kevin Godley. "They build you up and then take you down. When a new band comes along they attach themselves to them but after a while they get bored with them and start slagging them off. The business moves so fast they've got to do well to keep up. It is really down to the people who listen."

Whatever *New Musical Express* thought about *How Dare You!*, the album would go on to become one of the year's bestsellers, entering the UK album charts at No.5, where it would peak, during a seven-month chart run that included 11 weeks in the Top 10. It would go on to become the sixth bestselling new album of 1976 in the UK. *How Dare You!* did even better in the *New Musical Express* charts, the band relishing the irony when the album hit the No.1 spot in the paper's chart. Outside of the UK, *How Dare You!* would give 10cc their biggest hit album to date in many markets, reaching the No.1 spot in New Zealand – where it spent 31 weeks on the charts – going Top 5 in Canada and Sweden and reaching the Top 10 in Norway and the Netherlands, where it peaked at No.9 during a five-month chart run.

What made 10cc's commercial success the more remarkable was that it had been achieved without the aid of image or gimmicks. "We have never really gone out to get a particular following," said Graham Gouldman at the time. "We're not going to alienate anyone. It's better to have a wide audience. You can't knock success, yet critics try to knock you if you get popular in the charts." 10cc started rehearsing at Shepperton Studios in January 1976 for their upcoming European tour. The group were anxious to concoct a new set, having tired of the last one on their US tour. "We're going to attempt to do the whole of the new album," predicted Gouldman. "We'll know in rehearsal stage if it's going to work or not."

In the event the band would include eight of the nine tracks from *How Dare You!* in their set, with only the title track getting the bum's rush. When rehearsing Don't Hang Up the group decided to carry through the theme of the song by having Kevin Godley sing through a microphone placed in a telephone receiver while sitting at a table at the front of the stage. It took them a few weeks to figure out a way to do it. As usual, Paul Burgess joined the band to help them recreate as closely as possible their studio sound.

"On stage we have to compromise. Obviously, you can't do everything like the records," said Burgess. "But that is where I come in, to help give them as full a sound as possible on stage. When 10cc do an album, I have a listen and work out what part I can play towards the live show. Working live with this band you certainly move about a lot on stage, switching instruments. There's nothing worse than sitting on a drum stool for two hours at a time. People criticise them, saying they're only a recording band and can't do live what they do on record, but they can't have been looking or listening properly."

Didn't he ever get frustrated with his background role? "Not really," said Burgess. "I've been doing more and more each tour, and this time round had a few solos which compensated a bit. Basically, I'm freelance, but 10cc have first option. It is great working with four superb writers. I'm not a writer, never have been. I'm quite content as I am. It's a great life. I'm well looked after."

During their time at Shepperton, 10cc gave an interview and appeared on the front cover of *New Musical Express*. The purpose of the interview was to give the band the opportunity to pick out and discuss what they believed to be the best tracks from their four albums to date. The group singled out 12: Rubber Bullets, Fresh Air For My Mama and The Dean and I from *10cc*; The Wall Street Shuffle, Old Wild Men and The Worst Band In The World from *Sheet Music*; One Night In Paris, I'm Not In Love and The Second Sitting For The Last Supper from *The Original Soundtrack*; and I'm Mandy Fly Me, Rock 'n' Roll Lullaby and Don't Hang Up from *How Dare You!*.

While there were one or two surprising omissions – Somewhere In Hollywood springs immediately to mind – the 12 tracks were a good overview of 10cc's best work to date and represented some of the most sublime and influential music of the previous four years.

"Secretly, I desire us to raise the standard of popular music, but it does tend to sound a little bit pretentious," said Lol Creme at the time.

10cc's upcoming UK tour was their biggest to date, playing to a combined audience of more than 100,000 people over 33 concerts in 16 cities, including three sell-out nights at London's Hammersmith Odeon. The tour opened in fine style with a great performance at Sheffield City Hall on February 2.

"If 10cc are the worst band in the world then what price the likes of the Bay City Rollers?" wrote Ben Nielson, reviewing the concert in *Melody Maker*. "10cc made a mockery of the song – for sheer invention they must be among the best bands in the world." While done in a jokey manner, some of the group's onstage banter that night reflected the differences of opinion within the band that had surfaced during the making of the *How Dare You!* album.

"This song has absolutely nothing to do with me or Lol," said Stewart introducing Iceberg. "This song has *everything* to do with me and Kevin," countered Gouldman.

As on their previous tours, Lol Creme's comedic skills were once again put to good use. Creme's *pièce de résistance* this time around was his introduction to I Wanna Rule The World, where he talked of world domination in the style of a German dictator – dubbed, wittily, Herr Creme by the band – while accompanying himself on timpani drums for added dramatic effect.

Unfortunately, the tour was dogged by ill health early on, with Creme and then Eric Stewart both succumbing to the flu epidemic that was sweeping the country at the time. Things came to a head as the tour reached the Glasgow Apollo.

"We knew that Lol and I were ill," recalls Stewart. "We had a doctor come over to pump us full of antibiotics and vitamins and we were lying on two hastily prepared beds under the stage for the rest of the afternoon. We rehearsed briefly and thought we could do it. On the night, however, I got through maybe three songs and my voice packed up. I apologised to the audience and said we couldn't continue, but we'd come back at the end of the tour, and would repay anybody who wanted their money back."

Eight shows, in Glasgow, Edinburgh, Newcastle and Leicester had to be postponed before the tour resumed in Cardiff. Back on the road the band generally played a two-hour set.

"We've done a longish set usually," said Godley. "It has grown according to audience reaction of course, but usually about two hours ten minutes, and including a mixture of just about everything we've done."

Reviews of the concerts were again mixed, with the main criticism remaining 10cc's approach of attempting to faithfully recreate their records rather than reinterpret them live.

"We go on, we don't do a flash show," said Eric Stewart at the time. "We're not all lights and banging and explosions and dry ice. We go on and do a musical show which is a fair representation of our records. So, the only criticism that can be levelled at us, which people occasionally do, is that we do approach things in a cold way to get things right on stage. Which is something we've got to learn ourselves."

Conversely, critics that accepted the band's approach to live music gave them rave reviews. Phil Sutcliffe, reviewing one of the band's Hammersmith concerts for *Sounds* described what he saw as a "superlative display by one of the best bands in the world … one night with 10cc is like a year with any other band."

The UK tour continued, with John Tobler catching them at the Oxford New Theatre for his review in *Zigzag* magazine. "10cc in probably 90% of their set were a visual improvement on an aural delight. Their playing was a joy and their singing was impeccable and their use of lights, a lot of lights, was without equal in anything I've seen for some time."

On March 12, Phonogram released I'm Mandy Fly Me as the band's next single. Although one of 10cc's finest creations, I'm Mandy Fly Me wasn't usual hit single material. At over five minutes in length, and with no chorus, it was a bold but inspired choice, no doubt influenced by the success of more adventurous singles such as I'm Not In Love and Bohemian Rhapsody at the time. The gamble paid off and the song was a big hit, reaching No.6 in the UK charts and staying there for three consecutive weeks, providing 10cc with their eighth Top 10 hit. Readers of *New Musical Express* would vote it their sixth favourite single of 1976. In Ireland, the song was even more successful, reaching No.3, where it also stayed for three consecutive weeks.

The group might have thought that *How Dare You!* lacked any obvious singles, yet the album had yielded two Top 10 hits. In fact, 10cc were unintentionally turning into one of the most consistently successful singles bands of the decade, which was ironic given their apparent desire to be viewed as more of an 'album' band. "We don't actually record a specific single, we record a collection of tracks for an album and then try and pick out which is the most commercial for the time," said Stewart at the time. "But quite frankly I wouldn't worry if we never had another hit single. It would be nice to be in the position of, say, Pink Floyd where you know if you release a good album it's going to be a smash, whether it's two years after the last one or not. We would rather concentrate on albums."

One track from the new album destined never to be released as a single was Head Room, which was banned by London's Capital Radio. "10cc's Head Room will not be played," said Capital's programme controller Aidan Day at the time. "We would not consider playing it. I heard the record and formed the opinion that it is unsuitable for general programming."

At one point there was talk of releasing Don't Hang Up as a third single from the album. In fact, Godley and Creme actually made some drawings for a potential accompanying promotional film, but nothing ever came of it.

Following their UK tour, 10cc ventured into Europe in March and April, where their popularity was growing. The band played concerts in Sweden, Denmark and the Netherlands, and their first ever gigs in Norway and Germany. "In Germany we broke some new ground," said Kevin Godley. "It was pretty good apart from a couple of dates that were in the middle of nowhere."

They found themselves in hot water, however, introducing I Wanna Rule The World onstage. "When Lol goes into his bit about wanting to dominate the world we thought we had better be a bit careful," said Gouldman. "So, we substituted Winston Churchill for Adolf Hitler and it was worse than ever! We heard that one paper printed a headline like 10CC CALLED AUDIENCE NAZI SWINES – which just wasn't true."

Kevin Godley didn't help matters during a radio interview in Hamburg. "The interviewer asked us to say something in German on the radio and Kevin said, 'Blitzkrieg'," recalls Stewart. "The interview ended very quickly after that!"

On a more positive note, the band played what they felt to be one of their most memorable gigs on the German leg of the tour. "It was a gig we did in Munich," recalls Gouldman. "We got to the venue and it was a club rather than a concert hall. Promoters aren't always honest! There was a certain faction of the band that wanted to pull the gig, and there was another faction of the band that said, 'If we pull it, the fans won't blame the promoter, they'll blame us. Let's do the gig, go in with half the lights and half the equipment.' So, we did and it was one of the best gigs we ever played. It was so intimate. We were all sweating and the adrenaline was pumping. It was one of the best, best, best nights. It was absolutely brilliant."

As usual, the band was on the receiving end of a few practical jokes by their road crew.

"For Don't Hang Up, Kev would come off the drum kit and he'd sit at a table at the front of the stage and sing the song through a microphone that we'd put into a telephone, so that he could sing down the phone," says Zeb White. "Wherever we were, we'd always put something local onto the table. So, when we were in Frankfurt, we put a couple of frankfurters into a vase on the table. In Amsterdam, we put a couple of tulips into the vase. Then we got bored with just putting out a chair. Some nights it would be a bloody great big three-seater settee. Other nights there'd be a hat and coat stand or an umbrella stand. Kev would have no idea because we would put it all out in the dark. We'd blackout the stage and we'd all sneak on and lay it out and he'd walk down from the drum kit and find his way to the chair but he had no idea until the lights came up. Of course, by that time he'd started singing the song so he'd suddenly see two frankfurters in a vase and have to try and keep a straight face and get through the number."

In Stockholm, Eric Stewart entertained the crowd with a few bars of Mamma Mia in homage to the city's chief musical exports. In Copenhagen the band felt they'd played one of their best ever gigs. Overall, the band's European tour had gone well.

"All the places we had been to before were sold out, which was encouraging," said Graham Gouldman after the tour. "Many of the halls there are smaller though. It's a bit like starting again and that's not always pleasant. It's quite similar to the situation in Britain about two years ago."

10cc returned to the UK in late April to play the concerts they'd had to cancel earlier in the year due to ill health. In Edinburgh the band found themselves in trouble again, this time for taking the piss out of The Bay City Rollers. "It turned out that Les McKeown was in the audience!" said Creme at the time. "I hope he didn't take offence; it was only meant as a piece of fun. Someone told me he laughed, or was it he left, I couldn't quite make it out!"

10cc concluded their UK tour with three sell-out nights at the Glasgow Apollo. The customary end-of-tour pranks were once again in evidence on the last night of the tour. Support group Chas & Dave were the first to suffer at the hands of Zeb White and the crew.

"Dave had this acoustic guitar that was his pride and joy," recalls White. "Every night of the tour he would say to the road crew, 'Please be very careful with this guitar.' So, on the last night of the tour we thought we'd have some fun. We went out and bought a really cheap acoustic guitar and the plan was to swap it with Dave's guitar at some point in the show. We had rigged a small explosive charge to the cheap guitar and were going to detonate it on stage to wind Dave up, who'd think his precious guitar had gone up in smoke! We waited for the right moment, and just as Dave went to pick up his guitar, we pressed the detonator. But instead of a small bang there was this huge explosion! We'd obviously put too much explosive in the charge, and it blew the guitar to pieces, nearly taking Dave's right arm with it!"

Later that evening, it was the turn of 10cc themselves to be on the receiving end of a few practical jokes.

"Lol used to play timpani drums when he was introducing I Wanna Rule The World," recalls White. "That night we put two mackerel there instead of beaters. Just two slippery fish to play with! And we all had firefighting asbestos suits and headgear on in the wings just to wind them up. We'd also sawn one of the legs off the table that Kev used for Don't Hang Up and put the leg back on and attached a piece of cord to it, so that when Kev finished the song and put the phone down, we'd pull the cord and the table would collapse."

Despite the practical jokes, the gigs in Glasgow marked a real highpoint for the band, especially the last night of the tour.

"It was a magic night, one of the best gigs in my life actually, we had a ball and over-ran until the manager of the theatre threatened to turn off our power," recalls Stewart. "I said, 'Do you want a blood-bath on your hands?' and he backed down. Sheer magic!"

The shows marked the end of their extended European tour. "It's been a long haul," said Gouldman. "Originally there were two separate tours, the UK tour and the European one. But because of the flu thing it turned into one long one with three legs!"

Their final live engagement was a festival appearance in the Netherlands on May 22 at Oorfestival on a bill including Nils Lofgren, Eric Burdon and Gentle Giant. The gig, at the DHC football stadium in Delft, attracted a capacity 20,000 audience.

Looking ahead, Gouldman predicted the band's next moves, including their next live dates.

"It'll be about six months or so I guess. We're going on holiday for a while and then we're going to do some work in the new studios," he said. "Obviously we've got a few ideas about what we want to do but I'm not really sure if they'll reach fruition yet. It could be a double, though. We're thinking of aiming at that anyway."

CHAPTER 14

A COMPROMISE WOULD SURELY HELP THE SITUATION

FOUR YEARS ON FROM THEIR FORMATION, 10CC HAD BECOME ONE OF the UK's most successful bands with a string of Top 10 singles and albums behind them. Success was important to the group and they compared their own progress with that of their contemporaries.

"We analyse ourselves a hell of a lot and we discuss the progression of other bands in terms of success, not in terms of musical quality," said Eric Stewart at the time. "You see bands rise like rockets, whereas we creep up there slowly all the time. It's funny, you feel sometimes that you're never gonna be quite in that same league, although you know deep down that your music is better than most of the people in that league."

10cc's continual refusal to adopt an image or stick to a well-defined musical formula made it more difficult for them. "We do run the risk of losing our audience by moving away from what they want all the time," said Lol Creme. "But if that happens, it happens, you can't stand still."

Few bands at the time could claim to be enjoying as much commercial success and critical acclaim as 10cc. And the awards kept on coming. At the Dorchester Hotel in London on May 26, 1976, I'm Not In Love won no less than three Ivor Novello Awards, for 'Best Pop Song', 'International Hit of the Year' and 'Most Performed British Work'. Eric Stewart was further taken aback when actor and director Richard Attenborough approached him later that night. "He came up to me and said that he was glad that we'd won the award because he was a big fan of the band," recalls Stewart.

The hat-trick of Ivor Novello Awards was a remarkable achievement by anyone's standards and the latest in a long line of awards vying for a place on the group's mantelpiece. Eric Stewart had even been nominated for a Grammy Award for his engineering work on *The Original Soundtrack*. 10cc's future looked so bright you needed sunglasses and, in Strawberry South, they had a new state of the art, purpose-built studio in which to innovate to their heart's content. A band of 10cc's size now needed to pencil recording sessions into the diary months in advance. Godley and Creme felt that some of the spontaneity of their earlier work was now missing as a result. They looked to Strawberry South as a way of returning to that earlier spontaneity.

"The new studio will not be run like a commercial studio," said Creme at the time. "It will be available for hire when we are out of the country, but it isn't designed to be hired out really. The idea is that if at five o'clock on a Tuesday morning I feel like dropping in to put something down, I can do so. 10cc started like that, with a studio that we just fell into and experimented in, and our records used to be more experiments than anything else; and that was because we had studio time and equipment to play around with, and that's what we're getting back to with the new studio. We're taking stock and going back to square one because that was the most exciting period for 10cc. I think we're in a little bit of a rut at the moment and we want to get back to that exciting period, which was almost an art school period."

10cc's self-contained modus operandi was one of the band's strengths. But, at times, it also left them a little isolated and detached from what was going on around them. Looking back, Kevin Godley feels this was a flaw in the band's make-up. "I remember at the time Bruce Springsteen was exploding," he recalls. "And we said, 'It's old fashioned rock 'n' roll, how come he's huge?' For a simple reason. In this music world that we live in, 'heartfelt' and 'real' is going to beat 'clever' and 'contrived' every fucking time. Sorry, boys, that's just how it is. In the end it's about whether you connect with people or not and we didn't realise that and I think it was partially because we didn't listen to what was going on, we weren't connected, we thought we were just so fucking great, just carry on doing what we do and it'll all come to us. But it pays to be aware of what's going on."

It's unclear how aware the band were of the emerging punk rock movement. On June 4, 1976, The Sex Pistols played Manchester's

Lesser Free Trade Hall to a crowd of 40 people largely made up of future members of the next generation of Manchester bands, such as Buzzcocks, Joy Division, The Fall and The Smiths. The show would have a profound influence on them all. When The Sex Pistols played in Manchester again on July 20 they performed a new song, Anarchy In The UK. Shortly after, they made their debut TV appearance performing the song on *So It Goes*, a new music show filmed in Manchester hosted by Tony Wilson. Also making their debut on the same show was a prog rock band called Gentlemen, who had approached Paul Burgess to perform with them for their appearance. Burgess was impressed with the band, and particularly their guitarist Rick Fenn, but in the end, despite rehearsing together, they had reverted to their original drummer for the performance of their song My Ego's Hurting Me. Gentlemen and The Sex Pistols represented two polar opposites of music coming together.

"Punk and prog rock were like matter and anti-matter and I was utterly convinced that it was punk that was destined for instant annihilation," says Rick Fenn. "How wrong I was. Within a fortnight they were as big as The Beatles while Gentlemen, and prog rock generally, spiralled into a black hole."

John Lydon – now restyled as Johnny Rotten – might well have loved 10cc's first album but The Sex Pistols' visceral brand of rock 'n' roll couldn't have been more different from 10cc's style of music. It was a point that crossed the band's mind at the time. "We thought, 'How do we compete with this? What are we going to do? This is raw, this is sheer 'Fuck Everything'!'" recalls Stewart. "I couldn't listen to it actually, but it did make me think about what I was going to write again. But then I thought, 'You're not competing with this, don't walk in the studio with a pin in your nose and try to be outrageous, that's not you.'"

Recording of 10cc's fifth album was due to start in July 1976, which meant starting to write new songs almost immediately. "It's frightening to think that in three weeks' time we're going to have to start thinking about writing a whole pile of new material," said Lol Creme at the time.

But first the band took a well-earned holiday in the South of France with their families. On June 13, the group visited Bill Wyman of The Rolling Stones at his villa in Vence, in the hills above Nice.

That evening they went to see The Stones perform at Le Parc des Sports de l'Ouest in Nice. At the gig 10cc were asked if they were interested in supporting The Stones at the Knebworth Festival on August 21. 10cc were in two minds about whether or not to play the gig.

"We were warned not to do it," said Eric Stewart at the time. "I was talking to Paul McCartney about it and he said, 'You don't go second on a bill to The Stones, there's no way they're gonna let you get away with it.' But we saw them in the South of France, and had a nice chat with them, and they said, 'Why don't you do the show with us?' so we agreed to do it."

The car journey on the way back from the gig proved eventful. "I dropped Lol and Graham off and I was driving with Kevin," recalls Stewart. "He said, 'I can't carry on with the touring. It's not fair on my wife, Sue. Either she comes on tour with us or I stop touring.' At that point I seriously wondered whether 10cc would ever tour again."

Godley was getting fed up with the pressure that the band's touring commitments were putting on his personal life. "There was an unspoken group rule that wives didn't come on tour," recalls Godley. "I thought, 'Fuck that! I'm a person. The group owns me in so far as I write, I perform, I go on stage, but who I associate with and when and where is my business.' I didn't want to have any rules like that but I didn't want to force a Yoko Ono situation and demand that my wife came on tour with us. My life and my job were pulling against each other and I wanted to move the goalposts. When you're four guys together against the world, and then you start having relationships with people and get married, it exerts different pressures on that unit. Eric had never been hampered by that pressure because he was already married by the time 10cc started, as were Graham and Lol. But I was getting to the stage where I didn't want to be away from my wife."

In fact, Godley and Creme were both beginning to tire of the whole 'write-record-tour' treadmill. The last four years had been hectic. The group had written, recorded and promoted four albums and played some 200 concerts without a major break. How many bands today could boast such prolificacy? The pair also felt under pressure to continually pull rabbits out of hats and come up with something that topped what they had done previously.

"You've got this horrible thing in the back of your mind that says it's got to be better than what you've done before," said Creme at the time. "That's the biggest pain of all."

Six months on from its release, Lol Creme looked back with mixed feelings on the last album: "*How Dare You!* wasn't as good as it could have been," he said. "Everybody asked how we could follow up *The Original Soundtrack*, but we should have been able to improve on it easily; we've only got ourselves to blame."

Kevin Godley shared this view: "I think the album's too easy going, too middle-of the-road in the sense that we weren't trying hard enough," he said at the time. "It was a good album by a lot of standards, but for us we didn't get any buzz out of it, although we kidded ourselves that we did when it was released. But now it's a considerable time since the album came out, and you can stand back and look at it from a distance and see how it stands up against the other albums we've had out, and it certainly doesn't have the fire and inspiration of even our first album. Our records do sometimes tend to be a little clinical, probably because of the perfection thing. If we lose a bit of perfection and gain a little bit of feel, then it can't do anyone any harm. That's for us to decide – see what happens when we've tried it. But there should be more feel there, I think."

The pair were even critical of their own writing contributions, chastising themselves for repeating the first verse of Head Room rather than writing a new one. They also considered Don't Hang Up a failure. "We feel that what we had to say could have been put over better," said Godley at the time. "There's a habit we've got into in 10cc of using puns, which come automatically now. It's a habit that's very, very difficult to get away from, and which we were trying very hard to get away from in that song. It's too easy. It's almost a formula, which we're dead against. I think structurally it was a failure – it *sounded* structured. The whole point about structure is that it shouldn't sound as if it's been put together. It's like a Gene Kelly dance routine. When you look at it it looks great. It shouldn't look as if it's hard to perform. For me a perfect example of what we're talking about is an earlier song called The Dean and I. I think that was the perfect structure, whereas Don't Hang Up was more angular, talking in visual terms."

Looking back, Godley wonders if all the changes in the record detract from the emotional pull of the song. "It was trying to be too smart," says Godley. "We clevered ourselves into a corner."

It was a lucrative corner, though; 10cc had been lined up to record the music for an American advertising campaign for Revlon cosmetics. The ad, for Revlon's Natural Wonder Longlash mascara, was recorded at Strawberry in early July. At the time, Godley and Creme were getting closer to realising their ambition of bringing the 'Gizmo' to market. Musitronics planned to launch the 'Gizmo' in 1977 and Godley and Creme were keen for 10cc's next project to be a showcase for the 'Gizmo''s capabilities prior to its launch.

"It turns out that it's incredibly versatile, so we feel that's the direction we'd like to push the future music in, using this instrument," said Godley at the time. "It offers so many different sounds that it's too good to be ignored."

In addition to being the focus of the next 10cc album, they suggested that the accompanying tour could perhaps feature guest appearances from the world's best guitarists, each playing excerpts from the album on a 'Gizmo'. Eric Stewart and Graham Gouldman were far from sold on the idea. They saw 10cc's future rather differently, wanting to get on with the band's fifth album, using the 'Gizmo' as they had in the past to embellish their songs, rather than make the 'Gizmo' itself the focus of the record.

Unable to come to an agreement over the direction of 10cc's next album, a compromise solution was struck. Godley and Creme would spend a few weeks working on a 'Gizmo' demonstration record as a solo project at Strawberry North. In the past, Eric Stewart would have engineered any sessions at Strawberry, but this time Godley and Creme wanted a different approach, being concerned that Stewart had become too domineering in the studio. "We had said to Eric that we didn't want him to engineer it because we wanted it to be a separate project from 10cc," said Lol Creme at the time. "We didn't want to insult him as an engineer but we just wanted it to be separate from the group and therefore we asked Martin Lawrence to do it. He's got a tremendous amount of patience, which he needed. No matter how good Eric is he would have to admit that his patience has got limits and his limits are different from our limits."

While Godley and Creme got down to business at Strawberry North, Stewart and Gouldman started writing songs for the next 10cc album. They penned three new songs: a slow, bluesy number called The Things We Do For Love; a song about a career criminal addicted to prison life called Good Morning Judge; and the ballad People In Love. The plan was for the quartet to reconvene when the 'Gizmo' record was complete. But as work on Godley and Creme's solo project began in late July, what started life as a demonstration record for the 'Gizmo' soon developed into a fully blown album.

"It's a sort of experiment that Kev and I are doing," said Creme at the time. "Kev and I wanted to do the first definitive 'Gizmo' album, and we thought that if there was a best time to do it, it was now, so we set a few weeks aside and started experimenting to see the different sounds we could get out of it. We've been playing it seriously for two weeks on this album and it's really expanding. It'll probably end up as more than one album."

The pair found that the project changed their writing style. "We're writing in a completely different way now," said Godley. "We used to sit down at a piano, write a few words and get a song. Since having the 'Gizmo' everything we're recording is being made up as we go along because we hear something good and say, 'Let's put it down.'"

Freed from the constraints of needing to bounce their ideas off their bandmates, and lubricated by copious amounts of hashish, Godley and Creme were greatly energised by the experience of working on their own. "Lol and I were a little gang and always had been," says Godley. "We'd immersed ourselves in 10cc for a few years but by now we were reverting to being a little gang again, two mad people against the world. Ensconced in the studio, with a load of dope and a 'Gizmo', we were having a whale of a time."

With the 'Gizmo' project now likely to be "more than one album", Godley and Creme were keen to take some time out from 10cc, so that they could work on their record without the prospect of a new group album and tour looming over them. Stewart, Gouldman and the band's management and record company didn't like the idea. Putting 10cc on ice for six months was viewed as potential commercial suicide at the time. Instead it was suggested that the quartet should regroup to record a new 10cc single, to keep the band in the public eye. With some reluctance, Godley and Creme agreed to temporarily leave their project for a few weeks in order to work on the single and to fulfil 10cc's commitment to play at the 1976 Knebworth Festival, as special guests of The Rolling Stones.

When 10cc reconvened at Shepperton Studios in mid-August to rehearse for the gig it was clear that Godley and Creme's hearts really weren't in it. As the band worked out what songs to include in their 85-minute performance they decided to include one of Stewart and Gouldman's new songs, Good Morning Judge, in their set. They also elected to hire a mobile studio to record it, and their performance, at Knebworth. Strangely, the band also dusted off an old Hotlegs track, Run Baby Run, for inclusion in their Knebworth set.

As they prepared for the gig the group couldn't resist the opportunity to have a bit of fun at The Rolling Stones' expense. They hired a 60-foot crane from which they planned to suspend an enormous nose and droopy Zapata moustache above the trademark giant lips that The Stones used on stage. However, promoter Freddie Bannister failed to see the funny side.

"The stage was in the shape of Mick Jagger's lips, it was a huge affair," recalls Bannister. "When we arrived at Knebworth one day, just before the soundcheck, it was to find that 10cc had arranged for a crane to be in place and were busy lowering a very large drooping moustache and a large nose over these lips. It looked like Groucho Marx. And we hastily put a stop to it."

The concert on August 21 attracted an audience of 250,000 people. The festival kicked off with performances by the Don Harrison Band, Hot Tuna, Todd Rundgren's Utopia and Lynyrd Skynyrd, who were one of the highlights of the day. Backstage, the likes of actor Jack Nicholson and Paul McCartney mingled with the bands. 10cc had been scheduled to play an 85-minute set, between 5.15pm and 6.40pm. However, as the band's road crew readied the stage for 10cc's performance they discovered that none of the settings from the soundcheck seemed to be working properly. A two-hour wait ensued while 10cc's road crew tried to fix the problem. "It was really embarrassing," recalls Stewart. "It was worse for us because we were blamed for the delay. We had to sit behind those amps for two hours waiting to go on."

The longer the delay went on, the more restless the crowd became. One member of the audience relieved his frustration by clambering onto the stage and masturbating in front of the huge crowd. The relief was only short-lived, though, as he jumped off-stage and broke both his legs. A local paper would later wittily report, "During a technical delay at Knebworth, a young man had entertained the crowd single-handedly."

It didn't interrupt 10cc's road crew who were still trying to identify the cause of the technical issues, of course. Concert promoter Freddie Bannister suspected the delay was all just a ruse by 10cc to secure a night-time slot to showcase their light show. After all, it was a trick they'd been accused of before at the Reading Festival in 1974. With tensions rising backstage at Knebworth, 10cc were in danger of being thrown off the bill. "It almost came down to an ultimatum," said Rolling Stones tour manager Peter Rudge at the time. "We allowed them 40 minutes for a changeover but when it far exceeded that I went crazy."

Rudge asked 10cc to limit their set to an hour. Finally, at 8.30pm, they were forced to take to the stage, despite the sound problems not being fully resolved. "To this day, I can hear the jeers that greeted 10cc," says journalist Mark Ellen. "Three years later I asked Eric Stewart what had happened. 'Blame Keith Richards,' he told me, coldly. The Stones' guitarist, the world's thirstiest party animal, had apparently been refreshing himself enthusiastically all afternoon and, by eight at night, had been declared incapable of performance and carted up to the stately home for a snooze. In order to buy a little time, The Stones' road crew had thoughtfully sawed through the cables that connected the public address system and it had taken more than an hour for 10cc's mob to splice them back together again. A cunning plan that allowed Richards to sober up and put the blame squarely on someone else."

Whatever the reason for the delay, once on stage, it was clear that 10cc had either misjudged the occasion or were not ideally suited to an outdoor gig of this magnitude. One Night In Paris was never likely to be a festival crowd-pleaser yet the group decided to open their set with the song. "We opened with One Night In Paris because I think we just wanted to do the opposite of what was expected; but I don't think it worked," recalls Gouldman. "It was a bad day. We were delayed by about two hours and we were getting upset. There were technical problems and, of course, no one blamed The Stones, they blamed us. The sound was very strange on stage and I remember it as a very lacklustre performance."

Bootleg recordings of the gig confirm Gouldman's recollections are accurate. Aside from the sound problems, the delayed start to the gig had meant that the group had been forced to cut their set short. More worryingly, the band seemed rusty after three months off the road. "That was a new track that we haven't learned yet," Lol Creme told the crowd after they'd finished Good Morning Judge. The band's set finished strongly with a well-received I'm Not In Love but their encore of Rubber Bullets was padded out to nearly 13 minutes of banal boogie including a momentum-sapping timpani solo seven minutes in. In terms of how to approach a support slot at a major music festival, 10cc had just given a masterclass in how *not* to do it.

"What was needed to revive the flagging spirits of all on both sides of the stage at Knebworth was a set featuring short, sharp renditions of the band's most popular material. And it wasn't forthcoming," wrote *Sounds*. "10cc sounded fragmented and haphazard," and "made often disastrous attempts at opening up into just one more goodtiming rock combo. Not a wise step. It's not that 10cc played badly – on the contrary. They simply didn't fizz and sparkle as much as I believed they ought. Perhaps even the Worst Band In The World suffers from stage fright too."

A couple of days later, 10cc returned to Strawberry North to begin work on a new single, as the finishing touches were still being applied to their new studio, Strawberry South, in Dorking. Despite having performed Good Morning Judge at Knebworth, they decided to work on the ballad People In Love, arguably 10cc's first proper love song. Devoid of musical twists or ironic touches, the song didn't go down well with Godley and Creme. "What used to happen was that we'd all sit round a piano and whoever wrote a particular song would demonstrate it to the other two," says Godley.

"As the first bars of People In Love came out, my heart began to sink. Lol and I thought, 'This is a standard, boring, middle-of-the-road song. It's not really 10cc. It's a weak attempt to repeat I'm Not In Love again'. We reverted to type. There were the two art school students in a huddle and the two commercial brains in a huddle. It was the straw that broke the camel's back. I think that Lol and I had enjoyed our taste of freedom. We'd spent our initial three weeks working on the 'Gizmo' project and we thought, rather pretentiously, 'What we're doing is art; what we're doing is something important, something significant; this is just pop music!' There was a bit of that going on."

By now 10cc were functioning as two duos, rather than a cohesive unit. The tension that had crept in during the *How Dare You!* sessions quickly returned. To make matters worse, Godley and Creme felt that Eric Stewart was becoming a little too overbearing in the studio. But the main problem was that the pair simply hated People In Love. "Eric and I knew that Kev and Lol weren't crazy about the song and that's an understatement," recalls Gouldman. "This was probably the first song that Kev and Lol really didn't like at all and maybe we should have just ditched the song."

Proving that 10cc had ceased functioning as a cohesive unit, each member of the band was given the task of recording their own version of People In Love.

"There were four versions of that song, each of us going in the studio and recording the song the way we thought it should be," recalls Eric Stewart. "We were each given four tracks to complete and then we put them all together as well. It could have been one of those things that turned out brilliantly, but it didn't. It sounded horrendous." Gouldman concurs: "We all spent quite a lot of time doing our individual parts and we played it all back and it was a mess."

10cc took a break from recording on September 7 to attend a lunch at the Orangery in Holland Park, London to celebrate what would have been Buddy Holly's 40th birthday. The celebration was organised by Paul McCartney, who had recently acquired the publishing rights to Holly's songs, and was attended by a veritable *Who's Who* of British rock music, including Elton John, Roxy Music, Queen and Eric Clapton. Gouldman remembers Clapton still making disparaging comments to him about For Your Love at the lunch. He also recalls an atmosphere that afternoon between the band's members that continued as they headed back up to Strawberry to try and finish off People In Love.

"We went back to Manchester, played People In Love, and just looked at each other and said, 'That's it. We can't possibly continue like this,'" says Stewart.

It was clear that something had to change.

"I went round to Lol's house a few days later and said, 'Where do we go from here?'," recalls Stewart. "He said, 'I think we need to discuss this amongst the four of us.' So, the next day I got the train up to Manchester. When I got there, Kevin, Graham, Lol and Harvey all said, 'We don't think this is working, Eric, we would rather you left the group.' I was kicked out the band, much to my surprise! They thought I was becoming too domineering in the studio, it was beginning to get on their nerves. But when you're totally committed to something, you sometimes don't consider other people around you, you're blinkered and you don't realise it, until somebody pulls you up and says, 'Hey, hold on!' I was pretty shattered by the news. As far as I knew, Lol, Kevin and Graham were going to carry on and do the 'Gizmo' album as the next 10cc project. But it soon became quite clear that Kev and Lol really didn't want Graham involved in it either. So, two weeks later, I got a call from Harvey saying, 'I think you and Graham should carry on as 10cc because it doesn't look like the 'Gizmo' project is going to work with Graham.' Lol later said to me that the last thing in the world he wanted to do was carry on as 10cc, or carry on with me or Graham, at the time so the whole meeting had been a bit of a sham."

By this stage, Godley and Creme had decided that they were going to leave 10cc. This time a 'Truth Session' was not enough. The split was irreconcilable, despite the best efforts of Harvey Lisberg and Ric Dixon over the next few weeks to keep the two sides together. "There was one point when it was very much like a divorce," recalls Gouldman. "Lawyers and managers trying to keep you together but it was obvious that as far as Kev and Lol were concerned, they'd discarded 10cc. They'd used it as a stepping stone and wanted to move on."

The divorce analogy would be used frequently over the coming years to describe the split. "It was like a divorce I guess," says Lol Creme. "It was extremely difficult and in a way it was made even worse because we decided to leave when the band was so huge worldwide. People understand more if things are going badly, but we had to follow our instincts and leave."

Everyone inside the 10cc set-up was shocked by Godley and Creme's decision. Everyone, that is, apart from the duo themselves.

"It may have seemed sudden to everyone else but we'd been planning it for some time," says Creme. "When 10cc first happened, we decided to give it four or five years, because we were already interested in a lot of other areas, and always planned to move on at some point."

Couldn't the duo have worked their way around the problem, remaining within 10cc but taking time out to work on their solo projects? Surely 10cc had reached a point in their career when this was at least feasible. "The democracy of the band was probably what killed it in the end," says Godley. "It was the kind of democracy that was derived from a northern work ethic – all for one and one for all. It didn't allow for the expansion of the individual; it didn't allow them to go away and learn something and bring it back to the party. Other bands, like Roxy Music, managed to allow for the expansion of the individual and still keep the band going by saying, 'You need this time, go and do what you need to do. There's always Roxy Music to come back to,' which was a very sensible way to do it. But we didn't do that; we couldn't, for some unknown reason. In order to grow, we had to leave, painful as it was."

In hindsight, Kevin Godley and Graham Gouldman have both wondered whether they could have dealt with the situation differently. "In retrospect, and Kevin and I have talked about this, we should have been a bit more mature about it," says Gouldman. "We could have stood to have a year off and let Lol and Kevin do the 'Gizmo' album, to get it out of their system, and then got back together again as 10cc. Eric and I could have done other things ourselves, either together or with other people; there were always plenty of things on offer. But, unfortunately, we didn't have that maturity then. If we'd had a bit more give and take on both sides maybe we'd have stayed together longer. We should have worked it out somehow."

The split was acrimonious, made worse by the close bonds between the group's members. Graham Gouldman had known Kevin Godley since their primary school days, some 20 years earlier; Eric Stewart and Lol Creme were brothers-in-law yet wouldn't speak to each other for years after the split, placing an incredible strain on family and friends. "The break-up was very sensitive and I feel that it's a very personal thing," said Creme shortly after the split. "It's been a difficult break-up. I'm related to the guy (Eric Stewart). He's my brother-in-law and to have to say to the guy, 'I'm not going to work with you anymore because we have different ideas how we should work' is very difficult." "It wasn't amicable," confirms Stewart. "It all got pretty heated at the time."

News of the split was initially kept within the 10cc camp. When Phonogram told Godley and Creme on October 16 that they needed to have their solo project finished by January, so they could start work on the next 10cc album, they clearly had no idea that it was never going to happen. The band's publicist, Tony Brainsby, was one of the first people outside of the 10cc organisation to be told about the split. On November 4, Brainsby was up at Strawberry for a planning meeting for Godley and Creme's project. He met the Phonogram team at Stockport railway station, along with broadcaster Paul Gambaccini, who had been asked to write sleeve notes for the project. He took Gambaccini aside to tell him the news.

"Tony Brainsby begged me not to reveal 10cc had split in half," said Gambaccini. "Only then did I realise that it was to be Kev and Lol's breakaway album and not just a pleasant way to spend three months while Eric and Graham push pens across paper down south. I felt ill on the platform at Stockport station. The whole nature of the project has changed and all the Phonogram people at today's planning meeting don't even know. I felt crushed that Kev and Lol never bothered to tell me. They must have assumed I knew."

The split left a big question mark hanging over the future of 10cc. Godley and Creme wanted the name dropped, remembered for what it was and not, as they put it, "dragged into the gutter". Gouldman and Stewart's relationship had been damaged by the whole episode of the latter being asked to leave the band. Now they had to decide if they could patch things up and carry on as 10cc. The duo's credentials as writers, producers and musicians were not in doubt, but 10cc was a four-part equation whose success could in part be attributed to the synergy created by the differing aspirations of the Stewart/Gouldman and Godley/Creme axis of the band.

"The original 10cc was a chemical fusion of two parts that never looked compatible," wrote Harry Doherty in *Melody Maker* sometime later. "The cool commercial business and melodic sense of Eric Stewart and Graham Gouldman held the more extreme artistic and experimental aspirations of Kevin Godley and Lol Creme in check, while Godley and Creme forced Stewart and Gouldman to strive for greater perfection. It was, of course, this incompatibility that finally drove them apart."

This might have been a slight oversimplification but in essence it hit the nail on the head. Had the band split after the *Sheet Music* album, Godley and Creme would have gone on to record an overlong 20-minute version of One Night In Paris, while Stewart and Gouldman would have recorded an inferior version of I'm Not In Love without the haunting voices. The strength of 10cc was the unique chemistry that resulted from the synergy between both sides of the equation.

Although both parties were sufficiently multi-talented to function successfully as duos, both halves of the band would ultimately miss each other's input more than they would perhaps care to admit.

CHAPTER 15

FEELING THE BENEFIT

IRONICALLY, WHILE 10CC HAD BEEN IN THE PROCESS OF FALLING APART, the band had won their biggest accolade to date. During the autumn of 1976, BBC Radio One had mounted a search for the UK's all-time favourite record. It was the biggest listeners' poll of its kind at the time, generating over 100,000 votes from members of the public. The survey revealed that 10cc's I'm Not In Love was the nation's favourite record of all time, with Rubber Bullets also placed at No.62 in the Top 100 list.

Stewart and Gouldman were still grappling with their dilemma, though. "We talked long and hard about whether we had the moral right to retain the name," says Gouldman. "After all, it was 50% of the band leaving."

To answer the question in their own minds, they decided to record together to see if it sounded like 10cc. "We thought the best thing to do was go into the studio and record," recalls Stewart. "If it sounds like 10cc then great, if it doesn't then we knock it on the head, we become something else."

So, towards the end of October 1976, with Paul Burgess making his studio debut for 10cc on drums, Stewart and Gouldman set to work in their new studio, Strawberry South, on Good Morning Judge, the song the original line-up had previewed at Knebworth two months earlier. The studio itself was still in the final stages of being completed and their new purpose-built wraparound desk, designed by Eric Stewart and Tony Cockell of Formula Sound, had yet to be installed. So, recording started using a hired, portable 24-track Neve desk.

Echoing the jailhouse rock theme of Rubber Bullets, Good Morning Judge told the tale of a career criminal who becomes addicted to prison life and commits crimes just so he can get back behind bars. In the studio, Stewart and Gouldman gave the song a makeover from the version played at Knebworth. Out went the rather aimless and rambling structure. Stripped of its padding the song was honed to less than three minutes, marking a return to the short, playful songs of the band's debut album. The traditional, bluesy feel of the track at Knebworth was replaced with a bouncy funk-pop backing, which was embellished with the kind of studio trickery for which 10cc were renowned. In particular, Stewart multitracked his slide guitar licks and treated them with studio effects to create a unique, futuristic sound. Typically inventive, and with its state-of-the-art production, the result was vintage 10cc. With its deft vocal harmonies, it was actually hard to tell that Godley and Creme weren't playing on the track.

Suitably energised, Stewart and Gouldman started work on a second track, The Things We Do For Love, in November. The song had originally been about suicide, the remnants of which can still be heard in its opening lines. However, it evolved into something quite different, a semi-autobiographical love song. "I remember walking through the rain and the snow when I lived in Manchester and we didn't have a telephone," says Stewart. "I had to go and find a phone box to ring the girl who was about to become my wife, and the phones were down, and it was snowing, and these vivid pictures are there. If you put them in a song, a lot of people identify with a similar situation."

The Things We Do For Love had started life as a slower, bluesy number when it had been played to Godley and Creme while they were still with the band. Having decided to speed the song up, the new version wore the pair's pop sensibilities on its sleeve. Nevertheless, it was a perfectly crafted pop song of the highest order. With the added benefit of Stewart and Gouldman's studio skills, the pair knew they were on to a winner.

"We got about two-thirds of the way through the song," says Stewart. "I'd put my lead vocal down and a few other things, and I started putting some backing vocals down, triple-harmony things, and as I walked into the control room Graham said, 'It's a smash.' Just at that moment the whole song clicked."

Delighted with both Good Morning Judge and The Things We Do For Love, Stewart and Gouldman took the decision to continue as 10cc. Like Godley and Creme on their 'Gizmo' project, the pair were relishing the freedom of working on their own.

"Once you get a taste of it it's very exciting," said Stewart at the time. "I'm more excited now than I have been since the *Sheet Music* album. It's a great feeling and I don't want to give it up."

In fact, having decided to carry on as 10cc, Stewart and Gouldman used the band's second album as inspiration for their new record. "Graham and I went back to *Sheet Music* and said let's have a look at that album and find out why it was such a good album," said Stewart at the time. "It was so diversified, so different in its own way but coherent."

With Harvey Lisberg and Ric Dixon retained as their managers, Stewart and Gouldman signed a new five-album deal with Phonogram. Former record boss Jonathan King, who had negotiated a 4% royalty on all future 10cc recordings when the band had left his UK Records label, was given a choice of whether to receive his royalty on future Stewart/Gouldman recordings or future Godley/Creme recordings. He chose the former.

An official announcement was made towards the end of November 1976, to announce that Godley and Creme had left the group. The now defunct *National Rock Star* broke the story on its front page under the headline 10CC BREAK UP – NOT IN LOVE: "After four years together one of Britain's most important bands has parted down the middle – Lol Creme and Kevin Godley are leaving to work together while Graham Gouldman and Eric Stewart are being joined by drummer Paul Burgess to keep the name 10cc alive."

The paper printed a tribute to 10cc the following week, describing them as "Britain's most creative band since The Beatles." The music press gave heavy play to the 10cc split, with some critics dubbing the new incarnation of the group 5cc, much to Stewart and Gouldman's chagrin. Some rumours suggested that Godley and Creme's departure was, in fact, only a temporary measure. "That's quite incorrect," said Harvey Lisberg at the time. "It's impossible to say what the distant future might bring but, as of this moment, they are not thinking of working with 10cc again."

Eric Stewart and Graham Gouldman were more concerned with the future. They, and Phonogram, were keen to keep 10cc in the public eye. Despite having only just started work on their new album, it was felt that The Things We Do For Love would make an excellent post-split single to signal that 10cc were still in business.

"We felt instinctively that it was the right thing to do, that it would be a hit," says Gouldman.

Despite their confidence in the song's hit potential, the pair went to extraordinary lengths to maximise its chances of success. "The Things We Do For Love was mastered as a radio record in the cutting room," said Stewart. "We played around with it a long time to make sure it would come over on radio in a very special way. It's no big deal. There are two ways to mix a track. Either you mix the track for the guy with the big speakers and a superb system, or you mix it for 99% of the public who listen to the radio and have quite reasonable stereos. We mixed the track for the 99% with reasonable stereos."

Coupled with a new song, Hot to Trot, on the b-side, The Things We Do For Love was released on December 3 to positive reviews. "Whenever well-loved faces leave a band it always seems as though replacing them will prove impossible and Lol Creme and Kevin Godley will be sadly missed from 10cc's line-up," wrote *Melody Maker*. "But, from the evidence of this single it's obvious that whatever Eric Stewart and Graham Gouldman do as a duo, those familiar chart-topping sounds will flow. Another smash hit."

Gouldman's prediction in the control room at Strawberry South was soon proved right. The Things We Do For Love became a huge hit, enjoying an 11-week chart run and reaching No.6 in January 1977. The band had chalked up their ninth Top 10 hit, giving Stewart and Gouldman the confidence boost they needed. Kevin Godley was less enthused, allegedly frisbeeing his copy of the record into a derelict Manchester tenement by way of protest. To him, and to some 10cc fans, The Things We Do For Love was too pop-orientated, too far away from 10cc's philosophy of avoiding traditional songwriting conventions and subject matter.

In January 1977, Stewart and Gouldman gave their first major interview since the split to Geoff Brown of *Melody Maker*. Asked how the new album was going, the pair observed that there had been a notable change in the mood of the songs they had written and in their recording style. "The material's much more 'up' and the change in the style of recording is that we seem to be more natural and direct," said Stewart.

The interview shed some light on the different aspirations of the Stewart/Gouldman and Godley/Creme songwriting partnerships of the original line-up. "When writing a song I've always wanted to get to as many people as possible," said Stewart. "Some people call it middle-of-the-road but I think of it like The Beatles were middle-of-the-road. That sort of middle-of-the-road I would love for 10cc. I'm not interested in appealing to three guys in Outer Mongolia, who get off on a particular freaky lyric you've put in. I want to get to as many people as possible and the direct way is the way you actually talk to each other. So, write it down that way. We write much faster because we write it as we say it, instead of trying to find a new way of saying it."

"It's rarely a radical rethink," said Gouldman. "If it needs that, we usually say, 'Forget it.' But I never feel that I have to go out of my way to be different. I think we do that on a production level, sometimes it's apparent, sometimes it isn't. But in the actual writing I've got to like it, Eric's got to like it. If one of us doesn't then we've got to change it."

The pair felt that the original line-up had got into an experimentation for experimentation's sake rut.

"Experimentation became the norm for us, so it wasn't an experiment any more," said Stewart. "I think things got slightly jaundiced. But now it's more of a challenge because it's just the two of us and we've got a lot to live up to."

Back at Strawberry South, among the completed tracks was a new version of People In Love, the song that the original line-up had attempted to record prior to the split. A straight ballad, it was very different from the type of song previously associated with 10cc.

"We've found that we can write that sort of song really well," said Stewart at the time. "We love ballady-type things and we love romantic lyrics, which for 10cc the four-piece might be considered a little twee and boring. Now we haven't got that problem anymore and we certainly will be writing more of that type of song."

The original line-up had attempted to set the song to a quirky arrangement to counteract its relative simplicity. This time around,

Stewart and Gouldman went for a more direct approach, not that the song was easy to record. The pair made several attempts to record it before leaving it and coming back to it again later: "Somehow, eventually we got the right combination, the same instruments, but suddenly the timing hit," said Stewart. "When we got the take it was magic."

Stewart and Gouldman's decision to revoke the original line-up's philosophy of avoiding love songs wasn't the only change in direction they were planning for the band.

"It's bloody easy to write ambiguous songs because you find something sacred and knock it," said Stewart at the time. "That's really easy. We could write a dozen songs like that every day and we also find it very easy to do puns, which is another thing we're starting to be more careful with."

Ironically, one of their new songs, I Bought A Flat Guitar Tutor, took 10cc's love of puns to new heights, the song's lyrics cleverly echoing the chords of the song. Set to a jazz arrangement, the song lasts less than two minutes ensuring that the joke doesn't outstay its welcome, acting as a smart interlude on the album. Equally inventive was Honeymoon With B Troop, a song that had its bizarre subject matter rooted in fact.

"I remember reading something about some scout guy doing this," says Stewart. "He actually got married and took the cub pack on honeymoon with him to France. It's about what happens to him. It's a crazy song."

Honeymoon With B Troop was one of the highlights of the new album and demonstrated that the spirit of 10cc was still alive and well. In less than three minutes, the song is crammed full of twists and turns and clever wordplay as the ardour of the honeymooners is frustrated by the couple never being alone. Sitting with a tent-pole what a bloody jamboree, indeed! Elsewhere, the pair displayed their knack for writing about the most mundane of subject matter and turning it into something interesting with You've Got A Cold. The song had started life at, of all places, an airport.

"We were striding along the walkway towards an aeroplane which was due to take us to Amsterdam and then suddenly Eric started sneezing," says Gouldman. "He just couldn't stop and he set up this incredible rhythm. I couldn't help joining in too but I wasn't sneezing, just singing. A bit later on, when Eric had stopped sneezing, we put some words to the rhythm and came up with You've Got A Cold."

Joining them in the studio to record the song was keyboard player Jean Roussel. Potential new band members were being sought and, feeling that they needed a keyboard player in their new line-up, Roussel was tried out. He wouldn't become a permanent band member, instead recommending they approach Tony O'Malley of the recently split Kokomo. There were also rumours circulating at the time that Justin Hayward would be joining 10cc.

"It's possible that Justin may guest with Eric and Graham on their new album, which is now half-completed," said Harvey Lisberg at the time, "but I've no reason to believe that he will be joining them permanently."

Hayward would later reflect on the opportunity to join 10cc.

"I'd often thought of that because I've known Eric since we were sixteen, seventeen years old," says Hayward. "But I think if I was going to do that I should have done it, say, back when they first started as Hotlegs, which was when they really started having some success. Eric is such a strong personality, and I'm a pretty strong personality, and Graham, I think it would have just been too heavy and I think they were right to do as they did."

One person who was definitely approached about joining 10cc was guitarist John Miles, who had recently enjoyed Top 5 success with his single Music. "We thought we could do with another strong writer/guitarist in the band," recalls Gouldman. "But his manager said he was too big to do it, and then we gave the idea up."

Back at Strawberry South, Stewart and Gouldman were working on the album's tour de force, a new 11-minute piece in three parts called Feel The Benefit. "The song title was inspired by the sort of thing your Mum says to you when you are small, 'Take your coat off or when you go out you won't feel the benefit,'" says Gouldman.

To write Feel The Benefit, Stewart and Gouldman pieced together a number of riffs and musical ideas that hadn't been fully developed into proper songs in their own right. The guitar riff to the song's middle section, A Latin Break, had actually been written for the *How Dare You!* album but hadn't found a home until now. "After we'd written most of the tracks for the album we had some bits and pieces left over and we just put them all together," says Gouldman. "We did it in a very unconscious way, we didn't plan it meticulously. We just did it and it worked out great."

Among the fragments of song ideas that they pieced together was the opening chord sequence, which was clearly influenced by Dear Prudence by The Beatles. Recording Feel The Benefit marked 10cc's most ambitious project since One Night In Paris.

"It goes through six different phases of changes within the song," explained Stewart at the time. "It's very exciting to do something like this, because for something to last 11 minutes and hold your interest all the time it's got to be bloody marvellous, it's got to be fabulous. It's another challenge."

With Strawberry South still in the process of being built around them, recording the song proved even more challenging. "I was singing the lead vocal on Feel The Benefit and the whole studio started to shake," says Stewart. "We thought something weird was happening with the monitor system. We went outside and a guy with a power roller was flattening the parking lot and shaking the whole building. We had to wait half a day for that."

It was worth the wait: Feel The Benefit would go on to become one of 10cc's best-loved album tracks, not to mention the centrepiece of their live stage show, complete with its extended 90-second guitar solo from Stewart at its close. To add that final epic touch to the song, Stewart and Gouldman decided to use an orchestra and drafted in Del Newman, who they had previously worked with on the Neil Sedaka sessions and the more recent Blue Guitar single, to score the orchestral parts.

"I really enjoyed writing for tracks that gave me a challenge and allowed me to use techniques that my formal training had taught me," says Newman. "10cc's Feel The Benefit was one such track."

The orchestra was recorded at Threshold Studios in London.

"I still remember the thrill when I heard the opening section for the first time when the score grows and grows and opens out to that magnificent crescendo before the lead vocal starts," recalls Stewart. "The first violinist came up to the control room to listen for any changes he thought we may need in the balance and he turned to me and said, 'Eric, I know this may sound a little trite, but I think the song you have here and Del's arrangement is some of the best modern music I have worked on for a long, long time.' I was very chuffed and sat there beaming! I still get a great buzz when I listen to the opening, just as the strings enter, it's spine-chilling, especially in the studio on vast monitors. I wish everybody could hear it like I did then."

An orchestra had never been used on a 10cc record before. That role had previously been the domain of the 'Gizmo'. Stewart and Gouldman's approach was simple – if you want the sound of strings, then use strings, demonstrating the two different perspectives in the group's original line-up.

After the disappointment surrounding their lack of success in America in 1976, Stewart and Gouldman were particularly gratified to see The Things We Do For Love scaling the US charts. By the end of March 1977, the record had climbed the charts for 12 successive weeks and had now broken into the Top 10. The success of the single put pressure on Stewart and Gouldman to rush-release the next 10cc album.

"We were getting telegrams from Phonogram saying, 'Where's the album? We've got a record that's going to be Top 5,'" recalls Stewart. "We said, 'Screw it, we're going to take our time with it and be happy with it ourselves and hope the single slows down enough on its upward climb to give us breathing space.'"

By now the album was nearing completion. Of the other new songs, Marriage Bureau Rendezvous illustrated Stewart and Gouldman's skill with song construction. Casting an observant eye at dating agencies, the character in the song finds himself bombarded with choices in his introductory questionnaire before getting ready for his big date squeaky clean from his baths and smelling like he's '*drowning in a sea of cologne*'.

While Marriage Bureau Rendezvous was romantic in outlook, complete with an appropriately happy ending, Modern Man Blues was just the opposite. After finding a walkout note from his wife saying that his dinner was in the cat, the song's protagonist decides to enjoy his newfound freedom by well and truly painting the town red. The raunchy musical backdrop marked another departure for 10cc.

Stewart and Gouldman had decided on a title for the album

early in the recording process, having noticed a road sign on one on the bends on the southbound stretch of the A24 on the way into Dorking.

"There was a road sign near to the studio that said, 'Deceptive Bends'," recalls Gouldman. "It struck us as quite a subtle phrase for the Department of Transport, so we decided to use it as the title for the album."

It also seemed an appropriate phrase, given the deceptive bends that the band's path had taken over the past six months. Retaining the services of Hipgnosis to design the album cover, Stewart and Gouldman had requested a positive, romantic image when briefing them back in December.

"On the way home from the studio the first night that I'd seen Eric and Graham, I got to thinking about *Deceptive Bends* as a phrase," says Storm Thorgerson. "I began to free-associate and make simple connections and deductions. I cast aside anything to do with bends and curves in the road as too obvious. I rejected any ideas about deceiving the viewer with things that were bent but looked straight as idle trickery. As a result of this I considered the other possible meaning of bends ... and the bends of a diver came immediately to mind. I thought immediately of those divers' suits from the 20s or 30s and how amazing they look, not only for their bizarre metallic helmets but also for the whole 'monster' feeling that they evoke. Since you can't see either the face or the body you've no idea what the occupant really looks like. And then it wasn't long before I felt that the deception of *Deceptive Bends* referred to the person in the picture, not to the person looking at it. The diver is deceived by his own bends and fantasises freely. Since the band wanted a positive design it had to be an uplifting fantasy, such as emerging from the waters of the deep with his arms full of treasure. Perhaps he'd imagined himself rescuing the girl of his dreams from a watery death."

The photo shoot of the diver holding the girl proved quite eventful given the weight of the diving suits, borrowed from the Siebe Gorman company.

"The diver's helmet was incredibly heavy and we had no air supply for the man inside," says Aubrey Powell. "In the hot studio it became quite unbearable for him, especially as he was holding the girl. We had to keep stopping, taking the helmet off, and then putting it back on again – it was a bloody nightmare."

In casting the girl for the front cover, Graham Gouldman had suggested the American actress Jessica Lange but she had turned down the assignment. Instead, in order to give them more options to choose from, two different girls were used – one of them the model Nina Carter – who were photographed in the arms of the diver wearing green dresses, red dresses and even no dresses! Stewart and Gouldman also had to don the divers' suits for their inner sleeve portraits.

"I admired their chutzpah," says Powell. "They were trapped in those helmets for quite a while, feeling stifled and claustrophobic. And the sweat is real. Art for art's sake!"

The final album cover was a composite of 3 different images: the diver holding the girl (shot in the studio), the jetty and background divers (shot on location by the River Thames near Hammersmith) and a sea and sky landscape (from a photo library). The result was striking and would go on to be voted No.1 sleeve design of 1977 by *Music Week*.

As Eric Stewart mixed *Deceptive Bends* at Strawberry South in March 1977, it was clear that while Godley and Creme's surrealism and quirky humour were missing, many of 10cc's best-loved traits remained firmly intact: the inventive song ideas, the exquisite hooks, the articulate and often clever lyrics, the superb production values, the vocal harmonies. It was a remarkable achievement in the circumstances given that they had just lost 50% of the band. The pair had ably risen to the challenge of continuing 10cc, spurred on by their '5cc' detractors.

"The chemistry of 10cc definitely changed because it was just the two of us, it was bound to," says Gouldman. "Maybe we were a bit more romantic, and not quite as abstract as Kevin and Lol. But I think what happened was we were upset, and then we got angry and when we're angry, we get very creative. We got all this flak – 'It's 5cc, the better half have gone' – and rather than getting upset by it, we thought we'd get even."

Spirits were high as the release of the album drew near. The Things We Do For Love had peaked at No.5 in the US charts in mid-April and was on its way to selling 1.3 million copies during its

19-week chart run, going on to become one of the bestselling singles of the year in America. Finally, it appeared that 10cc's career was back on course in the US. In fact, with global sales of over 3 million copies, the song would actually overtake I'm Not In Love as 10cc's biggest worldwide hit to date, also reaching No.1 in Canada, No.2 in Ireland, No.5 in Australia, No.13 in the Netherlands, No.23 in New Zealand and No.24 in Belgium.

Deceptive Bends was released by Phonogram at the end of April to largely positive reviews.

"Let's forget all the jokes about this band now being called 5cc," wrote Jim Evans in *Record Mirror*. "Kevin Godley and Lol Creme are no longer part of the band, but the music emanating from the depleted ranks is as polished and confident as ever. A distinctive band that would blow most others out the studio – in both the musical and perfectionist stakes."

Colin Irwin's review in *Melody Maker* concurred: "Weep not for 10cc. It's a surprisingly up and happy album, which counters the past criticisms of them being too negative and pessimistic, even cynical. To this end they've sacrificed much of the cleverness, both in lyrical structure and instrumental arrangement, but this isn't necessarily to their detriment, for that wit was fast becoming tired. With another beautifully clean production, it has the freshness *How Dare You!* lacked."

Other critics were less convinced.

"It seems that the group's talent is spread a bit more thinly on the latest offering," wrote *Sounds*. "Perhaps the real value of the previous line-up was that in having four active writers involved in playing on each track, every corner of the songs was under much closer scrutiny. There are moments on this album when you can feel a gentle breeze blowing through what used to be a tightly woven mesh of ideas."

Unsurprisingly, *New Musical Express* didn't like the album at all but did at least offer begrudging praise: "It's a tribute to their production finesse that such a lucidly textured record as this can be made with combinations of just organ, piano, guitar, bass, drums and vocals. And unlike Queen's 'no Moogs' rider, the objective for 10cc is always the end product, not a display of clever cleverness in its achievement. Of course Eric Stewart is a meticulous, coherent guitarist and an even better singer, but I just can't shake off this feeling that there wasn't actually any reason for making *Deceptive Bends* ... they've got nothing very stimulating to play and even less to say. It all sounds very pretty. It's all fantastically performed and produced – it really is. But I think they did it for the money."

At least they were being consistent – they had criticised *How Dare You!* for exactly the same reasons. Commercially, *Deceptive Bends* was highly successful, spending five months in the album charts, including eight weeks in the Top 10 and peaking at No.3, only outsold by *Arrival* by Abba and *Hotel California* by The Eagles. Ironically, the group once again did even better in the *New Musical Express* charts, where the album reached No.2. *Deceptive Bends* would become the sixth bestselling new studio album by a British group in 1977.

With a hit single, and now a hit album, it was clear that Stewart and Gouldman had survived the split in a way few critics had thought possible, particularly in a year when punk rock was supposed to blow the old bands away. Now the goal was to prove that they could make it on the road too.

CHAPTER 16

15CC

A SEVENTH-MONTH WORLD TOUR, INCLUDING 10CC'S FIRST EVER GIGS in Japan and Australia, had been lined up to promote *Deceptive Bends* and Eric Stewart and Graham Gouldman were looking to assemble a new band to take with them on the road. To avoid comparisons with the original four-man line-up, they wanted the shape of the new band to include another guitarist, a keyboard player and a second drummer, having already decided to extend full band membership to Paul Burgess. They were keen for 10cc to remain a group in its proper sense, not just the two of them supported by sidemen.

"We really want to keep the image of being a 'band'," said Gouldman at the time. "Not two people fronting an orchestra."

They opted not to advertise the fact that they were looking for new members.

"We just put the word out that we were looking and we got about 200 tapes as a result," says Gouldman.

In the end, all the musicians that they selected came via personal recommendation. They had approached keyboard player Tony O'Malley after the recommendation from Jean Roussel during the *Deceptive Bends* sessions. O'Malley had actually known Stewart and Gouldman from his days playing with the band Arrival. That group had morphed into Kokomo, who were renowned for soul and funk rather than pop and rock. As such, O'Malley was, on the face of it, a surprising choice for 10cc. But with Kokomo announcing they were on 'indefinite hiatus' in January 1977, O'Malley accepted Stewart and Gouldman's offer to join the band. Drummer Stuart Tosh, formerly of Pilot – who had enjoyed success with the singles January and Magic – had offered his services after reading in the music press that the original 10cc line-up had split up. He had been working as an in-demand session musician since the demise of Pilot, playing on albums by the likes of Roger Daltrey (*One of the Boys*) and The Alan Parsons Project (*I Robot*). Finding the right guitarist, however, proved more difficult.

"A lot of the tapes, from guitarists in particular, were very flash, very fast playing but we're more into a guy playing two perfect notes than 20 in a bar," said Stewart at the time. "A lot of people seemed to want to blind you with science, and that wasn't what we were looking for. We were looking for style and creativity more than technical know-how."

Paul Burgess felt he knew someone that fitted the bill perfectly. He'd been impressed by guitarist Rick Fenn while working on a session for the band Gentlemen. Coincidently, when Gentleman had made their appearance on the TV show *So It Goes* in August 1976, 10cc's The Worst Band In The World had been playing in the background as Tony Wilson introduced the group. Burgess played Stewart and Gouldman some of the band's recordings and, suitably impressed, Fenn was invited to meet them in London, where they were shooting the video for 10cc's next single, Good Morning Judge. Set in a courtroom, the video featured Stewart and Gouldman playing all the characters – the judge, the jury and the felon – with the storyline following the crimes outlined in the song's lyrics. They were filming one of these scenes when Fenn dropped by to say hello. "The first time I saw Eric and Graham they were all made up as two of the jurors they played in the video and looked very strange," he recalls.

Directed by Bruce Gowers – who had worked with 10cc on some of their previous promotional films and had directed the video for Queen's Bohemian Rhapsody – the video for Good Morning Judge was groundbreaking for the time and a real milestone in music video history, often overlooked when landmarks of the medium are discussed.

"This was quite avant-garde at the time," says Gowers. "Videos were mostly performances, and in this one, Eric Stewart and Graham Gouldman chose to be actors playing all the parts. In various get-ups, they are the judge, the entire jury, etc."

That night, Rick Fenn travelled to Dorking ahead of auditioning for 10cc the following day at Strawberry South. As the other musicians arrived at Strawberry the following morning he remembers Stuart Tosh turning up in a Rolls-Royce. Stewart, Gouldman, Burgess, O'Malley, Tosh and Fenn spent the day jamming together in the studio.

"I was amazed and flattered that, as far as I could tell, the recordings of my guitar playing and Paul's personal reference appeared to place me in the band from the get-go," recalls Fenn. "The jam session we had all together in the studio felt like a formality. We then sat and listened to *Deceptive Bends*, which was literally just mixed, through the glorious studio monitors. It was awesome and I was in this band! I couldn't believe it."

Convinced that they had found the right musicians to take with them on their forthcoming tour, a press conference was held at the Montcalm Hotel in London to introduce the new line-up to the press and announce the dates of 10cc's upcoming world tour. "If in that time the band starts to work as a really tight unit, that will be 10cc," said Stewart. "If it doesn't, we'll have to look for other musicians."

By the time of the press conference, Good Morning Judge was already scaling the UK charts. Supported by its groundbreaking video, which was screened on *Top of the Pops* to glowing reviews, and with the wonderfully titled Don't Squeeze Me Like Toothpaste on the b-side, Good Morning Judge would spend five weeks in the UK Top 10, peaking at No.5 in late May, giving 10cc their 10th UK Top 10 hit and a further boost of confidence for 10cc Mk II.

With the first date of their world tour less than four weeks away, rehearsals at Shepperton Studios were intense, as the group's new recruits learnt the 10cc material and got used to playing together as a band. Clearly still reeling from the '5cc' criticism, Stewart and Gouldman elected to only perform songs from the group's back catalogue that featured the two of them as writers. Included, therefore, were the likes of Waterfall, Ships Don't Disappear In The Night, The Wall Street Shuffle, The Second Sitting For The Last Supper, I'm Not In Love, Art For Art's Sake and I'm Mandy Fly Me. Missing from their set were Godley and Creme-penned hits like Rubber Bullets and album tracks like One Night In Paris.

"Obviously, there are some songs we just can't do, it'd be a rip-off," said Gouldman at the time. "They were so tied up in the four of us that I don't think anybody could do it the same way we did it. One Night In Paris for instance or Don't Hang Up, which was Kevin's voice. You can't substitute that, it's not right."

As rehearsals progressed, the new line-up was not afraid to re-interpret 10cc's past. Waterfall benefited from being extended and reworked. Better still was their treatment of Ships Don't Disappear In The Night, which was transformed into a powerful bluesy number, showcasing O'Malley's piano skills to great effect. O'Malley was even given the honour of lead vocal duties on Art For Art's Sake. However, Stewart and Gouldman really wanted to showcase new material from *Deceptive Bends* and thus included every track, bar one, in their new set.

For added dramatic effect, a short burst of film would be pro-jected onto a screen behind the band during the introduction to Feel The Benefit. Shot by Hipgnosis during the photo shoot for *Deceptive Bends*, the film brought the album cover to life.

10cc had originally been due to begin their world tour in America to capitalise on the success of The Things We Do For Love, but the new group hadn't been ready. Instead, the band's world tour opened on home soil at the Glasgow Apollo on May 27, scene of the orig-inal line-up's last indoor concert back in April 1976. Kevin Godley broke the ice with his erstwhile colleagues by phoning Stewart and Gouldman to wish them success with the tour.

Opening night was an understandably tense affair. How would the new line-up go down? How would the new band perform given the relatively short period of rehearsal time? Any fears that Stewart and Gouldman had were quickly dispelled. 10cc Mk II went down a storm.

"Before this tour, I wouldn't have even dared hope that the new 10cc could equal, never mind supersede, the feats achieved by the original band, but at the opening of their British tour in Glasgow at the weekend, the revitalised group went a long way towards es-tablishing their right to leave the past behind," wrote *Melody Maker*. "Put quite bluntly, the old band, on stage anyway, could not live with this one. The new band possess such diversity and musical prowess as well as a refreshing blend of experience and youth that the po-tential for the future rates as one of the most exciting British rock ventures in years. The audience were ecstatic at the end of the night.

The set the band play is much better controlled than on previous tours. Before, it started well but dipped badly in the middle and it was always a bit of a struggle to get the pace going again. This one is beautifully paced, climbing from one level to another easily. From the word go it's an up. But if there's one singular contrast between the new and old, it must be in the feel this new band has. The original band were forever faced with the criticism of lacking feeling, a justifiable argument that could not be levelled against this group. If Godley and Creme's departure took half the heart out of 10cc, they have been replaced by a soul, mostly in the form of Tony O'Malley. O'Malley, the ex-Kokomo man, injects an earthiness that was never apparent in 10cc before. He has brought new guts to Art For Art's Sake on which he handles the vocal, but his major contribution is on Ships Don't Disappear In the Night which is transformed from a straight rocker to a more ballsy funk-soaked masterwork. When 10cc split last year, they were faced with the cynical title of 5cc. After seeing this performance on Saturday night I would suggest that the same people now start calling them 15cc."

For Rick Fenn, that very first gig with the band in Glasgow was "the thrill of a lifetime." The reaction from audiences and critics was the same as the tour moved on to Aberdeen and then to Newcastle. "After only five dates I am so excited with the future," enthused Stewart at the time. "The old band was like a musical eunuch. It had no balls. This one is much healthier."

Stewart's comments had echoes of those he'd made about only losing their tambourine player shortly after Wayne Fontana had left The Mindbenders, and speak more to how painful the band's split was still feeling at the time. Still, it must have been gratifying to see the new band going down so well with audiences and critics alike. "I've never heard I'm Mandy Fly Me sung with such conviction as in Newcastle City Hall," wrote Harry Doherty in *Melody Maker,* also commenting that Eric Stewart appeared "a lot freer and more expressive on stage now, as if he's gained more confidence with the exit of Lol Creme. He's more into his music, once again showing that he's a criminally underrated guitarist, wrenching out solos that leave you speechless ... and even his vocal, which always has possessed that golden texture anyway, seems to have gained even more feel."

Doherty was equally impressed with Graham Gouldman: "His bass work on this tour is simply quite incredible, thumping out hard riffs on hard songs and flowing lines on the softer material ... but there's a solo he takes on Feel The Benefit which is absolutely breathtaking. I've never seen any solo so magnificently showcased."

The tour was going better than Stewart and Gouldman could possibly have hoped. "Ecstatic – that's the word I'm looking for," said Stewart. "The new band has been accepted." It was clear that the new group had established a strong rapport with each other, both on- and off-stage. "I feel that this band is much closer than the old 10cc were in the first nine weeks of their life," said Stewart. "Somehow we've got this tremendous rapport. We find we laugh at the same things and have so much in common."

The new band members weren't exempt from practical jokes played by the road crew. One particular favourite involved putting their vocals through a harmonizer and then feeding the result back through their monitor speakers on stage during the course of a gig. "Your voice would go up and down an octave," recalls Stuart Tosh. "The audience would never hear it, just you through the monitor. So, you're either sounding like Mickey Mouse or Barry White."

As the band's road crew got to know the new members of the band they were given nicknames. O'Malley would be affectionately nicknamed 'Tony O'Marlboro' because of his prodigious smoking habit at the time. During soundchecks, Stewart would change the lyric in Feel The Benefit to *'We'll feel Rick Fenn a bit'*. Both Stewart and Gouldman considered the new band to work much better than the old on stage. "There are things missing in the new act which were there in the old 10cc," said Stewart. "Lol in particular is one of the main things, but these have been replaced by things that are more important to me, like musical spontaneity. There's an integrated meeting of minds on stage now, which transcends the comedy bit we used to get into, which bugged me quite a bit. We are serious musicians, although we do like to laugh at ourselves. We are serious musicians and we want to be taken as such and not forever bring ourselves down."

"That used to happen," agreed Gouldman. "It was a sort of self-consciousness that came out in making funny remarks. We're *not* the worst band in the world anymore. That used to be our thing. It was protection.

We don't do that song anymore because we don't think we are that anymore."

Which was a shame, given that 10cc's self-deprecating humour was one of the band's most appealing facets. The tour continued around the UK, concluding with three sell-out nights at London's Hammersmith Odeon. Unfortunately, some of the band's guitars were stolen from their dressing room at the venue, including a very rare, vintage 1959 flame-top Gibson Les Paul Standard that belonged to Eric Stewart.

"I remember that Brian Robertson from Thin Lizzy came over with these three beautiful Les Pauls because he'd heard on the radio that I'd had one stolen," recalls Stewart. "He very kindly let me borrow his guitar for a couple of days until I got another one."

Despite this setback, the concerts themselves were a resounding success. All three gigs at Hammersmith were recorded for posterity while Bruce Gowers, who had recently shot the video for Good Morning Judge, filmed the final night of the tour for what was intended to be TV broadcast later in the year. While this didn't happen, footage from the show of Feel The Benefit would appear prominently in the storyline of Willy Russell's *The Boy With The Transistor Radio*, which premiered on ITV in February 1980. An hour-long edit of the gig itself would eventually be released on video as *10cc Live in Concert* in 1981. Gowers captures 10cc in fine form and shows the band obviously enjoying themselves, with Stewart and Gouldman smiling throughout. Clearly amazed by the response of the audience, the band return to the stage to repeat Modern Man Blues by way of a second encore.

"To say that 10cc were taken aback by their reception at London's Hammersmith Odeon on Saturday night would be something of an understatement," wrote Hugh Fielder in *Sounds*. "They had literally played themselves out of material and when the audience continued to bay for more after the encore they had to play the same song again because, as Eric Stewart explained, the new band didn't know any others. Come on now, they could have taken a chance and played Rubber Bullets. After all, even if the number had fallen flat on its face it wouldn't really have mattered. But 10cc didn't feel like risking anything, even on a second encore. I guess it's churlish to pick holes in what was a magnificent concert carried off at a technical standard that was well-nigh perfect. It's just that I would like to have seen them putting in a little spontaneous guts and spreading a little honest dirt on the gloss finish. Still, Jesus was there and he enjoyed it. It can't have been bad can it?"

The feud between the band and the *New Musical Express* continued apace. Eric Stewart silenced a heckler with the line, "Bloody *NME* journalists! I remember when it used to be a *music* paper." Nick Kent responded by describing the concert as "the most forgettable rock gig I've seen this year."

Having completed their UK tour in late June the band now had a gap in their schedule until the Australian leg of their tour began in September. If ever there had been a perfect time for 10cc to tour the US it was now, given they had just enjoyed their biggest hit in America with The Things We Do For Love and with *Deceptive Bends* gaining positive reviews in the press. *Billboard* said that Stewart and Gouldman had "produced a lavishly pretty and cosmically silly LP in the great 10cc tradition ... beautifully lush melodies and production surrounding slyly surrealistic lyrics." *Stereo Review* even gave the album an 'honourable mention' in its 'Record of the Year' award for 1977 "in recognition of a significant contribution to the arts of music and recording". Phonogram was supporting *Deceptive Bends* strongly with press ads in the major music publications and with high-profile poster sites, such as a special build on Sunset Strip in West Hollywood, Los Angeles. Keen to follow up on the huge success of The Things We Do For Love, Phonogram in the US had opted to release People In Love as 10cc's next single.

"I just hope we're not typecast," said Gouldman at the time. "No one track represents our album. We're not a middle-of-the-road, balladeering group. We hope that people don't think that's all we do because that affects what sort of audiences you have. We played one concert in Germany where we got an audience of middle-aged people expecting a group like The Carpenters. I'm Not In Love had been the biggest record we ever had and they didn't know anything else. They freaked!"

People In Love was well received by critics – "Another lush, poetic production from this revamped but still beautifully creative group" wrote *Billboard* – and went on to become 10cc's second consecutive Top 40 hit in America, while a third single, Good Morning Judge, gave the band a minor US hit in the autumn. Yet despite spending 34 weeks in the US Top 100 with their singles during 1977, *Deceptive Bends* only did moderately well, reaching No.31 in the album charts as part of a 20-week chart run. Not quite the breakthrough that 10cc might have achieved if they had toured America that summer to support their album and singles.

Instead, it was announced on July 7, that 10cc were going to record a live album as their next project. Appropriately, the album was to be recorded in Manchester over two nights at the Apollo on July 17 and 18. The gigs were only advertised once before selling out. As the band prepared for the shows Graham Gouldman decided to get back in touch with Bernard Basso, his former bandmate in The Whirlwinds and The Mockingbirds. He phoned Basso and invited him to hang out at the soundcheck for the first of the Apollo gigs. Basso politely declined.

"About an hour later there was a knock on the door," recalls Basso. "I opened the door and there was a guy stood there who must have been six feet tall and as wide as he was tall. There was this stretch limo parked outside my house with blacked-out windows. He said, 'I've been sent down by Mr Gouldman to pick you up and take you with me to the Apollo.' I thought, 'I ain't arguing with this guy.' So, he puts me in the car and we get near the front of the Apollo and there are hundreds of girls out there and they're screaming their heads off. They manage to get me in through the back door, so I go into the dressing room and Graham says, 'Now look, I haven't seen you for ages, so you're going to stay with me all day and chat about old times.'"

As showtime approached Gouldman had a surprise in store for Basso.

"Graham said to me, 'Come on, I want you to walk with me to the edge of the stage and remember what it used to be like,'" says Basso. "And the butterflies came back like it was yesterday. All the memories came flooding back. It was an amazing feeling."

Introduced by their friend from Piccadilly Radio DJ Andy Peebles, the gigs captured the band in fine form, although 10cc would ultimately also draw upon recordings from their Hammersmith gigs for the live album, which was to be called *Live and Let Live*. As Phonogram made plans to release the album later in the year, 10cc flew to Sydney on August 30 to prepare for the next leg of their world tour, which involved performing their first ever concerts in Australia and Japan. Although breaking new ground for 10cc, other British bands had included both countries in their itineraries as early as 1975. Queen had toured Japan in April of that year, while both Wings and ELO had toured Australia in the second half of 1975.

After 10 days of rehearsals and interviews, the tour opened in Brisbane at the Festival Hall before moving on to Sydney, where they played the Hordern Pavilion for three nights. The gigs received rave reviews.

"You don't know how difficult it is to describe a concert that was so good it had you in tears of joy," wrote Annie Burton in *Ram* magazine. "This new revamped 10cc are more polished, more exciting, and yes, ballsier than the 10cc of multiple record and single. They were simply amazing."

The tour moved on to Melbourne – for three nights at the Festival Hall – before travelling to Adelaide for two nights at the Apollo Stadium, where the rave reviews continued.

"10cc's live show is perfection," wrote Ian Meikle in the *Adelaide Advertiser*. "It's been so long since there's been a show to come near 10cc's. 10cc, the thinking man's pop band, thrives on perfection. Its recordings have always been tagged too clever by half. But now its live show – the new and improved line-up's first to Australia – is proving that what's done in the studio comes as easily on stage. An awesome achievement, as anyone familiar with 10cc's particularly intricate blend of pop-rock knows."

Not everything went so well in Adelaide, though. Tony O'Malley was caught in possession of marijuana, which presented the band with a problem. Next stop on the tour was Japan, where the authorities took a hard line on drug use. Knowing that O'Malley would be denied entry into Japan if he had a drug conviction, the band's management postponed his hearing in Australia until after 10cc had completed their Japanese tour.

The band's Australian tour ended in Perth at the 8,000-seater Entertainment Centre. It would go on to be voted 'Best Overseas Tour' of 1977 by the readers of *Ram* magazine, with 10cc achieving high placings in the 'Best Album', 'Best Single' and 'Best Stage Act' categories as well. The success of the tour translated into strong record sales, with The Things We Do For Love reaching No.5 and *Deceptive Bends* peaking at No.8, becoming the ninth bestselling album of 1977. Stewart was impressed by the Australian music scene.

"It reminded me very much of England in the mid-60s," he said. "Lots of live music shows on TV, lots of live bands in clubs that you can go and sit in and play with, something that has died here in the UK, unfortunately."

The band's Japanese tour kicked off on October 1 with the first of three sell-out nights at Tokyo's Sun Plaza Hall. A recording of their next performance, at the Kosei Nenkin Hall in Tokyo on October 4, would appear as the bootleg *Play and Let Play*. Overall, the Japanese leg of the tour was a big success, inspiring Eric Stewart to write a new song, Tokyo. Japanese fans would remain some of 10cc's most loyal. A fanzine, *City Lights*, was established in 1981 and ran for 20 years, while another fan in 1987 would set up a bar called 10cc in one of the narrow, dimly lit alleys of Shinjuku's historical Golden Gai area of Tokyo.

For Zeb White, the tours of Australia and Japan were a particular highlight of his time touring with 10cc.

"I think probably the most memorable tours we did were the first tour of Australia and Japan because it was all new to virtually everyone," says White. "I think that was really the pinnacle. Three nights in Sydney sold out, three nights in Melbourne sold out, as well as Brisbane, Adelaide and Perth. And the same reaction in Tokyo and Osaka. We even did a matinee show on a Sunday afternoon at, like, 2pm. That was done with hangovers. It was a very quiet show."

Back at home, 10cc had been nominated for a BRIT Award, a new initiative by the UK record industry to recognise the best of British music. In the first year of the awards, and to tie in with the Queen's Silver Jubilee, it was decided that the awards should recognise the best of British music over the previous 25 years. Four records were nominated for 'Best British Single of the last 25 Years': She Loves You by The Beatles, A Whiter Shade of Pale by Procul Harem, Bohemian Rhapsody by Queen and I'm Not In Love by 10cc. While I'm Not In Love would not go on to win the award (which Queen and Procul Harem shared), it represented an incredible achievement to be recognised by the industry as one of the four best British singles of the last 25 years.

Before embarking on the final leg of their world tour, Phonogram released the double album *Live and Let Live* on November 18, supported by a TV advertising campaign.

"When Lol Creme and Kevin Godley departed many, myself included, thought this would be the beginning of the end for the band," said Jim Evans in *Record Mirror* giving the album a four-star review. "But with this year's British tour the new 10cc proved that all was well. That without Creme and Godley they were still very much a force to be reckoned with. That as a live band they were: entertaining, lively and supremely confident both in stage presence and musical ability. And ally with this the fact that on stage they manage to approach the perfection they achieve in the studio … the outstanding tracks in the live perspective turn out to be Feel The Benefit and I'm Not In Love, the former being so catchy and irrepressible. In the field of song construction they're in a class of their own. Still. Perhaps the departure of Creme and Godley gave Stewart and Gouldman a needed kick up the ass. Whatever, this album is magic."

Live and Let Live went on to reach No.14 in the UK album charts and earn the band another gold disc. It also charted strongly in Europe, reaching No.7 in Sweden and No.8 in Norway, aided by the final leg of the band's world tour, which saw them play 14 gigs in Sweden, Denmark, Germany, the Netherlands, Belgium and France in November and December. The tour went well and 10cc's chart success went from strength to strength. In the Netherlands, The Things We Do For Love and Good Morning Judge were both Top 20 hits, ensuring Top 10 success for *Deceptive Bends*. The album also went gold in Sweden and reached No.1 in Belgium and Denmark, while in Norway it reached No.4 and spent 18 weeks in the Top 10. *Deceptive Bends* became 10cc's bestselling album to date in Europe and their tour gained rave reviews.

"Really this performance was perfect," wrote *De Waarheid* reviewing one of the band's two gigs at Rotterdam's De Doelen. "With this concert 10cc proved – actually not necessary – to be one of the real top groups of the 70s."

The band's new line-up had proven to be a strong live team,

gaining glowing reviews at all points of their world tour. As the year drew to a close 10cc appeared in the 'Best Live Act' Top 10 in the annual *Record Mirror* and *Melody Maker* readers' polls (also achieving Top 10 placings in the latter's 'Best Producer' and 'Best Arranger' categories). However, Tony O'Malley's drug conviction meant his future in the group was untenable.

"Tony got busted in Australia and we had another Japanese and Australian tour lined up and we knew that he wouldn't be able to return because of his drug conviction," recalls Gouldman.

As the band started their search for a new keyboard player, it was announced that O'Malley was leaving 10cc. O'Malley's background in soul music always made him a somewhat surprising choice of keyboard player for a band like 10cc anyway, which he himself acknowledged after leaving the band.

"I don't know why I joined them really," said O'Malley at the time. "I suppose it might have been because I had no income. I suppose it is totally at odds with anything I've ever played in. Like I've been so restricted. The numbers are so worked out that to sit down and play it is dead easy."

CHAPTER 17

CON SEQUENCES

OCTOBER 1977 FINALLY SAW THE RELEASE OF *CONSEQUENCES*, KEVIN Godley and Lol Creme's magnum opus. Recording had continued after the split at Strawberry in Stockport – now christened Strawberry North – but with the studio fully booked months in advance, Godley and Creme had to make *Consequences* between the hours of midnight and 10am, meaning they lived a nocturnal existence. To make the recording process even more surreal, the duo were also living out of a suitcase. With their homes and families now down in Surrey, the pair were based at the Hotel Piccadilly in Manchester city centre, sleeping by day and recording by night. Accompanying them in the studio were the 'Gizmo', their engineer Martin Lawrence and copious amounts of hashish. "The thing I remember most is a piece of Lebanese hash about the size of a triple cheeseburger," recalls Godley. "That kept us going through the long nights."

By early November 1976, they had completed the first 10 minutes of the record, with the 'Gizmo' used to impressive effect. Creating sounds that even Godley and Creme had not thought possible when they started work on the record, the 'Gizmo' simulates orchestral effects and emulates the sound of everything from a saxophone to an opera singer. With the theme of the album being 'Man's last defence against an irate nature', the 'Gizmo' is used to bring the four elements of Earth, Wind, Fire and Water to life, as floods, typhoons and other ecological disasters spread across the planet. The way the burial scene of an early victim is rendered is particularly affecting. The listener is placed inside the coffin as the sound of the inclement weather up above, and the priest's committal, is slowly drowned out as each spade full of dirt lands on the coffin lid.

By early 1977, Godley and Creme had completed the first album in what was now to be a triple-album set. "I remember playing the completed first album to Harvey Lisberg and Ric Dixon at full volume," recalls Godley. "They said, 'Wow! That's fantastic! We love it!' And then the two of them went into the studio area to talk. We left one of the microphones on, and heard one say to the other, 'What the hell was that all about?' And the other one said, 'I don't know, I thought it was fucking garbage!' They didn't have a clue what it was all about and, quite frankly, neither did we! It was the work of two very stoned people, whose eyes were on a mass of details, hoping that the whole would be worth more than the sum of its parts. We recorded a song that we sped up 15 or so times to create the sound of a fly going by. Incredible, minute details. But there was never a grand design; there were no foundations. We were building on clay and it fell apart. It was a grand folly."

The Flood is a great example of them obsessing over the brushstrokes and losing sight of the bigger canvas. They recorded the sound of a bucket of water being thrown against the wall of the car park at Strawberry more than 200 times in order to create a track that builds from the sound of a dripping tap into a full-on tsunami that washes away a band playing at a music festival. There are some deft touches, and the end is certainly affecting, as the human heartbeat submerged by the tsunami is slowly extinguished. And maybe there is a hidden joke in the piece – maybe it's actually 10cc getting washed away in the flood. The 'If you pray hard enough it might rain' sign-off from the band at the music festival echoes Creme's joke at 10cc's rain-drenched Cardiff Castle gig in 1975. And the riff that concludes the gig sounds suspiciously like a spoof of The Second Sitting For The Last Supper. Yet still, despite the technical accomplishments and in-jokes, there is simply not enough to hold the listener's attention for the full eight minutes. At times, *Consequences* sounds like the aural equivalent of watching paint dry.

In between recording sessions, the pair enjoyed a bit of light relief with some practical jokes at Peter Tattersall's expense. "There was this German producer coming over one Saturday morning to look at the studio with a view to using it for a client," recalls Zeb White. "So, we went out and bought all this mock-brick wallpaper and we pasted it over some metal frames to give the illusion that we'd bricked up the studio. We then sprayed graffiti over the walls with messages like GODLEY AND CREME RULE OK. We then set up a microphone in there to record Peter's reaction to it. Of course, when Peter walked in with this producer, opened the door and turned on the studio lights, he couldn't believe it! What we'd also done was buy a sheet of hardboard and covered it with green felt and sat it over the top of the pool table that we had in the cellar at Strawberry. We covered it with all sorts of things – sausages and mash, curries, beer cans. When Peter saw it he went absolutely ballistic! He rang Ric Dixon, who said he'd come down to the studio right away to see it for himself. Of course, by the time Ric got to the studio, we'd cleared it all up."

By March 1977, the *Consequences* project had been in production for almost nine months but still had no end in sight. With Barclay James Harvest booked into Strawberry between March and June 1977 to record what would become their *Gone to Earth* album, and having tired of living out of a suitcase, Godley and Creme needed to find another studio to finish their album. In fact, Strawberry North was so in demand that the studio had turned down a booking from Paul McCartney for recording sessions for the Wings album *London Town*. After Godley and Creme had left Strawberry, Cathy Redfern found a note addressed to her marked 'To be opened 25th March 1980'. It read: 'Our dearest darling Cathy toots. Do you still remember those two very silly Jews? Well this little note is to remind you of all the wonderful and miserable days we spent in that place, making lots of noise and coffee and cheese and joints. And we loved you very much, and all the other burkes and dools and fools who joined with us in our own little world of lunacy and havoc. We will always remember you little honey so don't forget us. Lots of love, Lol and Kevin.'

Godley and Creme decamped to The Manor, the first residential recording studio in the UK, and one also designed by Westlake Audio. Located in Shipton-on-Cherwell, just north of Oxford, the studio was owned by Richard Branson and was primarily designed for use by acts signed to Virgin, the label that 10cc had nearly joined two years previously. The move to The Manor coincided with the next stage in the album's development, which involved collaborating with the legendary comedian Peter Cook, one of the leading lights of the British satire boom of the 60s.

"We needed a story for the music to be built around," says Godley. "Phonogram approached Peter on our behalf and offered him a lot of money. He moved in with us at Manor Studios for about three months."

Godley and Creme had originally developed a story that involved a gambling game between four characters, each representing one of the four elements. Cook suggested adapting the storyline to be built around a meeting between a couple (Walter and Lulu Stapleton) discussing their impending divorce with their lawyers (Mr Haig and Mr Pepperman). A series of strange happenings interrupt the meeting as the environmental crisis that is gripping planet Earth rages outside. Inside the room the discussion focuses on irrelevancies such as hairpins, while they miss the significance of what is going on in the outside world. In many ways, it was a metaphor for Godley and Creme themselves, locked inside the studio focusing on their musical hairpins while the musical landscape shifted outside.

In the story the only person not fazed by it all is Blint, the musician living in the flat below, who saves the day with a belief in the power of music and the significance of the number '17'. Lots of speculation has been made about hidden meanings in Cook's play. Is the divorce analogous to the split of 10cc? The book, *How Very Interesting*, even speculates that the characters are caricatures of the four *Beyond the Fringe* cast members – Peter Cook represented by the alcoholic lawyer Haig, the vocal mannerisms of Walter Stapleton mimicking Alan Bennett, the stereotypical Jewish lawyer Pepperman sending up Jonathan Miller, and the musician Blint representing Dudley Moore. Others speculate that the four main characters each represent one of the elements: Earth (Stapleton), Wind (Lulu), Fire (Peppermen) and Water (Haig). Whether any of these theories have any basis in truth is another matter, but the storyline gave Godley and Creme a structure around which to build the rest of the album.

"The way we worked was totally spontaneous," says Godley. "We'd record a little bit of music in response to something Peter had said, and then play it to him the next morning. Then he'd go away and write something more. It was a very collaborative, experimental period, though, as I say, we didn't know what the fuck we were doing!"

The working patterns of Godley, Creme and Cook were quite different though.

"We were never in sync in terms of creative output," says Godley. "Lol and I would work until quite late – one, two or three in the morning – and get up late the next day. Peter, on the other hand, was an early riser. He'd be up and around by eight or nine in the morning, bathed, showered, fresh as a daisy. And he'd be in the studio, ready to boogie, by the time we staggered downstairs for breakfast at half-eleven, twelve, looking like shit. Of course, by the time we finally came to, he was going out of it, because he'd start drinking at midday. So, he was going down just as we were coming up, and we met, as it were, for a couple of hours in the middle."

When it came to recording Cook's play there was talk at one point of using Peter Sellers and Peter Ustinov to perform some of the parts. In the end, Peter Cook would play all the characters himself, apart from Stapleton's French wife Lulu – whose accent could almost have been one of *les girls* from One Night In Paris – who was played by Cook's wife, Judy Huxtable. Mixed in among Cook's play were a handful of new Godley and Creme songs, like *Five O'Clock In The Morning*, *When Things Go Wrong* and *Cool, Cool, Cool*, most of which would have sat comfortably on a 10cc album.

In April 1977, Phil Manzanera, who had formed the band 801 during Roxy Music's hiatus, joined the pair at The Manor. 801 were nearing completion of their album *Listen Now*, which featured guest appearances from the likes of Brian Eno and Tim Finn. Godley added backing vocals to four tracks on the album at The Manor, while Creme performed the 'Gizmo' on Flight 19 and Initial Speed. Also guesting on the 801 album was saxophonist Mel Collins – who had played with Tony O'Malley in Kokomo prior to their split in January 1977 – who was drafted in to play on *Consequences* on When Things Go Wrong.

One unexpected highlight for Godley and Creme was the guest appearance of jazz singer Sarah Vaughan on Lost Weekend.

"The song was very George Gershwin," says Godley. "We thought it would be nice to do it as a duet, so we wondered, 'Who would be good to sing it?' We both thought of Sarah Vaughan but thought, 'No chance!' But the record company fixed it. It was brilliant!"

In his autobiography *Spacecake*, Godley recalls Vaughan's memorable visit to the Manor in May 1977, dressed in a powder blue trouser suit and matching hat.

"She intrinsically understood the borrowed Porgy and Bessness of the song so there wasn't much to say," says Godley. "We made shy and awkward small talk for a while as the vocal microphones were being set up then shuffled around the piano to rehearse the song. My oh my … I suddenly found myself singing for *her*. Guiding *her* through the melody. A thrill, it has to be said."

Godley then took his place in the control room as Vaughan added her vocals to the song.

"I'd already recorded my parts so I could sit in the control room and marvel as she cranked up those pipes and blew me out of the water," says Godley. "For me it was the sublime vocal centrepiece of the album. The best song in a project where songs weren't that important."

As *Consequences* neared completion, thoughts turned to a launch plan. There was talk of the work being launched at the Royal Exchange Theatre in Manchester incorporating dance, drama and music. Harvey Lisberg had visions of a West End production and an international touring company. For his part, Lol Creme wanted the album launched with a concert featuring the world's greatest guitarists each playing an excerpt from the album on a 'Gizmo'. Ultimately none of these ideas would come to pass.

Godley and Creme had signed a new record deal with Phonogram after the split with 10cc and Ken Maliphant, the label's marketing director, had the unenviable task of deciding how to market the album. He opted to launch *Consequences* as a lavish boxed set complete with a premium price.

"Ken had this bright idea to release the album for £11, whereas Richard Branson said to us, 'If I was putting this out, I'd charge a fiver'," recalls Creme. "Ken was saying it had to be a posh tabletop item. We knew we were sunk as soon as he mentioned it; it was a complete disaster in terms of marketing."

Picking up on a theme from Peter Cook's play, where Blint

suggests a significance to the number '17', Phonogram decided to carry this through to launch, giving the album the catalogue number CONS 17 and a launch date of October 17. Prior to that, *Consequences* was previewed to critics and the Phonogram sales force in a domed 17th-century church – the Ronde Lutherse Kerk – in the heart of Amsterdam, with playback starting at the 17th second of the 17th minute of the 17th hour on September 17.

Everyone attending had to wear a badge with the words "I am prepared for the consequences". As they took their places expectations were high. After all, this was the album that Godley and Creme had felt it necessary to leave one of the world's most successful groups for. "You may like it, you may loathe it, but you can't afford to ignore ... *Consequences*," announced Maliphant to the massed gathering, while Godley, Creme and Cook watched from one of the balconies and, in Godley's words, "bit each other's nails".

With the 'Gizmo' sat before them in a glass case resting on black velvet, the record began. Reactions to it were mixed. Some loved it but others struggled to keep awake for the full 113-minute, movie-length duration of the record.

"Sounding like a cross between 10cc, Monty Python, middle period Moody Blues and the least linear moments of the Firesign Theatre, the record demands being listened to, but then, if the response of the sales team was any indication, refuses to give up much in return," wrote Michael Gross in *Rolling Stone*. "Bees buzz, Negroes hum the blues, Peter Cook, the British comedian, adds long segments of what one supposes to be comedy, and then the 'Gizmo' launches into action, impressive, but lacking any direction. Twenty minutes into the presentation, heads began dropping on breastbones and the, unintentionally, funniest moment of the record occurred when snoring came from the speakers as eyes closed around the room. Already there was a cloying sense that though the disc would go on, things would not improve. 'It's not a good omen when goldfish commit suicide,' quipped Cook in one of his various recorded personas. Nor is it a good omen when that was the best joke the record had to offer. For Lol and Kevin's sake, one left hoping *Consequences* would, at least, sell a few 'Gizmos'."

At the press conference afterwards, Peter Cook responded to

one critic's negative line of questioning by asking him what he did in his spare time. "Nothing," came the response. "Well, fuck off home and do it," said Cook. A French journalist then asked if the dialogue would be recorded in other languages and added that he found it quite boring. Later on, when asked if *Consequences* could be performed as a play, Cook replied: "Yes, it's called *Fuck the French*."

The perceived wisdom today is that the UK music press panned *Consequences* at the time, given its release at the height of the punk rock explosion. However, the reality was quite different. While *Sounds* felt that *Consequences* was "completely over the top", *Melody Maker* claimed, rather boldly, that it was "the most important and best album released in years" and *Record Mirror* described it as a "masterpiece". Unexpectedly, even *New Musical Express* saw some merits. "Against my better judgement, I find myself enjoying it," wrote Phil McNeil. "In fact, the set's faults are quite the opposite of what you'd expect. Rather than it being an over-ambitious attempt to mate diverse elements, the mating actually works extremely well, but the individual parts fail to stand up on their own … The best parts are exactly those where the songs, effects and dialogue work off each other. At a few points Godley and Creme achieve a cohesion virtually unrivalled in the annals of the concept album."

Such was the strength of Godley and Creme's reputation that they were given the rare opportunity of promoting their debut single, Five O'Clock In The Morning, on *Top of the Pops*, before it had even charted. Yet despite an appearance on the show normally being enough to guarantee a hit, the record still flopped.

Consequences was given a heavy promotional push by Phonogram. Press ads boldly claimed that it was "destined to be the most important musical event of the year" – quite a statement given the changing musical landscape of the time, with the release of *Never Mind the Bollocks* by The Sex Pistols only weeks earlier. Just to up the ante even further, cinema adverts for the album, voiced by Peter Cook, boldly posed the question, 'Will music ever be the same again?' The answer would prove to be a resounding 'Yes', as the public chose to ignore the album in their droves; *Consequences* would spend one week at No.52 in the UK album charts before dropping like a stone.

"Yeah, it went silver, or was it bronze?" joked Creme sometime later.

Consequences was an adventurous project, and the album certainly had its moments, but if *Deceptive Bends* lacked Godley and Creme's surrealism, *Consequences* appeared in far greater need of Stewart and Gouldman's editing skills.

"It had pieces of sheer genius," says Stewart. "But for me what it was missing was my input and Graham's input. We could have steered it to something that was more successful."

Peter Cook later joked that it was the album that nearly bankrupted Phonogram. He was only half-joking. The album had taken over 12 months to record and was rumoured to have cost £250,000 to make, half of it from Godley and Creme's own pocket! With hindsight, even Godley and Creme laugh at the pretentiousness of recording a triple album.

"It was like the bars being taken away after leaving the band. We went berserk," says Godley. "There were so many ideas waiting to come out, they came out indiscriminately."

Nor did it succeed, as Phonogram had hoped, in attracting listeners outside of the traditional pop/rock genre, despite attempts to market it as another *Tubular Bells*.

"The timing, the price, everything was wrong about that album," says Creme. "A lot of it was instrumental, which I suppose was a subconscious rejection of all the boxes we were put into with 10cc, all that witty, funny, ha-ha stuff. The timing was terrible because, overnight, the whole punk scene took off in Britain. No one wanted self-indulgent statements or 'artistic adventures in sound' like *Consequences*. But the biggest fault with it was the packaging, which was the antithesis of what was happening at the time. We came out after 12 months locked away making it, and The Sex Pistols were out there and we thought, 'What's going on?'"

"It was instantly invalidated," says Godley. "We were like two Japanese soldiers emerging from the jungle 10 years after the war had ended. The landscape had changed. We'd lost touch. We'd believed in our own myth, not that there was one for anyone but ourselves. We'd submerged ourselves in the womb of the studio, at vast expense, to come out with some amazing piece of art and we lost the plot. We'd been overtaken by events. Looking back, there are some interesting things on that album, but not six sides worth! Not enough to warrant the amount of effort and expense that went into it."

For some, the whole *Consequences* episode saw Godley and Creme disappear up their own ingenuity.

"They turned their back on huge success because they couldn't stand it," said Harvey Lisberg sometime later. "They were great, brilliant, innovative – and what did they do? A triple album that goes on forever and became a disaster." Art for art's sake indeed!

For some light relief, Godley and Creme joined Phil Manzanera's 801 onstage at Manchester University on November 2, making their first live appearance since Knebworth in August 1976. The gig was recorded and would be released twenty years later as *801 Manchester*. At the end of the month, the pair headed to America to start a tour of radio stations in support of the release of *Consequences*. In an interview with *Los Angeles Times* at the Beverly Wilshire Hotel, Lol Creme conceded how difficult it was for their record company to market the album.

"It might be hell to sell this thing," said Creme. "The record company can't use its normal system of selling because this is a mixture of music and dialogue and it can't really be categorised. There is no way of taking a cut off the record that is indicative of the rest of it. It's a difficult piece of listening. You have to put a lot of energy into it. You need two full hours with no distractions. It's not the kind of album you can use as background."

Reviews of the album in the American press were mixed. ONE GIZMO DOES NOT A TRIPLE ALBUM MAKE ran the headline in *The Washington Post*: "*Consequences* supposedly carries a running theme of man's struggle against the elements of nature but the material is too dispersed to allow one idea to connect three records and the entire concept seems to collapse from its own inertia," wrote Mark Kernis.

The album failed to chart in the US. The failure of the *Consequences* project was a major blow to Godley and Creme but affected the pair in different ways.

"Kevin was heartbroken, I don't think he's got over it yet," said Creme 20 years on. "He was really, really upset about the way it was received, like a big turkey, really. I didn't take it the way Kevin did, to be honest, because I loved doing it so much and I learned so much, got so much out of it, a totally selfish thing, I didn't give a shit, I really didn't. And I never have, to me it's the doing of something that's the vibe, it's not necessarily the result. It's always a bonus if what you do does well, but it's not that precious,you know. I've always thought like that. And I could see why it was laughed at; it does look like a pretentious pile of old stuff. We were self-indulgent pop stars, there's no question about it."

With their reputation, and personal finances, bruised by the experience, there was immediate pressure to get straight back into the studio to record a more commercial album.

"One day our management took us to one side and said, 'Listen boys, you've got to make a single album already, a commercial album'," says Godley.

Deciding to make an album that was the antithesis of *Consequences*, their original plan was to record it from start to finish in three weeks, a bit like the process for the first 10cc album five years earlier. They also wanted to scale things back and record the album in a small, local 16-track studio.

"We did it using 16-track partly as an anti-big-production thing really," said Creme at the time. "That was the main starting point, that it was going to be a lot simpler. We were spoilt working in what Strawberry had become, like The Manor. Not to knock them, they're superb studios, but you begin to rely on them. You know there are certain pieces of equipment there that you can plug in to get certain sounds and I think that limits your ingenuity."

Having heard that there was a small, 16-track studio called Surrey Sound Studios in a disused village hall in Leatherhead they dropped by one day to check it out. As they walked in they met the owner, Nigel Gray, who was sawing up some bits of wood to make an acoustic screen. After spending a day trying the studio out they decided to record their new album there. Not that the duo had any new material written as the sessions began in March 1978.

"We didn't have any songs written or anything beforehand," says Godley. "We sort of fobbed everyone off really, saying, 'Yeah,

Harvey, we've got plenty written.' We went into the studio and we didn't know what the hell we were going to do."

At first, the duo felt under pressure to follow the advice of their management and record a more commercial album.

"So, we went into the studio with the great intention of trying to do that but we can't actually do that, think commercial in the traditional sense of the word," says Godley.

According to Creme: "We did try for about an hour and a half, then it was back to just experimenting on tape, back to our old usual system."

The first thing that the duo recorded was a drum tape loop that would evolve into the song Group Life, which reflected their experiences in 10cc.

"That song was about how something exciting can become very mundane very quickly and that's how life in 10cc was becoming after only four years," says Godley.

Most of the songs would evolve organically from putting a sound, word or idea on tape and building on it rather than writing a song in the conventional sense. Only two songs, This Sporting Life and Business Is Business, were written as songs rather than built from experiments. Slowly, the album began to take shape after a slow start.

"It was weird really, because in a way we were still coming down from *Consequences*, which we put 110% of our lives into for a year and a half," says Godley. "The feeling while we recorded that was so intense that this was almost an anti-climax, going back into the studio to redeem your credibility, if you know what I mean. So, it was obviously a bit odd at the beginning, but as the tracks began to appear I think we got more involved. The atmosphere was strange because we were far from totally sure that we wanted to record at all, but we were obliged to do so because that's the way we make our living."

Their approach led the pair to christen the album *L*, like the learner plates on a car when you're learning to drive. "The title *L* was admitting we were learners again," says Godley. "We don't know what we're doing, take it or leave it."

As the sessions progressed, the duo found themselves sharing studio time with another band at Surrey Sound Studios.

Occasionally Nigel Gray would play them their work.

"What we were continuously searching for with a million over-dubs they achieved naturally in spades with guitar, bass and drums, and didn't Nigel enjoy rubbing our noses in it," recalls Godley. The band was The Police, who were recording their debut album *Outlandos D'Amour*.

As the songs began to emerge, Godley and Creme were pleased with the results, feeling that their songwriting partnership was continuing to improve. "Our writing has progressed so much since we started," said Godley at the time. "We've explored those stages of wanting to write songs like other people. People are always trying to emulate their favourites whereas we're not. We're always trying to develop our personality through the medium."

L was certainly Godley and Creme's most autobiographical set of songs to date. While Group Life reflected on their time with 10cc – complete with its spoof of Donna – other tracks looked back at their time at art college (Art School Canteen) and further back to their school days (Punchbag). Appropriately enough, the latter's tale of bullying pulled no punches. The duo retained their keenness to turn everything on its head and approach things from a different perspective.

"There's very little point in putting out a record that somebody else could have done," said Creme. "If you take the logical way out every time you come to a song, it could have been recorded by a hundred different people because they are in command of the same instruments and chord changes; so we try and push things a little bit further so that you couldn't have got that piece of music by anybody else on the planet. All the stuff that's out at the moment you can get by anybody."

After losing so much money on *Consequences*, Phonogram took a more hands-on interest in the new sessions, an approach that didn't go down too well with the dynamic duo. "People kept saying, 'Have you done any singles yet?'" says Creme. "That fucked us off a little bit. We were doing music that was coming out instinctively and there was this threat."

For their part, Godley and Creme protested that their attitude hadn't changed from the 10cc days and if it was acceptable then, why not now? "These people want us to be 10cc, a pop group, but they don't even know what 'tocc' should be now, when in fact that's what they've got, the spirit of what tocc was in the early days, good ideas and hooks, and they don't realise it," said Creme at the time.

If their relationship with Phonogram appeared strained, it was nothing compared to their apparently deteriorating relationship with Eric Stewart and Graham Gouldman, with press interviews increasingly acrimonious. In an interview with *Melody Maker*, Lol Creme claimed that Eric Stewart "wasn't a songwriter".

"There's a point in me and Kev where it's too ridiculous and there's a point in Eric and Graham, and anyone else who's a song-writer, where it's not even worth trying," said Creme. "Our threshold is much greater than theirs; we'll go a lot further before it's not even worth trying."

Stewart and Gouldman were equally acidic in press interviews. Stewart said he had no intention of giving *L* a listen. "I've no desire to," said Stewart at the time. "It's a funny thing. I heard the first side of *Consequences* as they were doing it just before the split, and that was the last thing I really wanted to know about anything they were doing."

Gouldman had heard both of Godley and Creme's albums. "It's very hard to produce them, I should think, because they're very single-minded," said Gouldman. "On their new album, there are flashes of genius, and then the next track is a real let-down. They attempt things that they shouldn't attempt because they're not jazz musicians. It's all these nice little abstract notes and it doesn't really work for me because it's not Oscar Peterson playing. But then other tracks are amazing."

Featuring guest appearances from Andy Mackay of Roxy Music on saxophone, and Paul Gambaccini performing a vocal cameo on This Sporting Life, *L* weighed in at a sprightly 34 minutes. Released by Phonogram in August 1978, it met with mixed reviews. *The Sunday Times* described it as "Brilliantly recorded, brilliantly sung, an album of dazing difference" while Harry Doherty in *Melody Maker* said "Come December, it'll be one of my ten best." Yet not all critics were so convinced: "Godley and Creme possess tremendous musical talent...but if only the pair of them would stop trying quite so damned hard to be the future of rock and roll...then their work could prove to be much more satisfying," wrote *New Musical*

Express. Sounds concurred, giving the album a two-star rating: "*L* will not re-establish Godley and Creme as a force to be reckoned with. Rather it will confirm that in their desire to be unique and original they are their own worst enemies. Last time they wrote a bunch of great songs and hid them away between reams of boring dialogue; this time they've written a bunch of great lyrics and thrown them away on arrangements of prissy complexity. Maybe next time they'll get it right."

While Kevin Godley looks back on *L* as his favourite Godley and Creme album, Lol Creme's view of it is much less positive.

"It was terrible," he says. "The doom on it was pervading. We were very depressed at the time. That album's got some solid ideas on it but I can't listen to it, it doesn't give me good vibes. It's morbid."

Commercially, *L* only managed to get five places higher than its predecessor, peaking at No.47 in the UK album charts. Godley and Creme didn't appear unduly bothered. "Unfortunately, we're not too removed from the Zappa approach, where if it sounds too commercial we'll stick the word 'fuck' in it. It's almost that," said Creme at the time. "If it sounds too obvious, we get upset and we deviate and that's what throws people."

Creme's outlook was a far cry from his view two years previously when he'd said he was in the business of communications, not art for art's sake. "Even to 10cc fanatics, the early spin-off works of Kevin Godley and Lol Creme seemed challenging," says Chris Roberts in *Prog* magazine. "Perhaps there was a strain of resentment – we wanted the art pop band back together, not two times 5cc. And while Eric Stewart and Graham Gouldman were dazzling us with Feel The Benefit, this more technology-fascinated pair gave the impression of disappearing up their own gizmo."

With the relationship with their record company strained, they parted company with Mercury and signed a new record deal with Polydor. Mercury tried to salvage something from the wreckage by editing down the full 113 minutes of *Consequences* into a single 41-minute album.

Music from Consequences contained all seven songs, plus three musical extracts, but it too failed to capture the public's attention.

In the end, the only passage from *Consequences* to reach a significant audience would be a 90-second extract used by advertising agency Collett Dickenson Pearce to provide a suitably surreal soundtrack to their iconic *Iguana* cinema ad for Benson and Hedges. Ironic that after all the blood, sweat and tears that had gone into their 'art' it would be as the music to a commercial that would give their music its biggest audience. Directed by Hugh Hudson, the ad would go on to be voted one of the "10 best cinema commercials of all time" by *Campaign* magazine.

The 'Gizmo' itself would also fail to live up to its expectations, despite some very high-profile supporters: Jimmy Page would play the 'Gizmo' on Led Zeppelin's In The Evening; Paul McCartney would use it on the Wings albums *London Town* and *Back To The Egg*; and Justin Hayward utilised it extensively on The Moody Blues' *Long Distance Voyager* album, including the riff on their hit Gemini Dream.

"You had to have just the right kind of phrase; otherwise it sounded awful," said Hayward. "And you had to overdub it many, many times but that's the sound made by the 'Gizmo'."

Musitronics chief Aaron Newman, and key people in the company such as Mike Biegel, believed in the instrument as zealously as Godley and Creme to the point of divesting their core business to focus efforts on the 'Gizmo', which was to be launched under the name, the Gizmotron, in August 1979.

"Everybody thought we were going to make a fortune from the Gizmotron, so we decided to sell off Musitronics," said Newman.

The business was sold to the ARP synthesizer company, who were to pay royalties on all Musitronics products sold, which Newman planned to use to fund his new venture, Gizmo Inc. They drafted in leading industrial designer Herb Ross to finalise the styling and design of the Gizmotron. All were pleased with the finished prototype, which Creme demonstrated at the Chicago Trade Fair. However, the business soon ran into financial problems when ARP went under. To make matters worse, the Gizmotron proved to be unreliable.

"We were blown away by the 'Gizmo"s potential, but in hindsight, we should have realised that it couldn't work," says Newman. "The 'Gizmo' had some physical limitations that you couldn't really overcome. For instance, we discovered that if we made them during the winter they wouldn't work properly in hot weather. It was the characteristics of the plastics, and none of us were plastics engineers. We were out of our realm."

With more sophisticated synthesizers now available to musicians wanting to emulate the sounds of strings, the Gizmotron proved to be a commercial failure. "The company went bust, and we just got very fed up with it and decided to shelve the whole bloody thing," says Godley. Newman subsequently went bankrupt and then suffered a heart attack. It's little wonder that Mike Beigel would later describe Musitronics' dealings with the 'Gizmo' as an "epic Greek tragedy."

"It really is a sad story," he said. "It led Musitronics to its own destruction."

For Godley and Creme it would mark the end of a 10-year association with the 'Gizmo'. Yet for all its ability to emulate other sounds, arguably the 'Gizmo's finest hour – or, more accurately, its finest 200 seconds – was not to be found on *Consequences* or any of its other high-profile guest appearances; it was the spine-tingling backing it provided to 10cc's Old Wild Men. Such a shame that the instrument's development had to have such tragic consequences for the original line-up of the band.

CHAPTER 18

FROM OCHO RIOS TO DORKING

NEARLY TWO YEARS AFTER THE SPLIT OF THE ORIGINAL LINE-UP, THE prospect of the four founder members of 10cc working together on a new record seemed remote. Yet David Rohl, formerly of the band Ankh and now chief engineer at Strawberry North, had succeeded in doing just that. Recorded over a two-year period, during 'dead time' at Strawberry, Rohl had created a Tolkienesque concept album called *The Eye of Wendor*, which was released under the name Mandalaband in May 1978. Among the lead vocalists guesting on the album were Eric Stewart (Florian's Song) and Kevin Godley (The Witch of Waldow Wood) but, on Elsethea, Rohl managed to combine a lead vocal from Graham Gouldman with idiosyncratic backing vocals from Godley and Creme. It was the closest 10cc fans were likely to get to the original line-up working together at the time.

Meanwhile, the five members of 10cc Mk II made their first visit to Strawberry North to record the Randy Newman-penned music for an American *Dr Pepper* advertising campaign. "They had a lot of big bands record for them," says Rick Fenn. "I don't think I've heard it since it left the studio!"

Anyone accusing the new 10cc line-up of selling out may have forgotten that the original line-up of the band had recorded the music to an ad for Revlon's Natural Wonder Longlash mascara back in July 1976. Money for God's sake, indeed. American recording engineer Elliot Scheiner visited Strawberry North to oversee the Dr Pepper session. Scheiner, who would go on to earn no less than 25 Grammy Award nominations for his work with artists such as Steely Dan and Beck, was himself an admirer of Eric Stewart's studio skills.

"I even tried to get Eric nominated for a Grammy for best

engineering on *Deceptive Bends*," said Scheiner at the time, who had the rare opportunity of gaining an insight into how Stewart operated in the studio: "There is no talking to him between takes. He seemed to know everything he wanted to do automatically and, during the session, he seemed to have most of the say. Graham was certainly a part of it, and everyone in the band pitched in, but it still seemed like Eric's the heavyweight."

Following the end of their world tour, the five members of 10cc had taken a break before starting work on their next album. Eric Stewart had gone on holiday to Barbados with his close friend Justin Hayward and their families. The holiday proved to be eventful. "One day Eric decided he wanted to go parasailing and so we headed off to the middle of the ocean to this raft," recalls Hayward. "Eric was very, very painfully parasailed up into the sky by a very fast speedboat and I was left on this raft with these three boys. Then one of the boys said to me, 'Hey, I really like those chains around your wrist, I'll give you a dollar for them.' So, I said, 'Well, no I don't think so,' and he said, 'Well, in that case, I'll cut your hand off and take them.' So, I then started to go into this ludicrous explanation about how I got them, and they were a present from me mum, and all of this, and it was a case really of dark and mysterious meets white and pale – and getting paler every minute in the middle of the Caribbean." Stewart landed back on the raft to hear the argument in full swing. "It was an amazing confrontation between black and white on this 12-foot piece of wood in the middle of nowhere!" says Stewart.

On his return home, Stewart finally moved into Colombe, the house that he had been having purpose-built in Walton-on-the-Hill near Tadworth in Surrey. A joint house-warming and birthday celebration took place in late January with the entire band attending, bar Graham Gouldman, who was in Jamaica. His holiday also proved to be memorable. "I was talking with a guy I met there about sports," says Gouldman. "I said, 'You must really like cricket,' and he said, 'No, man, I don't like it, I *love* it!'"

When Stewart and Gouldman reconvened to start writing songs for the new album, a casual conversation about their holiday experiences inspired one of their new creations. Stewart's experience when parasailing was incorporated into the verses while

Gouldman's conversation about cricket became the hook to the song's chorus. Rick Fenn recalls the early run-throughs of the song in the studio as the arrangement took shape; "I remember it being quite whimsical," says Fenn. "At one point Graham asked, 'Can I have go at singing this?'"

With Gouldman taking lead vocal, the song became 10cc's first attempt at reggae. Anyone doubting 10cc's ability to pull off a reggae pastiche was in for a rude awakening. The result was vintage 10cc, although not everyone would be seduced by its charms. Some critics would later express a view that it contained racist undertones, with its racial stereotypes and patois voices. That was certainly not Stewart and Gouldman's intention, given the song reflected their genuine love of the Caribbean. If anything, they were mocking the holiday-maker who visits the islands and tries, unsuccessfully, to go native. If the use of stereotypes and voices was misjudged at least they were being consistent – the French had received the same treatment on One Night In Paris three years earlier.

After some discussion about the song's title – Gouldman favoured I Don't Like Cricket while Stewart preferred Dreadlock Holiday – it was the first song recorded for the band's sixth album. As the sessions began at Strawberry South in February 1978, it was clear that the rapport built up during their six months on the road together was very evident, setting the tone for the rest of the recording sessions which was "a very happy album to make," Stewart recalls. "It was thrilling, a total joy from beginning to end," confirms Rick Fenn. "There was a great band feeling."

The album would be the first with the new line-up and as such would be an important one for 10cc. The new members of the band had proved themselves admirably on the road, combining to create a formidable live team, but the studio was 10cc's real home. While their talents as musicians were clear, none of the new band members brought proven songwriting skills into the group. Burgess didn't write; Tosh had not contributed to the songwriting in Pilot; and while Fenn would go on to develop his writing skills, he saw himself as more of a musician than a writer at this point in his career. Still, the new sessions would give the new members their first opportunity to inject their personality into the band and they were actively encouraged to do so by Stewart and Gouldman. "They made us very at home in the band," recalls guitarist Rick Fenn. "Musically it was very democratic in the studio. Although I think we would all bow to their considerable musical experience, we would all chip in ideas. We were encouraged to write and sing our little bits. It was a really good time."

Stewart and Gouldman, however, retained overall control. "Graham and I are in charge of the final product because that is what we do best," said Stewart at the time. "But nobody is stifled. We want the other band members to say their piece. And we try every idea that comes up because it might just be that spark of genius that we're looking for."

With Eric Stewart and Rick Fenn handling keyboard duties until a replacement for Tony O'Malley was found the band continued work on the album. One new Stewart/Gouldman composition, For You and I, was further evidence of the pair's declared intention to write more love songs. It would later be described as the greatest song Paul McCartney never wrote. Benefitting from Stewart and Gouldman's skill in the studio, the song is transformed from a basic, standard song into a 'soft rock' tour de force, courtesy of an atmospheric arrangement and a strong lead vocal from Stewart.

Take These Chains was a simple three-minute pop song on the surface but took a few unexpected twists along the way that added more of a 10cc flavour to it. The song's origins were interesting.

"I was talking to Linda McCartney one day and she said, 'How quickly can you write a song?'" recalls Stewart. "I said, 'Well, give me a line to work on and we'll see.' She said, 'Okay, how about: *I'd love to love you but my hands are tied.*' So, I went away and wrote the song with Graham."

More traditionally 10cc was The Anonymous Alcoholic, a humorous account of a guy who disgraces himself at the office party, having ignored the promises he has made to himself never to drink again. The group segue into a disco section in the middle of the song, with a humorous nod to the Memphis Horns courtesy of Rick Fenn's Dorking Horns, as the protagonist tries to chat up his boss's wife, before reverting to a suitably sombre tone as he wakes up in the morning with no job and the mother of all hangovers. If one section of the song sounded familiar to 10cc fans, it was because Stewart and Gouldman had recycled the melody and lyric from Get It While You Can, an earlier b-side, for the song's chorus. Purists who pointed to this as evidence of 10cc's declining standards were clearly overlooking the fact that this tactic was nothing new for 10cc – parts of Fresh Air For My Mama from their debut had been recycled from the Hotlegs period.

Somewhat surprisingly, the new album would only feature four new Stewart/Gouldman compositions, although a fifth, Nothing Can Move Me, would appear as a future b-side. Elsewhere, for the first time on a 10cc album, Stewart and Gouldman wrote independently from each other, with five of the album's tracks being solo compositions. It would be the start of a gradual fragmentation in the Stewart/Gouldman partnership, each side coming in with songs that were fully formed rather than collaborating on them together. Stewart contributed Tokyo, a tribute to the city he had fallen in love with during his visit the previous autumn, as well as two songs that dealt with the subject of erotic fantasy – Everything You Wanted To Know About!!! and Shock On The Tube. The latter tells the story of a commuter who dozes off while travelling on the London Underground, waking up to find his fantasy has been just that – a dream.

"I was driving with a friend of mine and he said, 'I got a hell of a shock on the tube today,' and I thought, 'What a great title for a song,' and then I went away and fantasised a bit about this man coming home and then suddenly this vision sits down next to him and goes into this very weird happening, which is the story of the record," says Stewart. "It's just a fantasy."

Gouldman's two solo compositions both concerned the downsides of life on the road. From Rochdale To Ocho Rios dealt specifically with the disorientating lifestyle of being on tour – the 'It's Tuesday, so it must be Munich' syndrome. Life Line reflected the pressure that 10cc's increasingly global work commitments were placing on Gouldman's marriage.

One of the interesting dynamics of the original 10cc line-up was when they swapped songwriting partners. Stewart and Gouldman tried the same tactic with the new line-up, with the former partnering with Stuart Tosh and the latter with Rick Fenn. The anti-Communist Reds In My Bed, an Eric Stewart/Stuart Tosh creation, was inspired by a visit to the Berlin Wall.

"Looking across that wall gives you a depressing feeling that hits you right in the gut," said Stewart at the time. "I heard a story about one guy who actually got himself built into the shell of a car so that he could escape."

This, and other stories, made their way into the lyric, with Tosh also singing lead vocal on the track when the band came to record it. Less impressive was Rick Fenn's collaboration with Gouldman, Last Night, one of the weaker tracks in the new set. Another Gouldman/ Fenn collaboration, The Acapulco Kid, would be recorded by the band but never completed, and remains unreleased to this day.

In March, a replacement for Tony O'Malley was found in the shape of Duncan Mackay, former keyboard player with Cockney Rebel and, more recently, Kate Bush. Mackay had been a recommendation of Rick Fenn and joined 10cc at Strawberry South a third of the way through the new sessions.

According to Stewart, Mackay fitted in "like a dovetail joint" and immediately gelled with the rest of the band. Mackay would even get a songwriting credit for his collaboration with Stewart on Old Mister Time and, like the other members of the band, would go on to earn himself a nickname by the road crew, in his case 'Drunken Mackay', because of his partiality for a few drinks.

With much of its subject matter revolving around their travels during the previous year, the band decided to call their new album *Bloody Tourists*.

"The title came from a badge that was being sold in London at the time," says Stewart. "It said something like, 'Don't ask me, I'm not a bloody tourist, I live here.' I thought that *Bloody Tourists* would make a good album title."

It also seemed appropriate, given the band's recent bout of globetrotting.

"It's called *Bloody Tourists* because *we're* bloody tourists," said Gouldman at the time. "When we started doing the album it became apparent that a lot of the songs, quite coincidentally, were about being away from home, either on the road or on holiday. We did so much work last year, and so much happened to us, that it was worth writing about."

While 10cc's first two albums name-checked iconic Americana, the reference points this time around were places: London (on three songs), Jamaica (on two songs), Russia, Tokyo, Amsterdam, Hollywood, Acapulco; while Australia is alluded to in Life Line. Gouldman even references his home in Rochdale and the band's studio in Dorking on From Rochdale To Ocho Rios.

Once again, Hipgnosis were asked to work on the album cover for *Bloody Tourists*. "Storm came up with an idea of somebody who is reading a map, it blows in their face and they can't see where they are going," recalls Aubrey Powell. "The notion of travelling without really being there, or looking without really seeing, is the inspiration behind this picture. The tourist stares at the map; the wind blows it back in his face. He is seeing 'blind', never noticing or appreciating any place he visits. And what's interesting about that is the juxtaposition between somebody reading a map because they're lost and yet it's blown in their face so they can't see where they are going."

Thorgerson suggested various scenarios for the front cover. One of them featured a driver in a car with a map blown in their face. The chosen design, however, was of a disorientated tourist on an idyllic Caribbean beach unable to see the wonderful scenery around them for the map that is obscuring their view. Rather than use stock imagery Hipgnosis insisted that the image be shot for real on location, so Powell, accompanied by his girlfriend, was dispatched to the Caribbean.

"We set off to Barbados and got there but I could not find the right location," says Powell. "It sounds mad but I couldn't find somewhere where there was a nice cove with the right trees. I got lots of shots but I just didn't think I'd cracked it."

While in Barbados, Powell was happy with some shots he had taken for the cover of Dreadlock Holiday, which was scheduled to be the first single off the new album, but still hadn't nailed the cover shot for *Bloody Tourists*.

"Then on the way back to England we went via St Lucia and as the plane was touching down I saw right by the airport the ideal bay that I'd been looking for," recalls Powell. "I said, 'That's it!' We had a stopover of about four hours, so we literally grabbed the gear and ran to the beach, which was on the perimeter of the airport – you could do that in those days – and went to the sea, I stuck the camera in the sand on a tripod, set it on automatic and we took the photograph like that."

Powell, wearing his own shirt and jacket, donned a facemask that featured a carefully scrunched up map glued onto a plastic party mask with an elastic band and set his camera on timer. In the background his girlfriend can be seen enjoying a dip in the Caribbean Sea.

"When I got it back I was too small in the picture so I was cut out, made bigger, and stuck back on," says Powell.

Back in the UK, Hipgnosis took a photograph of 10cc for the inner gatefold sleeve. The picture shows the band as bloody tourists at an airport awaiting their next flight.

"The idea was to give this sense of travel," says Powell. "Their whole thing about *Bloody Tourists* was because that's what they felt like, because you never saw anything. You never actually see the place at all. You live in this cocoon, this bubble, and rock 'n' roll bands all complain about that, particularly those gruelling tours of America city hopping every day. You get into this hotel room, gig, plane, hotel room, gig, plane… and after a while it drives you a bit mad. And also, you're all locked together which does create tensions. So, the idea of the inside cover was simply to give this sense of air travel – with all these little lines showing little airplanes in all different colours – to give this sense of being trapped within this framework, this wire cage of air travel. On seeing this shot, Graham Gouldman exclaimed: 'Said in one picture what it was like to be on tour'."

The finishing touches to the sleeve were completed with George Hardie's graphics including what would become a new 10cc logo, using a star within the zero of the band's name. A giant neon version would be made for the group to use on their forthcoming world tour.

With the album completed, Stewart and Gouldman took the opportunity to upgrade Strawberry South to make it even more attractive for outside bookings. "We took out a loan to extend the studio and make it bigger," says Stewart. "We also built sleeping accommodation upstairs."

The first group to use the studio were Manchester band Sad Café, who had formed from the ashes of Mandalaband and gone on to release two albums without any major commercial success. Having signed a management deal with Harvey Lisberg, they had engaged Eric Stewart's services as producer to help deliver their commercial breakthrough. Stewart's connections with the group could be traced back even further than their Mandalaband days to his time with The Mindbenders. "At that time I admired a singer called Paul Young, then in a band called The Toggery Five," says Stewart. "He became lead singer with Sad Café, who eventually asked me to produce their records."

As recording of Sad Café's new album began at Strawberry South in July 1978, initial signs did not bode well. "We started working on the album and a strange thing started happening," says Stewart. "One by one, each member of the band came up to me in the control room when the others were elsewhere and said, 'I think we should do the song like this.' After a few days, I sat them all down and said, 'Look, I can't work like this, with each of you coming to me separately with different views on how we should tackle the material. I'm producing this album. Let me get on and produce it!' After that it worked out really well."

Aside from Young's vocal talents, Stewart was also impressed with the band's keyboard player, Vic Emerson, and would enlist his services on future projects. The sessions resulted in the *Facades* album, and among its highlights was the ballad Every Day Hurts, which Stewart felt would make a strong single. The album would be the start of a series of projects involving production and film work that Stewart and Gouldman would undertake, independently, outside of 10cc over the coming years. Other members of the band would also be free to work on extracurricular projects once they'd completed their 10cc commitments. Having worked on Kate Bush's debut album before joining the band, Duncan Mackay would continue to work with Bush, performing on her *Lionheart* album that summer.

That year the Strawberry empire was set to expand further with the opening of a third studio, Strawberry Mastering, designed to be one of the most advanced mastering facilities in the world. Located at 30 Strutton Ground in Westminster, London, the facility opened its doors during the summer of 1978 with the slogan 'Strawberry's for Afters'. Melvyn Abrahams, who had mastered 10cc's previous records and scratched his name on the run-out vinyl of most of them, was appointed managing director of the new venture. One of the first albums to benefit from Strawberry's fruits was 10cc's *Bloody Tourists*, but over the coming years Strawberry Mastering would be used to master albums by the likes of Led Zeppelin, Eric Clapton, Electric Light Orchestra, The Eagles, The Jam, The Cure, Elvis Costello, New Order, Prince, Dire Straits, The Pretenders, Roxy Music, Rod Stewart and their former bandmates Godley and Creme.

With the Sad Café project completed, the 10cc machine was being geared up again, with Dreadlock Holiday – chosen ahead of I Don't Like Cricket as the title for the song – released on July 21 as the band's next single, with a non-album track, Nothing Can Move Me, on the b-side. The single received good reviews.

"Dreadlock Holiday is a worthy addition to the long line of classic singles to have gone out under the 10cc banner," wrote Colin Irwin in *Melody Maker*. "It's got a fairly authentic reggae beat and even the lyrics mark a return to their former high quality tongue-in-cheek style said *Record Mirror*.

The group made a video, directed by Storm Thorgerson, with the less-than-tropical setting of the Dorset coast near Charmouth standing in, unconvincingly, for the Caribbean. The video received its premiere on the *Kenny Everett Video Show* on August 7.

At first, however, the prospects of a hit didn't look good.

"For two weeks nobody wanted to play the song," says Stewart. "Then suddenly it's a complete switch. Everybody turned around and said, 'Wow! What a great record!' and it sold half a million copies in four weeks."

With the record entering the Top 20, the call came to appear on *Top of the Pops*. 10cc had either been touring or recording when their last three hit singles had charted and so promotional films had been shown rather than the band appearing in person in the studio. As the first single with the new line-up it was a great opportunity to present the identity of the band to the British public. The appearance helped Dreadlock Holiday into the UK Top 10, where it would spend the next seven weeks. With the record still climbing the chart, *Bloody Tourists* was released by Phonogram on September 8.

"Stewart and Gouldman miss the adventure of Godley and Creme but like all good tourists you don't need too much adventure to have a damn good holiday," said *Record Mirror*, giving the album a four-star rating. The review was particularly complimentary about the album's closing track: "Everything You Wanted To Know About!!! is absolutely superb, with the hard sound of the 10cc guitar and the striving backbeat of the drums, into quiet harmonies and then back to the cutting guitar chords, harsh but harmonious."

Hugh Fielder in *Sounds* commented that 10cc had "got back to something approaching their former reputation with *Bloody Tourists*. Both Shock On The Tube and The Anonymous Alcoholic are clever and incisive and up at the top you get the odd 10cc gem. Dreadlock Holiday is one of them. I don't like it, I love it. The other classic is Everything You Wanted To Know About!!! which is a tough, brittle little rocker concerning a young man's first lay. Not exactly a novel topic but it's handled with genial talent, the words racing the melody line all the way through."

New Musical Express was less impressed. "Cool, sophisticated pop remains the core of the group's music," wrote Graham Lock. "You notice I say core and not heart. 10cc have been consistently accused of sounding contrived, soulless, artificial and *Bloody Tourists* has exactly these flaws. There are the customary lush harmonies, soothing vocals, and tantalising hints of gorgeous tunes that flit in and out of the convoluted structures and technical polish. They never had a lot to say, but now they insist on saying nothing in as many different and intricate ways as they can think of."

Melody Maker wasn't overly impressed either. "*Bloody Tourists* is a good, solid pop album," wrote Harry Doherty. "It signals the end of 10cc as a threat to the elite establishment and the beginning of them as a masses band."

Former bandmates Kevin Godley and Lol Creme seemed to share this view. "I've heard *Bloody Tourists* and it's great for what it is," said Godley at the time. "It just doesn't happen to be my kind of music."

Despite the frosty column inches, Kevin Godley kept in touch with his erstwhile colleagues. "We saw Kev the other night," said Stewart at the time. "We had a good old rap, you know. He's all right. We're okay. He's pleased for our success and we're highly disappointed about *Consequences'* lack of success because we know the amount of work that went into it. The only thing they lack is a producer to control them. There's a massive talent there but you've got to harness it in some way."

Some critics felt that the lyrics on *Bloody Tourists* carried a lot less weight than they had on previous 10cc albums. "Well, the subject matter's different," said Gouldman at the time. "We're not in a particularly cynical mood, at the moment. If every album we did was a cynical album, I think people would get bored with that. There are so many sides to 10cc, and I don't think we've ever repeated ourselves. Every record could possibly be by a different band, in a way."

Eric Stewart was less diplomatic: "You get in this strange situation, where you release two or three albums and the media start pushing you down as a cynical band. You release an album that isn't cynical and they say, 'What happened to the old cynicism 10cc used to have?' I mean you just can't win, it's a pile of shit. We've never been downright doomy and depressive about anything. I think that since the group split it's been a very positive direction all the way, being up."

What *Bloody Tourists* did have in abundance was warmth. Each track was beautifully recorded and featured some of Stewart's finest vocal performances to date. *Bloody Tourists* was unashamedly a pop album and a very good one at that. There were no pretensions to it being *The Original Soundtrack Part 2*. As such it marked a sensible move with the times, given the prevailing musical climate of the day.

"There's a lot more experimentation on *The Original Soundtrack,*" agreed Gouldman at the time. "I'm not going to defend us, all I'll say is that we don't consciously say, 'Let's make a commercial album that's gonna sell 5 million,' we just write the songs we feel like writing, that's all. It's coincidence that it works out that it's commercial; some people like commercial and some don't, but we're perfectly honest with ourselves, we just write what we want to write and if we want to write long drawn-out pieces on the next album then we'll do exactly that. We've always done what we've wanted to do and we've never said, 'Right, now the record sales have gone down in this area and that area we must look at the charts and see what's happening and copy this and that.' We've never done that."

The pair also stressed that there was still a great deal of experimentation in the studio.

"We still work the same way in the studio, we still experiment to the same degree as we always did," said Stewart. "Maybe the music has become more acceptable these days and maybe some critics don't think we're experimenting as much as we did, but we do. We spend a lot of time because every track has got to sound different to us. We do agree that this album is more immediate."

Proving that the band couldn't win, other critics censured them for still overgilding the lily and dubbed them the 'Professors of Pop'.

"That nickname is meant to be derogatory, but I consider it a great compliment," said Stewart. "We do analyse, we do create in a very technical way. Our aim is to achieve perfection."

Commercially, *Bloody Tourists* was a huge success. It entered the UK album charts at No.8 and would peak at No.3 as part of a 15-week chart run, earning the band another gold disc. To promote the album around the globe, 10cc were set to embark on their biggest world tour to date, an eight-month jaunt taking in over 70 concerts in Europe, America, Canada, Australia and Japan. Rehearsals began at Shepperton Studios in August, with the new show drawing heavily from *Bloody Tourists*, with 10 of the 12 tracks getting an airing.

"We will be doing most of the new album, all the obvious hit singles and a few of our favourite album tracks," said Gouldman.

Again, the group only played songs from the pre-split days that featured Stewart and Gouldman as writers. In fact, of the 17 songs that featured in their new set, only five were from the pre-split era, demonstrating how self-sufficient the new line-up had become in only two years. One song getting a makeover in rehearsals was Art For Art's Sake, which was extended to over 12 minutes through a new coda that gave Rick Fenn and Duncan Mackay the opportunity for solos, and featured Gouldman on lead vocal. Mackay's playing style was very different to that of Tony O'Malley. While O'Malley's style was soulful and based primarily around piano and organ,

Mackay's was more intricate and saw him utilising a range of different keyboards, including the Yamaha CS80 polyphonic synthesizer, to add colour and texture.

10cc's live show eschewed the growing trend for onstage gimmicks such as lasers in their stage act.

"We like visuals to enhance rather than take over," said Gouldman at the time. "You can overdo it. People come away from our concerts saying it was great music rather than saying, 'Weren't the lights terrific?' Our lights are there just as a background to us. They're not on a par or ahead of us."

However, the band did employ the talents of Kenny Everett to introduce them on stage via a short burst of film. With footage of Concorde being projected onto a giant screen, Everett's voice-over delivered a unique take on the pilot's traditional pre-flight announcement: *Attention please! Good evening, ladies and gentlemen, the brain now leaving Platform One is yours. Please fasten your safety belt and extinguish all lighted substances. Our hostesses will be passing amongst you throughout the trip to fondle your doobries and if you look under your seats you will notice the legs of the person behind you. We wish you a pleasant trip and welcome you to 10cc.*

On stage the band continued the 'bloody tourists' theme by playing in front of a palm-fringed backdrop, on sand-coloured carpet, while the tour programme was branded 'The Official Tourist Guide'. A variation of the *Bloody Tourists* album cover, showing a driver with a map obscuring his view, was shot by Hipgnosis for the tour programme. Look carefully and you'll see it's a map of the UK, with the cities on 10cc's itinerary circled.

The band's world tour kicked off in Stockholm on August 25 and was set to run through until March 28 in Tokyo. 10cc's popularity now meant they could fill huge venues such as the Stockholm Ice Stadium, Gothenburg Scandinavium and Copenhagen Idrætsparken. Their new album and single took the band's success to new levels across much of the world. In the Netherlands, Dreadlock Holiday spent four weeks at No.1 as part of a 17-week chart run, going on to become the fifth bestselling single of the year. It was also No.1 in Belgium and New Zealand, No.2 in Australia and Ireland, No.3 in France, No.5 in Switzerland, No.7 in Norway, No.11 in Germany – where it spent 23 weeks in the chart – No.16 in Sweden and No.18 in Austria. *Bloody Tourists* was equally successful. In the Netherlands, the album reached No.2, gaining a platinum disc in recognition of over 100,000 copies sold. In Sweden, the album hit No.3 and went gold, as it did in Denmark. In Norway, it peaked at No.4 and spent 16 weeks in the Top 10 alone.

Back on the road, Stewart and Gouldman proved once again to be the antithesis of your average rock 'n' roller.

"Neither of us has ever gone out with Britt Ekland," joked Stewart. "We do wreck hotel rooms when we're on the road but normally we phone ahead and book one specially. It seems the decent thing to do, and that way the hotel manager often joins in and has a bit of fun as well. It's difficult coming down from being onstage, especially as now we feel like 15cc."

Variations on this old 10cc in-joke came thick and fast every time the band hit the road.

"We don't smash hotels, we redecorate them. It's one of our hobbies," joked Gouldman.

Underneath it all, Stewart and Gouldman's approach was very businesslike.

"We try to put everything we've done back into the business one way or another," said Stewart. "We don't retire to the South of France in a million-pound villa and all that. We try to put it back into the business. The studio in Stockport, as well as helping us, was to help other musicians who, like us, were getting fed up with having to go down to London and having to pay London prices for studio time. We want to do other things. But the priority will still always be 10cc."

The UK leg of the tour comprised 19 concerts at 11 venues around the country, performing to a combined audience of more than 100,000 people. The tour opened at the Liverpool Empire on September 3, to rave reviews.

"Whatever the reservations about 10cc's new album *Bloody Tourists*, there's immense gratification in the way they've applied themselves to stage performance," wrote Colin Irwin, reviewing the concert in *Melody Maker*. "It's two years since the 'Gizmo' chopped them in half, and while the loss of Creme and Godley has inevitably denied them much of their inspired flair, the new line-up has learned to communicate with warmth in a way that the old band, born and bred in the studio, never achieved. Liverpool reacted with ecstatic enthusiasm to the opening night of the band's second tour since the change ... two hours, ten minutes that included a few fraught moments yet ultimate triumph. Another opening, another show. Liverpool was impressed."

After Liverpool, the tour took in three nights in Birmingham – where Stewart's "guitar playing sparkled and his voice was in great shape", according to Hugh Fielder in *Sounds* – and three nights in Manchester, before culminating with two sell-out nights at London's vast Wembley Arena. The gigs confirmed their status as one of the UK's biggest bands but also gave ammunition to critics who wanted to accuse 10cc of selling out.

"A band of this size with this equipment and crew is really expensive to keep on the road," said Gouldman at the time. "We want to get to as many places as possible, so we have to play bigger venues. The implication has been that the bigger you get the more bland, the more middle-of-the-road, the more commercial you become. But these things happen. The Beatles were worldwide great. I'm not comparing us to The Beatles in any way, but there's a very high-quality musical band that just appealed to everybody and nobody criticised them for it. I do detect a certain dislike of big bands. The only meter you've got for your success is that the box offices are full and that your records are constantly gold records."

The two concerts at Wembley Arena coincided with Dreadlock Holiday reaching No.1 in the UK singles chart. With *Bloody Tourists* riding high in the album charts, the gigs concluded a truly memorable week for the band, a return to the peak of success that 10cc had enjoyed during the summer of 1975.

"With *Bloody Tourists* we were on the crest of a wave again," says Stewart. "We were up there at the top once again."

To cap it all the London gigs went well.

"You can touch the magic tonight," enthused Eric Stewart at the first of the Wembley shows.

Karl Dallas, reviewing the concert for *Melody Maker*, seemed to agree.

"Sometimes, if it doesn't break it, a split can make a group. One thinks of Genesis, who have moved to occupancy of the centre of the world stage since they seemingly lost their most creative talent. And 10cc, divided in two, seem to have achieved a similar break through the barrier. Of course, one must acknowledge that a lot of what made 10cc so appealing – the ability of Messrs Stewart and Gouldman to produce pop for the thinking man, lyrics and tunes with easily identifiable hooks that make for chart success, plus un-expected twists and turns which repay more careful listening in tranquillity – is still with the band."

The band's second Wembley gig was interrupted when Kenny Everett walked on to the stage pushing a wheelbarrow full of gold discs for Dreadlock Holiday and *Bloody Tourists*, which he pre-sented to the band. With 10cc riding a peak of success across Europe, the band now set their sights on finally replicating that success in America.

CHAPTER 19

SPEED KILLS

THREE YEARS ON FROM THEIR LAST VISIT, 10CC WERE STILL KEEN TO break America, although their past experiences had left them wondering what they had to do to succeed there. "We've toured there, played good gigs, gotten tremendous reviews but we just can't break that bloody market," said Stewart shortly before the tour. "We'll release a single that goes to No.1 and then nine months later we're cold." Despite this, the band believed that they had perhaps their best chance of success this time around.

"There's always a pressure to break the American market and I think with this album we've got a good chance," said Stewart. "For the first time we've timed it so that it'll be out in America six weeks before we get there. In the past we've actually released the album four weeks after we've gone."

Having been disappointed with the support that Mercury had given *Deceptive Bends* in America – "Mercury poisoning," as Gouldman joked – 10cc had signed a new record deal in the US with Polydor, whose responsibility it was to push *Bloody Tourists*.

"We've changed record companies in America because we thought we weren't having the success we deserved," said Stewart. "So we're with Polydor now; we are also distributed over there by RSO who are really hot at the moment. So, we're hoping that their distribution, the new record company, the new album, which we feel is very 'up' and immediate, we hope all these factors will contribute to us cracking the American market."

With Polydor's support, the band had high hopes that America would finally succumb to their charms. *Bloody Tourists* seemed more in tune with the American market and gained very good reviews. *Trouser Press* described it as: "Warmer, fuller, and more convincing than anything 10cc has done before. Their ceaseless appropriation of every pop idiom imaginable is no longer mere cleverness, but an effective use of sonic expertise. Although *Bloody Tourists* may not rival *Some Girls* or Muhammad Ali for comebacks, it does signal the resurgence and metamorphosis of a bloody good band." *Circus* were equally impressed: "A spirited collection of pure pop and roll un-cluttered by the defiantly experimental high jinks of founding but now departed members Kevin Godley and Lol Creme. The sonic subtleties of For You and I, a majestically atmospheric ballad, and Take These Chains recall both the classic *Sheet Music* and the first post-Godley and Creme album *Deceptive Bends*." *Billboard* said the album "ranks as the group's most stimulating in some time. The tracks combine clever hard-edged rock with a melodic base and in-telligent lyrics. Most cuts display 10cc's wry sense of humour which cuts through the superb vocal and instrumental passages. A very tasty package."

The logistics of getting 10cc's gear across the Atlantic for their North American tour was a feat in itself. Nine tons of equipment – including two drum kits, nine guitars, seven keyboards, 35 micro-phones, two mixing desks, not to mention miles of cable – was packed into a 40-foot-long container at Strawberry Studios in Stockport by Zeb White and the band's roadies. It was then taken by road and loaded onto the container vessel *Manchester Courage* and shipped to Montreal, where it was taken by road to Winnipeg and unloaded at the Playhouse Theatre, where the band was based for several days of rehearsals.

While their equipment was en route, there were some encour-aging signs from across the Atlantic. Dreadlock Holiday entered the American and Canadian singles charts, while For You and I was chosen as the theme song to the film *Moment by Moment*, starring John Travolta – white hot after the twin successes of *Saturday Night Fever* and *Grease* – which was due to open a couple of weeks before Christmas.

The North American tour opened at the Winnipeg Arena on October 16 in front of 7,000 fans. It was a great start, followed by arena dates in Edmonton and Calgary, helping Dreadlock Holiday into the Canadian Top 30 and *Bloody Tourists* to become the band's biggest-selling album in Canada, where it was awarded a platinum disc. As 10cc played its first dates in the US, Dreadlock

Holiday was sitting at No.60 in the singles chart and climbing. In Phoenix, Arizona, the band had a visitor in their dressing room after their show at the Symphony Hall.

"There was a knock on the door and we opened it and there was Billy Joel standing there," recalls Stuart Tosh. "He came to, not apologise, but to say he kind of used I'm Not In Love on his track Just The Way You Are."

Joel, and legendary producer Phil Ramone, had borrowed the vocal technique from I'm Not In Love on Joel's breakthrough hit Just The Way You Are, which had reached No.3 in the US the previous year and would go on to be voted 'Record of the Year' and 'Song of the Year' at the 1979 Grammys.

As the tour crossed America, the band gained good critical reviews. One of the highlights was their gig at the Uptown Theater in Kansas City, where 10cc had enjoyed strong airplay – with Dreadlock Holiday reaching No.2 on KBEQ's airplay chart and *Bloody Tourists* peaking at No.4.

"All in all it represented a major advance in 10cc's mastery of the stage, as they tightened the pace by phasing out medium-tempo and off-beat numbers, filled out arrangements that once seemed thin and explored their freedom to toy with their stage sound. It's noisy and exuberant," wrote *Trouser Press* of the band's concert in Kansas City. "We're tighter, stronger, more powerful," agreed Stewart at the time.

Yet there was a growing feeling that the band was treading water in the US. The tour saw them playing in the same-sized auditoriums as on their last tour three years previously. Back at the Santa Monica Civic Center, they gained mixed reviews. *Cashbox* gave them a great review saying that they had "won the hearts of a sell-out crowd with its tight musicianship and its well crafted songs … Together they are one of the most entertaining rock outfits touring, able to blend cleverly or stand out on thoughtful solos."

The Los Angeles Times was less positive: "10cc's basic strength and appeal are as writers, arrangers and to a degree performers of a distinctive brand of rock. But Wednesday they seemed to fancy themselves supreme instrumentalists, offering a numbing array of atmospheric excursions. With all the captivating elements at its disposal – the range of styles it employs is breathtaking, Stewart's McCartneyesque voice is charming, its wit is sharp and literate, the arrangements are wonderfully versatile – this approach should serve as nothing more than an occasional change of pace."

Moreover, some of the dates on the tour failed to sell out, indicating that, if anything, 10cc's career was going backwards in the US. Stewart failed to hide his frustration when the band played to a half-full audience at New York's Palladium Theater.

"I hope all *three* of you enjoyed the show," said Stewart sarcastically towards the end of the gig.

"Although obviously disappointed with the low turnout 10cc went out with a bang of an encore," wrote *Billboard*. "A true show stopper, The Second Sitting For The Last Supper exploded with jackhammer intensity and brought the night to an impressive end."

To make matters worse, radio stations weren't picking up on Dreadlock Holiday in sufficient numbers to prevent it from stalling prematurely at No.44 in the American charts. 10cc had fallen victim to the radio-programming set-up in the US where radio stations played specific types of music. 10cc were technically a 'rock' band, with a 'reggae' single, thus falling between two stools. The failure of Dreadlock Holiday was repeated with *Bloody Tourists*, which peaked at a lowly No.69 in the US charts, despite the good reviews, the support of Polydor and RSO, and the tour.

Once again, 10cc had failed to break America. This time, Stewart and Gouldman decided that enough was enough. "You had that silly thing where just over the border in Canada we had a hit with Dreadlock Holiday, but back in the States we couldn't get a sniff," says Stewart. "We were so pissed off with the reaction that we went back to England to lick our wounds and said, 'Forget America, let's concentrate on Europe.' And we concentrated on every other market apart from America after that, and it was a mistake in the long run because we had massive success in virtually every other country. It's a market that I feel 10cc should have cracked. It's a regret personally that we didn't pursue it, but we couldn't really tailor the music for them. They said, 'You've really got to live there – go and do a tax year,' but I thought, 'Sod that! I've worked all my life to settle down here! I'm not going to be kicked out of the country.'"

At least the tour ended on a high note back on Canadian soil. The band's appearance at the Civic Centre indoor arena helped lift Dreadlock Holiday up to the No.1 spot in Ottawa's Top 30. The tour concluded with arena gigs at the Toronto Maple Leaf Gardens Concert Bowl and the Montreal Concert Bowl at The Forum, where the band played to an audience of 9,000 people. The concert was recorded for the *King Biscuit Flower Hour* and a handful of tracks would later surface on the bootleg *Cold Outside, Warm In Here*. At the hotel after the gig, the traditional end-of-tour party was in full swing.

"We had a bit of a party back at the hotel," recalls Zeb White. "For some reason, people started throwing glasses of water at each other. After a while, the glasses of water became ice buckets filled with water. The next thing we knew, a full fire hydrant had gone off which flooded two floors of the hotel! In the middle of the night they had to evacuate the next two floors of the hotel as well because water was seeping through. It was quite funny because we were all English apart from the American tour manager Jim Sullivan. When the police asked, 'Who's in charge here?' everyone pointed at Jim and said, 'He is!' So he got dragged off and the next day we just got the hell out the country!"

Around the world Phonogram had chosen different tracks from *Bloody Tourists* as follow-up singles to Dreadlock Holiday. For You and I would become a minor hit in the US and Canada, and From Rochdale To Ocho Rios a minor hit in Australia, yet neither succeeded in emulating the global success of its predecessor. The same fate awaited Reds In My Bed, which was the choice of follow-up single in the UK, despite the support of a video filmed during their recent stay in Los Angeles which was deemed too controversial to receive many showings on TV.

The anti-Communist Reds In My Bed probably didn't go down too well behind the Iron Curtain. Yet it was unlikely that many would have noticed, given that 10cc's records were allegedly banned in the Soviet Union on the grounds that the band were "neo-fascists." The rationale for this was supposedly a result of the English letter "c" being equivalent to the letter "s" in Russian and Ukrainian. This meant that "cc" was pronounced "ess ess", leading the Komsomol to believe that "Ten SS" somehow referred to Hitler's secret police.

Ironically, 10cc were themselves behind the Iron Curtain at the time, filming a 90-minute TV special for Polish television in Warsaw. "It's supposed to be syndicated throughout the Eastern bloc," said Stewart at the time. "It will be fantastic if it is!"

The experience of shooting the TV special proved to be quite surreal. "Right from the outset – the Aeroflot flight over there – it was like going back in time," recalls Rick Fenn. "It was a very bleak place though it was very impressive how they'd rebuilt Old Warsaw. But it was cold and grey and the first time I'd seen that divide between the 'proles' and the 'elite'. In our hotel there were 'dollar shops' where you could buy anything, but the shops and department stores outside were post-apocalypse. Long queues on the street where people didn't even know what they were queuing for. The director of the TV show had us all over to his home for dinner where we probably ate his year's supply of meat. We certainly drank his year's supply of vodka and reeled back to the hotel in a terrible state. The next day – filming day – we all had the worst hangovers any of us can remember."

Despite the hangovers, filming progressed well, at least until the director asked for a costume change. "At a certain point in the filming we were asked if we would wear black polo-necked sweaters," recalls Fenn. "First we thought they wanted to film our heads and somehow 'float' them in but it soon dawned on me that they hadn't really caught up with that sort of technology and I had to convince Eric and Graham, with some difficulty, that actually, they just wanted us to look like their idea of a pop band which was something from the mid-60s. Matching polo necks. Freddie and The Dreamers. We put a stop to that."

On their return home, 10cc had been lined up to play a prestigious one-off concert for the BBC's annual *Old Grey Whistle Test* Christmas TV and radio broadcast. The gig, on December 22 at London's Wembley Conference Centre, was due to be filmed, with edited highlights broadcast simultaneously on BBC2 and Radio One between 10.05pm and 11.00pm on Christmas Eve, introduced by Annie Nightingale. However, as the gig approached, there were fears that the threat of industrial strike action from a BBC technicians dispute may disrupt filming. The band decided to press on regardless, even when the two-day strike went ahead on December

21 and 22, meaning that the show wasn't filmed. Despite this, 10cc's gig at Wembley that night was a great success, with many in the band believing it to be one of the best concerts they had ever played. Critics seemed to agree. "The more I think about it, the more 10cc both musically and conceptually seem set to become the Pink Floyd of the 80s," wrote Mike Nicholls in *Record Mirror*. "While the last few albums have shown an increasing preoccupation with lyrical themes, technically they have also reached a degree of clinical perfection unimaginable when Lol Creme and Kevin Godley were in the band."

BBC Radio One broadcast an hour-long 10cc special on Christmas Eve, hosted by Andy Peebles, in place of the originally scheduled Wembley show. As the year came to an end, there was much cause for positivity in the 10cc camp. While the musical direction of the band was less experimental than the original line-up, Eric Stewart and Graham Gouldman had steered 10cc towards even greater commercial success. As 10cc broke for Christmas, the whole of 1979 was mapped out for them. Eric Stewart would mix Sad Café's *Facades* album at Strawberry South in January and then he and Graham Gouldman would make a special guest appearance at London's Royal Albert Hall on January 30 to perform I'm Not In Love with the London Symphony Orchestra in support of their platinum-selling *Classic Rock* album. 10cc would then travel to Leysin in Switzerland in mid-February to appear as guests of Abba in a TV special that was to be filmed by the BBC and broadcast globally that Easter. Subsequently, the band would embark on the Australian leg of their world tour, where they'd just enjoyed their biggest-selling single and album, with Dreadlock Holiday reaching No.2 – as part of a 19-week chart run – and *Bloody Tourists* reaching No.3. Then 10cc would play six dates in Japan, concluding at Tokyo's Sun Plaza Hall on 28th March. There was also talk of more dates in the US in the spring.

After their world tour, 10cc were lined up to write and record the soundtrack to the animated feature film *Animalympics*, due for release the following summer to coincide with the 1980 Olympic Games. 10cc were also due to appear in a film themselves, a movie called *Rock On*. "We're going to be stuck on Mount Fuji singing one of our songs," said Gouldman. "There's about 10 other bands in the film and rumour has it that Ken Russell is going to direct it."

On July 9, 1979, 10cc were scheduled to reconvene at Strawberry South to start work on their seventh studio album, to be completed by October for release early in 1980.

"It's going to be a very important album for us," said Gouldman at the time. "I'm really conscious of this 'commercial' thing that's been tagged onto us. We'll make a conscious effort to do something different. We've not consciously played it safe but looking back on it we have been commercial. I don't know why. It just happened that way. But I think it's a good time now to start looking to spread our wings again."

The rest of 10cc were equally enthused about the future.

"We've all sorts of interesting things in mind," said Stuart Tosh at the time. "There's so much potential in this band."

Sadly, that potential was about to be struck a savage blow. On the night of January 25, 1979, Eric Stewart was critically injured when his BMW 3.0 CSL sports car skidded on black ice and somersaulted off the road at Reigate Heath in Surrey.

"I'd been to a party at Duncan Mackay's house, had probably had a little too much to drink, and wasn't wearing a seat belt," recalls Stewart. "I'd dropped my wife, Gloria, at home and for some reason I was going to pop into the studio, although to this day I can't remember why. The road was extremely slippery but I wasn't driving fast at all. Going about 40 miles per hour, I went off the road. The car somersaulted and hit a wall. My head went through the windscreen and everything went black. Fortunately, a nurse had seen it happen. She saved my life by taking me quickly to a hospital and keeping me awake along the way. That evening, 40 cars went off the road on that same bend."

The fateful bend was ironically close to the stretch of road that had inspired the *Deceptive Bends* album title two years earlier. Stewart was taken to hospital at Redhill in Surrey.

"Eric is conscious and his condition is improving but we do not know yet the extent or seriousness of his injuries," said a spokesperson at the time. Stewart's injuries would turn out to be both extensive and serious and include a fractured skull, brain damage, a temporary loss of feeling down the left-hand side of his body and serious damage to his left eye and to the hearing in his left ear. The shocking news of the accident, and Stewart's injuries, slowly reached his bandmates.

"It is very upsetting and I don't want to talk about it," said Graham Gouldman at the time.

Alarmingly, at Redhill General Hospital, Stewart's condition worsened as it was discovered he was suffering from Stevens-Johnson syndrome – a reaction to the high dosage of sulphur-based antibiotics he had been given. "I had a violent allergic reaction to them," he recalls. "The antibiotics nearly killed me, not the accident! I definitely had a near-death experience. I felt very warm and safe and saw this bright light. I was drifting in and out of a coma. The very first thing I remember after coming around was a nurse leaning over me saying, 'Mr Stewart? Can you speak? There's a phone call for you.' She passed me the phone and a voice said, 'Eric? It's Paul.' I said, 'Paul? Paul who?' The voice said, 'Eric, it's Paul McCartney.' I couldn't remember anything. I said, 'Paul McCartney? That name seems familiar.' And all of a sudden, things started coming back to me. I said, 'Paul, how are you?' He said, 'Never mind how I am, how the hell are *you*?' We chatted and he asked if I fancied getting together, working with him, and right then, I'll never forget, I knew I was going to recover."

Understandably, the whole experience had a profound effect on Stewart's outlook on life. The following year, Stewart and his wife Gloria would welcome a second child, a son called Jody, into the world. In the meantime, news of Stewart's accident prompted Lol Creme to break the three-year silence between the two brothers-in-law.

"It was the first time that Lol and I had spoken since the split," says Stewart. "I told him that the reason I was so pissed off with him was because I hadn't wanted to see 10cc disbanded at a time when we were so successful. I said to him, 'I thought you were crazy and I was angry that you were damaging what I'd worked so hard to create with the studio. I couldn't talk to you after you ditched such a fantastic set-up.' But you can't carry around that sort of grudge forever, so we started talking again."

For 10cc, in the short term, the accident meant pulling out of the band's TV appearance with Abba – where they were replaced, at short notice, by Roxy Music – and the cancellation of their Australian and Japanese tours. And, in the medium term, a period of uncertainty, as it was unclear if Stewart would fully recover.

With the severity of Stewart's injuries unknown, Paul Burgess, Rick Fenn, Stuart Tosh and Duncan Mackay were all advised that 10cc was to be put on hold and it was suggested that they pursue solo projects. Burgess would work on a succession of Martin Hannett-produced albums with John Cooper Clarke (*Où est la Maison de Fromage?*; *Disguise In Love*; *Snap, Crackle and Bop*; *Zip Style Method*); Mackay would continue to work with Kate Bush (*Never For Ever*) and The Alan Parsons Project (*Eve*). Gouldman too sought solo work. One project allegedly saw him approached by Polydor to write a hit single for The Jam.

"There was one time with The Jam when the label started talking about getting the guy from 10cc to write a song for us because they thought we needed a single," recalls Paul Weller. "It was after *All Mod Cons*, when we hit a dip, and they were talking about us being dropped so they got 10cc to write a song for us. Luckily it was shit."

Gouldman was approached about writing the theme song to the upcoming Farrah Fawcett-Majors movie *Sunburn*, a project that didn't go down too well with Stewart.

"Graham visited me at home, where I was convalescing very groggily, three weeks after my car crash to see how I was getting on," recalls Stewart. "He mentioned that he was going to record the theme song to a film called *Sunburn*, which he did with the rest of the guys. I remember being a bit hurt thinking, 'That was quick. I've only been out of action for three weeks and he's in the studio without me.'"

On April 4, Gouldman began a three-day session at Strawberry South to record Sunburn, using Fenn, Burgess and Mackay as session musicians. When talk came of releasing the song as a single, it was suggested that it be done under the 10cc name.

"I got a call from Harvey saying that they wanted to release the record as a 10cc single," recalls Stewart. "That really pissed me off. I thought it was very opportunist. When I listened to the song I thought it was bloody awful. I phoned Harvey and said, 'You can't do this to me! You can't release this as a 10cc record!' So, it was released in Graham's name but the whole episode really hurt me."

The incident would serve to further fracture the relationship between Stewart and Gouldman. With Sunburn now scheduled for release as a solo single, Gouldman returned to Strawberry South on May 2 to record the b-side, Think About It, again with Fenn, Mackay and Burgess in support. The following day, the same musicians convened at the studio to shoot a video for the single, the footage from which would be interspersed with clips from the movie. Eric Stewart dropped into Strawberry South to say hello to the rest of the band while the video was being shot.

"Rick's jaw dropped to the floor when he saw me," recalls Stewart. "He threw his arms around me and said, 'Eric! You're okay! It's so good to see you!' It really cheered me up."

However, the experience soon turned sour. "When they started playing back the track I got this terrible pain in my head," says Stewart. "One, from the fact that the track was so bad, but more seriously from my left ear. It was at that point that I realised that I'd damaged my hearing in the accident."

Stewart would need an operation on his left ear, followed by a period of three months away from any kind of loud noise. "My doctor told me that if I wanted to recover I must stay away from racing cars and loud rock music," said Stewart. "When you consider I am a professional musician and my hobby is motor racing, you can imagine what kind of hell a restriction like that can be."

With Stewart convalescing, Gouldman's single Sunburn was released in June 1979 and started getting airplay. It entered the lower reaches of the singles chart a few weeks later, leading to an invitation to appear on *Top of the Pops*. "We did a pre-record, and were very excited because an appearance on *Top of the Pops* almost guaranteed a hit," says Gouldman. "We were waiting for the show to go out but then the Wimbledon coverage ran over, and the show never saw the light of day. I was devastated. No *Pops*... no hit!"

Sunburn stalled at No.52 in the UK but hit the Top 30 in Australia and the Top 40 in the Netherlands. While Stewart was out of action, it had been agreed that Graham Gouldman would write the soundtrack to the *Animalympics* film as a solo project.

"It was the first full-length feature film I'd ever done, and the soundtrack consisted of both instrumentals and pieces with words," says Gouldman. "I worked with a storyboard, which is basically a big book with pictures of every sequence, so you can take a look at that and devise the mood and the song immediately. It's a big help. And I would say to the director, 'If you could have any song in here, a song that exists, what would you have?' I was looking for clues basically. He would say, 'A Who song or a Beach Boys song' or whatever it was. And then I would just go away and write it. Working with cartoons is easier in a way, because if I'd written a song which was a few seconds over the allotted time, they would simply draw a few extra frames and extend that sequence."

Gouldman recorded the album at both Strawberry North and South in July 1979, again using Rick Fenn, Paul Burgess and Duncan Mackay of 10cc as session musicians. He then moved on to A&M Studios in Los Angeles to work on the orchestral parts, which were scored by movie soundtrack veteran Jimmy Haskell.

"I welcomed the opportunity of working in a different studio," said Gouldman at the time. "Having been involved in Strawberry Studios I tend to become a little insular about recording studios."

Of the 10 songs recorded for the project, the standout track was the poignant Love's Not For Me, a worthy addition to the Gouldman songbook, set to a simple acoustic guitar and accordion arrangement, the latter courtesy of old 10cc acquaintance Mike Timoney. Elsewhere, Gouldman experimented with African rhythms and chants on Kit Mambo and with synthesizers and sequencing on Bionic Boar, giving Duncan Mackay a field day with his keyboards. Less successful was disco workout Go For It, which was unlikely to have given Nile Rodgers and Bernard Edwards any sleepless nights at the time.

Gouldman's *Animalympics* soundtrack album was released by Phonogram in March 1980. Yet, while the cartoon animals in the movie competed for their sporting prizes, the real Olympic Games, due to open in Moscow on July 19, was in disarray. With 65 countries, including the US, boycotting the games because of the Soviet war in Afghanistan, the impact of the *Animalympics* movie was undermined. Although the film would premiere at the Miami Film Festival it would not get a domestic release. However, it did become successful on video and on TV.

Closer to home, life in the band had taken its toll on Gouldman's marriage to his wife Susan, which had irrevocably broken down.

"I was spending three-quarters of every year away from home," says Gouldman. "I had two marriages: to the band and to Susan. Later she said that if it had been another woman she'd have had something to fight against but she couldn't compete with the music. I was very depressed after the divorce and plunged myself into my work. But better to pick up a guitar than a bottle."

Fortunately, the divorce itself wasn't acrimonious.

"Luckily my children never saw a bitter side of divorce because it was very amicable and I stayed up north while they were young," says Gouldman.

The experience would inspire a number of new songs over the coming years, the first of which, I Hate To Eat Alone, would appear on the next 10cc album. In the meantime, the huge worldwide success of Dreadlock Holiday had earned Stewart and Gouldman another Ivor Novello Award nomination, for 'International Hit of the Year', although this time around they would lose out to The Bee Gees for Stayin' Alive.

As the new decade dawned, chart pundits were busy compiling lists of the bestselling singles, albums and artists of the 70s. Unsurprisingly, 10cc featured heavily throughout: *The Original Soundtrack* was among the UK's Top 100 bestselling albums of the 70s; 10cc were cited as one of the 10 most successful singles acts of the decade, estimated to have sold more singles in the UK than artists such as Elton John, David Bowie and Queen. I'm Not In Love continued to be voted the 'greatest single of all time' by the British public, coming top again in London's Capital Radio's annual 'Hall of Fame' poll. When Manchester's Piccadilly Radio marked their fifth birthday by presenting their top 261 records of all time, I'm Not In Love again topped the chart. 10cc also had two other songs in the Top 20 (I'm Mandy Fly Me at No.18 and Dreadlock Holiday at No.19), with The Things We Do For Love, The Wall Street Shuffle and Art For Art's Sake also in the list. It was interesting that all six of these 10cc songs were Stewart/Gouldman compositions.

With no new 10cc album in the pipeline, Phonogram planned to release a 'greatest hits' compilation. Once again, Hipgnosis were given the job of designing the sleeve.

"The manager, Ric Dixon, actually gave me the job over the phone," says Storm Thorgerson. "The lads, he said, were too busy to get involved. After all, it was a repackage, so it didn't warrant the same care and enthusiasm that a new album with new songs would. 'Do whatever you like and then convince the band that it's okay,' he said. So I thought about a collection of great hits, displayed visually."

The resulting design was crammed full of visual puns, playing with the idea of 'big hits' – a boxing glove, a Mafioso 'hit', a hammer, a bank job, *Titanic* hitting the iceberg, the assassination of Julius Caesar, William Tell's arrow hitting the apple, a sparrow killed at Lord's during a cricket match in 1936. Even the band themselves get in on the act, pretending to have a punch-up on the back cover. According to Thorgerson, designing the cover was "in some ways pure 10cc – taking a wry approach albeit a bit silly, verbally connected, pilfering history and lots of fun."

George Hardie was responsible for creating the layout using a combination of stock imagery and elements created specifically for the cover. The background image on the front cover was an old Victorian print of the state opening of parliament, hand-coloured in the bottom right and doctored to show Queen Victoria taking a swipe at Prince Albert. Hardie, and illustrators Jeff Cummins and Mick Brownfield, created some of the illustrations, while the *Titanic* was shot in a water tank at Shepperton Studios using polystyrene icebergs, and a bank in Mayfair was shot through a car window for the bank job image in black and white and then hand-coloured green. With Hardie leading most of the work, the Hipgnosis team, in their words, "stayed home and copped the money."

Released in September 1979, and supported by a £250,000 TV and poster advertising campaign – the former voiced by Kenny Everett with the strapline, continuing the 'big hit' theme, of 'Every track's a knockout' – *10cc's Greatest Hits 1972–1978* featured all 12 of the band's hit singles from Donna right through to Dreadlock Holiday, and received universally good reviews.

"Every track here is a gem," wrote Mike Nicholls in *Record Mirror*, giving the album a five-star rating. "This wackily packaged conglomerate stands as testimony to one of the greatest and certainly most creatively inspired pop-rock outfits of all time."

Harry Doherty was even more glowing in his praise in *Melody Maker*, and wrote, "A great album this: twelve songs, twelve hits. I can't think of any other contemporary group this decade who can claim such an achievement. 10cc's feats are numerous. They championed the short pop song at a time in the early 70s when it was decidedly unfashionable to do so ... then, not only were they content to produce songs with great hooks but dared fit them with a brand of lyrical expertise that was unique in itself. And so we have the definitive compilation, an album of daunting perfection."

As usual, the *New Musical Express* view was more jaundiced. "The one consistent element running through the present collection is their immaculate grasp of technique – always exact, almost exquisite, always precise. And often lifeless. The great risk in making music by artificial insemination is that if the hooks don't get ya then nothing else will. If 10cc never had pretensions to being anything but intelligently synthetic, always placing form before feel like pop scientists, then at least they began with an evil humour which made their music human."

Greatest Hits 1972–1978 returned 10cc to the UK Top 10, where it stayed for five weeks, reaching No.5 and remaining in the album charts for five months, eventually earning the band a platinum disc. With the album riding high in the charts, Eric Stewart's convalescence was further aided by the success of Sad Café's Every Day Hurts, the first single from *Facades*. Reaching No.3 in October 1979, the single would give Sad Café the commercial breakthrough they had been seeking and would go on to become one of the biggest hit singles of the year, selling over 600,000 copies. *Facades* would also make the UK Top 10, and go on to sell over 100,000 copies in the UK alone, spawning further hit singles in Strange Little Girl and the Rolling Stones pastiche My Oh My. Naturally enough, Stewart was signed up to produce the band's follow-up album.

In the meantime, with Gouldman working on his solo projects, Stewart was approached about projects of his own. French singer Mireille Mathieu sounded him out about producing her next album but, after an awkward meeting in Paris with Mathieu and her sister, Stewart demurred. While in Paris, Stewart met up with the French director Just Jaeckin, who was a huge fan of I'm Not In Love. He asked Stewart to write the soundtrack for his next film *Girls*. Stewart agreed, once he'd been convinced that it wasn't in the genre of Jaeckin's previous films.

"It's directed by the guy who did *Emmanuelle* and *The Story of O*, not that I'm moving into the soft porn market!" joked Stewart at the time. "It's a regular film called *Girls*, a sort of French *Saturday Night Fever*, broadly speaking. They want all the songs in English which is just as well; it would have been difficult writing them in French!"

Stewart would write much of the soundtrack with Duncan Mackay with a plan to record the music at Strawberry South in October and November, in parallel with 10cc's new album.

As Stewart and Gouldman contemplated the group's next move, they could feel content in the knowledge that 10cc's commercial success had gone from strength to strength under their guidance. The band's bestselling single and album worldwide had now been recorded post-split and, with Dreadlock Holiday, they had achieved 10cc's third UK No.1. And it was Stewart and Gouldman who had written the songs that appeared in radio stations' popularity polls, such as the six 10cc songs voted by Piccadilly Radio listeners in their Top 261. Unfortunately, Eric Stewart's near-fatal car crash had temporarily halted the band's progress, and the mid-to-longer-term effects of his injuries on his musical abilities remained, as yet, unknown.

CHAPTER 20

VIDEO KILLED THE RADIO STAR

THE FORTUNES OF 10CC MK II STOOD IN STARK CONTRAST TO THOSE OF
Kevin Godley and Lol Creme, whose career had failed to get off the
ground since leaving the band. "The years after 10cc felt a bit like
being in the wilderness," says Godley.

Disillusioned with the music business, the pair decided to dust
off their drawing skills having parked them for the past decade. "We
felt like retreating behind a couple of quiet drawing boards with
some Indian ink and doing something," says Godley. "The 'something' turned out to be an illustrated book, a parody of the rock 'n'
roll lifestyle featuring short stories and pen and ink observations of
the absurd world we'd inhabited for the last few years."

They would work on the book, to be titled *The Fun Starts Here*,
over the next two years. They'd also devise the sleeve concept for
the album *Turn of a Friendly Card* for the Alan Parsons Project.
Before resuming their own musical career, Godley and Creme produced and played on Mickey Jupp's album *Long Distance Romancer*
at Basing Street Studios. They would also produce a single for
Big Den and The Random Band, a cover version of Lee Dorsey's
1966 hit Working In The Coalmine. Now, having parted ways with
Mercury, Godley and Creme signed a new five-album deal with
Polydor Records. Their first album on their new label, *Freeze Frame*,
was once again recorded at Surrey Sound Studios in Leatherhead,
and featured some notable guest appearances, including Paul
McCartney.

"I asked him if he fancied being on a track," recalls Creme. "Before
I knew it, there he was; he came down to Surrey Sound and sang on
Get Well Soon. It was such a thrill."

Also appearing on the album was Roxy Music guitarist Phil
Manzanera, who the pair had worked with on his 801 project and

who lived up the road from Godley in Chertsey. Manzanera would later describe the duo as the two most brilliant musicians he'd ever worked with.

Sharing studio time with Godley and Creme at Surrey Sound were The Professionals, the group formed by Steve Jones and Paul Cook after the break up of The Sex Pistols. When they vacated the studio, Creme noticed that his vintage 1959 Les Paul 'Goldtop' guitar had gone missing. Jones, a self-confessed kleptomaniac, had stolen the guitar and sold it off to fund his heroin habit. "I was addicted to doing it," says Jones. "I didn't care who it was. I just had a mission."

Many years later, Jones would phone Lol Creme to apologise for his actions. "I've been straight for a long time now and one of the things I do is make amends to people I come across," says Jones. "I thought he would be upset, but he was thrilled that I was straight. Probably wasn't as thrilled when it happened."

The highlights of *Freeze Frame* were a handful of songs that would comfortably have sat on a 10cc album (Mugshots, Freeze Frame, Get Well Soon). As with *L*, Kevin Godley sang most of the lead vocals on the new album. "This was a weird transitional time for us, as Lol and I were in the middle of switching our musical personas," says Godley. "The front-line was stepping back to let the back-line up front because Lol wasn't into fronting anything anymore. He'd done his rock star tour of duty in the band and his head was more into recording and writing."

Elsewhere, the pair continued to innovate and experiment, albeit with mixed results. I Pity Inanimate Objects saw them experimenting with a vocal harmonizer. "We thought, 'What happens if I vocalise these words in a monotone – do an entire song on one note – and get Lol to play my vocal on the harmonizer keyboard?'," says Godley. The end result was technically impressive but ultimately pointless, being so discordant it was impossible to love. Another track, Brazilia, saw them adopt the approach they had attempted when recording the original version of People In Love with 10cc. "What we did with Brazilia was, after we made a simple rhythm track, each of us – including Phil Manzanera – would come in independently and record something we wanted to hear," says Godley. "I would go in one evening to tape my vocal bits and pieces, then Lol, and then Phil, with none of us hearing what the others had done. Then we played it all back to see what happened. The take that's on the album is it. Obviously with things that almost worked we had to slide them left or right a bit or clean out of sight. It's an interesting process, the element of chance."

It was an interesting experiment but it lacked cohesion and sounded disjointed and unfocused. There are some incredible moments but not enough to sustain interest over the song's six minutes. More coherent was An Englishman In New York, which explores the "madness and hypocrisy and contrast and extremes" of life in the Big Apple. The song was chosen as the lead single from the album but, sensing they were low down the pecking order of Polydor's promotional team, Godley and Creme came up with the idea of making a video to help promote it. They developed an eight-frame storyboard and sought finance from Polydor to make it. To their delight, Polydor agreed, on the proviso that they work along-side an established video director, Derek Burbidge. The one-day shoot for An Englishman In New York proved to be a life-changing experience for both of them.

"We were hooked," says Godley. "This video lark flicked a big switch in our brains. It was just as addictive as music, if not more so. We assimilated all the video and film basics we'd ever need on that one incredible, indelible day."

The post-production process marked the moment when they fully realised the potential of the new medium. "It was when we got in the edit suite that it all really came to life for us," recalls Creme. "It was like being in a recording studio – but for your eyes. That's when we looked at each other and said, 'We could have some fun here!'"

An Englishman In New York was a hit everywhere the video was shown, reaching No.4 in Belgium, No.7 in the Netherlands, No.25 in Germany and the Top 20 in Australia. It was a different story in the UK. Music with wit and intelligence was so out of favour that it seemed Godley and Creme couldn't get arrested. "This is a stun-ningly clever record, brilliantly arranged and bursting with verbal twists and little jokes," wrote *Smash Hits*. "I think I'll throw it in the bin."

The reviews of *Freeze Frame*, which was released in October 1979, were equally damning.

"Old enough, bored enough, cynical and uninspired enough to let their obsessive hailstorm of academic imagery completely cloud the remaining rags of their vision, Godley and Creme at last make a music to match," said *New Musical Express*. "It sounds something like this: endless stacks of freezer-fare noises, dehydrated, crunchy, flat and soulless; vocals force-fed through pitch modulators, strangled like rusting I-Speak-Your-Weight machines or fuzz-boxed to extinction; over-treated hunks of *Original Soundtrack*-type operetta, musicals, rambling acoustic guitar and anaemic rock 'n' roll. It's an odious racket, an expensive waste of time."

Without an obvious follow-up to An Englishman In New York on the album, Godley and Creme released a one-off single Wide Boy in April 1980 featuring Roxy Music's Andy Mackay on saxophone and Laurence Juber of Wings on guitar. Arguably one of their least characteristic songs, it appeared to be an attempt to sound like a New Wave record. In contrast, the accompanying video, again directed by the duo, was infinitely more interesting, featuring several groundbreaking visual techniques that had never been seen before. Having been impressed with their video work, fellow Polydor labelmate, Steve Strange was interested in creating a video for his band Visage's next single Fade To Grey.

"He asked the record company, 'Do you think Kev and Lol would do one of those promo films for my song?'," says Creme. "We said, 'We'd be delighted' and we did. And they gave us a budget of something like £2,000. But it got us started."

For two men whose childhood ambition had been to get into film, getting behind the camera was a dream come true. "For years we've wanted to make movies," said Creme at the time. "The song Somewhere In Hollywood on *Sheet Music* was about the frustration of not being able to make our own movies. That's why we had an album called *The Original Soundtrack*. We couldn't get behind a camera, but we did at least have access to a tape recorder. We have a need to express ourselves visually. That's why all the songs we did with 10cc were visual. We thought the more success we got as a band would make it easier to get into movies, but it doesn't work like that. The more success you have with a band, the more responsibilities you have to work with that band. So, in order to get into films, we realised one of the things we'd have to do was leave the group. So we did, but it still took us three or four years to get behind a camera."

The video for Fade To Grey worked well – helping the single become a Top 10 hit throughout Europe and as far afield as Australia and New Zealand – but, with the commercial value of videos still unproven, Polydor baulked when it was suggested that the pair make another video for Visage's follow-up single Mind of a Toy. "At that point record companies were sceptical about the value of these videos," recalls Creme. "They were saying, 'We're not sure that we want to spend any money on a new video for the next song.' And we said, 'I have to tell you that on Tuesday Visage were No.52 in the German charts but after they showed the video it's now No.2. And we got £12,000, I think, to do the next video."

The videos for Fade to Grey and Mind of a Toy helped promote the band's music to a wider audience with the latter earning Godley and Creme a 'Best Video' award at the very first UK Video Awards. To their delight, they were soon asked to direct videos for other artists, who felt more comfortable being directed by fellow musicians rather than directors from a conventional background. "Most of them had come from movies, TV or documentaries and acted like they were slumming it," says Godley. "They had no intuitive 'feel' for music let alone how musicians think. Acts began to approach us for all the above reasons and suddenly we had a whole new career."

Having worked on videos for the likes of Toyah (I Want To Be Free, Thunder In The Mountains), Joan Armatrading (The Weakness In Me, When I Get It Right) and Status Quo (Something 'Bout You Baby I Like), it was their next video for Duran Duran's Girls On Film that really put them on the map as directors. Filmed at Shepperton Studios on August 13, 1981, the video consciously courted controversy by featuring women in various states of undress acting out male fantasies including pillow fights and topless mud wrestling. It was all part of a master plan to get the band noticed. "We were very explicitly told by Duran Duran's management to make a very sensational and erotic piece that would be for clubs, where it would get shown uncensored just to make people take notice and talk about it," says Godley. "In the States at that time there were a number of clubs opening that had screens and music videos were being played on them. So, you didn't have to think about censorship. You could actually show stuff without having to worry about it too much."

The video also coincided with the launch of MTV in America on August 1, 1981, which would serve to step change the importance of music videos as a vehicle for artists to promote their new material. The video for Girls On Film was perfect for the new channel. "It had glamour, it had polish, it had sex, it had good-looking boys, it had girls sliding on poles," says Godley. "These were the ingredients that made it MTV-able."

For Godley and Creme, the opportunity to be in the vanguard of this new creative frontier was thrilling. "There were no rules about making videos," says Godley. "It was a very young industry. No one really knew what a video was supposed to be. So, we thought we could make it be anything we wanted it to be. It was tremendously exciting at the time."

They saw directing videos as an ideal stepping-stone to one day fulfilling their ambition of sitting in the director's chair of a movie. "From the outset we looked on promos as an apprenticeship," says Godley. "We were learning how to make films at other people's expense."

Ironically, just as their career as video directors was taking off, they finally enjoyed their first taste of chart success in the UK as a duo, five years on from quitting 10cc. After the commercial failure of their first three solo albums, Godley and Creme now found themselves with a big hit on their hands. They were in the middle of shooting a video for Toyah when someone told them that their new single, Under Your Thumb, was at No.30 in the charts. It was the first Godley and Creme composition to be a UK hit since 10cc's The Dean and I eight years previously. Given their lack of commercial success they hadn't got around to directing a video for their own single. So, when they got the call to appear on *Top of the Pops* later that week they found themselves making their first appearance on the show for four years. By the time they reappeared on the show two weeks later, Under Your Thumb was at No.6 in the charts and still climbing, eventually peaking at No.3 and spending four weeks in the UK Top 10. "That song was a fairly traditional writing system for us," says Creme. "I came out with some chords and at that point Kev automatically comes out with some words. And once you've got that clue, that 5% inspiration, the rest is hard graft. But you know the general direction because the tone of it is haunting and the mood of it suggested a ghost story."

Recording had taken place at a new 16-track studio built at Creme's home in Leatherhead, which he called Lymehouse Studios. Musically, the new album – which they called *Ismism* – saw them swapping their electric guitars and drum kits for synthesizers and drum machines, the latter partly the result of Godley suffering from a slipped disc at the time, which meant it was painful for him to play the drums and required him to programme his drum parts on a Linn drum machine.

"Lol would come and pick me up in his car and take me to the clinic to have acupuncture then I'd go back to his place and lie on the sofa," recalls Godley.

Godley's condition would also inspire some of their new songs, such as Snack Attack, which demonstrated that their ability to use wit and wordplay hadn't deserted them. "Eating was difficult," recalls Godley. "I was hungry and I couldn't eat anything – I was fantasising about food. I didn't know it would turn out as a spoken-word thing, but I had to do something. If I can't eat it, I'll write about eating it. Early rap/hip-hop? We were there – Rhythm and Jews."

The protagonist in the song is so hungry he will go to any lengths to satisfy his cravings, including selling his soul to the Devil for a T-bone steak. Elsewhere, there was a return to the pastiches of the early 10cc days with the Motown-flavoured Wedding Bells – complete with a clever lyric that is almost the inverse of Tracks Of My Tears as our hero decides his girl is not, in fact, the 'permanent one' – and the 50s send-up Sale of the Century. The pair's creative juices had begun to flow after a party at Kevin Godley's Tara House to celebrate his 35th birthday, where they had decided to secretly tape record the guests. They hit upon the idea of using what they had recorded as the backdrop to a new album. "It just seemed a good idea," said Creme. "You put on a party at a party and then you have a party! But in the end, we found we couldn't use the actual soundtrack from Kev's party, so we reconstructed it ourselves, using all the mannerisms. There are certain stereotypes that always go to parties – the pain in the arse telling us we should be doing something else, the two gays walking hand in hand ..."

In the end, the idea was condensed into one song, The Party. Typically inventive, the track contains a string of cameos from different guests at the party, including one who gives them some career advice, namely to forget about making videos and get back to writing hits such as '*I'm Not In Paris and The Dean and Me*'.

It was good but could have been brilliant had they had a producer to edit and focus the track, in the way Stewart and Gouldman used to in 10cc. You can imagine Gouldman pleading with his former colleagues to 'use the best bits' and bring in the song's chorus earlier than the five minute mark where Godley and Creme defiantly choose to introduce it. Still, such was the duo's enthusiasm that the rest of the tracks came together very quickly afterwards.

"I'm very happy with the whole album," said Creme. "It makes all the difference if you're enjoying yourself; all the best records to me are the ones where people seem to be enjoying it. You can feel it in the grooves. I enjoy listening to this album much more than I do some of the others."

Critics saw *Ismism* as a return to form for Godley and Creme, while the success of Under Your Thumb revived interest in the duo and helped the album into the Top 30. Godley and Creme's newfound success was ironic, given that they had been unmoved by the prospect of recording another album, wanting instead to concentrate on their new career as video directors.

"We were trying to get out of rock 'n' roll, we were concentrating on video," said Creme at the time. "But having this work in such an enjoyable way, it makes you want to try and get back. In a way, it's nicer than success with 10cc, because the band was trying to conform to an image in music and it became work, which is why we left. But it started out like this, doing it for fun, and then it took off."

Still, in interviews journalists couldn't help but ask the million-dollar question: had the duo ever regretted leaving 10cc? "No. Never. Not for one moment. I've never regretted anything," said Creme categorically.

Did they see much of Stewart and Gouldman these days?

"No, we haven't really kept in touch with the other guys," replied Creme. "I know what they've been doing but I didn't go to the gigs or anything. I wish everybody success. It's a much better climate when everybody's getting on with what they want to be doing. And we've been lucky. We took a massive cut financially when we left the band, but up to now everything we've done has been commercially successful except the music. Now that's successful too – it's like the icing on the cake."

Three-quarters of the original 10cc line-up were reunited briefly on BBC Radio One's *Round Table* programme, where Eric Stewart and Graham Gouldman were reviewing the week's new releases and were joined on the line by Kevin Godley after they'd reviewed Godley and Creme's next single, Wedding Bells. The song would give the duo another big hit, reaching No.7 in December, also breaking through in Ireland, the Netherlands and Australia, where it reached the Top 30.

In the meantime, The Boomtown Rats had asked Godley and Creme to produce their next album. Journalist Richard Williams had once written in *The Times* that The Boomtown Rats might turn out to be the "10cc of the 80s", although the band had not lived up to its early promise. Backing tracks were recorded at Ibiza Sound Studios with Godley and Creme at the helm, but the sessions didn't work out as well as planned.

"We just weren't on the same wavelength," recalls Godley. "The way they were used to working was completely different to us. We would tackle one track at a time, whereas they were used to putting loads of backing tracks down and working on top of them. It was down to different work practices more than anything else. We weren't producers as such. We were too focused on the craft as opposed to the feel, which is an issue, period. The thing about a good producer is that you have to get the best out of your act in the studio and take what they do and go with it to a certain extent. You can throw a few curve balls at them. But don't bring your own way of working to the studio because this isn't about you, it's about them. And I think we failed them in that respect."

Tony Visconti was drafted in to finish off the album, *V Deep*, which was finally released in April 1982. Marginally more successful was Godley and Creme's production of Blue Rondo A La Turk's single Klactoveesedstein, which was a minor hit that year. They also worked with Jona Lewie, producing and playing on the intriguingly titled album track Cream Jacqueline Strawberry.

Godley and Creme also finished work on *The Fun Starts Here: Out-takes from a Rock Memoir*. The book featured drawings and text satirising the rise and fall of a fictitious rock musician. It was a great opportunity to parody the world of rock 'n' roll and to put their art school training to good use. Any similarities with persons living or dead were, presumably, fully intentional – "From Manchester to the Hollywood Bowl, from lead guitar in Roy Brodkin and The Rapiers to a Major Rock award, from obscurity to plaster cast immortality in the Hall of Fame, his life was the ultimate rock and roll dream ... now Lol Creme and Kevin Godley reveal the inside story of a legend for today – a man whose career says everything there is to be said about the people, the music and the business of rock and roll. And every word might be true ..."

One of the drawings in the book shows superfan Corin, whose breasts have been signed by her rock star idols. Her right breast bears the autographs of Kev and Lol along with the likes of Jimi Hendrix and Dennis Wilson; her left breast bears two signatures, one is that of Paul McCartney, the other is in the handwriting of their former bandmate: *To Corin, Keep on suckin, love Eric. Xxx*

CHAPTER 21

ARE YOU NORMAL?

WHILE 10CC WERE PREPARING TO RE-ENTER STRAWBERRY SOUTH TO record their seventh album, their original studio in Stockport was proving to be a great asset for the next generation of Manchester bands. Many of these groups were signed to a new local independent label called Factory Records, co-founded by Tony Wilson, who often employed the talents of producer Martin Hannett.

"Why had those early Factory releases had that magical Hannett sound?," asked Wilson. "The young genius had been able to plug in his digital thingy into the outboard racks of a major world-class studio that was in Stockport – Stockport ladies and gentleman, Stockport, because 10cc were a Manchester band and they had taken the proceeds of the delicious I'm Not In Love and had reinvested in their home. Reinvested. Built a fuck-off studio. Respect. (Sorry about the Don't Like Cricket song, but otherwise, massive respect.)"

One of the first bands to sign to the label was Joy Division, who arrived at Strawberry in April 1979 to record their debut album, *Unknown Pleasures*, with Hannett producing.

"Tony Wilson always gave massive credit to 10cc for putting Strawberry in Stockport," says the band's Peter Hook. "The way he saw it, they'd reinvested the money they made from their music back into Manchester. He was right. Thanks to them we had one of the country's best studios on our doorstep, and we were pretty excited about it: our first foray into 24-track recording."

The recording sessions proved to be eventful. At one point in the proceedings, Hannett is said to have stood up on his chair claiming he could see a golden halo.

"It's a gold disc, Martin. 10cc, I'm Not In Love," pointed out Joy Division frontman, Ian Curtis.

"I'm not in 10cc, am I?" asked Hannett.

"No, Martin, you are in Stockport," replied Curtis.

A year later the band would return to Strawberry to record Love Will Tear Us Apart. The song's title was allegedly an ironic reference to Neil Sedaka's Love Will Keep Us Together, the original version of which, of course, had also been recorded at Strawberry, eight years earlier, with 10cc backing him. While Joy Division recorded the song, an up-and-coming Irish band dropped into Strawberry to meet up with Hannett. The band was U2 and they would return to Strawberry later that year to record their second single, 11 O'Clock Tick Tock. Twelve years later, they'd begin a long-standing creative relationship with Kevin Godley.

Meanwhile, in August 1979, 10cc started work on their seventh album at Strawberry South. It had been well over a year since the group had finished *Bloody Tourists* and, sadly, the long lay-off showed. "It took nearly a year, really, before we could work together again and it's amazing how quickly the wind can go out your sails," says Rick Fenn. "When the band reconvened somehow everything got knocked off-centre by Eric's terrible car accident. Obviously, Eric did but the whole band did too. It showed in the writing also. The spirit wasn't there when we were recording that album, I remember that quite well. It wasn't as good as before. That's just an opinion but it seems to be quite widely shared."

It would be hard to disagree with Fenn's assessment. A lot of the new material was simply not up to scratch. Maybe the need to write songs for a new 10cc album, as well as for two film projects, meant that their songwriting skills were spread too thinly? Perhaps the band were rushing back into the studio too quickly; after all, it was only six weeks later than they had originally planned to start recording their seventh album, despite Stewart's seven months of recuperation. Either way, new songs like Dressed to Kill were uncharacteristically nondescript. Even the group's better ideas weren't delivered with their usual aplomb. The idea behind Lovers Anonymous – an Alcoholics Anonymous organisation for people addicted to love – was inspired; but, frustratingly, Stewart and Gouldman failed to fully exploit the song's potential and compounded the felony by burying it in a bland arrangement. 10cc seemed to have their lost their mojo. "I remember things being a bit lacklustre," recalls Gouldman. "It was kind of like, 'It's not sparkly and bright anymore.' It had lost its magic. Maybe we should have stopped then or taken a year off or something."

Musically, the rapport that had contributed to the warmth of *Bloody Tourists* was far less evident this time around. The group weren't working as tightly as a unit as they had done on that album. Stuart Tosh, now living in New York, only contributed backing vocals to the sessions. More significantly, the impact of the fracturing relationship between Stewart and Gouldman cast a different atmosphere in the studio.

"When we reconvened it was tense," recalls Fenn. "There was a strange energy, a very different energy recording that album than *Bloody Tourists*, which was incredibly optimistic. I never talked about it with Eric but, looking back, I think he felt aggrieved that Graham launched himself into solo projects so soon after the accident and there was a bit of tit-for-tat going on. I think Eric saw this as Graham's megalomania. I don't believe it was anything of the sort. Graham just likes to work and he got offered nice jobs. We really had no idea how long Eric would be out of action. In fact, for a while, we didn't know for sure that he'd ever be back in action. It was a scary time. I wish Eric had talked it all out. We might have been able to clear the air, but the cloud hung over the making of the whole album."

Stewart and Gouldman also had differences of opinion over some of the new songs. "Graham was splitting up from his wife at the time and came into the studio with what I thought were very depressing songs, like How'm I Ever Gonna Say Goodbye and I Hate To Eat Alone," says Stewart. "I really didn't think we should record them as 10cc but they meant a lot to Graham, so they ended up on the album."

They might have ended up on the album but Stewart's involvement with both songs in the studio would be minimal, only contributing percussion to the latter, and nothing at all to the former, his absence put down to being 'out to lunch' in the accompanying liner notes. Despite Stewart's reservations, Gouldman's wistful I Hate To Eat Alone was arguably the best song on the album and one of 10cc's most autobiographical tracks to date.

Gouldman's observations on life after divorce were so well observed that they had to have been inspired by real-life events.

Stewart had brought in two new songs of his own to the sessions, I Took You Home and the standout Make The Pieces Fit, which ruminated on the mysteries of love in fine style. The band's recording of the latter featured great guitar work from Fenn, simple acoustic backing from Gouldman and a strong lead vocal performance from Stewart.

Of the new Stewart/Gouldman compositions, only It Doesn't Matter At All really passed muster, illustrating that at least the pair hadn't lost their knack of turning out gently affecting love songs. Elsewhere, the group set their caustic sights on some well-deserving targets, albeit with mixed results. One Two Five took a swipe at disco's mechanised 125-beats-per-minute tempo.

"Eric and I were saying that people were so into disco that they'd need a disco-ectomy to get rid of the disco in them," says Gouldman. "We were getting fed up with everything being computerised, with beats-to-the-minute and drum machines." Unfortunately, Stewart and Gouldman wasted their opportunity to send up the disco genre with the song. Lyrically, One Two Five just didn't hit the target.

Better was LA Inflatable, which ridiculed the shallowness of life in Los Angeles, and its obsession with the superficial: teeth, hair and 'curves that shouldn't be there'. However, as with many of the new tracks, it lacked the killer 10cc production.

Ironically, arguably the most characteristically 10cc song on the album featured neither Stewart nor Gouldman as songwriters. Welcome To The World, a collaboration between Duncan Mackay and Rick Fenn, packed a lyrical punch and twist of irony of which the original line-up would have been proud as they point the 10cc finger at unscrupulous politicians more interested in winning votes at the next election than tackling the real issues. Underneath it all, the message again was a serious one: are our children welcome to the world?

Of the band's other members, only Rick Fenn's writing skills are in evidence elsewhere – on Don't Send We Back, a song about the uncharitable reception received by the Vietnamese boat people in Britain at the time, and on How'm I Ever Gonna Say Goodbye, his collaboration with Gouldman. Despite the band's long lay-off, the writing talents of Messrs Mackay and Tosh were notable by their absence. Welcome To The World aside, the new members of the band weren't coming up with the goods on the writing front. As such, the 'new' 10cc line-up was overly reliant on Stewart and Gouldman. With Eric Stewart not yet firing on all cylinders after his car accident, this proved to be a flaw in the band's make-up.

Stewart's underperformance is most evident from his mix of the album. Previously, his skills as a sound engineer, and his mixes of 10cc albums, had been one of the band's greatest assets. The new album, however, wasn't sonically in the same league. Whereas Stewart's previous mixes had been detailed and vivid, the new album sounded muddled and flat. Even the revolution-ary half-speed mastering facility, recently installed at Strawberry Mastering, couldn't bring much-needed life to the grooves of the vinyl.

In fact, the group were so short on inspiration that they didn't even have a specific idea in mind for the album's title. Eventually they settled on *Look Hear?*, a play on words that again referenced the visual nature of the band's music. As usual, Hipgnosis were given the task of designing the sleeve.

"The band asked for 'something different'," recalls Storm Thorgerson. "I never really have a clear idea of what that expression means. So, we suggested a design with no images – sacrilege! Images were our business. Instead we proposed just words. Big words like headlines but done rough, no neat fonts, no colour. White type on black backgrounds. Plain as could be. The words would be ques-tions to involve the viewer in some degree of dialogue. First up was the T-shirt, which read on the front 'Are you coming' and on the back 'Are you going', no question marks, no punctuation. Just big, fractured, slightly clumsy lettering."

For the front cover of the album, Hipgnosis suggested posing the question 'Are you normal.' While making for an arresting cover, it also gave the impression that this was the title of the album, rather than *Look Hear?*, which would create confusion for record buyers later on. The idea was carried through to the record label itself, with the question 'Are you ready' on Side 1 and 'Are you done' on Side 2.

Having initially suggested using words rather than images for the cover, Hipgnosis couldn't resist developing the idea visually for the poster insert that would come with initial quantities of the album. They conceived an image of a sheep lying on a psychiatrist's couch. "The question 'Are you normal' led to the idea of normalcy and what could be more normal than a sheep, all of whom tend to follow each other," says Thorgerson. "But to be normal you'd need a lengthy dose of psychotherapy, hence the sheep on the couch undergoing intensive treatment, set against the vast sea of the unconscious, namely the wild ocean."

Of course, this being Hipgnosis, they insisted that, for artistic reasons, the image would need to be shot in Hawaii, where the waves and the light would be just right. Not unsurprisingly, Phonogram baulked at the idea of Hipgnosis flying out to Hawaii to shoot the image, particularly as it didn't even feature prominently on the front cover of the album. Instead, the record company suggested shooting it in Brighton, or perhaps North Wales, as an alternative. Amazingly, with 10cc's support, Hipgnosis managed to win the argument and Aubrey Powell was soon dispatched to Hawaii to capture the shot. Powell was en route when he realised he hadn't actually checked that there were any sheep on the island. To his dismay, a call to the Department of Agriculture in Honolulu revealed that there weren't any! Eventually, Powell discovered that there were a few sheep on the island, part of an experimental farming community attached to the university.

"Just as well," says Powell, "as Hipgnosis had persuaded 10cc to part with a load of cash to fly me 7,000 miles to the North Shore, where some of the largest surfing waves in the world are found, to photograph a sheep on a leather psychiatrist's couch on the beach."

Having enlisted the services of one of the university's sheep, Powell assumed that the couch would be easy to come by.

"I didn't bother to ask about it," says Powell. "Now, neither Freud nor Jung ever went to Hawaii and I discovered why. No couches. I had to have one built and spent the best part of five days catching the rays, swimming and hanging out whilst awaiting delivery."

Having sheared, shampooed and pedicured the lucky sheep, the day of the shoot finally arrived. However, the sheep seemed as enthusiastic about the shoot as the band's record company and kept hurling itself off the couch into the sea nearly drowning itself in the process. "Two large dogs and a snort of Valium calmed the beast and enabled me to take the shot," says Powell. "The look in the sheep's eyes says it all: 'Fuck you, British boy – Aloha and out!'"

Back at Strawberry South, there was another dynamic causing disruption in the studio. Eric Stewart's recording of the soundtrack to the film *Girls* at the same time as 10cc recorded their new album added to the strange atmosphere. Needing a ballad for his soundtrack album, Make The Pieces Fit, one of the strongest songs on *Look Hear?*, was switched to now feature on the *Girls* soundtrack, weakening the new 10cc album. To the rest of the band, *Girls* seemed to be a full-on collaboration between Stewart and Duncan Mackay, who had co-written most of the incidental music for the project. However, *Girls* would ultimately be released solely in Stewart's name, and not as a joint Stewart/Mackay effort, causing some tension between the two parties, which would eventually contribute to Mackay's departure from the band. In the end, neither the film or soundtrack album would be released in the UK, although Polydor issued two singles, Girls and Warm, Warm, Warm, in 1980.

"The trouble was that when they dubbed the French dialogue for the English version they used really dated words," says Stewart. "So, you'd have this incredibly cool bloke coming out with, 'Yeah, that'd be groovy, man.' The film lost its entire meaning so they didn't bring it out here. It was quite big in Europe, though."

With *Look Hear?* completed in December 1979, Stewart spent the first couple of months of 1980 back at Strawberry South producing Sad Café's next album, their follow-up to *Facades*. While the album, *Sad Café*, would spawn a couple of minor hits with La Di Da and I'm In Love Again, it would fail to emulate the success of its predecessor, although the band would remain a big live draw.

With solo projects completed, thoughts turned to the release and promotion of 10cc's seventh album. An edited version of One Two Five was chosen as the lead single from the album, coupled with Only Child, a new Stewart/Gouldman collaboration not featured on the album. The single met with poor reviews. "This two-years-too-late reference to disco's mechanised 125 beats per minute lacks the sprightly cynicism that was once this band's trademark," wrote

New Musical Express. "10cc seem to have lost sight of all their inspiration," said *Smash Hits.* "This sticky ditty sounds like an album track from five years back."

A significant budget was assigned to make an accompanying video for the single, to be directed by Russell Mulcahy, with a storyboard based around the 'disco-ectomy' idea that had inspired the song. Shot at the end of February 1980, the finished result illustrated why Mulcahy would go on to become one of the leading directors of the music video age. With prime-time slots for the video booked on TV programmes such as the *Kenny Everett Video Show*, hopes were high for another hit. The band was invited to make an all-important *Top of the Pops* appearance but declined, suggesting they show the video to One Two Five instead. It would prove to be a mistake. The BBC, preferring artists to play on the show rather than show their videos, demurred. Without the support of *Top of the Pops*, or sufficient radio airplay, One Two Five disappeared without a trace, failing, amazingly, to even scrape into the lower reaches of the UK Top 75, despite being 10cc's first single release in nearly 18 months and their first of the new decade.

"I don't know whether you can compute what will be a hit, I know I can't," says Stewart. "Looking back, whenever we tried to write anything that would fit with what was happening in the charts at the time we've failed miserably. The minute we've gone away from it and had a bit of fun we've come up with great stuff. That's a lesson we learned round about the disco era. When The Bee Gees were having success with stuff like Jive Talkin', we tried to do a disco track called One Two Five, based on the beats-per-minute of disco, so we were having a bit of a piss-take of it anyway, but it was a dismal failure. Nobody actually got the joke except us!"

Its fate was compounded by some poor marketing by the band's record company, who released solo singles from both Eric Stewart (Girls) and Graham Gouldman (Love's Not For Me) at the same time, both of which had to compete for attention with 10cc's new single. Still, the failure of One Two Five came as a big shock to the band. The lead single from all previous 10cc albums, *Sheet Music* aside, had yielded a Top 10 hit.

Look Hear? was released by Phonogram on March 28, supported by a radio advertising campaign featuring *Not The Nine O'Clock News* comedian Rowan Atkinson, which was quickly banned after complaints that it was offensive. At the same time, full-page ads in the music press posed questions such as 'Are you clean', 'Are you afraid' and 'Are you listening', along with the slogan 'This is going to worry you all day.' 10cc fans had every right to be worried all day by the contents of the album, yet *Look Hear?* managed to gain some positive reviews.

"All we have come to expect from 10cc, with or without Godley and Creme, is here in abundance," wrote *The Sunday Times.* "Highly literate music that remains accessible due to those fiendishly catchy hooks that are embedded in the complex mix. It is vintage 10cc: quirky bass vocals, searing rock numbers, floating pop ballads, a dash of reggae. Nobody produces more intelligent music and I Hate To Eat Alone, I Took You Home and It Doesn't Matter At All are classics. Melodic, original songs performed with skill and precision. The subject matter embraces loneliness, disco music, LA, love and the boat people. Not to be missed."

Sounds concurred: "The best album under the 10cc banner since *How Dare You!* and the first indication on plastic that the 'new' line-up does have an impetus of its own. For all that Stewart and Gouldman remain inveterate tunesmiths, the occasional writings of the other cc's are now helping to give the band a character of its own. The love songs of the old firm have a distinct atmosphere about them, although they rein back on the wondrous sound fantasies. Stewart's studio skills can always create and deliver ordinarily literate stories of break-up and loss with appealing melancholy. So that's Stewart and Gouldman back to a high level of understated craftsmanship. But 'best track' honours go to Duncan Mackay and Rick Fenn. Welcome To The World comes in on a Wakemanesque surge of synths then cuts away into urgent funk propelled by the dirtiest bass I've ever heard from Gouldman. That takes care of the action but the words are quite a surprise, with the new team as precise with the irony as the original quartet used to be."

Other critics were, rightly, more critical.

"A reasonably pleasant, innocuous collection of pop songs but it doesn't deserve to breathe in the racks alongside their innovative best, lacking the sense of purpose and conviction of the more recent *Deceptive Bends*," wrote Colin Irwin in *Melody Maker*. "Most of the tracks here are hummable and subtly infectious – with a bit more drive I Hate To Eat Alone and It Doesn't Matter At All might even make it on a higher plane – but so what? There are plenty of other bands – Squeeze spring immediately to mind – who operate in this straight pop field with a greater sense of fun and urgency and without the pretentiousness of something grander. Many of the ploys of *Look Hear?*, the use of counter-harmonies and alternating tempos, are throwbacks to the early days but there's a desperate lack of freshness and humour which made them so exciting then. LA Inflatable about the shallowness of LA and Lovers Anonymous, about unhappy relationships, show promising ideas frittered away in tepid arrangement. Mostly they seem to have little to say at all. It makes you wonder if 10cc believe in themselves anymore."

Look Hear? had its moments but it badly lacked the humour, invention, hooks and production values of 10cc's previous work, a view that has not dimmed with time, as a listen to the 2008 reissue of the album will testify. It remains, by some margin, the weakest album of the band's career. Aside from the substandard material it was clear that, from a production point of view, the group were beginning to sound dated. For the first time in their illustrious history, 10cc sounded in need of a producer.

Commercially, *Look Hear?* was only moderately successful, reaching No.35 and becoming the first 10cc album since their debut not to make it into the UK Top 10. It was the first 10cc album not to achieve silver status, selling less than 60,000 copies in the UK. When the band's next single, It Doesn't Matter At All, flopped too, it also became notable for being the first 10cc album not to contain a hit single in the UK. The group themselves might well have wanted to be thought of as an 'album' band, but the reality was that 10cc were more noted for their singles. Hit singles had been the lifeblood of 10cc's success and the relative failure of *Look Hear?* demonstrated how important hit singles had been in selling 10cc's albums.

Claims that 10cc's declining commercial fortunes were somehow affected by the impact of punk rock and new wave in the UK are wide of the mark though. Genesis, who released their new album in the same week that 10cc released *Look Hear?*, would reach No.1

with *Duke*, while contemporaries such as Queen, Roxy Music, David Bowie and Abba would all enjoy No.1 albums in 1980. Had *Look Hear?* been good enough, there is no reason why it shouldn't have charted as high as 10cc's previous albums.

Having been unhappy with Mercury's marketing of *Deceptive Bends* and Polydor's marketing of *Bloody Tourists* in America, 10cc signed a new record deal in the US with Warner Brothers, who felt that the artwork for the album would confuse record buyers. So, an alternative album cover was conceived, featuring the sheep-on-the-psychiatrist's couch image that Aubrey Powell had shot in Hawaii. Quite how this image linked to the title *Look Hear?* is not clear, as it was borne out of a discussion on what constituted normality. Still, the album gained some positive reviews.

"Wit, charm and pop sensibility have always been hallmarks of the 10cc style and *Look Hear?* is no exception," said *Billboard*. "Taking on a variety of topics this sextet handles them with humor and taste. The departure of Lol Creme and Kevin Godley from the band some time ago has not proven disastrous as this effort shows its creative juices are still flowing."

Despite the reviews, the album cover change and the new record company *Look Hear?* only managed to limp to No.180 in the US album chart. As 10cc's next world tour was being mapped out, it was decided to drop a proposed North American visit during the summer from their schedule. Instead, the tour would kick off in April with the band's biggest European tour to date, taking in 36 concerts in Germany, Denmark, Sweden, Norway, Switzerland, the Netherlands, Belgium, the UK and Ireland up until the end of May. There would then be a hiatus before the Australian leg of the tour kicked off at Perth's Entertainment Centre on October 20, followed by two nights at Adelaide's Apollo Stadium, four nights at Melbourne's Festival Hall, three nights at Brisbane's Festival Hall and concluding with four nights at Sydney's Hordern Pavilion. The band would play to over 60,000 Australian fans across the 14 dates. Then on November 15, 10cc would begin an extensive nine-date tour of Japan, taking in Tokyo, Yokohama, Nagoya, Kyoto, Osaka, Fukuoka and Sapporo.

10cc's 1980 live set featured 17 songs, only four of which were from the band's pre-split days, including a medley of Rubber Bullets,

Silly Love and Life Is A Minestrone for their encore, the first time these songs had been played live since Godley and Creme's departure. The group decided on a more elaborate stage set for the new show. They employed the services of Simon Woodroffe, who designed a giant 30-foot model of a reel-to-reel tape machine that would sit behind the band while they performed on stage. The prop was intended as a dig at critics who believed that 10cc used backing tapes on stage to recreate their sophisticated studio sounds.

"It's tongue-in-cheek," explained Ric Dixon at the time. "As so many people think the band use tapes. In actual fact the only time they use one is when the thing spins. I mean it's a bit difficult for the boys to make aircraft noises!"

The reels on the giant machine rotated at the two points in the band's set when backing tapes were used – at the start of I'm Mandy Fly Me and for the vocal backing of I'm Not In Love. The road crew put the prop to another use, however. "We carpeted it and had chairs in it and one of the crew had a hammock in it," recalls Zeb White. "It was on three floors and we had a bar and a lounge area and we had a darts room. After we'd set up a gig we'd all be in there. We called ourselves 'The Pod Club'. But the band knew nothing of it."

The world tour opened on April 10 at the Hamburg Congress Centre. For all the concern about the new album, the tour again impressed audiences and critics alike. A recording of 10cc's appearance at the Rheingold Hall in Mainz on April 30 captures the band in fine form, with many of the new tracks from *Look Hear?* coming across much better on stage than their anaemic versions on record. In Europe, *Look Hear?* performed well. In Norway, the album gave 10cc their highest chart placing to date, reaching No.3 and staying in the charts for 19 weeks, 11 of those in the Top 10. *Look Hear?* also reached No.14 in Sweden, No.18 in the Netherlands and No.40 in Germany.

The band's UK tour began at the Glasgow Apollo before moving on to Newcastle, and gained great reviews. "If when the original 10cc split four years ago Godley and Creme had retained the group moniker and the other two had gone out as Stewart-Gouldman or some such, how much of a difference would it have made?" pondered Ian Ravendale in *Sounds*. "Would the Godley-Creme cc be selling out City Hall for two nights while Eric and Graham failed

to shift the units? In a set just short of two hours the pace never fal-
ters. They were responsible for some of the great pop songs of the
last decade and prove it by pumping out every last one of them. It's
taken the new 'Tens' a couple of years but they've finally done it.
This is one excellent live show."

10cc's continuing draw as a live attraction was demonstrated
when their two concerts at the Manchester Apollo sold out within
an hour of going on sale, requiring the addition of a third date at
the venue. During one of the band's Manchester shows there was
a gentle sway to the giant reel-to-reel tape machine as 10cc played
their set. "It was one of the road crew getting his leg over inside the
tape recorder while the group were on stage," recalls Zeb White.

Still, the failure of the new album was a severe shock to the
system for a band as used to success as 10cc and the tour saw them
slightly less sure of themselves, a tenser affair than previous outings, with less onstage banter. TV cameras followed 10cc on their
dates in Birmingham and Brighton, filming a life-on-the-road documentary that would be screened by the BBC in early 1981. The film
showed the band's road crew setting up one of their concerts and
demonstrated the amount of behind-the-scenes preparation that
goes on before a gig.

10cc's UK tour culminated with two sell-out nights at London's
Wembley Arena. "Why didn't you buy the new album?" asked Eric
Stewart at one point in the proceedings. Stewart answered the ques-
tion himself a couple of years later when he conceded that *Look
Hear?* had "none of the magic of the past".

10cc then concluded their European Tour by performing their first
ever shows in Ireland, playing two nights at Dublin's RDS Simmons
Court Centre.

There had been talk of 10cc appearing as special guests of The
Beach Boys at the 1980 Knebworth Festival on June 21 on a bill that
also included Santana and Mike Oldfield. It would have been a great
opportunity to exorcise the memory of their disastrous appearance
at the 1976 Knebworth Festival, with 10cc's current live show much
better suited to a large festival than that of the original band four
years earlier. Sadly, negotiations fell through and the gig continued
without 10cc's participation, notable for being Brian Wilson's last
appearance with The Beach Boys in the UK.

With the next leg of the band's world tour not due to start until October in Australia, there was a period of hiatus for 10cc. In the meantime, the economics of the band's European tour were raising some eyebrows.

"We'd decided to be more democratic and pay the other guys in the band a percentage of the takings from the tour, rather than pay them a wage," says Stewart. "Every concert was a sell-out but when we finished the tour, Graham and I realised that we'd lost money on it! The costs of running that tour had been astronomical. The hotel bills, the size of the road crew, all the equipment. Graham and I couldn't believe it!"

With record sales declining, and touring on this scale becoming less financially viable, Stewart and Gouldman started to question 10cc's future. Supporting four other musicians in the band on an ongoing basis would become more and more of a challenge. With the group's future uncertain, a band meeting was convened in Manchester on August 8, where Paul Burgess, Stuart Tosh, Rick Fenn and Duncan Mackay were advised that 10cc were breaking up. It was reminiscent of the meeting that Eric Stewart had been summoned to in September 1976 when he was asked to leave the band.

"It was a real shock," recalls Fenn. "I think we were given the distinct impression that 10cc was over. Whether or not at that time Eric and Graham had intended to come together again to record and continue touring remains a mystery but, frankly, in spite of the massive disruption it obviously caused us, I never resented them for demoting us. Probably some did, but as far as I was concerned, continuing as a two-piece after Kev and Lol left would have been the smart thing to do. I think it was pretty magnanimous of them to have four of us come in and share the glory. For a double live, and two studio albums we had been notionally afforded equal status – not money, that would have been crazy – and this at the peak of the band's commercial success. Heady times. I only wish that this seismic change in the band's structure, which like I said, was reasonable enough, had been discussed frankly and openly."

10cc's upcoming tours of Australia and Japan were duly cancelled, the second time in less than two years that fans in those countries had been disappointed by the cancellation of a tour, and the former members of 10cc sought future employment. While no public announcement about the split would be made, Mackay's manager would advise the music press that his charge was leaving 10cc to pursue a solo career. Mackay would record a solo album, *Visa*, at his home studio that same month and play keyboards on Camel's album *Nude* at Abbey Road. Rick Fenn contacted Mike Oldfield through a mutual acquaintance and by September 1 was rehearsing with him for some upcoming tour dates, initiating an association with Oldfield that would last for many years, on tour and on record. Fenn would even be the inspiration for the song Family Man, which he co-wrote with Oldfield and other musicians working on the *Five Miles Out* album. The song would later be covered by Hall and Oates and reach the US Top 10 in June 1983. Paul Burgess would go on to record with Magna Carta (*Midnight Blue*), Camel (*Stationary Traveller, Dust and Dreams*), Jethro Tull (*A Classic Case*) and The Icicle Works (*Permanent Damage*) and tour with Joan Armatrading.

With 10cc having effectively been put to bed, Eric Stewart had time on his hands to collaborate with friends, such as Justin Hayward.

"Eric and I were in Strawberry South one night," says Hayward. "We ended up recording the backing track to a song called Goodbye." The song would eventually appear on Hayward's solo album *Moving Mountains*.

Now it was time for he and Graham Gouldman to contemplate life outside of 10cc.

CHAPTER 22

WE'VE HEARD IT ALL BEFORE

HAVING EFFECTIVELY BROUGHT 10CC TO AN END AT THE BAND MEET-
ing in Manchester in August 1980, Eric Stewart and Graham
Gouldman each started work on solo projects. Gouldman booked
Strawberry North for three weeks in November 1980 to record
some new songs, with Paul Burgess, Rick Fenn and keyboard player
Marc Jordan joining him for the sessions. Among the tracks they
worked on were Don't Ask and You Do That For Me. A later session
would see drummer Simon Phillips and Sad Café keyboard player
Vic Emerson joining Gouldman in the studio to record Survivor
and Tomorrow's World Today. Emerson would also make an important contribution to another new Gouldman song, the ballad
Lying Here With You.

Stewart recorded solo material too, booking time at Strawberry
South in January 1981, also employing the services of Paul
Burgess for the sessions. Among the tracks they recorded were Les
Nouveaux Riches and Don't Turn Me Away. Yet, by early 1981, it
seems that Stewart and Gouldman were having second thoughts
about putting the band to bed. "We weren't sure whether it was
a good idea to continue as 10cc," says Stewart. "But we were still
contracted to make another two albums for Phonogram and
because the next album was due to be our 10th, we decided to
keep 10cc going." The plan was to bring together the tracks that
Stewart and Gouldman had started work on independently and
finish them off together. "We do hope that we will have a new 10cc
album issued in April," predicted Ric Dixon, rather optimistically,
at the time.

However, with Stewart and Gouldman both lined up for solo
projects – the former working with Paul McCartney, the latter producing The Ramones – it soon become clear that this deadline

wasn't achievable. It would be June before they could get together finish off the next 10cc album.

Before their solo projects they did have one engagement as 10cc – a special performance of I'm Not In Love to help mark the re-opening of The Palace Theatre in Manchester. Attended by Prince Charles, the Royal Gala show on March 22 featured Manchester artists from the world of theatre, opera, ballet, comedy, rock and classical music. As Manchester's most successful band of the previous decade, 10cc marked the occasion by performing a unique rendition of their most famous song, this time accompanied by the Hallé symphony orchestra.

"The thrill of playing I'm Not In Love with the Hallé orchestra and a full choir was a real blast, I loved that," says Stewart.

Following the gig Stewart worked with Paul McCartney on his next album, which saw the former Beatle reunited with George Martin, himself an admirer of 10cc, who cited I'm Not In Love as one of his favourite songs. The sessions started in the aftermath of John Lennon's assassination, with McCartney still slowly coming to terms with the death of his former songwriting partner. At one point there was a moment when the reality of the situation seemed to finally catch up with McCartney.

"He said, 'I've just realised that John has gone. He's dead and he's not coming back'," recalls Stewart. "And he looked completely dismayed, like shocked at something that had just suddenly hit him." Stewart was energised by the experience of working with McCartney and Martin: "It's been wonderful watching them in the studio," said Stewart at the time. "They have this obvious rapport and total respect for each other. And it's lovely to hear them coming out with these little anecdotes about, 'Oh, remember that track we did on *Sgt Pepper*? Or *The White Album*? Remember when we did that, George?' And George will say, 'Yeah'. It's great to see all these ideas coming out again. And, I mean, I'm sat there just listening to it all and picking up thousands of ideas."

Initial recording had taken place at Air Studios in London but some of the sessions for the album would be recorded at Strawberry South, making the experience even more special for Stewart. One particularly memorable session saw the arrival of Stevie Wonder to work on the track What's That You're Doing?

"Just from hearing me talking Stevie said, 'Hey, you're the guy that sings I'm Not In Love. I love the way you sing that song.' It was just such a buzz for me to have Stevie at Strawberry, talking about songs that I'd written," says Stewart. "On one session, Paul, Stevie and I were making music until the early hours of the morning. It was one of the most beautiful moments of my life."

Stewart would ultimately appear on seven tracks on McCartney's acclaimed *Tug of War* album, which would reach No.1 on both sides of the Atlantic upon release in April 1982. Arguably Stewart's greatest contribution was the vocal harmonies on Take It Away. *Stylus* magazine would later comment: "The voices in this mastery of overdubbing are simply Paul, Linda and 10cc's Eric Stewart, but thanks to Stewart's vocal arrangement may well be the most gorgeous piece of vocalization this side of the chorus closing 10cc's own I'm Not In Love."

Graham Gouldman, meanwhile, had started production on the next album by American punk rockers The Ramones. "I was surprised when they approached me to do the project because their music was so different from what I was known for," says Gouldman. "I was wary but I do like a challenge. I asked Joey Ramone, 'Where do you see our paths converging? I'm an English pop guy and you're American punk guys.' He said, 'We think our songs are like yours.' He was talking about the songs I wrote in the 60s – they loved people like The Yardbirds. They felt that their songs had the same sort of inspiration. I could dig that."

The band's previous effort, *End of the Century*, had been produced by Phil Spector but had not succeeded in giving The Ramones the commercial breakthrough that their record company were seeking. The group themselves were in meltdown at the time. Relationships between the band's members were strained, with differences of opinion over what direction their music should take. The group were keen to work with Steve Lillywhite on the new record but their lack of commercial success meant that their management and record company had the bigger say. Sire Records label boss Seymour Stein was advocating Gouldman and, with him on board, his new charges checked out their producer's band.

"We listened to the 10cc albums and they sounded good," says Johnny Ramone. "Not what we like, but they sounded good."

In March 1981, Gouldman flew to New York to produce the album at Media Sound Studios, a former Baptist Church on West 57th Street. However, the first day in the studio on March 31 didn't bode well, with Gouldman's pop sensibilities clashing with the band's punk ethic. "I knew I was in trouble immediately when Graham said, 'Your amp is buzzing too much, you have to turn it down'," recalls Johnny Ramone. "I said, 'Oh boy. That's gonna be a problem. No one's ever said that to me before.'"

In total, backing tracks to 15 songs were completed over a three-week period. At one point there was talk of recording a cover of Gouldman's For Your Love during the sessions but, unfortunately, this idea was not progressed. Gouldman's approach throughout was to take a fairly light touch. "We changed arrangements slightly," says Gouldman, "but it was basic stuff like, 'Let's put an end on this song rather than fade it, let's double up on the chorus at the end, try bringing the harmonies in the first chorus rather than the second.' I did come up with harmonies but I had to keep those fairly simple. If I suggested a guitar part and showed it to Johnny, it had to sound like it came from him, or he wouldn't play it. Which I understood."

As the sessions progressed the band warmed to their producer. "He was always a gentleman," says Johnny Ramone. "He changed a lot of the songs: 'Here's a nice chord for the bridge, you should be playing a minor chord rather than a major chord,' things like that. He had ideas for harmonies and guitar parts that could be over-dubbed. He also thought of bass parts."

Joey Ramone even namechecked 10cc in the song It's Not My Place (In The 9 to 5 World) alongside Lester Bangs, Phil Spector, Jack Nicholson and Clint Eastwood.

With the backing tracks completed, singer Joey Ramone flew to England with Gouldman to record his vocal tracks at Strawberry North in Stockport. "Joey, bless him, was very, very finicky about getting things right," recalls Gouldman. "He used to twist his hair with his left hand, and he would sidle up to me and put his head to one side and say, 'Graham, is it too late to change that thing?' I'd say, 'Yeah, of course'. This would happen time and time again. It was his record so I always gave him the chance to change things. He cared very much about his work."

With the unlikely trio of Gouldman, Russell Mael from Sparks and Ian Wilson from Sad Café adding backing vocals, the album was mixed at Strawberry South in May 1981 and then mastered at Strawberry Mastering. Gouldman thoroughly enjoyed the experience of working with the band.

"I loved doing it," says Gouldman. "I expected to have a lot of trouble with them, but they were very cooperative and conscientious and quite finicky. That blows their entire image! They were ultra-professional. It was a good album, and apparently it sold well, but I'm not really known as a punk producer. I didn't get any offers to produce the next Clash album!"

Maybe not, but the album, titled *Pleasant Dreams*, gained some excellent reviews upon release in July 1981. *Rolling Stone* gave the album four stars, while *Creem* described it as "a masterpiece". In the UK, the reviews were equally positive.

"Ladies and gentlemen, Graham Gouldman meets The Ramones, making for one of the most inspired matches in recent times," said *Record Mirror*. "The guy who wrote hits for The Yardbirds and The Hollies while still in his teens should have been drafted in yonks ago. The effortlessness with which he switches from a pop to a rock sensibility suits The Ramones down to the last G sharp. Possibly the best thing about Gouldman is that he never outstays his welcome, so when he does pull the odd trick it sticks out superbly."

New Musical Express was equally enthusiastic.

"*Pleasant Dreams* is that LP The Ramones have always dreamt of making. A whole album of wholly realised songs, framed with non-stop pop expertise by producer Graham Gouldman," said Cynthia Rose. "Gouldman's obvious understanding of how the mid-60s hits so beloved of this band were structured – a cut called This Business Is Killing Me recalls Bus Stop, the hit he wrote for The Hollies during his post-Mindbenders stint as a songwriter. Another real surprise is the way he's re-shaped The Ramones sound (by bringing both drums and Joey's vocals right upfront, holding the guitars well back and maximising the band's *esprit de corps* through harmony) – not to tamper with but to enhance the explicitness of their world view."

Somewhat surprisingly, with Stewart and Gouldman still working on their separate projects, Phonogram announced the release of a new 10cc single, Les Nouveaux Riches, in May 1981. Written by

Eric Stewart, it was one of the songs he had recorded at Strawberry South at the start of the year and it is unclear whether Graham Gouldman performs on this version of the record. While the song's title hinted at a return to form – the subject matter an ideal and deserving target for 10cc's caustic wit – the song failed to hit the target lyrically or musically, lacking the punch and wit that had previously been the band's trademark. It was the kind of song that would have been kicked into shape by Godley and Creme had they still been with the band, and would have benefited from an injection of their wicked sense of humour to help really stick the knife in.

Given that it was the band's first new music in over a year, it was surprising that Phonogram decided to release it with so little fanfare: no video, no TV appearances, no promotion. Unsurprisingly, the song received little airplay and failed to put 10cc back on the hit trail.

"All sugar and no substance, and surely their weakest ever," wrote *Record Mirror*.

The following month, Eric Stewart and Graham Gouldman reunited to finish off the next 10cc album together, their approach informed by their recent solo projects.

"It's refreshing to do different things, you always learn something you can inject into 10cc," said Stewart, while Gouldman's experience of producing The Ramones made him "come back to 10cc with a more simplified approach".

10cc would effectively now be a duo, with Stewart and Gouldman drawing upon whatever musicians they needed in the studio or on the road. The next album would be an important one for the band, with the aim of getting them back on track after the disappointment of *Look Hear?* Still, the omens looked good. Stewart and Gouldman had triumphed over adversity before, responding to Godley and Creme's departure with *Deceptive Bends*, an album with a strong sense of purpose that had given them the confidence to continue as 10cc. Now, four years on, they had the opportunity to demonstrate that sense of purpose once again.

However, one major factor made the task much more difficult this time around. By now, the Stewart/Gouldman partnership had seriously fragmented. With most of the backing tracks recorded independently from each other, the pair now started collaborating on each other's songs, changing certain lyrics, melody lines, vocals and even titles in each other's work.

"We rewrote parts and played on each other's things," recalls Gouldman. "On a lot of the stuff it worked quite well because we still had the attitude of trying to make each other's stuff better."

Gouldman's lead vocal on Lying Here With You was re-sung by Eric Stewart, a wise move given Stewart's plaintive vocal style, while You Do That For Me was almost totally reworked lyrically and melodically to become Action Man In Motown Suit. To avoid confrontation between the two of them, the pair employed the tactic of referring to a fictional character, dubbed "that bloke in Outer Mongolia", who represented the kind of obsessive fan who would pick up on absolutely anything that wasn't up to scratch.

"If one of us thought that the other could sing or play something better, we would say, 'It's not good enough for that fucking bloke in Outer Mongolia. He'll notice that you've played the wrong note or sung it out of tune.' It stopped things getting confrontational in the studio," says Stewart. In fact, the tactic of referring to "that bloke in Outer Mongolia" to avoid confrontation in the studio wasn't new. The band's original line-up had employed this device too. This time around, Stewart and Gouldman would go on to express a special thank you to "that bloke in Outer Mongolia" in the credits of the new album.

At this point in the album's development, Stewart and Gouldman collaborated on some new songs. Overdraft In Overdrive was a humorous account of a man in dire financial straits. The protagonist in the song has the last laugh, however, when his rich Uncle Sam passes away and he inherits a fortune. Memories took a wistful look back at the innocence of childhood, to first loves and endless summers, with the pair also sneaking in a reference to Nights In White Satin in the lyrics. Notel Hotel was a return to 10cc's cinematic lyrical style. The song's paranoid hero checks into Room 1059 of the hotel and looks for hidden meanings and mysterious circumstances in everything he sees.

As thoughts turned to a title, Stewart and Gouldman decided to call the new album *Ten Out of 10*. It was supposed to be a nod to 10 years in business for 10cc and this being their 10th album. Which made perfect sense except for the fact that it was actually their *eighth* album, released a year before their 10th anniversary. Pedantry aside, the title was a far cry from the self-deprecating wit of some of their early album titles. *Sheet Music* indeed! The album cover, this time designed by Visible Ink following the dissolution of Hipgnosis, brought the storyline of Notel Hotel to life, and saw Stewart and Gouldman balancing precipitously on the outside edge of the 10th floor of the building, while the bellboy and the girl from the song also feature.

It was important that *Ten Out of 10* re-established 10cc after the disappointing chart performance of *Look Hear?* and a hit single would be critical to the album's chances of success. However, 10cc and Phonogram had different ideas about which track to release. Stewart and Gouldman were keen on Lying Here With You. "I thought the song was wonderful," says Stewart. "I thought it was the best song that Graham had ever written and should have been released as a single but the record company didn't agree."

Phonogram opted instead for the weaker Don't Turn Me Away. Released in November 1981, with Gouldman's Tomorrow's World Today on the b-side, Don't Turn Me Away was very pretty and easy on the ear.

"This is nice," said *Smash Hits*. "Pretty and nice. And well recorded too. What more do you expect from a 10cc single these days? A moody sax solo. You've got it. Twice."

It almost sucks you in until you realise, at about the moment the saxophone solo emerges into the mix, that you have heard this kind of track many times before, just never on a 10cc record. Never before had the band sounded so predictable. UK record buyers resisted its sugar-coated charms and the song failed to chart.

Ten Out of 10 was released on November 27 and, unfortunately, suffered a similar fate, although once again the album would do better elsewhere – reaching No.17 in Norway, No.24 in Sweden and No.31 in Canada – and eventually going on to sell over a million copies worldwide. However, calling your album *Ten Out of 10* was a gift for critics who, unsurprisingly, gave the record a very different kind of rating.

"Quite stunningly bland," wrote *Record Mirror*.

"They've clearly lost the spark of earlier discs, when the sad songs were heartbreaking and the funny ones wicked," wrote *Trouser Press*.

Worst of all was Colin Irwin's review in *Melody Maker*: "How much longer must this once glorious name be dredged out and fed through the works like a recycled sausage?"

Ten Out of 10 was a considerable improvement on its disappointing predecessor and has aged well, remaining an enjoyable listen today. The playfulness of Overdraft In Overdrive, the pathos of Memories, the intriguing narrative of Notel Hotel, the melodic simplicity of Lying Here With You are all appealing. But the record has too many 'filler' tracks. Songs like Survivor and Listen With Your Eyes had fewer ideas contained within them than could often be found on previous 10cc b-sides. Elsewhere, Les Nouveaux Riches showed their attempts at humour falling flat. At best, the album delivered a 'six out of ten' rather than the full marks of the title. Musically, the album veered dangerously close to middle-of-the-road, while lyrically it had little to say. Where were the trademark twists and turns? The album showed the band lacking direction and focus. It just wasn't up to the standard expected from 10cc.

Part of the problem seemed to be Stewart and Gouldman's resistance to change and refusal to move with the times. The new technology that was becoming available to musicians at the time – digital synthesizers and samplers such as the Fairlight – should have given 10cc a field day in the studio. Instead, the group sounded entrenched in the 70s, lacking inspiration and looking increasingly out of place in the music scene of the 80s, which was ironic given the band's reputation for being at the cutting edge of recording techniques. There was certainly no shortage of targets for their sardonic wit. The emergence of the pop video, satirised by the BBC TV series *Not The Nine O'Clock News* with their Nice Video, Shame About The Song spoof, would have been an ideal target for 10cc – and a tongue-in-cheek dig at their erstwhile partners.

The group also badly needed a producer. Gouldman recognised this, but Stewart felt the band should continue to produce themselves. Both were in-demand record producers in their own right, so why did they need external help, reasoned Stewart. *Look Hear?* and *Ten Out of 10* provided the evidence for the counter-argument. Looking back today, Gouldman concedes that both albums weren't up to scratch.

"I can't listen to those albums, really," he says. "There were some good songs on those records but it wasn't a happy time. We weren't facing up to the inevitable – to the fact that it was over. We should either have tried to change direction, which we didn't, or got someone else in the band, which we almost did. The albums weren't really bad, there was always the integrity, and the production values, but in retrospect, I find them rather dour, rather lacklustre. That's why I thought we should have got someone else in, to kick us up the arse. We didn't see what was going on around us; maybe we should have got a producer at that point."

The opportunity to work with another writer/producer presented itself when their American record label, Warner Brothers, refused to release *Ten Out of 10* in its original form.

"They wanted more of an American flavour to the album and were keen for us to work with an American producer or writer," says Gouldman. "When they suggested Andrew Gold I was over the moon. I'd always adored his work and reckoned he would be a kindred spirit. He seemed as if he was a Beatlemaniac and certainly an Anglophile."

Gold had a stellar musical pedigree. Born in California to musical parents, he was a virtuoso multi-instrumentalist, who had played a big part in Linda Ronstadt's breakthrough and had worked in the studio with the likes of Art Garfunkel, Jackson Browne and James Taylor before enjoying hits of his own with Lonely Boy, How Can This Be Love, Never Let Her Slip Away and Thankyou For Being a Friend. However, Gold's solo career had stalled after the failure of his fourth solo album *Whirlwind* in 1980. Lenny Waronker, then head of A&R at Warner Brothers, thought Gold would be the perfect man to bring a more American flavour to 10cc's new album and called him to sound him out.

"He asked if I was a fan of 10cc and I told him that indeed I was, very much," said Gold. "He said the band had a new album they were releasing called *Ten Out of 10* and he was of the opinion that, although the album was very strong, it might benefit the US audience to have a few additional cuts tailored more for the American ear. I said it would be an honour if the band said okay. I spoke to Graham and Eric by phone and soon I was in the UK co-writing and co-producing three tracks for the album, which was a blast to do and turned out very well. During the course of my three-week stay, Eric, Graham and I fell in love as it were. We listened to records each other liked and realised we had very similar tastes."

The collaboration with Gold worked well and spawned three new songs. The Power of Love sounded more contemporary than much of the band's recent output, benefiting from an atmospheric intro and a strong production. Run Away was a love song in the finest Stewart/Gouldman tradition, the perfect showcase for Stewart's plaintive vocal style. And while We've Heard It All Before tried a little too hard to return to the 'wacky' 10cc songs of old, at least it saw the welcome return of the band's humour, as they put the music-by-numbers programming style through the mill.

Stewart and Gouldman were both energised by the sessions and enjoyed the dynamic of having a third opinion in the band. Aside from being another source of musical ideas, it also served to relieve some of the tension between the two of them. In fact, so pleased were they with the collaboration that they decided to ask Gold if he wanted to become a permanent member of the group.

"During the sessions, Eric and Graham asked me to join 10cc," said Gold. "I was very flattered, it was like a dream come true, but for various reasons, which now seem dumb to me, I demurred in favour of pursuing my own career and returned to America."

All three songs, plus Gouldman's Tomorrow's World Today, replaced four of the original tracks including, strangely, Lying Here With You, on the US version of *Ten Out of 10*. Memories was also re-mixed for the US release, although the result was inferior to the UK version. However, despite the changes, America remained unconvinced and the album failed to arrest 10cc's declining popularity there.

The outlook was more positive in Canada where the band scored a Top 40 hit with Don't Turn Me Away, helping *Ten Out of 10* climb to just outside the Top 30 in the album charts. At the same time Eric Stewart and Graham Gouldman were preparing to take 10cc back on the road for the first time in almost two years. Nearly 20 years in the music business, and they were still looking forward to another live tour. "There's nothing to touch the feeling when you're walking out on stage to a sold-out audience," said Stewart at the time. "You hear that roar – it's like a drug. After something like five months in the studio, you're dying to show people what you've done."

Stewart and Gouldman were joined on the tour by 10cc stalwarts Paul Burgess, Stuart Tosh and Rick Fenn, with Sad Café's keyboardist Vic Emerson – who had guested on the *Ten Out of 10* album – filling the role vacated by Duncan Mackay. Emerson would form part of 10cc's live line-up over the next two years.

"I got on very well with Eric and 10cc had the same management as us," says Emerson. "I think I only missed one 10cc gig in that period. For two years I was in both bands."

The group's '10th Anniversary Tour', as it was dubbed, opened on February 19, 1982 at the Birmingham Odeon, and comprised 21 concerts, including two sell-out shows at London's Hammersmith Odeon. The Power of Love was released as a single to coincide with the tour, coupled with a new song, You're Coming Home Again, on the b-side. But despite being 10cc's strongest single since Reds In My Bed, and with an accompanying video directed by Storm Thorgerson, it failed to chart.

Back on the road, 10cc once again gained good reviews.

"While their former musical colleagues Godley and Creme are now deservedly reaping the benefit of hit singles, 10cc – Eric Stewart and Graham Gouldman – haven't had a big-selling single for some time now," said *Music Week*. "However, they are proving via their latest UK tour that they are still very much two of rock/contemporary pop music's best contributors. Six years after the departure of Godley and Creme, which many people thought could mean an early demise for 10cc, the band have gone from strength to strength musically, even if record sales have been a little disappointing."

The tour proved that, despite the patchiness of their last two albums, 10cc were still capable of cutting the mustard live.

"I'm Mandy Fly Me was delivered beautifully and received rapturously," wrote Garth Pearce in *The Daily Mail* under the headline REVVING AT 10CC. "Art For Art's Sake, injected with several minutes of superb jamming, proved that something fresh could be added to a firm favourite. After that the sheer self-assurance of the band took over. As a team, they work hypnotically."

Extra dates were added to the tour to keep up with demand, including a third London show at the Wembley Conference Centre, scene of the gig that should have been filmed for the Christmas 1978 *Old Grey Whistle Test* broadcast but wasn't, owing to a technician's dispute at the BBC. This time the gig, on March 16, would be filmed by former *Top of the Pops* director Phil Bishop for future broadcast on the soon-to-be-launched Channel 4 TV station. Ten minutes of the concert were shown on national TV in America on the *Don Kirshner Show,* and the show would subsequently be released on video as *10cc Live at the International Music Show.*

There was a strong feeling that Run Away should be released as 10cc's next single. Coupled with Action Man in a Motown Suit from the *Ten Out of 10* album, the song was released by Phonogram on July 16. A strong ballad, Run Away continued the recent improvement in the band's singles and deservedly gave 10cc their first hit of the 80s when it entered the UK singles chart on almost exactly the 10th anniversary of the band's first hit, Donna. Unfortunately, despite climbing 14 places the following week, Run Away stalled prematurely at No.50 in the charts. Had the record sold just a few more copies and crept into the lower reaches of the Top 40, the story might well have been very different. The band would have secured an appearance on *Top of the Pops,* the song would have been heard by a wider audience, helping it to climb further up the charts and serving to restimulate interest in 10cc. Unfortunately, its chart placing was lower than the song merited.

The big hit in the UK that summer was Come On Eileen by Dexy's Midnight Runners, a band that had asked Eric Stewart to produce them earlier in the year.

"That Come On Eileen is a very commercial track," said Stewart at the time. "They sent me a demo tape and asked me to produce them but I turned it down. Didn't think I could add anything to it."

With 10cc's promotion of *Ten Out of 10* having run its course, Eric Stewart and Graham Gouldman once again took up solo projects.

CHAPTER 23

FOOD FOR THOUGHT

AUGUST 1982 SAW THE RELEASE OF A SOLO ALBUM FROM ERIC STEWART. Originally to be titled *Roots Are Showing*, the album – now titled *Frooty Rooties* – featured a 1952 painting by American pin-up artist Gil Elvgren on the front cover.

"I've been working on it on and off over the last two years," explained Stewart at the time. "Basically, it's a collection of new songs done in the recording style of the 60s. I've used the same sort of guitars, microphones and amplifiers. I went out and bought a set of guitars that I knew I was going to need. On one track I trace my roots by using different types of guitars and amps."

The track in question, Guitaaaaarghs, moves through five phases, each focusing on a different musical style, from modern jazz through country blues, rockabilly, psychedelia and rock, with Stewart using a different guitar and amplifier set-up for each section. It gave Stewart the opportunity to pay homage to his guitar-playing heroes.

"There's a maple neck Telecaster for the James Burton solo, a maple neck Strat for a Lowell George/Ry Cooder affair, a 1957 Gibson Byrdland for the Scotty Moore licks and a Gibson L5 for that Eddie Cochran sound," says Stewart.

Most of the tracks on the album showcased Stewart's love of rock 'n' roll and the blues. The highlights of the album, however, are the tracks that veer closer to the spirit of 10cc. Make The Pieces Fit was a remixed version of the song that had originally been destined for *Look Hear?* but had gone on to become the standout track from Stewart's 1980 soundtrack album, *Girls*. It was a beautifully written, and beautifully sung, Stewart song of the highest order.

Doris The Florist was even better – an exquisite, touching and well-observed song about a florist, with Stewart adopting a wistful falsetto: *'She whispers to the flowers the people never buy / Her sorrow seems to know the bouquet left behind.'* The two songs arguably rank with Stewart's finest and stand head and shoulders above the rest of the album, which, as the title suggests, revisits Stewart's bluesy roots. The resulting sounds of songs such as Rockin' My Troubles Away and Strictly Business were light years away from the British musical landscape of 1982. In interviews at the time, Stewart acknowledged the changing face of the British music scene.

"I like to diversify on albums but 95% of the record-buying public seem to want an LP to sound the same the whole way through," he said.

More in the 10cc mould was a three-part piece called The Ritual. "I wanted to do something that wasn't a three-minute single," says Stewart. "I took the idea of someone going into a club and what they were doing there. Their ritual, walking in, spotting someone they liked the look of, asking them to dance and taking it from there." While not in the same league as One Night In Paris or Feel The Benefit, it is a tribute to Stewart's musical prowess that he manages to create such rich textures – particularly his use of vocoder voices and strings – almost single-handedly, drawing only on assistance from Paul Burgess for the drum parts.

"Eric Stewart follows in the footsteps of many other members of big-name rock bands who have ventured the path to solo success," wrote *Music Week*, awarding the album a three-star rating. "There's more than a passing shade of 10cc with some of the tracks of course but generally there's a lot of musical variation and the album should enjoy moderate success." *Smash Hits* was less charitable: "Snazzily recorded, expertly performed chunks of unremarkable, 10cc-flavoured fudge, peppered with the odd slice or two of equally unremarkable rock."

While record buyers proved to be indifferent towards *Frooty Rooties*, Stewart was enjoying the success of his association with Paul McCartney, whose album *Tug of War* had achieved considerable critical and commercial success. Having played on the song in the studio, Stewart was asked by McCartney to appear in the video for the single Take it Away, which was filmed on June 23 at Elstree Studios in Hertfordshire. It was rumoured that in between takes,

Paul and Linda McCartney, Stewart and other members of the band – Ringo Starr, Steve Gadd and George Martin – entertained the 600 specially invited members of the Wings Fan Club, playing extras for the crowd scenes, with rock 'n' roll standards such as Lucille, Peggy Sue, Send Me Some Lovin', Twenty Flight Rock, Cut Across Shorty, Reeling and Rocking and I Love Her So. The video, starring actor John Hurt, helped the single to reach the Top 10 in the US and the Top 20 in the UK.

The collaboration with McCartney worked so well that Stewart was asked to guest on his next album, *Pipes of Peace*, with recording sessions taking place at Abbey Road in September and October 1982. Again, the album featured an all-star cast, although one musician that Stewart didn't get a chance to work with was Michael Jackson.

"Every so often Paul would tell the band not to come in the next day," says Stewart. "Jacko would only work with Himself."

Meanwhile, Graham Gouldman had gone from the sublime to the ridiculous by taking up an offer to produce an album for an artist about as far removed from The Ramones as it was possible to imagine – Irish singer-songwriter Gilbert O'Sullivan. Recorded at Windmill Lane Studios in Dublin, Gouldman also sang and played guitar on the record, alongside contributions from former 10cc colleagues Paul Burgess and Duncan Mackay. Among its highlights was the self-deprecating Has Been.

"I enjoy Graham's work on this very much," says O'Sullivan. "At his suggestion, this is the first and only time I put the middle from one song into another. That was something he used to do with 10cc." Gouldman's influence can also be heard on the standout track, If I Know You – O'Sullivan's dig at a former lover. Gouldman gives the song a quirky, syncopated rhythm, which underlines the tale of betrayal. More in the 10cc mould was Live Now, Pay Later.

"Good work from Graham," says O'Sullivan. "He was well into his vocal harmonies; that's his thing. Some of it came out a bit more 10cc than perhaps it would have with Eric, but in for a penny, in for a pound."

The album, *Life and Rhymes*, was released in October 1982, preceded by the single Bear With Me, which featured a cameo appearance from Gouldman in the video.

Now with their solo projects completed, Stewart and Gouldman contemplated 10cc's next move. Neither were particularly enthused about the prospect of making another 10cc record, despite being contracted to Phonogram to deliver one more album. It felt like 10cc had run its course after 10 years in business. However, they were persuaded otherwise.

"We got a call from Brian Shepherd, the MD at Phonogram, saying he'd like to meet up with us," recalls Stewart. "When Graham and I got into his office he played us Private Investigations by Dire Straits and, afterwards, he said, 'I think that you guys still have another great album in you and are capable of doing something this good. Why don't you go away and write an extended piece?' So, Graham and I agreed to do another 10cc album and we went away and wrote 24 Hours."

It said a lot about 10cc in 1982 that they needed the intervention of their record company, and the music of Dire Straits, for inspiration. Still, Shepherd's suggestion to explore a less conventional approach was in keeping with the original spirit of 10cc. If *Ten Out of 10* had been full of songs that conformed to traditional songwriting conventions, with clearly defined verses, choruses and middle eights, 24 Hours saw Stewart and Gouldman once again experimenting with song construction. The result was an eight-minute *tour de force*, with well-observed lyrics on human life over the course of a day and night in a big city. In a way, there were echoes of One Night In Paris – complete with the sound of the city at the start of the song – albeit with the action taking place over a 24-hour period rather than just one night.

The pair also wrote two other extended pieces. Taxi! Taxi! was an eight-minute gem filled with musical and lyrical twists and turns that traced the anticipation and realisation of a romantic encounter, while The Secret Life of Henry told the story of a commuter with a very different persona in the workplace to the one at home. Clearly inspired, Stewart and Gouldman penned their best set of songs in years, all written together, with none of the 'solo' compositions that had graced the last few 10cc albums. The improvement in quality control, particularly in the lyric department, was striking. Americana Panorama contained some of the band's sharpest lyrics for some time, as they put the American Dream through its paces, with references to corrupt politicians like Nixon, the assassinations of JFK, Martin Luther King and John Lennon and the stockpile of nuclear weapons. Another new song, Working Girls, tackled the subject of sexual discrimination in the workplace.

As the writing sessions continued, a theme began to emerge. From the commuter with the double life in The Secret Life of Henry to the nightlife of City Lights, each song was like looking through a different window of life in the city. As such, Stewart and Gouldman decided to call the album *Windows in the Jungle*. With The Moody Blues ensconced at Strawberry South for nine months recording their album *The Present*, 10cc found themselves back in the position of not being able to book time in their own studio. They returned to Stockport to record their new album at Strawberry North, for the first time since *How Dare You!*. The sessions were to be engineered by Martin Lawrence who, exactly five years previously, had worked with Stewart and Gouldman's former bandmates on their *Consequences* project at the studio.

Recording of 10cc's ninth studio album began towards the end of October 1982. Although former 10cc cohorts Stuart Tosh and Rick Fenn both guest on the album, *Windows in the Jungle* saw Stewart and Gouldman working alongside new musicians, including some of the finest session men in the world. American drummer Steve Gadd was drafted in to play on some tracks, having impressed Eric Stewart during the recording of Paul McCartney's *Tug of War* album. When a jet-lagged Gadd arrived at Strawberry to start work on the sessions it prompted some rare rock star behaviour in the 10cc camp, with Stewart and Gadd snorting cocaine every night during the first week of recording. "When I played back what we'd done, it was awful," says Stewart. "Never again!"

Thankfully, recording became more productive and Gadd's distinctive drumming style worked well on tracks such as 24 Hours and Feel The Love, for which he suggested a different arrangement. "Graham and I played the song to Steve, and he said, 'Why don't we try this song in a reggae style? I love Dreadlock Holiday and I've never recorded a reggae track before.' So, we tried it and it worked out great and Steve's drumming on it was just incredible," says Stewart.

Simon Phillips, who had worked on the sessions for the *Ten Out of 10* album, filled the drum stool on other tracks. Conspicuous by his absence was Paul Burgess, who had originally been due to appear on the record. "I was due to start back in the studio, so I phoned up and they said, 'Oh, yes, we've just started today and we've got Steve Gadd in,'" recalls Burgess. "And to add insult to injury they were using my drum kit!"

The incident would serve to sour relations with Stewart and Gouldman. Despite the strain, Burgess was reunited with the duo early in 1983 to start rehearsals for a major 10cc tour of the UK. With Rick Fenn, Stuart Tosh and Vic Emerson completing the touring line-up, the itinerary was larger than their 1982 schedule, taking in 28 concerts at 23 venues around the country. Their stage backdrop was a cityscape consistent with the theme of their forthcoming album, while their set included Run Away and previewed three tracks from their forthcoming album – Feel The Love, City Lights and 24 Hours. The latter was released by Phonogram as 10cc's new single to coincide with the tour, but despite being a fine song, and a brave choice, it was far from radio-friendly and, at over seven minutes, received little airplay, despite a 'jukebox' version issued by Phonogram which divided the song into two parts. Unfortunately, the song only made No.78 in the UK charts.

Back on tour, at least, 10cc continued to please audiences and critics alike.

"Refreshing bursts of new material gave a hint of exciting things still to come from a band which appears to be aspiring to a second era of success," wrote *Music Week*, reviewing one of the band's sellout concerts at the Hammersmith Odeon.

One man not enjoying himself as the tour progressed, however, was Paul Burgess, who was becoming increasingly disillusioned following Stewart and Gouldman's snub at the start of the *Windows in the Jungle* sessions. To make matters worse, Burgess didn't like a lot of the new material.

"To make room for the new tracks they ditched some of the old numbers, which just happened to be some of my faves," says Burgess. "I didn't like the new stuff much. So, you see, musically I didn't enjoy the tour much." Things came to a head during the European tour that followed their UK dates. Burgess continues,

"We did a festival in Denmark. I actually said I didn't want to do it, but the message didn't get through until far too late, so I ended up doing that – and that was the last one I did." The gig, headlining the legendary Roskilde Festival in Denmark, attracted over 60,000 fans. It marked the end of a 10-year association with 10cc that had started back in August 1973 during the group's very first time out on the road.

Following the tour, Stewart and Gouldman reconvened at Strawberry North to put the finishing touches to *Windows in the Jungle*, with Rick Fenn adding guitar parts to a few of the tracks and Mel Collins adding saxophone. Vic Emerson and old acquaintance Mike Timoney would also guest on the album.

Despite encouraging the band to experiment with song construction, Phonogram now felt that there were too many extended pieces on the album and not enough potential hit singles. As a result, Stewart and Gouldman collaborated on a new song, Food For Thought, which worked the food-as-a-metaphor angle cleverly, revisiting 10cc's historic love of puns and wordplay. They recorded it at Strawberry North – with Stuart Tosh playing drums on a 10cc track for the first time since *Bloody Tourists* – and the song replaced The Secret Life of Henry on the album.

To design the sleeve for *Windows in the Jungle*, Stewart and Gouldman turned once again to Storm Thorgerson, now trading – rather unfortunately – as STd following the dissolution of Hipgnosis. Thorgerson created a design that featured three die-cut windows on the front cover that revealed images from the inner sleeve that related to a particular song on the album. Each 90-degree rotation of the inner sleeve enabled a different song, and associated images, to be revealed.

Mixed by Martin Lawrence in May 1983, *Windows in the Jungle* marked a return to form for 10cc. The record begins with the sound of jungle drums – lifted from Kit Mambo, a track on Gouldman's *Animalympics* soundtrack album – abruptly juxtaposed with the sounds of the urban jungle: car horns, traffic noises, and pneumatic drills. Adding another dimension to the album was the way in which the songs were cleverly interwoven. The intro to 24 Hours recurs during the fade-out of Taxi! Taxi!; the piano motif of Feel The Love reappears subtly in Working Girls; the saxophone riff at the end of Yes I Am! segues into the central riff of Americana Panorama.

10cc and Phonogram both recognised that a hit single was what was needed if they were to re-establish the band. It was decided that Feel The Love afforded them their best chance of success and plans were laid to release it as 10cc's next single. To aid its success, Phonogram sanctioned a large budget for an accompanying video. When directors were considered, Lol Creme and Kevin Godley were suggested. Enough water had passed under the bridge in the seven years since their split for all parties to agree to the 'reunion'. On June 27 1983 the four original members of 10cc got back together to work on the project. It was the first time that all four of them had seen each other since September 1976.

"It was great to do the video for Eric and Graham," says Creme. "It was like old friends seeing each other again; it was a shame the record didn't do more."

Released at the beginning of July 1983, Feel The Love failed to get 10cc back on the hit trail at home, only reaching No.87 in the UK charts despite a heavy promotional push. In Europe, however, the story was very different. In Belgium, Feel The Love reached No.13 while in the Netherlands the record became one of 10cc's biggest hits to date, reaching No.7 that summer.

Back in the UK, 10cc had been lined up to play two special concerts at the end of August. The first involved participating in the BBC's 24-hour *Rock Around the Clock* TV special and featured a live half-hour broadcast from The Regal Theatre in Hitchin. With Jamie Lane filling the drum stool vacated by Paul Burgess, the band performed a six-song set and received a tremendous reception.

The second gig, performing at the Penwith '83 Festival in Cornwall, as special guests of Meatloaf, was less successful. It was supposed to be the biggest ever gig staged in that county with an expected audience of 30,000 people and a bill that featured Aswad and Chuck Berry as well as 10cc and Meatloaf. The theory was that such contrasting artists would cater for the varying tastes of holidaymakers in Cornwall for the August Bank Holiday. It didn't work though, attracting a crowd of only 12,000, meaning that the organisers could not pay the performers their full fee. While most of the bands accepted the situation and agreed to play, Chuck Berry allegedly insisted on being paid up front in cash before he'd take to the stage. For Eric Stewart, he was excited to see one of his childhood heroes playing live and watched Berry's performance from side of stage.

"I wish I hadn't," says Stewart in his autobiography *Things I Do for Love*. "His guitar was way out of tune, he didn't bother to tell the band backing him what key he was playing in, and just slammed his foot on the floor of the stage when he wanted them to start or stop the song. He just didn't care and kept grinning at the crowd as if to say, 'Yes I know that this is crap but I really don't give a damn!' Here was one of my all-time heroes being such an asshole to his audience – why oh why? So sad."

After performing at Penwith, 10cc flew out to Australia to play their first gigs there in almost six years. First up was an appearance at the Rock For Rock's Sake Festival at Coomera in Queensland, followed by two nights in Newcastle and then two nights in Sydney.

Windows in the Jungle was finally issued by Phonogram at the end of September. It was, rightly, described by *The Times* as a "return to form" and was easily the band's best collection of songs since *Bloody Tourists*. In parts of Europe it was also the band's most successful album since *Bloody Tourists*. In the Netherlands, 10cc's career was enjoying a new lease of life following the Top 10 success of Feel The Love. *Windows in the Jungle* reached No.7 and even spawned a second major hit single in Food For Thought, which reached the Top 30 that autumn. The band made a headlining appearance at the Veronica Rocknight, in front of 10,000 fans, at the Ahoy Arena in Rotterdam at the end of September. The concert, an important one for 10cc, was filmed and broadcast on TV throughout Europe. Hit records, sell-out concerts. 10CC HAVE BEEN RE-BORN proclaimed one Dutch magazine headline.

Back in the UK a few days later, the story could not have been more different. *Windows in the Jungle* slipped into the lower reaches of the album charts, peaked at No.70 and then turned belly-up. The band embarked on an 18-date tour, consciously taking in more out-of-the-way destinations that had been absent from their recent outings, but the tour didn't go well. Even the band's

Hammersmith Odeon gig was disheartening, with Eric Stewart being assaulted on stage. It was the kind of incident that happens to a band when it is down on its luck. The tour ended inauspiciously on October 20 at the Margate Winter Gardens. It was to be their last gig together.

"We never actually discussed it, we just parted company," says Gouldman.

Both men had a distinct dread of living off former glories. "It was turning into a situation where we were going to become one of those nostalgia bands going round on package tours," says Stewart. "So, we agreed that if that was all that was left for us then we'd just shelve it for a while and leave it alone."

The straw that broke the camel's back was that Stewart and Gouldman had just delivered the strongest 10cc album in some time, had enjoyed considerable success with it outside of the UK, but found it largely ignored by both their record company and the record-buying public at home.

"The music scene was changing drastically at the time," says Stewart. "Maybe people had gotten used to us and we weren't being daring enough. In fact, I think somebody said at that time, 'If you released I'm Not In Love now, it would be a flop'."

Still, 10cc had survived the punk explosion seven years earlier, a seismic change far more significant than the changes taking place in the music scene in the early 80s. And in 1983 artists such as Pink Floyd, Genesis and David Bowie were still having No.1 records. For some reason, 10cc's music now seemed out of step with the rest of the music scene. They wouldn't, or couldn't, adapt their style with the times.

"We were probably a bit tired of it by then," reckons Stewart. "You really need success to fuel you. Maybe we were a bit out of step at the time, maybe we were a bit short of motivation."

Graham Gouldman has his own theory: "We were becoming too safe, too comfortable for the record-buying public. Plus, we hadn't changed that much, which didn't help. That style of music had had it."

Whatever the reasons, the facts were simple. 10cc had never really recovered from Eric Stewart's near-fatal car accident.

"After my car crash, this bloody great machine we'd invented called 10cc stopped running," as he acknowledged.

Coincidence or not, 10cc's career had begun to stall after the accident in 1979. With a few exceptions, the band had never hit its stride in the years that followed, despite Stewart and Gouldman's eternal optimism.

"Even as things were getting bad we thought, 'It's gonna be all right, don't worry about it, it'll be great,'" says Gouldman.

Simply put, the fun had gone out of being 10cc.

"It wasn't fresh any more," says Stewart. "We were just going through the motions. It wasn't exciting any more. Besides, we'd been working together as a production team before 10cc at Strawberry North and we started that in about 1969, so it was time for a break."

CHAPTER 24

SEPARATE LIMOS

THE DEMISE OF 10CC COINCIDED WITH THE END OF STRAWBERRY SOUTH
and Strawberry Mastering. Despite remaining an in-demand studio
– for the likes of Paul McCartney, Cliff Richard, Gerry Rafferty, The
Moody Blues, China Crisis, Gary Brooker, Thompson Twins and
The Police – the economics of Strawberry South didn't stack up.
Looking back, Eric Stewart reckons, "We poured too much money
into it and couldn't get enough out of the studio's earnings to cover
those costs." When the bank called in their loan in 1983, Strawberry
South went into liquidation. Unable to find a buyer for the studio,
the building was sold to a builders' merchants while Dave Gilmour
of Pink Floyd bought a lot of the studio equipment. Sadly, the
inside of the building was plundered in the process.

"Monitor speakers were just hacked out of the wall and all that
lovely Westlake building was just smashed to pieces," says Stewart.

Among the debris were the original reel-to-reel master tapes of
10cc albums recorded at Strawberry South, such as *Deceptive Bends*
and *Bloody Tourists*. "They were just left in a pile while things like
water pipes had burst, people had ripped sinks out and taken them
home with them," says Stewart.

When the master tapes were discovered, Zeb White was des-
patched to salvage what he could. Sadly, it would appear that some
of the tapes, particularly *Bloody Tourists*, had been irreparably damaged, as subsequent digital transfers of the album would never do
justice to the album's audio fidelity.

Happily, Strawberry North would fare much better, playing host
to the initial recordings of the next generation of Manchester bands.
New Order recorded their debut album *Movement* at Strawberry in
April/May 1981, with Martin Hannett once again in the producer's chair. When Joe Moss, manager of The Smiths, offered to put

up £225 to book Strawberry for a day for the group to record their debut single it was, according to Johnny Marr, "beyond exciting". They recorded Hand In Glove on February 27, 1983, returning to Strawberry in October to record their second single, This Charming Man, which gave them their first Top 30 hit. In mid-1985, The Stone Roses recorded tracks with Martin Hannett for what was supposed to be their debut album, including an early version of I Wanna Be Adored. The sessions were scrapped at the time but released 10 years later as *Garage Flower*.

Elsewhere, Manchester bands such as Buzzcocks (Everybody's Happy Nowadays), James (*Jimone, James 2*) and The Durutti Column (*Without Mercy, Another Setting*) all made important early recordings there. Strawberry also attracted groups from beyond the city, including The Sisters of Mercy, Echo and The Bunnymen, The Icicle Works and The Colourfield, whose frontman Terry Hall, formerly of The Specials and The Fun Boy Three, was a big fan of 10cc. "I love 10cc," says Hall. He relished the opportunity to work at Strawberry and to come into contact with people who had been involved in the 10cc story, including Paul Burgess, who would play drums on the album *Virgins and Philistines*, and studio receptionist Cathy Redfern, of 'big boys don't cry' fame. "I had this image of her as Joan Collins from her voice on the record," says Hall. "On Day 2 there, she popped her round and said, 'Just going out for chips. Anyone want chips?'"

Yet, despite Strawberry's ongoing appeal, it became increasingly difficult for the studio to keep up with the changing nature of the recording industry. In March 1986 it was announced that Strawberry had been sold to Nick Turnbull, of rival studio Yellow 2, for £200,000. The sale marked the end of Stewart and Gouldman's 18-year relationship with the studio, although Strawberry would continue to play an important musical role with bands such as Happy Mondays and Inspiral Carpets recording or mixing there.

By then, both Stewart and Gouldman were embracing life after 10cc. For his part, Gouldman had formed a new musical alliance with Andrew Gold.

"When Eric and I decided to call it a day, Andrew was the first person I contacted," says Gouldman. They discussed the idea of working together on some new songs. Equally enthused by the idea,

Gold travelled over to the UK to spend a couple weeks writing and recording demos at Gouldman's house near Rochdale, where he had recently installed a small £5,000 home studio incorporating a Fostex B16 16-track recorder and Allen and Heath mixing desk. The first song that they wrote together was a 60s pastiche called Don't Break My Heart. They enjoyed their collaboration so much that Gold extended his stay and the scope of the project expanded to record an album together, rather than just demos, at Gouldman's home studio.

"Andrew originally came over here planning to stay for two weeks and ended up staying for seven months," recalls Gouldman. "We recorded an album at my house in Cheshire, which is a great album, and we had the greatest time. I loved working with Andrew. I found a kindred spirit."

Among their new songs was Separate Limos, which seemed to draw upon Gouldman's recent experiences by charting the rise and fall of 10cc. Elsewhere, their songs reference the roots of their progenitors, with the unlikely pairing of Wilmslow and Malibu both mentioned in the lyrics. They were so pleased with their recordings that they decided to seek a record deal. Despite their years of experience in the music business they were still apprehensive about playing their new songs to record companies. "We feel very much like a new band," said Andrew Gold at the time. "We're dead nervous about everything." Given his contacts there, it made sense for Gouldman to play their new songs to Phonogram. "When we took the initial tapes down to our record company we were really frightened," said Gouldman at the time. "And it was kind of refreshing to feel that. There was nothing blasé about it. It's not just a 'something we'll do', we're deadly serious about it."

Phonogram signed the duo and planned to release Don't Break My Heart as their first single in May 1984, coupled with the James Bond spoof JB in Arabia. When Gouldman and Gold considered what to call their new band, they decided on the moniker World In Action. "Don't ask me why we chose that name," says Gouldman. "I have no clue now."

The single failed to chart but was released again in July 1984, this time under the new band name of Common Knowledge. It suffered the same fate, despite making a video that reflected the transatlantic nature of their alliance. When follow-up single, Victoria, flopped too Phonogram started to get cold feet and decided to shelve the Common Knowledge album. "Our record company dropped us but we still believed in our collaboration," says Gouldman. "So, we went back to Andrew's house in Los Angeles, wrote a load more songs and then came back to London and played them to Peter Robinson at RCA and he said, 'Great. I love this stuff'."

Having signed to RCA, Gouldman and Gold sought a producer who could give their new songs a fresh and modern feel. They chose to work with 25-year-old Phil Thornalley, formerly of The Cure and fresh from production duties on Prefab Sprout's indie classic When Love Breaks Down. Ironically, while recording that song, Thornalley had felt there was something missing from the production until he hit upon an idea inspired by 10cc. "I was panicking really," says Thornalley. "I think it wasn't until the 11th hour that I thought of looping Wendy Smith's voice to create those kind of washes, which is a trick I'd learned from 10cc who had come up with it for I'm Not In Love."

While preparing to record their first album for their new label, Gouldman was approached in May 1985 to produce a new version of You'll Never Walk Alone in honour of the 56 people who died in the the Bradford City football disaster. Released under the name The Crowd, the single reached No.1 in the UK and Ireland in June 1985, raising £132,000 for the burns research unit at the University of Bradford.

Recording of Gouldman and Gold's new album was to take place at RAK Studios in St John's Wood, London. With Gold still based in Los Angeles, the logistics of working together with Gouldman weren't always easy, particularly given Gold's aversion to flying (as reflected in his earlier solo song Endless Flight). Asked where the band's base of operations was, Gold would later joke, "On a 747 over Iceland".

With Thornalley at the helm, recording began with Gouldman and Gold performing all the instruments themselves. "I recall we were newly 'synthesizered' and '80s conscious', which meant a lot of programming on my part and Graham doing some bass and all the guitars," said Gold.

One of the first songs recorded was Right Between The Eyes, an irresistible pop song of the highest order influenced by both Motown and Prince, and all were pleased with the end result. "We knew after recording Right Between The Eyes that it was a snappy little ditty and would probably be a single," said Gold. "I recall doing the vocal a zillion times. There was definitely a nod to Prince, who Graham and I were both fond of. In fact, toward the end of the song when I say, 'Dig it', it sounds like it was stolen straight from Pop Life. Graham did all the distorted guitar work and the rest was all drum machines and synths, which was the usual fare back in those days."

Having worked with Phil Thornalley on most of the album, Gouldman and Gold self-produced three tracks themselves. These songs were partly recorded at Strawberry Studios in Stockport, marking the last time that an original member of 10cc would record there. As the album neared completion, thoughts turned to whether it should be released under the Common Knowledge banner or under a new name. In the end, after discussions with Peter Robinson, they decided on the latter.

"We changed our name to Wax, which was an idea I had on a train ride," says Gold. "I had written down about 50 names and Peter liked Wax the best."

The first Wax single, Ball and Chain, was released in October 1985 but failed to chart, despite the support of a video and a variety of remixes released on multiple formats. Fortunately, the group's second single, Right Between The Eyes, was far more successful, going on to become a big worldwide hit upon release in early 1986, reaching No.1 in Spain, where it spent six weeks at the top, and the Top 30 in Belgium, the Netherlands and Ireland. In the UK, however, the song only managed to climb to a disappointing No.60.

Wax's debut album, *Magnetic Heaven*, was released by RCA in May 1986 and acted as a fine showcase for Gold and Gouldman's immaculate pop sensibilities. By working with an outside producer and embracing new technology, the pair sounded fresh and contemporary again, constantly belying their age. It was important to the two of them that Wax be seen as a brand new entity rather than a project by well-established musicians.

"In England, that would be a plus," said Gold at the time. "Because generally there's almost an ageism there, that if you're not twenty-five and completely brand new then people don't really listen seriously. The kind of music that we're doing is very different from 10cc or an Andrew Gold record. It's obviously a little more modern."

In America, RCA celebrated the release of *Magnetic Heaven* with a launch party in Los Angeles at the Hollywood Wax Museum, attended by radio stations and journalists. *Magnetic Heaven* would go on to spend 11 weeks in the *Billboard* Top 200, peaking at No.101 in the American charts, selling almost 100,000 copies, while Right Between The Eyes would spend 13 weeks in the US charts, peaking just outside the Top 40. The band's progress in the US was not aided by the need to adapt their name in America. "We had to call ourselves Wax UK, because there was already a funk group called Wax at the time," says Gold.

Listening to the album today, while the production is well and truly rooted in the 80s, it remains one of the better post-10cc projects by any of the band's founder members, even if its success at the time was insufficient to get Wax to tour. "We needed the record to be really successful in order to get on the road, and that never happened," says Gouldman. "But I'm very proud of what we did on that album."

Keen to build on their momentum, Wax started work on their second album in March 1987 at Westside Studios in London, this time with producer Christopher Neil. Whereas *Magnetic Heaven* had seen Gouldman and Gold playing all the instruments themselves, the new album was made with guest musicians, such as keyboard player Adrian Lee and vocalist Paul Carrack, both of whom would continue to work with Gouldman on future projects. Among the album's many highlights was In Some Other World, a biting attack on American TV evangelists. Another of the new songs, Bridge To Your Heart, had particularly stood out to Christopher Neil when he'd listened to the demos that Gouldman and Gold had made for the album. When the time came to record his vocal, Andrew Gold made a mistake when counting the song in. "One, two... one, two... a-one, two, three, four... hold it," said Gold, stopping the count-in.

Listening to it in the control room, Gouldman and Neil decided to keep the take as it was rather than re-record the count-in as it made for a more striking opening. In July, the song was released as the band's next single. Bridge To Your Heart gave Wax another big global hit, reaching the Top 10 in Spain, Sweden, Belgium and the Netherlands, and the Top 20 in Germany and Ireland. This time the single also made inroads in the UK too, and as the song entered the Top 30, the call came in to appear on *Top of the Pops*.

"When we were on *Top of the Pops* it was just great, we just knew we'd made it – again," said Andrew Gold. "Graham and I were similar in our goals. We both really concentrated on the singles, and when we had success we felt that we proved that even more mature musicians could make it in what was a very teenage scene."

Bridge To Your Heart went on to reach No.12 in the UK charts, spending three consecutive weeks at that position. Kevin Godley sent his former bandmate a telegram to congratulate him on the song's success.

Wax's second album was called *American English* and saw Gouldman reunited with sleeve designer Storm Thorgerson. Released by RCA in September 1987, the album gained good reviews. "Old stagers making a last chuck at a buck you think? Wrong! *American English*, their second album, is brilliantly witty, should-be-chart stuff in an honourable line from 10cc via Squeeze," wrote Q magazine, awarding the album a four-star rating. "The single Bridge To Your Heart is typical of their good-time brass and brashness, but with In Some Other World the same tone veils a vicious satire of American television evangelists. Slick rhymes and pungent puns reinforce the impression of inspired craftsmanship at work on every aspect of the three-minute song."

American English would chart in the UK, the Netherlands and Sweden – where it reached No.8. Wax's chart success now made touring a viable proposition and, in October, a backing band was assembled that included former 10cc cohort Rick Fenn on guitar. During rehearsals, Gouldman and Gold decided to not only feature material from both Wax albums in their set, but also songs from their respective back catalogues, such as Dreadlock Holiday and Lonely Boy, and even For Your Love.

"Wax is about Andrew and I and the songs we're writing today, but it's also about the songs we wrote yesterday or, in my case, the day before yesterday!" said Gouldman at the time. Despite over 25 years in the music business, his love of music remained undiminished. "I still get as much of a kick out of it today as I ever did," said Gouldman at the time. "If I stopped getting pleasure out of it, I'd stop doing it."

The band's UK tour in November 1987 proved to be a success with their gig in Harrogate recorded and filmed by Storm Thorgerson for posterity. It would finally see release in September 2019. Life was once again sweet for Gouldman. The icing on the cake was that he had met Gill, the woman who would soon become the second Mrs Gouldman. "I thought long and hard about marrying again," says Gouldman. "I didn't want to make the same mistakes again. But I loved Gill and that was it." The couple would go on to have two children together – Rosanna and Alex. Meanwhile, keen to build on their success, Wax started work on their third album, this time with producer Peter Collins at the helm. "Like us, he's very pop-orientated," said Gouldman at the time. "He's also very good if you need extra musicians. He always knows exactly the right person." Among these was rap artist Mr Magic, who guested on the closing track Credit Where Credit's Due – an alternative, musical way of presenting the album's credits. They even tried to get George Harrison to perform the guitar solo on Don't Play That Song but he wasn't available, so Gold recorded the solo in the style of the former Beatle.

With the album completed, Wax played a series of concerts in June 1989, supporting The Bee Gees on their arena tour of the UK. Again, audiences were treated not only to Wax songs but also to tracks from the Gouldman and Gold archives. However, Wax's next two singles, the ballad Wherever You Are and the more up-tempo Anchors Aweigh, both failed to chart. A similar fate awaited the album, called *One Hundred Thousand in Used Notes*, when it was released in September. Despite selling 2 million albums during their tenure in Wax, their relative lack of success caused a great deal of frustration to both Gold and Gouldman and put a question mark over the future of the band.

"Maybe we were just a little too late in our careers for things to happen, which is a great shame," says Gouldman. "Because I really believe that my partnership with Andrew was the most joyous and fun I ever had with anyone, musically speaking."

BELOW: Lol Creme, Kevin Godley and Peter Cook prepare to face the *Consequences*, November 1977 (Michael Putland/Getty Images)

CONSEQUENCES

RIGHT: Cover for Godley and Creme's triple album *Consequences* released in October 1977
(Cover design by Godley and Creme, reproduced by kind permission)

Lol Creme/Kevin Godley

ABOVE: 10cc once again try to break America, as part of their seven-month world tour, November 1978 (Michael Putland/Getty Images)

RIGHT: Cover for 10cc's sixth album *Bloody Tourists*, released in September 1978 (Cover designed by Hipgnosis, reproduced by kind permission)

US press ad supporting the release of
Bloody Tourists (Thanks to Dave Jarvis)

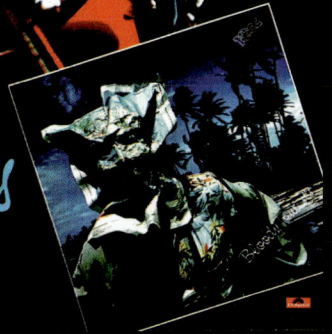

Two previously unseen outtakes from the *Greatest Hits 1972-78* photo shoot, June 5, 1979
(Photos by Aubrey Powell, reproduced by kind permission)

Two previously unseen outtakes from the photo session for 10cc's seventh album *Look Hear?*, January 31, 1980 (Photos by Aubrey Powell, reproduced by kind permission)

ABOVE: Aloha and out. Previously unseen photograph of a disgruntled sheep receiving hypnotherapy on a specially made psychiatrist's couch in Hawaii (Photo by Aubrey Powell, reproduced by kind permission)

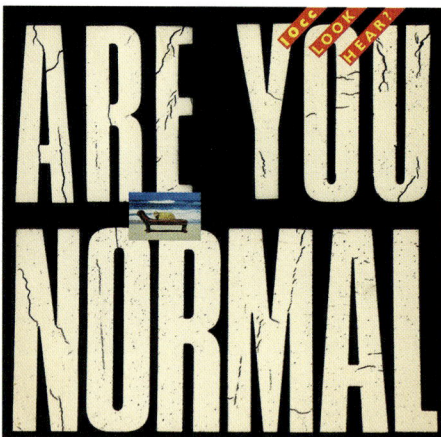

LEFT: Cover for 10cc's seventh album *Look Hear?*, released in March 1980 (Cover design by Hipgnosis, reproduced by kind permission)

ABOVE: Flyer for the band's gig in Ludwigshafen as part of their most extensive European tour, April 26, 1980 (Thanks to Dave Jarvis)

RIGHT: Cover for 10cc's eighth album *Ten out of 10*, released in November 1981 (Cover design by Visible Ink, reproduced by kind permission)

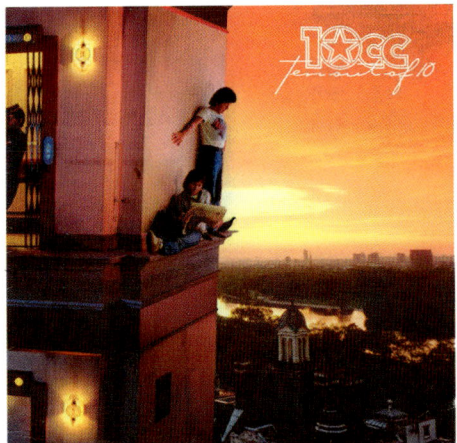

ABOVE: The original 10cc line-up
reunite to film the video for Feel The
Love, June 27, 1983
(Dave Hogan/Getty Images)

RIGHT: Cover for 10cc's ninth album
Windows in the Jungle, released in
September 1983
(Cover design by STd, reproduced by
kind permission)

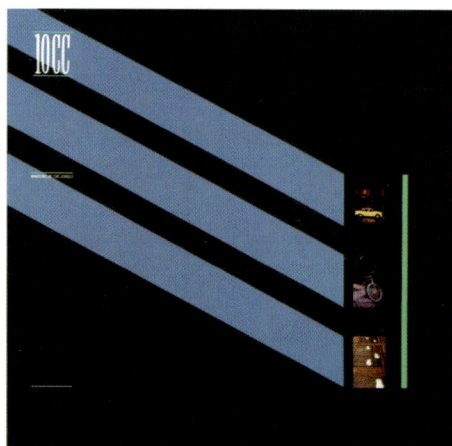

Eric Stewart films the video to Paul McCartney's So Bad during their five-year period
working together, January 13, 1984. (l-r) Ringo Starr, Eric, Linda McCartney, Paul McCartney
(Bettman/Getty Images)

ABOVE: Andrew Gold and Graham Gouldman film the video to Wax's first single Ball and Chain, October 21, 1985. They would go on to score two global hits with Right Between The Eyes and Bridge To Your Heart (Michael Putland/Getty Images)

OPPOSITE: Lol Creme and Kevin Godley direct the video for Frankie Goes To Hollywood's Two Tribes, April 21, 1984 (Express/Getty Images)

RIGHT: Changing Faces, the 1987 compilation album of 10cc and Godley and Creme hits which turned platinum and was instrumental in the band getting back together (Cover design by Graphyk, reproduced by kind permission)

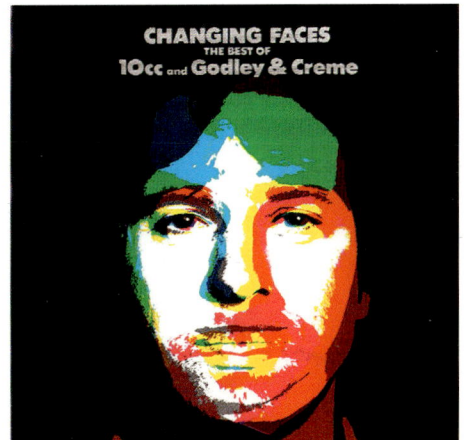

ABOVE: Graham Gouldman and Eric Stewart promote *Meanwhile* in the Netherlands, May 14, 1992 (Rob Verhorst/ Getty Images)

RIGHT: Cover for 10cc's tenth album *Meanwhile*, released in May 1992 (Cover design by Laurence Dunmore, reproduced by kind permission)

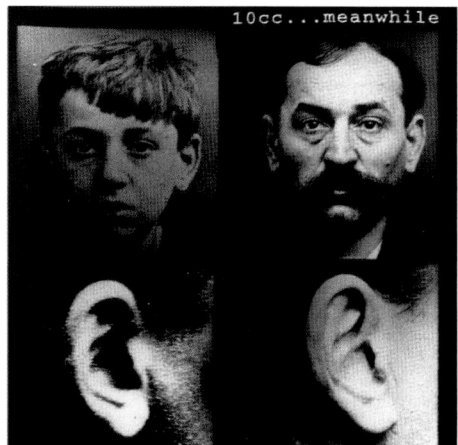

10cc...meanwhile

ABOVE: Flyer for 10cc's Japanese Tour in March 1993, their first time on the road in ten years (Thanks to Dave Jarvis)

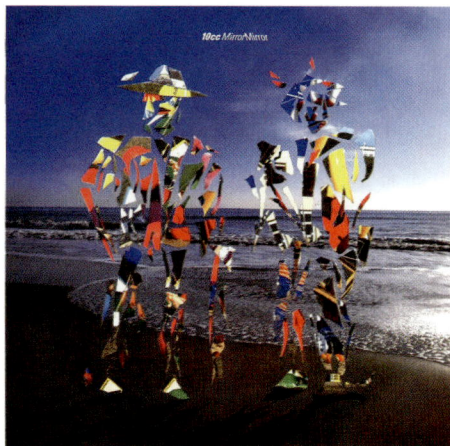

RIGHT: Cover for 10cc's eleventh album *Mirror, Mirror*, released in August 1995, although more like two solo albums rolled into one than a true 10cc album (Cover design by Storm Studios, reproduced by kind permission)

BELOW: Sir George Martin presents 10cc with an Ivor Novello Award for 'Outstanding Song Collection', May 27, 2004 (Richard Young/Shutterstock)

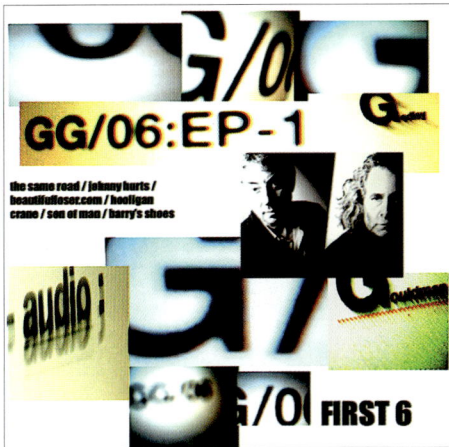

LEFT: Kevin Godley and Graham Gouldman launched their GG/06 project in July 2006 and released 6 songs together, including Son of Man which tells the tale of how 10cc formed out of the ashes of Hotlegs

BELOW: Cover for *Tenology*, released in November 2012 to coincide with 10cc's 40th anniversary, with the phrenology head inscribed with the band's influences (Cover design by Storm Studios, reproduced by kind permission)

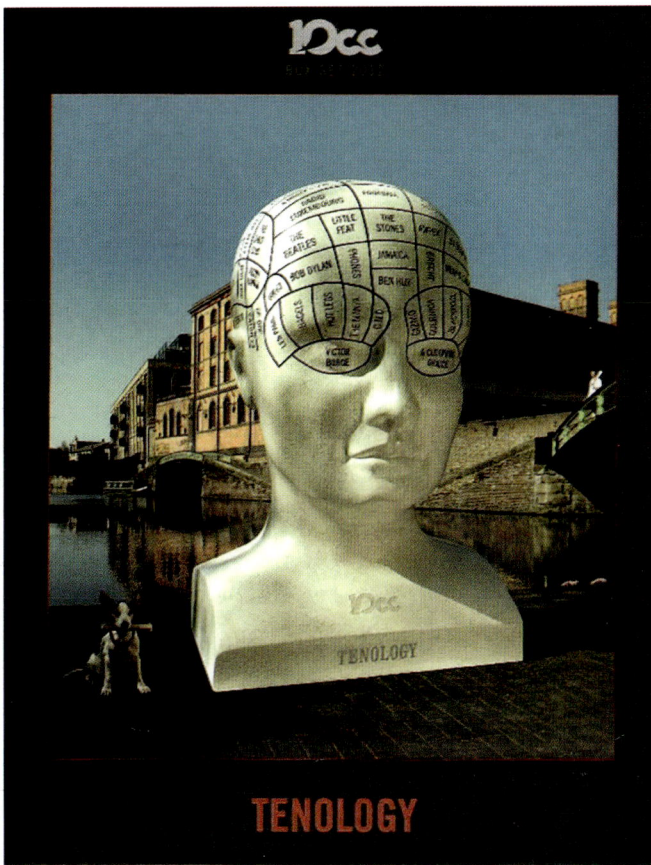

Eric at 75, a portrait taken by his son Jody, November 9, 2019 (Jody Stewart, reproduced by kind permission)

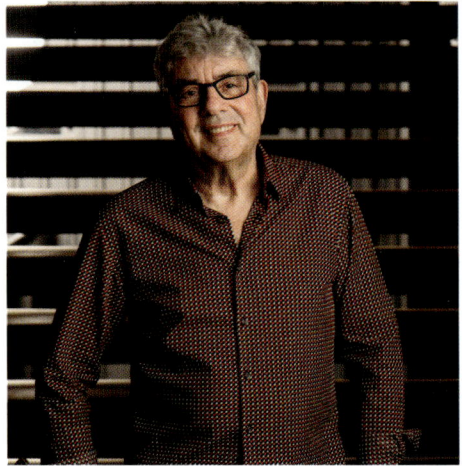

Graham promoting *Modesty Forbids*, released March 2020 (Reinout Bos, reproduced by kind permission)

Kevin continues to look for new angles (Sue Godley, reproduced by kind permission)

Lol performing at Cornbury Festival with the Trevor Horn Band, July 6, 2019 (Steve Thorne/Getty Images)

Following the end of 10cc, Eric Stewart had continued his friendship and musical association with Paul McCartney, appearing on the album *Pipes of Peace* and in the video for the single So Bad, which was a Top 30 hit in the US in January 1984. Unlike Gouldman, Stewart decided not to form a new group, and turned down the opportunity to join former Roxy Music members Andy Mackay and Phil Manzanera in a new venture called The Explorers.

"I was staying at my house in Barbados and I got a call from Andy and Phil, who were recording at Eddy Grant's studio," recalls Stewart. "They said, 'Do you fancy coming over to record some vocals?' So, I went over to the studio and I recorded some vocals, but I wasn't interested in joining them on a permanent basis in The Explorers. I didn't really see any point in a 10cc/Roxy Music supergroup."

Back at home Stewart had been approached by his friend Nick Mason, of Pink Floyd, to collaborate on some music for an advertising project. Stewart declined, instead recommending Rick Fenn, thus sparking off a musical partnership between Mason and Fenn that would yield film soundtracks (*White of the Eye*, *Tank Malling*), music for TV and advertising, and even a solo album, *Profiles*, which featured vocals by Dave Gilmour on its lead single Lie for a Lie. When Fenn and Mason were developing the soundtrack to a short film about Mason's life called *Life Could Be A Dream*, Stewart agreed to sing lead vocal on a cover version of The Crew Cut's Sh'Boom.

The first major post-10cc project that Stewart undertook was as producer of a new solo album by former Abba singer Agnetha Fältskog. The members of Abba had long been fans of 10cc, right back to when Anni-Frid Lyngstad covered The Wall Street Shuffle for her 1975 solo album *Frida Ensam*.

"In my days with Abba, I met Eric Stewart and 10cc a couple of times," said Fältskog at the time. "I've always been a 10cc fan, Eric's music stands for quality." Stewart and Fältskog met up that summer to start choosing songs for the album. They allegedly listened to over 400 songs, many of which had been submitted by friends of Stewart.

"Eric called several of his friends, who started working especially for me," said Fältskog. "I think it's an enormous honour that so many important people wanted to work on my album."

Among those answering the call were Roy Wood, Justin Hayward, Jeff Lynne, John Wetton and Geoffrey Downes. According to legend, Elvis Costello also submitted a song for the album called Shatter Proof but Fältskog elected not to record it. Stewart would contribute two new songs of his own – Save Me and a track that Fältskog would later describe as her favourite song on the album, the ballad I Won't Be Leaving You. He also collaborated with Fältskog on a couple of songs – I Won't Let You Go and You're There.

Recording began in September 1984 at Abba's Polar Studios in Stockholm, with a backing band that included Rick Fenn, Vic Emerson and Jamie Lane, who had played drums on 10cc's last tour, along with former Abba bassist Rutger Gunnarsson. In addition to his production work, Stewart played electric piano and sang backing vocals and would even go on to have a hand in designing the album cover. Backing tracks to 15 songs were recorded over the first two weeks before Agnetha started laying down her vocals.

"The singing isn't especially easy for me," said Fältskog at the time. "Sometimes I have to re-record my vocals for a song six times. Luckily, Eric is very patient. He has taken care that my voice has been committed to tape the best way possible, and we've also paid a lot of attention to the backing vocals."

While Stewart and Fältskog worked on her album at Polar Studios, her former bandmates Benny Andersson and Björn Ulvaeus were writing their musical *Chess* elsewhere in the building. Fältskog's album, to be titled *Eyes of a Woman*, was mixed in November but former Abba, and now Fältskog manager, Stig Anderson had reservations when he heard it. "Stig listened to the album the day we finished mixing and he called me the same night," says Stewart. "He said, 'Eric, I don't hear a hit!'"

Despite Anderson's reservations, the Stewart/Fältskog-penned single I Won't Let You Go would go on to reach the Top 10 in Sweden, Belgium and Poland, and the Top 30 in the Netherlands and Germany. However, Fältskog refused to do any promotional work to support its release in the UK, turning down invitations to appear on high-profile TV shows of the time, such as the BBC's *Wogan*. As a result, the song limped to a lowly No.84 in the UK.

"I was very disappointed that she wouldn't promote the single in the UK," says Stewart. "A real waste of all our efforts … I was really pissed off!" *Eyes of a Woman* would go on to sell an estimated 800,000 copies around the world, reaching No.2 in Sweden – where it turned platinum – the Top 20 in Norway, the Netherlands, Belgium, South Africa and Canada, the Top 30 in Germany and the Top 40 in the UK.

Having completed work on Agnetha's album, Stewart attended the UK premiere of Paul McCartney's movie *Give My Regards to Broad Street* at the Empire Theatre, Leicester Square in November 1984. Stewart's commitments to 10cc had meant he could only make a small contribution to his friend's movie when filming began back in November 1982. Stewart appeared in the film as part of McCartney's band performing the track So Bad, a title that aptly matched many of the headlines from critics when they reviewed the film.

"How's the new house, Eric?" enquires Ringo Starr, as Stewart pulls on his guitar in the film.

"It's alright," Stewart mumbles in response.

Such sparkling wordplay ensured the movie wasn't among the nominations for 'Best Screenplay' at that year's Oscars. The accompanying soundtrack album was more successful, with Stewart contributing backing vocals to the single No More Lonely Nights, which reached the Top 10 in the UK and US in October 1984.

Now, in the wake of the critical mauling of *Give My Regards to Broad Street*, McCartney's sights were set on making a credibility-restoring killer album as his next project. George Martin, who had produced McCartney's previous two albums, *Tug of War* and *Pipes of Peace*, had advised that he was planning to retire and would not be working on the next album. Martin sounded Stewart out about taking on the producer's role.

"George said to me, 'I think you should help Paul with his next album'," recalls Stewart. "I said, 'He's not asked me'. He said, 'Would you be interested?' I said 'Yeah'."

A few days later Stewart got a call from McCartney's manager, Steve Shrimpton, who invited him up to a meeting at MPL's office in Soho Square to formalise the offer. Stewart and his wife Gloria were having dinner with the McCartneys shortly after, when Linda suggested the two of them should write some songs together for the project.

"It started very casually with Eric," said McCartney at the time. "I just said, 'Fancy coming round one day to work with me on some songs?'" Stewart jumped at the chance of writing with the ex-Beatle. The plan was to sit across from each other with a couple of acoustic guitars. It was the first time that McCartney had written with a songwriting partner in this way since his work with John Lennon. Understandably, there was some nervousness on Stewart's part on the first day of the writing sessions.

"There was a bit of apprehension, of course, when we first sat down together with a couple of guitars because you're writing with a legend," says Stewart. Still, he and McCartney were both pleased with the first fruits of their new songwriting partnership.

"We started off with Stranglehold, putting rhythmic words in, using lyrics like a bongo, accenting the words," said McCartney. "We both enjoyed the experience."

"It worked out really well," says Stewart. "At the end of the first day Paul rang me at home to say, 'That was great. Same time, tomorrow?' So, I went back the next day and we spent the next four weeks or so writing songs together."

McCartney and Stewart would write 11 new songs together over this period, utilising a range of different techniques in the process.

"We tried different ways of writing," says Stewart. "It was a nice experimental method. Different songs were written in different ways." Arguably the standout track from the collaboration was the poignant Footprints.

"I'd driven through the snow," recalls Stewart. "It was really, really bad weather. Somehow, I got down to Paul's place and I said, 'What shall we write about today?' Paul said, 'Well, you give me a line and then I'll give you a line and we'll do it like that.' So, I said, 'It's beautiful outside' and we carried on from there. He came up with the next line and then I wrote the line after that and we wrote the whole song that way, without any music at this point. And then once we'd got something that looked like a set of lyrics we picked up our acoustic guitars again, face to face, and started playing some things that we liked instrumentally, chord sequences that were grabbing, and we had the song written in about four hours. It was really interesting."

A critical newspaper article that had clearly got under McCartney's skin inspired another new song. "I walked in another morning and I said, 'You look a bit tense' and he said, 'Yeah, I'm fucking angry'," recalls Stewart. "I said, 'What's the problem?' and he said, 'The press – what the hell gives them the right to tell me what to do with my life?' I said, 'What? Hold it. Write that down.' And we got Angry started."

A postcard inspired another new song, Yvonne's The One. "The song came about when Nick Mason of Pink Floyd sent me one of those Gary Larson postcards from the States, which said, 'When I first saw Yvonne, volcanoes erupted.' It was a classic line. I showed it to Paul and he said, 'Let's write the song,'" recalls Stewart.

Other postcards, of the British seaside variety, were part of the inspiration behind another song, Move Over Busker, which was filled with double entendres and references to the likes of Nell Gwyn, Mae West and Errol Flynn. "That's got a good American rock 'n' roll feel to it," said McCartney. "I think originally it was called Move Over Buster, which Eric and I thought was a bit ordinary. So, we just kicked it about a little bit and it came out 'busker', then that gave us more possibilities about wandering round and meeting people."

Stewart and McCartney demoed their new songs during the early part of 1985. Because of his conversations with George Martin and Steve Shrimpton, Stewart was under the impression that he had a production role on the album when recording commenced. McCartney, however, had lined up Hugh Padgham to co-produce the album, which didn't go down well with Stewart.

"It all got a bit sticky because he thought I'd wanted him to co-produce the album with me and I must have led him to believe that," says McCartney. "Then I said, 'Oh, we're getting so and so to produce it,' and he went into shock."

Padgham – who had produced albums by The Police, Phil Collins, Genesis and David Bowie – was delighted at the prospect of working on the project. "Of course, I was bowled over," says Padgham. "I was in my late twenties, still relatively young, young to the game. I thought this was just amazing. When he or someone couriered to me a cassette to the studio I went home incredibly excited to listen to those demos that he had done with Eric Stewart."

For Padgham, the project was even more appealing because Stewart was "a hero of mine from 10cc." However, he wasn't impressed when he heard the demos. "I can honestly tell you now that I was underwhelmed when I heard those songs," he says. "I thought, well, hang on, who am I to know, as a little 28-year-old guy, that Paul McCartney has given me these songs that are not very impressive? But what are you going to do when you've suddenly been asked to record an album with one of the greatest guys in pop music ever? You're not gonna say no, are you?"

Recording began in April 1985 at McCartney's Hog Hill Mill studio in Rye, East Sussex. To create a more spontaneous band feel to the sessions, the backing tracks were recorded with the nucleus of McCartney, Stewart and drummer Jerry Marotta all playing together in the studio at the same time. At first the sessions went well with McCartney enjoying playing with a band again in the studio.

"The first track we recorded was Stranglehold, with Jerry Marotta on the kit, Paul on bass and lead vocal, me on acoustic guitar, and Linda and I on harmonies," recalls Stewart. "It was a fantastic rhythm section and we were delighted with how the backing track turned out. When I got home that night I got a call from Paul saying, 'Brilliant, mate. I'm so pleased with how things are going. See you in the studio tomorrow.'"

On other songs, such as Pretty Little Head, the musicians would swap instruments. "I drummed on it, Jerry Marotta played vibes, and Eric Stewart played keyboards, so we all switched roles to send us off in a different direction," said McCartney. "Eventually you pull it back and make some sort of sense of it."

However, as the recording sessions progressed, the atmosphere in the studio became more fractious, with Stewart and Padgham having very different points of view on elements of the production. Something had to give, and six weeks into recording Stewart received a phone call from McCartney's production company, MPL.

"They told me there was a contractual problem," says Stewart. "Padgham's management had evidently decreed that he be sole producer. I was paid off."

Recording would continue sporadically over the next 12 months, with Pete Townshend, Phil Collins and Carlos Alomar all making guest appearances and with Tony Visconti and Anne Dudley working on the orchestral arrangements. However, as recording dragged on, relations between McCartney and Padgham also becoming strained. When the album was eventually released in September 1986, entitled *Press to Play*, its sleeve carried the credit 'special contribution by Eric Stewart'. The final tracklisting included six McCartney/Stewart songs – Stranglehold, Footprints, Pretty Little Head, Move Over Busker, Angry and However Absurd – while other collaborations, such as Write Away, Tough on a Tightrope and Hanglide would appear as future b-sides. A couple of other McCartney/Stewart songs were either recorded but not used (Yvonne's The One) or left unfinished (Don't Break The Promise).

Despite the inharmonious recording sessions, *Press to Play* became McCartney's most critically acclaimed album in years, receiving a four-star review in Q magazine. "There have, surely, been only three McCartney LPs in the last 16 years for which we should be eternally grateful," wrote Mark Ellen. "But let me amend that: here's the fourth. *Press to Play* sounds like all the most imaginative and workable elements of the other three shuffled together. Dependable coves like Pete Townshend, Phil Collins and Carlos Alomar add layers of professional varnish, and producer Hugh Padgham has pruned back the shrubbery but, more crucially, six of the ten tracks were written with Eric Stewart and, thus, benefit from a welcome measure of grit – McCartney's first serious crack at co-composition since Lennon."

Elsewhere in the magazine, journalist Chris Salewicz was equally enthused: "The principal strength of the new LP is the quality of the songs, six of which McCartney co-wrote with Eric Stewart, the former 10cc singer and writer of such classics as I'm Not In Love, a song that is almost a parody of a McCartney love ballad."

Rolling Stone viewed it as one of McCartney's better solo albums. "McCartney has always worked best with collaborators," wrote Anthony Decurtis. "Stewart pushes McCartney in some new directions, particularly on the dreamily abstract Pretty Little Head and the LP's grand Beatlesque finale, However Absurd."

Yet, despite the critical acclaim, *Press to Play* only reached No.8 in the UK and the Top 30 in America and throughout Europe, selling less than a million copies worldwide. None of the singles taken from the album would prove to be major hits, despite a big push behind the ballad Only Love Remains, which featured Stewart in the video and on stage alongside McCartney at the Royal Variety Performance in November 1986. *Press to Play* fell well short of being the commercial success that McCartney had been seeking and, 30 years on, he is quick to criticise the album as one of his weakest solo efforts. "It didn't really work out as well as I wanted it to although we did a couple of nice things," says McCartney. "But it wasn't a very successful album."

In 2017, *Uncut* published their *Ultimate Music Guide* to McCartney's career and concluded that *Press to Play* "ends with a run of McCartney/Stewart songs whose unforced charm suggests the partnership could have continued."

Ultimately, however, Stewart and McCartney's writing styles were perhaps too similar for a permanent writing partnership, although their friendship would endure and they would even go on to make more music together. McCartney would turn to Elvis Costello on his next album *Flowers in the Dirt*. In the meantime, by the time *Press to Play* was eventually released, Stewart had been approached about collaborating on another interesting project.

"I got a call from Steve O'Rourke, Pink Floyd's manager, who said, 'Dave Gilmour is looking for someone to write lyrics for the next Pink Floyd album, are you interested in writing some lyrics?'" recalls Stewart.

Gilmour was attempting to relaunch Pink Floyd in the midst of a very bitter legal dispute with Roger Waters, who had driven the concepts for previous Floyd albums. Gilmour approached a number of people to help nail the concept and lyrics for the next Pink Floyd album. "I'll give Gilmour credit," said Waters begrudgingly at the time. "When he devises a fraud, he goes to first-class talent for assistance."

Stewart was happy to get involved in the project. "I said, 'Sure,' so I met up with Dave, who said that the concept for the album was the human body," says Stewart. "He gave me some backing tracks of music he'd already recorded and I went away to write some lyrics for them. I worked on them for about 10 days and when I'd finished I phoned Steve and said, 'I'm ready to play some stuff to Dave.' He said, 'Well, Dave's a bit busy at the moment, send the tapes to me and I'll pass them on to him.' I thought that was a bit strange but, anyway, a couple of weeks went by and I hadn't heard anything, so I phoned Steve and said, 'What's going on?' He said, 'Well, Dave's decided to work on a different concept for the album now.' So, nothing ever came of it unfortunately."

Gilmour would ultimately abandon the idea of a central concept for the next Pink Floyd album, *A Momentary Lapse of Reason*, which was released in September 1987. By then Stewart had produced, and played on, sessions for a couple of up and coming bands. The first involved production work for a group called Flip.

"We recorded at the famous Abbey Road studios, meeting and working with some of my all time heroes, Eric Stewart of 10cc fame being one," says the band's Andy Kinch. "Eric played guitar and produced one of the tracks, Love Incognito. One outstanding memory from our sessions there was Eric singing a very special version of I'm Not In Love – just him on the studio piano."

The other project saw Stewart working with Scottish indie band Hearts and Minds, who were about to record their debut album for CBS and were searching for the right producer. "We were all thinking, 'Who might be good?' and Eric Stewart came to mind," recalls frontman David Scott. "He'd just worked on a couple of my favourite McCartney records and you just got the feeling he might be about and up for it. Unbelievably, when I called Annie Roseberry at CBS they'd had the same idea. As I recall, they called him up and he came to London later that week having loved the music. I remember right away he had big ambitions for the music and understood the kind of cinematic thing we were hoping for. And, of course, I was a huge fan of 10cc. So inventive and melodic."

The bulk of recording took place during the spring of 1987 at Britannia Row Studios in Islington, North London. "Any time you work with big names there is a bit of an adjustment period where you're going, 'Oh my God, he wrote I'm Not In Love,' but you get over that and just get on with it," says Scott. "Eric was great to work with, funny and talented and very generous in many ways. He was very strong on those sessions. I remember he focused a lot on tracking acoustic guitars and getting them to shimmer. He was tough when I did vocals and that was good too. We did some of the backing vocals together and that was a big boost to the confidence. It was a very good learning experience for me and I hope he would like some of the music I've made since."

Despite six songs being recorded during the sessions, only one – Turning Turtle – would see the light of day when it was released as a single in September 1987, albeit without success. By contrast, Stewart's first chart band, The Mindbenders, were enjoying something of a renaissance, with The Game of Love featuring in the 1987 Robin Williams film *Good Morning Vietnam* and Phil Collins taking his cover of A Groovy Kind of Love, originally sung by Stewart, to No.1 in both the UK and US charts towards the end of 1988.

In 1989, Stewart guested on what was originally intended as the 11th Alan Parsons Project album, but that would instead be released under the band name and album title *Freudiana*, with Stewart providing lead vocals on two tracks: The Ring and Upper Me.

It was now 10 years since his car accident and in that time Stewart had undergone numerous operations to try and save the sight in his left eye. By now the retina was so badly damaged that his eye specialist recommended that the eye be removed and replaced with a prosthesis. "I thought about this for a couple of weeks and gradually came to terms with his diagnosis," recalls Stewart. "We humans really don't want to give any of our 'bits' up do we? I called the specialist and told him to go ahead and within a week or so I went into hospital, was knocked out with a general anaesthetic, and my left eye was removed."

Following the operation, Stewart reflected on his future. After over 25 years in the music business he yearned for a change of lifestyle. Having always loved south-west France, he and his family set up home in an 18th-century petite manoir with 16 acres of land called Le Rausset on a high promontory overlooking the Dordogne River in 1989. With music taking a back seat, Stewart sought other interests.

"The loss of my left eye really made me want to prove something to myself," says Stewart. "A strange feeling of bereavement hit me after the eye was removed. So, I thought, 'What would be the craziest thing I could possibly do with one good eye?' Of course! I'll learn to fly an aeroplane!"

Having enjoyed a couple of lessons at a local airport near Bergerac, Stewart took a four-week flying course near La Rochelle in 1990. Despite successfully passing his pilot's test, he was told that with just one good eye he wouldn't be allowed to fly solo. Undeterred, Stewart visited a medical aviation specialist based at Heathrow airport where his sight was assessed and he was told that his peripheral vision was good enough for him to receive his full pilot's licence. Back at home, Stewart relished the opportunity to put his new licence to use. "I really did enjoy flying around the French skies," he said, "and especially when I got to fly in vintage aircraft such as the Boeing Stearman biplanes."

While he enjoyed non-musical pursuits, and with Wax seemingly coming to the end of its natural life, it seemed as if Stewart and Gouldman might be about to hang up their Gibsons and their Fenders.

CHAPTER 25

CHANGING FACES

WHILE ERIC STEWART AND GRAHAM GOULDMAN HAD BEEN STRUGGLING
to re-establish 10cc, Godley and Creme's career as video directors
had been going from strength to strength. Their work on Ringo
Starr's long-form video, *The Cooler*, became the official British entry
for the Short Film Palme d'Or at the 1982 Cannes Film Festival.
Given their growing reputation, it was a natural progression to be
asked to direct TV commercials. One assignment saw them direct
an acclaimed 50-second TV ad for Wrangler jeans. The ad saw the
duo recycle some of the groundbreaking visual techniques they had
used in their own Wide Boy video; they also provided the music
(That's What's Going On).

In between their video projects, Godley and Creme occasionally
found time to reacquaint themselves with a recording studio. Their
1983 album *Birds of Prey* was an electronic record that saw the duo
again using synthesizers and drum machines. While it had some
memorable moments – such as the haunting Madame Guillotine
– it also sounded at times like a contractual obligation and a distrac-
tion from their real passion of directing videos. The video shoot in
Los Angeles for the accompanying single Save Me A Mountain was
more eventful, albeit for near-disastrous reasons.

"We were shooting this riot scene where Kevin tries to calm
down the prisoners, but they ignore him and start throwing these
hammers past him at the guards," recalls Creme. "Suddenly he collapsed, and an impressive trickle of blood spread across the floor.
Well, naturally I thought it was an Oscar-winning performance, if a
little over the top. But when I yelled, 'Cut!' and he didn't move, we
suddenly realised he'd been hit for real. It was pretty scary."

While *Birds of Prey* failed to follow up the success of *Ismism*, their
next video project saw Godley and Creme working with a band that

had come a very long way since they'd first met them while sharing studio space at Surrey Sound Studios back in 1978. By now The Police were arguably the biggest band on the planet and about to release their fifth album, *Synchronicity*. Godley and Creme were signed up to direct the videos for three singles from the album and were given a pretty free hand. "I trusted them completely because they'd been musicians," says Sting. "I handed it over to them and let them do what they wanted."

With a budget of $75,000, the first video that they directed for The Police was for Every Breath You Take. In preparing for the video, Godley and Creme had seen some old black and white films from the 40s, such as Gjon Mili's classic short film *Jammin' the Blues*. They hit upon the idea of recreating the look and feel of a smokey jazz club jam session for the video. In a striking case of synchronicity, Sting had seen the same films and had a similar idea.

"We were all thinking along the same lines of a 40s jazz jam session look," says Godley. "We shot it at the Charlie Chaplin soundstage in Hollywood in black and white, keeping it very 'hard', so there were no greys. We enhanced that contrast look in the edit as well."

The video went into heavy rotation on MTV, contributing to its global success. The elegant simplicity of the video meant it stood out from the crowd on the channel. "The first video I watched over and over was Every Breath You Take," says musician Richard Marx. "It was like seeing a Bergman film. Directors usually spelled out every word of the lyrics in a video, but this was the first video I knew that didn't do that. It was abstract."

For the video to follow-up single Wrapped Around Your Finger, Godley and Creme employed the video equivalent of an old audio trick from their 10cc days. "We filmed it at double speed, so that when we edited it at normal speed, the band were all moving in slow motion, but their mouths were in sync to the track," says Creme. "It worked really well, but of course during the actual shoot itself, all you could hear was this Mickey Mouse-type vocal."

The video for Synchronicity II placed the band in a dystopian setting with each member of The Police standing on towers made up of piles of guitars, amplifiers, drums and junk, with debris and papers flying everywhere. During filming, drummer Stewart Copeland's tower caught fire and the crew started to leave the building. Creme, however, told the director of photography to keep the cameras rolling regardless.

Their groundbreaking approach to their next assignment would prove to be one of their most acclaimed. "We got a call one day from Herbie Hancock's manager," recalls Creme. "The problem he had was that he couldn't get Herbie on MTV because, he said, they won't show black artists. He asked if we could come up with an interesting video idea that would have Herbie in it at the minimum one could, so that it would get played on MTV."

Godley and Creme were shocked to hear that black artists weren't being played on MTV and baulked at the brief, but Hancock was keen for his new single, Rockit, to be heard.

"I told Godley and Creme, 'Look, don't even have me on it, don't have any black people on it – just make it as white as any video they might show by Led Zeppelin or anybody'," recalls Hancock. "They laughed. They thought I was joking, but I wanted people to hear the music."

Rockit was a groundbreaking record, one of the first to feature scratching and other turntablist techniques. When conceiving equally revolutionary concepts for the video, Kevin Godley recalled a TV programme he'd seen recently that featured the work of artist Jim Whiting, who created robotic figures, made from spare parts he'd found on rubbish tips, that he brought to life using bursts of compressed air.

"We went out and found where Jim lived," recalls Creme. "We pulled up outside and we looked through the letterbox. There was a very steep set of steps. It all looked very Dickensian in there. But hanging on the wall were all these bits and pieces of arms and legs and God knows what. Jim lived with these things and he adored them. He treated them as his children. So, we came up with the idea of setting the video in a house and making it all look very domesticated, like the way Jim lived."

Godley and Creme's idea was to create a domestic situation filled with these extraordinary creations performing very ordinary tasks: watching TV, ironing, brushing their teeth. The domestic setting enabled them to weave Herbie Hancock subtly into the pro-ceedings, performing on the TV screen in the living room, while the robotic figures around him do their idiosyncratic thing. Whiting created some new robots for the video, but pride of place among his robotic creations was one he dubbed 'Veronica'. The final edit was unlike anything anyone had seen before in a music video and Godley and Creme were delighted with the result. Hancock himself, however, wasn't so sure.

"I looked at it and I had no idea what I was looking at," recalls Hancock. "I mean, it looked interesting but I didn't get it. I really didn't get it. And I was going, 'Is it any good?' They said, 'Is it any good? It's fantastic!' And so, I said, 'I hope so!'"

Godley and Creme were quickly proved right. The video went into heavy rotation on MTV and, along with Michael Jackson's Billie Jean and Prince's Little Red Corvette, helped to break the colour bar on the channel. The video to Rockit was so integral to the record's success that when Hancock was subsequently invited to perform the song at the 26th Annual Grammy Awards he asked if the robots could perform live on stage at the Los Angeles Shrine Auditorium with him too.

"Jim was thrilled with this," recalls Creme. "But he insisted that 'Veronica' travelled with him First Class on the way out to Los Angeles for the Grammys. She had her own seat, did Veronica. She was a star!"

Back in the video director's chair, further projects included work with Elton John (Kiss The Bride), Culture Club (Victims), Yes (Leave It), Paul Young (Everything Must Change) and the reunion with Eric Stewart and Graham Gouldman on 10cc's Feel The Love. There were also a few assignments that went astray. One involved flying to Los Angeles to discuss ideas for a video for Earth, Wind and Fire. However, the band didn't show up for the meeting. On their way out of the building the band's manager allegedly asked the pair how the meeting had gone.

"There was no Fire or Earth," deadpanned Godley. "But I think we just passed Wind on the way out."

In 1985, The Police's manager, Miles Copeland, had struck upon the idea of creating a new music TV show called *Rebellious Jukebox* and called upon the services of Godley and Creme to direct the pilot and several episodes. Set in a fictitious club, with the owner played by Meatloaf and the manager by Jools Holland, it featured comic linking passages in between performances by bands.

"Godley and Creme are the only directors who came out of the rock 'n' roll world," said Copeland. "And the whole idea is that the show is made by rock 'n' roll people. And if the people in the show love it, you've done the impossible."

Unfortunately, the public didn't share Copeland's enthusiasm and the show was canned after the first two episodes were screened on Channel 4. Continuing their relationship with The Police, Godley and Creme were invited to film some of the band's concerts on their *Synchronicity* world tour, including their performance at the Spectrum de Montreal on August 2, 1983 (subsequently released as *The Synchronicity Show*) and their two gigs at the Omni Coliseum in Atlanta on November 2 and 3, 1983. Later, while editing the footage of the latter in New York, they were having a drink in their hotel bar at Le Parker Meridien one night, when producer Trevor Horn came over to introduce himself. Horn was a long-time 10cc fan, who cited *Sheet Music* as one of his favourite albums and I'm Not In Love as one of his favourite productions. The song's influence can be heard on several Horn productions, such as Dollar's 1982 hit Give Me Back My Heart.

Having hit it off in the bar, the three of them dropped into Electric Lady studios in Greenwich Village, where Horn was working with Foreigner on what would turn out to be abortive sessions for their *Agent Provocateur* album. Godley, Creme and Horn started playing around in studio downtime on a track called Hit The Box, a song that put the sound of TV channel surfing to a beatbox rhythm that Godley and Creme had written while bored out of their minds watching TV in hotel bedrooms in the US.

"We had great fun," recalls Creme. "It was such a shot in the arm to do music for a few hours. We had forgotten what fun it was. We left at 7am, but we made arrangements to meet six months later and have some more fun in the studio."

In the meantime, Horn asked Godley and Creme to direct the video for Two Tribes, a new single he had produced for band-of-the-moment Frankie Goes To Hollywood.

"What was amazing about that particular project is that Frankie were extremely important at that time and were leaders in terms of pop culture in the UK," says Godley. "And thank goodness ZTT Records understood that that meant they could be a little freer in their thinking with regard to what was done. So, as well as doing the straightforward three-and-a-half-minute pop video for the song, we were allowed to stretch it beyond all recognition – much as they released numerous different mixes of the song, we were allowed to do a video mix of the song which bore no resemblance to any other production at all. It was kind of like a mash-up documentary, one with music in the middle. But we were allowed to experiment and try and push the boat out creatively, which was tremendous."

The original idea for the video had been to create a new sport with two sides of 20 people fighting against each other. This idea was ruled out on cost grounds so, proving that necessity is the mother of invention, they came up with a much better one – they'd have just two people fighting against each other. But not just any two people; the fight would be between the leaders of the US and the Soviet Union.

"Instead of having a war featuring millions of people we're reducing it down to the bosses of the two major powers," says Godley. "We've got Chernenko and we've got Reagan battling it out on behalf of their mighty empires."

A fight between lookalikes of the two major superpowers was a bold statement at a time when the Cold War was at its height, but it ensured that the video for Two Tribes was one of the most iconic of the period. Godley and Creme also directed the video to the group's follow-up single, The Power of Love. Shot entirely on location in Israel, while Frankie Goes To Hollywood were touring America, the video didn't go down too well with the band themselves.

"We weren't consulted or originally in it; we were touring the US," says Holly Johnson. "The record company obviously had its sights on the Christmas market, the chocolate box nativity theme is testament to that."

With videos such as Rockit, Every Breath You Take and Two Tribes on their showreel, it was only a matter of time before Godley and Creme were recognised for their work. They picked up the award for 'Top Video Directors' – as well as 'Top Video' for Rockit – in February 1984 at the annual *Music Week* awards.

"There is no doubt in my mind that they are the top directors in this country," said Geoff Coy, video manager at CBS. "Their creative ideas are far ahead of everyone else and this fact emerged strongly during the judging of the awards."

Even more significantly, when MTV hosted their inaugural Music Video Awards in September 1984 at Radio City Music Hall in New York, Godley and Creme were nominated for no less than 16 MTV Music Video Awards, eight for Rockit and eight for Every Breath You Take. Hosted by Dan Ackroyd and Bette Midler, the awards celebrated the best music videos produced between May 1983 and May 1984 and, on a memorable night for Godley and Creme, they won six MTV Music Video Awards.

In the meantime, six months on from their meeting in New York, Godley and Creme joined Trevor Horn at his SARM studio in London to finish off Hit The Box, the song they'd worked on at Electric Lady in New York. Yet while the song worked when the pair conceived the idea in America, where there were hundreds of TV channels, it felt strange back at home in a world of only four channels. When asked what other musical ideas they had, Godley and Creme played them the fragment of a song they had created back in the Hotlegs days starting with the refrain *'You don't know how to ease my pain'*. It was little more than a guitar riff and half a verse, but Horn liked what he heard. While Godley and Creme went off to play table tennis, Horn and fellow Art of Noise member JJ Jeczalik fed the chord sequence into a Synclavier.

"The two of them created this kind of rolling, rhythmic thing based on that snatch of a song we'd written and then Lol put those beautiful liquid chords all over it and there was something there," recalls Godley. "And then I was kind of sent into the studio and told, 'Sing what you've got' and, 'Sing this bit there', and then at some point it took on a life of its own without actually taking it too much further at all. It didn't need much to take what we had originally written and turn it into a really good recording. But, of course, we didn't realise that. It took somebody else to draw that song out of us. And that was a revelation. It said things can be simple and work. They don't have to be complicated."

In the studio, they found Horn to be something of a kindred spirit.

"He was even more of a perfectionist than we were in 10cc!" recalls Godley.

Wrapped in a typically state-of-the-art Trevor Horn production, Cry was released in the spring of 1985. The song reached the Top 20 on both sides of the Atlantic, as well as the Top 10 in Canada, Germany and the Netherlands, selling over a million copies worldwide. Cry also enjoyed a new lease of life when it featured prominently in the final six minutes of the *Miami Vice* episode Definitely Miami in January 1986, seen by some as one of the defining scenes of the series. It was perhaps no coincidence that the pair's biggest global solo hit involved an external influence, a factor that had been absent since their 10cc days. The success of Cry was greatly aided by its accompanying video, which was one of Godley and Creme's finest to date.

"Originally, we were going to film the British Olympic skaters Torvill and Dean skating to it," says Creme. "But they were unavailable, so we came up with simply cross-fading all these different faces into each other as they sing the song. Interestingly, the results also produced a series of interim 'half-faces' that don't even exist. We actually auditioned faces, and even used a few friends, like Trevor Horn."

Other video directors would copy the pioneering technique relentlessly over the years, most notably on Michael Jackson's Black and White video. In 2011, *Time* would include Cry in their list of the '30 best music videos of all time' saying: "The entire medium of music video owes Kevin Godley and Lol Creme an enormous debt." Looking back, Kevin Godley views Cry as one of his career highlights.

"This is the moment in my life when my two great loves, music and pictures, came together in a perfect way," he says. "We'd always made music and we'd always made pictures, but the two weren't always usually successful. Here we were able to fuse the two, and it became a huge hit and validated the commercial aspect of what we did. It's the whole package, that we had an idea that was visual and an idea that was aural, and they came together to create this entity called Cry. People still talk to me about it to this day. That was a fabulous moment for us."

As Cry reached its chart peak in the UK in May 1985, Godley and Creme were in Paris directing the video for Sting's solo single If You Love Somebody Set Them Free. Sting invited them to join him on stage that evening at his gig at the Théâtre Mogador.

"That night we did some backing vocals at his show for a laugh," recalls Creme. "On the way there, Bob Geldof was crossing the road. We stopped and offered him a lift. He was telling us he was on a mission to get a huge live show together. He said we should do it as we'd just released Cry. That was the only time I regretted I hadn't said yes to an invitation to play live; it was such an occasion."

Of course, that occasion was Live Aid. It could have been an opportunity to get the original line-up of 10cc back together to perform as part of the show at Wembley Stadium on July 13. Money for God's sake would have been an appropriate fundraising plea for the occasion. That said, big shows like this had never been 10cc's forte, as demonstrated by their performance at Knebworth nine years earlier. Instead, Queen would be widely regarded as the highlight of the day.

Still, the success of Cry led journalists to ask the duo if they planned to go out on the road.

"Go on tour? I'd rather face a firing squad," replied Creme.

Instead, Godley and Creme commemorated their 25th anniversary of making music together with the release of their next album, History Mix Volume 1.

"After working together in the music business for a quarter of a century we thought we'd celebrate by putting out a compilation album," says Creme. "But not our Greatest Hits LP. That'd be too obvious. So, we both decided that a 'Greatest Bits' album would be far more interesting and fun to do. So, we started going through all our old tapes and demos, and just generally dug around. It's really vinyl archaeology or recycled music. And people sent us stuff we'd totally forgotten we'd ever done. We got one old demo from Graham Gouldman with a note saying, 'Don't give up your day jobs yet!' At the same time, we didn't want to spend months and months on the project, so once we'd collected all the basic material, we gave ourselves a time limit of just three weeks to pull the whole thing together, including mixing it. It was a bit like blending a huge cocktail with a thousand different ingredients. We just took the whole lot and fed bits and pieces into the Fairlight system and sampled them. And we chose all the idiosyncratic bits that best represented us, so it was very enjoyable."

The album features samples of various songs from 10cc – Rubber Bullets, Life Is A Minestrone, I'm Not In Love, How Dare You, One Night In Paris, Sand In My Face and The Dean and I all feature – and their solo work, mixed up and mashed up and set to drum loops by JJ Jeczalik. It was a groundbreaking approach at the time and, when it works well, it works brilliantly. The vocal and piano samples from I'm Not In Love work particularly well, as does the clever linking passage from that song's *'Big boys don't cry'* section into the *'You make me wanna cry'* refrain of Cry.

Elsewhere, the results are pioneering but overlong, the pair once again lacking a good editor or controlling influence to give their brilliant ideas cohesion. Released in June 1985, the cover, like the first 10cc album, was designed by the duo themselves.

"There's my drawing of Kev and his drawing of me," says Creme. "The record company thought it was cheap and nasty but naturally we insisted! The whole idea behind the album was to have some fun and experiment a bit with 20 years' worth of music. It wasn't so much a big effort to make a hit album, as it was to bake an anniversary cake with all these different slices. Looking back on even the last few years is kind of interesting because of the sheer variety of stuff we've done – or possibly fucked up!"

The duo continued to work with a very diverse range of artists in 1985, directing videos for the likes of Eric Clapton (Forever Man), INXS (This Time), Thompson Twins (Don't Mess With Doctor Dream) and Go West (We Close Our Eyes). They also worked with Duran Duran again, on the video for their theme song to the next James Bond movie *A View to a Kill*, an assignment they rejected at first because they didn't like the song. But they couldn't resist the opportunity to work on a Bond movie.

"The film's producer, Cubby Broccoli, allowed us a pretty free hand, as long as we included some of the movie footage," says Godley. "So, we saw it as an ideal opportunity to build lots of gadgets in the Bond style and film the video on the Eiffel Tower. So, we had a van built with a false cake on top, and a bomb detonator disguised as a Sony Walkman, and the telescope that turns into a gun."

However, their request to kill off the band's keyboard player in the video was turned down.

"We weren't allowed to kill Nick Rhodes!" says Creme. "The record company didn't want tons of complaints from the fans."

Yet despite their success and critical acclaim, Godley and Creme were starting to sense a change in the world of music video. Just like the music business had done almost 10 years earlier, music video was now starting to feel safe and sterile, driven by financial considerations rather than creativity. When, in September 1985, Godley and Creme were awarded the prestigious 'Video Vanguard' award at the second annual MTV Awards in New York, for their services to the industry, Godley used his acceptance speech to make his point, and pulled no punches in doing so.

"I want to know why it is that every form of art that becomes commercially successful suddenly decides to play safe to maintain its success," said Godley. "Don't ask me, I work on a direct line to my heart not my wallet. But from where I stand I can see something beginning that doesn't feel right. It disturbs me. Where once there was imagination and excitement and invention and soul, now there is stagnation and overkill, I'm afraid. The videos are all starting to look the same. I watch them and I'm seeing a factory production line. That's money talking, easy money. It's safe, it's expedient but it's not exciting and that's what video should be all about."

It was an awkward moment for the powers that be at MTV, and host Eddie Murphy tried to make light of it. But the speech reflected Godley's heartfelt concerns for the industry he loved.

"MTV was the maker of the video boom and the destroyer," says Godley. "To accommodate 24-hour-a-day video TV they had to be churned out. Churn, churn, churn, your ideas being digested by this monster."

The first cracks were also beginning to show in the relationship between Godley and Creme themselves. "We were growing up, finally," says Godley in his autobiography *Spacecake*. "We now had different lives, friends and tastes and it was beginning to show. The best way to describe our working relationship at this time is the classic see-saw analogy … when one of us was up and leading the creative charge the other was down, marginalised and emasculated until the see-saw swung back his way … at least that's how it felt to me. In times past this was done in the name of bettering an idea and ego didn't come into it. Now after half a lifetime of togetherness and a million reefers it created friction."

The first time this came to a head professionally was when Godley was approached to direct Fashion Aid, an event at London's Royal Albert Hall on November 5, 1985 that brought together some of the world's top designers to raise money for famine relief. It was the first project that Godley had worked on by himself.

"I knew it would leave Lol isolated for a while, not a good place to be, but I had to do it," says Godley.

While the experience would prove nerve-racking, it was ultimately liberating for Godley. His working partnership with Creme would never be the same.

"We kept going for a good few years and we did some great work but it wasn't the same," says Godley. "The wound never healed completely but the scar was only visible to us. There was a subtle awkwardness there, a tear in the fabric of who we were. We never really talked about it but in the privacy of our own thoughts we both acknowledged it was irreconcilable." Despite their concerns about the state of the music video industry, the pair continued to direct videos and gain acclaim for their work with the likes of Lou Reed (No Money Down), Wang Chung (Everybody Have Fun Tonight) and Peter Gabriel and Kate Bush on their duet Don't Give Up. By 1987, however, they were becoming bored with the medium and only accepted a few assignments. One was for Peter Gabriel's Biko, which incorporated footage from the film *Cry Freedom*; another was an opportunity they couldn't resist, to work with former Beatle George Harrison on the video for his single When We Was Fab.

"I approached them," says Harrison. "I said, 'Go home and smoke something, listen to this and come up with an idea.' I was a bit nervous because Godley and Creme are a couple of loonies, particularly Lol. But it was very good, very funny."

Harrison became so enthusiastic about the concept that he decided to use the occasion for a bona fide Beatles reunion which, given the continuing legal battles over Apple, was by no means easy. At first, everyone agreed, including Paul McCartney.

"He was going to wear the walrus suit and play bass," says Godley. "But unfortunately, he pulled out at the last minute, and that's when we got Elton John to come down. Elton walks past George and the band carrying a picture of John Lennon. So, symbolically at least, all The Beatles are there. It was a lot of fun to do, and George and Ringo were both great to work with. In fact, George enjoyed himself so much that he told us we'd have to direct all his Handmade Films from now on!"

Making the leap from the small screen to the big one was what most excited Godley and Creme. Their work had attracted the attention of Creative Artists Agency, a top American talent agency who represented many of the world's most successful film directors. Sadly, all the scripts they were sent were, in Creme's words, "garbage". One project involved a potential big-screen adaption of Billy Bunter, with Godley and Creme allegedly getting as far as asking Elton John if he was interested in the starring role. To make matters worse, none of the Hollywood executives they met showed any interest in the idea that Godley and Creme themselves were pitching – a movie based on the music of George Gershwin.

Finally, though, it looked like they were getting close to realising their lifetime ambition. They were keen on a script called *Howling at the Moon*, a western that revolved around the last night in the life of American gunfighter John Wesley Hardin. After several years of frustrating on-off negotiations with a variety of Hollywood studios, Godley and Creme finally secured a $4m budget from FilmDallas.

Ahead of starting work on the project the duo reacquainted themselves with the recording studio. In contrast to the high-tech, sampled nature of *History Mix*, their new album saw the duo working with 'real' instruments again for the first time in nearly 10 years. "We were both getting really bored with what we call today's 'perfect mediocrity', all that high-tech perfection that has absolutely no soul," says Godley.

One feature of the new album would be the prominent use of harmonicas. "We were thinking along the lines of this film we're going to be doing, which is basically a western drama, and then thinking about music and sounds, and that sort of sparked off the idea of using harmonicas," says Creme. "We also decided to use other musicians on the album for the first time ever, to get back to a real live band feel, and that's when we started auditioning harp players. And to our surprise, we found that there's a huge range, everything from bass to treble, but that traditionally harmonicas are always played as solo instruments. They're never played in groups. So naturally we thought, 'Why not use a harmonica section?' And after auditioning a bunch of players, none of whom had ever played with another harp player, we finally selected two guys, Mark Feltham and Mitt Gamon, and began laying down rhythm tracks at my home studio. Next, we brought in three backing singers, George Chandler, Jimmy Helms and Jimmy Chambers, whom we'd met while directing a Paul Young video, and started building up the tracks. The interesting thing is that the more we got into the sounds, the more we began rewriting the songs to suit the singers or the harp players. To be honest, I was dreading the whole album-writing process again but this time we kept such a clear focus on simplicity and soulfulness that it all flowed together very quickly."

Ironically, some critics thought the harmonica sounds were sampled. "People have been suggesting it's full of sampled sounds, but it's all real and live," said Godley at the time. "There's not a fucking synthesizer anywhere on it. We tried that whole synthesizer/ Synclavier route a couple of years ago, and in theory it should work just like a video edit. But strangely, in practice, we found the whole process to be incredibly boring. There was no spontaneity, no personality. We hated it."

Working with other musicians and real instruments had brought back that lost spontaneity and the pair greatly enjoyed making the album. "We cut two tracks a day, and worked very civilised hours, 10am till 6pm, and had more fun doing this project than we ever expected," said Creme at the time. "Normally I hate an album I've just finished, but of all our solo albums, this is my favourite."

Released in February 1988, *Goodbye Blue Sky* was Godley and Creme's most critically acclaimed album for years. "This is a brilliant pop album from a deep well of music," wrote Phil

Sutcliffe in Q magazine, giving the album a four-star rating. "The unremarked single A Little Piece of Heaven, a cheery calypso, must have seemed the obvious chart teaser for the 'ex-10cc duo'. But it gives barely a clue to the LP's dark scope. The dynamic is Godley and Creme's autographed silken vocal harmonies banged up against mainstream rock 'n' roll. Harmonica and Hammond organ make the mood: street sleazy in Crime and Punishment, raunchy riot-goin'-on for Big Bang, grooving down-the-dustpipe in Last Page of History. Meanwhile they sing the small-world big-problem blues. Those three songs cover respectively the decay of modern civilisation, the creation of the planet and destruction of the same by nuclear war. *Goodbye Blue Sky* is deeply serious, offering heartfelt prayers to God with a frequency which some may find upsetting, yet Kev and Lol still have the wit of word and sound to make their pessimism bearable, friendly in fact."

Sadly, the album failed to dent the charts in the UK, although the duo were more successful in Europe, where the single A Little Piece of Heaven reached the Top 30 in Germany, Austria, Switzerland and the Netherlands.

In the meantime, filming approached on their *Howling at the Moon* project. Kevin Godley described it at the time as "the major thing that we've been working towards for the past 27 years" such was its importance to him. "I'm saving up for my jodhpurs and megaphone as we speak," he joked.

Filming was due to start at Los Colinas Studios in Dallas, with actor Gary Busey playing John Wesley Hardin.

"It's been a real bitch to pull this together," said Creme at the time. "The main problem was that the script for *Howling at the Moon* is essentially a dramatic western and no one in Hollywood wanted to touch a western. They all told us it was box-office poison. We really got fucked around and became very pissed off and disenchanted with the whole business at one point. But we were determined to do this project, and it's actually all come together really well. Robbie Robertson is going to do the soundtrack, and Trevor Horn will produce it, so at least it'll sound good!"

Godley and Creme had spent a long time in pre-production, working on detailed storyboards of every scene, which they drew by hand.

"It took us a month to do but it'll save a lot of time and money in the end, because now we know exactly what we're doing," said Godley at the time.

Sadly, the project was destined never to be. A few days before filming was due to begin, the film's star, Gary Busey, had a near fatal accident while riding his motorbike in Los Angeles.

"Gary was almost killed in an accident on his Harley and so filming was cancelled," says Godley.

Clint Eastwood's *Unforgiven*, released a few years later, would take over $150m at the box office and prove that westerns were no longer box-office poison. With their own filmmaking ambitions on hold, Godley and Creme directed a TV documentary about the assassination of John F Kennedy called *The Day The Dream Died* that would at least inspire another filmmaker. The documentary cast serious doubt on the official version of events and would later be described by Oliver Stone as the "inspiration" for his feature film *JFK*.

Wanting to expand the possibilities of the music video, the duo unveiled a new concept that they called 'Videolas'. They booked themselves into Olympic Studios for five days to see if it was feasible to create audio and visual at the same time. The results were mixed and released as *Mondo Video* in 1989.

"They're not promos, but what we call 'Videolas'," said Creme at the time. "Each one is about 20 minutes long and will marry a musician like Sting with a Ken Russell, or a Peter Gabriel with a visual artist. And they'll be collectibles not just exclusively aimed at rock 'n' roll. Video is such a great medium, but it really hasn't been used much outside that pop/rock format. We definitely plan to cut down on music promos, but this is an area we'll keep contributing to."

It was an interesting idea but one that never gained momentum. By now Godley had taken on another project by himself, creating a seven-minute film for an environmental charity he had co-founded called ARK to get across their message about 'fighting for life on Earth'.

"The finished film, starring the magnificent Dawn French, was designed to explain in simple terms the environmental concerns facing planet Earth," says Godley. "My vision was a few steps ahead of current technology but a few steps behind our budget, which was zero. That said, everyone worked their nuts off to help me bring it to life, regardless."

As with Fashion Aid, the experience of working on his own was highly energising for Godley.

"I enjoyed that sense of freedom and knowing that I no longer had to factor in someone else's opinion was liberating and more addictive than any drug," says Godley. "I'm reminded of the feeling that Lol and I experienced together many years before when we left 10cc to explore new ground. It was the same feeling, the same impetus, the same need for independence. Once you start doing things on your own you find you don't have to check with someone else all the time. I was gaining in confidence. By that stage Lol and I were beginning to move in different directions. Godley and Creme were beginning to fall apart. We were starting to get competitive with each other. What had started as healthy competition was now becoming paranoid. There was more of a power struggle going on. The freedom wasn't there anymore. It was time to knock it on the head."

Godley decided it was time to dissolve the Godley and Creme partnership. He went to Creme's house to deliver the news.

"It was unpleasant but it was a cathartic moment," says Godley.

For two men who had been friends since childhood, working independently from each other would take some getting used to.

"I spent 27 years with Kev and I love him dearly," says Creme. "But he felt he had to have a change of lifestyle and that's fine. We never fell out."

CHAPTER 26

MEANWHILE

ERIC STEWART AND GRAHAM GOULDMAN HAD BEEN INUNDATED WITH offers to reform 10cc throughout the 80s but had turned them all down, having absolutely no desire to live off former glories. "We could work 365 days a year doing that nostalgia crap," says Stewart. "Our old manager was forever ringing us up saying Japan is offering millions of yen to tour there and we'd say, 'Oh God, Harvey, no!'" By 1987, the band's former record company, PolyGram, were planning a new compilation album, which brought together 10cc's greatest hits with Godley and Creme's best post-10cc work, effectively covering the 13-year period from Donna in 1972 through to Cry in 1985, plus a new Phil Harding remix of Snack Attack thrown in for good measure. With its title, and cover design, inspired by Godley and Creme's video for Cry, *Changing Faces* was released in August 1987 supported by a TV advertising campaign. Its success exceeded all expectations, reaching No.4 in the UK album charts and becoming their eighth Top 10 album as part of an 18-week chart run, including five weeks in the Top 10. More significantly, it proved that there was still a massive market out there for 10cc's music.

Part of the reason for the success of *Changing Faces* was that it marked the first time that 10cc's music had been widely available on the new Compact Disc format. PolyGram started issuing 10cc's back catalogue on CD, prompting the question of how well the band's music had stood up to the ravages of time. The answer was very well indeed. *Q* magazine gave four-star ratings to both *10cc* and *Sheet Music*.

"Their debut included the merciless 50s pastiches Donna and Johnny Don't Do It plus Rubber Bullets and The Dean and I, the filmic mini-epics which established that their own satiric and sophisticated style could also be chart-hot stuff. Apart from the singles, long forgotten tracks like Ships Don't Disappear In The Night and The Hospital Song were just as exuberant: diamond-bright of mind and guitar, ecstatic of harmony. And then, remarkably, *Sheet Music* was even better... one of the great pop albums of all time."

Elsewhere, 10cc were being cited as an influence by a new generation of British bands such as Tears for Fears, World Party and Prefab Sprout. "I can hear it in the songwriting of Prefab Sprout," says Gouldman. "They take the same sideways look at life, and they're very melodic and complicated, with lots of changes. And ABC's *The Lexicon of Love* was really excellent. Like them we never limited ourselves. In fact, we went out of our way not to limit ourselves. We always got criticised for being too complex, but better that than too conservative. We got bored easily, so we had to do things that kept us interested."

Prefab Sprout mainman Paddy McAloon, and his close friend Dave Brewis, of The Kane Gang, were both admirers of 10cc. "I was a major supporter in the early days and rate their first three albums very highly, especially *Sheet Music*, a brilliant album," says Brewis. "It wasn't the most fashionable thing in later years but I kept listening to them. When I met Paddy, he expressed a liking for them, especially the sound. Eric Stewart's production and the whole sound and arrangement thing they had going was incredible, especially considering the gear they worked with. I know Paddy likes the sound of I'm Mandy Fly Me and I played him Old Wild Men when I got it on CD. Some of their stuff is really out there and risky."

San Francisco band Jellyfish were another of the group's many admirers. "10cc were a huge influence," says the band's Roger Manning. "They modelled pop as its highest art form. They were a British Steely Dan in that way." British one-hit wonders Boys Don't Cry even named themselves after the spoken words from the middle section of 10cc's most famous record (and not The Cure record of the same name).

By August 1989, *Changing Faces* had sold over 300,000 copies in the UK and PolyGram laid on a celebration lunch to present platinum discs to the band. The event was attended by three-quarters of the original line-up, with only Lol Creme, now living in Los Angeles, absent. It was the first time that Stewart and Gouldman had seen each other since they put 10cc on ice, back in 1983. "We didn't see each other for six years," says Gouldman. "It was as if without 10cc there was no reason. That's how it was. Nothing happened that brought us together."

That said, both of them had kept up with what the other had been doing. Stewart had not found Wax to his taste: "I thought it was very poppy and not in a way I particularly liked. I found the lyrics very sugary." For his part Gouldman had liked Pretty Little Head but hadn't been particularly impressed with the rest of Stewart's collaborations with McCartney: "Good but not the greatest thing I've heard."

PolyGram had taken the unusual step of commissioning some market research to find out what the Great British public thought about the prospect of a new 10cc album. The findings were extremely positive, confirming that 10cc were still very fondly remembered and ranked alongside the likes of Pink Floyd in terms of prominence. In short, they loved the idea of a new 10cc album. Armed with this information, Polydor boss David Munns tried to persuade the band's original line-up to get back into the studio.

"They tried to get the four of us together again, but Kev and Lol really weren't interested," says Stewart. With Godley and Creme having just gone their separate ways it was the worst possible time to try and reunite all four of the group's founder members. At first, Stewart and Gouldman weren't convinced about the idea either.

"We'd all been moving in different directions and I think that we'd resisted the idea of making a new album," says Gouldman.

The timing of the offer, however, coincided with Gouldman and Gold's decision to scrap Wax. "Coincidentally, two weeks before the lunch Andrew and I had decided not to carry on with it anymore," says Gouldman. "We felt that we weren't having the support we thought we deserved and that although we wanted to carry on writing together, there must be some kind of fault in our Wax partnership as artists. So, the 10cc offer seemed providential."

The more that Stewart and Gouldman considered the offer, the more receptive they became. In the end they agreed to 10cc's second coming. "The two of us thought, 'Yeah, we've got a lot of ideas we want to get out, let's do an album,'" says Stewart. "We thought if it works, great. If it doesn't we'll hold our hands up and walk away. Neither of us needed the money after all." Still, it didn't hurt that Polydor were offering big money for the re-union: "Our record company made us a very generous offer," confirms Gouldman.

Stewart and Gouldman signed a new five-album deal with David Munns at Polydor. "It's going to see us through to our pension," joked Stewart at the time. As an added bonus, Godley and Creme agreed to 'guest' on the first of these albums, in return for Polydor releasing them from their contractual obligations as a duo.

With 10cc reborn, Eric Stewart and Graham Gouldman spent the summer of 1990 writing songs for their comeback album. Neither were sure whether the chemistry between the two of them would still be there, seven years on from their last writing sessions together, and at first it looked like the spark had gone.

"The first day we tried to write together it just didn't happen," recalls Stewart. "So, we took a break and spent hours listening to current music that we liked by people like Chris Isaak and Prince. The next day it just flowed. The first song we wrote was Welcome To Paradise: we realised that we'd opened Pandora's Box again!"

Delighted with the result, Stewart and Gouldman continued apace. "Every day we were coming up with new ideas and they were getting better and better as far as we were concerned," says Stewart. "And they sounded like 10cc songs again."

Gouldman was equally enthused: "It was exactly like it was when we worked together all those years ago. The chemistry was still there, we really enjoyed it. We wrote about 22 songs in a three-month period, so we felt confident that we could still do it."

Among their new songs was The Stars Didn't Show, a homage to the pair's musical heroes. "Eric and I were talking about heroes and the fact that there weren't any real heroes any more," says Gouldman. "The people on the bedroom walls at the time were very transient, without any longevity, and we thought it would be nice to write a song about all our heroes, people like Roy Orbison, although nobody's actually named in the lyric."

They were writing songs at Gouldman's house when there was a knock at the door. "It was someone collecting for charity," recalls Gouldman. "I gave some money and mentioned it to Eric. We started talking about pop stars whose charity work was motivated more by career progression than good causes and we wrote the song

Charity Begins At Home about it." The song was the latest in a long line of sacred cows for 10cc to target and the pair grasped the opportunity with both hands. Equally nimble of wordplay was Fill Her Up, which commented on the social pressure that women are under to conform to physical stereotypes, and the pair don't pull any punches, including a dig at Jane Fonda's expense.

Some of the other new Stewart/Gouldman creations were more autobiographical. Wonderland was inspired by the birth of Gouldman's daughter, Rosanna, and revisited an old 10cc theme – the innocence of childhood. Something Special was a humorous song about a guy who will go to any lengths to please his girlfriend, even if it involves shoplifting, stealing coins from the poor box or holding up a bank.

The standard of the new songs confirmed that the chemistry between Stewart and Gouldman was still very much there. It also proved that, as far as 10cc is concerned, the pair usually produce their best work when writing together. As previously demonstrated on albums like *Deceptive Bends* and *Windows in the Jungle*, the quality control was always higher, the attention to detail in the lyric department sharper. New songs like Green Eyed Monster showed this off to good effect. The song's protagonist is convinced that his wife is having an affair and his paranoia fuels itself. Lyrically, Stewart and Gouldman show their class in the details and demonstrate a playfulness missing from some of their latter period 10cc work. The pair themselves were highly energised by their collaboration. "When Eric and I started writing again it was an absolute joy," says Gouldman. "It was brilliant and there was a real magic to the demos that we recorded together."

Stewart also decided to dust off one of the unfinished songs that he'd written with Paul McCartney for the *Press to Play* album. Completed for the new 10cc album the Stewart/McCartney/Gouldman-penned Don't Break The Promises ironically delivered much less than it promised from such a stellar writing credit.

News of 10cc's reformation was broken by *Manchester Evening News* in October 1990, although they incorrectly claimed that Stewart, Gouldman and Creme had signed up for the reunion, "were recording new material in France" and "will tour America in the New Year". In actual fact, thoughts were turning to who should produce 10cc's new album. Having discussed a variety of possible candidates, they struck upon the idea of working with former Eurythmic, Dave Stewart.

"We asked him to produce the album but he was too busy," says Stewart. "He called back and said, 'I'd love to do it, but I'm tied up for the next year.' Unfortunately, we couldn't wait that long, so we started thinking about other producers."

Among those considered were Trevor Horn, Jeff Lynne and Gary Katz, the man credited with producing Steely Dan and Donald Fagan's acclaimed *The Nightfly*, one of Eric Stewart's favourite albums. "I loved those American sounds from the late-60s/70s, Steely Dan-type records," says Stewart. "They were crystal clear and every sound was beautifully recorded." Katz was approached and was available to produce the album. It was hoped that his influence would also give the album a more American flavour, theoretically offering 10cc a better chance of finally breaking the US market. One other advantage of working with Katz was that he owned his own studio in New York, which was ideal given that recording at Strawberry was no longer an option.

In January 1991, Stewart and Gouldman flew out to New York to start work on their new record. Their arrival coincided with I'm Not In Love riding high in the US charts again, courtesy of a cover version by Will to Power that had just reached the Top 10. The backing tracks for 10cc's tenth studio album were to be recorded at the legendary Bearsville Studios in Woodstock, upstate New York, with Stewart predominantly playing keyboards and Gouldman switching from bass to electric guitar. They were joined at Bearsville by drummer Jeff Porcaro and bassist Freddie Washington, both session men of the highest order.

"It's the first time we'd ever worked with American musicians," says Stewart. "But the atmosphere in the studio was just fantastic and it was great working at Bearsville because people like Bob Dylan and The Band had recorded there. The place just has an extraordinary atmosphere, you can actually feel the vibes."

Stewart and Gouldman played the demos of their new songs to Katz, Porcaro and Washington to see which ones made them sit up and listen. Some didn't make the cut, like Why Did I Break Your Heart, but most did, and together the quartet recorded the backing tracks to 13 songs. The sessions also saw an unscheduled guest appearance from New Orleans blues legend, Dr John.

"I was trying to play the piano part to Something Special and I said to Gary Katz, 'What I'm trying to do is play like Dr John,'" recalls Stewart. "He said, 'Why don't we just get Dr John in?' Within a few hours, he was in the studio with us. He ended up staying the whole night and playing on a few of the tracks."

Unfortunately, the collaboration with Katz turned out to be far from harmonious. "We got an indication that something was wrong right at the beginning," says Gouldman. "I remember that we were in the car with Gary going up to Woodstock and Eric said, 'We've written some new stuff, we'd like to play you the tape in the car.' Gary said, 'Let's listen to it tomorrow, I'll listen to it then,' and Eric and I both sort of looked at each other."

The relationship worsened as the recording sessions moved on to River Sound, the studio Katz co-owned with Donald Fagan on East 95th Street in New York City, where the vocal tracks were to be recorded. "I came to do my first vocal track and he wasn't even looking at me, he was on the phone," says Stewart. "He asked me to do four takes and said he'd sort the best takes for each line of the song. I said, 'Hold on, that's not how I work. I want to sing the fucking song, not let someone piece together the best bits later on.' So, we had a terrific row about it."

The mood in the studio was lifted by the arrival of Kevin Godley, who had agreed to guest on the album in order to get out of his existing recording contract with Polydor. "I was flown out to New York to do my bit," says Godley. "I'd resisted doing it for a while but then I thought, 'Fuck it! It could be a laugh.' The three of us had a lovely reunion breakfast on day one. As I recall all the basic tracks had already been recorded so it was myself, Graham, Eric and producer Gary Katz for two vocal-heavy days. I do recall a strange atmosphere in the studio. An intangible awkwardness. Everything sounded 'great', everyone got on 'great' but there was an essential ingredient missing. I also sensed Graham and Eric growing apart. Gary Katz was acting as a political as well as creative buffer, keeping personalities as well as music on course. It was fun, because I didn't have any responsibility. I just had to go in there and sing. It was enjoyable seeing Eric and Graham again; it was enjoyable singing again; and it was enjoyable not having to be part of it again. It was fun."

Godley recorded backing vocals to Welcome To Paradise and Charity Begins At Home, and even sang lead vocal on one track, The Stars Didn't Show. Recording continued in Los Angeles – at Schnee Studio in North Hollywood and Village Recorders in West Los Angeles – where they were joined by Lol Creme, who contributed backing vocals to six of the tracks, most prominently on Wonderland. "We very quickly got back into the same situation," says Gouldman. "It was lots of fun, lots of banter and joking around and going for the old harmonies."

Unfortunately, with relations between Godley and Creme still a little strained, the four original members of the group were never actually all together in the studio at the same time. With neither Godley or Creme interested in re-joining Stewart and Gouldman on a more permanent basis, the three tracks on which all four of them appear – Welcome To Paradise, The Stars Didn't Show and Charity Begins At Home – were the closest there was ever likely to be to a reunion of the original 10cc line-up.

Stewart and Gouldman's stay 'somewhere in Hollywood' proved eventful. "We were invited out to dinner by Steve Lisberger," says Stewart. "Before we went out to dinner he said, 'I want you to come out and meet a friend of mine.' So, we went out to this lovely house and it belonged to Bette Midler. We met her and she sat there and sang The Things We Do For Love. It was brilliant. She knew every word and she said, 'I love that song. Will you write me a song like that?' We were very flattered. Then, at dinner, Steve said, 'I've got another proposition for you, guys. How would you like to produce The Beach Boys?' We said, 'Wow! Are you serious? We'd love to.' He said, 'Well, let me just explain the situation to you. They don't talk to each other anymore. You'd have to meet them separately to get their agreement for you to do it and each of them would do their bits separately in the studio.' He went on for about half an hour and then he said, 'I've just talked you out of it, haven't I?' And we both nodded and said, 'Absolutely. Forget it. You can't possibly produce somebody in that way!'"

While in Los Angeles, Andrew Gold dropped into the studio to guest on Charity Begins At Home, while seasoned session men like guitarist Michael Landau and keyboard player David Paich were drafted in to add some finishing touches. By the time tracks like Welcome To Paradise were complete, they featured a small army of musicians playing on them. While they were all musicians of the highest order, perhaps inevitably the end result veered towards the anonymity of session players rather than the distinct personality of a band. With guitarists as gifted as Stewart and Gouldman in the group, why were session men like Landau and Gordon Gaines drafted in to add the solos?

By the time the album was finished it had allegedly cost £750,000 to make, using five recording studios and 19 guest musicians. It was a far cry from the self-contained *modus operandi* of the original line-up at Strawberry 20 years earlier.

With recording completed, the initial mixes of the album were put together in America. Stewart, however, was unhappy with what he heard. "I hated it," says Stewart. "It didn't sound like 10cc. It sounded like the Hollywood version of 10cc, with lots of expensive echo." Eventually, the master tapes were brought back to London for the album to be remixed at Trevor Horn's studio, Sarm West, by Steve Macmillan, who had recently mixed Seal's debut album. Eric Stewart also mixed several tracks himself.

Gouldman recalls: "Mixing took a long time because there were Gary's mixes and then there were Eric's mixes and then we were going to mix the mixes and that took forever, as did the artwork, which we weren't particularly happy with, and then the video for the first single…"

Having decided to call the album *Meanwhile* – inspired by a casual remark made by Lol Creme who had asked, 'Well, what have you been doing meanwhile?' – Stewart and Gouldman turned to Laurence Dunmore to design the cover. Dunmore's design featured an archive photo from the Prefecture de Police in Paris that showed a picture of a man as a child and in old age. While all his features have changed, the ear alone remains the same, signifying the continuity in 10cc's music. Despite the frustrations making the record, both Stewart and Gouldman were taking 10cc's comeback very seriously. "Of course we're serious about this, we wouldn't have made the album otherwise," said Stewart at the time. "We feel that there are at least four or five singles on it, and if the album does become a big success then we may well go out on tour again. We wouldn't consider it at the moment, though, because we wouldn't want to go out on the back of nostalgia. We're completely serious about it. The way I see it there's a void in the market that we can fill. The public are desperate for some songs, real lyrics, beautiful guitar playing. You know, when I've told people there'll be a new 10cc album, they say, 'Thank God for that!' These aren't friends, they're just people who recognise me in the street. They say, 'Great, we could do with some proper music again.' If those people are any measure, we could have another successful album on our hands."

Gouldman was equally enthused, preferring to consider 10cc's future rather than the band's past. "We talk about it because people keep asking us about it," he said. "I must admit that the 60s and 70s were exciting times and I've got a lot of affection for the period, but it's important to look forwards. That's why I'm so excited about the new album. I really do believe the songs are the best we've ever written."

Unfortunately, new Polydor boss Jimmy Devlin, who had just taken over the reins at the label following the promotion of David Munns, didn't share their enthusiasm. Devlin didn't think that the album sounded like a hit and sanctioned a marketing budget of only £7,500 to promote it, a severe setback to 10cc's comeback plans. To add insult to injury, pre-release hype from Polydor suggested that the album was a full-blown reunion of the original line-up, which angered Stewart and Gouldman.

"It's not the original 10cc line-up," said Gouldman at the time. "Kev and Lol guest, but they didn't do any writing. They're basically just on backing vocals."

Lol Creme was also unimpressed with the hype. "All these stories harm me in the work that I'm doing now," he said. "The advertising world thinks you're not taking them seriously when they read stories that you're getting involved in music again, but this is the way I've earned my living for the past 12 years! I have no interest in getting involved in the music business again. If I was I wouldn't go back and re-join the group I was involved with in 1976, I'd do something in a totally new way. 10cc are part of my past, not part of my future."

The first fruits of 10cc's new sessions were unveiled when Woman In Love was released on April 21, 1992 as 10cc's comeback single, coupled with the non-album track Man With A Mission. It was the band's first new music in nine years, but with little money to promote it the single gained minimal airplay and failed to chart in the UK.

Dedicated to Gouldman's father, 'Hyme the Rhyme', who had died during the making of the album, *Meanwhile* was released by Polydor on May 11. "Not quite the 10cc comeback, really," wrote *Q* magazine, awarding the album a three-star rating. "While Eric Stewart and Graham Gouldman were dead keen, Kevin Godley and Lol Creme could only make it for the studio sessions, crucially kiboshing the former four-way spice of their writing. So, *Meanwhile* is only halfway there. Green Eyed Monster, Don't Break The Promises and Woman In Love flow along pleasantly, contrasting with Stewart's plaintive, romantic voice and Gouldman's hard rock guitar lines, treats enhanced by the production of former Steely Dan knobsman Gary Katz. But there's not enough of the old acid wit and satire except on Charity Begins At Home where, boldly incorrect, they give the post-Live Aid scene a kicking."

Former *Melody Maker* journalist Colin Irwin reviewed the album for *Rock World* magazine: "Gouldman and Stewart are adamant. This is a new beginning, not a nostalgia trip, and fair play to them for that. They always were skilled and indeed ingenious songwriters and there's no reason on earth why they shouldn't compete on even terms with the young guns of the 90s. *Meanwhile*, sadly, doesn't quite cut it. It's classy and crafted; everything except the unexpected. We are being harsh. There are some magical moments to lift it all. The wondrously offbeat honky-tonk piano on Something Special for one thing; the dark irony and irresistible chorus line of Welcome To Paradise for another. Here, in flashes, is vintage 10cc. But these moments aren't frequent enough to compensate for some disappointing anonymity. Close but no cigar."

There were plenty of classic 10cc moments on the record: the middle eight of Woman In Love; the piano motif of Something Special; the chorus of Welcome To Paradise; the acid wit of Charity Begins At Home; the humour of Fill Her Up; the craftsmanship of Green Eyed Monster. Perhaps the only thing missing was the killer production treatment that had made their earlier music so exciting. The production of *Meanwhile* sounded flat and lifeless, leaving the listener wondering what kind of job someone like Trevor Horn or Thomas Dolby could have done in the producer's chair. Dolby's production on Prefab Sprout's 1990 album *Jordan: The Comeback* shared the invention and detail that characterised 10cc's 70s work. He would have made an excellent, and inspired, choice.

Although a second single, Welcome To Paradise, was released during the summer of 1992, backed with two other songs from the Bearsville sessions, Don't and Lost In Love, Polydor again did nothing to promote it and despite being one of the best tracks on the album, and a strong single, it too failed to chart.

While largely ignored by their record company at home, Polydor's Japanese counterparts had more faith in *Meanwhile* and expressed an interest in giving the album a promotional push. "We spent two years making that album and I wasn't going to see it die without a fight," says Gouldman. "Japan picked up on it and asked us to go out and do some promotion, which Eric and I did."

Stewart and Gouldman flew out to Japan in November 1992 to promote the album. The promotional work paid off. Woman In Love started getting picked up by radio stations, spending 11 weeks in the Tokyo Hot 100 airplay chart, including several weeks in the Top 30. *Meanwhile* would go on to become 10cc's most successful album to date in Japan, where, Stewart explained, "We were in the charts for 27 weeks with our album and with the singles." The group's chart success prompted a Japanese concert promoter to enquire about the possibility of a 10cc tour. "We thought, 'To hell with it, why not?' We'd always said no, but this time we thought we could have some fun," says Gouldman.

The pair returned to the UK to assemble a backing band and plans were laid for a Japanese tour. The call went out to former 10cc cohorts Stuart Tosh and Rick Fenn. Fenn was enjoying success at the time with a musical he had co-written with Peter Howarth called *Robin, Prince of Sherwood*, which had just opened in the West End. New recruits Steve Piggott on keyboards and drummer Gary Wallis completed the group's onstage contingent and, in February 1993, 10cc's touring line-up began rehearsals for the tour. Graham

Gouldman found that he barely had to rehearse the old 10cc songs: "It's all come back to me. It's amazing, just like riding a bike."

The band's 1993 stage set mixed classic hits and album tracks with new material from the *Meanwhile* album. Strangely, Stewart and Gouldman also decided to include two Beatles songs, Paperback Writer and Across The Universe, in their set. With 10 albums' worth of 10cc material to choose from, this was something of a disappointment.

The Japanese tour opened on March 22 at Tokyo's Mielparque Hall, with Eric Stewart dedicating The Stars Didn't Show to the memory of drummer Jeff Porcaro, who had died in August 1992, aged thirty-eight. Both of the band's Tokyo concerts were filmed and recorded for posterity, as they marked 10cc's first gigs in nearly 10 years. Polydor in Japan would subsequently release them as a double live album called *10cc Alive* and a video would also be issued. The six-date concert tour was a great success, helping to extend *Meanwhile*'s chart run. With the 10cc machine up and running, Stewart and Gouldman agreed to undertake a UK tour in June.

"We thought it would be silly to waste all this time and effort on rehearsals and not to do an English tour," said Gouldman.

Surprisingly, given their dread of being sucked into the nostalgia trap, the tour was dubbed *The Classic Hits Tour ... And More*, with publicity focusing on hearing the hits of the past rather than advertising that 10cc were back in business as a going concern. Although understandable in order to get bums on seats, audiences suspicious about 'nostalgia' packages, often featuring none of the outfit's original members, may very well have believed this to be the case for 10cc too. The result was half-full auditoriums on some nights of the 20-date tour.

For those that did attend the concerts, few could have been anything but delighted to see Stewart and Gouldman back in action; most fans had given up hope of ever seeing 10cc live again. Some even considered the band's 1993 touring line-up to be one of 10cc's finest. "When other people who know tell you, 'This is definitely the best-sounding band you've ever had,' I take notice of it," says Gouldman.

10cc's 'homecoming' gig at the Manchester Apollo was a particular high point of the tour. Cathy Redfern, of 'big boys don't cry' fame, was in the audience and went backstage after the gig to say hello to Stewart and Gouldman. Three nights later the band found themselves at London's Hammersmith Apollo, where they treated the audience to a full version of Rubber Bullets during the encores. Adrian Deevoy, reviewing the concert for *The Times*, was less enthused.

"Trumpeted as the *Classic Hits And More* tour, 10cc's first outing for a decade delivered the promised hits but was profoundly lacking in the 'more' part of the equation. The diminutive Eric Stewart, in dark glasses, played up the role of songwriting *eminence grise* to the hilt. Graham Gouldman worked the all-smiling thumbs aloft angle with conviction. Yet for all the melodic gymnastics and intricate arrangements the show was uncomfortably sterile. Even the band's best-loved number I'm Not In Love was performed too fast, while the keyboards reduced the song's multi-layered foundation of gently breathing chords to an ugly wheezing. It was only with the encores that the band appeared to loosen up. Rubber Bullets, like its subject matter, was hard and bouncy, while Life Is A Minestrone was consumed with relish."

Anyone sensing tension between Stewart and Gouldman that night was not imagining things. When Stewart introduced his partner sarcastically as "hit songwriter, Graham Gouldman" at one point in the proceedings, he was referring to the third in a series of 'Lifestyle' articles that Stewart felt credited Gouldman with setting up Strawberry Studios, of being the writer of I'm Not In Love and being the "Brains behind 10cc".

"We had already discussed these sorts of articles and the anguish they caused and had agreed that we wouldn't do any more of them," says Stewart. "So, I was seriously pissed off that morning to find that Graham had done yet another 'Lifestyle' article, and again taken sole credit for things I had developed or co-written in my years with 10cc. We had a heavy talk in the pub that afternoon. Graham said that he hadn't said these things, but he couldn't tell me why he hadn't credited me for my input in the writing, singing, playing, engineering and production in 10cc, and he refused to try to get the newspaper to print a retraction. In retrospect, I know that I shouldn't have let the article ruin the gig for me. It was very unprofessional, and I felt wretched at the time, but I should have realised that the people I care about know me well enough and are aware of my role in 10cc. Unfortunately, at the time I thought it was my problem and I had to sort it out, but I came to the conclusion that it was Graham who had a serious problem with his own perception of the part he played in 10cc, and his way around this was to give these dreadful 'Lifestyle' interviews."

The UK tour was followed by gigs in Europe, where *Meanwhile* had been relatively successful. Woman In Love had been a minor hit in the Netherlands and the group performed a major outdoor concert in August at the Veronica Beach Party, which was filmed for TV and broadcast throughout Europe. Back in the UK, 10cc headlined the Chiltern Music Festival on July 16, supported by Boy George.

With their concerts over, Stewart and Gouldman found themselves reflecting on the events of the previous 12 months. Despite their Japanese and European success, 10cc's UK comeback could in no way be described as successful.

"The British singles market waxes and wanes, it changes so drastically and so rapidly," said Stewart. "It's difficult to keep up with it. If your single isn't a hit, your album won't be a hit."

Yet the story could have been so very different. A more inspired choice of producer could have enlivened the songs on *Meanwhile* and given the album a more contemporary feel. Equally significantly, a decent marketing campaign would have alerted the hundreds of thousands of fans who had bought *Changing Faces* to the fact that 10cc were back in business with a brand new album. This should have revived interest in the band, ensuring that their comeback tour played to full houses in major venues across the country. Most importantly, the debt that the British music scene owed 10cc would finally have been acknowledged. Instead, their record company dropped 10cc.

"Polydor did not renew their option, mainly due to *Meanwhile* not being successful in England," says Stewart. "It wasn't even released in America, and that's the main reason why we had Gary Katz produce it in the first place, to break into America."

Looking back, Gouldman has mixed views on the album.

"The whole premise of the album was wrong," he says. "Eric and I should really have been controlling everything with our people. Just because you have the finest musicians in the world doesn't make it the finest album in the world. These guys were playing with every band in the world, brilliantly, but it wasn't *our* band. It was thrilling for us while we were doing it but in retrospect it was a big mistake. Maybe we should have gone back to me, Eric and Paul Burgess at that point. I don't listen to that album much. It's too dark."

CHAPTER 27

DIFFERENT PLANETS

FOLLOWING THEIR SPLIT IN 1989, KEVIN GODLEY AND LOL CREME HAD each adopted a change of lifestyle. Creme relocated to Los Angeles to embark on a new career as a director of TV commercials. His first assignment was for Chrysler, shooting no fewer than 17 TV ads for their Plymouth car brand. Star of the ads was singer Tina Turner. "I was so nervous, it was my first ever job on my own," recalls Creme. "I was desperate to make a good job of it."

Turner's manager, Roger Davies, was more interested in persuading Creme to direct the video for her next single, The Best. "It was the last thing I wanted to hear about," says Creme. "I wanted to be concentrating on these motor cars and how I would film them and put Tina in there and make it all look marvellous."

Eventually, Davies twisted Creme's arm but only on the proviso that the video was shot in secret. "I didn't want the Plymouth people to know I was doing it because they'd be extremely pissed off if they found out I was thinking about anything other than their 17 commercials, so we did it at night over a weekend out in the desert," says Creme.

While Creme would continue to direct the occasional music video, for the likes of Seal, Tom Jones and Sting, directing commercials would be his main focus while living in Los Angeles, for brands such as Miller Lite, UPS, Audi, Moneygram, Radio Shack, Nissan and NYNEX. But when the opportunity arose to fulfil his lifelong ambition of directing a full-length feature film it was impossible for Creme to turn it down. Having read through hundreds of scripts he came across a quirky comedy set in Jamaica called *The Lunatic*. It told the tale of a good-natured madman called Aloysius who talks to trees and cows and finds love with an overweight, oversexed German tourist.

"I read this script and as soon as the tree started talking I said, 'Hello, this is interesting.' This just suits my sense of humour," said Creme at the time. "I did it because there is space for these films in our entertainment industry. We have got plenty of violence and sex in movies. There is some violence and plenty of sex in this but in a delightful way."

Released in February 1992, *The Lunatic* gained only mixed reviews – "You know a film's in trouble when a tree has all the best lines," wrote *The Washington Post* – but there was praise for Creme's direction. "Director Lol Creme gives his (Aloysius) communions with nature a joyous, cracked quality," wrote the *Los Angeles Times*. "Even though Creme is a rock-video veteran, *The Lunatic* is refreshingly pokey and unslick. It seems to move with the same rhythms as the Jamaican lilt."

Creme would also direct the pilot episode of a new TV show, a comedy called *Limboland*. It aired in the US in August 1994, but a series was not commissioned by the network. By now Creme was also back making music again, co-writing, performing and producing songs – alongside Trevor Horn masquerading as Trelvis Hornsley – for the BBC TV comedy series *The Glam Metal Detectives*, which spawned the UK Top 30 hit single Everybody's Up! in 1995. The project saw him working with his son, Lalo, who had followed in his father's footsteps into the music business with his own band Arkarna. "How could I say that he should not go into entertainment – see the world, have fun, get loaded in every possible way – when it's given us and our families such a wonderful life?" said Creme at the time.

A few years later, when Trevor Horn reactivated Art of Noise, he invited Creme to join him, alongside founder members Paul Morley and Anne Dudley, in this latest incarnation of the band. Together they worked on a new album that fused modern drum 'n' bass rhythms, with adaptations of music written by the classical composer Claude Debussy. "We've taken eight of his songs and added new sounds and these amazing new computer-generated rhythms," said Creme at the time. "The openness, the sublime harmony and melody of Debussy's music sits exquisitely on rhythm. I'm sure he's turning in his grave but it's developed into a lovely, lovely piece of music."

The resulting album, *The Seduction of Claude Debussy*, was released in June 1999, preceded by the single Metaforce, which featured rapper Rakim. Art of Noise played a series of gigs to support the album, including a performance at the Coachella Festival in California that September. Footage of this show, and other gigs in Chicago and London, would be released on the DVD *Into Vision* in 2002. Creme also put his art school training to use and fused it with the latest technology to create a series of stunning digital artworks which, for a time, were available for sale through his website.

Kevin Godley had also been branching out into new areas. Having co-founded the charity ARK, Godley was becoming increasingly concerned with environmental matters. One day he was approached by the BBC about a project that he would later describe as "the most significant piece of work I've done in the field of music on film."

"I was asked by the BBC to conceive a film featuring musicians from diverse cultures singing and playing together to illustrate global harmony and to act as a fitting finale to their environmentally themed *One World* fortnight," says Godley. "This was to be a true example of World Music. The Beeb's initial thought to mount a Live Aid-style concert felt like a wasted opportunity to me and, as I'd had this vague notion of a 'chain tape' floating around my head for a while, I pitched it to the international TV powers that be fully expecting to be booted out the door, but they green lit it on the spot. I then had to figure out how to make it happen, and the fact that I actually did mystifies me even more."

Travelling the world to film and record musicians on location sounded simple on paper but presented many technical challenges for Godley, producer Rupert Hine and engineer Stephen Taylor.

"Existing technology for film sound at that time was restrictive in terms of recording music," says Taylor. "These days you could have an audio interface, a laptop, a bundle of microphones, headphones, maybe a playback speaker and there's your system – you have everything you need there."

Armed with a small mountain of equipment, they took their virtual studio on the road, with stops along the way in New York, Los Angeles, Rio de Janeiro, Africa, Helsinki, Leningrad, Paris and the UK. The idea was that each new musician they met on the journey would either have to come up with something that followed on from the previous artist's contribution, or add to what was already there, to create what Godley described as a "musical chain letter". In total, over 400 musicians contributed to the project, including both established Western artists – such as Robbie Robertson, Sting, Peter Gabriel, Lou Reed, Bob Geldof, Suzanne Vega, Dave Gilmour, Chrissie Hynde, Afrika Bambaataa and Godley himself – alongside World musicians such as Johnny Clegg, Salif Keita, The Chieftans and the Leningrad Symphony Orchestra.

One World, One Voice was screened by the BBC on May 26, 1990 and broadcast simultaneously in 25 countries to an estimated global audience of over 650 million people. The resulting album was released in June 1990 and reached the UK Top 30.

As he embraced new projects, Godley sold Tara House to musician Vince Clarke in 1990 after 15 years as his home. He and his wife, Sue, bought Heronden Hall in Tenterden, Kent. Godley remained at the forefront of music video, working with the likes of Blur (Girls and Boys), Bryan Adams (Can't Stop This Thing We Started), Paul McCartney (C'mon People), Sting (Fields of Gold), Eric Clapton (My Father's Eyes) and Kate Bush (The Man I Love). "I loved working with Kevin," says Bush. "So imaginative and great fun."

However, the band that he would have the most enduring relationship with was U2. Godley had first met the band when he'd attended the charity premiere of *Rattle and Hum* at the Empire, Leicester Square in August 1988. Six months later, when Godley and Creme had presented the award for 'Best International Group' at the BRIT Awards at the Royal Albert Hall the winners had been U2. "Unfortunately, the boys can't be here because they're out there grafting," said Creme. "So, I'd like to take this opportunity to award Kevin Godley the prize for 'Best International Group'."

Bono then called Godley to discuss the band's next video. "They'd just finished *Achtung Baby*, and they'd done one video already, and wanted to know if I'd be interested in doing the next, which was Even Better Than the Real Thing," says Godley. "I've probably done some of my best solo work with them."

The video was shot in February 1992 and featured U2, and their own lookalike band The Doppelgangers, as well as some groundbreaking 360-degree camera work that would go on to win two

MTV Music Video Awards including 'Best Group Video'. The collaboration with U2 worked so well that when the band took their landmark *ZOO TV* show on tour, they asked Godley to capture the spectacle on film.

"It was a dream directing job that gave me an unprecedented amount of freedom to express myself on film within the confines of a live rock show," says Godley. "Nothing was sacred in *ZOO TV*. Every preconception could be trashed and every media mangled and I'm pleased to say I did my fair share of both."

Godley would go on to direct a string of acclaimed videos for U2, including Lemon (1993), Numb (1993), Hold Me, Thrill Me, Kiss Me, Kill Me (1995), Sweetest Thing (1998), Stuck in a Moment You Can't Get Out Of (2001) and Until the End of the World (2002). His services were also secured for some of the band's side projects, such as Adam Clayton and Larry Mullen's theme song to the movie *Mission: Impossible* and Bono's duet with Frank Sinatra on I've Got You Under My Skin. The shoot for the latter proved problematic but ended on a high note with Ol' Blues Eyes singing Strangers In The Night to Godley's wife, Sue, over dinner at a Mexican restaurant in Palm Springs that evening.

No assignment was bigger, however, than when Godley was approached to direct the video for a brand new single by The Beatles. Real Love, from their *Anthology* project, saw the three remaining Beatles building on one of John Lennon's unfinished demos. By this point, Godley had worked on video projects with George Harrison (When We Was Fab), Ringo Starr (*The Cooler*) and Paul McCartney (C'mon People), also filming a pre-concert film for the latter's 1993 *New World* tour. The film courted controversy by showing graphic images of animal cruelty in support of vegetarianism, a cause close to both McCartney's and Godley's heart. Because of the tight secrecy surrounding The Beatles project, Godley was not given a complete version of the finished track during editing of the video, so he privately overdubbed his own voice in place of some absent vocal lines for reference purposes. "So, when the guys looked at my rough edit they were listening to John, Paul, George, Ringo and Kev," says Godley.

This slow, rough mix of Real Love, complete with Godley's vocals, later appeared on various bootlegs. A couple of years later

Godley reunited with McCartney in less happy circumstances, directing the tribute for his late wife Linda. The show at London's Royal Albert Hall in April 1999, featured the likes of George Michael, The Pretenders, Elvis Costello, Neil Finn and McCartney himself. Godley's film *Here, There and Everywhere – A Concert for Linda* was screened on BBC1 later that month.

Meanwhile, Polydor's decision to drop 10cc left a big question mark over the band's future, particularly with relations between Eric Stewart and Graham Gouldman once again strained. With 10cc back on hold, Stewart took up an invitation from Alan Parsons to guest on his solo album *Try Anything Once*, contributing lead vocals to two tracks, Wine From The Water and Siren Song, while Gouldman resumed his songwriting partnership with Andrew Gold and guested on Gilbert O'Sullivan's album *Every Song Has Its Play*.

If you listened hard enough it was possible to hear 10cc's influence still evident in the music scene of the day. When Mike Mills of R.E.M. developed the outline of a new song with the working title of Hey Love he used I'm Not In Love as his blueprint.

"It's one of my favourite production sounds ever," says Mills. "When you add the sentiments that are expressed in it and the way the background vocals go with it, it's just perfect. I'd always loved the song and just the feeling of the background vocal sound, it was something we'd never tried. Scott Litt and I had been talking about 10cc and how cool I'm Not In Love is as a song. And Scott said, 'I bet we can do something which has that sound.'"

As the band started to record the song at Bearsville Studios, Litt recorded Mills as he sang different notes, then played them back on a mixing board, with each fader controlling a separate note, like 10cc had done on I'm Not In Love. Mills then played with the faders to create his own unique choral backing.

"I just played my voice and brought in the notes that needed to be there, very haphazard and random," says Mills. "I could never play it the same way twice."

As recording continued in Miami, Michael Stipe developed lyrical ideas for the song and by the time his vocal was added at Bad Animals Studio in Seattle the song was called Fuck Me Kitten. Actress Meg Ryan, who was filming *Sleepless in Seattle* in the city at the time, visited the group in the studio. "Meg Ryan came by and she just loved the song," recalls R.E.M.'s Peter Buck. "But she said, 'You know, when I grew up if the word 'fuck' was in the title and it was on the cover, I couldn't buy it in my town.' And we thought, 'That makes sense.' You want to reach people. You don't want someone to arbitrarily say, 'You can't hear this.'" By the time it appeared on R.E.M.'s next album, *Automatic For The People*, the song's title had been changed to Star Me Kitten.

In 1993, producer Trevor Horn, a long-time fan of I'm Not In Love, helmed the recording of a new version of 10cc's best-loved song by The Pretenders for inclusion in the Demi Moore film *Indecent Proposal* while The Fun Lovin' Criminals took their more radical reworking of the song to just outside the UK Top 10. By now, the song had spawned over 50 cover versions.

"There's a lovely version by Richie Havens, just him and an acoustic guitar, in a very raw fashion. It's wonderful," says Stewart.

Less pleasing were the inferior cover versions that had become hits for Will to Power and Johnny Logan. But even those stood head and shoulders above what many, including Graham Gouldman, feel is the nadir of all I'm Not In Love covers.

"I remember once seeing Petula Clark doing this disco version of I'm Not In Love," recalls broadcaster Stuart Maconie. "It was one of the most rancid moments in pop history because here's this record whose beauty is its kind of understated charm, ethereal romanticism; and there's Petula hoofing it up. I thought, 'You've not really understood this song have you, Pet?'"

Elsewhere, critics noted 10cc's influence on the music of Ben Folds Five, such as on The Last Polka, from the band's eponymous debut album, which had musical echoes of One Night In Paris. At least, critics outside the US noticed. "Oh yeah, but Americans don't know that 10cc stuff at all," says Folds. "I was always relieved when people said, 'Man, that bit sounds like the Doobie Brothers.' I said, 'Yep, exactly.' It's easier that way."

On the other side of the world, 3 The Hard Way were enjoying considerable success with their single Hip Hop Holiday, which reached No.1 in New Zealand and the Top 20 in Australia, in 1994. The song borrowed heavily from 10cc's Dreadlock Holiday but unfortunately the group had not secured the rights to use the song, meaning that Eric Stewart and Graham Gouldman allegedly received all songwriting royalties from the record.

10cc's Japanese success had prompted one of the country's major record labels, Avex, to ask Stewart and Gouldman if they were interested in making another 10cc album. The company had recently set up its UK operations and were looking for a major act to sign to their label. While Gouldman was keen, Stewart initially turned down the offer.

"I refused at first, partly because I hadn't worked with Graham for a long time and partly because I thought it was bordering on necrophilia to resurrect the 10cc name yet again," says Stewart. "Harvey Lisberg then asked me if I minded Graham putting out an album as 10cc on his own. Of course, I hit the roof! This didn't go down well. Harvey then persuaded me to at least give it a try."

By now, the Stewart/Gouldman partnership had deteriorated to the point where they could not face collaborating together, so they worked on their songs independently of one another. "By the time we started work on this album, I think Graham and I had lost all respect for each other's input," says Stewart. "That's really why we recorded our own songs separately. When I'd got a demo through of the songs that Graham wanted to put on the album, it included songs like Now You're Gone, The Monkey and the Onion, Grow Old With Me. I said to Graham, 'I can't possibly work on these songs with you, they are too depressing. I don't think they're good enough,' but Graham said, 'There might be some songs of yours that I don't like but they're our babies and I want to see them through.'"

Stewart started work on his songs at his home studio in France. When he went through his old tapes looking for new song ideas, he found the outline of a track that he had recorded in his home studio with Paul McCartney back in 1988. "Paul had been round at my house, we'd had a really good wine-laden meal and he said, 'Let's have a mess in the studio,'" says Stewart. "When I had the offer of the new album, I went through the old tapes and found it. I thought it would make a great song."

Stewart was to be proved right. The song would become Code of Silence, one of the highlights of the new album and one of Stewart's finest solo efforts. He also decided to resurrect Yvonne's The One, an unused McCartney collaboration from the *Press to Play* writing sessions, and set it to a reggae rhythm. McCartney would make a guest appearance on both tracks, contributing keyboards to the former and rhythm guitar to the latter.

Among Stewart's other new songs was Margo Wants The Mustard, which had been inspired by a woman he had met while on holiday in the Caribbean with his friend, racing driver Alain de Cadenet, and their families. "I'm sat in my house in Barbados and Margo was a lady cooking for us," says Stewart. "Alain poked his head round the door and said, 'Hey, Eric, Margo wants the mustard.' It immediately clicked in my head – what a great idea for a song! Why? Because you turn it into anything. It's not just for the food, it's for her life, a bit of spice, she needs something exciting to happen. If you're a songwriter by profession, a phrase like that can kick things off. In 10cc, a lot of our songs were kicked off that way. Life Is A Minestrone was just a line Lol and I heard on the radio."

Everything Is Not Enough was the result of some soul-searching on Stewart's behalf, as he questioned whether the material side of his life was affecting the spiritual side. "I was at the point where I was saying, 'Theoretically I've got everything I need, but is the material side of my life actually killing the spiritual side?' And in my case I thought it was, and I didn't need three houses, I didn't need a collection of racing cars, I haven't got a Picasso but I didn't need one – I could go and look at one and say, 'That's great!'"

Meanwhile, in London, Graham Gouldman had been hard at work on his new songs, with Adrian Lee, who he'd worked with previously on Wax's *American English* album. "I decided I needed to work with someone who was a keyboard player and who was good with computers," said Gouldman. "Originally Adrian was going to be my sidekick but when I went to work with him it worked so brilliantly that it became obvious to me that his involvement was going to be more than just being a sidekick, so I made him co-producer on my stuff."

The pair worked together on new tracks, many of which Gouldman had written with songwriting partners other than Eric Stewart. "On this album the real departure is that we worked with different writing partners," said Gouldman at the time. "I've known

Tim Rice for years, and he was always threatening to send me some lyrics, which turned out to be The Monkey and the Onion."

Another song, the soulful Peace In Our Time, was written with Steve Piggot, who had played keyboards on 10cc's 1993 tour, while Ready To Go Home was Gouldman's latest songwriting collaboration with Andrew Gold, a song inspired by the recent death of his father.

"When we started writing it, we had these chords that sounded very spiritual to me, like a hymn," says Gouldman. "My Dad had passed away, and Andrew had lost his Dad, and we were talking about the legacies – what we're left with, what we're going to do and where we're going to go, and how we have to be accepting. We'd been talking about the positive side to death. If someone's ill for a long time, it's a release for them to go. The legacy they leave behind becomes more alive, certainly in my father's case. The lyrics are more abstract. They're not just about one experience."

When it came to recording the song, Gold guested on guitar and put down a guide vocal, which, to his surprise, made it onto the final cut of the record.

"When Graham and I wrote the song, I sang the vocal just as a guide," says Gold. "In fact, the vocal track was only the second take we did. I thought that when the tape was played to Eric he would re-record the vocal, but it was left with me doing it."

Stewart liked the song but found it too slow. He suggested re-recording it in a reggae style but this idea was not progressed. In fact, none of the tracks on the new album would feature Stewart and Gouldman actually playing on them together, much to the disappointment of fans, who viewed the record more as two solo albums rolled into one than a genuine 10cc offering. Even the two Stewart/Gouldman writing collaborations that appear on the record were left over from the last album.

"Graham and I wrote Take This Woman for *Meanwhile*," says Stewart. "The song was originally about a guy in church not wanting to get married, but we changed it around. Why Did I Break Your Heart? was also written for *Meanwhile*; we played it to the musicians on that album but they didn't go for it. I rearranged the rhythm and Avex liked it for the new album."

One positive aspect of the new record was the production, which sounded more vivid and colourful, more in keeping with what was expected from a 10cc album. A lot of credit for the overall lush sound of the album can be attributed to Adrian Lee, who, after working with Gouldman, ended up working on Stewart's songs too.

"Avex loved my tracks but said they wanted to change some of the sounds on them, because they thought they were a bit crude," says Stewart. "Adrian did some lovely re-MIDIing of the sounds. The physical playing is still what I played but he put some gorgeous sounds on there."

In fact, Stewart was so impressed by Lee's input that at one point he could see him in a future incarnation of 10cc.

"For a while back there, I had this vision of 10cc being me, Graham, Andrew Gold and Adrian Lee," says Stewart. "Back to the 'three Yids and a Yok' of the early days. By bringing in people with very good musical brains like Andrew and Adrian, you wouldn't have had the confrontation that you can get between two people. That was the great thing about the original four-piece 10cc. It's much easier to be democratic when there's four of you, it's impossible when there's just two of you."

As the album neared completion, thoughts turned to a title.

"Graham and I each submitted a list of titles to Avex," says Stewart. "At one point I wanted to call the album *Different Planets*, because by this stage I thought that Graham and I were operating on different planets, but Avex liked one of the other titles I had suggested, which was *Mirror, Mirror*. The title had been inspired by an agony aunt column I'd seen in an American magazine. I thought that *Mirror, Mirror* would make a great title for the album, very reflective of our two personalities."

To design the album cover, Stewart and Gouldman reunited with Storm Thorgerson, the former Hipgnosis man, who had first worked with 10cc on *Sheet Music* 20 years earlier.

"Storm went away and created this image of these two guys made up from shards of broken mirror for the cover," says Stewart.

Thorgerson gave both characters a name – 'Eric' and 'Graham'. While Avex planned the release of *Mirror, Mirror*, Stewart and Gouldman had been presented with yet another award for I'm Not In Love, this time in recognition of 3 million airplays on American radio. Expressed another way, the song had clocked up the equivalent of a staggering 34 years of continuous airtime!

"People say to us, 'You must be really fed up, you must have sung I'm Not In Love thousands of times,'" says Gouldman. "But it doesn't seem to matter, it's kind of got a life of its own that it's always a pleasure to sing and play."

Such a pleasure to sing and play, in fact, that they found themselves playing an acoustic version of the song for a television programme, a performance that would inadvertently make its way onto the *Mirror, Mirror* album.

"We went into Metropolis Studios in London to film a documentary about 10cc for TV," says Stewart. "While we were in there, the guy doing the interview said to Graham and me, 'Play us one of your hits as a simple thing, just the two of you.' He asked us to do I'm Not In Love acoustically with just a guitar and a piano and we said, 'Yeah, let's have a go.' We sat down and did it very quickly and the take that went out on *Mirror, Mirror* is exactly the take as we did it. It was right off the cuff. There's nothing else on there except for two voices, guitar and piano. We went back into the control room to do the interview and listened back to what we'd recorded and everybody went, 'This sounds great, you should put it out as a single.'"

Avex felt that an acoustic version of I'm Not In Love would be a great way of generating press coverage about the return of 10cc. Stewart and Gouldman themselves were not overly enthused by the notion, though.

"I didn't like the idea at all," says Gouldman. "A 20-year-old song to introduce a new album containing 13 new songs from 1995!"

Eric Stewart had actually dismissed the idea of I'm Not In Love in an acoustic setting in an interview as far back as 1989.

"People have played and sung things to me occasionally and there's a magic in it, the melody is interesting and it grabs your attention," said Stewart that year. "And people do say that you can recognise a great song just played on an acoustic; but if I played I'm Not In Love on an acoustic I don't think it would live. I mean, it was written on an acoustic but it just doesn't live that way."

It's a shame that Stewart and Gouldman didn't listen to their instincts. The new version of I'm Not In Love did them no favours, lacking all the magic and charm of the original, while adding nothing new to the song. Of course, Eric Clapton had proven with his unplugged version of Layla that classic rock songs could be reinterpreted successfully in an acoustic setting. But, stripped of its haunting vocal backing, the new version of I'm Not In Love just didn't come up to scratch. Looking back, Gouldman concedes that the new version was "dreadful". Still, the strength of feeling at Avex persuaded Stewart and Gouldman to reconsider and the song was lined up as 10cc's next single.

"There was a lot of pressure on us to put it out," says Gouldman. "At the time we thought of it as a means to an end, to help sell the rest of the album, but it was just pathetic. Not one of our finest moments."

To relaunch 10cc to the music press, Avex lined up a special gig at The Captain's Room in the Lloyd's of London building on February 16, 1995. In front of 350 specially invited guests, Stewart, Gouldman and Rick Fenn performed acoustic versions of The Things We Do For Love, Dreadlock Holiday, I'm Mandy Fly Me, The Wall Street Shuffle and I'm Not In Love, plus Take This Woman, Margo Wants The Mustard and Ready To Go Home from their new album. The gig helped to secure 10cc a large number of radio and TV appearances to coincide with the release of the acoustic version of I'm Not In Love on March 6. Champagne corks popped a week later when the single entered the UK charts at No.29 – 10cc's first Top 30 entry since Dreadlock Holiday in 1978 and the band's 14th chart hit. Stewart was driving back from a weekend in Bath with his wife Gloria after celebrating their 29th wedding anniversary when he heard the news.

"It's a knockout," said Stewart. "It's a long time since we've been in the charts as 10cc."

Momentarily, it seemed as if Avex's grand plan was going to work. Unfortunately, the expected Top of the Pops appearance didn't materialise and the single dropped down the charts the following week. Still, at least the song had charted and thoughts turned to a follow-up.

"There are so many possible singles we could go for, for different reasons," said Stewart at the time.

Eventually they decided on Ready To Go Home. "It's a very,

very strong track and we got great feedback from America on it, and that's the main reason we've decided to release it," said Stewart at the time. "It's breaking out in cities in America already, which is great."

In the meantime, 10cc had been lined up to undertake a tour of Japan. "We're currently rehearsing for a tour which we start in Japan on May 24, and when we come back we do Europe and we're setting up a UK tour as well," said Stewart at the time. "So once the machine is in motion we'll tour this year as long as we can, a world tour hopefully with America, if this breakthrough that we've got there happens."

The Japanese tour saw Stewart, Gouldman, Rick Fenn and Stuart Tosh joined by drummer Geoff Dunn and keyboard player Alan Park. The set-list featured all the classic hits with four songs from *Mirror, Mirror* and two songs from *Meanwhile* plus a few surprises, such as Sand In My Face from 10cc's very first album, a song that hadn't been played live by the band in 20 years. Unfortunately, while things were going well in Japan, 10cc's US breakthrough didn't materialise. In the UK, Avex postponed the release of Ready To Go Home, losing the momentum that had been gained from the press coverage generated in support of the acoustic version of I'm Not In Love. The much-hoped-for tours of the UK and America were cancelled, as they were not felt to be viable without new hit material.

Mirror, Mirror was finally released in the UK in August 1995, but by this stage many fans had snapped up the American and Japanese imports that had been available since March, and which had received a one-star rating in Q magazine: "Stewart and Gouldman do little more than devalue 10cc's good name with menopausal self-pity. The inclusion of I'm Not In Love (Rework of Art Mix) suggests equine necro-flagellation."

At the time, Phil France, the band's label manager at Avex, had proposed that they film a TV special for VH-1 as 10cc's next project. "Phil suggested we do a live album in front of an audience of fellow musicians, celebrities and assorted press, playing 10cc songs old and new," says Stewart. "We asked George Martin to produce it and he said he'd be delighted to do it. We were going to record it at George's Air Studios."

Stewart and Gouldman planned to use an orchestra to back them on certain tracks and needed an arranger: "So, I asked John Paul Jones to do the string arrangements," says Gouldman. The former Led Zeppelin bass player, who had worked with Gouldman back in the 60s, wasn't the only former collaborator that they had in mind for the project.

"We were going to do the album with guests," says Gouldman. "The idea was that if we did Bus Stop, for example, we could get Allan Clarke or Graham Nash to come and sing it with us."

Unfortunately, Stewart and Gouldman had differences of opinion over the set-list for the project. Gouldman wanted to include some of the pair's pre-10cc songs, such as Bus Stop and A Groovy Kind of Love, but Stewart saw it differently.

"Eric, Harvey and myself had a meeting in London but we couldn't agree which songs should be included," says Gouldman. "Eric had finally agreed to do A Groovy Kind of Love on it, and I wanted to do two or three of my songs, but Eric thought it'd be too retro. I just thought we had such a big body of work that we could nod to it."

Unable to come to an agreement on the project, Stewart and Gouldman put 10cc back on indefinite hold. Still, with 10cc's 25th anniversary looming, Harvey Lisberg tried to get the four original members of 10cc back together again to record a song for a new greatest hits album. One of Lisberg's ideas was to get them to re-record Neanderthal Man.

"Harvey called me up and said, 'I think the band should get back together again to record a new version of Neanderthal Man,'" says Kevin Godley. "I said, 'Why? No way! What on earth for?' But I went home and ended up writing a lyric on my laptop. I wrote this thing called Son of Man, basically about the way the band formed and how it worked. It was quite nice; it worked quite well. So, I thought it might be interesting to record it, so I spent a couple of days in Dublin with Gavin Friday and we messed around for a while, but nothing came of it. There's a half-finished track lying around somewhere."

Instead, the band's anniversary was commemorated by the release of *The Very Best of 10cc* in March 1997. The album received some stunning reviews, confirming yet again how well 10cc's music had stood up to the test of time. "Virtuosic, cinematic, brilliant," wrote *Mojo*, describing 10cc as the "cleverest pop band of its generation ... Pop music this good is a miracle. Respect due, listen and learn, we're in the presence of greatness."

The Very Best of 10cc reached the UK Top 40 and would eventually go on to earn the band a platinum disc. Kevin Godley wanted to mark the band's 25th anniversary with a TV documentary of his own. "I called it *Wrong Number*," says Godley. "You know, the story about 10cc being the average male ejaculation. Well, that's a pretty sad story for four guys, isn't it? The other reason for calling it *Wrong Number* was that I noticed that the first and last tracks by the original 10cc, Donna and Don't Hang Up, both featured telephones in the songs."

Unfortunately, Godley's 10cc documentary never made it beyond pre-production. "It's very difficult to get interest in one-off ideas for music programmes, unless they fit into a series," says Godley. "It's a shame, because I had quite a novel way of doing it in mind. If it ever comes to fruition, it will be good."

Digitally remastered CDs of 10cc's classic albums followed later in the year, including rare b-sides as bonus tracks. Sadly, the damage done to the mastertapes of *Deceptive Bends* and, even more significantly, *Bloody Tourists* was very evident on these releases. Despite this, the albums received glowing reviews. Paul Lester, in *Uncut* magazine, described 10cc, *Sheet Music* and *The Original Soundtrack* as, "Five-star records all," and awarded four-star ratings to *How Dare You, Deceptive Bends* and *Bloody Tourists*, citing the latter as "Seventies pop close to its very best". Even Godley and Creme's 'grand folly' *Consequences* was hailed a "lost masterpiece" in the 'Classic Albums Revisited' feature in *Uncut* magazine: "*Consequences* remains the outstanding, misunderstood musical legacy of extraordinarily gifted artists ... the Coen brothers of rock."

While Harvey Lisberg hadn't succeeded in getting all four of 10cc's founder members together for the band's 25th anniversary, he would play an important role in getting half of the original line-up to create new music again for the first time in over 20 years. Graham Gouldman had written a song with Italian songwriter Claudio Giudetti but couldn't nail the lyrics.

"I mentioned this to Harvey and we were talking about potential lyricists for the song," says Gouldman. "And Harvey said, 'What about Kevin Godley?' I said, 'It would be great if he'd do it.' Anyway, Kevin heard the track and liked it and agreed to do it."

Gouldman sent Godley a copy of the backing track but at first his songwriting partner was a bit rusty.

"I wasn't used to writing to order from a tape recorder," says Godley. "So, I phoned Graham and said, 'Why don't you come over to my place and we'll have a go.' And we cracked it in a couple of days. We were really pleased with it. There was still a spark there. It was like riding a bike. It was fun to do – just jumping on the bike and riding again."

Godley's lyric for the song, which was titled Just Another Day, dealt with the theme of suicide, not the usual subject matter of your average pop song, but then again neither was the subject matter of their last collaboration on 10cc's Iceberg back in 1975. The experience of writing together would prove to be an important stepping-stone towards further Godley/Gouldman writing collaborations in the future.

"We both really enjoyed writing together again," said Gouldman at the time. "We both said it was like no time had passed by. It was such an enjoyable thing to do that we're probably gonna write some more stuff together."

CHAPTER 28

LIVE AND LET LIVE

WHILE LOL CREME HAD PLAYED THE OCCASIONAL GIG WITH ART OF Noise, of the four original members of 10cc it was only Graham Gouldman who really missed life on the road. At first he'd play a few one-offs, such as a special gig at the Subterranea Club in London alongside Neil Finn and Roddy Frame for the Jools Holland-hosted BBC TV series *In the Round*. Having only met each other an hour before the gig, the resulting performance was wonderfully spontaneous, the set-list crammed full of some of the best songs from the previous four decades: from Gouldman's 60s classics like Bus Stop and For Your Love, through to gems from 10cc, Aztec Camera and Crowded House. Towards the end of the concert, Finn, Frame and Gouldman start jamming with each other, with the audience treated to a unique version of I'm Not In Love, with harmonies courtesy of Finn and Frame.

Having teamed up with Rick Fenn to perform acoustic sets at the Green Room in London and Ronnie Scott's in Birmingham, Gouldman decided to commemorate 10cc's upcoming 30th anniversary in 2002 with a tour featuring a full band. "I realised I missed playing on the road, and I wanted to do it," says Gouldman. "I didn't want to call it 10cc, because it wasn't. It was something I had a hankering to do more for the pleasure of it; I didn't think it was ever going to be a great money-spinner."

In November 2001, Gouldman sent a letter to Eric Stewart advising him of his intentions. "Obviously the band won't be called 10cc," wrote Gouldman. "And I will make every effort to ensure that promoters and venues bill the show clearly as me presenting 'the music of 10cc' so there can be no misunderstandings."

Gouldman set about pulling together a band for the tour. He got back in touch with Paul Burgess, who he hadn't played with in almost 20 years, and signed up Rick Fenn. New recruits Mick Wilson and

Mike Stevens completed the line-up, with Wilson taking on lead vocal duties for the songs originally sung by Eric Stewart and Lol Creme. They toured the UK in 2002 billed as 'Graham Gouldman celebrates 30 years of 10cc'.

In October 2003, now known as 'Graham Gouldman's 10cc', the band undertook a tour of Australia and, in July 2005, a tour of Japan – this time as '10cc featuring Graham Gouldman and Friends', a billing that was also used for a UK tour in February/March 2007. Yet, despite Gouldman's intention not to go out as 10cc, it was impossible to stop some promoters using the band's name as a shorthand to sell tickets, which created issues for Eric Stewart. "I got a whole boatload of emails to my website saying, 'Where were you? I bought a ticket for 10cc and there was only Graham Gouldman there,'" says Stewart. "So, I had to send out a general email on my website and said, 'I apologise for this but please don't blame me. Myself and Lol Creme have never been asked to do a tour by anybody. No-one has ever asked us if we'd like to tour with Graham Gouldman. You go along and if you feel you've been cheated, ask for your money back. If you don't feel like you've been cheated, that's always up to you. You pays your money and you takes your choice."

While some fans were disappointed at Stewart's absence from the shows, others enjoyed the opportunity to hear 10cc's music live again. There were certainly some deft touches to enjoy, such as Rick Fenn's sublime Floydesque guitar work on a new intro and outro on Art For Art's Sake; and the moment in Donna when the usual sound of an old-fashioned telephone ring is wittily replaced with the annoying ringtone of a mobile phone. Critics were certainly impressed with the musicianship on show.

"Combining harmony vocals worthy of The Beach Boys with the sort of super-slick musicianship associated with Steely Dan is one thing in the recording studio," said David Sinclair in *The Times* of their gig at London's Shepherd's Bush Empire in March 2007. "But as they rattled through The Wall Street Shuffle, The Things We Do For Love, Life Is A Minestrone and Art For Art's Sake, the friends proved themselves able to reproduce such feats with ease. And by the time they cruised towards the finishing line with I'm Not In Love, Dreadlock Holiday and Rubber Bullets, the sheer weight of hits had produced a momentum that was irresistible."

While Eric Stewart was absent, Gouldman did manage to coerce another original member of the band to join him onstage at a couple of the shows. In Cardiff and London, Kevin Godley walked onstage, without fanfare, during Old Wild Men, one of 10cc's very best songs, and not heard live since Knebworth over 30 years earlier. "I had no idea what to expect," says Godley. "I just stepped up to the mic for the second verse and I thought everyone would go, 'Who's the old geezer?' but it was like 'Yes!!!' It was amazing."

"Hi honey, I'm home!" said Godley when the song was over. The whole performance, including Godley's guest appearance, was filmed for posterity and lined up for release on CD and DVD to be titled *Clever Clogs*.

Gouldman and Godley weren't the only members of 10cc keeping the band's music alive. For a bit of light relief, Lol Creme had formed a 'pub band' with his friend Trevor Horn. They enlisted fellow producer Steve Lipson, songwriter Chris Braide and drummer Ash Soan in the venture, with a view to playing a few low-key gigs just for the fun of it. Calling themselves The Producers, they played their first gig together at the Barfly in Camden Town in November 2006, and included 10cc's Rubber Bullets and I'm Not in Love in their stage set. It was 30 years since Creme had last performed these songs live, at the final gig performed by 10cc's original line-up at Knebworth in 1976.

By the time The Producers played their second gig in February 2007, they were starting to debut their own material alongside the cover versions. A single, Barking Up The Right Tree, sung by Creme, was released later in 2007, with the band playing intermittent gigs and enjoying the experience of playing together so much that they started work on an album at Trevor Horn's SARM Studio in Basing Street, Notting Hill in London.

Gouldman, meanwhile, was about to release *Clever Clogs*. By now, he seemed less concerned about overtly using the band's name, effectively releasing it in May 2008 under the 10cc banner, complete with a new band logo and artwork by long-time 10cc collaborator Storm Thorgerson. Featuring extensive bonus features, including interviews with Gouldman and Thorgerson, *Clever Clogs* received good reviews.

"Purists may baulk at the fact that this incarnation includes only Graham Gouldman," wrote Chris Roberts in *Uncut* magazine. "You can't argue with the songs though", giving the DVD a four-star rating. The release created further tension between Stewart and Gouldman, who had said up to now that promoters had been responsible for using the 10cc name. "He said that it wasn't his fault, it was the promoters," says Stewart. "I thought that was a bit odd because he then releases a live CD and calls it 10cc. And it's not 10cc! That's got nothing to do with the promoters."

Whether or not Gouldman has the moral right to use the 10cc name in this way is a subject that divides fans, in the same way that fans were divided when Godley and Creme left the band. Whatever the reservations about Gouldman's use of the band's name, it seemed to be doing 10cc's legacy some good. And, at every show, Gouldman assiduously credits the writers of each song as he introduces them in the set, thereby fully acknowledging the contribution of his former bandmates. Audiences and critics alike certainly seem to enjoy the experience, as evidenced at the group's gig at London's IndigO2 in May 2008.

"Although I approached this show with a degree of cynicism and suspicion, it was washed away by the experience of watching Gouldman and his expert band work their way through 10cc's catalogue," said David Cheal in *The Daily Telegraph*. "Gouldman, now 61, must have played some of these songs thousands of times, but he looked fresh, sharp and enthusiastic as he and his four bandmates opened the evening with Wall Street Shuffle and went on to perform what was effectively a greatest hits show ... an unexpected pleasure."

Since then, Gouldman has taken his band all over the world several times, including tours of the UK, Ireland, Germany, Austria, the Netherlands, Belgium, Switzerland, Sweden, Norway, Denmark, Iceland, South Africa, Japan, Australia, New Zealand, Canada and even shows in New York and Moscow. They have also played numerous festivals – GuilFest, Cornbury, Hop Farm, Cropredy, Rewind, Weyfest, Hyde Park, Wychwood – and 19 arena gigs in Germany as part of the *Night of the Proms* tour alongside groups like Tears For Fears, who were also fans of the band. "10cc are probably the main reason we agreed to do this leg," says Curt Smith. "Roland and I are big fans, especially *Deceptive Bends*."

Early in 2011 Gouldman participated in the BBC TV series *Songwriter's Circle*, alongside Fran Healy of Travis and Canadian songwriter Ron Sexsmith, filmed at Bush Hall in Shepherd's Bush, London. "I loved that, because I met Ron, who I was a fan of," says Gouldman. "I was delighted to meet him and we kept in touch. And I love his work. A lovely guy too."

The gig saw a memorable performance of The Things We Do For Love, with Sexsmith joining in on the harmonies. "I used to sing that in the back of my parents' car," Sexsmith told the audience.

Gouldman celebrated 10cc's 40th anniversary in 2012 with more touring. As the band prepared for another tour, they settled into their rehearsal studio in North London. Unbeknown to Gouldman, in an adjacent room in the same rehearsal studio, The Producers were trying to get to grips with 10cc's The Dean and I. As both bands took a break they ran into each other in the communal area of the rehearsal room and Lol Creme and Graham Gouldman came face to face with each other for the first time in nearly 10 years. "I had a very nice chat with Lol," says Gouldman. "It was good to see him."

One of the highlights of Gouldman's subsequent tour was a memorable night at London's prestigious Royal Albert Hall on his sixty-sixth birthday. Paul Carrack made a guest appearance with the band to perform I'm Not In Love, while Kevin Godley guested again, suggesting a new twist on the band's first ever single, Donna, to commemorate the occasion.

"I was thinking of the context of the show but I was thinking, 'Maybe people are bored to death of the song, it's our first record. How can we make it stand out and be a little bit special?'" says Godley. "And I was thinking about some street-corner doo-wop bands I'd seen in America and how accomplished they were and I thought, 'Well this song was part of that tradition.' Strip away all the pretend tremolo guitars and do it as if we were a vocal doo-wop band on the street. It worked extremely well." Godley also performed Old Wild Men and Sand In My Face with the band and even played drums on Rubber Bullets. He loved the experience.

"The Albert Hall was extraordinary," says Godley. "It was magical. I felt 25 years younger. Shame I didn't look it!"

In 2013, Gouldman stripped things back by taking an acoustic show called *Heart Full of Songs* on the road. The tour gave him the opportunity to perform songs spanning his entire career, from the hits he wrote in the 60s through his work with 10cc and Wax and beyond. "It's interesting how some songs work and some don't, so we don't do those," says Gouldman. "It's a much more intimate show; I talk a lot more about the songs as well." He enjoyed the experience so much that he undertook a full *Heart Full of Songs* UK tour in 2014, 2017 and 2020.

Eric Stewart hadn't played live since 10cc's Japanese tour in 1995. He nearly performed I'm Not In Love at the tribute concert for Sad Café singer Paul Young at the Manchester Apollo in December 2000 but pulled out of the gig, although he would contribute to Young's posthumous album *Chronicles*, released in 2011. However, in February 2014 Stewart would make a rare guest appearance at the Music Producers Guild Awards, in support of Trevor Horn, who was being recognised for his 'Outstanding Contribution to UK Music'. Stewart performed I'm Not In Love with Horn and his band The Producers at the ceremony. It was the first time that Stewart and Creme had performed together on stage for nearly 40 years. "Playing and singing I'm Not In Love at the MPG Awards was a real buzz, and having Trevor Horn and Lol Creme, Seal and Anne Dudley in the 'backing group' was a real thrill for me," says Stewart. "People in the audience like Bill Wyman, and many other greats from the past, coming up to me and complimenting me on the song, and its performance that evening, was the biggest thrill of all."

The Producers would continue to perform live, now known as The Trevor Horn Band, with memorable gigs at the Shepherd's Bush Empire in March 2015, Cornbury Festival in July 2015 and at the Wickham Festival in August 2016.

Graham Gouldman's 10cc toured again in 2015, this time performing *Sheet Music* in its entirety followed by a greatest hits set. Some of the songs from *Sheet Music* hadn't been played live in 40 years; other tracks had never been played live before at all. "When I started rehearsing them, I realised why," says Gouldman. "They're so complex and arguably not concert-friendly. They demand to be listened to, something like Clockwork Creep, there's so much going on for it. There's people in the audience who know every track intimately on *Sheet Music*, but the people who only know the hits have a slight look of bewilderment on their faces."

Once again, he asked Kevin Godley if he'd like to be involved but this time he declined. Instead, he agreed to create a unique video for Somewhere In Hollywood. "I offered to re-record the vocal to minimal instrumentation and make a film of myself singing it so the band could accompany my projected image on stage," says Godley. "Of course, I ended up throwing in a few visual atmospherics to enhance the overall look. Mind you, the thought of a 20-foot close-up of my face fills me with horror so I'm glad I never got to see it in situ."

Godley would go on to make two further films for Graham Gouldman's 10cc that were unveiled on the band's 2019 UK tour. By then, in addition to his own touring commitments, Gouldman had toured the world as part of the 13th iteration of Ringo Starr's All-Starr Band playing 40 dates in Belgium, Czech Republic, Denmark, Finland, Germany, Monaco, Netherlands, Israel, Italy and the US.

"I have to pinch myself when I'm onstage and I'm singing away and I look to my right not more than two feet away is Ringo Starr," says Gouldman. The set-list included three 10cc songs: The Things We Do For Love, Dreadlock Holiday and I'm Not In Love.

"I just love performing," says Gouldman. "I'm lucky, my working life, I get to do the three things I love the most: songwriting, recording and playing live. Never a day goes by when I do not appreciate how lucky I am to do that."

CHAPTER 29

WRONG NUMBER

FOLLOWING THE END OF 10CC IN 1995, GRAHAM GOULDMAN HAD continued his songwriting partnership with Andrew Gold, releasing a 'new' Wax album in 1997. *The Wax Files* brought together six new songs, two previously unreleased tracks from the archives, and a selection of songs from Wax's three albums. New songs like Does Anybody See You? and Touch and Go were some of Gouldman and Gold's finest collaborations to date, proving that their 15-year songwriting partnership was still fruitful. Their very first collaborations, for the unreleased Common Knowledge album in 1984, finally saw the light of day in September 1998, when the album was released, along with three new songs, as *Commonknowledge.com*.

Gouldman collaborated with a variety of other songwriting partners in his post-10cc years. "It's very difficult to get songs placed as a songwriter because so many artists write their own songs," said Gouldman at the time. "So, I've made a conscious decision to write with artists or producers for specific projects."

Such projects saw him writing with the likes of Cerys Matthews, Marti Pellow, Gary Wright, Paul Carrack – on his 1997 single The Way I'm Feeling Tonight – and with Peter Cox and Peter-John Vettese on the song Soul Rising, which would be recorded by Joe Cocker on his 1999 album *No Ordinary World*. Another project saw Gouldman writing with Gary Barlow. "The first time I met Graham was in 1998 while starting work on my second solo album," says Barlow. "We spent two great days at my studio in Cheshire. In our session we wrote two songs." The first of these songs, Stronger, was released as Barlow's next single and would go on to reach the UK Top 20 in July 1999.

An invitation from his music publisher to take part in their annual writers' week would be the catalyst for Gouldman to participate in further songwriting collaborations. The idea was to bring together a diverse group of songwriters in a remote setting to get them writing songs together in a variety of different permutations. Gouldman was among 15 songwriters including Chris Difford of Squeeze, Kirsty MacColl, Lamont Dozier and Suggs from Madness who met up at Huntsham Court, a country house in the rolling Devon countryside. After breakfast on the first day, the group were split into five teams, each containing three writers. Gouldman was paired up with Difford and Suggs.

"Suggs came up with this title, There Was A Day, and that was it," recalls Gouldman. "We were off and running. And I had this sort of guitar figure, and we just sort of ran that." After dinner, each team played their new songs to the wider group. "Even for an old cynic like me, that first night was tear-inducing," says Suggs. "Just hearing a song that people have written that same day is brilliant and strange."

Combining Gouldman's melodic touch with Difford's deft lyrics, the song even manages a neat reference to I'm Not In Love in the chorus. Later in the week Gouldman was paired up with Kirsty MacColl. While nothing emerged between them from the Huntsham Court sessions, it sparked off a songwriting partnership that would blossom afterwards. "We get together, write loads of bits, and then she goes away and picks the bits she wants to finish, writes some lyrics and then we get back together to finish off the songs," said Gouldman at the time. "She's great to work with." Of these songs, Treachery – complete with a neat lyrical twist about an artist stalking a fan who has switched their allegiance to another artist – would appear on MacColl's next album, the excellent *Tropical Brainstorm*, while Things Happen would appear as a b-side. Unfortunately, any further collaboration was curtailed by MacColl's tragic death in the December of 2000.

Having now amassed a large catalogue of new songs, written with a variety of songwriting partners, Gouldman decided to record a new solo album as his next venture, the long-awaited follow-up to 1968's *The Graham Gouldman Thing*. "I've been waiting for that one to drop out of the charts before starting work on the next one," joked Gouldman.

The album, wittily titled *And Another Thing*, was released in October 2000. Recorded in London, Los Angeles, Nashville and Genoa, it brought together songs old and new including a reworking of You Stole My Love, his 1965 single with The Mockingbirds. Gouldman wasn't afraid of reinventing the past, replacing the original middle eight with one originally written for another of his old songs, Schoolgirl. The highlights of the album, however, were a couple of new songs. There Was A Day, Gouldman's collaboration from the Huntsham Court sessions, features co-writers Difford and Suggs both guesting on backing vocals. The other highlight was the haunting Walking With Angels, written in Nashville with Gordon Kennedy, inspired in part by a charity trek through Israel where Gouldman felt very connected with his late father.

Also included on the album was Just Another Day, the song that he'd written with Kevin Godley back in 1997. However, the version that appears on *And Another Thing* has Godley's lyrics replaced with a new set written by Frank Musker. "I've never really had a very commercial mind," says Godley. "I've always written lyrics that were a bit edgy or a bit different, and that was the case here. Everyone said, 'We can't sing about suicide on a single.' Stuff like that." A hidden track at the end of the record strung together all the questions Gouldman gets asked in interviews: *'What comes first, the music or the words? / Do you still see Kev and Lol? / Did you split amicably, you and the lads in 10cc?'*

Meanwhile, Eric Stewart had spent most of his post-10cc years happily pursuing non-musical goals. In particular, he and his wife bought and renovated a succession of houses in south-west France, with Gloria utilising her skills as a garden designer and dealer in French decorative artefacts and textiles. Occasionally, Stewart would lend his vocal talents to a musical project, such as the 1996 Alan Parsons album *On Air*, or dabble in his home studio. One day he found himself working on a song for a friend.

"A good friend of mine, Vic Norman, had his 30th wedding anniversary coming up, so I thought it would be nice to give him a special anniversary present," says Stewart. "So, I wrote this song for him and his wife, called The Norman Conquest (Part 2), and recorded it at my studio in France. I transferred it onto CD, made a little cover for it and sent it to him. He phoned me back and said,

'Eric, this is great! Why don't you release it?' The more I thought about it, the more I realised that there was a good idea for an album there, where each track was written about a different friend of mine, telling their own particular story."

With no specific release date in mind, Stewart worked at his own pace when inspiration took him, playing all the instruments himself. With the working title of *My Dear Friends* many of the songs reflected Stewart's relationships. The importance of friendship itself is explored in A Friend In Need, arguably the strongest track on the album. Five years on from its original impetus, with the album nearing completion, final overdubs were added at Dave Gilmour's Astoria Studio – located on a houseboat on the River Thames – where Sam Brown, Helen 'Aitch' McRobbie and Louise Marshall added backing vocals to several of the tracks.

Having now settled on *Do Not Bend* as the title, the album was released in April 2003 with a cover featuring a picture taken by his son, Jody. The album marked Stewart's 40th year in the music business and an initial limited-edition run included bonus tracks and sleevenotes featuring words of support from former collaborators such as Paul McCartney, George Martin, Neil Sedaka and Alan Parsons. *Do Not Bend* is mainly the sound of Stewart having fun in the studio, as reflected in the song The Gods Are Smiling. "It reflects my own euphoric state of mind," says Stewart. "I have finished my album at last and I'm pleased and excited about my music for the first time in a long time. I am enjoying my life very much, and my family are all progressing nicely along their own paths."

There are some strong moments on *Do Not Bend*, and Stewart's voice sounds great throughout, but at times the songs are swamped by the overuse of steel drums, synthesised brass sounds and drum machines. "It's slightly surprising that his made-at-home solo efforts sound so mechanised and dated," wrote Chris Ingham in *Mojo*, awarding the album two stars. "He retains a distinctively witty and allusive lyric style and his creamy vocals are instantly identifiable and attractive, particularly on the gentler pieces. But these songs needed the nurturing attention of real instruments to give them soul, rather than the brittle, one-man-and-his-computer digital clatter Stewart has conjured here. Shame really. Next time Eric, get your acoustic out."

Kevin Godley remained active in music video, working with the likes of James (Tomorrow), The Charlatans (Forever, A Man Needs To Be Told), Keane (Is It Any Wonder?, The Way I Feel), Will Young (Leave Right Now), Katie Melua (Nine Million Bicycles, I Cried For You, The Flood) and Snow Patrol (Crack The Shutters). Yet, despite his success as a video director, there were sometimes frustrations with the process.

"I love directing music videos but ideas get filtered through an army of producers, art directors, casting, camera department, wardrobe, editors, special effects, blah blah blah, etc. etc., before they exist, so spontaneous it's not," says Godley.

Godley had the urge to make new music again and decided to work with a collaborator he already knew. Having worked together on Just Another Day seven years earlier, he turned to Graham Gouldman, thus providing yet another unexpected, but very welcome, twist in the 10cc story. So, why Gouldman?

"In a nutshell ... unfinished business," says Godley. "In all the years that we've known each other we've only written three pure, Godley/Gouldman songs. That, and a desire to find out if the music muscle still worked with someone I enjoyed and didn't have to spend weeks getting to know."

Gouldman readily accepted Godley's invitation to collaborate.

"I was delighted when he called to suggest we write some songs," says Gouldman. "When I asked, 'Why?' He said, 'No reason ... just to do it and see what happens.' A good enough reason for me. What followed was a series of writing and recording sessions where the remit was – No Remit. Something like the early days when we wrote and recorded for ourselves with one ear half-cocked for something that broke the mould. I always figured Kev had the best voice in the band, ironic then that he never sang lead on a 10cc single ... even I managed that!"

The pair started writing together in January 2004 and continued whenever they had a break in their schedules. Both were energised by the experience. "It was exhilarating to hear a haunting, Mr G chord sequence, wrap some words around it and feel something actually come to life, in real time, again," says Godley.

The first song that they wrote together was The Same Road, a tale of "a burned-out, homesick, American executive, snarled up in traffic on the Westway, who fantasises about finding a soul mate in a pressurised, loveless world."

"At the time, we weren't sure if it was for us or another artist," says Godley. "Lyrically, it draws on seeing people trapped in offices all day, fantasising about finding something better. Of the five in the can, so far, it's probably the sweetest tune but the most derivative lyric."

As the pair wrote more songs together, a less derivative and more distinctive writing style began to emerge. Among these songs was the stunning Beautifulloser.com, an eight-minute tour de force reminiscent of 10cc epics from the early days, albeit with a subject matter that concerned very 21st-century issues.

"Beautifulloser.com is real," says Godley. "Felt like shit. Looked like shit. Felt like my career was over and I was about to spiral down the plughole when I heard someone on TV use the words 'beautiful loser' and it rang a deep, dark bell. I grabbed something and held on. I wouldn't get sucked into oblivion until I wrote this down. What if there was a website where rich and talented people end up when they have nothing left? A site where the cruel, empty or simply curious could log on to witness their humiliation and, if they were really lucky, death. The way things were heading it didn't seem that far-fetched so, not being technologically gifted or sick enough to build the real thing, I wrote a lyric. The words spewed out in a week. Lots of them. A man is haunted by his younger self and filled with regret at turning into the online business monster that, unwittingly, creates the circumstances for his old friend's death. Couldn't stop the words or the ghosts. They're still coming two years on from recording the song. A tiny edit removing the phrase 'And her face shows every line she's taken' regrettably made the cut flow better. I know the song is about me but am I the haunted man or the suicidal woman? Two things I learned writing and recording it... I need collaborators to bring the best of the worst to the surface and I still can't do brevity."

Other tracks included Johnny Hurts and Hooligan Crane, a song that revisited the theme of bullying from Godley's schooldays, complete with an alluded reference to his school's motto ('Delapsus Resurgam') written on the tie. Unlike the *'spotty, specky, four-eyed, weedy little creep'* who exacts his revenge on his tormentors in I

Wanna Rule The World, this time the bully himself feels remorse for his actions and takes his own life.

"These tracks are pretty lean by our previous standards," says Godley. "They're more heartfelt, focussed, less layered and lyrically they're tougher."

The pair decided to make these songs available to download via their own website, rather than wait until they had a full album's worth of material ready. Calling themselves GG/06, the website was launched in July 2006.

"All hail the democracy of the internet," says Godley. "You don't have to be young, safe and predictable to find an audience anymore. And we're definitely none of those."

A fifth collaboration, Son of Man, saw them working on the lyrics that Godley had tried to write 10 years previously in telling the tale of the band's transition from their pre-Hotlegs days through to the formation of 10cc. A Godley/Gouldman collaboration, featuring cameo appearances from Eric Stewart (being asked in a 1981 interview on BBC's *Swap Shop* how the group was formed) and Lol Creme (singing the chorus to Neanderthal Man), it symbolically features all four of the band's original members.

A sixth song, Barry's Shoes, followed in 2007 and was set right back where it all began, as teenagers in Manchester, Jewish boys sat in the synagogue thinking about a bigger world outside where "shoes were more important than God". It marked the first time Godley had got back behind a drum kit to record since *Goodbye Blue Sky* in 1988.

"I forgot how demanding it was, especially when you haven't played properly in about 20 years," says Godley. "It wasn't like riding a bike. It took me a day to get back to basics. It was so much more rewarding than drum programming. I was looking forward to it, it was very exciting. I thought I would be a physical wreck the next day, but I was fine."

While Godley and Gouldman had other songs in various stages of development, further collaboration was made more logistically difficult when Godley and his wife Sue decided to move home to County Wicklow in Ireland in 2008. "I love it here in Ireland," says Godley. "I'd done quite a bit of work here over the years and enjoyed being here. What I like about this country is that culture is a part of people's everyday lives. Everybody wants to be a writer or a singer or a musician. In England, everybody wants to be famous. There's a big difference. This is a good place to be."

While music continued to take a back seat to his other pursuits, Eric Stewart released a new solo album *Viva La Difference* in January 2009. "The title track itself is about the fact that people are different," says Stewart. "Why the hell should we be asking people to all be the same? I love the fact that we're different. Viva la difference! That's the sort of message in that particular track."

This time, Stewart eschewed drum machines in favour of real drums, courtesy of local drummer Alain Merlingeas. "It's got a bit more of that old vibe that I used to like with the 10cc records, especially the early ones where we were recording on eight-track," says Stewart. "One of the down sides of modern recording is that we've got endless choice now, of how many tracks, and you don't have to commit anything. I think it sometimes clouds the issue of what you were trying to do. So I've been restricting myself to 16 tracks and if it doesn't sound right, then I've got to find a way of making it sound right, and ditch stuff from it that may be not needed. I'm being very careful with the blend of sound on the tracks and ensuring the instruments don't get in the way of each other, which can happen so easily. One of the biggest faults I find on a lot of modern recordings is that they just blitz them with sound so heavily; you can't see the wood for the trees. Where, if you listen to something gorgeous and simple, like the early Beatles tracks, or Presley, you've got three guys and one guy singing, with a bit of spring reverb or something, and it sounds beautiful and powerful. We sort of lost the ability to do that, with the technology becoming so complex, so I'm heading a bit back in that direction, and looking for that warm, warm sound."

Viva La Difference is again the sound of Stewart enjoying the pursuit of his own musical vision. There are still several songs that sound like he is exorcising his own personal demons, but elsewhere Stewart proves he is still capable of taking listeners aback with some of his subject matter, such as on Down By The Palace, where he gives the British Royal Family a kicking, or Gnome Sweet Gnomes, which sticks the knife into morally bankrupt Swiss bankers. The standout track, however, is We're Not Alone as Stewart contemplates his wider place in the universe. "It's an important song for me," says Stewart. "We'd just celebrated the birth of our first grandchild, a lovely boy called Christian. I was looking at him one day and thinking really far-out thoughts as to what goes on in the universe. I looked at his innocence and thought, 'Surely we can't be the only people around.' And that's where I got the idea for We're Not Alone."

In 2012 Lol Creme's band The Producers were finally about to release their debut album. Originally to be titled *Studio One* then *Watching You Out There* and even, at one point, *The Path of Sydney Arthur*, the album finally appeared as the more prosaic *Made In Basing Street*. One of the songs, Freeway – inspired by the experience of driving at night in Los Angeles – saw Creme recycle a guitar riff he'd developed back in 1970 for the Hotlegs song Suite FA. "That riff had been going around in my head for years and I thought that it was too good not to use it again," says Creme.

Outside of playing together in The Producers, Creme continued to work with Trevor Horn on a variety of musical projects. Take a look at the credits and Creme's name appears as backing vocalist, musician and even, occasionally, songwriter on albums by Rod Stewart, Tina Turner, Tom Jones, Cher, The Pet Shop Boys, Lisa Stansfield, Kate Bush, Robbie Williams, Seal, Olly Murs and The Overtones. He would even make a few live appearances, participating in the 'Produced by Trevor Horn' tribute concert at Wembley Arena in 2004, with The Pet Shop Boys at The Mermaid Theatre in 2006 and with Robbie Williams at the BBC Electric Proms at London's Roundhouse in 2009.

Graham Gouldman continued to enjoy participating in writers' weeks. One session saw him partnered with two country songwriters, Kevin Montgomery and Beth Nielsen Chapman. "I've been stalking Graham Gouldman since he was nineteen and I was not even born yet because his writing is just so superb," says Chapman. "I think maybe my favourite song of all time is The Things We Do For Love, so to get to meet him my mouth just dropped and I couldn't believe I was getting to sit in a room and write with him." The trio came up with Come To Mine, which would appear on Chapman's album *Hearts of Glass*. Another songwriting session saw him collaborate with Tom Fletcher and Danny Jones of the band McFly on the track I Got You, which would appear on their No.1 album *Wonderland*. The 40-year age gap between them didn't seem to be an issue.

"Once you get a couple of blokes together with acoustic guitars, you are just two blokes with guitars rather than one being old enough to be the other's father," says Gouldman. "Age has not stopped me doing anything I did when I was a lot younger. I enjoy what I do so much that that keeps you young."

As Gouldman started compiling material for a new solo album he knew that ill health would prevent a major contribution from his close friend Andrew Gold, who was suffering from renal cancer. Gold seemed to be responding well to treatment, so Gouldman was shocked when he received a call in June 2011 telling him that his friend had passed away. "I found out he'd died of a heart attack when his ex-wife called me as I was at the airport, coming back from Holland," says Gouldman. "He was a great communicator and a marvellous person. He was unique not only as a musician, a Jack-of-all-trades and a master of all of them, and everybody loved him. He was a big man with a big personality. I'm not quite accepting of his death even now. I can't grieve properly until I accept it, so it was important for me to be able to write something about him."

Gouldman found himself discussing Gold during a songwriting session with Chris Braide, who had recently been working closely with Lol Creme in The Producers. "We had been talking about Andrew, who Chris was a great fan of, and we decided to write the song about him," says Gouldman. "Chris lives in LA so we finished the song via Skype and email. I recorded my vocal, acoustic guitar and a ukulele in London and sent the tracks to him in LA. I was expecting him to call me to discuss how the song production should proceed. Instead, he sent back a complete recording with the parts I had sent him and all the harmonies and instruments that he put on. I was completely blown away by what he'd done. The outro that Chris sings reminded me so much of Andrew's voice that it brought me to tears."

The resulting song, Daylight, was released in June 2012 as Gouldman's next single, exactly a year and a day after Gold's death. It was taken from Gouldman's solo album, *Love and Work*, which he dedicated to his great friend. According to Gouldman, love and work, "are the two most important things to me and the album is one of the most important things I have done. It has come at a significant time in my life as well and the cover reflects that."

The cover saw Gouldman once again reunited with sleeve designer Storm Thorgerson and featured a picture of a baby sitting on a rocking horse – a droll reference to Gouldman being an old rocker. "This was all new material but performed by an old hand," says Thorgerson. "It was like something brand new on an old nag so we put a baby on an antique rocking horse, which seemed to suit Graham to a tee; it also allowed us a pun on his initials (GG)."

Among the songs on *Love and Work* was one that told the tale of how he met his future third wife, Ariella. "We were set up by a mutual friend," says Gouldman. "I didn't know it was a set-up. Ariella walked in and I thought, 'Mmm, she's nice…' and while we were having our curry, I could feel a kind of 'thing' for her. The four of us in the party agreed to go out for another meal but the other two dropped out and that's when it really all started."

The experience would be immortalised in the song Ariella, complete with a great rhyming couplet as she asks him for a recommendation in the curry house: '*I said "I'm going for the jalfrezi" / I thought she'd order korma but she went for something warmer / That ticked all the boxes for me.*' A further song, Memory Lane, followed after he'd taken Ariella around Manchester to show her where he used to live and went to school.

"When we returned to London, as we had such a lovely day, which was so uplifting, I wrote that song as an expression of the day's experience," says Gouldman. *Love and Work* was released in August 2012 to very positive reviews. *Q* magazine said the album "sees Gouldman recapturing the crafted elegance of his best work", *The Spectator* called it "a masterclass in pop songwriting", while *Uncut* claimed "*Love and Work* blends seamlessly with Gouldman's best work".

"I'm very proud of it," says Gouldman. "It was a labour of love but the reviews have been great. I knew it was never going to be a chart-topper or anything like that but I'm very proud of it. I had so much pleasure making it. The people I work with, they're all great people and I like them and there's joy in it and the sun shines in it and it makes a difference. I think if you're unhappy, for any reason, it kind of seeps into the grooves."

Meanwhile, in Ireland, Kevin Godley continued to break new ground and, ever the innovator, created an app called Youdio which gave any musician with an internet connection the opportunity to easily collaborate with others anywhere in the world and make music and videos. The idea for the app had its roots back in the *One World, One Voice* project that Godley masterminded in 1990. Back then, Godley had been frustrated with the limitations of the technology, which restricted ongoing collaboration.

"It irritated me that the music couldn't continue, that it was fixed in stone," says Godley.

Twenty years later, the technology had moved on significantly to the point where it was possible to effectively create a global recording studio in the cloud. That made it possible to create an app that gave aspiring musicians the opportunity to collaborate, be that with other up-and-coming musicians or more famous names such as Ronnie Wood, Dave Stewart, Phil Manzanera, Stewart Copeland or Taylor Hawkins of the Foo Fighters.

"Technology for me is the new Beatles," says Godley. "They were all about change, innovation and pushing things forward. Technology can do those things too."

Godley also remains a campaigner for change on a broader scale. He directed the video for the We Are Not Afraid campaign, which aimed to raise funds for the refugee crisis and victims of religious and political violence.

"Irrational hatred is a cancer of humanity's own design," says Godley. "To succumb would mean the failure of our species."

Released in November 2016, the video featured almost 200 musicians and actors – including Robert De Niro, Bruce Springsteen, Brian Wilson, Keith Richards, Robert Plant, Nile Rodgers and Elvis Costello – all holding up signs with the slogan 'We are not afraid'.

One ambition that Godley has yet to fulfil is to direct a movie, although he has come close on several occasions. First there was the aborted *Howling At The Moon* project back in 1988. Then in 1997, he wrote a screenplay with Adrian Deevoy called *Where The Treetops Glisten*. It was a one-room drama, similar to *Twelve Angry Men*, based around a television production company in America.

"It was about the future of television," says Godley. "At the time we first wrote it, it was science fiction but most of the things we wrote about have come true."

The screenplay has since gone through six drafts and remains on the shelf. Another close encounter with the big screen involved working with author Richard La Plante on a screenplay for his book *Hog Fever*. After several years of failing to get backing for the movie, La Plante resigned to record it as an audio book instead.

"I'm dribbling into a microphone in a tiny LA sound studio, trying to record an audio book of my memoir *Hog Fever* and the sound engineer looks as bored as I feel," recalls La Plante. "Then a thought hits me like the crack of thunder from a V-Twin exhaust. 'Shit, why don't I do the *Hog* screenplay, not the book, and get real actors in, sound effects, rock music, the works? I'll phone my writing buddy, Kevin Godley – the Scorsese of music video – and we'll call it an … ear movie.'"

The idea was to create "a pure audio experience with music plus all the production values of a movie but without any pictures." In a way, the idea of an "ear movie" had echoes of *Consequences* and its goal to be a "movie for the blind".

"The whole thing takes place in the consulting room of a psychiatrist, played by Terence Stamp," says Godley. "I ended up directing him live over Skype from County Wicklow while he was in Los Angeles. I have to imagine that's never been done before. To direct Terence Stamp was a hell of a thrill for me."

The project was also notable for its soundtrack, which featured the first set of songs that Godley had written entirely by himself. The Bad & The Beautiful had originally started life as a lyric for a GG/06 song but had remained unfinished until now. Other songs included Work Song, Just Write and Confession. "Everything I've done over the years has been a collaboration of one form or another, because I don't play an instrument," says Godley. "I sing and I play percussion, but I don't play guitar and I don't play keyboards. For some reason, I managed to write some songs for this project, which is essentially a play about a middle-aged biker looking for his lost youth via the Harley Davidson legend."

At the time of writing, Godley is working on a future movie

project, with the working title of *The Gate*, based on a true story in the life of Orson Welles. As Welles looks back on his life he thinks about the time he visited Ireland, aged sixteen, and bluffed his way into his first professional acting role at The Gate Theatre in Dublin. "It's the story of how a young boy found himself, as told by a man who lost himself," says Godley, who also started work on his first solo album, *Muscle Memory*. It had been inspired by two instrumental tracks he was sent, from two people he'd never met, asking if he'd be interested in writing melodies and lyrics for them and turning them into songs. "I pulled both tracks into Garageband, set up a microphone and started reacting to them," says Godley. "And they were both really exciting things to work on."

The first, from French DJ and EDM artist Luke Mornay, resulted in Expecting A Message, which Godley describes as "a gospel song about alien abduction. Obviously." The second, from John Moulder, became the Bowie-esque Periscope. The experience had reignited Godley's desire to make music again. But how to approach it from a new angle? "It wouldn't have been right to hook up with Graham again for a number of reasons – because we'd done it and I don't live in England anymore, so that makes it geographically difficult," says Godley. "I was looking for a way to stimulate, to get the juices flowing again so I could feel it as opposed to just do it. And doing those two tracks I thought maybe this idea can translate to a longer piece."

Godley launched his campaign in August 2017 seeking submissions of musical backing tracks in "any genre, any tempo, any mood, but please don't send me anything too predictable!" He was sent 285 backing tracks with a view to picking 12 to be recorded for *Muscle Memory*.

With a career that has involved art, music, inventions, video and apps it was little wonder that Godley was approached to write an 'interactive memoir' of his life. The result, the highly entertaining *Spacecake*, was published as an e-book in March 2015 to rave reviews. Crammed full of interactive content, there are links to rare recordings – including the very earliest Godley and Creme demos from the late-60s – as well as video content. Reflecting Godley's eclectic career, the front cover proclaims, 'The book of the film of the song of the app of the…'

The experience of writing his autobiography left Godley with a revelation. "Jesus … I've just realised something," he concludes. "Records? Radios? TVs? Tape recorders? Cameras? Musical instruments? Fuck me! In the end, I did go into the family business."

Eric Stewart also took the opportunity to write his autobiography and, like Kevin Godley, opted to publish it as an e-book crammed full of interactive content, including some outtakes from the *Press to Play* sessions with Paul McCartney, and footage of Stewart and Lol Creme reminiscing about the old days. Entitled *Things I Do For Love*, it was published in March 2017 with each chapter dedicated to the various loves of his life: family, music, guitars, cars, houses. Stewart doesn't pull any punches and doesn't shirk when discussing the more painful moments of his life: the split of the original 10cc; losing his left eye in his car accident; and his fracturing relationship with Graham Gouldman.

"Most of me rewriting what had happened in those particular circumstances was rather sad," says Stewart. "There was, and still is, something inside me that will rise to the challenges that those things threw at me. I found that I could work my way around problems like these, and still do. As I said in the book, 'Life is not always a bowl of cherries', and still isn't, but I can usually find a sensible way through the problems that still occur. Thinking positively!"

So, did Stewart learn anything about himself in the process of writing his autobiography? "The major thing that is obvious, I suppose, is that I have been a very, very lucky guy," he says. "Just being in the right place at the right time, especially getting the job as lead guitarist with Wayne Fontana after his own guitarist didn't show up at the audition with Philips Records. I realise now that I was always very open to all possibilities that were offered to me."

Stewart's autobiography was followed by a two-CD compilation of his solo works, with material taken from each of his four solo albums plus his, to all intents and purposes, solo contributions to 10cc's *Mirror, Mirror* album. Stewart took the opportunity to use modern technology to remix some of his old songs.

"It was quite exciting listening to all the original analogue tapes again, and thinking, 'Can I improve on these songs?'," says Stewart. "I thought I could really improve on the sounds that were there on those multitrack tapes. I used the far-superior digital 'plug-ins' to finely tune the sounds and feel of the songs and was really thrilled when I took them out of my studio and played them in my car. Sat in the car, the sounds were so superior to the original recordings in that I could hear all the instrumentation, and lyrics and backing vocals, and guitar solos so much better now."

Originally with the working title *Eric's Head Revisited*, it was eventually released as *Anthology* in July 2017. At its best, songs such as Make The Pieces Fit, Doris The Florist, A Friend In Need and We're Not Alone are among the finest recordings made by the band's four original members and provide a welcome opportunity to appreciate Stewart's solo work. *Super Deluxe Edition* would go on to rate it one of the 10 best box sets and reissues of 2017.

"It works beautifully and I played this to death in the summer months of 2017," wrote Paul Sinclair. "Stewart has everything. A brilliant musician, his songwriting chops are matched only by his production skills – everything *sounds* great and there are some wonderful arrangements, styles and rhythms on show. His lyrics are spot on too – full of wit and humanity. I would love to live in a world where sets like these make it to the higher reaches of the chart. Highly recommended."

After writing songs for nearly 50 years, Graham Gouldman was inducted into the Songwriters Hall of Fame in New York in June 2014 in recognition of his huge body of work. Asked to perform a song at the ceremony, Gouldman had the task of picking just one from his entire catalogue. The song he chose was Bus Stop.

"I'm so proud to be the recipient of such a prestigious and coveted honour," said Gouldman accepting the award. "I've also been lucky enough to work with some wonderful collaborators. And, of course, my fellow 10cc members, Kevin Godley, Lol Creme and especially Eric Stewart, with whom I wrote so many of the band's most famous songs."

Further recognition followed when the BMI presented Gouldman with their BMI Icon award in October 2015 at London's Dorchester Hotel, where he performed I'm Not In Love with Lisa Stansfield. The BMI Icon award is given to songwriters who have had "a unique and indelible influence on generations of music makers".

"Graham Gouldman is a musical force whose legendary catalogue has had a massive international impact on pop music for five decades and counting," said Brandon Bakshi, Executive Director of the BMI. "Both his remarkable creative contributions as a longtime songwriter and member of the beloved band 10cc and his success penning hits for iconic bands of the 60s, define Graham as a true BMI Icon. We're extremely proud to honour him for his artistry and undeniable influence in shaping the genre."

Gouldman received an even greater accolade when he released a new six-track EP *Play Nicely and Share* in September 2017. "I played it to my grandson, Max, and asked him what he thought," says Gouldman. "And he said, 'Grandpa, it's almost as good as The Beatles!' Now that's an accolade!"

It was also very apt, because Gouldman enlisted the talents of former Beatle Ringo Starr when recording a new song, Standing Next To Me, which told the tale of his experience on the road as part of the All Starr Band. This, and other treats such as All Around The World and the jazzy That's Love Right There, were included on a new solo album *Modesty Forbids*, which was released in March 2020. Nearly 60 years after forming their first bands, the members of 10cc were still adding new chapters to their illustrious story.

CHAPTER 30

OLD WILD MEN

WHILE 10CC MIGHT NOT HAVE EXACTLY COME BACK INTO FASHION there has certainly been a change in the way the band are perceived over the second decade of the 21st century. Perhaps the original impetus for this was the 'Guilty Pleasures' movement, which championed music that it wasn't fashionable to like. What began as a five-minute slot in DJ Sean Rowley's BBC Radio London show in 2004 evolved into what *Esquire* magazine called "a fully-fledged, all-singing, all-dancing pop music phenomenon", involving its own club nights and compilation albums. The first compilation album featured 10cc's The Things We Do For Love.

"10cc are the reason I started the whole 'Guilty Pleasures' thing in the first place," says Rowley. "When it first started people were coming up to me and going, 'What are you doing all this ironic stuff for?' and I was like, 'I'm really, really not being ironic'. And that was really important for me in the beginning when we were setting out the stall, so to speak. It was basically saying, 'We do actually really love this.' If we were being ironic I would have gone slightly insane."

Slowly, it has become acceptable to profess your love for 10cc and more and more artists have cited the band as an influence. "Right at the beginning of Kaiser Chiefs we were all listening to the best of 10cc," says the band's Simon Rix. "I really like them because they are quirky but in a very pop way. Something that we try to achieve." This can be evidenced on tracks like I Predict A Riot, a song that the band's manager describes as "10cc meets The Clash".

Another band singing 10cc's praises were The Feeling. By now there was no reason to feel guilty at all about music you loved. "There are no guilty pleasures anymore," says the band's lead singer Dan Gillespie Sells. "You're allowed to like Andrew Gold, ELO, Supertramp or 10cc. It's really liberating."

"10cc were amazing," says the band's bassist Richard Jones. "Their stuff was so varied," says drummer Paul Stewart. "Everything from reggae (Dreadlock Holiday) to soft-rock ballads (I'm Not in Love)." In a serendipitous twist of fate, Graham Gouldman's son even played a big part in The Feeling's breakthrough.

"My son Louis worked for Universal Records as an A&R man," says Gouldman. "He discovered The Feeling. It was a quite a coincidence. When he met them, they didn't know who he was but they told him that 10cc were a big influence on them."

10cc's back catalogue has continued to be repackaged and released with compilation albums charting strongly around the world. *The Ultimate Collection* in Norway and *10cc Collected*, a TV-advertised triple-CD collection, in the Netherlands both reached the Top 20. 10cc's legacy has not been so well served by their former record companies in the UK, however. Jonathan King has relentlessly regurgitated the material from 10cc's first two albums into countless compilation records. The best of these, *The Complete UK Recordings*, was awarded a five-star review from *Uncut* magazine upon release in 2004: "If you only buy one reissue this year make it this super technoid missing link between Zappa and ZTT," wrote Paul Lester.

Universal Records – who now own 10cc's Phonogram catalogue – seem content to repackage the band's material with cheap artwork, superficial sleevenotes and appalling quality control, as evidenced by *Greatest Hits … And More*, a two-CD set released in the UK in November 2006. So poor was the quality control on this compilation that Feel The Benefit actually runs a full minute longer than it should because it plays at the wrong speed! A further compilation, *The Very Best of 10cc*, was released in April 2009. Even critics who regarded the band's music highly were critical of these releases.

"The core catalogue of 1970s' hits is pretty well perfect," wrote Paul Du Noyer in *The Word*. "So, it's a shame that this CD reissue is shunted out to the market with such an utter lack of love. There have been plenty of 10cc compilations before. It would have been nice to raise the stakes a little, and perhaps rectify some of 10cc's historic anonymity. Instead the disc arrives without a sleevenote or any pictures of the band. How can record companies complain that punters are deserting the CD medium when they can't be bothered to add a modicum of value? Or even accuracy? I warmly recommend this music. But, personally, I'd head for Spotify."

With the band's 40th birthday approaching, Universal finally planned the box set that 10cc so richly deserved. Titled *Tenology*, this time Eric Stewart, Graham Gouldman, Kevin Godley and Lol Creme were all consulted on the tracklisting; longtime fan and *Guardian* journalist, Paul Lester interviewed all four of the band's original members and contributed an 8,500-word essay for the accompanying booklet; and Storm Thorgerson was commissioned to provide the artwork, some 38 years after first working with 10cc.

"I had an idea that since they were like cultured pop that we should use a phrenology head like the Victorians and inscribe the influences on the music in the compartments drawn on the porcelain bust," says Thorgerson. "The references all come from the band themselves and the head is a little bigger than a Victorian one. The head was taken to a canalside in recognition of the Manchester Ship Canal, which is where the band come from. A cricketer on the bridge reminds us of Dreadlock Holiday and the dog with a bone reminds us that there are many telephone references in 10cc's music." Among the references inscribed on the head are Radio Luxembourg, Scotty Moore, Gene Kelly, school bullies, the JLB, art college, the Oasis club, The Beatles, The Beach Boys, the USA, the 'Gizmo' and three Yids and a Yok.

This time the music itself was properly remastered and sounded more vivid and detailed than previous digital transfers. There are even a few rarities thrown in for good measure, including the original line-up's failed attempt to record People In Love shortly before the split in 1976. A few other rarities make it onto the album too, albeit unintentionally. Alternative versions, featuring early mixes of Don't Turn Me Away and Run Away, appear by mistake and while inferior to the final versions give something new to diehard fans. The fifth disc in the set was a DVD of the band's videos and rare TV appearances.

Tenology is not perfect – the tracklisting and sequencing is flawed in places and including the edited version of the band's masterpiece I'm Not in Love is utterly inexcusable – but it would be churlish to pick holes because, for once, the overall project was given the care and attention that 10cc deserve. *Tenology* was released in November 2012 and received excellent reviews.

"Now that we have finally broken the connection between guilt and pleasure when it comes to music, it's time to reappraise these stalwarts of the 1970s pop charts," wrote *The Independent*. "And though the odd irritating single makes it on to this four-CD-one-DVD celebration of their 40th birthday, there are enough album tracks and b-sides to make the case that what we actually had in 10cc was a British Steely Dan: clever, funny and funky as hell when they wanted to be."

The Daily Express said 10cc's songs "demonstrate a skill in pop songwriting that has rarely been equalled before or since" while *Metro* was equally positive: "After years of being dismissed as arch, pompous studioholics, it's gradually become acceptable, fashionable and perhaps obligatory to worship at the shrine of 10cc. These sensationally talented Jewish-Mancunians moved from daft doo-wop pastiches to sophisticated studio rock, marrying Tin Pan Alley craftsmanship with high-end studio craft."

A further box set – *Before, During and After: The Story of 10cc* – appeared in July 2017. While its purpose of exploring the music of the band's members before and after their time with 10cc gave it a point of difference, the outcome was disappointing. Despite new cover art from Kevin Godley, the compilation itself was lazily curated. Two of the four discs simply regurgitated earlier releases, even down to the sequencing: Disc 1 is literally 1979's *10cc's Greatest Hits 1972–78* while Disc 3 is 2003's *Strawberry Bubblegum*. With so many gems from the pre-10cc period widely unavailable, it marked a missed opportunity. Where is Baby Not Like You, the song Lol Creme penned for Gouldman's band The Whirlwinds? Or the singles released by Gouldman and Godley's group The Mockingbirds? Where are the early Godley and Creme songs from The Yellow Bellow Room Boom or Frabjoy and Runcible Spoon days? Or the Stewart-penned tracks for The Mindbenders? Or even Today, the Hotlegs song that featured all four of the future members of 10cc? Not to mention any of the unreleased demos in the Strawberry vaults.

Despite their critical revival, 10cc have not seen their back catalogue treated with the same respect as other artists. While other bands have seen the anniversaries of their landmark releases celebrated with new 5.1 surround mixes and the inclusion of previously unreleased live material, rare tracks and outtakes, none of 10cc's albums have received this treatment. Where was the 40th anniversary edition of *The Original Soundtrack*? Tracks such as One Night In Paris and I'm Not In Love cried out for a 5.1 mix; add in live versions of The Second Sitting For The Last Supper, Flying Junk, The Film of My Love, One Night In Paris and I'm Not In Love as recorded in Santa Monica in November 1975 but never officially released until now; and throw in some rarities such as a version of I'm Not In Love featuring the original discarded middle section. Clearly Universal feel there is not a big enough market for it. Yet *The Original Soundtrack* continues to be cited by bands such as Everything Everything as a major influence.

"This album is deceptively complex and proggy," says the band's Alex Robertshaw. "They are masters of caricature and very accomplished songwriters in loads of different-sounding genres. Perhaps they don't know what genre they are, and they don't fit in anywhere, and they have a humorous side, and they are really really good, but that sounds a bit too like us! I'm Not In Love I'll readily admit to being probably my favourite song."

Over 40 years on from its original release, I'm Not In Love remains 10cc's most enduring legacy, as acknowledged by *Q* magazine who included the song in their February 2019 round up of the most influential records of all time. British radio DJ Mark Radcliffe devoted a chapter to the song in his 2019 book *Crossroads* in which he seeks out the moments that changed music forever. He describes I'm Not In Love as a 'masterpiece' and marvels at its 'sonic sumptuousness'. The song has been played well over 5 million times on American radio alone, and continues to inspire new generations of musicians. UNKLE tried to recreate the song's vocal effect on In A State, even inviting Graham Gouldman to guest on the track, as a nod to the debt they owed 10cc for borrowing the vocal-layering technique they had pioneered.

"After the big string crescendo, there are six different singers, including Graham," says UNKLE singer Richard File. "We got them to sing each note of the chord; then, we layered them and bounced them all to solid tracks in Pro Tools. Imagine if you are playing a mixing desk as you would a piano, but each note comes up on a fader, and as you bring them up, they create a chord. It is a warm, beautiful sound. In the end, there are 128 voices."

In 2010, indie band Gayngs even released a whole album, *Relayted*, that was inspired by the song. "I'd been listening to a shit-load of 10cc and I was just like, yeah, I want to do something like this," says the band's Ryan Olson.

The album gained a five-star review in *The Guardian*, prompting the paper to call I'm Not In Love "the most influential song of 2010". Two years later, Ben Folds Five would also pay tribute to 10cc's most famous record on the track Sky High from their Top 10 US album *The Sound of the Life of the Mind*. "That's exactly what it was, a nod to that," says Folds. "10cc essentially invented an instrument on I'm Not In Love and we used that instrument, which is singing aahs in the key of the song, looping them and sending them all through the board. It's like having a Mellotron of your own band ... a 10cc-atron! It's the most intense, amazing sound."

In 2014, The Ting Tings also tried their hand at recreating the song's vocal backing on Communication from their album *Super Critical*. "We were watching this documentary on 10cc," says the band's Katie White, "and how they recorded I'm Not In Love and how they recorded their vocal and every note and the whole spectrum of chords, and then they played the huge old mixing desk like a keyboard, and we were like, we've got three weeks, when in our lives are we ever going to be in this kind of studio where we can experiment and have a bit of fun rather than rush. So, we did that. We have a song called Communication where we did the whole 10cc approach to it and played the whole mixing desk like a keyboard."

The influence of I'm Not In Love can be heard on records by the likes of Daft Punk (Nightvision) and every year brings new cover versions in a bewildering range of styles. Reinterpreted as a jazzy torch song by Julia Fordham or performed in a trip-hop style by Olive; expressed from a female point of view by Tori Amos (from her US Top 5 album *Strange Little Girls*) or given an indie make-over by Camera Obscura; there's even a punk version by The Father Figures, a ukulele version by Joe Brown and a piano version by Rick Wakeman. Among the more conventional interpretations, by artists such as Queen Latifah and Rick Springfield, is arguably the finest cover of the song: Diana Krall's reading, for her 2015 album *Wallflower*, benefits from a gorgeous string arrangement courtesy of producer David Foster, while Krall's distinctive voice carries the song's emotional pull perfectly. In 2017, former Primal Scream backing singer Denise Johnson released an acoustic version of the song that worked much more effectively than 10cc's own 1995 acoustic re-tread while Kelsey Lu recorded a haunting version for her 2019 album *Blood*.

The song has been a staple of artists' *Late Night Tales* albums, with groups like The Flaming Lips and Groove Armada including it in their sets, and DJ David Arnold recording a new version of the song in 2016 with female Irish duo Song Sung. "*Late Night Tales* each need a cover version," says Arnold. "I'd been playing I'm Not In Love in my sets so I thought I'd do it with the girls. It turned out it's one of their favourite tracks of all time, so they knew it inside out, knew all the harmonies. Keefus and I worked on the music in my studio, then sent them the track. Because it was a last-minute thing, it was the only track where I wasn't there to record the vocals, but they knew the track so well they were able to hire a room and go in and do a really good recording of the song."

Bands like The Thrills and LCD Soundsystem have used the song as walk-on music at their gigs. "Of course, I'm Not In Love, which has very little to do with the rest of their catalogue, is amazing," says LCD Soundsystem's James Murphy. "But I also love Good Morning Judge, which is pretty funky, so is The Dean and I and Art For Art's Sake. The Things We Do For Love was totally a radio classic when I was a kid. The Worst Band In The World is sampled by Dilla on *Donuts*. I love 10cc." Their influence can also be heard in the music of bands as diverse as Hot Chip and Field Music. "I quite like the proggy end of 10cc like Don't Hang Up from *How Dare You* – it's a masterpiece," says Field Music's Peter Brewis. "That's definitely something we aspire to." When, in 2019, Tim Burgess's producer mentioned that one of his new tracks reminded him of *Sheet Music*-era 10cc, Burgess excitedly tweeted that he could think of no higher compliment.

10cc's music has been used as part of the soundtrack to countless TV shows such as *Luther*, *The X Files*, *My Name is Earl* and *The*

Office. Even lesser-known album tracks have been featured, such as Marriage Bureau Rendezvous from *Deceptive Bends*, which can be heard in the finale of Stephen Merchant's HBO series *Hello Ladies*, and One Night In Paris in the Season 2 opener of *The Marvelous Mrs. Maisel*.

Unsurprisingly, Hollywood has featured 10cc's music in movies such as *The Virgin Suicides*, *The Social Network*, *Running with Scissors*, *Halloween 2*, *Snatch*, *Bridget Jones: The Edge of Reason*, not to mention the memorable opening scene from *Guardians of the Galaxy* featuring I'm Not In Love. The song finally reached No.1 in the US during the summer of 2014 as part of that film's highly successful soundtrack album, which has sold over 2.5 million copies around the world. The Things We Do For Love has now been played over 4 million times on American radio and been covered by the likes of Gregson and Collister, Amy Grant and Tina Arena, who recorded the song for the 2014 Christmas campaign of Australian retailer David Jones, with proceeds donated to the National Breast Cancer Foundation.

The abundance of hooks in 10cc's songs mean they are a gift for being sampled. Lloyd Banks, part-time member of G-Unit, sampled The Dean and I on the track When The Paint Is Peeling from his platinum-selling, US No.1 album *The Hunger for More*. Influential hip-hop producer J Dilla sampled The Worst Band In The World prominently on the track Workinonit and Johnny Don't Do It on Waves, on his acclaimed album *Donuts*, recorded shortly before his untimely death. Elsewhere, their songs have been widely sampled such as: Rubber Bullets (Thee Tom Hardy's Always In Command), Brand New Day (Kankick's To The Ghetto), I'm Mandy Fly Me (D-Sissive's All My Friends Are Dead), I'm Not In Love (Roc Marciano's 76), Baron Samedi (Nottz featuring The Alchemist's The 1ne) and Tokyo (SebastiAn's Arrival). 10cc's songs have featured in some memorable 'mash-ups'. Go Home Productions paired I'm Not In Love with Marvin Gaye's Let's Get It On to stunning effect on Marvin's Not In Love, while Mighty Mike mixed the song with Gotye's Somebody That I Used To Know to create Not Somebody That I Used To Love; Good Morning Judge was wickedly mashed up with Michael Jackson's Smooth Criminal on the witty Good Morning Judge Melville around the time of Jackson's court case; while Dreadlock Holiday was paired with Destiny's Child's Independent Woman. I'm Not In Love was also mashed up with Michael Bublé's Home and Daniel Bedingfield's If You're Not The One in London radio station Magic FM's successful TV advertising campaign.

Unsurprisingly, 10cc have spawned several tribute bands around the world. In New Zealand, a 12-piece, all-female group called 10dd were formed in 2010 and perform a cappella versions of not only 10cc's biggest hits but also more obscure album tracks such as Head Room, Iceberg and Rock 'n' Roll Lullaby.

The band's contribution as producers and musicians on other people's records remains highly regarded. When Justin Hayward was compiling his 'best of' album, *All the Way*, in 2016 he went to great lengths to track down the original Eric Stewart mix of Blue Guitar, as recorded with 10cc in 1974.

"I was overjoyed to find that," says Hayward. "I knew it was good, in the original form and mix. So, Graham Gouldman and I went to try and find that original Eric Stewart mix. It was unadulterated, clear and brilliant."

Godley and Creme's video work remains groundbreaking and is still inspiring bands today. When Elbow wanted a video for their single Gentle Storm in 2017, lead singer and chief songwriter Guy Garvey wanted to emulate Godley and Creme's video for Cry. "Gentle Storm reminded me of something, but I couldn't work it out for a bit, the yearning and the sparsity of the sound," says Garvey. "When I worked out it was Cry, I asked the rest of the band if they remembered the video, 'cause it was such a seismic event as a kid. I realised that a lot of people wouldn't know the track or the video, even though they were both so important to me." Garvey, who cites *How Dare You* as one of the first records he ever bought, called Kevin Godley about recreating the Cry video for Gentle Storm. At first Godley baulked at the idea.

"Why would he want something that was already out there?" says Godley. "Then I realised 'out there' really meant out there since 1985, and a whole generation or three wouldn't have seen the original, or have a clue who Godley and Creme were, so to a world of millennials it would probably be, 'Who the fuck?'" Among the changing faces featured in the video for Gentle Storm are the band, actor Benedict Cumberbatch and Godley himself.

Even the 'Gizmo' has been enjoying something of a renaissance. Intrigued to know what the sound was at the beginning of Led Zeppelin's In The Evening, Aaron Kipness started to collect old Gizmotrons once he'd discovered the source of the sound. Eventually he hit upon the idea of reverse engineering the device in order to create a new version of the 'Gizmo'. In 2013, a small team of engineers, armed with the original patent drawings and these original Gizmotron samples, started work on creating a next-generation model using modern materials and manufacturing methods. The end result was the Gizmotron 2.0, which was launched in February 2016, once again offering guitarists the promise of infinite sustain and the ability to create orchestral sounds. The initiative was supported Kevin Godley, who gave his blessing for the 'Gizmo' to be brought back to life. Now anyone wanting to create their own Consequences can purchase their own 'Gizmo' from gizmotron.com, while listening to a new podcast on Godley and Creme's triple album that was launched in April 2019 by musicians Sean Macreavy and Paul McNulty. That same month an image created by Godley and Creme for their ill-fated project appeared as the front cover of the Chemical Brothers album No Geography and a CD reissue of Consequences followed in August. And, if that wasn't enough, even the band's football records for Manchester City remain in high regard by Noel Gallagher. "Every time I see him he praises our brief 'football' period to the high heavens," says Godley.

Since the millennium then, 10cc have finally begun to receive some of the credit that they so richly deserve. Uncut magazine described them as "the greatest British pop group of the post-Beatles era". Even more significantly, their extraordinary body of work was acknowledged with a special Ivor Novello Award in recognition of their 'Outstanding Song Collection'. Eric Stewart, Graham Gouldman and Lol Creme proudly accepted the award from Sir George Martin at the Grosvenor House hotel in London, with only Kevin Godley absent from the proceedings.

The band's production expertise was recognised in 2009 when they featured in BBC Radio Two's The Record Producers, a series of special programmes exploring the work of legendary record producers. All four of the band's members contributed to the programme and Eric Stewart provided original multitrack recordings of Donna,

Rubber Bullets, The Wall Street Shuffle, Life Is A Minestrone and I'm Not In Love that were dissected and analysed by record producer Steve Levine. Aside from giving a fascinating insight into the band's recording process, it also highlighted that there were still a few surprises in the archives, such as the original middle eight of I'm Not In Love with the lyrics that were scrapped in favour of the '*big boys don't cry*' refrain.

Broadcaster Stuart Maconie acknowledged the band's quirkier side on his BBC Radio 6 show, *The Freak Zone*. Subtitled 'Oddly and Creme' the programme revisited some of 10cc's, and their band members', more obscure and avant-garde moments.

Then, in December 2015, BBC Four screened an hour-long TV documentary on the band, *I'm Not in Love: The Story of 10cc*. It again featured contributions from all four of the band's original members alongside the likes of Trevor Horn, Graham Nash, Stewart Copeland, Dan Gillespie Sells, Paul Gambaccini and Tim Rice, and was well-received. "The film isn't just about one song, of course, but it just so happens that that one song does kind of encapsulate the 10cc story," wrote *The Guardian*. "That they were essentially two bands in one (and would go on to split into two); that they were pioneers, innovative and inventive, pushers of limits; that they made some of the best, cleverest, craftiest songs; and that their impact and influence would last long and strong. I used to be ever so slightly embarrassed about loving 10cc; I now realise, after seeing this excellent documentary, that I was silly to feel embarrassed."

The legacy of Strawberry Studios was celebrated with an exhibition called *Strawberry Studios: I Am In Love*, which opened at the Stockport Museum in January 2017. The exhibition, the brainchild of Strawberry authority Peter Wadsworth, celebrated the 50th anniversary of the opening of the studio, and not only highlighted the work of 10cc – including various items loaned by the band – but also acknowledged the debt that the next generation of Manchester bands, such as Joy Division, New Order and The Smiths owe to Strawberry. Originally intended to run for a year, *Strawberry Studios: I Am In Love* attracted over 20,000 visitors over the first 12 months, leading to an extension until the end of September 2018.

Former drummer of The Fall, Paul Hanley, wrote an excellent book – called *Leave The Capital* – that waxes lyrical about the contribution of the members of 10cc and Strawberry Studios to the Manchester music scene: "If the achievements of the four members of 10cc are bracketed together, they are truly staggering," writes Hanley. "Between them they wrote and performed several of the most important songs of the 60s, enjoyed massive success in the 70s as both a singles and albums band, created one of the decade's most innovative and best loved records, and kick started the video revolution in the 80s. On top of that, and arguably even more importantly, they bequeathed Manchester a proper world class recording facility that was affordable even to impoverished independent labels." Stockport band Blossoms, also fans of 10cc, have even vowed to reopen Strawberry Studios if they make it as big as they hope.

While the reevaluation of the original 10cc line-up gathered pace, though, it appears that the band's post-split output remains sadly unloved, despite highlights such as *Deceptive Bends* and their reputation for being a better live band. It's almost like it never happened. "This period has been literally written out of the band's history," says Rick Fenn. "If I was in any doubt about that, seeing the recent BBC documentary – brilliant in so many ways – finally confirmed that, in the eyes of Graham, Eric, and Kev and Lol (rather more reasonably) and the length and breadth of the world media, I have never been a member of 10cc. The three albums that said otherwise must have been wrong. But I get it, and I will always be deeply grateful to Graham and Eric for bringing me in and for being able to play my small part in the extended history of 10cc."

Across the pages of this book, musicians as diverse as Paul McCartney, Abba, Tears For Fears, LCD Soundsystem, Kaiser Chiefs, Elton John, R.E.M., Trevor Horn, Terry Hall, John Lydon, Everything Everything, Axl Rose, The Feeling, Genesis, A-ha, Phil Spector and Field Music have all paid tribute to the music of 10cc. Yet, despite the improvement in the band's reputation, it still remains some way off what it should have been. Of course, Jonathan King has his own theory as to why 10cc don't get the credit they deserve. "To this day, I think they are one of the most underrated and underestimated bands and the worst thing of all is that they could have been ten times bigger," says King. "If I'd kept them and they'd stayed with me it would have taken me a bit more time but I would have broken them. I would have continued to develop them in the right way and stopped them being obsessed with how much more money they could make and the other things. We would have gone on having fun and it would have gone on getting better and better. And they had the talent and the ability and the musical skills because the four of them all had different areas that were strong, that they should have been one of the ten biggest bands of all time and, unfortunately, they're not. In history now, they're one of the 50 biggest bands of all time I think you could say."

The band's manager, Harvey Lisberg, expressed his own theory on 10cc's standing when interviewed by Johnny Rogan for his book *Starmakers and Svengalis*. "I think they should have been bigger," said Lisberg at the time. "The only reason why they weren't, aren't or ever will be is because of their snobbery. It was absolutely impossible to convey one ounce of creative feedback to 10cc. All you could say was that you didn't like something. They believed they knew it all. And they had a lot of success. You don't argue with people who are turning out No.1's. But, in my heart, I felt that if only they had put on sequinned jackets or got something additional that the kids could have got off on – then they could have been as big as Pink Floyd."

Kevin Godley, in his Foreword to this book, explained why the band could never have taken the approach of donning sequinned jackets. He has his own more plausible theory as to why 10cc don't get the credit they deserve.

"It used to piss me off but I understand it now," says Godley. "I think it's less to do with music and more to do with personality and style, or lack of it in our case. People, on the whole, like their rock stars to live like rock stars. If we'd looked or acted like Pete Doherty, we'd have been deemed cool. But we didn't. 10cc didn't OD, wear make-up, kill anyone, do smack, change sex, drink their own piss or commit suicide. No dysfunctional mythology = unmemorable. That's how it is."

While many 10cc fans have dreamed of Eric Stewart, Graham Gouldman, Lol Creme and Kevin Godley getting back together to work on a brand-new project, the moment now seems to have passed, although it is rumoured that the four original members of the band were made a very generous offer to reform to play 11 arena gigs in the UK in 2013 in venues such as London's O2. Sadly, the likelihood of the original line-up ever working together again is extremely remote. Even getting Stewart and Gouldman to collaborate again seems highly unlikely given the nature of their relationship.

"Eric and Graham are good people – it's a shame they can't see that in each other," says Rick Fenn.

Looking back on the special four-part chemistry that made the original line-up so exciting it is clear that each member of the band brought something unique to 10cc beyond their accomplished songwriting, production and playing skills. Godley drove their inventiveness, constantly pushing the envelope, asking 'What would it be like if … ?' and steering them away from anything that sounded too predictable; Creme brought a playfulness to the band, bringing a sense of humour and fun to the fore, that ensured they never took themselves too seriously or veered towards pretentiousness; Stewart, as the resident engineer and studio whizz in the band, was able to push the studio to its limits, conjuring beautiful soundscapes from the creative ideas that were flying round in the studio, helping to define their cinematic sound; and Gouldman, with his ear for melody and a great hook – "Just use the best bits" as he would joke – ensured that there was always a healthy balance between art and commerce in 10cc's music. Together they created a style of music that was utterly unique. And, of course, in Strawberry Studios they had their own sandpit to play in, their own laboratory to experiment in.

As Rob Steen, who writes for *The Sunday Times*, said about 10cc: "Snappy of melody, sneering of tone, they were England's answer to Steely Dan, only wittier. Plundering, parodying and pastiching every known nook and cranny of popular music, they unearthed something entirely, irresistibly and gobsmackingly unique. A re-evaluation is well overdue."

One of the original intentions of this book was to stimulate a reappraisal of the band; to prove beyond reasonable doubt that 10cc's contribution to British pop music has been significant and that it deserves to be acknowledged and not overlooked as is still so often the case at present. 10cc may not be the world's bestselling band or the most influential; they were never the voice of a generation and there are many artists who've had a far greater cultural impact. But, over time, it does at least seem as if a growing number of people finally appreciate the uniquely original, inventive, witty, intelligent and melodic music of the worst band in the world.

And, as for everyone else, well ... *we're working on it*.

AFTERWORD BY ERIC STEWART

WE WERE CHILDREN IN OUR OWN TOY SHOP. I HAD MY VERY OWN studio and my mates joined me to have a ball, making strange sounds that people thought were quite good. In fact, they even went out and bought them in great numbers, enabling me to make my studio bigger and better, and the people bought even more of our silly sounds and life was wonderful.

But then two of my friends wanted to go and play on their own and I was very sad, and told them so, but they still went and we carried on, and we sold some more records, but it wasn't the same anymore. I missed the wacky brains of my two friends and I think they missed me too.

Still, life goes on. Ob-la-di, ob-la-da as the dark man said to Paul.

AFTERWORD BY GRAHAM GOULDMAN

WHEN I WAS ELEVEN YEARS OLD I WAS GIVEN MY FIRST GUITAR AND from that moment on I dreamed of being in a world-famous band.

Although I had written hit songs for other artists in the 60s, it looked like I would never make it onto *Top of the Pops* myself. Then in 1968 I met Eric Stewart, who asked me to become a partner with him in Strawberry Studios in Stockport. Two old chums of mine, Kevin Godley and Lol Creme, joined the party and soon the four of us became the 'Jack of all trades' at the studio.

After a good Chinese meal, and spending too much time on other people's records, we decided to become a band ourselves. 10cc were born. There we were: four accomplished songwriters, musicians and singers, plus Eric's engineering skills. We soon became a powerful self-contained unit. We had four incredibly exciting and creative years together and, even when Kev and Lol left the band in 1976, Eric and I continued to have success all over the world.

The preceding pages reflect that whole period. We have all given as accurate a description as possible of what those days were like, although some of our memories may be a little unclear. It is only after reading this book myself that I realise how important and influential 10cc were. I hope you enjoyed reading it as much as we enjoyed making it happen.

10CC

GROUP LIFE

1OCC CHRONOLOGY

1972

May Eric Stewart, Graham Gouldman, Lol Creme and Kevin Godley record Donna as a b-side for a potential single Waterfall. Jonathan King offers to release it on his UK Records label and christens the group 10cc

June Neil Sedaka records his album *Solitaire* with Stewart, Gouldman, Godley and Creme at Strawberry

Aug [4] Donna released b/w Hot Sun Rock

Aug [11] John Peel plays Donna for the first time on his radio show [*Friday Night is Boogie Night*, BBC Radio 1]

Sep [23] Donna enters the UK Top 50 giving 10cc their chart debut

Sep [27] 10cc film an appearance on *Top of the Pops* performing Donna [broadcast BBC1 Sep 28]

Oct [11] 10cc film an appearance on *Top of the Pops* performing Donna [broadcast BBC1 Oct 12]

Oct [18] 10cc appear on *Lift Off with Ayshea* performing Donna [ITV]

Oct [21] Donna peaks at No.2 in the UK and stays for two weeks

Oct [25] 10cc film an appearance on *Top of the Pops* performing Donna [broadcast BBC1 Oct 26]

Nov [18] Neil Sedaka's Beautiful You, recorded at Strawberry with 10cc, peaks at No.43 in the UK

Nov [24] Johnny Don't Do It released b/w 4% of Something

Dec [4] 10cc appear on *TopPop* in the Netherlands performing Donna [AVRO]

Dec [27] 10cc appear on *Lift Off with Ayshea* performing Johnny Don't Do It [ITV]

1973

Feb/Mar Neil Sedaka records *The Tra-La Days Are Over* with 10cc at Strawberry Studios

Mar [24] Neil Sedaka's That's When the Music Takes Me, recorded at Strawberry with 10cc, peaks at No.18 in the UK

Mar [30] Rubber Bullets released b/w Waterfall

May [3] 10cc film an appearance on *Top of the Pops* performing Rubber Bullets [broadcast BBC1 May 4]

May [4] 10cc appear on *Lift Off with Ayshea* performing Rubber Bullets [ITV]

May [24] 10cc film an appearance on *Top of the Pops* performing Rubber Bullets [broadcast BBC1 May 25]

Jun [1] Rubber Bullets is played during the end credits of *Top of the Pops* [BBC1]

Jun [7] 10cc film an appearance on *Top of the Pops* performing Rubber Bullets [broadcast BBC1 Jun 8]

Jun [16] Neil Sedaka's Standing on the Inside, recorded at Strawberry with 10cc, reaches No.26 in the UK

Jun [22] 10cc appear on *Top of the Pops* performing Rubber Bullets [repeat of earlier recording, BBC1]

Jun [23] Rubber Bullets reaches No.1 in the UK

Jul [27] 10cc's debut album *10cc* released

Aug [9] 10cc film an appearance on *Top of the Pops* performing The Dean and I [broadcast BBC1 Aug 10]

Aug [10] The Dean and I released b/w Bee in My Bonnet

Aug [25] 10cc appear on *Disco* in Germany performing Rubber Bullets [ZDF]

Aug [26] 10cc begin first ever UK tour at DOUGLAS Palace Lido, with Paul Burgess augmenting their line-up on drums

Aug [28] STOKE Heavy Steam Machine

Aug [30] 10cc film an appearance on *Top of the Pops* performing The Dean and I [broadcast BBC1 Aug 31]

Aug [31] SWINDON Brunel Rooms

Sep [1] *10cc* enters the UK album charts

Sep [7] BIRMINGHAM Barbarella's

Sep [8] Neil Sedaka's Our Last Song Together, recorded at Strawberry with 10cc, peaks at No.31 in the UK

Sep [12] 10cc film an appearance on *Top of the Pops* performing The Dean and I [broadcast BBC1 *Sep* 13]

Sep [15] The Dean and I peaks at No.10 in the UK

Sep [15] FOLKESTONE Lea Cliffs Hall

Sep [16] COLCHESTER Woods Leisure Centre

Sep [20] TAUNTON County Ballroom

Sep [20] The Dean and I reaches No.1 in Ireland

Sep [22] *10cc* peaks at No.36 on the UK album chart

Oct [6] Neil Sedaka's *The Tra-La La Days Are Over*, featuring 10cc as
   musicians and co-producers, peaks at No.13 in the UK

Oct [6] LONDON Queen Mary's College

Oct [11] LONDON Greenwich Borough Hall

Oct [12] MARGATE Dreamland

Oct [13] PLYMOUTH Guildhall

Oct [20] BRISTOL Yates Entertainment Centre

Oct [23] HOVE Town Hall

Oct [26] HEREFORD Flamingo Ballroom

Oct [27] LONDON London School of Economics

Oct [28] MANCHESTER Hardrock

Oct [29] STAFFORD Top of the World

Nov [3] SCUNTHORPE Baths Hall

Nov/Dec 10cc start to record their second album at Strawberry

Dec [8] CANTERBURY Kent University

Dec [14] GLASGOW University

Dec [16] GRAVESEND Lions Club

Dec [20] 10cc film an appearance on *Top of the Pops* performing Rubber
   Bullets [broadcast BBC1 Dec 25]

Dec [22] HASTINGS Pier Pavilion

Dec [28] LIVERPOOL Top Rank Suite [supported by Queen]

Dec [29] LOWESTOFT Pier

1974

Jan [4] Paul McCartney starts producing his brother's album *McGear* at
   Strawberry Studios and shares studio time with 10cc as they continue
   to record their second album

Jan [9] 10cc appear on *Lift Off with Ayshea* performing The Worst Band in
   the World [ITV]

Jan [19] The Worst Band in the World released b/w 18 Carat Man of
   Means

Jan [20] 10cc appear on *Sounds on Sunday* [BBC Radio 1] performing Oh
   Effendi, Sand In My Face, Somewhere In Hollywood, Rubber Bullets,
   Headline Hustler and The Worst Band In The World

Jan [26] LONDON Regent Street Polytechnic

Feb [6] 10cc film an appearance on *Top of the Pops* performing The Worst Band in the World [never broadcast]

Feb [8] 10cc film an appearance on *Top Pop* performing The Worst Band in the World [broadcast AVRO Feb 25]

Feb [18–23] 10cc begin their first US tour at ATLANTA Richard's

Feb [25–Mar 2] BOSTON Performance Center

Feb [26] Footage of 10cc performing Old Wild Men is shown on *The Old Grey Whistle Test* [BBC2]

Mar [3] Radio and press interviews in New York

Mar [5–7] ROSLYN, My Father's Place

Mar [8] Tour party for press at The Colony, 61st Street and Madison Avenue, New York

Mar [9] NEW YORK Academy of Music*

Mar [11] CLEVELAND Agora Ballroom*

Mar [13] PARSIPPANY Joint In The Woods

Mar [14] GREENVILLE Thiel College Passavant Center [with Badfinger]

Mar [15] Kevin Godley is taken ill with tracheitis and the rest of the tour is cancelled. While Godley recuperates, Stewart and Creme holiday in St Lucia, Gouldman in Los Angeles

Mar [25] *Don Kirshner's Rock Concert* is broadcast featuring 10cc performing Sand In My Face, The Dean and I, Fresh Air For My Mama, Headline Hustler and Rubber Bullets [syndicated]

Apr [1] Neil Sedaka's *The Tra-La Days Are Over* album certified silver in the UK

Apr [13] Justin Hayward records Blue Guitar with 10cc at Strawberry

Apr [20] 10cc film an appearance on *See You Sunday* performing The Wall Street Shuffle and Fresh Air for My Mama [broadcast BBC1 Apr 21]

Apr [27] YORK University

May [15] 10cc appear on *The Bob Harris Show* performing Old Wild Men, Clockwork Creep, Silly Love and Oh Effendi [BBC Radio 1]

May [16] Rubber Bullets wins 'Best Beat Song' at the Ivor Novello Awards at the Grosvenor House Hotel, London

May [17] LONDON Central London Polytechnic

May [18] BIRMINGHAM Locarno

May [22] 10cc film an appearance on *Top of the Pops* performing The Wall Street Shuffle [broadcast BBC1 May 30]

May [24] The Wall Street Shuffle released b/w Gismo My Way

May [24] 10cc's second album *Sheet Music* released

May [25] HARLOW Central Park

May [28] 10cc begin their second US tour at DETROIT Cobo Hall [supporting Ten Years After]

May [30] CAPE COD Coliseum* [supporting Johnny Winter]

May [31] NEW HAVEN Veterans Memorial Coliseum

Jun [1] NEW YORK Madison Square Garden [supporting Johnny Winter]

Jun [2] PROVIDENCE Palace Concert Theater [supporting Slade]

Jun [5] ATLANTA Municipal Auditorium [supporting Slade]

Jun [7] MIAMI Gusman Philharmonic Hall [supporting Slade]

Jun [8] ST PETERSBURG Bayfront Center [supporting Slade]

Jun [11] KANSAS CITY Memorial Hall [supporting Robin Trower]

Jun [12] ST LOUIS Kiel Auditorium [supporting Slade]

Jun [13] LOUISVILLE Convention Center [supporting Slade]

Jun [14 & 15] LOS ANGELES Shrine Auditorium [supporting Ten Years After]

Jun [15] *Sheet Music* enters the UK album chart at No.21

Jun [16] ORLANDO Jai Alai Fronton Hall [supporting Slade]

Jun [18] CHARLESTON Municipal Auditorium

Jun [19] KNOXVILLE Civic Coliseum

Jun [20] DETROIT Masonic Temple [supporting Slade]

Jun [21] CHICAGO Auditorium Theater [supporting Slade]

Jun [23] TORONTO University [supporting Steeleye Span]

Jul [6] DUNSTABLE California Ballroom

Jul [7] LONDON Rock Proms at Olympia National Hall [supported by The New York Dolls]

Jul [7] 10cc appear on *Sounds Interesting* [BBC Radio 3]

Jul [13] The Wall Street Shuffle reaches No.10 in the UK

Jul [26] SUNDERLAND Locarno

Jul [31] TORQUAY Town Hall

Aug [1] BARNSTABLE Queens

Aug [2] PLYMOUTH Guildhall

Aug [14] 10cc appear on *Slaom-Show* in the Netherlands performing The Wall Street Shuffle [BRT TV]

Aug [17] EASTBOURNE Winter Gardens

Aug [21] 10cc appear on *In Concert* performing Silly Love, The Wall Street Shuffle, Baron Samedi, Old Wild Men, Oh Effendi, Fresh Air for My Mama and Rubber Bullets [BBC2]

Aug [23] Silly Love released b/w The Sacro Illiac

Aug [23] READING Festival

Aug [29] 10cc appear on the BBC's *Radio 1 Club Special*

Sep [1] DOUGLAS Palace Lido

Sep [4] 10cc film an appearance on *Top of the Pops* performing Silly Love
   [broadcast BBC1 Sep 5]

Sep [12] GUILDFORD Civic Hall

Sep [13] LONDON Rainbow Theatre

Sep [14] MANCHESTER Free Trade Hall

Sep [15] COVENTRY Theatre

Sep [17] NEWCASTLE City Hall

Sep [18] PRESTON Guildhall

Sep [19] 10cc appear on *45* performing Silly Love and The Sacro Illiac
   [ITV]

Sep [21] HULL City Hall

Sep [26] 10cc film an appearance on *Top of the Pops* performing Silly Love
   [broadcast BBC1 Sep 27]

Oct [1] *Sheet Music* is certified silver in the UK

Oct [3] LEICESTER De Montfort Hall

Oct [4] BATH University

Oct [5] *Sheet Music* peaks at No.9 in the UK

Oct [8] PORTSMOUTH Polytechnic

Oct [9] SOUTHAMPTON University

Oct [10] WARWICK University

Oct [11] SALFORD University

Oct [12] LEEDS University

Oct [12] The Wall Street Shuffle reaches No.1 in the Netherlands

Oct [15] HUDDERSFIELD Town Hall

Oct [17] EXETER University

Oct [18] BRADFORD University

Oct [19] HULL University

Oct [20] BRISTOL Colston Hall

Oct [21] SHEFFIELD University

Oct [22] OXFORD Polytechnic

Oct [25] LUTON College of Technology

Oct [26] NORWICH University of East Anglia

Oct [30] CARDIFF University

Nov [1] SWANSEA University

Nov [2] MANCHESTER University

Nov [7] CHELMSFORD Chancellor Hall

Nov [8] NOTTINGHAM Trent Polytechnic

Nov [9] ISLEWORTH Borough Road College

Nov [23] Silly Love reaches No.7 in the Netherlands

Nov–Jan 10cc record their third album at Strawberry Studios

1975

Jan [18] Richard Branson offers 10cc £100,000 to sign to his Virgin record label

Jan [31] Branson offers £200,000 to sign to Virgin as bidding war with Phonogram ensues

Feb [10] 10cc sign a five-album deal with Phonogram worth $1m [announced Feb 13]

Mar [1] *Sheet Music* is certified gold in the UK

Mar [5] 10cc's third album *The Original Soundtrack* released

Mar [5] 10cc begin UK tour at LEEDS University

Mar [6] SHEFFIELD City Hall

Mar [7] SOUTHPORT New Theatre

Mar [8] MANCHESTER Free Trade Hall

Mar [9] HANLEY Victoria Hall

Mar [10] PORTSMOUTH Guildhall

Mar [11] PAIGNTON Festival Hall

Mar [12] EASTBOURNE Congress Centre

Mar [14] NEWCASTLE City Hall

Mar [15] DUNDEE Caird Hall

Mar [16] GLASGOW Apollo

Mar [17] EDINBURGH Usher Hall

Mar [19 & 20] LONDON Hammersmith Odeon

Mar [21] 10cc appear on *The Old Grey Whistle Test* performing The Second Sitting for the Last Supper [BBC2]

Mar [21] Life is a Minestrone released b/w Channel Swimmer

Mar [21] BIRMINGHAM Odeon

Mar [22] BOURNEMOUTH Winter Gardens

Mar [22] *The Original Soundtrack* enters UK album chart at No.6

Mar [23] LEICESTER De Montfort Hall

Mar [24] CARDIFF Capitol

Mar [25] SWANSEA Brangwyn Hall

Mar [26] 10cc film an appearance on *Top of the Pops* performing Life is a Minestrone [broadcast BBC1 Mar 27]

Mar [29] SOUTHEND Kursaal

Apr [1] *The Original Soundtrack* is certified silver and gold in the UK

Apr [1] MANCHESTER Free Trade Hall

Apr [4] 10cc begin first European tour at BRUSSELS University

Apr [5] GOTHENBURG Concert Hall

Apr [6] STOCKHOLM Concert Hall

Apr [8] LUND Olympen

Apr [9] COPENHAGEN Tivoli Concert Hall

Apr [10] 10cc appear on *TopPop* in the Netherlands performing Life is a Minestrone [AVRO]

Apr [10] 10cc appear on *Top of the Pops* performing Life is a Minestrone [repeat of earlier performance]

Apr [11] NIJMEGEN De Vereenigen

Apr [13] GRONINGEN De Oosterport

Apr [14] AMSTERDAM Carré Theatre

Apr [23] 10cc film an appearance on *Top of the Pops* performing Life is a Minestrone [broadcast BBC1 Apr 24]

Apr [27] OXFORD New Theatre

Apr [27] 10cc appear on *Sounds On Sunday* [BBC Radio 1]

Apr [28] BRISTOL Colston Hall

Apr [29] BIRMINGHAM Odeon

Apr [30] GUILDFORD Civic Hall

May [1] LIVERPOOL Empire

May [2] LANCASTER University

May [3] Life Is A Minestrone reaches No.7 in the UK

May [4] CROYDON Fairfield Hall

May [17] *The Original Soundtrack* peaks at No.3 in the UK

May [23] I'm Not in Love released b/w Good News

May [28] 10cc film an appearance on *Top of the Pops* performing I'm Not in Love [broadcast BBC1 May 29]

Jun [12] 10cc appear on *Top of the Pops* performing I'm Not in Love [repeat of May 29 performance]

Jun [25] 10cc film an appearance on *Top of the Pops* performing I'm Not in Love [broadcast BBC1 Jun 26]

Jun [28] I'm Not in Love reaches No.1 in the UK while 10cc have two albums in the UK Top 10 for three weeks: *The Original Soundtrack* and *10cc*

Jul [1] I'm Not in Love is certified silver in the UK

Jul [2] 10cc film an appearance on *Top of the Pops* performing I'm Not in Love [broadcast BBC1 Jul 3]

Jul [12] 10cc headline at CARDIFF Castle [supported by Thin Lizzy and Steeleye Span]

Jul [26] I'm Not in Love reaches US No.2 and stays there for three weeks

Jul [28] 10cc begin recording their fourth album at Strawberry Studios [through to Oct 3]

Aug [20] 10cc appear on *Musikladen* in Germany performing I'm Not in Love [ARD]

Oct [16] Cover shoot for fourth album *How Dare You!*

Oct [25] 10cc begin North American tour at NEW YORK Beacon Theater followed by launch party at Le Jardin, 110 West 43rd Street, New York

Oct [26] MONTREAL University Sports Center

Oct [27] QUEBEC Palais De Congress

Oct [28] OTTAWA National Arts Center

Oct [29] PROVIDENCE Rhode Island College

Oct [30] NEW BRUNSWICK Cooke College

Nov [1] DETROIT Michigan Palace

Nov [2] YOUNGSTOWN Tomorrow Theatre

Nov [3] INDIANAPOLIS Rivoli Theater

Nov [4] ST LOUIS Ambassador Theater

Nov [5] CINCINNATI Emery Auditorium

Nov [6] CLEVELAND Allen Theater

Nov [7] CHICAGO Riviera Theater

Nov [8] ST PAUL Civic Center

Nov [9] MILWAUKEE Uptown Theater

Nov [13] VANCOUVER Queen Elizabeth Theater

Nov [14] PORTLAND Paramount Theater

Nov [15] SEATTLE Paramount Theater

Nov [15] Justin Hayward's Blue Guitar, recorded at Strawberry Studios with 10cc in April 1974, peaks at No.8 in the UK

Nov [16] SPOKANE Coliseum

Nov [17] YAKIMA Capitol Theater

Nov [18] MEDFORD Armory

Nov [19] REDDING Civic Auditorium

Nov [21] Art For Art's Sake released b/w Get It While You Can

Nov [21] SAN FRANCISCO Winterland

Nov [22] FRESNO Warnors Theater

Nov [26] SANTA MONICA Civic Center [recorded for *The King Biscuit Flower Hour*]*

Nov [27] PHOENIX Celebrity Theater

Nov [29] DALLAS Convention Center Theater

Nov [30] NEW ORLEANS The Warehouse

Dec [2] 10cc film an appearance on *Top of the Pops* performing Art for Art's Sake [broadcast BBC1 Dec 4]

Dec [3] ATLANTA Civic Center

Dec [4] BALTIMORE Orpheum Theater

Dec [5] PHILADELPHIA Tower Theater* [2 shows]

Dec [6] BOSTON Orpheum Theater

Dec [17] 10cc film an appearance on *Top of the Pops* performing I'm Not in Love [broadcast BBC1 Dec 25]

Dec [18] 10cc appear on *Top of the Pops* performing Art for Art's Sake [repeat from Dec 4]

Dec [19] John Peel plays I'm Not in Love as one of his 15 favourite singles of the year [BBC Radio 1]

1976

Jan [1] Listeners of London's Capital Radio vote I'm Not in Love their favourite song of all time

Jan [5] Photo shoot with Lord Lichfield

Jan [9] 10cc's fourth album *How Dare You!* released

Jan [14] 10cc film an appearance on *Top of the Pops* performing Art for Art's Sake [broadcast BBC1 Jan 15]

Jan [17] Art for Art's Sake peaks at No.5 in the UK

Jan [31] *How Dare You!* enters the UK album chart at No.5, where it peaks

Feb [1] *How Dare You!* certified gold in the UK

Feb [2] 10cc begin UK tour at SHEFFIELD City Hall*

Feb [3 & 4] MANCHESTER Free Trade Hall

Feb [5] Eric Stewart and Lol Creme taken ill with flu during a gig at the Glasgow Apollo leading to postponement of 8 dates

Feb [14 & 15] CARDIFF Capitol

Feb [16] BRIGHTON Dome

Feb [17–19] LONDON Hammersmith Odeon

Feb [20] PORTSMOUTH Guildhall

Feb [20] 10cc appear on *Don Kirshner's Rock Concert* in the US with pre-recorded performances of I'm Not in Love, Art for Art's Sake, Head Room and Don't Hang Up [syndicated]

Feb [21 & 22] BIRMINGHAM Odeon

Feb [24 & 25] BRISTOL Colston Hall

Feb [26 & 27] LIVERPOOL Empire*

Feb [28] CROYDON Fairfield Hall

Feb [28] 1976 Grammy Awards in Los Angeles with Eric Stewart nominated for 'Best Engineered Recording' for *The Original Soundtrack*

Mar [1 & 2] OXFORD New Theatre

Mar [3 & 4] IPSWICH Gaumont

Mar [6 & 7] LEICESTER De Montfort Hall

Mar [8 & 9] EDINBURGH Usher Hall

Mar [12] I'm Mandy Fly Me released b/w How Dare You

Mar [25] Video for I'm Mandy Fly Me premieres on *Top of the Pops* [BBC1]

Mar [28] 10cc begin European tour at OSLO Njårdhallen

Apr [1] GOTHENBURG Concert Hall*

Apr [2] *How Dare You!* peaks at No.1 in New Zealand

Apr [2] STOCKHOLM Concert Hall

Apr [3] COPENHAGEN Tivoli Concert Hall

Apr [5] AMSTERDAM Carré Theatre

Apr [6] ROTTERDAM De Doelen

Apr [7] HAMBURG Musikhalle

Apr [8] OFFENBACH Stadthalle

Apr [8] Video for I'm Mandy Fly Me is shown again on *Top of the Pops* [BBC1]

Apr [9] ERLANGEN Stadthalle

Apr [10] MUNICH Theater An Der Brienner Strasse

Apr [10] I'm Mandy Fly Me peaks at No.6 in the UK and stays three weeks

Apr [12] MANNHEIM Rosengarten Musensaal

Apr [13] WINTERTHUR Eulachhalle

Apr [19 & 20] NEWCASTLE City Hall

Apr [21 & 22] ABERDEEN Capitol Theatre

Apr [24–26] GLASGOW Apollo

May [22] 10cc headline OOR POPFESTIVAL in Delft, the Netherlands [supported by Nils Lofgren, Eric Burdon and Gentle Giant]

May [26] I'm Not in Love wins three awards at the Ivor Novello Awards at the Dorchester Hotel, London

Jun [13] While on holiday in South of France 10cc meet up with Bill Wyman of The Rolling Stones and then see the band play at Parc des Sports de l'Ouest in Nice. They are asked to support The Rolling Stones at Knebworth

Jun Kevin Godley and Lol Creme start recording a demonstration record for the 'Gizmo'

Jul [3] 10cc record music for a Revlon advertising campaign at Strawberry

Aug [21] 10cc support The Rolling Stones at KNEBWORTH Festival*

Aug [23] 10cc start recording a new single People in Love at Strawberry Studios

Sep [7] 10cc attend Paul McCartney's Buddy Holly celebration lunch at the Orangery, Holland Park, London

Sep Kevin Godley and Lol Creme leave 10cc

Oct Eric Stewart and Graham Gouldman, along with Paul Burgess, start recording at Strawberry South. After recording Good Morning Judge and then The Things We Do for Love they decide to continue as 10cc

Nov [27] Announced in the music press that Godley and Creme have left 10cc

Dec [3] The Things We Do for Love released b/w Hot to Trot

Dec [16] Video for The Things We Do for Love premieres on *Top of the Pops* [BBC1]

1977

Jan 10cc continue to record their fifth album at Strawberry South

Jan [6] Video for The Things We Do for Love shown again on *Top of the Pops* [BBC1]

Jan [15] The Things We Do for Love peaks at No.6 in the UK

Jan [20] Video for The Things We Do for Love shown again on *Top of the Pops* [BBC1]

Feb [1] The Things We Do for Love certified gold in the UK

Feb [2] *10cc* certified silver in the UK

Feb [2] *100cc – The Greatest Hits of 10cc* is certified silver and gold in the UK

Feb Peter Cook starts work on Godley and Creme's solo album at The Manor Studio, Oxfordshire, UK

Mar [31] Video shoot for Good Morning Judge directed by Bruce Gowers

Apr [1] Paul Burgess, Rick Fenn, Stuart Tosh and Tony O'Malley join
Stewart and Gouldman at Strawberry South to audition for 10cc

Apr [8] Good Morning Judge released b/w Don't Squeeze Me Like
Toothpaste

Apr [26] The Things We Do for Love reaches No.5 in the US

Apr [28] The Things We Do for Love is certified gold in the US

Apr [28] Press launch confirming Burgess, Fenn, Tosh and O'Malley as
new members of 10cc at the Montcalm Hotel, London

Apr [28] Video for Good Morning Judge premieres on *Top of the Pops*
[BBC1]

Apr [29] 10cc's fifth album *Deceptive Bends* released

May [9] Rehearsals for upcoming tour begin at Shepperton Studios

May [12] Video for Good Morning Judge shown again on *Top of the Pops*
[BBC1]

May [21] *Deceptive Bends* peaks at No.3 in the UK

May [27 & 28] 10cc begin UK tour at GLASGOW Apollo

May [28] Good Morning Judge peaks at No.5 in the UK

May [30 & 31] ABERDEEN Capitol Theatre

Jun [1 & 2] NEWCASTLE City Hall

Jun [3] SHEFFIELD City Hall

Jun [8] LIVERPOOL Empire

Jun [10] STAFFORD Bingley Hall

Jun [12 & 13] MANCHESTER Belle Vue

Jun [14] CARDIFF Sophia Gardens

Jun [15 & 16] SOUTHAMPTON Gaumont

Jun [18–20] LONDON Hammersmith Odeon [recorded for live album
Live and Let Live, last night filmed by Bruce Gowers]*†

Jun [23] AMSTERDAM Jaap Edenhal

Jun Deceptive Bends certified gold in the Netherlands

Jul [1] Good Morning Judge certified silver in the UK

Jul [5] People in Love released b/w I'm So Laid Back, I'm Laid Out

Jul [7] Announced that 10cc will record a live album in Manchester

Jul [16 & 17] MANCHESTER Apollo [recorded for live album *Live and Let
Live*]

Jul [21] *Deceptive Bends* certified silver in the UK

Aug [10] *Deceptive Bends* certified gold in the UK

Aug [30] 10cc fly to Sydney ahead of their first Australian tour. *The
Original Soundtrack, How Dare You!* and *Deceptive Bends* all certified

gold in Australia

Aug [31] Video for People in Love shown on Marc Bolan's series *Marc* [ITV]

Sep [3-4] Rehearsals at BRISBANE Festival Hall

Sep [5] 10cc begin Australian tour at BRISBANE Festival Hall

Sep [7] Eric Stewart and Graham Gouldman are interviewed on *Flashez* [ABC TV]

Sep [8–10] SYDNEY Hordern Pavilion

Sep [15, 16 & 18] MELBOURNE Festival Hall

Sep [17] Godley & Creme's first solo album *Con sequences* press launch at Ronde Lutherse Kerk in Amsterdam

Sep [20 & 21] ADELAIDE Apollo Stadium

Sep [20] Tony O'Malley arrested in Adelaide for drug possession

Sep [24] PERTH Entertainment Centre

Oct [1–3] 10cc begin Japanese tour at TOKYO Sun Plaza Hall

Oct [4] TOKYO Kōsei Nenkin Kaikan*

Oct [7] OSAKA Festival Hall

Oct [17] Godley and Creme's *Consequences* released

Oct [18] I'm Not in Love is one of four nominees for 'Best British Single of the last 25 years' at the first BRIT Awards ceremony

Nov [2] Godley and Creme guest with Phil Manzanera's 801 at Manchester University

Nov [18] 10cc's first live album *Live and Let Live* released

Nov [24] *Deceptive Bends* certified gold in Sweden

Nov [25] 10cc begin European tour at STOCKHOLM Concert Hall

Nov [26] GOTHENBURG Scandinavium

Nov [27] LUND Olympen

Nov [28 & 29] COPENHAGEN Tivoli Concert Hall

Nov [30] HAMBURG Congress Centre

Dec [1] DÜSSELDORF Philipshalle

Dec [2] FRANKFURT-OFFENBACH Stadthalle

Dec [3] HEIDELBERG Stadhalle

Dec [4] MUNICH Schwabingerbraeu

Dec [5] ERLANGEN Stadhalle

Dec [6 & 7] ROTTERDAM De Doelen

Dec [12] PARIS Pavillon de Paris

Dec Tony O'Malley leaves 10cc and the band search for a new keyboard player

1978

Jan [7] *Live and Let Live* peaks at No.14 in the UK

Jan [10] *Live and Let Live* is certified silver and gold in the UK

Feb–Jun 10cc record their sixth album at Strawberry South

Mar Duncan Mackay joins 10cc replacing Tony O'Malley

Apr Strawberry Mastering opens in London

May [12] Mandalaband release *The Eye of Wendor* featuring guest
appearances from all four original members of 10cc

Jul [1] *Deceptive Bends* certified gold in Canada

Jul [3] Eric Stewart begins producing Sad Café's album *Facades* at
Strawberry South

Jul [21] Dreadlock Holiday released b/w Nothing Can Move Me

Aug [7] Video for Dreadlock Holiday premieres on *Kenny Everett Video
Show* [ITV]

Aug [7] Rehearsals for upcoming tour begin at Shepperton Studios

Aug [16] 10cc film an appearnce on *Top of the Pops* performing Dreadlock
Holiday [broadcast BBC1 Aug 17]

Aug [18] Godley and Creme's second solo album *L* released

Aug [26] 10cc begin European tour at STOCKHOLM Isstadion

Aug [27] GOTHENBURG Scandinavium

Aug [28] COPENHAGEN Idrætsparken

Aug [29] MALMO Folk Park Festival

Aug [31] 10cc appear on *Top of the Pops* performing Dreadlock Holiday
[repeat of Aug 16 performance, BBC1]

Sep [1] Dreadlock Holiday certified gold in the UK

Sep [3] 10cc begin UK tour at LIVERPOOL Empire

Sep [4–6] BIRMINGHAM Odeon

Sep [8] 10cc's sixth album *Bloody Tourists* released

Sep [8 & 9] ABERDEEN Capitol Theatre

Sep [10 & 11] EDINBURGH Usher Hall

Sep [13 & 14] NEWCASTLE City Hall

Sep [14] *Bloody Tourists* is certified silver in the UK

Sep [14] 10cc appear on *Top of the Pops* performing Dreadlock Holiday
[repeat of Aug 16 performance]

Sep [15] BRIDLINGTON Spa Pavilion

Sep [16–18] MANCHESTER Apollo

Sep [16] Godley and Creme appear on *Sounds Interesting* [BBC Radio 3]

Sep [19 & 20] BRISTOL Colston Hall

Sep [21] 10cc appear on *Top of the Pops* performing Dreadlock Holiday [repeat of Aug 16 performance, BBC1]

Sep [21] SOUTHAMPTON Gaumont

Sep [23] Dreadlock Holiday reaches No.1 in the UK

Sep [23 & 24] LONDON Wembley Arena

Sep [25] BRIGHTON Centre

Sep [26] *Bloody Tourists* is certified gold in the UK

Sep [30] *Bloody Tourists* enters the UK chart at No.8

Oct [1] *Bloody Tourists* is certified gold in Canada

Oct [7] *Bloody Tourists* peaks at No.3 in the UK

Oct [7] Graham Gouldman and Duncan Mackay appear on *Swap Shop* [BBC1]

Oct [16] 10cc begin North American tour at WINNIPEG Arena

Oct [18] EDMONTON Concert Bowl at the Coliseum

Oct [19] CALGARY The Corral

Oct [21] PORTLAND Paramount Theater

Oct [22] SEATTLE Paramount Theater

Oct [23 & 24] VANCOUVER Queen Elizabeth Theater

Oct [27] SANTA ROSA Veterans' Memorial Auditorium

Oct [28] BERKELEY Community Theater

Oct [29] STOCKTON Civic Auditorium

Oct [30] Film video for Reds In My Bed at Burbank Studios

Oct [31] LOS ANGELES

Nov [1] SANTA MONICA Civic Center

Nov [3] SAN DIEGO Fox Theater

Nov [4] PHOENIX Symphony Hall

Nov [4] *Bloody Tourists* peaks at No.2 in the Netherlands and stays there for four weeks

Nov [5] ALBUQUERQUE New Mexico University

Nov [8] DALLAS Convention Center Theater

Nov [9] KANSAS Uptown Theater

Nov [10] MINNEAPOLIS Orpheum Theater

Nov [11] Dreadlock Holiday reaches No.1 in the Netherlands and stays there for four weeks

Nov [12] WHITEWATER MILWAUKEE University of Wisconsin

Nov [13] DETROIT Ford Auditorium

Nov [15] DAYTON Memorial Hall

Nov [16] CLEVELAND Music Hall

Nov [17] BUFFALO Kleinhans Music Hall

Nov [18] READING Astor Theater

Nov [19] STONY BROOK State University of New York

Nov [20] POUGHKEEPSIE Mid-Hudson Civic Center

Nov [22] PITTSBURGH Stanley Theater

Nov [23] PHILADELPHIA Tower Theater

Nov [24] NEW YORK Palladium

Nov [24] Reds in My Bed released b/w Take These Chains

Nov [25] Dreadlock Holiday reaches No.1 in Belgium and stays three weeks

Nov [25] Video for Reds in My Bed premieres on *Tiswas* [ITV]

Nov [25] PASSAIC Capitol Theater

Nov [27] TORONTO Maple Leaf Gardens Concert Bowl

Nov [29] OTTAWA Civic Center

Nov [30] MONTREAL Concert Bowl at The Forum*

Dec [3] Dreadlock Holiday reaches No.1 in New Zealand and stays three weeks

Dec [13 & 14] 10cc film TV special in Warsaw

Dec [22] LONDON Wembley Conference Centre [due to be filmed by the BBC but prevented by a technicians strike]

1979

Jan In the Netherlands, *Bloody Tourists* is certified platinum and Dreadlock Holiday certified gold

Jan Eric Stewart mixes Sad Café's album *Facades* at Strawberry South

Jan [25] Eric Stewart is seriously injured in a car accident

Feb [1] *Bloody Tourists* certified platinum in Canada

Apr [4–6] Graham Gouldman records solo single Sunburn at Strawberry South

May [3] Video for Sunburn filmed at at Strawberry South

Jun [1] Gouldman's Sunburn released b/w Think About It

Jun [5] Photo session for *10cc's Greatest Hits 1972-78*

Jun [6] Gouldman films an appearance for Sunburn on *Top of the Pops* [BBC1, never broadcast]

Jul [10] Gouldman begins recording of the soundtrack to the film *Animalympics*

Aug [7] 10cc start recording their seventh album at Strawberry South [through to Dec 13]

Aug [19] Graham Gouldman appears on *Star Special* [BBC Radio 1]

Sep [8] Gouldman appears on *Rockpop* in Germany, performing Sunburn [ZDF]

Sep [21] *10cc's Greatest Hits 1972–1978* is released

Oct [12] 10cc film an appearance on *TopPop*, the Netherlands, performing I'm Not in Love [AVRO]

Oct/Nov Eric Stewart records the soundtrack to the film *Girls*

Oct [26] Neil Sedaka's *Laughter and Tears* certified platinum in the UK

Nov [1] Every Day Hurts certified silver in the UK

Nov [3] Sad Café's Every Day Hurts peaks at No.3 in the UK

Nov [10] *10cc's Greatest Hits 1972–1978* peaks at No.5 in the UK

Nov [15] *10cc's Greatest Hits 1972–1978* is certified silver and gold in the UK

Nov [30] Godley and Creme's third album *Freeze Frame* released

1980

Jan [1] *10cc's Greatest Hits 1972–1978* certified platinum in the UK

Jan/Feb Eric Stewart produces Sad Café's next album at Strawberry South

Jan [31] Photo shoot for next 10cc album

Feb [2] Sad Cafe's Strange Little Girl, produced by Eric Stewart, peaks at No.32 in the UK

Feb [26] Willy Russell's *The Boy with the Transistor Radio* premieres, featuring Feel the Benefit prominently in the storyline [ITV, repeated Sep 11]

Feb [27] One Two Five video shoot with Russell Mulcahy directing

Mar [7] One Two Five released b/w Only Child

Mar [8] Graham Gouldman appears on *Tiswas* [ITV]

Mar [8] Godley and Creme's An Englishman In New York reaches No.4 in Belgium and stays five weeks

Mar [12] Sad Café's *Facades* is certified silver in the UK

Mar [17] 10cc start rehearsing for their upcoming world tour

Mar [27] Premiere of the movie *Animalympics*

Mar [28] 10cc's seventh album *Look Hear?* released

Mar [31] Video for One Two Five premieres on *Kenny Everett Video Show* [ITV]

Apr [10] 10cc begin European tour at HAMBURG Congress Centre

Apr [12] BERLIN Hochschule Der Künste

Apr [12] *Look Hear?* peaks at No.35 in the UK

Apr [13 & 14] COPENHAGEN Falkoner Theatre

Apr [15] GOTHENBURG Scandinavium

Apr [17] STOCKHOLM Isstadion

Apr [18] DRAMMEN Drammenshallen

Apr [19] Sad Café's *Facades*, produced by Eric Stewart, peaks at No.8 in the UK

Apr [20] AARHUS Veijlby-Risskow Hall

Apr [21] VEJLE I Drottens Hus

Apr [22] FRANKFURT Jahrhunderthalle

Apr [23] MUNICH Circus Krone

Apr [24] DÜSSELDORF Philipshalle

Apr [25] 10cc film an appearance on *RockPop*, Germany, performing One Two Five and It Doesn't Matter at All [broadcast ZDF May 10]

Apr [26] Sad Café's My Oh My, produced by Eric Stewart, peaks at No.14 in the UK

Apr [27] ZURICH Congress Centre

Apr [28] STUTTGART Liederhalle

Apr [28] One Two Five peaks at No.9 in Norway

Apr [30] MAINZ Rheingoldhalle*

May [1 & 2] THE HAGUE Congress Centre

May [3] AMSTERDAM Jaap Eden Hall

May [4] BRUSSELS Forest National

May [5] The BBC announce that they'll film behind-the-scenes footage on 10cc's upcoming UK tour

May [7] Premiere of film *Girls* in Paris

May [12 & 13] 10cc begin UK tour at GLASGOW Apollo

May [14 & 15] NEWCASTLE City Hall

May [17–19] MANCHESTER Apollo

May [19] *Look Hear?* peaks at No.3 in Norway and spends 11 weeks in the Top 10

May [20 & 21] BIRMINGHAM Odeon

May [22 & 23] BRIGHTON Centre†

May [23] It Doesn't Matter at All released b/w From Rochdale to Ocho Rios

May [24] IPSWICH Gaumont

May [26 & 27] LONDON Wembley Arena

May [29 & 30] DUBLIN RDS Simmons Court Centre

Jun [25] Sad Café's *Facades* certified gold in the UK

Aug [7] Rick Fenn, Paul Burgess, Stuart Tosh and Duncan Mackay advised 10cc are splitting up

Oct [20] Sad Café's Eric Stewart-produced eponymous album released

Nov [1] Sad Café's *Sad Café*, produced by Eric Stewart, peaks at No.46 in the UK as their single La Di Da peaks at No.41

Nov [3–21] Graham Gouldman begins recording at Strawberry North with Paul Burgess, Rick Fenn and Marc Jordan

Dec [22–31] Gouldman continues recording at Strawberry North with Simon Phillips and Vic Emerson

1981

Jan Eric Stewart starts recording tracks for a solo album at Strawberry South

Feb [9] *Sad Café* certified silver in the UK

Mar [7] Eric Stewart appears on *Swap Shop* after premiere of *On the Road with 10cc* film [BBC1, repeated Aug 1982]

Mar [22] 10cc perform I'm Not in Love with the Hallé Orchestra at the Palace Theatre in Manchester, as part of a Royal Gala celebrating the theatre's reopening

Mar [31] Graham Gouldman starts producing The Ramones at Media Sound in New York, while Eric Stewart works with Paul McCartney on his next album

May [5–8] Joey Ramone records vocal tracks for *Pleasant Dreams* at Strawberry North

May [22] Les Nouveaux Riches released b/w I Hate to Eat Alone

Jun/Jul 10cc complete recording of their eighth album at Strawberry North and South

Jul [18] Graham Gouldman appears on *Pop Quiz* [BBC 1]

Jul [20] The Ramones release *Pleasant Dreams*, produced by Graham Gouldman

Sep [17] Godley and Creme appear on *Top of the Pops* performing Under Your Thumb [BBC1]

Sep [29] Godley and Creme appear on *TopPop,* the Netherlands, performing Under Your Thumb [AVRO]

Oct [1] Godley and Creme's Under Your Thumb certified silver in the UK

Oct [12] Godley and Creme's fourth solo album *Ismism* released

Oct [17] Godley and Creme's Under Your Thumb reaches No.3 in the UK

Oct [24] *Ismism* peaks at No.29 in the UK

Nov [6] Eric Stewart and Graham Gouldman appear on *Round Table* [BBC Radio 1]

Nov [10] *Swap Shop* performing Don't Ask and Don't Turn Me Away [broadcast BBC1 Nov 14]

Nov [13] Don't Turn Me Away released b/w Tomorrow's World Today

Nov [14] Eric Stewart and Graham Gouldman appear on *Swap Shop* [BBC1]

Nov [21] Photo shoot with Lord Lichfield

Nov [23] 10cc appear on *TopPop,* the Netherlands, performing Don't Turn Me Away [AVRO]

Nov [27] 10cc's eighth album *Ten Out of 10* is released

Dec [1] Godley and Creme's Wedding Bells certified silver in the UK

Dec [26] Wedding Bells reaches No.7 in the UK

1982

Feb [3–16] 10cc rehearse for their upcoming 10th anniversary tour, with Vic Emerson of Sad Café replacing Duncan Mackay

Feb [19] The Power of Love released b/w You're Coming Home Again

Feb [19] 10cc begin UK tour at BIRMINGHAM Odeon

Feb [20] SHEFFIELD City Hall

Feb [21] LIVERPOOL Empire

Feb [22] BRISTOL Colston Hall

Feb [24] PRESTON Guildhall

Feb [25] GLASGOW Apollo

Feb [26] ABERDEEN Capitol Theatre

Feb [28] EDINBURGH Playhouse

Mar [1] NEWCASTLE City Hall

Mar [2 & 3] MANCHESTER Apollo

Mar [5] ST AUSTELL Cornwall Coliseum

Mar [6] SOUTHAMPTON Gaumont

Mar [7] CROYDON Fairfield Hall

Mar [8] BRIGHTON Centre

Mar [10 & 11] LONDON Hammersmith Odeon*

Mar [12] POOLE Arts Centre

Mar [13] OXFORD Apollo

Mar [14] LEICESTER De Montfort Hall

Mar [15] IPSWICH Gaumont

Mar [16] LONDON Wembley Conference Centre†

Mar [17] BIRMINGHAM Odeon

Apr Graham Gouldman produces Gilbert O'Sullivan's *Life & Rhymes* at Windmill Lane Studios, Dublin

May [24] Ringo Starr's *The Cooler*, directed by Godley and Creme, screened as the official British entry for the Short Film Palme d'Or at the Cannes Film Festival

Jun [23] Eric Stewart films the video for Paul McCartney's Take it Away single at Elstree Studios

Jul [16] Run Away released b/w Action Man in Motown Suit

Jul [27] 10cc film an appearance for *6:55 Special* performing Run Away and Dreadlock Holiday [BBC2]

Aug [13] Eric Stewart's solo album *Frooty Rooties* released

Aug [14] Run Away peaks at No.50 in the UK

Sep Eric Stewart works with Paul McCartney on his next album

Oct [1] We've Heard It All Before released b/w Overdraft in Overdrive

Oct [18] Gilbert O'Sullivan releases *Life and Rhymes*, produced by Graham Gouldman

Oct [23] Graham Gouldman appears on *Saturday Superstore* [BBC1]

Oct [25] 10cc begin recording their ninth album at Strawberry North

1983

Jan [27] *10cc Live at the International Music Show* premieres [Channel 4]

Feb [14] 10cc start rehearsing for their upcoming tour

Mar [1] 10cc begin UK tour at ABERDEEN Capitol

Mar [2] EDINBURGH Playhouse

Mar [3] NEWCASTLE City Hall

Mar [4] SHEFFIELD City Hall

Mar [5] NOTTINGHAM Royal Centre

Mar [6] LIVERPOOL Empire

Mar [8] LEICESTER De Montfort Hall

Mar [9] IPSWICH Gaumont

Mar [10] BRIGHTON Centre

Mar [12] SOUTHAMPTON Gaumont

Mar [13] CROYDON Fairfield Hall

Mar [14] PORTSMOUTH Guildhall

Mar [15] CARDIFF St David's Hall

Mar [16 & 17] LONDON Hammersmith Odeon

Mar [18 & 19] BRISTOL Hippodrome

Mar [20] POOLE Arts Centre

Mar [21] ST AUSTELL Cornwall Coliseum

Mar [22] NOTTINGHAM Royal Centre

Mar [23] OXFORD Apollo

Mar [24] PRESTON Guildhall

Mar [25] HARROGATE Centre

Mar [26] SCARBOROUGH Futurist Theatre

Mar [27 & 28] MANCHESTER Apollo

Mar [29 & 30] BIRMINGHAM Odeon

Apr [1] 24 Hours released b/w Dreadlock Holiday [Live] and I'm Not in Love [Live]

Apr [28] Godley and Creme's fifth album *Birds of Prey* released

Jun [11] 10cc film an appearance for *Freddie Starr's Showcase* performing Feel the Love and I'm Not in Love [broadcast BBC1 Jul 12]

Jun [16] 10cc film an appearance for Granada TV performing Feel the Love

Jun [27] Eric Stewart, Graham Gouldman, Lol Creme and Kevin Godley are reunited for the first time since the split to film the video for Feel the Love

Jun [27 & 28] Rehearsals for Roskilde appearance with Duncan Mackay on keyboards

Jul [2] 10cc perform at ROSKILDE Festival in Denmark†

Jul [8] Feel the Love released b/w She Gives Me Pain

Jul [19] 10cc appear on *6:55 Special* performing Feel the Love and I'm Not in Love [BBC2]

Aug [18] 10cc film an appearance in the Netherlands performing Feel the Love

Aug [26] Soundcheck for BBC2's *Rock Around the Clock* with new drummer Jamie Lane replacing Paul Burgess, and Vic Emerson back on keyboards

Aug [27] HITCHIN Regal Theatre†

Aug [30] 10cc perform at PENWITH Festival [supporting Meatloaf]

Sep [3] 10cc begin Australian tour at COOMERA Rock for Rock's Sake Festival

Sep [5 & 6] NEWCASTLE Workers Club

Sep [9 & 10] SYDNEY Selina's

Sep [17] Feel the Love reaches No.7 in the Netherlands, and spends 6 weeks in the Top 10

Sep [19–22] Rehearsals for upcoming tour with Jamie Lane

Sep [29] 10cc film an appearance on *TopPop,* the Netherlands, performing Food for Thought [AVRO broadcast Oct 8]

Sep [30] 10cc's ninth album *Windows in the Jungle* released

Sep [30] ROTTERDAM Ahoy Arena†

Oct [1] *Windows in the Jungle* reaches No.7 in the Netherlands

Oct [3] 10cc begin UK tour at NORTHAMPTON Derngate

Oct [4] READING Hexagon Theatre

Oct [5] NORWICH Theatre Royal

Oct [6] HALIFAX Civic Theatre

Oct [7] WARRINGTON Spectrum

Oct [8] BOSTON Haven Theatre

Oct [9] LLANDUDNO Astra Theatre

Oct [10] MIDDLESBOROUGH Town Hall

Oct [11] SOUTHPORT Theatre

Oct [12] YORK University

Oct [13] DERBY Assembly Rooms

Oct [14] CRAWLEY Leisure Centre

Oct [15] BOURNEMOUTH Winter Gardens

Oct [16] CHIPPENHAM Goldiggers

Oct [17] LONDON Hammersmith Odeon

Oct [18] EASTBOURNE Congress Theatre

Oct [19] WORTHING Assembly Hall

Oct [20] MARGATE Winter Gardens

Oct [22] Food For Thought reaches No.18 in the Netherlands

1984

May Graham Gouldman and Andrew Gold release the single Don't Break My Heart under the band name World In Action. They re-release it in July and change their name to Common Knowledge

May [18] Godley and Creme direct the video for Two Tribes by Frankie Goes To Hollywood

Sep [3] Eric Stewart starts producing a solo album for Agnetha Fältskog of Abba at Polar Studios in Stockholm

Sep [18] Godley and Creme win five awards for their Rockit video for Herbie Hancock and one award for their Every Breath You Take video for The Police, at the first MTV Music Video Awards at Radio City Music Hall, New York

1985

Jan Gouldman and Gold release second single Victoria as Common Knowledge, but the album they have been working on is shelved

Feb Eric Stewart and Paul McCartney record demos of the songs they have written together

Apr Eric Stewart starts recording with Paul McCartney for his next album

Apr [22] Agnetha Fältskog releases her Eric Stewart-produced album *Eyes of a Woman*

May [11] Godley and Creme's Cry reaches No.19 in the UK

Jun [9] Graham Gouldman-produced You'll Never Walk Alone by The Crowd, recorded to raise funds for the Bradford City Disaster Fund, reaches No.1 and stays there for two weeks

Jun [14] Godley and Creme's sixth solo album *History Mix Vol. 1* released

Sep [1] You'll Never Walk Alone certified silver and gold in the UK

Sep [13] Godley and Creme win the 'Video Vanguard' award at the MTV Awards at Radio City Music Hall, New York

Oct [14] Gouldman and Gold, now trading as Wax, film the video for their debut single Ball and Chain

Nov [5] Kevin Godley films Fashion Aid event at the Royal Albert Hall, London

1986

Mar [5] Strawberry North is sold to Nick Turnbull

Mar [31] Wax release Right Between The Eyes

Apr [21] Wax's debut album *Magnetic Heaven* released

Aug [22] Paul McCartney's album *Press to Play* released featuring six co-writes with Eric Stewart

Sep [8] Wax's Right Between The Eyes reaches No.1 in Spain

Sep [18] *Press to Play* certified gold in the UK

Oct [10] Graham Gouldman appears on *Singled Out* [BBC Radio 1]

Oct [25] Graham Gouldman appears on the Manchester edition of *City to City* [BBC Radio 1]

Nov [24] Eric Stewart performs Only Love Remains with Paul McCartney at the Royal Command Performance at Theatre Royal in London

1987

Mar [2] Wax start recording their second album [through to May 20]

Jul [6] Wax release Bridge To Your Heart

Aug [17] Wax appear on *Top of the Pops* performing Bridge to Your Heart
[BBC1]

Aug [23] *Changing Faces* released

Aug [29] *Changing Faces* enters the UK album chart at No.11

Aug [29] Wax's Bridge To Your Heart reaches No.12 in the UK

Aug [31] Wax's second album *American English* released

Sep [2] *Changing Faces* certified silver in the UK

Sep [7] Wax's second album *American English* released

Sep [10] Wax appear on *Top of the Pops* performing Bridge to Your Heart
[BBC1]

Sep [11] *Changing Faces* certified gold in the UK

Sep [19] *Changing Faces* peaks at No.4 in the UK

Nov [11] Wax begin 19-date UK tour at NORTHAMPTON Derngate
Centre

Nov [27] Wax gig at HARROGATE Conference Centre[†] is recorded and
filmed by Storm Thorgerson of Hipgnosis

1988

Mar [7] Godley and Creme's seventh album *Goodbye Blue Sky* released

Mar [12] Godley and Creme's A Little Piece of Heaven reaches No.12 in
Belgium

1989

Jun [14 & 15] Wax begin a UK arena tour supporting The Bee Gees at
London Wembley Arena

Aug [31] *Changing Faces* certified platinum in the UK

Sep [22] Wax's third album *One Hundred Thousand in Used Notes* released

Oct Polydor present 10cc with platinum discs for *Changing Faces* and try
to get the four original members of the band to record a new album

1990

May [26] *One World, One Voice* – brainchild of Kevin Godley – broadcast
in 26 countries to a global audience of 650 million

Oct [10] *Manchester Evening News* reports that 10cc are to reform

1991

Jan 10cc start recording their 10th album at Bearsville Studios in upstate
New York

Apr [14] 10cc film an appearance on *Countdown* performing I'm Mandy Fly Me [Veronica Broadcasting Association]

Jun [6] *The Very Best of 10cc and Godley & Creme* peaks at No.10 in the Netherlands and certified gold

Sep [28] 10cc film an appearance in The Hague, Netherlands

1992

Apr [21] Woman in Love released b/w Man with a Mission

May [11] 10cc's tenth album *Meanwhile* released

May [13] 10cc film a TV performance in Brussels performing Woman in Love

May [14] 10cc film an appearance on *Countdown* performing Woman in Love [Veronica Broadcasting Association]

Jun [8] Welcome to Paradise released b/w Don't and Lost in Love

Nov [18] 10cc interviews in Tokyo on a Japanese promotional tour

1993

Mar [2–15] Rehearsals for their upcoming tour with line-up including Rick Fenn, Stuart Tosh, Gary Wallis (drums) and Steve Piggott (keyboards)

Mar [22] 10cc begin Japanese tour at TOKYO Mielparque Hall†

Mar [23] KAWASAKI Club Citta

Mar [24] TOKYO Gotanda Yu-Port Hall†

Mar [26] FUKUOKA Crossing Hall

Mar [27] OSAKA Sankei Hall

Mar [28] NAGOYA Club Quatro

May [29] UMEA Festival, Sweden

Jun [2] 10cc begin UK tour at RHYL New Pavilion Theatre

Jun [3] PRESTON Guildhall

Jun [4] YORK Barbican

Jun [6] GLASGOW Concert Hall

Jun [7] SUNDERLAND Empire Theatre

Jun [8] DERBY Assembly Rooms

Jun [9] LEICESTER De Montfort Hall

Jun [10] BIRMINGHAM Symphony Hall

Jun [11] LINCOLN Ritz

Jun [12] MANCHESTER Apollo

Jun [14] CROYDON Fairfield Hall

Jun [15] LONDON Hammersmith Apollo

Jun [16] GUILDFORD Civic Hall

Jun [17] SOUTHEND Cliffs Pavilion

Jun [19] SWINDON Link Leisure Centre

Jun [20] READING Hexagon Theatre

Jun [21] IPSWICH Regent

Jun [22] CARDIFF St David's Hall

Jun [24] GUERNSEY Beau Sejour

Jun [25] JERSEY Inn on the Park

Jul [16] CHILTERN Music Festival

Aug [8] SMUKFEST Festival, Denmark

Aug [21] VERONICA MUSIC BEACH PARTY†

1994

Aug 10cc start recording a new album but Graham Gouldman and Eric Stewart each record their tracks separately

Oct I'm Not in Love is certified as having been played 3 million times on US TV and radio

1995

Feb [13] 10cc perform I'm Not in Love and Take This Woman acoustically on *James Whale Show* [ITV]

Feb [14] 10cc perform I'm Not in Love acoustically on *Pebble Mill* [BBC]

Feb [15] Session at BBC Maida Vale studios for BBC Radio 2 programme *Well Above Average*

Feb [16] 10cc perform a six-song showcase gig in LONDON at Lloyd's of London Captain's Room

Mar [6] I'm Not in Love (1995 Acoustic Session) released b/w Blue Bird

Mar [9] 10cc perform I'm Not in Love acoustically on BRMB radio

Mar [11] *Well Above Average: The Continuing Story of 10cc* [BBC Radio 2]

Mar [17] 10cc perform I'm Not in Love acoustically on Metro radio in Newcastle

Mar [18] I'm Not in Love (1995 Acoustic Session) peaks at No.29 in the UK

Apr [16] LIVERPOOL Empire

Apr [17] 10cc perform I'm Not in Love acoustically on radio in Reading

Apr [28] 10cc perform I'm Not in Love acoustically on *Littlejohn Live & Uncut* [ITV]

May [1] 10cc begin rehearsals for upcoming Japanese tour with Stewart, Gouldman, Fenn and Tosh joined by Alan Park (keyboards) and Geoff Dunn (drums)

May [24] 10cc begin Japanese tour at TOKYO Shibuya Kokaido

May [25] NAGOYA Diamond Hall

May [27] OSAKA Kousei Nenkin Kaikan

May [28] 10cc perform on Radio Osaka

Jun [3] ESBJERG Rock Festival, Denmark

Aug [21] 10cc's 11th album *Mirror, Mirror* released

1996

Feb [27] *King Biscuit Flower Hour* released, the first official live recording of the original line-up, captured in Santa Monica in November 1975

Sep [9] Digitally remastered *The Original Soundtrack* released

1997

Mar [24] *The Very Best of 10cc* released

Jul [7] Digitally remastered CDs of *How Dare You!*, *Deceptive Bends* and *Bloody Tourists* released

Jul [29] Graham Gouldman and Rick Fenn begin a two-week residency at the Green Room at the Café Royal. Andrew Gold joins them onstage on Aug 2

1998

Feb [23] Graham Gouldman begins a residency at Ronnie Scott's in Birmingham with Rick Fenn, Jamie Moses and Mick Wilson

Jun [6] First-ever 10cc convention is held in Stockport

Aug [24] Graham Gouldman and Andrew Gold's album, recorded as Common Knowledge in 1984, is finally released as *Common Knowledge.com*

1999

Mar [17] Graham Gouldman's 10cc appear on *National Lottery* TV show performing Dreadlock Holiday [BBC1]

Apr [18] *Here, There, Everywhere: The Concert for Linda McCartney*, directed by Kevin Godley, is televised [BBC 1]

May [10] Graham Gouldman begins a residency at Ronnie Scott's, London

Jun [28] Art of Noise, featuring Lol Creme, release *The Seduction of Claude Debussy*

Jul [2] Graham Gouldman, Neil Finn and Roddy Frame appear on *Songwriters' Circle* [BBC 2]

Jul [24] *The 10cc Story* is aired [BBC Radio 2]

Oct [9] Art of Noise play at the Coachella Festival in California

2000

Oct [2] Graham Gouldman's second solo album *And Another Thing* released

Oct [11] Graham Gouldman presented with the prestigious Gold Badge Award from the British Academy of Songwriters, Composers and Authors at the Savoy Hotel in London

2001

Nov [16] Graham Gouldman writes to Eric Stewart to advise him of his intention to put together a show to celebrate and perform the music of 10cc

2002

Apr [26] Graham Gouldman, along with Paul Burgess (drums), Rick Fenn (guitar), Mike Stevens (keyboards) and Mick Wilson (vocals, percussion), begin 26-date UK tour to celebrate 30 years of 10cc

2003

Apr [7] Eric Stewart's second solo album *Do Not Bend* released

Jul [1] *Strawberry Bubblegum*, a collection of pre-10cc Strawberry Studios recordings, released

Sep [16] Bus Stop is certified as having been played 3 million times on US TV and radio

2004

Jan Kevin Godley and Graham Gouldman start writing songs together again

May [27] George Martin presents 10cc – represented by Eric Stewart, Lol Creme and Graham Gouldman – with an Ivor Novello Award in recognition of 'Outstanding Song Collection' at the Grosvenor House Hotel in London

2005

Sep [12] London radio station Magic FM launch TV advertising campaign featuring a mash-up of 10cc's I'm Not in Love, Michael Bublé's Home and Daniel Bedingfield's If You're Not the One

2006

May [8] Lol Creme performs backing vocals with The Pet Shop Boys at the Mermaid Theatre in London

Jul [4] Kevin Godley and Graham Gouldman launch GG/06 with four songs available for download: The Same Road, Hooligan Crane, Beautifulloser.com and Johnny Hurts

Nov [6] *Greatest Hits and More* is released, containing fifth GG/06 track Son of Man

Nov [28] Lol Creme performs Rubber Bullets and I'm Not in Love with his band The Producers at the Barfly in Camden

2007

Mar [9] Kevin Godley joins Graham Gouldman's 10cc onstage at Cardiff's St David's Hall

Mar [16] Kevin Godley joins Graham Gouldman's 10cc onstage at London's Shepherd's Bush Empire†

May [2] Blue plaque unveiled at 3 Waterloo Road in Stockport to commemorate Strawberry Studios

Oct [16] The Things We Do for Love is certified as having been played 3 million times on American TV and radio

Oct [23] GG/06 release their sixth track Barry's Shoes

2008

Mar [1] *10cc Collected* triple album peaks at No.15 in the Netherlands

May [12] Graham Gouldman's 10cc *Clever Clogs* DVD released

Oct [7] Bus Stop is certified as having been played 4 million times on US TV and radio

Nov [28] Graham Gouldman's 10cc begin a 19-date Night of the Proms arena tour in Germany along with Tears For Fears and Robin Gibb

2009

Jan [8] Eric Stewart's third solo album *Viva La Difference* released

Apr [20] *The Very Best of 10cc* released

May [4] 10cc feature in the BBC Radio 2 series *The Record Producers*,
including new interviews with all four original members of the band
Oct [6] I'm Not in Love is certified as having been played 5 million times
on US TV and radio

2010
May [20] Graham Gouldman presents Neil Sedaka with a Special
International Ivor Novello Award at the Grosvenor House hotel

2011
Mar [4] Graham Gouldman, Ron Sexsmith and Fran Healy appear on
Songwriters' Circle [BBC Four]

2012
May [10] Kevin Godley joins Graham Gouldman's 10cc onstage at
London's Royal Albert Hall, on Gouldman's 66th birthday
June [25] The Producers album *Made in Basing Street* released
Aug [6] Graham Gouldman's third solo album *Love and Work* released
Nov [19] 10cc anthology *Tenology* released to mark the band's 40th
anniversary

2013
July [23] *The Very Best of 10cc* is certified gold in the UK

2014
Feb [13] Trevor Horn is presented with the 'Outstanding Contribution to
UK Music' award by the Music Producers Guild, with Eric Stewart
joining he and The Producers onstage at the Park Plaza Riverbank
Hotel to perform I'm Not in Love, the first time he and Lol Creme
have performed together since Knebworth in 1976
June [12] Graham Gouldman is inducted into the Songwriters Hall of
Fame in New York City
Aug [25] Digitally remastered CDs of 10cc's *Ten Out of 10* and *Windows in
the Jungle* released
Oct [13] The Things We Do For Love is certified as having been played 4
million times on US TV and radio

2015

Feb [5] Graham Gouldman's 10cc begin UK tour performing *Sheet Music* in its entirety followed by a greatest hits set with a special video contribution from Kevin Godley on Somewhere In Hollywood

Mar [5] Lol Creme performs with the Trevor Horn Band at London's Shepherd's Bush Empire and performs three 10cc songs

Mar [16] Kevin Godley publishes his e-book autobiography *Spacecake*

Aug [29] Kevin Godley joins Graham Gouldman's 10cc onstage at Proms on the Pier in Dun Laoghaire

Oct [19] Graham Gouldman is awarded a BMI Icon by the BMI at London's Dorchester Hotel

Dec [4] BBC Four broadcasts *I'm Not in Love: The Story of 10cc* featuring interviews with all the band's original members [repeated Jul 2016, Jan 2017, Sep 2017, Mar 2018]

2016

Feb [3] Launch of the Gizmotron 2.0, a new and improved version of Godley and Creme's original 'Gizmo'

May [11] Eric Stewart attends the memorial for Sir George Martin at St Martin-in-the Fields in London

Aug [8] Kevin Godley launches his website

2017

Jan [27] *Strawberry Studios: I Am in Love*, a year-long exhibition celebrating 50 years of Strawberry Studios opens at the Stockport Museum

Mar [15] Eric Stewart publishes his e-book autobiography *Things I Do for Love*

Mar [31] *The Very Best of 10cc* is certified platinum in the UK

May [9] Graham Gouldman's 10cc appear on *Later … With Jools Holland* [broadcast BBC2 May 9 & 12]

Jul [21] Eric Stewart compilation album *Anthology* released

Jul [28] 10cc anthology *Before, During, After – The Story of 10cc* released

Aug [2] Kevin Godley announces intention to record a solo album *Muscle Memory* and invites musical collaborators to get involved

Sep [8] Godley and Creme anthology *Body of Work 1978–88* released

Sep [22] Graham Gouldman six-track EP Play Nicely and Share released as he undertakes the Heart Full of Songs UK tour

Nov [24] *Listen People: The Graham Gouldman Songbook 1964–2005* released

2018

Feb [22] *Strawberry Studios: I Am in Love* exhibition extended to September 2018 due to popular demand

Jun [2] Graham Gouldman joins Ringo Starr's All Starr Band for the start of a 41-date World Tour performing The Things We Do for Love, Dreadlock Holiday and I'm Not in Love

Jul [13] Kevin Godley receives honorary Doctor of Arts degree from Staffordshire University

2019

Mar [7] Kevin Godley unveils two films – for Son of Man and I'm Not In Love – that he has made for Graham Gouldman's 10cc

Apr [12] The Chemical Brothers use an image created by Godley and Creme for their *Consequences* project as the front cover of their album *No Geography* in the same week that Paul McNulty and Sean Macreavy launch their *Consequences* podcast

Jun [26] Apple launch a new TV ad in India for the iPhone XS featuring Dreadlock Holiday as the soundtrack

Aug [9] Caroline International release remastered CD of Godley and Creme's *Consequences*

Sep [27] Cherry Red Records release *Wax Live In Concert* CD/DVD recorded in Harrogate in November 1987

Oct [11] *The Mindbenders Live On Air 1964-66* released featuring archive recordings of the band in session for the BBC

10cc singles

1. Donna b/w Hot Sun Rock (UK Records, August 1972) Highest chart positions: No.2 in the UK, No.2 in Ireland, No.2 in the Netherlands, No.4 in Belgium, No.7 in France, No.10 in New Zealand, No.53 in Australia

2. Johnny Don't Do It b/w 4% of Something (UK Records, November 1972) Highest chart positions: No.21 in New Zealand, No.22 in Belgium

3. Rubber Bullets b/w Waterfall (UK Records, March 1973) Highest chart positions: No.1 in the UK, No.1 in Ireland, No.3 in Australia, No.10 in France, No.17 in New Zealand, No.17 in Belgium, No.18 in Germany, No.43 in Italy, No.73 in the US, No.76 in Canada

4. The Dean And I b/w Bee in My Bonnet (UK Records, August 1973) Highest chart positions: No.1 in Ireland, No.10 in the UK, No.10 in France, No.21 in New Zealand, No.61 in Australia

5. The Worst Band In The World b/w 18 Carat Man of Means (UK Records, January 1974) Highest chart position: didn't chart

6. The Wall Street Shuffle b/w Gismo My Way (UK Records, May 1974) Highest chart positions: No.1 in the Netherlands, No.4 in France, No.4 in Belgium, No.9 in Ireland, No.10 in the UK, No.38 in Germany, No.87 in Canada, No.103 in the US

7. Silly Love b/w The Sacro Illiac (UK Records, August 1974) Highest chart positions: No.7 in the Netherlands, No.10 in France, No.20 in Belgium, No.24 in the UK

8. Life Is A Minestrone b/w Channel Swimmer (Mercury, March 1975) Highest chart positions: No.6 in France, No.7 in the UK, No.7 in Ireland, No.12 in the Netherlands, No.15 in Belgium, No.48 in Australia, No.104 in the US

9. I'm Not In Love b/w Good News (Mercury, May 1975) Highest chart positions: No.1 in the UK, No.1 in Ireland, No.1 in France, No.1 in Canada, No.2 in the US, No.3 in Australia, No.4 in New Zealand,

No.5 in Belgium, No.5 in the Netherlands, No.6 in Norway, No.8 in Switzerland, No.8 in Germany, No.17 in South Africa, No.26 in Italy

10. Art For Art's Sake b/w Get It While You Can (Mercury, November 1975) Highest chart positions: No.4 in Ireland, No.5 in the UK, No.5 in France, No.6 in New Zealand, No.61 in Australia, No.69 in Canada, No.83 in the US

11. I'm Mandy Fly Me b/w How Dare You (Mercury, March 1976) Highest chart positions: No.3 in Ireland, No.6 in the UK, No.18 in Sweden, No.25 in New Zealand, No.44 in Germany, No.50 in the Netherlands, No.60 in the US, No.62 in Canada, No.62 in Australia

12. The Things We Do For Love b/w Hot to Trot (Mercury, December 1976) Highest chart positions: No.1 in Canada, No.2 in Ireland, No.5 in the US, No.5 in Australia, No.6 in the UK, No.13 in the Netherlands, No.23 in New Zealand, No.24 in Belgium

13. Good Morning Judge b/w Don't Squeeze Me Like Toothpaste (Mercury, April 1977) Highest chart positions: No.5 in the UK, No.7 in Australia, No.12 in the Netherlands, No.12 in Sweden, No.20 in Belgium, No.23 in Germany, No.47 in Australia, No.69 in the US

14. People In Love b/w I'm So Laid Back, I'm Laid Out (Mercury, July 1977) Highest chart positions: No.40 in the US, No.74 in Australia, No.90 in Canada

15. Dreadlock Holiday b/w Nothing Can Move Me (Mercury, July 1978) Highest chart positions: No.1 in the UK, No.1 in Belgium, No.1 in the Netherlands, No.1 in New Zealand, No.2 in Australia, No.2 in Ireland, No.3 in France, No.5 in Switzerland, No.7 in Norway, No.11 in Germany, No.16 in Sweden, No.18 in Austria, No.30 in Canada, No.44 in the US

16. Reds In My Bed b/w Take These Chains (Mercury, December 1978) Highest chart position: didn't chart

17. One Two Five b/w Only Child (Mercury, March 1980) Highest chart positions: No.9 in Norway, No.19 in Germany, No.29 in the Netherlands, No.85 in Australia

18. It Doesn't Matter At All b/w From Rochdale to Ocho Rios (Mercury, May 1980) Highest chart position: didn't chart

19. Les Nouveaux Riches b/w I Hate To Eat Alone (Mercury, May 1981) Highest chart position: didn't chart

20. Don't Turn Me Away b/w Tomorrow's World Today (Mercury, November 1981) Highest chart positions: No.38 in Canada, No.49 in

the Netherlands, No.94 in Australia

21. The Power Of Love b/w You're Coming Home Again (Mercury, February 1982) Highest chart position: didn't chart
22. Run Away b/w Action Man In Motown Suit (Mercury, July 1982) Highest chart position: No.50 in the UK
23. We've Heard It All Before b/w Overdraft In Overdraft (Mercury, October 1982) Highest chart position: didn't chart
24. 24 Hours b/w Dreadlock Holiday (Live) / I'm Not in Love (Live) (Mercury, April 1983) Highest chart position: No.78 in the UK
25. Feel The Love b/w She Gives Me Pain (Mercury, July 1983) Highest chart positions: No.7 in the Netherlands, No.13 in Belgium, No.76 in Australia, No.87 in the UK
26. Woman In Love b/w Man With A Mission (Polydor, April 1992) Highest chart position: No.55 in the Netherlands
27. Welcome To Paradise b/w Don't / Lost In Love (Polydor, June 1992) Highest chart position: unknown
28. I'm Not In Love (1995 Acoustic Session) b/w Blue Bird (Avex, March 1995) Highest chart position: No.29 in the UK

10cc albums

1. *10cc* (UK Records, July 1973)
   Johnny Don't Do It / Sand In My Face / Donna / The Dean And I / Headline Hustler / Speed Kills / Rubber Bullets / The Hospital Song / Ships Don't Disappear In The Night (Do They?) / Fresh Air For My Mama. Highest chart positions: No.36 in the UK, No.201 in the US
2. *Sheet Music* (UK Records, May 1974)
   The Wall Street Shuffle / The Worst Band In The World / Hotel / Old Wild Men / Clockwork Creep / Silly Love / Somewhere In Hollywood / Baron Samedi / The Sacro Illiac / Oh Effendi. Highest chart positions: No.9 in the UK, No.15 in the Netherlands, No.81 in the US
3. *The Original Soundtrack* (Mercury, March 1975)
   One Night In Paris / I'm Not In Love / Blackmail / The Second Sitting For The Last Supper / Brand New Day / Flying Junk / Life Is A Minestrone / The Film of My Love. Highest chart positions: No.3 in the UK, No.3 in France, No.5 in Canada, No.15 in the US, No.37 in New Zealand

4. *How Dare You!* (Mercury, January 1976)
How Dare You / Lazy Ways / I Wanna Rule The World / I'm Mandy
Fly Me / Iceberg / Art For Art's Sake / Rock 'n' Roll Lullaby / Head
Room / Don't Hang Up. Highest chart positions: No.1 in New
Zealand, No.5 in the UK, No.5 in Canada, No.5 in Sweden, No.7 in
the Netherlands, No.10 in Norway, No.26 in Finland, No.47 in the
US

5. *Deceptive Bends* (Mercury, April 1977)
Good Morning Judge / The Things We Do For Love / Marriage
Bureau Rendezvous / People In Love / Modern Man Blues /
Honeymoon With B Troop / You've Got A Cold / I Bought A Flat
Guitar Tutor / Feel The Benefit. Highest chart positions: No.1 in
Belgium, No.1 in Denmark, No.3 in the UK, No.4 in the Netherlands,
No.4 in New Zealand, No.4 in Norway, No.4 in Sweden, No.8 in
Australia, No.28 in Finland, No. 31 in US, No.78 in Canada

6. *Bloody Tourists* (Mercury, September 1978)
Dreadlock Holiday / For You and I / Take These Chains / Shock on
the Tube / Last Night / The Anonymous Alcoholic / Reds in My Bed
/ Life Line / Tokyo / Old Mister Time / From Rochdale To Ocho Rios
/ Everything You Wanted To Know About!!!. Highest chart positions:
No.2 in the Netherlands, No.2 in New Zealand, No.3 in Australia,
No.3 in the UK, No.3 in Sweden, No.4 in Norway, No.12 in Germany,
No.26 in Finland, No.58 in Japan, No.69 in US, No.74 in Canada

7. *Look Hear?* (Mercury, March 1980)
One Two Five / Welcome To The World / How'm I Ever Gonna
Say Goodbye / Don't Send We Back / I Took You Home / It Doesn't
Matter At All / Dressed To Kill / Lovers Anonymous / I Hate to Eat
Alone / Strange Lover / LA Inflatable. Highest chart positions: No.3
in Norway, No.14 in Sweden, No.21 in the Netherlands, No. 35 in the
UK, No.40 in New Zealand, No.40 in Germany, No.72 in Canada,
No.180 in US

8. *Ten Out of 10* (Mercury, November 1981)
Don't Ask / Overdraft In Overdrive / Don't Turn Me Away /
Memories / Notel Hotel / Les Nouveaux Riches / Action Man In
Motown Suit* / Listen With Your Eyes* / Lying Here With You* /
Survivor* (US version replaces * with The Power of Love, Run Away,
We've Heard It All Before and Tomorrow's World Today). Highest
chart positions: No.17 in Norway, No.24 in Sweden, No.31 in Canada,

No.49 in the Netherlands, No. 209 in the US

9. *Windows in the Jungle* (Mercury, September 1983)
24 Hours / Feel The Love / Yes I Am! / Americana Panorama / City Lights / Food For Thought / Working Girls / Taxi! Taxi! Highest chart positions: No.7 in the Netherlands, No.70 in UK, No.97 in Canada

10. *Meanwhile* (Polydor, May 1992)
Woman In Love / Wonderland / Fill Her Up / Something Special / Welcome To Paradise / The Stars Didn't Show / Green Eyed Monster / Charity Begins At Home / Shine A Light In The Dark / Don't Break The Promises. Highest chart positions: No.39 in the Netherlands, No.84 in Japan

11. *Mirror, Mirror* (Avex, August 1995)
Yvonne's The One / Code Of Silence / Blue Bird / Age Of Consent / Take This Woman / The Monkey And The Onion / Everything Is Not Enough / Ready To Go Home / Grow Old With Me / Margo Wants The Mustard / Peace In Our Time / Why Did I Break Your Heart? / Now You're Gone / I'm Not In Love (1995 Acoustic Session). Highest chart position: No.46 in Japan

Eric Stewart albums

1. *Girls* (Polydor, May 1980)
Girls Opening Music / Girls / Disco Grindin' / Switch le Bitch / Aural Exciter / Warm, Warm, Warm / Tonight / Snatch the Gas / Your Touch Is Soft / Trouble Shared / Discollapse / Make The Pieces Fit

2. *Frooty Rooties* (Mercury, August 1982)
The Ritual / Make The Pieces Fit / Never Say 'I Told You So' / Night And Day / All My Loving Following You / Rockin' My Troubles Away / Doris The Florist / Guitaaaaaarghs / Strictly Business

3. *Do Not Bend* (Strawberry Soundtracks, April 2003)
You Can't Take It With You / A Friend In Need / The Gods Are Smiling / Fred And Dis-Audrey / I Will Love You Tomorrow / Sleeping With The Ghosts / Rappin' With Yves / Norman Conquest II / No No Nettie / Mr Decadent / Do The Books / Set In Blancmange / A Human, Being / You Are Not Me

4. *Viva La Difference* (Strawberry Soundtracks, January 2009)
Gnome Sweet Gnomes / It's In The Blood / Friends Like These / Down By The Palace / Do Not Bend / Millennium Blues / Viva La Difference / We're Not Alone / Word Of The Mouth / Sleep At Night / Can't Get Enough

Further listening:
Anthology (Cherry Red, July 2017) 31-track, two-CD collection featuring the best of Stewart's solo albums, with many songs remixed by Stewart for this compilation

Graham Gouldman albums
1. *The Graham Gouldman Thing* (RCA, July 1968)
   The Impossible Years / Bus Stop / Behind The Door / Pawnbroker / Who Are They / My Father / No Milk Today / Upstairs, Downstairs / For Your Love / Pamela, Pamela / Chestnut
2. *Animalympics* (Mercury, March 1980)
   Go For It / Underwater Fantasy / Away From It All / Born To Lose / Kit Mambo / Z.O.O. / Love's Not For Me (René's Song) / With You I Can Run Forever / Bionic Boar / We've Made It To The Top
3. *And Another Thing* (Dome, October 2000)
   You Stole My Love / Walking With Angels / Dancing Days / Just Another Day / Sometimes / There Was A Day / Heart Full Of Soul / Ready To Go Home / Single Tonight / Walkin' Away / Can Anybody See You?
4. *Love and Work* (Rosala Records, August 2012)
   The Halls of Rock 'n' Roll / Daylight / Ariella / Then It's Gone / Let Me Dream Again / Lost In The Shadows Of Love / Battlefield / Cryin' Time Again / Any Day Now / Puttin' My Faith In Love / Black Gold / Memory Lane
5. *Play Nicely and Share* (Rosala Records, September 2017)
   Let's Get Lost / Come To Mine / Do You Wanna Go / Rave On / Just Like Yesterday / Play Nicely And Share
6. *Modesty Forbids* (Lojinx, March 2020)
   Standing Next To Me / That's Love Right There /All Around The World / It's Not You It's Me / What Time Won't Heal / Different Times / Wake Up Dreamer / Russian Doll / Hangin' By A Thread / Waited All My Life For You / New Star

Further listening:
Listen People: Graham Gouldman Songbook 1964–2005 (Ace Records, November 2017). A 24-track collection featuring cover versions of Gouldman songs, including by The Mockingbirds, The Hollies, The Yardbirds, Cher, Morrissey, Kirsty MacColl and McFly

Kevin Godley and Lol Creme albums

1. *Consequences* (Mercury, October 1977)
   Seascape / Wind / Fireworks / Stampede / Burial Scene / Sleeping
   Earth / Honolulu Lulu / The Flood / Five O'Clock In The Morning
   / When Things Go Wrong / Lost Weekend / Rosie / Office Chase /
   Cool, Cool, Cool / Cool, Cool, Cool (Reprise) / Sailor / Mobilization
   / Please, Please, Please / Blint's Tune (Movements 1–17)

2. *L* (Mercury, August 1978)
   This Sporting Life / Sandwiches Of You / Art School Canteen / Group
   Life / Punchbag / Foreign Accents /Hit Factory / Business Is Business

3. *Freeze Frame* (Polydor, November 1979)
   An Englishman In New York / Random Brainwave / I Pity Inanimate
   Objects / Freeze Frame / Clues / Brazilia (Wish You Were Here) /
   Mugshots / Get Well Soon

4. *Ismism* (Polydor, October 1981)
   Snack Attack / Under Your Thumb / Joey's Camel / The Problem /
   Ready for Ralph / Wedding Bells / Lonnie / Sale Of the Century /
   The Party

5. *Birds of Prey* (Polydor, April 1983)
   My Body The Car / Worm And The Rattlesnake / Cats Eyes / Samson
   / Save A Mountain For Me / Madame Guillotine / Woodwork /
   Twisted Nerve / Out In The Cold

6. *History Mix Vol.1* (Polydor, June 1985)
   Wet Rubber Soup / Cry / Expanding The Business / The 'Dare You'
   Man / Hum Drum Boys In Paris / Mountain Tension

7. *Goodbye Blue Sky* (Polydor, March 1988)
   H.E.A.V.E.N. / A Little Piece Of Heaven / Don't Set Fire (To The
   One I Love) / Golden Rings / Crime & Punishment / The Big Bang
   / 10,000 Angels / Sweet Memory / Airforce One / The Last Page Of
   History / Desperate Times

Further listening:
Body of Work 1978–1988 (Caroline International, September 2017)

Kevin Godley and Graham Gouldman (GG/06)
   First 6 (Originally downloads from GG06.com)
   The Same Road / Johnny Hurts / Hooligan Crane / Beautifulloser.
   com (July 2006) / Son Of Man (Nov 2006) / Barry's Shoes (Oct 2007)

Kevin Godley

1. *Hog Fever* (Escargot, November 2015)
   The Bad and The Beautiful / Work Song / Just Write / Confession
2. *Muscle Memory* (State 51 Conspiracy, 2020, www.kevin-godley.com)
   [provisional listing at time of printing] All Bones Are White /
   Periscope / One Day / 5 Minutes Alone / The Bang Bang Theory /
   The Ghosts Of The Living / Hit The Street / Song Of Hate / Cut To
   The Cat / Bullet Holes In The Sky / Expecting A Message

Further listening:

The Mindbenders: *A Groovy Kind of Love – The Complete LPs & Singles
   1966–68* (Cherry Red Records, 2010)
*Strawberry Bubblegum: A Collection of pre-10cc Strawberry Studios
   Recordings* (Castle Music, 2003)
Hotlegs: *You Didn't Like It Because You Didn't Think Of It* (Grapefruit
   Records, 2012)

10cc Set-lists

1974 US Tour – Boston Performance Center (27/2/74) Speed Kills / Sand
   in My Face / Donna / Oh Effendi / Waterfall / Headline Hustler /
   Silly Love / The Wall Street Shuffle / Rubber Bullets / Fresh Air For
   My Mama / Run Baby Run
1974 UK Tour – London Rainbow Theatre (23/9/74) Silly Love / Baron
   Samedi / Old Wild Men / Fresh Air For My Mama / Donna / The
   Sacro Iliac / Ships Don't Disappear In The Night (Do They?) /
   Somewhere In Hollywood /Speed Kills / Oh Effendi / The Wall Street
   Shuffle / The Worst Band In The World / Rubber Bullets
1975 US Tour – Santa Monica Civic Center (26/11/75) Silly Love / Flying
   Junk / Baron Samedi / Old Wild Men / The Sacro Iliac / Somewhere
   In Hollywood / Donna / Ships Don't Disappear In The Night (Do
   They?) / I'm Not In Love / The Film Of My Love / Art For Art's Sake
   / The Worst Band In The World / Neanderthal Man / The Wall Street
   Shuffle / Rubber Bullets / One Night In Paris
1976 European Tour – Liverpool Empire (26/2/76) Art For Art's Sake /
   Silly Love / Lazy Ways / Rock 'n' Roll Lullaby / The Worst Band In
   The World / The Second Sitting For The Last Supper / Old Wild Men
   / Iceberg / Don't Hang Up / Head Room / Ships Don't Disappear In
   the Night (Do They?) / The Sacro Illiac / I'm Mandy Fly Me / I Wanna

Rule the World / The Wall Street Shuffle / I'm Not In Love / One Night In Paris / Rubber Bullets

1976 Knebworth Festival (21/8/76) One Night In Paris / The Worst Band In The World / Good Morning Judge / Silly Love / Don't Hang Up / Old Wild Men / The Wall Street Shuffle / Neanderthal Man–Run Baby Run / Ships Don't Disappear In The Night (Do They?) / I'm Mandy Fly Me / The Second Sitting For The Last Supper / I'm Not In Love / Rubber Bullets

1977 World Tour – Tokyo Sun Plaza Hall (1/10/77) The Second Sitting For The Last Supper / You've Got A Cold / Honeymoon With B Troop / Art For Art's Sake / People In Love / The Wall Street Shuffle / Ships Don't Disappear In The Night (Do They?) / I'm Mandy Fly Me / Marriage Bureau Rendezvous / Good Morning Judge / Feel The Benefit / The Things We Do for Love / Waterfall / I'm Not In Love / Modern Man Blues

1978 World Tour – Dallas Convention Centre (8/11/78) The Wall Street Shuffle / Ships Don't Disappear In The Night (Do They?) / Shock On The Tube / I'm Mandy Fly Me / Old Mister Time / Dreadlock Holiday / Art For Art's Sake / For You And I / From Rochdale To Ocho Rios / Feel The Benefit / Reds In My Bed / Good Morning Judge / Everything You Always Wanted To Know About!!! / The Things We Do For Love / I'm Not In Love / The Second Sitting For The Last Supper / Modern Man Blues

1980 World Tour – Mainz Rheingoldhalle (30/4/80) LA Inflatable / The Wall Street Shuffle / One Two Five / I'm Mandy Fly Me / Lovers Anonymous / How'm I Ever Gonna Say Goodbye / Good Morning Judge / From Rochdale To Ocho Rios / Art For Art's Sake / It Doesn't Matter At All / The Things We Do For Love / Don't Send We Back / Dreadlock Holiday / Feel The Benefit / I'm Not In Love / Rubber Bullets–Silly Love–Life Is A Minestrone (medley) / Roll Over Beethoven

1982 UK Tour – Manchester Apollo (2/3/82) Good Morning Judge / The Wall Street Shuffle / Don't Ask / I'm Mandy Fly Me / The Power Of Love / The Things We Do For Love / Don't Turn Me Away / From Rochdale To Ocho Rios / Les Nouveaux Riches / Dreadlock Holiday / Lying Here With You / Memories / Feel the Benefit / Art For Art's Sake / I'm Not In Love / Rubber Bullets–Silly Love–Life Is A Minestrone (medley) / The Second Sitting For The Last Supper / Roll Over Beethoven

1983 UK Tour – London Hammersmith Odeon (10/3/83) Rubber Bullets–Silly Love–Life Is A Minestrone (medley) / I'm Mandy Fly Me / 24 Hours / The Wall Street Shuffle / Run Away / The Things We Do For Love / Good Morning Judge / City Lights / Art For Art's Sake / Lying Here With You / From Rochdale To Ocho Rios / Feel The Love / Dreadlock Holiday / I'm Not In Love / Feel The Benefit

1993 Japanese Tour – Tokyo Mielparque Hall (22/3/93) The Wall Street Shuffle / I'm Mandy Fly Me / Good Morning Judge / Welcome To Paradise / The Things We Do For Love / Across The Universe / The Stars Didn't Show / Art For Art's Sake / Paperback Writer / Shine A Light In The Dark / Feel The Benefit / Dreadlock Holiday / I'm Not In Love / Rubber Bullets–Silly Love–Life Is A Minestrone (medley) / Slow Down

1995 Japanese Tour – Tokyo Shibuya Kokaido (24/5/95) Art For Art's Sake / I'm Mandy Fly Me / Welcome To Paradise / Good Morning Judge / Take This Woman / The Wall Street Shuffle / The Stars Didn't Show / Margo Wants the Mustard / Sand In My Face / Code Of Silence / Ready To Go Home / The Things We Do For Love / Feel The Benefit / Dreadlock Holiday / I'm Not In Love / Rubber Bullets–Silly Love–Life Is A Minestrone (medley) / Johnny B. Goode

Graham Gouldman (pre-10cc songbook)

A Little While Back / Because You're There / Behind The Door / Better To Have Loved and Lost / Bus Stop / Chestnut / Come On Plane / The Cost Of Living / Crickets / East West / Evil Hearted You / The Flight Of The Mockingbird / For Your Love / Gimme Love / Going Away / Going Home / Growing Older / Happy, That's Me / Harvey's Theme / Have You Ever Been To Georgia? / Heart Full Of Soul / Hey Mom, Hey Dad / I'm Gonna Take You There / I'm 28 [AKA Geting Nowhere]/ I Can Feel We're Parting / Imaginin' / I Never Should've Kissed You / The Impossible Years / It's Alright Now / It's Nice To Be Out In The Morning / The Joker / The Late Mr Late / Leisurely Age / Lemon and Lime / Listen People / London Look / Look Through Any Window / Love Is Just A Game / Madelane / The Man With The Golden Gun / Marcel's / My Father / My Story / Naughty Nippon Nights / No Milk Today / Nowhere To Go / Oh Soloman / Ooh She's Done It Again / Pamela, Pamela / Pawnbroker / People Passing By / Sad and Lonely / Safari / Santa Claus / San Tokay / Sausalito (Is the Place to Go) / Schoolgirl / Skit Skat /

Some People / Stop! Stop! Stop! (Or Honey I'll Be Gone) / Susan's Tuba / Tallyman / Tampa Florida / That's How (It's Gonna Stay) / Together / Travellin' Man / Ulysses / Uncle Joe The Ice Cream Man / Upstairs, Downstairs / Wheel Spin / When He Comes / Who Are They? / Why Say Goodbye / Wicked Melinda / Willie Morgan / The World Is For The Young / You Stole My Love

Kevin Godley and Lol Creme videography

Godley & Creme: An Englishman In New York (with Derek Burbidge, 1979) / Godley & Creme: Wide Boy (1980) / Visage: Fade To Grey (1980) / Visage: Mind of a Toy (1980) / Status Quo: Something 'Bout You Baby I Like (1981) / Ringo Starr: Private Property, Attention, Sure To Fall (combined in the short film *The Cooler*) (1981) / Toyah: I Want To Be Free (1981) / Joan Armatrading: The Weakness In Me (1981) / Joan Armatrading: When I Get It Right (1981) / Toyah: Thunder In The Mountains (1981) / Duran Duran: Girls On Film (1981) / Godley & Creme: Wedding Bells (1981) / Graham Parker: Temporary Beauty (1982) / Asia: Heat of the Moment (1982) / Asia: Only Time Will Tell (1982) / 10cc: Feel The Love (1983) / Any Trouble: Touch and Go (1983) / Culture Club: Victims (1983) / David Sylvian & Ryuichi Sakamoto: Forbidden Colours (1983) / Elton John: Kiss The Bride (1983) / Godley & Creme: Save A Mountain For Me (1983) / Herbie Hancock: Rockit (1983) / Herbie Hancock: Autodrive (1983) / The Police: Every Breath You Take (1983) / The Police: Wrapped Around Your Finger (1983) / The Police: Synchronicity II (1983) / Yes: Leave It (1983) / Frankie Goes To Hollywood: Two Tribes (1984) / Frankie Goes To Hollywood: The Power of Love (1984) / Paul Young: Everything Must Change (US Version, 1984) / Godley & Creme: Golden Boy (1984) / Artists Against Apartheid: Sun City (with Jonathan Demme and Hart Perry, 1985) / Duran Duran: A View To A Kill (1985) / Eric Clapton: Forever Man (1985) / Go West: We Close Our Eyes (1985) / Godley & Creme: Cry (1985) / Godley & Creme: Wet Rubber Soup (1985) / Graham Parker: Wake Up Next To You (1985) / Howard Jones: Life In One Day (1985) / INXS: This Time (with Peter Sinclair, 1985) / Sting: If You Love Somebody Set Them Free (1985) / Thompson Twins: Don't Mess With Doctor Dream (1985) / Huey Lewis and the News: Hip To Be Square (1986) / Jana Pope: Don't You Hear Me Screaming (1986) / Lou Reed: No Money Down (1986) / Patti LaBelle: Oh, People (1986) / Peter Gabriel & Kate Bush: Don't Give Up (1986) /

Rob Jungklas: Boystown (1986) / The Police: Don't Stand So Close To Me '86 (1986) / Ultravox: All Fall Down (1986) / Wang Chung: Everybody Have Fun Tonight (1986) / Go West: I Want To Hear It From You (1987) / Godley & Creme: A Little Piece of Heaven (1987) / Peter Gabriel: Biko (1987) / Godley & Creme: 10,000 Angels (1987) / George Harrison: When We Was Fab (1988) / And Why Not: Restless Days (1989)

Kevin Godley videography
Fine Young Cannibals: Don't Look Back (1989) / Band Aid 2: Do They Know It's Christmas? (1989) / Wet Wet Wet: Sweet Surrender (1989) / Erasure: Blue Savannah (1990) / Bryan Adams: Can't Stop This Thing We Started (1991) / Bryan Adams: All I Want Is You (1991) / U2: Even Better Than The Real Thing (1992) / Bryan Adams: Thought I'd Died and Gone To Heaven (1992) / Sting: Fields of Gold (1992) / Moodswings and Chrissie Hynde: Spiritual High (1992) / Garland Jeffreys: The Answer (1992) / U2: Numb (1993) / Frank Sinatra & Bono: I've Got You Under My Skin (1993) / Paul McCartney: C'mon People (1993) / Blur: Girls and Boys (1994) / Gavin Friday & Bono: The Name of the Father (1994) / Dave Stewart: Head of Stone (1994) / East 17: Steam (1994) / Kate Bush & Larry Adler: The Man I Love (1994) / U2: Hold Me, Thrill Me, Kiss Me, Kill Me (with Maurice Linnane, 1995) / Deep Forest: Deep Forest (1995) / Whale: I'll Do Ya (1995) / The Beatles: Real Love (1996) / Adam Clayton & Larry Mullen Jr: Mission: Impossible (1996) / Gavin Friday: You, Me & World War III (1996) / Phil Collins: Dance Into The Light (1996) / Forest for the Trees: Dream (1997) / Tonic: Soldier's Daughter (1997) / Garland Jeffreys: Sexuality (1997) / James: Tomorrow (1997) / Eric Clapton: My Father's Eyes (1998) / Kele Le Roc: My Love (1998) / U2: The Sweetest Thing (1998) / Boyzone: When The Going Gets Tough (1998) / Boyzone: You Needed Me (1998) / Helicopter Girl: Subliminal Punk (1998) / Phil Collins: You'll Be In My Heart (1999) / The Black Crowes: By Your Side (1999) / Ronan Keating: When You Say Nothing At All (1999) / Boyzone: You Needed Me (1999) / The Charlatans: Forever (1999) / Wyclef Jean & Bono: New Day / Warchild (1999) / Gabrielle: Rise (1999) / Alabama 3: Woke Up This Morning (2000) / Sting: After The Rain Has Fallen (2000) / Rod Stewart: Into Your Arms (2000) / U2: Stuck In A Moment (2000) / Marti Pellow: I Wanna Be Close To You (2001) / Gabrielle: Out of Reach (2001) / Him: Pretending (2001) / Zucchero: Baila (2001) / Zucchero: I'm In Trouble (2001) / The Charlatans: A Man Needs To Be Told (2001)

/ Ronan Keating: If Tomorrow Never Comes (2002) / Ronan Keating
& Lulu: We've Got Tonight (2002) / Scarface featuring Faith Evans:
Someday (2002) / Will Young: Leave Right Now (2003) / The Rapture:
Sister Saviour (2003) / Haven: I Wouldn't Change A Thing (2004) / The
Corrs: Summer Sunshine (2004) / Kealer: Cry (2004) / Lisa Stansfield:
Treat Me Like A Woman (2004) / Bryan Adams: Flying (2004) / Ronan
Keating & Yusuf Islam: Father and Son (2005) / Ben Adams: Sorry (2005)
/ Katie Melua: Nine Million Bicycles (2005) / Jamie Cullum: Mind Trick
(2005) / Katie Melua: I Cried For You (2005) / Shayne Ward: That's My
Goal (2005) / Brothermandude: Automatic (2006) / Keane: Is It Any
Wonder? (2006) / Mojo Fury: The Man (2006) / Snow Patrol: Crack The
Shutters (2008) / Boyzone: Better (2008) / Katie Melua: The Flood (2010)
/ Gavin Friday: Able (2011) / Graham Gouldman's 10cc: Somewhere In
Hollywood (2015) / Hozier: Better Love (2016) / Elbow: Gentle Storm
(2017) / Tom Chaplin: Still Waiting (2017) / GG/06: Son of Man (2019)
/ Graham Gouldman's 10cc: I'm Not in Love (2019) / Keane: The Way I
Feel (2019)

Lol Creme videography
Tina Turner: The Best (1989) / Tom Jones: If I Only Knew (1994) / Sting:
I'm So Happy I Can't Stop Crying (1996) / Art of Noise: Dreaming in
Colour (1999) / The Producers: Barking up the Right Tree (2007) [+ *The
Lunatic* (Island Pictures, 1992)]

Strawberry Studios
Notable records recorded/mixed at Strawberry Studios North
(*part-recorded, **mixed only)
10cc: *10cc* (1973), *Sheet Music* (1974), *The Original Soundtrack* (1975), *How
  Dare You!* (1976), *Live and Let Live*** (1977), *Ten Out of 10** (1981),
  Windows in the Jungle (1983)
A Certain Ratio: Houses in Motion (with Grace Jones, unreleased) (1980),
  *To Each...*** (1989), Won't Stop Loving You** (1990)
Barclay James Harvest: *Early Morning Onwards** (1972), *Baby James
  Harvest** (1972), *Octoberon** (1976), *Gone to Earth* (1977), *XII* (1978),
  *Live Tapes*** (1978), *Eyes of the Universe* (1979)
Bay City Rollers: *Once Upon a Star** (1975)
Buzzcocks: Everybody's Happy Nowadays (1979), Strange Thing** (1980)
The Charlatans: Indian Rope (1991)

The Colourfield: *Virgins and Philistines* (1984)

John Cooper Clarke: *Me and My Big Mouth* (1981)

Crispy Ambulance: *The Plateau Phase* (1982)

Cutting Crew: *The Scattering** (1989)

Sandy Denny: *Rendezvous** (1976)

Durutti Column: *The Return of the Durutti Column** (1980), *Another Setting* (1983), *Without Mercy* (1984), *The City of Our Lady*** (1987)

Echo and The Bunnymen: Jimmy Brown, Bedbugs and Ballyhoo, Over Your Shoulder (1985)

Godley & Creme: *Consequences** (1977)

Graham Gouldman: *Animalympics** (1980)

Happy Mondays: *Bummed*** (1988)

Justin Hayward: Blue Guitar* (1974)

Kitchens of Distinction: Quick as Rainbows (1990)

Hotlegs: Neanderthal Man (1970), *Thinks: School Stinks* (1971)

The Icicle Works: Hollow Horse (1985)

Inspiral Carpets: Island Head** (1990), Beast Inside (1991)

James: Jimone (1983), *James II* (1985)

Joy Division: *Unknown Pleasures* (1979), Transmission (1979), Love Will Tear Us Apart (1980)

Syd Lawrence Orchestra: all albums recorded 1969 to 1984

John Lees: *A Major Fancy** (1972)

Magazine: *Magic, Murder and the Weather*** (1981)

Mandalaband: *Eye of Wendor* (1978)

Magna Carta: *Midnight Blue* (1982)

Mike McGear: *Woman* (1972), *McGear* (1974) produced by Paul McCartney

The Mock Turtles: *Turtle Soup** (1990)

Mud: *It's Better Than Working** (1976)

Pauline Murray: *Pauline Murray and the Invisible Girls* (1980), *Pauline Murray* (1981)

New Order: *Movement* (1981)

OMD: Electricity** (1979)

Oscar: *Oscar* (1974), *Twilight Asylum* (1975), *Cobblestone Heroes* (1976)

Quando Quango: *Pigs & Battleships* (1985)

Ramases: *Space Hymns* (1971)

The Ramones: *Pleasant Dreams** (1981)

Sad Café: *Fanx Ta Ra** (1977), *Misplaced Ideals** (1978), *Olé* (1981)

The Scaffold: *Sold Out* (1975)

Neil Sedaka: *Solitaire* (1972), *The Tra-La Days Are Over* (1973)

Sisters of Mercy: Body and Soul (1984), *First and Last and Always* (1985)

The Smiths: Hand in Glove, This Charming Man (1983)

Eric Stewart: *Frooty Rooties** (1982)

Stone Roses: So Young** (1985), *Garage Flower** (1996)

U2: 11 O'Clock Tick Tock (1980)

Wax: *Magnetic Heaven** (1986)

Notable records recorded/mixed at Strawberry Studios South

10cc: *Deceptive Bends* (1977), *Bloody Tourists* (1978), *Look Hear?* (1980), *Ten Out of 10** (1981)

Gary Brooker: *No More Fear of Flying** (1979)

China Crisis: *Difficult Shapes & Passive Rhythms** (1981)

Gonzales: Move it to the Music (1979)

Graham Gouldman: Sunburn (1979), *Animalympics** (1980)

Justin Hayward: Goodbye (1980)

Paul McCartney: *Tug of War** (1982)

The Moody Blues: *The Present* (1983)

Patrick Moraz: *Time Code** (1984)

The Police: *Zenyatta Mondatta*** (1980)

Gerry Rafferty: *Sleepwalking** (1981)

The Ramones: *Pleasant Dreams*** (1981)

Cliff Richard: *Now You See Me, Now You Don't* (1982), *Silver* (1983), *Dressed for the Occasion*** (1983)

Sad Café: *Facades* (1979), *Sad Café* (1980)

Shakatak: *Drivin' Hard** (1981)

Eric Stewart: *Girls* (1980), *Frooty Rooties** (1982)

The Strawbs: *Heartbreak Hill* (1978)

Thompson Twins: Make Believe (1981)

Rick Wakeman: *Sea Airs** (1989)

Hit Factory

Some 112 hit singles around the world have been written (w), produced (p) and/or performed (m) by Eric Stewart [ES], Graham Gouldman [GG], Lol Creme [LC], Kevin Godley [KG] or All [10cc]. Here's a list of the hits, artists and highest global charting positions

KEY: *Date* / Song (Artist) / Peak (Country) / 10cc member (m) musician, (p) producer (w) writer

Jul '63 / Hello Josephine (Wayne Fontana & The Mindbenders) No.46 (UK) ES (m)

May '64 / Stop, Look and Listen (Wayne Fontana & The Mindbenders), No.37 (UK), ES (m)

Oct '64 / Um, Um, Um, Um, Um, Um (Wayne Fontana & The Mindbenders), No.5 (UK), ES (m)

Feb '65 / The Game of Love (Wayne Fontana & The Mindbenders), No.1 (US), ES (m)

Mar '65 / For Your Love (The Yardbirds), No.1 (CAN), GG (w)

Jun '65 / Heart Full of Soul (The Yardbirds), No.2 (UK, CAN), GG (w)

Jun '65 / Just A Little Bit Too Late (Wayne Fontana & The Mindbenders), No.20 (UK), ES (m)

Sep '65 / She Needs Love (Wayne Fontana & The Mindbenders), No.32 (UK), ES (m)

Sep '65 / Look Through Any Window (The Hollies), No.3 (CAN), GG (w)

Oct '65 / Evil Hearted You (The Yardbirds), No.3 (UK), GG (w)

Jan '66 / A Groovy Kind of Love (The Mindbenders), No.2 (UK, US), ES (m)

Feb '66 / Listen People (Herman's Hermits), No.3 (US, AUS), GG (w)

May '66 / Can't Live With You, Can't Live Without You (The Mindbenders), No.28 (UK), ES (m)

May '66 / You Stole My Love (Mike Furber), No.36 (AUS), GG (w)

Jun '66 / Bus Stop (The Hollies) No.1 (CAN, SWE), GG (w)

Aug '66 / Ashes to Ashes (The Mindbenders), No.14 (UK), ES (m)

Oct '66 / No Milk Today (Herman's Hermits), No.1 (AUS, NET), GG (w)

Nov '66 / Behind The Door (Cher), No.74 (CAN), GG (w)

Dec '66 / East West (Herman's Hermits), No.5 (NZ), GG (w)

Dec '66 / Pamela, Pamela (Wayne Fontana), No.5 (AUS), GG (w)

Apr '67 / Going Home (Normie Rowe), No.11 (AUS), GG (w)

Aug '67 / Tallyman (Jeff Beck), No.30 (UK), GG (w)

Aug '67 / The Impossible Years (Wayne Fontana), No.72 (AUS), GG (w)

Sep '67 / The Letter (The Mindbenders), No.42 (UK), ES (m), GG (p)

Jul '69 / Sausalito (Ohio Express), No.64 (AUS), GG (w)

Jun '70 / Neanderthal Man (Hotlegs), No.1 (FRA), ES/KG/LC (w, m, p)

Oct '70 / Neanderthal Man (Idle Race), No.2 (ARG), ES/KG/LC (w)

Dec '70 / The Man From Nazareth (John Paul Joans), No.25 (UK), ES/
      KG/LC (w, m, p)

Apr '71 / Susan's Tuba (Freddie and The Dreamers), No.1 (FRA), GG (w)

Sep '72 / Donna (10cc), No.2 (UK, IRE, NET), 10cc (w, m, p)

Nov '72 / Johnny Don't Do It (10cc), No.21 (NZ), 10cc (w, m, p)

Nov '72 / Beautiful You (Neil Sedaka), No.43 (UK) 10cc (m)

Feb '73 / That's When The Music Takes Me (Neil Sedaka), No.18 (UK),
      10cc (m)

May '73 / Rubber Bullets (10cc), No.1 (UK, IRE), 10cc (w, m, p)

Jun '73 / Standing On The Inside (Neil Sedaka), No.26 (UK),
      10cc (m, p)

Aug '73 / The Dean and I (10cc), No.1 (IRE), 10cc (w, m, p)

Aug '73 / Our Last Song Together (Neil Sedaka), No.31 (UK), 10cc (m, p)

May '74 / The Wall Street Shuffle (10cc), No.1 (NET), 10cc (w, m, p)

Jun '74 / Liverpool Lou (The Scaffold), No.7 (UK), LC (m)

Aug '74 / Silly Love (10cc), No.7 (NET), 10cc (w, m, p)

Apr '75 / Life Is A Minestrone (10cc), No.6 (FRA), 10cc (w, m, p)

May '75 / I'm Not In Love (10cc), No.1 (UK, IRE, CAN, FRA),
      10cc (w, m, p)

Oct '75 / Blue Guitar (Justin Hayward & John Lodge), No.8 (UK),
      10cc (m, p)

Dec '75 / Art For Art's Sake (10cc), No.4 (IRE), 10cc (w, m, p)

Apr '76 / I'm Mandy Fly Me (10cc), No.3 (IRE), 10cc (w, m, p)

Dec '76 / The Things We Do For Love (10cc), No.2 (CAN, IRE),
      ES/GG (w, m, p)

Apr '77 / Good Morning Judge (10cc), No.5 (UK), ES/GG (w, m, p)

Aug '77 / People In Love (10cc), No.40 (US), ES/GG (w, m, p)

Sep '78 / Dreadlock Holiday (10cc), No.1 (UK, BEL, NET, NZ),
      ES/GG (w, m, p)

Jan '79 / For You and I (10cc), No.82 (CAN), ES/GG (w, m, p)

Jan '79 / From Rochdale To Ocho Rios (10cc), No.65 (AUS),
      ES/GG (w, m, p)

Jun '79 / Sunburn (Graham Gouldman), No.26 (AUS), GG (w, m, p)

Sep '79 / Every Day Hurts (Sad Café), No.3 (UK), ES (p)

Jan '80 / Strange Little Girl (Sad Café), No.32 (UK), ES (p)

Feb '80 / An Englishman In New York (Godley & Creme), No.4 (BEL),
    KG/LC (w, m, p)

Mar '80 / One Two Five (10cc), No.9 (NOR), ES/GG (w, m, p)

Mar '80 / My Oh My (Sad Café), No.14 (UK), ES (p)

Jun '80 / Nothing Left Toulouse (Sad Café), No.62 (UK), ES (p)

Sep '80 / La Di Da (Sad Café), No.41 (UK), ES (p)

Dec '80 / I'm In Love Again (Sad Café), No.40 (UK), ES (p)

Sep '81 / Under Your Thumb (Godley & Creme), No.3 (UK),
    KG/LC (w, m, p)

Nov '81 / Wedding Bells (Godley & Creme), No.7 (UK), KG/LC (w, m, p)

Nov '81 / Don't Turn Me Away (10cc), No.38 (CAN), ES/GG (w, m, p)

Mar '82 / Klactoveesedstein (Blue Rondo A La Turk), No.50 (UK), KG/
    LC (p)

Jul '82 / Take It Away (Paul McCartney), No.7 (NET), ES (m)

Aug '82 / Run Away (10cc), No.50 (UK), ES/GG (w, m, p)

Oct '82 / Tug of War (Paul McCartney), No.53 (UK, US), ES (m)

Apr '83 / 24 Hours (10cc), No.78 (UK), ES/GG (w, m, p)

Jul '83 / Feel The Love (10cc), No.7 (NET), ES/GG (w, m, p)

Oct '83 / Food For Thought (10cc), No.18 (NET), ES/GG (w, m, p)

Oct '83 / Say, Say, Say (Paul McCartney), No.1 (US, CAN), ES (m)

Dec '83 / Pipes of Peace (Paul McCartney), No.1 (UK), ES (m)

Jan '84 / So Bad (Paul McCartney), No.23 (US), ES (m)

Oct '84 / No More Lonely Nights (Paul McCartney), No.2 (UK, IRE),
    ES (m)

Mar '85 /I Won't Let You Go (Agnetha Fältskog), No.6 (SWE),
    ES (w, m, p)

Mar '85 / Cry (Godley & Creme), No.8 (GER), KG/LC (w, m)

May '85 / One Way Love (Agnetha Fältskog), No.37 (GER), ES (m, p)

Jun '85 / You'll Never Walk Alone (The Crowd), No.1 (UK), GG (p)

Nov '85 / Spies Like Us (Paul McCartney), No.7 (US), ES (m)

Apr '86 / Right Between Your Eyes (Wax), No.1 (SPA), GG (w, m)

Sep '86 / Press (Paul McCartney), No.21 (US), ES (m)

Oct '86 / Stranglehold (Paul McCartney), No.81 (US), ES (w, m)

Nov '86 / Pretty Little Head (Paul McCartney), No.29 (BEL), ES (w, m)

Dec '86 / Only Love Remains (Paul McCartney), No.7 (CAN), ES (m)

Aug '87 / I'm Not In Love (Johnny Logan), No.6 (BEL), ES/GG (w)

Sep '87 / Bridge To Your Heart (Wax), No.3 (BEL), GG (w, m)

Nov '87 / American English (Wax), No.29 (BEL), GG (w, m)

Jan '88 / A Little Piece of Heaven (Godley & Creme), No.12 (BEL), KG/
   LC (w, m, p)

Oct '89 / Anchors Aweigh (Wax), No.95 (UK), GG (w, m)

Mar '90 / Sailing (Rock Against Repatriation), No.89 (UK), KG (m)

Mar '90 / Soledad (Roé), No.15 (FRA), ES/GG (w)

Aug '90 / I'm Not In Love (Will to Power), No.7 (US), ES/GG (w)

May '92 / Woman In Love (10cc), No.55 (NET), ES/GG (w, m)

Jul '92 / Cry (Lisa Edwards), No.5 (AUS), KG/LC (w)

Apr '93 / I'm Not In Love (The Pretenders), No.74 (CAN), ES/GG (w)

Jan '94 / Hip Hop Holiday (3 The Hard Way), No.1 (NZ), ES/GG (w)

Nov '94 / If I Only Knew (Tom Jones), No.11 (UK), LC (m)

Dec '94 / Wherever You Are (Michael Ball), No.88 (UK), GG (w)

Mar '95 / Everybody Up! (Glam Metal Detectives), No.29 (UK),
   LC (w, m, p)

Mar '95 / I'm Not In Love (Acoustic Session) (10cc), No.29 (UK),
   ES/GG (w, m, p)

Feb '96 / The Things We Do for Love (Amy Grant), No.41 (CAN),
   ES/GG (w)

Dec '96 / In Your Wildest Dreams (Tina Turner), No.2 (A), LC (m)

Jul '97 / I'm Not In Love (Fun Lovin' Criminals), No.12 (UK), ES/GG (w)

Sep '97 / The Way I'm Feeling Tonight (Paul Carrack), No.84 (UK),
   GG (w)

Jun '99 / Stronger (Gary Barlow), No.11 (FIN), GG (w)

Jun '99 / Metaforce (Art of Noise), No.53 (UK), LC (w, m, p)

Aug '02 / Love Da Sunshine (Intenso Project), No.22 (UK), ES/GG (w)

Nov '03 / In a State (UNKLE), No.44 (UK), GG (m)

Aug '04 / Cry (Kealer), No.84 (UK), KG/LC (w)

Feb '05 / Treat Me Like A Woman (Lisa Stansfield), No.36 (A), LC (m)

May '06 / I'm With Stupid (Pet Shop Boys), No.8 (UK), LC (m)

Jul '07 / I Don't Like Reggae-ton (Pachanga), No.34 (GER), ES/GG (w)

BIBLIOGRAPHY

THE MAJORITY OF THE SOURCE MATERIAL FOR THIS BOOK IS TAKEN FROM exclusive interviews conducted by the author with Kevin Godley, Graham Gouldman, Eric Stewart, Paul Burgess, Rick Fenn, Harvey Lisberg, Jonathan King, Zeb White and Aubrey Powell.

Thanks to David Scott for sharing his recollections of working with Eric Stewart with his band Hearts and Minds.

Thanks to Simon Barber and Brian O'Connor for allowing me to use material from their excellent *Sodajerker on Songwriting* podcast series, including interviews with Kevin Godley, Graham Gouldman, Neil Sedaka, Ben Folds Five and Blossoms.

Thanks also to John Birch for giving me access to his interviews with Phil Thornalley and Dave Brewis.

Other important source material for the book includes:

George Tremlett: *The 10cc Story* (1976)

Hipgnosis: *Walk Away René* (1978)

Alan Lawson: *It Happened in Manchester* (1991)

BBC Radio 2: *Well Above Average* (1995)

BBC Radio 2: *The Record Producers* (2009)

Howard Sounes: *Fab: An Intimate Life of Paul McCartney* (2010)

Malcolm Wagner: *George Best and Me* (2010)

BBC Four: *I'm Not in Love – The Story of 10cc* (2015)

Kevin Godley: *Spacecake* (2015)

Eric Stewart: *Things I Do For Love* (2017)

Aubrey Powell: *Vinyl. Album. Cover. Art* (2017)

Paul Hanley: *Leave The Capital* (2017)

Harvey Lisberg: www.harveylisberg.com

Kevin Godley: www.kevin-godley.com

Other source material:

Record Mirror: interview with The Mindbenders by Norman Jopling (20/8/1966)

Newsweek: Male Plumage '68 (25/11/1968)

Melody Maker: Hotlegs interview by Andrew Means (25/7/1970)

NME: interview with James Johnson (21/10/1972)

Zig Zag: interview with Neil Sedaka by John Tobler (4/1973)

Melody Maker: interview with Richard Williams (14/4/1973)

Record Mirror: interview with Mike Beatty (2/6/1973)

NME: review of *10cc* by Ian MacDonald (28/7/1973)

Melody Maker: review of *10cc* by Richard Williams (28/7/1973)

Record Mirror: review of *10cc* (28/7/1973)

NME: interview by Ian MacDonald (11/8/1973)

Record Mirror: interview by Mike Beatty (25/8/1973)

Record Mirror: Douglas Palace Lido concert review by Danny Wilson (8/9/1973)

Melody Maker: Swindon Brunel Rooms concert review by Kevin Halligan (8/9/1973)

Melody Maker: interview by Geoff Brown (22/9/1973)

Rolling Stone: interview by Paul Gambaccini (8/11/1973)

Rolling Stone: review of *10cc* by Greg Shaw (22/11/1973)

Disc: review of The Worst Band in the World by Rosemary Horide (19/1/1974)

Sounds: interview by Bill Henderson (9/2/1974)

Melody Maker: interview by Geoff Brown (16/2/1974)

NME: interview by Nick Kent (16/2/1974)

Connie De Neve: *Sheet Music* press release (5/1974)

Melody Maker: review of *Sheet Music* by Colin Irwin (18/5/1974)

NME: review of *Sheet Music* by Ian MacDonald (18/5/1974)

Disc: review of *Sheet Music* (18/5/1974)

Record Mirror: review of *Sheet Music* by Chris Poole (25/5/1974)

Melody Maker: interview by Geoff Brown (25/5/1974)

Sounds: review of *Sheet Music* (25/5/1974)

Record Mirror: interview by John Beattie (1/6/1974)

NME: interview by Steve Turner (29/6/1974)

Disc: interview by Andy Blackford (6/7/1974)

NME: article on the 'Gizmo' by Stan Henderson (20/7/1974)

Sounds: review of Silly Love by John Peel (24/8/1974)

Melody Maker: interview by Geoff Brown (12/10/1974)

Melody Maker: Isleworth concert review by Andrew Warshaw (23/11/1974)

Melody Maker: review of *The Original Soundtrack* by Colin Irwin (1/3/1975)

NME: review of *The Original Soundtrack* by Charles Shaar Murray (1/3/1975)

NME: interview by Charles Shaar Murray (15/3/1975)

Record Mirror: review of Manchester Free Trade Hall concert by Martin Thorpe (15/3/1975)

Melody Maker: review of Life is a Minestrone by Colin Irwin (29/3/1975)

Melody Maker: review of Hammersmith Odeon concert by Geoff Brown (29/3/1975)

Melody Maker: interview with Karl Dallas (5/4/1975)

International Musician: interview by Caroll Moore (5/1975)

Rolling Stone: review of *The Original Soundtrack* by Ken Barnes (19/6/1975)

Disc: interview by Rosemary Horide (28/6/1975)

Melody Maker: review of Cardiff Castle concert by Brian Harrigan (19/7/1975)

NME: review of Cardiff Castle concert by Charles Shaar Murray (19/7/1975)

Melody Maker: interview by Harry Doherty (20/9/1975)

Rolling Stone: interview by Paul Gambaccini (25/10/1975)

New York Times: review of New York Beacon Theater concert by John Rockwell (27/10/1975)

Los Angeles Times: review of Santa Monica Civic Center concert by Richard Cromelin (11/1975)

Record Mirror: interview by David Hancock (13/12/1975)

NME: article by Charles Shaar Murray (20/12/1975)

Melody Maker: interview by Chris Charlesworth (27/12/1975)

International Musician: article on Strawberry Studios (1/1976)

Melody Maker: review of *How Dare You!* by Geoff Brown (10/1/1976)

NME: review of *How Dare You!* by Pete Erskine (10/1/1976)

Record Mirror: review of *How Dare You!* (10/1/1976)

NME: interview by Andrew Tyler (7/2/1976)

Melody Maker: review of Sheffield City Hall concert by Ben Nielsen (7/2/1976)

Streetlife: interview by Bill Henderson (21/2/1976)

Melody Maker: article on censorship (21/2/1976)

Melody Maker: interview by Geoff Brown (28/2/1976)

Zig Zag: interview by John Tobler (4/1976)

Melody Maker: interview by Harry Doherty (7/4/1976)

Record Mirror: review of Glasgow Apollo concert by David Brown
    (1/5/1976)

Sounds: review of Knebworth concert (28/8/76)

Beat Instrumental: interview by Peter Douglas (9/1976)

International Musician: interview by Ray Hammond (11/1976)

Melody Maker: interview with Eric Stewart and Graham Gouldman by
    Geoff Brown (22/1/1977)

Sounds: review of *Deceptive Bends* by Hugh Fielder (30/4/1977)

Melody Maker: review of *Deceptive Bends* by Colin Irwin (30/4/1977)

Record Mirror: review of *Deceptive Bends* by Jim Evans (30/4/1977)

NME: review of *Deceptive Bends* by Phil McNeil (7/5/1977)

NME: Good Morning Judge video review by John Bell (7/5/1977)

Record Mirror: interview by Tony Bradman (7/5/1977)

Melody Maker: review of Glasgow Apollo concert by Harry Doherty
    (4/6/1977)

Melody Maker: interview by Harry Doherty (11/6/1977)

Sounds: review of Hammersmith Odeon concert by Hugh Fielder
    (25/6/1977)

NME: review of Hammersmith Odeon concert by Nick Kent (25/6/1977)

Circus: interview by Kris Nicholson (21/7/1977)

Rolling Stone: interview by Paul Gambaccini (28/7/1977)

Adelaide Advertiser: review of Adelaide Apollo Stadium concert by Ian
    Meikle (21/9/1977)

Melody Maker: review of *Consequences* by Harry Doherty (24/9/1977)

Paul Gambaccini: *Consequences* sleevenotes (10/1977)

Sounds: review of *Consequences* by Tony Mitchell (15/10/1977)

NME: review of *Consequences* by Phil McNeill (29/10/1977)

Record Mirror: review of *Live and Let Live* by Jim Evans (3/12/1977)

Los Angeles Times: interview with Godley and Creme (4/12/1977)

De Waarheid: review of Rotterdam De Doelen concert (7/12/1977)

Washington Post: review of *Consequences* by Mark Kernis (9/12/1977)

10cc Appreciation Society: newsletter (2/1978)

Studio Sound: article on Strawberry Studios (5/1978)

10cc Appreciation Society: newsletter (6/1978)

Record Mirror: review of Dreadlock Holiday (29/7/1978)

Melody Maker: interview by Colin Irwin (26/8/1978)

Record Mirror: interview by Robin Smith (2/9/1978)

Record Mirror: review of *Bloody Tourists* by Jon Frewin (2/9/1978)

Melody Maker: Liverpool Empire concert review by Colin Irwin (9/1978)

NME: *Bloody Tourists* review by Graham Lock (16/9/1978)

Sounds: Birmingham Odeon concert review by Hugh Fielder (16/9/1978)

The Evening Standard: interview by Barry Cain (9/1978)

Melody Maker: review of *Bloody Tourists* by Harry Doherty (23/9/1978)

Sounds: review of *Bloody Tourists* by Hugh Fielder (23/9/1978)

Melody Maker: Wembley Arena concert review by Karl Dallas (9/1978)

Sound International: interview by Ralph Denyer (10/1978)

Los Angeles Times: interview by Richard Cromelin (29/10/1978)

Circus: interview (7/11/1978)

Record Mirror: Wembley Conference Centre concert review by Mike
   Nicholls (6/1/1979)

Trouser Press: interview by Peter Olafson and Jim Green (4/1979)

Beat International: interview by Tony Horkins (7/1979)

Record Mirror: review of *Greatest Hits* by Mike Nicholls (1/12/1979)

Capital Radio: *Meet the Music Makers* (12/1979)

Tony Jaspar: *The 70's A Book of Records* (1980)

Melody Maker: review of *Look Hear?* by Colin Irwin (29/3/1980)

Sounds: review of *Look Hear?* by Phil Sutcliffe (29/3/1980)

Record Mirror: interview by Mike Nicholls (4/1980)

Sounds: Newcastle City Hall concert review by Ian Ravendale (5/1980)

Ian Ravendale: interview with Justin Hayward (6/1980)

Kevin Godley and Lol Creme: *The Fun Starts Here* (1981)

NME: review of Pleasant Dreams by Cynthia Rose (11/7/1981)

Melody Maker: interview with Godley and Creme by Colin Irwin
   (17/10/1981)

International Musician: interview with Eric Stewart by Max Kay (10/1981)

Music Week: interview by Geoff Goy (18/2/1982)

Music Week: review of *Frooty Rooties* (23/10/1982)

Record Collector: article by David Thompson (3/84)

Record Collector: article by David Thompson (4/84)

Billboard: interview by Paul Grein (12/4/86)

MTV: Paul McCartney: Rock 'n' Roll Legend (8/1986)

Q: review of *Press to Play* by Mark Ellen (10/1986)

Q: interview with Paul McCartney by Chris Salewicz (10/1986)

Rolling Stone: review of *Press to Play* by Antony DeCurtis (23/10/1986)

Johnny Rogan: *Starmakers and Svengalis* (1988)

Q: review of *Goodbye Blue Sky* by Phil Sutcliffe (2/1988)

Pulse: interview by Iain Blair (4/1988)

Q: interview by Phil Sutcliffe (6/1988)

Guitarist: interview with Eric Stewart by Tony Hicks (2/1989)

Replay: interview by Chris White (4/1992)

Rock Compact Disc Magazine: interview by Paul Lester (5/1992)

Rock World: interview, and review of *Meanwhile*, by Colin Irwin (6/1992)

Daily Mail: interview with Graham Gouldman by Moira Petty (4/6/1993)

The Times: review of Hammersmith Apollo concert by Adrian Deevoy (18/6/1993)

Independent: interview by Jim White (2/1995)

Record Collector: interview by Peter Doggett (6/1995)

Mojo: interview by Sylvie Simmons (7/1995)

Guitarist: interview by Tim Slater (8/1995)

Q: review of *Mirror, Mirror* by Andrew Collins (3/1995)

Rob Steen: interview with Graham Gouldman (1995)

Q: review of *King Biscuit Flower Hour* by Kit Aiken (2/1996)

Uncut: reviews of *How Dare You*, *Deceptive Bends* and *Bloody Tourists* by Paul Lester (4/1997)

Mojo: *The Very Best of 10cc* review by Chris Ingham (4/1997)

Richard Branson: *Losing My Virginity* (1998)

Uncut: review of *Consequences* and interviews by Kit Aiken (3/1998)

Storm Thorgerson and Aubrey Powell: *100 Best Album Covers* (1999)

Ira Robbins: *Pleasant Dreams*: reissue sleevenotes (2002)

BBC Radio Wales: interview with Eric Stewart by Alan Thompson (2003)

The Sunday Times: interview with Eric Stewart (13/4/2003)

The Sunday Times: interview with Eric Stewart (30/5/2004)

Christopher Sandford: *McCartney* (2005)

Randolph Michaels: *Flashbacks to Happiness: Eighties Music Revisited* (2005)

Pitchfork: interview with Kaiser Chiefs (4/4/2005)

Sound on Sound: interview with Eric Stewart by Richard Buskin (6/2005)

Record Collector: interview by Terry Staunton (12/2006)

The Word: interview with Kevin Godley and Graham Gouldman by Paul Du Noyer (3/2007)

The Times: review of Shepherd's Bush Empire concert by David Sinclair (3/2007)

Storm Thorgerson and Aubrey Powell: *For The Love of Vinyl* (2008)

The Daily Telegraph: review of London Indigo2 concert by David Cheal (5/2008)

Magnetic Heaven: reissue sleevenotes (2009)

Keith Altham: The Yardbirds and the Cereal Killer (2009)

Del Newman: *A Touch from God* (2010)

Croydon Municipal: interview by Bob Stanley (2/11/2011)

Singing Bassist: interview by Anders Lundquist (20/11/2011)

Prog: article by Paul Lester (12/2011)

Vintage TV: interview with Lol Creme (2012)

Peter Hook: *Unknown Pleasures* (2012)

Jewish Chronicle: article by Paul Lester (27/12/2012)

Graham Nash: *Wild Tales* (2013)

Mojo: review of *Space Hymns* by Martin Aston (5/2013)

Record Collector: Roger Taylor interview by Paul Lester (12/2013)

John Lydon: *Anger Is An Energy* (2014)

Songwriting: interview with Trevor Horn (24/2/2014)

Prog: article by Malcom Dome (6/2015)

Classic Rock: The making of I'm Mandy Fly Me by Dave Ling (9/2015)

The Guardian: review of *I'm Not In Love: The Story of 10cc* by Sam Wollaston (5/12/2015)

Shindig: interview by Michael Bjorn (4/2016)

Uncut: The making of Rubber Bullets (7/2016)

Uncut: LCD Soundsystem interview by John Lewis (9/5/2017)

Malcolm Wyatt interview with Graham Gouldman (21/9/2017)

Wall Street Journal: interview by Marc Myers (25/11/2017)

Classic Rock: interview with Paul Lester (12/2017)

Classic Bands: Hugh Padgham interview by Gary James

Mark Radcliffe: *Crossroads* (2019)

INDEX

ROLL OF HONOUR

The publishers gratefully acknowledge the contribution of everyone listed below, whose generous support helped bring this project to fruition.

Ulla Åkerström, Darren Allen, Gregory M. Alonzo, Cord M. Altes, Omar S. Amin, Grahame Anderson, Olov Andersson, Brian Andrews-Rowley, Hubert Annen, Janet Arbuthnott, Bev Ashwell, Bruce Attenborrow, Stevie Axeman, David Ayre, Jan Backenroth, Hans Baeyens, Richard Banham, Joe Barbour, Willy Barden, Dark Barker, Mike Barrington, Stuart Batsford, Frans Baunsgaard, Mel Beattie, Philip Bentley, Robyn Bierton, Big bad Pad, Finn Bjelke, Lysander Bjølgerud Wear, Michael Björn, Christine Bonner, Rob Bousfield, Hans Brakenhoff, Virginia Bravo, Stian Brekke, Dave Brennan, Desiree Bromwich Hughes, John Bruinsma, Fabrizio Burelli, Mark Bursa, Paddy Butler, Mike Butter, Andrew Button, Andrew Cakebread, Nigel Calderley, Maria Canderudh, Luca Caretto, Gary Carolan, Barry Carr, Gary Carter, Jan Cees Noord, Henrik Thor Christensen, Kenneth S. Clapton, Pete Clarke, Al Clewlow, Russ Clewlow, Andrew Cole, Richard Collins, Brian Collishaw, Leslie John Collison, Nigel Collyer, Mark Colton, John A. Convey, Donald Roy Cooper, G. S. Cooper, Shaun Nicolas Corry, David Coulter, Mike Crane, John Mark Crosby, Hervé Dandois, John Davies, Paul Davies, Podge Davies, Campbell Devine, Fernando Di Donato, Steve Doty, Tom Drysdale, Paul E. Dunne, Phil Duscovitch-Davis, Andrew Dutton, Rosemary Ebling, Daniel Eggenberger, Bosse Ehnsiö, Robert Eiba, Jacques Engler, Dale Everett, Calum Ewen, Brian Fagan, Glyn Fearby, Peter William Ferguson, Niels Flintrup, Ali Foeger, David Forrester, Stephen Foster, Neil Fox, Rainer Frilund, Nick Fuller, Nick Gazeley, Jaak Geerts, Lars Wilcken Gertsen, Dave Gilbert, Tom Gillitt, Gjalt, Uncle Reet Glass, Jose Gomez, Dave Goodall, Lynne F. Graham, David Green, Sue Green, Anthony Greenman, Peter Gustafsson, Dave Guyers, Graeme Hammond, Stephen Hammonds, Sarah Hampson, Ralph Hansel, Bjarne Hansen, Jonn-Stian Hansen, Helen Harland, Zoe Harris, Paul Harrison, Greg Hart-Davies, Peter Haworth, Graham Heeks, Noch Hendrik, Michael Herbert, Marc Herold, John Heseltine, Colin Hesketh, Paul Hibbard, Hillyfaekillie, Ulf Hoberg, Grant Hobson, Ruben Hoffbeck, David Hoffman, Kenneth Holm, Mike Holt, Lee Hopkins, Henrik Houborg, Colvin Houston, Angela Howe, Bob Howell, Dr. Mark Hughes, Frank Hull, Gareth Hunt, Mark Incley, Dave Ingram, Edgar Jakobs, Tony Jaras, Peter

Jenkins, Lars Johansson, Russell Jones, Vivian Jones, Wim de Jong, Ruud Jongens, Phil Judge, Paul Kaufman, Inoue Kazuhiko, Connie, Chris & Andrea Keen, Richard Alan Keeves, Martin Kelly, Paul Kerr, Phil Kirk, Jo Kjorstad, Peder Kleis, Inge Kuijt, Sunil Kumar, Jerry Lamberth, Jim Lawn, Jeff Lawrence, Peter Leeson, Toni Lehto, Graham Anthony Lever, Tim Levey, Paul Lewis, David Lightfoot, Graham Long, Alexey Luganskiy, Phil Lukes, PerPer Lundberg, Stewart Mackie, Sean Macreavy, Patrick Maes, Per Magnusson, Mark Mahoney, Maurice Manington, Jim Markey, Marleentje, Richard Matthews, Robert McAlpine, Alex McCambley, Tam McCrae, Calum John McGregor, Stephen McKay, Patrick James McManus, Alan McQuatters, Steve Mercer, David Middleton, José Miguel, Michael Mohan, Eric Montfort, Thomas Monument, David Morgan, Wayne Morgan, David Morris, Kate Mulcahey, Stephen Murphy, Mike Nawas, Martin Nielsen, øivind nilsen, Eugene O'Clark, Patrick O'Neill, Ann Oakley, Atsushi Ono, Craig Owen, Fred Owen, Akihiro 'Iriomote' Oyama, Stuart Padmore, Phil Parker, Stephen Pearson, Mikko Pellinen, Graham Penson, Doug Perkins-Ball, Torbjorn Pettersson, Paul Phillips, John Pike, David Pinder, Claus Poulsen, Simon Poulter, Rich Price, Charles Priestley, Paul Rab, Steve Redford, Norman Reid, Evyatar Reiter, Gareth Richards, Ben Richardson, Carolien Rietveld, Thomas Riha, Murray Robbins, Paul Robinson, Michael Roesmann, Lauretta Roper, Fred Rosenkamp, Tuomas Ruikka, Ian Rushbury, Miles Salisbury, Rickard Sandby, Dick Sax, Hans Scheffler, Ronald Schepper, Michael Schoeneburg, Malcolm C. Searles, Jon Sharp, Karen Shaw, Pete Shaw, Peter Michael Sieker, Karen Simpson, Peter Sinnige, Joe Skade, Hans Sloot, Graham Smith, Rob Smith, Simon Smith, Clark Snyder, Adam Southward, Gareth Spero, Rob Stanley, John Steele, Dr. Uwe Ingo Steinorth, Christopher Stephenson, Mikael Stigell, Tony Still, Peter Stillwell, Howard Stone, Ian Street, Mark Poul Stubbs, Michael Svensson, Alan Sweeney, Chris Taylor, Rob Tijdeman, Stuart Todd, Graham Tomlinson, Steven Toomey, Steve Truman, Roman Tschopp, Knut Tungesvik, Andrew Turner, Nicholas David Turner, David Twitchett, Uncle Bernard and The Loose Change Buskers, John Upton, Martijn Vaassen, Bernard Vallee, Henk van der Sluis, Ronald van Klooster, Dave Verey, Rudy Vervecken, John Waddington, Laurence Wake, David Ward, Iris Weatherley, Matt Signia Alpha Webster, Daniel Werkelin, Micke Werkelin, Sarah Whelan, Jack White, Peter C. Whitfield, Gudrun Widmark, Gary Wilson, Jonathan Wilson, John Wilson, Esa Wirta, Alan V. Wiseman, David Wood, Melanie Wood, Phil Wood, Jim Woodford, Kingsley Wright, Lorraine Young, Philip T. Young.

THE COMPLETE SHORT STORIES

The Works of Patrick O'Brian

The Aubrey/Maturin Novels
in order of publication

MASTER AND COMMANDER
POST CAPTAIN
HMS SURPRISE
THE MAURITUS COMMAND
DESOLATION ISLAND
THE FORTUNE OF WAR
THE SURGEON'S MATE
THE IONIAN MISSION
TREASON'S HARBOUR
THE FAR SIDE OF THE WORLD
THE REVERSE OF THE MEDAL
THE LETTER OF MARQUE
THE THIRTEEN-GUN SALUTE
THE NUTMEG OF CONSOLATION
CLARISSA OAKES
THE WINE-DARK SEA
THE COMMODORE
THE YELLOW ADMIRAL
THE HUNDRED DAYS
BLUE AT THE MIZZEN
THE FINAL UNFINISHED VOYAGE OF JACK AUBREY

Nautical Novels

THE GOLDEN OCEAN
THE UNKNOWN SHORE

Other Novels

CAESAR
HUSSEIN
TESTIMONIES
THE CATALANS
THE ROAD TO SAMARCAND
RICHARD TEMPLE

Short Fiction

BEASTS ROYAL
COLLECTED SHORT STORIES

Non-fiction

MEN-OF-WAR: LIFE IN NELSON'S NAVY
PICASSO
JOSEPH BANKS

Anthology

A BOOK OF VOYAGES

Poetry

THE UNCERTAIN LAND AND OTHER POEMS

PATRICK O'BRIAN

The Complete Short Stories

HarperCollins*Publishers*

HarperCollins*Publishers* Ltd
1 London Bridge Street,
London SE1 9GF
www.harpercollins.co.uk

HarperCollins*Publishers*
Macken House, 39/40 Mayor Street Upper
Dublin 1, D01 C9W8, Ireland

Published by HarperCollins*Publishers* 2023

1

These stories were mostly written in the first half of the twentieth century
and characters sometimes use offensive language or otherwise are described
or behave in ways that reflect the prejudices and insensitivities of the period.

A catalogue record for this book is available from the British Library.

ISBN: 978-0-00-852543-9

Set in Adobe Caslon Pro

Printed and bound in the UK using 100% Renewable Electricity
by CPI Group (UK) Ltd

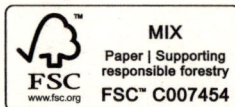

Contents

CONTENTS

Foreword

My introduction to Patrick O'Brian's short stories occurred during my first visit to my parents' home at Collioure in 1955. My stepfather Patrick and my mother lived in fairly dire but happy poverty in an upstairs flat (actually a room – I slept in a sort of cupboard) close to the harbour. Patrick was little known as an author in those days save to the cognoscenti, but never allowed disappointment to deter him.

At that time I had read none of his published work, despite the fact that much of it was written for young people. Fortunately our tastes in many respects followed similar courses, particularly an intense love of the long eighteenth century. However, the only one of his published works I recall his sharing with me at the time was his first collection of short stories, *The Last Pool* (1950). I read them with avidity, and particularly enjoyed his affectionate parodies of early Irish saga and hagiography, 'The Green Creature' and 'The Virtuous Peleg'. Especially charming were delightful touches, like the angel whose neat agility saves the worldly Peleg from tumbling into the pit of Hell:

And the angel at the bottom of the chasm peered up through the shifting fog and altered his feet, and as he caught Peleg he said, 'There, easy now, Peleg ...'

Although I had at that time yet to visit Ireland, Patrick's stories' vivacity, humour and touches of brogue rang true. No reviewer then suspected that he was not Irish, and he possessed a wonderful innate capacity for absorbing other cultures at an imaginative remove.

Patrick acquired his skill in writing short tales at a very early stage of his literary career. Having completed his first novel *Caesar* (1930) at the precocious age of twelve, he turned his hand to short stories. Initially they were aimed at the flourishing children's market and were published in collections such as *The Oxford Annual for Children*, which made ideal Christmas presents. These early tales often featured brave but doomed wild animals, and in 1934 he published his first collection *Beasts Royal*. I suspect that his largely lonely and to some extent harsh childhood propelled him into identification with the graceful creatures of his imagination. However, there is nothing mawkish or sentimental about his animals, birds and even a whale ('Skogula'), who all too often come to a grisly and unjust end.

During his teenage years in his family home at Lewes, Patrick developed a keen eye for the majestic landscape of the South Downs and lofty sea-cliffs beyond. Later, when he and my mother decamped after the War to their tiny cottage refuge in Snowdonia, Patrick took up fishing, shooting and following the local hunt. Several of his early stories were drawn from these experiences, as was much of his evocative novel *Three Bear Witness* (1952).

Other tales include characteristically magical passages reflecting Patrick's love of the landscape and the natural order. He had paid an extended visit to Ireland in 1937, from which stemmed his deep love of the country, its people, and scenery.

> There was no clear line of demarcation between the sea and the land: they merged vaguely to an indeterminate region, a flat and sodden country, flat, flat and limitless as far as sight could reach. Through the mud of this country three old rivers slowly ebbed and flowed, losing their nature of land streams without ever gaining the character of inlets of the sea; they were joined by a thousand outfalls from the bog, and all this water crept secretly through a pale vegetation of fat-leaved plants and unnatural grass ('On the Bog').

It was largely the grim Welsh winters that made Patrick and my mother seek refuge beside the warm Mediterranean in the summer of 1949. Seven years later he published a further collection of short stories, under the telling title *Lying in the Sun* (1956). These too were in large part autobiographical. When I came to investigate them for the first volume of Patrick's biography, I was delighted to find that they not only reflected Collioure, its environs and its people, but included forays into his own fears and wish-fulfilment. 'The Lemon' recounts the protagonist's destruction with a hand-grenade of a noisy night-club beneath their flat in the Rue Arago. I recall the offensive night-club and can imagine the therapeutic effect of the tale's climax:

It went off with a great orange flower of light that blossomed momentarily in the whole street. I pushed back the electric fuse and went silently upstairs, pursued by the familiar smell of dust.

There was no possibility of detection. All the neighbours would be at their windows, not looking down the stairs.

Before the rapturous reception of *Master and Commander* in 1970 and its successors in the series, Patrick often found it easier to place his short stories in newspapers and journals. A sudden flash of inspiration could not always be absorbed into a pending novel but might be satisfactorily employed as the basis of a succinct tale. Thus his short story 'The Walker' begins with the unnamed protagonist's vividly-evoked stroll along an unidentified stretch of cliff and seaside, which after some pages leads into a dramatic episode in the lives of some nearby inhabitants. Every step of this stroll is familiar to me from retracing the itinerary on the outskirts of Collioure. I have little doubt that it was during one of these walks that Patrick gained his inspiration for the tale, which he then blended with his routine stroll. Much the same procedure can be detected in others of his short stories, and there may well be additional instances unknown to me.

'Samphire' recounts deteriorating relations between a newly-married young couple, in whom I recognise my mother and unfortunate father. Again, Patrick's regular bouts of ill-health inspired 'A Minor Operation', while 'The Voluntary Patient' describes the mental suffering of a psychiatric patient tortured with remorse for an unspecified crime. I wonder who that could have been?

It is curious that Patrick did not publish more short stories set in the historical past, given his unrivalled skill in that genre. The only exception, 'The Centurion's Gig', published in 1968 among Christmas tales in *Winter's Tales for Children*, was in fact a skilfully-concocted extension to his early children's naval novel *The Unknown Shore* (1959), which could fit seamlessly between chapters five and six of that work.

Among Patrick's unpublished works (now held in the British Library) are a couple of historical tales. They might have sprung from the *Boy's Own Paper*, for which they were possibly intended. The first is a stirring tale of the crusades, in which the valiant hero is accompanied by a gallant comrade 'Sir Padraig of Kerry', in whom may be recognised the youthful author. The other, also untitled, concerns a young poacher and wicked eighteenth-century squire. There is no indication that he ever sought a publisher for the two stories, and I suspect Patrick was conscious of their juvenile inadequacy. He was clearly finding his feet in the historical genre of fiction, and it was only later that his wonderful skill in recreating an authentic historical past came to fruition.

It is clear that Patrick loved the delicate skill involved in short story writing, just as he enjoyed composing poetry, both of which seem quite often to have been written for his own and my mother's delectation, without any necessary move towards publication.

It is good to see the entire collection of Patrick's short stories, bound here in a single volume for the very first time, which I fancy would elicit a wry smile of satisfaction from their devoted author.

Nikolai Tolstoy, 2023

The Complete Short Stories

I

The Return

———⊶⊷———

All day the fly had been hatching, and where the stream broadened into a deep pool between two falls the surface was continually broken by the rising of fish, broken with rings spreading perpetually, crossing and counter-crossing. It was a perfect day for the hatch, mild, gentle and full of life. Under the willows on the far side of the pool ephemerids drifted in their thousands, and the trout jostled one another in the shade of the willows, drunk with excitement and greed. Great heavy-headed cannibals with harsh, jutting under-jaws came from their stony fastnesses beneath the fall to rise at the fly; tender young trout rose beside them and took no harm.

All down the length of the stream the trout made holiday: they added a fresh, water-borne note to the incessant, imperceptible noise of the country, a note quite distinct from the purl of the water over the big pebbles above the fall, and from the sharp punctuation of the splash of the diving kingfisher, who flashed up and down his beat, darting ever and again on some minnow or tittlebat, some half-transparent fishlet that strayed up into danger from the green, waving forests in the stream's bed.

The best part of the stream lay between the ruined mill and the bridge: a path, some little way from the water, but roughly parallel with it, ran through the grass from the mill to the bridge. On the other side the woods came down to the water's edge, where huge pollard willows stood knee-deep in the stream making deep quiet bays for chub and quiet-loving fish. Formerly the underbrush had been cut back for the comfort of fishermen, but now it was over-grown, and the riot of young fresh green was brave in the sun.

Immediately below the pool the stream ran with a deeper note, flowing faster through a more narrow course, being constricted by worn rocks, which it could surmount only when the winter rains came down. Here the bridge spanned it in one leap; an ancient stone bridge it was, exquisitely lichened and its lines all rounded with age. There was an appearance of vast solidity about the bridge; it was massive and immovably firm, but it had a won-derful grace. A few self-sown wallflowers, tawny yellow, grew in its sides, and the sun was upon it now. The road that the bridge carried on its back ran clean a little way into the wood, but after the first bend it was lost and overgrown, for it was quite neglected.

The kingfisher perched on a stump close by the bridge to preen itself in the sunlight. It took no heed of the trout, nor of any of the innumerable sounds that came from hidden places all around it, but all at once it froze motionless on the stump, with its head raised questioningly. Then it sped down the stream in a blur of blue-green light, low over the water.

A little while after a man came down the lost road through the wood. At the bridge-head he paused, blinking in the sudden light. The trout stopped rising; a dabchick dived silently and swam fast away under the water. The pool held still to listen. Treading softly over the encroaching moss, the man came on to the bridge: he leaned over the coping and stared upstream. He was a tall, thick man, with a red face and black hair, quite gross to look at, and urbanized now: on his shoulders he carried a knapsack and a rod. After some minutes he looked down at the stones on which he leaned: initials and dates were scratched and cut into them. He knew almost to an inch where his own should be. They were there, J.S.B. in bold, swaggering letters, deeply carved, with a date of many years ago and a girl's initials in the same hand coming after them. Mary Adams: how very clearly he remem-bered her. A glaze of sentiment came over his eyes. A pace along the bridge there was J.S.B. and E.R.L., more discreetly this time, and, lower down, J.S.B. and T.M. There was a little cushion of moss spreading over the T.M.: he flicked it off and stood up. She had always called him Jeremy in full.

At the far end of the pool a trout rose, with a clear, round plop. The kingfisher flashed under the bridge and vanished upstream. The man walked on over the bridge to the path that led to the mill. From the path in the meadow he could see the stream, but from far enough away that he would not put the fish down.

He sat down in the sweet, dry grass and threw off his knapsack. He put the joints of his rod together, and it quivered pleasantly in his hand: from the pockets of his knapsack he drew old tobacco tins, a reel with an agate ring, his fly box; his fingers seemed too coarse for the tiny, delicate knots in the translucent cast, but the knots formed and the fly was on – a grannom. At last he stood up and whipped the rod in the air: he worked the line out loop by loop; it whistled and sang. He cast his fly at a dandelion clock, and after a few casts the fly floated down and broke the white ball. Satisfied, he walked gently towards the stream; for some time there had been a recurrent heavy swirl under the alders on the far side. Kneeling down – for the day was bright and the water scarcely ruffled – he worked his line out across the stream and cast a little above the rise. His fly landed clumsily in a coil of the cast; the trout ignored it, but did not take fright. When it had floated down, Jeremy twitched it from the surface and cast again. This time it landed handsomely, well cocked on the surface, and as it came down his hand was tense with anticipation; but the trout took another fly immediately in front of it. The third cast was too short, and the next began to drag, and the fly was half-drowned. He switched tiny specks of water from the grannom and cast again; still the trout let the fly go by, and a snag bore it over to a sunken branch. Delicately he tweaked and manœuvred with his outstretched rod, but the barb sank into the wood and held firm.

Will it give? he said, or will I go round and free it? Come now, handsomely does it. He lowered the top of his rod and pulled through the rings. The line stretched and the branch stirred: all around the trout were rising. He gave it a sudden, brutal jerk and the fly shot back across the stream, carrying a white sliver of wood on its point.

I did not deserve that, he said, taking the little piece off, I did not, indeed. He walked some way up the pool, waving his rod as he went. At haphazard, he cast to a small rise by the near bank, hardly pausing in his stride. At once the trout took the fly and went fast away with it in the corner of his mouth. The little fish was game enough, but he was finished in two mad rushes: he played himself, and came rolling in on his side, still defying the hook, but with no more power to fight it. The fisherman took another like the first a little higher up, beyond the pool. They were both about half a pound – small for that stream – cleanly run and game, but stupid.

After he had put the second fish into his bag, he rested; there was a crick between his shoulders from the unaccustomed exercise. He squatted on his heels, and almost without knowing it he filled his pipe as he gazed over the water: the kingfisher passed again, and in the woods a garrulous jay betrayed a fox.

It was just at this place that he had taken his first trout, tickling under the rill for them with Ralph, who was simple, but who could poach like an otter. The march of the years between those times and now effaced the unhappy days of his boyhood and adolescence, and now that he knew the value of the happiness of the days that remained to him that his former, smaller self had lived in a golden world. He had so little to show for all that he had lost; and sudden, intense regret for it took him by the throat for a moment.

He took off his shoes and socks, laid down his coat, and rolled up his trousers. The water was surprisingly cold as he waded into the stream; he could feel its distinct movement between each toe and the edged stones hurt his feet. He walked on the beds of water plants, sinking his feet to the ankles in the brilliant green: at each step he could feel innumerable tiny hoppings against his soles. The last time he had walked that way the water had been well up his thighs, he remembered, and in the middle the current had sometimes plucked him off his feet. Above him there was a small pool, with a stone rill above and below it. A crayfish exploded before his white toes, shooting through a cloud of silver minnows. Three or four small trout flitted from the weed-beds as he walked, speeding up the open, clean lanes between the orderly weeds; there seemed to be no other fish, but he knew the ways of these trout, and he waded quietly to the bar of stones, where the water came through fast from the pool. The force of the current had washed out a deep hollow here, and the water was too deep to stand in.

The sun had passed well over noon-height, and a deep shadow lay slantwise down the wall of stones beneath the water. Nothing could be seen there, but middle-aged Jeremy, standing thigh-deep at the edge of the scoop, leaned over and passed his hand along the stones, feeling gently into the interstices. Almost at once his fingers touched the firm, living body of a trout: the fish, working in the strong current, moved a little to one side. It was not frightened. He touched it again, drawing one finger up its side, feeling the strong, urgent thrust as the trout pushed continually upstream to hold its position. As his eyes grew used to the deep shadow, he could see the trout's tail, moving steadily to and fro. Carefully he continued to stroke its unresisting body, working the fish into the grip of his fingers: as soon as he could gauge the full length of the fish he knew that it would be too big for one hand, so he brought the other down, changing his foothold as he did so. The trout started and moved restlessly, but the quiet stroking of its belly on each side calmed it. Up and up the fingers stole, now touching the gills for a moment, then lingering. He drew in his breath, made his whole body tense and ready, and then with an instant grasp behind and under the trout's gills he flung it over his back on to the bank, where it sprang and curved in the sun. Grinning like a boy, he waded in a slow hurry back to the edge, killed his fish – a good fish, a very nice fish indeed – and sat down to dry his feet on a handkerchief.

He was hungry now, quite suddenly and unpleasantly hungry. He collected dried grass and twigs: the thin blue smoke of his fire rose straight up high into the air. He fanned it until it had a red heart, and he gutted two fish. He washed them in the stream and cut a green withy: coming back to the fire's black circle, he spitted them and lapped them with a piece of string to keep their bellies in. He twirled the ends and cooked his trout until their skins were wrinkled and golden and their pink flesh showed through the cracks in it. He had a broad leaf for a plate and bread and butter and a screw of salt from his bag. Being rather greedy by nature, he buttered and salted the fish with great care and ate them and the crusty bread in alternate bites, so that the taste came fresh and fresh: and at the end he slit out the little oval pieces from the cheeks of the trout and toasted them on the last piece of crust, so that the morsels spattered for a moment in the heat. After he had wiped his fingers and his mouth, he lay on his back in the soft, cushioning grass with his head under the shade of a bush, and all around him there was a murmur and a drowsy hum, and he slept.

When he woke up the sun had gone down three parts of the way to the horizon. Long shadows stood across the stream, and in the broad motes that came through the trees the spinners still danced in their hosts.

The fisherman raised his head and ran his fingers through his hair: he had not meant to lose his time in sleep, but here he did not mind the loss so much as he might have done on another stream; for he was here on a pilgrimage.

He walked back along the stream so as to fish up the same stretch again, and at the end of the pool by the bridge he saw a big rise – no splash, but the big, swirling ring that it is such a pleasure to see. The trout was on the farther side, well out in the open water, so it was necessary to creep up to an alder and, kneeling precariously on the edge, to cast left-handed from a long way off. Tentatively he worked a long line out, feeling his way across. A capricious little breeze, with no fixed direction, had arisen while he slept: the bushes behind him were a continual anxiety, and his knee kept slipping on the rounded edge of the bank. With his mouth closed tightly, he breathed heavily through his nose and concentrated on the flying line: his fly weaved back and yon, like a detached speck over which he had some occult control. The fly sped out and out, and still further; it was a very long cast. He shot the line, checked its run and bowed his rod; its forward motion stopped and as naturally as a dropping ephemerid the fly touched the surface, precisely where he had wanted it. The trout came straight at it, took it hard and vanished in a series of rings that spread out well across the pool before the fisherman raised his rod in a gentle tightening of the straight line. At once there was a great jar on the line as the trout jerked against the pull and sent the hook right home. The reel screamed, the rod curved, the line raced out. The trout leapt, not once but six times, showing clear a foot above the water at each leap. The man scrambled away from the insecure bank and stood in the water: his rod was thrilling with life under his hands. Three-pounder at least, he said it was, perhaps four, and Aah, would you? he said as the trout turned and dashed for the willow roots. His rod curved almost to a half-circle, checking sideways. The trout leapt again, slapping the water; it changed direction and shot up past him to the other end of the pool, into the deep stones beneath the rill. He could not reel in fast enough, and the line was still slack when the trout reached the stones.

Deep down in the calm water at the side of the rill the fish lay, beneath weeds and a tangle of drifted wood. Anxiously he twitched on the line; it was as dead as if it were tied to a rock. He was almost sure that it must be round the wood if not round the deep weed as well, but with his rod far out on the one side and then on the other he tried to stir the trout. There was no result, no feeling of life. With his rod pointing at the fish, he thrummed on the line, pulled and eased, did everything he knew, but it was entirely of its own foolish will that the trout moved in the end. Moved by some fancy, it turned round from its hole in the rocks and headed downstream with fresh strength. The cast strained shockingly: a green streamer carried away from the weed-bed, the line snaked free through the floating debris, and he was still on to his fish. For a dangerous minute the weed dashed through the water after the trout, but its stems parted before the cast.

Again the reel sang and the line fleeted away in spite of his checking finger and the straining rod: it was a heavy fish and a

9

strong one. When the line was gone to the first knot in the backing, the trout was the whole length of the pool away; he dared not let it run any further, so he stopped the line dead for a second; it stretched and he let it go slack. The trout stopped, leapt twice, but went on under the bridge, down through the dark tunnel of swift water, and the fisherman's heart sank. But he ran down the bank, now in the water, now out of it, stumbling and panting and sweating. The line was fraying against the stone foot of the bridge both this side and that; the strain was unwarrantable, and still the trout was running. He reached the bridge, with a couple of yards of backing on his reel, and the fish curved across to lie under the shade of the far bank, with its gills opening wide and fast.

Jeremy had been under the bridge; he knew its dark-green slipperiness and the almost certainty of a ducking. The rod might break too. However, there was nothing for it: he pushed his rod through, tip foremost, and bowed his head under the arch. The pent-in water took him behind the knees and nearly had him down at once: its note changed as soon as he was under the bridge. Then the trout began to rush across the stream again, and in his flurry of spirit he was through the bridge and on the shingle the other side before he had had time to think about it.

The heavy strain of the angled line had tired the trout, and its rushes were now much shorter, and they lacked the irresistible fire of the first. He made line on it fast, and fought it hard, never giving it a moment to recover. He thought he had it once, and pulled it in towards the bank as it lay inert upon the water, but before he had got it more than halfway it revived with a desperate rush and very nearly broke him against a stone on the bottom.

The trout lay on the bottom and would not move: the fisherman had been so near success and failure that he grew over-cautious now. He knew that his cast must be in a bad way, and he dared not pull until a sudden feeling of desperation nerved him to it. The fish had recovered, and it had learnt cunning. It meant to go through the bridge again, and he only stopped it with a strain that came within an ace of snapping the cast at the worst fray. Then he saw the line coming back and he scrabbled his way fast up the bank to keep the strain, reeling in as he went. I know I shall trip, he said, and that will be an end to it: but his good fortune was with him, and he kept his feet among the bushes and lumps. He kept the fish on the top now and bore masterfully on it, because there was no other way. Its strength ebbed in short rushes and a few angry leaps; the continual pressure was breaking its heart, and at the end it lost its head, used up the last of its strength in an unavailing burst and rolled sideways in the water.

He reeled in it very cautiously over the shingle where he stood ankle-deep. He was between the fish and the water as it grounded; there was a wild flurry and he had it out jerking and gasping on the grass in the last golden sunlight of the day.

He took the draggled fly from the corner of its jaw – it had nearly worn free in the fight – and he stood above the fish, gazing at it with satisfied admiration. It was a perfect fish: he looked down on its small, well-formed head, the gleaming pools of its eyes, and the golden yellow under the delicate white of its throat, and it lay there quiet with labouring gills. He must weigh a good four pounds, he said, drawing his finger down the fine, pink-flecked line that divided its belly from its gorgeous spotted sides. The fish bounded at his touch, and lay still again. He saw its strong shoulders, the saffron of its fins and the splendid play of colours over its whole glowing body, and he could not find it in his heart to kill the fish. It was the day and an undefined symbolism that worked upon him too.

Bending to the water, he held the trout upright with its head upstream: it was certainly four pounds. Its gills opened and closed and the cool water laved through them: for minutes he held it so, until fresh life and a little strength flowed into it and it lashed free. The trout almost turned belly-up a little way out, but more strength came to it. It turned into the stronger current and sank down to the waving green. He could see it there plainly, working gently under the soft shelter.

He wound his reel and packed his rod. The first owl cried and he went over the bridge: he went away, through the woods by the lost road, in the dying light.

The Last Pool

—⊗⊗⊗—

'This is the last pool,' he said again, as he stood by the side of it with the water running over the toes of his waders. He had said the same thing at each of the five pools below it, and he had meant that if he did not catch a trout he would go home. Each pool in turn had yielded nothing, not even a rise to save the face of his resolution. Each time he meant it more, and now he meant it entirely: beyond this pool was a long flat stretch of river, difficult to fish and notoriously barren; to circumvent both it and the small private lake beyond meant a tedious hot walk in waders already too warm for comfort.

The last pool was certainly the best pool for size and looks; it stood high above a series of chaotic rapids, and an almost unbroken rim of rock enclosed it. At the top end the river came clear over a wall of black basalt four or five feet high, curving over in green water before it broke into two main cascades that came down in foam to the pool. Even now, after weeks of drought, the top quarter of the pool was white, and the water had a menacing roar to it. The outlet was one single column of racing water, a broad mortal jet that came through a black gate of rock in the pool's lower rim; it was from this that it had its name of Goile-adair, or, as some said, the Kettle. The sides of Goileadair were sheer-to, and down the middle of it was a shingle bed, piled there by the two competing falls above. The highest part of the shingle was out of the water now, and quite dry.

There was a sombre air about this last pool – little colour, for the valley just here narrowed to a gorge with a great deal of naked rock to its sides. The Scots pines that had taken footing in the crag to the left showed darkly above, and the flash of the falling water accentuated the black polish of the half-sunken rocks. In Conan's time they drowned lepers here.

The gorge was beautiful, this man, this James Aislabie, observed to himself; but it was a harsh, grim kind of beauty, God forbid. He sat down on one of the smooth rocks that marked the end of the pool, the edge of the cleft that let the water out; the river slid fast and silently between these rounded edges, its surface curved and tense. It ran over his dangling feet with an insistent pressure and a grateful coolness; and in ten minutes the all-pervading roar that filled the gorge no longer reached the threshold of his hearing.

At the top end a yellow wagtail perched on a flat stone and stood bowing there and bobbing, and as James Aislabie watched the bird – a fine bird in the glory of his feathers – a fish leapt out of the foam a little to the one side of it. It was a small white fish, a sea-trout of perhaps half a pound or less, but it was a sight pleasant enough to a man who had fished long hours in the heat of the day without the sight of a fish at all.

All day long the weary length of the river, with its difficult, reed-grown banks lower down, and the beat of the sun on his back: the disastrous lowness of the water, with its shining surface and his cast lying awkwardly curled upon it, and his hot boots and the grinding strap on his shoulder. The bad, short, laboured casts as his arms grew more and more tired, the glare on the water as his eye followed the place where his fly ought to be, and the swirling water. When he lay in bed thinking about fishing he did not recall these things, nor the flies cracked off, pulled off, dropped, lost high up in trees.

He considered the best way to fish this pool, and he thought about changing his fly. He had no confidence in the fly he was using and none in the only other fly he had left, which was far too big. However, he cut off the one and tied on the other: it was more a gesture of piety than anything else. The name of the fly escaped him; somebody's Fancy, or possibly Indispensable, he thought, as he pulled the knot tight round the black, shining eye. It seemed but decent to do the thing correctly, although his belief in his motions had almost wholly gone.

His faith in the day's fishing had gone in three stages. At first, on the flat, easy stretches of the lower river, he had been keenly expectant, had made each cast with extreme care: he knew that some fair sea-trout, two- and three-pounders, had been caught within the week, and he hoped with each new cast that he should see the white flash of a turning fish and hear the scream of his reel. Then as the hours passed he had begun to hope rather desperately for just one fish, one, to save him from the wretchedness of having nothing at all. He pictured to himself the beauty of the fish, its gleaming sides, its black spots, the square tail and the fine, strong head, the heft of a good one dead in his hand. The vision grew clearer and more desirable still as he became more and more certain that he was going to catch nothing. It seemed, towards the end of the day, so very unlikely that any fish should want to take an artificial fly tied to a piece of gut; it was so improbable that there were any fish in that river, that if it had not been for some nagging persistence in the back of his mind he would have gone home about tea-time.

The feathers were smoothed, the cast was tried; he stood up and worked out a good line, facing the falls at the top of the Goileadair. His arm was rested, and he cast well; the line shot handsomely through his fingers, and the new fly dropped into the eddy at the outer side of the right-hand fall. It settled for a moment while the current carried down the slack; Aislabie's hand, as though it had an eye, took the line and drew it in, while he stared after the racing spot on the surface that should cover his fly. He was just about to lift his line off the water when some tiny variation stopped him. Was the cast moving a trifle across the current? It was, and the movement increased. With a quiet, smooth firmness it glided across and then upstream: there was a swirl under it that checked his quick strike. Aislabie stood there with the coiled line in his fingers.

'Wait. Oh wait,' he whispered, and he let a coil slip out through the rings.

Then came the pull; a firm pull, rather than the jerk of a little fish. Aislabie struck, with a straight, tight line; he struck too hard from over-anxiety. He had not finished the lashing upward stroke before his rod sprang to violent life. The rod top whipped down to the water, and two coils of line shot from his detaining fingers, and the reel gave a flying screech. In the middle of a pool a huge fish flashed three-quarters of its length into the air: it shook its head, poised there for an instant and fell sideways. In that instant Aislabie had seen every spot on it – the impression burnt itself in as a flash of lightning does. A silver, fresh-run cock-salmon, the heaviest he had ever seen alive. He had even seen the gleam of his cast between the strong beaked jaws.

Before the splash had settled it leapt again, clear of the water this time, and stood on its tail, worrying its head from side to side. Aislabie dropped his rod top: his hands were trembling so much that he could hardly find the knob of the reel, and his heart hammered in the back of his throat. His mind was devoid of coherent, conscious ideas: there was only a sort of cold exultation.

Then came a period of short, frenzied rushes across and across the pool, while Aislabie did nothing but endeavour to keep a tight line. This was not too difficult, as the fish went to and fro across the middle water, keeping roughly the same distance from him. His sense returned, and with it the depressing certainty that he was going to lose his cast for sure and probably most of his line as well. His reason conscientiously told him that only a silly man would hope to land a thirty-pound salmon with a short trout rod and fifty yards of line, a 3X cast and a little fly that a salmon should never have touched.

A salmon had no right to be there: only three, and small fish they were, had been taken in the river in the past twenty years. The top of his desire had been a two- or three-pound sea-trout, weighed by a friendly scale.

His body and the rest of his mind fought the salmon with every particle of skill and resource he had. A wild hope began to glow there in his heart; he put a stronger check on the fish, and the salmon responded with a strength that made the running line bite into his fingers.

So far the salmon had made no attempt to run up or down stream, and at present the only danger lay in the long, dividing finger of the bank of shingle between the incoming falls: if the run took the cast across one of its stones and then the fish were to turn, the cast would surely break. He became aware of this at the same moment that he saw the salmon turn just below the surface at the right-hand side of the pool and rush directly at the spit of shingle. Its shoulders were barely covered and he could see the wake it made, curving away right-handed to cross the tip of the spit. Plainly the salmon meant to go up into the deep hole at the foot of the left-hand fall. This would do two things: first, the curving rush would carry the line, if not the cast, over the bare rocks; and second, it would in all probability run the line clean off his reel, in which case it would tauten, stretch to the breaking-point in an infinitesimal fragment of time, break at the weakest point – he had a fleeting vision of the knot joining cast and line – and leave him with a still, lifeless rod.

As the wake neared the point, he leaned his rod out to the left horizontally and checked the racing line with all the force it could bear. The rod bent and quivered to the butt and the salmon's curve flattened perceptibly; it cleared the point several feet below the bare stones, but still the fish bore up right-handed. Aislabie could check no more. Suddenly he let go altogether, and his reel ran out free and screaming. He felt the knot between line and backing pass up through the rings, knocking as it went, and a bitter wave of disappointment welled up around his heart. There was very little backing – he had been careless – and that little was frayed and stiff. He could not gain any distance by wading into the pool; it was neck-deep a foot from where he stood.

The salmon took no notice of the slackened pressure; it sped on into the boil of the fall, to the topmost limit of the pool, and dived into the deep, slack water on the further side of the fall, the inward side under the falling water. There it lay, with its side and belly fins spread and its gills working violently: from time to time it worried, nuzzled against the water-worn rock, trying to dislodge the fly; but the hook was well home.

Aislabie stood there with a couple of yards of backing still on his reel, and for the first time he felt a reasonable hope. He had little enough ground for it, since the line was angled about a rock, and the salmon, should it wish to stay where it was, could not be moved. Still, ambition swelled up and took entire possession of him, so that he could hardly breathe. He saw the fish dead on the shore and wiped the loose scales from his hand – he would have to tail the salmon, for he had neither gaff nor net: he settled in his mind how to attach it to his bicycle.

The salmon, angered and disturbed by the thrumming that the taut line made in the fall, moved across the current and then quite slowly down into the quieter water. Aislabie left it alone until it was farther down than the shingle bed and then he bore gently on the line. The salmon, fiery as ever, hurled itself into the air twice, skittering along on its tail, and rushed straight across to the right-hand pool and back. It paused a moment, and then started a savage, exhausting series of short runs up and down the left-hand half of the pool. Had it not kept to the far side, right under the steep bank, the line would have crossed the middle bar every time, and it would certainly have parted. As it was, Aislabie, standing as high as ever he could, was just able to keep a straight line and a continual slight check on the salmon. Then, when the fish came over again to the hither side, he could bear more strongly against the pull, and now he felt that the salmon's first splendid flush of strength had gone.

His greatest fear was that if he should manage to tire the fish to a dangerous point, it would go downstream, through the pouring lip of the pool, down the strong column of water, and there, among the precipitous black rocks, he could not hope to hold it for a moment.

Time rushed by, marked only by the passage of crises; twice he had slipped on a mossy piece of stone, once the salmon had bored into the only small patch of weed in the pool, and many times his line had dragged perilously over the bare rocks. Long ago he had noticed, with a hurried glance at his top ring, that the sun had left the trees. By now he felt that he knew the fish intimately well, could foretell its reactions, could think in front of it. It was a stupid, angry fish, he thought, with little of the sharp wit of a trout; a clever fish would have been off in less than five minutes. His own reactions, the working of the rod, the instant reeling-in, the varied check, were quite automatic by now; he did not think of them at all. As the fish began to tire in good earnest, to make shorter rushes, he pressed it harder and harder, allowing no moment of rest. Often as it turned he saw the white of its belly.

'It will go down any minute now,' he said, and with half an eye he marked three loose stones. He shuffled one between his feet, and when the salmon turned heavily down the current he had it there to throw with his free hand. It was his one chance, a remote chance, but his luck was with him. The salmon was near the surface, just above the very strong rush of current, and the stone splashed six inches from its nose. It turned and ran upstream.

Quite soon after this the salmon began to tire so much that it was rolling in the water, and he could draw it towards him ten and twenty yards before it would run. At last he brought it into the side, curved with exhaustion and seeming half-dead. He towed it gently up the bank to the one place where the rock ran down to within a couple of feet of the surface. With slow, blundering haste he changed his rod to the other hand, knelt down, muttering 'Calmly, calmly ...' and made a foolish, impetuous grasp at the salmon. His fingers slipped incapably on the scales, and the salmon shot away with enormous power. The rest and the touch of his hand had renewed its courage and strength. He had known it, he said, and a lowering premonition of failure had been upon him as he knelt.

It was a weary battle now; his strength seemed to have gone into the fish. The consciousness of his own ineptitude tired him more than anything else. He realized now that his arms were as heavy as they could well be, that his reeling hand was about to be seized with a cramp, that he was going to make some last fatal error.

With a headstrong wilfulness, he bore on the salmon, disregarding his frail, frayed cast. The fish sank in the depths, and he pumped it out with the force he would have used with tackle fit for a salmon. His foolishness answered; the salmon made a last flagging run, tried three leaps, each weaker than the last, and lay drifting on the surface.

Now that he could see victory, Aislabie's desperate courage left him; he wasted vital time gaping, tied in an agony of indecision. His body and mind were so tired that he could hardly think.

The salmon came drifting down on the current on the near side of the pool. It was not going fast, for it was not in the main stream, but to one side of it. The fish passed him, and he stood impotently staring: it was downstream of him now, drifting towards the out-pouring fall, drifting faster. A queer eddy took the inert body, swirled it out of the current into the slack water of an overhung bay just to the one side of the fall's top.

With an awakening gasp he came out of his trance and ran heavily down the bank to the rock over the bay. He dared not draw the salmon along the bank now, so near the strong current, for he had left it so long that its strength might well be reviving, and one stroke of its tail would carry it into the run, over the edge and away. He knew that he must tail the fish there as it lay or lose it.

The rock on which he stood overhung the water by four or five feet; three feet down, below the usual high-water mark, a narrow sloping ledge jutted out. The fish was on the top of the water, filling this little cut-off basin, a demi-lune made by a backward swirl from the fierce stream that ran at right-angles to its mouth. He put his left foot down to the water-polished ledge – there was not an honest sharp edge of rock anywhere – put his right leg out behind and knelt on the smooth rock, facing up the pool. His right hand, holding his rod, stretched as far as it could over the flat top on which he had been standing.

He was oppressed by a sense of strong, present danger, and

when he was in position he paused to collect himself. Peering down, he saw the fish from its dorsal fin to its tail; its head was under the rock and out of sight. It had sunk lower, and now lay in some two feet of water. Just above the tail fin he saw a faint band of lighter scales, the place where his hand had grasped before.

Now he let his arm down to the water, and as he touched the surface he felt his left knee move. There was a patch of dark wet moss under it, and the rubber of his waders was slipping gently on it, downwards. The movement was very gradual, but the slightest motion of his body increased it. He brought his hand back to steady himself, but all his weight was on his left knee, and his hand found no resting place to thrust upon. He put his rod down, quite gently, for any abrupt movement would be fatal, and sought with terrible eagerness for a hand-hold; there was none anywhere in the compass of his reach. His right elbow stayed him for a moment, and by a huge muscular contraction he seemed almost to recover his poise. But his elbow could not grip on the mossy rock; the tuft of moss and grass on which it relied slid from under it, and he felt his weight swaying over on to his unsupported left side. He knew he was falling then. It was quite impossible to get his balance again, and even the smallest movement made him slide a minute, sickening, irrecoverable distance. His right hand, as though working by itself, still searched every inch of the smooth rock for a hold. There was none. He slid further. His whole body was tense to the extremity of its power, and the tension was unbearable. It was a relief when he fell at last – he no longer had to do anything now; it was decided for him now. He observed that his reason was working perfectly well although he was terrified and sweating with the fear of death.

'Right,' he said aloud, and let himself go. His hand, already under water and within a foot of the salmon's tail, dropped right on to the lighter patch of scales: he gripped with a kind of furious reaction just as his face hit the water and his mouth and nose filled chokingly.

The salmon gave a vast, galvanic lunge which momentarily checked his downward fall so that his body was asprawl when it hit the dark racing water. His face was set in a horrible grimace, but his fragmentary thought 'Oh God, the speed ...' had no horror in it.

It was like coming out of an anaesthetic. He was quite happy, and he was aware that he was conscious before he opened his eyes. As he had supposed, there were people around him, and they were talking, although at a great distance still. He looked placidly at the grey shingle alongside his cheek and somewhat out of focus because of its nearness, he saw the battered head of the salmon.

They were wrangling softly about where the priest was to be found, and Dr Niel said again, 'I tell you he will certainly be at Tobin's – we sent for him – my own patient, for all love. Hurry now, Jack, will you? You can take the poor man's bicycle from by the bridge ... Surely to God it must be the biggest fish that ever ran up this river.'

Aislabie smiled secretly: a voice said, 'He has come to,' and another, so anxious and kind, 'Can we ease you, Mister, as you lie?' The doctor was speaking too in a professional voice; but Aislabie could not bring himself away from his deep innermost glow; he smiled again, and drew in the smell of the fresh-run fish.

3

The Green Creature

━━⬗⬖⬗━━

They say of the Lake Orbhuidh that it was inhabited by a creature called the ancient green creature, which was however of the form of a young woman. This one was not of the human kind, but had been there in the old times when there were serpents; and although she could have most shapes it was her nature to be of the shape and mind of a young woman and to live in Orbhuidh. It was her nature too to require the blood of men four times in every hundred years: it was so that if she could not come at it she would grow old and hideous, whereas she was exceedingly beautiful and desired above all things to remain so. For her ordinary diet she would have the form of an otter or a fox and in these shapes she hunted with great skill and cunning, so that it was supposed that a host of foxes and otters lived in the neighbourhood of Orbhuidh, and they all of a wonderful cunning. Her delight in the way of flesh was a young child, but for her main purpose a grown man it had to be, or a good youth at the least, full of hot blood.

It was the trout of the lake that kept her beautiful beyond all power of words. They were golden, splendid fish and numerous past the ability of man to number them, and the men would for ever be coming up from their valleys and over the bare hills and the harsh mountains to fish for them, and from time to time a man alone and by himself would see the fish rising in the lee of the round island of Orbhuidh, and having caught nothing he would put off his clothes and swim towards the island. The

nearest way they would swim, those who could swim; there were
not many, but always some, and clearly if they were not the good
swimmers they would choose the nearest way, which was from
the end of stepping stones that led out into the deep water. Along
these rocks they would go, jumping like goats on the far ones at
the end and holding their rods with care. Then, from the last,
which was above the deep water, the man would always stand for
a moment with his rod like a spear high in his right hand and
holding his nose with the other and he would close his eyes and
go into the water with a small leap with his feet first. He would
always plunge down with something of a splash and a rush of
bubbles and he would never come up. You would never see the
top of his head coming up black through the water and his hand
holding his rod coming first, because she would have him fast
down there. Woven about with strong green long weeds he would
be and she holding him and pressing him down with strength.

For seven hundred generations of men she was undiscovered
for certain, although there was always a strong suspicion on the
place by reason of its nature and appearance. But in that year
she had so weary a time with a fat grocer who could hardly sink
even of his own will that she made an error and left his clothes
where his grieving relatives found them. They knew very well that
he had not made away with himself, for besides being rich and
happy he had many convenient places for so wicked a deed near
at hand without climbing mountains that were steeper for so fat
a man than for others.

From that time on Orbhuidh had been blacker in the people's
minds and few came up to fish, and they in crowds together, and
the wives and mothers of those disliked the taste of the trout
from Orbhuidh.

Great care she took to improve the fishing, and an admirable
sight it was to see her come over the dew in the shape of an otter
with a fine living trout held in her mouth so delicately that he had
not a scale bruised. She provided new stock so, and destroyed the
old tyrants in the deep holes, and the lake was better kept than
the Lord Lieutenant's, so that men passing on other avocations

would see the surface of it like a simmering pot with the big trout rising for ever. So in time the fishers grew in number again, but for a generation and more not a man or a boy would dip in his toe.

In those days Daniel Colman lived down there in Kilronnen, or he did at least when he came home in the holidays now, and had all his days as a boy: and he was without doubt the strongest man of those parts, which, moreover, were unusually famous for strong and learned men. From his earliest days he had been of a great strength and nimble too, not a staring, hidebound ox of a fellow like some, and no boy nor young man could come near him in the hurling, and he would dance, in his carnal days, until no person, male or female, could stand up with him any longer by reason of the heat and the fatigue. He could also play the fiddle with strong melody and he was kind in his heart and good-natured to a fault. It was a terrible blow to the young women of Kilronnen when it was known that Daniel had gone to the seminary to be a priest, but the truth was that his vocation was so powerful that candles lit by his bed and bells rang from time to time and there was no withstanding it.

There his tutors distrusted his lively eye and his straight back, but they delighted in his learning, for he had an elegant turn in that way which they had not expected. In so short a time that a man would be ashamed to name it, he had read the library through, and the Rector buying new books by post and rail apart from what could be obtained in the town. Daniel was so powerful a reader that he bent the very covers off the books and scattered the leaves like chaff winnowing out the learning, and every last bit of it he kept, so that in the holidays he was able to reply to every question that they asked him and the entire barony was edified with the elegance of his learning and the powerful flow of his speech.

Towards the end of his time at the seminary he was seen to grow thoughtful and pale, so that his appearance was more in keeping with the black of his coat. The Rector shook his head at the sight and feared that the seminary would lose its ewe lamb, which was the term he used for Daniel by way of ornament. And when he came home for his last holiday his face grieved his kind aunt and his uncle, who was bent in years and without a son or the hope of one now indeed. It was then that he declined the hurling and the dancing and withdrew himself to walk alone in the uneasy time of the night, and they offered him diversions in vain. But one day, looking fondly at his old rod, he said that fishing had always been his joy and was also the occupation of certain Apostles in the young days of their life as well as the delight of Popes and Emperors. His kind aunt was glad that he would take a reasonable diversion, but when she found that he meant to go for a trout in Orbhuidh her heart failed her suddenly and if she had not been under the awe of his learning she would have spoken a long while against it.

It was a long, hot way up the valley and over the bare hills and the harsh mountains, but his great strength and the nimbleness of his person carried him without a pause to the dark shores of Orbhuidh. He was a wise fisherman, and he sat quietly on the dark shores to see were the fish rising and where, and to see what fly there might be in the air or upon the water.

Now, when he first came there was never a fish to be seen, not one circle on the water, and there was no fly; but after he had sat awhile, looking at the beauty of the lake, though it was a strange beauty too and not what every man would choose to look at by himself alone, he saw a gillaroo of an outrageous length leap clear of the water just under the round island of Orbhuidh where the wind had left a calm place. The splash that it made caused the snipe to fly from the bog, and from the mountain it echoed again. So large a trout had never been seen in Orbhuidh, and it was a charming sight for a man furnished with a rod.

Daniel Colman began to fish then, and he fished with all his might. He was certainly the strongest fisher that had ever fished Orbhuidh, and his rod was twenty feet long. He had a great black line and a gut of ten yards with thirteen eminent flies upon it of a variety of colours and of every size as well as the tail fly, which was a murrough of his own tying. He threw eighty yards at a cast, and each as straight as a ruler, but did a fish rise to any one of his flies? He cast further: he cast ninety and a hundred yards, with his line whistling over the heather behind him and close by his ear and his rod groaning like a pine forest in a tempest of wind, and he fished deep and slow as well as quick on the surface, but for all the fish he caught he might have been fishing on the smooth grass of the shorn meadow behind his kind aunt's house, where she spread the linen.

Daniel Colman went three times round the lake, quite round it, casting with every step that he made, but his casts were as fruitless as they might be, and in the middle the gillaroo was joined by three others. Then Daniel sat upon a rock at the nearest place to the island and watched them rising there; they were feeding with the appetite of lions devouring good Christians, and it was upon some fly that was blowing off the island, and each was big enough to carry away a small child. His heart burned at the sight and his breath came short.

'I must be on that island,' Daniel said, and he put off his good black clothes, folding them decently in order upon a clean rock and weighting them down with another against the wind. It blew warm and delightful on him as he stepped out over the stones that led towards the middle of the lake. Between the far ones at the end he had to jump like a goat, and he held his rod with care. The last was big and flat: it was the place where so many men had taken their farewell of the sun, and he stood upon it. Under the hang of the rocks the ancient green creature twisted her weeds together nervously and wished he would come on and not wait there, causing her to delay the refreshment of her beauty, holding her breath with anxiety.

He did not hold his rod in one hand and his nose in the other, nor did he make a small leap into the water with his feet going first. He threw his rod far in like a javelin and dived cleanly after it, parting the water with his pointed hands, for he was the strong swimmer of Kilronnen.

The ancient green creature was hardly ready for this, but she was quick-witted and she shot from under the rock like a pike and caught him by the heel. He kicked her off, but there she was above his back and his limbs were wrapped about in long green weeds and she was pressing upon him with strength. Daniel, with his learning, knew directly that this was no human creature, so he stopped struggling at once and held his wind until he was black in the face and his features were much disordered.

Now with his first few kicks and sideways lashes, before he took thought, he had raised white-topped waves upon Orb-huidh and the green one had naturally supposed that he was in his death agonies, so she towed him quietly to her cave with a pleased smile, thinking of the benefit to her beauty his strong blood would surely be.

On the sanded floor of her cave she pulled him above the water mark and when he was sure that he was on dry land he let out his breath with a great sough like a bull.

'Your soul to the devil, Daniel Colman,' she cried in a great taking. 'You are still alive, I find.'

'I am that,' he said, sitting up and draining the water from his ear; and he added: 'Thanks be to God.'

'Well, it is not right indeed,' she said. 'You had better go back into the water now.' She said this because she, like all of them, had no power to put a man in, only to drown him there.

'I will not,' said Daniel Colman, and he sat with his back to the wall of the cave.

For a long while they sat like fools, without a word to say, and then she in a sudden fury came raging at him to drive him into the water, with threats and outrageous curses most terrifying to hear. But she was exceedingly beautiful in her face and her figure so elegant too that he smiled and told her to hush and he said: 'We may as well be civil as not.'

'Do you wish to be turned into a beast, young man?' she cried, dropping large tears of rage.

'Now hush again,' said Daniel. 'I know you very well, and it is many learned and ancient books I have read concerning your powers and the powers of other devils.'

' Do you call me a devil, in my own house?'

'You will never deny that you are related to fiends?'

'A person may be related to fiends without being a devil, I believe.'

After some time Daniel said, 'It is the strange house where a stranger sits fasting. There are many houses where the people of the house understand civility better than that.'

'And there are some people with better breeding than to sit there mother-naked and with no more shame than a crawling child,' she said and threw him the old fishing coat of the farmer of Athanrighe which was hanging on a nail apart from the others. It was a blue coat, with short tails.

'It is by reason of my profound learning that I am unashamed,' replied Daniel, but he blushed as he put it on.

She gave him the side of a kippered trout: it was five feet long, and the half of it bent the thick wood which it hung upon.

'We understand civility very well,' she said.

They sat with the kippered trout between them and in a little while they were speaking as kindly as two Christians and passing the victuals and the drink to and fro quite easy and complaisant. He did not say a grace aloud out of delicacy for her feelings, but when he had eaten all he could he thanked her and that many times. With the meal away, they talked about fishing, and he told her about the salmon, which she had never seen, and he described them in such true and laudible terms that her eyes glittered with desire to be among them.

'And why are you never there at the bar of the sea when they are running strongly, or in the falls where they leap?' he asked.

'You know very well,' she said, 'or your learning is not what it should be. You know very well that I may not go beyond a day's journey from here and that I must be here in my place at noonday or lose my beauty.'

'Well there is a great deal of that: more than I have ever seen among all the women of the christened kind.'

She was pleased at that, for, apart from a few low fiends and things of that kind, she had received no compliments on her exceeding beauty, although she had wished them often and often.

'Tell me, though,' said Daniel, 'who told you that?'

'It was him, of course,' she said, nodding her head towards the mountains.

'Who? What name do you call him?' But she would not answer. 'Will you whisper it?' he asked, but she could not. 'Is it Aog?' She nodded, with her eyes staring for the roof to fall in and large cracks to appear on the floor.

'Well, Aog,' he said, and a big, deep laugh came out from his throat. He spat delicately out of the door and said again with a loud mock in his voice, 'Aog. I supposed it was old Thunder-and-Lightning up there who told you that big lie. And it was he telling you that your beauty would fade without strong blood to keep it up, I have no doubt?'

'It was too.'

'And it was that old left-handed fool – his soul to the devil'– he spoke in a powerful, bold voice, nodding towards the mountain – 'who told you the false word of hell; it was he telling you that it had to be men, four in a hundred years? And that his thunder would crush the mountains and his lightning strike through the bowels of the hill if you broke your troth with him?' She nodded, pale at the horror of his speech. 'And it was on account of the high mendacious babble of that one,' he said, spitting from him again, 'that you drowned the grocer of Ballymor, a member of the Council, and drank his blood. And so many others too, the pity of it? And he with no more power over your beauty than the fish in the lake.' He waited a pause, and said, 'Listen now, bring me that troth here.' She got up trembling all aghast and brought it.

'I thought it would be so,' he said, turning it over and dandling it in his hands, 'a very cheap one, and of poor quality at that. Now will I tell you about Aog, the old cheat of the world, the father of lies?'

'If you please,' she said, and folded her hands, 'for I see you have the learning, and the great learning.'

'He has seen all of you grow kind to men because of the love they have to your exceeding beauty, and one by one you have all gone away from the watery places except yourself and one or two more in County Roscommon and one in some foreign place, Greece I think it is, and he has come up with this tale on his black tongue the way you must do this and do that, so that you will always see men as your enemy and prey and always be here, where they will never see your shining beauty.' There was a far thunder in the mountain, but the roof stayed whole and the floor did not crack on any part of it, and Daniel spread his hands in a derisive manner to put a mock upon Aog.

'Look at this troth,' he said, 'and see how I break it.' It shivered in his big square hands and she cried out and fell down on the sanded floor with terror: but he picked her up very kindly and said, 'The old thief was too mean ever to give you a name, I am sure. However I will give you the name of Kate, which is also a name of exceeding beauty, and now you must follow me and be christened into mortality and leave this un-Christian drinking of blood which is neither respectable nor serviceable to your beauty. And we shall take my uncle's farm, he being old and bent now, and sometimes we shall go down to the river by the sea for the salmon.' He turned a strong look on her, and said with a windy sigh, 'For now I shall never make a priest.' And she bowed her head and followed him out of the cave.

4

The Happy Despatch

―――⟨∞⟩―――

Slieve Donagh on the east and Ardearg on the west hold a valley between them as lovely as any valley in the world. The nearest road is a great way off, however, and the valley is beautiful without praise.

A man standing halfway up the side of Ardearg would see the whole of the valley at once, from the high curtain of precipitous rock that closes the upper end to the curious, bar-like round of hill at its mouth. This bar is pierced by a single cleft that lets the river through, but the cleft is wooded, not to be seen, and the bar hides the valley from the lower world. On each side of the valley's head stand the tall mountains, rising nobly, each in a smooth, steep slope to shale, naked rock and savagery; their ridges, equal in height and unbroken, form the valley's sides. From his vantage point, the observer would see the soaring sweep of the top of the valley, the steep flanks whose slope ends suddenly in the flat green of the bottom: there would be half a mile of swimming air between him and the other side, and this would give him a feeling of immense height. He would see with the utmost clarity the meandering course of the Uisge, whose source is here at the foot of Slieve Donagh.

The Uisge, the bright stream, was high and running fast between its banks; two and three days before it had been over them, flooding the bright green bed of the valley and scouring the rock pools clear. The fishing in this highest stretch of the river was not at all good by most standards. There was no possibility of sea-trout above the falls in the cleft and the brown trout were tiny, elusive fish, never above four or five ounces in weight and mostly half that size.

It was this that made it possible for Woollen to be fishing there. The lower water had some value and was let to an angling association. On account of his extreme poverty, Woollen belonged neither to this association nor to any other: indeed, there were times when it seemed to him that he hardly belonged to the human race at all, the more the pity, for he was a sociable creature by nature. He was an incongruous figure, with his mild sheep-like face and bowed, apologetic shoulders, here in this fierce valley – a valley that must have looked the same before ever the Firbolgs came into it – primitive and harsh, a place for cruel and bloody slaughter.

Woollen was as unsuited to the neighbourhood as he might well be. He was an Englishman, and it was widely known that he was, or had been, a Freemason. This was an unusually devout parish, and Fr. Tobin a bitter Anglophobe.

Woollen had a wife, a deathless shrew. There was something wrong with her that caused her to lie the day long on a sordid stuffed couch, from which she screamed abuse in an untiring, metallic voice, rendered piercingly sharp by long wear. Her face was a disagreeable purple and flour lay thick upon it; her body, of ponderous bulk, was covered with a deep layer of pale grey fat. She did not wash: she had many disgusting personal habits. Woollen had married her in haste a great many years since; she had been employed in an inferior boarding-house at the time. As for Woollen, he had been gently bred, of no particular family, but a gentleman. An elderly, ailing parson had brought him up, had disliked him nearly all the time, and had seen him into the Army with querulous relief. With neither connections nor abilities, he had found his way into one of the nastiest of infantry regiments, and he had passed several unenviable years in association with a number of third-rate subalterns who, sensing his timidity, had from the first used him ill. He had been their butt, and they had shown an ape-like ingenuity in making him wretched. Some of them had traded on the kindness of his stupid heart.

When he had thrown up his commission to join an acquaintance in a commercial undertaking, they had said that he would be rooked, and they were right. The businessman from Manchester, who had promoted a company with a registered office and documents bright with seals, and who had allowed Woollen to come in on the ground floor with the title of Director in Charge of Army Contracts, had taken his small patrimony and his gratuity within six months. All that was left to him was the income of seventy-two pounds a year that an aunt, his last known relation, had left him in trust.

He was, as he very soon discovered, wholly unemployable – these were the bad days, the very bad days – so he had taken the advice of a sort of friend, the senior captain of his regiment, and had come to Ireland with the intention of living in rural ease, keeping hens and so on, in a cottage on the estate of the captain's cousin, Harler.

It had taken nearly all Woollen's loose cash to transport himself, his vile wife and their few possessions to this far, hidden corner of County Mayo. He had been deceived again: the cabin was barely habitable, the possibilities of making money from tomatoes, mushrooms or eggs were non-existent, and the reputation that he brought with him of being a friend of the Harlers damned him. This was a district that had suffered terribly in the troubles, and at least one Harler had been proved an informer. Two sons of the family had been in the Black and Tans. The paltry estate was now managed at a distance by a Harler who was some kind of a broker or attorney, a heavy, unshaven, loud-mouthed fellow who met all complaints, all requests for repairs, with blank indifference.

Woollen, of his own act, had effectually closed the door of silence upon himself. He had thought it best to maintain his status by a certain stiffness – after he had asserted his gentility, he could unbend to the two or three half-gentlemen of the neighbourhood. He never had the opportunity. His poverty was quickly discovered and they felt themselves outraged. Even the poorest of his neighbours considered himself affronted. Woollen had picked up a glaze of military stupidity in the Army and a kind of superficial arrogance – a protective colouring of which he was wholly unconscious – and this unconciliating manner, added to his horrible wife, his native stupidity and to his other overwhelming disadvantages, rendered him perhaps the loneliest man in the county. Years of slow misery had passed since he first came. All his ill-informed ideas and schemes for making a little extra money had come to nothing: worse, many of them had cost invaluable pounds. Those which had not been downright foolish had wrecked on the indifference or open hostility of his neighbours. They would not teach him anything, and, being town-bred, he knew almost nothing of any value. His pig had died; his attempt at goat-keeping had been disastrous, for the animals had strayed incessantly, and after they had accomplished a great havoc he found them mutilated in the Irish fashion. His hens had gone, victims of a family of stoats: long after the event the memory could bring a choking disappointment. Seventeen pullets, so carefully bred up, fed at such cost, cosseted by him from chicks to the point of lay, housed with such pains, all slaughtered for fun within a few minutes. His beehives had been tipped over so often by unknown hands in the night that he was hardly sorry when the survivors died of Isle of Wight disease. So the list would run on; every enthusiasm, each fresh plan frustrated by lack of knowledge, want of a few pounds, evil fortune; perpetual failure, unending poverty.

It would not have been a gay life alone: in the company of his wife it was hell. That unlovely woman lay, wrapped in a mauve thing, on her creaking stuffed couch, with a malevolent blur in place of a mind. Directly she was legally married she had resolved never to do a hand's turn again her whole life long. She had deceived herself as to her husband's resources, but with incredible persistence she maintained her resolution. She was a teetotaller. She lived almost entirely upon tea and bread and margarine. She was unbelievably ignorant, and her tiny mind had narrowed with the passing years to the point of insanity.

Through countless nights of dumb, aching misery Woollen had revolved plans for removal, for going away to some happier place where children would not shriek after him with stones, to some English backwater, somewhere where he could do something; but every fresh day had shown him their impossibility. Poverty had brought him there, and poverty chained him there. Long ago he had made an arrangement for his tiny income to be sent to him in weekly sums; it was the only way, he had found, of keeping out of debt – it should be stated, with great emphasis, that he had a single-hearted regard for what he conceived to be his duty, and a simple honesty that would put nine men out of ten to shame at the judgment seat. From this weekly sum it had never yet been possible for him to save twopence.

Mrs Woollen hated fishing. It had been the subject of countless disgusting rows, bellowing, smashing quarrels that had left him shattered in spirit and her exhilarated. Once she had broken his rod, and he, moved out of himself, had beaten her almost to insensibility with the butt-end. This had earned him one undisputed day's fishing a week, for a deep voice had warned him, against his convictions, never to apologize for this outburst, nor, indeed, to refer to it.

The day was Thursday, and this Thursday had dawned fair. He had risen before the alarm clock rang, as excited as a boy, and he had walked the four miles up the river with an eager impatience. The locals were sure that he fished the preserved water, and they would willingly have sworn to it; the water-bailiff often hid up for him. But Woollen had never in his days of life put a fly upon forbidden water. As he walked he averted his eyes from the pools with their widening circles of invitation, and pressed on to the ravine at the bottom of the high valley.

At the top of it, hot and panting, he was in his own place. The lower river, with its chequer-work of farms and small-holdings, was out of sight; his own prison and incubus too. Above there were the impassive mountains, which had always seemed friendly to Woollen, and there was hardly a sign of man. The high valley was notorious for the bog-evil and the poverty of its grazing; no walls divided it – in this it was singular – and the only sign that men had ever been in the valley was a mound with a circle of stones on the top of it. The mound was regular, thirty or forty paces round and five feet high. By some it was called the Torr an Aonar, because it was supposed that an anchorite had lived there, though indeed the stones had been piled by hands that knew nothing of the Cross. Formerly the mound had been at a considerable distance from the water, but the stream changed its course in very rainy winters and now it ran fast round half the mound, following the curve of it.

Immediately below the mound was a large pool, the best in the upper stream; several times Woollen had seen a trout in it that must have weighed over a quarter of a pound, and twice it had risen to his fly. At present he was still a long way from the mound, fishing the quiet middle stretches. The fish were coming up well – rising a little short, some of them, but already he had caught five. One had been too small even for this stream, but two were gratifyingly heavy. He had missed a dozen or more, but that was nothing to a man so habituated to misfortune.

He stalked along now, casting well forward with each step. He was throwing a longer line than was necessary, mostly for the pleasure of seeing it go out straight before him; he was casting easily and well, with a slight, constant breeze at his shoulder to lay the cast out flat. His mild, foolish face had an unwonted happiness on it. He talked gently as he went, in a voice a little above a whisper.

'Behind the rock, in the calm place . . . no, nobody there . . . try each side.' His fly was going down just where he wanted it, on the spot he was looking at each time. To the right of the rock the fly danced down the edge of the main current; there was a silver flash under it and Woollen struck, whipping the fish into the air, well out on to the bank. He had found this to be the only way of taking these mercurial little trout, but it still came hard to him to strike with such force and speed. The fish sprang and sprang in the grass until he reached it; it was of due size and he killed it, not without a qualm for its beauty. Thousands of trout he must have caught by now, and still, each time, he had to justify himself for the final killing.

He smoothed his fly, a red quill in the last stages of decrepitude, and looked over the length of his cast. It had a great many knots in it, most of them clumsy, for he was not a man of his hands, and it was uncommonly short. Both cast and fly would have to last a great while yet, as Woollen knew with a deep certainty. Few things would have given him greater pleasure than a five-pound note to be spent without remorse of conscience in a good tackle shop.

He went on, along the right bank, fishing steadily. The sun came out hot on the back of his neck. For a long stretch no fish came up, and he saw that it must be about noon. Lunch was cold new potatoes and a white pudding – good for a hungry man. He ate it with his back against the deep bank, where the Uisge came down through a series of rocky pools. The warmth beat down upon him; new-sprung ferns shaded his head with a green, sweet, shade, and he dozed for a while.

When he woke up the sun had gone in again and the day was overcast, though still warm. His first cast brought out a better fish than he had caught all the morning, and the omen held true. The three rock pools, generally good for a rise apiece, yielded seven fish, not one of them under two ounces. It was odd, Woollen observed aloud as he arranged the fish according to size on the grass, gazing at them with a childish complacence, it was odd how one's standards changed: he had fished some of the English chalk streams where a half-pound fish was as a minnow; now he was delighted with two-ounce fish. Anything much smaller than that was rather disappointing, but these did in truth look like real trout; small ones, indeed very small ones, but the real fish for all that.

He went up the river slowly now, for the fish were coming up in a most gallant and determined rise. The Uisge had little trout, but there were many of them on a good day. By the time he reached the pool under the mound his cloth bag was heavy in his pocket, and he had lost certain count of his fish, a thing that had not happened to him since he came into Ireland. He was on the opposite side to the mound, and as he stood at the foot of the pool he saw that the flood had bitten deeper into the round of the Torr an Aonar; there was a deep scar of bare earth, and the low scrub that had lined the far bank at the top was now in the water, most of it lying sideways with branches tearing the water, still anchored by the roots.

He wanted to cast diagonally up the pool, straight for the mound, for the deepest water was just under it, and there he had raised his good trout before. Formerly he had cast up from where he stood now, dropping his fly into the little smooth place on the far side of the incoming current – a natural weir brought it in with some force – so that it poised momentarily before dragging across and down. Now, with this change, the piece of slack water was very much enlarged, and might hold nothing; also, the half-submerged tangle of dwarf willow and bramble, with all the rushes and grass that it had gathered, made the cast a dangerous one. He was undecided still when he saw a rise in the eddy; he could not see whether it was his fish or not, but he made a couple of air casts, feeling his way across the pool, and then dropped his fly neatly into the middle of the slack water. But he had too long a line out, and when he struck with the rising of the fish he could not whip it cleanly from the water. It darted instantly into the tangle, and before he could reel in, the line was fast knit.

Woollen crossed the pool at the bottom and came round to the tangle. It was awkward to get at it, because of the slope of the mound, which ran straight into the water here, but with a good deal of trouble he pulled the whole weedy mess up on to the side. The trout was only a very little fish, not the big one at all. Woollen took it carefully in his wet hand and worked the hook out. He went up to the bank overhanging the slack water so that he could put the fish into a quiet place out of the run of the current. Much more of the bank had caved in than he had supposed, looking from the other side. He knelt and held the little fish in the hollow of his hand under the water; it stayed there for a moment before shooting away into the waving green bed, out of sight.

When he had disentangled his cast and line he began to

examine the altered bank, so that he should know the new lie of the pool another day. Huge slices of spongy black earth had been undercut and lay at the bottom with their long grass streaming. One slice had not quite parted; it hung with a deep wide crack between it and the still solid land. Woollen pushed it with his foot and it went over, quite slowly, with a watery sough. The water was shallow under it, and the black earth lay half awash. Woollen was still looking vacantly at it when there was a slight rumble – tremor rather than sound – under his feet and a great stone slab fell flatlings into the thin water and mud, scattering them far out across the pool. Immediately after there was an indescribable rushing noise as a hundred thousand gold coins gushed on to the slab piling up like wheat, cascading, flowing, flowing. All at once the gush stopped: one last coin rolled down, slid down the side of the pile and rang on the stone.

Woollen had not moved. His breath suspended, his hand to his mouth; his throat was stiff, could not swallow, and his heart was doing strange things even before his reason had grasped the reality of what was before him.

Two things stabbed into his mind; one the word 'escape' and a thousand implications behind it, the other the dreadfulness of the coins on the far side dribbling down to irrecoverable loss in the deep water. With a violent, epileptic jerk he leapt to rescue them. There was no need: they lay in a few inches of water on the side of a turf that had gone in before. The surprising chill of the water checked him, and he stood there gasping, with his sense coming back. Bending, he peered under the dark bank: the earth had fallen away from a stone chest buried deep in the mound; three sides of it and its lid still stood there, canted outwards by long subsidence to such a degree that no single coin remained. The fourth side and a long sliver of flawed stone from the bottom of the chest had fallen under the immense weight of the gold. His mind digested this while he drew breath, and at once he was back with one foot on the bank and the other on the stone slab, saying, 'Easy now, old Woollen. Steady does it,' and picking up gold with both hands. He worked with immense speed at first, but as his natural phlegm began to reassert itself even in the smallest degree he arranged them in neat piles, counting as he did so.

His first wild flurry of spirits, painful in its intensity, calmed, to be succeeded by an all-embracing happiness. This vast hoard was his. He had not the first glimmering of a doubt there. Plans formed and reformed with lightning rapidity in his head; he lost count of the hundreds. He came up on to the bank among the piles to count again, and he suddenly found himself trembling with weariness.

The sun came out, and the gold sent back its light, not a coin but what was brilliant; no tarnish, no obscuring dust. Woollen sat among the heaps, passing the gold through his hands. It was not Armada gold, as he had expected; there were a few Roman aurei, some Greek staters, among them coins of a beauty that struck him even then, and a mass of thick, unintelligible rounds that he supposed to be Oriental. There was no silver, no bronze. Gold; all gold.

He knew that he could not possibly carry a tenth part of it, and while he was weighing in his mind the ways of dealing with it he was possessed with the idea that he might already have been seen – some lurker in an illicit still, some chance wandering youth in the mountainside. He did not ever suppose that there might be other things in the valley watching him, measuring his breath, weighing his shadows; silent things like a round bank of fern or a crag at a vantage point, incessantly recording, communicating with each other, collating, storing up.

There were stills in the neighbourhood, he knew very well. The gleam of the hoard – how it flashed and shone; it would catch a man's eye five miles away. With a chill on his soul he covered some with his coat, strewed the broken tangle over more, tore up bushes to cover the rest. He stared searchingly at the mountains, down the two ridges; there was no movement, only a kestrel hanging in the wind. The valley behind him was empty.

'I must not dig. They would see the marks ...' His mind's voice trailed off in an anguish of frustration. Illumination came:

he sprang down into the water again and tore lumps from the fallen earth. Then leaning under the still overhanging bank to the great chest he levelled its floor with clods, piled it high with gold, built up a wall of stones and turf to serve for the fallen sides, and crammed the chest again. The slab, lest it should draw notice, he moved with a strength that he had never known before, and plunged it into the deep swirling middle water.

Some gold remained, enough to buy half the County Mayo. He dug among the bushes, in spite of his fear; he dug with his hands and slashed the roots with his knife. There was little trace when he had done. By now his mind was running fast and clear. 'I will go over to Ballyatha,' he said, 'and I will sell four or five at Power's there. Then I will buy some decent clothes and have dinner at the Connaught. To-morrow I will send some to the big London dealers, and when I have the money . . .' There were so many possible variations that his mind stumbled in a happy indecision.

He was ready. A dozen very thick coins weighed down the pockets of his coat. The sun was well down the sky but if he hurried he could reach Ballyatha in time. It was clearly essential that he should not be cheated of one day's happiness; it was less clear how getting to Ballyatha affected the safety of everything, but he was entirely certain that it did. The way was over the pass between Slieve Donagh and Ardearg, right up the valley and over the curtain of rock that closed its upper end. A chasm, not six feet wide – a man could touch each side with outstretched arms – and twenty yards long formed the pass, and below it on the far side was the town.

There was no path: he toiled upwards with his eyes fixed on the skyline. When he had gone a quarter of a mile he spun round, ran in long bounds downhill to the water, to the chest, grasped handfuls of gold, stuffed his pockets, his trout-bag, hurled the fish away. Then, breathing in great uneven gasps, he turned his face to the pass again and forced his labouring body up and up, on for ever, always uphill and the short grass slippery like glass.

He must get there in time, everything depended on it. The

weight was more than he could bear and the pass was infinitely high above. The sun hurried down. Woollen, the unfortunate man in all his days, pressed on and on, and still the everlasting hill stretched above and beyond him. A despairing glance over his shoulder at the sun as it dipped made him stumble and fall. The wind chilled his soaking body. On and on: not to look up: on, on, on. He did look up, and the pass in the dusk was before him.

But in the pass he met the keeper of the hoard.

5

The Virtuous Peleg

———⊗⊗⊗———

Every year a great concourse of people come to the place they call Kevin's tomb in the mountains and they pray him to intercede for them, for although he is not a saint upon the calendar – he is not that Kevin, but another – he is much revered in those parts which is no doubt a great solace to him as he burns for ever in the extreme torment aggravated as it is by every device and artifice known to the fiend of hell. The pilgrims suppose him to be well placed to intercede for them, in which they are right, by far the most of them being false lechers, damned in every inch.

Kevin was a young man when he first lived in the beehive cells that stand around Deara. He had no inclination to the warfare which was the occupation of his sept, nor to work, and equally none to women; he was as soft as a cat and sober in his discourse and he slept inordinately, which made him fat despite the diet of Deara. In the first years of his life with the holy monks he was unable to avoid a small share of the work, but when his young cousin Peleg was allowed to join him this was no longer the case, which was a consolation to Kevin.

Peleg had little enough inclination in his nature to work, but he revered his cousin, who had an awful and persuasive way, and had been held up to Peleg as a man perfect all the days of his life, and daily young Peleg forced his nature and conquered this aversion and cleaned the cell and tilled the apron of garden and carried stones from the common field. The carrying of them, even

the huge square ones, was easy enough for Peleg, being the length
and breadth of an ox as he was, and that of the larger kind.

They did not hold Peleg in much estimation at Deara, for he
had no learning and if they had known he was incapable of his
letters even, Peleg would have been put out of the beehive cells
and they would have made him go back to watching his father's
herd of swine, a meagre herd that was watched already by his nine
brothers.

Peleg was humble in his mind and freely acknowledged his
deficiencies; he studied meekness and told over his letters by day
and by night, but they ran by like water or the mist and he had
no hold upon them, which made him low in his spirits: his mind
would also turn of itself to young women, especially to the three
daughters of Turlough who were so kind and loving to him; and
whenever his mind did this he would leap up and plunge into
the deep pool to his neck and tell over his letters. Kevin told
him each time how wicked he was, and the monks would offer
to scourge him at any time, by day or by night, whenever he felt
himself invaded by the flesh or the Devil.

It was at about this time that news came to Deara of Brothen's
wonderful voyage to the Picts, how he went on a millstone that
happened to be on the shore, and he sleeping most of the way and
without oar, rudder or sail, and how he had baptized seven Pict-
ish kings in one day, eleven dukes with their families, with many
other nobles and four large fields of ordinary people.

The news edified the monks of Deara, as well it might; but it
seemed to Peleg that he noted a certain restraint, almost a sour-
ness like that you may see on the face of the second man when he
says how well the first has run. Peleg too felt that the honour of
Deara was in some way lowered by this success from the north,
and daily after he had returned thanks for the spread of the faith
he prayed that some one of the holy men of Deara might be
moved to take to the sea, to be wafted by ghostly hands to the
pagan coast, there to meet a bloody martyrdom with unflinching
delight or to convert fourteen kings with the numerous family of
each while the sun should stand in admiration and the day grow

long enough for the numbers of the common to pass the end of counting. He prayed especially that the reverend Kevin might be the chosen vessel: he prayed with fervour and his four bones were flayed and his blood soaked into the stone.

Days passed, and the monks of Deara looked at one another sideways and anxious, but none went near the strand.

Peleg watched Kevin for signs of a trance or an exaltation perhaps, but Kevin still moved slowly and slept the day long in his cell, waking to eat or to go through the motions of worship. The only hopeful sign at all was his increasing absentmindedness; for day after day now he would forget that the stir-about was for two and he would eat it all, as well as the nuts.

Many days Peleg fasted and that apart from the usual fasts of Deara which were known in all the Christian world: it was for his soul's health, as he found one evening, it being Friday and his birthday. There was an angel sitting on the heap of stones by the side of the common field that Peleg was picking for ever.

'Now, Peleg,' said the angel. 'God and Mary to you.'

'God and Mary to you and Patrick, sir,' replied Peleg, with good manners all over his ugly face.

'I have two messages for you, Peleg,' said the angel, and he stuck a moment in his speech, and Peleg could see that the messages had flown out of his memory and it was a question whether he could get them back or no.

'I have two messages for you, Peleg,' he repeated, slowly and leaning upon the importance of his words.

'I am much obliged for your kindness, your reverence,' said Peleg. 'It must have been the weary road, the day being close and thunder coming.' It was a little at random that he was talking, to save the angel from embarrassment.

'Now I will tell you what it is, Peleg,' said the angel, getting up off the heap of stones. 'Should you like to try a couple of falls with me? You was always the one for wrestling, I think.'

'If it would not be too forward in me, sir, I should welcome it of all things,' said Peleg. 'To try a couple of falls with your honour would give me all the pleasure in life.'

45

The angel stretched his arms and stamped his feet; he was a cheerful angel, the sort St Paul warned women about, and Peleg thought he had taken drink upon the way.

'I shall dust your jacket, mind,' said the angel, and he was right, for in five minutes he had put Peleg down on the flat of his back three times with a bang that made the dust fly up.

'Now sit down upon the stone, joy,' said the angel, 'for you are pale in the face, I see, and I will tell you the two messages. The first is, "Heaven helps those as help themselves," and the second is, "There are those who seem more than they appear to others or themselves notwithstanding the appearance of some as they would appear in the first place; or the contrary."'

Peleg thanked the angel many times over, and asked might he hear the blessed words again.

'Why, no, Peleg,' replied the angel slowly, getting himself ready to go. 'I doubt it would be exactly right for me to repeat them, being the way it is. But they will certainly echo again, and bear the most elegant fruit.'

So Peleg walked with the angel to the edge of the field, where the path came in, and said, 'If your reverence chooses to take the road, the path that crosses the bog by those willows is the best, and the second house on the way is Seamus's, where is the best refreshment and easy bedding, with butcher's meat every day of the week almost.'

'I know it,' said the angel. 'I was there on my way.' And he said as he went, 'Health and glory and salvation to you, Peleg,' and Peleg replied, 'A hundred thousand thanks to you, your reverence, and glory and health and happiness for ever to you.'

The messages did indeed re-echo in Peleg's mind, they churned about until the inside of his head was full of night, and there was no sense in it. He went wandering over the bog in a daze until it was dark, and then he went vacantly into his cell where Kevin was asleep, and lay down on the hard floor.

He could not remember going to sleep, but he woke up very suddenly in the dead hour of the night, his mind a blaze of illumination: there was a little sickly moon but enough to see by and he looked closely at Kevin who was in the very depth of stupor and his mouth open. Peleg eased up his chin gently to improve his appearance, and gently, like a woman, gathered him up in his clothing as he lay there and carried him out of the cell. As he had often done, he struck the lintel with his bowed shoulders and bore off a handsbreadth of skin, but the pain did not discommode him nor the prodigious vast weight of his cousin and his bulk overflowing.

The dew was thick on the grass and his footsteps showed clear, running straight to the strand. There were boats there, and three millstones of different sizes, but millstones were for the beneficed clergy, abbots, bishops and deans, and Peleg put Kevin into a little neat curach. The sleeping Kevin groaned and settled himself and Peleg sat on a thwart while the tide swept them out and away on the far, broad ocean.

For hours and hours Peleg sat there in a holy calm, contemplating the beauty of the calm sea, for it was like a small pond in its calmness and there was the long path of the moon behind them. The air was warm and sweet like hay to smell and the curach slipped through the quiet water, creaking a little and the water making a little slipping noise under it.

Dawn came up with the glory of heaven and still Kevin slept. Peleg longed to wake him so that they could be speaking of the voyage; sometimes he moved with more noise than he needed, and sometimes he coughed, but it was not until just before tierce that Kevin moved. The fat man gaped stupidly at Peleg, with his mouth dragged open, and when Peleg bade him rejoice because they were on the sea moving fast with the push of unseen hands towards the heathen shore he made no reply. He stared wildly round the pale bowl of the sky, green and grey where it met the sea all round and no land, no land at all; unending waters stretching away and away to the edge of the world and the sun glittering on them. He moaned aloud as he sat there crouched, and Peleg told him of his angel and about the glory of their approaching mission. Kevin made no answer, but when Peleg said he thought they might sing a loud prayer, he leapt up and stood balancing in the curach as it rocked and screamed curses at Peleg with the worst words in the world so that Peleg wondered how he had ever come to know them: and Peleg grew weary of hearing Kevin staining his soul and he rocked the boat the way Kevin was not expecting it so he fell in over the edge and swam in the sea among the fishes of the deep, and monsters came into his mind as well as the fear of drowning. So Kevin was in a great taking and nearly dead from his various fears and the furious amount of salt water he had taken in while shouting under the sea and breathing there too, and he spoke civilly to his cousin Peleg to have him into the curach again, which Peleg did, though with difficulty.

Now Kevin lay in the bottom of the curach weeping with cold and so frightened that he had not the look of a white pudding, far less a man, and Peleg sat on the tail end of the boat thinking, while he trailed his hand in the water.

A little spirit came back into Kevin as the sun dried him and he asked had Peleg brought any food, but Peleg had not brought any food; then he said they ought to go back because he had no licence from his superior to be converting heathens and because there was a book in his cell of great power and efficacity and he did not know how he could turn them from their heathenish ways without its help, and if Peleg would turn back now he would get the book and the licence from his superior as well as some relics and they would start again in a more respectable vessel than a common curach stinking of old fish the way it did, and dangerous with its thin, leaky sides.

'There is no sail, reverend Kevin, nor oars, nor a rudder to turn with: furthermore, we are impelled by unseen hands.'

So Kevin lay down again in the bottom of the boat and groaned until the sun went down into the sea behind them and night spread over the waters and still the curach slipped on with the push of unseen hands.

In the morning the sun was in front of them again and at their side was a grey island rising high out of the sea: Peleg awoke from a kind sleep and there by the side of the curach was a seal

48

watching for him to wake. He blessed the good seal, which was his custom, and the seal brought him a fish to his hand.

The island was full of sea-birds, white, black and pied, as full as a hive of bees, and their screaming awoke Kevin, who said they were fiends and cursed them. He wished to go on to the island to escape the sea and would have swum, for they passed very near, but he saw the seals as thick as a fair and he was afraid. 'They are fiends,' he said. 'The sea is full of fiends.'

The island sank into the sea behind them, but before it was quite down they saw land ahead stretching far to the either hand Presently Peleg could discern the mouth of a broad river, and the curach went up into it, over the bar with no more than three inches of water covering it at this state of the tide, but that so godly quiet that they slipped over with no danger, and now Peleg saw on his left hand a sandy waste and on his right hand a rich, fruitful country, green and red where the soil showed.

Kevin's heart and courage had grown since they had crossed the bar, and he was talking when the curach grounded gently in the sand of the right-hand shore. The jar threw him flat on his face, so Peleg picked him out of the boat and put him on the dry sand, where he sank down in a heap, gasping. Peleg looked and he saw the neat curach turned about already and running easily through the water, which had waves now, though small. He watched it going on the broad waters and he felt a small quell in his heart, but only for a moment, he being maintained by the zeal of his mission.

They went up the shore, Kevin blaming Peleg very bitterly for letting the curach go, and into a green wood, where Peleg lit a fire, having returned thanks, and he cooked the fish, which was a mullet; and the heathen of those parts surrounded them in the bushes.

The first they knew of the heathen was a terrible howling and an ululating that would have daunted the heart of an emperor, it was so near and the men unseen. Then there was a shower of arrows and stones that tore the green leaves and the heathen rushed in upon them. They were painted orange and they carried long, bare knives and it was the way they had to flay all strangers on their coast. Peleg and Kevin without drawing breath for one peaceable word sprang, leapt and sped through the trees and beyond inland with all the agility in the world, running so fast they passed the startled deer, and the heathen ran after them to have their hides, but their heathenish cries and howling delayed them, whereas Peleg and Kevin ran without a word, seeing they needed their breath and could not be sparing it in hallooing and bawling aloud.

It was a wonder to see the fat man run with his face and belly quivering and shaking like the bag of a cow, but soon he faltered and cried out to Peleg, who took him by the hand and they raced over the strange country with flying strides and the heathen drawn out behind them, howling angrily in the distance, angrier as the distance grew.

For hours and hours they ran until they came to heathery land, high and rolling, with standing meres and bogs and they could see clear miles behind them with nobody following. It was a harsh and desolate country, and its brooks ran dark between black, steep banks. White mist curled in the lower parts and already with the coming of the night the mist was rising to cover the whole country.

On the top of a craggy piece they lay in a cave, a great deep cave that went back and back, and Peleg's mind troubled him because he had avoided his martyrdom and because he had uttered no peaceable or godly word to the heathen. Kevin wept from exhaustion and lasting terror and the pain of his feet as well as for the memory of the grey mullet uneaten by the woodland fire: he uttered a few watery prayers and slept in his moaning. But Peleg remained waking, working in his mind, and when the devils of the waste-land came they found him awake.

The sight of so many fiends at once appalled Peleg beyond the power of speech, and Kevin turned the colour of lead, with never a word in his mouth, though it opened and closed. The devils sat about the cave, quite easy, and lit it up with the effulgence of their persons.

The captain of the devils, a grand spotted one, spoke in a loud commanding voice to Peleg and said: 'Now, Peleg, we don't want but two words with you, just renounce the Trinity at once, if you please, and we'll cry quits.'

But Peleg said never a word, and he made no answer again when the captain of the devils said, 'It is only a form, you know; there is nothing to it, at all.' So the devil grew angry and sent for a rack and a portable furnace and when they had put down the rack, together with a variety of instruments like iron flails and saws which the messengers brought of their own motion, with a ringing clash on the floor and had set up the furnace the way the cave stank of brimstone the captain nodded to Peleg and said, 'We'll sort you directly, my man.' Then he turned sharp on Kevin and gave him the same order and he said, 'Kevin, stand up at once and renounce the Trinity out of hand,' and he stamped fire.

Kevin stood up at once, but Peleg cried to him to have courage. The devil nodded to a great hairy thing of uncertain shape that had been standing behind Peleg's neck all this time, breathing on him, and it struck him down and gagged him. He lay and heard Kevin renounce the Trinity and everything else he could lay his mind to, and indeed Kevin blasphemed until even the devils stretched their eyes and looked behind them.

'It's all very well,' said the oldest hob-devil to the Captain secretly behind his hand like a man at a fair, 'but we shan't have his soul for certain like this: he must be damned of his own will, you know.'

The Captain said, 'Sure, you're right, my dear, but if he's got a soul at all there would be hardly any taste in it, or flavour, as you might say. We'll not spend anything on getting it, so. However, try an ordinary temptation or two by all means, if you're so inclined.'

Then they turned to Peleg and threatened him like black-guards, but Peleg said, 'You old blackguards, the back of my hand to you all.'

Then they had him to the rack, but it was too small by half for one of his length, and even when they had it wound right up it hardly stretched him above an inch. So they started on him with their flails, but they had small confidence in them, seeing that Peleg's father had always beaten his sons whenever they did wrong with a holy rage far beyond the emulation of devils, and Peleg had often done wrong in his young days – nearly every day, indeed. When they were tired and had spoilt three of their fails they stopped and took Peleg into an inner cave. There they made him sleep and let him rest while they considered of what they should do. He woke up to find the three daughters of Turlough in the cave, they who had been so kind and loving to him before he went to Deara after holiness, and a voice said in his ear that he could have whichever he chose as a reward for his fortitude. But the devil himself could not have told the confusion in Peleg's heart at the sight of the three together, by reason of the passages he had had with each separately, and Peleg blushed fiery red and hid his face. The she-devils who personated the daughters of Turlough thought themselves scorned and they stepped out of the cave with bitter anger and said they had no business with geldings, nor with unnatural men, they said.

This put the devils out of countenance, for they saw they were improving Peleg's chance of salvation hour by hour, and this was poison and death to their minds. When they had tempted him with meat and drink and fire and water as well as with gold and silver and the promise of land with no success, they said he must be more holy than he looked, and the great scholar of the world, no doubt.

'There is only one way with these scholars,' said the Captain and he called for a pen. For seventy-three days they kept Peleg by while the Captain worked fourteen and fifteen hours a day and his claws grew long and curved for want of the wear of exercise and fiends ran hither and yon with sheets of paper at every hour on the heather of the waste-land. At the end the Captain had two books written, the one of elegant poems so lewd that they would have been a danger to St Anthony, and the other, in fine elm boards with silver clasps, a book of homilies so eloquent that they would have struck Chrysostom dumb, and they poisoned through and through with the creeping poison of a heresy so persuasive that no ecclesiastic much under the degree of a saint could have withstood it.

They put them by Peleg while he slept and they penned him up with them and a good, clear light and a reading desk and no other kind of diversion at all until his beard grew to the middle of his chest and they judged he had had time to damn himself. But Peleg had only opened the books once apiece to see were there capitals painted on gold with every variety of colour and beasts interlacing, but there were not, the Captain having no turn that way, and he had closed them without taking more thought, for his strength was not in reading and indeed he could not exactly recall above half a dozen of the letters themselves at this distance from Deara. He had spent his time in mortification and prayer and learning the meekness that he lacked, and particularly in praying for his cousin Kevin, which had done his own soul so much good that it was now practically white and in better shape than it had been since he was first capable of sin.

It was on a Friday that the Captain sent two devils to the inner cave to fetch Peleg, and when they opened the door they understood how it was with him and they turned grey and stood there abashed. Now Peleg had had plenty of time to collect himself and to consider what he would do and he was accustomed to the sight of fiends, however plain. He came at them briskly and struck their heads together for the glory of God so hard that they gave out a sound like a mallet on wood and no other but lay there like sacks. And he stepped over them and came to the outer cave where the Captain of the devils was waiting and the Captain saw how it was with him and stood up, grey in his colour and shrinking. Peleg struck him down for the glory of the Trinity and bent him back so that his horns, which were his pride and joy, locked in the long curl of his hoofs, and Peleg bowled him in a hoop out of the cave and down the slope to a bottomless mere, where he lies still, mopping and mowing for ever in a powerful rage and heating the waters of the mere so that neither fish nor frog can live there, far less breed, whereas before it was the great place for the snigging of eels.

Then he took his cousin Kevin from the corner of the cave and asked had any of the other devils a word in their mouths, but they standing mumchance and looking meaner than any book can say he gave them all a great devastating curse and walked out into the light of the day.

He walked with his head in the air for seven miles, glorying in the verdant world and the blue of the sky and longing for some honest meat, and Kevin followed him with the meanness of hell showing in his face. Then Peleg remembered his humility and made Kevin go in front, and they came to the edge of a chasm. This chasm was a furlong across and far deeper and it barred their way, and as Peleg stood there on the edge considering it and marvelling at its black depth and the wafting fog in it Kevin thought of the thirty bags of gold and the life-long idleness and safety for ever that the oldest hob-devil had promised him by the holiest oath if he would do Peleg a mischief, and he considered too how that he was already damned for sure, and, trembling all over, he crept behind Peleg and with a desperate moan he hurled his weight on Peleg's back and Peleg fell with his two hands outstretched grasping the air.

Before Peleg had fallen a yard the fiends of hell were upon Kevin and they snatched him away to their own place, he screaming like a stuck pig about their oath and they laughing white-hot tongues of fire.

And the angel at the bottom of the chasm peered up through the shifting fog and altered his feet, and as he caught Peleg he said, 'There, easy now, Peleg.' And he put him down and looked kindly in his face and said, 'Sit down upon the flat rock, Peleg, for you are pale in the face, I find.' 'God put a flower on you, joy,' said Peleg, and thanked him with all the civility at his command and many elegant turns of speech.

The angel let him breathe awhile and said, 'Stand up now, Peleg, for I have a message for you. It is you must go down to the sea again, to the heathen of the pagan shore, and there are fourteen kings of the pagan shore to whom you must preach the faith, for now there is virtue in you. That is the message: and now we shall take a glass or two together, for I have a bottle conveniently near at hand, and it appears that I will not see you again until I stand with my trumpet to sound you in over the mossy walls of Paradise.'

6

The Curranwood Badgers

———∞∞∞———

Mr Burke had a pack of foxhounds and he drank a bottle of wine a day, but for all his glory he was never able to bully or flatter Joseph Quinn into growing citrus fruit in the William and Mary orangery at Curranmore; so when the obstinate old Fenian died he imported a Welsh gardener, named by his aunt. She lived conveniently near to Holyhead, and she recommended Moses-Henry Williams from a personal knowledge of twenty years, during which he had made the thin acid ungrateful earth of Plas Pwll flower like Eden before the Fall, if as may reasonably be supposed Eden was planted with heathers of every variety, azaleas and rhododendrons.

In those days of depression it was hard for a man to find a place: the big houses were closing everywhere, Plas Pwll among them, and butlers, footmen, grooms, gardeners and valets joined the desolate queues outside employment exchanges; so Moses-Henry tore up his roots, left the gardens to go back to bramble, nettles and furze, with the yew-hedges spiring, bracken heaving up through the gravel and his frames vanishing in a sea of fool's parsley, and boarded the midnight packet with his son Gethin, their possessions done up with horticultural twine: a widower, alas, and he had never learnt how to pack, far less to wash, cook or sew. A tearing-up of roots indeed. He had never travelled farther than Bala; he had never been out of the sound of his own language: he was a deacon in the chapel at Rhobell-y-Big (Strict Ebenezer), and he had relatives in all the hill-farms behind.

It would have broken his heart, but for the rich Munster earth, the unlimited stable-manure, the warm soft air, his half-acre of glass, and the spontaneous ease with which everything grew, including the pineapple, the peach and the coveted orange.

For young Gethin it was harder still. He left his first and only love at Rhobell, his flame undeclared, without their having exchanged more than conscious looks and a fairing; and although he was kept hard at weeding his heart flew back across the sea to his native slates and the cold drifting rain, to the gaunt farm-house that sheltered Angharad, and to the hay-barn where they had sat side by side, their hands almost touching, talking politely through the hours of an infinitely welcome storm from the west.

Then again, Gethin's schooling had been all in Welsh: his mind was monoglot, and the Irish household abashed him with their unhesitating flow of English, as pure as a book. Their ways, their food and the flatness of their country amazed him; and when he saw the men hurry out on Sunday to start a hare he felt the world's foundations crumble.

The cook, who had eighteen nieces to marry and all the young men emigrating in droves leaving nothing but wicked old bache-lors behind, and who loved to see young people happy, took him to a ceilidhe. She had known a convert make an excellent hus-band, or a husband at least; and there was no time to be lost, poor decent young fellow. But Gethin could make nothing of the thumping music, the pipes and the fiddle, still less of the dances, the floor trembling under him; and although the girls were so fresh, sweetly-spoken and modest, he had nothing whatsoever to say.

His solace apart from a knee-harp of his own manufacture, was the company of Mr FitzGibbon, the huntsman, himself a recent arrival in the Curranmore demesne, Aloysius FitzGibbon from Cork. He had travelled far out of Ireland, as a trooper in his youth, when there were horses in the cavalry regiments, and then as a hunt-servant to various English packs: he understood much of what Gethin had to say, and as to the Welshman's Protestant-ism, he delivered his opinions at length in the kitchen. Between his wheezes, chuckles and parentheses on oecumenical progress ('the back of my hand to the priest the wrong way about, arsyversy – give me fish on Friday and the comfortable Latin') the words 'an oppressed people too, so they are' and 'kept their language itself, so they have, by damn' recurred again and again; and it was understood that the constancy of the Welsh in one respect might to some degree compensate for their changeability in another, and that they were not so utterly damned as Orangemen or Freemasons. 'Though to be sure we must pray for them buggers now,' he said with a sigh, before coming back to the Welsh 'great fellows too, in the poetry line'.

FitzGibbon was long past mark of mouth, and what with whiskey and bawling at hounds his voice was a creaking whisper: a short, broad-shouldered, round man with a scarlet face set in wrinkles of mirth. His riding was now largely a matter of balance, a continuous miracle, but he hunted Mr Burke's hounds with passionate zeal, with skill and success; he killed a wonderful number of foxes a year, and the death of each was a fresh joy to him, a triumph never staled. He loved almost everybody around him, a most affectionate creature, so much so that the Kingdom of Thomond was filled with his likenesses, some tall and others short, but none under ten for virtue had been thrust upon him at last.

It was strange that he and Gethin should have taken such a liking, for Gethin had never seen a hound in his life, far less climbed on to a horse and his soul shuddered at the scream of a hare. However, he loved Mr FitzGibbon, and often after a long day he would go to the kennels to help feed the hounds, facing the ghastliness of flayed cows long dead, hanging blue and rain-soaked in chains from a tree, the swollen sheep, the quarters of an ass.

His father disliked the dogs – Calvinism and foxhunting do not run together – but he could not dislike FitzGibbon when he came to their cottage in the evening and laughed and wheezed in the corner seat, a party of pleasure in himself; and when Gethin asked for a holiday to go and draw the badgers of Curranwood with the huntsman he did not object.

The badgers had been increasing these last few years: they

were turning up in places where they had never been heard of, and many a fox had gone to earth in an unsuspected sett, or had retreated into the fastness of an old holt newly enlarged. The worst badgers of all, said Mr FitzGibbon, were those who lived in Curranwood; they were unreasonably prolific; they were dead-bent upon peopling the country with more of their kind – little doubt they were Jews. And if the poacher Edmund Colman were to be believed, they were rogue-badgers as well, taking pheas-ants' eggs, chicks, leverets, partridges, rabbits, poultry, even small lambs, for the love of God. Edmund was probably right, since he watched his rivals more attentively than the keeper could do, he being so taken up with trying to circumvent the whole Colman family and the Quinns and indeed most of the male part of the village.

It was a long stretch to Curranwood, over the Sliveen bog and into the hilly country beyond, and as the kennel-boy cried off at the last minute – his Da was not feeling quite well in his bowels, the typhoid maybe – it was not that he himself was afraid: he did not care for Curranwood at all; had often been to it free and volunteerly for eggs, when at school – Gethin walked there by himself. He was glad of the solitary walk, partly because it would lead him through a patch of sweet-gale on the bog, a reminder of home, but even more because he had a poem turning about in his head.

His steps helped to beat out the metre, and in the open coun-try he tried how it would sound.

Over the Irish sea the moon hangs like a red hawk.
   It has caught my heart as the red hawk catches a warm quivering mouse:
   The small blood rains down.

The moon hangs over the Irish sea like a looking-glass.
   Angharad, my eyes strain up till the tears rain from them:
   When will they see yours shining there?

He varied it this way and that, inverting the lines, shifting the pause; and it was not from want of labour that the poem was still far from what he knew it might be – what it had been indeed when he first dreamt it – by the time he came to the place where he was to wait for Mr FitzGibbon. But his mind was not in its best dispositions, being in a forward-looking state of excitement, reaching out for the events of the day. He had heard of badgers for ever, but he had never seen one and he would have walked ten times the distance for the off-chance of a glimpse. He was not at all sure what drawing implied: he imagined it meant something in the nature of driving them away; but the abstract notion of death caused him no particular concern.

The place where he waited had been called Curranwood only these last few generations; before that it had an Irish name, and people still sometimes called it by the rough equivalent, the *kind* or *gentle* place, which was in itself a way of avoiding the still earlier heathen name, one that referred more particularly to the mound in the middle.

An ancient wood, one of the few remaining pieces of the forest that had once spread so far over the island: it had never been cut, never tended in any way in the past; and it was left untended, almost unvisited now. It had not changed since the last wolf in Munster retired there to die: the returning Firbolg would have found it the same. Occasionally Conn Leary, the quickset man, would grub round the edge when he was pressed for an order, and the keeper looked through it at times; otherwise the wood was never disturbed except when Mr Burke's hounds came there, the earth-stopper, or guests desperately keen for a cock.

It was a mixed wood, seen from outside, with ashes in the place where Gethin stood, alders down by the stream, and hazel; but its heart was all oak and had been for ever: low spreading trees, from hollow shells a thousand years old to saplings or the springing twig of the year. Young trees and old: yet the feeling was one of immense and hoary moss-grown age. That was the first feeling. The next, following without a pause, was that the wood was curiously silent; and not only silent but hostile.

Gethin stood in an open place where a ghost of a path led in among the ash-trees, and when he had felt this uneasiness upon him for some time he put it down to the ashes, with their poisonous drip. Nothing wholesome would grow under ash-trees, he knew: he would move farther into the wood.

Beyond a slope studded with toadstools – violent translucent slime-covered witch's jelly and a colony of white boys, now in viscid decay – he came to a place where the trees stood wide enough for fern to grow; and as he sat there he wished he had not set out so soon. There would be a long wait now, and already his poem seemed flat and cold, not worth turning in his mind, far less saying aloud in this silence. He made another about foxes in a rigorous old metre, more an eisteddfod exercise than a poem; but even as an exercise it was not much good, and it had the word silence in it, which he disliked.

Presently he found that he was thinking not about how to avoid the word silence but about trees and how very much more alive they were than they seemed. No one was afraid of a single tree, standing by itself. Nor of a dozen: nor of an orchard: nor of any number of planted trees. But a grove, an old grove of say a hundred, might have its particular feeling, its own air inside it; and this was far more than a grove – a wood, and a very ancient wood.

All at once it occurred to him that what he was looking at, the trunks, the boughs, the twigs branching for ever was not the true living part, the knowing and living part; they were only the creature's inverted lungs hanging there. The head, the being itself, was underground. A tree was certainly an underground creature, a thing of the dark; and its true members were the roots, intricate past imagination and creeping extremely fine far beyond the spread of the boughs.

And yet that was not right, either: a single tree was hardly a creature at all, not a being in itself: that was why it was not formidable. The whole wood, all these trees together with their roots mingling in the closest communion so that the entire floor was a network, *that* was the real being, huge, silent, a single, listening being.

No doubt it was worse when they were all of the same kind: the same message passing through. And here there was nothing whatsoever but oak. As he said *worse* he realized that he dared not move. His neck was stiff: it would be extremely dangerous to turn his head. His senses were all on the stretch and he could hear very slight noises, so slight that they accentuated the dark, living silence – a crack behind him and to the left, a rustling. But it was not the noises that frightened him: what it was he could hardly yet name, although the name flickered on the edge of his unwilling mind.

A pigeon came gliding in, landed above him; then catching sight of Gethin's candle-white face it clattered out of the tree with an explosion that nearly made him sick. Yet this broke the spell of rigid listening; and not long afterwards he heard a familiar sound in the distance, Mr FitzGibbon cursing Yellow William, the ass. At once his terror receded, dwindling back into the wood before him; he stood up without the least precaution, and although one leg had gone numb he hopped and stumbled along so fast that he was there on the path as the ass entered the wood.

FitzGibbon had three couple of terriers with him and a puppy he had brought back from its walker: a crowd of everyday creatures, smelly and welcoming; particularly Gethin's favourite dog, the little square bitch that shared his supper and often brought her fleas into his bed, Biddy by name. 'There you are, boy, God love you,' he said. 'Let's sit down in the shade.' He wiped his scarlet face with his handkerchief, looked round and asked 'Where's Tom?'

'He is looking after his Da, who has the typhoid to his bowels maybe.'

'He is looking after Bridey Colman more likely, the jackeen. I'll cut him, by and by – put an end to his capers – Jesus, Mary and Joseph, I can hardly spit for the heat.' He sat down to wheeze under the ash-trees, and winked at the ass's pannier, saying something barely coherent about bottled porter, the fewer the better fare, a bite of cheese, and mind the old crow now Gethin avick.

When he had gasped and drunk and grown cooler he said, 'Tell me a poem, boy, till I drink up my porter.'

Gethin put Biddy off his knee, cleared his throat for the right bardic moo, and said

'Little foxes at the bottom of the cliff,
Young foxes playing in and out.
I let my breath go at last
And instantly they are old hard foxes, motionless.
I breathe in again – no foxes there at all
Only silence, and a feather turning in the breeze.'

The old man chuckled and said it was as good as the Latin almost: would Gethin tip him the English of it, now?

As they passed up through the wood Mr FitzGibbon showed Gethin the signs of the badgers, their high-roads, their filth-pits, the places where they stood up like cats, sharpening their claws; he pointed these things out in grunts and wheezes, shouldering his way along the badger-path, and it was not until they reached the first sett that he turned round, took the iron bar and the spade and said pleasantly, 'I hope we kill the little old bugger in here. Younge Crambo needs blood.'

This was the first time that Gethin had known for sure that death was of the party, though the zeal of the dogs might have told him so at the edge of the wood. He said nothing, but listened while FitzGibbon described the loss of a cub in this very place at the end of a day, a cub he had particularly wanted to kill because the young entry too needed blood, the tonic of the world. 'Cubs, now, you don't want to be massacring cubs or breaking their hearts – just split up the families – but some blood the young 'uns must have.'

It was a new holt on a hazel-bank, not at all obvious, because the freshly-dug earth hardly showed between the nut-trees; and then there were rocks too, which stopped the badgers mining far down. But FitzGibbon pointed out the tracks, the odd wisps of bedding; and in any case the terriers' passion showed that this was no ordinary place.

The chief entrance was between two rocks, and ferns covered the hole, sweet-scented ferns. FitzGibbon gave Gethin the dogs and went grunting down on all fours, parting the fern and thrusting his head in as far as it would go, as he sniffed for the reek of a fox. Now the terriers knew he was in earnest and they bawled louder still, scrabbling the earth, pulling like horses, strangling themselves. The huntsman raised his purple face and called out for Teague, and the minute the terrier was loosed (a low dog with a great lunt of a head, a primitive Sealyham) it ran to him silently. Aloysius picked it up, whispered privately into its ear, and put it to. Teague thrust straight in and vanished.

FitzGibbon listened for a while and then he called for Biddy, the dog with the cruel scar on her face: she shot down after Teague and all at once the other dogs fell silent. They sat there at Gethin's feet, rigid, pricked up, trembling continuously, while the huge hound puppy wandered about so deeply ignorant that it took no interest in anything but twigs and an odd bit of filth, like a child taken to Rome. Some underground noise set them shrieking again and one of the couples broke from his hold – he had no sort of authority over the dogs at this point, though they liked him. FitzGibbon caught them with an off-hand sweep and held them dangling as he listened below. Apart from a slate-pencilling the other two were quiet, and Gethin could hear Biddy's characteristic scream, muffled under the earth. Suddenly Teague reappeared, having come up from another hole. His hair was roughed the wrong way and his white had turned black-ish-brown: he ran busily through the bushes.

FitzGibbon slipped another dog, Crambo. Time passed, poised between crisis and boredom, an attenuated war: sometimes there were thumps below ground, sometimes a dog showed unexpectedly before darting below. Then at last came Biddy's frantic marking voice and at once the noise redoubled as Teague joined her. FitzGibbon turned from the mouth of the holt and nodded in a pleased, significant manner, winking and jerking his head sideways. Gethin could not interpret the look at all, but he felt his excitement mounting.

The din came closer: the badger was beginning to drive the dogs, a heavy boar badger for sure, a hard fellow with a deadly gripe. Now FitzGibbon was calling down the hole – 'Loo, loo into him, boy. Break him and tear him, then. There's a Teague. Go to him, Biddy. Bind hard to him, boy. Both sides, both sides, d'ye hear me now?' – a continual stream of words, and oaths against the badger. But the badger drove them: Biddy came right out, with the red blood flowing, and Teague could not face him alone. He retreated; the noise died down. Now he was in a lower tunnel: he had thrown up a mound of earth, blocking the passage, and the dogs were the wrong side of it.

There followed a long, long pause, with nothing but muted scuffles and grunts below. In his excitement Gethin had edged right up to the huntsman and they exchanged nods at every renewal of the underground noise. Now they heard Biddy again, marking to him; she was keeping her distance, while the other dogs found their way through the maze. The badger was moving steadily along a tunnel that stretched away to the left: at first they could hear Biddy under their feet, then they followed the sound along and through the hazel-clumps to the outcropping rock at the back. Here she was joined by Teague and Crambo. Together they made a continuous din, and when they came to a stay, a stay proved by banging with the spade, FitzGibbon gauged the place carefully and clearing himself a space he drove down into the earth. His coat was off, his round back bowed to the work: the soil flew from the hole. His breath grew short, his face more scarlet still, the sweat ran fast, but his eyes were blazing and he never paused as he hacked through the roots and flung up the earth. A yard down his spade rang on a great flat stone: now the din was close and incessant, a growling and snarling beneath the higher-pitched roar. 'The crow,' said FitzGibbon, reaching behind him. He had the tip of the bar under the stone: he heaved it loose and then high on to its side. It swung up and Gethin saw his badger at last, the striped head lifted, eyes blinking in the sudden light.

Then they were all down on him. At the worst Gethin had not expected this – the harsh grunting of breath, the thudding, the blows; the silence under the terriers' din.

At last he looked again. Mr FitzGibbon was brushing the earth from his clothes, wiping his face on his handkerchief, his hands on the grass; the dogs were still round the badger, growling as they dragged its limp body this way and that over the ground. He turned his pleased, innocent, engaging old face to Gethin and said, 'If I hadn't fetched him a puck with the spade, he had Biddy destroyed, the way she was under him.' His voice was so much the voice of everyday life, so devoid of evil or wicked excitement, that Gethin felt the world come back into order, the hellish chaos fade like a nightmare. Surely all this was natural enough, part of the woodland scene? The big puppy was rolling on its back biting the leaves on either side. But when Gethin tried to speak he found that his voice was not under control.

FitzGibbon picked up the spade and his coat and they left the trampled devastated sett. Speaking in snatches over his shoulder he said they would try the big holt, the place they called the Shee in the old days, a hundred years ago, before Saint Patrick or Nebuchadnezzar; not that he expected they should do much, it being as huge as the underground railway in London. 'Was you ever in London, boy? The wicked great city, with no kind acquaintance – not to be mentioned in the same day as Cork. Still it has this railway, runs under the ground.' But it would stir them up, the old thieves, and maybe persuade them to go on to Mr Costelloe's land: they hated disturbance. And indeed it was likely they might find an outlier and chop him before he got into the maze. 'Or labyrinth,' he added, after a pause.

Gethin, carrying the heavy crowbar, cold and hard, walked some paces behind; and as he walked the guilt pressed down on him like a physical weight. He had done a horrible thing: a great unjust wrong, and a hideous wrong. He was one with the Devil. And now he was walking along behind Mr FitzGibbon, going on to another such blasphemous sin. He had no power to call out that it was evil. And as his mind cleared so that he understood this, he also found his old dread growing upon him again, in spite of the company: the company that was no company – he was utterly foreign to them.

Mr FitzGibbon had stopped: they were at the main sett and he was pointing out the features of it. 'That's the old Shee itself,' he said. A bald mound fringed with nettles and elder: a heap of grey moss-covered stones: all round, the ancient oak-wood, crowding in towards the central space, the trees standing so close they shut out the evening sky.

Innumerable generations of badgers had changed the symmetry of the great mound; innumerable generations had dug here, and the spoil-heaps themselves stood as high as a man. They were still digging too: in two or three places the fresh earth showed plain.

Gethin had no animosity towards Mr FitzGibbon, made no judgment on him or his dogs; he only felt a sick apprehension of what was to come. The day was turning in spite of him. There was nothing he could do and when FitzGibbon said should they go round to look at the queer old stone he followed without a word. FitzGibbon was telling him about his boyhood in Cork – not a local boy at all – *he* had not come off the bog – old-fashioned ways – and there they stood in front of a domed cylindrical stone, dark, a yard high, faintly covered with interlacing bands. As they reached it a magpie flew out of an elder and FitzGibbon broke off to stare for its mate. The minutes went by, and no second bird. 'By damn,' he cried, striking his spade into the ground. 'There's the end of our luck, the bloody old bird. The bloody, mongrelly bird.' Gethin heard him curse the wood, the rotting bloody old wood, and the dogs, the glum parcel of sods – no keenness, no fire in these dogs – they should be given a meal of mustard, once they were home. 'And you've lost your tongue, young fellow. Is it the colic so sudden, the gripes? But I dare say,' he added, good humour returning, 'I dare say you have a poem in mind.'

He paused, looking at the low yellow sky, and the silence gathered in: the dogs gazed up into their faces. Gethin's extreme distress had affected the bitch he liked best: the others had caught it from her – it was spreading fast. He had some vague notion of this, but how much of it was himself and how much the wood Gethin neither knew nor cared. 'I was going to tell you about that stone,' FitzGibbon said, 'but sure I'll do that another time.' And raising his voice to its habitual pitch he cried 'Hoick, a Teague, hoick a Biddy, get along forard. Hiyo, hiyo, hiyo. We'll try the first sett.'

It was a big open hole, unconcealed, the earth sandy and clean. He put Hector and Cutty to it, but they would own nothing there: went in, came out again with a busy, attentive look. He put them in again. This time they went a little farther before they came out, and while they were down Teague started to dig at a small hole to one side; he disappeared, and all at once Biddy let out an eager screaming, shriller than her usual note. Yet when she was slipped she made nothing of it at all: in and out all the time, whimpering – she seemed to have forgotten her trade.

'She had a kiss she didn't like the last time,' said FitzGibbon without conviction. 'She prefers that kind by the post.' He peered and smelt at the little hole. 'It's the queer smell here, so it is,' he said. 'Maybe a fox is after dragging something down.'

The day had lost its meaning, certainly all sense of zeal; and Gethin felt that FitzGibbon's strong sense of the world, his unquestioning acceptance, was yielding now: abruptly he cried out 'Late it is, Mr FitzGibbon. Late it is. Shall we go now, before it is too late altogether?'

The effort made him tremble. FitzGibbon did not answer directly, but looked up at the sky again. A long pause, in which the dogs moved about: they would not stay down, but for Teague. The hound puppy sat close by Gethin, pressed to his leg. 'Maybe you're right, too,' said FitzGibbon at last. 'We'll just wait on Teague, and if he don't find ...' The hound lifted its head in a howl. FitzGibbon leant over and gave it a staggering cuff. 'Ah, you miserable sods.'

The wait drew on and on. At times Teague could be heard, and FitzGibbon called down to him. 'Have you something there, boy? Loo into him, Teague' – a remnant of eagerness, automatic, mechanical now. The shadows darkened under the trees.

Even FitzGibbon had fallen dead silent – not a murmur of comment, no interchange, no winks, not a word of encouragement – when the dog yelled out close at hand, in the big hole itself. A roaring, rushing din immediately by them and the uncoupled terriers flew straight to the noise, the appalling furious noise. The hound puppy fled, white under the trees, and howled as it flew. Then there they were in the flying earth and dust at the mouth, all the dogs backing out: FitzGibbon on his knees, reaching far in, dragging on two terriers and roaring 'Grip to him, Teague. Hold fast to him, Cutty.' His left hand gave suddenly: the dog shot back, landing on Gethin's knees, a mess of blood and earth where its head had been. The next moment FitzGibbon reared up and backed from the hole, still grasping Teague's hindquarters and bowels.

He turned his face to Gethin; it was yellow, with the dirt and the bristles of beard showing clear. The dust died in the burrow. The appalled dogs snuffed at the blood and licked their lips, squatting tight. Over the whole open space silence came in, so strong that little falls of earth could be heard in the sett. FitzGibbon looked uncertainly from the hole to his blood-covered hand, whispering 'Bloody Christ, bloody Christ, bloody Christ.' He glanced quick over his shoulder twice, crossed himself, felt for his handkerchief and said, 'We'll get home now, if it's not too late.'

7

It Must Have Been a Branch, They Said

⸺◦◦◦⸺

The meet on the prodigious sweep in front of Chaytors was one of the great events of the season: it was one of the very grand packs that met there, and it was a social event of capital importance.

McAdam, sitting on his bay hireling, watched everything attentively. His day with the Rutland was costing him a lot of money, and he intended to have the value of it. He counted the gorgeous red men several times without reaching a firm total, because their coming and going in the door of the house confused him. He was sorry for this, for he wished to be exact in his account afterwards, and this seemed to him a significant figure, especially when you consider the cost of maintaining a pink coat in the shires. However, he had in his mind the exact tally of the boxes he had seen, a very fair conjecture of the number of second horses, and a multiplication sum for the huge silent cars that hooted with such a note of insufferable condescension at the people who followed on foot.

There were many people in tweed and many villagers: they got out of the way of the horses and the motor-cars. Some of the mounted figures spoke to the villagers: they spoke with a kind of cringing bonhomie, and the villagers, nervously aware of their gaping relatives, replied shortly, with an air of surly indifference. They would not be brought out, nor trapped into an opinion.

No communication took place between the red coats and the

tweed coats, however; none between the horses and the bicycles. McAdam had never seen this in such an exaggerated form before, although he often – indeed generally – followed on foot in his own country. He very well knew the feeling of superiority that a man on a horse feels over the unmounted world; when he had ridden out of the dealer's yard that morning he had felt towards foot-followers as an habitual cyclist feels towards bicycles when he is driving a car for a change, but this exhibition made him feel like bowing to the tweed coats and waving his hat with wreathed smiles to the dun macintoshes. He did not move his hat or bow, smiling: in such an assured and self-possessed atmosphere, it would have taken a great man to do so.

No one had spoken to him, horse or foot: he had not expected it, being a stranger; but he would have welcomed a civil word. There was plenty of conversation, and the rich people spoke very loudly indeed, so without being guilty of any improper listening McAdam learnt something of the country they were going to hunt and the morals of the field.

'This is about the only show left where men still look better than women,' said a voice behind him. The voice sounded so near and so confidential that McAdam looked round, with a half-smile on his face, ready to look pleasant in case he had been addressed.

A man and a woman were behind him, a youngish man on a great big flashy chestnut with white stockings, and a woman on a nervous, elegant brown mare; they were obviously members of the Rutland, as obviously as if they had worn the button in their noses. It was very obvious, too, that McAdam had not been spoken to. The big man's expression hardened to an inimical, contemptuous stare, and McAdam's half-smile faded at once; he looked awkwardly away and gazed between his horse's ears.

Almost at once, moving his hands in a vain attempt to look easy under the stare that he still felt directed at him, McAdam dropped his crop. No man looks dignified in such circumstances, and it was doubly unfortunate for him that hounds should have moved off just as he was dismounted and grovelling. He had his crop in his hand and a foot in his stirrup, and his horse, excited by the general movement, was going round from him, so that he hopped foolishly.

'*Will* you get out of my bloody way?' said the man on the big chestnut, pushing his horse forward. McAdam floundered into his saddle as the chestnut's shoulder struck the bay and nearly threw him down: only a positively acrobatic twist saved McAdam from sprawling backwards on the gravel.

For a long time as they tittupped to the covert McAdam watched the big man's scarlet back bobbing up and down in front of him. Then someone else edged his horse between them, and soon a tradesman's van, coming out of a farm gateway separated them still further.

The incident had been trivial enough, and McAdam was not the sort of man to brood over it unduly, but there had been something so insulting in the man's look and voice, so gratuitously offensive, that McAdam would have had to be a meeker man than he was to swallow it without a good deal of resentment. The big fellow was of a type that McAdam had always disliked; large-featured face set in sulky, contemptuous lines, more ready to look unpleasant than pleasant, a face that showed generations of good feeding and an unsmiling, unfounded confidence in its own superiority; the whole on a strong, heavy body. It was a face and type that McAdam associated, perhaps unjustly, with the word Guardee – almost certainly without justice, for he had never known anyone in the Guards who had been at all like it.

The big man's name was Wilkes. By the time they reached the covert McAdam had pretty well forgotten him, at least with the front of his mind, and he was anxiously trying to count the field. It was an impressive sight indeed; there were truly magnificent horses among them, and although some of the people riding them were neither very good horsemen nor particularly lovable souls, their general effect was decorative in a high degree.

The covert was quite small, but McAdam was surprised with the speed hounds found and pushed their fox out of it. He had stayed with the majority on the hither side, and as he let his horse go with the cavalry charge that followed the gone away at the far end, he remembered the neatly folded sack he had noticed by the gate into the wood, where the knowing, round old huntsman with Weller's face had taken his pack not so many minutes ago.

Now, as he crammed his hat down on his ears, he began to feel the nature of his horse: it had been plain from the first that the bay loved hunting, had grown old in it; you could see that from his attentive knowledgeable air, the cock of his ears at the twang of the horn in the wood, and the unhesitating determination to get away in front as he heard hounds running.

There was a recently laid hedge just ahead; the hedger was by it even now, with his billhook in his hand and an angry, Bastille look on his face: you could see the other side level and innocent of ditch; everyone in front of him took it quite happily. As McAdam approached the hedge he felt his horse shape its stride: he was aware of an acute fear that either he or his horse would fail. The bay gathered himself too early, changed step, gathered himself again, and took the little hedge with the air of one surmounting Mont Blanc. McAdam stuck on, despite the hard, slippery saddle, for he was at least a competent rider – better, that is, than he thought himself. But it was plain, as much from the horse's air as from the lack of power and elasticity in the leap, that this hedge represented the bay's limit, or something very near it.

The next, a hairy brute of a hedge, already had two gaps in it, and the bay, ears well forward, made for the larger without any prompting from McAdam. They scrambled through with a determined lunge in a shower of twigs and made directly for a distant gate in the next field, a gate already crowded by riders whose horses could have jumped a steeple.

They soon understood one another perfectly well: they both wanted to see as much of the hunt as possible, but McAdam lacked the skill and the horse the strength to take a dashing line, so they used gates and gaps wherever they could, hurried down lanes and generally behaved in a very scrubbish, undignified manner. It was economical and it repaid; they were up a few minutes after hounds had run their fox into a drain.

There followed a sad business in the drain, and McAdam, who hated this side of hunting, withdrew to eat his sandwiches. He got into conversation with a groom who was there with a second horse, and learn a great deal about the surrounding country. The groom was a cousin of the huntsman and he was full of information; he told McAdam that the next covert to be drawn would be Jarretwood, and he described the nature of the place and the usual lines that Jarretwood foxes took. 'They'll have to work to find him and put him away, though: not like t'other one,' he said with a grin. He promised McAdam that if he followed him he would not go far wrong, adding that he had to take care of the horse he was riding for his master, and that he supposed Albert, meaning McAdam's mount, who was perfectly well known to him, would not mind taking it fairly easy too.

He followed the groom to Jarretwood, and took up his stand at a point of vantage that the groom showed him. The field had thinned out very much and the scene was now far less gay than it had been outside the first covert. Even if there were twice as many people on the far side as there were on this, McAdam observed, it would hardly be called a big field any more.

He was standing on a knoll above the covert, a big furze covert on the side of a wide stretch of sandy common: there was never a tree to justify the name of Jarretwood, only two great round islands of furze, joined together by a narrow belt to make a rough figure of eight. The groom had told him that a fox would often break one side or another of this narrow joining piece; it was evident that others knew this, for a good many people, as well as McAdam, were stationed where they could command a good view of it. Behind McAdam lay the waste of common land; short, rabbit-kept turf, a few bramble thickets and nothing else for miles, a wonderful place for a gallop: before him, downhill beyond the furze, was a little more common and then good fenced pasture running down to the flat land. It was obviously part of a rich estate; the rail and post was white and trim, the notices warning off trespassers stood squarely and exactly spaced. Below this, on the flat, there was a fair amount of plough, some wood, and here and there an almost invisible sunken lane between tall, stout hedges.

The groom had assured McAdam, with as much certainty as if he had arranged it with the fox, that if the huntsman put in at the bottom, the fox would take to the higher country. Perhaps he might have done so if they had got him away quickly, but they drew right up through the covert, ran a little way on a heel line, and worked right through again before they induced him to go, and then he stole away unseen at the very bottom. He went straight down, and when hounds at last struck his line, the best part of the field was left.

McAdam followed the lead of the groom and many others through the narrow piece of furze, and as they cleared it they heard hounds on their right. At this point the zeal of the groom's horse, a most enviable mount, overcame its rider's discretion; they went away with the clear intention of joining the first flight, and McAdam saw them no more.

It was a good scenting day, and hounds fairly tore along down through the pasture. Albert, encouraged by his rest and rendered desperate by their distance from hounds, took the rails in fine style, and for the first few intoxicating minutes McAdam rode as straight to hounds as though his horse were worth five hundred guineas and he a steeplechaser of high renown. Then Albert rapped hard as he was going over, pecked on landing, and McAdam went over his shoulder as neatly as could be wished. He landed soft and easy but a tumble of that kind is never very pleasant, and he felt both shaken and sick as he opened his eyes (he always closed them whenever he fell off a horse) and got to his feet. Albert was standing within a few paces of him, with a kindly expression on his long face. They set off again, much more soberly, and found a gate leading into a lane. It was the lane that divided the higher pasture from the plough, and as McAdam rode down it, the hedge on the plough side grew higher and higher, so that he could not see over it at all. Then, quite a long way on, there was a cross-roads; the left-hand fork seemed to be in the right direction, but there had been so many twists and turns that he could not be sure any longer. Time was slipping away fast, and he knew that if he did not get away in the right direction very soon, he would be left for good.

Until he had fallen off he had always been fairly near other people, most of them with the unworried look of men full of local knowledge, but now the world was suddenly empty. He took the left-hand turning after losing five minutes in the vain hope of hearing hounds or seeing someone who might know where they were. Now the hedges grew higher on either hand, and still the road meandered: once or twice McAdam rode out into the middle of a field to get a clear view and recover his bearings if he could, but the landscape was diversified and ambiguous and soon he could no longer persuade himself that he had any idea of his true direction.

'Well,' he said, 'I have seen the Rutland kill a fox: it is true that it was not very handsomely done as these things go, but I have taken part in a fine burst as well, and no doubt when I read the account of it next week I shall learn where they got to – a famous point, I am sure it will be – and it is probable that I shall recognize many of the landmarks mentioned in it.' He spoke to himself in this way to cloak the sore disappointment that was welling up in him and the intense frustration that he felt at the racing passage of time – the vital minutes had added up to a sad total by now.

Far ahead he heard the welcome noise of a car; it was coming in his direction. His heart leapt with recovered hope and he stopped the car. A man with spectacles thrust his head out of the window; he had a green suit on and a wool tie. In reply to McAdam's question he said, 'I abhor blood sports,' in a loud, angry voice. And, withdrawing, he said, 'Dressed-up sadists.' As he took his foot off the clutch the engine stalled, as he had forgotten to change down. He started it again, but his happy glow was spoilt, and he felt McAdam watching him as he wrestled with the car.

McAdam was saddened by this, for he always felt that he ought to have some ready answer, and none ever occurred to him until long after. Strong, unexpected disapproval put him at a loss: he knew that he was not a sadist, but he felt all the difficulty of proving a negative whenever the Pharisees attacked him. While he was riding quietly along the grass verge of the lane thinking out one or two good replies, it appeared to him that the road was familiar, and he looked about him attentively. He was back again almost where he had started from, and he saw that if he carried on round the thicket on his left he would come in sight of the common again.

He had hardly made quite certain of this before he heard hounds again, behind him. The fox had run a ring – he was already in the covert again, resting when he should have been running. They came nearer, one high-voiced bitch speaking all the time and the rest crashing in at intervals. They crossed the road a hundred yards ahead. Albert stood like a statue, and McAdam clenched his fists with delight: it was one of those glorious reversals that one so often prays for and which sometimes happen.

The pack crossed in a moment, with eyes for nobody; nothing mattered but their urgent quest. They ran fast up the slope towards the covert, a compact body, intent and deadly earnest. McAdam swung up the hill again, and for a few minutes, to his inexpressible satisfaction, he was alone with the pack. But then a long-legged soldier passed him, and the huntsman, followed by three or four: even so, McAdam, by dint of running up the last stretch to save the labouring of Albert, was with the first few when hounds ran into their fox a little way the other side of the covert. He was there, indeed, before the Master, whose august figure, purple in the face and covered with mud, came up on the finest horse in the country some five minutes later.

By this time Albert had nearly had enough: he was willing and eager to go on, but there was no spring in him – he was no longer up to a full day. Hearing the name of the covert they intended to draw next, McAdam decided to go along, for it was a famous covert, one that he had always wanted to see, and then, having seen it, to make his way back to his lodgings, which were nearer there than here.

As they waited about on the high common they were joined by others, among them Wilkes, the tall, objectionable man, who was in an evil temper and very hot. He and his horse were not on good terms, and the chestnut's front was covered with foam. He came up quite near to McAdam, turned as if to ask him a question, but checked on recognizing him; he treated McAdam to an offensive stare, a stare so offensive that McAdam felt inclined to resent it with some equally offensive remark. He could think of nothing to say, however.

As they rode slowly away to Langmore Hanger, McAdam reflected upon this man's conduct: his former irritation revived, and in spite of himself he found it swamping his happiness that his good fortune had brought. There was something so damnably pleasant about Wilkes's whole appearance – his very being was an offence to McAdam. Wilkes felt much the same, only with a heavy, dumb malignance that was habitual to him, and a sort of lowering contempt. Their horses seemed to share this strong, spontaneous antipathy: Albert laid his ears back as the chestnut drew away, and there was a vicious look in his eye.

Wilkes cantered on to talk to one of the men in front: after a few minutes he passed on to the Master. McAdam was delighted to see that he got precious little change there; after a short exchange, Wilkes turned away, obviously wishing he had not spoken. He saw that McAdam was watching him.

As they approached the covert McAdam saw the square tower of Lowood Church appear on his right hand, and he knew that he now had his bearings exactly, and that he could get home easily. Langmore Hanger was a beautiful wood, with well-spaced, tall timber and great banks of rhododendrons: it had three main rides and many more cross lanes.

They took a very long time to draw the hanger, and after some time McAdam joined a small group of people at the place where the middle ride cut one of the cross lanes. He found that he was intruding on what was apparently a family group, but his embarrassment was relieved by a great crash of music up at the top of the wood. There was a distant hallo and the family galloped furiously up the ride. McAdam waited for a moment and then turned Albert's reluctant head away along one of the narrow paths.

He was going through a hazel coppice near the edge of the wood when he heard voices shouting in one of the rides: they were men who had been left on the wrong side. One was asking where they had gone, and the other replied that he thought they had turned left-handed, but that he was not sure. A little while after he heard the rush and thrum of a galloping horse behind him; Albert quickened his tired pace nervously.

McAdam turned in his saddle to peer back: he had a queer feeling of inevitability in his heart. It was Wilkes, of course. He pulled his horse up hard and brutally hard as he saw McAdam slowly going along the narrow path.

'Will you get out of my bloody way, you goddam sod?' he shouted, and the tone was so grossly insulting that McAdam's face flushed sudden red with anger, although the words made no more impression on him than rain. He turned Albert's head sharply and stood across the path. No ready words came to his tongue, but his face spoke plain.

'Will you get out of my bloody way?' repeated Wilkes, backing his horse.

McAdam made no reply, but shifted his crop to his right hand and gripped it just above the thong. His horse was trembling and switching his ears back and forth.

'Out of my bloody way,' shouted Wilkes in a higher pitch, and, striking hard into his horse, he charged down the path: a branch knocked his hat off as he came, with his whip hand up to shield his face and his whip ready.

Albert stepped sideways just before the impact, pressing the hazels back. McAdam struck backhanded, hard and true, and he hit Wilkes above the eyes with immense force. The beak of his crop went in. It smashed right in. The blow killed Wilkes. It killed him in that moment and he was dead as he fell. His head was flung backwards and he fell between the horses: their hoofs smashed him. The chestnut reared before it bolted, and it left

Wilkes lying there in the churned black earth, lying there on his back dead without a twitch: his arms were flung out, and his hands, palm upward, were spread wide open.

McAdam looked at him without particular emotion; he had seen too many dead men to worry unduly about this one, and he felt no regret then or at any time after. He looked composedly up and down the path: there was no one: there was no sound in the wood at all. He was the only living man there.

From far out in the open country came the music of the whole pack, running on a breast-high scent. McAdam turned his horse's head and rode out of the wood.

8

The Slope of the High Mountain

———⊗⊗⊗———

Snow had fallen in the night and it lay on all the ground above five hundred feet, showing brave in the sun and making the sky so blue that it was a living pleasure to look at it.

To the men walking fast up the Nantmor road the sharp cold was a pleasure too, for their hurry had warmed them to a fine heat. They had already come some miles over the mountains before they had struck the metalled road, along an ancient track that wound among the high bogs, often ambiguous and always hard to be found: they had followed it without losing it, but it had taken time above their allowance. They were hurrying, therefore, with the fear of lateness behind them, and their nailed boots rang quick on the hard road, and they steamed in the frosty air.

It was to a meet of foxhounds that they were hurrying, a meet right under Snowdon, at ten o'clock. Moel Ddu was on their left, and Moel Hebog after it, and the snow lay well down their sides; the men could not see Snowdon yet, for the hills shut in the top of the valley. The cruel black rocks of the Arddu rose sheer on the right hand, and the Nantmor river ran fierce below them. Far along on the road ahead a man was walking fast: he was a dark figure, dressed in black, incongruous among the rocks, and he was singing passionately. It was a hymn in Welsh and he was a shepherd: presently he vanished at a turning in the road, and although they heard his singing high up among the stunted trees they did not see the man again.

The road continued to rise and soon there were no more trees on either hand, and the black rocks showed harsher. The top of the valley was desolate with the gigantic spew of a dead slate quarry, high and lonely on the deserted road. Marching lines of square pillars showed where the aqueduct had run: many of them leaned strangely, and some had fallen. Huge, unprofitable slate rocks lined the road, holding back the black hills of jagged spoil.

The men had spoken little for the last half-hour, but now they said to one another that the road would soon turn to the left, and Gonville began to talk about how birds cannot tell how fast they are going in the air if there is a cloud or no light at all. Brown did not believe what he was told, but he was unable to refute it. Gonville, aware of his disbelief, went on in a dogmatic tone, telling him more about the birds of the air and the way they know nothing except possibly by magnetism. However, Brown did not quarrel with him, and when the road turned to the left all thoughts of wrangling went out of his head.

Right before them was Snowdon, sharp and brilliant in the sky, with Lliwedd jutting fiercely on the right and deep new snow over all, sparkling nobly in the sun. New clean snow, unspoiled by runnels, and Snowdon's eastern face looked smooth by reason of the depth of the snow.

They were looking at Snowdon from a fair height and with a deep valley between: this waste of air below and before them gave the mountain an altitude and a majesty far beyond the amount of its height in feet. The sun was behind them, and it shone on the incisive, spectacular ridge that joins Lliwedd and Snowdon, separating the peaks with a great sweep of hard shadow.

It was a sight to make even a dull man's heart leap and exult, like sudden good news or a lost thing found.

The way was downhill now, down into Nant Gwynant, with the big lakes one on either hand and the river joining them. The hard walking they had done had caught up with the clock, and when they came down into Nant Gwynant, to the Glaslyn and to the gate leading up to the farm of Hafod Llan they were before their time. For all that, anxiety harassed them as they waited by

the gate where the milk churn stood, and they discussed the mis-
adventures that might have happened, the possibility of a mistake
in the time and of an error in their route – suppose, they said, the
Captain has gone up by another way? But when they had been
worrying themselves for a quarter of an hour the car and the
trailer passed them and swung up the cart track to Hafod Llan.
They ran after it and came up as the Master was going into the
farmhouse to ask after his fox. There were a few other people, and
the farm children stared at them and the hounds.

Eight couples were there, stretching and walking about: there
was a strong smell of hounds everywhere. The outraged farm dogs
bawled from a distance, but offered nothing more. The hunt terriers ran busily to and fro; all hard-bitten and many with recent
scars and bald patches. The hounds were mixed. There were Welsh
hounds, fell-hounds, and crosses, and there was an English bitch
with a noble, judicious head who looked strange among the slim,
fine-boned creatures around her. Benign hounds they were, but
not effusive like some; Ranter, Rambler, Ringwood, Driver and
Melody, Drummer, Marquis, and Music, the surest of them all.

The Master came out of the farmhouse. He was of an ancient
family, and his people had hunted this country above three hundred years. He had a falcon's nose and eye, and his moustache
curled with a magnificent arrogance. He wore a very old cloth cap
and a torn Burberry which concealed his horn and the whip he
carried over the shoulder of his jacket. He spoke to the huntsman
in Welsh and they moved off towards the Gallt y Wenallt, the
mountain behind the wood.

When they came to a gate at the bottom of the wood the
Master turned off downward and the huntsman, with the field
and the hounds, went up through the copse. Hounds were soon
out of sight among the trees, and Gonville and Brown pushed
themselves to keep up with the long-legged huntsman. Soon they
reached the snow where it lay thin and melting in the open spaces
between the trees: they climbed quickly past the height where
it was melting and came out at the top of the wood. As they
cleared the trees a hound spoke below them, and they paused

for a moment. Hounds passed up through the wood, working intently, but with very little sound; they were moving quite fast, and when another hound spoke – a deep-mouthed hound it was – they were far along.

The men had reached a path, and they followed it. It ran up from the wood to the top of a bluff, an almost sheer cliff that rose high above the woods. They could see hounds below them when they reached the top of this bluff and they stopped in a sheltered place – sheltered, because the wind, a small wind that came off the snow, bit very sharp and hard, they being in a sweat with the hurry.

They had come round the shoulder of the Gallt y Wenallt out of the sun, and here it was much colder. The face of Wenallt, running steeply down to Llyn Gwynant, was on their left: below them, at the bottom of the mountain, was a deep belt of trees; above the trees, a long sloping scree that stretched up to the foot of the cliff. Below the wood was the still lake and its river, and beyond the lake the ranks of bare mountains marching away one behind the other.

Hounds were working across the scree just below the snow; they were coming slowly up, and dubiously. However, they puzzled it out across the rocks, up through the heather in the face of the cliff, for the scent lay there, and up almost to the men crouched in their bit of lee.

Now they were hunting more confidently, and it was a rare delight to watch them packed close together with their heads down and almost touching and their backsides wriggling as they carried the line over the hard places, and how they ran streaming out over the easy ones. Down they went again, much faster than they had come up, down and into the wood.

Then the waiting men heard no more for a long time, nor saw anything. Brown talked to the huntsman, a young, tall Welshman who swore in English; he had most of the terriers with him, and the old white bitch nipped precisely into Brown's lap. The other terriers crawled in the snow, for the pleasure of scratching their bellies against its crust. The huntsman carried a long pole and he wore old blue breeches: he told Brown that the Master would be below the wood, and that if the fox were a Cwm Dyli fox, as he supposed – but as he was speaking there was a crash of savage music in the wood. They all stood up in silence, and directly hounds were speaking again, singly and in a choir. They were running fast. In a minute or two the huntsman said that they had either got him going or they were very near to him, and in that moment the fox came up out of the wood, up to the clear edge of it. A dark brown fox was he, big and rangy, a long-legged fox. He looked up at the men far above him, and plainly they could see him deliberate as he stood there, looking up and damning their eyes. The fox looked down and trotted away along the top of the wood, inclining rather upward to the mountain – a low-pitched diagonal up the great sloping apron of Wenallt.

As the fox went away clear of the wood the huntsman sprang down the face of the cliff and holloed him away with great shrieking hooicks: he went down with a wonderful agility, going too fast to fall, and the snow flew up from his feet. The fox did not hurry for all that, but went steadily on: the men could see him between the rocks and low pieces of broken wall, and once or twice he looked up with a fleeting glance. The huntsman was crying to his hounds to lay them on, but they came up rather slowly, and by the time they were running on the line the fox was farther away than a man would have supposed possible.

He was going toward Cwm Dyli, it appeared, Cwm Dyli, far up at the top of Nant Gwynant, higher up than Llyn Gwynant, and right round the whole mass of the Gallt y Wenallt the men must go to get there.

This mountain, this Wenallt, is the end of the mass of Snowdon on the Nant Gwynant side – the deep valley and the lake define the mass. The mountain faces the lake squarely. Its top part is craggy, but not pointed: two arms run down from the top, arms that would embrace the lake if they ran further, but the one that shelters Hafod Llan is broken by the cliff and the wood swallows it, and the other, the far one towards the top of Nant Gwynant, peters out in the dead ground at the marshy top of the lake.

Between these arms and below the crags of the top is a vast

stretch of ground, a table tilted to an angle of fifty-five degrees and more. The men must cross this stretch. They were already about two-thirds of the way up it, and the intention of the first man was plainly to go straight across. The rest of the field followed, for he knew the country well. As soon as they left the rock of the cliff they found the going very hard. The sloping face was covered with thin wiry grass growing in shallow soil, and the grass lay under an inch or two of snow. Everywhere there were rocks and stones, nearly all on the surface, and none to be relied upon for a handhold. The snow was too shallow to tread into steps, and it was of that coarse, crystalline sort that makes a foot slip as ice does; much of the stuff was hail. The grass was no help either; the way it lay was all downhill, so it would not hold a foot up, and its roots were so poor in the red scratching of soil that a very little pull brought the whole handful up.

They came to a wall, a wall that ran down the mountain to the wood, one of the innumerable walls that intersect the summer sheep-walks there; it accentuated the angle of the slope, and if Brown had not heard the cry of hounds in front of him he would not have followed the leader over the wall, but would have looked for another way.

It was worse the other side. Brown had not brought a stick – he preferred to have both hands free for climbing – and he missed it sorely now. Gonville was a little way behind him; they were too far apart to talk, and even if they had been closer the difficulty of their way and their hurry would have kept them silent.

For a little way there was the likeness of a path, but this vanished after it had led them well out on to the face of Wenallt. The slope grew a few degrees steeper now, and now they crept painfully and slow. It was a cruel slope: a man could hardly keep his feet standing quite still on it.

From time to time Brown looked down to the distant wood, over the great sheet of white, a sheet that he could now see to be full of boulders that jutted sharply from its surface.

They were all crawling along with their left hands to the snow, sometimes with their whole bodies pressed to it, all with a strong uneasiness. The real present fear, with no interposing doubts or comforting illusions, did not strike into Brown's heart until he saw a flat stone that the man in front of him had dislodged go sliding easily down, easily and then faster, throwing snow from it like a ski, and at last crashing into an ugly great black rock far, far down. Just after this the man in front turned left-handed directly up the mountain, going up a gully with the help of his iron-pointed stick: he was aiming for a saddle that led behind the rounded brow of the peak. He did not speak to Brown – he was too much occupied for that – and Brown stood considering.

He did not like the look of the way up. He kicked the rounded clogs of rammed snow from his boots; they clogged every few steps in this stuff. He looked forward, and again the cry of hounds raised his heart: the slope was surely easier in front, and indeed he must have come over the worst, and by God there was no going back over that stretch. Below him, a great way down, he saw a figure at the far end of the wood; it was the Master, and he was looking steadfastly up to a point on the other side of the shoulder of Wenallt that was in front of Brown.

If they have run him in round there, said Brown, I shall be the first up. He looked round before he started forward and saw Gonville spread-eagled in a bad place; another man was holding out his stick for him to grasp, and it was obvious that they were going back. Brown waved; he felt secretly rather pleased. His fear had receded, and although he knew, with his head, that he was in danger, the real starkness of it had gone. I may slip or fall, he said in effect, and that could be fatal – probably would be – but these are things that happen to other people.

The first ten paces were easy and the next quite plain, but then he saw bad ground ahead and he judged that he must go down a little to get along at all. The huntsman came into sight just below the snow; he was walking with the terriers along the diagonal line the fox had taken. He had been hidden for most of the time by a drop of ground that did not show from above. This confirmed Brown in his plan, and he decided to go down to the good ground and then across to intercept the huntsman's path as he crossed the far arm of Wenallt. Just at this point the ground went down in steps, still grass-covered: these he negotiated, with his face downward. Below the steps the slope was terrible, but there was no retreat. It had looked just the same, or better, from above. I will go down on my bottom, he said; a little farther down and then across. The immensity of the stretch below him, the snow ending in shale and the far, far trees; the huge sweep sickened him.

He shuffled down – come, it's not too bad, he said, but while the words were still in him, and he in an awkward position with his legs stretched out and his weight on his elbows and heels, he began to slip. With a furious, controlled energy he gripped into the grass and earth. It tore away without hesitation. Flat on his back, he went; he went with his arms out and his crooked, tense hands scrabbling for a hold, failing, then pressing fiercely on the sliding snow, stemming, breaking, but impotently and in vain, for he was going faster. Faster: with a terrible certainty the momentum increased: the seconds of controllable speed had passed. It is happening to me, he said: and Now for it, he said, as he passed into a hurtling rush down; but still he hunched his shoulders to protect his head and forced his hands into the snow. The sense of responsibility was gone and with it his fear: he expected one dark blow, a smashing blow and the end, but not without a certain constancy of mind.

His feet were against a rock, a firm rock. It was all over; and he was still, unmoving and unhurt. He lay for a moment, for some minutes, breathing and looking at the sky. He was wet, soaked through and through; the whole of his back was wet through and the caked snow was forced into his clothes. Was he hurt? No, he was not hurt. His hands were strange to him, but he was not hurt – all whole. He got up, trembling and shaken: he did not think very clearly now, in this strong reaction.

The trees were a good deal nearer: Brown was halfway down the mountain-face. He could not see the others when he looked up, nor could he be sure of the place where he had started. He looked down, but the huntsman was no longer to be seen.

He felt that there was a strong necessity to go on, not to stop, not to make anything of it. He thought slowly: perhaps he had been stunned, had been unconscious for a while without knowing it? How otherwise could Emrys have vanished like that?

He went on a few steps farther down to look from side to side: no man could he see, but there was a neat precipice, only fifteen or twenty feet deep, but sheer, and if he had not fetched up where he did he would have gone over it without any sort of doubt.

This shocked him unreasonably and he turned his face to the dark crags above him. How he longed for the rough, strong rocks, firm and true; their steepness was nothing, he said inwardly, for they were reft and fissured and it was like going up a ladder.

Without thinking any more he started to move up. From where he was the crags seemed continuous right from where the grass ended to the very top, and once the rock was gained it did not look at all difficult to go up over the summit of Wenallt.

His new way was easier than creeping sideways across the mountain, but it meant going on all fours, and soon the snow had so numbed his battered hands that all the strength left them. They would hardly even open and close, so when he reached the first of the rocks he could not go up. He rested a long while before they recovered, and in a few minutes that he took in climbing the first stretch their strength went again. Again he rested, this time under an overhanging rock where sheep had stood years beyond counting in hard weather. By some freak his sandwiches had escaped being crushed into a mess, and eating them brought Brown back to common things and to a comforting sense of ordinariness – a feeling that had been quite stripped from him for some time before. He was shivering in his soaked clothes, soaked in front now as well as behind, for he had groped upward through deeper snow on his hands and knees; but his courage was fairly well as he came out of the sheep's place.

He could see three separate masses of rock above him, and no more: he would be climbing them, he could see, in the right direction – that is, his path would carry him over toward Cwm Dyli, and he reckoned that from the top of the third crag he would see round into the valley on the other side.

The first crag was steady, exhausting climbing, not difficult, but needing continual strong effort. At the top of it was a stretch of open shale before the foot of the next crag. This was anxious going, very, for the snow was far thicker at this height, and it was not a pretty task to creep over unseen shale pitched at that angle and with that vast amount of world below. Brown set himself to it, and worked up along the edge of the scree, where he knew the bigger stones would be lying under the snow.

His good fortune brought him up to the top, under the second crag, trembling with the effort. He had to wait for his hands again, and now for the first time, as he squatted out of the way of the little breeze, cramps seized him with force and anguish, so that he grunted aloud. Now his heart began to falter a little, less at the pain and the fear that they might grasp him again when he was crucified on a rock than at the new appearance of the crag above him: rocks that had appeared to be joined when he decided to climb them now had showed themselves to be far apart, separated by stretches of snow that might conceal anything, stretches that tilted shockingly, so that some of them looked almost vertical.

However, he hoisted himself up the nearest rock, and reached for the next handhold; it was a high, flat rock-face that he was going up now, and he had to walk up it with his feet while he held on with both hands. As he looked down to see whether his right foot was well placed, looking down with his chin in his chest, he saw beyond his foot black rock and snow stretching down forever, then that horrible plane slope, and infinitely far away the trees and the lake. These he saw upside down, and he sickened at the sight. With a convulsive, wasteful effort he struggled to the top and lay there. He knew that he must not look down any more, for his courage was beginning to go, and with it his freedom from the terror of height.

It was while he was on the third mass of rock, worming himself across a gully to a climbable rock, that he came face to face with a hound. It was Ringwood, obviously coming down from the top. He was followed by others: they looked momentarily at Brown and went on. Even with four legs they found it hard, and one slipped twenty feet and more while Brown watched them. He no longer minded about hounds: all that he wanted, and the huge want filled him to the exclusion of all else, was firm ground, level ground, under his feet and the sky in its right place over his head.

The topmost piece of the third crag was an ugly, out-leaning breast of rock with a narrow cleft in it. The strength of his hands was gone again, and as he stood wedged in this cleft he thought he was going to fall at last. He did not fall, though he swayed backward; his elbow held, and with his chin ground down to the top of the rock and a chance grip for his knee he came up to the top. Kneeling there, almost sick with the muscular effort, he saw that what he had climbed was a false crest. Beyond and above him stretched three hundred feet of nearly perpendicular rock, interspersed with gullies and patches of shale. A wide tract of flattish ground that led back from the top of the false peak had hidden all this from him as he stood below: even now what he saw as the top might not be the real summit.

Without allowing himself to formulate anything about this, Brown began to walk across the dead ground. The gesture was very well, but after he had climbed a little way cold despair overtook him. This was worse than the mountain below: the rocks were farther apart, the bare, smooth slopes steeper and wider. It was unclimbable; his strength was almost gone and there was no way down.

When he came to a platform with a sheltering slab over it Brown stopped. The last phase of climbing had had a nightmarish quality; not daring to look down any more, he had won the last fifty feet at the cost of cruel labour and intense apprehension with each movement. All the time stark, naked fear had been on him, and it was on him now, and he knew that it was a rightful fear.

For a long time he squatted, inert and unfeeling. A cramp revived him and he noticed that the sun had come round the edge of the mountain. The sky was still the same unclouded perfection of a sky that it had been in the morning. He did not know the time – could not guess it, either. His watch had stopped when he had gone down.

Now that he was wholly determined not to go on he felt better. He looked down, pressing his back against the firm rock, and he experienced that sense of flying that comes with some kinds of giddiness. This passed, and he surveyed the country below him. He had come a long way; the trees were even more distant. A feeling of utter, desolate remoteness filled him: he seemed quite cut off from the world. But so long as he was no longer going to drive himself up he did not mind very actively: no more fruitless crawling up, with knees and hands slipping and every movement perilous, arduous beyond bearing: to be left alone, that was the thing.

How kind the weather has been, he said after a great timeless pause; if it had blown hard or snowed some more I should have gone before now. How long would it be? he asked; but made no reply.

Far, far down, a little above the wood there was Gonville running with the immense strides of a man going downhill; he was crossing from right to left. Brown could recognize him by the yellow waterproof jacket that he was wearing. He ran to the wall at the end of the wood and stood by the gate.

Brown's heart went out to him in a kind of envy and a desperate longing to be down there. The thought of shouting came to his mind: on a still day like this he might make himself heard down there. But he dismissed the thought, and in a few moments the whole pack came running fast along the wall toward Gonville; Brown flushed at the sight and stood up to watch them tear along the top of the wood and vanish on his right. By the time he sat down again Gonville had disappeared.

He relapsed into the same dull, marooned feeling; he repeated that it would not be possible to go down the way he had come up, but he did not care very much. Time dropped slowly on and on, and nothing at all happened: no change, no movement.

Two ravens flew out above him from Lliwedd over the lake, flying with steady wing-beats whose sound came down to him. The front one was almost silent, but the second bird spoke all the time in a guttural monotone, *gaak gaak gaak*: occasionally the front bird replied, deeply, *gaak*. They flew straight away from him in an undeviating line for his home.

The warmth of the sun was grateful to him: in spite of the sodden coldness of his clothes his spirits rose under it, and presently he was aware of being alive again, with an active mind and his apathy gone.

When he made his great discovery he felt a fool; he could have blushed for it. Ever since the sun had come round the shoulder of Wenallt it had been melting the snow fast. The snow-line on the horrible slope, his chief dread, had been retreating steadily for a great deal of the time that he had been climbing – had crept up after him. Inexplicably, when he had looked down he had never looked for it nor seen it. But by now the slope was free from snow almost to the foot of the crags. A vast sense of relief, of ignominious anticlimax filled him. Without waiting, he let himself down from his place, he let himself down like a sack and he fell safely. He slid and scrambled recklessly down the shale and it submitted to this. He defied the black rocks now and in minutes he threw away the height that he had won with such pain. Twice he slid deliberately down long stretches of snow, squatting on his two feet; the first time he pulled himself up on a rock on the calculated edge of destruction; the second time he let himself go down the last snow of the horrible slope and did not stop until he was on the clean grass. He kicked the last snow from under his boots and ran down the grassy innocent slope laughing like a boy, down to the thorn trees and down safe and happier than Lazarus to the lovely wood and the lake with the blue sky over them, and in ten minutes the real knowledge of naked fear had left him again.

9

The Long Day Running

The first song Lemuel Kirk ever learnt was John Peel; he loved everything about it; he knew all the words, and he often made the palm-trees tremble with his view halloo. He had longed to go out with a fell-pack from his earliest days; and now that he was settled in Wales he had the opportunity of fulfilling this ambition – indeed, of surpassing it, for the country inland was made up not of fells but of mountains.

His predecessor at the hospital, a Welshman with a wide acquaintance in the surrounding counties, gave him an introduction to the master of a famous old pack that hunted them, and in the autumn a postcard came to tell Dr Kirk that hounds would meet at Hafod Uchaf on Thursday, at half past nine.

The dogs were a mixed body – fell-hounds, Welsh hounds, a beautiful English bitch from the Pytchley, and almost as many terriers as foxhounds: small terriers of different colours, most of them whiskered and hairy, all coupled with heavy chains. The Master was followed by a personal dog, an old cross-bred black retriever that farted every few minutes and that took no notice of anyone. The Master himself was a spare, remote man with a hawk nose, a curling moustache and a piercing blue eye: his horn could be seen under his Burberry and he carried a long-lashed crop slung over his shoulder. Something had occurred to vex him, which disturbed the rest of the field; but he greeted Kirk kindly, and hoped that they would be able to show him some sport. Gerallt

Williams, the huntsman, had brought his son to the hospital for a course of treatment, and Kirk already knew him. And there was a weather-beaten woman whom he recognized as one of the magistrates who had fined him for a motoring offence in the summer. The rest of the field he had never seen, to his knowledge: some local farmers and artisans; a tall soldier called Major Boyd, some other 'educated' men; a schoolmaster with a hard-faced virgin at his side. They were all dressed in strong, shabby clothes; they all wore boots; they all carried sticks. Kirk felt too new altogether, except for his boots – they at least had seen service during his long walks in August and September.

Little did Kirk know about hunting, and the apparent competence of the others disturbed him. Following at all seemed to him to imply a moral duty to keep up, to go through thick and thin, and to be in at the kill. He could not possibly expect to distinguish himself in any way, still less to be given a brush; but he did hope to avoid disgrace. He was the only black man in those parts; and apart from that these people seemed to him stand-offish – it would be painful to expose himself in front of them. Yet perhaps this was no more than a question of language: many of the patients from the hill farms and villages needed a Welsh-speaking nurse to interpret for them when it came to the finer points; and in his farther walks he had noticed how people avoided conversation, not to display their imperfect English.

At this point the farmers were all speaking Welsh – the word *llwynog* kept recurring; the Master spoke Welsh or English indifferently when he spoke at all. 'For Christ's sake let's cut the cackle, Dwch anwyl,' he said, pulling a watch from his waistcoat. 'If he don't choose to meet my bloody hounds prompt, let him go and – himself.'

They moved off, the huntsman; the lean pale pack, smelling strong of hound; the Master and his familiar spirit, farting as it went; the shabby field.

As they came into the high valley, the fox slipped up over the edge of it and away. He went with no hurry, picking the easy path through rocks and shadows, and if it had not been for two sheep that started violently, making the shale rattle on the mountainside, he would never have been seen. A big dog-fox, long-legged and uncommonly dark: he paused on the skyline, on the edge of the steep slope, and looked down before he vanished.

There were half a dozen of them there at the far end of the lake and more strung out along its barren shore, all staring up at him: the hounds were farther on, where a fall came down to the water at the head of the valley. It made no difference to the fox that he had been seen, because the dogs were already working along his drag among the black rocks; but it pleased the followers – Kirk's heart leapt with delight.

This was Cwm Llyn Du, a great bowl of a valley like a crater with a quarter of its wall broken away at the lower end; it had high steep sides, so sheer that on the two arms before the break the grass could only just get a footing, while the top end was savage, bare and sterile.

The pack was on the true line, with Bashful and Melody out in front; and its meandering path showed exactly the way the fox had gone up some hours before. This was a fair scenting day up here, and suddenly as they came to the place where he had been lying, Melody bawled out with passionate conviction, then four or five more all together, and they were away with a splendid wild crash of music, all close together with no doubt or hesitation, sweeping away in a tight white line, noses down, running fast.

Kirk stood entranced for a moment, but already the followers were toiling up to that far-away crest, taking different lines, all of them steep the moment they left the water. Out to the right there was the long-legged huntsman with four of the terriers. Running along the flat Kirk came up behind him; but Gerallt went so fast with his long legs and his ceaseless springing stride that Kirk could stay with him only by putting all his closest attention to it, taking advantage of every easy step, watching the huntsman's feet in front and above, concentrating all the time. The least stumble jerked the breath out of him, losing distance; sometimes he was on all fours; often he seized the grass with his nearer hand to help him along, always too far behind to relax his concentration for a moment. He saw almost nothing of the hounds as they hunted up and along the side and over the rim at the very nick in the rock where the fox had stood, but all the time there was that lovely remote barbarous din to keep him tearing along like a boy. He meant to keep with Gerallt if he possibly could, both as an expert fox-hunter and as his only acquaintance – the Master was too awful a figure by far – and already there was a tacit understanding between them: most of the followers hunted in pairs.

Kirk saw the top of the ridge coming at last, and he fairly ran up the last stretch. Gerallt was already there, gazing down at the great sweep of country the other side.

Below them stretched a tumult of rounded hills, a heaving ocean of rock frozen and set aeons ago. From high above, from this Craig Llyn Du where they stood, the roundness was strikingly apparent, although from below nothing of it could be seen. The lower hills sloped down to the shining face of Llyn Cidwm far in the distance – Llyn Cidwm he knew – and beyond the water the mountains rose dimly, merging into the general grey of a dull overcast sky, cold, with rain threatening and the worse threat of low cloud: already the bare head of Moel y Gigfran had wisps passing over it.

Most of the other followers were on the ridge. The woman magistrate's hair straggled somewhat, but on the whole they all looked surprisingly composed. 'They must have hearts like steam-engines,' reflected Kirk, privately feeling his own.

There was no sign of the hounds. Once the distant clamour of the sheepdogs of Rhaiadr Mawr made all heads turn, and once a movement of sheep far below half deceived them: then the Master spoke briefly to Gerallt and they began to move down towards a jutting crag that would command the ground directly beneath them – a wide tract that was invisible from the ridge of Llyn Du. From here they saw a man far below, a small dark figure pointing away towards the lake with repeated emphatic jerks of his stick.

'He's gone for Moel y Gigfran,' said Gerallt, in a voice between statement and question: the Master nodded, and they turned northward, keeping along a high broad undulating ridge with outcropping pillars of granite. Presently the followers were scattered over a furlong or two, with Gerallt and Kirk somewhat ahead, taking the higher ground. They were not going so fast now by any means, and Gerallt told Kirk about a noson lawen where he had sung penillion all last night to Maire Votty's harp. 'Up until three I was, and home by the light of the moon, four miles over the old mountain.' He sang one or two of the penillion, and a stanza from *Timotheus cries*. Kirk had loosened up now; his second wind had come, and as he swung along over the close turf he felt a great well-being – he could go on for ever – he would be in at the kill! They went up and down, up and down, but there was nothing steep, and Gerallt was not pressing himself.

Now there was a distinct cry of hounds before them, and every face lightened: it was clear they were in the right road. Then from a knoll Gerallt saw them and pointed them out, a line of long white dots, like sheep, but moving fast and continuously. The wind was increasing now, blowing from behind them, snatching the noise of the hounds from their ears; but when the wind slackened, or when they were under a lee, they could hear it plain – clearly the hounds were quite near their fox, pushing him along handsomely.

At a given point the Master came to a halt, with the followers ranged at various distances from him; and they all gazed up at the massive side of the Moel y Gigfran. It seemed a terribly long way off to Kirk, and he could hardly distinguish the hounds at all by the time they ran over the ridge, over the back of the bald mountain, away from the lake. There was some talk about the line the fox would take – a flood of place-names, for every rock, pass, pool or bothie had its name – and presently Gerallt started away again, bearing left-handed: the Master and most of the others stayed in the shelter of the crag, a few more in a dell below, and Kirk hesitated, unwilling to attach himself to the huntsman too obviously – to appear to cling. A few minutes later the tall soldier, followed by the schoolmaster and the virgin, struck directly up towards the top of the mountain, while another group went away diagonally for the ridge. Gerallt was already a small active form, moving through the heather in the middle distance. The Master sat down and lighted his pipe. Kirk stood irresolutely a little longer and then dropped down from the crag in the same direction as Gerallt.

Soon he was out of sight of all the rest, both before and behind. To his right he had the high irregular side of the mountain and to his left the valley, with the road far below and the lake: he was going along a rough, boulder-strewn plain, a great step or terrace half-way up the side of the Moel.

Presently it seemed to him that he had been on his own a long while, with nothing but the wind and the emptiness around him – too long, and he was increasingly afraid that he would never be with the hounds again. It was a world given over to the raven: a pair of them passed high over it, communicating through three miles of air, steadily croaking one to the other. He might have been alone in it – no sign of men at all – for although he caught distant glimpses of the road it was so remote that it belonged to another planet entirely, another life. The ground, which had been reasonably plain in the distance, now proved to be full of bogs, some standing in defiance of nature on the slope, and with rocky clefts that needed care and circumspection – pitiably slow. It called for a great deal of effort too, and in time it warmed him finely in spite of the searching wind: he was wiping sweat from his face when he saw Gerallt far up on his right, much higher than he had expected and farther away than he had supposed possible. It was heartening to see him at all however, and Kirk turned directly up the main slope. The lie of the land was now such that the valley, the sweeping great valley Nant Cidwm, was shut out of his view, and only the rising hulk of the mountain with the racing drifts of cloud on it remained to show him the way.

The stimulus of the sight of Gerallt died after he had gone another cruel hard mile, and on the top of a viewpoint that showed him nothing but a thousand acres of desolation and the dislocated skeleton of a sheep he stopped to take breath and to consider. There were so many ways they could have gone without his seeing them, and the likelihood of his being still in the right direction was very small. For the last long stretch he had been working round the side of Moel y Gigfran, climbing and turning among rocky gullies, going where he could rather than where he would, and now he was by no means sure which way round he was. The mountain seemed to rise in both directions, and he stood there in a state of tired despondency, undecided and wet-foot, with disappointment welling up.

He stood long enough for the cold to get at him, so that he was glad to be moving again. But he went heavily now, with no spirit, and his sad mind had already returned to the prosaic road so far below and how he should reach it and the paper-work that would be waiting for him at the weary end when he came round a shoulder of the mountain and saw the hounds and the followers not two hundred yards ahead.

They were grouped among a tumbled mass of boulders in a sloping waste of shale – the backside of the Moel – and the hounds were lying here and there upon the rocks, licking their paws or staring vacantly. Kirk's face creased with instant joy: his heart beat double-time. He walked up, looking as unconcerned as he could manage.

This was the Ddear Felin, an ancient fox and badger strong-hold; and in the middle of the boulders he could see the bowed back of the Master, head and shoulders down a cleft between two yellow rocks. Gerallt's head was also down the hole, his body arched over the Master's: they were listening intently. Major Boyd sat by the earth, holding a tight mob of terriers: an empty couple showed that some of them had already been put to. One thin black-and-tan bitch barked unceasingly and every now and then all the others would join in, screaming and bawling. When they were not pulling, reared on their hind legs, they sat trembling all over, whining shrill. Boyd's temper had improved with his walk; he told Kirk that they had run their fox in, that Bellman had marked him true for quite half an hour, and that it would be the Devil's own job to bolt him. He suggested that Kirk should post himself on that tall rock down there to view him away, if the terriers could make him budge.

The boulder was rough and harsh – a pleasure to creep up after all the treacherous wet slate of the other side – and from its flat top Kirk surveyed the whole of the earth, a mass of loose rock ten yards across and running twenty down the slope; some of the boulders that formed it were as big as a cart, but most were smaller; and many of these had obviously been moved before – they showed raw yellow underneath. Above the earth shale ran up clear for three or four hundred feet: below, the slope was less, and there was some grass and heather among the rocks. On the far side from Kirk, the way he had come, there was the shoulder of the mountain, and it broke the full force of the wind: behind him still more shale stretched away, its lower edge ending in much the same kind of grass, heather and bog, scattered with boulders fallen from the high crags of the Moel y Gigfran. Above the shale nothing but bare rock, vague in the thickening cloud.

Other followers were posted here and there on vantage-points, and Kirk saw with satisfaction that there were not so many now as there had been. In the lee of a crag the women were mending a torn skirt with safety-pins. Clearly it was his duty to watch the broken ground below him, a gully whose nearer end was hidden from the rest, and for the first quarter of an hour he stared eagerly, rarely taking his eyes off to see what they were doing at the earth. Then his nearest neighbour began to eat his lunch – a turkey's leg with crusty bread. The sight brought an instant, painful salivation, a grind in his stomach, and Kirk realized that he was shockingly hungry. Cautiously he dragged his sandwiches from an inner pocket, still keeping his eye on the gully; but what with the business of separating the wet conglomerate and of keeping insist-ent hounds from eating the pieces before he could get them to his mouth – gently insistent hounds, but tall and pervasive – his very close attention dwindled. He engulfed the food, a wretched pittance, mostly bread with cake-crumbs ground into it from his repeated falls; and by the time it was gone all the warmth he had generated on his way up had left him. Now the wind was a continual enemy; no crouching or huddling would escape it, and soon it pierced even into his protected middle parts. His eyes watered as he stared at the gully; his hands, reaching for his pipe, were too numb to do more than fumble impotently at the buttons; his neck and shoulders were rigid with shivering. He looked enviously at Gerallt and the Master, now shifting masses of rock, scarlet with exertion. They had changed terriers – the magistrate had charge of the disgraced muddy couple – but still the little dogs were not doing very much: all cry and no wool. A Jack Russell kept skipping about on the top, searching and searching for a new entry – she thought nothing of the place where the others were, four or five of them who kept up a muffled bawling and scuffling deep underground. Kirk watched her with an apathetic stare: he had never been so cold in his life.

The present seemed always with him, and this vile wind. The man on the far side seemed to be suffering even more, cupping his frozen ears with an unconscious look of pure misery.

The Jack Russell was screaming away, bouncing over the rocks with desperate energy, yelping at every bound: nothing of this pierced Kirk's numbed mind for two beats of time, then everything was movement – hounds streaming down and round the far shoulder, the men all standing, bolt upright and motionless, the Master shouting to the highest of them all, incomprehensible words in the wind – and he realized that the fox had stolen away, had crept an unbelievable distance from the earth before breaking, and although he had passed close by two or three hounds only the terrier had seen him.

One of the farmers was already racing up the crag at the corner of the shale: at the top he paused and pointed, with a shout flung back over his shoulder. A moment later the hounds swung right-handed, all giving tongue, and they came back into view.

Kirk stared ahead of them, searching the heather for the fox. To his intense surprise he found himself hoping that the fox was well ahead – that it should at least have a fair run for its life. Indeed, that it should get away.

The whole pack crossed on the flat ground three hundred

yards below, and behind them the white terrier, yelling still. The whole pack in deadly earnest: there was not a hound but spoke, and the music echoed from the Moel behind and a ragged cliff in front, echoed and reverberated, though torn by the wind. Its beauty had a devilish, pitiless quality, thought Kirk; yet when the hounds checked at a bog over to the right and fell almost silent, his excitement faded; and when almost immediately afterwards they hit off the line again with a splendid crash, he felt a wild exultation.

It looked as though the fox were making for a small earth farther along at the bottom of the shale, but they were pressing him too hard and he ran on past it, on and round. They were running so fast that they were out of sight in a few minutes; and presently they were out of hearing too, the wind being foul.

The followers waited to see whether he would turn left-handed again into the high broken country behind the Moel, and Kirk took the chance to peer into the earth. He could see nothing but tumbled rock with here and there a brown shrivel of small fern or a handful of crude harsh red earth. It seemed quite impossible that a fox should have got away so far without having been seen.

There were still two terriers down, and Gerallt stayed to bring them out. Major Boyd started up the shale in a sloping line for the ridge: another group went along the bottom in the direction the fox had taken. The Master watched them go, then turned back the way Kirk had come: as he left he spoke to Gerallt – a word over his shoulder, torn away by the wind. Gerallt understood it, however, and laughed.

When they were alone Gerallt asked Kirk to hold the remainin terriers, and bent to the earth. Without looking up he said, 'So you came along then, Doctor?'

'That's right,' said Kirk.

The terriers were wedging one another far down under the rocks; they could be heard quarrelling, and nothing Gerallt could do would bring them up. Eventually he and Kirk and the other dogs walked away from the earth together: two minutes later the terriers came out, matted and entirely changed in colour.

They set out after the Master, and now Kirk was glad that Gerallt was going fast; in a little while warmth flooded through him, reanimating all but his hands and ears, and he could enjoy being alive once more. They were going directly away from the obvious line, but it was clear that if the fox carried right round the top of the Moel this course would bring them out charmingly.

Once they were round the shoulder they caught the full force of the wind, colder now by far, and the first handful of rain came driving flat along it. Kirk and Gerallt turned up their collars at almost the same moment: it was not much of a protection, to be sure, but they treasured that two inches of dry neck.

It was a long while before they saw the Master again. He was walking rapidly up a distant slope, away from them and below, strangely foreshortened. He and they were going in almost exactly the same direction. 'Surely,' thought Kirk, 'this is a good sign.' For now to him *good* once more meant being with the hounds, hunting the fox and eventually killing him.

Ever since they had come round into the wind and they had been travelling diagonally towards the Cidwm valley: hard going all the way, and Kirk had to put so much physical and spiritual energy into keeping up with the huntsman that he had little time to inspect his own attitude towards the fox, towards the fox's fate. Once on an even slope he made an observation about 'wanting to have his cake and eat it'; and another time, when Gerallt was untangling the terriers, he recalled the same ambivalence at a bullfight – his pleasure when the goaded bull hurled a torero into the crowd: but no more than that.

The mountainside stretched away behind them, and now they were looking down again into Nant Cidwm, with the lake almost behind them. They must be in the next county by now, thought Kirk, glancing at his watch. It had stopped, however; stopped hours or miles ago, some unremembered fall having sprung its works.

The Master was sitting under the lee of a rock with his black dog, watching his hounds work along a dry ravine. The scent was poor down there, the day growing so precious cold, but they were working it out cleverly, all close together, with their noses down and their bottoms wriggling eagerly. After a while the Master said that young Lucifer was shaping well – he might be quite a good dog yet. They carried the line right across, and at the far edge of the ravine they started running again, a hound with a deep mouth speaking all the time. Still they bore away right-handed, and it seemed that the fox was running a true ring, a great elliptical path with the Moel at its centre, irregular in places but always tending back to its beginning.

The walked now on the inside of this ring, keeping the hounds in view for a good while. Since they were on the higher ground, they could see the hunting of the pack to perfection, and Kirk was so taken up with doing this and with remaining upright that by the time the hounds ran clean away he no longer had the least notion of where he was – from this high table-land he could see not a single familiar shape: north and south were buried in the clouds.

Some time after the pack had disappeared the three men sat down on a knoll: now and then they heard the dogs, and some-times, from the movement of sheep, they could tell where they were. Kirk could not make out why they sat there, why they did not go on after the hounds; but he was happy to sit, and what strength his mind still possessed was taken up with thoughts of food.

A quarter of an hour later they were going along at a great pace, pushing in a straight determined line across the country: the reasons for this move were utterly obscure – Kirk thought he must have dozed momentarily in spite of the cold, because he had suddenly started up to the sound of urgent Welsh, and then immediately afterwards they had set off. 'Without sleep, there is no waking,' he said, nodding to himself. 'That's logic.'

Time passed, and his hunger with it. From time to time as they traversed this stony wilderness they paused to listen, and it seemed to Kirk that they were anxious now. At last, far ahead, they heard a hound, a single deep bell-like voice. They stopped to make certain, for the wind had often made a noise like baying as it eddied in the higher crags; and indeed there it was, clear and certain, directly forward.

'It's marking in the Ceunant he is,' said Gerallt: or rather he put out the words as a suggestion. The Master waited a moment longer and then nodded. They went on faster still and presently four or five hounds met them, young hounds, capering idly about. The pack had run their fox to earth; they had grown tired of waiting and they were scattering abroad. Unless the marking hound stayed where he was, the fox was lost.

Gerallt called them in and ran forward, bounding like an enormous hare and bawling 'Yo mark her then, Countess. Yo mark her then, Ranter. Ooick, Ranter, yo mark to him, boy.'

Some of the hounds that had broken back began hunting away to the right on a frivolous line and now the Master's voice joined in as he lifted them off it. 'Aah, you bloody rebels. Lucifer, Lucifer, you bloody sod. God damn and blast that bloody Lucifer.'

Kirk heard the twanging of the horn as he toiled up the slope, and all at once there he was on the edge of the Ceunant, an abrupt, unexpected cleft, a narrow gorge, a shale and grass slope running down to jagged rocks and a white stream far below: it wanted only a few more vertical degrees to be a precipice. Gerallt was already far down its face, scrambling and sliding at a breakneck rate, still roaring like a bull. He was making for an outcrop of grey rock that jutted from the slope, with three good hounds below it, marking still – Ringwood, Countess and Ranter.

Half consciously Kirk noticed the care with which the hound in front of him launched itself over the edge: nothing much, but a horribly significant little check that made him feel sick as he too went over. It was worse than he had thought, the farthest limit of what two feet could manage; but his stick, his nailed boots and two or three providential rocks kept him from plummeting headlong to the distant stream, and with a last wild rush he reached the outcrop. Here, with the flat top firm under his feet, he found that his body was trembling all over – that the height had made him so dizzy he could hardly stand.

The Master was there immediately after him; without a pause

he passed his terriers to Kirk and slipped down to join Gerallt below. A double note of the horn brought the stragglers racing in from the far side, and now the terriers were put to. The earth was a long cleft in the base of the rock, a cleft that ran up until it became a hair-like crack. The terriers below were madly excited; they set up the wildest bawling, and before he was aware the little brutes that Kirk was holding hurled themselves at the edge and very nearly had him over. He braced himself against their pull, squatting on the rock, and he yelled at them; but they took no notice of his voice, nor of his stick, though he rapped them hard.

From this position he could see nothing: he did not mind that at all however – the near prospect of being plucked over that edge had quite daunted him. The sheer twenty feet and the plunging slope below had woken all his latent vertigo: his stomach heaved: the landscape turned.

Presently he heard Gerallt's voice calling him. The terriers, who had grown resigned, instantly redoubled their fury, heaving him towards the break. He thumped them brutally and edged to a place from which he could see the huntsman.

'Would you come down here just a minute, Doctor?' he asked. 'May I let the terriers go?'

'Oh no indeed. You must not let the terriers go, Doctor bach.'

It was a hellish experience. Where the rock met the shale was the only way down, and it was vertical – only a few widely-spaced and uncertain stones to give any footing at all. Without the right use of his hands and with the terriers liable to hurl him off his balance at any moment, it seemed impossible. However, this time his low, savage, earnest cursing impressed the dogs: he dangling them ruthlessly by their collars, dragged them over rock; and, gravity and good luck helping, it was done. He came into the comparative safety of the slope under the outcrop: Gerallt handed him those terriers that were not already underground and recommended his going back to the top, as the best place for watching for the fox to bolt. Kirk faced the return with a kind of desperation; in fact it was far easier than the descent. The terriers pulled eagerly, and he clawed up after them.

With all these dogs milling about it was hard to find a firm place to sit: but with brutal dragooning he did clear a good recess, a recess with a grip for his heels, some way back from the hideous edge; and there he sat. He could not tell what was happening below without peering over – an impossibility until this vertigo could be mastered – so there he stayed, feeling his bruises, reflecting upon giddiness and its unreasonable panic, and staring vacantly at the terriers until the Master's voice called for more by name. Kirk did not know any of their names, but he slipped those who seemed most eager to go. He seemed to have done right, for there was no sound of reproach, and some minutes later the Master called for another couple, adding 'That Tory had a grip on him now.' Kirk was left with the two quietest: old bald-faced bitches with few teeth between them, who had been brought only because it broke their hearts to be left.

He felt the dizziness recede, and the illogical dread; and to test the effect of height again he stood up. He had taken two paces towards the edge when he saw the fox on the shale twenty yards below the earth, running hard and fast in a bunched-up long-legged gallop, its tail held up in a curve.

Instantly he bawled 'Gone away', and there again was the Jack Russell with another terrier by her, flying over the rocks But every hound had been idling on the far side, and although they were laid on with might and main they were slow away, and with intense relief Kirk saw the fox racing between the boulders right down towards the stream before they began to run on his line.

This time the terriers were all out directly, all but one, and they did not wait for him. The fox had run straight up the Ceunant for a quarter of a mile, then up the side where it was very bare and rocky, and so over the ridge behind. They talked a little as they followed – the atmosphere was different, now that there were only the three of them left – and the Master said that until this last minute he had supposed they had changed foxes, had put up a fresh fox by Llys Dafydd; but now he saw that it was the same. Gerallt said that Countess had marked very well, and the Master agreed – she was a nice little bitch.

The wind met them again at the top of the ridge with even greater force: they saw hounds on the other side of the valley, working slowly up the far slope: far more slowly now.

'It's this damned cold wind spoiling the scent,' said the Master.

They went down, across the marshy bottom and up the other side. Up and up the other side: it seemed unending, and the muscles on the front of Kirk's thighs hurt so much that he thought they must refuse their duty. He poled himself up with his stick, working out each step ahead: and there was the top, the strain gone as though he had dropped a heavy load. He paused a moment to look at his meaningless watch and breathe deep, staring round the grey, indeterminate landscape. The others were twenty yards ahead now, and he broke into a shambling run to catch up. Down the hill, then up another. How he wished they could stop, if only for a minute. To sit in the shelter of a rock long enough to smoke a small pipe out . . .

How interminably the upward slope climbed on! How he hated the steadily marching backs in front of him. Now a wall, a stone wall with a strand of old barbed wire on top of it; and the terriers had to be helped over. Kirk went last, and by the time he had leapt down, jarring every fibre of his being, the others were well beyond it, going fast. Again the stumbling run, the trip and fall, before he joined them.

Another wall – this mountainside was checkered with them, great unsteady dry-stone barriers – another slope. But at least this slope was down and for a few hundred yards it changed the strain, until the long fore-reaching jolt made a climb almost welcome again. Now the hounds were at a check in the wet dead ground at the bottom and the men paused to let them work. With Bellman and Ranter and the cleverer hounds leading they cast round and about on the far side, but it was some time before they could hit off the line again. Kirk was happy to see the others sit on stones as willingly as he did himself and show evident signs of fatigue: he had begun to think them immortal. As the ghost-like hounds wafted to and fro he felt a hint of strength coming back into his legs: he might, if pushed, manage to get up again. Now Ranter hit the line; Countess owned it too, and some other hounds; and although they were no longer speaking with that old passionate conviction, they ran straight, all together, and up the other side.

It was not until he was half-way up the next slope, climbing a wall again, that Kirk recognized the familiarity of the darkening countryside. They were mounting towards the Craig Llyn Du, going painfully up the way they had come down so very long ago. Here the scent was patchy; the hounds had to puzzle out the line almost yard by yard, and now they hardly spoke at all. Slowly they carried it up and up, right to the great curtain of rock; and as their white forms zigzagged up the steepest part Kirk fell behind. His lungs and heart seemed to be bursting, and although he was climbing still it was only because of a check that he was able to come up with them. Up up and beyond to the edge of the bitterly cold lake from which the water fell so far to Llyn Du. Up here the ice was forming, and the crust tinkled underfoot.

From the high lake the hounds came back along the stream to the falls, and now it seemed that they had certainly lost their fox. It took them twenty minutes to work over the bare rock in the howling wind, but at last Countess, casting ahead as far as the heather, spoke on the true strong line – the fox must be failing, his scent growing fatally strong – and the others came to her. They ran fast down the length of the fall, checked for a short while at the bottom and then while the men sat and watched them they ran with a fine cry along the shores of Llyn Du and over the lower edge of the valley that enclosed the lake, down to the broken country out of sight.

They must be very near him, thought Kirk as they began to go down. Down, from rock to rock with here and there a patch of heather; they dropped fast, ten times faster than the weary road up, and when they reached the bottom Kirk reflected that he might as well have stayed below all the time. More usefully too, for then he could have gone along to see which way they had taken in the difficult country beyond: his heavy mind was obstinately fixed on the notion of the chase.

They splashed along – it was marshy here – and both the Master and Gerallt were listening – they were uneasy – the hounds had fallen mute too suddenly. Had they run into their fox? He was sure they had not.

The lake was far longer this time; there were waves on it and a yellow foam on the leeward shore. It took a long time to reach the place where the sloping ground began; and there they were met by several hounds coming slowly back, quite at a loss and dispirited. No sound of any marking, and indeed Ranter, the most steadfast hound in the pack, joined them a moment later, with Countess and Bellman. It was clear that the unceasing bitter wind had been too much at last – the failing scent would not lie; and when they came to a little ravine with a path running through it the Master said, 'Well, I think I shall go home now, Doctor. Where did you leave your car?'

'At the end of the road,' said Kirk. He was standing with his back to the wind, facing one of the many sudden upthrusts of rock that lined the hillside: on the face of it, seven or eight feet up, were three ledges, two bare and one with heather growing. On the heather-covered ledge there lay the fox. Dead-beat, wet, matted, flattened. Kirk closed his mouth suddenly with an audible intake of breath: he peered furtively at the Master's tired, drawn face and turned away from the ledge in case it should be obvious where he was looking. The Master bent to his horn and blew a lovely note, long and true; then another: the fox did not stir.

At last they were moving down the path, the huntsman in front, then a long string of hounds with more joining them from either side, then a bunch of sober terriers, many of them carrying a leg, then the Master with his old black dog moving stiffly, then Kirk; they went down the rocky defile with their heads bowed against the wind, down to the long road home.

10

Naming Calls

⎯⎯∞∞∞⎯⎯

At the head of a high, barren valley stood a cottage; it was so high in the bare mountains that it was something of a shock to see it there at all. For mile upon mile all round it the rocks stared black and desolate in the falling rain, and on the heather and the green bog a few sheep worked hard for their living. The wild land ran right up to the door-sill of the cottage (Llys Dafydd was its name) and it was plain that no man had ever tried to make a patch of garden there. No, it was not in any way a farming house: the sheep of those parts had to look after themselves without shepherds, and no good crop would ever come from what little earth there was, it being so shallow and harsh. It was, indeed, one of those many rough houses – barracks, they are called, even when they have but one or two little rooms – that were scattered among the hills by prospectors for slate or copper. This was one of the few with a roof still, and the young man who was in it now had put glass to its windows again.

Llys Dafydd was wedged into the steep side of the valley out of the weather: it stood on a platform of rock, a platform covered with fine, down-like turf, and it looked out over a mere. A stream trickled down behind it, conveniently near at hand, and two faint paths led to its door. The left-hand path ran to the deep, fern grown hole where the miners had tried their luck under the shoulder of the mountain – had tried it in vain – and the other went down and down to the remote village which stood at the end of the road.

Abel Widgery had taken Llys Dafydd for two or three reasons; the most important was that it was necessary for him to spend the long vacation reading hard, essential, indeed, if he were to stand any chance of a good degree. Scarcely less important to him was the opportunity of bird-watching. The bare hills were full of wheatears; there were whinchats and stonechats lower down, and pied flycatchers in the woods. Buzzards and ravens were common, and peregrines were not rare.

The renting of Llys Dafydd had proved almost insuperably difficult: William Williams, Rhobell y Moch, to whom the mountain belonged, had declined answering his letters on the score of imperfect English, and it was only through the good offices of Evans the Post, working at two removes, that even the most tenuous agreement had been reached. However, the first days of July had seen him installed, rucksacks, sleeping-bag, patent stoves and all. Cae Uchaf had very kindly brought the heavy things in a cart, and the first week had passed in ceaseless activity; bookshelves, the windows, the defective chimney, the unfamiliar cares of housekeeping, these had kept him busier than he had been in his life. The weather had been good all the time, and Widgery looked forward to a perfect summer.

On Saturday morning, the seventh day of his tenancy, he woke with the sun, straight from a deep sleep to complete consciousness, and got up from his bed on the hard floor feeling strong and active, happy for no immediate cause. As he was dressing a bird flew by the window, dark, instant shadow, and above the roof another cried with a loud, ringing voice. He dropped his tie and stood still; that was no jackdaw, he said, and the second bird came down past the window. With infinite pains he crept to the window, to the lower corner of it, and slowly raised his head. As his eye came up to the level of the glass he checked: his heart came thump into his throat, for there was a chough on the short grass just outside. The sun was just into the valley and it shone full on the bird: Widgery had never seen one before, and he would never have believed the brilliance of the bird's scarlet legs and beak. It was so close that he could see into its eye. The chough was busily working on the turf: it walked, almost ran, three or four paces backwards, listened, then drove its slender beak in and out of the turf, right in and out as fast as a starling, or faster. Widgery, filled with precarious elation, hardly dared look at it directly, for fear that it should become aware of him. At the edge of his field of vision he saw the other chough, walking nearer. They were untidier birds than he had expected from the pictures, less sleek, more like small, unkempt rooks.

A quarter of an hour passed. The choughs liked their diet, and in time Widgery's knees, which were thin, began to hurt him. He moved, with great caution and without frightening the birds; when they flew away, which was within a few moments after he had moved, it was of their own motion. Widgery was guiltily conscious of a mixture of feelings in which relief played a not unimportant part. Now that the birds were gone there was a feeling of anticlimax, but he knew that if they had stayed very much longer he would have thought of driving them away. He was discontented with himself, and he prepared his breakfast in an offhand, sluttish manner. While he ate the bright morning clouded.

This day was to be the beginning of his reading programme, but after he had washed up he had no inclination to read. The pages went slowly over, and in the end he found that when he had finished a paragraph he had no idea what had been said, although he had conscientiously formed each word with his lips. He closed the book and started on his lecture notes: they seemed either trivial and obvious or obscure to incomprehensibility. His eye roved vacantly and slid down to his watch; it was unthinkable that so few minutes should have passed, but when he held it to his ear the watch was ticking.

The rain started, and almost at once he heard drips coming through the roof. That was the end of his reading. Everything had to be moved to avoid the drips; a pool grew in the middle of the floor.

Widgery passed the rest of the day, a very long day, going over and over the old ground of his lecture notes. His acquired knowledge had never seemed so unprofitable, and by the time he lit the lamp he knew that he had done little or nothing of use.

In his enthusiasm, he had excluded from his baggage any books that could be described as amusing, and now he was reduced to writing letters until he could and decently go to bed. In all his letters he described the choughs, never failing to point out that such a thing could never have happened in any but an extraordinarily remote place. He had no need to exaggerate the loneliness of Lyls Dafydd; it was in a far sort of country, unfit for the habitation of any man but a hermit, a man able to struggle with loneliness and devils.

Sleep kept very far from him after he had blown out the lamp. The steady noise of the rain and of moving waters outside would have been sedative after a time, but there were the incessant, uneven drips, drips of all tones and pitches, some near, some quite distant, probably from the eaves, dripping into the puddles outside. After a long spell of determined stillness, with vacant mind and relaxed body, he resigned himself to waking and let his mind run idly where it liked.

It chose, as it so often did, to run over those shameful occasions which he would most have liked to blot out, those dreadful things that made him blush in the dark: the joke he had made which the unsmiling company thought to be in poor taste, the time when he found himself impotent, his arrival in a suit when everyone else had a dinner-jacket on – these, and many like them, repeated their well-known lines, no word forgotten, no humiliating nuance overlooked, every possible consequence magnified. He forcibly diverted his thoughts to other things, to the stories of various books. From one of them his now sleepy mind glided off to a scene in which he was a minor actor. He was in a vast, low-ceilinged kitchen with an uneven, red-bricked floor: there was a pump at one end and a range at the other, glowing nobly through its bars in the dusk. In front of the fire was a hip-bath, filled with soapy water that steamed in wisps; on each side of the fire was a comfortably shaped woman in a brown wooden armchair. One was his Nanny and the other her sister, the woman of the house. Nanny's knees and lap were swathed in towel and he was being dried. They were in that house, a farm-house, because of the death of Abel's father, a formidable, roaring tyrant – it was only since he had gone to the university that Abel had begun to realize that there must have been something very strange about his father's life, and stranger still about his death, and the manner of it.

Nanny and her sister were talking, and Abel, stooping to see under the hot brass top of the fire-guard, was watching a potted-meat jar melting in the stove; with the liveliest satisfaction he saw a drop form, gather globular weight and fall, still with an interior glow, into the ashes. It left a long tail behind, like treacle. Then the fire fell inwards and spoilt everything. Mrs Holt was saying, 'When the end come, did Mr –' and Nanny stopped her mouth at once. 'Tut, now, Abbie,' she said. 'Naming calls, you know. God between us and harm.' She added the last with an involuntary glance over her shoulder, and Abel felt a thrill of exquisite horror run through him.

He recaptured the feeling now; the words had an awful value of their own, and the course of years had enhanced this. He repeated them now, with a sense of growing insecurity. He felt a powerful temptation – temptation, because he resisted it as though it were an evil sin – to say his father's name aloud. He made a strong effort and changed the current of his thought.

In the early morning he dropped into a series of uneasy dozes, and he dreamt of the far-off horror of his father, and he shouted, so that he awoke suddenly, with the sound of his cry still in the room.

With a sudden burst of energy, he got up and lit the lamp, and in the light the terror of nightmare receded and his sense of proportion returned. He knew that he must have been talking in his sleep again, as he had done from his school-days. He dozed off, with the lamp still alight.

The morning was dark and the rain had increased when he woke; it was coming down in big drops, and a south-west wind was driving it across the valley. The mountainside that lay over against his window was laced with a dozen new white torrents, and the trickle that ordinarily ran so peaceably by the wall ran now with a high and masterful sound. He found that a stream had started under his own roof; it welled up between two of the slabs that made the floor and ran out under the door, where it made a spreading pool. This meant another rearrangement of the room, and in the doing of it he dropped the matches into the pool and trod upon them heavily.

Before coming to Llys Dafydd he had drawn up an exact time-table, which disposed of every minute of his day. He made a conscientious attempt to follow it now, but it would not answer, and before long he was gazing out of the window, with his elbows on the sill and his legs astraddle to avoid a growing pool.

The valley was worth watching: a solid mass of grey was racing over it, with hardly a rift to show how fast it was going. At frequent intervals the heavy squalls of rain marched up and across the valley, their slanting lines plain; whatever they covered they blotted out. The higher part of the ridge opposite was hidden, but the cross-wind, which from time to time sent a howling gust directly up the valley, tore the cloud-covering into whirling eddies and the black rock showed through. The wind made an increasing, strenuous noise, very tiring to hear.

Abel watched one of the regular cataracts; it had swollen overnight into a considerable waterfall, but the wind never allowed it to come down the main drop. As soon as the white stream reached the top of its precipice the wind whipped it into spray and flung it back, far up the mountainside. Occasionally a lull would let it come halfway down in a wavering curtain before it was torn off again, but most of the time it ran to the edge and then off at a mad angle into the air.

It was very impressive indeed, and Widgery leant there for a long, long time. In time his mind quite abstracted itself from the scene outside and wandered off into the vaguest day-dreams. 'Naming calls', he found himself repeating, and as he said it he was conscious of a strong disinclination to turn from the window to the gloom behind. He did turn, however, and having pottered idly among his books for a little while he began to prepare a cold lunch for himself. It was necessarily cold, for the match heads had quite disintegrated, and he had no others.

After lunch he read again, with a little more gain this time, and he plodded on to the end of the afternoon's programme, although his eyes were pricking with tiredness and his mind heavy and unreceptive. Loss of sleep always made him feel like this, and now, when he closed the book he closed his eyes too, for they hurt, and his head ached: he was asleep in a few minutes.

An extraordinarily loud gust woke him. He went to the window, stretching and yawning; the wind had increased, and it was tearing the water from wherever it lay on the mountain; there was not a puddle that could stand five minutes before a blast whipped its surface back into the air. It was impossible to see now which was rain and which was not: the air was full of water, and every standing rock streamed without cease on its windward side. The wind was backing and the gusts that came up the valley came more directly and with greater force. They could be heard and seen as distinct entities: far down to the right there would be a howling roar, higher than the continuous sound that filled the air, and a darker patch would be seen moving furiously up the valley, flattening the battered heather and hurling the old sodden dead fern of last year high into the air, and stretching the arms of the sparse thorns to the utmost limit. The shallow mere below the cottage with its thin fringe of low rushes was almost invisible in the flurry; it had no surface – one minute the water was scooped away and the next it was hurled back.

Widgery heard one gust coming directly for Llys Dafydd, and he half crouched as it struck. The air went strange in his ears and the whole fabric of ponderous stone shifted under the blow. The extreme pressure lasted long enough for him to be certain that the roof was going, and then he was left, staring and frightened, but unhurt. It was like being missed by a bomb.

He could not settle again after this, but took his chair to the window; before, he had been exhilarated by the storm, but now he was seriously uneasy; it was getting out of all bounds. His alarm, plain physical fear, sent another dread out of his mind. All day that phrase had either run through his head or had stayed in the back of his consciousness, and he had been full of a nameless apprehension. He had wished that he had asked Carter to come with him: as a cure for loneliness he had talked aloud, and had tried to sing, but the result had been so false and dispiriting that he had stopped.

Now the night began to fall. He looked at his watch to see whether this was the growing storm or the end of the day, and he found that the watch had stopped. He wound and shook it, but it would not tick, no shaking or manipulation would make it move: it was dead, and he had lost a companion. The tick of a clock or a watch is a matter-of-fact, usual companion, a great relief on occasion, and now it had deserted him. The wind was dying with the going down of the sun, but as is so often the case the force of the gusts increased powerfully. Many passed Llys Dafydd, for it was cleverly placed among its sheltering rocks, but three struck it with full force. Each was of enormous and increasing strength, and each left him crouching and shaken. The third was succeeded by an interval of calm as extraordinary as the blast; there were a thousand sounds of water, but it seemed as though something immense had been turned off, and the water was as nothing.

Widgery sat listening, with a strained anxiety. An instant horror caught his breath. There was something outside the door, he said. A long pause followed and he sat tense, leaning slightly forward, rigid in his chair. He could hear the beat of his own heart. The wind returned, but underneath its noise he heard the sound that made his neck stiffen and his hand come halfway to his mouth. The twilight faded, and still he sat rigid, listening and listening.

High up on the mountainside a vast mass of rock, undermined at last by the scouring torrent that ran under its foot, moved with a tiny forward motion and a deep, prodigious grind: its several parts reft one from another and the whole slid, plunged, hurled itself down the scree with a terrible, thunderous, menacing crash that lasted for whole minutes. It roused men in the far distant farms, but Widgery's straining ears separated it instantly from that which he was listening for and disregarded it. He was listening for a little grating sound, no more, but horrible beyond words.

'What did I say in my sleep?' he asked for the hundredth time, though he knew very well now.

There was an old cough outside, a little scratching rap and the door creaked with a pressure that was not that of the wind. A pause that lasted beyond counting came after: he knew that he must not take his eyes from the door, though even its outlines were going in the dark; they wavered and took on strange forms. This space seemed endless before he knew again that something was going to happen. The scratch, a little grating knock, a pause, then a battering, furious smashing on the wood, the frail wood, and there no more than a hasp to keep it. Abel shrieked high and the door burst open, swinging wide and shuddering on its hinges.

II

The Dawn Flighting

———⌾———

The night was old, black, and full of driving cold rain; the moon and the stars had already passed over the sky. But anyhow they had been hidden since midnight by the low, racing, torn cloud and the flying wetness of small rain and sea-foam and the whipped-off top of standing water. Dawn was still far away: from the dark east the mounting wind blew in gusts; it bore more rain flatlings from the sea.

Bent double, with the breath caught from his mouth, a man struggled against the force of the living wind. He walked on the top of a sea-wall that guarded the reclamation of a great marsh. At this point the wall ran straight into the teeth of the wind for a long way; there was no shelter. He had to walk carefully, for the mud had not frozen yet, and it was treacherous going. Behind him his dog, an old black Labrador, picked its way, whining in a little undertone to itself when the way was very dirty.

A great blast came, halting him in mid-stride; he staggered and stepped back to keep his balance. The dog's paw came under his heel and there was a yelp, but he heard nothing of it for the roaring of the wind. He leaned against it, and it bore him up with a living resilience, suddenly slackening, so that he stumbled again. The false step jerked a grunt out of him.

Thrusting his chin down into the scarf under his high-buttoned collar and shifting the weight of his gun, the man pushed on. All his mind was taken up with his fight; every long, firm step was a victory in little. The hardness of his way and the unceasing clamour at his ears had taken away every other thought. He was hardly aware of the places where the driven wet had pierced through, above his knees, down one side of his neck, and on his shoulder where the strap of his cartridge-bag crossed over. Earlier on he had been inked by the weight of the bag and by the drag of the gun in the crook of his arm, but now he did not heed them at all; the wind was the single, embracing enemy.

At last the sea-wall turned right-handed, running along the south face of the saltings. At the corner he stooped and slid on all fours down the steep side into the lee. At once it seemed to him that some enormous machine had stopped; in the quiet air he breathed freely, and sighed as he squatted in the mud. The Labrador shook itself and thrust its muzzle into his relaxed hand. Absently the man felt for its ears, but the dog was insistent; the custom must be fulfilled. When he had changed the hang of the strap on his aching shoulder the man searched under his mac-intosh among the scarves and pullovers for an inner pocket; he found half a biscuit and his pipe. The flare of the match in his cupped hands showed his face momentarily, in flashes, as he sucked the flame down; it showed disembodied in the darkness, high cheekbones and jutting nose thrown into distorted promi-nence. The foul pipe bubbled, but the acrid tobacco was instantly satisfying; he drew and inhaled deeply for a few moments.

'Well, that's the first leg,' he said to the dog as he got up. He went on under the lee of the sea-wall, walking heavily in the deep, uneven mud. Further on there was a place where he had to leave the wall to strike across the marsh for a stretch of open fresh water: there was only one path that led to the mere. At this time of the year the marsh was impassable except by this track, for the land-water had deepened the mud so that a man could sink out of sight in it almost before he knew he was in danger.

Anxiously he counted the time that he had taken walking along the southern wall; if he missed the path he would not get across the marsh for the dawn flighting. He crossed an old, broken sea-wall that joined the other, and he knew that he was near the path. When he climbed to the top of the wall to look for the three posts that would give him his bearings he felt an abatement in the wind: it blew less furiously, but it was colder now – certainly freezing. A flurry of sleet stung his cheek. The wind was veering to the north-north-east. He found the posts and the track; he was glad, for it was easy to miss in the dark, when all that could be seen looked strange, even monstrous.

The dog went before him now, finding out the tortuous way: sometimes a single bending plank led through the deep reed-beds, loud in the wind: treading on the planks stirred the marsh smell. Once there was a rush of wings, and desolate voices fled away piping in the darkness. They were redshanks or some kind of tukes – inedible, and his half-raised gun sank.

Now the wind was at his back; it was blowing itself out in great gusts. A thin film of ice was skimming the top of the puddles, and a more querulous note sang through the reeds. He looked over his shoulder, scanning the eastern sky for the first cold light: there seemed to be a lessening in the darkness, nothing more. He pushed on faster: the way was a little easier now.

Presently large dim shapes came up out of the blind murk before him; they were the trees surrounding the mere. He stopped to take his bearings again, and then he went on cautiously. The ground rose a little; there were brambles and patches of alder, laced through and through with rabbit tracks. Ahead a buck-rabbit thrummed the earth, and three white scuts bobbed away. Very carefully the man came through the undergrowth among the trees: a flick of his thumb and finger brought his dog in to heel. There might well be duck down on the water. Choosing his steps and crouching low in the bushes and then in the reeds, the man slipped down the bank, down the sheltered way, and crept secretly into the butt of cut reeds at the pond's edge.

After a little listening pause he stood slowly up, holding his breath and staring with wide-opened eyes through the shoulder-high reeds. Still a little bent, he peered intently over the water. There were no duck; only a little grebe swam and dived unwit-ting on the mere. He slowly relaxed, and sat down on the rough, unsteady plank stool in the butt.

He stretched and shook himself, for he was still desperately tired from getting up at two o'clock in the morning, and his eyes prickled. He looked to his gun, wiped a clot of mud from its barrels, and propped it carefully in the corner of the butt by his cartridge bag; he was warm now in the shelter of the reeds, and he settled himself comfortably to wait for the dawn flight of the wild duck.

Now that he was in the butt, time seemed to begin again: for the whole of the way out across the marsh it had stopped. He had been trying to race the dawn – quite another thing. By and by he pulled out a packet of bread and cheese, with an apple against thirst, for the marsh water was sulphurous and brackish. He ate bite for bite with the dog, but absently, with his senses on the stretch.

By imperceptible degrees the sky lightened, so that when he looked again he could see halfway across the water. The lake had formerly been a decoy: the hoops for the duck-pipes still showed in the overgrown channels, and a cottage, half-sunk and unroofed, marked where the wild-fowlers had kept their gear.

He was unready, for all his vigilance, when the first duck passed over: one hand was scrabbling in his pouch, the other holding his pipe. With his unlighted pipe in his mouth and his gun in his hands, he listened again: the sound was high above, a sound hard to convey. There was a creaking in it, and a whistling. His ears followed the sound, and the dog stared up into the dim quarter-light. The noise circled round the mere twice, coming lower. Mallard they were, by the sound, and they were coming down. The butt stood on a spit of land with the length of the pond lying out on each side, so that the duck would come in across. He stood with his back to the wind, jiggling his forehand nervously and biting hard on the stem of his pipe. Down, and up again: he caught a glimpse of them, five mallard. They came round lower, the flight-note changed and they braced hard against the wind to land. Up went the gun and his fingers poised delicately round the triggers. The sound of wings rushed closer: he saw the duck, picked the right-hand bird, steadied, and fired, swinging his second barrel into them as they crossed so quickly that the two tongues of flame stabbed the darkness almost at the same moment. There was a splash in front of him, then a threshing in the water. His hands, working of themselves, broke the gun and thrust new cartridges into the smoking breech. He stared up, waiting for the duck to circle overhead, but they swung wide out of range, and he heard them go. The Labrador stood rigid, ears pointing: Fetch, he said, and the dog flung itself into the water. It was back in a minute with the mallard held gently at the shoulder. Stooping, he let the dog put it into his hand, and as he straightened a disturbed sheldrake passed over, gruntling as it flew. It circled the mere twice and came down with a long splash: he had caught a glimpse of the breadth of its wings and had heard its small noise, for the wind was dying now, and he was nearly sure that it was a sheldrake. The bird swam close to the butt, safe in its uneatable rankness, so close that he could see the nob on its beak: he was glad to see it, for it would bring the other duck down.

He lit his pipe, crouching in the bottom of the butt, with his head on one side for the sound of wings. Presently they came, a flight of mallard, and above them, close behind, half a dozen sharp-winged widgeon. The mallard came straight down, sweeping right across in front of the butt with their wings held against the wind and their bodies almost upright; they tore up the water, each making a distinct tearing sound, and settled at the far end of the decoy. At once they changed from things of the wind to earth-bound, quacking ducks, awkward and lumpish in the water. The widgeon, more wary, went round high and fast: they seemed to suspect something, but the duck on the water reassured them, and they dropped down, slipping sideways down through the air on stiff, decurved wings, on the one slant and then on the other, like aeroplanes that have come in too high.

They came straight at the butt, as if to skim over it and land the other side. As he brought his gun up for the difficult shot they saw him and lifted: he fired at once. The first barrel jerked the bird a yard higher and clipped feathers from its wing; the second missed altogether. With a loud and rushing noise, the mallard got up. He stared impassively after the flying widgeon, not allowing himself any emotion, for he was a choleric man, and if he let himself start to kick and swear he might carry on and spoil his whole morning with rage, as he had done before.

Automatically he reloaded, sniffing the sharp, sweet powder smell: the mallard wheeled back over the pond. He took a chance shot at the lowest and winged it. It came down in a long slope into the brushwood on the other side of the decoy. The dog went after it, but could not reach it, for the bird was in a tall, dense thicket of brambles. The dog came back after a long time and stood bowing in deprecation: the air was quite still now, and the mallard could be heard moving over on the other side. He cast a look round the low bowl of the sky, now almost white, and saw no birds: he walked quickly round the mere, for he hated to leave a wounded bird for any length of time. The brambles ripped through to his flesh, but he got the duck and gripped it by the neck. A strong pull, and the bird jerked convulsively and died.

He looked up: three widgeon were coming over, high and fast. with their pointed wings sounding clear. He flung himself on his back in the rushes. They were right over his head as he raised his gun: the movement was plain, in spite of the rushes, and they lifted high. It was too long a shot, but he fired his choke barrel at the middle bird, making great allowance ahead. The bird seemed to fold, to collapse in the air: it fell like a plummet and hit the ground a yard from his feet so hard that he felt it strike. He stared at the duck with an unconscious grin of pleasure; for it was a wonderfully long shot. He picked it up and smoothed its beautiful ruffled breast with his finger. With a sudden, unforeseen leap, the widgeon came back to life; it almost sprang from his loose hands. He killed it and went back to the butt.

It was a bird worthy of a good shot; a fine drake it was, nearly as big as the mallard in the corner. He smoothed its yellow crest: its blue legs and beak were brighter than any he had seen.

Far away there was the deep boom of a punt-gun. That will get them moving, he said, and the dog moved its tail. A big mixed flight came in: with good fortune he got four barrels into them, killing two mallard and a shoveller. He regretted the shoveller, for by his private rules they were not to be shot. There was something about their coral and prussian blue and white bib and tucker that combined with their disproportionate beaks to make them look too much like agreeable toys. But, firing so quickly, he had not distinguished it.

For half an hour after that, while the first rays of the true dawn showed, the duck flighted in great numbers over the marshes. He shot a brace of teal right and left, a feat that consoled him for many bad misses, and he killed another widgeon and three mallard. But he was not shooting well: the duck were moving very fast, and his tired eyes were strained by the changing light. After seven successive misses – one bird carried away a deadly wound – he felt a wretched frustration welling up. By now the watery sun was showing a faint rim over the sea. All at once he felt very weary; unshaved, dirty and weary, with his eyes hot.

A little time passed and the sun came bodily up. The flighting was over, and he bent to his bag. As he stowed each away he smoothed it with care; he put the exquisitely marked teal on the top and strung the bag up. It was barely a quarter full: he had not done at all well. He knew that on such a good day he should have killed many more. He counted the big pile of empty cartridges against his bag, and he thought of the long walk back. He always had a feeling of reaction after he stopped shooting, when the taut excitement died rather ignominiously away, and now there was a strong vexation of spirit upon him as well as that.

'Oh well,' he said, and slung the bag on his back. He could see far and wide over the marsh now; beyond the sea-wall the masts of the fishing boats showed clearly in the sharp air. It was freezing now for sure. Towards the sea he saw a ragged skein of duck weaving and drifting like a cloud: there was none over the marsh. A curlew cried despairingly over his head; breaking its heart, it was.

The wind had quite died. Stiffly, with a lumbering gait, he went back towards the sea-wall with his dog padding quietly after him.

From far away there came a sound over the marsh on the still, frozen air: he looked round and above, but he could see nothing. The sound grew stronger, a rhythmic beating, strangely musical, and he saw three wild swans. The light caught them from below and they flashed white against the cold blue. High up in the air, their great singing wings bore the swans from the north: they flew straight and fast with their long necks stretched before them.

The rhythm changed a little, sighing and poignant, and a leaping exaltation took the man's heart as he gazed up at them, up away in the thin air.

The beat changed more, and now they flew striking all together, so that their wings sung in unison as they went over his head. He stood stock still watching them, and long after they had passed down the sky he stood there, with the noise of their wings about his head.

12

The Trap

———∞∞∞———

Luke Carpenter stood at the edge of Barton Wood, peering hesitantly into the twilight. There was a new, trim gate in front of him, and by the side of the gate a board gave notice to the literate that man-traps awaited the trespasser. Luke was no great scholar, though he knew a great L when he saw one, and an N; but he knew about the man-traps. He had seen the terrible wounds that Lory Fisher had taken from one, wounds that had destroyed one leg and maimed the other, so that he had been transported with a pair of crutches. It is true that public feeling for some miles around was so strong after, that they had not set the traps for the whole of the rest of the season; but now the steel jaws were waiting again, tense and hidden, somewhere in the dark undergrowth there where the pheasants were.

Ordinarily Luke would have leant on the gate to stare into the wood, but now he stood with his shoulders hunched a little way from it; his stance was unnatural and his broad, red, stupid face had the dismayed look of a detected thief. It was his intent to go into Barton Wood and take a pheasant from it. At least, that had been his intention when he left his cottage, where Nellie sat with a frightened look on her pretty face, waiting for their first baby: old Mrs Reid was there, mumbling and waiting. He could not bear the house any longer.

She was prettier now than she had been when he married her, three months ago in the mouldering dank church, and the parson disapproving so that you could feel him with every word; and even then she had been so pretty that Luke, sitting on the other side of the fire, would exclaim 'Taw!' after a while of gazing at her, and would slap his leg and scrape his chair. Her mother had been a love-child – a younger son of the Big House – but they had never noticed her, if, indeed, they had ever been sure of her identity, for the younger son had been killed in his first engagement and had told nobody about the state of his affairs. Nellie, however, had inherited a delicate beauty, and if she had not been a kind, soft-natured girl she could have done exceedingly well for herself instead of yielding to Luke's dumb, longing gaze and the three hideous fairings he had bought her in the days when he had two pennies to jingle together.

The regular sound of a trotting horse interrupted not Luke's thoughts, for he was not thinking – did not think very often – but his irresolute uneasiness. He listened for a moment, plunged into the ditch, realized that a horseman could see him there, and scrambled out again on to the road, where he began walking with a dreadful affectation of ease and purpose. A man cannot walk comfortably with a birding-piece held under his stiff arm, rigid down his side under his smock; nor, unless he is a right poacher, can hc go along with his ordinary unconscious slouch when the drum of hooves may mean that some one of the parish gods is hard behind him. Luke was not a poacher, he was too timid, and except as a boy after rabbits he had never been out on a blowy night like this, with intent in his heart.

The noise was upon him, and instead of turning to gape as he would have done at any other time, Luke went doggedly on, as if by not noticing he would be immune from notice; and when the Squire gave him a good night he was suddenly inspired to answer in an assumed voice, a voice so loud and extraordinary that the Admiral turned in his saddle at the sound.

The horse was out of sight and hearing before Luke recovered his wits enough to turn upon the road and go back to the gate. There was no reason why he should choose this of the many gates, but the flurry of spirits in which he had been all day long, and the indecision, made him cling to any settled oddment of plan as to an established guide.

THE TRAP

It was terrifying that the Squire himself should have seen him,
for the Admiral had, as Luke knew very well, a good memory for
a man's face, and it was well known that he would rather lose an
ounce of his own blood than a brace of his pheasants. Ever since
he had come to his estate on the death of his brother – an event
which coincided almost exactly with his reaching flag rank and
unemployment in the Navy – the Admiral had settled down to
being a country gentleman with the same restless determination
with which he had harried the French. He had at once seen that
the old system of farming was inefficient; much more could be
produced by enclosure and labour at wages would be much better
for the lower sort of people than their old vague, complicated
subsistence: he had set about enclosing with such vigour that
already the commissioners had parcelled out the whole waste,
and the final division of the rest was only awaiting a trifling
adjustment of boundaries between the Admiral and Mr Ellis, the
other big landowner. It was hardly to be wondered at that the
Admiral was unpopular in the village, for the disappearance of
the common land had changed the lives of the common people
from an arduous but reasonably well-fed and happy existence to
an arduous, hopeless, wage-bound drudgery. It was not this, however, that made them hate the Admiral; they accepted it as inevitable, for they had seen it happening throughout the country for
years past, and it was only the gentle, unacquisitive nature of the
old squire that had preserved them from the cruel march of the
times: the enclosure seemed to most of them impersonal, official,
and the farmers explained that it was for the good of the country.
What they hated was his importing of a Scotch bailiff and his
ferocious preservation of game. His long training in the rigorous
discipline of his service – he had gone away to sea when he was
twelve – and long periods of independent command, together
with a passion for neatness and efficiency did not qualify him
to agree well with his slow-moving, dull and apparently stupid
tenants. When they would not see what was for their own good
he lashed out with evictions, and they retaliated upon his coverts.
The Admiral increased the number of his keepers-strangers, with

no friends in the neighbourhood, and a brutal lot some of them were. Already he had two of the older men and five young ones – Tom Cole hardly more than a boy – sent over the sea to New South Wales: and there was that horrible fray in the park itself when the keepers got John Finch down and killed him between them in the dark. There were two men in gaol, too: four of them rotting in gaol. And the families on the parish, with all the bitter shame of it, and the new paid overseer, Campbell, the bailiff's brother-in-law, with his raw, skinned face and his legal turn of mind, enjoying his work, loving the power.

Still the poaching had increased. The Admiral had some of the finest partridge country for miles, and his pheasants were known in London: in his brother's day six famous shots had shot all day for an election dinner, and the carts had been piled high with a number of birds so great that none but the actual counters believed it; yet the birds seemed as plentiful as ever when next they shot. There had been poaching in those days, too, but it was mostly boys doing it for fun, a cottager wanting an occasional something for the pot, or one or two steady old hands who never overstepped the mark of what was tolerable.

Now the Admiral was ashamed to ask his grander friends to fag so far for so little, for now the poaching was vicious, systematic and commercial. New poverty, revenge and opportunity had turned almost every parishioner under the rank of farmer into a poacher, and the birds were wild, scarce and fast vanishing.

The London road came through the village; the coaches stopped at the Champion of Wales, whose landlord was a deep file and a knowing one, and the coaches and wagons took up hampers of game right through the season, and a month or so either side of it. The landlord was a substantial man, one of the few voting freeholders of the borough, and neither the Admiral nor Mr Ellis could touch him. He was a good man to the poachers. It was known that he had paid the lawyer who had saved Jem Harte at the Assizes when they went to swear his life away, and every man in the village knew that he had perjured himself when he had proved old Billett's alibi. There were two gangs of poachers in the village, and the landlord dealt with them by wholesale. He had their nets and engines where no warrant would ever find them, and for the occasional hands it was known that the fowling-piece in the little room behind the tap was always to be had without the asking, and that if it were put back with a brace of pheasant or a hare in the box underneath, the man who put it would find something at the bottom of his beer.

It was strange that the keepers and all but those who knew should have supposed that Luke was one of the most desperate of the poachers, for until that very day he had never gone into the little triangular room. They had supposed that he must be because his cottage lay far out of the close-huddled village, right by the best pheasant covert on the estate, and because he had taken the enclosure so cruel hard. It was all of a piece with Luke's general fortune that his father should have been an encroacher on the waste, and that his cottage should have had no legal existence – or at least so little that Luke was not allotted even the odd patch of ground that the other cottagers were given as a compensation for the loss of what was the basis of their livelihood. His two cows and the promising calf, his famous geese – uncommonly heavy birds, always – his pig, all had gone, because the land was taken from under them, and there was nothing for them to eat. His cottage appeared to be still his, as far as he could tell, but now thy were talking of cultivating the big field – Moor Field – right up to the door of it, taking in his very garden.

He had got up, once, at the meeting of the commissioners, standing there in his best smock, with his great red face (almost girlish, it was, and smooth) and a prepared piece on his tongue, and he had tried to tell them that long before he was born his father had been allowed his place by the other commoners, and that he, Luke, had followed his father, and that although there were no writings (they always wanted to be shown writings) he had a true right: and he had finished by saying that he had always been a hard worker and that he hoped he would always do his duty. They had heard him quite kindly, concealing their weary impatience, and had tried to explain; but it was almost another language that they spoke, and he never knew why he had lost his patrimony.

Now eggs, bacon and beer, milk and cheese and butter were no longer there by nature as they had always been all his life; now they had to be bought at the shop, and the money for the cows and the unseasonable geese and the rest was gone, and Luke would sooner have passed the gateway of Hell than the door of the shop where Davies, with the new prosperous, angry, pursey air sat with his book of accounts.

There was still firing, though now sour looks were cast at a faggot, and the garden had potatoes and green-stuff, so with that and what little day-labour a man could get in disturbed, troubled times, with men at every farmer's door, they had so far kept off the parish. The weight of the future pressed continually upon Luke, and in these days there was always something of an uncomprehending, frightened look about his face in repose. The future with three mouths to feed was – he could not say what it was, but he pushed open the gate and walked into Barton Wood.

It was darker and quieter in the wood, and the wind was less. The sun was somewhere behind the low bank of cloud on the western horizon, or perhaps it might have sunk already, for the light was certainly going, and as he walked quickly down the glade a pigeon came in to roost, pitched into a tree, saw him, and went out with a great clatter of wings.

Here was a hazel thicket, just out of sight of the road; here he stripped off his smock, rolled it up, hid it. He had on his father's old snuff-coloured coat, and he showed but vaguely among the trees as he stepped out of the bushes with the fowling-piece in the crook of his arm.

Three steps more into the long glade and he stopped: the resolution that had brought him here, right on to Tom Tiddler's ground, was failing. With a sudden thump, his heart sprang: lup dum, too loud. Something had squeaked behind him. He was rigid, not looking round, and it came again, a high scream. Just this had frightened him so many times before: when he was a little boy, gathering sticks, it had frightened him. His mother had told him that it was two branches crossed, grinding across each other with the swaying of the wind and often he had seen the truth of it, white patches on high old branches: but was it always the wind in the branches? Was it that now?

It was: with every gust of wind it came, and it did not move. He went on, along the open glade. Here there was no fear of traps, and he had a faint hope that he might see a bird on either side – he often had when he had come this way in the evening as a boy. But now the birds all roosted farther from danger in the thicker cover, where Sir John had planted the evergreens. Over in that direction he heard the cock-cock-cock of a pheasant, and he knew that he would have to go down, past the pond and over there, if he wanted to be sure of the sight of a bird.

The glade led to an open place where was the keepers' hut, the place where the beaters met and received their instructions when the Admiral shot. Here was Yellow George's gibbet, hung with mummified or rotting weasels, stoats, owls, a merlin and the last battered remnants of an osprey. They called him Yellow George because his service in the Indies had given him a yellow face. He was a proper villain of a man, bullying (he had been a sergeant in *Caligula* when the Admiral was her captain) hateful and envious, servile to his master and a cruel driver of those under him; a bloody-minded man. He was brave, however, and trustworthy as a gamekeeper; he truly hated poachers, and he never sold his game.

Luke dared not go within sight of the hut in case there should be anyone there: he had to branch off to the left, making a cast through the wood to hit the path leading from the hut down to the pond. At first there was space among the trees – mostly beeches, and clear below – but soon there were bushes, undergrowth, hiding places for traps, and he had to quest his way with anxious care in the fading light. The path, when he found it, was more overgrown than he remembered it years ago, when he used often to go down with firewood to his auntie at Church End: his godmother she was, in fact, no kin; but he called her his auntie. In these days, of course, no children went down the path.

Down its tortuous length he went, feeling before him with a

slim hazel; he had hardly the concentration left over to listen or to watch abroad, but when he came to a well-remembered open place, where there were still the wet heaps of sawdust on which he had played as a child, from this place of brambles and fern he saw twenty or thirty pigeons lift suddenly on the wind from the trees at the top of the wood, up behind him and towards the far end, away from the road. They were disturbed; any fool could see that. He knew that he was not alone in the wood, but the knowing of it did not weigh on him so much, for he had never thought he was: his fear had all the time peopled the shadows with silent malignants, watching him with knowledge, ready to come out at their own time: there had been sweat on his back from the moment he passed the gate.

Down, and into the solemn darkness of the trees again, down to the pond, where the reeds bent in the wind. The light was going fast, and although the sky was still bright, when he looked at his feet he could hardly see. There was no danger of a trap here in the open, and he went faster. There were bats over the pond, although it was so late in the year. He had had a game bat once. Now here, on the level ground the other side of the pond, the trees began again, and in front of them ran the wall. It was a strange wall to find in the middle of a wood like this: they said that it had cost Sir John (who thought that his head was made of glass) a thousand pound a mile. There was but one gap in it even now, after all these years, and the deep ditch on this side was still unchoked.

It was a difficult leap, with the gun in one hand and just the narrow strip of earth at the wall's foot on the other side: if he had not leapt it so often before he would never have adventured upon it now. The breathless flying moment, the twist and grip on the wall were just the same. His free hand sought the familiar holds unguided, and he climbed to the top of the gap – the top, because although some of the wall was fallen there was still a fair height of it standing, strong and broad enough to stand on. He was in the very act of jumping down when he saw the trap under him – actually launched, his balance gone. With a wild fling of his arms, a writhe, a last convulsive effort as his foot left the stone he flung himself sideways of it and clear by two feet. He fell into thick brambles, but the stir of his blood was such that he never minded their laceration and tore free, still holding the gun.

The trap crouched right under the shadow of the wall, half buried and veiled with careful fern: only the wind had shown it, momentarily baring a toothy that gleamed in the last light. He stood by it, breathing heavily, as strongly as a cart-horse after a hill, and as his tumult of spirits died down he felt a kind of desperate, excited confidence mount in his heart. He stared at the thing, plucked away the fern and stared at it naked. Its evil jaws were full a yard long: Yellow Jack had been filing the teeth sharp, and now they shone bright. Its curved gape was wide enough to grip a barrel. In its jaws, near the hinge, was a wooden block designed to prevent them from snapping right to: they were to remain still so far apart that they would not take a man's leg off clean. There was a wire running from the plate that set the trap off to the warning pistol – a blank, loud bang that would tell the keepers of their success.

Luke had known gins all his life, and this was no more than a big one: the thing he did not understand was the pistol; he dared not take it off and uncock it, nor spring the trap and set it off. For a little while he considered: if he found what he wanted up in the evergreens he would have to come back this way; it was the safest way, and there was his smock. If they heard his shot in spite of the wind, he would need to come back fast (for he was in no mind to make a night of it – just one bird, or at most a brace, and away without dwelling) and this was the only place to get over.

He put his hands to the trap: it was surprisingly light. He lifted it gently to the left of the gap – not the brambles side – to the left, bore it without a jar, one finger under the plate, as far as the reach of the chain. He put it down as delicately as if he were balancing it. It was clear of the path to the gap, but he resolved to go wide by it on his way home.

Now uphill again through the trees: he was beginning to tire, for he had been working at sunrise after a three-mile walk to Clotton, where there was half a day's setting of quick to be done for Mr Ellis on the new farm. An owl swept noiselessly over his head, weaving through the branches. There was a dog barking somewhere: the wind brought it in snatches. Was it from Church End, or were the keepers out? No poacher's dog would ever make a noise like that.

Here were the evergreens beginning: the nature of the wood changed; there was no more undergrowth, only a few spindling plants, pale and feeble, under the dark shadows. He mounted the slope and left the sheltered hollow; the wind kept all the wood in motion: there was sound everywhere.

Now he crept slowly, bent and peering up to catch the branches against the sky, hoping for the solid shape of a roosting pheasant, black against the bright grey. His feet were silent on the moss: he held his gun stretched forward in both hands. His eyes flickered down momentarily to pick his path, then strained back to the branches. His mouth was wide open.

There – there it was. Or was it not? Black and fat across the branch: it swayed again. An old nest? He crept nearer. A pheasant: there was its tail. A pheasant for sure. His heart was at it again as he brought up his piece, thump, thump, thump, and his arm trembling. Was this right? He had hardly fired off a gun before. Nearer: must not miss. Nearer the mark. He half lowered the gun, crept hunched and bent, staring fixedly at the bird, stepped right on to a dry twig. The pheasant burst out of the tree with a shocking clatter and a raucous scream – an explosion, a rocket, a warning to the whole parish. Luke stood dumbfounded, still crouched, still half-pointing. As disappointment and mortification seeped in, the muzzle of his fowling-piece sank to the ground.

There was a cocking on his right and a cocking before him. The barking came again. Was it nearer? God send it was not Yellow George with his great Newfoundland dog, like a hairy ass and savage. No, that was only a cur, far off. His sense came flooding back, and he went softly forward.

He was hard by the birds before he saw them. On a low branch they were, and if the cock bird had not stirred, grumbling, Luke would never have known, for they were too low for him to get them against the sky without almost kneeling. At the sound he stopped still, as still as a hunting animal, then turned slowly. The branch was still, being a thick and low branch, right in front of him and trending away, so that he was on the flank of the birds.

Up came his gun, slowly, slowly, and he was glaring down the barrel, glaring, and his lip bitten hard. His thumb had the hammer and at the click of the sere the cock bird moved again. Now as his finger jerked with all his force on the trigger and his eyes shut with the same movement, the heavens burst, exploded with an enormous universal bang in his ear. He did not fall, despite the blow the overcharged piece had dealt him: he staggered back a pace, and the stunning passed from him and he opened his eyes; the singing died in his ears.

There was a flapping, flailing under the tree. He darted forward, and as he gripped the pheasant he kicked another on the ground. He drew the bird's neck, and in that instant he heard a clear, authoritative whistle blown somewhere in the wood towards Church End. There was a third pheasant running from him, trailing a wing. He stuffed the two birds into his pockets, hesitated a moment and turned back for the pond. The whistle shrilled out again behind him, nearer than it was.

He ran, too fast for wisdom, and as he ran he ran faster. There was blood on his hands now; only pheasant's blood, but he was armed by night, and that was hanging. That was a hanging matter, and no pardon; every countryman knew that.

He tripped on a stump and fell headlong. The yellow lights sprang behind his eyes, and he lay there gasping a moment, half-winded. In spite of his foolishness, he had been coming in something like the right direction, downhill, down to the long wall and the pond. But he was too far along for the gap: he must turn left-handed and still down. There was a noise behind him, along the slope, nearer the right way for the gap. If they should reach the gap first he was lost, hemmed in, caught for sure, and he an armed man by night. The idea of Nellie came on him with a terrible poignancy, and he saw her as clear as noonday light.

Fast down, down and to the left. They were moving too, very

fast, tearing down. They? Or was it but one man? He was silent now, the hunter. Was he on the path above the gap, waiting for Luke to come on to it? He could not have reached the gap yet. Luke tried to hear through the pounding in his ears, but there was wind, wind all the time.

Where was he? Luke stood pressed to a tree, straining his eyes into the darkness and the moving shadows. No sight of him, no sound: the hunter was waiting for him to move. Or was he silently creeping up? Luke slid away from the tree, bent double, moving with huge care: rustling fern and dried leaves, thunderous even with the wind.

'Hey!' The sudden hail froze his heart with terror.

'Hey!' The terribly loud voice shattered him again. 'I see you there. You there: I can see you. Come out now. You had best come out of that before I blow your head off. Come out of it. I can see you.' Yellow George.

Luke could not bear it. He flung himself down the hill, sobbing; and the shot banged out behind him. One pellet stung red hot in his arm, the rest pattered and slashed in the trees above.

Flying down, leaping and flying, on and on down the slope, the branches whipping his face: he felt his legs weakening, they seemed to be going stiff and weak, and always Yellow George came crashing on behind him.

Weakening: what man can run on a diet of potatoes and hog-swill?

There was the gap in the wall, clear despite the darkness, the line of it clear against the shining water of the mere beyond it. Twenty yards and Yellow George, crashing and shouting, almost on his back. He could feel the claws almost on his back and the hot breath. He was on his knees and up again, labouring, with his mouth wide and his eyes fixed, starting like those of a hunted deer – no fight in him, flight, only flight and no strength to fly. A God-sent burst of speed, the wall, something deep saying *The bramble side, the bramble side.* The wall, and the roughness of it: up, fling over.

The bang behind him was nothing to Luke: when it pierced

his mind some minutes later he thought Yellow George had fired on him again: the clash of the trap he did not hear, for it was deadened.

Luke lay in a fern brake only a few yards off the path, lay crouched like a beast with the breath pumping in and out of him. The merciful time passed, and some measure of sense and strength came back to him. There were whistles again – the keepers who had heard the alarm pistol. They were far over yet, towards the lodge, but Luke's reason, shouting through the haze, told him it was time to be going. He had the fowling-piece, safe by a wonder, and the birds were warm and heavy in his pockets.

Up the path now, the thin, winding path whose turns he knew. And Yellow George below lay in his silent agony, with the sweat dripping off him, waiting for the poachers to come and serve him out if he made a sound.

Luke was in the glade, in the thicket of hazels, and his smock was on him again. To the gate and the road, almost unconsciously, though still with caution and the awkward walk, a hundred yards on the open road, then down the old cart track that wound secretly to the back of the inn: so to the village and the warm, bright windows of the taproom. Bright squares in the mist, and the big oblong as the door opened for a man to come out.

They looked up as Luke came in from the little triangular room, looked up and looked down again: they looked studiously away, averting their eyes, turning their heads away, and the hum of voices started again, but falsely now. The landlord fixed a sharp look on him and beckoned.

'Wipe tha face, Luke,' he whispered as he gave him a mug, and Luke smeared the blood on his pallid forehead with the tail of his neckerchief. The landlord wet his cloth and wiped him clean.

'Now drink it up, and get along home,' he said, and Luke set to his beer, the big quart laced with gin, and it went warm to his heart before he set it down. Then, with the last sip swilling on the pewter bottom, he turned it up, and there was the thin, cold heaviness of a guinea in his mouth, hard between his teeth, heavy and cold on his tongue.

13

The Little Death

He had never felt that sense of having been there before so strongly: climbing up the ladder to the platform, he knew perfectly well that the top rungs would be scaly and harsh, and that there would be a box, a dark green box on top of it.

There was no box.

He pushed up the trap door at the top and awkwardly, holding the gun in his left hand, clawed up on to the bare rectangle of planks: there was no box. However, the newness of being up there carried his mind directly on, and he looked eagerly about.

For years he had wanted to see what it would be like from the platform, and it was pleasant to find that the reality surpassed his old expectation. He was among the tree tops, up in the delicate, gently waving part of the trees, and all the branches tended up, reaching towards him. There, to his right, was the sharp white ribbon of the road seen at intervals through the dark pines, and there was the shooting-brake in the gateway: on his left were the ordinary trees of the wood; some, like the birches immediately under him, were shorter than the truncated pine that supported his stand, and these he could see from top to bottom, wonderfully graceful and delicate, although their leaves were going. Most of the trees on the left hand were about the same height as the platform, or a little higher, but here and there a tall beech or one of the noble ashes for which the wood was named rose high above the rest.

He stepped to the edge of the unrailed platform, and, repressing a first hint of vertigo (the platform was in gentle motion), he looked over the edge to the shadows, where the keeper still stood, the white of his upturned face showing far below: forty feet, or was it sixty? These heights were very difficult to judge: at any rate, it was high enough for the man's face to be small, like an egg, and for his voice to come floating up strangely.

'Mr Grattan? The horse is under the far side.'

'Under the far side, is it?' He did not know at all what the keeper meant, but he was not going to show his ignorance: the keeper had already glanced at his gun, an old common, long-barrelled hammer-gun it was, of Belgian make.

There were two big hooks fixed underneath, and groping under the platform Grattan found a trestle – obviously a thing to sit upon. He pulled it up, and he was setting it square on its feet when the keeper called again, telling him that the pigeons usually came in from the right. Grattan thanked him, and watched him go away: for a few paces he could see the keeper's feet before his head and behind, fore and aft, a queer, long stride it looked, before he was under the trees and out of sight.

The trunk of the pine ran up three or four feet above the stand, and it was pleasant to have it for his back as he sat upon the trestle. The sound of the keeper's going died away, and the returning quiet brought back with it that remoteness that had been with Grattan all day, that feeling of being at one remove from life, or rather from one's surroundings, so that they look as little real as the back-cloth of a pantomime, and it would not be surprising if they were to sway gently with a bellying wave from behind. It was something remotely like one of the stages of drunkenness when a man seems to stand a little to one side of himself, listening to what he says and watching him, but without a great deal of interest.

All day it had been with him, but that was not remarkable for it had waited upon him now and then from boyhood, and since he had come home from the war it had been at his elbow most of the time. Nobody knew about it: he had not told anybody, and indeed if he had wanted to he would have found it very difficult to describe what it was, the thing that interposed itself between him and ordinary life, so that with an indifferent eye he saw everything strange, so that sounds and impressions came through to him as if they travelled more slowly: the something that gave him an inner life of far greater reality than that which went on around him at the same time and in which he took part with the rest of him. It was not to be defined, this inner life; it had little to do with conscious thought; it was a kind of awareness and a withdrawal to another plane of existence. And always, from the very first time that he had known it, a boy walking along the tow-path on a summer's evening in the shadow of the heavy, dusty green of the trees, twenty years ago, always there had been something of anticipation in it. In the last year this had increased, and now, today more than ever, it was a sense of growing, inevitable crisis – something outside himself for which he was waiting. It was something that he awaited calmly, for in this everything was slow and calm, but it was of vast importance and his being was keyed up and up for it.

He could not, on the few occasions when he had (almost impiously, it seemed) tried to formulate some ideas upon it, he could not even put any name to its nature, but today he was more certain than ever of its imminence. It would happen to him without any doing on his part: it was at once desirable and terrible.

The existence of this more real life did not prevent him – never had prevented him – from living at his common level: this very afternoon he had felt a strong inclination to decline the brown holland bag that his aunt had lovingly made him for his cartridges, as a surprise; and he had been ashamed of the appearance of his gun among the lovely hammerless ejectors carried by the other guests. However, he had neither put the cloth bag down nor concealed it in his pocket, and as a penance for these impulses he had worn it until he had forgotten it. Nowadays he forgot things very quickly; even the excitement of this invitation to Langton and the near-certainty of a job on the estate, which had made such a flutter at home, had left him almost unmoved after half an hour, although but a few years ago it would have kept him in a turmoil, partly pleasant, but increasingly alarming as the day grew nearer: for Mr Clifton's Langton was a very grand place indeed, quite the grandest in a county full of big estates. His uncle and his three aunts (dear, kind people: he had lived in their celibate house nearly all his life) had always talked, interminably and vaguely, of great things for him; they had foreseen, foreseen. Entirely without influence themselves they attributed to it a mystic value. With significant, worldly nods they had approved his first boyish acquaintance with the children of the local magnates. So suitable; they said to one another, pluming and settling in their upright armchairs. Few things had given them greater pleasure than the chance that made their nephew a friend of young Clifton: they had served in the same squadron, and in the short time before Clifton had been killed they had grown very much attached to one another. The invitation to shoot pigeons at Langton and the offer of some as yet undefined employment with the old agent were consequences of their friendship: the old aunts had seen it as an opening of long-closed doors.

But all this was wonderfully remote now: Barringham and Langton seen through the wrong end of a telescope, wonderfully remote; the aunts and his uncle and the garden, little moving figures in the garden with no meaning, hardly names even. And the quiet flooded back into the wood, and his mind retreated, moved back and back and back. He sat bowed on the trestle, with his mouth open, with his eyes – wide, staring eyes – fixed on a knot: his gun lay across his knees, held inertly by a passive hand.

There was so much quiet in the High Ash wood that even the bang of a gun away before him did not dispel it, nor the quick left and right behind. The creaking flutter of two wood-pigeons coming in to the dark pine just to the right of him pierced through to his mind, but it made no impression: the birds settled noisily, with the trunk between them and him. He was quite still, his breathing slow and shallow: his eyes did not move from the knot.

The dusk gathered under the trees, dark pools where the peeling birch trunks showed white. They were having good sport along the edge of the wood, just inside the belt of pines, and the guns were going fast: the pigeons were moving continually up and down the long, dark tract, uneasily in flocks and swift single birds clipping fast to their night's rest. They were filling the trees all around Grattan, heavy, fat birds that looked too big for the twigs they landed on, fat heavy wood-pigeons that walked, hopped, flapping among the twigs and branches to solid perches, and smaller stock-doves with them, many in the trees and many passing overhead.

In some part of Grattan's bowed head there was a picture of a pale, clear sky, quite clear above an unending floor of white cloud, and in the sky was an aeroplane falling and falling, falling for ever. It turned as it fell in its dying, broken fall, and each time it turned full to him he saw the Hackenkreuz on its wings. He went close to it, and he could see the German's face, expressionless and closed. They were quite alone in the sky. Grattan watched impassively and said, He is not going to bail out. I think he cannot bail out.

A trail of black smoke shot from the Messerschmitt before it plunged into the white floor of cloud, and the black plume stood, poised on a narrow foot that stayed momentarily firm in the sudden vortex of the swirling white, after the machine had disappeared; and he was saying aloud, While I live I shall never kill another living thing.

But all this was only in the forefront of his mind; behind it he was withdrawn, and there was a very slow current of thought going on between the two: up there, above the cloud, he had known that he had been there before, knew just what the black smoke would look like over the billowing hole in the cumulus. The very words that he had said had had a used feeling and an accustomed sound: they had been formulated, like a prayer. Here, on the platform, he had known what it was going to be like. There was no box, of course; but the box had been there once. If he got up he would see the place where it had stood. But that was by the way: the *déjà-vu*, which had once made him so uneasy, was only a side issue, something that came at the same time as the withdrawal: all that mattered was what was coming.

As he stirred unconsciously he made the legs of the trestle grate on the platform: now a fat wood-pigeon was staring and bending, peering at him with a round eye, bowing and staring like an alderman about to cross a road. The bird's suspicions were confirmed, and it clattered out of the tree, followed by a cloud of others: the noise jerked Grattan into the living present, and he stood tense on the platform, with his gun ready to spring up. The light was almost gone: he could not see the tiny disturbed goldcrest that went Tzee tzee so loudly in a branch within his hand's reach.

A returning pigeon – some had not believed, and had only circled once – fluttered against the clear sky at the very top of a tree right before him. He had cocked his gun automatically as he stood; now he pulled both triggers, firing down into the dark shadows, and watched the horrified bird flash dodging away. The scent, delightful from old association, the scent of the powder came up as he broke the gun and dropped the smoking empty shells on the stand, stopping them from rolling off with his foot. Then he fired another two barrels, and did the same: That should do for the keeper, he said, and sat down again.

Again the quiet came back, the curtain dropped fast, and now his mind was glowing with active suspense: it even invaded his body: his heart beat and his stomach was constrained just as it had been with him and he a young boy in his first love. Now it was here, here and coming on him.

He stood up slowly, with his gun hanging open in his right hand and his left hand wavering to his lips.

But it did not come. There was only the soft wind and the far-off voice of old Mr Clifton: 'Grattan, we're going along now.' The words drawn out, calling to carry, and the lights and the gentle whine of the car, that died to a throb.

He made no reply, but turned in the darkness.

14

Samphire

———— ✦ ————

Sheer, sheer, the white cliff rising, straight up from the sea, so high that the riding waves were nothing but ripples on a huge calm. Up there, unless you leaned over, you did not see them break, but for all the distance the thunder of the water came loud. The wind, too, tearing in from the sea, rushing from a clear, high sky, brought the salt tang of the spray on to their lips.

They were two, standing up there on the very edge of the cliff: they had left the levelled path and come down to the break itself and the man was crouched, leaning over as far as he dared.

'It *is* a clump of samphire, Molly,' he said; then louder, half turning, 'Molly, it *is* samphire. I *said* it was a samphire, didn't I?' He had a high, rather unmasculine voice, and he emphasized his words.

His wife did not reply, although she had heard him the first time. The round of her chin was trembling like a child's before it cries: there was something in her throat so strong that she could not have spoken if it had been for her life.

She stepped a little closer, feeling cautiously for a firm foothold, and she was right on him and she caught the smell of his hairy tweed jacket. He straightened so suddenly that he brushed against her. 'Take care,' he cried, 'I almost trod on you. Yes, it was samphire. I said so as soon as I saw it from down there. Have a look.'

She could not answer, so she knelt and crawled to the edge. Heights terrified her, always had. She could not close her eyes;

that only made it worse. She stared unseeing, while the brilliant air and the sea and the noise of the sea assaulted her terrified mind and she clung insanely to the thin grass. Three times he pointed it out, and the third time she heard him so as to be able to understand his words. '. . . fleshy leaves. You see the fleshy leaves? They used them for pickles. Samphire pickles!' He laughed, excited by the wind, and put his hand on her shoulder. Even then she writhed away, covering it by getting up and returning to the path.

He followed her. 'You noted the *fleshy leaves*, didn't you, Molly? They allow the plant to store its nourishment. Like a cactus. Our native cactus. I said it was samphire at once, didn't I, although I have never actually seen it before. We could almost get it with a stick.'

He was pleased with her for having looked over, and said that she was coming along very well: she remembered – didn't she? – how he had had to persuade her and persuade her to come up even the smallest cliffs at first, how he had even to be a little firm. And now there she was going up the highest of them all, as bold as brass; and it was quite a dangerous cliff too, he said, with a keen glance out to sea, jutting his chin; but there she was as bold as brass looking over the top of it. He had been quite right insisting, hadn't he? It was worth it when you were there, wasn't it? Between these questions he waited for a reply, a 'yes' or a hum of agreement. If he had not insisted she would always have stayed down there on the beach, wouldn't she? Like a lazy puss. He said, wagging his finger to show that he was not quite in earnest, that she should always listen to her Lacey (this was a pet name that he had coined for himself). Lacey was her lord and master, wasn't he? Love, honour and obey?

He put his arm round her when they came to a sheltered turn of the path and began to fondle her, whispering in his secret night-voice, Tss-tss-tss, but he dropped her at once when some coastguards appeared.

As they passed he said, 'Good-day, men,' and wanted to stop to ask them what they were doing but they walked quickly on.

* * *

In the morning she said she would like to see the samphire again. He was very pleased and told the hotel-keeper that she was becoming quite the little botanist. He had already told him and the nice couple from Letchworth (they were called Jones and had a greedy daughter: he was an influential solicitor, and Molly would be a clever girl to be nice to them), he had already told them about the samphire, and he had said how he had recognized it at once from lower down, where the path turned, although he had only seen specimens in a hortus siccus and illustrations in books.

On the way he stopped at the tobacconist on the promenade to buy a stick. He was in high spirits. He told the man at once that he did not smoke, and made a joke about the shop being a house of ill-*fume*; but the tobacconist did not understand. He looked at the sticks that were in the shop but he did not find one for his money and they went out. At the next tobacconist, by the pier, he made the same joke to the man there. She stood near the door, not looking at anything. In the end he paid the marked price for an ash walking stick with a crook, though at first he had proposed a shilling less: he told the man that they were not ordinary summer people, because they were going to have a villa there.

Walking along past the pier towards the cliff path, he put the stick on his shoulder with a comical gesture, and when they came to the car park where a great many people were coming down to the beach with picnics and pneumatic rubber toys he sang, *We are the boys that nothing can tire: we are the boys that gather samphire*. When a man who was staying in the same hotel passed near them, he called out that they were going to see if they could get a bunch of jolly good samphire that they had seen on the cliff yesterday. The man nodded.

It was a long way to the highest cliff, and he fell silent for a little while. When they began to climb he said that he would never go out without a stick again; it was a fine, honest thing, an ashplant, and a great help. Didn't she think it was a great help? Had she noticed how he had chosen the best one in the shop, and really it was very cheap; though perhaps they had better go without tea tomorrow to make it up. She remembered, didn't she, what they had agreed after their discussion about an exact allowance for every day? He was walking a few feet ahead of her, so that each time he had to turn his head for her answer.

On the top it was blowing harder than the day before, and for the last hundred yards he kept silent, or at least she did not hear him say anything.

At the turn of the path he cried, 'It is still there. Oh jolly good. It is still there, Molly,' and he pointed out how he had first seen the samphire, and repeated, shouting over the wind, that he had been sure of it at once.

For a moment she looked at him curiously while he stared over and up where the plant grew on the face of the cliff, the wind ruffling the thin, fluffy hair that covered his baldness, and a keen expression on his face; and for a moment she wondered whether it was perhaps possible that he saw beauty there. But the moment was past and the voice took up again its unceasing dumb cry: Go on, oh, go on, for Christ's sake go on, go on, go on, oh go *on*.

They were there. He had made her look over. 'Note the fleshy leaves,' he had said; and he had said something about samphire pickle! and how the people at the hotel would stare when they brought it back. That was just before he began to crouch over, turned from her so that his voice was lost.

He was leaning right over. It was quite true when he said that he had no fear of heights: once he had astonished the workmen on the steeple of her uncle's church by walking among the scaffolding and planks with all the aplomb of a steeplejack. He was reaching down with his left arm, his right leg doubled under him and his right arm extended on the grass: his other leg was stretched out along the break of the cliff.

Once again there was the strong grip in her throat; her stomach was rigid and she could not keep her lip from trembling. She could hardly see, but as he began to get up her eyes focused. She was already there, close on him – she had never gone back to the path this time. God give me strength: but as she pushed him she felt her arms weak like jelly.

Instantly his face turned; absurd, baby-face surprise and a shout unworded. The extreme of horror on it, too. He had been half up when she thrust at him, with his knee off the ground, the stick hand over and the other clear of the grass. He rose, swaying out. For a second the wind bore up his body and the stick scrabbled furiously for a purchase on the cliff. There where the samphire grew, a little above, it found a hard ledge, gripped. Motionless in equilibrium for one timeless space – a cinema stopped in action – then his right hand gripped the soil, tore, tore the grass and he was up, from the edge, crouched, gasping huge sobbing draughts of air on the path.

He was screaming at her in an agonized falsetto interrupted by painful gasps, searching for air and life. 'You *pushed* me, Molly you – *pushed* me. You – *pushed* me.'

She stood silent, looking down and the voice rushed over her. You *pushed* – you *pushed* me – Molly. She found she could swallow again, and the hammering in her throat was less. By now his voice had dropped an octave: he had been speaking without a pause but for his gasping – the gasping had stopped now, and he was sitting there normally. '. . . not well; a spasm. Wasn't it, Molly?' he was saying; and she heard him say 'accident' sometimes.

Still she stood, stone-still and grey and later he was saying '. . . *possibly* live together? How can we *possibly* look at one another? After this?' And sometime after it seemed to her that he had been saying something about their having taken their room for the month . . . accident was the word, and spasm, and not well – fainting? It was, wasn't it, Molly? There was an unheard note in his voice.

She turned and began to walk down the path. He followed at once. By her side he was, and his face turned to hers, peering into her face, closed face. His visage, his whole face, everything, had fallen to pieces: she looked at it momentarily – a very old terribly frightened comforting-itself small child. He had fallen off a cliff all right.

He touched her arm, still speaking, pleading. 'It *was* that, wasn't it, Molly? You didn't push me, Molly. It was an accident . . .'

She turned her dying face to the ground, and there were her feet marching on the path; one, the other: one, the other; down, down, down.

15

The Clockmender

———⬥⬥⬥———

Suddenly he was awake. His waking had the abrupt complete-
ness of an electric light, entirely off one second and entirely on
the next. This was no warm transition from a confused doze to
a partial consciousness of the world, an awareness that would
begin with the pillow, the position of his relaxed body under the
bedclothes, and that would work slowly outwards to a comfortable realization of the world, with himself in it, each piece falling naturally into its accustomed place. No. This was an abrupt
and full awakening from a profound sleep; and the world that
presented itself was naked, instantly concrete, sharply defined
and entire.

He knew at once that there was no hope whatever of drifting
off again, and he realized with horror that the grey light in the
room could not have been there much above an hour. He looked
over the edge of his bed at the pair of chronometers on the low
table: on each severe dial the steel hands showed five twenty-five.
Some disturbance, some chance noise had cheated him of three
hours of sleep.

It was a tragedy. He would have to get up very soon, for in a
short time the insistent restlessness of his body would make bed
intolerable and he would be forced into waste of another day,
another cruelly lengthened day.

Three hours more to serve. It was a tragedy: and it was so
unfair. He had spun out the evening until well past ten o'clock,
and he had won the right to sleep until eight or even nine. He

had gone on polishing the new-cut pallets of the Knibb clock until they were almost beyond perfection, burnishing the faces with a slip of agate – four thousand lengthways strokes to each of the four angles. Two hours and thirteen minutes, timing each stroke by the beat of a half-seconds pendulum. That had earned him his rest, surely.

But no. Here he was at half-past five, irrevocably awake and committed to the day. Something tapped on the window and scraped across the glass: that must have been it, he thought, looking round; the long thin branch from the wisteria: it should have been pruned years ago, when it was a stray twig; but now it had grown long enough to reach the windowpane as the cold wind of the dawn dragged it against the side of the house.

He had planted that wisteria himself when first he had the place. In those days he had been up with the first light – he had been up *before* the first light – for he had often switched on the lamp as he dressed. He had dressed in his gardening clothes at once, to lose no time.

He had dressed then: he had willingly gone through the process of putting on all those garments, selecting, buttoning, tying, turning right-side out, doing-up; every day he had accepted the series of motions that would have to be reversed at night. At that time he had been able to accept the drill of left arm – right arm, left leg – right leg, left foot – right foot, and its perpetual repetition. And the prospect of it had never kept him daunted in his bed: he remembered his eager getting up – springing up – in spite of his warm sleepiness, from a bed where he had gone to sleep still working out the details of the garden. Of the kitchen garden, mostly, for although he had a brave show of flowers it was the parallelograms of the kitchen garden that fascinated him – the drilled rows of the potatoes and the cabbages – and he would lie fighting against sleep while he carried out the mental arithmetic designed to show the total yield of his thirty-five rows of main-crop potatoes, if each plant yielded an average of three and a quarter pounds.

He remembered that now, as a fact: but he could no longer

comprehend the once-vital urgency that had made it a fact; he could not feel that there was anything at all in common between the young man who had so enthusiastically worked out the cropping-plan for a seven-year rotation; who had, as the winter days grew short, dug the last double trenches by the light of a hurricane lamp to be doubly ready for the longed-for spring. Nothing in common between the man who had dug and cherished the garden and the one who now had not even visited the lower plot, the head-high jungle of nettles and fool's parsley, for months and months. Yet there was a physical continuity: the body was the same. And it was the same bed in which he lay. The wisteria, too, was a speaking witness. He had planted it, a straggling whipple, over the buried carcass of an ass, and now its trunk was like a grey python on the wall and its untended branches rapped against his bedroom windowpane.

One day, perhaps, he would go down through the tangle of roses to the kitchen garden and see whether among the rank growth below the apple-trees he could find the remains of his hives. It would be interesting to know if any of the colonies had survived. Once, nearly three years ago it must be now, he had seen a swarm clustered like an uncoloured shining bunch of grapes on the handle of a forgotten spade. They might have been from his own bees.

He would go down. But at the thought of actually doing it, of fixing a time for doing it, of dressing in order to do it, so great a physical repulsion seized him that to escape he turned his head further down into his pillow and fixed his eyes on the glass window in the side of the chronometer case.

The cylindrical hairspring contracted, swelled, contracted, the pulsation of a metal heart: he could not see the slow, even swing of the balance-wheel, but behind the links of the fusee, taut between the helix and the drum, he caught the recurrent flash of the scape-wheel pinion: the soft gleam of brass in the grey light was like the ever-returning wink of a lighthouse, impersonal, utterly reliable, continuing an indefinite series that drew out towards infinity; and in time the beautiful monotony steadied his mind. Now he could think more evenly of the prospects of the lengthened day.

They were horrible. But they were not so horrible as thinking of the garden and of all those other things that had once filled his life. Some of them he had cut out deliberately: he had amputated them when each in turn had threatened to grow into an exclusive obsession. Seeing his friends, for example; and his exact system of economy – that had been one of the hardest, but he had succeeded in the end, and now his rows of account books, with every item of expenditure balanced against each incoming penny, had remained unopened these many years. It had been so delightful to calculate the market cost of the garden produce: the bees had had their ledger too: and it had been such a keen triumph to deny himself for the reward of carrying over a surplus from one month to the next. But now he spent as he chose, not even taking a note of it; and in the second drawer of his desk the dividend vouchers piled up, still uncounted; and somewhere there was a clip of uncashed cheques.

This amputation had been successful, but it had required a dreadful effort: other things had fallen away of themselves. He had deliberately shut his door to callers, but he had never of set purpose opposed himself to books or music. Yet the one was as successful as the other, and it would now mean as much forbidden and indeed impossible effort to open the piano and play as to open the door and engage in conversation with a casual visitor.

They had shredded away, all these things – all positive action, all doing, had retreated obediently to the other side of what was tolerable. When he got up now, he would slip on his dressing-gown. More than that would be – he wrenched away from the thought.

What do fleas do when they are not biting? he wondered. Or dogs, when they are not fighting, eating or being taken for a walk – house dogs? They must fall back into the stagnant pool of time. What a universal cruelty, repeated throughout an infinity of members, to be suspended in the fantastically deliberate flow of time, with no possible escape but the even greater horror of the farther limit, where there was no time at all. For very small creatures perhaps it would be worse: a day might be a year for them, by reason of their size.

Oh the days and the unending hours, he thought, turning his head from side to side. Yet all the time one's body lived eagerly in the flow: hair and nails – every night his unwanted beard thrust up another hundredth of an inch; and continuously, without a second's pause, his skin renewed itself, thrust on by innumerable subtle needless combinations of blind vitality.

Why should the clocks alone have stayed? There seemed to be no reason for their permanence, but in the next room, among the desert of unopened books, there was his workbench, clean, sharp-angled and precise with its rows of tools, broaches, dies and taps, throws, pliers of different shapes and sizes, all ranged so exactly that by now he could pick up each separate tool without taking his eyes from his work. This perfect arrangement called for years and years of use, but then of course he had begun years and years ago. To begin with the old grandfather in the hall could not be made to go: the watchmaker in the village was ill, so he had tinkered with it himself. A common thirty-hour movement, no more, but the simple mechanism, the wonderfully clear train of cause and effect, fascinated him and when he eventually mastered it, when the clock was ticking comfortably, he felt the strangest triumph. He bought books on clocks and even began to collect them in a small way: with the pleasure they brought him came the reproaches of his conscience – it was excessive and disproportionate to spend twelve hours a day for a week in wrestling inexpertly (he was inexpert then) with the escapement of a repeating verge – but in this case, and in this case alone, the reproach died of itself. The proposition that clocks should go was unanswerable. It was of absolute importance that they should go, should measure time exactly, and he concentrated all his powers to the task. He also bought more clocks.

'Well,' Dr Provis said, almost the last time he ever came to the house, 'I suppose it is a harmless way of killing time.' The remark was approving in substance but it was delivered with a kind of sneer: resenting this, he countered with a shrug of his shoulders and a half turn of his body. 'Ha, ha,' he replied. 'I think there is a difference, Provis, between *killing* time and *measuring* it.'

And then again, the full significance apart, this was an activity in which he could control all the factors: for clocks, rightly adjusted, would go; they had none of the intolerably frustrating imponderables of living things, yet for him they were alive enough. They exactly suited him; and his somewhat inhuman persistence suited them.

But in the last eighteen months the area of his pleasure had contracted. By now he had a very high degree of skill; he could cut a pair of pallets for any escapement the old clockmakers had ever made, and in case of need he could even produce a new scape wheel. But a new scape wheel was now a few hours' work: once it had been the toil of weeks, and once he had felt a tingling elation as the new wheel first revolved, ticked, and swung the doubtful pendulum. And by now he had an example of every variant; there was no new principle to be explored, and by the rules of his conscience he could not clutter up his house with clocks that would essentially be no more than duplicates of those he had already. Nor, now that he had the highest degree of manual ability, could he interfere with a clock that was going perfectly. Once, with no more than a half-imagined hint of irregularity, he had felt justified in stripping a clock and searching over every part of it, perfecting as he went; but he could not do so now. It must not be blind activity, doing for the sake of doing: it had to have the dignity of an end in view. That was a discipline which he must never, never break, or the whole thing would fall into an incoherent mockery.

He could do it all now, verge pallets, deadbeat pallets, ordinary anchor pallets . . . abruptly he remembered his evening's work. To make a long night's sleep more sure he had stayed up to finish the pallets of the small Knibb clock. He had finished the work entirely: he should have kept it for today. Without it the grey hours stretched away in an endless plain without anything at all to break the horrifying blank.

He lay there with the utter vacancy before him, and if no relief had come he might have screamed at last. But at a few minutes to six the arm lifted from the locking plate of the Graham bracket clock; the detent wheel spun three-quarters of a turn; the hoop wheel moved the distance of two pinion leaves; the clock was ready to strike six. It was immediately followed by the others. His practised ear heard the cocking of the clocks, and a springing hope made his thin heart beat.

There was no hope from the Knibb clock: that would be going accurately, with no shadow of a doubt. It was perfectly in beat and he had regulated its pendulum to the last hairs-breadth: he knew that clock. But it seemed to him that in his sleep he had heard the Tompion drop a stroke, as if the locking plate were worn: it had given trouble seven years before. Unless it were a dream it would be the Tompion, and it would probably have happened at three – he heard them through his sleep, he knew. And if that were so it would now strike five, not six. Five strokes instead of six: it would be an escape, a reprieve for one more day at least.

He listened intently, breathing shallow not to make a noise. The hands of the two chronometers crept in perfect unison towards the point of six. In the next room an assembly of long-case clocks, bracket clocks, wall clocks and table clocks stood poised to bell out the time. Only the equation clocks and the big regulator would not say anything: they had no bells. The others, the converted Cromwellian lantern clock, the early Fromanteel, the Tompion, the Graham deadbeat, the Mudge, the Quare, the Harrison, had all raised their striking trains. They stood there in no order, here and there about the book-lined room: he cared nothing for the beauty of their cases and some rested on rough trial benches, stripped of their hoods and covered from the dust with glass bell jars. Their ticking filled the room with a strange, depressingly urgent confusion of sound as they flicked the present by. Brass and iron insects, horrifying in their nakedness and numbers, perpetually eating time.

He waited, and as the moment drew nearer and nearer he clenched his fists under the bedclothes.

The first clock dropped and whirred; the pin gathered the tail of the hammer and bore down upon it. The first stroke rang out pure, but the second was lost in the clangour of the other clocks, whirring, striking faster or slower, all bawling out that it was six, pinning the moment down.

Straining his head up from his pillow he followed the deep, smooth tone of the Tompion through the competing din. At the fourth stroke his expression changed, and at the fifth his face lost its humanity. Now there was the racing pause between the fifth stroke of that one bell and the sound of the sixth, if it should ever come. The pause lengthened at last beyond the possibility of another stroke – it had missed for sure; but until the last of the clocks had finished, the Graham with its melancholy toll, his face did not change. Only then, when the last sound had died to a humming in the bell, did he allow his strained-up head to move. It sank down, and his eyelids fluttered over his eyes; but in another minute he was up, his fingers twitching with activity. He threw the dressing-gown over his shoulders and shuffled quickly to the door: and as he opened it he lowered his head to conceal the pale smile on his face.

16

Not Liking to Pass the Road Again

⸺⸺⸺ ⧜ ⸺⸺⸺

The road led uphill all the way from the village; a long way, in waves, some waves steeper than others but all uphill even where it looked flat between the crests.

There was a tall thick wood on the right hand for the first half: for a long time it had been the place of the Scotch brothers. They were maniacs, carpenters by trade, Baptists; and one had done something horrible to his brother.

I have forgotten now why I thought that only one brother still lived in the wood: perhaps I had been told. I used to throw things into the wood.

At first they were small things, bits of twig or pebbles from the middle of the road, the loose stuff between the wheel tracks; I threw them furtively, surreptitiously, not looking, just into the nut bushes at the edge. Then I took to larger ones, and on some bold days I would stand in an open wide part of the road flinging heavy stones into the wood: they lashed and tore the leaves far within the wood itself. It was a place where there had been a traction engine and where they had left great piles of things for the road.

Quite early in the summer (there were a great many leaves, but they were still fresh and the bark was soft and bright) I was there and I had two old chisels without handles; they were brown and their cutting edges were hacked and as blunt as screw drivers, but their squared angles were still sharp. I had gashed a young tree with one, throwing it; it had taken the green bark clean from the white wood.

I had them purposely this bold day prepared, to throw them in with desperate malice – I was almost afraid of them then. I did not throw them far, but flat and hard and oh God the great bursting crashing in the wood and he came, brutal grunting with speed.

Before my heart had beat I was running. Running, running, running, and running up that dreadful hill that pulled me back so that I was hardly more than walking and my thin legs going weaker and soft inside.

I could not run, and here under my feet was the worst hill beginning. At the gap by the three ashes I jigged to the left, off the road to the meadow downhill, and I sped (the flying strides) downhill to the old bridge and the stream full-tilt and downhill on the grass.

Into the stream, not over the bridge, into the water where it ran fast over the brown stones: through the tunnel of green up to the falls I knew the dark way. I knew it without thinking, and I did not put a foot on dry ground nor make a noise above the noise of the water until I came to the falls and then I stepped on a dry rock only three times all the way up the wide mouth. It is easier to climb with your hands and feet than to run on a bare road. And I came out into the open for an instant below the culvert on the road, a place where I could look back, back and far down to the smooth green at the foot of the old bridge.

It was still there, casting to and fro like a hound, but with inconceivable rapidity. Halfway up the meadow sometimes to hit back on the line, so eager, then a silent rush to the water's edge and a check as if it had run into a stone wall: then over and over again, the eager ceaseless tracing back and fro. Vague (except in movement), uncoloured, low on the ground.

There was a cart on the road now, well above the ruined cottage, and I went home. I changed my boots without being seen – they had kept the water out for a long time, although I had been up to my knees at once; in the end the water had come in down from my ankles, quite slowly.

That night and afterwards, when I told the thing over to myself I added a piece to make the passing of the road again more bearable. In the added piece my mother came in and said that we were all to be careful when we went out because there was a mad dog. 'Hugh was found on the old bridge,' she said (Hugh was one of the farm boys), 'at the foot of the old bridge, with his face bitten. They have taken him to hospital, but he will not speak yet.'

17

The Voluntary Patient

⎯⎯⎯⎯⎯⎯⎯⎯⎯

'What is that noise?'

'Which noise?'

'Like a dog howling. There it is again.'

'Oh, that. It is only Mr Philips. He is upstairs this afternoon,' she said with a satisfied smile. 'We have been a little troublesome, and we shan't come down until we are in a better mood. "You can't do this to me," he said, "I am here on a voluntary basis, you understand, and can leave whenever I choose, upon giving proper notice."'

They both laughed, and the second woman, still tittering, said, 'Always the same old tale. But which is Mr Philips? The one who looks out of the window?'

'No. Isn't he a scream? No, this is the one with the fiddle I told you about. You haven't seen him yet – he is at the back.'

'Well, why doesn't he play his fiddle?'

'He has quite given it over, and spends all his time writing. I said to him the other day, "Mr Philips," I said, "why don't you give us a tune?" No answer. Just scribble scribble scribble, as if his life depended on it.'

They both laughed again, and the second woman said, 'You get all the funny ones.'

'Not that he's as funny as some, but he does get some funny ideas. "Make the punishment fit the crime" is his latest.' She hummed a bar and they both sang.

'La di da di da di da
Make the punishment fit the crime.'

'How do you mean, though?' asked the visitor.

'Well, he says all this psychosomatic stuff – you know what I mean?'

'Of course I do.'

'Don't be offended, love. He says it is all part of the same thing, and you bring it on yourself?' The visitor grinned and nodded, and the tall, black-haired woman went on, 'It's all part of the same thing, he says. Oh, we get it by the hour sometimes, and then he writes it all down.'

'You do have more fun than we do,' said the visitor crossly. 'On the accidie side they are a dull, mumchance, pompous lot, all puffed up with their own importance.'

'Oh. I don't know,' said the other in a modest tone. 'Here,' she added, leaning sideways and picking up a closely written sheet, 'this will tell you all about it. It will make you howl.'

The visitor, a woman with sparse sandy hair and a dead-white transparent skin, flushed so that the redness could be seen mounting above the rounded protuberance of her forehead and far into her scalp. She took it greedily, but she said at once, 'This is not the beginning.'

'It doesn't matter: it's all the same.'

'". . . and as no two crimes are exactly the same,"' she read aloud, '"so every punishment is unlike every other punishment. When a man wakes in the night and finds his head filled with remorse and bitter, old regret, if he chose he could reflect that no other man in the world would be suffering precisely that remorse nor exactly that regret: it might be quite as vain and sterile and long-lived, but it would not be wounding him with the same sharp terms. Of course, he would not choose to do so, for he would be too busy dodging about inside his mind, trying to escape – unless, that is, he were occupied with feeling the wound to see how much it still hurt and trying to persuade himself that there was virtue in mere remorse." He, he, he,' went the sandy woman;

but putting her glass on the paper she said with an affected prim indifference, 'He writes very neat.'

'I don't know that that's the best piece,' said the other, peering at the writing upside down. 'There was a good one I meant to show you the day before yesterday.'

'From Mr Philips?'

'No, the pale fellow.'

'He's another funny one, isn't he?' she said abstractedly, as her eyes ran down the paragraph below the round of the glass's foot.

'"So in sinning you create your own punishment,"' she read. '"In the act of the particular and unique sin the compensating punishment is born: it is inevitably born, and it always exactly counterbalances its cause."'

'Does he ever put any address?' she asked, breaking off.

'No: he's one of our new boys. They haven't let on yet.'

'Has he told you what his trouble is?'

'No. But you would have screamed the other day: they were asking him about his eyes and I couldn't help hearing. Osborne says, "And what about this shadow in the left-hand field of vision, Mr Philips?" And he says, "Oh, it's nothing much." So Osborne says, "But it is still there, I collect?" And he says, "I'm afraid so. Do you attach any importance to it?" – trying to put him off, you know. Then Osborne hums and haws about sciasis for a bit, tips old Prince the wink, and leaves them together. Old Prince, of course, begins to lay on the soothing syrup right away – dear, kind old man, butter wouldn't melt in his mouth.'

Both the women laughed, slapping their thighs and rocking to and fro. The dark one controlled herself first and said, 'A drop more, love?'

'I don't mind if I do,' she said, holding her fingers to the glass. 'Ta.'

At this moment the black-haired woman was called out of the room and the visitor, dangling her tongue into her gin, but not sipping it, read on over the rim of her glass.

'"It is not the observer who must be asked, but the sufferer. To the observer it must appear that there are many identical crimes, which may or may not have identical punishments. If we take the ordinary crimes, lying and theft, it can be said that in every case the criminal is punished by being a liar (for obviously it is not the punishment of being disbelieved that counts – that is no more than a haphazard retribution for lack of skill) or by being a thief, by inhabiting the mind and body of a thief: but that is a merely superficial view. Take as an example the commonest criminal of them all, the selfish, disagreeable man: this sufferer, heavy under the self-inflicted punishment of an everlasting evil temper fixed into his body by his indulgence in unpleasantness, can point out a thousand significant differences in his punishment as compared with the next man's; the weight of his sour life presses on innumerable points of sensitivity that no other man can have. It is the same with the ordinary hysterias, neuroses, and psychosomatic diseases. Yet it is true that in this range we do have an apparent similarity: the enormous differences, the differences that instantly convince the most casual observer, come from huge and monstrous crimes. It is these that cause the monstrous births upon the other side. I think of the horrible thing at the bottom of the Last Judgment at Albi: that must have been created, automatically created, by one appalling crime alone. That crime may have been called by the same name as other crimes (Judas' sin is nominally shared by the latest petty traitor) but obviously it was as unique as its result. This thing at Albi could never possibly have served to counterweight two crimes: it was made by one alone. Bosch and Breughel, too; they show the harmony and equipoise . . ."'

Her eyes skipped down the lines until a capital began again. "'It comes to this: each of these acts adds another to those things that live in Hell – *creates* it. It creates a new fiend."' A pleased smile spread slowly across her face: she nodded her head, staring intently at the blank wall in front of her.

'What was it?' she asked, as the door opened again.

'Oh, nothing. Only the brimstone going out. But as I was saying, old Prince sits himself down and goes on and on in his quiet, soapy voice – gets very confidential and friendly.'

'He is a proper card, old Prince.'

'Yes. He likes to see how far he can make them go. If only he can get them to go down on their knees and blubber the whole thing out while he does you know what behind them, it sets him up for a fortnight. Sometimes he borrows Ambrose's outfit, but the pure jam is when he can firk it out of them voluntary, sobbing in mother-bull's bosom. Anyhow, this time he gets our gentleman on to his hobby-horse about this psychosomatic business and rewards and punishments and so on; then after a bit he breaks off and says, "But this figure that you think you see, Mr Philips, it has no certain form?"

'"No!" he says, as quick as that. Then he hesitates and says, "No. No. It is only dark. Always behind me, as I told you; and when I turn it goes."

'"It always goes? Vanishes?"

'"Yes."

'"Always?"

'"Yes. Well, that is to say . . ." He hesitates, and old Prince looks grave and sympathetic, very interested and kind. ". . . that is to say, almost always. But once I turned too quick and I thought I saw it then."

'"Was it – forgive me if I seem indelicate – was it a dreadful thing?"

'"I hardly know what to say," says Philips, pretending to blow his nose and dropping his handkerchief. "Not really, perhaps Not in itself. I thought it was the shadow of a barn – the sharp line and the corner."

'"Just that? No more than that?"

'"The shadow of a barn. The side going up so sheer and the angle of the roof."

'Old Prince leans back in his chair, looks at his watch. And coughs. "Shadows, my dear sir, he says, rather impatient but covering it up, you see . . ."'

'He's a cunning one, old Prince.'

'". . . shadows," he says. "We all know how a horse will shy. We all know, too, how our bodies can deceive us, and especially our eyes. An unwise indulgence, a late supper, and we are apt to dream at night and to have our faculties disturbed the next day. Singing in the ears, spots floating in the air. They tell me it is the liver." And he looks at his watch again. But our Mr P. is getting very agitated, gripping the arms of his chair so that the whole floor trembles.

"'Don't go," he cries – as if old Prince had any intention of going – "I should like to ..." He bogs down there; but after a minute he says, "I had an interesting talk with Father Ambrose the other day."

"'Oh indeed?" says Prince, very solemn. "Well, I am sure it must have done you good. My dear colleague has a brilliant understanding: I only wish he could be here more often. But they keep him so very busy, you know."

"'Your colleague? But I thought you were ...'"

"'Why, yes. Father Ambrose is my colleague. In my humble way I fulfil a dual function here. I am very proud of my connection with him: he is a wonderful person, and I have learned a great deal from him. I am sure he must have done you good?"

"'Yes, yes," he says, "Father Ambrose was very kind – wonderfully patient – most considerate."

"'May I ask what you talked about?"

"'It was mostly the same subject that we have just been discussing. But he is so sympathetic that I ventured to put it on a personal plane."

"'I see. I see. You told him everything?"

"'Yes."

"'Everything?"

"'Yes."

"'So of course he was able to reassure you completely?"

"'It was not a regular confession, you understand," says Mr P., still holding off.

"'No. I quite understand. But, however, he was able to reassure you."

"'Yes."

'I thought that was the end, but after a while old Prince leans forward and says, "My dear Philips – I hope you do not mind me calling you that – my dear Philips, I am afraid that you may have some unexpected reserve. Unfortunately Father Ambrose will not be back for some considerable time, but if I can be of any service to you, I am entirely at your disposition."

"'It was after my talk with him that I turned and saw it clearly," blurts out Mr Philips.

"'Dear me," cries Prince, and I knew he was so near a fit of the giggles that I nearly went off myself, although I was alone in the corridor. But he goes on very grave and earnest. "Dear me, you must have found that very disturbing."

"'I can't bear it. I can't bear it," he says.

"'Now, now, my dear Philips; let us be calm. Calm. I am here to help you: you know that, don't you? Let us look at it this way: as it happened after you had had your, your 'talk' shall we say, with Father Ambrose, there cannot possibly be any connection between this and your former – what term shall we employ? – your former visions. For as I understand it you told Father Ambrose *everything*? The account was quite complete?"

"'Yes. But perhaps it was not valid."

"'If it was complete it was certainly valid. There were no omissions?"

"'Oh no. Certainly not – no voluntary omission at all."

"'Perhaps some little suppression almost unnoticed at the time, which has occurred to you since?"

"'I don't think so. No. But I can't bear it – I can't. It is getting so much worse."

'Prince calms him down a little and then says, "Perhaps if we were to run over the main points of your conversation with Father Ambrose you might find it helpful, and it is possible that you might bring something fresh into your memory, something that you unconsciously kept in the background before. As I am sure you have noticed, our memories are extraordinarily unreliable, and they have a strange capacity for hiding things that we do not wish to remember. Yes, I am sure that that would be our best course: but may I beg you to be frank? I am sure that you will realize that complete frankness is of the first importance."

'"You are very kind. But I am afraid of trespassing on your good nature. I kept Father Ambrose here for hours."

'"Not at all, not at all. Now I think – yes, I am sure of it. I think you would be more at your ease if you were to kneel here, facing the window. I shall be able to hear you perfectly well. Remember, you cannot be too minutely detailed."

'So Philips gets down on the floor and puts his face against the cushion of the chair old Prince has been sitting in and old Prince stands behind him in the middle of the room, bending up and down on his knees and going like *that* with his hands.'

'He, he, he.'

'But instead of beginning, he jumps up again and says, "Do you feel that my theory of punishment is sound, Mr Prince?"

'"Eh?" says old Prince, rather put out and giving him a dirty look under his eyebrows. He hadn't expected that, and nor had I; but he recovers himself and says, "A very interesting theory, Mr Philips, very interesting indeed. But these are terribly difficult questions and I am sure that our best course is to do as I suggested. Shall we begin at the beginning?"

'Of course, he wants to get him down on his knees again, and for a moment he does go down. But then he bobs up again and stands there wringing his hands as good as a play. "I can't bear it," he keeps saying, "I can't bear it."

'"There now, my dear Philips, let us collect ourselves. Let us be calm. I will be just here behind you, and I will listen without interruption, I assure you. And we must bear in mind the absolute necessity for complete frankness, must we not?"

'Old Prince is looking very ugly, but Philips is half turned to the window and doesn't see a thing: he keeps moaning "I can't bear it. I can't. I can't."

'Prince sees that it is no good going on with that line, so he hands him back into his chair, waits until he has come off the boil, and then, after a little while, he says in a thoughtful voice, "The shadow of an upright wall, and the angle of the roof. Now let us reflect. What, by your theory, could have called that into being?"

"'It is not only the line and corner now. I didn't tell you. I didn't like to say," he gasps.

"'There is something else?" murmurs old Prince, to help him on.

'Philips whispers something, but what it was I could not catch: the next thing is old Prince saying, "Perhaps you could give me a general idea, eh?"

'But "I can't name it," he says, jerking his head over his shoulder.

"'Just some hint – ?" says old Prince, for our man is very near the point now, and old Prince is all hot and excited. But it won't do: he has pressed him just an inch too far and at that point our man sticks. He can't bring it out, and it's no use, although Prince soothes him and soft-soaps him for half an hour and more. You would have screamed. If you had been there I would never have been able to hold out.'

'Was he cross?'

'He was livid, my dear. He got out of the room all right in the end, still the dear old gentleman; but he gave me such a look as he shoved by.'

'He doesn't like to fail. But he'll have him next time.'

'Oh yes, he'll have him next time. But he likes it first go off, and this was rather a special one.'

'I wish I had seen it.' She paused for a while before adding, 'You have all the funny ones.'

'We've been lucky recently. There's another comic in the upper wing who –'

'What was that noise?'

'Which noise?'

'Like a dog howling.'

They both listened. The inhuman cry swelled to an enormous volume and after an instant's silence a furious trampling shook the ceiling of the room.

A slight frown creased the forehead of the black-haired woman, and she stood up, very tall and solid over the rickety table. 'The students?' she said. She stood considering for a moment with her lips pursed, while the hellish din continued overhead. 'Yes, the young devils must be teasing him. Old Prince said he might give them leave.'

A moment later she said, 'They've left him now.' She turned to a cupboard, took an instrument out for herself and handed another to the visitor.

'We'll go up too, shall we?' she said

'Oh *yes*,' cried the other, jumping full of glee, 'and we'll make him say who created *us*.'

And laughing they hurled themselves out of the room and raced up the stairs, screaming with laughter that flew before them to the door of Mr Philips' private room.

18

Billabillian

———⦵———

Cornelius O'Leary slid the last ten pieces of eight into the canvas bag and put it down again under the table with a grunt. The total was the same as before, when he had checked and re-checked it; but he was glad to have the confirmation fresh in his mind: it would not do to make a mistake.

He sat down in front of the neat arrangement of papers and reviewed them anxiously: there was nothing missing, and he could find but one thing to do – he ranged the row of weights on the right-hand edge of the table in a still more exact line of descending size. He wished the captain would come, but he knew very well that a good half-hour must elapse before he heard his step on the companionway. Cornelius had begun his preparations far too soon: even before the anchor had roared out in Sumbawa Road at dawn he had started laying out his bills of lading, cargo lists, and books. The ship, the *Trade's Increase*, lay under the shelter of Bloody Point, cut off from the ocean swell, and for once the wide, brass-bound table held his ranks of weights, his piles of coin, his strings of cash, his rulers, and his pens as firmly and as solidly as though it had been on dry land. It was all ready, and he wished the captain would come.

It had been a long voyage, a hundred and eighty-three days from the Pool of London, and Cornelius was burning to be ashore: but he knew that he must not move from the cabin until the captain had come below to inspect his papers, and until between them they had concluded the payment of the billabillian with the captain of the port. He averted his gaze from the porthole and began to repeat his tables again. Ten pecooes, one laxsan; ten laxsans, one cattee; ten cattees, one uta; ten utas, one bahar.

Yet although he could shut out the sight of the crowded harbour inshore, with its forest of masts, curving bamboo yards and rattan sails, he could not prevent the warm scent from drifting in and breaking through the dutiful, ordered line of calculations in his head. It was a heavy, indefinable smell: he could distinguish all the spices, but there was the scent of the tropical land, green leaves still wet from the warm rain of the night, and a thousand other things without a name.

They had smelled it first far out to sea. He had come on deck from the stifling cabin where old Mr Swann lay speechless and twitching under his heavy rugs, and in the milk-soft air he noticed it at once. One of the sailors had said, 'Do you smell that? We shall make our landfall in the morning.' And as Cornelius stood leaning on the rail, breathing the clean and scented air and watching the phosphorescent wave glide smoothly from the bows to the white fire of their wake, the sailor had added ominously, 'The tide is on the make. But it will ebb when the moon dips down: he will not see the light.'

They had buried the old man in sight of land, sewn up in canvas and with heavy shot at his feet: he had slid quietly off the grating and had vanished with hardly a splash in the clear green water, leaving a trail of white bubbles. He had been out of his right wits since they had left the Cargados Shoals, that fetid and toothless old man without a nose, but he had been kind when he was not ill, and Cornelius, thinking of him now as he looked at an entry in the dead man's hand, felt ashamed that he was so cheerful and excited.

A general roar on deck broke across his train of thought: he looked up, and there, framed in the wooden square, was a brown girl, her face and her bare breasts pointing up to the rail. She was holding a basket of fruit to show, and as she stood in the unseen boat, gliding from right to left, the ripple of the water, reflected from the side of the *Trade's Increase*, flickered over her satin body.

The crew were shouting a babel of encouragement, praise, and invitation: Cornelius heard the loud smacking noise as one kissed his hand, and the girl's cat face smiled. Cornelius had heard that the heathens went about with almost nothing on, and he was charmed to find it true: he felt the strong stirring of his blood, but as he heard the bellowing of the mate he blushed and restrained himself from going over to the porthole and craning out. There was a padding of bare feet on deck and then the renewed hammering as the men went to work again on the hatches.

He stirred uneasily in his chair. Would the captain never come? Beyond the porthole there was a square of brilliantly sunlit world, all the more dazzling for the darkness of the cabin: the calm dark blue of the road, with the ships lying spaced out; the paler blue or the harbour with the close-packed fleet of junks and proas; the cascade of green on shore, not very far away; and the sun over the whole of it was the sun of the land, warm and golden with dancing motes and heavy with the scent. They had coasted for a week, but still his nose was sharp from months at sea, and he drew in the air with a deep, savouring breath; it was as heady as wine, and it stirred him to the heart. Would the captain ever come?

But he imposed on his face the serious look of a man – a man with great responsibilities – and repeated, 'The Java tael is two and a quarter pieces of eight, and that is two ounces English.' He laid his hand over a paper whose edges were curling in the sun and went on, 'The Malay tael is one ounce and a third: but the China tael is one ounce and a fifth. So the China tael is six-tenths of a Java tael exactly.'

Yes, he had all that by heart. All the currencies, weights and measures of the East Indies and the Spice Islands at his fingertips. And he knew his bills of lading by heart, too: there was no need for this array of papers. He could tell precisely what they had in their cargo and where it was stowed, without his lists. But they had to be there; it was orderly and correct, and their neatness gave him a feeling of solidarity and accomplishment. He was sure that the captain would be pleased. He had seen little of him, but from what he had seen, he knew that the captain liked exactitude: Cornelius had already been commended for know-ing how many barrels of powder there were without having to go and count them. That had been a little while after Cornelius had been moved from the *Clove* to the *Trade's Increase* because of Mr Swann's illness, and just before the captain himself went down with the calenture that, together with scurvy, had attacked the whole ship's company when they were making their northing from the Cape. It had been a sickly ship from the start of this long and dangerous trading voyage, and they had all thought that the captain was going to die. But every morning and every evening, except for the days of the great storm, they had heard the psalms coming from his cabin, and just before old Swann sank for good and all, the captain reappeared on deck, thinner than ever, pale in his black coat, silent, but very much in command. He had at once had the guns run out – they were still a match for any Dutch ship, in spite of their losses – and had had two men flogged who were slow and remiss.

'You are a lucky devil, Teague,' said the mate to Cornelius (the mate was lax in his expressions). 'You have all the luck in this ship, I believe.'

In a way it was true. Both the men over him had died: Wilson of the calenture in Saldanha Bay and at last old Swann; and when their consort the *Clove* had vanished in the storm, Mr Rolfe and the merchants' factor had vanished with her, leaving Cornelius and the mulatto clerk as the only men, under the captain, for the trading, which was the heart and being of the venture.

It was lucky; but it was not entirely unforeseen. 'Old Swann will not last beyond the Cape,' his uncle had said, 'and with any right chance the Dutch will knock one of the others on the head. In three or four voyages you will be on your own, and then, if you have the wit to escape the fever, the Dutch, the Spaniards, the Portuguese, the Sea-Malays and the Java pox, you will make your fortune, if you keep my advice in mind. Then you can sit at your ease like a lord on Fiddlers' Green.'

Cornelius had not looked for his luck; he had been heartily sorry for the occasions of it; yet having it put between his hands, he meant to grasp it. All the way across the Indian Ocean he had conned his instructions, had gone through and through Mr Swann's lists, had counted and re-checked his chests of Spanish silver, his moidores, ducatoons, sequins of Venice and gold mohurs, had dived and wriggled his way through the fantastically mixed cargo in the holds; he had learned all he could from the mulatto, part Malay, part Portuguese, part Javanese; and he had read his uncle's advice until he knew whole paragraphs by rote. But he had not been able to win the confidence of Popery, the mulatto; and he regretted that, for he was a friendly soul. Perhaps if he had made the whole voyage in the *Trade's Increase* he might have done so, but he had sailed beyond Madagascar in the *Clove*; and with the sinking of that ship he had lost most of his intimate friends. It was not that this ship's company was unfriendly or reserved – far from it; but Popery, or Sawney Bean, as some called him, remained aloof, in spite of their common religion; for Cornelius was a Catholic, and that, in a time when it was death for a priest to be found in England, would ordinarily have been a tie. However, Cornelius could not hang out his beliefs aboard an English ship – he had learned that much caution – and perhaps Popery did not know of them: perhaps, too, he resented Cornelius having charge of the papers: he may have hoped for promotion for himself. Perhaps it was just that he was a proud, injurious Portingale.

Again there was a mounting tumult of cries on deck, and Cornelius heard a dull crash on the other side of the thick wooden wall behind him. After a moment of dead silence came the first mate's furious shriek, 'Get your ——— boom out of my shrouds, you whoreson black ape,' then the captain's cold, harsh voice cutting through the oaths and counter-shouting: 'Mr Williams.'

The mulatto pushed his blue face through the door. 'Captain not coming yet,' he said, and closed it again.

The sound of shoving, fending-off, the orders, the groan of wood and the gurgling of churned water was succeeded by the startlingly close vision of a high, recurved prow in Cornelius' porthole: clinging to the prow were three bearded Arabs, shaking their fists at the deck of the *Trade's Increase*. They were like angry prophets, and they were so close that Cornelius could see their yellow, blood-shot eyes straining from their heads in fury as they shot their stream of words up through the air. There were more prophets in the waist of the dhow, but they were silent: they glared with dumb rage or watched in motionless indifference as the dhow laboured past the *Trade's Increase* with her enormous sweeps. Cornelius noted her armament: only four guns; three brass serpentines and a demi-culverin: the *Trade's Increase* could sink her with a single broadside.

The falsetto and the bass of the Arabs died away, to rise again as the dhow tried to make her way against the tide between two junks moored inshore: now the shouting was increased by the shrill howl of Cantonese, but Cornelius' attention was distracted by a flash of scarlet beyond the junks, a flash of scarlet threading through the masts of the proas by the landing stage, and the beating of a drum.

That, he thought, must be the heathen duke: the rajah, as they called him here. Unless it could be the prince's officers for the customs. No: the scarlet was on shore, not coming out to sea. On shore under the palm trees. They were playing a strange, harsh, screaming music there. Would the captain never come?

Again Cornelius turned his mind from the delights of the unknown shore to the papers in front of him.

'Some report, these Islands were once in Subjection of the King of Ternate, but whatever they once were, now they are a sort of a Common-wealth,' his uncle had written in his clerkly hand ('No tropes or elegant turns, you understand,' – looking contentedly at his work before he had handed it over to his nephew – 'Nothing but a plain, thorough-stitch account. Tropes are for learned men, not half-merchant, half-sailor, half-witted swabs like super-cargoes.' But he was quite proud of his writing, nevertheless; Cornelius had little penetration, but he knew that much.) '... sort of Common-wealth; yet there is one Supreme Officer, whom they call a Subandar, that appears at the Head of the State, and has the Trouble of Managing, but not the full Power of Disposing of any Public Affair, without the good Liking, and intervening Approbation of the People.

'Their way of dealing is by Bahar and Cattee: the small Bahar is ten Cattees of Mace, and a hundred of Nutmegs; and the great Bahar a hundred of Mace, and a thousand of Nutmegs. And the Cattee here is 5 Pound 13 Ounces English; the prices variable.' This was not Sumbawa: it was Banda, and the *Trade's Increase* would not be there until they had laid in their cargo of pepper; but Cornelius read on.

'The Commodities requested here are Broad Cloth, Stammel, Calicoes black and red, China boxes, Basons without Brims, light colour'd Damasks, Taffatees, Velvets, Gold Chains, Plate Cups gilt, Head-pieces damask'd, Guns, Sword-blades, but not such as are back'd to the Point. There's a great deal of Profit in bringing Gold Coyn hither; for you shall have that for the value of 70 Rials in Gold Coyn, that will cost you 90, if you pay in Rials ...' Frowning with concentration, Cornelius placed the rimless basins in his mind: they were stowed under the forepeak, beyond the cases with the small blue beads.

'You have at this Place some of the best Benzoin perhaps in the World, and in great Plenty; and the glorious Gems of Pegu shine here likewise. There's vast quantity of Silver in Bullion, that's brought hither from Japan; but Rials of Eight are more in request, and will bring in Bullion ¼ of a Rial Profit. All your broad Stammel Cloth, Iron-works, and fine Looking-Glasses, are things that take exceedingly here, and Saunders, Sapon, Camphire, Amber, Elephants' Teeth, Rhinocero's and Hart's Horn; to which add Honey, Spanish Soap, Sugar Candy, all sorts of Leather, Wax-Candles, and Pictures. Only as to Pictures, the larger they are the better, but they are not so much for Faces, as Landskip, Representations of War, amorous Intrigues, some remarkable Story of comical Fancy, as the Painter's Invention guides him.'

Cornelius turned on: he had all that in his head. At Soocadanna the weights are the mass, the coopang, the boosuck and the pead. At Soocadanna, diamonds. 'They are gotten as Pearls are, by Diving; and the River most celebrated for the Search and

Discovery of them is the River Lane; such a one as which any Prince that had it in his Dominions, would not have very much cause to complain, if it yielded the Country no Fish. All the trading Part of Mankind being fond of this precious Commodity, the Place never wants a Crowd of Ships, Praws and Juncks ... yet the Place is in the height of its charming Lustre in April.'

But one should watch the weighers always, they being Chinese, and apt to favour their own countrymen, in any commodity from rice to dragon's blood.

Cornelius turned back the pages and memorized the piece on civet, bezoars, and musk. 'Musk. There are three Sorts of it, black, brown, and yellow; of which the first is stark naught, the second good, and the third best of all; it ought to be the Colour of the best Spikenard, and of so strong a Scent, as to be rather offensive than otherwise, especially if tasted, when the Fumes of it seem to pierce violently into the Brain, and search the Head at a wonderful Rate.'

His uncle had opened a drawer in the Chinese cabinet and had given him a piece of yellow musk to smell. 'Does that go to your scalp, boy? Does that make your essence quake, eh? Does that clear your intellectuals?'

'Yes, Uncle John, sir.'

'I hope it does, indeed,' – shaking his head doubtfully – 'for I am sure they want a vivifying spark. It's the headpiece that counts, boy,' he had said, patting him on the shoulder, 'You must think judiciously and quick. Tell me now if you remember the customs at Sumbawa.'

Cornelius put his hands behind his back and repeated, 'There is the prince's custom called chukey, which is eight bags upon the hundred, rating pepper at four pieces of eight the sack, whatever price it bears. Then there is the billy, the billy . . .' His voice trailed away.

'Hell and death! The billabillian, moon-calf: the billabillian, you mumchance Tom a'Bedlam brain-sick zany. Swab, to forget the prime foundation of them all. Here, take the page and spell it out.'

"'Then there is the Billabillian,'" read Cornelius, "'which is this: If any Ship come into the Road laden, the King is to be immediately acquainted with the Sorts, Quantities, and Prices of the Commodities in her, before any part can be landed: upon which he sends his Officers to the Ship to look narrowly into her and takes of all the Sorts what he likes, perhaps at half your Price, or it may be something better, according as you can agree. So if you lade Pepper, you pay for every 6,000 sacks, 666 Rials, or else are obliged to be the King's Chapman for as many thousand sacks, at one half, or three fourths of a Rial more than the Current Price of the Town. The Dutch indeed go a more com-com –'"

'Compendious, my boy,' said his uncle, nodding pleasantly at the word.

"'The Dutch indeed go a more compendious way to work; and to avoid the trouble of the Duty and the Searching, agree with the Officer so much in the Gross, for the Lading of the Ship, which is generally about seven or eight hundred Rials.'"

'Remember that, Cornelius. Remember that, and you will make your fortune yet. It is not your whoreson sixteen shillings a month that will give you all this – ' He waved expansively at the comfortable room with its Cordova-leather hangings and its carved plaster ceiling with the Virtues and a Cornucopia; and his wave carried Cornelius' mind beyond the windows to the walled garden with its espaliered fruit trees, and out of the garden to the meadows that sloped gently down to the Thames, where his uncle would sit with his pipe in one hand and a glass in the other, watching the ships going up to London from the sea, or listening to the bells from Dartford over the water, or Gravesend.

'– it is not your whoreson pay: it is the billabillian that you ought to go down on your knees and thank the Lord for. That and your own trading afterwards – afterwards, mind – when the ship has had her due.'

'But Uncle John, sir,' said Cornelius nervously, 'it is – is it quite right?'

'Blood and damnation!' cried the old gentleman, turning from red to blue. 'What have we here? A snuffling, canting, talking-through-the-nose Puritan? A Praise-the-Lord-with-Joyfulness Shufflebottom like the poxy, snivelling French dog of a conventicle-haunting text-splitter I kicked out of the Goat and Com passes the other day? Rot the boy. Of course it is quite right. Do you think I would do it if it were not? Blast your eyes.' He fumed in silence for a while; then recovering his good humour and his normal scarlet face he went on, though with still a trace of the exasperation that talking with Cornelius often brought into his voice, 'It is good for the merchants, good for the prince's officers, good for the captain and good for the supercargo. Everybody, apart from a few sickly rogues who should never have seen the light of day, much less been breeched, everybody does it. Why, kiss my hand, I remember Evans, of the *Roebuck*, when he was sent off for cloves to Pulo-Temba, making himself a purse out of the Sabandar's duty there and another out of the rooba at Timor. He kept it close, he and his captain, until he was knocked o' the head in a fight at Jakarta, and then he told us before he died. He was a great man, and his merchants gave him a piece of plate worth fifty pound, as a gratification for looking after their trade so well, in the year 'twenty-three. And he was one of those quiet dogs – no Java girls, no arrack for him – never moved without an Amen in his mouth and the Good Book in his pocket. That's a good man, I believe? He'd bury you a dead seaman as trim as any parson in the land. No, no: you will see old Swann, if he lives the voyage, or Adams if he don't, give the prince's officer, the rajah's Arapotee, as they say in those parts, a round five hundred pieces of eight for the *Clove's* billabillian. And the prince's officer, this Arapotee, will give him a quittance in his hand for nine hundred, or maybe a thousand clear, and he will share the difference with the captain: you will get a score to yourself if you stand by, and the next voyage you will get more, and more the next after that, until in the end, with God's blessing, you will have it in your own hands to make the shares. Then, if you keep clear of the Dutch in the Sunda Straights, half a dozen voyages will make you, and you can set up for a squire by land.

'Dear Lord,' he said, blowing out a cloud of smoke some

minutes later, 'If Captain Johnson of the *Clove* could hear you a-doubting of the billabillian, he would have you overboard when you were five minutes out of soundings, or keep you to sell to the Sultan of Cayalucca. You must indeed want wit, my poor moon-calf nephew, not to understand that it saves the merchants' goods and money. If you open your hatches and break bulk among those land-sharks – for all those heathens are thieves inveterate, knowing no better – you lose a good eighth, seeing they all have twelve hands apiece, like their idols. And at the end of it they give you no thanks for having made them search, and they buy up half your cargo for their king at their own price, which is a sinful waste. No: it saves the merchant's pocket, and it makes a wastrel venture a profitable voyage. It gives the Arapotee a noble present. It gives the captain and the supercargo a rightful bounty on their wages – and nobody, not even the merchants, expects them to wind their way across the world's great sea for hardtack and a few ha-pence. No: they may take the billabillian, and they may trade afterwards once the ship has got her belly full: that's right and just. Don't you be wiser than the rest of the world, Cornelius, and don't you let your captain suspect he's gotten a formal, psalm-singing precisian aboard when you come to be on your own, or by God, it will be the last voyage you ever make.'

He was benign and calm again by now. When he was not blue in the face with rage he was always kind. He had taken in his widowed sister and her little brood of Papists – and a dangerous charge it might always be – and at this very moment, thought Cornelius, working out the change in time for the longitude, he was probably singing all the decent words he knew of a song while Sue and Bridget piped along beside him. He was choleric at times, that could not be denied, and he hated Puritans like poison, though he never went farther into the parish church than the bell-tower; but these were only squalls on a gentle sea. And it was not only a rough, careless, sailor's kindness that bound Cornelius to him; it was much more. For example, he had not only found his nephew his place in the *Clove* and his outfit, but he had spent days and weeks in drawing up his pages of advice: it was the fruit of great experience, and to the day Cornelius sailed he kept adding notes. There was one here now, beautifully written in the margin of the pages about Timor. 'Balee, to the westward of Lambock, in 8 degrees of south Latitude, yields great Plenty of Wax, which is made up in large Cakes, from eighteen to thirty Rials to the Peecul, as the Time serves. There's a great deal of Deceit, very often, in this Commodity; and to be sure that you are not cheated, the best Way is to break it, and see whether it looks agreeable within. The Wares to be carried hither, are Chopping-Knives, China Frying-Pans, China Bells, small Bugles, Porcelains, colour'd Taffatees (but no Blacks), Pieces of Silver beaten flat and thin, and of the breadth of one's Hand; and your Broad Cloth of Venice Red and all your Coromandel Cloths are topping Com-modities here; but the most vendible sorts are the Gobarees, the Pintadoes, and the fine Tappies of St Thomas. There may be good Profit made of the Trade to this Island, in the Teeth of the false Dutch, for the Chinese have given four for one, to some of our English that ventur'd with them thither.'

His uncle had written that in front of the roaring fire at Christ-mas, but Cornelius, thinking of him now, saw him sitting in his meadow, listening placidly to the Dartford bells and waving the stem of his pipe to count the changes. Then he realized that it was something on shore that had brought this image so sharp and clear into his mind. He raised his head and listened: yes, in that queer, tip-tilted temple under the flaming trees someone was beating on a gong, a rhythmic boom-boom-boom that came echoing over the water like the passing bell at home.

'The Dutch were highly disgusted at our coming hither, and as inquisitive to know who directed us to this Place, threatening all with Plagues and Death,' he read. But he could not keep his mind to his book. He looked out to the brilliant light again, to the diminished world, yet so much more brilliant and animated for its confining frame. The gong in the temple was beating still, and a little wind was moving the palm trees: the splashes of moving colour up behind there must be the market place, where the men from the European ships, the Chinese junks and the Arab dhows met with the Malays, the Formosans, and the Javanese. If only the captain would come he could go ashore. Cornelius had a desperate feeling that tomorrow it might all be gone: he was so longing to be there that he could hardly sit.

'Mr O'Leary,' said the captain, 'have you the lists for the after-hold? And the papers for the customs men? They are putting off from the shore.'

'Yes, sir. Here is the after-hold.' Cornelius dropped it in an excess of zeal: he was nervous of the tall, yellow-faced captain, and he was not used to being called Mr O'Leary.

'Very good, Mr O'Leary,' said the captain, nodding over the list of bales. The mulatto came in and stood by the porthole, looking out and darkening the sun. 'Customs man coming soon,' he said. 'Billabillian.'

The captain did not answer, but looked among the papers for the lading of the *Trade's Increase*.

'Here it is, sir,' cried Cornelius, divining the captain's wish. 'But we will not need it, except for show,' he said, with a laugh and a knowing wag of his head. 'I have put the chief officer's present on the locker sir, and fifty strings of cash for his men.'

'Present?' said the captain. His back was to the light, and Cornelius could not tell from his voice whether he was pleased or not by this display of efficient promptitude.

'Yes, sir, a looking-glass, a case of spirits, and one of the boxes of opium, sir, like Mr Swann said.' He spoke with confidence; he remembered Mr Swann's words exactly. 'That should please the black bastard's heart,' he said, in imitation of Swann.

'Mr O'Leary,' said the captain, sharply.

'I ask pardon, sir,' said Cornelius, going red and drawing the top of his shoe up the calf of his left leg. After a moment he said, 'I drew up this little paper of the billabillian, sir. It should make us four hundred pieces of eight, give or take a score eitherway.'

After the briefest hesitation the captain took the paper in silence: as he looked at it he said nothing.

The awkwardness that had arisen with the captain's 'Mr O'Leary' did not fade away. Cornelius felt it strongly. Had he

PATRICK O'BRIAN

made the captain's share large enough? Surely: it was twice what Uncle John had said. He was conscious of the mulatto's fixed stare: he said, 'I have counted out the six hundred reals in the two bags under the table.' Then, feeling that he had to say something more, he added, 'They are damnation heavy,' with an embarrassed laugh.

'Mr O'Leary,' said the captain again, but automatically, without meaning. He had turned a little to the light, and Cornelius could see that his little deep-set eyes were still scrutinizing the slip of paper. Was it not clear? He had set it all down exactly, and had headed it Billabillian, with two lines ruled under it and the date.

'Is the sum taken away rightly, sir?' he asked, into the continuing silence. A boat rowed by with squeaking oars, and its shadow passed over the ceiling.

'The subtraction is correct,' said the captain. 'It is all quite clear.' He seemed to notice the mulatto for the first time, and pointed silently to the door; the mulatto went out, giving Cornelius a strong, but incomprehensible look as he passed by him.

'Tell me, Mr O'Leary,' said the captain in the same toneless, contained voice, 'how do you spell your names? Write them at the bottom here.'

He put the paper on the table, and Cornelius, confused and obscurely unhappy, wrote his name below the sum. Cornelius O'Leary.

'Thank you,' said the captain, sprinkling sand on the signature and folding the paper into the pocket of his black coat.

'May I go ashore when we have finished, sir?' asked Cornelius, smiling hesitantly, as he looked up into the captain's strange, withdrawn, inimical face.

'When next thou goes ashore,' whispered the captain, with a sudden cold ferocity, 'false thief, it will be –'

Popery knocked at the door, opened it. Behind him there was a man in a gorgeous sarong. The mulatto stood aside, and said, 'Billabillian.'

19

The Soul

With the full moon hidden, but only just hidden, the world was lit by a gentle light, enough to see the great features of the land, the rocks, the line of wild mountains, and the shape of the coast. There was no wind, no wind at all, and the soft clouds hung low, smooth, united and unmoving; they never parted for the stars to shine through, but it would not have been called a cloudy night; they were not positive enough for that. The warmth came up from the ground, from the side of the hill, from all around, an enveloping warmth in that still air.

As she had but just left the cemetery, where the cold lingered among the cypresses, among the angular white tombs and the high pigeonholes where the poor dead lay, she rested on the wall above the cliff and let the grateful warmth soak in.

This, she thought, must be very like what the ancients believed the end of the world to be – the flat world, that had an end. The dark cliff dropped a hundred feet, perhaps two hundred, to an unmoving sea: on the water there was no reflection; a faint haze deadened it, and no sound came up. There was no horizon. The sea and the sky joined perhaps, but they were lost.

It was as if she looked into nothing, into infinity. Only a light far out, a round light with no path on the sea, and that gave even more the impression of unending waste beyond.

A poor soul, she thought, would have to go down the path that was before her, the cliff path, and walk out over that space to the light, beyond all words remote. It would be a perfectly smooth desert, and your feet would not find a surface, not a hard surface. Perhaps for some distance you could walk easily, but then for an unmeasurable time you would labour – dream-walking – with a huge mental effort for no gain.

Although it was so empty from here, you might pass a silent, pale soul working out some cruel meanness, some tyranny that had not been paid for with more than a moment's uneasiness before. You might pass: but was there anyone she could pass?

The light was infinitely remote. But it was no good waiting: all the hope that there could be was in the traject; and in the faint light she bent to see the winding of the path.

20

On the Bog

— ⧓ —

'It is time to be moving,' said Boyle.

'What? What?' cried Meagher, starting wildly out of his sleep – a cry of alarm.

Boyle made no reply, but flashed his lighter to look for the leg of the tall thigh-boots beside him; indeed there was no need for a reply, since the momentary gleam showed the whole scene at once, the interior of a reed-walled butt, guns, a game-bag, duck-boarded floor, the wooden bench. The flame also lit Boyle's handsome face, exaggerating its high arrogant nose and the morning beard; and in this brief flash Meagher's being fell back into its present context.

They had lain out on the bog all night, so that they could get out to the far end for the geese, for the dawn-flighting, well before daybreak and well before any keepers were moving.

Of course it had been Boyle's idea entirely. In Jammet's a man was prating about geese, great skeins of greylags brought down by the hard weather, and turning to Meagher Boyle said, 'How should you like to have a shot in the morning? I know a capital place, and you are the great wildfowler, I believe.'

Meagher was pleased, flattered with the notice and the preference – particularly the preference, because toad-eating Clancy was there, eager for any invitation that might be going; and although he had been up at a party all night before he said he would be very happy indeed – 'wildfowling is meat and drink to me'. They left at once, walked over the river to Boyle's place

– Meagher was one of the few who had been there – and loaded gun-cases, cartridge-bags and tarpaulin into the car.

'It is the devil we have no dog,' said Boyle. 'Clancy spoke of a labrador.'

'Oh, that was only his froth and pride; he has never owned so much as a cat in all his life. I'll act as the dog,' said Meagher, laughing.

Boyle sent him for cartridges with a five-pound note and as soon as he came back they drove straight out of the town. A long drive, too fast for conversation with the hood off, fast along winding lanes and boreens, and Meagher was excited with the rushing air, pleased to be sitting there next to Boyle: then the stop in the lee of a turf-stack and the walk out, a great way across rough pasture as far as a dyke. 'We are not going in there, are we?' asked Meagher, reading a notice in the fading light. It was one of many posted all along the near bank forbidding trespassers, warning of mantraps, stating that dogs should be shot on sight.

'That is the general idea,' said Boyle. He felt for a plank in the rushes, laid it across, lifted the wire the far side, slipped through and stood waiting.

'I don't mind a bit of poaching,' said Meagher, 'but ...' He could not find an acceptable way of putting 'but only when it is fairly safe', so he said no more. This was certainly far from safe: he did not know which county they were in even, but they had run along two miles of park wall with an enormous house inside it before stopping, and now they stood in flat open country without a bush or a hedge for miles. The notices were fresh and trim; this was obviously a strictly preserved estate.

'Never worry about them,' said Boyle. 'You are only an honorary dog; and in any case geese and duck are not game. They are *ferae naturae* – they have no *animus revertendi*.'

Meagher could hardly reply to that. He walked on over the tussocky forbidden ground, looking as unconscious and confident as he could. They had not gone a hundred yards before a single partridge got up in front of them, a little to the right. Boley's gun leapt to his shoulder; he fired, and the bird hit the ground so hard it bounced twice. He said, 'I beg pardon, Meagher. That was really your bird. Just pick it up, will you, there's a good fellow.'

Meagher picked it up, glancing round in every direction; and he picked up two rabbits and a snipe as well before they reached downright bog with redshanks in the cuttings and curlews crying high overhead. Looking ahead in the twilight he could see tall reeds, dense cover that would hide their nakedness; but between them and the reeds lay an intricate series of channels, many of them newly dredged. Boyle led the way through, walking casual and easy like a tenant for life and a man who knows his way well.

'You seem to know your way well,' said Meagher.

'I used to come here in the old duke's time,' said Boyle. And some time later, pushing through the innermost reeds, he said, 'The old boy always did himself proud. Just look at this butt, will you? Now that's what I call a truly ducal butt. Benches, duck-boarding. There will be straw in that barrel; but suppose you cut some rushes as well – here is a knife. I will keep an eye lifted in case the duck start to move.'

Meagher could have sworn he had not slept at all that night. Certainly with his prickling eyes and general weariness he felt he had not. The greater part of it (all but the last twenty minutes in fact) he had lain listening to Boyle snoring on his back, listening to the desolate call of marsh-birds he could not put a name to, weird shrieks and groanings, and to the stir of the reeds as ice formed on them. He was not very cold as he lay there in his nest of rushes and straw under a piece of tarpaulin, but he was wet from below and hungry, and as the hours wore by he smoked until he had no more in his packet. He was a heavy smoker, deeply addicted to cigarettes.

It was partly anger that kept him awake, anger and resentment. They had not been in the butt half an hour before the duck began flighting, mallard, wigeon, teal, pintail, great numbers of them, and Boyle set up a fusillade, a firework display, an artillery battle, that must have been heard five miles off at least in this deathly calm air. Every shot made Meagher wretched, and by the time the movement was over and he had searched out a good score of birds he was in such a state of nervous indignation that he almost cried out, 'You invite me to shoot and without a word of warning to expose me to this sort of thing – you have no consideration at all.'

The only words that actually passed were Boyle's. He said, 'I think it is over: in any case it is too dark to see. I cannot wait to get at the geese. Good night to you, now.' No jocular or commiserating reference to the few ineffectual half-hearted shots that Meagher had let off; tact, that was the lay, a tact so obvious that it was, if not a studied offence, then at least most unfriendly.

Their acquaintance ran back a considerable way, so far that Meagher could say of Boyle, 'We are old friends: I have known him for years', but it had never really matured: there was too little in the way of candid interchange, too much reserve for that. Meagher admired Boyle's undeniable style, his offhand way with people, and his occasional lavish generosity; but he had few illusions; he knew that Boyle liked to have a companion – he had no girl, no permanent judy, preferring temporary drabs of the lowest kind – and as Meagher was generally available so he was the most frequently chosen. Then again he knew that although Boyle could talk freely about Stockhausen, Schwitters, Brecht, he was virtually illiterate: none of the things that interested Meagher concerned Boyle in the least: he would see the National Library, the Gallery and the Abbey go up in flames with cheerful indifference. Occasionally a wild, unpredictable gaiety would come over him and then he would lay aside his reserve, horsing around in Mother Daly's like a boy; but on the whole he was elusive – there was no coming close to him at all – and rather than friendship between them there was a kind of exasperated love on Meagher's side alone, a love not only for Boyle's thoroughbred grace, his elegance, his ability to cope with guns, rods, horses, waiters and girls, but also for his vulnerability. Boyle was a man who had to be on top: he had to excel in every field. Humiliation would destroy him – if a girl were to turn him down or if he were to scrape a bus as he shot his car one-handed through the whirlpool of College Green he would be undone. In some fields – in talk – Meagher could protect him; and to protect such a creature was a privilege, an infinite superiority. Boyle walked a perpetual tightrope, and although up until now he had never stumbled badly to Meagher's knowledge he was continually in danger of doing so, in danger deliberately created by himself. Blazing away as though he owned creation on preserved land stuffed with keepers: a perfect example.

As though he owned creation ... he must own quite a share of it, however. How much nobody knew, but certainly more than most of their circle, certainly very much more than Meagher, who lived by expedients – small journalism, a little reviewing, the occasional grant. Once he had taken Meagher and a couple of dreadful little bus-stop tarts to a house behind Enniskerry, letting himself in with his key: half had been ruined so long ago that trees grew twenty feet out of it, but the rest was deeply comfortable, though dusty – carpets, huge leather chairs, mahogany – and the drive was kept up. He also had a tower in the County Clare, where he fished: but many of them claimed to have towers in the County Clare and what really impressed them was this visible car, the sight of him coming out of the Kildare Street Club, and his beautiful cigarette-case, made of gold. The car might be uninsured, the tower a myth, but the case was there all the time.

Money: that was the great trouble. When they went out, who picked up the restaurant bill? Who paid for the drinks, the petrol, the tickets? Usually Boyle was delicate, but he had a sadistic streak in him and sometimes he could make Meagher feel all the difference between a man with fifty pounds in his pocket and one with a packet of pawn-tickets done up with an elastic band. There were times when instead of offering a lift, a dinner-jacket, a loan, he would compel Meagher to make the direct request; once or twice he had casually borrowed one of Meagher's precious pounds and had forgotten to repay. Odd little meannesses too, such as disappearing for a moment and coming back with a freshly-lit cigarette. No doubt they arose from a dislike of being sponged on, of being manipulated; and fellows like Clancy were shameless at sponging.

Yet in spite of all this they laughed at many of the same things; they enjoyed the same films; they could be companionable enough; they had fun; and surely, said Meagher, fundamentally Boyle had a liking for him, and respected his parts.

The liking was not apparent on either side at this moment, however. Something seemed to have happened to their relationship during the night, as though Meagher's resentment and silent injurious expressions had conveyed themselves into the other's sleeping mind; or as though Boyle had reflected upon Meagher's 'I do not mind poaching but . . .' and had filled in the gap, or upon his ignominious performance with the gun (Meagher was a countryman only by theory). While for his part Meagher could not see why he made all this coil about a mere dilettante, a sciolist, a dabbler. 'I am far more intelligent than he is, far better educated,' he reflected, plucking straw and rushes from his clothes. He may have a bodily, an animal intelligence – he is good at killing things – but surely to God a man is above a brute. He has read nothing at all.'

Here Boyle finished buckling his thigh-boots and walked out of the butt, leaving the game-bag for Meagher to carry: in the reeds outside he lit a cigarette, and at the smell of the returning waft Meagher's stomach gave an avid craving heave. He remembered not only that his packet was empty but that he had had neither dinner nor tea. To be sure, Boyle had eaten nothing either; but Boyle was well padded, whereas Meagher, who lived by his wits, was painfully thin. The gap of a meal told on him at once.

'Perhaps that is why I am feeling so very brittle all over,' he thought. 'That and two sleepless nights. And I dare say I have a cold coming on – to lie out all night in the wet, what a notion! – a bad go of flu.'

He followed Boyle through the reeds: they walked without speaking to one another, as though there were an acknowledged breach. Through the reeds round the lake and out on the far side; and here, stretching infinitely far beyond them, was the landscape of a dream, perfectly silent, perfectly still; the whole bog, with every rush and clump of grass upon it, was white with hoar-frost, and it gleamed gently in a suffused shadowless light that came dropping from the frozen air together with minute crystals of ice: no visible source for the light, no stars, no moon, only this high luminous mist. A world before the creation. An enormous flatness with no details in it, for the impression of light was illusory and at any distance everything merged into uncertainty; there was no one object that could be seized and defined apart from the sea-wall away to their left, the single firm line in this universal vagueness, a line that ran curving away for ever.

Boyle was screwing himself up to see his watch, to make the hands show in the darkness of his bosom. 'Just hold my gun, will you?' he said. A beautiful short-barrelled hammerless ejector, lighter by far than the old-fashioned brown keeper's gun allotted to Meagher.

'Can you make out the time?' asked Meagher, and to his shame he heard a placating note in his voice.

Boyle did not answer directly. In a cold impersonal tone he said, 'Only two hours to go. We shall have to step out if – oh for Christ's sake don't hold your gun like that, you silly whore! Don't you know you must never point your gun at anything you don't mean to kill?'

Meagher was on the edge of crying out that it was not pointed, that it was not loaded; but the shocking brutality of the assault, quite outside their habitual intercourse, choked back his lies and he followed Boyle in silence.

Two hours, he had said. Surely they had been walking more than two hours? The night seemed a hundred years old. The sea-wall was unchanged, the one firm thread in a shifting interminable dream; it stretched before and behind, a broad ten-foot earthwork with sluices here and there and every few hundred yards a set of posts, startlingly upright in a world so flat, like black exclamation marks signalling danger: each one might be an armed keeper. The idea of running away from a keeper, of labouring over the bog with a gun pointing at his back, was horrible to Meagher: and who could tell what Boyle might do, in such an encounter out here at the far end of the world with no one to see? He was a deeply bloody man. 'A whore, a pillar of ignorance,' said Meagher.

But although the sea-wall was still the same it no longer ran through the same country: now they had primeval saltings on their left hand and the deep mud of a tidal river, while on the right the sweet-water marsh shone and glittered with creeping water. A landscape even more inhuman, desolate and unearthly than before: vaster too, for now an increase in the light had brought the indeterminate sea into its farther rim. The falling aerial crystals had turned to penetrating wet, but so far this had not affected the whiteness of the ground. The frost still struck upwards.

The mud seemed deeper underfoot, however – it had long since filled Meagher's inadequate shoes; and certainly his sick hunger and abject craving for tobacco had grown immeasurably. He felt even more brittle and his lack of sleep had got into his red-rimmed bleared watering eyes, so that when he concentrated on a post it flickered and even waved its arms; his sense of smell and his hearing had become unnaturally sharp. He heard the whistle of a flight of duck before Boyle, as they passed high overhead. These must be the first birds of the dawn-flighting; so surely the day could not be very far off, and release from this nightmarish entertainment?

Certainly there was more light, even if it was only the rising of the moon; but at the next set of posts this did not prevent him from catching his leg in the barbed wire slung between them. He gave a strong kick to be free of it: the wire broke from the post and snarled right round his leg, the barbs running deep. It nearly had him down: he staggered on one foot, his loaded gun swinging in an arc, pointing now at Boyle's head, now at his loins as he walked steadily on. Meagher recovered his balance, laid down the gun, laid down the game-bag (it weighed forty pounds), and knelt to wrestle with the wire. Wet with drizzle and mud, his numbed hands merely fumbled, and in a sudden flare of anger and resentment he tore at the wire with all his force. It was no good. He was still held fast, ignominiously kneeling there with the mud soaking into his knees; and in a sudden collapse of spirit he crouched against the post, watching Boyle stride away. He knew Boyle was aware – it was a conscious back – and he knew Boyle would not turn unless he were called upon for help.

Meagher did nothing until he saw the small leap of a flame: Boyle had lit a cigarette and was waiting for him. Meagher forced his mind to be cold, followed the pattern of the barbs and disentangled them one by one, tearing the cloth as he did so. He picked up the bag and followed, limping: as he got under way so the glow of the cigarette moved on.

Long before he caught up, the cord of the bag was biting into his shoulder again and the weight of the gun was a torment: he was wet through and through; he was full of yellow rancour and spleen; but with something of the cunning of fever he said 'I shall keep up with him: even Boyle has not the face to smoke without offering me one if I am right by him – a guest, for all love!'

He could feel the paper cylinder between his two fingers and his thumb, the glowing end sheltered in his palm from the drizzle, the deep inhalation, the yielding of the tube at the very end, the red arc and the hiss as he threw it into the water.

Still the old night faded and little by little the marsh came to life – heart-broken cries as dim birds fleeted away; rails grunting and squealing in a reed-bed; far over the devilish yell of a vixen. 'Do come along,' said Boyle once or twice. 'We shall never get there in time.'

A little while after they had passed a patch of black quaking bog with a dead bullock in the middle, its peeling horns and part of its head showing above the mud, a brace of teal sprung from a flash of water to the right of the wall, rising fast, almost vertically. Boyle missed them right and left. He walked on, saying nothing, faster than ever; and Meagher could tell from the set of his back that he was bitterly crossed.

'Do come on,' he said again, and now the light was spreading fast from the east, showing the white carcass of a boat on the far bank of the river. 'All I ask is a couple of shots at the geese. Just one pitiful shot; and we shall not get even that at this pace.'

On, faster still: Meagher did not give a damn in hell for the geese or the prospect of shooting at them, but Boyle's failure had revived his spirits a little and he walked along with his resentment somewhat appeased. Yet at the same time the sense of unreality – this unearthly landscape, his own light-headed fatigue – grew on him: his mind wandered off to other places and times, to odd, disconnected fantasies of triumph, and when he returned to the present he found he had dropped behind. He also found that his anger was dead: weary tolerance had replaced indignation.

Boyle had left the sea-wall some way before the point where it turned right-handed, and he was making his way cautiously through the mud towards a plank that led to a dense screen of reeds. Meagher did notice a soft gabbling in the distance, but it meant nothing to him. He only saw that by going straight along the wall he would avoid the mud and come to the bridge as soon as Boyle, thus making up for lost time. He did not catch Boyle's backward signal – the flash of his hand he would have used to a dog – and he hurried along with a sudden quick softening and a resolution to ask Boyle openly for a cigarette, to accept the humiliation of doing so, to gratify him. This was to be an offering, a reconciliation, and he called out 'Boyle, I say, Boyle.' As he called he saw the furious gesture and ducked; but it was too late. There was a monstrous threshing of wings on the far side of the reeds and the geese, hundreds, even thousands of geese, lifted high out of range.

As if he were alone Boyle walked on through the screen, taking no precautions now, and he went along the edge of the turlough where the smell of geese lay heavy, looking at the droppings and feathers: after some time he emerged, much farther round the bend, and came back along the wall. Meagher ran to meet him: his apologies died in his throat at the look, not of intense dislike or anger nor even fury but of utter contempt. A frigid, objective, dismissing contempt like a blow, breaking even the most rudimentary social contract. And while Meagher was uttering the few words he could force out, Boyle's eyes wandered off, bored, uninterested: he reached for his case, opened it – it gleamed like a chalice inside – deliberately chose and lit a cigarette.

Beside them, lower than the wall itself, a huge pale-blue bird came gliding through the frozen air, shadowless over the white ground, never moving its wings: behind and a little higher came its mate, even larger, dark and forbidding. They turned their heads to look at the men but they never deviated from their course; and as they flew a silence spread over the marsh – duck and small birds had been stirring; now they were mute. Not a sound, not a movement. Meagher's sense of the world was so altered that he saw them with no surprise: in this universe huge pale sinister birds might very well pass within handsreach.

Boyle's gaze followed them, and then as he turned to go he glanced at Meagher again, noticed that he was still speaking, moved his mouth into a civil, well-bred rictus, and walked off.

Meagher walked along behind him: the distress of this look, so much more fundamental than the rough words at their setting-out, combined with the unreality of the scene, with the monstrous birds, the silence, the unbelievable final severing of their relationship and with his own state of physical wretchedness to shake him so that he hardly knew what he was at.

He walked on a mile, close at heel, the general pain separating into its various components. Rage predominated, and the extreme of humiliation – ultimate humiliation: the rage made him tremble; it knotted his throat and his stomach. The expression on his very pale face was strange to him, like a mask imposed from outside. Yet he still thought he was indulging in fantasy when he said 'But it is you are the fool, Boyle, to go out no one knows where with a man you humiliate: it is you are the fool to put a gun in his hands and turn your back on him and walk where he can push you down into the slime for ever, you whore.' And even when he had the brown gun up and quivering behind Boyle's head it still seemed only unreal show and mime, part of the abiding nightmare all round; but his finger curled on the trigger and squeezed as he cried 'Like that!' and the gun shot out an orange flame.

The unexpected bang and the recoil quite stunned him: it was not until the slow smoke cleared that he saw Boyle in the water, motionless now. Meagher slid down the wall and stood up to his knees, straddling the body and bowed as though to heave it out. Blood flowed from the shattered head, pouring and turning like smoke in the water, and through the eddies rose an enormous eel.

Silence returned: only the raucous panting of his animal breath. Then from far away on the motionless air over the bog came a sound. He looked up – the sky had turned pale – but there was nothing above him. The sound grew stronger, a rhythmic singing beat, and turning his appalled staring face still higher he saw three swans. The first light of the sun touched them from below and they flashed pure against the blue, flying straight and fast from the north with their long necks stretched out before them. The rhythm changed a little, sighing and poignant: changed still more, and as they passed high overhead their wings sang in unison, bearing his spirit away and far, far away.

21

The Passeur

———— ∞∞∞ ————

Behind the town there was a hill, behind the hill a mountain range; behind the range another range, behind that range an ancient wood, and in that wood there was a man.

The little rosy town, tight like a swarm of bees, with its roofs touching everywhere and not a foot of ground to be seen from above except in the great drum of the bull-ring, all this and the brilliant sea, the pure curve of the harbour and the row of fishing boats, has been described so often that there is nothing new to say.

The hill – the hills – behind, these too are so well known: the terraced vines, black gnarled points on a contoured, modelled chocolate pattern, a green blush, a blue-green incipient flood when they are sprayed, a full green solid mass, then gold and crimson on the hills according to the season: the olives and the pines: the gardens, flat with rigid squares wherever there are streams – the gardens with their peach trees and their apricots in the beds of green; trees like trees in samplers or on stocking legs, neat, trim, precise – these too are full of people and well known. Beyond the utmost limit of the vines, the garrigues covered with cistus and myrtle and Spanish broom, false lavender and asphodel, carpeted with thyme, dry, arid, wrecked by goats; here still there are people: the garrigues are known, known as well as the cork-oak groves that stand so nobly on the higher ground, crimson-lake when the cork has left their trunks. The trees are orderly, arranged in quincunxes and numbered in white paint:

men are there, if it is only twice in a year. Even beyond them, in the barren country, a few parched farmhouses keep their hordes of goats and walk them on the nearer mountain range: and that is not the end, for on the mountain live the cattle, belled but savage, and they wander free, bulls, cows and heifers, steers and calves, the whole crest of the nearer range is theirs, and the other side to the very edge of the unknown country.

This country starts with the second mountain range. The two are separated by a scorched and naked valley, wide and deep with sides that sheer abruptly into overhanging crags: for here the rock is granite. The harsh, crumbling micaceous schists are left behind, and with them that acid, chemical, volcanic sterility that brings to mind a slag heap, the poisoned wasteland of an industrial town. With the change of rock comes a change in vegetation; it is much richer, far more gracious. It is a country of forest trees except on the higher land where, when even the low holly and the dwarf juniper can no longer hold out against the wind, there is sweet turf like a lawn, covered with flowers. You would gasp to see them in an alpine garden, but here they are in such profusion that you cannot walk without treading on them; and then, wherever the grey and lichened rock shows through, or where the huge boulders stand uncovered, everywhere there are saxifrages crowding, cushions of delicate pink flowers, tight rows encrusting the gentle rock where they can hold a footing.

Here, in this intervening valley, there were no trees, however: the whole of it had been ravaged by a fire that burnt not only the undergrowth, the trees and every living thing that moved, but even the earth itself, searing it to the bare rock: and so it remains. The prevailing wind, the tramontane, swept over the distant ridge for all the days of the fire, and preserved the farther trees – prevented the fire from crossing the mountain. The forest reaches the top, therefore, and can be seen between the naked peaks, just overlapping into view.

The ravaged valley must be crossed: hours of break-neck scrambling and sliding down; a long traverse over the bottom; hours and hours of climbing up the other side. There is nothing but charred wood and ruin: a few blackened trees still stand, and where there is some trace of fertility left in the soil, there are blue thistles. Some wandering birds are there, that hurry through, and a few large green lizards; nothing else. But at the crest suddenly the new country shows itself and unfolds in a series of high, cut-off, unsystematic valleys, with the forest spread over all of them and running up and over all the peaks and ridges except the highest. It runs on and on, a dark green that smooths all angularities, on and away until the trees appear no larger than the smallest bushes seen from a distance; and in the end, before they are lost behind the higher mountains, they might be no more than a crop of darker grass, so uniform they are, and so united.

Once across the ridge you cannot look back and see the sea any more: it is the unknown country, and everything behind and known is cut off. There are trees before you, and on each side trees: and already you are among the first of the trees. This is the wood.

The man in the wood had crossed over the ridge that afternoon, bleeding from the thistles on his legs, striped with black where he had pushed through the rigid, scorched, dead trees, and choked with the black dust. On the ridge the trees stood wide on the turf – oak trees here – and he passed through them and down the slope, being swallowed by the wood almost before he realized that he was well in it.

He made his way down, where the oaks were thick and smaller on the steep slope, low, almost bushes, down, across the brown stream, and up again through the tall trees to the first of the downland crests, where the high timber stopped, diminished to a border of strong hollies, and those to low, neat, prickly bushes, as trim as if they had been shorn. There were little silvered junipers on the clean turf, and flowers everywhere – tiny yellow rose-shaped flowers. He had stayed up there for half an hour, standing exposed on a certain rock, and then returning he had plunged into the trees again.

He sat now on a slope above the stream, a little way inside the wood. Here it was beech wood, all beeches except for a few spindling hollies and one prodigious oak. The upper edge of the wood, with its belt of hollies and mixed lower trees was dark behind him, and in front the wood was grey.

When first he had passed through the sunlight had dappled the ground, and in the stronger light the carpet of dead brown leaves – no undergrowth, but only leaves – had shown red and umber, and a lively green had filtered through. Now the shadow of the mountainside had swept across the wood: it was light still but the night had never wholly left the wood and by the stream it gathered there again.

It was not a deep, a thick, wood, obscure or hard to penetrate: far on each side of him the grey trunks rose solemn to an unseen burst of green, but its grey silence was quadrupled by the dead trees that stood; still stood, though dead. From the hump of moss on which he sat it seemed to him that half the company was dead: it was not so, but dead trees stood on every hand. Some lay, felled by the wind, and many were there, flayed white and blackened by the lightning blast. On the ground, covering it high in some places, the branches lay, some mouldering to their last decay, some fresh, but all pale: in the living trees too there were dead branches, diseased limbs of their own or the arms of other trees which, falling, had caught and had not reached the ground, huge gaunt bones hung up in chains.

It was a wood in as natural a state as it could be, for no one had cut it, planted or touched it: it was too far, too isolated by the rocks and precipices for the charcoal burners even. But to him it looked unnatural, a wan Golgotha of a wood.

There were ancient trees that had died where they stood, and some had fallen, bringing down others: there were ancient trees that still lived, enormous slow eruptions that had been glorious but that now were three parts dead, massive limbs that towered up beyond the screen of leaves, dead and naked in the sea of green. There were very few young trees, and even those few were grey: everything was grey now, beneath the barrier of the leaves.

At the bottom of the slope, far down, a cataract in the stream sent up a continuous noise that made the silence stronger. He sat there, wondering if he would ever *hear* the trees, and he sat comfortably on his moss-buried rock, quite relaxed, leaning his head back against the broad stone, slowly drawing in fresh strength (it had been a cruel journey). His mind wandered at large; but it did not wander far, not so far that it did not return with an instant spasm when there was a sound behind him.

It was to his left, in the higher wood behind him. With his neck rigid he kept his head still; a movement is seen when stillness is not. And the sound was crossing behind him.

There are sounds made in spite of an intention to make no sound: they are not like common noises. There are small sounds made by large things, and they are different: a blackbird scuffling in dead leaves may make more noise, but it is not the same.

Now it was directly behind him: it must be nearly by the hollies, he said, with all his senses sharpened to the last degree, but strained backwards and his useless eyes unseeing. His mouth was half open, and his nostrils flared; he breathed, but very faintly.

The noise stopped. He grew more rigid, and his right hand, poised above his knee, slowly clenched to. From the first second he had known that something was in presence: now it knew; and this was the crisis now.

Then from the centre to the right, faster, and more quietly now: it was on his right side and his eyes, forced to the corner (but his head quite rigid still) pierced with all their force. The sound, now stronger, and his head jerked round; and there fleeting among the trees, the glimpse of a tall grey form, far bigger than the dog he feared.

Breathing normally again, and easy now against his rock, he closed his mouth: the tension died all over his body.

Cold: it was growing cold, and he gathered in his warmth, sitting closer, buttoned up his coat. With the creeping shadows the naked trunks stood barer still, with a light of their own under the darkening canopy.

Now he was leaning forwards, waiting actively: it was nearly time. He caught it at once, the low far whistle away on the right hand: he was half up, and across his field of view the tall grey wolf ran back through the trees, headed, fast but unhurried, almost noiseless.

The whistle again, and he answered; a clear, true whistle. A distant voice, well known, carried across on the silent air. 'Aa-oo, aa-oo,' and 'Aa-oo, aa-oo,' he answered.

Leaning on the silence he waited, and the words came clear, calling over the distance, 'Come back again, man: come back at the dark of the moon.'

22

Nicolas

⸺◦◦◦◦⸺

Before the Spanish war a woman came into this village, a fine, strong upstanding woman with her husband. They came from Spain and she was the daughter of a rich shopkeeper: she had married one of her father's workmen and her family had cast her off. It must have been a passionate family, and she must have known what its reaction would be, for she had removed all the things she valued most before the explosion. A more confiding daughter might have been thrown out into the world naked, but she and her husband ran away with three trunks and a domed hatbox.

It was difficult to see why she should have married him: he was an insignificant little pale man, perpetually worried and muddled – no particular character of any kind, nor good looks. She was nothing like that: in those days she was a handsome young woman, stocky and coarse haired, but with a lovely bloom then and magnificent eyes; and even then she had a masculine decision and force. She could have had the choice of the young men of her quarter, and she would have brought a dowry better than most, her father having only the two daughters. But whatever her reasons were, she chose Ramon, and she brought him up into France. It would be interesting to know the details of their flight, how the trunks were carried unseen (big wooden trunks like seamen's chests), how they found a priest to marry them without her parents' consent. It must have been in a church, because this was in Primo de Rivera's time, when there was no civil marriage. How did they manage for ready money, and their passports? But these details pass by unknown; they arrived here by the train and found a lodging in a house that belonged to the butcher in the rue Mailly.

They had no acquaintance here; they spoke no French, and although they came from near Valencia, where the language is not unlike the Catalan of the Roussillon, she had always spoken Spanish at home. There appeared to be no reason for their staying here and when they did, month after month, people began to say, as a cause, that Ramon was an anarchist. That did him no good among the patrons when he looked for work, and he was never able to find a settled employment. He was no good for anything that required strength or initiative and one wondered how he had earned his living before. In a village like this, which depends on fishing and vineyards, the choice of employment is small and the work is hard; hard and skilled.

Soon they began to sell the things that they had brought with them. The women noticed the absence of Pilar's gold cross, the gold cross that she wore to church: she went every Sunday at first, with a fine black dress and a mantilla pinned up on two combs at the back of her head and her good leather shoes clacking on the uneven cobbles. She went less as her pregnancy advanced, and after their son was born she went only now and then, almost furtively to the earliest Mass in the morning. Her mantilla had gone now, and the good black dress, and in common espadrilles she made no tapping over the cobbles.

They would have been much better advised to move further on, to Perpignan, where Ramon might have found steady work, because the town was full of Spaniards even then, and they stick together, employing their own people when they can. But for some reason Pilar was resolute in staying; perhaps it was some vow that she had made, or a feeling that the village would be lucky for them: it can hardly have been the beauty of the place, for she was as indifferent to that as the other inhabitants.

By the time Nicolas was born they were very much reduced. The kindness and the curiosity of their neighbours broke against her pride, her keeping-herself-to-herself; but Ramon was not like that and it was known that there was very little bread in the house. Sometimes they said that Spaniards were accustomed to living hard – 'a piece of bread spread with garlic is a regale for those people down there,' they said; and they said that everyone knew Spaniards would starve for a week to buy fine clothes and walk about on Sundays. They said that people should stay in their own countries. But there were women who felt for Pilar, and shook their heads sorrowfully when they saw her beginning to watch for the postman. He passed every day at about eleven with the box slung before him and the letters piled; and every morning after Nicolas was born Pilar was at her window by ten. But he always passed her door, and after two months Pilar stopped watching. She stopped singing, too, at that time. Before, the street had loved to hear her: all the morning, when the sun was in at their window she sang as she worked, her deep pure voice sounding through the street with no effort: she sang unconsciously, long, long flamenco songs with their strange barbaric cadences on a quarter tone. But after those days and days of long waiting she did not sing any more.

She could not feed her baby, and she did not seem to take much pleasure in him: it was lucky for Nicolas that Thérèse three doors away had a dead baby at the same time, or he would have gone as short of food as he did of maternal affection. It was not that anyone could have reproached Pilar with unkindness, or neglect. She attended to Nicolas with great care; he was always as clean as he could be kept, and his clothes in order; and she never screamed or rated at him like nine out of ten mothers do here nor dealt him those resounding slaps that alternate with great smacking kisses – the common penalty for being a child in Catalonia. It was just that she did not like him very much.

His father was devoted to him in his fond, weak fashion, and used to walk him about on his shoulder among the boats in the sun: but when the influenza came Ramon took it and died. Pilar did everything to keep him in the world – tisanes, the local healer with his mumbo-jumbo and his little ball of clay on a string, and even, at the very end, the doctor: but it was no good; he died gently in the night.

She felt it: yes, she felt his death and her loneliness, but not nearly as hard as she thought she would: her capacity for love was going, but she had this in exchange, that she did not feel the bitterness of sorrow any more.

It was after that that she found the first regular work that either of them had had since leaving Spain. It was not much – ten hours a day at the anchovy factory – but it was enough to keep them going, though it left her little of the day for her house, and less for her son.

They remembered her at the factory as a reserved, silent woman, not so much unfriendly as absent, sunk in upon herself. It was curious that she did not make herself unpopular, but she did not: her bourgeois origin and her withdrawal might have raised them against her, but for years after they spoke of her without any dislike or envy.

She aged rapidly after Ramon's death, as if it had been the parting of the last hope, and everything after it was desolation. She took to black at once, like the other women: a very ugly dress of dead black cotton stuff that drank in the light, a black piece on her head, thick black stockings and black espadrilles. At thirty-five she had the appearance of an old woman. She was still as strong as ever she had been, and a harder worker than before. She was up at dawn for the factory, and in the dusk of a long day one would meet her coming down from the mountain with a faggot of brushwood as big as her own body, high on her shoulders and held by a cruel rope across her forehead. With this load she would walk with a set, pale face down the dry river-bed, never pausing, though the sweat ran in her eyes. You would see her on the straight path down from the chapel through the olive groves, where the tramontane blew so cold all the winter long, walking steadily with this burden, overtaking one group of women after another, black twos and threes, all loaded, bent and chattering in their harsh-voiced patois. She would pass them with a brief '*Allez*', never stopping.

It was one of these great faggots that killed her in the end. She had been farther than ever for it that day, right up over the Pic Taillefer, and coming back she took a shortcut by the station. She was mazed with fatigue; her belly and back had a separate life of pain, and the rope cut so that the drumming in her ears drowned the thunder of the train.

Nicolas was sixteen by this time, a fragile, pale slip of a boy. Thérèse asked him to come into her house and kept him there for some months. She had always been kind to him: it was she who had been his foster mother at the start of his life.

But he would not stay. Thérèse's sons soon forgot to be gentle for his sorrow, and he was away. It was summer, and he slept by the boats or in the grass of the castle battlements. Thérèse fed him when she could, but in the day he was usually far away from the village.

Most people said he was simple, but they said that of anyone of their own kind who did not behave as they did. He was strange, of course, and he had been from a little boy, but if simple means stupid, he was never that. When M. Durand (who was very fond of him) was still the master at the school Nicolas had been ahead of the others in reading and writing: it was after M. Durand went and the new man came that it went badly. M. Guiton had no time for him, and when he began to stay away from school no one made any fuss.

He had been a solitary little boy, and he grew more solitary. The other children never thought he was one of them; they made game of him and he avoided them more and more, staying the day long in lost corners of the huge castle, or wandering alone in the mountains. He did this with wonderful secrecy while he was still supposed to be at school, but after his time for education was over his mother had let him go as he liked. She had spoken to the fishermen about taking him out with them, not with much hope of success, because she saw him much as they did. They were civil, but they had their own sons and nephews, and besides, there was the difficulty about his papers. She had nodded, and thought she would wait until he grew stronger in body and more ordinary. She thought that she would live forever.

Perhaps she would have made more of an effort if he had not found a piece of work for himself. It was not work as people understood it, but it was money. He carried the easel and colour box for a Swedish painter, who paid him a man's wages all the summer through. They had met in the mountains. The Swede, an enormous man, deep in fat and scarlet in the heat, was lame, short-sighted and clumsy. He was having a miserable time with his baggage as he fell and slid down a rocky ditch through the vines. He had taken it for a path – the brown bed of leaves gave it the level appearance of a path – and when he was halfway down he could go no further. For once Nicolas did not run away when he saw the man; he would have if the man had not been so obviously wretched, but this time he slid quietly up on the far side of a wall and looked at him close. The Swede was almost weeping with the heat and his unhappiness. The last fall had opened his colour box, and he was peering myopically among the knee-deep vine leaves for the little tubes and pots. A cloud of flies surrounded him, and the unremitting sun beat on his scarlet head.

They took a liking to one another after that first afternoon. The Swede was not a talking man – he spoke little French, anyway – but he was lonely, and he was pleased with the silent companionship of Nicolas. He thought the boy was beautiful, too; he admired his slim, frail body and his fine head. The villagers did not: there was something unmasculine about Nicolas. It was not that he was girlish at all, but he had thin, delicate bones and in his face there was the timidity of a wild animal, a wild but unarmoured, gentle creature.

He used to wait for the Swede at the place where the *route nationale* goes out of the village, and all through that summer they traversed the vineyards, the mountains and the pine woods. They hardly ever talked except at their midday meal. All the time the Swede painted busily, lunging at his canvas and mumbling as he stared at it with his eyes half closed. Nicolas watched him for hours and hours. He learnt to clean the brushes, and when the Swede in his agitation smeared the rocks with gouts of ultra-marine, flake white and crimson lake, Nicolas took a brush and worked the paint into patterns.

This was the beginning of his painting. The Swede did not encourage him or discourage him, but when he went away in the autumn he left him colours, brushes and several pieces of canvas-covered board.

Nicolas was a painter. The village was used to painters and had seen Matisse and his friends come down from Paris. The people liked paintings: they understood, too, that in Paris and other places a picture signed by Derain or Matisse would fetch a great deal of money, and this shed a hesitant aura of respectabil-ity over the painters as a class. For themselves they liked pictures that showed things as they were: no fisherman would tolerate bad drawing in the rigging of his boat, and no one would allow that the houses might be jumbled, or the number of the windows altered.

Nicolas provided the sort of pictures they liked: the streets were in the right order, the shutters were the right colours, the church clock would show the time, and every man could recog-nize his own boat. The queer perspective did not trouble them, and they did not notice, or overlooked, the landscape swimming on a plane that was not of this world, bathed in a strange light that was not from the sun.

They liked the pictures, and they bought them readily. They did not pay for them, of course, as if Nicolas were one of these *messieurs* from Paris. A hundred francs from the rich *vignerons* or *saleurs*; wine, baskets of fish, meals from the others, were the painter's fee. They always paid much more for the frames, but Nicolas was content, and they had the feeling of doing good at the same time. The butcher in the rue Mailly was one of his best patrons: he covered the walls of his parlour and had some paintings over for his bedroom and the shop at the cost of seven metres of boudin at different times and about half that length in *saucisse de montagne,* hard as a board and so peppery that one winked.

Thérèse sold his pictures for him when money was concerned: she was a good woman, and she bought him clothes.

They still thought him simple, but they did not make game of him any more: the boys who had been children with him were growing up, and the next generation were used to him and did not follow him in little straggling cruel bands. He still fled the village in the day, but now he had a place and a dry roof. There are three ancient towers behind the village, each on a hill, and M. Puig, whose vineyards surrounded one, let him have it – the use of it – for a large canvas with his own vines covering it from side to side.

As towers go it was a very small one, not much larger at the base than a very large tree. Formerly it had been much higher, and in the days when it was used for watching against the Barbary pirates it had possessed battlements on top: but now it was not above twelve feet high, and its ragged top showed like a broken tooth on the skyline. It had one domed room. The floor stood four or five feet above the level of the ground, and one approached the low, arched door by a series of little crescent-shaped steps, worn hollow by hundreds and hundreds of feet. There were three narrow, barred windows – very little light because of the great thickness of the wall, not enough to penetrate to the top of the domed stone ceiling: it vanished upwards.

When he was in this tower and the door closed, no one could tell whether he was there or not. The windows were too high to peer in through and the inside was too dark for anyone to see in by the holes in the door. It was paradise for Nicolas. He did not like being seen by anybody, and now he could close his door – it had enormous iron bolts that creaked into the stone holes. If he sat on the grass outside his tower he could see the whole length of the road from the village and both the paths that led into the vines: no one could approach unseen within half a mile. And from there, up on that hill, he had the whole village under him, a cup of rose-pink roofs huddled at strange angles, with vivid blue, green and orange shutters: there were the two other towers, and the shifting olive groves between. Far on his left was the Canigou, thirty, forty miles away, with snow for half the year: sometimes it was so close that he could have walked there in an afternoon, and sometimes it was not there at all. Behind were the dark mountains, Pic Taillefer and Madeloc with its tower: there were wild boars up there, and at night the smugglers passed with their silent mules, on the mountain path to Spain. The white road below him, with cars all day and lorries: beyond that the railway line and then the orange trees and cypresses. The tense arc of the bay and the illimitable sea, changed with every wind and sky. Boats from the harbour, coming in at dawn, and on the larger sea ships crawling with a plume of smoke. The fishing boats with lateen sails, and with the wind the schooners up from Spain.

At night the trains were louder: there were the high-pitched Michelines that hooted, the whistle of the local trains, and the roar and scream of the Barcelona express that swept at full speed through the station with an almighty thrust and shrieked before it plunged into the tunnel.

In 1939 the tubes of paint suddenly became more expensive, and the gendarme came to the tower to ask Nicolas for his papers. He came three times, but Nicolas never replied. He waited listening behind the door until he heard the heavy crunch of boots going away again. It was the adjoint at the *mairie* who got him in the end: he spoke to Thérèse, and Thérèse – he would always let her in – she made him come down with her.

There was a hopeless muddle about his identity. His parents had never regularized their situation; Ramon had not registered the boy's birth – he might have made some kind of declaration at the Spanish consulate, but nobody could find out. It was a strange thing to find in France, this total absence of papers, for they had not been illegal immigrants like so many of the Spaniards, and Nicolas had been to the *école communale*: but the village had had a wonderfully haphazard administration for many years, and now, continuing the tradition, they told him to go away. The adjoint stuffed the dossier at the back of a filing cabinet, together with the unused ration papers of the last war. The general impression was that Nicolas was a Spaniard – a Spaniard from the legal point of view.

The war was over so soon that they did not have time to worry about him again until it was all over.

He painted in those days; more than ever before. Paints had gone, and canvas too, but he had the paint that the fishermen used for their boats, and he used cardboard or pieces of three-ply. He was going his own road toward – toward what? He knew his own aims, and one can divine them, but it is hardly possible to explain. It would be an exaggeration to say that he became abstract, but his paintings became more and more simple, the forms existed for themselves alone; but above all the early quality of remoteness grew more and more pronounced until it pervaded all his pictures. They were flooded with light, always; he was pre-occupied by that; but it was as if they were lit by the light of the moon – yet not the moon with its indefinite, rather commonplace mystery; another light, as searching and as powerful as the sun, but not the sun. He had begun with an astonishing technical competence (it had frightened the Swede) but now he was leaving behind him everything facile; his work was growing harder, very much harder.

There was little food in those days: everybody knows that. But Nicolas had always lived on the edge of nothing, and the trains still ran and the white triangular sails still came in with the nets at dawn, and in the still night the lamparos gleamed at sea, strung like a necklace on the horizon.

Then the Germans came. They came in lorries in the autumn of '42. There were grey troops everywhere: you could not walk here; you could not walk there. Wire, guns, regulations.

They were the *mairie*: there were no young men left in the *mairie*. The adjoint was in Germany; the secretary too, and the mayor had died at Haye-les-Dunes. There was forced labour in Germany, the STO, and they caught René Delmas on the frontier as he was running from it: they had dogs. François Batlle and Pau Roig, Jean-Baptiste Maillol; they got Roger Pous at the Col d'en Jourda. Thérèse's son Michel, they got him: and the

Spanish guards turned back young Olive, even from Espolla, far over the frontier. Gypsies: they could not have gypsies and wanderers. They caught two in the woods of the Massane.

In the *mairie* they had all the papers straight, in order, regular. Everything was in order. But they worried about Nicolas. He had no papers.

For days and days a heavy, old, grey German pushed his bicycle up to Nicolas's tower; but Nicolas never answered to his call and knock.

Now, hard after the others, there were the black Germans in the village, the ones with shiny boots and high-peaked caps. They were sharp, much quicker: there was nothing to say to them.

News goes fast in the village; it went even faster then, and Thérèse heard that they had gone five minutes after they had left, three of the black Germans, and a little sleek crouching Frenchman with them.

She ran by the quick way, past the graveyard and through the cypresses and the orange trees where the fruit still glowed through the leaves. But she was old now, and slow, and when she reached the tower the door was open, open and swinging, lurching on one hinge, broken and swinging and the sun was on the empty floor of the tower.

Hans Brueckner on the Edge of the Sea

Four hundred times, and never twice the same: he had looked at the sea four hundred times, four hundred days in the morning, and each day it was different from the day before, from any of the days before.

In November, when first they had arrived, tearing down in packet lorries from Orleans, it had been the Mediterranean that he had expected, the quiet, tideless sea, blue past imagination and bathed in the light of the sun. Perhaps after the first weeks of excitement he had been secretly disappointed in the Mediterranean: it was too cold to swim with pleasure, although most of them did bathe, shouting and splashing on the beach reserved for the Germans; and the hard, dusty, sandless pebble beach was disagreeable, uncomfortable and wrong. Then there was the lack of rock pools – no tide, no pools – and only a strong and regular tide could have made the filthy habits of the villagers tolerable: they had drains, they had a proper collection of their garbage, but they made use of neither. Nowhere on the rocks could you go without some disgusting encounter, no hidden corner without its buzz of flies.

But he came to know it better: its apparent sameness was rudely broken by the winter storms, the sudden, violent storms that struck with no warning and threw the towering waves high on the castle wall; and ever after he had seen its unending variety, the nacreous days when the surface was lost and confounded with the light, the blazing noon of high summer when the milk-warm sea took on its deepest colour and the nights when the lapping waves shone with phosphorescence and every pebble glowed, when the bottom of the sea blinked with a thousand eyes, and when he could see his hands tearing flames of white fire in the black water as he swam. The calm days when the sea had meandering lanes, and the cloudless days of wind, the white horses on the blue.

He had come to know it better, but he had hardly loved it before today. Today it was a grey sea; grey, grey and immeasurably old. And on the sea the sea mist; at half a mile from the shore they joined: you could not tell which was sea and which was mist. Both grey, drained of all living colour. There was no living thing on the sea; no birds, no breath of wind, although the swathes of mist moved slowly. No waves, but a great quiet swell, and the curved water rose and fell. Quite silently: nothing but a measured sigh to make the silence more profound. From where he sat he saw a black rock, a savage point six feet above the surface; and then it vanished and the faint oily swirl was all to show that it had been there; no white, no trace of foam. And so it reappeared, quietly, with an inevitable steady thrust, black and sharp against the grey.

Behind him the low clouds had blotted out the mountains; only the low hills still showed, and with their new background their shapes were changed, new lines and a new significance. The clouds were still descending, spilling over from Spain through the passes, and on his right hand the high castle on Pic Naou stood half covered, with its central tower already lost.

The low and covered sky brought down the height above him, and the mist had drawn in the ring of the horizon; but still the world seemed larger. The silence, the knowledge of more sea unseen and mountains high beyond the hills; the world ran out beyond its bounds.

It was not sombre; nothing black or sombre. Not threatening at all: impartial, grave and silent, never ending; death's own image. The sea was death's own image.

Out there, beyond the mist, beyond the wall of mist, there was more sea. Grey and the same, with the same high, even swell: and there the whole horizon would be mist.

Hans Brueckner undressed slowly. He put the heel of his boots in a crack of the rock and drew them off. They stood, paired, by the neat square of folded clothes.

It was not cold. Awkwardly over the hard and jagged rock to the edge, and then cautiously because of the spiny urchins to the place where the deep sea came sheer up to a gulley in the rock. He balanced himself for a moment on his two hands over the water, waiting for the swell to rise to him, and then as it reached the height he let himself in, slid in with no sound.

The cold caught his breath, stiffened him for a second, and his head sank under, but he went clear of the rocks with the retreating swell and as his face rose he was swimming strongly and rising on the next swell.

For a hundred yards he swam without pausing, straight out with a long, easy stroke. The water was no longer cold. How wonderfully buoyant it was, after the Baltic; he could swim forever. When he turned on his back for the first time he looked behind him; he had only swum a disappointingly short way. He had expected the shore to have sunk in the mist already, but it was there as clear as if there had been no mist. The long jetty with the light on the end of it was still high enough above him to block out his view of the town, but he could see the fort behind the town and the gun emplacements on the cliff; and as he lifted on the swell he could see the top of the church tower rising above the jetty.

He turned again after ten minutes' swimming, and now there was haze between him and the town. It was all visible, perfectly visible, but softened and uncoloured. The jetty had sunk to its due proportion and now he could see the whole town in one sweep, the town and the faubourg; the long, straggling faubourg with its flat-faced houses, yellow, blue and faded rose with brilliant shutters, the colours all sun-baked and harmonized, but all dead and pale today; and the town tight-packed inside its wall, crowded on the in-curved hillside, a mass of pink roofs running up to the square bulk of Vauban's fort. In front of the faubourg the pure curve of shore, empty now; not a single boat was there. And between the town and the faubourg the huge grey pile of the castle, the Templars' castle, plunging straight down into the sea. An enormous mass of stone, a town in itself, with houses built inside its courts and pink roofs showing above the severe, high-sweeping curtain wall.

Then behind the town, its frame, the lower hills, all corrugated with the contour lines of vine; but fading now. The high Pic Naou had almost gone; the ghostly castle showed and went, and showed again. That was the place where they had taken the Belgians, just there in the olive grove behind the castle.

That memory had forced its way into his unwilling mind. He stayed for a moment, digesting it; looked once more at the town, the high strange clock tower and the walls, the house where he was quartered: all silent, motionless; no people. He turned in the water and faced the sea. The contrast surprised him; the land, the town, the faubourg and the hills had been so still and dead. But the quiet grey sea, with no lines, no sign that any living thing had ever been upon it, was utterly remote from the land, unrelated to the living world: not dead, but death itself. Its huge simplicity, how soothing and how lovely.

He was swimming far into it, on and on.

He swam quite slowly now; long and steady, practised strokes, untiring and unconscious. He was a good swimmer and once his body had the rhythm of the stroke he could go on a long time, without rest or thought. His mind was free, but it turned vaguely, with no clear subject, no ordered sequence until suddenly, as if from outside, his inner voice said, 'What are you doing?' With a sharp insistence it said, 'What are you really doing? Are you playing with suicide again, or are you at a real decision now?'

He hardly knew what to reply. His mind had been as grey and misty as the sea when he had started. He had not been in any great pain of spirit; indeed, he had been almost happy, with the beauty of the sea: there was no crisis of decision; he had slipped in almost without thinking about it, as if he had been moving half asleep.

'Yes,' said the voice, 'but a reason must be given: there must be a clear decision soon. Is this your playing with despair or is it not? Another bout of histrionics, spiritual masturbation? Or is this something honest for once?'

Hans Brueckner tried to find the true answer: he tried so hard, but where was his integrity? Everything was doubtful, coloured; and he had so often lied.

Three things were certain, and perhaps a fourth.

The war: he was not frightened for himself so much. The ultimate disaster was his side's defeat, and he saw its unmentionable shape in Italy and Russia and over Germany, everywhere; a blackness flickering all round the horizon. Whatever he might say at times he was identified with his own people: he was a German and a piece of Germany. To see his country go down in black ruin, bombed, smashed and overrun; the real, the German world undone –

Then for himself, for the Germans here, strung out along the coast, what would be defeat for them? There were so few of them, holding down a huge stretch of country, and so many French. There were the marquisards behind, all along the mountains to the Pays Basque, hundreds of them, and their numbers growing every day. The people in the village knew: you could see it in their faces; their talk was different, and their hate was stronger.

That hatred, how it had worn him down. All the time it was there, disguised quite often, the false smiles in the cafés and shops, the civil compliments on his French, but just as clear as the cold unwinking hostile stare of the fishermen, the older sailors who had fought before. That honest loathing and its counterpart, collaboration – co-operation praised by all official means. 'We build the new order together, side by side, shoulder to shoulder, our old enmity forgotten: soldiers in the same cause, we march to the light of a new dawn.' Perhaps there had been a time when he had believed in the new order strongly enough to have swallowed that. But, dear God, what a crew they were, these Miliciens, these

PPF, these RNP, in their comic-opera uniforms. It made you want to hold your breath when they came into the room, so as not to breathe the air that they had used. And the unctious civilians at the Préfecture, so supple and obliging. And the informers; every shape and size – anonymous, disinterested zeal, the preface to a favour asked – all sorts, and every day. How he despised them, how deeply; from the very bottom of his heart he despised them. Yet he had to work with them; he had to use them. He would so much rather have been a fighting soldier – he would have volunteered for the Eastern Front, anything, but he was pinned there in counter-intelligence, pinned by his almost perfect French and his fluent Catalan, and pinned by his thick-headed chief, who had just sense enough to know that he could not do without him.

If it had not been for that wretched decision to study the romance languages; if only he had specialized in a dead dialect instead of Catalan he might have been a plain, unworried soldier – or worried, at any rate, by straightforward enemies, bombs and shells.

But these little vicious Dagoes – you saw them at their best in bands of ten or more – these wretched pathological misfits, they were the reaction against the nation's loathing, the negative extreme of what was represented by the maquis. By them he could judge the depth of the hatred of the land: and how contemptible they were, and how abhorred. They did the things that made Schultz and Mueller flinch.

That hatred, oh it was unjust for him. He had been correct, more than correct, much more, and always. In the house where he was quartered he had shared his rations with the family, the old schoolmaster and his wife and daughter; he had been considerate and friendly from the beginning, but he had never really pierced below the wall of hatred. Even now, when long use had made him something like an ordinary member of the household, he knew that if it came to the point old Delmas would give him up to the nearest maquisard with joy in his heart: and that in spite of all he had done for them. He had smoothed their difficulties with the Kommandatur, he had practically told them that their nephew Joséph was going to be taken, and had said – not in so many words, but unmistakably – when the patrol on the Spanish frontier would be withdrawn to smarten up for the general's inspection. He had done that, and he had listened to the old man's tales of the time when he was a soldier, a French soldier occupying the Ruhr. He had known from the first that Delmas was a Communist, and he had assured his chief that the old man was harmless. Night after night he had heard the muffled do-do-do-doom of the B.B.C., and he had done nothing about it – indeed, he had listened himself after a while.

But more than all that, much more, he had loved Renée from the day he had first seen her, and he had never done a single thing to offend her. Even when he was drunk and burning afire he had never laid a hand on her. He had put up with her scorn and her cold hatred of his uniform. He had talked for hours about the real culture of his people, the inevitable disguising excesses of war, the basic friendship of Germany for France, the German admiration of French writing, painting, everything: it made no difference.

Everybody knew about his passion: Schultz laughed at him every day. 'Why don't you have the old man in for questioning?' he said, 'Or the girl and have it done out of hand?' Of course he could have done that: he had only to say one word and it was done.

He could have had any number of girls, and he never had one, so as not to offend her. They were there, plenty of them. Women whose men were away in Germany: they were poor, he was rich – that was all there was to it. There was no food on this coast, now that all the fishing boats were dragged up to the Place and chained there, and a boom stretched across the harbour mouth. Not that that was the sole reason: there were volunteer whores just as there were Miliciens, from that bitch-in-heat at the château to the half-wit girl at the patisserie who had poxed half the gunners of the artillery detachment before she died in abortion that winter.

No, it was wrong to say that it had made no difference. She had grown more tolerant. She had listened when old Delmas and he talked about Communism, and she had even come to talking to him herself, of her own accord. Progress until yesterday, and then finish. All over. She did the washing: he had asked her to wash his shirt.

That was after they had taken the Belgians in the olive grove, the two Belgians and their *passeur*. He had been called in to help with the *passeur*, who pretended not to speak French, only Catalan. Well, that was a bad afternoon. His chief was there, and Schultz and Mueller. No Miliciens, thank God, but still it was a bad afternoon. But was it so bad? In real honesty now, was it so bad? Of course he always hated the summons, but when it was all in train, wasn't there something? When Mueller was not there, with his bawling and screaming, nor any dirty little Dago swine whom he despised, before whom he could not indulge himself at all, and whose actions raised a dumb, hating protest in him, then, when it was all like that, was there no beastly, sickened joy in it all?

It was worse if you admired them: there were Communists who had passed through the office – hard, hard men, with not a word to say. There is a wonderful beauty in suffering.

If only he had been posted farther from the frontier the work would have been different, but here all the time there were people trying to escape to Spain. Escaped prisoners of war, young men on the run from forced labour, Frenchmen on their way to North Africa or England, airmen, English agents; they all came down to be smuggled over by these frontier peasants.

This *passeur* had been tough, too. He had not been in it for the money, like some; and he had other people to cover.

But it was the act of a fool, a fool, a fool to give her that shirt to wash. It was easy enough to do it yourself under a cold tap.

A little splash of water filled his mouth and interrupted his stroke. He was in the mist now: he rose in the water and looked all round, like a seal. Yes, it was what he had hoped; he had passed the door into the whole grey world. Sea, and the dome of mist. No hint of anything beyond; the two grey things forever, and the everlasting swell, and silence.

He found that he was getting cold, his stomach shivering as if he had not eaten for a long while. He broke into a rapid crawl, tearing through the sea until his breath came short and the cold was gone; then he turned again to a steady, rhythmic side-stroke, lying on the sea before each push, curling his head down to it as it made a pillow for him. The regular, profound, unnatural, trained breathing of a swimmer helped him to think.

His mind was back: the fourth point now. It was natural enough for a boy in the Hitlerjugend to lose his religious faith; that happened often enough, even with the Catholics. And for a young man at the university, with the sort of background he had, and his set of friends, it was easy enough to lose faith in the mystical side of National Socialism: you could do that and carry on with ordinary life without losing your integrity. The concealment, the necessity for deception, was damaging, but the core could remain. The more you had believed, of course, the more it hurt; and the more you tried to stave off disbelief the more your integrity might suffer, especially if you padded the blow by shifty compromise – picking out bits and pieces to believe in, like the obscene loathsomeness of the Jews, and the holy mission of the German race.

A sudden cramp seized him in the stomach; he doubled up and choked. It passed in a minute as he rubbed his muscles straight, but after it he lay floating on his back for a long time, relaxed and staring up. This was even more pure than the sea, more nearly absolute, the low, domed vagueness and nothing to be seen, no solid thing to touch; to float there, no weight, no hard thing, no lines. But the cold was coming back, and he must swim.

It was the association with the cramp that brought it into his mind, the sight that he had seen in Puig Oriole the week before. The straggling village, low houses on each side of the broad, empty *route nationale*, and down the middle a young man walking, his pale face with the dirt showing strangely, no expression on it, but terror and exhaustion showing in his whole body; walking stiffly between two Alsatians, big, mean-faced bitches. His trouser legs were torn to ribbons, and through the rags the wounds, a hanging strip of flesh. There was no man behind him. No need: the dogs would take him straight to the post. If he ran, or if he turned aside for a moment, they would kill him.

The young man – a boy – walking, staring before him, walking down the village street, and the people watching him from the doorways, silent.

Well, if you are guarding a frontier, it is as logical to stop a man with a dog as with a bullet or a stretch of wire. If he is to be taken to the post, it makes no difference who takes him there. To say 'You do not hunt a man with dogs' is sentimental clap-trap, if on the other hand you allow him to be hunted by a machine.

Collective responsibility: that was another phrase. He was *not* responsible, in any degree, for that young man walking between the dogs: he had protested against it with all the force of his character, although the emotion was illogical. No; he had not done anything. What could he have done?

But to go back: it is usual enough to lose faith. No one can be blamed for that. Dozens of the men he knew were no more nominal Christians, and dozens were no more truly Fascist now than they had been before Hitler. But what if you caught a new faith? What if you were spiritually and intellectually convinced of the truth of Communism and would not admit it? Or would admit it only to do nothing about it?

Those long talks with Delmas: had he not been driven from one position and another? The old man was clever, highly literate, but more than all he was burning with sincerity. He had an unassailable conviction, and he could explain his reasons for it. With him there was nothing that could not be questioned, and nothing that did not lead his way. It was no good bombarding him with the imperfections of the practice: he would admit them all and return to the principle, the basic theory, the one and only thing that mattered. He had used the English phrase 'Clear your mind of cant.'

And like the embodiment of his words there were the Communists they took. Hard men, hard and dedicated. Put them against the pimps in uniform, the Milliciens or the PPF, and what could you think?

But was the whole world wrong? Were Jews and Russians saints? Now he was tiring: he was shivering all over with a big convulsive tremor that started in the pit of his stomach and spread. His jaw quivered each time he opened his mouth to draw breath.

Three times, four times, he had overcome his resistance to the idea. Were not the relapses, the allegedly intellectual non-acceptance only the rationalization of his cowardice? What was he to believe of himself? Where would self-deception end? One skin peeled off after another – was there anything inside?

If it really was so, that he believed, then if he had some truth left in him he must act. That was clear: there was no possibility of a silent, passive acquiescence, 'I believe' and that is all. But was he made of that heroic stuff? And what good would it do? What could he do? And what would be the use? In five minutes he would be walking down the road to the post between two gaunt dogs. Hans Brueckner walking rigidly along the narrow path that the dogs judged right, all the miles to Buchenwald.

And all that for something that perhaps he did not really believe all the time.

This belief, was it a reaction against his desire to be safe? Oh he had thrashed it over and over and it was no good now, and he was glad, so glad to his soul for the sea.

24

The Lemon

A man who lives alone grows strange: and I have been solitary now, how long? Some years at least.

It is the peace he has, the room to develop. Most people are bound to observances; the clock if they are employed, the routine of a life in all events; but a man alone can live to himself, lie three days abed, work through the night, sit motionless for hours, think in the way he likes. He grows unlike the others; for a man must think to grow, and thought is a slow process, a cumulative thing that grows: you must not check it. But meals, visitors, and hot and cold, set hours, do check it. They dissipate the cloud, the haze inside which your mind can turn. The solitary man grows strange; but it is the strangeness of an adult among children.

It must be the right kind of man, of course. It is not every man who can live by himself: two of the other painters here are mad. With old Dupont it is probably a question of senility, no more; but Laforge is mad directly. He goes by with a quick shuffle, just not breaking into a run, and there is such a look of concentrated unhappiness on his face that if it were not so annoying you would be desperately sorry for him – providing you thought there was still a 'him' alive behind that closed-in, wretched face. The people in the street turn after him and stare. They make the usual gesture, and although they have seen him for a long time now they watch him avidly to find him worse. Presently they will shut him up, no doubt.

In madness, I understand, there is nearly always this misery:

not quite always, but certainly very often in the kind of solitary madness that I am thinking of. There is always – and this is the vital distinction – a loss of objectivity.

They also lose (a consequence, I think) whatever sense of humour they ever had. And that I do possess, as strong as it was when I was a child, to whom so very many things are funny, even the sound of words. The last time I had dinner with the Lemaîtres, Marie said that someone or other had a sponge factory, and the words themselves were so absurd – not the meaning, the words intrinsically – that they made me laugh and laugh and laugh, although I did not want to. I did not want to hurt Marie (I do not know her well, nor yet Lemaître) and it was not an explicable joke, *fabrique d'éponges*. It depended on the *i*, long and high, and the round *ponges*, and the particular air of solemnity. But I could not stop, though I turned my eyes away from their ludicrous wondering faces, faintly displeased behind their polite smiles: I swallowed a mouthful of scalding soup, dropped my napkin: but it was no good, the tears came into my eyes, and when the *fou rire* gained the others and they began to giggle too, I burst out and gasped and gasped until I was nearly sick and could not breathe. We said *fabrique d'éponges* and howled: sometimes we could say no more than *fab* ... It wrecked the dinner: but my God I laughed.

However, that is only a minor point: the essential is the insight, objectivity. I have watched a clock for hours, the wonderful peace of the pendulum's swing, and I have seen it swing left and right, left and pause, back across the nadir, rise and pause. And stop. Stop poised up on the right until I have let it go, to swing and tick, swing and tock. But all the time I have known just what it was, that my mind was spinning free and time was not. No loss of insight there.

And I have looked at my naked feet, bony and long on a chair before me, and I have seen the stigmata form, and from each crimson wound a rose.

Yes, I know that road: I am quite clear there. That is not what can do you any harm, nor make you unhappy. On the contrary,

I should say, all things summed up, that I was a very happy man. I was less so when I still roved after women, when that hunger and excitement drove me out; when a dark warm evening came and I was restless, could not settle until I had defined my need. But that was long ago. I have had all the common girls here, and some others too; Thérèse and Rose, Conchita and that Denise who made me ill. The fair one – Marie-Claire? Denise again? I never could recall her name. But since the fire went out, I have been happy, in my way.

Yet so much hangs on what you mean by that. A calm euphoria, an isolation: that is what I mean. A burrowing in, deep, deep down until you reach a kind of peace glowing inside a haze.

Sometimes it will not work; something goes astray. This morning it was like that. I was reading, and between the paragraphs the associations piled up, so that I was thinking on two or three separate levels; that is normal enough; every man does it who talks, and at the same time thinks of what he is going to say next, and at the same time bears in mind that he must not stay more than five minutes because he has an appointment, and at the same time sees a creature flying and says in some inner compartment, 'That is a wasp: it might sting.' It is normal, and with practice it can be developed.

As I say, I was following out these associations, and that usually settles down to a line of wordless thought which goes on while I read and after I have stopped, reaching, in the end, my happiness far down.

But this morning, the associations grew and multiplied; they were obstructive, unmanageable, and I became confused. Generally they act as planes, planes that dissolve, one behind the other, like my painting: though that is an inaccuracy, because like the sheets of colour in my work, they are not *behind* one another – that is not the relation at all. They are *different* planes; but I will not dwell on this.

This time there were two other features, both quite familiar, but now they were out of place. The first was that the whole thing was a game, a pretence that I could stop at any minute.

The whole thing, my sitting there, my being in that room, my existence indeed; that was a game. This feeling I have known for years and years, and sometimes I think it first arose from some dishonesty, from some insincerity and forcing of emotion. When I was a very young fellow I played at being in love, saying the words, making the gestures, while my heart pumped blood hard through my veins and real tears blurred my vision; but all the time I had a faint (not always so faint) glimpse of myself from a viewpoint generally in a corner of the room and I would say something more or less satirical – my corner-self would say it internally. Later, a good deal later, when I finally abandoned figurative painting, I worried about the honesty of my work, and I believe the worry, the question at all, was a proof that somewhere I was cheated, worked myself into an attitude where the self standing in the corner could rightly smirk and say, 'Oh behold the new-born Braque.'

There was more to it than that; much more, but these partial causes are very remote now. The important thing is that at times the feeling is very strong (it hardly ever leaves me entirely) and then my surroundings seem so impalpable, such a hollow pretence, that it makes me if not unhappy, at least confused. Ordinarily it is not unpleasant, rather the reverse: one can pretend to be going for a walk, to be talking in a friendly, sociable manner, to be living very cheerfully – it simplifies daily life very much. No: what I have said might have been the cause was not the cause at all. The two pretences are quite distinct, different in nature. The first was dishonesty; the second is not – it is a feeling that the illusion is slipping away.

The second thing that spoiled my reading and its consequences was a sense of having been there before. The words had a vexing half-familiarity, though it was a new book: now and then a whole phrase would be entirely known and (what was more troubling) my own reflection on the known phrase would come out pat like a sentence learned by heart. I knew what I was going to read, what I was going to say on discovering that I knew it, and my own rejoinder to that second discovery: and so on, seven deep.

My own comfortable, favourable mist or haze was now a fog. I no longer felt that at the worst I had only to stop pretending, stop playing this private game, to stop existing. I was getting lost, losing control: and to reassert the discipline of my mind I deliberately read a page of the book. That did very little. I got up and washed my hands and face.

I was sorry now that my cat had gone: I had had an affection for that distant creature although I knew it was a descent into emotion; and now I was sorry that the cat was not in the studio. I would have opened it a tin of fish if it had been there, and doing that would have been valuable.

I looked at the painting that I had up on the easel and I began to work on it mechanically. Soon I had spoiled the canvas, and I let my hand draw criss-cross lines.

The base and cause of the wretched state of my mind, I found, was a sort of dream that I had had in the night. It was about my neighbours.

They were good neighbours, below, in front and on each side. They were often very kind to me – took in parcels, told me the news of the quarter when we met, and when my cat was still here they were kind to her, too; gave her milk. I do not think they approved of my girls, but that was long ago, and I had always been very quiet, even then. They were working people, kind, sensible, tolerant. Good people, my neighbours: all except the man and woman who kept the restaurant on the ground floor. They were a bad couple; the man a flashy, smarmy-haired little pompous rat; the woman a short-legged, hard-faced shrew of about forty. I went there at first because I thought it would save trouble, and they gave me an omelette with a cockroach in it. They drank heavily, quarrelled and screamed until dawn sometimes. Their place was frequented by their friends and by foreigners on the spree, and they bawled and sang and shrieked above the blaring radio until four or five in the morning. The man was odiously ingratiating: the woman too: she had a high screaming laugh, more truly metallic than I have ever heard from a human throat. She could let it rip at will, and she did whenever anybody else laughed. It was quite false: she had never really laughed in her life except at a puppy drowning.

They had a waitress whom they did not pay: she made her living from tips and by whoring with the customers. All the sporting men of the place went there after her and you could hear them out-manning one another in deep voices and whooping cachinnation. She was a big wench, fairly pretty, crammed with high spirits. I would have had nothing against her at all, if she had not sung: but she did sing, every morning until lunch-time, while she cleaned the restaurant. She sang very loudly, very affectedly – she was being the quaint pretty girl scrubbing floors and not minding it, I believe – and on one note only. It was a false note, and the damned songs she sang penetrated windows, shutters, floors, everything.

There they were, a pretty crew; and the man had one trick that irritated me more than all the rest. He had an ugly little sign-board hanging on the wall, pointing to his restaurant, and every time he passed it he would set it straight. The gesture, indicating ownership, importance, the right to touch, was so automatic that he would do it without even looking to see whether the sign were straight or not. Sometimes he would go out, touch it without looking, and come back. I could have borne anything but that.

To return to this kind of dream of which I have spoken. They were making more noise last night than usual. I wondered whether my neighbours in front would get angry enough to throw a bottle: they did sometimes when the din had been intolerable for many hours past midnight. I felt angry for them: they and all the people around were working families who got up early. Many and many a time have I seen them come out, cross and bleary, robbed of their sleep and robbed of their full day's power by the screaming hooligans below. As time went on I grew angrier on my own account.

Then I was thinking in my chair for a long while. In separated waves the noise pierced through, but when I got up to find my bomb I was no longer angry. I was far within myself, but I recalled my anger, for myself and for those other people, and I examined it: it was very red, emotional and raw: roughly triangular.

My bomb was one of the small kind that we used to call a *citron*. I do not know its technical description, but it was a hand grenade, shaped like a lemon. I had kept one, because I liked its form. I found it in my box of different shapes, kicked off my slippers and went quietly downstairs. As I went down the shrieks and laughter increased. In the lobby inside the front door (it is always open except in the winter) there are the fuse-boxes for the whole house. I drew the white porcelain bridge that controlled the restaurant's electricity, and as their lights went out I heard the huge, anticipated shriek and the waitress's unbridled scream as one of the men grabbed her in the dark.

The electricity is always breaking down in this street, and everyone has candles ready. I waited a moment until I saw the dim glow reflected, and then I went into the street. In the darkness outside the open restaurant door I stood and looked in: the girl was out of the room; the rest were gabbling about a second candle. They were all drunk. The woman let out a burst of her cackle and I drew the pin. It was, I remembered, a seven-second fuse, so I counted five before lobbing it in. It was remarkable that the people looked at the bomb as it landed, and not towards the place it came from, as I had expected.

It went off with a great orange flower of light that blossomed momentarily in the whole street. I pushed back the electric fuse and went silently upstairs, pursued by the familiar smell of dust.

There was no possibility of detection. All the neighbours would be at their windows, not looking down the stairs.

Now the thing that worries me about all this was the moral aspect. The withdrawal of the fuse was an act of lunatic cunning that would never have occurred to me as myself. I do not think that I even knew which was the right box. But the fact that I did withdraw it is terribly significant: at some time in my journey downstairs my play, my pretence of being a man – and hence my control – must have merged into a sense of reality and uncontrol.

This train of thought must have started in the morning before

I sat down with my book, it must have started unconsciously when I looked down into the street and saw a mess of plate glass still heaped in the gutter and the people staring: and it must have been that that wrecked my reading, a deep, well-founded distrust of that single element in the dream – dream or physical reality, it does not matter which.

The essence of the matter is that the action of withdrawing the fuse was the action of a psychopath. And the consequences are bad. I do not mean the bodily consequences: detection is impossible. No; the consequences of an action that one recognizes as undoubtedly psychotic are that one must take measures against the possibility of a repetition: if once the lapse is established, to go on living would be criminal in an honest man.

And it is so soon established: one question is enough. 'Did you draw that porcelain bridge that holds the wire, and did you leave it so that you could push it back in the dark?' If the answer is yes, you must then say 'You did not know where the fuse box was: you know almost nothing about electricity. But your unconscious mind had noted the place and the function of the bridge; long ago, perhaps. It formed an intention, against the time when it could take over control. The intent was criminal. The thing that formed it must be cut off. The only moral issue now before you is the recognition of this fact.'

25

A Journey to Cannes

———∞∞∞———

Louis Durand had been kind to Kandinsky from the day they had first met in Paris, twenty years ago. At that time Durand had already finished with the Beaux Arts and lived in his studio waiting for his first exhibition, which would establish him, once and for all, as a new, significant force in painting. He had many admirers among the students and one of them had brought Kandinsky to see him. Kandinsky was very young, full of admiration for the wonders of Paris, but he was not very happy. At Julien's and the Grande Chaumière they made a fool of him : his abilities were slight, little more than a schoolboy's talent, and they called him a *pompier.* They made fun of his name, and as he had little or no physical courage they played cruel practical jokes on him. He appeared to be one of those timid people designed from birth to be a victim, and although he was studiously inoffensive he found oppressors at every turn. The notorious wealth of his family made him an easy mark: he was damned as a bourgeois from the beginning, and his elaborate easel, his array of brushes and colours excited anger and derision. When it was found that he would neither end money nor pay for more entertainment than he received he was universally condemned, and even those who might have hung on to him in the hope of eventual benefits turned against him.

He was introduced to Durand a little while before this pitiful avarice was discovered: the man who brought him thought that he would be doing Durand a good turn – it was a sincere gesture of friendship.

Kandinsky was deeply impressed by the pictures that Durand showed him, flatteringly impressed; and although he praised awkwardly Durand felt the genuine appreciation that came through Kandinsky's timid, self-conscious phrases. They were striking pictures. At that time Durand was working continuously, hours and hours every day while the light lasted; he was in the high flood of his youth, a he had no doubt of himself. He had great technical ability; his work was clear, sharp and underivative. There was nothing immature in it, and in those days he had, like a good demon at his elbow, a voice that told him when a picture was finished.

If people found that his pictures, with their brilliant planes of pure colour and their soaring geometrical forms, looked better in the shapeless disorder of a dirty studio than ever they did in a gallery or framed on a civilized wall, they did not tell him so then: nor did anyone say that the first effect of his pictures was the greatest; that the second, third, and fourth times one saw them their force appeared less and less, until after a few months they seemed to have little more significance than decorative pieces of colour on the wall. Nobody suggested that his theories required a far greater intellectual basis than he possessed to be convincing for long: nobody said that the ideas of cosmic equivalence, so exciting then, would appear old-fashioned to the next generation. Nobody said those things then, even when Durand was out of the room; and even in his deepest moods of depression Durand never thought them to himself.

However, it is pleasant to be admired, even when one is sure of oneself, and Durand was pleased with the fervour of Kandinsky's admiration. He felt a curious, protective affection for the little man, and when at their third or fourth meeting Kandinsky confided to him that his family kept him strictly to a small allowance – would buy him anything, rent him the best studio in Paris, pay for any amount of teaching and material, but would not part with a hundred francs over and above the stated monthly sum – even then, when it was apparent that he could not possibly buy a picture: Durand continued his friendship, asked him to the studio, showed him his new work, gave him a *gouache* from time to time, and helped him to paint a little better. Yes: he had been kind to Kandinsky; he had felt a real affection for him.

But all that was long ago, long ago. Kandinsky's father had died – that was before Munich – and Kandinsky had turned to the management of the family concerns. He had been away for a long time, in America, England, all over the place: the Kandinsky uncles and cousins had seen the swift development of his hereditary abilities, but Durand, when they met again, had been utterly disconcerted by the change in his disciple. Kandinsky had burst upon him with all the new strength of his character, the profound confidence of a man who not only has an account with a bank, but owns the bank itself.

Kandinsky was still the admiring, faithful Kandinsky of Montparnasse: he still thought that he considered painting the most important thing in the world; but Durand knew better. He astonished and wounded Kandinsky by the violence of his invective against the bourgeoisie: he said some very cruel things. He said that if Kandinsky had ever been able to paint better than the last of the *pompiers*, his conduct would have been worse than that of Judas; but that as it was, it was no more than a commonplace reversion to type.

He was very angry. It was not that he was jealous of Kandinsky's money, his huge hôtel in the rue Masseran, his château in the Dordogne or his streamlined Hispano-Suiza: he was bitterly resentful of the escape of the little man whom he had patronized. He was aware of the escape long before Kandinsky realized it, and he precipitated the realization by his outcry against it. The escape was a challenge to his values and to himself as a person: the ugliness and violence of his reaction frightened him; he had not thought of himself as a possessive friend, and he could not account for the pain that made him lash out so hard.

After a little while he refused to sell Kandinsky any more of his pictures: just before the war he could afford himself that luxury. It said a great deal for the sweetness of Kandinsky's character that this sop to Durand's pride was enough, and they were able to continue friends afterwards. It was a disconnected friendship, interrupted by the huge desert of the war, but they still wrote to one another, and now, in the dirty little third class carriage, Durand was travelling slowly through the arid hills of the Languedoc to visit Kandinsky in his villa by the sea.

On the rack over his head there was a portfolio filled with *gouaches*, and below them the awkward parcel of his four latest canvasses. He was going to let Kandinsky buy what he liked.

He was much older now, he said, and that old piece of vanity belonged to the past. The last time he and Kandinsky had met – that was three years ago, or nearly four – they had talked about their boyhood, in a comfortable, reminiscent way, and Durand had laughed at his dramatic damnation of all rich men.

For a long time Durand had examined this little monument to his own integrity; now that his youth was so far behind the monument stood out in a strange isolation. Its existence was illogical from the first, but it had taken Durand years to convince himself, by reason and logic, that the time had come for its disappearance. When you have gone through twenty years of crawling flat on your belly to a mob of greasy tradesmen you cannot sensibly maintain a romantic attitude like that. No monuments.

The last five years had been harder than all the rest: difficulties with the galleries, the misery of fawning for a little more publicity, the terrible increase in the cost of living, canvasses, colours, brushes, all beyond measure. Durand's being had crystallized early, as a young man; he did not change easily, and for him a hundred francs still seemed to mean what a thousand meant now.

You could not say that he was an unsuccessful painter: far from that. He had known a hundred times more success than all but a very few of his contemporaries. People knew his name in Paris, London and New York; knew it well. They would say 'That is rather like a Durand in the treatment of the colour, is it not?' Half a dozen important galleries and museums had pictures of his, and he would be mentioned with approval in any future history of French painting.

But they admired more than they bought: and there were

people who said that he was repeating himself. They said that he was doing the same old trick over and over again. They said that there had been no real development in his painting for the last ten, fifteen years – that no development was possible, that he was up a blind alley. They said that he was very clever, of course, and that he handled paint beautifully. He had met with a good deal of official approval – welcome, but disturbing; he knew that it must set the young men against him, and one day he heard a group of them referring to him as a waning painter. That was like a harpy, always with him: it worried him far more than the discreet failure of his last two exhibitions.

Then there was the unending series of ignoble shifts for money: it had been almost amusing and an adventure when he was young, but of late years it had grown more and more wearisome, disgusting. Drumming up attendance for an exhibition, the personal invitations, the little dirty arrangements with the newspapers, the urbane agony of the *vernissage*, the backscratching – oh he was sick of it. And sick to death of the tradesmen, the galleries run by bandits, cheats, reptiles camels. And sick of not daring to let his prices down for fear of frightening the snobs who respect only the ticket. And sick of opening the papers – the *Figaro* civil, but obviously disappointed; the *Monde*, polite in three lines while giving a paragraph to that charlatan from Paraguay; the – offensively gushing (that had cost two hundred copies paid for in advance and two quarter-page advertisements); *Les Arts*, still respectful, still not liking to condemn; but how different from ten years ago.

Money was so much more necessary now: a succession of unsatisfactory women – they cost money now, instead of being the companions, the breadwinners even, of former days. And adult tastes. If once you have got into the train of eating well, living like a creature of this century instead of like a caricature of Murger, the garret and the *choucroute garnie* lose their glamour. A bathroom, it becomes a necessity; you have to pay for it, and a painter, even a fairly well-known painter, is in a helpless position when it comes to making money. Everything depends on public opinion, on a few people who know and on a crowd of snobs. You cannot go out into the streets and scream: it would do no good; they would not believe you. But it is no good waiting until you are dead if you want the money now – the bandits, the bandits, the reptiles, the art dealers, that is what they wait for. They wait until a man is dead and cannot produce any more; then their property is safe and the prices go up: you cannot suddenly flood their market once you are dead. So you must circumvent them, you must have the right friends, the contacts among the rich industrials; you must be able to dress reasonably well, go to good restaurants, appear at the Biennale at Venice, meet the rich ones, be nice to them, entrap them, show them your studio, go through your paces, and when there is the awkward pause because they do not like to ask the price, you must carry it off so that there will not be a hideous embarrassment.

You might think that it would come easier with practice, easier with the years: but it does not. Still, in the end you become well broken to that side of a painter's life, more than broken, and although it galls it is really quite pointless to leave the very best contact in your life on one side, like something sacred. One is not, after all, a fetish-worshipper. No. So in the end you make a long, exhausting journey in a third-class carriage, accompanied by your personal harpy, with a bundle of *gouaches* dutifully tied up on the rack overhead, and the awkward parcel of canvasses under them.

A sudden icy doubt shot into Durand's mind. Suppose he does not like them? It was a long time since he had seen Kandinsky, and they had not written much in these last years. It was twelve months since Kandinsky's last note – a queer, uncommunicative scrawl – and it suddenly appeared to him that for a long time now Kandinsky had been going farther and farther from him, growing secretive, withdrawing by a conscious desire. He would have read the criticisms in the papers, of course, and Kandinsky knew enough to interpret them. But any painter might go out of fashion for a few years, for twenty years even: that did not signify. To a man who could really see what was in the work, who had followed its development with the closest interest, it meant nothing, the fluctuation of public opinion – contemporary opinion.

Kandinsky was not, never could have been, a painter of any sort of distinction, but he did understand painting: he appreciated it as very few could appreciate it. No: that was a silly suggestion.

But, he said to himself, if there had been any truth in it, if it could possibly appear for one moment that Kandinsky did not love the pictures, rejoice in them, he should not have one, no, not if he offered millions. Durand swore it, vehemently, again and again.

Outside the station the big car was waiting for him, but Durand sent it off with his baggage: he said he would walk up. He found a barber's shop and had a shave: since he had stopped being young he had discovered that he felt at a disadvantage unshaved. The rest in the chair and the hot towels refreshed him; he walked up to the villa much more cheerful, and as he reached the big garden the anticipation of his welcome, an excited, happy feeling, made him hurry. They were looking out for him, and the door opened as he reached the steps.

The butler was pleased to see him, hoped that his voyage had not been too tiring: M. Kandinsky was in the drawing room. The drawing-room door opened: Kandinsky stood in the white frame of it, and a woman behind him. With a quick solicitude Durand noticed that Kandinsky was bowed and old. The poor old fellow is ill, he said, and aloud, 'Edouard, my old Edouard, how are you?'

Kandinsky held out his hand, smiling. 'Well, Louis?' he said, 'How glad I am –'

He was smiling, very happily; but his head was not quite turned to Durand advancing up the white hall. Two yards, one yard apart, they were together; but still Kandinsky did not grasp Durand's outstretched hand. He did not take it for one second, two seconds; he did not take it until the woman, secretary, nurse, came from behind and guided his wavering hand into Durand's.

26

The Tunnel at the Frontier

———— ⊗⊗⊗ ————

Looking up he saw the sea at the end of the tunnel, the line of the horizon sharp, dividing the round mouth. On the sea, brilliant light, and a boat with a man in it, doing something with a net over the edge. Outside the tunnel the world was blazing with a white glare, but inside he could hardly see: there was a dull, sweating concrete path, and the walls curved, arching overhead.

What the devil was the sea doing at the end of that tunnel? The *sea*? From that he asked himself What tunnel? and he paused, walked slower, coming up from the abstraction into which he had sunk. The tunnel must have been familiar, or he would not have wondered about the sea. Did he usually walk along it the other way?

He recalled getting off the train, with a crowd of other people, their noise as they hurried through the tunnel with their feet echoing and flapping. They had hurried intently past him, although at first he had gone fast, imitating them. Now they had all gone and alone he went slowly: lagging still in his ear was the sound of the last people, their resonant feet before they left the tunnel to him.

It was like waking up from a strong dream, one so strong that for minutes you lie on the borders of the dream and reality and wonder which is which. But it did not clear: there at the end of the tunnel was the sea, stretched tight, the flood of sunlit air, and all enclosed by the mouth of the tube, a round patch of another world, infinitely remote, and unreal – not so much distance (though the tunnel was still long before him) as on another plane.

Slowly he went now, very slowly, his feet going of themselves. His mind was still heavy, turning slowly. It had been warm in the train: and everybody had got out.

There were books under his arm; it was cramped with carrying them. He had been reading a book in the train, wedged in the blind corner by the corridor: people were standing all the way; he had not been able to see out. He must have been reading a long time before he went off into this meditation. The book had been about a man – he moved his hand to look at the book's title, but it was much too dark in the tunnel. It had been about a man who had loved a woman and had married her, and they had lived very happily, part of one another for years and years, and she had died. She had been killed in the war: or had she died? Was he confusing it again?

She had died. That was why he was so unhappy, because he had felt for this man and woman in the book, and he had caught the desperate, everlasting sorrow of the man, the dreadful unhappiness that was with him all the time and when he woke in the morning instead of a real life this man awoke to a silent blank, an emptiness that filled instantly with the realization, fresh each morning after the interval of sleep, and the sorrow welling blotted out each fresh day. This man had no comfort, because he did not believe in a future life; no hope, and he could not be a coward now and cheat and alter the order of his mind. He lived in the same house and all day her things were round him: there was nothing in his life that they had not done together.

He had never liked other people much; they were so imperfect and dull by the side of her. But in a hateful world, with war and the threat of war every day at every turn, and tyranny, misery and oppression and grinding poverty of the spirit, he had been happy: and he was lost now, alone in it. Job had been blasted: but Job had a God. This man was quite alone. He had only his virtue and his courage, and his virtue and his courage were ebbing fast away.

They had been very poor, and the dreadful details had piled on him. When there is a body in your bed, do you lie with it or stretch out on the floor; when the body is the corpse of your love, I mean? He could not do what they had always said they would do: she was buried roughly by officials, casual, hard, inimical municipal employees, and his hate for them had kept him alive for days and days. But it sagged, flagged away, and he had to simulate the motions of rage to feel it at the last.

That was the book. That was the book: it had made him so unhappy.

He stopped dead, and the sound of his feet echoed as he stood still, staring at the sea, far sea. That was the book? Irresolutely he put his free hand to his eyes, wavered. That was the *book*?

He turned his back to the light and hurried back into the gloom, faster and faster, his feet alone and hurrying, faster until the echoes were confounded into the one dull noise of his flight.

27

Lying in the Sun

With his face cradled in the soft bend of his arm he could see nothing: but the strong glare of the sun filtered through the crook of his elbow and through his closed eyelids, filling his head with a red light. Behind him, or rather beyond his feet since he was lying on a beach, there was the faint and intermittent murmur of the sea, very small waves that curled and hissed a few inches up the pebbled shore. Above him and all round on every side the dome of the sky pressed down, hemming in and confining this world of brilliant light; there was no room for any air to move and even the sea was flattened by the weight of the day.

Some of the other people on the beach, however, were not conscious of the weight. They bathed, splashing, and ran about with cries; beyond his right shoulder, ten yards farther up the slope, a family of French women under parasols untiringly discussed their concierge, two or three of them talking at once. From time to time they shrieked orders to their children not to go too far, not to wet themselves, to keep their heads covered, and out of the medley of sound the children shouted back.

But the French voices pierced through indistinctly from a very distant world, remote in every way; and the only sound that he heard and accepted was the lapping of the sea.

If he were to raise his head a little and turn it he would be able to breathe more easily; but then the light would change to yellow, and he did not want that. He preferred the dim red, and he nuzzled his face a little deeper into his arms; the redness surged and for a time it was branched through and through with orange streaks. It settled, and he sank farther into his isolation.

This was like swimming in a tide of blood, he thought; or not so much swimming as having one's being in it. This would be the life of a foetus, bathed in dark redness and safe; the only sound in its world would be the throb of the blood, like the waves that he heard now, weak and faint but always there and always prevailing against the irrelevant shouts, the crunch of feet on pebbles, the women gabbling, the ice-cream seller's raucous voice, the thrum of the diving board and the splash of the divers. Those sounds were all so faint, dream-like and unreal; they did not impinge upon his inner world at all, so long as he kept his head right down. So long as he kept his head down he was safe; his limits were drawn in to the sound of the waves in his ears; the ball of red light in his head, and the feel of his forearm across the bridge of his nose – his world was contained by these three things, and it did not extend even to his body, sprawling there on the stones and slowly roasting under the sun.

But it was such a feeble refuge. He was so vulnerable in it, and he had no defence except pertinacity against such things as the gravel sprayed by running children. The children, the voices, the madly yapping, scurrying dog, they were all able to break in; yet he could defend himself to some extent – against those there was the barrier of numb remoteness and self-removal. The far more dangerous enemy, the enemy against whom he had no defence at all, lay just there on his left.

If he were to stretch out his hand, and not to the full stretch either but only half a foot, he would touch her side. Her right shoulder, probably, for she had turned over some time ago to 'do her front'.

She had only to move, to say, 'Darling, you aren't burning, are you?' to smash straight in. She possessed that power, was entitled to it, and several times already she had used it; once she had asked him to oil her back, once she had said that it was getting hot, and another time, having seen a French couple publicly embracing a little way along the beach, she had thought it would be fun and very 'Continental' to imitate them.

But it was a long time now since she had moved or spoken. She was taking her sunbathing very seriously; as she said, they had so few days left now that unless they wanted to go home without a tan they should spend every hour they could upon the beach.

The time was short indeed. She had prolonged it twice already in spite of protests from her home; but for all that there would be little time now for lying in the sun. They had arrived at the hotel within a day of each other, in the same storm of wind and driven rain. This had been going on, said the despondent guests, since Tuesday; on Friday, when he arrived, it had never seemed likely to stop, and on Saturday, when the girl came dripping from the station, it appeared to be set to foul for ever. The people of the town said that there would be no grapes at all that year – mildew in the vines and the cold rain-bearing wind blowing perpetually from the sea.

The rain poured from the gutters of the roof. Cactuses and palms glistened in the wet; the pomegranate flowers lay beaten in the mud. The hotel was not designed for indoor life; it was meant for sleeping in and eating meals. There was no sitting room and in the bedrooms the hard wooden chairs were shaped for holding bags and clothes. The inhabitants of the town, amazed by this weather (although they had it nearly every year), clustered in the cafés with their friends and stared at the racing sky or repaired their wine barrels and their fishing gear; but for the people in the hotel there was nothing to do at all. Those who spoke French joined together in sudden intimacy and talked with strange, compulsive freedom of their affairs, but these two spoke no French and obviously they were thrown one upon the other; and he, from idleness, boredom, and a feeling that it was 'the thing to do', had seduced her.

That is to say, he had adopted a gallant attitude, and very quickly he had been hurried by circumstances, by an untimely consideration for her feelings (for she was as serious as she was plain), by moral cowardice and by the utter impossibility of getting away,

into making declarations that he did not mean and into doing –
doing, that was the inescapable fact – that which he had only the
faintest desire to do.

If only the rain had stopped one day earlier . . . the recollection
of that unhappy, intensely self-conscious grappling made him
sweat, and echoing in his head there came her words, 'When we
are married, darling, we will read psychology together.' The echo
exactly reproduced the mincing refinement of her voice, and the
curiously artificial sound of 'darling'.

She knew all about psychology; she had 'done' psychology. She
was a schoolmistress. She wore spectacles. She was what they
called 'one of the quiet ones', and her convulsive ardours daunted
him. She went a queer, mad colour when she was moved; a whiteness appeared about her nose and her lips went blue; it seemed
that her heart was weak. She was awkward and superficially timid;
but she had an astonishingly high opinion of her own abilities and
she would recount, with satisfaction, the names of the diplomas
that she had won; she was also persuaded that men found her
irresistibly attractive and she said that she found travelling alone
a great trial because of their attentions.

If only she would go away he would be quite fond of her; he
would indeed, and he would do all he possibly could to be agreeable by post. But she would not go away. Not in this life. He would
have to kill her to make her go away. If he were to reach out now
he would feel her there, and if he were to look sideways he would
see her, fixed there and immovable.

He would see her round and satisfied face, her somewhat
positive expression fixed by years of her calling into a didactic
rightness that would nevertheless melt into a tender leer when
she saw him looking – a tenderness that would appear intolerably simpering and affected to his hostile eye. Or worse, an
arch coquetry, a privy beam of concupiscence. At all events, he
would see this red and peeling face with its cardboard nose-guard
against the sun and he would either smirk back at it or commit a
horrible brutality; her confidence was spectacular enough, but it
was so insecurely based.

Above the face he would see the bright cotton square – 'Real peasant-craft, with such a merry, sincere mood . . . don't you *feel* it, darling?' – and below it the long, thick expanse of body, somehow improperly exposed in a bathing-dress, not deformed in any way yet giving the impression of indecency; then the short, powerful legs, close-shaven and terminating in espadrilles made by 'such a simple, friendly peasant-body – so direct and uncomplicated – at one with the sea, the sun and the vineyards'. Those dreadful, carefully enunciated phrases, how easily they came tripping out and how complacently. 'Oh darling,' she had said when he had given her the monstrous little coral and cameo heart-shaped gawd, 'What a definitely *genuine* mood it has – and the lovely, lovely symbolism of the piece of coral – (solemnly) darling, what a wonderful person you are.' Then archly, winsomely, 'And is it really all for poor me, he, he?' And solemnly again, 'I will keep it for ever. It must have been made by some little sunny artisan who loved it. Wherever did you find it?'

He had found it under the paper that lined the cupboard by his bed, and Heaven only knew what uses it had served before; he had felt ashamed the moment he had given it, uneasy, irritated, and ashamed; it was so tawdry and her enthusiasm was so silly, and yet when she said, 'I will keep it for ever' there was so much true and human feeling rising painfully through all the nonsense that it had stabbed his conscience hard.

If only she would go away . . . But she would never go away. And if he looked sideways she would be there, holding her brooch, her damned 'for ever' brooch.

Yet perhaps if he looked sideways, if he looked sideways in point of fact he would not see the change he imagined; there would be no hurried rearrangement of the features into a romantic shape. Nor, if he reached out his hand, would he feel an answering reaction from her flesh. For nearly an hour ago her heart had given an odd triple beat and had then stopped. She had felt a confused exaltation which she had supposed to be a part of her radiant nervous state, something between sleep and dreaming, and she had never heard the guttural murmur that her dying throat had whispered out. Her right arm and leg had contracted momentarily, almost touching him; but they had relaxed at once.

Her body now lay under the sun much as it had done before. Her mouth gaped a little more than usual and her eyes were staring wide behind her sunglasses. If he looked at her closely he would see the blueness of her lips, but he was familiar with that and it would not strike him; he would also be deceived by the oil and the tan that she had already acquired – by the oil particularly because it gave a superficial gleam and because in places it had caught the dust (this tideless beach was very dusty) and that made the skin look inhuman anyhow.

And if he touched her he might still suppose her to be asleep. She was not rigid yet; and the sun still gave her warmth.

But cradled in his red dark secret world he did neither of these things. Although he knew that by now his back must be burning he lay there motionless, retracted and curled up.

The metallic voices of the large family to the right were now discussing lunch; they were calling the children with threats. There was a noise of furling parasols and the grind of their retreating steps at last. Now the chief sound in the forefront of the general, though diminished, clamour was a long stream of words in some Scandinavian language, all delivered at the same high, even pitch – a young man reading to his mother from a book.

From time to time all this seeped in, together with the sound of leaving feet, the long, sad whistle of the train far off – that must be the big express – and oddments of sound like the splashing of a stone or an isolated cry.

He went far, far down into his retreat, but all the time there was a part of his mind that was recording the noises by the sea and when he came near to the surface again he was in possession of two facts. One was that the beach was nearly empty now; the other, that she had not moved for such a very long while that she too must be burning in the sun.

She would certainly move quite soon. She would think he was asleep; she would pat him, and in a deliberately musical voice she would cry, 'Billy! Wake up darling!' She called him Billy, or Billy-boy; and his name was Hugh.

Yet on the other hand, if he raised his head and himself dispelled his safety, she could not break in. There would be nothing to break into. He began to count; he would reach a thousand slowly.

Away down the beach there was a grating sound as the rich people with the villa across the bay launched their boat – the grating and then the hiss as it took the sea. It was a huge silence after that.

At seven hundred and thirty-two he stopped, stopped instantly and flushed. His counting flew to the winds and he found that he was tingling all over with anticipation. Quite deliberately he raised his head, holding his breath and already straining his eyes round under his closed eyelids. He felt the crinkling of the burnt skin on his neck and then an intolerably brilliant flood of light blinded his opening eyes; they were distorted from his long pressing on them and all he could see as he peered so intently was a dark shadow by his side.

The long beach stretched away on either hand. There was nothing alive but a solitary gull, immobile at the farther end; in the dead stillness the sea was flatter still, and only once a single ripple made the faintest sighing on the stones.

He did not look again until his view was clear. There was nothing at his side. With a violent emotion that he could not define he saw that there was nothing, nothing but his own shadow and the hollow where she had lain, and in the hollow the cameo and coral brooch surrounded by a little heart of stones.

He leant over it, observed mechanically that it was flecked with salt, and furtively he picked up his clothes. With a bowed head he hurried silently across the burning shingle to the road; he was aware of no emotion clear in words, but as he reached the steps he realized with horror that his face was streaming with tears, and that as they fell upon the stone they dried there in little rounds.

28

The Path

—⊗⊗⊗—

I forget now why I went down the track alone: but I did, and Mary and my sister, the Franciscan nun, were to follow me in half an hour.

It was a poor little brown track, nothing more than foot-worn, which was surprising for so important a frontier. The frontier itself was one of those noble, striking barriers between one country and another; a high, long mountain up whose farther side we had toiled, insect-small and hardly moving in the vastness of the landscape, all the morning. Then there was the top with a breathing of new air coming over it, a new sky, and stretching indefinitely below, another world, vague and indeterminate in the haze so far below, stretching away forever.

In this middle state we could look back to see where the cities in the plain stood one behind the other, each with its pall of smoke, and from them every now and then a gleam of light flashing back from the glass of a moving car. But we were not much concerned with what we had left: it was what was to come that absorbed our whole attention. And yet I went on alone: I cannot think why; but no doubt we thought it best at that time. We said that we would meet again in the town. We none of us knew the town, and it appears now to be a hare-brained arrangement – so many opportunities for confusion, missing one another.

The path, as I have said, was a narrow track, winding and easy to lose at first on the bare mountainside, so very strange and foreign, so very unlike the farther slope. I had not expected this at all. However, I was too much occupied with the little, immediate details of our journey to take in more than the general impression of it, and now I have only a confused recollection of brownness, a warm and naked descent over a rolling mountainside, immense on either hand.

We had not been able to see the customshouse from up there, nor the town below, because of the fold of the mountain, but I had no doubt of the way. Though perhaps it is not exact to say that I had no doubt, because I was fortified and reassured when in a little while the path led between two embanked walls – obviously a road, constructed at one time with great labour, but never finished or carried up to the frontier itself.

I was carrying the pack, as I should have said before: and because the distance to the customshouse was not very great I had not troubled to swing it on to my galled back again; I carried it in my arms, like a baby. It was very inconvenient; it had always been too heavy – in all the upward climb it had grown heavier – and now it hampered me intolerably. I continually shifted my grip, but nothing would do: it would not rest easy, and when I came in sight of the customshouse and saw that they were closing I cursed the wretched burden, cursed it with all my heart.

By the time I reached the building all the doors were shut but one, a little side door probably meant for officials. I went through it without much hope, but nobody appeared to notice me and inside there was a scene of great activity. It was a very large shed with people in every direction, and I stood undecided for a time, not knowing what to do or where to go. Quite near me, on my left, was a kiosk, not unlike a paybox. It stood isolated there on the floor of the shed, and it drew my attention.

There was a priest in the kiosk, a big, pink-faced man with barely room to sort his forms and papers. I was in such a hurry of spirits that it hardly seemed extraordinary to see him there, nor was it very strange that at the sight of my passport he should speak to me in English. A part of the reason for my confusion and trouble of mind was that I had stupidly brought the other two passports with me instead of leaving them with my wife and my sister: I had been worrying about the necessity for explanations and the difficulty of them, and I was in a miserable state of indecision. He was so very helpful and unofficial that before we had exchanged half a dozen words I had shifted the whole problem on to him. He did not appear to find that there was any difficulty at all. As he turned the pages of the passports he said, looking at my sister's face, that he had often seen her; not in the flesh, he added, but in the papers – which, considering the universal spreading of the church, is not astonishing. I was astonished, however, and gratified as well: I felt that I was the better received for it, and that I myself had a certain reflected glory, not without material advantage in so clerical a country.

It was a pity, for the friendliness left his tone. He assured me that he would look after them when they came through, and towards them his voice was cordial: but for me he was no more than polite, and when I took my heavy pack to the inspectors I felt him looking after me.

Now the confusion again and the hurry: I must pass over this, and the bad revelations of my pack, so exactly rifled, turned inside out by expert searchers. (They were perfectly correct, always civil – I could not complain – and everyone was searched.) All that my head cannot recall precisely now: indeed, I must quite soon have lost the sequence of happenings and the thread – it was all so very important, and because I was so conscious of it I foundered in a welter of explanation, doubt, uncertainty – worry and confusion that did not clear (and will not clear now, at this great interval of time) until I was free on the mountain again.

From that time on, or rather from that *place* on, I have everything straight. It has been, after all, plain enough, uncomplicated.

There is this path, brown in an uncoloured world of hills: it is halfway up the side, running straight, never rising much or falling. It is trodden into the side of the hill and it winds continually as it follows the swell and curve of the mountain.

She started before me along this path, and I hurry to catch her up. It is easy walking, neither hot nor cold, and I go with long strides, fast and pursuing. I shall never catch her: I know that. I shall never catch her, however much I hurry – and I do hurry, press on hard without a moment's slackening of the strongest continual effort; and I go fast, for all the weight of my pack.

I shall never catch her: but I have this, that I am on the ground that she has travelled. The 'never catching', that is less important now: we are divided by the distance, but the path is our connection; and I shall never let the distance grow.

29

A Minor Operation

In Saint-André an English couple lived in the old town, down by the harbour. They were called Charlotte and Laurence Smith, and he earned his living by designing Christmas cards. She helped in the lean seasons by teaching English to the daughters of the tradesmen, who usually paid in kind: this was more convenient in the end, because it took away the sting of a money transaction, and since the shopkeepers had their goods at trade prices and were accustomed to dealing in large quantities, they gave her more than ever she could have bought with the money. But indeed, all the people there that they met appeared free-handed and kindly: they had not been there three months before the fisherman's wife in the house over the way began to bring papers of fish; and in season all the fruits of the country came up their stairs.

'There,' they would say. 'Profit by it. There are too many peaches in the garden this year.'

The Smiths made the return to the best of their ability. They burnt black in the vendanges, and they helped with the cherries: but still the balance was heavily against them.

They were a quiet, retiring pair, and it was difficult to see why they should have been so well-liked in Saint-André, among people who could be, and were, so hard to their own. It was partly their dog that made them so many friends: this was a terrier, Toby, an affectionate, well-mannered dog they had brought with them from Cornwall. They loved it dearly; so much indeed that at times they would reproach themselves for giving such affection to an animal – the transferred, disproportionate love of a maiden lady, they said, with some earnestness.

But it was not the dog wholly: there was something curiously charming about this young couple – though 'couple' is hardly the word, for they were virgins; virgins from principle, mystic and practical.

This state was less onerous for them than for others, perhaps, because of their low diet; but hard or easy, they kept to it. They had determined on it first from semi-religious, semi-aesthetic reasons, and in time these imprecise and emotional causes had been reinforced by the plain and worldly consideration of children. There were times in the spring when Laurence would have changed this, but he fought down the occasional beast, and they continued to cling to their status. An anomalous state, perhaps, but it had a strange, unearthly integrity, and it may explain some part of their charm. There was some thing there that was more than an artificially prolonged, desiccated childishness; they had a purity that was not mawkish (though it may have verged upon it) and in Charlotte the untouched, unawakened freshness had not passed.

When they had lived in Saint-André for some time Laurence's right hand began to hurt him. An almost imperceptible knob had appeared on his wrist, and now it increased: every week it was larger, and at last it began to contract the muscles of his hand when he worked and at night it would grow numb while he slept.

Being poor, they delayed the operation for a long time and would have delayed it longer but that an unexpected sum of money, unmortgaged, outside their budget altogether, came by the post in the morning, and Charlotte said, 'You must have your hand done at once.'

The doctor was calm, business-like. With no hesitation he repelled the half-implied question about cancer. 'No,' he said, 'this is just a little cyst.' He pressed confidently upon the boss, wriggled it. 'Does that hurt?' he asked.

'No, it does not hurt. Only the rest of my hand feels strange

– either dead or strained; and I was afraid – my hand is my living, you know,' Laurence said with an apologetic laugh.

'Yes. Quite so. Of course, you have let it grow too large, and now there is a certain amount of pressure. However, it is a very simple little operation – you want it removed, I take it?'

'Oh yes,' he said, faintly. The words 'operation' and 'remove' were so disagreeable to Laurence that he would have temporized, asked whether there was any danger in leaving it alone, whether exercises might not in time – but he was still so pleased at having his spectre banished that he said Oh yes, though faintly.

'It is hardly worth going into the clinic for it,' said the doctor. 'I have to go to see my brother-in-law about another patient this afternoon. He will have it out in a minute, and I can drive you back.'

When he reached home he told Charlotte that he would be going into the town with the doctor that afternoon: he spoke very casually – it was nothing of importance, he said in an offhand voice, but it would be just as well to have it seen to. He succeeded so well in dissembling his anxiety that in the end her calmness provoked him a little. He felt that although it was a sudden affair, unbrooded-upon, and although he had insisted that it was quite trivial, still it was almost unfeeling to be so easy about it, and to dismiss him without any flutter at all. At lunch, in spite of himself, he let drop a few ominous words, and he had the reward of seeing Charlotte turn pale and her eyes fill with tears. He repented of his triumph at once, and until it was time for him to go he laboured to reassure her. He was not nearly so successful as he had been in the first place, and although she was cheerful enough when they parted, he saw her, when he turned at the bottom of the stairs, with her face turned toward him, looking wan and doubtful.

It was a silent ride in the car. The doctor had to stop at half a dozen houses on the way, and anything like a connected conversation was impossible. Laurence was glad; he felt pensive and unwilling to talk: it was not that he was afraid – he was perfectly willing to go through with it – but the feeling that something disagreeable lay ahead made him low in his spirits.

The surgeon was a big man, authoritative and affable. He had an efficient, unpretentious manner that Laurence found comforting: he gave a cursory inspection to Laurence's wrist, said that it was only a little cyst and that he would 'whip it out directly'. 'You want it removed, of course?' he said, changing his jacket for a white overall. Even if he had been far more timid than he was, Laurence could not say no, not now, having been driven there in the doctor's car: but his yes brought the wall of immediacy so close that he could touch it with his hand.

It was oddly informal: Laurence sat on a stool by the little enamelled operating couch; the surgeon was at the far end among the sterilizers, making a clatter of instruments; Dr. Fabre stood in the open door between the consulting room and the surgery. The brothers-in-law were talking about Dr. Fabre's new house, and Fabre, from the kindly motive of including Laurence in the conversation, told him how many rooms there were, and how tedious the move would be. Both the medical men had shed that hieratic, pompous carapace which they usually presented to their patients, and Laurence found, with gratitude, that their chat did in fact divert his mind from the preparation of the implements.

'Would you like to lie down on the couch?' said the surgeon, who was now filing the neck of an ampoule.

'Just as you wish,' replied Laurence who until this time had sat with his bared arm on the table. 'I'm afraid you will find me a great coward with the injection.'

'Oh, it's nothing,' said the surgeon.

'What is it?' asked Dr Fabre.

'Stovocaine,' said the surgeon, advancing with a tray.

Laurence was glad to be lying down: he could not see, and now at all costs he did not want to see, the things on the tray.

The surgeon was swabbing his wrist with ether: immediacy was right next to him now, touching his hand.

He retreated as far as he could into himself, and listened to the animated talk about removers' estimates. There was a pause as the surgeon filled his syringe. He said 'Relax your arm,' in a professional voice, and suddenly, with unexpected force, he sent the needle home. There was the unnatural swelling pressure as he forced the liquid in; then the withdrawal.

'There. Not so bad, was it?'

'No indeed,' said Laurence, contriving to smile.

In the long pause that followed he made an observation about surgery in the days before anaesthetics.

The next needle passed through numb flesh, and after a while the surgeon set himself to begin. 'You are very nervous, aren't you?' he said, quite kindly.

'I'm afraid I am. It's foolish –'

'Just relax. You won't feel anything at all: nothing, I assure you, except the pressure.'

The tinkle of the instruments in the tray, and then the weight of the surgeon working: it was true, he felt nothing but the pressure. But what a pressure. It was growing and growing – so much greater than anything he had expected: as if the man were trying in a brutish fashion to drive through the bone and gristle of his wrist. And he could hear so horribly well. His hearing was unnaturally acute now, and now all his perception was in his ears. He could keep his body relaxed, his face without expression, submitting; but he could not command his ears, and they listened with feverish intensity.

He was sure that the surgeon was rooting, grubbing with a pair of blunt-nosed scissors, forcing and rooting. Laurence's face was cold with sweat, and he heard his own breath coming fast, faster; deep involuntary breaths that sounded like waves in his nose and throat.

'I must not be sick,' he said. 'I must *not* be sick.'

The darkness was flickering all round the patch of distempered wall that he had fixed with his eyes, a patch of wall with an old nail-hole on which he could concentrate. In and in: the darkness drove in and in around the nail-hole. He could still hear his breath, but it was coming from another body at his side: and far away the sound of another piece of steel, and the pressure renewed.

Now there was only the nail-hole visible. The darkness jagged round the edge of the circle: could he keep it there?

Dr Fabre was patting his cheek. Even before he opened his eyes Laurence was conscious of the position: he had fainted like a green girl.

'I'm so sorry,' he said, loudly, and he raised his head to the beaker of rum that Dr Fabre was holding to his mouth. The surgeon was still sitting there: it had been the briefest moment, Laurence thought.

The rum traced a fiery path down to his stomach, and stayed there, burning. He choked with the next sip, but he felt his forces reviving, gathering with enormous speed. He thought of making his excuses again – talking to show that he was quite well now; but on reflection he said nothing. 'It would be best to keep quiet about it,' he said.

'All right?' asked the surgeon, setting to him again.

Laurence was much more relaxed now. 'Perhaps it was my heart,' he thought. 'I ought to have told him about my heart. It would look so silly now.'

God above, what force that man must have in his hands. Or did the anaesthetic exaggerate the feeling of pressure? Now there was a hard, grinding sound, a sound that came into the middle of his head, and again he felt his breathing change. The darkness was coming again.

'I think he's going,' said the voice at his head.

'No, I'm all right,' said Laurence.

'Breathe deeply,' said the surgeon, still bent over the incision.

He did breathe deeply; but still the darkness gathered. He closed his eyes, but it was still there, flickering all round the circle. He must keep it back. The operation would be over in a minute; it could not last much longer. He must keep it back: he would keep it back. But he could not. It swept in; and the blackness filled his head.

He was still there. He could hear nothing, but he was still there, and time raced through his mind like a black ribbon. It raced faster and faster, so fast that he could no longer fix his attention on it: it was spinning so fast that he was giddy, and he felt his perception of it grow fainter.

It was still there, racing at an inconceivable speed, but dim, far down: then it was gone.

The surgeon raised his drawn face to Fabre. 'His heart was in a shocking state,' he said.

Fabre was grey and old now. 'Shall we try strychnine again?' he said. The surgeon nodded. 'Just ring through to the hospital and say I will be delayed,' he said.

It was stifling hot in the little room. They both had their coats off. The sterilizers were boiling furiously, unchecked, and the windows were covered with steam: in tacit agreement they had closed both the doors, and now the air was thick, unbreathable, heavy with the fumes of ether.

A long time after they unbent, straightened, and their rising showed the ugly, gaping wound below his heart. The surgeon switched off the powerful operating lamp and swept the pile of instruments into a tray.

'I shall have to go to the hospital all the same,' he said. 'There are three urgent cases.'

'I shall have to tell his wife,' said Dr Fabre.

They covered it with the surgeon's overall and went away. They should not have left it.

They had been gone two minutes, three minutes. The heavy front door banged behind them and Laurence, or rather 'Laurence', got up. He sat for a moment on the edge of the metal table, looking round the room, and then with a galvanic activity huddled on his scattered clothes. His shirt – they had cut his shirt open – hung slack on either side of him. It did not conceal the open, grey and blue unbleeding wound. Furiously he thrust his arms into his coat, ripping the lining: tie and collar he threw to the corner.

In the street be hurried, crossed under the wheels of a bus, and pursued by the scream of brakes and the oaths of the driver he pressed through the crowd.

He knocked into a man with a sack, cannoned off a lamppost,

and drove through the people, dividing them in a straight line, faster and faster.

He was on the white high road, running now, running with great leaping strides, a springing, tearing pace down the middle of the road, the white path where the shadows of the trees stopped in the dust.

Faster, faster, and the miles lay behind him: downhill with the road, dust thick on his open mouth.

Charlotte had had the kettle boiling an hour before she heard the foot on the staircase. The best cloth was spread: there were muffins for tea.

As she filled the teapot she heard stumbling below. Hurriedly she put down the kettle. 'The switch has gone wrong again,' she said, and to the dog who was standing there whining, tense, with its tail wagging fast, 'Quiet, Toby. Where's master?' She put on the switch at the top of the staircase and opened the door. She bent to see down and called 'Lory. How was it, Lory?' He was coming up to the first landing, awkwardly. The dog hurried down to greet him but at the landing it stopped, then flew on, barking and barking. He kicked it, bitterly: it fell, scrabbling down the stairs to the doorway. It went out of the door howling, and its howling went away down the street.

'Lory?' she called.

Up the last flight he came faster, much faster, swarming darkly up the staircase: she saw his face lifted to hers, and his eyes glittering.

She fell back in the doorway. He was there and upon her. Slam, slammed the door on him, crouching at the handle: but the key would not, would not turn, and as the door opened the desolate howl of the dog came up the staircase.

30

The Walker

—⦿—

In the country around this village it is not as simple as one could wish to find a pleasant, easy path for walking. The roads inland are all uphill, and although it is true that they lead through magnificent, dramatic country – bold, falling rock with terraces of vines and olive trees standing among the dried-up, barren mountains – they are roads that have to be climbed with attention: the landscape makes continual demands upon one; the winding, rock-strewn paths need perpetual care, and both these things interfere with the real aim of a walk, which for me is a half-conscious gentle physical exercise, the perfect accompaniment to reflection. I do not say that the countryside is anything but superb, and for one who walks to see magnificence these paths are ideal: but that is not my aim, and sometimes I long for an ordinary sober country lane, a way through the level cornfields or a towpath along a quiet river or a sea wall between salt flats and a marsh. Then there is the heat: for a big, heavy man that is important, and in the summer (it lasts from April to November here) all these roads are tilted to the blazing sun throughout the day.

The alternative is to walk along the sea. It is fresher in the summer, but there again it is not the kind of walking that I like best, for the sea is bordered by high cliffs: the sea comes right to their feet, and there is no way along the shore; one must be climbing or descending all the time.

When I was a little boy I lived for a time in a place where there was an immense stretch of sand, hard, pounded sand upon which you could walk for miles and miles. You never had to watch your feet on the level sand: walking was effortless, and the rhythm of your steps and the half-heard incessant thunder of the sea induced that trance in which one can go on and on for ever, singing perhaps, or talking to the air. There were shells, too, far better than the shells are here, delicately stranded at the watermark, and all kinds of sea-wrecked things, trawlers' floats, kelp, sea purses, spindrift, tarred or whitened planks of wood.

That is the sort of beach or strand that is lacking here; for here, as I say, there is no way along the sea except by the cliffs, and although they do sometimes go down to a little bay of shingle, it is only to rise again abruptly within a hundred yards. It is not a coast for general wandering: it is not a shore where one can stroll at all, and that is my only complaint against this place. I have no others. My lodgings are clean and orderly, the people are used to me, they are quiet and civil, and nobody interferes with my work or my set habits.

However, there is one walk that is neither violent nor exhausting. It is not a very good walk: it is an illogical, synthetic walk, but it is the best that I have been able to find and I have gone over the paths of it so often now that my feet find their way by themselves, leaving my mind free, to meditate or drift in vacancy, just as it pleases; and that is all that one can ask.

I go out of the back of the village, past the fort: for this is a bad part, for the quarter's rubbish dump is by the fort, and there is always a carrion smell and the thin dogs hunt about in shameful, mean-looking bands. The rubbish is supposed to be burned in that square concrete box, but although a cloud of stinking smoke drifts over it, the amount is never the less. I pass it and hurry over the bare drying-ground: the wind is almost always in the right direction, and as soon as I am on the level field the reek is blown away, so by the time I am halfway over it the unpleasant feeling has quite gone. This is the place where the women spread their washing out to dry, and in certain months of the year the men bring their nets to lie in the sun.

Beyond the drying field one must branch off to the left, to the

main road and follow it to the entrance of a broad cart track: this is
where the walk begins. The track dips down between high banks,
and very soon there are hedges on either side. These are the only
hedges for miles around, and if it were not for the prickly pears
that show here and there and the pomegranates that form part
of the hedge itself, one might suppose the track an English lane.
On the far side there are orange trees and vines, which destroy
the effect, but all around the farmhouse that stands on the downward slope an ordinary market garden gives the green in ordered
rows again – broad beans, cauliflowers and cabbages, lettuce, car-
rots, familiar plants. Farther down, the bushes close overhead and
the lane becomes a tunnel through the green; then at the bottom
there is the river. For nearly all the year the bed is dry, and even
when there is some water flowing it is always possible to cross dry-
shod. Now I turn to the right and follow the path downstream.
Here there are laurels, a few willows, tamarisks and those tall, thin
bushes that have purple sprays of flowers – the kind that bloom in
the late summer and draw flights of peacock butterflies.

Among the bushes there are dragonflies, for the river, flowing
underground, leaves stagnant pools in the hollows: and up and
down the river bed, low under the trees, innumerable swallows
dash through the light; there are martins, too, and in the evening,
when the bats are out and the swallows are no more than dark
blurs, more sensed than seen, the white bottoms of the martins
show, disembodied, weaving up and down.

I follow the river then, and come to its mouth. This is in one of
the little bays that I have mentioned: it stands between the cliffs
on either hand, a half-moon of shingle, with tall reeds at the back
of it and behind them an orchard of fig and orange trees. The river,
when it is flowing, hugs the right-hand side, cutting along at the
foot of the cliff itself, and the beach shows no sign of having a
river in it at all.

It is a shingle beach, with large pebbles at the back and small
ones by the sea. Nearly always there is a high-water mark of
broken reeds, bushes, driftwood and grass-like seaweed: this line
of vegetable rubbish (it is as much as two feet high sometimes)

stays unmoved from one big storm to another. Only at the equinox, when the wind comes straight in from the sea, do the waves beat in so far, and then there is nearly always rain inland, so that the river brings down more dead reeds and bushes, and these, being unable to drive out to sea, drift in the little bay and are thrown in to the same high-water mark.

It is only at these times, too, that the one boat that lives on that beach is hauled up far from the sea. It is a blue boat, shaped like those one made from paper as a child; the old man of the orchard uses it to fish for congers. He spends more time in his boat than working on his land, and it is said that he knows the rocks at the bottom of that bay better than most men know the rooms of the house they live in. But he is a savage old man, a solitary, and I do not speak to him nor he to me.

When I am on the beach I usually walk up and down it. It is not that it is agreeable to walk upon – the shingle is so loose and shifting that one's feet plunge deep and walking is painful – but it is the end of my walk. One must either go back the way one came (an unsatisfactory retreat) or else climb up the cliff, which is not walking any more. It is the cliff path that I nearly always take, up past the destroyed German searchlight and to the huge domed gun-emplacements home; but I walk up and down first to consider it.

I walk, naturally, by whatever water mark there may be. Not the high ridge-like mark of the great storms, for that so rarely changes, but by the sea itself; and sometimes, when there has been a swell, or a storm in Africa, there are shells or wreckage on the beach.

Once I found a wet brass ring. It had just arrived from who knows what rolling in the sea. It was a cheap ring, the kind that is sold in fairs: the sea had pitted it with eatings-out and dents, which gave it the look of vast antiquity. But in low relief on the flat part of it there was a swastika, and no doubt it had belonged to one of the Germans drowned here in the war. The ring filled me with repulsion, like a thing unclean: the round was so much the answering shape to the finger that had fitted it that I shuddered and threw it far into the sea, wiping my hands on the pebbles afterward. A human finger, by itself without a hand, is a disgusting thing. A human finger in the sea.

The pelvis that I found did not have the same effect. It was not long after the ring, and it lay within a yard or two of the place where I had picked it up: but I did not connect it with the Germans drowned – nor, indeed, with mankind at all.

It was by itself, white, dry and smooth, symmetrical and polished to inhumanity by the sea. It was only by a conscious effort that I could feel that this had been a piece of a man – only by running my hand round my own hip to my spine and tracing the same rise and curve that I saw on the bleached and diagrammatic bone in front of me. It had been in some way human, that was true; but is a shell the shellfish? This pelvis was very like a shell. Ordinarily, I suppose, a human bone would raise some emotion, some emotion resembling piety; it would be a disturbance of decency, a kind of profanation on the shore. But I felt no such emotion as I sat looking at this bone: I connected it with death, but with no particular death. A specimen in an anatomical museum could more easily have been clothed with living flesh than this white basin in the sun.

One's mental processes, and especially the wandering fantasies that pass through one's mind as one walks, are linked by a chain of association so slight that it usually cannot be traced. A bramble will claw out from a thicket: one pushes on automatically, and then in half an hour one will find that one has been dwelling on the Passion for the last mile of the road. That is why I speak of this bone: it provides the obvious and unfortuitous start for the recollections that unfolded in my head as I walked up the cliff path and high along the edge of the sea to the ruined batteries, where the camouflaged concrete still lies among the thistles and the asphodel, with its reinforcing steel rods all standing like the prickles of some prodigious monster of the earth.

When first I came to this village I lodged in a house belonging to an elderly couple named Joseph and Martine Albère. It was a large house, but I was the only lodger: it was a tall, gaunt place, always cold and damp, even in the height of the summer, and from the outside you would have said that it was uninhabited. But it was in good repair, a solid, middle-class house, much richer than the terrace-cottages in which most of the villagers lived: only the presbytery and the doctor's house were better; and from this I judged that the owner would be a man of some standing in the village. I learned, too, that my landlord was the owner and the equipper, the *armateur*, as they say, of three fishing boats: his boats, then, were the direct means of livelihood for nearly forty of the men of the place – a considerable proportion of the working inhabitants.

However, I soon gathered the impression that Albère was not a man of high standing. It is difficult to say how one forms an impression of this nature: it is built up of so many little things – gestures, tones of voice, a look cast backward, an avoiding eye – but in the end it grows into certainty. On the concrete, demonstrable side there was the fact that he never ran for municipal office, that he was president of none of the many co-operative or political associations and that he never appeared at any of the funerals or public feasts.

He seemed to be rich but unconsidered: a contradiction of common experience. At one time I asked myself whether in fact he was rich. Would a rich man take in a lodger? He did not seem to like letting the room I had; but when upon some trifling disagreement (he did not allow his lodgers the front-door key) I suggested that I should find a room elsewhere, he showed so much concern that I could not but suppose he was in earnest. He at once proposed a much lower rent if I would give up my point, and after a little more discussion I agreed to stay. This caused him a disproportionate satisfaction.

Then I learned that he had a fourth boat building on the stocks, which disposed of my idea that he was poor, for at that time a new boat was a very costly undertaking. As for the letting of rooms, that might indicate much or little: after all, in a big house one might let rooms to keep the house lived in, simply to prevent that decay that always comes in an empty place.

But still he remained a curious man to me. He did not like me, and he did not like having me in the house: yet he did not want me to leave it. The rent that I paid was a trifle to him even before he reduced it, yet he forced himself to be amiable to me, provided my room with the meagre best of the furniture in the house, and waited up every night to let me in after my evening walk.

He was a small, dark man, about sixty-five years of age: he was always carelessly dressed, dirty and unshaved, and his air of brutality contrasted strangely with the house he lived in. How did this brutal air appear? He was not obviously vicious; he spoke politely enough to me (though it was patently constrained) and I can only say that it must have been his lurching walk, the set expression on his face and the way he terrorized his wife that made me think, 'Albère? A brutish man.' His wife I hardly saw: she was utterly effaced, and she moved about the darkened house furtively, with the sound of a person who is trying to make no noise – this was when she was going about her obvious, everyday duties. She was much more like an imprisoned servant than the mistress of the house. Whenever she spoke to me he would appear and, whatever she was saying, she would stop and hurry downstairs. Yet I had the impression that in spite of this domination they were allies. Sometimes, in the dead quiet of night, I would hear them talking, two whispers, urgent and hurrying, that would answer one to the other in the basement of the house. They slept in the kitchen, and I do not think they ever used any other room.

When I had been there some time I learnt something of their habits. They did not sleep very much, and every few hours one or another of them (or sometimes both) would creep up to the top of the house, along the passage that traversed its length, opening every door softly and softly closing it again, then down the stairs to the middle landing, very silently past my door to the room beyond, and there they would pause, perhaps for as long as half an hour, before coming out, crossing quietly to the other side of the house, back to the stairs, and so down again to the hall and their kitchen.

But I have my nocturnal habits, too: and more than once

I have been there before them, fixed silent in a corner just off their trodden beat (for their patrol was so settled by long routine that their feet stepped in exactly the same places night after night), silent and unbreathing, watching their shadows.

However, this was much later: at first I merely noted that they never left the house together, and that when one was gone the other always waited in the hall or near it to open the door.

They appeared to have no relations. At least nobody ever came to visit them; and as far as I could see they were always in the house except when Albère was on the beach, conducting his business with the crews of his boats or when the woman was out for shopping. She never went to church: nor, of course, did he.

I had been there a long time before I found out what was the matter with them. It was a long time, for there were two difficulties in my way: the one was that the people of the village were not unduly open – they may know for generations, but they will not go out of their way to tell strangers – and the other, that I do not talk readily either. I do not go to cafés nor make acquaintance with the loungers on the quay. My form of recreation after my work is to walk. I like to go for long, uninterrupted walks.

Eventually it was a Dutch painter who told me what I had to know. He was a fat, exuberant man – spoke the language perfectly, having been brought up in Rheims – and he almost forced himself upon me. All he wanted was an audience: he loved to talk, and the smallest word of attention would keep him talking on the quay for hours. He was not my idea of a Dutchman. He knew all the fishermen and all the shopkeepers: he was hail-fellow-well-met with all of them before he had been here a month, and he stayed for a long time. It was a local man who told him about Albère: or perhaps 'local man' is inexact, for he was a waiter who had married a local girl and settled down here: he did not have the same sense of a closed community. The facts were common knowledge, and I often came across references to them afterwards. Albère was originally a sailor, a seaman employed on the packet boats that run between France and North Africa. On his ship, the *Jules-Bastide*, there were two other men from this village.

One night, about thirty years ago, the *Jules-Bastide* put out from Marseilles in a black gale of wind: there were very few passengers, for it was mid-winter, and most of those few went straight to their cabins. Only a few Algerian deck passengers huddled on the fo'c'sle, and one solitary priest, indifferent to the weather, stayed on the afterdeck. He carried a black valise wherever he went. When he went below for dinner he kept it with him, and afterwards, when he returned to the deck, in spite of the wild seas, he carried it still. He paced up and down in the gale, always carrying this valise. There were three men on duty on this part of the ship at this particular time, Albère and his two fellow-villagers.

In the morning the priest was missing. Nobody knew anything about it: the official inquiry revealed nothing whatever. There was even some mystery about the identity of the priest, as there had been a mistake in the list of passengers, and the person who had arranged for the priest's ticket could not be traced.

Shortly afterwards the three men left the sea. One bought a café in the town ten miles up the coast: the second took an important farm some way inland; and Albère bought the house where I was staying and the three fishing boats.

Within a year the first man and his wife were burned alive in a fire that destroyed their house and café. Two years later the second man, already overcome by misfortune in all his enterprises, lost his only son: the boy was killed riding a motor bicycle that his father had bought him. The man returned to this village by foot, walked to the graveyard, and hanged himself in the daylight.

Ever since, the Albères had been waiting for their turn. They had taken me in as some kind of protection (the lightning, they thought, would not strike a house where a just man lived) but still they did not think that my presence was enough: they were still in dread, and I remembered how one night, early in my stay, I had gone out about three in the morning (I had thought that it might be the beginning of the day of wrath, but when I looked at the stars I found that I was wrong: I had been unable to move Aldebaran) and I had unbolted the door without a sound. When I came back and closed it after me, I heard the stifled gasp that

Albère made as he stood silently behind the door, and in the moonlight from the landing window I saw that he had a gun. He muttered something about thieves, but, as I thought at the time, you shoot thieves down. Thieves had their hands cut off in former days; they were also stoned to death. Some thieves were nailed and hung up alive.

Nothing has ever given me a livelier pleasure than my realization that they had taken me in as a protection. And it came to me quite slowly, as I was walking by the river, that once again I had been chosen as the hand of God. After such a long time it had come again: all my anxious waiting was rewarded. The wickedness of my doubt was overlooked – for at times I had wavered – and now once again I was the elected vessel. I had hoped for so long; and to hope for such an election twice in one lifetime seemed presumptuous indeed. But now I was the hand of God again; the wrath of a jealous God who spoke through the prophet and ploughed the Amalekites into the ground. And without any knowledge I had been set there in my place for a long year past: oh, it was the sweetest realization in the world, this kindness done to me.

Clearly I knew that it was not for the murder I had been sent: no, no; it was for accidie. These wicked people had despaired of all forgiveness: they had hardened their hearts, and for that last wickedness they were to be destroyed in this world as they were already damned in the next.

I waited for the dream that would direct my hand: it had been so clear before. It had been so clear and explicit, and twice repeated, on the last occasion, the sawing of the blasphemer in Newtownards. But it did not come at once this time, and in my lightness of spirits I could not sleep. Between half-past three and four o'clock they were on the upper corridor, together; and the spirit of delight was so strong in me that I could not resist the pleasure of running out with my black coat over my nakedness, barefoot up behind them. They were in the far room, listening; I was fast in the black shadow of the corner, and as they crept by I sprang on them shrieking, 'The priest, the valise, the priest, ha ha ha ha ha.' I leaped and sprang, but with the shrieking and the laughter I could hardly run as fast as they did. They were some way ahead, the man before the woman, and I am a very big, heavy man; but I cut them off at the head of the stairs and hunted them into the farthest room: I howled and howled in the room. And I let them escape me there while I ran to leap and shriek all through the house. Then I had them on the stairs half down, the man dragging the woman by the arm. They were trying to reach the door, and the laughing nearly choked my breath. From up there I few, I say I *flew*, and smashed them down on to the far stone floor.

But it was finished then. It was finished almost before it had begun. I had meant a full night's inspired, enormous ecstasy, and I had wasted it in half an hour. Before it had started it was done: they had died without a mark; and I had not set the sign.

31

The Flower Pot

Wind. It had been blowing all night and now with the rising of the sun it increased, backing a little to the south-east and hurling furiously in from the sea in uneven gusts. The village was built with its back to the north wind from over the mountains and this wind from Africa found it defenceless: in the narrow streets dust and sand flew in blinding vortices; little stones slashed on the glass like hail, and somewhere in an empty house an unfastened shutter slammed and slammed with the noise of a loud gun.

Hermann and Ludwig rose early, though they had not slept well all through the night because of the wind: twice Hermann had got up, the first time to close the window, the second to bring the flower-pots in from the window-sill. They rose early, and when they opened the shutters they saw that the sea was not coming in in high waves, but was held flat by the wind; the grey, hurried ripples had their heads whipped off in spray before they could rise to the height of a wave. There was so much spray and sand in the air that the wind was visible, and it obscured the low sky. In the street below people hurried, bowed and close in to the side; they bowed against the wind and then it would turn with redoubled force and stagger them from behind. A dustbin lid rolled up and down the cobbles, sometimes bowling like a hoop and sometimes carried along flat; it made a hollow, melancholy noise.

The flower-pots stood in a row on the floor: it was necessary to move them to make the bed. There were cactuses in most of the pots, Maltese Crosses, Moses' Heads and the long, straight, prickly kind with neither branch nor curve, which have so strange a flower in their season: the largest pot had carnation slips, just starting to root and push with a fresh living green. Six cuttings and not one failure.

'You ought to fasten those pots with wire,' said Ludwig. 'I know,' said Hermann. 'I meant to do it yesterday.'

He ranged the smaller pots over by the dressing-table, but there was no room for the carnations. He put their pot back on the window-sill, grunting at the weight. He closed the window again, hurriedly.

He was at the far end of the bed, holding a corner of the sheet when a fresh gust hit the street: it was so hard that the air in the room changed – it was like the explosion of a bomb; the instant before the overwhelming crash of sound the pressure changes in your ears. They stopped, half crouched, and their hearts beat in anticipation and dread. The right-hand shutter slammed with enormous force, rebounded, and the wind nailed it to the wall again.

The big pot had had its edge just over the sill: the shutter had struck it. The pot rocked in against the window-frame and then out, right out.

Hermann saw it go and cried out, 'Oh oh . . .' His hands jerked across the bed towards the window. Then there was a complete silence.

They were at the top of the house, a tall thin house, forty feet above the crowded street.

Ludwig darted a look of hatred at Hermann's horrified, paralysed face. Hermann put it there, the great clumsy fool, the careless, careless swine. Now there would be a dreadful scene with those disagreeable restaurant people downstairs. And the lovely plants. Six lovely cuttings, the best carnations in the world; just rooting, doing beautifully. He had planted them with such care. They would have flowered this year. And the pot smashed and all the earth wasted. Big ugly beast. With his hairy, coarse great hands.

Hermann stood in the same forced, constrained attitude,

motionless all the length of the silent pause. His big, open face kept its expression of horror, like a single photograph cut from a strip of film: but behind his face, through all the interminable rushing pause, his mind raced, its different layers spinning a compressed, intensely vivid pattern. He heard the crash, the shock: not the explosion of the pot on the stones, but the duller sound of its hitting a man. Then in the instant before the cries in the street, the small clatter of the broken shards falling with the man. He saw the man, sprawled on his face, half in the gutter, and the gaping wound in his head, his torn shoulder. The man quite still, and the dark blood just starting to flow across the stones, a pool, and the rivulet into the gutter: the running people, foreshortened from above, and the cries. The screaming of the couple from the restaurant; the gathering crowd: then everybody pointing upwards.

An enormous feeling of guilt overwhelmed him. One minute's care on any of the hundred days before, and it would all have been perfectly well: he knew he should have done it: he had said it, had said it, had said it.

A man struck dead. A fisherman – no one else to keep his family. The news going home and the bitter misery now and for ever.

The guilt, familiar always, but in a new shape now, swelled and swelled to fill and terrify his mind.

Oh you careless, careless fool: you wickedly, criminally careless fool. Nothing left but to give everything you have to the people and get yourself out of the world.

The shouting and the pointing in the street, the angry shouting: he would have to go down, try to explain in French, try to apologise. The police, the questioning, searching, their life ripped open for everyone to stare at. Their shelter gone. And only yesterday it had been so beautiful, peaceful, happy at last. They were settled and now everything, every single thing was disrupted and spoilt for ever.

And spoilt for Ludwig, poor Ludwig – all spoilt: and he had smashed poor Ludwig's flowers.

A man struck dead, or maimed for ever: struck down and by his fault. The great wave of hatred rising from the street. The foreigners at René's have killed *père* Matthieu. The pointing and the great just wave of hate; and his head only, peering from the window, peering down to meet the hatred and the pointing.

The rush, the downward multiplying rush, malignant fall, the heavy deadly silent thing: oh would it never end?

32

The Party in the Cave

———— ❦ ————

For Charles and Mary de Salis

This was the Spain of the first days of the Republic; and although Edward had heard great things of the new freedom he was not prepared for the atmosphere of happiness, excitement and energy that he found all the way across from Santander, where he landed, through Aragon to Jaca, where he taught in the summer school, and thence to Catalonia and the sea.

He would hardly have recognized it as the same country as the Spain he had known before: all the way across he met the change, this newly-liberated hope, this un-Spanish enthusiasm; for now was the honeymoon of the Republic, before the illusions died and before the Communists organized their strength. It was all so fresh and vivid: it was like the enthusiasm of a delighted child, and it was very touching.

One reason why this Spain was so unlike the country which he had seen in his childhood and during his holidays from school and the university (he had relatives in Spain, and went out every year) was that in the solid, well-established circle of his people's Spanish friends he had only met the families of high officials or wealthy businessmen, whereas now he was mixing with students, teachers as young as himself, writers, painters, journalists and Utopians with the dew still shining on them. But even so, with every allowance that could be made, it was another world, and he was happy in it.

He was of an open, friendly disposition, and although as a professed liberal he was a little earnest and solemn when he thought about the responsibilities of his creed, he was a cheerful creature for most days in the year. At this time he had every reason to be cheerful. His summer course had been a success, he had enough money not to worry about his holiday, and here in Palafox he had already met so many agreeable acquaintances. There was his friend José, with whom he was staying, and José's cousin Antonio, who had come from Madrid to start a co-operative school for the grown men and women of the district. It was a school where those who knew their letters taught those who did not, and where those who had a book read it out to those who had never possessed one: it was a place of boundless enthusiasm and good will; the strong, intelligent, able pupils had built it from the foundations to the roof; there were no desks yet, but they would come, together with paper, ink, pens and the paradise on earth.

Edward and Antonio had made a blackboard in the afternoon: at least, it was a board, and it was black; for some reason it would not take chalk nor hold itself square, but tomorrow it might very well improve by itself. For the moment they were more occupied in singing with the stationmaster, the nephew of the priest, two fishermen, the leader of the Anarchists of Palafox and four husky pupils from the school.

Although they had drunk little more than fruit juice and fizzy beer they were all somewhat elevated, half drunk with the lasting exhilaration of the time and the sense of their unity; but Edward was not yet sufficiently unselfconscious to join in with the full extent of his lungs. He was still a little too much aware of the other people in the café and of the crowd in the rambla: he was perfectly happy, but he would keep his voice, such as it was, for later in the evening, when they would all go up to the cave with melons. In the meantime he opened and closed his mouth with a faint mooing, as he did during the hymns in church at home.

It was growing late, and they were only waiting for Estéban with his guitar and Raimundo.

'Sing, Edward,' cried José in his ear.

'He is too poor to sing,' said Diego, smiling kindly at him across the table. 'It is well known that Englishmen are too poor to sing.'

'There is wit,' said the older fisherman. 'How will he answer that?'

'The frog sings, although she has neither hair nor wool,' said Antonio.

'Here is Estéban,' said all the men who were facing the street. 'Adeu, Estéban. Estéban, how are you? Have you mended your guitar, Estéban? Where is Raimundo?'

'He is coming after,' said Estéban. 'He has met two foreigners and he is finding them a room. We will not wait for him.'

They streamed out of the café, bought their melons at the comer stall where the twenty yards of cobbled rambla petered out into naked river-bed, and began to climb the dusty, stony path up through the olive-groves to the brow of the cliff. By the time they were at the top the light had begun to fade from the valleys, and already the little harbour far below them had a violet haze, a violet pool floating over the tight-packed roofs.

In the deep natural cave under the Moorish watch-tower it was deliciously warm: the sun had been beating into its mouth throughout the earlier part of the afternoon and now it had reached the perfect state between hot and cold. The kindly warmth of the rock made it feel soft, and Edward, sitting there in the gentle gloom, was suddenly conscious of being entirely happy. It was partly a physical happiness: he could feel the whole of his body relaxed and easy; he was aware of his arms and legs – their well-being and separate euphoria – and all his senses were wonderfully acute. The smell of the thyme drifting up from the warm cliff-face and wafting into the comparative coolness of the cave was far stronger than usual, and much more sharply distinguished from the acrid, piercing scent of the dried-up land behind: there was the honey-scent of the alyssum too, and the all-pervading sea. And his hearing was extraordinarily keen: he could hear the deep thrum of the guitar's thickest string and the slightly false vibration of its wooden body, although Estéban was barely stroking it with his thumb as he searched dreamily for the beginning of the song.

He found it presently, and humming to supply the notes of the missing cord, he drifted into the *habanera* that Edward liked best of all the songs they sang up there. The fishermen and one of the pupils came from the village where they sang this habanera, and quietly, one after another, they fell into the pattern of the sound. It was a long, long song, with in definite repetitions, and by the end they were all singing. Edward did not think that he was making anything more than a gentle hum until the last verse, when the shortness of his breath showed him that this was not the case: but they had all been singing so truly together that no one voice stood out.

They went straight from the habanera to the song called 'The Four Cats', all in perfect agreement and without a pause: then to the song of the Old Man and to the ballad of the gypsy girl and the *Guardia Civil*. It was in a pause in this last ballad that Antonio, who was sitting in the mouth of the cave, said that Raimundo was coming up the path with two other men.

'They must be his foreigners,' said Estéban.

They finished the song, but when it was done they did not begin again. They lay quietly about the cave, eating slices of water-melon and talking in undertones. Far out on the curving horn of the land the lighthouse had already begun to wink: three flashes and a pause, coming again and again, with a remote and impartial certainty.

The whole evening was violet now, and star after star pricked out, each one unseen until it was fully there.

They lay there, placidly listening to the footsteps on the loose stones of the path, and when Antonio said, 'They are turning by the white rock now,' his words fell into a comfort able pool of acquiescent silence.

Edward heard the faint stir of the strings of the guitar as Estéban moved, and in another moment the mouth of the cave showed three clear-cut silhouettes against the sky. The short one was Raimundo: the other two were tall, and one had a queer, misshapen darkness on his back, an accordion on a sling.

They were out of breath from their climb, and for a moment they stood there, outside, and the comfortable people inside looked at them. But this was a very short moment, and directly Raimundo was introducing them, Franz and Alois, introducing them and naming the dim forms in the cave.

Edward was unwilling to change the luxury of his position, but it was necessary to stand up solemnly and shake these powerful hands. Everybody shook hands, and it was at once apparent that the two German students were guests – distinctly guests and that they were to be invited to sit down in defined and certain places.

They spoke good Spanish, and they were not embarrassed. They asked to try Estéban's guitar, and they said that one of the strings was broken. They gave an account of their travels – they had been given lifts all the way down from Göttingen – and they asked to be told the occupations of the people in the cave – were they students? Were they interested in the works of Garcia Lorca? What did they think of Unamuno, whose works were very much appreciated in Germany?

When they were told that Edward was an Englishman, the taller one swung up his accordion and played the tune 'Tipperary', singing fragmentarily, 'It's a long, long way ...' He played with finished precision, and after the last slow chords he laughed and said in English, 'The jolly students at Göttingen play that often.'

They were both highly efficient musicians, and when they had played two patriotic Spanish songs and 'Ach du liebe Augustin' and 'Gaudeamus igitur' they offered a selection of the flamencos which they had heard in Granada and arranged themselves.

'Ah, Granada and Sevilla,' said Alois with a sigh, combing his hair back from his forehead. 'There was a Swedish gentleman there who showed us the lemon-trees growing and took us two hundred kilometres in his car and gave us dinner.'

The flamencos had a relentless, metronomic beat, but the lieder which followed were beautifully sung, and afterwards, when

Estéban and one of the fishermen sang a *habanera* the Germans pleased them by listening with the closest attention and writing down the words and music by the flare of matches that lit the cave with a portentous and dramatic light.

It was quite dark now, and now the strangers no longer seemed like particular and separate guests. They were quite confident – they were no longer those who had been invited on civil sufferance from outside – and they lay at their ease, reaching uninvited for the melon slices like the rest.

Yet at some point after their arrival, perhaps at that indefinable moment when they had become a part of the now enlarged and altered body – when they, becoming part of the community, had changed its nature – the tension in the cave had begun to grow. Edward was not an exceptionally sensitive man, not even today, when all his sympathetic faculties were on the stretch, but for a long time now, as the night wore on, he had felt the electricity in the atmosphere: it increased imperceptibly: it was becoming unbearable. He had not spoken for half an hour, except to answer a direct question: the cave was not silent, however, for the foreign Spanish rarely stopped an organized question-and-answer that did not flag. Edward paid little attention to the voices or the matter, which was mostly folklore, local customs and the rest, but for some reason he was sharply aware of José, unseen at his side, and of the fishermen behind him in the darkness.

There were swift currents of hostility in the cave; but it was not Edward and the Spaniards against the foreigners. It was disunity and chaotic, pointless malice.

It was no words that acted as the catalyst nothing that he could define, no horse-play that turned bad. But there was a cry on his right, a hoarse malignant shout, and somebody hit him on the throat.

Hands were snatching at the melon heap. The guitar gave a great twanging bang and Edward was slapping at a vague confusion before him.

In the blind melee there were no words, just blows: a wild anarchy, and they were pushing, thrusting through enemies in the dark. A piece of melon-peel caught him across the mouth: he confusedly thought its coldness was a wound: and in that moment the struggling mass reached the mouth of the cave. Free from the walls they fled, stumbling and rushing in the darkness at a breakneck speed, each in his own direction and alone.

33

The Overcoat

—❦—

He had got up half an hour earlier than usual. The thought of the board-meeting at eleven o'clock had come directly into his mind when he woke and he had not been able to stay in bed for his warm, meditative, customary half-hour: it was an exciting thought; he had plenty to say and the right to say it now. They would listen to him with respect: he would have power in his hands, and there at that long table he would use it. It was an exhilarating prospect, and he could not stay in bed.

The household was disturbed by this break in the order of things; they saw him from the kitchen windows walking up and down the path by the rose beds. He himself was aware of the difference, but for him it was a good difference and the sound of the coffee-mill pleased him; it was a clear sound out there in the garden, unlike the muffled reverberation that reached him in bed every ordinary morning in the year.

His turn in the garden, the freshness of the air, gave him an appetite and he took three whole cups of coffee instead of one and a half – another change to mark the day. It was still early when he had finished, and he decided to walk to the office. It was fresh; just cold enough, he thought, to make his new overcoat necessary. It was a beautiful overcoat, warm, admirably cut, and it held him up, gave him straight, square shoulders and a good, continuing sense of well-being. He would have been sorry if the day had been a little warmer.

How pleasant it was walking in the thin sunshine, a brilliant, unwarming spring sun that sent golden bars through the lopped plane-tree: lining his avenue. The trees stood orderly, exactly spaced, with their amputated stumps raised in a drill as precise as the town council's saw could make it. There were a few untouched branches left, and if the weather continued so they would be out in green bud within the week.

Down the avenue, across the canal and into the town: bright yellow tram-cars jangling, passing one another in the broad streets, and cars passing the trams. There were not many people about: it was still early, but the working-men had vanished into their factories an hour ago and the office people had already begun their day; only here and there a worried young man hurried, turning and re-forming his excuses.

It was disagreeable to see them, vexing: nothing could be easier than punctuality – bicycles, buses, trams – just that minimum of self-discipline. If an employer, a company, engages a man to work from eight till six and pays him for it, the employer has a right to those hours: it is as dishonest to subtract from that time as it is to sell short weight. Just that minimum of discipline, but how rare nowadays – even now in this difficult time, when discipline and a new order and strength were more than ever necessary.

The flower-stalls in the Opera-house square changed the current of his thoughts. Brilliant daffodils, mimosa, baskets of pure colour; and the smell of jonquils.

He crossed the square without waiting, there was so little traffic; only a tram and a couple of military lorries in sight. The tables were out on the pavement, and the waiters were sprinkling, sweeping, setting out the clipped trees in their green wooden tubs. A few men were already there, reading their papers, drinking coffee: he noticed with satisfaction that they all had overcoats.

Outside the Ministry of Propaganda there was a continual coming and going of uniforms. As he saw them he involuntarily straightened his back, noticed it to himself and smiled. But he went on holding himself rigid: that was how a man should stand; it was the outward sign of an inner discipline.

These new uniforms. They were unfamiliar to him: very smart

and soldierly, but he did not understand the insignia yet – must look into it. Were these officers or not? They looked like officers, but he could not be sure.

The clock was striking as he passed the sentries. All the clocks: he could hear them taking it up all over the town. He had plenty of time to spare, and he could indulge himself in a little detour before going on to the office. It was always a pleasure to look into the jewellers' windows, and now that he could walk in if he chose – he would not choose, but *if* he did – the pleasure was something more, an active excitement, no longer a detached appreciation. There was much more to be seen too, now, with so many sudden alterations and money changing hands so fast and the refugees selling cheap.

There were a great many of these grey uniforms. They were new. He had not seen them before Wednesday or Thursday last. Double Sam Browne, revolver, breeches and boots. They would have been cavalry when he was a boy, but they were all gone, the horses – that was a pity. Perhaps some armoured regiment? Or were they soldiers at all? They were tall, upstanding fellows, picked men; most probably they were one of the new formations.

Two of them were coming down the empty pavement towards him. Great big men; the girl between them did not reach their shoulders. A tart. No. She was a youth-leader. She had trousers on and a tight sweater: exaggerated breasts pointing forward and the badge on the tip of one. Rubber, no doubt. That traveller had told him you could buy them in all the shops these days.

They were talking and laughing very loudly, strung across the pavement. They could not be drunk so early in the morning? No, just Spring and high spirits. You have to allow for high spirits in the young; and these were certainly officers. They had gold bars on their sleeves.

He turned to look in the window. Church plate, mostly. You could get some very old things in church plate. The window had just been dressed and they had not put the price tickets on; how irritating. The rock-crystal thing – a pyx, ostensory, what did they call it? – might look very good with a concealed electric light in it shining through, a bedside lamp. The foot was probably silver-gilt, not gold.

The two men and the girl were looking in the window too. He saw her face reflected: she looked exactly like that telephonist they had discharged last year, the one who was always being rung up by her young men. They were talking very loudly still, laughing about a big amethyst ring in a corner of the window, a bishop's ring. They were saying something about chastity and the amethyst, and laughing. He stole a sideways glance at the girl's breasts. They must be rubber – he had never seen any so – What would it be like to? She was between the men holding them each by the arm, squeezing them into a tight group of three heads bent to the glass. She wanted them to buy her something; she was playing at wheedling them, an exaggerated child's voice, baby-talk. Did they both?

Now they wanted to see the rest of the window. It was a small window, not room for four to stare: he would have left it to them, but the shopman was just putting the price tickets on and to-day, big and square in his new overcoat, he said he would stay one minute to see the price of the rock-crystal thing. He did not have to dodge about like some people; he and his kind were equal partners in the new order in fact, in the last resort they were the controlling partners. The officer next to him did not turn his head; he put out his arm, a grey military arm across the chest of the new overcoat, and still talking swept him back, great strength but half exerted. The three moved down, filling the brilliant window.

Behind them on the pavement he stood. He had staggered, off his balance, unresisting, and he stood behind them, just behind their backs.

His breath was stopped; he was drawn up, tall and rigid, his neat gloves folded in his right hand. He had been pushed. *Pushed*. He had never pushed anyone in his life. He had *never* broken the social contract. He was as strong as any man, with a board-meeting in front of him and his overcoat his guarantee. He was a director, he would scream it. He had been thrust, assaulted, violated. These were not drunken soldiery, unshaven, out of hand.

They had not secretly shouldered him, pushed him like men in a queue, unadmitting. Naked, naked, it was naked: they had pushed him. Oh the Ministry would ring. Oh the Ministry would ring. Those broad, smooth grey backs, criss-crossed, unconscious, talking and laughing with their whore. They would be stripped, reduced; the Minister would hear of this.

But he had been pushed. He must resent it. What sense of order was this? Speak sharply, command redress, apology, what the Devil? Allow such a liberty, such humiliation? Sit down under it? Beyond anything. At once: now, at once.

He looked left and right, glaring, for witnesses, support and public condemnation – outrage. Two men passed, glanced in curiously: a taxi asked him mutely, Cab sir?

In, slam the door. The tart's face turned; so lewd, triumphant.

His voice was repeating the office address, and his hands gripped, turned and gripped one inside the other; but where was comfort? Not in the number and the street's name though he grasped at that, one thing stable, fundamental; that at least had not been pushed away, that was not a cardboard foundation to be pushed away. At least, not yet. And old and shrunk, sunk, an old man, he repeated it, huddled there in his coat too large.

34

The Stag at Bay

———— ∞∞ ————

Edwin, as the long and briefless years trailed on, devoted himself more and more to lecturing and journalism. At the moment he was labouring over an article on marriage for a women's magazine – 'Let it be chatty and smart. And rather profound – *human*: you know what I mean? And you can be wistful if you like; old, battered, experienced. But not more than fifteen hundred words.'

The article was proving much more difficult than he had expected. It was not for lack of raw material – pinned to the wall in front of him was a list of smart things that had already been said about marriage – and it was not for lack of experience or thought. Marriage was a subject that he had thought about a great deal, deeply, and he had supposed that the profound part of the article would be the easiest: yet although he was in the right mood, costive and solemn, the words would not form themselves into an orderly and harmonious procession. They remained in his head, swirling in grand but indeterminate shapes; or if they had any concrete existence at all it was in the form of scrappy notes, odd words jotted down: *marriage iceberg – sunk – top quarrels – corruption in state.*

Not from lack of experience: he was married himself and at this time he felt more than usually married, for not only was he immersed in this article, but Julia had left him again, had gone back to her mother, and he was conscious of this all the time, if for no other reason than that the place was in such a mess. He never cleared it up on these occasions, partly on what he called principle and partly because it gave him such a moral advantage to be found in a slum, with every crock and pot unwashed and dishes piled on the floor, bed unmade, laundry sprawling abroad. He would not deliberately make a hole in his sock; but he would not prevent it, either. And yet he would not consciously welcome the hole; he would say tut-tut over it and inspect it with distaste: still less would he acknowledge that he piled the dishes in an unnecessarily picturesque confusion. His recognition of his moral advantage took place on some remote and not very savoury level of awareness: the piling of the dishes was traditional in the helpless male – any comic strip would bear that out, and besides there was the principle Man works not in House – and it was quite unconscious when it was quite fair: it was quite fair of course because Julia was in the wrong; therefore it was totally unconscious.

Marriage iceberg. Somewhere he had read that seven-eighths of an iceberg is always submerged and that it is only the remaining eighth that one sees; and this he meant to liken to marriage, the visible berg corresponding to the squabbles and superficial disharmony and the vast unseen majority serving as a figure for the profound unity and deep affection that must always subsist, etc. A church-going expression covered his face: he nodded gravely, and bending over his desk he began to write.

His pen stopped, started again, faltered and limped: he crossed out the whole paragraph and began afresh. He must make it quite plain about the underneath of the iceberg being really there.

Slow, slow. The cat, which standing at the door had asked three times to go out, now paced deliberately into his bedroom.

It was a slow article to write. Julia had slammed the door behind her just after the smart pieces had all been collected and as the first words were being written, 'We all know Mr Punch's advice about marriage ...' Yet the first section, the chatty part, had scarcely been completed before she had given Edwin grounds for divorce, and she was not by habit a flibbertigibbet, a fly-by-night, an itching palmer; neither loose nor fast. Her motives had been mixed: sizzling vexation of spirit, a conviction that nothing mattered; but also curiosity. She wanted to know, to really know, what adultery was like.

The article was still bogged down in the second, or human, part when, pursuing her research with an ardour that could no longer be attributed to revenge or a spirit of inquiry, she increased his grounds to a most liberal extent – to expansive and park-like grounds in which the horned beasts could be seen wandering at large.

At the beginning of the profound section she was in bed with horrible old Anthony Limberham, her cousin, to whose busy prayer she had yielded at three o'clock on Tuesday afternoon. She was quite accustomed by now to his faintly incestuous sheets – to their moral significance, that is – but not to the flagrant luxury of their hem-stitching, nor to the sinful depth of the carpet that met her feet when she got up. The unashamed magnificence of Anthony's flat, his delighted pursuit of the sins of the flesh, the huge and beautiful meals (no shopping, cooking, washing-up) they both ate so greedily, the flowers, the scent, the lovely clothes, all these refreshed her soul like rain after drought. She sloughed the anxiously contriving housewife, dropped ten years from her appearance, and responded to his cheerful obscenity with an assured impudence that no longer shocked her inner mind. Her eyes shone; she looked pink, virginal and inviting; her hair curled naturally; in all her life she had never felt so well.

Her sense of fun, much discouraged by life with Edwin and the hundred best books on the seventh floor of a cold-water walk-up, came suddenly to life again, and Anthony, scarlet in the face and wheezing, watered it with gin. She was going to the dogs – such agreeable dogs.

In the morning the tide of washing-up reached Edwin's desk itself, and at eleven a little congealed bacon-fat obscured his views on the state. These views had got into the article because they seemed to him to follow naturally after the piece about ice-bergs: he had expressed them forcibly, at some length, and with particular feeling today. He found them satisfactory and comforting even now, although the bacon-fat had reduced them to a kind of aphoristic précis: '. . . corruption in state, however bad, always occurs over basis of working integrity – unseen, unheard, taken for granted. – Crime not crime if normal; and once it becomes normal, unthinkable dissolution of the state.'

Scraping some of the grease off with the paper-knife he commended himself for not being angry. He thought of ringing up his mother-in-law's house and telling Julia that she was forgiven: he thought of clearing everything away completely. But he sickened at the prospect of the actual effort; and then it really would be too Quixotic to throw away so much advantage. Magnanimity had its limits: and after all he had not been . . .

What exactly had he meant to forgive her for? His memory, usually so very precise in such matters, could not supply the grievance at once, and even after bungling about among the files for some time it could come up with nothing better than general disrespect, inattention, or answering back. There was no heinous crime, like the unmended drawers of the last great row. The prefect-Edwin was inclined to mercy; fright and the possibility of dismay were beginning to creep through the levels of consciousness and he was growing less absolute. But there was such a great deal of washing-up.

'Or we have a very fine oryx, sir,' said the shopman.

They looked thoughtfully at the noble, leaping symmetry of the polished horns. 'No,' said Anthony, after a moment, 'What I really want is a stag, and, to be precise, a royal with at least twelve points.'

'Don't be pedantic, Anthony,' murmured Julia, with a blush. She turned away and gazed under the arm of a polar-bear at the hurrying traffic. '. . . a long way before you find a royal, sir. We used to see them often in the old King's time, but now I'm afraid you'll have to go a long way . . .' the shopman said, bowing them out.

A long way, a long way, but they found it at last in the limbo of an auctioneer's back room.

'A very fine 'ed, if I may say so,' said the warehouseman, hurring on the stag's eye and shining it with his handkerchief: it gleamed, brilliant among the dust and cobwebs that veiled the long muzzle, as bright and expectant as a natural in a bus. 'A very fine 'ed, sir,' repeated the warehouseman, polishing the other eye, 'And I dare say it was his pride in his days of life.'

He stood aside to watch Anthony, who had borrowed a clothes-brush, and who was busily grooming the stag with it, going shshsh-shshsh like an ostler. The preposterous old satyr, purple as he bent to polish the antler, winking at Julia through the tangle of tines, made the warehouseman nervous and talkative. 'A very fine 'ed and worth every penny of two, twelve, six which I couldn't take a penny less – the horn alone is worth twice the sum named for the manufacture of fancy goods – penknife handles, sir, carving forks. And when ground is used for the cure of certain female ailments as no doubt your good lady knows, sir: I am a married man myself, ahem. Oh sir, you may say "Oh, it is a very old article." Why, yes, sir, it *is* an old article and who denies it? But a horned stag is a very old article by nature. In its nature, sir, a stag is an old article.'

'Yes, yes,' said Edwin to the telephone, looking dutiful and attentive into the distemper three inches from his nose. 'Yes, Lady Dogge. Yes: yes. I'm very sorry, Lady Dogge; but it's finished now, Lady Dogge. Oh, please don't say that, Lady Dogge. No, Lady Dogge. Yes, Lady Dogge. Good-bye, Lady Dogge.'

'The bitch,' he said, but not very loud. He sat down quickly to his desk and read through the manuscript. 'It will do,' he said, without conviction, and crammed it into an envelope.

He hurried down the shallow flights of stairs, iron-bound cement in a chocolate-painted well that clanged and echoed, down to the wan hall with its lavatory tiles. The porter came out of his booth and watched him down the last four flights.

'Good afternoon,' he said to the porter, as he put the envelope into the slit. 'Is there any post?'

'Where's Mrs?' said the porter, staring up the stairs.

'She's away at the moment.'

'Oh. Visiting, isn't it?'

The porter was also the deputy hangman for the south-east region and the tenants had to humour his independence.

'Yes,' said Edwin. 'Has the postman been?'

'No,' he replied, putting his hand over his coat-pocket. 'No, I don't think. But there is a parcel for you. Mrs is leaving it this morning.'

'Then why did you ask where she was?'

'Oh I did not, Mr; and it is a big old parcel,' said the porter, suddenly changing his tone to one of close affection and laying his hand on Edwin's sleeve as if to test the quality of the cloth, 'I can have the string, isn't it?'

The porter had already unwrapped the greater part of the stag, and Edwin finished the unpacking there in the booth: then grasping the polished shield upon which the head was mounted he began his upward journey. At the third flight he had to change his hold, for the shield was too slippery and the head too heavy in front; but taking the creature round the neck he balanced the weight better, and although it was momentarily disagreeable to put his face against the old rough hairiness he soon grew accustomed to it and after a flight or two he did not mind at all. They went up, cheek by jowl, very well balanced, and with the same noble antlers shading them like an open-work umbrella; and as he climbed – far happier than when he had gone down – Edwin reflected upon this token of his wife's esteem, this mute forerunner of her prompt return.

'I had almost begun to think –' he confided to the stag. And 'It will be very useful,' he said to himself as he opened the door, 'and although it is far too large and spreading for the lobby, I will fix it solidly to my bedroom wall after I have done the washing-up, and I will hang my clothes on it at night.'

35

The Falling Star

———— ⨳ ————

"'Since first I saw your face,'" the young man sang, writing a train of notes. 'No,' he said in an ordinary speaking voice, 'No . . . "Since *first* I saw your face."' He hummed the new version and altered the notes.

That had been on a Thursday in September: the seventh: and she had appeared in the crowd at the door of the Saltons' studio. She had stood there, trying to place her hostess and looking as lovely and improbable as a lily in a potato-patch. It was extraordinary that everybody did not stop talking to gaze at her as he did, open-mouthed, and so absorbed that when Lucy Salton asked him to look after her as she knew no one, he hardly understood her and she had to repeat herself.

"'I resolved,'" he sang, "'to honour and renown you.'"

That was the meaning of the pile of songs on the table and the manuscript of the sonata still open on the piano.

"'If I now be disdained'" – but of course that was nonsense: and it might bring bad luck to score it so sadly. He knew that she ought to disdain him, but she was far too kind: she had no idea of her own worth, nor of her beauty. Last time she had not been very well: she had a headache, and he had been boring, tactless and awkward, as usual. He should never have made that remark about the pamphlets – he did not mean it, but he felt he had to say something, and he hoped it might turn out amusing, but it had been stupid, denigrating and pompous, as well as being quite against his own convictions. However, it had passed over: she was very forgiving: she would not remember it for five minutes. it did not matter.

"'If now I be disdained'" – but in a cheerful unbelieving voice – "'I wish my heart had never known you.'"

He tried the variation on the piano, standing there with his right hand spread over the keyboard while he looked out of the window on to the leafless pattern of the plane-tree, looming from the silent, motionless fog. The notes fell one after another, pure and intolerably sad.

"'What? I that loved and you that liked ... '" No, no, no. It would never do. There must be no belief in it. He wrote again: an F sharp and a fall of grace-notes would take the curse off it. It must sound as though the singer feared nothing – cool, detached, amused. A confident lover pretending to be dismayed.

The door slammed below and heavy feet pounded on the wooden stairs. Could it be Matthew already? He darted to the door and peered down.

'Hallo Peter,' called the voice from the darkness, moving rapidly upwards.

'How pleasant to see you, Matthew,' he said, standing back from the door. He waited for Matthew's news, but the short, dark man flung himself down in a chair and said, 'Did you see the review in the *Witness*?'

'Yes,' said Peter, 'it was quite good.'

'Are you trying to be funny?'

'Well, it said "talent" and "promise". Compared with their usual ...'

'Talent and promise. The usual smear words. And that piece about learning the use of – oh, what the hell. I'd rather be flayed by the gutter-press than praised by it any day of the week. The fore-runners are always crucified. But at least they might have the courage to sign their dirty little articles. I should like to know the bastard who said "obligatory disregard for convention".'

Peter made a sympathetic noise, but he did not prolong the conversation. He waited anxiously in the discontented silence.

Matthew picked up the scored sheet and stared at it. 'This another of your songs?'

'Yes.'

'But it was set hundreds of years ago.' Pointing to the dedication he said, 'Do you suppose Teresa is going to prefer your version to the Elizabethan's?'

'Perhaps not. But I hope she may like it.'

'Hm. Are all these other ones for her?'

'Yes. But don't crumple them, Matthew, there's a good fellow.'

'All right, all right.' He continued to stare at the sheet in his hand, 'I know this one,' he said. 'There was an earnest do-gooder who tried to make us dance roundelays or whatever it is when you put woollen garters with little bells on your legs and caper about flashing your false teeth and spectacles at one another. And he got a parcel of little arty lick-spittles to sing madrigals with him in the bicycle shed. This was one of them.' He began to chant aloud. '"What? I that loved and you that like" – that's always the situation – "shall we begin to wrangle?" – of course you will. By the way, Teresa can't go with you this evening: I did my best for you, but she's got to see a sick aunt. "No, no, no," – that's what you say – "my heart is fast" – he calls it his heart, the half-wit – "and cannot disentangle." It could easily enough if the girl weren't unwilling and inaccessible.' He paused. 'Listen, Peter,' he said, leaning forward, 'can I speak to you frankly? Brutality is supposed to be the duty of a friend.'

'Well,' began the pale young man, turning back from the window.

'It is the kindest thing in the end,' continued Matthew, 'and you might as well be told now as find out later. You're wasting your time running after Teresa. No. Don't get excited. Try to think with your brain instead of your loins – or your heart as I dare say you call it. It's nothing very important: it's just that she is not your type at all, and you aren't hers. You won't get any further with her by turning up every other day and whining that she ought to love you because you love her. Nothing in the world bores a girl worse than that.'

'Is that what she said? Did she tell you that?'

'No. Of course not. But I've got eyes in my head and I've had a good deal more experience than you. I know the type, Peter: it's no use. And anyhow it's not worth looking tragic about. You wouldn't like it if you had her.'

'It's not a question of "having". You don't even begin to under-stand . . .'

'Oh yes I do. Though I suppose you think you're of another flesh. You still really believe that it's all a matter of sighs and soul-mates and talking about music, don't you? With maybe a little surreptitious fondling on the side. It astonishes me that a man of your age can carry on in that way, like a retarded adolescent. You start by building up an image – it is just like this anaemic little song. "Where beauty moves and with delights" – she's quite good-looking in a plutocratic sort of way, but so would anyone else be who could afford to put a working-man's yearly wages on her back. And as for her wit – my God. She's got a brain like a dried pea. "And signs of kindness bind me." She's about as kind as a crocodile.'

'Really, Matthew, you . . .'

'No, it's always the same dreary thing. You're just the same: there's about as much genuine emotion between you as would fill a thimble. It's always the same with you rich people.'

'Rich?'

'You don't have to work for a living do you?'

'Not exactly.'‘

'Then you're rich. If you had started down the mine at twelve, you'd know what rich means. But you've no idea, none of you. If you were put in a narrow seam you'd come out raving mad, not just bandy-legged. That's what money gives you – straight legs. And you don't even know it: you think it's normal to have straight legs.' He stretched out his own and looked at them, flexing his knees sideways.

'They really do look quite all right, Matthew,' said Peter. 'But I thought you said it was rickets.'

'Rickets and going down the pit. Those are two things you

people buy exemption from. But you pay for it. Oh yes, ha, ha. You pay for it. You're so coddled against reality that you no longer have any genuine emotion. You wouldn't write pretty songs about a thin-blooded girl if you were sweating down there at the coal-face, half-naked, with the roof crumbling over your head. You wouldn't think about her at all. No. Your class only have little half-hearted self-pitying abortions of feeling: a strong purge and a tart who knows her job would cure it all by tomorrow. That, or an honest piece of work – though that might kill you. You only feel with your hearts, as you call them. We lower classes feel with our guts, too: our whole bodies. If we want a girl we go and take her. We live a whole life.'

Leaning over the tablecloth and looking sideways at the girl on the red plush beside him, Matthew pursued his theme. 'What sort of a half-baked conception of life can your sort of people possibly have? You are more intelligent than most of them, Teresa, but even so I don't suppose you have been able to learn anything of any value at all.'

The waiter hovered. 'The *ris de veau* is very good,' he suggested, cocking his head on one side.

'What's that? Rice?'

'Isn't it sweetbreads?' said the girl. 'I mean, I don't know. Let's have a chop.'

'There, you see,' said Matthew, as the waiter went away, 'you know the French they write on menus: but you've no more idea of your own identity than this roll. Do you know what an aneroid barometer is?'

'It's the thing you tap in the hall.'

'Exactly. You tap it and then the needle jumps backwards or forwards: you tap it to get an answer. It's insensitive. It doesn't know until it's asked and even then it only gives you a rough average of the state of affairs as it was some time ago. Now take the lower classes, as you call them –'

'But I don't, Matthew.'

'Oh yes you do. We smell and we eat peas with our knives. I'll show you when the dinner comes. But compared with your dumb aneroids we are water barometers. Do you know what a water barometer is?'

'No, Matthew.'

'It's made of very simple materials: nothing fancy, no gilding. Just a huge glass tube about the height of the gallery up there, with water in it and a vacuum in its sealed top. An enormous version of the old-fashioned straight mercury barometer. It isn't pretty. But my God it works. The pressure of the atmosphere varies every second: you'd never know it from an aneroid, but this thing shows it. It's sensitive: it knows what it feels. You don't have to tap it. The top of the water is never still for an instant. When it isn't shooting up and down by a foot or so an hour, it is pulsating, quivering, alive – fully alive. That's me, a tall, upright cylinder, quivering and alive.' He looked sideways at the girl and laughed.

'I don't have to spell it out to you,' he continued. 'You may be only an aneroid by birth, but at least you have made some progress. You don't have to be told – ' His gesticulating hand knocked against the vase of flowers and a stream of water shot across the tablecloth, soaking the bread in its pierced basket and dripping soundlessly into the carpet. 'Damn the thing,' he said, 'this perpetual sniffing at the sexual organs of vegetable is a typical class-perversion. You have no time for it if you go own the mine at half-past four in the morning and sweat dark blood in the belly of the earth. The workers have no time for beating about the bush: if we feel an emotion we feel it strongly and register it at once. Now listen, Teresa,' – sliding his hand along the plush seat to hers – 'I need you: I need you. Not because you are good-looking, but because you've got intelligence, real strong intelligence buried somewhere down there under all your class-prejudices. It's for my work I need you. You could help me.' His face looked cold, hard and determined, but his hand gripped hers with painful strength, grinding the sapphire ring against the emerald. 'I'm not going to woo you, as they call it,' he said. 'I'm not going to send you pretty-pretty songs or vegetables on heat. I'm not going to insult your male intelligence with any of that round-about obscene symbolism. I want your body, of course,' he added, pressing her hand again and sweating a little on the wings of his nose, 'with a precise and localized urgency, but it is your mind that . . .'

In the lonely dusk, far away, Peter sang, 'I sent thee late a rosy wreath'. He had indeed. It looked rather like one of those rings of holly that people hang on their door-knockers at Christmas, and it had cost a week's living. He had asked the shop not to make it look too funereal: but had they entirely succeeded? It had a thick base of moss mounted on a frame of wire; and the wire showed through on the worn place where he had carried it.

'We common people are direct,' said Matthew. 'We are like trees. Have you ever seen an elm in flower? It comes bursting red through the soot of the Black Country, and it stands there proud and outstretched in an act of fertility that goes on all through the spring. That is the difference between my sort and the others. *They* send you a dried, sterile cut flower, pretending that it means something else. *I* offer you a full-grown, virile tree, unashamed and undisguised. I am an elm in flower.'

'Oh Matthew,' she said, dropping her eyes.

36

The Handmaiden

———∞∞∞———

'So, it is settled, then?'

'Yes. It is settled,' she said; and since she was a woman who liked to cope with difficulties at once she stood up and walked straight to the door.

'You're not going *now*, are you?' cried Edward, in an unbelieving tone.

She turned in the opening and smiled. 'Never mind, Edward my dear,' she said, to smooth away the unhappiness she thought he was concealing. 'It really won't be anything at all. I don't mind it.'

'Oh,' he said, and there was a pause. She stood looking back, for the oh still hung up in the air, inconclusive; but all he said was, 'I was just wondering, in that case, whether you would mind coming back by the village. I am right out of tobacco. Since you will be in that direction ...' The untimeliness of his request seemed to become more apparent as he uttered it and his voice trailed away, ending in something between a cough and a laugh, with the word 'anticlimax' thrown in.

'Of course,' she cried, keeping the surprise and disappointment out of her voice and nodding too vigorously. 'A box of Henry Clays and a yellow tin of panatellas.'

What an extraordinarily crass thing to produce, she thought, walking rapidly up the path: but perhaps he had meant to say something quite different. Perhaps this something else had turned out to be in the wrong key altogether while it was actually on its way – emotional or dramatic – and he had hurriedly sub-stituted this awkward piece about cigars. That must certainly be the case, for no one could call Edward blockish. How stupid not to have thought of it at the time. But that had been altogether typical of the discussion: polite, oh so considerate, ham-handed. At the very moment when they most needed to be even closer than usual they had somehow flown miles apart and had found themselves obliged to make blundering, muddled signals across the painful gulf with no common language any more.

How had it begun? And who had started it? She could not tell; but she felt the cold of loneliness and she walked faster up the hill. She had been married for more than ten years now, and she was no longer equipped for individuality: everything in what she thought of as her only genuine life had been doubled and made real by sharing, and this solitude was desolation itself. 'Mrs Grattan,' she murmured, emphasizing the Mrs: and a little later, 'I am in a silly, silly flap.'

At the top of the path she stopped, turned round and sat on a hummock. Their house lay below her, and she gazed studiously down upon it, calming herself with an enumeration of its charms; there were plenty of them, in all conscience; and once the water was piped from La Higuela there would be even more. Lawns . . .

La Higuela. She raised her eyes to look in the direction of the hidden village, and because they had been staring down for so long she saw the whole landscape with a sudden freshness – the col-ours all tuned sharper, the perspectives subtly changed, everything much more important. No longer blunted by familiarity; the view acquired a mysterious significance: a false significance, perhaps, but for the moment this was a portentous landscape, one that might be waiting for some huge event, the Second Coming or the Antichrist, a chariot of fire, the Annunciation.

The feeling of imminence passed almost as soon as she had formulated it; but the freshness stayed. This was how they had first seen the country: rounded bosomy little hills in the fore-ground, all neatly planted with almonds, precise little trees on a pink ground, like embroidery; beyond them, filling the middle distance, an ocean of olives; and then the sierra, sharp against the sky. She let her eyes run from the far left, run steadily along the deserted scene, strangely empty and uninhabited apart from the innumerable host of the olive-trees, along the crests beyond, some snowy and remote, some craggy and quite near; from left to right, taking in the ruined castle, the half-seen abandoned monastery (it had a lovely baroque court, grass-grown and silent, invisible from here), the crumbling triumphal arch among its cypresses, until she reached the hermitage. Here she paused for a moment, gazing affectionately at its little rounded apse, and then swung her head full right for the dramatic contrast, the spectacular set-piece that never failed to come off – the dazzling sweep of sea, the whole pure curve of the bay with the mountains running down to the Mediterranean at the far end, the long coastal plain, bright green with sugar-cane and checkered with different-coloured fields (they were already cutting in some places), the villages flashing white, the round walled town on its mole-hill, the Moorish fortress on the island, and all along the shore the white hem that meant there had been a storm in Africa.

This was how they had first seen it. There was the same even all-embracing light from the sun behind her, gently warm in the soft unclouded midwinter sky, ripening the bananas and the custard-apples and reflecting colour so brilliantly that she could see that the cloth hanging from a window three miles away was blue. Even the flecks of sail on the luminous sea might have been the same, unmoved.

One change there was, but it lay below her, not in the general scene: they had found the house dead and now it was alive. That made a great deal of difference, she thought, looking down on it as objectively as she could. In all this vast expanse of country there were only about seven houses visible, and two of them were ruined. A landscape had to have living houses in it (the remote toy villages of the plain did not count), and this was a living house, beautiful, reasonably-sized, deep in its own land for privacy, built round a patio and surrounded by gardens; and although from this plunging angle she could see little but its pale tiles – nearly all their pink drained out by the sun – she could place the arches of the covered walk exactly and each wrought-iron screen, each well-proportioned opening on to the outside world. The two courts lay open to her view; but so, she noticed with distress, did her little walled garden. Or at least parts of it: all the lily-bed and most of the tamarisks. They had overdone the trimming of the trees, which was a bore, because the walled garden was where she sunbathed; and much as she liked the local peasants she had no wish to play Susannah to any yokel's elder, however picturesque. They would have a pool there, she reflected. When the water came from La Higuela, or a fountain at the very least; and what was now a tawny patch would be real grass, and Irish green.

She was above the house but no great way from it through the air, quite near enough to hear the singing. It was Conchita, of course. After a moment she attended to the song, a flattened version of a record the radio had been plugging these last months, and shrugged with a slight impatience. Conchita could sing fla-menco so beautifully . . . but it was no use going on and on. She must be singing in the drawing-room. How odd. Conchita had a strong sense of the proprieties, stronger than Paula Grattan's, and she had never been heard to utter except in the kitchen or the court outside it. She *was* in the drawing-room: Paula saw the window open and a mop come out. What of it? She said, faintly disgusted at having stared so long to prove her tiny point. What *did* it matter? Yet it added a little to her returning sense of – not exactly of displeasure, which sounded pompous, but of *not being pleased*. And although she went on in a more equable state than she had started out, this feeling came back to her more than once in the course of her walk.

It was a damned thing, this going to La Sartén. A damned thing. But it was no good anticipating the encounter. She knew what she had to say, had rehearsed it several times: why go through the whole process twice in the same day?

She walked along the sandy road through the olives, trying to keep her mind serene and blank; and for a while she thought she was succeeding. She took an intelligent interest in a hoopoe that was obviously wintering here, well north of its usual limits, a charming cinnamon-coloured bird with black and white bars that walked busily, short-legged, in front of her, rising every now and then to flit a hundred yards farther on, raising its crest each time it took off or landed; but then she found that her fingers were picking convulsively at her balled-up handkerchief and must have been doing so for the last half mile.

They had talked over their plan so often and for so long now that it had come to seem quite reasonable, even quite ordinary: no longer wildly abnormal, grotesque, impossible to phrase with any decency. Surely, with each encouraging the other, they had distorted their perspective? Now that she was alone, actually walking along the cart-track to La Sartén, with no one to prop up her conviction, the whole thing was beginning to look to her as it must look to the rest of the world. Or was she being stupid again?

Now that it was becoming a practical issue, a matter of immediate action, with such disconcerting speed, the whole thing seemed to her profoundly distasteful. An ugly business. Was it so in fact? Was she not merely trying to shirk the interview ahead? How much was plain jealousy?

The house came in sight. She found herself dawdling, looking with an exaggerated interest at the olives, their ancient trunks split, rent in three, sawed and mutilated over the centuries, standing images of torture, confined in round walls like well-heads, imprisoned; but each with its boughs inhabited by a luminous aerial being that lived on the wind.

This would never do. Half-consciously she checked her hair, face, clothes; and achieving a real silence of mind for the first time that day, she walked straight on through the trees.

Mrs Grattan sat on a straight-backed black chair that had been set for her where the beaten earth met the hearthstone: on her right an immense pot hung darkly over a glow in the cavernous fireplace; to her left the twilight held two or three women dressed in black: aunts. Only in front, sitting on a broken chair and two boxes was there a clearly visible group – Conchita's mother, a female cousin, and another aunt. They were all dressed in black cotton, with black shawls, black stockings, and black rope-soled shoes; they all had eyes screwed up and watering, red-rimmed from their work in the shifting glare of the olive-leaves; they were all of the same indeterminate age, between forty and eighty; and she could not certainly tell one from the other. Her chair-leg was slowly sinking where an undetected spill of soup had softened the ground, and a good deal of her attention was taken up with keeping her balance and at the same time concealing the fact; but enough was free to have received a number of impressions – the oilcloth on the round table smelt just like the oilcloth in the kitchen at Killeen: the hens that walked in and out seemed to be house-trained: the ornaments were of a fair-ground tawdriness past belief: the everyday pots were fit for a museum: they did their washing-up in what must surely be an alabaster sarcoph- agus. The anecdote about the health of an unknown child at a great distance was drawing to a close, and with it the period of necessarily-wasted time.

Very well, she thought, so this is it. At least I have a better lead-in than I could have expected. In an unemphatic voice she said, 'As you know, ladies, there are no children in my house. My husband and I had always hoped for a child, but now the doc- tors say we shall never have one. It is I who am barren, not my husband. We had thought of adoption, but you cannot tell whose child it might be; and it rarely succeeds. What we hope is to find a young woman of good character and a very respectable family whose parents will allow her to bear my husband a baby. We know that this might injure the young woman's chances of marrying, but we should provide her with a handsome dowry. We have often discussed it . . .'

Yes: very often. It was her suggestion in the first place: she had never forgotten Edward's delight at her supposed pregnancy long ago, nor the way he had sung about the house, laughing and saying, 'Now we shall not all die.' And apart from that there were so many, many reasons: everything in favour of it.

And now this had seemed the perfect – not *opportunity*, that odious, exploiting word, all wrong – but rather combination of circumstances. This family was healthy, desperately poor, and manless, having been on the losing side in the civil war; they were anti-clerical and therefore not subject to the priest; the girl herself was clean, beautifully built, and now that she had been fed properly, outstandingly attractive. How brutish and ugly it all sounded: but those were the raw facts, and they were unchangeable.

Ugly. Yet in their own private language it had all become so quickly stylized, dulcified, attenuated; they had been facetious about the patter of little feet, the happy event, bawds, interesting condition, the onlie begetter.

Then again they had had one of their enthusiasms about Conchita and her family; had been silly, attributing all sorts of earthy virtues to them. Why were they both still so silly, after years and years of adult life? She did not even like these people at all, she reflected, looking at them. Those who were in the light might just as well have been in the dark: there was nothing to be told from those closed, lined, concerned faces. Dim, dim creatures, almost extinguished by the burden of their life. No human contact. She could not tell what they thought of the proposal nor what they thought of her.

Having said what she had to say right to the very end, she sat there, physically relaxed now that the chair had stopped sinking, but exhausted and empty. The sun, coming in at a wider angle, lit the side of her small head, still held up quite straight: with her ash-blonde hair and her grey eyes, and with a composed, even remote expression on her face, she looked incredibly distinguished; and, in that dark, huddled room, incredibly foreign. She also seemed indifferent to the outcome of her speech.

The aunt who spoke the heaviest dialect was still going on and on about some place of pilgrimage far away to the north, in the Pyrenees, where childless people went on foot, climbing the mountain to couple with their heads in a holy saucepan: at least that was what it sounded like. She could only be sure of understanding Conchita's mother, who spoke something like standard Spanish.

What did they think? Many and many a time had she inveighed against the Spaniards' stupid affectation of being high and proud, of never smiling, of concealing their emotions in this silly, theatrical way; often had she wished to bang their heads together and make them behave naturally; but never so much as now. 'They caught it from the Moors,' she repeated, and all at once she became aware that for some minutes past she had been driving her wedding-ring into the knuckle of the opposing finger with painful force. Her hands were clasped on her lap: she looked at them. They clasped, loosened, moved over one another, and clasped again. Dear me, she thought, I am *wringing my hands*: so people really do: I am *amazed*.

The hoopoe was still there, drinking at a pool left from the autumn rain: it lowered its long curved beak, raised it vertically, closed its eyes and swallowed glug-glug-glug, like a hen. 'Lord,' she said, 'what wouldn't I give for a drink! A stiff one.' For a while she hesitated between the cold, roborative kick of a martini and the immediate lift of whiskey: gin was the right thing for a bawd, however, and she would have it the moment she reached home. She could see the misted glass with the olive looming faintly through and a sliver of lemon from their own untreated tree: a bowl of pine-kernels too, and some salted almonds. Conchita was very good with drinks. Edward had taught her the whole ceremony.

How astonishing that she should have come from La Sartén, thought Paula: practically a cave-dwelling. In her maid's uniform – long black dress, frilly apron, cap and streamers – she looked like a drawing from an old bound volume of *Punch*. To be sure, the clothes were natural enough in Spain, where so many things looked as though they had escaped from the nineties; but Conchita also behaved like a maid in one of those archaic pictures. You would have said she was the product of generations of good service, trained by the housekeeper of some big place in the country: she looked so much the part that it was absurd to hear

Spanish coming from her mouth rather than a gentle brogue. Modest, good, and oh so pretty. It made one smile to look at her.

It *was* astonishing. But at one time she had thought it even more so: in those days she had thought Conchita quite the prettiest, brightest girl she had ever seen, and had meant to teach her to read – to bring out her innumerable latent virtues, intelligence, taste and all the rest of it. How grossly unfair, and at this point how horribly suspect, to blame the child for not being what she had never claimed to be: Conchita might be rather stupid, resistant to learning, a besotted and firmly illiterate watcher of the television, but she still remained pretty, diligent, honest, industrious, reliable … And she could sew beautifully, insisted Paula Grattan, topping the hill above their house, and as for washing – 'Oh my God,' she whispered, stock-still on the hidden path.

Clear below her in the small walled garden stood a figure wearing a familiar housecoat, poised there in the sun. Another squeal pierced up through the still air, and as she uttered it Conchita darted into the tamarisks. The soft branches waved; from beneath their feathery covering came another cry, the excited whoop of amorous pursuit and ritual flight. For a moment the girl reappeared at the edge of the tamarisks, struggling, the blue coat held by unseen hands in the bush, pulled open and showing her long white legs, her belly, her high young bosom. Then she toppled beneath the heavy foliage: shrill protests, diminishing; a slap. Silence.

Her first reaction was incandescent anger. She stood rigid there with her fists and her teeth clenched and all the foul words she had ever heard rushed through her mind. 'In *my* garden,' she said hoarsely. 'In *my* garden – in *my* housecoat – under my very eyes, the bitch.'

Her knees were trembling and she sat down, turning her head away from the garden. She scrabbled blindly in her bag for a cigarette: her face was set and very pale.

She could not light the cigarette and she threw it impatiently away. Her whole being was seething with fury and malignance:

a torrent of disconnected ejaculations raced through her injured spirit: 'Couldn't wait for it – the putrid little whore – the odious, lecherous bastard – bald and fat – I always thought she was a tart – sly, sly as a cat – a cat on heat – in my own garden, the swine – turning the house into a brothel.' But all this only served to relieve her immediate rage; beneath it a monstrous suspicion was taking form, thrusting up through the anger.

How long had this been going on? Had they been making a fool of her since the beginning? Did they do it every time she went out? She remembered Conchita's singing 'the moment they had the house to themselves'. But with a far deeper stab she returned to the knowledge that Edward had asked her to go round by La Higuela: under the stress of her interview she had entirely forgotten about his cigars and she was back long before they could have expected her. Had he really done that? Had he really sent her out of the way? She could almost swear she had seen a handful of cigars in the box last night when she was tidying round his chair. In that case it *was* just a pretext; his painfully awkward words were . . . oh surely not? The mounting cold put out her anger: her intelligence swept the declamatory nonsense to one side and began to probe the real question. She searched back and back into her memory: who had started the idea in the first place? Who had renewed it when Conchita arrived? She thought *she* had. Most probably, though she could not remember the occasion. But had it been planted in her mind? She wanted the truth, nothing else at all; but it was terribly elusive. Even in this last discussion, which had brought things to the plane of action and which had ended so clumsily, who had been the real initiator? Where had this dreadful lack of sympathy come from? At one time she had thought it was from her own suppressed jealousy; was it really from his awareness?

Suppose he had already got the girl with child, wouldn't he then send her off for this ghastly interview so as to have it all legalized after the event? This was a new theory that came forcing itself in, together with a bitter resentment of the heartless insensitivity that *could* ask her to walk another couple of miles after such a party, that *could* agree to her offer to make all the arrangements singlehanded, that *could* send her to say, 'My husband wishes to use your daughter for breeding purposes. What will you take for her virginity?' without a scrap of moral support. Though indeed he spoke almost no Spanish, cried another of her voices; and it was true that he – it was not fair to . . .

She brushed all that aside and with passionate concentration she burrowed through the history of words, gestures, moods, tones of voice, to find the truth; but she could not ever be sure that she had it; she could not ever be sure that she was not successfully lying to herself, either believing what she wanted to believe or insisting upon martyrdom.

She turned her head from side to side: she could not keep her mind needle-sharp and cold. She was too tired, dispirited, and sad, sad. The renewed desolation of loneliness struck her with infinitely greater force and she bowed her face into her hands: tears ran between her fingers to the dusty ground.

In time she returned to the ordinary, demanding world. She was disgusted with the scene she had made and with the poisonous, dirtying, ugly things she had said; she was disgusted with the whole thing and she was weary through and through. But while she was repairing the worst of the havoc done to her face ('My God,' she said to the little mirror, 'what a wreck') she found that her judgment had fixed rock-hard upon a decision. She would go down to the house and find out whether there were cigars left in that box or not. If there were not, if it was empty in fact, then he might just have yielded to a sudden burst of goatishness: *that* she could cope with – that would be a recognizable Edward. But if there *were* . . . why then she would have been a complacent fool for all this while. She would have been genuinely deceived and she would have to make a fundamental reassessment, since the Edward who could send her (she prayed she was not blaspheming him) on such an errand, and for such a purpose, would be a stranger to her, a man she had never really known; perhaps even an enemy. Everything she had ever heard about cold duplicity

318

in marriage came back to her: tales of unsuspected change, malevolence, concealed bitterness.

But she had to know. She had to know one way or the other. And suppressing a little habitual whimper to Edward (her invariable recourse in unhappiness till then), she walked down the path.

Before coming to the door itself she made a noise; she was ashamed of doing so, but she had to – it would not be bearable to catch them, to stumble right on to the beast with two backs and meet its hatred. So shoving the iron garden-gate to and fro she advertised her presence: a harsh metallic clangour.

She did not know quite what she had expected, but it was certainly not the front-door half open and Conchita's face peering through the gap. Sickened by the noise she had made – the grating of the iron had pierced through and through her aching head – and perhaps encouraged by the scared little face, she walked straight forward, brushing her hands.

The girl stood back, retreating into the hall. She was still buttoning her black dress and at the same time trying to confine stray wisps of hair. She was ivory pale, and Paula Grattan could hardly make out what she was saying.

Paula's senses were unnaturally acute: she was aware that there was something here she had not expected at all, a tension in the house that did not match with her own. The hypotheses raced through her head and she was already more than half way to the answer when, glancing over her shoulder, she saw a slim youth glide away by the garden wall.

Conchita followed her eyes: stifled a despairing cry but not a flaming blush. Paula caught some distracted words about 'a cousin, who happened to be passing by', and turned away to gaze at the maiolica on the hall table while she mastered her own feelings and let Conchita do the same. Without turning round she asked where Edward was. He had gone to the village for tobacco – he had none left – had started a little after the señora – he meant to surprise her on the road.

Listening attentively to this, Paula chose her most beloved vase, the roundest, as an offering. She closed her eyes and let it drop: the pot exploded like a bomb. 'When you have swept up the pieces, my dear,' she said, 'be very kind and bring me a martini in the drawing-room. And Conchita, you must take great care with men; it is terrible what they can do to a woman.' She walked along the hall towards the door, called, 'Never mind about the drink,' and hurried out of the house on Edward's track.

37
The Thermometer

They had nothing whatever to say to one another, and between them the silence grew so massive that it could almost be seen: on the one side of it small boy – of what age? He had asked, but the reply had slipped his mind. Below the age of puberty, no doubt, he reflected, taking the short trousers as evidence, and by so much the more removed from humanness: but how much below it? A squat and meagre child. It might be anything. If it had been a specimen – and it looked not unlike some of the swarthy things his colleagues dissected – it would have had a label with all the relevant information. What the devil could he do with it, do with it? His mind trailed off into an habitual repetition.

The boy saw a vast column of authority on the other side, omnipotent and grey. Grey the vague clothing that draped the massive form, grey the enormous trousers, untidily folded like an elephant; and the huge stone face, expressionless and everlasting, was also grey. The boy was not conscious of having stared, yet he knew that grey hair not only covered that head, but also, in a horribly fascinating way, burst in tufts from the ears, and even appeared, unnaturally straggling, on the bridge of the nose. The only exception to this rule of grey was the eyes, which were watery blue with red margins: the boy did not look up, of course, but he was aware of these eyes, gleaming weirdly through the thick, distorting lenses of a pair of thin steel-rimmed spectacles, looking across the silence at him – down at him, from a height of about a yard above his own head and at a distance exactly equal to the length of the piece of Turkey carpet on which they stood. At the same time, but from different heights and distances, Koch, Pasteur, Ehrlich, Creighton, Beale and Muller, in frock-coats, beards and steel-rimmed spectacles, dignified, hairy and inhuman, gazed out from the walls into the middle of the room, adding to the silence.

The boy was oppressed by the silence, but not every much He was not answerable, and so long at he stood still with fidgetting, picking, staring, sniffing, gaping, biting his nails, stooping, gnawing the inside of his mouth or turning his toes in, he could not be blamed. At least, he could not be blamed by the rules; and he was willing to credit his cousin once removed (for those enormous hair-backed hands which were now holding a watch on the blurred upward horizon of his field of vision belonged in fact to his paternal grandfather's nephew) with decency enough to observe the rules, if only at first. Being not to blame, therefore, he was free to argue out the pattern of the carpet and to absorb the various smells of the room – tobacco, books – the room was lined with them below a certain height and their backs gave off an odour of glue, dye and buckram: new books and shiny quarterlies – warmed town air and above all chemicals, pungent and unfamiliar.

At one time during the silence Mr Carew had taken his watch out of his waistcoat pocket with an indistinct notion of holding it to his cousin's ear; but a moment's reflection had told him that this gesture would be quite unsuitable in the present case and he was in the act of closing it when his mind strayed off to its repetition of 'do with it, do with it', and from that point to a less uneasy general meditation, if not to a temporary mental stagnation.

The watch remained open in his hand: it was a hunter, and its outer cover stood at right angles from the dial, while between the two the leaf-thin inner cover caught the light in a double gleam. The whole looked like an exotic flower: the boy watched it with his eyes deliberately unfocused and somewhat crossed to make the golden image swim. But it vanished suddenly and with a triple click as Mr Carew cleared his throat, returned entirely to the present, and said, 'Well, I suppose you would like to rest after your journey? Yes, I am sure you would. And here is the paper, if you would like to look at it . . . through the door.'

When he opened the door he had a stupefying impression of blindness and being unable to breathe, for instead of the air and light that had always met him on the other side of every door there was a curtain, and because his eyes were unprepared for anything so near they could not make it out. An arm stretched suddenly over his head and he automatically dodged his head under his upraised elbow, but it was only Mr Carew reaching for the curtain. 'Against the draughts,' said the deep voice on high as they passed through the dust-smelling folds.

He found himself alone, holding *The Times*, in a new room. Mr Carew would come back at four 'when he had been to the Institute' and then 'they would have a cup of tea together and talk over the future.' The heavy brown curtain had fallen at the word 'future' concealing Cousin Carew; but almost at once it had stirred and billowed; the enormous form had partially emerged and looking upwards he had met the queer, magnified pale glare full in the eye, all the time the huge voice was saying with an artificial lightness and certainty, 'Of course I need not say that I am sure that nothing will be touched.'

So he stood for some time, quite still, while this unpleasant and even shocking introduction to the room receded from the present. It was a cold, stark room, lit by the north light which flooded in through a window whose panes were made of ground glass: this blind but shining quality in the window, together with the *portière* that masked the door, gave the inside of the room and everything that went on inside it, a very special feeling of insulation- a deaf and inner world. It was an improbable room: that is to say, no person that he could conceive could ever have lived in it, although it possessed a shining, black, horsehair couch. It was the kind of room that could only be accepted: but he saw at once that it possessed extraordinary attractions. He walked over to the couch, on which it was supposed that he would recline, sipping *The Times* and dozing, until four o'clock; it was high and slippery, but at the second attempt he scaled it, and sat there dangling his legs. So much was required of him in politeness to the fiction that he was tired after his journey: he also unfolded *The Times*.

It was not a room into which a man accustomed to children would have introduced the little boy. Cradled in its basket under the main laboratory bench stood a carboy of sulphuric acid, ten gallons of brimming vitriol, while above it nitric, hydrocyanic, oxalic, hydrochloric, malic, formic and hydrofluoric offered their possibilities of fuming experiment and sudden death in a neat range of Winchester quarts. On a shelf to the right of the bench a large jar of caustic soda in cigarette-like sticks provided the same end by a different means: the strychnine was on the top of the cupboard, however, and almost out of reach.

And then from the opposite point of view, the incubator held cultures and living tissues that were the fruit of long months of preparation – a hand playing with the long rod of the thermo-static control, or even idly fondling its shining counterpoise, might falsify the results of a whole series of experiments – and apart from the incubator there were scores of appliances, instru-ments, switches, dials and complicated arrangements of glass, all functioning and all vulnerable: it was decidedly unsuitable in every way.

He listened. One did not live with Mrs Clapp for long with-out becoming tolerably sly, and he listened for a good while. Yet this was little more than an automatically-taken precaution: he did not really believe that Cousin Carew would lurk in the pas-sage, creep to the door, turn its oiled handle silently and flung it open to catch you in some forbidden pursuit, such as staring in the looking-glass. Cousin Carew would indulge in any excesses he chose (subject to the rules), seeing that he had the power to do so; but he was so much larger than even Mrs Clapp's most spiteful predictions had foretold, so bodily vast and spiritually overwhelming, that these excesses would be of the Sodom and Gomorrah kind or nothing at all – fire, brimstone and annihila-tion at the least; nothing trifling like waiting at the door.

Still, he listened; and it was not until ten slow minutes had gone that he slipped down and began his first, tentative, tiptoe exploration of the room. It was a five-sided room with the couch flanked by glass-fronted bookshelves along one wall, and as he proceeded anti-clockwise round it he came first to the long, high microscope table, with its tall and unlikely stools. There were two microscopes on it, one under a glass bell. Next came the curtain that hid the door, then a white cupboard with a white metal trolley in front of it, then a bare expanse of the third wall. Here was a picture, the only one in the room: it was a large picture, and in it an immense and bearded figure waded knee-deep in the sea, bowed under the burden of a curious great slab, which he was carrying from right to left. No one could say where he was carrying it to, but he was going very carefully, in order to keep it flat, because the top of the slab was a garden: you could consider the slab as a kind of stone tray – a very large one, because the garden was big enough to have quite large trees growing in it, and it was full of people of the ordinary size. They wore robes. Some were dancing but those who were nearest were lying on their sides, *letting water pour out of jars over the edge.* They were holding the jars in a loose sort of way, but they were not really taking any notice: they were not even looking where it was going. They did not look over the edge: nor did anybody else up there. Perhaps they did not know that they were being carried and if so they were a stupid lot.

How did they get water up there, being detached? And it was so silly to show it always pouring out like that: it would not last any time. Some of it might be dribbling on to the giant. Was it meant to be Cousin Carew? How would they ever be able to renew their water? Perhaps when he had waded a bit farther he would come to an enormous rock and he would smash them all down on it. If it was meant for Cousin Carew, why the beard?

It was an unsatisfactory picture really, and presently he moved on, still undecided. Here was the beginning of the long, white-tiled laboratory sink that swept round the shallow angle to the fourth wall of frosted glass, where the main bench showed its array of laboratory glass – retorts on tripods, upright tubes clasped in iron tongs, red rubber tubing, corks with glass tubes coming through them, bottles joined by the middle, by the neck, by the bottom. Bunsen burners. By comparison the fifth wall was dull: it only had the incubator, a microtome and a centrifuge that happened to have had its handle taken off.

His tour lasted some time, quite long enough for the peculiarly cut-off, contained atmosphere of the silent room to have impinged upon him and to have given him the beginning of that feeling of total privacy that was essential for glee in him.

The third time round he climbed the rungs of one of the stools and sat upon the horse-hair eminence – Mr Carew had a passion for black upholstery stuffed with horse-hair – looking at the microscope, the rows of test-tubes in their racks, each with its sloping field of jelly, speckled or striated, the rows of slides, the parade of dropping-bottles, aligned by size from the right and all pointing their noses to the left. Basic Fuchsin, he read on the nearest, while he was wondering how to look down the microscope without touching it. What was Fuchsin, and how could it be Basic? The microscope was not very difficult; but he had to kneel on the stool and put a hand on each side of the stand to have his head poised right over the eyepiece. But it was a disappointing tube. At first he could see nothing whatever, and even when after long peering he made out a dim grey round down there, with the shadow of his eyelashes crossing and recrossing its surface, it was not very exciting: and if it had not been for the potency of the words 'Looking through a microscope', he would not have hung over the unlit instrument for two minutes, let alone a quarter of an hour.

The picture yielded no more at this examination than it had at first. The water still poured in unaccountable vexing waste from the jars, the gigantic Cousin Carew forged carefully on through the deep, bent under his careless load. Surely he would chuck the whole thing off when he got out really far? It was impossible to tell from his expression, however, which was inscrutable and old.

He was moving slowly away from the picture, bowed, with lumpish motions, looking inscrutable and old, when he noticed a small looking-glass by the sink. He hurried to it and leaning over the sink to bring his face as close as possible to the glass he gibbered silently for a while. Then he dragged down the lower covers of his eyes until a great deal of red showed, and afterwards he stretched his face sideways with the palms of his hands hard and long so that his eyes almost vanished and the tight skin over his nose and cheekbones showed yellow against the blueish tumescence of his distorted lips; this was his most accomplished face; but before it reached perfection and the utmost limit of the stretch his eyes always lost their ability to see and he could only guess the ultimate effect.

He throttled himself dull purple with his tie, investigated the gaps in his teeth, and settled down to his usual intercourse with this rare, most treasured and best companion – rare, because of Mrs Clapp's aversion for mirrors.

He leant close and imitated Mrs Clapp for his own applause. Tightening his lips and narrowing his eyes he said, 'Now then, now then . . .' But his invention failed him and for his portrait he fell back on a list of words, *combinations, drawers, undergarments, noblesse oblige*, which were typical of her, and unmentionable words which she said openly, like crutch, armpits, nostril. Article. Mrs Clapp called a chamber-pot the article. There was one under his bed; but he was not allowed to use it.

He protruded his lower jaw, and in defiance of Mrs Clapp he said the oaths Damn, belly, dung, Devil, bloody. His reflection applauded this daring flight, but the words were hardly out before he felt uneasy, for the last two were blasphemy and they had been clearly said, not mumbled with the possibility of casuistical excuse.

This momentarily chilled his enjoyment; he turned away from the looking-glass and that mirror-world in which he was somewhat compromised, and moved into the clear middle of the room, where he span until he was dizzy – the best way he knew of changing an unwelcome Bow of thoughts and averting the evil chance.

Staggering, he reached the main bench along the blind but

luminous window, the bench with the retorts, the air-pump, the flasks, phials, alembics and tubes, and the Bunsen burners. One of these had a pilot-light, a minute plume of stiff blue flame, and laying his head sideways on the zinc-covered bench to steady himself he saw that the flame possessed a little ghost of dancing air, like the few candles he had been left alone with. They had been utterly absorbing: he had burnt the matches from the tray of the candlestick, burning them at each end and dipping them in the pool below the foot of the flame so that they would burn again, on and on, until at last the candle died, a tiny blue flame with no yellow left, a bishop's hat, floating on the pool right down in the socket – a flame that would become too small and delicate to be touched or helped with the charred end of a match, a flame that would go on nevertheless, existing with no more light than would just illuminate the pool of wax and the busy circulation in it, detached almost entirely from the wick, but which finally, for no reason – certainly for no incautious breath of his – would gather itself from below, draw up a hairsbreadth higher and vanish upwards, leaving him stiff, cold and still partially hypnotised.

The flame of the Bunsen burner was very good indeed: it did not have the supernatural qualities of the candle, but in some ways that was just as well, and in active burning powers and robustness there was no comparison at all. He had defeated his conscience at once: his hard-learnt caution had resisted, but step by step it had given way, and now, waiting for the mercury in the thermometer to creep down, he placidly directed the tongue of flame down-wards, flattening it against the zinc table-top. Again the metal sweated mysteriously under the heat: it should have dried, in the course of nature, but it sweated, and the drops, running viscidly into one another, smelt vile like a gas-works. To his right lay the unscattered ashes of what little he had found to burn in this aseptic place – two matchsticks, half an inch of discarded rubber tubing, a little paper, some horsehair and the chips from a pencil sharpening and to his left the thermometer, with its obedient life.

It was an unusually long thermometer, graduated to four

hundred degrees, and by now he had perfected a ritual in which he made the quicksilver mount stage by stage to the very top, to the unmarked space above the highest score. He had done it a great many times already, driving it up by the power of the flame, with a continuous murmur of command and warning – an incantation that worked certainly – and now he was waiting to do it again. Unfortunately, it would now come down nearly as quickly as it would go up, and that meant too long a wait between the necromancies.

It had just been lying there, this thermometer, naked on the bench about eighteen inches from the burner with the pilot-light; and even now it was not above a foot from its original position. Long before, when his caution still was jagging across his pleasure, he had pointed out that his retreat was secure: he had only to turn the tap with one motion, put down the thermometer with another and make three steps towards the couch to be as safe as if he had lain there all the afternoon.

It would be cool now, he thought, setting the burner down on its base: but it was not; the silver still showed quite high in the stalk, and its downward movement was now so slow that it could hardly be seen at all. He blew on it and the mercury shrank a little: it had nearly reached the thirty mark, and when it did it would only have ten more to go, because the ritual could begin when it reached twenty, the point at which he had found it. But how it crawled.

With some surprise at his stupidity, in not thinking of it before, but with more pleasure at having thought of it now, he darted over to the sink, dribbled the cold tap on to the thermometer and saw it contract to ten degrees.

He was so pleased. This would allow him to command the quicksilver in both directions, to say 'Zadkiel sink down' as well as 'Rise Zadkiel'. He filled a beaker at the tap and carried it carefully to the bench, holding the thermometer across his mouth like a stick.

He turned the burner higher, and hurrying his liturgy he made the mercury race up count by count: at the end, by the four hundred mark itself, he was quite mute. His sallow face was pink and his eyes shone as he held the tube, now a solid bar of mercury, over the cold water. His gaze was fixed on the silver column as he lowered the bulb into the beaker: as soon as it touched he would see the quicksilver shoot right down. Not breathing, he let it carefully to the surface of the water: there was a sharp hiss, the bulb and the lower inches of the thermometer shivered, and he saw the column separate into an unconnected row – dashes of mercury.

At first he could not understand what had happened. Then, in spite of the fragments of glass, he would not. It was too dreadful to be true; and he stood there motionless, quite ashy pale; his mind was so beset, and so shocked, that for a long time he could not tell what he thought, nor what he felt except the presence of disaster. He stood there holding the tube very carefully, waiting for it to come right again: and more and more the awful suspicion that it might not ever come right flooded into him.

It still might not be true, or not wholly true: there was hope, he thought, when he was thinking again after the first full shock; and softly he turned the Bunsen burner out, tiptoed to the sink and with infinite attention he poured the water off the quicksilver and the little mess of glass.

He tried and tried again, but the pieces would not stick with spit; the quicksilver would not run back into the tube at all; and while he was pressing a piece of glass against the broken end another two inches came away and shattered on the floor. Yet still at the very bottom of his mind he believed that something beautiful would happen that would enable him to put the healed thermometer very gently down exactly where he had found it and go and sit on the couch until the end of the day. It went slowly, this belief, and he did not see it flicker out; but immediately afterwards he understood that the catastrophe was whole and real, and that his attempt at piecing together the fragments could never succeed.

He accepted this dully, and after one or two faint gestures of protest he stopped even trying to complete the impossible jigsaw: the pieces, ten large ones and innumerable fragments, lay arranged in front of him; what was left of the quicksilver was in the beaker to his right, and the broken thermometer lay across behind the smallest fragments. All he had to do now was to wait: in the exhaustion of his spirit he felt quite numb, and now, if he had been a crying child, he would have wept, long, with his head down on his arms. But he was dogged still, and after a long time he began a sort of little dreary joyless game of spillikins, arranging and rearranging the pile of fragments with the longest splinter.

A remote, muffled noise somewhere outside wrenched him alive with a tingling jet of fear, and he realized what he was waiting for – that he was waiting for the end of the afternoon and that the end of the afternoon was really coming, and that then the door behind the curtain would open.

He hurried to the couch and sat on it, holding the newspaper, a symbol of obedience. If only it had not happened: once he could almost have persuaded himself that it had not, or that it would all come right, but there was no hope of that now. It was too late: and everything began to seem much worse, the enormity even greater, and with a violent new sense of worry he feared that perhaps he had broken the microscope too.

He had not: he went to it, and it was not broken. But what did that matter? It was no comfort. The thermometer was and the microscope might as well have been: it made no difference.

If he picked up the microscope and smashed it and the Basic Fucshin and all the pointed bottles? And then smashed the ground-glass windows and found a way out? He stared round and round, breathing deeply.

He was feeling sick. He was going to be sick. For a long time he hung over the sink with the tap running: he took a drink in his cupped hands. Now he was very cold and his desperate apprehension seemed to have been swallowed up in the misery of being sick: yet the first sound revived it, and now that the twilight was beginning to make the frigid windows more important in the room his jangling nerves caught the faintest sounds or invented them. It must surely soon be four o'clock?

Yet time went on and on and on. Shut away in that darkening room, sealed from the rest of the world, he felt that it had gone wrong, as it sometimes had before – time had gone wrong when he had been lost, and once in a waiting-room. For a good while there had been no sound, and he was beginning to dull the edge of full reality again when with an appalling explosion a telephone bell shrieked out.

It seemed to be coming from over by the window, but he did nothing about it: he stood in the middle of the room, clasping and unclasping his hands while the noise battered his head. Behind him the curtain swelled and parted and let in a great stream of golden light with the huge dark man in it.

'In the dark! Why . . .' He heard the words mingling with the dreadful bell, the thumping fast strides, a little crash of glass and the click of the telephone.

'Hallo? Yes, but just hold on a minute. I'm in the dark and something has fallen over. Philip, put on the light, will you? By the door. To the right.' And screwing up his eyes he saw Cousin Carew leaning on the bench, still vaster in his overcoat. 'No, nothing at all,' he was saying. 'It was only that I knocked a thermometer off the bench with my coat and trod on it. Nothing of any importance. I was afraid it might have been the ureometer. I say I was afraid it might . . . no, no, nothing of importance. A thermometer. No. No. It was only a thermometer.'

38

The Centurion's Gig

The wind went down with the sun, and presently there was nothing but a hot air wafting out of Africa. It was just enough to fill the sails of the *Wager* as she stood south-south-west under her courses, topsails, and topgallantsails, exactly in the wake of her next in line ahead, that elegant rakish forty-gun ship the *Pearl*; but it was not enough to send the least breath down into the suffocating depths where the *Wager*'s midshipmen had their being.

The midshipmen's berth in H.M.S. *Wager* was low, cramped, awkward, and crowded; and therefore, it was in these latitudes – not far to the north of the tropic of Cancer – uncommonly hot – a perfectly normal state of affairs in the Royal Navy; but the young gentlemen, the midshipmen, the master's mates, and other such low forms of life that dwelt there, had seen fit to make it very much hotter, first by eating a supplementary two pounds of salt pork a head in honour of their guests, Mr Palafox of the *Centurion* and Mr Shovell of the *Gloucester*, and then by launching into a most passionate argument about when the century would end.

'It is so staringly obvious to even the very weakest understanding that the nineteenth century will begin on 1 January 1800,' said James Campbell, staring round the table and automatically ducking as the Atlantic swell sent the heavy brass lamp swinging at his head, 'that I am amazed any poor clot-polled gowk should think it worth his breath to deny it. Amazed, amazed.' And indeed he looked tolerably amazed, for the punch that was supposed to be quenching the pork-raised thirst had been given a double ration of naval rum, by way of celebration, and its fumes were fast mounting to his head, giving him a very glassy and stolid expression indeed.

Three voices from the gloom instantly broke in with three different but very heated refutations, and above them all could be heard the piping of William Teape, the youngest of the company – he was but twelve, though he had been on the books of his uncle's ship these last three years – crying, 'It all started with the year nought. You must count the year nought!'

It so happened that all these people exhausted their breath at the same moment, and in the momentary silence Jack Byron said to the surgeon's mate, 'What do you make of it, Toby?' The surgeon's mate was peering intently at a scaly creature about three inches long that had dropped from the beam above his head and that was now eagerly devouring the piece of cheese he held towards it on the point of a lancet. 'Why, I take it to be a form of Willoughby's great chaenomastrix,' said Tobias Barrow.

'No, no. I mean what do you make of it – when will the century end?'

'What century?'

'Why, the century we have been talking about this last age – this century, our century. It ends in 1800, does it not? With 1801 as the first of the next. It stands to reason.'

'Dr Price,' said the surgeon's mate, taking a sip of punch to refresh his mind, 'the great Dr Price, as he is properly called, for his eminent talents and particularly his transcendent skill in civil calculation, was applied to, to settle the astronomical, or chronological, or grammatical, or metaphysical point in question – for it partakes of all these qualities . . .'

'Have a banana!' cried a great spotted youth named Cozens, banging the table with delight at his own wit. 'Haw, haw!'

'Though why you should worry your heads about the matter puzzles me, I confess,' said Toby, glaring sharply at them through his thick spectacles, for Willoughby's great chaenomastrix had taken offence at the noise and had darted into the bosom of the sleeping Mr Shovell of the *Gloucester*, 'seeing that it is only 1740 now, and to judge by your manners, your gross beastly appetites – or shall I say bulimies? – and what I know of your healths, not one of you is likely to survive six months, let alone sixty years.'

'Never say that, soul,' cried Cozens, who was in fact to leave his bones on a desolate frozen shore before his next full year was out. He spoke in a suddenly uneasy voice, for he had been bred to the sea (which Tobias Barrow had not), and like so many sailors he was deeply superstitious: indeed the whole berth fell so gloomy all at once that Jack Byron thought it his duty to say to their guest, 'Mr Palafox, sir, would you care to take a turn on deck? It's most uncommon hot below.'

'With all the pleasure in the world,' said Peter Palafox; and then remembering his manners he added, 'though this is the most elegant berth, sure, for comfort and amenity, that ever the heart of man could desire.'

'Lard above,' said Jack, stepping on deck, 'it's hotter still.'

They stood for a moment on the port gangway, and the ghost of a breeze coming in over the bows made them gasp. Jack and Peter glanced instinctively up at the sails, and at that moment the foresail shivered. 'That bowline!' called an angry voice from the quarter-deck, though even before that the bowline had started to guilty life and the bridles were plucking the weather-leech taut. The *Wager* was as close-hauled as she could be, pointing up between four and five points of the wind, which was the best she could manage. She was a comfortable ship, a converted East Indiaman, but she was not much of a sailer, particularly close-hauled, and now although she was keeping her station a cable's length astern of the *Pearl*, she had made rather more leeway than the rest of the squadron, which could therefore be seen from her deck at an angle, a stately line of ships stretching away over half a mile of sea, their crowded sails pink with the reflected glory of the sunset – the *Severn*, the *Centurion*, the *Gloucester*, the *Pearl*, with the victuallers to leeward and the fast-sailing *Tryall* to windward, watching for the Spaniards who might have set out from Cadiz

335

in pursuit, for the squadron was bound for the Horn, to pass into the Great South Sea, there to take, burn, sink, and destroy any of His Most Catholic Majesty's ships they might fall in with, and to harass his subjects and possessions in Chile, Peru, and all points west of the Isthmus of Panama. What with battles, shipwrecks, and above all the ravages of the scurvy, few of the members of the squadron were ever to see Portsmouth again: but fortunately sailors are an unreflecting race, and now with abundance of confident good spirits and speaking in a high, carrying voice, Jack Byron gave Mr Palafox his views on how the squadron, and the *Wager* in particular, ought to have been handled.

'All this standing for hours on the same tack is a great error,' said he. 'We'll be in with the loom of the land presently, and everybody knows how that sets you inshore directly – that is to say eastward, whereas we ought to make our southing as soon as we possibly can.'

'I suppose the Morocco coast won't lie much above twenty leagues away, at all,' said Peter Palafox, nodding eastward over the rail.

'Just so,' said Jack. 'We must be off Salee at present. So what we ought to have done was to make our southing in short boards far to the west, for these long tacks close-hauled are only a kind of seesawing – they will bring us back over precisely the same piece of sea tomorrow; and that is what I should have said two days ago, if they had asked my advice. In such an unweatherly old tub as this ...'

'Mr Byron,' called a voice from the quarter-deck behind them.

'Sir?'

'Pipe down.'

This threw a certain damp upon the conversation; but after a while Tobias Barrow said privately to Jack, 'Do you think we might be indulged in the use of the long-boat again?'

'Why, certainly,' said Jack. 'But on second thoughts,' he added, casting a look over his shoulder, 'it might be better to go into the *Centurion*'s gig. If agreeable to Mr Palafox?' The gig was, for the moment, Mr Palafox's kingdom, for he was delivering the

commodore's orders throughout the squadron – orders to rendezvous at Madeira in case they were scattered. 'With all my heart,'
he said, swinging over the rail into the chains and hauling on the
painter to pull the boat alongside.

'I will just hurry downstairs and bring up my little net and
a jelly-bag,' said Toby. 'With so placid an ocean it is possible,
just possible, that we may light upon yet another pedunculated
cirripede.'

'Would he be making game of us, now?' asked Peter Palafox,
who was very quick to resent anything like an affront.

'Never in life, upon my word and honour,' said Jack. 'You would
never believe what a learned cove he is – reads Greek for the joy
of it, has filled our cabin with curious flayed monsters in spirits
of wine, and has never spent five minutes of daylight below since
we left the chops of the Channel in case he might miss some
sea-fowl, in spite of being as sick as a dog every time we meet
the slightest hint of a sea. And now ever since we have reached
these latitudes he has spent every night in the long-boat, staring
at the things that light us, like a cat at a vase of goldfishes.'

'Well, I honor learning, the Dear knows,' said Peter. 'So he's
not the great seaman, at all?'

'Lard no. He had never seen salt-water, never smelt the bilges
of a ship, till I brought him to Portsmouth at the beginning of this
commission. He is my particular friend, you know – you should
see his prodigious curious collection of serpents at home – and
I have brought him into the Navy by way of making his fortune.
But I should never call him a seaman: no. He looks upon the
whole ocean as a museum of natural curiosities; why, the other
day he desired the first lieutenant to put the ship about because
he fancied he spied a turtle. I try to keep an eye on him and make
him understand our ways, but he's in the moon three parts of
the time, parsing his Sanskrit verbs.'

'What did your first lieutenant say?' asked Peter, with an inward
smile.

'Oh, our Mr Bean is as good-natured a man as ever breathed,'
said Jack, 'and he's beginning to know Toby by now – knows he

would never do it for a cod. But he did not choose to put about, I must confess.'

'You astonish me, sir,' said Peter Palafox. 'And so your friend has a serpent, by land?'

'A vast number of serpents, I do assure you – carries 'em in his packet. "Admire my new serpent," says he, plucking one forth and waving it under your nose. The one he gave my sister measured two yards and an inch.'

'How I should love to see a serpent,' said Peter.

'Han't you ever seen one?'

'There's never a snake in all Ireland,' said Peter Palafox with a sigh. 'Not so much as a cobra's child nor yet an asp.'

'Toby,' said Jack, 'Mr Palafox tells me there are no serpents in Ireland.'

'No indeed,' said Toby, 'poor people, poor people. No moles either, and only one kind of crow.'

Jack and Peter stepped down from the chains into the gig, received Toby's trawl, his dredge, his jelly-bag (for animalculae), his hand-net, a variety of pots and cans, and lastly his person. He was a clumsy, awkward creature, descended no doubt from some stock other than the nimble ape, and his way of coming down the *Wager*'s side was to hold his breath, close his eyes, clench his teeth, and let himself drop, trusting to gravity to get him down and to Providence to preserve him from drowning in the gap between the boat and the ship's side; though this time, it must be admitted, he gave a kind of cataleptic jerk as he let go.

Fortunately the gig was at the height of its rise and both Peter and Jack were natural born seamen; they collected him and set him upright in the stern-sheets. 'That was better, I believe,' he said, staring round with modest triumph. 'Was you amazed at my leap, Jack? I am becoming quite the mariner.'

Peter Palafox let go and they went slowly astern, to be brought up aft of the long-boat with an almost imperceptible jerk, so little way did the *Wager* have upon her. Down there on the face of the water there was a delightful freshness, a marvellous atmosphere for meditation and repose. They handed all the gear into the long-boat and sprawled at their ease in the gig, trailing their hands and feet in the lukewarm sea.

The sun was well down now, and only the highest of the western clouds showed that he was still to be seen from the top of the sky; night was sweeping up fast from Africa, so fast that the stars were coming out in scores rather than one by one. Jupiter first, a great blazing round, and then the fixed stars, all rather farther over to the north than they were at home, leaving room on the southern rim of the sky for quite new constellations, Corona Australis, Ara, and low down the topmost stars of the Southern Cross. From far over the water there came the sharp tang-tang of two bells in the last dog-watch, probably from the *Severn*; the sound was repeated in all the other ships, and in the silence they could even hear it from the little *Tryall*, far up to windward. In the *Wager*'s great stern-lantern there appeared a small glow that rapidly became a splendid effulgence, lighting up the great sweeping curve of her driver and the tall figure of Captain Kydd, standing with his hands behind his back, staring up into the sails.

'There will be a heavy dew tonight,' observed Jack, nodding towards Jupiter.

'Maybe that will make it a little cooler,' said Peter, who had rolled his coat into a pillow and who was now quite ready to go to sleep.

'Can it be . . .?' cried Toby, starting to his feet. 'Can it be?' he cried, pointing and putting his foot on the gunwale to crane up a little higher. The gig lurched under his sudden movement and he instantly fell over the side face-first, without the slightest motion to preserve himself. They seized him as soon as his upstretched hands reached the surface and hauled him in, spouting pints of pure Atlantic. 'Infinitely obliged,' he gasped, as Peter Palafox wrung the sea out of the skirts of his rusty black coat and dried him with a handkerchief. 'Most kind.' He leapt up again. 'Easy, now,' they said, steadying him. 'I was not mistaken,' he cried, stabbing the air with incredible eagerness. 'A whale!'

'There she blows!' roared a voice from the *Wager* above them – Henry Doggett, who had been pressed out of a Hull whaler, and who now flew up to the maintop to regale himself with the sight of a whale, until a bosun's mate with a rope's end persuaded him to return to his duty below.

Staring out over the sea in the direction of Toby's pointing hand, Jack and Peter saw nothing, nothing whatever but the long oily swell with here and there a little ripple as the light air touched it. And then, perhaps a quarter of a mile away, a double jet shot up fifteen feet and stayed there in the motionless air while you might have counted three: there was the easy heave and roll of something dark, then a broad spread tail appeared, stood motionless for an instant, and so vanished, leaving the sea as apparently deserted and uninhabited as it had been before.

'We shan't see him again,' remarked Jack, sitting down.

'Why not?'

'They always sound deep when they put their flukes up like that – stay down perhaps half an hour and come up a vast way off.' They listened to him with profound attention, and Jack, pleased with being an authority on whales, added his remaining piece of lore. 'Their throats are so small that a penny loaf would choke them, however.'

This had much less success. Mr Palafox turned away with the air of one who is being trifled with: how could a whale come by so much as a Wood's halfpenny, let alone any greater coin, for all love? And Tobias Barrow returned to his rapt contemplation of the place where the whale had been. 'I am penetrated,' he said after a while, '*penetrated* with admiration. What happiness to see a whale! I have beheld Leviathan.'

The twilight was darkening now, and the lights of the ships ahead mingled with the blaze of stars that reached quite down to the sea; the *Wager*'s stern-lantern filled what faint wash the ship possessed with a river of light, and from the warm dimness behind the lantern came the squeak of a fiddle as the watch below took their ease on the fo'c'sle.

Already the cold unearthly phosphorescent gleams were showing in the sea – pale flames here and there that would presently join, giving every rippled surface a coruscating life of its own.

This was the beginning of the night, a new world; and countless myriads of creatures were mounting towards the surface. Toby put out his trawl and his jelly-bag, and some ten minutes or so later he said, 'You will not think me ungrateful, Jack – you will not think that I repine at my lot – when I say how I should like to see him again, just once more?'

Scarcely were these words out when there was a kind of welling-up to the sea, an eruption as it were, a boiling that tilted the gig to the edge of destruction. Then a great sigh seemed to fill the world, and they were surrounded by warm air and spray. The gig rocked back, and they were confronted with an impossibly enormous presence, a vast, black, gleaming, streaming face, an immeasurable countenance, rank upon rank of whalebone, a clearly-defined lighter lip, and then, as sharp and distinct as a heart could long for, a small round lively eye, tiny in all that bulk, but brimming with intelligence. Then an impression of unending length as the whale heaved up its shoulders, rolled and dived. And lastly his tail, detaching itself in a leisurely manner from the sea, rose up and up with its broad black flukes poised before it came down with a splash that soaked them through and through, swamped the boat, and sent the whale darting down to sup upon a host of pteropods and shrimps.

'I could have touched him, Jack,' cried Toby, when he could speak again – when emotion no longer choked him and he could utter intelligible words. 'I could have touched him, I swear.'

'It would have been an infernal liberty,' said Jack, baling away for dear life. 'Come now, Toby, bear a hand, I beg, and scoop some of this water out, as we are doing. It looks so much better in the sea. And Toby, I must insist upon your moderating your wishes. I know how it will be,' he added gloomily, addressing Peter Palafox, 'the next thing we know and he'll be calling for a roc, or a chimaera, or the great sea-serpent itself. And then we shall be in a pretty state of confusion, I believe.'

Aboard the *Wager* no one had seen or heard anything whatsoever: their prodigious drama had passed unnoticed, for all the *Wager*'s people were staring fixedly at the *Pearl*, who was repeating the commodore's signals with a hoist of lanterns. The only hint of human concern for them was a cross, anonymous voice in the darkness that wanted to know 'what all the splashing and assing about in the boats was for'; but it did not press its inquiries, and presently, after the changing of the watch, everything fell wonderfully silent.

'Only yesterday luminous squids seemed to me the height of human felicity,' said Toby, after a long pause. 'But now they will be precious small beer. I am very happy to see them, however,' he observed, peering down through the water, where a darting like a swarm of comets showed the passage of those same enterprising creatures.

Jack swam up from his soft, warm, overwhelming sleep, realized what Toby had said, replied, 'To be sure' and sank back again. He was aware, without knowing how, that Peter Palafox was already fast asleep in the bows; and for his part, although he once more heard Toby address him on the subject of whales – the benignity to be detected in their gaze – their length – their probably weight – their diet – reflections upon Jonah – he did not open his eyes again until a pale light told some vigilant part of his mind that it was dawn.

He sat up, feeling splendid, cool at last, and wonderfully rested, though still wet, either from their swamping or from the prodigious dew: but he was almost immediately conscious of something gravely amiss. He stared round to make out what it was, and the answers presented themselves at once. In the first place the gig was in the midst of a thick fog: and in the second it was quite alone. The white world that surrounded them was wholly and totally mute; and the gig's painter drooped alongside, limp, attaching them to nothing at all. No wonder he had not heard eight bells in the middle watch, when he should have woken. He glanced round to see whether his companions were there. They were there, right enough, draped in the unlovely attitudes of sleep, with their mouths open. For a moment Jack was almost afraid to wake them.

'Toby,' he said, softly. 'Toby.'

Toby opened his eyes. His pale and usually serious, thoughtful expression suddenly blazed with delight. 'The whale, Jack. Do you remember the whale?'

'I do indeed. But where's the *Wager*?'

Now it was Toby who stared about. 'Why,' he said, 'it was there when I went to sleep. I remember tying the rope again by the light of its great lantern.' He went exceedingly red. Jack cocked an eye at him, but said nothing: the words 'tying again' had told him all he needed to know. He had the greatest admiration for Toby's mind, and he loved him dearly; but he had seen Toby's knots. 'The fact of the matter is,' said Toby in a low voice, 'that I saw what I conceived to be a particularly interesting object up the pointed end of the ship – in the event it proved to be only an unusually bright patch of phosphorescence – and I thought no harm in undoing us and clawing along by a variety of projections on the ship's side to see. I did the rope up again with extreme attention, I do assure you Jack.'

Jack nodded, fanning the mist with his hand as though to dispel it. 'As soon as this burns off,' he said, 'I dare say we shall see her lying becalmed a few hundred yards away.'

For a little while they let all the possible consequences of the situation sink in: then, both stirred by the same thought and both turning with the same movement, they looked round at Peter Palafox. There he lay with his head partially buried in his coat and his mind racing along the green roads of his native land on an unbiddable left-handed horse, terrified that he might not reach his ship in time to join the Navy and take part in all the delights it held in store. They were exceedingly unwilling to wake him: they would infinitely have preferred that he should sleep on until the dissolving of the fog showed the *Wager* lying there with limp, dew-dripped sails, within easy hailing distance.

The dissolving of the fog showed them nothing of the sort. Its attenuation to mere vapid mist, the appearance of a suffused blueness above them, and the dispersion of the last wafting veils by the rising sun took half an hour – thirty minutes in which their ears strained for the slightest sound or the slightest glimpse of the ship, and strained in vain; thirty minutes in which their hearts sank lower and lower. By the end of this time the whole bowl of the sky was clear – not a cloud upon it; and the whole round of the horizon was clear too. They lay in the middle of a great blue disc of sea, and there was not a ship or a boat or anything whatever to break its even surface upon the whole of its vast extent.

Just as the sun in setting had swallowed the breeze, so in rising it brought it back again. The glassy surface ruffled over, and with a sensation of quite extraordinary anguish Jack thought of the *Wager* heeling to the breeze under a press of canvas, fetching the white wake of the *Pearl*, and the whole squadron racing away in a long line far, far to the south.

'Jack, I am infinitely concerned ...' murmured Toby, and for some reason they both looked guiltily round at Peter Palafox. He was sitting on a thwart, wide awake, and his mouth was poised for whistling: as they turned, however, he unpoised it, and said with a smile, 'Good day now. How charmingly cool it is, too.'

'Here's a pretty kettle of fish,' said Jack, blushing; and Toby said, 'Mr Palafox, I am infinitely concerned, but it seems that through my negligence in fastening the rope I have cast us all away.'

'Well, never be in such a taking, joy. It could happen to anyone, I am sure. Think of Saint Brendan – he was from Clonfert, not far from us. Or Saint Ruadan, who crossed the ocean in a villainous little small meal-trough, whereas this is as solid a gig as ever a man could look for. Though it makes my heart black to think how I gave the water-keg to the cooper to mend.' He looked thoughtfully into the empty locker. 'How far off the coast of Africa do you suppose we might be?' he asked.

'Fifty miles, perhaps,' said Jack.

'But surely the ship will turn round directly they find we are gone?' cried Toby. They both looked at Jack, who was by far the most experienced in naval ways.

He shook his head. 'Captain Kydd might signal the commodore – he probably will,' he said doubtfully, 'but upon my word

I can't see him putting about just for a gig that has gone astray, not with every day as valuable as it is. I know I should not, if I were commanding a squadron upon such urgent service.'

There was a silence while they digested this. 'They were going to tack in the middle watch,' said Peter. 'Now suppose we went adrift about midnight, and suppose there has been no shift in the wind, and suppose 'tis about one or two bells in the forenoon watch now, why then we should see their topsails a couple of leagues, say, due south or thereabouts about noon. So if we pull south or a little west of south, we shall cut right across their path.'

'Very true,' said Jack, 'if we had anything to pull with.'

'Oh, oh,' murmured Peter, with a sudden piercing recollection of their wild prodigal thrusting of oars into the long-boat, together with everything else that might hinder their luxurious sprawling.

'Furthermore,' said Jack, 'you're forgetting their leeway. *Wager* was steering south-south-west a half west, but her true course was at least a point and a half off; and if this goes on,' said he, as the freshening breeze sprinkled them with little drops from a chopping wave, 'they will have the topgallants off her in ten minutes' time, which will mean another whole point . . .'

The conversation grew more and more technical, quite out of Toby's reach, and he sat there in silent misery, only rising once, to be sick over the side as discreetly as possible, until they had finished.

This took a long while, a very long while: for a great deal was at stake – everything, indeed; and a wrong decision could lead to a protracted and very horrible death. In the end they decided to remain where they were until the evening, in the hope that the squadron, beating up into a contrary wind and lying no closer to it than the least weatherly ship of them all, would pass again on the opposite tack at least so close that they might be seen from the masthead. And then, if they saw nothing by twilight, they would rig the best jury-mast they could, using the gig's top-strake and their shirts for a sail, and make for Gibraltar.

'Africa is nearer,' said Peter Palafox.

'Why truly, so it is,' replied Jack. 'But what happens to people cast away on the Morocco coast? They are either knocked on the head by the Moors directly or else they are sold as slaves. Or else they run ashore on the edge of a vast howling waterless desert and wander up and down and perish miserably. Besides, the wind has been fair for Spain these last three days, and they say it won't change till the dark of the moon. With this breeze we could run it down in what – four or five days?'

Peter looked grave. 'Sure, it's the only answer,' he said: but he scanned the southern horizon with an even greater longing than before.

The sun climbed up the sky, and the freshness left the breeze. By noon the morning seemed to have begun quite six weeks ago – a remote, unpleasant memory. Time passed slowly, slowly, and with every minute the air grew hotter. Once, at about eleven o'clock, Toby had seen a turtle, apparently sleeping on the surface; but he had not liked to mention it.

'You may strike me down if ever you see me without a needle again,' said Jack. 'I shall always carry a dozen in the handle of my knife.' He was laboriously sewing their shirts together, pricking the holes with a sharpened splinter and threading them through with a yarn from the unlaid painter.

At last the sun reached its height, passed over the meridian, and began its unbelievably tedious downward course. According to their calculations this was the most favourable time for them to see the white gleam of topsails against the southern sky; and although these calculations had very little solid fact behind them, every heart in the gig was painfully wrought up. No one spoke, or very little; for not only were they far too concerned with staring over the sea until they could scarcely make out anything at all, but even a very little talking increased the enormous thirst that had been parching them for as long as they could remember.

One o'clock. Two o'clock. Three. Four, and the gig was filled with very slowly disappointed hope, too bitter to express.

'Perhaps we had better set about starting this strake,' said Jack, tapping the gunwale with his knife. 'It will be a long business.'

'Sure it's a desperate . . .' began Peter; but he checked himself and began to consider how best to work something like a mast out of the living timbers of their boat without weakening it too much. Neither Jack nor he had any liking for their task – no heart for it at all, and they pondered long and gloomily over its technical difficulties.

'Jack,' said Toby in a tone of hesitant triumph, 'is that a sail over there?'

'Yes!' cried both Jack and Peter in the same instant, staring rigidly away to the east, not to the south at all. Then Jack said 'Yes' again, but in a woefully doubting, crushed kind of voice.

'What's amiss?' asked Toby.

'Wait a minute,' said Jack, wishing to make quite sure. 'No top-sails. No topmasts. She's lateen-rigged. A polacre.'

The polacre was coming along very fast, with the wind on her beam, steering a course that would carry her some way north of the gig. Her three immense triangular sails showed up sharp and clear, each like the dorsal fin of a shark – three sharks crowded close together and racing over the sea. 'She must be running close on ten knots,' he muttered. She was hull-up already. Peter gathered their sewn-up shirts and he stood on a thwart to wave them.

'Wait a minute,' said Jack.

'Why?' cried Peter in amazement.

'Well, the fact of the matter is . . .' said Jack, and paused, still staring under his hand at the long low black hull. 'The fact of the matter is, she's a Salee rover.'

'Oh, oh, oh,' said Peter, dropping the shirts.

'What of it?' cried Toby. 'Are the men of Salee never to rove, forsooth? A most eligible vessel – a very pretty vessel, indeed.'

'They are Barbary pirates,' said Jack.

The three of them gazed at the Salee rover, and their hearts were filled with a strange turmoil of feelings.

'They sacked Baltimore not a great while ago,' said Peter. 'And one of them sheltered from a westerly under Inishkeeragh; they landed in the morning and killed all the men in the village – cut their throats in the street – and they hanged the priest in the chapel there with a hog beside him. They carried off the women and the middling children, and when they left they fired every roof and stack and barn in the place. You'd never believe the desolation. There was a Dutch renegado among them, a man with a yellow beard, and he was the worst of them all, they say.'

They sat down, still gazing at the polacre; in the last five minutes she had run off at least a mile, and now every detail was clear – the short, forward-raked masts, the immense curved yards, and the high bow-wave she threw up gleaming white on either side.

'She's seen us,' said Jack. The corsair's long single deck was crowded with men, an improbable number of men, and now there was an agitation among them, a swarming into the bows and up the shrouds – dark arms pointing, turbaned heads staring towards them.

'If she don't put her helm a-lee directly she'll never fetch us on this tack,' observed Peter.

The stir aboard the polacre increased, but still she held her course, and the heads of three watchers in the gig pivoted steadily from right to left as they followed her. From right to extreme left, when their heads could turn no more unless they changed position altogether and faced north. This they did unconsciously, moving as through in a dream. Now their backs were to the wind and the corsair was directly downwind of them, rather above half a mile away: they could see a man in a red turban waving both arms, as though he were in a terrible passion.

'Do you think . . .' began Toby, but as he spoke the polacre flew up into the wind and came about on the starboard tack.

'That's the strange thing to do,' said Peter, frowning.

'A rum go altogether,' said Jack. Obviously there were divided counsels aboard the polacre, for if the corsairs had merely altered course and run up to the windward of them they could have tacked and picked up the gig at their leisure. But as it was they were pointing up into the wind so much that the polacre could hardly get along, and even so it was not sure that her course would bring her to the boat. It was as though the Moors had hesitated again and again, and as though they were now trying to snatch up the gig in the shortest possible time.

'They are counting upon the way we make with our drifting,' said Jack. 'I dare say with this breeze we shall go a hundred yards down-wind in the next half-hour. But why do they cut it so uncommon fine as to rely on that? Why?'

Answer came there none until Toby, whose eye had involuntarily followed the passage of a Madeiran petrel overhead and southwards, muttered in an uncertain, troubled voice, 'May I say there is another sort of ship over there?'

'Where?' they cried, spinning round to see a brig bearing down on them, a brig that any normal person would have recognized as the *Tryall*, although she was a mile and a half away. She was coming down at a great pace with a brisk following wind – perfect for a square rig – and she had all her canvas abroad, even her topgallants, which was uncommonly brave in such a breeze. Jack glanced from the brig to the polacre and from the polacre to the brig. 'Upon my word I don't know,' he said. The brig was a great way off, but she was coming down like a racehorse: the polacre was horribly close, but she was beating up at barely three knots, if that. Furthermore, although she was as close-hauled as she could be it was not quite certain that her course would carry her to the gig. But at all events the situation was clear at last: the polacre had hesitated because of the brig – her topgallants must have been visible from the polacre's masthead long before they could have been seen from the gig, even if the gig's crew had been looking in the right direction – and then at the last moment the Moors had decided to make a dash for it, to sweep up the gig, go about and run on the larboard tack, for sailing on a wind she could run three miles to the brig's one.

'Faith, I cannot tell, either,' said Peter. 'But one thing's sure – we must stop our drifting. Mr Barrow, my dear, will you cast your jelly-bag astern and haul it in with all your might while we make a drogue?'

He and Jack seized the shirt-sail, made its corners fast to the unlaid painter, working with incredible speed and co-ordination, carried it to the stern, flung it as far as their line would allow, let it sink, and then hauled. The sail opened like a parachute: the gig moved towards it: their drift was checked – reversed. This was not unnoticed aboard the polacre, which was less than two hundred yards away, and the angry roar from aboard her was an unmistakable command. Jack snatched the jelly-bag – its extra line gave them a longer haul – and they flung out their drogue again and again and again. Then something skipped in the sea beside them and passed between Jack and Toby with a shrill hum.

'They're firing a patarero,' observed Jack, casting the drogue.

The next ball hit their gunwale, flinging up slivers of wood, and a second later there was a volley of musketry from the polacre: white splashes appeared all round the gig.

'Come on,' cried Peter, diving into the sea. The others hesitated – they could not swim, but the flash of the patarero made up their minds, and they slipped awkwardly over the side, grimly clinging to the tholepins and straining up with their chins. The firing stopped: and now after their furious activity with the drogue they could look around again. It was not an encouraging sight: the brig was still a quarter of a mile away, and she did not seem to be moving quite so fast, whereas the polacre was slipping easily towards them, terribly close – perhaps the wind had shifted a trifle. Fifty or sixty dark faces lined the rail, and their talk came clearly over the water, excited and harsh. A tall man was standing on the rail, one hand holding the shrouds, the other swinging a grappling-iron.

Their three heads turned back to the *Tryall*, as though begging for a sign. And the sign came: a puff of black smoke on the fo'c'sle, instantly torn away by the wind, and then the deep boom of the *Tryall*'s bow-chaser, accompanied by a wonderfully heartening cheer from her crew. The ball pitched short, between the gig and the polacre, ricocheted in a high leap, and passed through the polacre's foresail, leaving a neat hole.

'There's a chance, there's a chance,' screamed Jack. The polacre's helmsman had let her fall off a little at the sound of the gun, but now he brought her up, and the Moors all gave an answering cheer.

Another bang, another cheer from the *Tryall*: but they never saw the flight of the ball. Another, that kicked up a white plume a few yards from the polacre's forefoot. Another, and they heard it pass singing high overhead.

Jack broke one of the tholepins as he tried with all the strength of his mind and body to force the *Tryall*'s shots to strike home: Peter was speaking in a steady, conversational tone beside him, but in Irish: Toby was repeating the Miserere psalm. The Moors' faces were very clear now, and so was the white grin of the black man with the grapnel. A chopping wave broke over Jack's head, but he cleared his eyes again just in time to see the taut perfect triangles of the polacre's sails dissolve in total confusion. A high shot, just grazing the mast, had cut the mainsail halyard and the yard had come down with a run. The Moors instantly started the fore and mizzen sheets, the helmsman bore up, and the polacre ran straight down the wind. In two minutes they had cleared their deck, and hauling their wind they went limping fast away towards Africa. And five minutes after that the *Tryall* backed her topsails, coming neatly into the wind alongside the gig.

The gig's crew were pleased to be given huge quantities of tea and water and wine; they were pleased to eat again and to be able to oil their scarlet sunburnt backs; but once the first enormous relief was over they were almost equally pleased – or pleased on another plane, to put it more exactly – to find that it was not *they* who were considered the poor helpless lost boobies. The unhappy lieutenant temporarily in command of the *Tryall* had wandered from his station in the night and had been frantically beating to and fro in search of the squadron; and since Peter Palafox was the bearer of orders for him from the commodore, to be delivered in the *Centurion*'s gig, and since the said orders had in fact been delivered in the manner specified, there was a very strong likelihood that when the squadron reached the rendezvous mentioned therein – to wit, Madeira – then everything would pass off perfectly well, with no wry looks or harsh words on the part of any of the superior officers. Indeed, so persuaded were Jack, Peter, and Toby of this prodigiously comforting truth that their confidence returned to an almost overwhelming degree, and as they ate their second enormous supper of the day they kindly gave the *Tryall*'s solitary midshipman hints and advice on the care of open boats on the high seas, when delivering orders about a somewhat scattered squadron.

When the young man, duly impressed, had gone about his duties, Jack yawned, stretched, and remarked, 'I think I shall turn in. Hot again, ain't it?'

'I make no complaint,' said Peter, with a grin.

'It *is* hot,' said Toby. 'Really the most favourable sort of weather for observation . . . Jack,' he added, with a certain hesitation, 'I have noticed that as there is no room for the gig on the deck of this otherwise most commodious, agreeable vessel, they are towing it behind. Now do you think – it being understood, of course, that I touch nothing – that we might be indulged . . .?'

39

The Rendezvous

———⟨∞⟩———

Clearly umbrellas must often blow inside-out (how many times
has one not had to tack violently in the turbulence at a street
corner, grasping the mast with both hands and just, but only just,
succeeding in dipping the rim under the current?) yet all my life
I had never seen one. There it lay, a smallish umbrella, neither
particularly a man's nor a woman's, in the shining, wet-running
street, well away from the tumultuous gutter. It was not an old
abandoned thrown-away umbrella – everyone has seen *them* –
but a fairly new one: you could tell at first glance that it was mal-
formed in some way, but it was not until you saw the metal ribs
sticking through the respectable bright cloth that you understood
it had been blown inside-out and that its defeated owner had
made an attempt at folding it again before realizing that there
was no hope and laying it deliberately in that position, parallel
with the street, in nobody's way, relinquishing it kindly, perhaps
with a certain respect.

One's eye takes these things in at great speed (I was running
at the time), and all the faster if there is any sense of crisis, any
amorous excitement or impending catastrophe: afterwards one's
mind has to plod along rationalizing the eye's instant answer, its
explanation of the problematical wreck, the overturned car, the
domestic scene in a lit window as the train runs by. The sense of
crisis was there, as well as the other factors, for the town was on
the edge of disaster. The heavy rains of the last three days had
been followed that morning by a stupefying downpour: warm

353

rain hurtling down in drops of far more than natural size and between these drops a fine mist of shattered water. The earth could take up no more and already the river was a great cambered churning ochre mass from bank to bank, tearing furiously at the bridge, and by the Prefecture the orderly canal had drowned its trim brick walls, while the municipal oleanders, their roots ten feet below, jerked their highest leaves, their tallest twigs, among the filth and rubbish on the uneven, breakneck surface. And apart from the general crisis I had my own as I ran splashing past this umbrella. The Paris express would leave (if it were still running) in eight minutes: the station was a quarter of an hour away, and there was not a taxi to be seen anywhere in this flooded town.

There is something odious, almost unclean, in picking at one-self, slapping labels on to emotions and behaviour – peering through your own keyhole and perhaps at the same time putting on a show for the voyeur. However, there is no doubt a discredit-able side to this perpetual missing of trains: and the running, the sweat (and how I sweated under my mackintosh in that steaming heat) only makes it more discreditable still. The cast-iron alibi, even to one's own court of conscience (but I *ran*, I ran all the way to catch it), grows less convincing in the hundredth repetition, particularly when it carries on into dreams.

Sweating and soaked I saw the express pull out and gather momentum as I burst from my last-minute cab. The red lights on the back of the last carriage swung round the curve and vanished – oh familiar nightmare – and I sheltered in the station buffet with its coffee-urns, its silent, frightened waitresses, the thun-der of falling rains, sirens, apocalyptic candles in the gloom (the electricity had failed), the deep roar of running water everywhere.

However, by the time the next train left, the slow train, feel-ing its way over the flooded plains where only the embankment stood above the water – the vineyards all drowned – I was almost dry: though it was impossible to say the same for my book, or for her letter, or for the bundle of notes, of money (a source of great satisfaction to me) that I had thrust into my pocket for this ren-dezvous and that had soaked up the water to a surprising if not to a dangerous extent. And by the time I was in Paris the whole sky was blue – not so much as a cloud, not even on the southern rim.

I had already missed my connection and the essence of the rendezvous. of course: there could be no Cossack hat at the far end of the platform – did she still wear that hat, or had worms fattened on the Persian lamb? – no tall head stretching taller still behind the ticket-collector, no pale-blue eyes looking cold and remote until they flashed into recognition. Should we have shaken hands, kissed? Stood lumpish, undecided, muttering 'How well you look – not changed in the very least', each waiting for the other to make the spontaneous unstudied gesture, to define the relationship? Should I have been able to control my voice? That had haunted me ever since I opened her letter.

So I had missed the essence of the rendezvous; and as for tele-phoning in London, hearing that mortal ringing tone in an empty flat, counting thirteen, counting thirteen again before hanging up, I could do that just as well from Paris. But there was still a train to Dieppe I could catch if I hurried, and at that juncture it seemed to me I ought to go through all the required motions. In that phoney histrionic voice which comes booming out when in fact far deeper real emotions are there below, I said it was right that I should die by inches in a call-box at Victoria rather than in an archaic booth at Austerlitz – that it should in common respect for her cost me two new pence rather than ten new francs.

This time I reached the train by racing through the barrier and although two doors would not yield I wrenched the third open and leapt in as the whistles blew and red flags waved. An empty compartment, smelling of dust, with views of Bayeux, Caen, a grisly watering-place, and three graffiti: *Couple criminel, vomi par la cité, faiseurs d'orphelins*; *Je t'aime, Nicole*; and *Vive moi*.

For the first quarter of an hour or so the railway from Paris to Dieppe perpetually crosses and re-crosses the river: you see it now on the one side and now on the other, and far off through the window a toy Eiffel Tower where you do not always expect it. It was while I was sitting in the carriage that I worked out this piece about the umbrella, its significance (shield, broken, carefully laid aside) and its obvious connection with missing trains; and when at about tea-time we stopped on a blank stretch of line I had little hesitation about getting out. Little hesitation, but still some: the sewing of my right-hand or should I say right-foot shoe, over-taxed by my paddling in it and by its stewing hours of heat in the waiting-room, had started to come undone.

It was not so much that the sole had come frankly off, flapping downwards, as that the upper part had begun to rise; yet it seemed to me that by now the relative movement had stopped, and as I had always wanted to see this piece of river close to I opened the door and dropped on to the stones that make the permanent way: rough, pointed stones, flecked with oil and tar, of a kind to be seen nowhere else. It was an odd feeling to lay a hand on the lower edge of the tall train and to know that I was still in touch with it, that I could still become an integral part of it, and that if I chose not to do so it would move off, *exit left, gasping and heaving*, leaving nothing between this side of the line and the river but transparent air: at the bottom right-hand corner of the carriage, in gold on the brown background, stood the single word Purge.

The river was exactly as I had hoped it would be. There are so many places that can only be seen from a train – landscapes as absolute as the moon, railway-cuttings filled with cowslips, and grave-eyed badgers pacing there between them. Here was the broad Seine, full but not flood-full, rolling from brim to brim, and on my right, where Purge had been, the long spit of a tree-covered island coming to a point in the middle of the stream. A motor-barge pulling a string of lighters was thrusting up through the current towards the far side of the island, and on the near side a bright blue and red ship with the Belgian flag came floating down. It was a great wide view that I had, though not distressingly large – none of the dehumanizing expanse that you see from an aeroplane: perhaps two miles upstream to where the island merged into the general blur, and somewhat less to a curve that shut off the water in the other direction. Just before this curve I could make out a hard line that I believed to be a weir; and if I was right, then, oh joy, there would be five acres of detergent foam, and swans swimming in the Tide.

It was all that I could have wished. Warm, still, gentle, luminous air a mild, veiled sun; the light brighter in some places than in others – Seurat near to, Claude Lorraine farther off. Before I moved the bow-wave of the motor-barge had vanished behind the island and a woman had hung out a line of bright washing on one of those that it towed. Some other vessels had come into sight here and there and not very far from the bank I could now make out the necessary fisherman, his heavy green boat moored against a background of reeds: but although there might be all this light and movement the whole effect was that of a uniform silence. Nothing that moved moved abruptly; there was the gliding continuity of the water and the swimming of the boats, and what human motion there was was small and doll-like in the distance. The angler never stirred.

I found the old tow-path and began to walk downstream, with the very agreeable sensation of being wafted along, of being part of the general flow. Of course, the sides of the path were somewhat overgrown, but a bare white track ran down the middle of it, and no doubt it would take me as far as Rouen if I let myself go with it long enough.

The hard line was indeed a weir, a weir that I knew well from the train, and it had its solid park of froth ending in a rounded point from which the current plucked islands and white ribbons, carrying them far down the river, out of sight; but no swans, except for a disappointing grey cygnet on the other side. This was an area I knew intimately well, from having gazed at it out of the windows of another world, but my knowledge was partial, based upon another sense of time and distance, and it did not extend to names. It did not extend to the great works with chimneys and open ironwork towers beyond the stream, either (I must always have looked too fixedly at the weir); but I was not surprised to see it, for there were many such things, vast inhuman enterprises that seemed to work themselves, spread out arbitrarily along this river. The drifting smell persuaded me that it was a chemical works; yet

357

as far as I could see the world was unaffected by it. The chimneys bore their plumes of smoke, the unnatural reek came across the air; yet the river flowed and the trees stood up round and green, as though the two entities were entirely independent of one another. How different this will be, I said with a little skip, when I come to the burning fields.

But they were far away. First I had to follow the Seine round a noble bend that curved back on itself in a more than S, and this took me upwards of an hour: an S that the train annihilated by drawing a dollar stroke across it at eighty miles an hour. Dutch barges in the middle, with their fags; a very long low vessel with its body awash and a ridiculous wooden house perched up on one end – French; another Belgian, riding high with its screw churning white; yet not a sound did I hear until the very tail of the S, when a magpie flew from a bush on the left and trailed far out over the river, cackling as it went. Until then there might have been a deafness on the world.

Now for the first time plain agricultural land came down on the river on my side of it. Fields, divided by post and wire; leys; a fair amount of stubble, some of it already ploughed; neat heaps of dung; no people – just the fields and in one of them an empty cart. Another turn: meadows with lapwings calling over them, and along the river-bank (propped by piles, black baulks of timber, at this point where it was so deep) the tall dipping gallows of a row of fish-traps, archaic things like lateen masts, some with their baskets hoisted up, others dipping attentively. Beyond them lay an empty ferry-boat, moored to a wavering pier; and here a road came down to the river, a cart-track from a village or from the small collection of farms whose dark outbuildings I could make out behind a line of trees. Another mile, with an easy path under my feet; a few boats, and nothing else moving in the world except for one moorhen that jerked its neck among the reeds.

Now I was coming closer to my Sodom: already there were some sickly willows on the bank, by no means as sweet a green as those on the farther side, and a far greater profusion of the rank yellow weed called Stinking Willy. A train went by on the other bank, running at full stretch for Paris, and it gave me a pleasant feeling of being both here and there – a feeling slightly marred however by a lingering impression of guilt that I did not choose to identify at that moment; the association of trains and morose delectation, no doubt. The vegetation was thinning out; even the harsher kinds of grass had a stunted, lightless, sullen look; the naked earth showed more and more, a damp, soured desert: and here at last was my burning field. A great long rectangle, perfectly neat, perfectly level, and it was all made up of a black, coke-like substance, lying there in unspeakable profusion and emitting trails of smoke, yellow rising fumaroles, small pink fames here and there, and sometimes, where the smoke was darkest, a dusky crimson glow. No wire round it, no fence. No warnings: apparently no road. I had always wanted to smell it, and now, since the movement of the air was against me, I eagerly climbed from the towpath to the first black crunching scoriae. I could not stalk about on it as I had promised myself, because my gaping shoe would let in some furious spark; but I did take a few triumphant paces, and immediately the heat rose up through my soles.

Bare earth with a sulphurous efflorescence came next, then sparse foul shrubs, twitch, and rose-bay willow-herb in seed. Gradually the trees improved – taller, more sprightly. Almost all traces of my burning field had gone by the time I came to these allotments late in the day, these oblongs of kitchen-garden huddled together, speckled with tool-sheds made of old shutters, railway sleepers and metal advertisements; a scene that could only be explained by the presence of some industrial village hidden behind the rising land.

And now there were figures in the landscape, a group of youths clustered strangely behind one of the little sheds. They were near enough for me to see the black leather jackets, the big shining buckles, the unmistakable hair, the thickness of the frontal bone, the deep unluminous skin, and the shot-gun that the tallest had in his hands. They broke up on seeing me, some running, all moving rapidly away from the bothie; then they slowed to an exaggeratedly casual film-cowboy stride, with many an evil look backwards. In the first moment the group – they had certainly been breaking into the shed – had lost much of its cohesion, but by the time they had passed through the remaining allotments they had regained it, and with it all their bold inhumanity. Their direction, as far as they had any direction, was down the river, and for some minutes we all walked slowly towards Rouen. Slowly, because that was their pace; and slowly, because I had no wish to catch them up.

The river was beginning one of its smooth splendid curves again, bearing away to the left, and this bend enclosed a vast half-moon of marshy land, intersected by palely shining ditches and a much larger reed-lined canal. 'I shall cut across the bend,' I said, 'for although there is nothing against stepping out and passing through the midst of them, I do not choose to do so.' All lies, all lies, of course; there was everything against walking through the midst of them, for we were not indifferent; a relationship had already been established, and its rays were darting to and fro – fear, dislike and contempt on my side, and malignance, revolt and bloody dissatisfaction on theirs.

It was a great mistake, a bleeding error: I had none of the local sureness of a man of those parts, one who knew his way among the ditches and whose knowledge would have given him an assured countenance even through the back of his head. I had hardly begun my uncertain blundering through the reeds before I turned from a spectator to a quarry.

There was no overt move for a little while and indeed the knowledge of the situation did not spread to all minds and to all levels of awareness without a considerable delay. Besides there was a gap in time, a parenthesis, in which they shot a magpie (they shot at everything that moved), winged it, and thrashed about after it as it ran, hopped and fluttered, sometimes, poor bird, skimming to a moment's safety in the reeds on the far side of a broad ditch.

But soon enough there I was, going faster and faster along my predetermined chord while one straggling line of youths hurried shouting along the towpath and another, more compact, launched out across the marsh on a course that would intercept mine unless I either ran or deviated to the left. I deviated, all right. My chord became a curve, and the curve sharpened sensibly as the gleam of gun-barrels in the fading light caught my eye. At some point, unseen by me, the sun must have sunk into a band of haze low over the trees beyond the river, and now the white light of the evening was shining from all the water in the bog. Steadily on, with the marsh-smell rising to my nose and the marsh-mud (viscous, dark) packing into the gap between the sole and upper of my shoe, working under the arch of my foot. On, on. What dreadful galvanic energy possessed those youths, what superabundant activity, unnecessary life!

In front of me stretched a surface far wider than I had expected: this was the canal that drained the middle of the bog; and it looked very deep. Some ditches I had leapt, without too great an air of flight (I thought) and some I had crossed on planks. But here was no bridge that I could make out, and if I were seen attempting to jump it – it might just be done – then there would be no disguising the situation. The leap would be an open acknowledgement that the thing had turned into a hunt and myself into a legitimate prey. Besides, I did not know which side of the canal they were: they might have crossed it by the bridge that must certainly exist at the far end, where the canal fell into the Seine. Staring round did me no good, for here I was among the reeds, and their feathery heads cut off my view. An irresolute step took me away to the left along the canal, and here, just past a low-spreading willow-tree, there rose up an enormous shape. Straight up into the air it rose and after a stab of pure terror I recognized the broad wings and shape and colour of a heron: at once the shape diminished to a natural size. The slow beating flight rose and turned into the evening breeze from the river, mounting languidly, as herons will.

Then came the double bang-bang of the gun and the heron slanted down in a long glide towards the river-bank. There was a confused shouting and bellowing of orders, raucous, ugly,

near-hysterical, and then another shot. I made my way fast along
the canal, keeping down among the reeds and the willows, and at
length I paddled my way into a particularly dense clump of bul-
rushes that stood around a little subsidiary pond. Here I squatted
on a tussock of that wiry grass which stands dry in the wettest
places. There was the best part of the shell of some bird's egg
under the tussock next to mine, and one could still see the bent-
lined hollow in which it had been laid. 'Tranquillity,' I said; and
I noticed that the light was too dim to make out the colour of
the shell. To some degree I was still unwilling fully to admit that
I was hiding; but in reply to the commonplace observation 'these
things just don't happen – you are upset, nervous, all on edge' my
memory produced details of gratuitous acts of this very nature
and repeated them over a long period. And when I heard movements and voices again in front of me – that is to say further
along the canal than the point I had reached – my whole being
at once acquiesced and compressed itself into a smaller space,
eyes glaring, ears and nostrils stretched: no doubt it also emitted
a quarry's smell. And I was surprised to find my hand creeping
towards my wad of notes: I had not consciously thought of them
since the train, so very long ago. There was the faintest wetness
still to be detected in their heart.

'There! In there!' shouted a voice, and someone threw a clod of
earth into the rushes and the water: but it was twenty or thirty
yards away. Still, this full admission was very bitter, and beneath
the humiliation I felt a surly glow begin go rise.

It might have grown into something very rough and careless in
time or with a sudden emergency, but it had certainly not reached
that point yet, and I lay as close as a hare. As far as I could tell
they were scattered promiscuously over the marsh – some of
them shouting a great way off – and they seemed to be skirmish-
ing about in twos and threes. What I could not make out was
where the gun might be.

Nor, when at last I came out of my hiding-place, could I make
out which way round I was. West I could tell, for there was
the remaining yellow glow; but the closer lie of the land escaped

me – the canal no longer seemed to be running in the right direction, and the chess-board ditches (as far as they could be seen at all in this dying glimmer, faintly helped by a weak-backed moon) had been slewed round so that they no longer pointed out my way. There were a few voices still to be heard, mostly quite far off. They no longer had the fierce zeal of the earlier stage, but still I went on cautiously, working in what I thought was the direction of the river; and when I heard a cry of 'Look out! There he is!' I turned at once.

The frightened tone was cordial to me, so was the sight of shadowy figures fleeting away from me over the marsh; but still I edged off into cover, since they might be running straight to their friends.

Now there was a great deal of that foolish ululating oo-ooh that townspeople keep up so in the country: but quite commonplace now, none of that implacable passionate intensity that you hear when hounds hit off the line – silly human beings was all And I supposed, as I sat on my heels in a hollow, that they had gathered again, at least into two bands; though there was some isolated whistling and bawling over to the left.

The weak moon had gathered spirit: it had put out the Pleiades and it shone on every watery stretch. A heavy dew was falling: wet piled upon wet.

'If only I had a piece of string,' I said, 'how much easier it would be.' My sole was now a true drooping sole. I had to raise my foot six inches higher than I should ordinarily have done, to prevent it from stubbing on the ground; and at every step I grasped with my toes – a useless, unnecessary, and (after a thousand repetitions) a very tiring action.

My direction was unsure – quite vague. I had thought of making my way back to those allotments and thence to my hypothetical village, but on reflexion I preferred the towpath, and it seemed to me that if I kept on a general westerly course I must come to it in the end. It must surely be over there; and yet here was a metalled road, a meaningless road, if ever I had seen one. What was my right course now? On the far side, beyond still another ditch, stood a sign-post. I could have sworn that even a newspaper would have been legible in this brilliant moon – at least the headlines – but when I walked across (the road-grit sharp under my ridiculous foot) I found that I could not make out a single word. By now I was not going to leap another ditch with my shoe in that shape merely to learn, perhaps, that I might not deposit ordure there, so I considered for a while; and seeing that the road seemed to slope a little to the right, I went down it: in a quarter of a mile it brought me to a raised bank, and as soon as I had walked over it there was the Seine, there were the lights of some great installation far over on the other side, and between this bank and that two boats crossing on the black water. They hooted gently to each other as they passed, and their washes crossed reciprocally, the ripples showing in the light. The river was flowing the way I had expected it to flow – how comforting – and where I stood the metalled road ended in a gravelly place with a small ferry, just large enough for a single car. And here was the towpath: I started along it – so much easier than the broken surface of the bog, and presently the whole ludicrous, painful incident, which had already diminished wonderfully, dwindled into a foolishness long past.

It did not revive even when my mind was jerked from its mild inward rambling by a sound that it told me was caused by a bullock churning about in a wet pasture, frightened by its own shadow. But it did revive in all its full strength, it did shock my heart to a momentary halt and wring my stomach tight again when I saw the youth bolt upright by the mast of a fish-trap. The moon was shining full upon him. Was he dim-sighted, half-witted, a nyctalope, to suppose himself invisible? Had he read in a book that if you stand quite still you cannot be seen?

Quite still he stood, and as I came closer I could see the moon shining blue upon his teeth – a black hole of mouth and then these teeth. In that light his face seemed drained, eyeless, and sweating cold, for what could be seen did also glisten.

My foot had made the smallest pause when I saw him, hardly measurable it was so small, because I knew that the entire situation was reversed, utterly reversed; and I came on with my awkward lame-duck gait.

'Have you a piece of string?' I said.

No answer. No movement. The line of barges that had been following me passed by and I saw him silhouetted against the navigation lights.

'Have you a piece of string?'

His eyes showed in the moonlight, a sudden gleam (had they been closed?), and in an abrupt harsh rush he said, 'Yes, a whole ball of string. A whole ball of string. Twine.'

'Why does he carry a whole ball of twine with him?' I wondered as I sat down. I said, 'What is the name of the next village?'

'Bougival,' he answered gently, very soft.

'Bougival,' I said, seeing the map quite clearly now. 'Ah, Bougival. Why, yes, of course, it must be Bougival, the place where lettuces are grown. I shall telephone from there.'

40

The Chian Wine

When first he came to Saint-Feliu the middle and indeed the
dark ages still hung about the streets, while the beach was classical antiquity itself. The village was so heavily fortified, with two
castles, five towers and a massive surrounding wall – so heavily fortified against the Spaniards, the Algerine corsairs and the
inhuman people from the neighbouring province that there was
little room for the three thousand inhabitants. In the course of
centuries they had crammed their houses into narrow winding
lanes, so close that their roofs, viewed from the nearby hills,
resembled a swarm of bees, with never an open place to be seen.

Hanging from his window over one of these deep lanes in the
hope of air – he had been ordered to the Mediterranean for the
air – Alphard saw a world he had imagined long past and gone:
in those days mules paced by; women with loads poised on their
heads – heads that turned slowly, with infinite grace, to watch
the town-crier as he beat his drum and announced death or the
arrival of goat-cheese in the market-place. Tumblers appeared, a
family of dumb acrobats; they spread a dusty mat on the cobbles
and tumbled there in the street, turning somersaults and con-
torting their lithe dusty bodies until it seemed they must come
apart, while their dumb, thin-faced children looked up with open
hands to the windows, catching the sparse shower of little coins:
and at All Hallows a Basque brought his dancing bear – they
slept together, by arrangement, in the cellar of Alphard's house.
The life of the village went on in the street. At noon the men lit

366

fires of vine-cuttings outside their doors, and the smell of grilling fish wafted up; family quarrels also came out into the open, and once he saw a stone-faced woman bring a chair and sit outside a door all day and half the night until her husband should come out. Every morning the women carried pots of filth mixed with ashes to the edge of the sea; every morning they and their daughters went to the pump recessed into the opposite house for water; every evening the grandmothers came back from the hills loaded with an immense faggot, held by a band across their foreheads. Every evening the ass that belonged to Alphard's landlord picked its way through the people, through the innumerable dogs and cats, and walked up the ladder-like stairs, followed some minutes later by its master, a man with a fair-sized vineyard and a market-garden, and one of the few who did not go out with the fishing-boats. The fishermen all had vineyards too in the terraced hills behind; and as peasants they lived by the rhythm of the sun for half the year, rising before dawn and sleeping in the heat of the day; in the due seasons they worked, sprayed, sulphured and pruned their vines, and every autumn, when the grapes came home in narrow carts or in eared tubs slung to the saddles of hump-backed mules – brass-studded, old crimson saddles – the streets ran purple and the smell of fermenting wine hung over the town. But as fishermen they lived by the moon, rising according to its motions and gathering in the darkness at the gate that gave on to the open strand. Sometimes they came back at moonset, sometimes not until the bell was ringing for high mass, but more usually at dawn; and when, as it often happened, the cock upstairs made sleep impossible, Alphard would go down to watch them.

It was here on the beach that the ancient world showed purest: with his back to the town he could forget the two or three thousand intervening years. The sea was timeless, of course; and apart from the baroque church on his left the shore-line too was quite unchanged. The long, brilliantly-painted, high-prowed boats with pagan symbols on their bows might have been launched for the siege of Troy: the men who sailed them, rounding the jetty under their archaic lateen sails or sweeping in when the breeze failed them, might have been bringing back the Golden Fleece. In fact they usually brought anchovies; and when the catch was heavy they would heave to there at the edge of the sea, picking the silver fish out of their nets, tossing them into baskets. They would then carry the baskets up the beach – a line of men in red Phrygian caps and washed-blue drawers staggering abreast through the shingle with these gleaming fish between them, while their house-cats came running out, tails erect, each to its own basket. One day, when he was watching, a fisherman handed him a small amphora: after the south-east gales they often came up in the nets, tearing the delicate mesh, and usually the men broke them on the gunwale to make sure they would sink for good; but this was a neat little jar; it had done no harm; and Joseph thought Monsieur Alphard might like to have it, the seal being still intact.

It was indeed: beneath the incrustations of the sea the wax stated that Aristolochus of Chios had made this wine; and beneath the seal the wine, or at least a liquid of some sort, could be heard and felt. 'I shall try it some day,' said Alphard, setting it on a tripod from the hearth. 'Wine of the nth Olympiad! I shall try it one day, when I have good news.'

Now ten and twenty years had passed, a generation and more, and the wine still stood among the books, its seal unbroken. Alphard himself looked much the same, though his hair was greyer still, his sight was dim, his taste for music and for reading had almost gone, and even his longing for salvation; and his long solitary walks had shrunk to an occasional stroll along the jetty: his heart was quite shrivelled with habitual woe and its consequent selfishness; but he still cared for his everlasting bird and for the mice that came for its seed. He still looked with automatic eagerness for a letter in the morning, although by now he would not have known what to do with it if it had come; he still divided his morning, after early mass and the post, between *Le Monde* and the *Gazette de Lausanne*, lunched at home with his bird on a piece of cheese, dined at the Café du Commerce, and then sat for

an hour or two over his coffee on the terrace, watching the pas-
sers-by and the sea beyond. He had become inured to the tragedy of growing old; his jets of rebellion had faded, and he knew
that presently he too must die – he could hear the crier's voice
announcing it before the goat's cheese and the eels. Yet still for
the children of the village Monsieur Alphard in his dark, shabby
suit was as unchanging and as little noticed as the clock-tower.

But Saint-Feliu had changed, changed almost out of recognition. Pert white houses had sprung up outside the walls, with
red-brick well-heads over nothing, gnomes, plastic storks; drains
carried the filth into the viscid sea, now spoilt at last; water ran
in every house; bottled gas or electricity had replaced the faggot-
bearers; the braying of the conch was no longer heard, announcing a haul of mackerel, to be given to anyone who chose to bring
a dish; what was left of the fishing-fleet ran on diesel-oil, distributed by a scarlet pump in the sea-gate itself, and the well-
clothed younger generation no longer spoke the ancient tongue.
At the autumn fair of the patron saint raucous microphones had
replaced the human voice; the bear, the magpie that picked your
fortune from the cards, the sword-swallower, the performing
fleas, the fire-eater, were no longer to be seen, nor the pig-faced
woman; and the hand-cranked roundabout had given way to an
enormous whirling mass of supersonic planes. Hotels abounded
– the Café du Commerce was now the fifty-roomed Comman-
derie du Soleil – and in high summer the villagers wandered like
strangers among the tourist hordes: out of an obscure sense of
shame the men had laid aside their red caps and broad sashes and
the women their white lace coiffes. The ass and the poultry had
long since vanished from Alphard's house. After a marriage the
sheets no longer hung from the window: no ribald voice called up
'How much for a pint of pigeon's blood?'

'Yet still,' he said to Halévy as they sat there after dinner, 'the
spirit of the place is quite unaltered. This is not the Spanish
coast, whose soul has gone, quite gone. Whatever you may say,
these people have kept their integrity: this is a true, an eternal
microcosm . . .'

'When I used to come here as a boy,' said Halévy, 'Louise made the best fish soup known to man – pounded lobster-claws, a sea-devil's liver, the garlicked bread singing from the pan. Now she has hired a fellow with a tall white cap, and the soup comes out of a packet: I detected the criminal industrial crumbs, uncooked, this very evening. And this is not even the tourist-season. There is no excuse. No: it breaks my heart to contradict you, but these people have lost their sense of beauty. The doctored wine alone, and what they buy from me, must convince you of that. Here too the past has died: two thousand years of tradition have died! There is no bridge between the jet-age and the past.'

'Monsieur le Curé,' cried Alphard, rising from his chair and bowing to the cassocked priest, 'good evening to you. There,' he said to Halévy, 'there is your bridge – one of your bridges. The Church has not changed.'

Halévy smiled, raising his shoulders and spreading his hands; but he only said, 'He seems an excellent man, to be sure; it does me good to see him.'

Alphard felt the strength of Halévy's tactfulness and the naïvety of his own remark in the present circumstances, and he cried, 'Not changed essentially, not here, I mean. The vernacular is so close to Latin any way that it makes little difference. The natural piety of the village is the same as it always was. Take my grocer Fifine, for example: she has sugar blessed on Saint Blaise's day, and whenever you have a sore throat she gives you half a dozen lumps – *gives* them, I say. Because to sell a blessed object would be gross impiety. There is your true medieval spirit, vigorously alive in the midst of electric refrigerators. Or take our curious vespers this day week, in which they have used the vernacular ever since the night of time.' He paused, recollecting that the traditional proceedings at Saint-Feliu on Good Friday were far too truly medieval to describe to Halévy. He was an Avignon Jew who had recently opened a small gallery outside the sea-gate, not far from the church, where he exhibited a few young painters and bought antiques for his brother's shop in Paris. He was old and fat and he had a mane of white hair; he meant to retire to

Saint-Feliu, with the gallery for fun. Hitherto he had known the village only in the summer.

'What is so curious about your vespers?' he asked.

'Or take our bull-fight at Assumption,' said Alphard, feigning not to hear. There is continuity for you ... and apart from anything else, these people are still at the mercy of the sea for one half of their living and of the sun for the other half: they dare not presume, or go whoring after other gods. They must keep the ancient ways, so long as the ancient ways keep them. But speaking of continuity, I should like to show you my jar of Chian wine one day. The seal is unbroken – a seal pressed at least two thousand years ago! We might even try it.'

Halévy did not follow the sequence of these observations – how could he? – but he saw that Alphard wished to change the subject, and he said that he should be very happy to see and even, if he were allowed, to try the Chian wine. 'I shall be back before Easter, to get the place ready for the tourists. First I have to go to Gosol, where a man tells me his cousin has a Romanesque Virgin he might sell. I doubt the story very much. A true twelfth-century Virgin is scarcely to be hoped for today – all that were portable have already been sold. But I shall go: I love those strong, pitiless faces, even when they are fakes.'

Good Friday's dawn could not be seen for the clouds coming up from the south: a hot brooding day with a great many flies about. They even came into the cool depths of the church where Alphard was listening to a foolish young Dominican rattling away – an involved, enthusiastic sermon about ecumenism. The friar was in favour of it, but that was all his hearers could make out, since the reasoning was tenuous in the first place and the preacher had lost even that thread early on. The greater part of the congregation sat quietly as the excited, electrically amplified voice went on and on, booming from loudspeakers hung in the aisles. The acoustics were poor, but even if the Dominican had been content with the voice God gave him most of the older women would not have understood his French. They stared before them in a mild, holy stupor, watching the candles flicker or the choirboys scratching themselves as they read their comics: they did not seem to mind the flies, either. Alphard wondered at their patience. He himself had outlived his desires or had seen them dwindle into mere velleities – nothing mattered very much – but he had not outlived testiness, and as he brushed away a cluster of heavy, sluggish flies he muttered 'frying in Hell ... frying in Hell.' He had had the greatest respect and affection for John XXIII as a man, but as a pope he thought him utterly disastrous – the results of his actions were utterly disastrous. Temerity, wild zeal, enthusiasm ... Could it really be true that he was a freemason, a Communist?

The tedious friar came down from the pulpit at last, but he contrived to give the mass a new-fangled twist at the very end: if Alphard understood him right he asked for the congregation's blessing.

'At least one will know what to expect this afternoon,' he said indignantly, dipping his hand into the dried-up stoup. 'That will be a comfort.' Their old priest would be taking the traditional vespers, as he always did: a dear man, untouched by modernism – nothing histrionic there – no innovations to be feared. The moment he passed the door heat enveloped him completely; it was as though he had walked into a physical substance, for now the sirocco had set in. The flies were thicker still, hatching in multitudes from some hidden filth; and looking up to the ominous sky he saw that the mountains behind the town had that particular livid glow that often came before a storm.

'I hope it will not spoil the children's day,' he said. Not that he liked children: and most of the present crop, born since the village had grown so much richer from the tourists, were rough, aggressive, ill-mannered. They despised their illiterate parents; and their worshipping illiterate parents gave them far too much money. Far too much to the adolescent boys especially, who shrieked about the village streets on mopeds. Not that the girls were much better: a bold, gum-chewing, confident set. It seemed an unhappy generation for all its wealth; old and hard so very young. But still he hoped their day would not be spoiled. It was a particular ceremony, essentially for them; and it linked them with a very distant past – to the Crusades, in all probability. Many of them were dressed up for it already. He saw Fifine, leading her niece and her hulking great nephew by the hand. The children (if the hairy Albert could be called a child) walked stiffly, their arms away from their fine new clothes, and the free hand of each held an enormous rattle, of the kind that whirls about its stem. Both looked over-excited, and there was a glow of anticipation on their aunt's Visigothic face as she steered them through the throng.

A few yards farther on the shutters of the gallery were up, but to his surprise Alphard saw Halévy in the door, sweeping vigorously. He was bare to the waist and sweat ran through the grizzled mat on his bosom: he was wearing a beaded skull-cap, however, presumably against the dust. Averting his eyes from the mat, Alphard said, 'Are you back already?'

Halévy said that in fact he was – that he had found no Madonna – four hundred miles in pursuit of a myth – and that he was profoundly discouraged.

'Come and try my Chian wine this evening,' said Alphard. 'Come at half past six.'

'I should be very happy,' said Halévy. 'Thank you. Such a privilege.' They talked about the weather – Halévy said the mountains made him think of El Greco – and while they were talking a horseplaying band of youths and boys, throwing sand and stones at one another, lurched into them. 'Jean-Paul, what are you about? Dédé, say you are sorry to the gentleman,' cried Alphard.

No apology, no reply: only a 'tough guy' look.

'Ill-mannered brutes,' he said. 'Really, I am ashamed for the village. I beg your pardon.'

'They all seem over-excited today,' said Halévy. 'All the children. What are those rattles they are carrying, and why the saucepans?' But before Alphard could reply, he went on, 'Oh, I have a horrible piece of news for you. The municipality has forbidden sardines to be grilled in the street: it seems the tourists do not like the smell.'

'They may forbid until they grow black in the face,' cried

Alphard, flushing. 'The past will have its rights. The past will rise up and have its rights.'

Alphard was not used to receiving guests, and after his lunch and his siesta he spent a considerable time setting his room in order, brushing the table, cleaning two glasses, moving chairs, angering the bird. Outside it was even hotter, dustier, and more oppressive. He was late for vespers and he slipped into a side-chapel: the ceremony was perfectly familiar to him now, although it had seemed so strange twenty years ago, and he 'found his place' as it were, without hesitation. The remaining psalms and antiphons followed their universal course and then the ancient local variation began, in the vernacular – the Magnificat and its antiphon, followed by the curé's address. Alphard understood the language pretty well, and as the address never varied year by year he followed it with ease: yet it was not really a very interesting address, except on historical grounds, being an allegory showing the relationship between the Church and the unbelievers under the outward likeness of the conduct of the lion towards the ass, taken straight from a medieval bestiary; and as the curé's triple r's and explosive participles rolled round the church Alphard's attention wandered. Sometimes his eyes strayed over the shrouded form of Saint Eulalie, following the ecstatic baroque swirl beneath the sheet; sometimes he looked at the instruments of the Passion, the lance, the sponge, the cruel pincers, hanging unveiled beyond the saint; and sometimes he gazed at the packed congregation. On most days their conduct left a great deal to be desired; awe and even common respect were wanting, and the people, above all the children, usually whispered, giggled and stared about. But now, in spite of the heat, the flies, their new clothes, and the temptation of their rattles, whistles, saucepans and drums, they were exemplary; every year they delighted in the piece about the lion, and this year their interest was even greater. Leaning forward in their seats they listened with the keenest attention to the unvarying description of the beast: 'His head is the head of a king and he has a terrible neck and a mane and his chest is vast and square:

he holds his great tail high above the ground. His flattened legs come down to his huge feet, which are divided, with long hooked claws . . . the ass alone resists him, braying there in the wilderness.'

The curé never used the microphone, and his fine deep voice filled the church, each word as distinct as a stone. The description was done and now the allegory was to be unfolded and made plain: here he might well have lost his grasp upon his hearers as he went on, right through the list; but they knew the climax was coming, and they never stirred. '. . . and the tail of the lion is justice, divine justice high over us. The lion's leg is flattened, and here we see the coming of the Passion: the shape of his foot is God's own sign that the world is to be held by the clenched fist. The sharp crooked claws are vengeance against the Jews; and the ass, who is the evil ass but the Jews? With the terrible face of a lion He will appear to the Jews when He judges them, for they damned themselves . . .'

Now the tension was growing to its height. Alphard had heard this twenty times and more, but he too leaned forward on his chair.

'For they damned themselves: the Jews betrayed their king.' In the momentary pause all the children drew in their breath; every mouth was open, every tongue shaped to form the sound of D; and the moment the priest cried 'Death to the Jews!' they all burst out 'Death to the Jews!' an enormous shrilling, instantly drowned by the even greater din of rattles, whistles, saucepans, drums as they rushed in a body from the church, leaving the adults to listen to the collect, read in a mild and unemphatic routine voice.

To recover from the shattering din and to avoid the racing bands of children as they howled and whistled in the streets, blind with excitement, Alphard usually walked on the jetty for half an hour; but today he went straight back along the beach towards his house. The sirocco had dropped: a brooding calm.

There was indeed something unusual about the general hubbub: less of the high small-child piping and more of the crack-voiced adolescent bawl, with here and there a woman's shriek and the bass roaring of a man. But Alphard's mind was far away until

375

he reached the diesel-pump. Here there was a dense crowd, an impenetrable swarm – every youth and child in Saint-Feliu – and something was terribly amiss. The fun had turned oh so sour: the smell of a bull-fight or worse. In the heat and the dust and the shouting he tried to push through: somewhere in the middle of that tight mob outside Halévy's gallery there was a rhythmic crash; and striving, thrusting his way through the smaller children on the fringe he saw half a dozen great boys swinging a baulk of wood, a launching stretcher from the beach, swinging it end-on against the door – a battering-ram. All round the edge there were women screaming, grasping at their own children: astonished men and dogs came running. Alphard shouted 'Jean-Baptiste, Jojo, put it down – stop, stop at once,' but as he tottered there, children underfoot, children pulling at his legs, the door gave way and there was Halévy, terribly pale, his white hair streaming, with an antique, bell-mouthed gun in his hands. A high triumphant roar, the shriek of rattles, a shower of stones, and he fired. Alphard went down. Had he been hit? No. But the swarm of children struggling over him three-deep kept him in the dust and by the time he struggled to his feet it had happened. The jet of diesel-oil played straight into the shop: Alphard stood there, bumped into, unsteady, tossed from side to side, amazed, tears running down his face, shouting 'Stop, stop, stop,' and the flames shot up, straight into the windless air, mounting high, high under the black and swirling smoke, an enormous fire.

The men were there, hitting, kicking, turning off the pump. Alphard turned away and he came face to face with a small beaming round-faced child who had not yet understood the change, a child that danced still, marvelling at the fire, waving her rattle and chanting 'Death, death to the Jews.'

41

A Passage of the Frontier

The threat from the north grew stronger, and the stateless persons and undesirables began to move towards the Mediterranean and the southern frontiers. Then suddenly, overnight, the full danger was there, immediately at hand: blind tanks roared down the motorways, endless lines of trucks full of infantrymen, guns, the political police; and far ahead of them all parachutists were setting up roadblocks, directing the military traffic, requisitioning houses, carrying out the first arrests. All trains were stopped, all main roads, bridges, tunnels closed.

Now plans that needed more than a few hours for their execution were abandoned; now the nearest road was the only road; and before dawn on Friday a hired car put Martin down at the end of a charcoal-burner's track on the high slope of the Coma du Loup.

They would have preferred to get him out of the country by way of Switzerland, but that was impossible now: all frontiers were closed to those with no legal identity. Encantats was the only solution, a small Pyrenean smuggling centre inland from Andorra, even higher and more remote. It possessed no motor-road into France, but as even the mule-track was guarded they had him set down in the Coma du Loup with a drawing of the smugglers' path and a carrier-bag of food; and Jacob lent him a hard-weather coat. The driver also had an envelope of paper money, to be handed over at the last moment; but he did not see fit to hand it over – he turned his car, throwing up loose earth, bark and scraps of charcoal on the blackened ground. Martin made stiff, inadequate gestures to guide him – stiff because he was still cramped by the long night's headlong flight.

The driver took no notice until the car was round; then he put his huge face out of the window, and through the smoke and steam he shouted, 'You follow the river. The ford is the boundary. Cross and follow the right-hand stream. You can't miss it.'

'Thank you very much,' said Martin. 'Good-bye.'

'The stream on the right,' said the driver, holding up his left hand. 'I've never been there myself, but you can't miss it.' He gave Martin a cold nod, crashed the gear home and jerked off down the track. The car was gone in a moment, but for some time it could still be heard, winding down through the trees in the dark-ness. Martin did not move until the sudden chatter of a jay star-tled him into motion, breaking a spell that might have lasted until the rising of the sun. He picked up his paper bag and began to climb through the trees.

This was near the top of the forest: he had passed up through the last half-mile of beeches, and now on the higher slope it was all pines, scaley pines standing steep from the mountainside. On his right hand the broad stream ran fast and deep, fall and pool, fall and pool all the way, and the brown water racing between high banks of rock.

At the beginning, under the beeches, there had been a clear path, indeed several paths; but up here the pine-needles did not hold the track. There were great heaps made by ants with wander-ing lines among them that might have been made by any number of beasts; but nothing like a distinct trail. The slope increased, and soon he was gasping; and as the day grew warmer, so green clouds of pollen began to drift through the forest, an enormous vegetable act of love. He came to a rocky shoulder where the trees grew sparse – no canopy to shut him in – and far over he saw the opposing mountain-flank, smoking green as though the whole forest were on fire.

In another hour he reached a level stretch of the river, a place where he could reach the water and wash and drink at last.

Drying, he sat on a grey boulder and picked raspberries. They grew all along among the rounded boulders, now that the trees were thinner, together with columbines and yellow lilies. Out there in the stream, where a fallen trunk had made an island, stood another lily, a tall purple spotted one whose petals curved back to touch its stem; and lying among the leaves at its foot, a blue crumpled packet that had held cigarettes. Nearer, in the gin-clear water, a rusting sardine-tin. 'Might this be the ford?' he said, and looked more attentively at the banks. Yes, certainly this was a place where one could cross, perhaps the first he had seen between the deep-cut banks; and certainly people had been crossing here for years and years, since the steep rock on the far bank was worn into steps. And farther up another stream joined this, as both the drawing and the driver had said.

So this was the frontier itself. He stepped into the water, unbelievably cold, and stood for a while with a foot on either side of the middle-line: then he waded over, to another country.

It feels much the same, however, he said, looking back to the bank he had left. The same trees over there, the same wild falls of rock, furred over with dry grey lichen; and a very small bird continually flitted to and fro across the water, busily from tree to tree, minding him no more than if he had been a cow.

Where it ran along the difficult course of the right-hand stream, the path was clear again; and often whole stretches of the bare mother-rock were trodden out into a smoothness that showed the grain and inner colour of the schist; but sometimes the steady upward sweep of the mountain was broken by broad level steps where the river soaked promiscuously among the bushes and the swampy earth, the coarse hummocks of grass and sour brown pools; here, and even more in the frequent steep gulleys, the path would divide, wander and dwindle into unmeaning ribbons. Yet time and again when he seemed to have lost it for ever his hand would reach out for a branch whose bark was already worn to the wood, or as he leapt a small ravine his foot would land in a place worn deep by other men. The path always reappeared, and it led him high, high towards the last thinning-out of the trees; now they stood wide apart, each one lower, with its under-branches touching the now frosty ground, and each looking older by far. The whole character of the forest had changed; the trees no longer hemmed him in, but stood casually, with junipers between them and even broad glades of low pink-flowering rhododendrons or open grass, studded with unopened gentians.

Then came one last belt of ancient twisted moss-clad pines, hardly more than bushes, and abruptly he was out of the trees altogether: they were ruled off as though by a line, and the sky, no longer patches of light above the branches, spread wide overhead. An enormous sky; vivid and brilliant beyond anything he had imagined: these hours of climbing had kept his head down, and now the immensity of this vast bowl overwhelmed him.

Another five hundred feet over the bare grass and he sat down to gaze round the world. His heart was pounding and his breath came short – visible breath that lingered in the unmoving, frigid air – and for some time his gasping body would scarcely let him comprehend what he saw: it was as though he were contemplating a brilliant but entirely foreign universe. Yet in time it resumed an intelligible form: there was his dark forest, sweeping down in wave after wave to the dim lower clouds; and beyond the great valley to the north rose answering mountains with rounded tops. Somewhere in the hidden land between them must be the last remote village and the road. It was an enormous landscape, on a scale that quite abolished hours or miles, but this was not the half of it – behind him the high mountain cut off the rest of the world. To his right as he turned there were two soaring peaks, joined by a ragged curtain-wall; they were very dark on this northward side, and the snow that lay in their deep gulleys showed with a deathly light; they had screes and beds of shale hanging on their steep sides or running down to the chaotic rocks below, and the screes were cold and grey, severely inanimate. But on his left the solitary peak had caught the sun. Every detail of its warm brown and ochre cliffs was clear, and in this brilliant clarity it might have been no more than an hour away, but for the golden cloud that floated between him and the nearest spur. Between these mountains, and due south of him, there appeared the upward edge of a wilderness of rock that threw up uncounted peaks; their grey northern sides were powdered with snow, and deep snow lay here and there in streaks. These raised, distant peaks were all he could see of the waste beyond. 'The necessary pass will be clear, no doubt,' he said, 'once I can survey the whole.'

The cold seeped into him from below; the air bit his ears and nose; and when at last he felt for the map his hands were numb The single mountain was certainly Malamort, and it was beyond it, on the sunward side, that he must go, through a gap between the mountain and the chaos to the south: he could see no gap, but his drawing showed the path, a line winding up to the shoulder of Malamort. The gap must be there, and it must be exactly to the south-east, hidden by some nearer crest. With a sudden eager desire to know what was on the other side of the limiting ridge, to find the pass, to be moving in this silent enormous world, he started up the slope, a smooth alp dotted with pale boulders like gigantic sheep.

It was a rounded slope whose skyline mounted pace by pace with him, false crests in an interminable series, and it was steep; yet he hurried up it, sometimes chuckling, sometimes singing loud; and where the slope was less he ran in bounds, waving his arms and singing louder still. The grass thinned and the bare earth showed more as he gained height, gritty earth among pale grass, dirty and crushed from the snow that had left it a few days ago. Now and then he slipped and fell; but he fell easy on the wet sloping ground; it did not affect his elation nor his speed and in time he gained the true ridge at last, with its long wave of standing snow. Here he fell silent: now he was standing in the sun, astride of a vaster world by far, because the last two thousand feet had brought up mountains on every hand, and he was above them all, above everything except Malamort; and clean round the horizon these mountains rose and fell, a brown infinity. The great valley on the north was gone, obliterated by the miracle of breeding cloud, rounded white masses rising below him into the middle air, forming slow whirlpools and momentary towers. Once the whole gleaming ocean parted from top to bottom, and he saw a heightened fragment of the common world – thread-like roads, the railway-line, a winding river, the huddle of a town with smoke, the minute patchwork of fields. But with the closing of the clouds and their continual mounting there was nothing on that side but the great ranges as they stretched away, illimitable against the lower sky, rising from the rising sea of white: but on this side, the new, southern, sunlit side, no clouds; nothing but a desert of broken rock, brilliantly lit yet dark and even black in places, with sheets of snow and many lakes, black-rimmed, shining water in the hollows; screes everywhere, and rarely a touch of green. The wilderness filled all the middle distance, and beyond it the saw-edged ranges ran on and on: the mountains of Aragon, no doubt, and perhaps those of Navarre.

The snow under his feet was crusted, granular and hard; it was pocked with old rain and powdered with a dust of earth, but beneath the crust it was the purest white. Its taste was thin – insubstantial – yet it left a burning in his mouth.

Virgin snow: there seemed a want of piety in walking upon its unbroken smoothness; and never was there such a world for piety – it might have been created yesterday. Others had not felt the same, however. Twenty yards away to the left footmarks crossed it at its lowest point. What is more, they continued beyond the present limit of the snow; and these compressed footprints were still unmelted; they ran on, a series of white dots pointing straight to a cleft under the sheer rock-face of Malamort, a slit perhaps an hour away, hardly to be seen at all in the blaze of the sun without their help. For this necessary pass, this Portal Nera, lay in the deep shadow among black, impassable rocks.

Once he was across and fairly on the southern slope, the sun warmed him through and through, comforting him to the bone. The gentians were open here, stars and trumpets, fields of them, and the air was like good news: he said, I could go on for ever.

He walked with long, reaching strides, on and on: yet the sun climbed and the pass barely moved. The air was stirring now, and a black vulture rose in spirals on a thermal current until it was no bigger than a lark: the bowl of the sky turned an even intenser blue. This was perfect walking, these miles of level or slightly downward path, almost like a slow gentle flight or even levitation after the grind of the ascent: slowly the pass changed shape, and to his left the peak soared higher still, growing until it filled the eastern quarter of the sky.

For long stretches he watched the alternate reappearance of his feet and the even flow of the ground beneath. Once he looked up at the clatter of a band of chamois crossing a scree a mile away to the west, and once he followed the flight of a large white butterfly with red eye-spots on its wings; but upon the whole he kept his head down, in a floating dream.

The third time he looked up he was in the very entrance of the pass, and he saw a man in a grey cloth cap, a surly red-eyed man with his legs wrapped in coarse brown paper from knee to ankle: he was sitting on a dark boulder in the shadow of the cliff, beside a shapeless load, or burden. He asked Martin had he the right time?

'I am afraid I have not,' said Martin, 'but it is early yet, I am sure.' He sat down and watched the man as he knotted two broken ends in the sacking of his load.

'Whore of Babylon,' said the man, forcing the knots tight; and he muttered continually as he turned the bundle over and over to verify the fastenings. 'What is your name?' he asked.

'Martin Kaftan.'

'Where do you come from?'

'France.'

'Where are you going? Are you alone? Do you know anyone in Encantats?'

Martin answered these questions, and after a pause the man, pretending to inspect his burden still, drew out a knife. He feigned to cut the loose end of a string and said, 'You know nothing about the mountain. Look at your shoes. I dare say you have a good many pairs of leather shoes in your house,' he added, with a cunning leer. Martin looked at his shoes: their soles were shining

383

from the grass; they were indeed quite unsuitable. 'Come,' said the man, 'let me scratch them with my knife.'

With the shoes in front of him he did not scratch them yet, but pushed up his sleeve and began to shave the hair on his forearm. The hairs skipped under the edge, leaving a bare, mown tract of skin. 'Sharp,' he said. 'That's what I call sharp.' He was looking uglier now, with white spittle between his lips, his eyes were squinting with excitement, and the defect in his speech grew more pronounced. He said, 'You are afraid to be on the mountain alone with all that money and your fine coat. Let me feel your coat. What have you got to eat?'

Martin laughed, leaning back against the rock. He said, 'How would I be afraid on the mountain, my dear? And no one can rob me on this journey, because I was robbed before I began. The coat is not mine, and I left all my food at the top of the forest, by mistake: a chicken, bread, and a bottle of wine. What is your name, pray?'

'Joan,' said the man, vaguely. He seemed to be coming out of his fit, and although he said 'No', when Martin asked him whether he had anything to eat either, after a little while he brought out a flat black loaf and two onions and unslung the greasy leather bottle he wore on his shoulder. He scratched a cross on the loaf, cut off a piece and gave it to Martin with one of the onions; and when Martin held out his hand for the knife to slice the onion he passed it without reflection. He also passed the wine.

Munching fast he told Martin how good he was: uniquely good: took no advantage of the situation as any other man might, nay *would*, for the laws of God were not observed and God Himself had never reached these parts. 'There was the izard-hunter from Politg – they cut his throat in this very pass before he could say hail Mary and Espollabalitris ate his balls.'

'What are izards?'

'Izards are what you make chamois-skin out of: where were you brought up, God forbid? But I should never have eaten any Christian's balls. I am too good,' he said with his eyes closed tight, and he pressed Martin to eat more, to drink as much as he could.

'Drink, man, drink. I do not reckon the cost,' he said, squirting the jet into Martin's mouth.

'You are very kind,' said Martin, when the skin was empty. 'I hope you will find my chicken, in time, and the bottle. They are in a paper carrier-bag, on a rock where the trees begin.'

'Never mind, never mind if the bears have had them. I can go all day and night without refreshment, to help a poor man. I do good, but I never mention it. There are hundreds and thousands down there' – jerking his head backwards – 'who owe everything to me: but I say nothing.' Shading his mouth he whispered, 'There are evil tongues down there,' and nodding vehemently he set to scratching the shoes, raising diagonal weals on their soles with the point of his knife.

'Thank you very much,' said Martin, making to put them on.

'No, no. Let me,' cried Joan, cramming them on to Martin's feet and lacing them with terrible force. He grew excited again when he described the course of the path as it led on to the Cami Real, the great mule-track, confused in his description, obscurely angry and contentious; his ugliness was increasing fast, but when Martin said he supposed the burden must weigh a great deal Joan turned off directly to tell what he could carry, compared with common men. And indeed when Martin lifted it, meaning to help it on, the weight was staggering. Joan thrust him aside, swung it up with one hand, looped it on with a sordid web and stood displaying himself with angry satisfaction. 'Watch me,' he cried, setting off at a furious pace up the hill. His voice came fainter: 'You have never seen anything like it. But this is nothing to what I can do, Mother of God.'

'Thank you for telling me the way,' Martin called after him; but Joan ran on and on, without another word.

For two hours more the path ran sweetly round the shoulder of Malamort, dipping to a lake: other paths had joined it, coming from valleys to the east, but they were obviously less important; and in any event this lake was marked upon his drawing; it had been named by Joan. All that he had to do now was to walk left-handed round its shore, climb by the stream the other side, reach the high snowy ridge beyond, find the westward pass above two small lakes, and so drop to the road.

The great hollow, a ring two miles across, was surrounded by cliffs on three sides; they had beds of shale at their feet, and in three places they were broken by streams coming from the higher ridge. Three streams, and one of them a waterfall; yet clearly the first was his. It was much larger; it was directly on the other side of the lake; and there had been no mention of his crossing water.

The fourth side was filled by a marsh, covered with cotton-grass, and among the boulders on its edge grew a low, fern-like plant in great profusion; the last year's growth, brown, dry in the sun, and fragrant, made the softest resting-place. He sat down and gazed at the water, his whole body relaxing at once, limp, boneless and pliable: the lake had no banks, in the ordinary sense – there were just these falls of rock, and then, without transition, water. It had no vegetation in it or round it: no clouds passed overhead, no birds. No breeze touched its surface. It seemed that there was no life here, only sky, rock and silence; but presently he saw rings spreading, and later he heard the splash of a rising trout. There were other sounds too: stone avalanches rumbling in the distance; the thunder of rock falling from the cliffs, several times repeated, and startling at first. He watched the rings form, spread and intersect; he dozed, awoke, dozed again, and fell fast asleep in his bed of fern.

It was a nearer rock-fall and the cold that roused him. The sun had left the water, the whole bottom of the ring, and now it lit only the upper half of the eastern cliff: already the air down here was sharp. There was no time to be lost, and quickly putting on his shoes he hurried round the lake. He climbed fast up along the bed of the first stream, but the shadow climbed faster still: before he had reached the ridge the lower sky was violet, and the arch of the day was closing towards the west. He had seen nothing like a path for the last hour, but now the snow was coming closer, and surely he would find it there.

Indeed, there it was, a track slanting westwards across the snow, almost exactly where his anxious theory had placed it. But alas, when he came to it there was clearly something wrong – too slender, far too neat – and when he bent in the fading light he saw the mark of cloven hoofs. This was the path, and no doubt the habitual path, of a numerous band of chamois. Certainly it was: ten minutes later he rounded a bluff with the breeze in his face and came full upon them. The group exploded, racing away, leaping skip-skip-skip down and across an impossible rock-face, so that he was in dread for their legs and necks.

However, they were gone, safely gone, before he could even count them, and his anxiety returned to himself; the twilight was mounting fast to these regions, and the only hint of real path that he could see led upwards, still higher, to no pass that he could discern among the massive peaks ahead.

'Yet it may very well drop again suddenly,' he said. 'It may very well show me the pass in half an hour; and as soon as I am on the road I shall find a shepherd's hut. Joan spoke of one where the road leaves the forest, and two not far from the chapel.'

On. Higher and higher, winding where the rocks would let him rather than where a fading sense of direction urged him to go on. He often fell now, once losing his hold on a scree and sliding down a hundred feet with stones falling all around and beyond him. Eventually, with his breath gone, his strength going, and a deep cut in his side, he found himself creeping in the near darkness along a snowy ledge with a sheer face on his right hand and a precipice on his left.

The snow had melted away from the rock-face, where the sun had warmed it, leaving a passage wide enough to stand in – wider in places – and then, on the outward side of the ledge, a firm white mass as high as a counter. He leant on this counter, surveying the night as it rose from the east – Mars blazing already, even the small stars pricking out, but never a hint of the moon – and the dark shapes of the mountains looming against the sky. 'I am far, far too high,' he said. 'But I cannot go any farther. Snow is said to conserve the warmth: I shall try to find a wider place, and there I shall lie.'

Fifty yards along the ledge turned sharply: he was observing,

'And if it does not, then I shall run up and down until the day,' when he heard a snort, a muffled, hurrying sound ahead. At the same moment he caught a goatish smell, and his feet were treading in dung. 'So this is where the chamois sleep,' he said. 'How wise.'

It was the most sheltered place that could be wished at this great height: beneath the counter there was no wind at all; some warmth still emanated from the cliff, and the smell soon passed unnoticed. His body was so tired that the rock seemed soft at first, and he lay there in a half-doze, watching the stars as they swept over the narrow trench above.

A long, long night, however, with an increasing cold that reached to his heart at last. By two o'clock it seemed to have been going on for ever. But at least he was beyond hunger, and his thirst he could satisfy from the snow. When the stars were paling he fell into a tormented sleep, cramped and uneasy, but so deep that the sun was as high as the Malamort before it woke him.

'It is over,' he said, shading his eyes from the glare and unscrewing himself from the tight ball in which he had lain. 'It is over at last.' He got on to his knees, then to his feet, and as he slowly straightened so the pure revivifying sunlight darted straight into his upper half: his blood began to flow, the tension and shivering died away as the heat pierced deeper and deeper; his teeth no longer chattered. He took off his soaking blood-stained filthy coat and stood back against the warm rock with his arms spread wide and his eyes closed. All around him there was the drip of melting snow.

Now his shirt was dry and even his frozen spine was supple; he leant his elbows on the counter and looked out. Below him, cloud. Nothing but that white sea of impenetrable cloud, rising to within five hundred feet of his ledge. Mountains thrusting through it – to his left the familiar praying hands of Malamort – and a perfect sky above. He said, 'They will lift in time,' and his eye caught a white-splashed shelf of rock below, within spitting distance below. Three bearded vultures stood upon it, the parents and their huge blowsy child, sluggishly preening themselves and waiting for the day to warm. His gaze made them uneasy, and presently one cocked its head upwards, shuffled to the edge and launched itself silently into the void. The others followed, and for a moment he saw six great sharp-winged forms gliding over the clouds, the birds and their close-following shadows.

'I have slept with vultures too, I find,' he observed; and wedging its sleeves into a horizontal crack he spread his coat to dry.

There was no attempting to move except upwards, which was absurd; so during the hours in which the cloud slowly boiled and rolled in upon itself below, sometimes sending off long streamers but never breaking, he also dried his trousers and his handkerchief, luxuriating in the heat as they hung.

Gradually the unseen waterfall to his right increased in sound and volume as the sun unlocked the higher snow and ice; and when at last the cloud began its definitive rise, the jet came into sight, a single arch of water shooting out from a broken cliff and plunging into the whiteness, now only a hundred feet below.

Tenuous vapours were drifting overhead: all the sharp definition of the cloud was gone. The sun dimmed, and a moment later it was no more than a white ball in the enveloping fog. He put on his good dry clothes, grateful for their warmth, and relapsed into timeless waiting.

Would the cloud continue to rise? Or would it hang about the mountain-tops all day, all night, perhaps for weeks on end? A small shining beetle climbed laboriously about the pellet-shaped droppings and the compacted masses of izards' dung. Several times it fell on its back, waving its legs, and each time he set it on its feet; but it seemed to possess no sense of purpose or direction.

The cloud lifted. It took a great while to do so, but it lifted and the last stage was as dramatic as the raising of a curtain. A hint of thinning, and then suddenly it was overhead, completely overhead, revealing the lower world, whole, clear and plain.

There, immediately below him, was the forest. There, on the flank of a valley, was the road, rising to a saddle to the west. There was the river. And there, on the grassy slopes above the forest, he could see minute shapes that must be grazing cattle. Poring over this landscape spread below him he made out three shepherd's huts, all far away, the nearest being close to the upper limit of the trees, between the forest and the road, on the far side of the river. From one blue smoke was rising; and each had a strange brown square in front of it, like a field.

There too were the small lakes, far away to the east; and there to be sure he saw the path, so well trodden by the herds down there that it might have been a road. He had not gone so far wrong: the general direction had been right. Only he was three thousand feet too high. And his precipice fell half that distance without a break. How to get down it? Along the ledge in the hope of its joining that far shoulder? Back the way he had come, trusting to find a way along its foot? There were not so many hours of daylight left, with the tall mountains cutting off the sun so soon, and the best way he must find, or he was lost in sight of home.

Backwards, forwards, sideways, up and down, climbing, sliding, sometimes falling, it was not until the evening sky flushed red that he was down to the two small lakes, fetching them at last by a long tack that lost him an hour and more. 'But once I am round this pool,' he said, forcing his exhausted body through a bog, 'I am certainly on the one true path: then if I do not fall again I may very well get there by night. And surely I shall not fall upon the road itself?'

Five minutes later he missed his leap on a shifting rock; but the fall sent him sprawling on to the undoubted path, and now it was only a question of clearing his head, gathering himself together, choosing the right direction, and going on and on for some hours. 'Providing the shepherd is at home,' he said.

Past the lakes, on, and a long haul, to the first of the trees, strangely familiar with their hanging moss in the deepening twilight; down through the trees to the river and the ford. The swift icy current, knee-deep and more; the slippery stones in the darkness. He said, 'Shall I ever make this last half-mile?' as he paused long on the farther bank, searching for strength to stand up again. There was only a plain meadow between him and the light of the open door, but now the cruel frost came dropping from the sky and he was as weary as a dying man.

Ahead of him stood the herd, packed into the trampled square in front of the hut – mares with their mule foals, cows, heifers, beasts, some sheep, two goats, two pigs, with a mist of soft breath rising from them all – a guardian dog at each corner, huge woolly dogs with steel-spiked brass collars. They had heard and smelt him coming since before he crossed the river, but they said nothing: only one young subsidiary dog slunk close behind his legs and gibbered its teeth uneasily; and he walked very slowly past them towards the door.

It was open to let out some of the smoke, and it showed a glowing stone-built room. There were two fires blazing inside, one on the hearth, another, a small and clear fire of juniper, burning on a stone shelf beside the bench; and this bench, this broad wooden platform against the back wall, filled the entire width of the hut. The shepherd lay there on a deep pile of sheepskins, and he was reading in a book. One arm held it to the light, and the other lay round the lamb that slept against his side. A very old bitch and some cats filled the rest of the bed.

The very old bitch grunted as Martin appeared in the door, and the shepherd turned his eager smiling face towards him. 'Have you come?' he said, closing the book, disengaging the lamb, and beginning to rise. 'And have you come at last? You are the Christ? I have been waiting and waiting for you.'

'No, my dear,' said Martin, leaning against the jamb. 'I am not the Christ.'

'Are you not?' said the shepherd, touching his arm. His face clouded painfully; but he said, 'Lie down on the warm bed, while I milk a cow.' He looked searchingly into Martin's face again and said, 'And are you indeed not the Christ? Yet the dogs never spoke; and this is the time. No? Well,' – smiling once more – 'then I shall not have to kill the lamb.'

42

On the Wolfsberg

When she came out of the mindless, ruminating state that walking often induced she found that the moon had risen: a gibbous moon behind hazy cloud, but enough to flood the world with diffuse light. She also found that she had no notion where the road was going to, nor why she was walking along it so eagerly, nor indeed who or where she was.

As far as she could tell she had never seen these vast rolling mountains, with their moonwards sides gleaming a soft grey and their deep coombs as black as velvet and the white ribbon of a road that ran on and on, vanishing behind spurs and shoulders but always reappearing higher up on the next flank beyond until at last it was lost in the general merging of cloud and sky and moonlight.

'This is the damnedest thing,' she said, amused, 'I have absolutely no notion of . . .' She looked attentively at the road: it was a metalled road, but clearly few people ever used it – plants stood knee-high in the middle, and brambles reached from either side, flat on the surface. The even slope ran upwards, with no hint of its destination ahead, no high perched village, no lights anywhere, high or low: all around the vast field of view, nothing but these soft hills for ever, limitless peace and silence; and on her right a dark mass with jagged peaks against the sky.

'I must have been lying in the grass,' she said uncertainly, picking dry wisps and fern from her clothes. 'But where? When? How come?' There was no answer at all; a vagueness like that of the grey mountains; but a placid vagueness – she was not particularly concerned or upset even when a concentrated effort brought no response.

'The great thing in these cases is not to press,' she said. 'It is like trying to force a tune – if you leave it alone, five minutes later or perhaps the next day you will find the whole orchestra booming away in your head, apropos of nothing. I have only to let a few synapses clear and I shall be able to call myself by name. I shall be able to fill out an hotel card – surname, Christian name, maiden name, date and place of birth, profession, nationality.' She walked on, whistling Death and the Maiden in an undertone, and presently she was floating along at her former steady pace.

'Amnesia, amnesio,' she sang, after a while. 'What a caper. How much is there left? A great deal, I find: speech centres unaffected, technical memory unimpaired.' She repeated the alphabet, the cranial nerves of the dogfish, the list of elements. 'I am a woman, of course; I never had any doubt of that. Youngish: sound in wind and limb.' She glanced at her hand. 'No ring: but that's not evidence. And I am *myself*, that's sure. What I am looking for is the label.' Her mind flitted away in a long digression – how much was label a component of identity? How much epoch, nationality, with all their values and associations? Take the social context away from a parcel of reflexes conditioned by that context and what remains? Something, nevertheless: the size of a dried pea or even smaller, but irreducible and enough for the statement *I am me* to carry some conviction.

'However,' she said at last, 'my sex is certain, and the time is the present, whatever that may mean: the question is, what is myself doing in these mountains?'

Here the road led her round to the westward side, still warm from the sun, and wafts of aromatic air surrounded her. 'I can't put a name to these smells,' she said, 'nor can I attach them to any sort of association: I don't know them at any level. So I must be abroad.' This reasoning was confirmed when she found a milestone by the road. 1.3 km, clear in the moonlight. 'Kilometres. So this is certainly Abroad, as I said.'

Far away, carrying a great way, there came the call of a mid-wife toad, repeated at solemn intervals: 'Ayltes obstetricans,' she murmured; and reflecting upon the immense silence in which the sound was produced – a silence that seemed part of the moonlight and the huge expanse of shadowed mountain – she concluded that she must herself be an urban creature, used to a continual background of noise. 'Some time ago, a mile back perhaps,' she observed, 'I heard running water on the far side of the valley; and that amazed me too.'

For an indeterminate time, still walking steadily, she contemplated the peaceful infinity of rounded hills below her, the slope falling sharply from the road, and the mountains above and beyond her: it was not in any way a hostile landscape nor, though bare of trees, a savage one; but rather detached, almost irrelevant – a landscape for vague wandering rather than incisive thought. 'You would say the farther side was as clear as day,' she said, 'but when you look close everything is uncertain. The folds merge together; there is no telling where one begins and the other ends – as soft as clouds from an aeroplane. These mountains . . .' All at once she cried, 'Mountains! In my very last letter – such a pompous letter – I wrote "leaving geology and everything else aside, from a strictly anthropocentric point of view, mountains are there as an analgesic." It was my very last letter to – ' And looking at them the name was almost there, hovering half-formed in her throat; but it faded, no longer to be grasped, before she could bring it to the level of perception. 'Never mind,' she said. 'I shall catch it unawares, in time.'

Yet time had lost its usual flow, and indeed almost all its meaning: that is to say, in so far as time differed from mere succession. A raucous voice from the sky startled her, breaking her train of thought – a voice that wound about, trumpeting overhead. 'Heavens!' she cried, peering up. 'What can it be? No owl ever carried on like that.' A farther trumpeting to the north, and the voice drew off to join it. Her wits returned and she said, 'Why, *Nycticorax nycticorax*, of course. But it might have been an ostrich, judging by the row . . . Amnesia: it is an obvious refuge

394

from distress, from an intolerable situation: everyone knows that. But I feel no particular distress; no heartbreak, no depression. Only a pleasing melancholy, engendered by this prodigious wild romantic prospect. And perhaps a sort of bruised feeling ... I suppose,' she cried, laying her hand upon her bosom, 'I suppose I have not been knocked on the head and raped, with all that grass on my back?

'No, of course I have not: everything is perfectly intact. And I do so despise women who are perpetually being raped, or almost raped, or in situations where they might have been raped – trains, cabins, lifts, lonely woods – the lot.'

The road was turning slowly out of the light of the moon: for another hundred yards she still had her faint shadow for company, and then it was gone. In the soft darkness only the white track could be seen, and with nothing, not even moths, to distract her mind, she thought more about this feeling of a bruise. It was in her heart, and as she probed its nature it was so very like a physical pain that she could almost define it anatomically.

None of this helped her in her search for a label, but it did take away from her amusement. By the time she walked out of the darkness nothing sharp or clear had flashed into her mind, yet enough of an atmosphere in some way connected with this bruise had drifted near enough to the threshold of apprehension for her to say, 'If it is as bad as all that, I do not want to find it. Just let me walk along like this.' Another waft of scent drifted across. 'I love this road.'

The scents were extraordinarily varied; there was one as sweet as orange-blossom but far more piercing, another like pot-pourri, and one that must surely have been rosemary; and she thought she had been entirely taken up with her attempt at classifying them when she saw a piece of paper on the road.

Her automatic cry, 'Let it be nothing symbolic, for God's sake. No more of those square old symbols,' showed her that in fact some part of her mind had been running in quite another direction. 'No more symbols,' she went on nevertheless, 'and nothing *directed*: I have had digs enough to last me the rest of my life.

If it says anything in the line of *expense of spirit in a waste of shame* I shall blaspheme.'

It was not of that nature at all. Tilting it to the best light she made out a set of diagrams, possibly directions for solving a Chinese puzzle, an interlocking wooden ball.

She opened her fingers, let it plane gently to the ground, and walked on. But the realization that some busy autonomous process had been burrowing in that direction took away the very last of her amusement: she felt an anxious, dreary expression settle on her face and she found that the elasticity had gone from her stride.

Her whistling was a failure too. 'It occurs to me,' she said, after a long course in the darkness, two miles at least, 'that the reason why I do not really care where this road is going is that I do not care where I am going either: not a damn, alas.'

Moonlight again, even brighter now; and with the change of light there was some subtle alteration in the atmosphere, the landscape and the sky – a certain air of menace. She noticed it at once, but she said, 'Nothing can threaten me; nothing can threaten me now.'

She must have reached some kind of pass, for now the road no longer climbed. After a quarter of a mile of flat it began to slope down, still in this noiseless silvery everlasting universe, the easiest road in the world to follow. And although at present the silence had something frozen and indeed inimical about it, she sank deep into its cold heart.

Down and down, so detached from her body that she could have left it to float on ahead, and so removed from any ordinary consideration that the wolf did not cause her any extreme surprise.

He was a big wolf, lean, long-legged and gaunt, and he was drifting along on the mountainside above her and somewhat behind, moving silently on a track parallel with her own. He reached the inky shadow of a rock, and she saw his eyes gleam green.

It did not surprise her very much; and although at first her heart beat hard and quick and she felt weakness in her knees, this died away and she and her pursuer moved on steadily, the wolf paying no overt attention to her and she watching him out of the corner of her eye as he loped through the clumps of thyme. Presently she heard a soft dump as he leapt down on to the road, crossed, and took up his position on her left, still a long stone's throw away, neither gaining nor losing ground.

He was easier to see now, and although the moonlight never gave a really sharp view of him at any one time, the countless glimpses built up a perfect image: he was enormously strong.

'It would be a laugh if he turned out to be no more than a prodigious great dog,' she said, and she was surprised to find tears running down her face. 'But it is more likely he is just some damned symbol, longing for a romp.'

She wiped away her tears and sniffed, and at the sound the wolf's ears pricked up. They walked on. Half a mile later she called out 'Hey!' and the wolf froze, so that she could see him perfectly: a huge brute, quite six feet long with his mangy tail; and in spite of his silver flanks he looked indescribably mean. After some repetitions of this he sprang up on to the road and followed immediately behind, his shadow clear on the whiteness; and sometimes he snuffled on her track. But she was growing bored with the wolf, bored with watching, bored with tension.

At last anger flared up: she turned and cried, 'What kind of a goddam symbol are you, anyhow?' At this point the wolf was sniffing about a milestone: he kept his eye on her and deliberately cocked his leg. 'A symbol cocking its leg, for God's sake,' she exclaimed. 'I never knew wolves did that. Unless indeed it is symbol upon symbol.' She picked up a stone and walked back along the road: the wolf crouched, rigid, glaring. She called out, 'Here's for you, *Canis lupus*,' and as her arm whipped up she knew who she was and that Hugh Lupus was an empty selfish man, hollow and false: false through and through. The knowledge came faster than the flying stone.

43

Simon

———— ⪦⪧ ————

Simon, reading on the hearth-rug, looked up and asked: 'What is a whoremonger?'

'I don't know, my dear,' said his mother, absently, poking the fire: and when she had the logs just so she added: 'but I believe it is pronounced hore, with no w. What is that book?'

'It's an enormous history of England, about Cromwell.' The news of the pronunciation of whore drove history from Simon's mind, for it shed a sudden and brilliant light on odd scraps of conversation he had heard in the kitchen, scraps that children are more likely to pick up than others. 'Maggie is going with Alfred now . . . Maggie is going with Mrs Gregory's William . . . Maggie is going with George . . . Maggie goes with soldiers from the camp.'

'That Maggie,' said Mrs Hamner, the bearded cook, 'is now the village whore.'

The word, formerly connected only with frost and aged heads, instantly took on a meaning more consonant with Mrs Hamner's disapproving tone, since from the context of Cromwell's remark it was clear that whore and harlot were the same creature. Simon knew all about harlots, except for what they actually did, and he was charmed to be so well acquainted with one in the flesh. It was like knowing a phoenix, or Medusa.

'I shall go and tell Joe,' he said to himself, and although the fire, the hearth-rug and the after-tea comfort were wonderfully attractive, he closed the book and hurried out.

Joseph was his elder brother, a heroic figure, already at the university, who spent these evenings of the vacation out with his gun, shooting the odd early rabbit along the edge of Barton wood or the pigeons as they came in to roost. Simon sometimes went with him, to pick up the dead birds, and he had noticed how cheerfully he could greet Maggie if they met, and she coming home from work: familiar greetings. Christian names, laughter. Joe would be delighted to know that she was the village whore, or harlot.

The question was, where would Joseph be? There were many possibilities. Barton being a fair-sized wood; but in the end he decided on the corner jutting out into Half-penny Fields, where the path from Wansbury and its glove-factory meandered across the pasture to the village. There might be mushrooms there, and in any case Joe would probably come back that way when it was too dark to shoot.

Simon, big with his news, reached the corner far too early; there were no mushrooms, and although two white scuts fled away into the undergrowth there were no birds coming in yet. Simon lingered for a while, wondering what harlots really did and trying to hoot like an owl through his fists, their thumbs joined tight.

Presently he heard a couple of shots far over on the left-hand side. Joseph must be shooting the pigeons feeding on Carr's broad stretch of kale, unless indeed it was the Carr boys themselves. No. It must be Joseph – the Carrs were at a football match far beyond Wansbury – and he must come back this way. Simon was certainly not going to walk along the wood to meet him and be cursed for putting down all the rabbits; nor would he cut across, with the likelihood of missing him in the thick stuff. He would fool about here, looking for a straight wand that would do for a bow until Joe appeared.

Simon was an enterprising, birds'-nesting little boy, and in this part of the wood he had found a wool-lined crow's nest last spring as well as many of the frail transparent rafts upon which pigeons laid, and of course, the ordinary thrushes' and blackbirds' along the edge. He knew the place quite well. Yet fairly close to the path there was an oak he had never particularly noticed, not a promising tree for nests; but now, with so many leaves already fallen, at a modest height he saw a rounded mass that might well have been a squirrel's dray. With its twisted, nobly old trunk the oak was easy enough to climb until he could reach the branches, and although the dray was too old and sodden to be of any interest, Simon, on coming back to the crown, observed with delight that the oak's trunk was hollow. And not only hollow, but provided with a hole at the bottom, through which the evening light showed plainly: one could drop down inside the tree, down on to the deep bed of leaves, push them away and shout out of the hole, terrifying, or at least astonishing, one and all. If only the tree were right on the path rather than some way into the wood the effect would be prodigious; but even so it would still be very great. An eldritch shriek might help, since it would make people look in the right direction.

He lowered himself carefully into the hollow, hung from the edge at arm's length, let go and dropped, dropped much farther than he had expected, into the leaves. They too were far deeper than he had thought they would be, and much wetter. Under the top layer, brown and dry like breakfast-food, came first a porridgy mass and then a vegetable mud, knee-deep. Already his shoes and stockings were hopelessly compromised, and he had scarcely realized the depth of this misfortune before he found that clearing the leaves did not enlarge the hole for more than the handbreadth of dry on top. That was why the rest was like so much thick and indeed fetid soup; it was stagnant, enclosed. He scooped what could be scooped to one side and, no longer minding his shirt or jersey, tried to thrust his head through the hole. Even forcing it with all his might, there was no hope.

Rubbing his excoriated ears he sat on the dry part and said: 'I must climb up inside with back and feet, like mountaineers in a rock-fault.' But the mountaineers he had read of did not have to contend with slippery rotting wood, nor with very short legs. There was one roughly three-cornered space where he could get a hold and gain three or four feet before slipping, but after that it was impossible – the width of the trunk was greater than his outstretched body – and the daylight at the top was of course far out of leaping reach.

When he had fallen half a dozen times he sat for a while, gasping and collecting himself. His bare knees were bleeding; this was nothing unusual with him – they were generally scarred – but it was difficult to see how they could have been barked in a glutinous hollow tree. Not that it signified. As he sat there he found he was trembling, and a new kind of fear – not worry or frustration or dread of reproof but a cold, deep, unknown fear – began to stir about his heart or stomach.

The sound of a muffled shot calmed it for a while. 'Joe can't be long, and I shall roar out,' he said, and he contemplated the dingy wall reflecting that if only he had not lost his penknife he might have cut hand-holds in the soft wood. Quite suddenly he saw that the wall was no longer clear: daylight was fading fast, the evening cloud gathering.

Another double shot. It seemed nearer – Joe was on his way back and if he could not be made to hear before he passed, there was no help, no help at all.

Simon began to shout, much too soon, 'Ooh-hoo, ooh-hoo, Joe, Joe. I'm in the tree. I can't get out. I'm in the tree. Joe, Joe, Joe . . .'

The noise of the shouting inside the tree and its urgency made him begin to lose his head and he leapt at the wall like a frightened, indeed a frantic, trapped animal, eventually falling back exhausted, sitting there and frankly weeping, great racking sobs.

They calmed in time – there was little light now at the top opening, none at the bottom – and once again, but with dread-filled and reasonable purpose, he began his shouting. Yet the sound of his utmost efforts was now a coarse whisper, no more; and even when he heard Joseph and Maggie walking along at no great distance, laughing and talking – 'give over, now, do' – he could make nothing better than a high thin pipe and a faint battering on the spongy wood.

'What was that?' asked Joseph.

'It was only an old cat, or an owl. Come on.'

'It might have been Simon, playing a game.'

'Ballocks. Come on, if you want it. I can't be home late again: we'll go to the barn.' Their voices died away. Simon tried two more strangled, almost silent cries and gave up.

The anguish of bitterly disappointed hope and underlying terror slowly gave way to a torpid misery; he was cold, too, and soaking wet.

There was one more revival, one more fit of wild-beast leaping at the wall, and then of heart-broken tears, and then a deeply unhappy resignation, huddled for warmth in the least wretched corner.

Overhead it was full night now, stars in the darkest blue. And presently an edge of moon. There was some very small comfort in the moon, though the rising southwester bellowing through the trees added still more to the pervading threat. Yet, as he looked, the piece of moon was shut out – broad shoulders in the open crown of the tree, and Joseph's anxious voice: 'Simon? Simon?'

'Oh, Joe . . .' said Simon in a recognizable gasp.

'Reach me up an arm, will you, old fellow?'

Children's Stories

44

Skogula – the Sperm Whale

———— ⬤⬤⬤ ————

In the warm seas where squids, octopi, and the like flourish and grow fat, a large school of sperm whales were feeding. Deep down near the sea-bed Skogula, a young bull whale, was pursuing a squid, which, having exhausted all its sepia, was now shooting backwards by means of its long arms, which it used like oars. The whale caught it, and rising to the surface he swallowed it with every sign of enjoyment. He dived again, and swimming along just a few fathoms above the bottom, he looked out for food, but as he was swimming along rather a cold current he could not find any. So after a while he changed his course and swam towards a rocky place where the sea-bed sloped suddenly upwards. Locating an octopus he made for it. His quarry, however, saw him and ejected a black cloud, disappearing into the ripped-up side of a sunken ocean-going tramp lying on the sea-bed under many fathoms of water. The decks harboured hundreds of crabs and shellfish which had come for the dead bodies of the crew years before, and because of the great quantities of crabs, the octopi lived both in and around the ship in great numbers.

As the whale passed a few feet above the deck, looking for the octopus, the skeleton of a man lashed to the wheel shifted in the current, and the skull rolled down the sloping deck, dislodging some crabs who lived inside. As the crabs came out the whale saw the whip-like tentacle of the octopus shoot out after them from the broken window of the charthouse.

The whale swam down and seized the tentacle, hoping to drag the octopus out by it, but the arm snapped off short, so he rose to the surface and spouted several times. He could see the rest of the school of whales lying awash a short distance away.

Just then his mother rose near him, finishing a squid. She was one of the seven wives of the leader of the school. Her husband was a great bull in his prime, fully sixty feet long, who ruled the school with a rod of iron, or rather with his ten-foot ivory-clad under-jaw, with which he had fought his way to the head of the school (in his youth) and had held that position ever since.

Like the other whales, Skogula's mother was looking rather anxious, and he wondered why, for he did not know, as the others did, that his father had decided that the school should migrate farther south.

Skogula's mother was particularly worried, for she knew that he would have to swim with the school for long distances and the pace set by his father, as there were no young calves in the school at the time, would be quite fast. She did not know whether Skogula would be able to stand it.

But he continued ignorant until the next morning, when his father swam right round the school, then he sounded and coming up again at a great pace, he leapt clear of the water and, with a great splash, took up his place at the head of the school and started off southwards.

For a long time they swam steadily, rising to spout every few minutes, until the leader heard, very far off the cry: 'There she blows!' He could not see the ship, being unable to see far in air, but he knew the cry, having been harpooned once. He was very much alarmed, as Skogula could see, and began to take in vast quantities of air, spouting noisily.

The whaler was lowering boats; Skogula could just hear the sound of men rowing them, and a moment later his father dived, showing his great tail for a second before he disappeared; the rest of the school followed him and they all sank to a great depth.

After some time had passed, Skogula felt in need of air, and wondered when his father would go up to the surface. But the leader did not rise, so Skogula left the school, meaning to catch them up later, and rose to the surface.

He emerged near one of the boats, and spouted at once. He did not see the boat as it was behind him. As he was spouting the mate in charge of the boat edged it close enough, and the harpooner seized his first harpoon and stood up in the bows. He was poised for the cast when a clumsy hand at tub oar fouled the whale rope. This spoilt the harpooner's cast, and his iron, which lodged just above Skogula's left fin, had no force in it. Then the whale dived.

The harpooner darted an angry glance at the clumsy hand, and seized the second harpoon, which was lashed to the first by only a short length of rope; he threw it overboard, as the whale was already under the surface.

The second harpoon, however, went skimming along over the water, following Skogula's blind rush, and it foul-hooked a second boat, engaging firmly in its side. The boat swung round, but the barb held fast, so that the first harpoon tore out of Skogula's side.

Meanwhile the school had risen some distance away, and Skogula, when he had calmed down a little, went towards them and found that he had not been missed by the others. Meanwhile the boats were returning to the ship, as a dense fog had risen.

But from that day on, Skogula never trusted boats again. The school only rested for a few hours before the leader ploughed on again, and by nightfall they were a great way from the old feeding grounds. For a long time the whales continued in this way, sometimes passing ships from which their leader always hurried them away at a great pace, and they were never attacked. In time Skogula lost a lot of his extra fat, and drew on his blubber reserves.

At last, after a longer swim than usual, the leader stopped, for Skogula's father knew this place very well, having led the school there more times than he could count, for he had been born there.

Skogula lay awash for some time before he began to look around, as he was very tired. Then he raised himself a little higher out of the water so that he could see that he was in a sort of deep lagoon which was bounded on his left by a crescent of tiny islands. These extended in a serrated half moon to meet another crescent formed of white rock, stretching from a slightly larger island which had a little vegetation.

The islands were too small to support any men or animals other than a few seals, sea-elephants, manatees, and dugongs, who lived on the fish which abounded there.

But birds lived there in thousands; on the main island legions of penguins waddled about, and myriads of gulls dwelt on the smaller rocky islands.

Besides the gulls, there were also frigate birds, boobies, solans, albatrosses, swallow terns, albacores, and many others, including one old fishing eagle, blown there from the north in a great wind.

Skogula found that there was excellent food to be had in the lagoon, where the squids grew to a much larger size than those which he had found in the old feeding ground.

But he was disappointed to find that the octopi were no better than those which he had eaten before, though he was glad to find that there were more of them.

A long time passed while the school lived in the lagoon, feeding well and growing fat and contented.

Skogula was dozing at the surface, digesting an unusually large dinner of squids, one day, when a small school of sperm whales approached the lagoon. They were led by a remarkably large young bull, who made for the main entrance of the lagoon.

Skogula's father saw him and swam out to meet him, circling round in a large sweep; these tactics puzzled the newcomer, who soon laid himself open to a side attack. As he did not turn quickly enough, the older bull charged at once, tearing a piece of blubber from the other's side.

Then Skogula's father dived and attacked the newcomer from the other side. Soon the water around the younger bull grew pink, and sharks approached from all sides. After a little time, however, the newcomer managed to get face to face with his antagonist, and in a moment their great jaws were interlocked. After a while they broke away, and the newcomer managed to get a hold on his enemy's left fin, crushing and crippling it.

Skogula's father creamed the water all round with the lashing of his tail, and then he charged forward again, and the fight continued furiously. After a lot of ineffectual butting, the whales got their jaws interlocked again, and they raged up and down until they passed beyond Skogula's sight; but he could trace their path by the movements of the dense cloud of hoarsely screaming gulls, who followed them, but soon he lost sight of even the gulls, though he could hear the whales beating the water into foam a great way off.

Some time later the younger bull returned alone to the lagoon, though he was badly wounded in a score of places. Skogula never saw his father again. He might have been killed, but that was not likely. He had probably been badly beaten and, if so, he would go away from the school for ever up to the northern seas.

Of course, the victorious survivor took over the command of both schools, which soon merged into one large one, and under his leadership they followed just where his fancy prompted him.

The whales had gone great distances before under their old leader, but now they went even farther afield, never resting in the same place for more than a week. Skogula had fed in the Indian Ocean in one month and off Zanzibar in the next.

But before a great time had passed, Skogula began to notice that the new leader was not nearly so pleasant as his father had been; he was bad tempered and loved to bully the younger whales, who all came to avoid him as much as they could.

Once, as Skogula was pursuing an octopus near St. Helena, the leader snapped it up in front of his nose. This was an insult, but Skogula thought that it would be unwise to attack the aggressor, as he would not have a chance and would only be hurt and driven from the school, so he turned aside to look for another meal.

This occurred again on the next day and the next, until at last Skogula grew quite used to it. A long time passed, during which time the whales had gone a great distance. But as they did not travel in any kind of formation as they did under Skogula's father, some of the smaller cows and calves were eaten by sharks.

Two of the larger bulls who had swum far from the rest were

also attacked by giant swordfish, and one was killed. Skogula was once attacked by three of them when he was feeding. They attacked from below, trying to thrust their swords into his soft underparts, and he was forced to leap clear of the water to avoid them.

As he came down, he lashed out furiously, and by a lucky stroke managed to hit one of them on the side of the head with his tail, killing it at once.

Meanwhile the other two were attacking him from the front. One charged at his head, and the other attacked him from the side; the first merely bounced off, but the other buried his sword just above his right fin, and Skogula spouted dark red blood. His temper was now fully aroused, and for the first time, using his full strength, he lashed with his tail hard enough to blind his enemies, and then turning, he bit one right through the middle of the body and the sharks who were waiting all around tore the wounded swordfish into fragments. The survivor was now joined by another swordfish, and they harassed Skogula from behind, but the whale whipped round with astonishing agility. He snapped furiously at them, but missed, and was forced to leap into the air again, for they had got underneath him. On coming down, he dived deep with the fish in full pursuit.

Skogula had taken in enough air to stay down for a long time, so he went very deep, and at last the swordfish gave it up. Skogula was badly hurt, and as he swam back to the school he felt at least three places in his tail where the swords had gone right through. It took him a long time to recover, but when he did, he knew as much about fighting swordfish as any whale, for he had thought out, in a dim way, defensive tactics for the future.

He was able to put the plans into execution before long, as he was attacked by five very large swordfish when some distance south of the Cape. He took his opponents quite by surprise, killed two, and chased the others for a long way.

After his victory over the swordfish Skogula began to realize his strength, and he started to look rather strangely at his leader when that whale took away his food; and his thoughts turned towards the possibilities of challenging the tyrant, defeating him, and taking command over the school. In his imagination he saw himself the leader of the largest school in the sea, holding undisputed sway over all their doings.

At length the whales began to move eastwards until, after many months, they were lying some distance off the coast of Brazil. On the way they had lost three big bulls and one cow, all four taken by whalers.

By this time Skogula had reached the length of fifty-nine feet, and was still growing, and the leader had long ceased to take away his food.

After a few days the school began to go northward, and soon they encountered a current of water that was nearly fresh; it came from the Amazon, and the whales found it very difficult to swim in.

Skogula thought he must be ill as he lurched and rolled, almost losing control in the unsupporting water. This was not at all to the liking of the leader, who soon turned south again.

During the last few months, Skogula had become increasingly friendly with an attractive young cow called Miska. He had seen her first when looking for cuttlefish, and had felt attracted to her from the first, and she liked him quite well.

When the sea was all phosphorescent, as it often was, they used to chase each other, lobtailing and leaping out of the water as all the whales used to do in pairs, but only at night when the water splashed up like liquid fire.

But as the school was nearing Cape Horn the leader began to take such notice of Miska that Skogula began to feel quite uneasy.

By the time the whales had reached a good feeding-place off the Falkland Islands, all the rest of the school knew that Miska was wavering between Skogula and the leader.

As Skogula did not know half the tricks which whales use when they fight together, he felt a little apprehensive; he also knew that if he put the fight off too long, Miska would get tired of waiting and go over to his rival. So on the next day, when all the whales were at the surface, Skogula summoned up all his courage, and swam across the water to his enemy.

Miska watched him with an anxious yet pleased expression, for she was very gratified at the idea that all the fuss was over her.

Skogula, on nearing the leader, felt fearful, but he put on speed and butted the other in the side. His adversary had been expecting this, and quickly wheeled round to meet Skogula. The other whales retired to a short distance. As the leader came shooting towards him Skogula felt paralysed for a moment, but in an instant he launched out ploughing up big waves on each side as he surged through the water. The whales met with a dull thud, and Skogula saw his enemy half roll over. This was only a trick, but he rushed in to be met by a gleaming row of teeth, which instantly closed on his flanks just below his side fin. Frantic with the pain Skogula tore himself away, and then charged in again snapping furiously.

The whales were enveloped in a flurry of white foam as they raged to and fro, beating up the water with their tails.

The great waves that they made reached an object which was lightly wedged between two rocks. This object floated when a big wave lifted it lightly off the rocks, and it bobbed up and down in the sea.

The fighting whales could hardly be seen for the splashing, but things were not going very well with Skogula, for the blubber was torn from the sides of his head in great strips and he had lost quite a lot of blood. The other had got some nasty furrows down the sides of his head; he was not having things all his own way.

But Skogula was beginning to tire, and it was all he could do to keep face to face with his enemy. The round object was getting nearer and nearer to the whales. Skogula began to attack furiously, for he felt his strength was giving out.

He scored a great slash down his opponent's side, ploughing up the blubber. A moment later they had their jaws interlocked and they tore the water into a thin spume in their fury.

Skogula was half over in the water as his opponent pushed him backwards, when he felt an awful pain and a sharp crack as two of his big teeth gave way and tore out. Suddenly the other broke away and backed for a fresh charge, and though he had suffered rather badly, losing three teeth, he was still much fresher than Skogula.

As the other broke away Skogula had received a terrible wrench which had dislocated his jaw; he snapped feebly and it hurt. The other bull charged, but was met firmly and retreated again. Skogula knew that he could not go on butting to keep the other off, and sooner or later he would have to give way.

His adversary was lobtailing, bringing his great tail down on the water with a sound like that of a gun. Skogula eyed him apprehensively for a moment, when he caught sight of the object which had floated quite near. But he had no time for watching it, for the other was charging with his under-jaw snapping up and down.

The swirl which he made, reaching the ball, brought it right across his path, and the attacking whale bit at it in his anger.

Instantly a great wall of green water shot up with a sky-splitting explosion, and Skogula was rolled over and over by the terrific force of it and felt his jaw slip back into position. A moment later a shower of blood-stained water and blubber and bones rained down from the sky – all that was left of Skogula's enemy – the sixty-four foot sperm whale, after the contact mine had done its work.

45

A Peregrine Falcon

―――❦❦❦―――

A female peregrine falcon surveyed with justifiable pride the two eggs she had just laid. They were a dull reddish brown with beautiful mottling, and as they lay in the untidy, scrappy eyrie they looked very pleasing.

The falcon eyed them approvingly, and then sat down on them and fluffed out her feathers to keep them warm. Her mate the tiercel returned to the nest in the evening; he brought no food as he had not expected the eggs. Having scolded and flapped about a little, the mother gave the eggs into the charge of her husband, and sailed off in search of supper.

She flew out over the Newhaven marshes and saw a heron flapping slowly home; she dropped out of the sky on to the startled bird, who gave a squawk of dismay and sank to the ground.

The peregrine observed the sharp, upturned beak of the heron, and soared up again. She was too hungry to wait and battle, so she mounted higher in wide circles until the marshes appeared as a flat mud-patch below her, and the downs which surrounded them like green hillocks stretching away to the sea in the south and the weald in the north.

On the banks of the Ouse, which meandered through the marshes, her wonderful eyes detected a movement. Folding her wings she dropped like a stone until she was near enough to see a water-rat, who, unaware of his fate, was eating a small beetle.

A shadow glided over him, and he looked up in alarm, but too late, for in a split second he was rushing up into the air in the powerful claws of the bird.

A speck hung high in the air above her claimed the peregrine's attention; she glanced at it with a swift, sideways motion of her head, and recognized another peregrine, a stranger who lived near Pevensey. Higher still than this bird, far out of human sight, soared the stranger's mate.

They both saw her and slanted down out of the sky in huge circles as they manoeuvred for position in the fading light. The first peregrine was anxious, and increased her great speed, flying homewards towards the Newhaven cliffs where her eyrie and eggs were guarded by her mate. Suddenly the Pevensey tiercel stooped, dashing downwards with the rushing sound of a rocket.

She rolled sideways as he approached her, and down he went, spinning a good thousand feet before he could check.

The Newhaven bird had scarcely recovered her balance when the tiercel's mate attacked her from the side, striking heavily above the right wing. A cloud of feathers were scattered, but the falcon's terrible claws failed to grip, and she broke away, wheeling high for another attack.

The Newhaven falcon saw the tiercel coming up again, and with a harsh scream she dropped the water-rat, and circled rapidly higher, receiving the female's second attack with a quick double roll which confused her enemy for the moment, and it gave the harassed bird time to mount higher.

As the other peregrines sheered off, the tiercel dropped down after the water-rat, which he secured before it reached the ground. His mate flew off towards Pevensey, while he circled to gain height. The Newhaven bird did not want to lose the water-rat, and bore down on the tiercel, who fled away towards his mate. They both flew away towards Pevensey, the female circling and covering her mate's retreat.

The Newhaven falcon was feeling too hungry and tired to chase them, so she flew high over the downs to find a rabbit.

She had no luck with the rabbits, however, as they had become extremely wary through years of attacks from owls, peregrines, kestrels, and sparrow-hawks, who were all very fond of rabbit meat.

Sailing over Caburn the peregrine became aware of a pigeon about a quarter of a mile away flying rapidly towards London.

Her hopes rose, and mounting rapidly to a great altitude she exerted every effort, and gradually overtook the pigeon.

The pigeon flew quickly, cleaving the air with the inherent swiftness of generations of pigeons, but the falcon flew quicker, and stooped on the pigeon with enormous speed, coming down squarely on its shoulders, driving her great claws into the soft body.

On returning to the eyrie, the falcon found her mate still on the eggs; she shuffled him off (he was a good three inches shorter) and inspected her eggs closely: they were all right, and she settled down on them for the night. On the next day the tiercel flew from the eyrie early in the morning and returned about noon with a small rabbit, which he gave to his wife. He brought in more food during the day. About four o'clock the tiercel relieved his mate at the eggs; and she stretched her cramped wings, flapping and screaming at the edge of the eyrie.

Far below her on the beach, a man heard her, and looking up he saw the ledge on which the eyrie was built. Having preened herself in the sun the falcon glided off the ledge and flew away to the marshes.

The plovers all fled before she came near, for they had become cautious from long experience.

She flew low over the long grass, and started a jacksnipe, which shot away, corkscrewing and turning in its own inimitable manner. The falcon caught the snipe when it tried to double, and ate it on the ground.

She flew back slowly towards the eyrie. When she came near enough she heard the tiercel shrieking and calling harshly.

Hastening her pace the peregrine approached the nest from the sea. She saw a man taking her eggs.

He was an oölogist, a great enemy of birds, who had seen her stretching her wings earlier in the day.

He had lowered himself over the cliff from a rope tied to a tree, and had fastened a safety line round his waist.

The tiercel had not been able to save the eggs, which the collector had just put for safety in his mouth. The mother falcon stooped at the man's head with great force, knocking his thick cloth cap off, and wheeling again for another attack.

The man turned pale, he had not thought it serious enough a matter to hire a helper, and he was alone. The tiercel flapped furiously about his head, and the oölogist was too busy keeping the terrible talons from his eyes to climb to safety.

The tiercel drew off for a moment, and the oölogist quickly replaced one egg, thinking to distract the parent's attention, and he started climbing.

He had not hauled himself a dozen feet, however, before the mother, who had mounted to a great height, stooped. The man's hands were holding on to the rope, so she caught him full in the face.

With a shriek he lost his hold and fell, the thin safety rope snapped, and he fell to the rocks below.

The out-going tide washed him out to sea.

46

Wang Kahn of the Elephants

———❧———

Wang Kahn was chief of all the elephants who were piling teak for the Amalgamated Teak Company. He was a mighty bull in the prime of his life, and he was extraordinarily skilful with the great teak logs that came floating down the river from the forests on their way to the coast and the Company's headquarters.

His mahout, Moti Lal, was the grandson of Wang Kahn's first mahout, and the son of his second. For three generations Moti Lal's family had ridden Wang Kahn, and the great elephant loved his mahout and Little Moti, the mahout's only son; and as they both loved Wang Kahn they were all three very happy.

He was standing in the shade of a tree, with Little Moti between his ponderous feet.

'Lift me up, fat pig,' said the child, and in a moment he was on the elephant's broad back, where he was as much at home as on the ground. Presently Moti Lal came out from his hut, carrying a pot of arrack, a very powerful spirit brewed from rice; Wang Kahn loved arrack, and he came from under the tree with his trunk outstretched.

'Descend, O worthless child, and go and see that no one steals the melons,' cried Moti Lal, giving the elephant the arrack.

Coming down by way of the tail, Little Moti went to guard the ripening melons, and his father mounted the elephant.

He was one of the very few mahouts who never used the

ankus, or iron elephant goad, but guided Wang Kahn by speaking to him or by tapping the sides of his head with his feet.

Wang Kahn was very wise, perhaps he was the most wise of all the elephants; at any rate Moti Lal thought so when he saw how he responded to the slightest word or touch.

They went down to the river where the other mahouts had assembled the remaining nine elephants. Moti Lal noticed that the great teak logs were coming down the river in greater numbers than usual, and he shouted across to another mahout, 'Are they sending down an extra consignment?'

'No,' replied the other, 'there was a block up by the Tulwar station, and this is the result.'

Just then a party of men arrived with a fresh load of logs to be floated down to the company's headquarters some 200 miles down the river.

The white superintendent, who rejoiced in the name Smith, rode up on his elephant and gave orders to concentrate on getting the fresh teak into the water.

'But, tuan,' said an aged mahout, 'there will be a jam.'

'Don't answer me, man,' cried Smith, who was young, and raw, and considered himself above taking advice from a native.

Until noon they worked on the new logs, huge thick trunks twenty feet long, which the elephants handled with a remarkable skill, as they had a perfect sense of balance.

When they knocked off for the siesta (no work was done in the great heat of the noon-day sun) and returned to the elephant lines, the logs were going downstream in perfect order, though rather tightly packed.

When the heat of the day had passed, the elephants were taken into the forest for clearing and hauling new timber down to the river. The elephants all loathed clearing, because they had to grub up roots with their tusks, and scuffle about in harness, dragging great tree-trunks and things.

Moti Lal did not like his son to come down to the river, but he always let him come into the forest on Wang Kahn's back.

They were rooting up a tree stump in a dusty clearing when the alarm siren, the signal of a jam in the river, shrieked from the river bank. Before any order was given Wang Kahn had put Moti Lal on his back and set off for the river.

They found an extraordinary turmoil in the river; on a rock which stood just clear of the water about a quarter of the way across the river there was wedged a great log, and behind it there stretched a mass of logs all heaving and swaying with the force of the stream.

The whole river, from bank to bank, was covered by a wedge-shaped jam, all dependent on the one great log which lay across the stream against the rock; more logs were being brought down every minute, and if the jam were not released very quickly the logs would form themselves into a dam, and flood all the low-lying country round the river for miles.

The river piled up more and more logs behind the block, and Smith strode up and down the bank, very scared, and bawling for Wang Kahn. At last the elephant arrived, and Smith ordered Moti Lal to make him move the big log which was at the apex of the triangular wedge. Slowly the elephant waded in, he had seen at a glance that the thing to do was to give the log a sharp tug to set it afloat again, and then rush back again to the bank before all the timber came rushing down with the terrific force of the pent-up river behind it.

Guiding him carefully through the water, Moti Lal brought Wang Kahn to the log, and they were just about to pull, when Little Moti, who had been forgotten in the turmoil, fell into the river.

The boy could not swim very well, and no one could possibly swim in the welter of rushing logs if once Wang Kahn released them. His father plunged in after Little Moti, shouting to Wang Kahn, 'Hold the logs, *hathi-raj*.' The elephant had heard and understood. Moti Lal had not seen that the great trunk which held the wedge had slipped a little, and was almost free of the rock.

The elephant had felt the log slip a little, and he knew that there was a danger of the whole jam giving way before Moti Lal could reach the bank. He felt the weight increasing enormously as more logs were piled on the back of the wedge, and he knew that if he wanted to reach the bank alive he would have to go at once, and quickly at that.

Little Moti was struggling and frightened, but his father had got hold of him, and they were slowly nearing the bank.

From the corner of his eye Wang Kahn could see this, and he set his mighty shoulder at the base of the log and pushed with all his great strength. It did not give an inch; things were worse than they had appeared, and the elephant could not hold the mass back for more than a few minutes at the most.

The swimmers had passed out of his sight now, and his only anxiety was that they should be able to gain the bank before he had to let go.

He straddled a little wider, and strove fiercely against the shifting logs whose weight was slowly pushing him back; grunting and exhausted, he made a great effort, and gained an inch. Just then Moti Lal crawled out on to the wet mud of the river bank, and shouted to Wang Kahn, who heard, and trumpeted as he went down in the maelstrom of crashing logs.

His body was washed ashore next day, far down the river, almost unrecognizable.

47

The White Cobra

A pipal-tree grew in the open space about which the houses of the village of Kurasai were built. It was in the hollow roots of this tree that a cobra had his dwelling.

Every evening, when the people of the village assembled in the open space to talk, the elders set a dish of warm milk at the roots of the tree for the cobra to drink.

In many of the villages of the Punjab there are such cobras, but this one was peculiar in that it was white, with curious markings. It had first been seen on the eve of the feast of Krishna, so it was called Vakrishna, and it was looked upon as a possible incarnation of the god.

The inhabitants of Kurasai were Hindus, but they were tolerant people, and therefore they welcomed a Mohammedan snake-charmer, who turned up one evening, and said that he had come from Peshawar on a journey south. The fact was that Hussein – for such was his name – had heard of the white cobra, whose fame had spread, when he was performing with his snakes at a feast given by a petty rajah some forty miles south in Fakirpur, and, on hearing of it, had instantly desired it.

On the same evening that he arrived he came to give an account of himself to the headman in the open space, which was also the court of justice for that village.

Slowly he led the conversation round to cobras, of which, he said, he was inordinately fond. Now it happened that at this time the headman's youngest son came with the warm milk for

Vakrishna, but the snake would not come out on account of the stranger.

The headman was chary of speech concerning the white cobra, towards which he bore himself reverently, being a Hindu, so Hussein did not press the matter, but announced that he would be staying for a few days to rest for his journey.

The headman would only say that the cobra had brought the village good luck for some years, and the village priest bore him out in this, pointing out that the crops in Kurasai were better than those of any village for miles around. 'Not that we are at all wealthy,' he said hastily, as he saw Hussein listening attentively, 'but we manage with economies.' Then he turned the talk to more general matters, and the priest, eager to show the villagers the depth of his learning, questioned Hussein on certain points of the faith of Islam.

It transpired that Hussein was a Sufi – a freethinker, as opposed to the orthodox Shiahs. This at once raised him in the estimation of the villagers, whose neighbours towards the north were strict Shiahs, and great cattle thieves.

On the next day Hussein did not speak of snakes at all, but discussed the Government; he agreed with the headman in condemning it, and so, by the next day, he felt sufficiently confident to speak freely about the white cobra.

He learnt that it was at least a hundred feet long, and that it spoke with the voice of trumpeting elephants; but it was plain that the simple villagers wished to impress him, so he was suitably impressed. At fifty miles he had heard of Vakrishna as a great snake which was longer than five large pythons, and as impalpable as the mist; by twenty-five miles the cobra had shrunk to a snake as long as three pythons, which habitually ate tigers; and at ten miles it was only a great snake which could kill an elephant. Yet all these reports contained the same assertion that the cobra was white, so Hussein bided his time.

That evening, when the warm milk had been set down in front of the little hole from which the snake used to come Hussein offered to give a free performance with his snakes.

He set down the basket with the snakes in it and squatted before it; the villagers sat round in a ring.

The Mohammedan blew a thin, squeaky tune on a kind of globular flute, and presently the lid of the basket began to rise. It fell off sideways, and a cobra's head appeared in the opening. The tune grew faster, and the snake shot up a foot or so, swaying in time with the tune.

Soon two other snakes appeared, and they crept out of the basket on to the ground. The crowd was quite silent, and the only sound that was to be heard was the shrill piping of the snake-charmer.

The three cobras shuffled vaguely, half coiled, with their heads about a foot from the ground.

Suddenly the tune changed, and the snakes began to dance. They traced strange patterns on the dust, weaving their heads to and fro, moving incessantly.

Hussein heard the faint hiss that he had been expecting, and turning ever so slightly he saw half the length of Vakrishna pro-truding from the roots of the pipal-tree.

The hood on the cobra's neck was half open, and its curious markings showed distinctly on the strangely white skin. Hussein caught his breath, for he saw at once that it was the real thing, that great rarity, a truly white cobra.

Slowly he let the music die down; he had seen all that he wished.

As the music became fainter and more slow the snakes danced less swiftly, and at length they sank to the ground. Quickly Hussein picked them up by the neck and thrust them back into the basket.

All that night the snake-charmer lay awake, thinking of the white cobra. He knew that if he took it away he would not get twenty miles, for there was no railway, and the hue and cry which the villagers would certainly raise would catch him before he could dispose of his treasure. By daybreak, however, he had thought out a scheme. He had noticed that they were repainting the dak-bungalow with white paint. At noon he went there and took a little pannikin full of the white paint, and during the siesta, when everyone else was asleep, he took one of his own snakes and painted it white.

It was very difficult to keep the snake still, but Hussein was safe enough, as the cobra's fangs had been drawn long ago. At last the snake was fairly white all over, and nearly dry, but it was in a furious temper, and although Hussein had drugged it before starting, he was hard put to it to control it by the time that he came to try to paint Vakrishna's markings on it.

At length the task was completed, however, and the finished product might easily have been taken for Vakrishna in the dusk. In the night when the rest of the village was asleep, the snake-charmer crept to the pipal-tree, and squatting by the hole he played certain tunes on his pipe very softly. It was a long time before the snake took any notice, but by the time the moon had risen, Hussein heard the dry rustling sound that a snake makes when it moves, and he saw the cobra's eyes gleaming in the entrance to the hole. In the moonlight the white snake was almost invisible, but Hussein could see its shadow quite clearly.

Very slowly Vakrishna slid out into the open.

From beneath his loose cloak Hussein took the body of a young rat; he laid it on the ground and shuffled backwards into the deep purple shadow of the pipal-tree.

The cobra's head glided towards the rat, and then, with an incredibly swift movement, Vakrishna snapped it up and swallowed it. Hussein could see all this by the light of the full moon, he could even see the rat going down the snake's body, and he went back to bed well satisfied.

In the rat's body the snake-charmer had put a certain drug, because he could not handle the cobra while it was conscious, as its fangs had not been drawn, and it did not know him.

By the next day the painted snake became more furious than ever, as the paint made it extremely uncomfortable.

Hussein knew that the drug would act at about noon, so he made his plans for departure, telling the headman that he would be continuing his journey in the afternoon, when the heat of the sun had died down. So far his plan had worked perfectly, and the only thing that worried Hussein was the behaviour of the painted snake, which was ominously calm.

When the great heat of the noonday sun had driven all the villagers to shelter, the snake-charmer went to Vakrishna's tree with a hooked stick. Quickly he drew the limp, unconscious snake out, and put it into a sack, from which he took the substitute, and put its nose to the hole in the tree.

The painted snake seemed disinclined to go in, so Hussein trod on its tail; it disappeared into the pipal-tree.

Hussein strolled back to his room by a devious way. No one had seen him. He gloated for a while over the white cobra, and then put it into a special basket by itself.

He packed up his belongings and set out, passing by the pipal-tree, where he could see the painted snake's head at the entrance to the hole. He tapped it on the nose, and it shot back into the hollow roots.

He had gone some ten miles by nightfall, and he slept in a village with one arm round Vakrishna's basket.

Towards morning he was awakened by the headman of Kurasai, who was bawling in his ear and beating him with a stick.

They all set on him, and dragging him into the road they beat him until he was unconscious. They also broke his baskets, releasing his trained snakes, and they took away Vakrishna.

The priest, apparently more compassionate than the rest, stayed to revive him, and when he came to his senses, Hussein asked him how they had found out.

'A little before sundown,' said the Brahmin, 'when all the village was assembled, your snake came out, and before our eyes he cast his skin, and I, picking it up in its entirety, clearly perceived the fraud, as the paint flaked off.' And with this the compassionate man beat Hussein more grievously than the others, leaving him for dead.

48

Shark No. 206

———⌘———

Number 206 was a tiger-shark, a long, lean man-eater, the terror of pearl-fishers and coral-divers. When he was very young he had been taken out of the sea in a net by a scientist in the Ichthiological Observatory, and a ring with the inscription T.S. 206 on one side and the observatory's address on the other had been fastened in his gills and he had been entered in the books as shark No. 206.

Since then, however, he had had time to grow into the huge fish that was known as the Devil by the native pearl-divers of the Island of Waitoa in the South Seas.

The lagoon in which the pearl oysters bred was not very well protected by its storm-battered coral reef, and at high tide the sharks could come in with the rollers as they went over the half-submerged reef. The ground sharks and the bottle-nosed sharks could easily be frightened by splashing, or at the worst they could generally be kept off with a long knife, or if that failed they did not usually kill their victim, but only took an arm or a leg. But neither splashing nor a knife could deter a tiger-shark, nor would one ever be contented with an arm and give the wretched man a chance of life; they would take the whole man, leaving only scarlet water behind.

No. 206 was particularly dreaded by the pearl-divers; he would not stop for anything, and always got his man.

He would rise up from the oyster-beds like the shadow of death, and if once he reached his victim the man was dead.

He did not stay in the lagoon of Waitoa, however, as there were many other sharks, and the divers were very cautious.

One day, when a whaler called at Waitoa, 206 followed it as it left, and fed on the scraps which were thrown overboard.

The twenty-foot man-eater was not proud, and he would eat bad salt pork or potato peelings with the humblest dog-fish; he would often eat the humble dog-fish too.

No. 206 was always hungry; he would eat anything, including tin cans; given time he could digest them, and even thrive on them. The only time that his immense appetite was quite sated was when the whaler, which was in luck, caught three great sperm whales. They were towed along by the ship, and 206, in company with a host of other sharks, fed long and full, and the two little pilot fish which guided him to his prey became fat and slow.

The whaler, however, sailed south until she came to the icy Antarctic seas where the great whales bred, and thither the tiger-shark could not follow her, as he was used to the tropical seas in which he had been hatched.

He left the whaler when another ship crossed her path and followed the new ship, which was a slow, grain-carrying four-masted sailing ship, schooner rigged. She was from Sweden, and her name was the *Björn Anderssen*.

The tiger-shark followed her for many days until it happened that a Friday fell on the thirteenth of the month.

Now as Friday the thirteenth was notoriously a bitterly unlucky day, the wooden-legged sea-cook on board the *Björn* had felt justified in fortifying himself with rum, and he left his galley to go forward to the fo'c'sle, where one of the hands was known to possess a bottle.

Hardly had he left his galley when the *Björn* ran her head into a comber and shipped a green sea; the waist-high wall of water swept the cook overboard.

The watchful pilot fish darted ahead of the shark. Following his two brightly-coloured guides, 206 came upon the unfortunate sea-cook struggling in the water.

The triangular black dorsal fin cut the surface, travelling

incredibly fast towards the doomed man; five yards off the fin disappeared, and the shark's white belly flashed in the sun as he turned over to engulf the man.

The cook had seen his death coming for him in the shape of a great fish, and he had fainted before it reached him, so he did not feel the fierce teeth as they sheered through flesh and bone like butter.

It was all over before a boat could be launched, and all that was left to tell of the unfortunate sea-cook was a rapidly dissolving red stain in the sea.

The cook's wooden leg troubled the tiger-shark for some time, but he soon forgot it.

The next day the sailors took a great barbed hook and bent it to a thin steel cable, and fastening a lump of salt pork to it they threw it overboard.

No. 206 was the only large shark following the *Björn* so they felt fairly sure of hooking the right fish.

The sight of 206 – and, for that matter, of any shark – was not at all good, unlike his nose, which was marvellously keen, and so he always let himself be guided by his pilot fish, who lived with him, sheltering behind his gills in times of trouble.

They had keen sight, and the shark could easily follow their brightly-coloured bodies, although he guided himself towards his prey to a considerable extent by his sharp sense of smell.

When the salt pork was dropped overboard the pilot fish darted forward, leading 206 to the sinking meat.

The sailors could plainly see the pork in the calm, clear water. All at once the tiger-shark glided out from beneath the keel and took the meat. The sailors all pulled on the cable together in order to strike the hook well into the shark's mouth. It lodged firmly between two of his many rows of teeth.

As soon as 206 felt the hook he dived, but the seamen had the cable wound round a winch, and that checked the cable, pulling the shark up short.

No. 206 tugged for some time before he understood that he was held by the cable. Meanwhile the sailors were winding in the line on the winch. For a few moments the shark let himself be dragged upwards, and then the sense of danger penetrated into his bewildered brain.

Instantly he set his great weight against the upward motion, but still the men gained, drawing the cable in foot by foot, rewinding it on the winch.

No. 206 felt frightened for the first time in his life, and he lashed the water desperately, pulling against the hook. He did not gain, but he stopped the winding of the cable. He could not keep up the tension, however, and slowly the rewinding recommenced.

The bo'sun went below for an axe with which to cut the shark's spine when they had it on deck.

Fighting every inch, the tiger-shark was slowly nearing the surface when he realized that if he did not get off the hook quickly, he would never get off it at all.

The pilot fish were circling distractedly, but they were quite useless now.

Suddenly 206 gave way and shot up to the surface, flying clear of the water in a prodigious leap. He came down with his full weight on the taut cable.

The great jerk unseated the winch, which tore free from the deck and flew over the side, carrying with it three of the men who were holding the cable.

Instantly the bo'sun, who had an axe in his hand, ran to the nearest boat and cut the ropes holding it to the davits.

He and the first mate jumped down into it and reached the men before 206 had finished wondering how he had got free, for the hook was still in his mouth.

The iron winch, sinking rapidly, gave a hard downward pull on the hook, which tore free, taking some teeth with it.

It took the shark some time to realize that he was free of the hook, but when it got through to his confused brain he went back to his old place under the keel of the ship, where his pilot fish rejoined him.

Strangely enough he did not associate the ship with danger, but only salt pork, which he decided never to touch again.

The sailors, when they saw that the shark still followed the ship, took a stouter cable and hook.

The master, however, insisted that the capstan should be used, for although he fully agreed that the cook should be revenged, he hardly liked to account for the loss of another winch to the owners.

On the next day they dropped the pork overboard as before, and the whole crew from the captain down watched it as it sank. No. 206 came from under the keel, but he would not touch the meat.

Even when it was thrown over with the offal from the galley he picked it out and would not touch it. For three days the sailors tried to make him bite, but without success.

He had got it firmly fixed in his head that salt pork was not good for him.

Then one of the ship's three cats died, and the captain had the idea of changing the bait. Accordingly the cat's body was thrown overboard one clear morning.

No. 206 came from beneath the keel and snapped it up without the least suspicion. Instantly the hook struck hard, and the shark knew that he was caught again.

He dived so quickly that the sailors were taken unawares, and let about twenty fathoms of the cable go over without checking it. This gave 206 a good start, and he streaked under the keel, hoping to break the line against it. But it was too stout, and soon he felt the steady pull of the turning capstan. He had got to the other side of the ship, though and with the cable stretched tightly against the keel, the sailors found that they could not haul the strong fish in by hand, so they fitted the spars to the capstan, and, leaning against them, they turned it as if they were raising the anchor.

> Judah! Judah! Idaho!
> Four black ladies all in a row,
> And one come out of Mexico . . .

they sang as they stamped round. The tiger-shark felt the slow, irresistible force, and he was obliged to give way to it.

Inch by inch he was dragged under the keel again and slowly up the other side.

When there were only about two fathoms of water left over his head he tried his spectacular leap again.

Up he shot in a shower of spray, and he gleamed in the tropical sun for a moment, a perfect curve over the blue sea; he came down with a splash that drenched the sailors, but the thick cable and thicker hook held fast, and in another moment he was hauled clear of the water to the tune of the shanty.

He lashed about in a perfect frenzy of rage, and splintered the rail as he came over the side. When they had got him on deck the men hardly knew what to do with the raging devil which they had hauled out of the depths.

The bo'sun with his axe was knocked flying, to land unconscious in the lee-scuppers.

The heavy fish plunged to and fro on the deck, springing about with almost supernatural strength. He scattered the hands, and it looked very much as if he would get over the side again. The captain dived into his cabin, and came out with a rifle in his hands. Taking as careful an aim as he could at the bounding shark, the captain let it have an explosive bullet in the head.

But 206 died hard, and it was not until the fifth bullet had thudded into his furious brain that he lay still.

They cut him open, and retrieved, among other things, the cook's wooden leg, a gold watch, three sovereigns, and the ring numbered T.S. 206, which the captain sent back to the Ichthiological Observatory with an account of its recovery.

49

Python

———— ⊗⊗⊗ ————

In the humid depths of an African jungle the heat of midday struck down on to the tropical foliage and made even the sodden ground steam.

At noon there was not a sound except the monotonous hum of countless insects; all the animals were sleeping. Suddenly a shrill, almost human scream roused the hordes of monkeys which swarmed in those parts. The scream was followed by the querulous chattering of hundreds of the little beasts. One of their number had been caught by a python.

This python was a huge snake, fully thirty feet long, and as thick in the middle as a man's thigh; he would eat anything from a frog to a man, but he preferred monkeys.

Very slowly he would creep up a tree, looking so like a strand of the great parasitical creepers that even the keen-eyed monkeys were deceived, and when he reached a suitable branch he would lie along it and wait for his food to come along.

This python's particular hunting-ground lay along the banks of a swampy river. Here game was plentiful, and the python had lived well for many years. More years, indeed, than he could count, for although he was an intelligent beast, he could not recall happenings which took place before about ten castings of his skin.

His only rivals were leopards, who took monkeys; and the crocodiles in the river, who took the deer when they came down to drink in the evening. The python had long cherished a grievance against one particular leopard, who was constantly poaching on his preserves, and also against one huge, fat old crocodile who lived solitarily in a pool over which hung many trees.

This crocodile, not content with stealing the monkeys who fell into the water when the python had missed them at his first strike, had also snapped up drinking deer from under the python's very nose.

One day, therefore, when he had just finished changing his skin, a painful process, the python, who was feeling discontented, decided to do away with both of his enemies as soon as possible.

He thought that he would deal with the crocodile first, as the leopard generally hunted at night. When he had finished his monkey, which he swallowed whole, the python dropped ten feet of his body on to a branch below. He curled his tail round this lower branch and dropped the rest of his length down to it. This branch led, like a road, to trees which in their turn led to the river.

Thus the great snake went fully half a mile without touching the ground. Throughout his own hunting-ground the python knew similar roads which led to all parts of his domain.

When he reached the river the python drank deeply and had a swim to loosen his new skin, which was rather tight.

He swam very fast, without effort, with about twenty-five feet of his length under the surface, and his head raised above it. He swam down the river to the pool where the crocodile lived. The whole river was inhabited by crocodiles, but none of them cared to touch the python when they saw him swimming past.

When he came near the pool he lowered his body in the water until only his head and a few inches of neck was visible above the surface. But for all that the old crocodile, stretched out on a mudflat near the bank, saw him out of one eye.

The crocodile was a blunt-nosed mugger, a villainous old man-eater who was fully the python's equal in years.

Lying on his mudflat with his mouth open and the crocodile-birds hopping in and out of his teeth, the mugger saw the python, but did nothing.

The snake gained the bank and went up an overhanging tree.

There he coiled himself in the crotch of the tree and watched the crocodile. They watched one another without winking for more than an hour; the snake because he had no eyelids with which to wink, and the crocodile because he felt the intense animosity of the python, and was too suspicious to lose sight of him for a second.

The day wore on eventlessly, but a little before dusk a baby monkey fell out of a tree next to the python's; it lay on the ground whimpering, but its mother was too terrified to come to it, as she had seen the python move.

As the little monkey hit the ground the mugger slid noiselessly from his mudbank and reached the shore with hardly a ripple to show that he had moved.

For the moment the python had gone right out of his mind, for if there was anything for which the mugger would swim a mile, it was a baby monkey.

The crocodile waddled awkwardly but rapidly up the bank, and snapped up the monkey. On the land he was at a disadvantage; he knew it, and was turning to go when the python dropped on him.

For a moment the snake's great weight crushed the breath out of the mugger, and he did not move.

Instantly the python flung two coils round the crocodile's mouth, and held it closed as in a vice. The crocodile knew that if he did not reach the water before the snake had coiled about his tail and body, he would never survive the fight.

He made a desperate effort, and digging his stout claws into the sand he shuffled towards the river.

But the sand gave way beneath him, and the python had his tail curled round the trunk of a tree, so the mugger did not gain a foot. He lashed furiously with his powerful tail, but the python put a coil round it for all that.

Then the crocodile tried tearing at the snake with his strong claws, but there was not an inch of the python within reach.

He knew then that his only hope was to lie flat against the ground to prevent the python from coiling round his body.

Imperceptibly the coils about his head and tail tightened, and the python began to draw him farther up the shore by pulling on the tree round which he had coiled his tail.

The mugger felt himself being dragged backwards, and made a despairing effort. The python's tail lost its hold, and the two plunged into the river, closely intertwined.

By the time they had got to deep water, however, the snake had put three coils about the crocodile's body.

The mugger fought desperately, tearing at the coils with all his strength. But it was of no avail, the coils tightened, his spine broke, and he died.

When he had made sure that the mugger was dead, the python swam to the shore, leaving the body to be eaten by the other crocodiles. On examining his wounds he found that although his new skin was torn in two or three places, the crocodile had not hurt him at all badly.

Towards nightfall he heard a leopard's coughing roar behind him in the forest. He went with his usual unhurried speed towards the noise, and soon he came to a branch on which he picked up the leopard's scent. He knew at once that it was not his enemy who had passed there, but another leopard.

Until moonrise he waited in a tree in which he had often seen the leopard, and a little after the full moon came up he saw him trotting along on the ground between the trees, evidently following some trail.

Very quietly he followed the leopard, gliding from tree to tree more like a wraith than a thirty-foot python.

The scent was strong, and the leopard never hesitated until he came to a clearing. In the middle of the open space a kid was tethered. The leopard sprang noiselessly into a tree; he had not seen the python.

The leopard crept to the end of a branch which overhung the clearing. The python climbed to a similar branch immediately above the leopard, who was completely absorbed in watching the kid. The great cat crouched flat against the branch; its spotted skin was almost invisible in the moonlight dappled with the

shadows of twigs: only the tip of its tail moved, twitching feverishly from side to side.

The python saw the great muscles between the leopard's shoulders swell and tauten as he prepared to spring, and the snake
knew that the time had come to strike.

Accordingly he wound five feet of his tail round the branch,
and prepared to let the rest of himself drop and coil about the
leopard. But the leopard sprang a second before the python had
expected, and the snake missed his aim.

The leopard streaked on to the ground and sprang at the kid.
Before he reached it, however, he was knocked head over heels
backwards, for a rifle bullet hit him as he was in mid-air. A white
hunter had tethered the kid there as a trap for the leopard, and he
had been waiting since midday in a machan which he had built
in a tree close by.

The leopard was killed at once, and after a second shot to make
sure, the man came awkwardly down from his tree, for he was
cramped by his long vigil.

He carried a revolver in his hand in case the leopard was only
shamming. He came just under the tree in which the python had
recoiled himself, and having made certain that the leopard had
really passed out, he put the revolver back in its holster.

The python liked men; they tasted like fat, soft monkeys. He
had already eaten three.

The hunter never had a hint of the python's presence until he
felt a coil round his chest. He made a dash for the open, but the
coil tightened, and quickly the python hitched two more round
him.

In a second the coils were so tight that the man could not draw
breath, let alone call for help; but he still had one arm free, and he
plucked furiously at his revolver.

The snake let the rest of his body down to the ground, and
tightened the coils a little more. Some ribs gave way and the man
felt himself losing consciousness, but he made a prodigious effort,
and pulled the revolver clear of its holster. The python threw three
more coils round his legs, and tightened them. If he had not been

so worn out by his fight with the mugger he would have finished his puny adversary much sooner. He raised his head to the level of the man's face in order to throw a coil round his neck.

This was a fatal mistake; the man raised his revolver with his free arm and blew the python's head off.

There was a pause, then the coils slackened and lost their grip, falling away from the hunter.

The white man blew a whistle for his native servants, who were encamped nearby, and collapsed. They carried him back on a litter, for many of his ribs were broken.

On the next day, being of a frugal turn of mind, he had the python skinned as well as the leopard; the python's skin became handbags, and the leopard's a hearthrug.

50

The Condor of Quetzalcoatl

One of the highest passes in the Andes runs past an ancient temple of Quetzalcoatl, a great god of the ancient Aztecs, who is still worshipped by some of the Indians, and this pass is called the Pass of Quetzalcoatl.

For about a mile at its highest point, this pass is a ledge barely a yard wide in places, which runs like a tiny crack across the face of an immense precipice.

The Andes rise above the pass up into the clouds, and the precipice falls sheer away from the ledge down into a valley of pines an incredible distance below.

There was another ridge high above the pass, a small piece of rock jutting out from the face of the precipice. It was entirely inaccessible to anything without wings, and on it there lived an immense condor.

This condor was famous throughout the mountainous country about the pass, and the Indians called him the condor of Quetzalcoatl; he was easily distinguishable from other condors by his enormous wing-spread, which marked him as a giant even among such huge-winged birds as his fellow condors.

The pass of Quetzalcoatl was rarely used since the Spaniards conquered South America, for the gold mines to which it led were hidden so well by the Indians that they have never been found.

About once a month, however, the little Indian village sent a load of moderately rich silver ore south over the pass to Pontrillo, where it was exchanged for the various things that the Indians wanted.

The ore was carried by a train of about a dozen of the sure-footed llamas which the Indians have used since time immemorial as pack animals.

An old Indian called Pepe usually took the llamas over the pass, as he knew it very well. The village also sent him because he had a shrewd eye for a bargain, and would get more value for the silver ore from the merchants of Pontrillo than anyone else.

Now it happened that for about a week before the llama train was due to cross the pass, the condor of Quetzalcoatl had been having very bad hunting. Indeed, he had not had a full meal for some days.

As he wheeled effortlessly thousands of feet above the pass, cutting great circles in the clear air, he noticed Pepe leading the heavily laden llamas.

The Indian saw the condor, and he waved to the bird, for he knew it quite well, having watched it every time he crossed the pass. It gave Pepe a curiously pleasant feeling which was at the same time slightly melancholy, to see the great condor wheeling up on motionless wings into the intense blueness of sky.

As the llamas came to the very narrow part of the ledge which ran under the condor's eyrie, Pepe stopped watching the bird, and concentrated all his attention on getting his heavily laden animals safely across the dangerous part of the pass.

The llamas were loosely roped, head to tail, so that they should keep in a line, but the rope was very thin, so that if one fell the rope would break, and the falling llama would not drag all the others with it.

Just at the very thinnest part of the ledge the rearmost llama slipped, and fell on to its knees, hurting itself quite badly. Its load was too heavy for it to get to its feet again, so Pepe crept back along the edge of the pass, pushing the llamas against the face of the rock to enable himself to get past.

Hung motionless on the wind, the condor's keen eyes marked every detail of the accident.

Pepe was having some difficulty in getting the llama to its feet, and as he pushed between it and the sheer rock, one of its hind feet went over the edge.

The condor turned his head to the earth and shot down a thousand feet, then he steadied himself, and stooped in an immense curve, striking the llama in the middle of the back.

The condor came down at a tremendous speed, but so accurate was his judgment that he shot between the animal and the rock face, passing immediately over Pepe's head.

The llama tottered for a moment, and then fell from the ledge, overbalanced by its heavy load. The thin rope broke with a clear snap. Pepe saw the llama turn several times in the air; it seemed no larger than the palm of his hand when it struck the ground.

The condor dropped after it like a plummet, and Pepe cursed it by all the saints of Christendom and by all the gods of the Inca pantheon. Then he scrambled along the ledge to the head of the train, and led them carefully over the dangerously narrow path.

When they reached the part where the path widened into a safe road, Pepe let them take their own way, and strolled along behind, cursing the condor.

The dead llama had belonged to Pepe; it had been one of the three which he had bought some time ago. The rest of the train belonged to the other villagers.

Pepe arrived in Pontrillo before sunset, but he was distracted by the thought of his loss, and made a very poor bargain with the astute merchants.

He set out before sunrise the next day, for it was a full day's journey home.

The llamas were only lightly laden with the things from the town. They passed under the eyrie at high noon, and Pepe saw the condor sitting there, full gorged and motionless.

He threw a stone at the bird, but the eyrie was far out of reach, so he shook his fist, and cursing the condor, passed on.

The villagers were sympathetic enough not to comment on the very poor bargain Pepe had made with their silver ore, but for several days he was quite morose, brooding over his loss.

In a month's time the llama train set out again; Pepe had armed himself with a long stick, as there were no firearms in the village.

The condor had been looking out for the llama train for some time, and he followed it at a great height until they came to the dangerous part of the pass, when the bird swung into the wind and hung quite still over the thinnest part of the ledge, watching every movement of the llamas very keenly.

Pepe urged his animals right in against the face of the rock, and walked behind them, watching the condor.

He felt quite sure that the condor would attack the rearmost animal again so he prepared for it, giving the last beast a light burden so that it would not overbalance.

He kept the llamas at a trot so as to get them past the dangerous ledge quickly. He looked at the condor, who was so high that he looked like a floating black feather.

Suddenly the great black bird raised his wings over his head, and dropped; he had seen the foremost llama getting nearer the edge. He checked at a thousand feet above the pass, and paused, judging that there was not quite room to swoop between the llama and the precipice.

Pepe saw what the condor was aiming at, and ran along the ledge to the front of the train.

There was only just room for him to stand on the edge and push the front llama back; this took all his attention.

He heard a rush of wings as the condor stooped on him. He caught a glimpse of broad black pinions, and then he knew that he was falling.

His only feeling was one of intense surprise as he saw the llamas on the pass apparently shooting up into the heavens.

Then he turned in the air and saw the ground rushing up at him incredibly quickly. He had no time to be afraid before he struck it.

The last thing he saw was a huge blue butterfly that flashed past him.

The bewildered llamas made their way back to the village after two days. The villagers, headed by Pepe's son, Iturrioz, set out to look for him. They knew his skeleton by his necklace of red Indian gold; there was nothing else to know him by, for the twenty-three great condors who had followed the condor of Quetzalcoatl had only left the larger bones.

On his father's skull, Iturrioz swore a feud against the gorged bird, who sat on the edge of his eyrie, looking down with glazed eyes, and holding out his wings for the sun's warmth.

Iturrioz went to the ruined temple of Quetzalcoatl and made a sacrifice, spilling blood and salt, for the condor was sacred to the god. Then he went home, and going to his hut he took his bow from beneath the eaves.

Iturrioz was a famous bowman, and he, with two other young men, did all the hunting for the tribe. He took five arrows that had belonged to his grandfather that were only to be used in blood feuds. These arrows were of cunning workmanship; and they were tipped with jasper.

On his thick, powerful bow, Iturrioz put a new string, and then he put the arrow heads to soak in a small pot of cura, a most potent venom.

He set out along the pass early in the morning of the next day. The sun was high by the time he came under the eyrie. The condor was nowhere to be seen.

The Indian squatted down and waited patiently, leaning against the warm rock.

As time wore on and the condor did not come, Iturrioz chewed at a leathery tortilla, still squatting with his great bow across his knees.

He had never seen a firearm of any kind, and, although he had heard of them, he did not really believe in their existence.

At times he thought he saw a speck high in the sky which might have been the bird, but otherwise no living thing stirred. There was no sound of any kind, nor was there any wind.

For some time Iturrioz considered the possibility of reaching the eyrie far above him, but he soon abandoned the thought, for the rock rose sheer; it did not offer the least foothold.

It would also be next to impossible to shoot the condor in its eyrie, for the projection offered a complete shelter from an arrow.

The condor did not return before nightfall, so the Indian left the dangerous part of the pass and went back to a spot where he had left a blanket. He rolled himself in this and slept until daybreak.

At sunrise he rose and went back to the village. There he took a very young llama, which he led along the pass of Quetzalcoatl. The condor was sailing slowly down the gentle wind some way below the pass, but he saw Iturrioz and the llama and wheeled into the wind, climbing rapidly. He soared high above the ledge, and poised himself motionless on his broad wings.

The Indian tied the llama to a long rope, and squatted down on the ledge in the same place as before. The young llama wandered up and down the ledge, for the rope to which it was tied was long enough to let it go a good distance from Iturrioz.

Twice it came so near the edge that the condor started to dive, but each time the bird checked, and each time Iturrioz sank back, releasing his bow with a twang.

The third time, however, the young llama presented a perfect target for the stooping condor.

The bird swooped from its great height; the Indian stood erect, perfectly still, with his arrow drawn to his ear.

The condor grew nearer and larger, and Iturrioz heard the rush of its wings. Then he loosed his arrow, the aim was true, and the jasper-headed arrow passed clean through the bird's body, so strong was the bow.

The condor, jerked out of its course, screamed, and missed the llama. It shot down past the ledge, and then wheeled slowly up, hoping to gain its eyrie.

With lightning rapidity the Indian shot his remaining four arrows into the condor. He shot so quickly and so true that the four shafts were all in the air at one time, and they all found their mark.

The condor almost reached its eyrie before it died in the air. Then it circled down; the huge outspread wings supported the dead bird for a time, but soon it slipped sideways and hurtled down.

A drop of deep red blood fell on the ledge, where it dried quickly in the fierce sun.

51

Old Cronk

———— ⋙∞⋘ ————

A heron was flying slowly over the marshes a little before day-break. There was light enough to fish by, and the four clamorous youngsters in the nest at home would soon be wanting food.

The country people who lived in and about the marsh knew the heron well, because of his remarkable size and age.

They called him Old Cronk, because of his voice. Landing on the edge of a stream he began walking slowly along the water's edge, peering into the water.

A frog swam jerkily into Cronk's sight, and the heron shot his long beak into the water with lightning speed, spearing the frog through the middle of the back.

Swallowing the frog into his crop, Cronk stalked on. Coming to a little pool, he stopped at a clump of kingcups, and drew up one leg under him, waiting for something to come along.

The white morning mists were melting away as the sun came up before Cronk saw anything. It was an eel, swimming slowly along the bed of the stream with a wriggling, snake-like motion. Cronk's eyes brightened, and he stiffened with a barely percepti-ble quiver of his crest.

Down shot the spear-sharp beak, and the eel flew up into the air, impaled on the point. With a quick jerk the heron flung it off, catching it again with an open beak.

The eel joined the frog in the heron's crop. Fearing that the disturbance must have startled all the other fish in the stream, the bird waded to the bank, where he gave a little jump, and launched

446

himself into the air, flying with firm, steady wingbeats along the course of the stream until he came to another pool, larger and deeper than the first.

Here he landed on the bank, and waded slowly into the pool until he stood in about a foot of water.

Waiting for the inhabitants of the pool to settle down again after the slight disturbance that he had made, Cronk surveyed the pool. It was about twenty feet across, the stream led into it at one end, and two smaller streams led out at the other.

The heron had not fished in this pool very often, as the water was muddy, and it was not easy to see the fish.

For about half an hour the heron stood on one leg, stock-still, as if in deep meditation.

A roach rose at a fly a little across the pool, and the soft 'plop' that it made sounded clear in the still morning air.

A fat bream rose lazily to the surface near Cronk's feet, and swallowed a little insect that was struggling in the water.

Cronk jerked the bream into the air, and a second later it had joined the frog and the eel in his crop.

The wavelets subsided, and the heron settled down again to watch. A school of roach entered the pool from one of the smaller streams.

Cronk strode through the water with a purposeful air, making no disturbance. The soft brown mud at the bottom covered his toes as he waded a little deeper. With his long neck outstretched, Cronk waited for the roach to come a little nearer. Slowly the roach came within reach, and the bird raised his head to strike.

Then there was a rush as a great pike shot up from a deep hole, and snapped up one of the little fish.

Cronk had struck at the roach before he had realized the size of his adversary.

His beak had shot in after the roach just half a second before the pike had swallowed, and Cronk saw that he had got more than he could manage.

The pike snapped his strong mouth on Cronk's beak, and pulled. The heron was taken off his guard for the moment, and almost lost his balance, but he flapped wildly with his wings and regained it, jerking twice with his beak to dislodge the pike.

Cronk dropped the roach, and was backing towards the land when the pike, who was in a furious rage, having been hurt by the heron's beak, rushed snapping at his legs.

The heron darted down his beak to defend his legs, and jabbed the fish in the side. Undeterred, the pike seized Cronk's right foot and pulled him over on one side. The heron lost his balance and fell with a squawk and a loud splash, thrashing the water wildly with his wings. Somewhat alarmed by the terrific splashing that the heron made, the pike drew off, watching warily.

Cronk was badly shaken and flustered by falling over, and in his attempts to regain his balance he got out of his depth, and was forced to swim.

He could swim, but he did not like it, especially as he knew that he could not fly until he got to the land.

The pike, a very fierce old fish, weighing between twenty-five and thirty pounds, had lived for many years in the deep hole in the middle of the pool.

He was now thoroughly roused, and wanted to get Cronk over the deep hole in order to be able to drag him down by the foot and drown him. The pike had killed many moorhens and mallard in this way.

Getting between the bird and the bank the pike broke water with a loud splash, hoping to terrify Cronk into swimming deeper. But Cronk was far too stout a bird to be terrified by splashes, and he shot his beak at the pike, catching him, by a lucky chance, in the right eye.

The big fish beat the water into a foam before diving to bury his head in the soft mud.

The heron took advantage of the pause to swim towards the bank. Feeling land beneath his feet, Cronk began wading to the side. He heard the pike shoot clear of the water just behind him. Owing to his eye injury the pike had quite missed Cronk's foot, and he snapped his powerful teeth on empty air.

Wheeling, the heron struck two lightning blows into the great fish, completely transfixing it; he jerked his beak free and reached the bank.

The pike sank writhing, to float up dead a little later on his side.

Cronk shook himself, and hopped into the air, flapping strongly with his broad wings.

He flew slowly, because he was tired, but soon he saw the trees of his ancient heronry coming into sight. He gave a loud 'Cronk! Cronk!' and quickened his pace. A few moments later he landed lightly on the great untidy heap of twigs on which his mate and four young ones awaited breakfast.

52

Gorilla

———⊗⊗⊗———

Four great apes sat in a tree at noon. They were gorillas, one huge male, his wife, and two small ones. A fifth gorilla, the smallest, was scratching up roots on the ground.

From where he sat, high up on a sort of flat nest or platform of branches and twigs, the big gorilla smelt man. He gave a grunt, and his son on the ground swung up into the tree.

The fierce glare of the noonday sun scarcely penetrated the dense tropical foliage of the forest, and a steamy twilight prevailed except in the occasional clearings.

The largest of the apes had encountered men before, and he had killed two quite easily, but he did not understand them, and so he feared them in a dim, resentful way.

The scent grew weaker, and died away, but none of the gorillas left the trees until well into the afternoon. When they were in the trees they were at home; they swung from branch to branch by their great arms as lightly as gibbons. On the ground they felt lost and out of place. They walked awkwardly on their stumpy bow legs, keeping almost erect by leaning their knuckles on the ground. They shuffled uncomfortably, using their long arms as stilts, when they tried to walk upright; they went faster on all fours.

When it rained, as it often did, they were very miserable if they were on the ground, because they slipped, and stepped in puddles and mud, which they detested, being cleanly creatures. So they always went up to their nest to shelter from the warm downpour, and sometimes they had to sit there for hours, watching the rain.

The father had sometimes tried to make a roof to keep the rain from dripping on to him, but he had never quite succeeded.

Sometimes when they were feeding far from their usual haunts they would meet other gorillas, but they avoided them as a rule. Once when they had encountered a solitary, morose old gorilla, he had attacked one of the younger ones, and the big male had gone to his rescue. The two gorillas had faced one another on the ground, half erect, roaring and beating their huge chests. The younger ape had slipped back to his mother.

On that day the two males had contented themselves with roaring, and had not fought, but about a month later the old gorilla had passed under a tree in which his former adversary was hiding. Before he had had time to know what was happening, a great weight had struck him in the back, and fierce teeth had met through his neck, and he was dead. His enemy had remembered, and had hidden on purpose.

The gorillas could talk, although their words were few and difficult to distinguish from grunts. In their guttural, throaty speech the big male was called Urrgh.

Once Urrgh had had three wives, but two had been speared to death when the gorillas had been raiding the sugar canes near a native village. On that occasion Urrgh had killed two men by tearing them to pieces with his hands.

On their platform the gorillas had made heaps of dried fern leaves and grass, from which they made themselves comfortable beds. From the time when he had smelt men until late in the afternoon, Urrgh occupied himself with making a bed.

He selected tufts of soft grass from the main heap and took them to the corner of the nest nearest to the trunk of the enormous tree, then with the greatest care he arranged them to his liking. When he had finished, something in the bed displeased him, so he tore it to pieces, and started again.

Suddenly a change in the wind brought back the smell of man. This, combined with the failure of his bed, annoyed Urrgh, and he got up on his stumpy legs and roared a great deep-throated roar, and thundered on his chest with his clenched fists – the sound was like that of a muffled drum. Then, stopping, he cuffed his wife, and went on with his half-made bed.

His wife, offended, went down to the ground, where her offspring were grubbing up roots.

The veering breeze carried away the smell of men, and the gorilla concentrated on his bed.

Suddenly he saw something glint in the bushes on the ground. He looked down to the little clear space where his family were scuffling about – they had noticed nothing. He looked again, and saw a number of men crouching in the shadow of a thick bush.

He knew that there were more than four, because he could count up to four, but no more.

He was too curious to see what they were doing to give the alarm at once. The thing which he had seen glittering was the barrel of a rifle.

There was a white hunter with five black servants. They were out to catch a young gorilla alive, and they had a net for that purpose.

The wind was blowing into the faces of the hunters, so the gorillas on the ground had no hint of their presence.

One of the smaller apes was gradually nearing the edge of the little clearing; quickly the net shot out and covered him. Instantly Urrgh gave a great bellow of warning and swung down towards the ground. His wife and the other young ones reached the platform as Urrgh reached the ground.

On the ground he paused for a moment, beating his chest. The hunters had all their work cut out to overpower the powerful young gorilla in the net. Suddenly Urrgh charged; scrambling along, now on all fours, now erect, he went faster than a man can run.

The white hunter fired twice; the first bullet missed, but the second struck Urrgh in the shoulder. It did not stop him, however, and before the white man could fire again Urrgh tore the rifle from his grasp, twisted it up like so much rubber tubing, and launched himself at the men.

Two of the natives broke and ran, but the remaining three threw their heavy spears. One only grazed him, but the other two pierced him through the chest. He did not stop for all that, and seized the nearest native in his great arms. He finished the wretched man in a few seconds, but by that time the others had fled, carrying their captive still in the net.

Urrgh dropped the corpse and began to pursue the fugitives. After a moment he stopped, and plucked at the spears. In the heat of the battle he had hardly felt them, but now he felt the pain and roared, pulling at the spears. One came out easily, but the other was barbed, and the head broke off short.

He shambled back to the clearing, where his wife came down to him. She licked his shoulder, and after a few minutes they set off on the trail of the hunters.

They could see the track easily, for the running men had beaten down the undergrowth in their hurry.

The apes swung through the branches after the men, and after a bare minute of hard going they came within sight of them. The hunters were on the bank of a river, just getting into a canoe. They pushed off as the apes came roaring down to the water's edge.

They still had the young gorilla, and the current was far too swift for the apes to cross by swimming.

They returned to the trees, and raced up and down trying to find a place where they could cross. At last they came to two great trees whose branches interlaced over the river. Urrgh and his mate hurled themselves across, and cast about for the trail again. It was some time before they found it, and Urrgh was weakening from loss of blood, but his rage kept him on.

By nightfall the gorillas reached the hunter's camp, which was in a clearing surrounded by large trees. The natives were just beginning to make up the fire for the night, and the white man was standing under one of the trees lighting his pipe.

The young gorilla was in a portable cage. The white man knocked out the dottle of his pipe against his heel, and filled it again.

From a leafy branch just above him a great hairy hand reached down . . . he never uttered a sound when he dropped, because his neck was broken.

The natives saw his death in the twilight, and ran; they would fight in the daylight, but not in the dark.

It was the work of a minute for the two full-grown gorillas to smash the light cage. As night fell the three fled back through the branches to their platform.

In the night Urrgh became feverish, and dreamed of great gestes. He fought with his shadow in the light of the moon, and fell backwards from the platform.

He was dead by the morning.

53

Rhino

————— ⦾⦿⦾ —————

A rhinoceros was resting beneath a tree. The blazing African sun was beginning to go down in the west, but the heat was still at its worst, and the dusty plain, sparsely covered with scrub and small trees, shimmered in the heat-haze.

On the rhino's back a dozen small birds hopped to and fro. They were the only living things whose presence the rhino could tolerate, for he was constitutionally ill-tempered; but he liked the birds because they kept away the big stinging flies, and, better still, they removed the boring parasites who burrowed into his thick, tough hide, and made his life miserable.

The sight of any other creature except these birds filled him with unreasoning annoyance, and if it stayed near him his annoyance would turn into rage, and he would charge it even if it were a lion.

His sight was very poor, but his acute sense of smell made up for that. His short sight made him suspicious of everything which he saw moving, and sometimes he would root up a bush that had been moving in the wind on the off chance that it might be some animal.

He was afraid of nothing on earth, but there was not an animal in the bush who would care to try its chances against him.

When he came down to the water-hole in the middle of the plain everything made way for him, from the lions downwards.

Once a lion had tried conclusions with him; it had not lived to tell the tale.

The rhino was a terrible fighter; his immense weight, his remarkable speed when he charged, and above all the single long horn on the top of his snout, combined to make him almost invincible. Once he had got his ponderous body under way his great weight gave him an unbelievable velocity, and at the height of his charge the rhino could outpace a galloping horse.

The pride of his life was his horn. The long, sharp, tapering projection curved slightly backwards; it was unrivalled as an instrument for ripping up his opponents.

He spent a great deal of time in stropping it against the trunk of the same tree against which he rubbed himself, with the result that all the bark of the tree near the ground disappeared.

In much the same manner as a bird whets its beak on a twig, the rhinoceros sharpened his horn against the tree, keeping it sharp for any emergency.

His greatest strength lay in his shoulders, so when he threw up his head the force of the jerk was so great that anything that he had impaled on his horn was thrown high over his back. He kept himself practised at this by grubbing up bushes and small trees, so that the part of the bush in which he lived was freely dotted with dead, dry trunks and branches; it also helped to work off his ill temper.

His only rival in the bush was another rhinoceros, who lived some way to the north, and who was the only animal who had ever beaten him. This was in a fight for a remarkably well-made female rhino.

He had not been quite at his prime at the time when he was beaten, but the defeat had preyed on his mind, making him more than usually morose.

A strong north wind had been blowing all day, but as the sun's heat grew less, it dropped, and a little before sunset a light south-west breeze blew across the plain.

The breeze carried with it a smell which puzzled the rhino. He sniffed the wind meditatively; he could distinguish the scent of the mixed herd of wildebeest and zebra which wandered habitually in the south of his part of the world in that season; that was the prevailing scent, but there was also the musty, somewhat fetid odour of a lion, probably attended by a few jackals and hyenas; it was none of these smells, however, that disquieted the rhino, for he was quite used to them, and knew what they were; it was another smell which he did not know that puzzled him.

It was vaguely like that of another rhinoceros but it was subtly different; it was obviously not that of any carnivore or else it would have had that slightly musty savour that the meat-eating animals always carry about with them.

The rhinoceros decided to investigate the scent, and he went up the wind with his usual surprisingly nimble trot.

Everything got out of his way, for his anger was not lightly to be incurred.

He came to a belt of trees and paused, for the light breeze had failed. In some thick grass nearby he picked up the trail again, for the tall grass held the scent very well, so that he could follow it without lowering his head.

It was evident that about a dozen of the animals had passed there, and that they were not far away, for the scent was very fresh.

Suddenly he came out of the trees, and there, showing plainly against the skyline, were eight elephants.

They were looking straight at the rhinoceros, for they had heard him coming through the trees. There were two bull elephants, one very old, and the other in his prime; they were accompanied by two cows with two half grown, and two very young calves. The rhino's first feeling was one of intense surprise and curiosity; then almost immediately he felt annoyed that these animals should be in his part of the bush.

This annoyance turned into rage as he began to scratch the ground with his forefeet. The rims of his little eyes grew red, and he twitched his ears to and fro.

Seven of the elephants faded silently into the trees, and the big bull remained in front of the rhino, about a hundred yards away from him.

The elephant's colossal ears were outspread, and he held his trunk stiffly out in the air, sniffing. His great tusks shone in the golden sunlight.

The elephant's eyes were no better than the rhino's, but in the clear light of the setting sun they could see one another plainly.

The rhinoceros flicked his little pig-like tail about for a moment, and then, tightly curling it over his back, he lowered his head and charged with a high pitched squeal like the whistle of a train.

The earth shook as he thundered towards the elephant, who coiled back his trunk and bent his forelegs somewhat to prevent the rhino from dashing beneath him, and disembowelling him with a sweep of his horn. The rhino came down on the elephant in a cloud of dust; the elephant turned his great shoulder to take the shock and to avoid the rhino's horn.

They met with a dull thud; a cloud of dust flew up, and the rhino, deflected from his course by the elephant's movement, careered on into a sapling, which he crushed flat.

He had not expected the elephant to withstand his charge, but it did not dismay him at all. He turned, and charged again.

They met shoulder to shoulder again, and this time the elephant slid back a little at the impact.

The elephant could not receive the charging rhino on his tusks, as the great speed and weight might snap them, for they were very long compared with the rhino's horn.

At the third charge the rhino scored a long gash down the elephant's side, and he turned quickly to follow up this advantage, but the elephant had turned more quickly, and bore down on the standing rhino, trumpeting shrilly.

The rhinoceros staggered at the shock, and nearly fell, and before he could recover the elephant gored him furiously. Both tusks pierced him, but neither found a vital spot; before the elephant could press his advantage, the rhino ran in under the scarlet tusks.

The elephant slipped, and fell squarely on top of the rhino, knocking all the breath out of his body, and not leaving him any room to use his horn. Before the rhino could get breath to rise the elephant scrambled off him and, kneeling, struck in with his tusks.

Fortunately for the rhinoceros one tusk glanced off his tough hide, and the other missed him altogether, ploughing up the hard earth about an inch from his head.

Regaining his feet, the rhino backed away; and the two great beasts stood glaring at one another.

The sun set with the suddenness peculiar to tropical lands, and in the afterglow the rhinoceros circled round the elephant, seeking a good place from which to charge.

With their weak eyes both of them were having difficulty now in seeing one another clearly.

Finding a sandy hillock, the rhino lowered his head and charged. The elephant was standing in the shadow of a tall bush; the charging rhinoceros could hardly distinguish between elephant and shade, so his earth-shaking charge missed the greater part of its effect, as he struck the elephant a glancing blow. His great pace prevented him from pulling up, and he went crashing away into a thicket of thorn bushes.

He pulled himself out, grunting, and galloped back. The elephant had disappeared. In the gathering shadows the elephants had noiselessly slipped away into the trees; the rhino had not heard them go, for with their soft, padded feet, the great brutes could move like shadows.

The strengthening wind kept the scent of their retreat from the rhinoceros, who stood bewildered in the shadow where the elephant had stood, and where his own blood marked the place of the fight.

He peered into the dusk, but saw nothing. Then with a grunt he swung round and made for the dense mass of thorn bushes in which he slept.

He felt quite happy, for his wounds were not very serious, and they hardly troubled him; he thought in his own vague way that he had kept his part of the bush against the invaders. The fight had worked off all his moroseness; he was thoroughly satisfied with himself.

As he went, everything, from the prowling lions downwards, made way for him. Tomorrow, he thought, he would show that other rhinoceros in the north what fighting really meant.

54

Jehangir Bahadur

———— ✺ ————

Although Hussein was by profession a snake-charmer, he had been born a mahout, and until he had made things too hot for himself in the Public Works Department he had worked with the elephants which his father had ridden before him.

Hussein, after an extremely varied career, decided to settle down on the land and end his life in peace. He had neither land nor money, but, as he said, even the eagle is born without feathers.

While he was travelling about the Punjab with his snakes he encountered a regiment going north up the Grand Trunk Road with all its guns and impedimenta. Hussein followed the soldiers among the camp sutlers, and when they encamped he prepared his snakes for a performance.

Nevertheless, until they had fed he did not approach, for there is a native proverb which says 'Never speak to a white man until he is fed.' After their meal, however, the soldiers were disposed to be amused, and Hussein gave his performance in an open space before the tents.

Soon after the sun set, and the snake-charmer wandered away to the native lines to look for a bed. He learnt that there was straw to be had for two pice in the elephant lines, and he went towards the place where about twenty elephants were tethered for the night. There he encountered the chief of the mahouts, who gave him straw for a bed.

When he had secured his bed with a piece of rope he turned

to go, but the chief of the mahouts cried out, saying, 'The price, O son of Eblis!'

'Old man,' replied Hussein, 'who gave thee leave to sell the Government's straw, expressly purchased for the greater comfort of my lords the elephants?' and with this he went away, bearing his straw to a secluded spot towards the end of the lines.

'Now,' said the chief of the mahouts, 'I clearly perceive that that man is fundamentally evil, and that this is an unfortunate day for me.' But he did not pursue Hussein, for he was an old man and disliked tumult.

Hussein made a kind of nest in his straw and burrowed into it. He slept soundly until a little before dawn, when one of the elephants who had slipped his picket ropes woke him by taking the greater portion of his straw.

Hussein sprang up, abusing the elephant in the tongue of the mahouts. It drew back, ashamed; for an elephant is most sensitive to abuse in language which it understands, but none outside the mahout caste understands the peculiar *hathi*-tongue in which elephants should be admonished and rebuked.

The elephant became ashamed of itself, and shuffled backwards into the shadows. It was a bull elephant, with tusks ringed with silver bands that gleamed in the half light.

Hussein went back to his bed, but there was not enough to sleep in, so he gathered up his basket of snakes and went over to a fire which some of the early rising camp followers had kindled.

From one he borrowed some cold boiled rice wherewith he broke his fast. The man who yielded up his rice was a Jat, a farmer from the rich corn lands some way farther north, who had come into the camp to sell fowls. He was a simple man, and Hussein borrowed a rupee from him.

After his meal Hussein went back to the elephant lines to look at the elephants, for his breeding had given him a true appreciation of the great beasts. On the way he came across a man selling sugar cane, and he bought several of the sweet, juicy sticks.

He came to the elephant lines, and almost at once he recognized the one who had eaten his bed by the silver rings about his tusks. The elephant knew him at once, and looked sheepish; then it reached out its trunk and touched him on the arm, and Hussein knew that he had known this elephant long ago.

He thought for a moment, and then it came back to him in a flash; it was Jehangir Bahadur, who had come to his father for training when Hussein was a youth. He had been very fond of Jehangir for the five years that he had known him, although he was naturally most attached to Muhammed Akbar, the elephant which his grandfather, his father, and himself had served – indeed Hussein had not left the service until Muhammed Akbar died.

Jehangir had recognized him as soon as he had seen him in the full light, and he gave a little gurgle of delight, bending his fore-legs until his head was almost on the ground, with his trunk curled back over his forehead.

When they had stroked and patted one another, Hussein sat between Jehangir's front feet and fed him with the sugar canes in the shade of his flapping ears.

Presently a man came along the lines, and seeing Hussein he cried, 'Man, stand afar off, for this is a lordly elephant, and one who is by no means to be fed by lowly people.' And Hussein answered, saying, 'O *bahinchute*, since when have the drovers of beasts called themselves mahouts?' for he saw by the man's caste mark that he was no mahout, but a mere herder of cattle.

'Nevertheless,' replied the man, somewhat abashed, 'I am the temporary attendant of the mighty one.'

'Has he then no regular mahout?' asked Hussein.

'No, for he will suffer none to remain with him for more than a few months. It is said that he seeks a previous mahout, and will never be satisfied until he finds him.'

'These are true words,' replied Hussein, 'you may fetch me water, a brush, and some arrack. This is an honour, for I am he whom Jehangir Bahadur has waited. On your head and heart.' Now the man was taken aback by Hussein's air of authority, and straightway he went to fetch that which was commanded. The water and the stiff brush having been brought, and the arrack having been set aside in a pot, Hussein washed Jehangir all over very carefully, cleaning his great ears tenderly, and plucking the small stones and thorns from his feet.

When he had done he gave Jehangir the arrack to drink; by this time several other mahouts had come, and they said, 'Who is this?' They learnt that Hussein was Jehangir's first mahout, and they said, 'These things are as they should be.' For they had spent their lives among the elephants, and they understood them.

One asked Hussein why he did not rejoin the service, and he replied that he had left it quickly for certain imperative reasons, and that he would find it hard to get back again.

'But this is an exceptional case,' said an old mahout, 'and Jehangir will undoubtedly pine if you leave him again. I will speak to the chief of the mahouts myself.'

And all the mahouts said, 'This is just.'

But when the chief was brought he looked sourly upon Hussein, for he recognized in him the man who had tricked him out of two pice the evening before, and he said, 'Now this is without doubt an evil man, a *bût-parast*, and one whose female relations have no noses; who is he to consort with us?'

'But Jehangir will perish if he goes,' said one of the mahouts.

'That is not so,' replied the old man, 'for I shall make him my own especial charge.' And with this he caused Hussein to be ejected from the camp.

Jehangir could not help him, as he was shackled with chains to prevent him from wandering again, but as Hussein was hustled away the elephant trumpeted and raged.

Hussein dared not return to the camp on account of the enmity of the old man, but in a week, when the regiment moved north again, he followed it, and saw Jehangir pulling the guns with the other elephants. He was very troublesome, however, and constantly stopped among crowds to look for Hussein.

The chief of the mahouts rode him, and wielded the iron ankus unmercifully, so that Hussein, watching from afar, raged furiously.

When it came to the place appointed, the regiment was split up, certain of the elephants being sent north with the guns, and the others being returned to south with various burdens.

Among those who were sent back was Jehangir, for it was feared that he would go *musth* and run amok.

The chief of the mahouts went north with the other elephants where he was killed by reason of a stone that fell on his head as he passed beneath a bridge; so Hussein was able to see more of Jehangir. He followed the returning detachment, giving performances with his snakes whenever he could.

In a few days he approached the man who commanded the mahouts, and asked to be taken on, but the man refused, saying that he had been warned against Hussein as a wicked man who sought an opportunity to do evil.

Hussein had no money wherewith to bribe the man, so he cried out to heaven that this was an injustice, hoping to catch the ear of a white man, but the other man shouted louder, and men came running who beat Hussein with their *lathis*, and throwing him into a dry ditch forbade him to come near the elephants again. That night he stole to the lines and lay at the feet of Jehangir; the elephant lifted him up on to his back, and Hussein whispered his troubles into the broad waving ears.

When he slept from weariness, stretched on the elephant's back, Jehangir shuffled to the limit of his chains, and then strained slowly against them; he put his mighty strength into the task, and presently Hussein was awakened by the clear, sharp sound of snapping iron. The noise was not enough to alarm anyone, so none saw the elephant slip away from the lines like a grey shadow, moving without a sound.

Hussein lay still for a moment, somewhat confused. Then he felt Jehangir moving under him, and he sat up. The elephant had come out on to the road, and was moving rapidly towards the south, where the thick forests lay within a mile of the road. Jehangir left the road, and went into the deep elephant grass which bordered it; he stopped, and stuffed a bunch of tender leaves into his mouth.

'Turn, Light of my soul,' said Hussein, very frightened, 'turn and go back before they find that you are gone. They will say that I have stolen you.' Jehangir remained motionless. Hussein slipped to the ground and argued with the elephant.

'If they catch me now they will send me to the jail for many years, and I shall die,' he said.

But Jehangir only gurgled, and his eye took on an obstinate gleam. 'Turn back before it is too late,' repeated Hussein.

'I cannot hide you, and they will catch us and put heavy irons upon you.' He stormed, but Jehangir only ate leaves, and rolled his head: he pleaded with the elephant, and wept at his feet, but Jehangir only ate wild sugar cane and stood upon three legs to rest the fourth.

At length Hussein stood speechless, and Jehangir reached out his trunk and putting his mahout up on his back again he set off towards the forest.

Then the mahout gave in, and guided the elephant on to a path which led more straightly to the deep woods. He urged Jehangir to his full speed, a peculiar loping shuffle, which took them along at a great speed; for, as he told the elephant, they would have to go far before dawn in order to have a chance of getting clear away. With his tireless gait the elephant gained the virgin forest before the moon had set, and by dawn they were so far away from the camp that Hussein felt safe; nevertheless they kept on until noon, when they rested by a river.

Hussein lay on the warm sand and thought out a plan. He decided to lie hid until the hue and cry died down, and then to go as far south as possible, keeping away from the towns; then he thought that he would travel slowly about the country, hiring Jehangir and himself to clear away trees and to do work for which a well-guided elephant is essential. He had encountered men who owned an elephant and who travelled like this, so his appearance would give rise to no suspicion.

He decided that he would do this until he had amassed sufficient money to buy land and to settle down with Jehangir who would be able to do the work of many bullocks without feeling it.

Hussein lived in the forest with Jehangir for some weeks before he thought it safe to move up the river to where he knew the Grand Trunk Road crossed it on a bridge.

He altered Jehangir's appearance as much as possible, scrubbing off the Government broad arrow, and paring away the Government number from the nail of his right fore-foot; he also took the silver bands from the elephant's tusks and put them on his wrists as bracelets to make himself look respectably wealthy.

They made their way slowly up the river until they came to the road, which Hussein meant to cross so as to avoid observation, but the first thing they met as they crossed an unfrequented stretch was a man on a Goverment elephant.

This was the same man who had caused Hussein to be beaten some time before. They recognized one another at once, the man bawled, 'Stop thief', and urged his elephant forward, beating with his heavy ankus.

Hussein leaned forward and spoke to Jehangir, who burst into a tremendous gallop. There was open country the other side of the road thinly interspersed with trees. Jehangir charged across the road and thundered away over the plain. The man set his elephant in pursuit, and the two rushed furiously away towards the west.

Very soon Hussein saw that Jehangir was losing ground, so he pulled up, and the two elephants faced one another.

Suddenly they both charged, and met head-on with a thud that shook the ground. Forehead to forehead they pushed furiously, each trying to force the other backwards.

The two mahouts hurled abuse at one another as their mounts strove with all their great strength.

His opponent was gaining a little, being somewhat heavier, so Jehangir, getting a foothold in the loose soil made an immense effort, so great that his fore-feet left the ground and he leaned with all his weight on his enemy, who began sliding slowly backwards, his feet slipping in the dust.

At the same moment Hussein leapt across on to the other elephant's neck, and seizing the mahout, he cast him down.

In another second Jehangir had defeated his opponent, thrusting him backwards and sideways; very quickly Jehangir backed, and then charged, ramming the other elephant in the side. He went over with a crash right on top of his mahout, who was struggling on the ground. Hussein had time to leap clear, and immediately he ran to Jehangir to stop him battering the other elephant to death. Jehangir obeyed at once, and Hussein, mounting on to his neck, guided him back into the forest.

Having concealed him in a clump of bamboos and forbidden him to move, Hussein went back to the dead mahout. There was nothing to be done for him; the falling elephant had killed him instantly, and in a panic had run back to his elephant lines.

Presently the people who saw him return without his mahout sent out a search party, who found the body, and Hussein, coming up as if he knew nothing about it, learnt that the man had been trampled to death by his own elephant, which he was known to have treated cruelly.

Nobody recognized Hussein or suspected him even when he appeared riding on Jehangir; it was a district in which he had never been before, and his story was accepted without the slightest question.

Once he was safely away in the south Hussein carried out the rest of his plan, and in time he bought three fields and a small house in which he lived very happily, although he was hard put to it to find a shelter for Jehangir in the rains.

55

Jellaludin

———✦———

Hussein, before he had acquired his elephant, had been a snake-charmer, and at that time he had possessed a mongoose.

Jellaludin, as the mongoose was called, on account of his whiskers, was quite good enough for Hussein's purposes. Hussein became quite attached to Jellaludin, for the mongoose was very intelligent, even if he was somewhat fat and lazy.

In time Jellaludin grew accustomed to Hussein's three tame cobras, all of whom had their fangs drawn, and although the sight of a strange snake made the fur rise all along his back, he quite liked the three lazy old snakes who lived in Hussein's flat-bottomed basket.

During the heat of the summer it was Hussein's custom to follow the white people up to the hill stations, for they always paid well if they were amused.

He did not confine himself to giving performances with his snakes, however; he also used his snake-charming powers to free houses from snakes. He did it in this way: first he would make the acquaintance of some tradesmen who knew all about the white people, and from them Hussein would find out which of the sahibs had wives; then he would go to the houses of these sahibs and bribe the *khansamah* to let him give a performance in the compound.

After the performance he would announce that he felt the presence of snakes in the house itself, and if this made a suitable impression upon the white people, he would offer to come back in the evening to catch the snakes – for a modest fee, of course.

Then he would go round to the servants' quarters, and get them, with a promise of commission, to secrete his tame snakes in the house. One – the largest – he always had put in the bedroom, another in the bathroom, and a third in any conveniently dramatic place. Towards sundown he would return, looking important, with a sack for the snakes, his flute, and Jellaludin.

In the house he would go from room to room, sniffing; when he came to the bedroom he would assure the memsahib that there was a cobra in the room, then he would squat down on the floor and, having produced Jellaludin from a fold inside his voluminous robes, he would play on his squeaky, globular flute, while the mongoose went round and round the walls, sniffing.

When he felt that the tension had reached its climax, Hussein would change his tune, and the well-trained cobra would glide out from beneath the pillow and swell out its hood, hissing furiously. Then Jellaludin, who knew his part quite as well, would dart at the snake and leap at its head; before any harm could be done, however, Hussein would rush at the cobra, and bundle it into his sack.

After he had gone from room to room, and collected his snakes, he could be practically certain of about four rupees from the grateful white people, and more if they were newcomers, but at least half of his reward had to go in commissions to the servants.

When there was a child in the house, however, he could always be sure of at least ten rupees, for if he had heard that there was a child, he would borrow trained snakes from any of the fakirs of his acquaintance who possessed them, so that he could produce as many as ten of the reptiles from all around the child's cot before its parents' horrified eyes. This was particularly well paid, though of course the commissions to the servants and the fakirs were higher.

The only thing that sometimes put Hussein off his stroke on such occasions was Jellaludin, who, though he did his best, could not always distinguish between the strange tame snakes and snakes that he was really supposed to kill; and then towards the end of the performance, when he had apparently slain nearly a dozen snakes to the accompaniment of furious leaping in the air, he became rather tired, owing to his fatness, and he was not quite so spectacular as Hussein might have wished, but on the whole things went off very satisfactorily.

Now it came to Hussein's ears when he was in Simla that the wife of the District Magistrate of Jullundur was known to be extremely fearful of snakes, and that her husband was very wealthy. This he heard from a sunyassi who had borrowed Jellaludin for a day; the mendicant had also remarked that the magistrate had two young children.

So Hussein, who had got all that could be expected in one season from the white people in Simla, packed up his snakes, his flute, and his few other belongings in an ancient piece of cloth, and, calling Jellaludin from under the thatch of the roof, he set off south.

After a certain time had passed he came to Jullundur, where he sought out one of his friends, a sadhu who dealt in curses of all kinds.

From the sadhu Hussein borrowed no less than nine assorted serpents, ranging from a small but venomous *krait* to an immense hamadryad cobra. They were all well trained, and Hussein spent a whole day in getting Jellaludin used to them.

All his usual preliminaries went well, and one evening a week after his arrival in Jullundur he began to extract snakes from the magistrate's house.

He had various less spectacular snakes scattered in the usual places, but he had at least six concealed about the magistrate's children's nursery.

He came to this room last of all, and when he had played his flute for a little while the snakes began to come out into the open. One flopped down from a tear in the ceiling cloth, two more came from a rat hole in a corner, and the great hamadryad came from under one of the cots.

At first everything went well, and Hussein had most of the

snakes in his sack before he noticed that Jellaludin was not doing his part at all well, indeed he looked quite languid.

The mongoose was so slow in dealing with the big cobra that before Hussein could very well say that Jellaludin had finished with it, another snake came out, and the white people, who were looking on, became most uneasy.

Hussein became rather flurried, and before he had dealt with it, the sixth snake came from the hole in the wall where the punkah came through. The white man leapt for his riding crop, and he killed the unfortunate snake by breaking its back. Hurriedly bundling the other two into his sack, Hussein cursed the magistrate bitterly in Urdu.

Unhappily for the snake-charmer, the magistrate knew the tongue perfectly, and replied in the same language; then he clapped his hands to call the servants, whom he told to throw Hussein out of the house.

This was done, and in the doing two of the snakes were hurt. The dead snake was the small blue *krait* belonging to the sadhu; it was said to be valuable on account of the various tricks it could perform. When the sadhu heard of its death, and saw two of his other snakes wounded, he cursed Hussein root and branch; and he also exacted ten rupees by way of compensation.

Hussein blamed Jellaludin bitterly, for if he had done what he had to do quickly, instead of being lazy, everything would have been well, and the white man would have given him at least fifteen rupees, and saying this, Hussein cuffed the mongoose repeatedly, threatening to drown him in a well.

Jellaludin felt the disgrace keenly and went off his feed, with the result that he grew quite thin.

Fortunately Hussein had saved his own three cobras, so he was able to keep going by performing with them, although the sadhu had taken all his resources.

He left Jullundur as soon as possible, and turned up, after wandering for some time, at Benares, where he hoped to pick up some information from the host of mendicants and wandering priests who thronged the holy city.

For two days he sat before the great temple of Kali, speaking with the crowds of assorted fakirs who resorted to it.

On the third day he saw an old friend of his, a sunyassi who cast horoscopes, and from him Hussein learnt that a group of English tourists would be staying at the house of the political officer in one of the small principalities, and that the rajah was going to give them a feast, as they were quite distinguished politicians.

Hussein knew that all kinds of entertainers would be wanted, so he went towards Kapilavatthu, the rajah's capital. On the way he encountered a company of dancers who were going to the same place, so he travelled with them, arriving at Kapilavatthu in a week.

After the feast Hussein gave a performance with his snakes which went off quite well. On the next day he presented himself at the political officer's house, having had ten trained snakes, which he had borrowed, placed in strategic points, and he announced that he would free the house from the snakes which he felt sure were in it.

The Resident had seen it done before, and he had a shrewd idea of how it was worked, but he thought that it would impress his guests, and might even stop the distinguished politicians talking for a little while, so Hussein was admitted.

First he produced snakes from the ceiling cloth – it was very striking to see a fat, writhing cobra wriggling out of the ceiling – and then he piped them out from underneath the white peoples' beds. After that he went to the large, white tiled bathroom, which was the joy of the Resident's heart, where he had his last two snakes concealed.

Hussein, having put them back into his sack, was beginning to make his preparations for departure, when he saw, to his horror, another snake creeping out of the drain-pipe.

It was a great hamadryad cobra, one of the most venomous of snakes. In the hope that it would go back when it saw the people, Hussein kept on piping with his flute; but the cobra came on, and by the time it was half-way out, Jellaludin, who had been sniffing about on the other side of the room, saw it, and darted forward.

Hussein was very much afraid lest Jellaludin should take it for one of the trained snakes, and only nip it gently in the neck, for if it did, the mongoose would undoubtedly be bitten, and if he could not find a certain herb to eat in time, he would certainly die.

This herb is only known to the mongooses, who run to find it if ever they get bitten in a fight with a snake, and when they eat it, it counteracts the poison, and they take no harm.

As soon as Jellaludin got near the snake, he realized that something was wrong, and he danced round on his toes, keeping at a safe distance.

The big cobra came fully out of the drain-pipe, and coiled itself so as to be ready to strike.

The mongoose darted round and round it, drawing slightly nearer. Suddenly the hamadryad struck, missing Jellaludin by an inch. It smacked against the white tiles with a sound of a cracked whip, and the mongoose sprang back out of reach.

Hussein could not go to his help, as the cobra would have bitten him, and he would have died within an hour.

The snake recoiled itself, and Jellaludin began going round it again. It turned steadily, watching for a chance to strike. It thought it saw an opportunity, but the mongoose was out of reach, and as the snake faltered for a split second, Jellaludin leapt at its head. He got a grip on its neck just below the hood – too low down – and the cobra, twisting its head managed to bite Jellaludin twice before its spine was broken.

Without pausing for a moment Jellaludin dropped the inert body, and leapt out of the open window into the garden; he had no time to waste if he was to save his life.

He saw a patch of neglected grass, and darted into it, sniffing eagerly. Soon he found that which he sought, and having eaten the bitter herb, he looked for water.

In the house the white man crushed the cobra's head under the heel of his boot, and Hussein put the body into a bag, for if Jellaludin was still alive he would love the cobra as a meal.

Barely waiting for his money, Hussein hurried out of the house.

He found the mongoose sitting on the gravel drive, licking

the bites. Seeing Hussein he trotted up and jumped on to his shoulder, from whence he crept into the inside pocket in which he always travelled.

Then Hussein knew that all was well, for if the mongoose had been going to die, he would have known it, and crept away to some quiet, dark place to die in peace.

When they reached the house in which he was staying, Hussein produced the dead cobra from the bag, and laid it in a quiet corner.

Jellaludin began at the tail.

56

The Salmon

〰

The salmon leapt again, curving up against the sheer drop of the waterfall. But he fell short, bruising his body against the black rocks: the moon had risen, and it shone on the gleaming scales that the salmon had left on the jutting rocks.

Since noon he had been hurling himself up the stream, striving to pass the salmon-leap into the clear running water which his mate had passed earlier in the day.

Now the fish rested on the gravel, sheltering beneath a shelving stone, his gills opening and closing jerkily; he was nearly exhausted, but a very deep instinct kept him facing the stream. He and his mate had come from the seas, back to this river where they had both begun life as ova.

How they found their way back is a deep mystery, but they had come, driven by a vague, immensely powerful longing that had drawn them through thousands of miles of water, for the purpose of spawning in the quiet, clear water where their ancestors had spawned before them.

After a pause the salmon came out into the swiftly flowing water, forced his way against the stream to the bubbling foot of the fall, and leapt: he fell back once more, and leapt again. Still he could not reach the top, but this time he reached the sacks which the keepers had put over the worst rocks to prevent the noble fish from injuring themselves, so he left no more scales to mark his failure.

PATRICK O'BRIAN

Again and again the perfect arc of his leaping body gleamed in the moonlight.

At last a very clean, high leap brought him over the edge, and he struggled into a deep backwater to recover his strength before pushing on after his mate.

He rested, motionless, on the sand beneath a rock that towered out of the water. For long, quiet hours he stayed there, while the sore places where his scales had been scraped off ceased hurting, and the weariness passed out of his body.

From higher up the stream came the whistling cry of an otter. An owl passed silently over the river, and innumerable little things made tiny noises along the banks.

The moon sank, and the stars swept over the sky. A breeze came with the dawn, and a green light came down through the rocks. The salmon stirred; then he passed into the main stream: a strong motion passed through his body, culminating in a powerful sweep of his tail, and the fish moved up through the water.

After a little the power of the stream slackened, and the salmon went faster. Towards noon he felt hungry and rose at an occasional fly on his way: at one point, where the stream was broad and sluggish, he paused in the eddy made by an old tree stump. From this place he could get any number of flies: some he just engulfed as they floated down: he only leapt now and then for a particularly choice insect.

On the opposite bank a man saw him rise. This man had been fishing since the early morning, but never a fish had risen to his fly.

Now he stiffened with excitement as he saw the big fish rise clear: with sure fingers he knotted a salmon-fly and a length of strong, pliant gut, thin and almost transparent.

He cast, and the fly swung out over the water: after a little while he got his range, and the fly swept over the surface just above the salmon. The fish eyed it, but he did not rise.

There was some little thing wrong with the flight of the fly that aroused his suspicions. It passed over his head again, but he still took no notice; instead he shot half out of the water and

476

took a passing blue-bottle. It tasted rank, and the salmon spat it out again.

Five times the man brought his fly over the eddy where the big fish rested, then he changed it for another.

The salmon half-rose at this new fly, but he checked at the suspicion of the flying line behind it.

After a time a swarm of black flies came down the river: he rose steadily at them, just popping his mouth out of the water, and engulfing them; he selected each one.

He let the false fly pass again and again.

A daddy-longlegs came blundering down about a foot over the surface. The salmon flashed out of the dark eddy: at the same moment the false fly struck him in the side, and he was foul-hooked. The sharp barb jerked into his flesh as he splashed down into the water, with the crane-fly in his mouth

The stabbing pain frightened him for a minute, and he streaked into the open stream.

The man had not seen quite what had happened because of the spray when the fish leapt, but he felt the line tearing through his fingers as the reel spun madly round, and instinctively he lowered the tip of his rod, giving the salmon his head.

Up shot the big fish, a silver streak in the sun, but the man was ready for it, and the line was loose and free. Three times the salmon leapt high out of the water; then he sank to the bottom. The hook was fast in his side, just behind his left pectoral fin.

Cautiously the man wound in his line, but as soon as the salmon felt the slight tug that showed that the line was taut, he shot away up the stream at such a speed that the reel screamed shrilly as the line streaked out again. The fisher followed as well as he could, stumbling over stones in his high boots.

He kept on winding in the line as soon as the salmon stopped.

Suddenly the fish doubled, and set off down stream: the rod bent like a bow, but the line held. The salmon broke the water quite near the man in a tremendous leap. He held his breath – it was the biggest salmon he had ever hooked; he saw that it must weigh a good twenty-five pounds if an ounce. The reel screamed again as the salmon went away up the stream once more. The fish doubled so quickly that the man had no time to reel in his line. The salmon felt that the slight tension was gone, and he sank into a deep hole under a rock to rest. The line grew tight again, and the man tugged gently: the fish did not move.

He dared not pull any harder for fear that the hook might break free, or that the line would go; so the man waited.

There was no sign of movement from beneath the rock for a long time, so the man held the rod in one hand while he groped for some chocolate in his breast pocket with the other. He ate it warily, ready to drop it and use both hands if the salmon stirred, but it did not.

At last he bent down and searched for a stone in the river bed: he kept his eyes on the rock, but his fingers found a good-sized pebble. He threw it carefully, so that it fell almost on top of the salmon: he threw another, and another. The third touched the fish, and it sped away across the stream.

The fight began again: all the time the man let the salmon have its head when it rushed up and down the stream, but as soon as the power of the fish slackened, the tension of the thin line pulled it in towards him.

Again and again the fish leapt, trying to break the line, and many times he tried to get it round a tree stump or rock so as to cut it, but always the angler's cunning foiled him.

At length the salmon grew so tired that he floated on his side, and the man wound the line gently in.

It was going to be a devil of a job to land a twenty-five pounder single-handed, but the man had his gaff ready, and as he was quite near the bank he felt sure that he could do it, particularly as he thought the salmon was played right out.

The salmon, as he lay limp on his side, felt strength coming back: he let the man pull him in until the last moment, when the gaff was stretched out over him – the steel red in the setting sun.

Then, with all his strength, the salmon leapt; the reel whirred for a second, and ceased abruptly – the line had broken.

The splash as the fish fell back seemed to come some time

later: it sprayed the man. The salmon, exhausted again by this effort, floated down the stream on his side, his eyes glazed and his gills open. The man waded in up to his waist and took a last chance with his gaff, but he slipped on a turning stone, and only grazed the salmon's side. The fish dived to the bottom, where he stayed for about an hour, when he went back to the dark hole to rest.

The man recovered his tackle and went home, dog-tired.

That night a pair of otters came down the river. They drove before them a young salmon. They swam as fast as the fish, but they could not turn so quickly, and sometimes they had to rise for air. One swam by the dark hole, silver bubbles flying from his fur, but the salmon in the shadows stayed still, and they passed him by.

The younger fish fled on down the stream until the otters were very close upon him, then he doubled and swam with all his speed back to the hole that he had noticed as he flashed down the river.

The gliding black shapes of the otters followed close behind him, and the larger salmon, seeing that the hiding place was dis-covered, shot away across the stream to the shade of some rocks.

He tried to shake off the younger salmon, who swam beside him, hoping that the otters would hunt the larger game.

But they did not: the smaller fish was harried away into the shallow water, where they settled him in a flurry of spray.

Then the otters carried their prey away to a flat rock. They only ate the best meat from the top of the neck – the rest of the salmon they left.

Meanwhile the first salmon pushed on up the stream: he knew that they would come back.

He came to another salmon-leap, but they had put padded rungs on this one, so he soon passed it into the higher water.

He was now in the higher reaches of the river, where there were clean sandy stretches suitable for spawning.

In the morning he found his mate.

57

Cheetah

———— ⚬⚬⚬ ————

I

Behind the great stables of the palace of a Rajah of one of the smaller Rajput states lay the quarters where lived the hawks, hounds, cheetahs, and other animals used for hunting. The men who looked after them lived in little huts round about, or in lofts over them; of these men, the only one who had not inherited his office from his father and grandfather was Hussein, who was therefore despised.

Indeed, Hussein had only been able to enter the Rajah's service by means of his elephant, Jehangir. Being unable to afford to feed Jehangir, Hussein had gone to the keeper of the Rajah's elephants, and, in return for his appointment, had left Jehangir to be used by the keeper of the elephants, provided always that he was well fed and looked after, and that he remained Hussein's property.

From his childhood Hussein had always had a way with animals, so he soon made friends with the young hunting-leopard that was to be his charge. At first all the other men looked on Hussein with enmity, for they regarded him an interloper; moreover, they were all Hindus but one, whereas Hussein was – nominally, at any rate – a Moslem. The one exception was a very old man indeed, a Mohammedan, who looked after one of the many cheetahs. The old man had four wives, one of whom – the latest and youngest – found favour in Hussein's eyes. She was the daughter of a Bikaneeri camel-man, who had given her to her

480

husband as part payment of a debt. She was a Mohammedan, but she wore a very light chuddar; her name was Fatima.

She and Hussein often talked over the balcony which ran along the back of the zenana. Hussein learnt that the old man was completely under the domination of his third wife, a very strict woman who would not let him take the opium to which he was addicted. She was furious if her husband ever took any notice of his other wives, and frequently threatened to poison them. Moreover, she controlled her husband's money, and would never allow him enough to buy opium. The old man was curiously terrified of this wife's displeasure, and though in a weak way he hated her for her strong will, he loved her as well.

Hussein wished to learn all that was necessary to train a hunting-leopard to provide good sport, and as no one would treat him as anything but an outsider, he decided to learn from the old man, and to bribe him, if necessary, with opium.

The next day when the cheetahs were being exercised Hussein walked in front of the old man, and ostentatiously dropped one of those little heart-shaped brass boxes with various compartments in which one carries hashish, bhang, betel-nut, or opium, according to one's taste. Picking it up, he let fall a few opium pills. At the time Yussuf – for that was the old man's name – said nothing, but in the evening he said to Hussein, 'I have a cheetah collar for which I have no further need: it would fit your cheetah perfectly.' And with this he scratched himself with an embarrassed air.

'Alas,' replied Hussein, squatting down before the cages, 'I am a poor man, and although I know that Shaitan needs a new collar, I am too needy to supply him with one fitting a cheetah of his quality; also I am a timorous man, and I dare not apply to the chief hunter for money, for he is prone to wrath.'

'Now I see that you are a deserving man, and modest,' said Yussuf, 'so I shall give you this collar. It is a poor gift, although the discerning eye might find some small merit in the chasing of the brass ring that encircles it. Indeed, now that I compare the unworthiness of the collar with the manifest excellence of the one to whom I address myself, I am overcome with shame to such

an extent that I can no longer think of offering you this bauble –
although it has a certain mere commercial value – as a gift.'

'Yet assuredly this would be a royal gift,' said Hussein uneasily.

'Even so,' replied the old man, 'but it is unworthy of you. However, I see a way out of the difficulty: in order to show the lack
of worth of this collar, I will exchange it with you for a certain
trumpery brass box which I saw you drop this morning.'

Without more words Hussein produced the box. Yussuf's eyes
gleamed, and he stretched out his hand.

'But I forgot,' said Hussein, as if moved by an afterthought;
'I have left certain pills in this box; I will remove them.'

'Pray do not trouble yourself,' stammered the old man eagerly;
'they may assuage various pangs that I feel after having partaken
too freely of dates.'

'But these pills are of no value for such pangs. They are more
concerned with giving ease to the mind, being made of opium.'
There was a pause as Hussein transferred them to another box.
Yussuf's face fell as he saw the last pill go, and he said with a
melancholy air, 'The Prophet never forbade its use; he only
referred to intoxicating liquors.'

'Allah's curse on all unbelievers,' said Hussein, conventionally.

'Just so,' replied the old man firmly, thinking of his third wife,
'but perhaps one of these pills might help a peculiarly heavy feeling that I can discern in my head.'

'It is possible,' said Hussein, handing him one, 'yet it may have
strange effects, such as producing hallucinations, or even boils.'

'Nevertheless,' replied Yussuf, swallowing the pill contentedly,
'it is good to mortify the flesh. My father told me that in Udaipur
he once saw a remarkably holy dervish completely covered with
boils. This holy man, dying became a famous *pir*, and the devout
still flock in great numbers to his tomb.'

'*Allahu akbar*,' said Hussein, and unrolled his rug towards
Mecca, for the sun was setting, and the hour of the evening prayer
was at hand.

After they had prayed, Hussein blew gently upon his smoul-
dering fire, and fanned it into a blaze, for the nights were cold at

that season. They made themselves comfortable about the fire, and Hussein led the conversation to the subject of cheetahs. Long into the night the old man spoke on their correct training, and on the way in which they should be made to hunt.

The one pill that Hussein had given him was not sufficient to send him off into a coma, for he had a strong head, but it was enough to loosen his tongue, and Hussein, listening eagerly, learnt a great deal.

The next evening Yussuf came again, and Hussein gave him another pill, and they talked until the moon set, when the old man, having taken a second pill when Hussein was not looking, went to sleep. Hussein had to carry him back to his house, where he pushed him gently through an open window. After that he was more careful, and kept Yussuf strictly to one pill an evening.

As time went on, it became the accepted thing for Yussuf to spend his evening with Hussein. To the questions of his third wife, the old man replied that he and Hussein discussed grave matters of the law of Islam, and that it was correct that the only two Mohammedans among the hunters should help one another as much as possible. In this way Hussein learnt a great many things about his new craft, and by the time the season for hunting gazelles came round, he felt confident that both he and Shaitan would do as well as most. Shaitan was a good-looking young cheetah with a very affectionate way about him; indeed, he was more like a dog than a cat. When he was still he looked a gawky beast, with legs too long for his body, but when he got into action all his clumsiness disappeared, and when he was going at his top speed there was nothing on four legs that he could not catch. Of course, the hunting-leopard could not keep up this great speed for long, so it was essential that he should be brought as close as possible to his quarry before being unleashed. It was in this that the skill and cunning of the hunter told, for a clumsy man could frighten an entire herd of gazelle by a false move, and a whole day's hunt would be spoiled.

The cheetahs were usually used to hunt gazelle, as very great speed was necessary to run them down, and no hound could get near them. But sometimes they were set at larger deer, or even at bustards.

The keepers of the hunting-leopards were divided into those who concealed themselves at some distance from the quarry, and let the cheetah stalk it down and hunt it in its own way; and those who led the cheetah, hooded and leashed, as near as possible to the quarry, and then released it to run it down in full view of the hidden spectators.

The first was the safer method, for the tawny, spotted leopard could find cover very easily; moreover, a cheetah would naturally be a better hunter than a man. But the second way was more spectacular, for the hunter, if he were skilful, could rely on the unhooded cheetah giving chase at full speed, whereas one who had stalked its own prey might easily leap at it from a bush, and the thrill of the hunt would be lost.

II

There was an immense plain near the Rajah's summer palace, which was one of the biggest preserves for gazelle and larger antelope in Rajputana.

One day at the beginning of the season all the court moved out to the summer palace, and towards the end of the baggage train the cheetahs with their keepers travelled in bullock carts. Hussein left Shaitan in the charge of Yussuf, and walked by the side of Jehangir, who might otherwise have been worried by the tumult and the noise. He spent a good deal of time every day with Jehangir, for neither of them had very much to do.

When everything had arrived at the summer palace, and Hussein had seen that both Jehangir and Shaitan were comfortable, he joined Yussuf, and they went in the company of the rest of the hunters to the great plains where the gazelles were to be found, for there was to be a hunt on the next day, and it was necessary for each man to know the place where he should hide.

The men disposed themselves cunningly among the bushes so as not to disturb the feeding deer, and they whispered together.

'It seems to me,' said Yussuf, 'that the gazelle are more timorous than formerly, and more watchful.'

'Perhaps the villagers have been harrying them.'

'After what happened last year, they would never dare to come within miles of the preserves.'

'That is true; it is more probable that the leopards have increased. I saw three half-grown cubs last year, but Khem Singh would not let me shoot them, saying that they would provide sport for the Rajah when they grew up.'

'Khem Singh is the son of a noseless mother: he thinks of nothing but the honour that he will obtain by driving out his leopards to be shot. He never considers us.'

'*Inshalla*! But did you hear the tale that is told of his wife's cousin?'

'A jocose tale; but I heard a better concerning his second son's third wife . . .'

At length the plans for the hunt were completed, and it was decided that some picked deer should be quietly separated from the herd, and driven across the plain opposite the Rajah's stand. At various points the cheetahs would be concealed, one for each beast.

The next day Hussein rose early with the rest of the hunters and went to his appointed place. He led Shaitan by a leash.

From his place Hussein could see down the bush-covered slope to the sandy plain, and over it to the belt of trees where the spectators were. He squatted down in a thicket; Shaitan sat by him, sniffing the air eagerly. They could not see a sign of the other hunters, but Hussein knew that old Yussuf was a little way to his right, and another man to the left.

For some time nothing happened, and Hussein settled down comfortably in the little grass-lined hollow that he had made for himself the day before. He stared vaguely out over the bushes, and tickled Shaitan's ear. All at once something in the bushes lower down the slope caught his eye; he looked more closely, and saw a tawny beast creeping flat on its belly between the bushes. At first he thought that it must be one of the cheetahs, but soon he saw that it was larger and more thick-set; then he realized that it was a wild leopard.

He watched it for some time before he was convinced; then, when he was sure that he was not mistaken, he decided to creep along to Yussuf, who would know what to do. If the leopard were left undisturbed it might spoil the day's sport by taking one of the gazelles and heading off the rest.

Hussein put the hood on his cheetah's head and tied the leash to a sapling. Then he began to crawl towards Yussuf. But by the time he was half-way there the gazelle had come into that part of the plain that lay between the slope and the trees. Hussein was in a particularly exposed position; there was no good cover for yards, and if he moved or made a noise the gazelle would certainly be headed back.

He crouched quite still, pressed against the ground. The little deer were uneasy, but not alarmed; they were trotting in fairly close formation towards a patch of tall grass some way to Hussein's right.

From the corner of his eye he could see that Yussuf had unleashed his cheetah, which was creeping down to the quarry.

Suddenly he saw three of the other cheetahs break cover and dash into the open. The gazelle were flying before them right past the leopard, going at a tremendous speed, with the cheetahs gaining a little. They were all quite close together. All at once the leopard gave a loud, hoarse scream, and leapt into the midst of them. At first nothing could be seen for the dust, and then Yussuf's cheetah shot away from the bushes and charged at the cloud of dust.

At its first leap the leopard had knocked one of the long-legged cheetahs over, and had cannoned into another. Instantly they all set upon the leopard, who disabled two so quickly that Hussein could hardly see what had happened to them before they fell.

Yussuf had not seen the leopard, and could not see it for the dust. He thought that the cheetahs were fighting among themselves, so he caught up his staff and ran down to separate them.

The leopard had dealt with three of its slighter adversaries before Yussuf reached them, so it was free to spring at the man. Hussein, following close behind, snatched up a stone, which he flung at the leopard, hitting it in the side; at the same time he hit it on the head with his staff, which broke in his hand. The leopard sprang. The old man went down heavily, striking his head against a stone. Hussein tripped over a root, and fell full on to the leopard, which turned under him.

For a second both were too stunned to do anything; then Hussein seized the leopard's throat and squeezed it with all his strength. The leopard grunted, and jerked convulsively to free its legs, which were under Hussein's body. At first they were entangled in the clothes, and Hussein pressed himself as hard as he could on to the leopard to keep them there. But there was a rending sound as its hind feet kicked free: Hussein felt its claws tearing the flesh of his thighs, and he crushed the throat between his hands furiously. For a moment he could hear the choked sound of the leopard's breathing, and the ripping of its claws.

The sinewy body beneath him writhed and jerked powerfully; the forefeet came into play.

Then others ran up; the Rajah himself shot the leopard through the head, and someone pulled Yussuf from beneath the two. He was half stunned, but not seriously hurt.

Hussein was in a worse way, and they had to carry him home in a litter. By the time he reached his quarters Yussuf was quite recovered, and he swore that Hussein had saved his life, saying, 'See what men are the faithful! What lions of the desert! Allah's curse on all unbelievers. By my father's beard, we shall be blood-brothers, and my women shall nurse him. *Inshallah!*' And although he was old enough to be Hussein's father, he performed the ceremony that made them blood-brothers, and took him into his own house, where his women, especially his third wife, who was grateful – for she loved her husband – and his fourth wife, Fatima, nursed him until his wounds were healed.

They sent for a famous hakim from Dacca, who gave Hussein a stewed toad garnished with texts from the Koran, and the Rajah sent his own physician, a Scotsman, who applied antiseptics, which were carefully wiped off as soon as he departed.

In spite of his doctors, however, Hussein recovered. When he was walking about again he was sent for by the Rajah, who had been greatly impressed by the incident, especially by his own part in it. At this time there were a number of Englishmen visiting the state, and the Rajah wished to show his own magnanimity, kindness, and other virtues, so Hussein was brought in, dressed magnificently in a gold-embroidered robe lent for the occasion. He knelt before the throne – the Englishmen and the rest of the court were on either side of it – and the court poet recited a long poem in Persian describing the deed – particularly the Rajah's part in it.

Then the prince drew a ring from his finger and threw it to Hussein, who uttered a long blessing on the royal house and its heroic head, giving all the credit for slaying the leopard to the Rajah.

The Rajah, who was in a good temper that day, was delighted when he saw that his visitors were impressed, and he said to his treasurer who stood behind the throne, 'Fill this good man's mouth with gold.' The treasurer looked rather sour at this, for finances were low as usual, but he pulled a fat purse from his waist and came to Hussein.

Hussein opened his mouth as wide as possible, and pressed his tongue down to make more room. The treasurer, a Bengali Brahmin, drew some coins from his purse and put them in; Hussein saw that they were copper, but he dared not say anything, contenting himself with glaring reproachfully at the treasurer. The latter, looking distinctly less bitter, filled the open mouth and retired.

Hussein closed his mouth with some difficulty, and struck his head on the ground three times before shuffling out backwards on his knees, according to the custom of the court.

Nevertheless, he was consoled by the fact that the treasurer had accidentally slipped in a gold mohur among the rest, and that the Rajah's ring was of good red gold, with a small, but sound, ruby in it.

58

The Snow Leopard

———— ⌘ ————

Bhotia paused, wiped away the sweat that trickled down his face, and bent again. He was cutting sweet grass for fodder against the autumn.

His kukri slashed into the tall, luxuriant swathes; at last he had got enough, and he tied it into a huge bundle with a withy. Then he set off for his house far up the slope of the kol.

It was half-way up one of those huge ravines that one finds all over Nepal. The rivers from the Himalayas cut tremendously deep gorges as they come down in spate with the melting snow from the lower slopes; on the higher slopes the snow never melts at all.

The little Gurkha staggered along under his huge load until he came to the stream where Dhorgoshi, his son, was waiting with another load.

Together they made their way up the great hill; as they went up and up they got free of the tropical heat of the deep valley, and they breathed more easily, for they were hill-men, and they loved the bite of the wind that came straight out of the Himalayas.

There was an amazing difference in the country as they got higher, for in a few miles it changed from the tropical jungle of the deep valley to the thin forest of the foothills; after they had gone up through the forest they came into the bare hill country where their home was.

There was another valley between them and the house, but in the thin clear air they could see right across very plainly. As

Bhotia let his load down on a rock he pointed; there were several ponies and mules outside their house.

'Is it Chetwynd sahib already?' asked Dhorgoshi.

'It must be; he has come quickly.'

They had not expected the Englishman for another day.

He was a soldier, very keen on hunting, who came up into the Himalayas every year, and always Bhotia was his shikari. Chetwynd was in a Gurkha regiment, and Bhotia had served under him in the Great War and in innumerable little frontier wars; they got on very well together, for they respected one another.

When they got across the valley they found Major Chetwynd waiting for them. After greetings had been exchanged – they were always the same, the ceremony never altered – Major Chetwynd said, 'You've grown, Dhorgoshi.'

'Yes, sahib, I am a man now' replied the boy.

It was Dhorgoshi's great ambition to go into the high hills as gun-bearer with his father and Chetwynd sahib; he had persuaded his father that he was old enough now, and it only remained for Chetwynd to give his permission.

Bhotia broached the subject in the evening: 'My worthless son wants to come with us, sahib,' he said. 'He will not be in the way, and he might be useful; I have taught him what little I know of shikar.'

'But surely he is over-young?'

'I was a man at his age, and I had killed a black bear with my kukri.'

Dhorgoshi's heart stood still while the major filled and lit his pipe; he could not speak in the presence of his elders. Then Chetwynd spoke between the puffs of smoke.

'Well, all right; I don't want to have a fellow I don't know.'

Dhorgoshi swelled with joy, but he said nothing.

Early next morning the preparations began; the bearers were sent back to Khatmandu, and the barest necessities were packed on to a wiry little hill pony. The kit was given a final overhaul, and in the afternoon they set out.

Every season Chetwynd went far up into the hills to a certain remote village, which he used as a base camp; some of the supplies had been sent up there earlier in the year, and they were in charge of Bhotia's cousin, who lived there.

It was an ideal country for record heads, because practically nobody hunted there. It is extremely difficult to get permission even to pass through Nepal, much less hunt in it, but Major Chetwynd had done the Rajah a good turn once, so he always got his permit.

Eventually they reached Khala Dyong, perched high up above the snowline, and so far north as to be practically in Tibet. The people were a strange mixture of Tibetans, Ghurkas, Mongols, and Chinese. Every year caravans would come down through the passes from Lhasa and beyond; one had been gone only a few days when Chetwynd arrived.

A merchant, who knew the Englishman, had left word of a great snow-leopard that had taken a yak half a day's journey north.

'I wonder,' he said to Bhotia, 'whether that is the same beast that took the big markhor we had trailed half the day.'

'I remember, sahib: his right fore-pad was scarred, so that the pug-mark had a clear line running across it.'

'You're right. It is very probably the same one; there would hardly be two of that size in the same place. We'll go after him to-morrow, if we can pick up a spoor.'

The next day, however, Bhotia's cousin reported some fine heads of ibex, and Chetwynd decided to go after them first.

They set out at dawn, and they found fresh slots quite soon. Bhotia said, looking at the tracks, that there was one really big male – possibly a record head – and four females, one of whom had a kid.

After more than an hour's patient tracking they rested under a great bare rock, and fed. Dhorgoshi took his food to the top of the rock, which was stuck in the side of a great valley, and squatted there.

Far across the bare rock and snow he saw something move. In the clear air he could see very clearly for a great distance.

Shading his eyes from the glare of the snow, he looked long and steadily at the moving shape. It moved up on to a hillock, and then it stood out clearly; it was an ibex, and even from where he was, Dhorgoshi could see that it carried a fine sweeping pair of horns.

Quietly he dropped down, and pulled at his father's sleeve. Bhotia looked where his son pointed, but he saw nothing, nor did Chetwynd until he took his field-glasses; then he said, 'Dhorgoshi's right, Bhotia – take a look.'

Bhotia took the glasses. 'What a head, sahib!' he exclaimed. 'We must get him.'

They stalked the ibex for an hour before they got within range. The big male was standing clear against the sky-line when they reached the other side of the valley. Very slowly Chetwynd raised his rifle; he took long and careful aim. A split second before he fired the ibex moved, and the bullet missed by a few inches. He sprang to his feet as the ibex was disappearing, and took a snap shot. There was absolute silence as they stood staring over the snow; then the echoes of the shots came back, one after the other.

They scrambled up the slope to the place where the ibex had stood. The goat's tracks were there, clear and fresh, but of the ibex itself there was no sign. It was as if it had dissolved into the snow.

On a rock Bhotia saw a spot of blood; he pointed without speaking. Chetwynd nodded, and they all set off along a high ridge in the direction in which the tracks led. Before long they came to a place where a glacier had cut a great furrow in the mountain-side. There was a fairly wide ledge of bare rock along the side of the precipice.

There was nothing to show whether the ibex had passed that way or not, but they followed the ledge along. It was strewn with great boulders, but the hillmen went right over them, and Chetwynd followed.

It was very tricky climbing, because there was a drop of several hundred feet down to the bottom of the ravine on one side and a sheer wall of rock on the other. Chetwynd scoured the ravine with his field-glasses, but he saw nothing. Then Bhotia found another splash of blood; it was fresh, so the ibex must have gone that way.

They pressed on, panting in the thin air. At last they caught sight of their quarry. The ibex was standing on the top of a boulder, watching them. As soon as they stopped it leapt clear over the edge of the precipice. It seemed as though there was no foothold for a fly, but the ibex leapt from rock to rock, standing on space no larger than a man's hand, and leaping down and down until it was out of sight in the narrow valley.

'Can we get down, do you think?' asked Chetwynd.

'Impossible; but we can climb up to the top of the ravine, and perhaps you can get a shot from there.'

'Right! Can you manage, Dhorgoshi?'

'Yes, sahib.'

It was a very stiff climb to the top; one slip would mean a fall and certain death.

Dhorgoshi gritted his teeth and forced himself not to look down. As he paused, spread-eagled on the almost sheer rock, he felt something very like panic, but he fought it down, and began to climb again. His foot could not find the hold it sought, and for a moment he thought he would have to disgrace himself and go down again. Then he felt Chetwynd's hand round his ankle, guiding his foot to the little ledge.

After that it was fairly plain going, and they reached the snow again in a few minutes. Chetwynd nodded to Bhotia and smiled. 'That was rather an anxious few minutes,' he said. 'I wasn't sure that I could make it at one time.'

Dhorgoshi loved him for not mentioning that missing foothold, and for acknowledging that it was a stiff climb. He tried to look unconcerned, but he felt his heart still hammering.

From where they were they could see the ibex standing behind a rock half-way up the other side of the ravine. Only its unmistakable horns and its hindquarters were visible, so Chetwynd decided not to risk a shot. They waited for the goat to move, but it did not, so they sat and ate some of the food that

Dhorgoshi carried. Suddenly Bhotia stiffened, looking fixedly at something at the bottom of the ravine.

'What do you see?!' asked the Englishman.

'I am not sure,' replied Bhotia. 'May I have the glasses, sahib?'

He looked again, and then handed Chetwynd the glasses.

'By gosh, it's a snow-leopard' he said after a moment. 'Have a look, Dhorgoshi.'

The young Gurkha looked, and he saw the snow-leopard creeping along from rock to rock towards the ibex. The long, thick, yellowish fur, spotted with black, toned in with the rocks and snow perfectly, but with the field-glasses Dhorgoshi could see that the snow-leopard was a huge beast – large even for the snow-leopards of those parts, which ran almost to the size of tigers.

'I'll bet a year's pay that it's the same beast that took our markhor last year,' said Chetwynd. 'It was just about here.'

He watched intently for some time, and then he took the cartridges from his rifle, slipping in another sort. 'I wish I had some heavier stuff,' he said, 'but I think this should stop him.' He lay down so as to get more certain aim.

'A very long shot, sahib,' whispered Bhotia. 'It will drop, and the wind is coming down the ravine.'

Dhorgoshi waited, the tip of his tongue protruding. He fixed his eyes on the slowly moving leopard.

The shot parted crisp and clear; the leopard jumped high into the air, coming down out of sight behind a rock; the ibex leapt away in a flurry of snow, and vanished.

Dhorgoshi bit his tongue. They hurried down into the ravine, scrambling down in the snow, and climbing more carefully among the rocks. They had had to go a good way along the ledge before they found a place where they could get down, so when they reached the other side of the ravine at last, none of them was sure just where was the rock behind which the leopard had fallen.

They climbed up to the level of the place where the ibex had been standing, and they worked along from there. The black rocks among the snow were all very much alike, but at length they found another ravine, much smaller, but quite deep, and very dark.

'He is probably down there,' said Chetwynd.

'Perhaps we . . .' Bhotia was saying; but his words were cut off by a great coughing roar behind them. The snow-leopard, very much alive, crouched for a second, its thick tail lashing; then it charged. Bhotia was knocked against a rock and half stunned. He knocked his son over, and Dhorgoshi scrambled to his feet, spitting out snow, to see Chetwynd lying under the snow-leopard.

Dhorgoshi tugged out his kukri and threw himself on the snow-leopard's back. He hacked with all his force at the neck. One blow was enough; the heavy razor-sharp knife went half through the thick neck. With a convulsive bound the snow-leopard leapt clear, and lay against a rock twitching.

Chetwynd, unhurt, reached his rifle in a second, and put a bullet through its head. Then he turned to Dhorgoshi, and held out his hand. Bhotia staggered up, beaming all over his face.

'I said he was a man, sahib,' he said.

59

Giant Panda

───❊───

Where the snow-crust was thin, bamboo shoots thrust themselves up into the sun. A vague shape moved about among them. All that was visible of the animal from a distance was disconnected black patches; indeed, the giant panda might have been so many stones naked in the snow; only when it moved did its great, bear-like form reveal itself.

The giant panda, a vegetarian epicure, shuffled slowly about, choosing the tenderest shoots: they were sweet and juicy, the sun shone brilliantly from the western verge of an immaculate blue sky, the great Himalayan peaks cast still greater violet shadows across the perfect snow.

Placid contentment had filled the panda all the while it was feeding: this content was suddenly marred as the panda caught an alien scent among that of the bharals that had been there some time before. It was a scent that the panda could not connect with anything that it had ever seen; it evoked no mind picture of any animal, yet it was disturbing.

Only recently had the panda come across this scent: sometimes it had come on the wind, and sometimes directly from curious tracks, wholly unlike those of any of the animals that the panda knew and accepted as part of the world: the scent was as disturbing as that of a snow-leopard, or of the pair of tigers who sometimes hunted right up into the snows – great, hungry, long-furred tigers whom the panda always avoided by miles when they came among the bamboo-groves.

The scent came, in point of fact, from a certain Bhotka, a hunter.

Bhotka, while the panda fed, was watching from behind some rocks; there was a considerable distance between them, but the exceptional clarity of the mountain air in the spring made it seem less.

Bhotka had heard of the great pandas: they were almost legendary among the villages sparsely dotted about the snow-fed rivers, but very few men had ever seen them, and many disbelieved in them altogether. Bhotka had, hitherto, relegated them in his own mind to the same category as the 'abominable snow-men' occupied – devilish beasts that undoubtedly existed, but not for ordinary men.

It was springtime, and the panda felt curiously irritable at times: it felt that its meal had been spoilt. The scent, which drifted low across the snow-crust, came from the track left by the hunter as he had followed the bharals up into the higher snows earlier in the day. The men of the villages from which Bhotka came were universally opposed to washing, holding it to be effeminate and unlucky, so the scent was an easy one to follow.

The panda had nothing more than a vague idea of finding out what it was that had walked among the young bamboos, yet even this curiosity was unusual in the panda, for ordinarily it was an animal that desired nothing more than to be left alone, and to leave everything else alone. It moved effortlessly and rapidly up the great slope; its gait appeared clumsy and even awkward, but in reality it was admirably adapted for the panda's line of country.

Bhotka had lost sight of the panda soon after it had left the bamboo, for a high ridge came between him and the farther slope. Suddenly the giant panda appeared over the crest of the ridge rather less than a quarter of a mile away. Its size quite paralysed Bhotka; as it came nearer its eyes, each ringed with a monocle of black fur, seemed to stare straight at him.

The hunter gave vent to a kind of bellowing moan and ran very rapidly away from the rocks where he had hidden. He was a brave man, and would have faced a snow-leopard with comparative equanimity, but this was too much for him altogether – it smacked of the supernatural.

The giant panda, intensely surprised, sat up for a moment like a bear, to see better; Bhotka flung one terrified glance behind him, and saw the great bulk of the giant panda upright against the setting sun.

The hunter ran like one hag-ridden until he came, gasping and groaning, more dead than alive, into his own village, where, when he had recovered somewhat, had poured out a truly marvelous tale – a tale that kept the children inside the huts for weeks, and made the hunters go out in groups of three or four for a considerable time.

Bhotka's tale suitably embroidered, spread among the villages, and travelled until it was picked up by a caravan of Mongols, who heard it at their camp fires while their camels shivered and snarled all round them.

Time passed, and the tale came to Peshawar, and to the ears of the English there. Somehow it still retained a part of that frenzied sincerity with which Bhotka had poured it out in the first place, and it carried conviction to one Fenwick, a great shikari, who was the fortunate possessor of a very considerable fortune.

Now it happened, by a curious quirk of fate, that a little before he heard the tale, Fenwick had been jilted good and hard, and he had taken it very much to heart: being nothing if not conventional, Fenwick instantly decided to get all the leave he possibly could, and to go and see if he could pot a giant panda, for so he correctly assumed Bhotka's snow-devil to be. He talked with several people who knew the country where the rare beasts were found, and one of them said that he knew of the village from which Bhotka came; this man said that it was considerably nearer India than the known haunts of the giant pandas, but he also said that that did not militate against its probability, for so little was known about them that it was impossible definitely to lay down any sort of boundaries for their country.

Fenwick also came across a body of scientific men, who had

come to India for a most learned society to take photographs of various rare species; these men, first one at a time and then altogether, begged Fenwick not to pot a giant panda if he found one, but to take films of it, or at the very least, to film it before killing it.

Fenwick pushed off early one morning, with all his usual impediments, and a small film camera as well.

In the high snows, while tales of its dreadfulness circulated among the villages, the giant panda and its mate made their home in a different cave a good way away from the place where Bhotka had seen it, for the incident had upset the panda, and as they both valued their solitude above all other things, they avoided the place.

As the warm weather came on, innumerable little streams flowed down to swell the rivers, which became torrents, and the young bamboo, on which the giant pandas fed, unlike their carnivorous ancestors, shot up apace. The pandas found plenty of good feeding places, and after a certain period had passed the she-panda gave birth to three cubs.

The ibex and the blue sheep and the shas came down from the high snows to find the tender young grasses and sweet herbs that grew wherever the streams ran. The little red pandas ran among the bamboo groves; they were not very much like their giant cousins, being much smaller and, moreover, they had tails, but they had the same type of head as greater pandas, and they had the same round faces.

To the very desolate country where the giant pandas lived, a snow-leopard came, because many markhors came there in the rutting season.

News of Fenwick's coming went before him, and it came to Bhotka, who travelled many days to offer himself as a guide or a gun-bearer, partly because he knew that the white men paid very well, and partly because he felt that he had lost prestige by running away from the giant panda. Fenwick welcomed him, because he was the first who brought him any definite news of the quarry he sought.

499

The snow-leopard had poorer hunting than it had expected in its new terrain, and it took to going down to the villages to raid the herds of little black cows that were kept there.

After a while it found a mate, and they made their lair in a cave a few miles from the pandas' cave. When the cub was old enough to travel, the giant pandas moved farther away from the snow-leopards, so that when Fenwick came to the place where Bhotka had seen the giant panda, there was not the least trace of it for miles around.

Very patiently Fenwick searched for some sign of his quarry, and he sent men out to seek among the bamboo groves for the panda's droppings, but there was no success. At last Fenwick began to give up hope, and decided to confine himself to getting a record ibex head, for when he had been looking for the giant panda, he had seen many fine heads.

Accordingly he and Bhotka went away early one morning, following a fresh trail; from the tracks it was obvious that there was one really big male and four females, one of whom had a kid. Afternoon came, and they rested under a great bare rock, and fed. When he had finished his food, Fenwick stood up to stretch; just as he stood up he saw something move in the distance.

Shading his eyes from the glare of the sun upon the snow, he looked long and steadily at the moving shape; it moved up on to a hillock, and then it stood out clearly; it was an ibex. He took his field glasses, and then he saw that the ibex carried a truly noble sweep of horns. Quietly he dropped down, and showed it to Bhotka, then they began stalking it.

It was more than two hours before they got within range. The big male was standing clear against the skyline when they reached the other side of the valley. Very slowly Fenwick raised his rifle; he took long and carful aim. A split second before he fired the ibex moved, and the bullet missed by a few inches. He sprang to his feet as the ibex was disappearing, and took a snap shot.

There was absolute silence as they stood staring over the snow; then the echoes of the shots came back, one after the other. They scrambled up the slope to the place where the ibex had stood. The goat's tracks were there, clear and fresh, but of the ibex themselves there was no sign. It was as if they had dissolved into the snow.

On a rock Bhotka saw a spot of blood; he pointed to it without speaking.

Fenwick nodded, and they set off along a high ridge in the direction of the tracks. Before long they came to a place where a glacier had cut a great furrow in the mountain. There was a fairly wide ledge of rock along the side of the precipice. There was nothing to show whether the ibex had passed that way or not, but they followed the ledge along.

Great boulders lay along it, but the Hillman went right over them, and Fenwick forced himself to follow, although they were coated with ice. It was very tricky climbing, because there was a drop of about two hundred feet to the bottom of the ravine on the one side, and a sheer wall of rock where the precipice towered up on the other.

However, they found another splash of blood, and that gave them heart. They pushed on, panting in the thin air; at last they caught sight of their quarry again. The ibex was standing on the top of a boulder, watching them. As soon as they stopped, it leapt clean over the edge of the precipice.

It seemed that there was no foothold for a fly, and Fenwick looked to see the ibex dashed to pieces, but it leapt down and down, standing now on a piece of jutting rock no larger than a baby's hand, and now on a crumbling piece of ice. Down and down it went until it was out of sight in the narrow valley.

The men could not possibly get down, so they climbed up to the top of the ravine in the hope that they might get a shot down. It was a very difficult and dangerous piece of mountaineering, but they did it, and from the top they could see the ibex standing behind a rock half-way up the other side of the ravine. Only its unmistakable horns and its hindquarters were visible, so Fenwick decided not to risk a shot.

They waited for the goat to move, and had some more food. Suddenly Bhotka stiffened, looking fixedly at something on the glacier at the bottom of the ravine; it was a snow-leopard –

the same snow-leopard that had annoyed the giant panda – and it was creeping flat on its belly towards the ibex. Through the glasses Fenwick could see that it was a huge beast, running almost to the size of a tiger.

The ibex caught the snow-leopard's scent, and leapt nervously on top of a rock, where it stood sniffing the wind. Fenwick took aim and fired; the shot parted crisp and clear, and the ibex fell off the rock; then it got to its feet, scrambled a little way, and fell again. It lay quite still.

The men ran along the edge of the ravine until they came to a place where they could get down to the glacier. They were half-way across the glacier, and quite near the ibex when they saw it move again. It made a last convulsive effort and ran a short way as the snow-leopard charged and leapt on it.

Fenwick cursed, and fired twice at the leopard; both shots missed, however, and the leopard swung the ibex over its shoulder.

The snow-leopard was running over the boulder-strewn ice some distance away before Fenwick had time to jam another clip into the breech; he jumped on to a rock, and took a snap shot at the leopard, hitting it in the near fore-paw. The leopard roared, and half-turned, but it changed its mind, and went on again without dropping the ibex. Fenwick slipped off the rock, and fell into a drift of powdery snow; when he had extricated himself, the snow-leopard was some way off – it had gained ground considerably.

Bhotka, who was nearer the leopard, kept up a volley of stones, hoping to make it drop the ibex, but it would not, and Fenwick was not using heavy enough ammunition to do it much harm.

They went on for about five minutes, then all at once the snow-leopard stopped, and looked round. It had come to a wide crevasse. It seemed to be pondering the wisdom of charging the men. Fenwick fired again, and Bhotka hit it with three successive stones. The leopard leapt across the crevasse, dropping the ibex as it did so. Then it disappeared among the boulders.

The crevasse was a broad one, and deep. The ibex lay at the bottom of it, looking remarkably small; there was obviously no hope of getting it. They had a very long journey before them, and it was getting late. They were angry and despondent. Bhotka paused, and looked at the snow-leopard's spoor.

'It is the same leopard that took three cows from a village some way from ours,' he said.

'I'll get that darned beast if I follow it for a month,' said Fenwick.

The next day they set out after the leopard, but they could not find it; they searched for a week before they found its spoor. It was plain from the pug marks that the leopard had been badly injured in its foot.

The wound had not healed cleanly; and it spoilt the leopard's hunting by cutting down its speed considerably.

For three days the snow-leopard had not fed, and then its mind turned towards the panda cubs. Ordinarily it would not have considered it for a moment, but its mate had just given birth to her cubs, and she had to be fed.

It was on the day that the leopard was going to the pandas' lair that Fenwick and Bhotka picked up its trail.

They were still a good way off when they heard the leopard's screaming roar, followed by a noise of great beasts fighting.

The leopard had waited until both giant pandas were out of the cave, and then it had darted in, picked up a cub, and made off as fast as it could. Pandas are usually quite silent, but the cub made a loud squealing, and its mother came racing over the snow. The leopard was hampered by its burden and by its wound, nevertheless, it was nearly a quarter of an hour before the she-panda caught up with it.

The snow-leopard dropped the cub, and turned; the she-panda charged silently. The force of the impact knocked the leopard backwards, and the panda was upon it before it could recover. But the leopard took advantage of being underneath, and clawed at the panda's belly, seeking to disembowel her. They rolled over and over in the snow, the leopard coughing, snarling, and roaring, but all the time the panda made no sound. The cub sat up and licked itself.

It was at this point that Fenwick and Bhotka came over the

rocks above the fighting beasts. They gasped, truly amazed. Quickly, with the shikari's instinct, they hid themselves behind what cover there was.

Fenwick thanked his Maker that he had slipped the cine camera into his hip-pocket, from where he was he had a perfect view of the terrific fight, and without cease he filmed the great beasts as they rolled to and fro in the reddening snow.

The position had changed; the leopard had scrambled on to the panda's back, and was tearing at her neck; her hide was tough and her fur thick, but the leopard ripped savagely through it. The panda threw herself on her back in an effort to dislodge the leopard, but she could not.

Fenwick was thinking of helping her with his rifle when the male giant panda came furiously up the slope. Fenwick gasped; even from Bhotka's description of the animal, he had never envisaged so huge a beast. The panda had its fur all standing out in its rage, and it steamed in the cold air because of the speed at which it had come.

Silently, like its mate, it charged the leopard, who sprang from the she-panda. The giant panda half reared as the leopard sprang, and clasped it about the shoulders. The leopard gave a coughing scream, tore madly at the panda's head, and then its spine cracked with a sound like a stout branch breaking. The giant panda dropped it, and went to his mate.

They licked one another and the cub most tenderly for a little while, and then they went away.

Fenwick covered the retreating pandas; it was an easy shot. All the hunter in him urged him to make a great reputation as a shikari in three simple shots, but somehow he felt that he could not.

His rifle wavered, and Bhotka looked at him expectantly: a little pressure on the trigger, and he would have at least one magnificent skin, and Fenwick knew it, but he lowered his rifle, smiled at Bhotka, and said: 'I've got all I want here,' patting the cine camera.

The pandas vanished over a ridge, and no man ever saw them again.

60

Noughts & Crosses

———— ⚇ ————

Several men were sitting around the fire in the smoking-room of their club; they were talking about narrow escapes and strange adventures.

'Well,' said Sullivan, 'I don't know that I have come in for much more danger than most, but I had a pretty unnerving experience once – funny thing, I was dreaming about it only last night; I often do. It was like this – but it's rather a long story –'

'Go on,' said the others.

'It was like this, then: a friend and I were out in Australia – '25 that would be. We were fishing for sharks all along the little atolls by the Great Barrier Reef in an old schooner that we'd bought for a song in the Islands. There were half a dozen Kanakas aboard for a crew, and we had a long-boat and a couple of dinghies. Our head-quarters were a little island called – oh, bothered if I can remember the name now, but it was a beautiful little place, absolutely the model of what coral islands should be – almost unreal, though, like the things they wangle at Hollywood.

'We used to keep quite a number of men there, Kanakas mostly, and a few Japs, to do all the things necessary for getting the shagreen into shape for trading. An old Chinese was overseer – he was no earthly good, but his cousin used to buy pretty nearly all our stuff at a fairly decent price, so we kept him on. The schooner was pretty ancient when we bought her, and soon it was evident that she would have to have the weed scraped off her hull, and have some of the worse leaks patched up. In those warm seas the weed grows very fast on the bottom of a ship, and it cuts your speed down badly after a while. She was not a big ship by any means – quite small, even as Island schooners go – so we thought we could careen her ourselves and do most of the work. We had an amateurish sort of run-way put together, and by getting all our men on the other end of a cable we managed to beach her.

'For a couple of days we got the Kanakas to clean her hull – it was absolutely encrusted. Meanwhile, we went out in the whaler with Billy, an Australian aboriginal; a wonderful man he was with a spear, too. I remember how he used to – but I'm wandering. Besides Billy, we had a young Japanese called Fujimoto, and a Kanaka from Samoa whose name I forget.

'We meant to go out to a little atoll where we had a hut and some stores, picking up what sharks we could on the way, and to come back by way of another island where there were some water barrels that we had left.

'The trip was to take a couple of days: by then the Kanakas would have cleaned the hull, and the holes could be patched – we preferred to do that ourselves.

'We set out in the early morning. The mast had been stepped, and we made pretty good way under mainsail and jib, the breeze coming over the quarter. The steering was rather tricky, but my friend knew the channels through the reefs perfectly.

'It was some time before we got out of the network of shallow, reef-bound lagoons, but when we reached the other side of the big reef, where you look down to the bottom through five fathoms of clear water, we kept an eye open for our fish.

'There's an awful lot of nonsense spoken about the man-eating propensities of sharks; I know there are fully a hundred types of shark – there may be many more than that – but only about half a dozen are man-eaters. Still, the tiger-shark of the Pacific is a really ugly customer, so is the white shark, and that hideous brute the hammerhead. We usually got the ordinary little fellows – about five or six feet long. Billy speared the smaller ones, and we got the rest with great lumps of meat stuck on hooks rather like those that butchers use, but with a barb.

'On the way out we didn't have much luck, and we had decided to stay out fairly late to see whether we could make up for it, when we noticed that the sky was looking very queer. In fact it was obvious that we were in for the very devil of a storm. If we had not unshipped the barometer while the schooner was being careened we should have been warned by the falling glass before we had started, but it had been put out of harm's way. We made straight for the atoll, and we had got the whaler well up the beach before the cyclone reached us.

'First there was a great howling wind that made the whole of the sea white with broken water, and then there came the most appalling lightning that I have ever seen in my life – it came flashing low over the sea, and it struck several palm-trees quite near us.

'The rain and the thunder seemed quite mild compared with the hissing, crackling lightning and the tremendous wind. It went on all night and half the next day. At noon, when the sun put in an appearance, we went down to the shore. There was an immense swell on the sea; the surf was indescribable. There was no chance of getting the boat away. Fortunately it had not been damaged; if it had been we should have been in a mess.

'Luckily there was a good deal of food in the hut, so we spent another night there. In the morning we managed to get the boat through the surf, and we set our course for the other island, where there were water barrels, and a tank that we needed for trying out the shark-oil.

'There were practically no fish in the shallow water; they all make for the open sea so as not to be smashed against the rocks, or carried on to the shore by the immensely powerful surf. But in the deeper water we saw many more sharks than usual, although this part of the sea was their favourite haunt. The first hook that we put out was snapped up almost at once by a big tiger-shark. It was a deuce of a job to get him into the side; but after a pretty hot struggle we got him there, and Billy was able to plant a harpoon into him. We always used a harpoon for the really big fellows, and this was the biggest we had struck so far.

'He towed us a good way out of our course, but we got him in the end. When we killed him he gave a last smack at the boat with his tail, and that jarred some of the cross beams so badly that a couple of small leaks showed in a few minutes. We went on towards Ataoloa, the island where the barrels were, towing the tiger-shark behind us – he was far too big to haul aboard.

'I don't know why it was, but the storm seemed to have brought more sharks to our usual haunts than ever. Even in ordinary weather the sea was what books call shark-infested, but now it seemed absolutely alive with them. Soon there were about half a dozen little fellows following us, taking bits out of the tiger-shark. Billy speared a couple very neatly, and the rest followed farther behind after that. It was late before we reached Ataoloa: we collected the barrels and the tank, which was a big, square, zinc affair – rather troublesome. It had been used quite recently for getting the oil out of the sharks' livers, and it hummed rather badly. Partly because of the late hour and partly because of the hum, we decided not to hang about too long, and to get back after an hour's fishing. We rowed out to the open water; there was a dead calm, so the sails were useless, and we cruised slowly about. Suddenly we noticed the smaller sharks which were following all sheering off; they were getting out of the way of a Port Jackson – one of the biggest and fiercest of all sharks – which was coming up like a shadow from the deep water.

'At first we thought that he was after the tiger-shark, but he hung about just under our keel, which was rather puzzling. A little later he was joined by another Port Jackson and a white shark, both huge fish, neither of them an inch under thirty feet long. After a little longer there were a good many blue sharks as well, none of them small.

'We could see deep into the clear water, and there was no doubt that there were an extraordinary number of them following us. The Kanaka and Fujimoto were getting a bit worried; they said that the sharks smelt the tank, and that they were mad to get at it. I don't know if a fish can really smell anything that is out of the water, but it certainly looked as if they were right. One thing

I am certain of, though, and that is that a shark will always follow if there is a dead man aboard, so it looks as if they could get the smell under water.

'We got a small fellow with rather peculiar markings on his skin, but before we could haul him in he was simply ripped to pieces. After that Billy and the Kanaka turned as white as they could, and they begged us to make straight for home. My friend said that we would stay out until we'd got one more – more from obstinacy that anything else – and then the Kanaka got rather above himself, and insisted on going back. This rather put my friend's back up, and he said he'd see them all to blazes before he went in without another fish. Billy sat quiet in the bows, and the Jap crouched against the side, muttering to himself. They were badly rattled. I was a bit windy myself, because I did not like the look of some of those big fellows under our keel. But my friend had red hair, and he was as obstinate as a mule. There was a hammerhead cruising about just by the tiger-shark – you don't often see them in those waters: they generally keep up north – and my friend pointed him out to Billy. The black fellow nodded, and poised himself in the stern sheets.

'I can see him throw that spear now; it was a wonderful cast. The hammerhead thrashed about furiously, but we got him into the side, and the Kanaka hit him on the head with the sledge-hammer that we always carried. Up came the Port Jackson and a couple of white sharks, but we had the hammerhead over the side before they could reach him. That seemed to infuriate them, and a second later the Port Jackson fetched us a great bang amidships with his tail, which rocked the whole boat so much that we shipped a good deal of water.

'"Let's get going," I said. My friend nodded, and we got out the oars – the sails were useless in the dead calm, as I said before. We had two pairs of oars, and between us we made the boat really move. The natives worked as I had never seen them work before.

'We had hardly got well under way before there was another bump under our keel, then another. It was almost as though we were on a reef.

'We had to start bailing after a while, and just then the hammerhead came to life again; it lashed about all over the place until I shoved it over the side with a boat-hook. But that didn't make any difference to the other sharks; they were determined to capsize us, and every other moment the boat would be jarred from stem to stern.

'"Cut the tiger-shark adrift," I shouted, and the Kanaka let it go in a second. They left us in peace for a few minutes after that, and we had time to get the boat moving really fast. We hoisted the sail to catch any little breeze that might come along. But in a few moments they were back again; great ugly devils they were, too. Even my friend began to get the wind up; he hit at one with his oar, and the next minute it was torn out of his hand, and he was almost dragged into the water. At the same moment there came a great smack under the keel, and the boat nearly went over. Water was simply pouring in now; some of the cross-beams had gone, and the floor boards were loosening rapidly.

'Another oar went – the Kanaka's this time – and we stopped rowing to bail for dear life. But it was no good; the water came in over the side every time we rocked badly.

'The boat began to settle. The gunwales were almost awash. Then suddenly it was all over: the boat slid quietly down from under our feet. There was a threshing of white water, and I jumped for one of the barrels: I never saw what happened next, but I heard three screams.

'When the foam had died down I looked round from my barrel, and I saw my friend in the water tank. He was bobbing about like a kid in a soap-box – even then it struck me as rather funny. I hadn't much time to think, though, because my barrel rolled over, and I was in the water again. I saw the flash of a white belly just under me, and I saw the shark's head shoot past. In a fleeting glimpse I noticed its eyes: there was absolutely no expression in them.

'My friend grabbed my arm and hauled me into the tank; there was just room for both of us to squat in the bottom.

'There was no sign at all of the natives – they had simply disappeared. Night fell very quickly, and soon it was dark. The sea was phosphorescent, and we could see the dorsal fin of one shark cutting a thin wake like a flame through the water. They left us alone during the night, and I went to sleep.

'In the morning we found that we were out of sight of land; there was nothing but blue sea all round, and a blazing sun that crept higher and higher.

'My friend was curiously silent: I think he was brooding over the thought that it was his obstinacy that had brought it all about. I was barefoot, and I only had a jacket and a Malay sarong on; he had khaki shorts and a shirt; our hats had gone.

'As the sun sailed up to noon height we noticed the heat rather badly – you see, the tank was about five feet deep, and the sun beating straight down into it had the effect of making the metal somewhat like an oven.

'We had neither water nor food; in my pockets I had my pipe, but no tobacco, and a pencil; he had a handkerchief.

'As I have said, the tank had been used for sharks' livers – we noticed that nearly as much as the heat. What a ghastly stench! I can smell it now.

'Added to this there was a heavy swell on, and although we were both good sailors, there was something about the heat, hum, and swell that combined to make us quite sea-sick. We covered the top of the tank with my sarong; the shade was a great boon, only it was very difficult to keep the sarong up there, as it was just too small. Of course, we were jammed up pretty close to one another, and that made things a bit worse, if possible.

'We had no way of moving the tank, and we should have had no idea where to move it to even if we had been able to make any headway.

'In the meantime we played noughts and crosses all over the inside of the tank with my pencil; I won a great deal of money – some three million or so, if I remember rightly. I never got it, though.

'The second day was exactly the same as the first, except that a shark tried to upset us, but we hardly rolled at all, being two-thirds under water.

'We played more noughts and crosses.

'It was not until the third day that we really noticed our thirst. By then neither of us could speak, our tongues being too swollen; but until we had reached that stage the lack of water was nothing of a hardship compared with the heat, hum, and swell. At noon that day I noticed that my friend was drinking sea-water. I would have remonstrated with him, but I could neither speak nor move by then, and he could only just crawl.

'In the morning of the fourth day, when the sun had begun to come over the edge of the tank, he went mad quite suddenly.

'He undressed, mumbling that it was a fine morning for a bathe. I managed, I don't know how, to trip him as he began crawling over the edge, and fortunately he was too weak to get up again.

'I think I was conscious for another whole day. It was one of the P. & O. ships that picked us up. An ocean current had carried us hundreds of miles on to one of the main shipping routes from Australia – it was really quite lucky.'

Sullivan laughed reminiscently. There was silence for a while. After a couple of whiskies he went to bed.

'I don't know why,' I said, 'but I feel certain that that story of Sullivan's is absolutely true.'

'It is,' replied Ross. 'I know, because I was the other man. We often play noughts and crosses still.'

61

Two's Company

I

The tender puffed busily away from the lighthouse to the relief ship. The two men who were left at the base waved for a long time; the ship was the last they would see of the outer world for three months. The lighthouse was almost the most lonely in the world: it guarded a dangerous reef in the cold northern seas. There were a few little barren groups of rock jutting out from the sea near it, but never a blade of grass grew there. Now and then a few wandering seals would come there, but usually they stayed away. The ships that passed kept far out in the clear sea, so that they were only vagrant ghosts to the men in the tower.

One of them, Ross, was a big broad Scotsman, and the other a thin tall Irishman called Sullivan. They had knocked about all over the world, often quarrelling, but sticking together, although they were as different as any two men could well be. Ross was a fairly typical Lowland Scot, hard, and very silent; he had red hair and a great jaw. Sullivan, on the other hand, loved a jest, and he had the gift of a free-running tongue born in him. They were both educated men, oddly enough; Sullivan had been to Trinity, and Ross to St. Andrews, where he had lived on Homer and a barrel of salt herrings. They had been to sea for a long time together before they had got this job, and at one time they had owned a small tramp steamer between them, but it had literally fallen to pieces when they were in the Islands, gathering *bêche-de-mer*.

They went up the spiral staircase to their room at the top. The lower part of the tower was filled with machinery for working the light, and with great stores of oil. Round the top of the tower was a platform, and at the bottom was another, considerably larger. The two men had been on the lighthouse before for a week, so that the other keepers could show them everything. They had bunks to sleep in, and one fairly large round living-room. There was a wireless set, but as the rocks all around and the great mineral deposits under the sea set up a great deal of electrical disturbance, it was not much use.

At first the two men were kept busy the best part of the day, for the tending of the lamp was not a simple matter, but after about a week they arranged things so that quite half the day was their own. They played innumerable games of chess, but Ross nearly always won, and Sullivan took a dislike to the game; he said there was no joy in it, and took to spending a good deal of his time fishing from the top platform, from where he could see deep into the water. There was a certain amount of kelp growing about the submerged reefs, so the fish came there, but usually Sullivan caught only little fish. It was late autumn when they had first come to the lighthouse, and as winter approached the migrating cod came past the reefs.

Sullivan was leaning over the rail one morning with his line held loosely between his fingers, when it was suddenly jerked away and went over the rail as if a shark had been on it. He had time to put his foot on the end of the line before it was all gone, and he began to haul it in. He pulled a cod to the edge of the lower platform, but he saw that even the stout sea line that he was using would not stand the weight of the fish. He shouted to Ross, who popped his head out of the round window.

'I've got a whale!' he shouted. 'Go down to the bottom platform and haul him in.'

Ross sped down the iron staircase and lugged out the cod by its gills, then he clasped the fish to his bosom and brought it in. They had cod for every meal until it went bad.

In the evenings they used to sit about the stove, for it was very cold at times, and talk; Ross did not say much unless he was arguing, but Sullivan could talk for two. They had not been there three weeks before there was a storm. Not an ordinary storm by any means, but a great roaring storm so strong that the spray of the waves was flung as high as the light itself. The roaring of the sea was so loud that they had to shout to one another to make themselves heard. All night the storm went on, but it faded away with the coming of the sun.

They went out on to the platform, holding tight to the rail, for the wind had not yet abated very much.

Suddenly Ross pointed down. Without a word Sullivan leaned over the rail, and saw the huge body of a whale wedged between a spur of rock and the concrete of the lower platform. The great seas had put it there after beating its life out against the rocks. There was a heavy swell on the sea, but no broken water, so they went down to the lower platform and looked at the whale for some time.

'We'll never be able to move it,' said Ross. A storm-blown kitti-wake flew by, and settled on the whale. Before dusk about twenty other birds were there, and in the morning a great host of gulls screamed over the huge carcass. All through the day more birds came; apart from the gulls, there were a fair number of little auks, strange birds with shrill voices. At first the men rather enjoyed the noise, it was so different from the endless rumble of the sea; but after a day or two, as they were leaning over the rail, watching the cloud of birds, Sullivan said, 'That screaming is getting to be rather too much for me.'

'Ay,' replied Ross.

With the gulls there came many sharks. The first on the scene was a big basking shark, fully thirty feet long; Ross saw it resting on the surface by the submerged part of the reef. After a little while it glided down through the water under the carcass and, turning on its back – Ross saw the gleam of its white belly – tore away a great strip of blubber.

It was not long before several hammerheads appeared, with two or three large Greenland sharks. At first they fed furiously, struggling to get at the whale, but after some time even their monstrous appetites were satisfied, and they rested all around on the sea-bed, dark, ominous shadows clearly visible from the top platform.

All the time more sharks came in. Even in Suez and the Islands the men had never seen more sharks, nor bigger ones.

It was Sullivan who suggested that they should fish for one.

'What should we do with it?' asked Ross.

'Oh, well, I don't know, but they are evil devils.'

In the chain locker they found a hook used for hauling things with a pulley.

'But it hasn't got a barb,' said Sullivan.

'If once we get that into his head,' replied Ross, 'and keep on hauling, it won't need a barb.'

They bent it on to a length of steel hawser, and that in turn on to a stout chain. Sullivan went down to the lower platform where he could reach the head end of the whale, and cut away a large piece of flesh. They put it on to the hook, and lowered it into the water. Ross called attention to a Greenland shark which was cruising past the tail of the whale. They waited until the fish had come close to the lighthouse, and then swung the meat in over its head. Nothing could have been more simple than hooking the shark; it rolled on its side and snatched at the sinking bait. They both pulled hard on the chain; then they were nearly dragged off the platform as the great fish felt the hook. Sullivan was half over the rail, and he felt the chain slipping through his hands.

'Put a hitch round the rail!' he shouted.

'I'll have to let go while I do it,' said Ross. 'Can you hold on?'

'I'll try.'

Ross whipped the chain round the stout iron support, and the strain was gone. 'The hook's well in,' he said. The shark lashed furiously, and the iron rail bent.

'I think we've bitten off more than we can chew,' said Sullivan. They both heaved on the chain. It did not give an inch. The shark lashed the water into a foam. Suddenly Sullivan had an idea; he turned and dashed into the lighthouse.

'Where did I put that revolver?' he shouted.

'It's in my kitbag,' answered Ross. 'Hurry up, or the fish'll have the whole railing off.'

Sullivan ran back with the revolver, a heavy '45. He plugged three shots into the shark without any noticeable effect except that at the sound of the shots the cloud of sea-birds rose like an inverted snowstorm.

'It's no good; the stanchion will go in a minute.'

'Let me have a shot,' said Ross. He emptied the revolver into the shark's body; still the fish tore at the chain.

'We'd better let the chain go,' said Sullivan.

They tried pulling again, but although they hauled with their utmost strength they could not bring the shark in. All the other sharks were attracted by the splashing. Eventually it pierced the dull brain of one of the hammerheads that the other was hooked; the hideous beast rushed in and bit a great piece out of the Greenland shark's side. Sharks prefer shark-meat to whale-meat, and soon a dozen of them were ripping the hooked fish to bits. The chain grew slack as the wretched shark was literally eaten alive. The men watched, fascinated.

'How very like men they are,' observed Sullivan.

'Don't be sententious; let's save the head. The gulls will clean the skull for us.'

In a little while the head and the skeleton were all that was left. The unfastidious sharks swallowed most of the bones, but the men saved the skull, with its great jaws and row after row of teeth.

II

One thing that got more on Sullivan's nerves than the ceaseless clamour of the birds was their habit of dashing against the great light in the darkness like moths at a candle; in the morning there would often be several bodies or, worse still, badly wounded birds lying on the top parapet. He was a tender-hearted man towards all animals – sharks excepted – and it hurt him to see the birds broken. He rigged up a kind of netting round the light and thus saved most of them, but one morning Ross, who had gone out first, called him up; there on the platform was a sea-eagle, stunned, but not dead. Farther round the parapet was a great skua tangled in the netting. It was badly hurt. Both these were much heavier birds than the usual gulls, and the netting had not been strong enough to save them. As they stood looking at the birds the sea-eagle recovered, quite suddenly; it screamed harshly and hopped into the air, but its left wing was damaged and it could not fly. Sullivan advanced towards it, saying, 'Pretty polly, pretty polly; there's a good bird.'

The good bird gave him one look of fear – Ross said that it sneered – and scrambled under the railing, hoping that its wings would bear it. They did not, however, and the eagle splashed into the sea. Sullivan ran down the spiral stairway to the lower platform. He crawled to the edge of the rocks and seized the eagle by the neck. He was none too soon, for a shark rose as he pulled the bird out. He had taken his coat off, and he wrapped it about the furious eagle, then carried it upstairs to their living-room.

Ross had worse luck with the skua: he disentangled it, and as soon as its head was free it ripped his hand open with its strong curved beak.

'Oh, ye ———— ye naughty fowl,' said Ross. Then Sullivan came out, and together they took the skua in. They wrapped it up in a curtain and put it by the eagle. The bundles heaved, but were silent.

The men had a good deal of work to do on the lamp, so they shut the birds in and left them.

'What do you suppose we can do with them?' asked Ross, polishing one of the innumerable reflecting facets.

'I remember a man in Galway who had one of those sea-eagles – ernes, we call them there; he had caught it up in the misty Isles when it was half-fledged. It got so tame that it sat on his shoulder, and caught him fish and conies. If I can tame this one it'll keep us in fresh fish all the year round.'

'What about the skua?'

'Well, that's your look-out; you took it. They are evil birds –
you'd better wring its neck.'

'Oh, I wouldn't do that: if you can tame your erne I can tame
my skua – it'll be something to do.'

On that day they first noticed that the whale was beginning
to smell.

They rigged up a couple of perches for the birds, and they lifted
them – they were still enveloped in the jacket and the curtain –
on to the wooden cross-beams.

'Can you find your fowl's feet?'

'No,' replied Sullivan. 'I think it's upside-down.' A moment later
one of the eagle's talons tore through the coat and grasped his arm.
Sullivan had put on a thick overcoat, but the claws ripped through
the cloth like paper, and he only just managed to keep them from
his flesh. At length they got the birds on to the perches, and they
put a stout line round the wood, tying the birds by the leg. Then
they took off the coat and the curtain. To their surprise neither of
the birds uttered a sound; they ruffled their feathers and blinked
in the light.

'Let's leave them to settle down a bit,' said Ross.

When they came back at lunch-time the birds screamed and
flapped their wings, but the men took no notice of them. While
they were eating Sullivan said, 'Do you remember that time when
we were stranded in Samarkand?'

'Shall I ever forget it?'

'Well, when we went east through Turkistan to Peking there
were some Tartars in the caravan who carried hawks on their
wrists.'

'I remember them; and there was that little squat chap – the
one with St Anthony's fire all over his face – who had a gyrfalcon.'

'That's right, Tzu-Lu was his name. I asked him once how
he managed that bird, and as far as I could make out he said that
he starved it so as to make it more sweet-tempered and docile.'

'That's a remarkably good idea; they used to do it over here
when everyone had a hawk; besides, it'll save food.'

So for some days the birds went without food, but they were used to it, and it took a long while for them to become anything like sweet-tempered, much less docile. The skua was the first to stop trying to rip everything that came in reach to pieces, and Ross gave it a piece of whale. The whale, by this time, was getting past a joke; the sharks and the gulls had removed a good deal of it, but there was still a mountain of flesh.

The eagle held out with gloomy dignity for a little while longer, but then it fed, too.

They devoted a lot of time to the birds, for they had little else to do half the day, and the lower platform was already uninhabitable on account of the whale. They had a bet on who should be the first to get his bird to feed from his hand. Sullivan won the bet, but he lost the top of his little finger. Still, after a time the birds became far more tame.

Meanwhile, life was becoming unbearable; the humming-bird, as Sullivan called the whale, reeked to the heavens. The birds were unaffected, but the men soon felt that they could not stand it any more.

'We must do something about it; it's worse than Kashgar in summer,' said Sullivan. 'What about covering it with some of the oil and setting light to it? That would change the stench, and it couldn't possibly make it any worse.'

'As soon as we lit it the heat would blow up the oil tanks: that's no good.'

They thought in silence for some time; then Ross said, 'It's the seventh today, isn't it?'

'Yes, but what about it?'

'There's a destroyer due to pass on the nineteenth; she'll dump a barrel with papers and things in it fastened to a buoy; we're supposed to take the dinghy out and get it.'

'I remember – those fellows told us about it. Lord, but it'll be grand to see a bit of news.'

'Well, if I can get that destroyer on the wireless I will ask them to let us have some powder, and we'll blow the stinker to pieces.'

'And ourselves too, I suppose?'

'No; we can set the charge against the rock in small quantities, and do it bit by bit.'

'That's more feasible than burning it, anyhow. Do you think the radio will do it?'

'I hope so, but if not, we can hoist a distress signal, and they'll maybe send in a boat.'

By the nineteenth they were almost dumb with sore throats, and Sullivan had curious yellow spots all over his body. They got nothing from the wireless but weak atmospherics, so in the early morning they hoisted a blanket and two red curtains from the highest point they could reach. All day one or the other was on the top platform with a telescope. Sullivan was there at about four o'clock with his erne on its perch beside him when he saw the destroyer's smoke on the horizon. He called Ross.

'I hope she comes near enough to see our signals before dark,' said the Scotsman.

It was almost dusk before the ship was near enough to the lighthouse for the men to be able to see the men on her decks. They saw the barrel and the buoy dropped overboard; the destroyer gave a hoot on her siren and put on speed.

'Ten thousand devils! They haven't seen our signals!' cried Ross.

They waved blankets from the parapet for about five minutes before Sullivan saw a string of flags run up on the destroyer.

'They've seen us, *laus Deo*,' he said.

'Where? Give me that telescope,' said Ross, whose eyes were not so good. 'Get that code book; I've forgotten how to read flags.' Even with the code book they could not make out the signal, because of the fading light. Together they waved a blanket, trying to send a Morse message. It was no good.

'Here, let's signal by the light,' said Sullivan, darting into the lighthouse. A few minutes later they had the great beam shooting out over the water. Ordinarily the light sent out flashes, two long, and three short, but there was an interrupter gear fitted, and Ross worked this while Sullivan went out on to the platform, standing with his back to the blinding glare. The stuttering

Morse shot out, and presently he saw the destroyer lowering away a boat.

'They're coming,' he shouted. The boat came over the heavy swell, threading through the half-sunk rocks. They brought it beautifully alongside the lower platform, and threw Ross a rope, which he made fast. The lieutenant in charge came on to the platform, holding his nose.

'Gosh, what an appalling stink,' were his first words. 'What did you signal for?'

'We want some powder to get rid of this foul whale – but come inside; it's not quite so bad at the top.'

The birds screamed and flapped their wings at the sight of another man, and the erne, who was walking about – they were tame enough to be let off their perches – bit him in the leg.

'Nice pets you've got,' he said, when Sullivan had taken the eagle away.

'Well, they were absolutely wild not so long ago; we'll teach them decent manners soon. Won't you sit down? We've got a spot of whisky somewhere, I think.'

'Thanks awfully. I wonder if the men could come in out of the stink?'

'Surely, I'll give them a hail. If you come out on to this platform you can see where the whale lies.'

'I don't know whether we've got what you want on board, but perhaps the armourer could dismantle a few shells,' said the lieutenant, after a while.

'I suppose it couldn't be towed off?' asked Sullivan.

'I hardly think it would be possible now that it is so very decomposed – better try blasting it,' replied the lieutenant, and he left as soon as he decently could.

It was dark by now, and they had to wait until the morning. The powder came in a bag, and there were several detonators with it. They went down to the lower platform to decide where to put the first charge. Eventually they rammed it down as far as they could between the whale's head and the rock: it was not a pleasant job, but it was better than putting up with the stench. They retired to the lighthouse, and pressed the handle of the detonator. There was a muffled roar, and a fountain of whale's flesh shot up. Sullivan went to the door.

'Wait till it's all come down,' said Ross. After a few moments they went out; the whale's head was entirely gone. By noon all the rest of the carcass that was above the water had been blasted to pieces.

III

In a little while the whale was only a memory; the sea-birds went away, but some of the sharks stayed about the reef long after the bones had been polished white.

The erne and the skua grew tamer and tamer; they would both take food quite gently from the hand, and Sullivan carried the eagle on his wrist, having improvised a hawking gauntlet from folded canvas. Ross went one better, and made a hood for the skua, so that it sat on his arm quietly, being blindfolded, like the hawks of former days.

The time for the coming of the relief ship grew nearer and nearer. Neither of the men wanted to leave the lighthouse, so Ross, who had resuscitated the wireless so that the atmospherics were not too bad, picked up a passing ship one night and spent the evening talking to the wireless officer aboard her. That evening was a particularly good one for transmission, and Ross sat in front of the Morse key with the earphones on far into the night.

Suddenly Sullivan said, 'Half a minute; let's get them to relay a message to HQ volunteering to stay on here for another spell. We could do something worthwhile with six months' pay.'

'Ay,' said Ross, and in a few minutes the message was tapped out. In an hour the answer came back. They could stay, and they would be given a bonus and extra leave; the relief ship would bring stores at the appointed time.

'I'd give the soul out of my body for a violin,' said Sullivan; 'see if you can get them to send a decent one, and a box of books that I left with that old woman.'

'And my pipes,' replied Ross.

The relief ship came and went. They were glad when it was gone, because they found that they were embarrassed when other people were there.

'I'm afraid we are getting rather thin-skinned in our old age,' said Sullivan, when the ship had left.

'It's morbid, but what does it matter?' said Ross.

From the first they realized that it had been a mistake to send for the fiddle and the bagpipes. Neither appreciated the music made by the other, and soon their nerves were getting ragged.

It was not long after this that they began talking to their birds more than to one another. Sullivan used to go up to the top platform with his sea-eagle when Ross occupied the lower one with his bagpipes and the skua.

The daily work and the birds kept them going, however, and a sort of lethargy that came over them made the days fly past.

One evening Sullivan spoke. 'Look here, old man,' he said, 'we must try to be a bit more human. Do you know we haven't exchanged a single word all day?'

Ross did not answer for some time, and then he said, 'Ay.'

Some time after this Sullivan was walking round the lower parapet when the erne spread its wings in the strong wind, as it had often done before, but this time it flew off his arm – the knot of the cord about its leg had slipped. The eagle sailed away in a wide sweep round the tower. Sullivan stood watching it; his heart felt cold. Then he dived into the lighthouse, seized a piece of meat, and ran out again. The erne was still circling slowly round the tower. Sullivan held out the meat in his gloved hand and whistled as the eagle passed him. It turned in its flight and came towards him; his heart stood still. The eagle landed lightly on his arm, shook out its feathers, smoothed them, and began eating the meat. Sullivan flushed red with joy, and he walked slowly into the lighthouse. Ross received the good news sourly. He was jealous.

'Lestris would do the same,' he said. The skua was called Lestris, and the erne Cuchulainn.

'I bet you a fiver it would not.'

'All right, we'll see.'

The skua did not come back to Ross's hand at once; it sat on the rail for some time. Ross stood stock still, so did Sullivan; there was a feeling of great tension. Then the skua hopped into the air, spread its broad wings, and sailed on to the outstretched arm.

That evening they talked freely: they were human again. Sullivan played Ross's favourite melodies on his violin – he was a really good player – and Ross did what he could in the way of Irish airs on the pipes. They made an agreement of mutual tolerance, and they praised one another's birds. But in a few days the old silence fell between them and they only spoke when it was necessary.

The birds grew accustomed to flying back to their masters, and one day Lestris, having caught a fish at the surface, brought it back. Ross was in high feather, but Sullivan felt annoyed, although he did not say much. He tried to indicate to Cuchulainn that he wanted the erne to bring in fish, but he could not get the idea across. The erne was puzzled; it knew that Sullivan wanted something done, but it could not tell what it was. There was an almost dog-like look in its fierce eyes, and Sullivan loved Cuchulainn for it.

One day, after Lestris had brought in three fish, he said to Ross, breaking the silence of several hours, 'Let's send them out together; maybe Cuchulainn will follow the skua's lead.'

'Ay,' said Ross.

The two great birds swept out over the sea; Lestris dived on a herring, and flew back to the lighthouse. Suddenly Cuchulainn realized what Sullivan wanted. The erne swept up in broad circles, rising without a movement of its great wings. The skua left the tower again and came up by the eagle.

Another herring rose to the surface, and both birds dived together. The skua snatched it from Cuchulainn's claws. The sea-eagle slashed at the skua, and the herring dropped into the sea again. The birds rose together, all idea of fishing gone. They closed, feathers flew, and they parted again.

Ross and Sullivan called and whistled in vain. Cuchulainn dashed at Lestris; in a second their talons were locked, and they fell fighting into the sea. The men rushed down to the dinghy, and rowed out in time to save the sinking birds. They pulled them apart, and rowed back. Neither of the birds was very badly hurt, though they both lacked a good many feathers, and one of Lestris's claws was badly wrenched.

That evening Sullivan played Bach, to Ross's great discontent, and Ross blew an endless dirge from his pipes. Ross gave up first, for lack of wind. He went up to tend the light; when he came down Sullivan was talking to Cuchulainn, stroking its neck. They sat down for supper.

'It was your darned bird that began it: I've a mind to wring its neck,' said Ross, after an hour's silence.

'You're a liar,' said Sullivan casually.

'What?'

'You are a dirty liar, a puling ——'

The table went over with a crash; Ross hit Sullivan over the mouth, and the skua croaked.

Then the fight began; they had been spoiling for it for months. They stood toe to toe, hitting as hard as they could. Neither attempted any defence; they just slogged with all their might. Sullivan went down, and Ross fell on top of him. They got up, and set to again. The table and chairs were splintered, and the birds screamed furiously. The oil lamp went over.

Just before it went Sullivan knocked Ross right out. He stood panting for a moment; then he turned and went out to see to the light. He came down the stairs again, wiping away the blood that flowed down his face. Ross was still unconscious, and Sullivan carried him to his bunk. When he was there Ross began to come round; his eyes had a mad gleam in them, and he struck out at Sullivan, who held him down firmly.

'Look here,' he said, 'we'll both go mad if this goes any further; we must hold on until the relief ship comes. We've been getting madder and madder these last two months. Pull yourself together, man.'

The fight cleared the air wonderfully. Together they cast the bagpipes and the violin into the sea. Oddly enough, they still kept very silent – largely from habit – but there was none of that rancour between them now.

The relief ship came, and it brought the new keepers.

'How did you like the six months on end?' they asked.

'Oh, very enjoyable, but perhaps a little too quiet,' replied Sullivan.

Before they went aboard they set Lestris and Cuchulainn free on the top parapet, and left them there.

They were talking to the captain below when the mate called down, 'Come up and have a look at these birds – they won't go away.'

Ross and Sullivan exchanged glances; then they went up. Cuchulainn and Lestris were waiting on the rail.

62

No Pirates Nowadays

———⚬⚬⚬———

I

'Speaking of furs,' said Sullivan, fanning himself with a folded palm-leaf, 'did I ever tell you of that Japanese cook I met while you were in Batavia?'

'We were not speaking of furs in the first place, and what has a Japanese cook got to do with them, anyhow?' asked Ross, leaning back against his camel saddle. The big Scot was too hot to fan himself.

Sullivan stretched his tall, lean body, and yawned. 'It was just an idea that passed across my mind,' he said.

'Not one of your ideas for making money?' asked Ross suspiciously.

'Well, as a matter of fact –'

'Ha! I was afraid of that. Now listen: you can take your idea and bury it. You'll have plenty of time to dig a nice deep hole before this Kaid of yours turns up with the money.'

'Arrah, don't let that be worrying your Scotch soul, my boyo –'

'Scots, please,' interrupted Ross; 'and you listen to me. Quite apart from the fact that we'll never see our guns or our money again, I'm sick of this beastly oasis, and I'm tired of dates for breakfast, lunch, and tea, with half a peck of sand for dinner. We're sailormen, and we ought to earn our living on the sea, not sitting by a puddle in a desert a thousand miles from the nearest port. So just you get it into your teak head, Sullivan that I dislike the sound of your voice when you talk about ideas.'

A little before moonrise the same night, five white mehari camels hunkered down at the oasis.

'Salaam, Kaid,' said Sullivan, greeting the Arab.

'Salaam alaikum, Effendi,' replied the Kaid, touching his head and heart. They exchanged a few remarks, and then, apparently as an afterthought, the Kaid mentioned that he had some money. His men brought leather bags and a rug. The Kaid rung the coins out on to the rug one by one, while Sullivan, knowing the breeding of the desert, affected not to count them.

Next day, as Sullivan and Ross travelled across the desert on the thoroughbred trotting camels that the Kaid had left as a present, the Irishman settled himself comfortably, and said, 'I don't want to rub it in, my good man, but if I were not a gentleman and the descendant of ancient Irish kings, I should say that there was something in my ideas.'

'Mphm,' replied Ross. For a long while they rode in silence.

'Ay,' said Ross, at last. 'More by luck than good management, though. We ought to stick to the sea.'

'Very true: now this idea of mine would be entirely on the sea.'

'Then you'd better tell me about it. You'll surely burst if you don't.'

'It was like this, then. Yamamoto, the cook I was telling you about, went down with pneumonia out beyond Medicine Hat, and I looked after him. He had been a sailor most of his time – he came from one of the northern Japanese islands – and a little before he died, he told me of an island way beyond Saghalien where the sea-otters breed: he was more than half Ainu, and his totem was the sea-otter, so he had never made use of the knowledge, but he passed it on to me, as a sort of payment for looking after him.'

'Sea-otters, eh? The fur is more valuable than ermine.'

'Yes. Next to chinchilla it's the rarest fur in the world. My idea is that we go and get some. We have got the capital now for a boat, and I have got a good many more details – that's just the bare outline.'

'What, go to Saghalien because of the babbling of a delirious Japanese cook? Blethering foolishness. Those parts are very poorly charted: and how do you know he was really talking about sea-otters, anyway? It was probably a moribund seal that his cousin's wife's brother-in-law saw. Tush! Stuff! If you find me wandering about in those latitudes calling "Puss-puss-puss" to imaginary sea-otters, you can call me a yellow-belly.'

II

The schooner pushed slowly through the fog: the soft chug-chug of her auxiliary engine echoed back from the blank yellow wall that surrounded her. The look-out man, who had been staring for hours into the dense whirling vapour, started as he heard a step behind him. He could hardly distinguish the dim form in the murk.

'You're a yellow-belly, Ross,' came Sullivan's voice through the fog.

'Och, you've said that twice today, man. D'ye think we shall ever be able to take our bearings again? It's four days since we've had a shot at the sun. And I'm afraid there's ice about by the smell of it.'

Sullivan sniffed the air. His keen nose detected that faint change that had already warned Ross.

'You're right,' he said. 'It's not far away, either. We must be farther off our course than I had thought. What do you make of the current?'

'I can't make it out at all. According to the chart there shouldn't be one here, but there's no manner of doubt that we have drifted a prodigious great way.'

'Have you seen anything at all?'

'Nothing all this watch. Is it eight bells yet?'

'Not quite. I'll get young Derrick to relieve you if you'd like to come below and work over my reckonings again.'

Derrick came on deck in response to a hail, and took over the watch. He was a strong, broad-shouldered boy, and big for his age, but he looked surprisingly young to be on a schooner in those dangerous seas. He was Sullivan's nephew, and they had picked him up at Kuala Lumpur, where his father had had a plantation, and where both his parents had died, leaving Derrick almost stranded. It had been a last-minute arrangement, much against Ross's cautious judgement; but, as Sullivan said, they could hardly leave the boy on his beam ends, and it would have delayed the voyage too much to have remained to make all the arrangements for sending him home to school. So, to Derrick's vast delight, he had been signed on, and, from the day he had got over his first bout of seasickness, he had worked hard and willingly, earning even Ross's good opinion, a thing which the Scot gave but rarely.

Below, in the saloon, Ross and Sullivan worked over their reckonings: for the third time they came to the conclusion that an uncharted current had swept them a good distance off their course. A hail from the deck interrupted them: Derrick said that he had heard the sound of another ship's engines. They listened: out of the fog there came the distinct sound of a throbbing screw.

'Ahoy, Li Han,' shouted Sullivan. 'Tell Svenssen to sound the fog-horn.'

'Fog-horn instantaneously it is, sir,' replied the Chinese cook. A moment later the melancholy bellow wailed through the fog. Surprisingly close, on the starboard quarter, came the answer.

'Stop the engine, Li Han,' shouted Sullivan, 'and stow the dictionary.'

Li Han went aft without a word, a little distressed at this reference to his treasured dictionary, from which he was teaching himself 'number one first chop' English. The engine spluttered and ceased; the other ship could be heard plainly moving towards them. 'Stand by to start up,' shouted Sullivan again, and he hailed the other ship. The answer came, 'Who are you?'

'The *Wanderer*. Who are you?'

'The *Santa Maria*. Can I come aboard?'

'Send a boat.'

They heard the splash of a boat being lowered, the gurgle of the oars, and then out of the wall of fog a jolly-boat appeared, not ten feet away.

The master of the *Santa Maria* came aboard. He was a big, immensely fat man, swaddled in two or three coats.

'How do?' he said, shaking hands. 'Can you give me our position? I've had no bearings for days.'

'Come below and have a drink,' said Sullivan, leading the way.

'Mphm,' muttered Ross, looking askance at the huge figure of their guest. In the saloon, Captain Jenkins – he introduced himself by that name, but he did not answer to it very promptly – gulped down three drinks in rapid succession, and poured himself a fourth unasked.

'I'm mighty glad I chanced on you,' he said. 'We've run out of everything except tack and bilge water, and we've sprung a leak that we can hardly keep under with the pumps going day and night. Perhaps you could bear a hand and let us have some stores?'

'Why of course. What's your cargo?'

'Soya fertilizer for Callao from Liao Tung.'

Ross had not spoken since they had gone below: abruptly he said, 'Didn't I meet you one time in Macao, Captain Jenkins?'

'Who? Me? No, never been in Macao.' He seemed a little uneasy, and hurried on to speak about the leak in his ship. Before he went they promised him some stores, and arranged to come over to see if they could help with the leak.

'There's something queer about him,' said Ross, when they were alone; 'I could swear I've seen him before.'

'Oh, there are plenty of rough-necks like him knocking about the China seas, working for Chinese owners. I've seen a dozen like him.'

'Mphm,' said Ross.

Towards the end of Derrick's watch the fog showed signs of lifting. The boy could see the *Santa Maria* fairly clearly: she was an ocean-going tramp, with squat, ugly lines, and the paint scaling off her sides. She was deeply laden, and she laboured in the swell. He gazed at her through his binoculars, and, as far as he

could see in the swirling mist, her crew at the pumps were all
Malays. Among other things he noticed that the paint of her
name appeared to be much fresher than that on the rest of her.
He mentioned this to Ross, who had just come on deck to have
the boat lowered away. Peering through Derrick's binoculars the
Scotsman said, 'Hmph', in a satisfied tone, and added, 'You've got
sharp eyes, lad. Jump into the boat and keep them skinned when
we're aboard her. There's something odd about that craft, or I'm
a longshoreman.'

Derrick remained on the deck of the *Santa Maria* when the
others had gone below to inspect the damaged hull. The serang
was an elderly Malay with an uncompromisingly villainous face:
he shook his head when Derrick spoke to him in English, reply-
ing, in Malay, that he did not understand the Tuan's language.
Derrick was about to repeat himself in Malay, a tongue which
he had spoken ever since he could speak at all, when he thought
better of it, and remained silent. A life-buoy had caught his attention: there was nothing odd about its shape, but the name on it
was 'S.S. *Firefly*, Macao'. The serang followed Derrick's glance,
and frowned: suddenly he pointed to the *Wanderer*, and shouted
in Malay, 'Get that life-buoy out of here, you sons of pigs.' Derrick saw that he was meant to look round, and he did so. When
he turned, the life-buoy had disappeared.

Down below Sullivan was telling Captain Jenkins that the leak
would not be serious once the pump sumps were cleared. Ross
remained silent and suspicious. By the time they had reached the
saloon again Jenkins had started questioning them about their
cargo and destination.

'We're on a pleasure cruise,' said Ross abruptly, interrupting
Sullivan, who was about to speak.

The breeze from the north-east, which had started to blow
in the fore-noon, had cleared the fog away, and they were able
to take their bearings again. Aboard the *Wanderer*, Ross and
Sullivan plotted their course afresh, and they found that they
had continued more or less in the right direction while they had
been drifting.

PATRICK O'BRIAN

'I tell you that ship isn't what she pretends to be,' said Ross, pushing aside the thumbed logarithm tables.

'You've always been a canny, suspicious sort of a devil, Ross: you mustn't take friend Jenkins too seriously. Possibly he is sailing under false colours, but there's many a man does the same when his ticket has been taken away from him. What does it matter to us, anyway?'

'Hmph. Did you mark his crew? There were half a dozen more men on that tramp than he could possibly use.'

'That's true.'

'And soya fertilizer doesn't smell like opium. Did you mark that?'

'No.'

'You were too busy smoking that cabbage-leaf cigar he pressed on you. But I trod on your foot when we passed his open cabin door.'

'And I saw the arms rack. Still, you might carry them if you were going to trade south and east. We've got an armoury, but that doesn't make us into pirates.'

'Whisht, man. Who said anything about pirates? I never committed myself to that extent: all I say is that a large crew of queer-looking scum, a heavy arms rack, and a cargo that smells like opium, is just a wee bit by-ordinary.'

Derrick came in to report the log readings.

'Did you notice anything aboard the *Santa Maria*, lad?' asked Ross.

'Well sir, there were one or two things,' replied Derrick, and he told them about the life-buoy. 'And another thing,' he added: 'when the serang came about the stores, he tried to pump Li Han for all he was worth, but I don't think he learnt much.'

Sullivan showed more interest; he shouted for Li Han, who came in and bowed.

'What did the serang ask you, Li Han?'

'Sir, he made inquiries in Malayan dialect concerning whereabouts,' replied Li Han, beaming.

'How do you mean, whereabouts?'

534

'Where we are about to come from and go to and what for, sir.'

'I see. What did you tell him?'

'Sir, I make replies inconsequential and evasive. Also similarly when he inquires exact strength of crew numerically.'

'Good. Was there anything else?'

'Indubitably yes, sir. The serang is making derogatory remarks, saying that we are poor and without face. But I rebuff him circumstantially and say that our face and prestige is so great that we have huge and lucrative mysterious project in hand.'

'Hm. All right, you can go, Li Han.' When the door had closed, Sullivan said, 'If you're right, Ross, poor old Li Han has given the show away trying to save our face. There's something wrong about the *Santa Maria*: I wish we hadn't fallen in with her just now. Still, we can keep a weather eye open.'

'But Uncle,' said Derrick, 'if they were pirates, why didn't they attack us when you and Mr Ross were aboard their ship? We shouldn't have stood a chance.'

'Pirates, my boyo? That's a strong word: you mustn't expect the skull and crossbones nowadays.'

'But you told me that strange things still happen at sea, Uncle Pat,' answered Derrick, going red in the face.

'And so they do. I have heard of men scuttling their ships for the insurance money, and even of men who've done that and been picked up and then thrown their rescuer's crew overboard, and saying that they found her abandoned after the storm in which their own vessel was sunk. But piracy in the old way – well, it's bending the long bow rather too far.'

'Ay,' said Ross. 'Don't worry your head about pirates, lad: go along and work out those navigation problems I set you.'

'Ay ay, sir,' said Derrick, and left them. But he carried with him the firm conviction that the *Santa Maria* was a pirate, and that his uncle thought so too. He was not far wrong, for when he had gone, Sullivan opened the arms chest, and started to clean an already spotless rifle.

'I tell you what, Ross,' he said, threading the pull-through: 'if our suspicions are correct, Jenkins would wait till we've pulled off our "huge and lucrative mysterious project", as Li Han would call it, before he tried any of the Jolly Roger business.'

The breeze freshened at sunset, and the *Wanderer*, without a reef in her sails, scudded cleanly before the wind on her new course. By the morning the *Santa Maria* was out of sight.

III

Some three days later Derrick was below, learning to splice a rope with Olaf Svenssen, the only other member of the crew besides Li Han, when Ross shouted 'Land ho!' from the deck. Derrick tumbled up, and stared at the clear, unbroken sea.

'Where?' he asked.

'On the port bow. Take the glasses.' Through the binoculars Derrick could distinguish a small black smudge among the clouds on the northern edge of the horizon.

'Is that it?' he asked.

'Maybe. We're going to have a look.'

Very slowly the smudge grew more distinct, until at last they could see the jagged rock peaks of the little islands quite plainly.

'If there are sea-otters on those rocks,' said Sullivan, 'we had better not scare them off by getting in too close. We'll anchor here and pull ashore to reconnoitre.'

'How do you catch them, Uncle? Like seals?'

'There doesn't seem to be any accepted way. They are too rare to be hunted much. Some of the Japanese set traps for them, but we'll go after them with a rifle: it's more sporting, and we can spare the young ones.'

'Providing there are any,' grunted Ross, sceptically.

They left Svenssen and Li Han aboard the *Wanderer*, and pulled for the shore. As they rowed nearer they could see that there were four islands, one some five hundred yards across, and the others much smaller. It was difficult to find any landing place, for the bare rock rose straight out of the sea to a height of ten to twenty feet. As they circled round to find a beach, Sullivan leaned on his oars and stared inshore.

'What do you make of that, Ross?' he asked, nodding towards a smooth, round head that was bobbing up and down just behind the backwash of the surf.

'Weel,' said Ross, staring too, 'I dare say it's a common seal, but we might as well follow it up.'

There was a swirl in the water, and the head disappeared, to come up again some distance away. They rowed quietly after it, and in five minutes they found themselves facing a little beach hidden between the jutting rocks. The animal went in on the back of a wave, springing clear of the wash as it broke. In a moment it had darted up the narrow strip of shingle and vanished among the rocks.

'Did you ever see a seal move like that, Ross?' asked Sullivan.

'Mphm. Let's get ashore.'

They climbed to the top of the island, to a peak from which they could see all round. It was an extremely bleak and desolate place; and there seemed to be no living thing on it. A chill wind blew.

'There's another beach down there,' said Sullivan, pointing to leewards, 'and there's this one. You take the far one, Derrick, and I'll scout around, if you'll lie up by here, Ross.'

They separated, and Derrick climbed and scrambled down to a small cliff overlooking the leeward shingle. He settled himself comfortably in a niche, and rehearsed in his mind all that his uncle had told him to do. 'You lie up, my boyo,' he had said, 'and have your rifle so that you can shoot without making much movement. If a beast comes up on shore, make certain there's not another one behind it before you shoot. Squeeze your trigger, and make sure the bullet has no corners to go round before you fire.'

Derrick turned up his collar: the rock seemed to grow harder and colder as he lay on it, waiting. At first he stared hard at the sea, hoping for something to come any minute, but as time went by his attention wandered, and he began to think about the *Santa Maria*.

It was not until the sea-otter was half-way up the beach that Derrick spotted it. His heart leapt into his throat, and he grasped

537

his rifle. The sea-otter was a very much larger beast than he had expected, being almost the size of a seal. It stopped to scratch its head in the middle of the beach. Derrick held his breath and drew a bead on it, aiming between the eyes, so as not to spoil the fur. His foresight was perfectly steady, and his aim dead true. He conquered an instinctive desire to shut his eyes, and squeezed the trigger gently. Nothing happened. He squeezed harder, and still nothing happened. He had left the safety-catch on. He moved an inch to release it, and the sea-otter stopped scratching. He slid his fingers round to find the trigger, fumbled for a moment, and lost his aim. Like a flash the sea-otter vanished into a breaking wave, and Derrick was left, ready to kick himself with annoyance, with a perfect chance missed.

From the other side of the island he heard three shots fired so rapidly that you could hardly have got a blade of grass in between them, as his uncle would have said. After that he heard two more from farther over on the south, followed, an hour later, by another from the beach. It was beginning to get dark, and it seemed plain to Derrick that he was going to go back empty-handed. He scanned the edge of the sea eagerly, but nothing appeared, and at length he heard the whistle that was to call him back. He gave a last look at the sea before getting up: there was nothing to be seen. He arose, and stamped his feet to get them warm. Startled by the noise, four sea-otters that had been lying on a ledge some twelve feet below him all the afternoon jumped down to the beach, and sniffed the wind.

Almost before he had thought of what to do, Derrick brought his rifle up and drilled the largest cleanly through the head. The rest dashed for the sea, and he shot another as it went.

For the next week they hunted systematically over the islands, getting good bags every day, until they were sure that the remaining sea-otters were all either young ones or breeding females.

As they rowed back with the last load of skins Sullivan said, 'This will be just about the biggest single cargo of sea-otter pelts that has come to Europe for the last twenty years.'

'Ay,' replied Ross. 'We've got a small fortune on board, but we've still to get it home.'

'I'd like to see anyone try to get them away from us,' said Sullivan, tying up to the *Wanderer*. 'We'll stow these, and then we'll lay our course for Yeddo at dawn.'

They were busy stowing the pelts – a difficult and tedious job – when Li Han came below.

'Svenssen begs to report, please, one sail to starboard bow, yes,' he said. 'He reports simultaneously distressing signals.'

Ross reached for his binoculars and went on deck; he came back in a few minutes and said, 'He's right; there's a steamer flying distress signals. She looks like the *Santa Maria*.'

'Does she, then? What's she doing here, two hundred miles off her course?'

'Hmph. That's what I'd like to know.'

'Better have a look-see, anyhow. She might be sinking, whoever she is.'

'Mphm.'

'Well, you might be wrong, and we can't leave her to founder.'

'If you're set on it, then, we'd better make sail.'

'Only thing to do. Don't you think so? You can't leave a ship in distress, can you?'

'Ah weel, I'll not commit myself to an opinion, but I've got a hunch about it.'

The *Wanderer* swung into the wind and tacked for the steamer. When they came nearer they could see that she was the *Santa Maria*, and Ross became very uneasy. In a few hours they were within hailing distance: they could see the Malay crew getting a boat ready, but there was no sign of Captain Jenkins. The boat ran alongside the *Wanderer*, and the serang came aboard with a note.

'Jenkins says he's very ill,' said Sullivan, reading the note, 'and that his serang can't navigate. He thinks there's another leak gaining fast on the pumps, and that the engines are faulty.'

'Mphm,' said Ross.

'We'll get salvage money if we take her into port,' said Sullivan; 'let's go and investigate.'

'I suppose we shall have to. The serang and another man had better stay here. Derrick, you give Svenssen and Li Han a rifle apiece and tell them to keep an eye on these two: we're going to leave them here as a precaution. Don't let Li Han tell them anything, and don't let anyone come aboard until we return.'

The serang and the other Malay were very reluctant to remain, but they had no choice. Derrick took them below to the galley and told Li Han to give them chop while he went to get the arms, Svenssen met him coming out of the saloon.

'Ay ban uneasy in mineself, Mr Derrick,' he said quietly; 'those Malays got each one a kris in his sarong. Ay don' laike their faces, neither.'

'Nor do I, Olaf,' replied Derrick. 'Do you think there's going to be a shindy?'

'Ay t'ink maybe. Ay seen plenty bad Malays. We better watch out, eh?'

They went back to the galley, where Li Han was trying to talk to the Malaya. Li Han's Malay was fragmentary at the best, and what little he knew was of a dialect different from that which the men spoke. Derrick could understand them as well as if they had been talking English. As he listened he blessed the idea that had kept him from letting them know that he understood their language when he was aboard the *Santa Maria*, for when Li Han left the galley, the serang said to his fellow, 'They are suspicious, Thaung.'

'What of it? So were the crew of the *Firefly*, but we cut their throats, and there were nine men aboard her, too.'

'What you say is true, Thaung. And we have the two big men already. It will be quite easy, but we must not let these three fools shoot any of us with their rifles.'

'Just as you say, serang. I shall cut the young one's throat myself: he has something of the look of the magistrate at Mallatengeh who hanged my father.'

'How delightful it is to have pleasures in store, Thaung. But we must ask the Tuan to let us keep the Chinese to cook for us. This fried rice is excellent.'

Derrick's blood ran cold as he listened, but with a great effort he made no sign. Did it mean that Uncle Pat and Mr Ross were already dead? He thought feverishly, wondering what to do for the best.

'When will the others be here?' asked Thaung, picking his teeth.

'The Tuan said just after sunset. They are to swim round one by one to the saloon porthole. It would not do to row over all together in a boat, because the pigs will be suspicious when the big men have not returned by then, and they might do some damage before they are killed.'

'How wise the Tuan is, indeed. They will not attack until they are all in the saloon together? There is no danger from the big men?'

'Just so. The Tuan will offer them drinks as soon as they are aboard. They will know nothing in two minutes. Then we shall throw them overboard when we have secured this boat.'

Derrick's heart leapt with relief: there was hope, he thought, if his uncle and Ross were still alive. At this point Li Han came back and started a polite, but aimless, conversation with the serang. Derrick saw that he would hear no more, so he went on deck to think out a plan of action. He walked up and down, racking his brains: he looked at the sun; it was nearer to the horizon than he had thought. There was not much more than an hour left before the sun would set, and the Malays would come slipping through the water with their krises ready for killing.

'I must do something,' he said to himself. 'If I made the saloon porthole fast they wouldn't be able to get in. But that wouldn't be any good. The first one would swim back, and then they would attack from all sides, and we could never hold them off.'

He turned over a dozen plans, but each one had a fault. At last he called Svenssen on deck and explained the situation to him. At first the Swede said nothing, then a grim smile spread over his face, and he said, 'We have a big rough-house, eh? There aindt no other way, I guess.'

'But that wouldn't save my uncle and Mr Ross, Olaf. Can't you think of any other thing to do?'

'Ay ban thinking, Mr Derrick, but there aindt no way out for any of us, Ay reckon. We yoost better kill all we can and trust in luck, eh?'

'It looks as if it would be the only way. I wonder if Li Han would have an idea. You go below, Olaf, and tell him to come up while you keep an eye on the serang.'

When Derrick had told Li Han of what he had heard, the cook said, 'Educated Chinese boy like me is not afraid of death, but find physical violence abhorrent. I go take opium pill, sleep till all finished. You like one piece opium too?'

'No thanks, Li Han. We've got to face it out. Go below and send Olaf up. I've got an idea.'

By this time the sun was almost touching the water. There was no time to be lost.

'Olaf, I've got an idea,' said Derrick; 'come along with me. It's our last hope. I'll explain as we go.' He ran to the saloon, gathering a coil of fine rope as he went. 'Bring a couple of belaying pins,' he shouted, as he tumbled down the companion way. In the saloon he flung himself on the furniture, clearing a space to roll back the carpet. 'Look, Olaf,' he said as he worked, 'here's a trap-door down to the hold. We must get it so that I can open it at once. Are all the hatches battened down?'

'Why, no. There's the aft –'

'You go and make it fast. I'll manage this. Leave me a belaying pin, and show a leg.'

Derrick was left alone; in the rapidly fading light he rolled up the carpet covering the trap-door, lugged the precious furs into a conspicuous position, and rearranged everything to look as natural as possible. He had hardly finished stowing the rope and belaying pin, when a faint scrabbling noise caught his ear. He crouched in the shadow by the porthole, grasping the heavy belaying pin. A brown hand slid over the rim of the porthole. Derrick heard the man grunt as he swung himself up. The Malay's head and shoulders wriggled through. Derrick held his breath until the man was half-way into the saloon, then, with all his force, he brought the belaying pin down. There was a crack as if he had driven a cricket

ball, and the man fell into the saloon, three parts stunned. He
grabbed for his kris, but Derrick jumped on him, and hit him
again. The Malay writhed under him, and got a wrestler's grip
on his forearm. The man was strong, and he was fast recovering
from the blow. Derrick fought madly, but he saw the gleam of
the raised kris. Olaf came in; he picked the Malay up as if he were
a child, and dashed him down again with appalling force. The
Malay lay still in a crumpled heap. Derrick staggered to his feet,
groping for the rope.

'Quick,' he said, 'before another comes. You stand by the porthole, and I'll tie them up.'

Derrick had barely closed the trap-door, through which he
had shoved the bound Malay, when another hand appeared at
the porthole; the head followed it, and Olaf struck. He seized
the Malay by the hair and flung him into the saloon: Derrick
roped his hands and feet together and rolled him down into the
hold. They waited in silence: for what appeared an age nothing
happened; then they heard a whisper in Malay.

'Are you there, Kelan?'

Derrick answered softly, 'Yes, come quietly.'

There was another thud, and Derrick closed the trap-door
again. Olaf grinned at him in the half light.

'We making out okay, huh?' he whispered.

'There's a chance now,' replied Derrick.

Two more Malays came and went down to join their fellows.
Then three came at once, whispering together. The first came
through confidently, and Olaf took him so fiercely by the throat
that he could not utter a sound; then he struck him on the back
of the neck with the edge of his hand, and the man fell silently:
he served the second in the same way; but the third asked for a
hand up, so Derrick reached out and took his hand, heaving him
up. Suddenly the Malay realized that something was wrong –
the hand was white. With his arm just through the porthole, he
reached for his kris, and stabbed as fast as a striking snake. The
knife pinned Derrick's forearm to the wood, but Derrick hung on
for a second, just long enough for Olaf to grip the man's hand and

pull him through. The Swede dealt with him, and turned to help Derrick, who was half fainting with pain. He wrenched the kris out of the wood and whipped his handkerchief round Derrick's arm above the elbow, tying it as tightly as he could.

'You aindt much good now,' he said.

Derrick forced a grin, and said, 'I can still shove them down. Hit 'em hard, Olaf.'

'Good lad,' replied the Swede, and turned to the porthole.

After that they were kept very busy. A head appeared; Olaf cracked it and flung the body over to the trap-door, where Derrick pushed it down and closed the lid. Derrick's arm was hurting badly, but the excitement kept him from noticing it too much. He lost count of the men at last. There came a long pause, and Olaf said, 'Well, Ay guess there aindt no more today. How your arm feels, eh?'

'Not so bad, thanks. If that's the lot, we'd better go across and see to my uncle and Mr Ross. Let's get –'

He broke off and spun round. The serang and Thaung stood in the doorway, covering them with their own rifles. Olaf flung his belaying pin and leapt: Thaung fired, and Olaf slumped down on the floor. The two Malays stared about them in the twilight, trying to grasp what had happened.

Derrick saw that he would be shot down if he moved: he stood still, waiting for the end. If only Li Han had kept his wits about him, he was thinking, when above his head he saw the Chinese cook kneeling on the skylight, trying desperately to open it. He had a steaming cauldron by his side.

Derrick knew that he must gain time. Suddenly he shouted out in Malay, 'Serang, wait for a moment. I will show you a great treasure.'

The serang started, and replied, 'Where? Show me at once, or I shall slit your throat.'

Derrick saw that Li Han had opened one of the catches. He started on a long direction.

'You must go down to the forward bulkhead –'

Li Han raised the last catch and silently raised the skylight.

He stood just above and behind the Malays. He lifted the great cauldron. 'Excuse, please,' he murmured: and poured the boiling water onto their heads. The serang's rifle went off, splintering the wood behind Derrick's head. Li Han leapt down on Thaung, knocking him out: Derrick caught Thaung's rifle, shot the serang in the shoulder, shouted to Li Han to raise the trap, and bundled the still struggling man down into the hold. He sat down, gasping to regain his breath. Olaf groaned, and sat up, rubbing his head: the bullet had nicked the side of his head, temporarily stunning him: now, apart from the nasty cut, he was all right.

The rest seemed simple by comparison. As they rowed over to the *Santa Maria*, Derrick asked, 'What became of your opium pill, Li Han?'

'Extreme terror and timidity prejudicial to exactitude,' replied Li Han, beaming. 'In my haste I mistake liver pill for desired article. Hence unusual valour and agility. But regret washing-up water now total loss.'

They crept aboard the *Santa Maria*, but their caution was unnecessary, for when they burst into his cabin they found Jenkins three parts drunk on his bunk. Ross and Sullivan were lying gagged and bound on the floor. Jenkins dropped his gun as they came in and turned very pale: in his terror he was a pitiable object.

As the gag came out of Sullivan's mouth he fetched a deep breath, and said, 'Well done, my boyo; we'd given you up long ago. Is the *Wanderer* all right?'

'Why, of course, Uncle – you left me in charge of her, you know. We disposed of the Malays in the hold.'

'Good lad,' said Ross, tying Jenkins's hands; 'I hope you battened them down. They're sure to steal the ballast otherwise.'

Ten days later the *Wanderer* sailed out of Yeddo harbour, leaving Jenkins and his crew behind them in prison.

'I told your pig-headed uncle that there would be trouble if we went aboard the *Santa Maria*,' said Ross to Derrick, as they leaned over the rail.

'Why did you go then, sir?' asked Derrick.

'Aha, my boyo,' shouted Sullivan from the wheel; 'it was the salvage money he was after; that's why he risked his Scotch neck. Ross, you're nothing but a yellow-belly. D'ye hear me? A yellow-belly. But I tell you what; when we were in Yeddo court-house I had an idea –'

'Mphm,' said Ross, winking at Derrick.

63

One Arctic Summer

It is a little more than a year ago now that I set out to look for Wetherill; he was lost, as you may remember, when he was trying to fly over the North Pole. I could never quite fathom why he had ever wanted to fly over it; the flight had already been made, and very efficiently, by all sorts of people before he tried. He had said, somewhat frivolously, that he wanted to know what it felt like to be in a place where the only possible wind was a south wind. Be that as it may, he was lost, and after a week I went north after him, because I knew that he was practically indestructible, and that he would almost certainly turn up eventually and call me a poor friend if I had not done something.

It was a weary business at first. I knew his route, so I went up as far north as the Finnish railways go, and then I went on beyond with five Lapps and a good many reindeer to the encampments of the nomad Lapps, and among them I sent inquiries in all directions. They are a peculiar crowd, the Lapps; they speak a horrible language that sounds all consonants, with every word about a yard long – far worse than Finnish, which is supposed to be one of the most difficult languages in Europe – and they have no idea of the value of money at all. I found this out very early, because I offered money rewards for any information, and none of them took any notice. They are absurdly wealthy, some of them, because they have enormous herds of reindeer, which they could sell, if they wanted to, to the Finns, but they are quite content with living in tents, and driving their huge herds all over the north of Lapland.

Personally I rather admired them for it, but it makes life difficult for outsiders.

One of the most difficult things was the language question,
but I got over that fairly well because I speak Russian fluently,
and in the old days most of them came under Russian rule, and
generally I was able to find one who could understand me. The
Christian Lapps treated me very well. They were extremely hos-
pitable, and they did everything they could for me, but most of
the Lapps are pagan.

Sometimes, as we went north, we passed villages, all of them
inhabited by Christian Lapps, and at one of these the five men
whom I had taken on at the beginning of my journey said that
now they would stay there, because they were tired of going on,
and because we were leaving behind the territory of the Christians, and going up into the land of the entirely pagan and almost
savage nomads. At first I tried to laugh them out of it, but either
they had no sense of humour or they hardly understood Russian,
for it had no effect at all; then I tried to persuade them, but they
said that they saw no reason why they should go on if they did
not want to, and that I could have my money back as they did not
particularly want it anyway.

This left me without anything very much to say, so we sat down
to reindeer steaks seethed in milk. One of the people in the village, when he heard what I was there for, said that he thought
that a man who was away hunting had said that somebody had
told him that something vaguely corresponding to an aeroplane
had passed that way some time before. This was the first clue that
I had picked up since I had left the places where Wetherill had
been in touch by wireless. It cheered me up immensely, although
I could not be sure that I had even the gist of what they were
trying to tell me, for their scraps of Russian were so very sparse
that anything approaching an unusual description of a thing of
which they only knew by hearsay was almost impossible. I had
to stay there quite a long while; they pointed out that they – the
villagers, that is – had all gathered there to meet one another for
a festival that was to come off later, and that while I was perfectly

welcome to stay as a guest, or borrow their reindeer and go away, they did not feel that the laws of hospitality demanded that they should form an expedition to take me north, or another to take me south again. At one time I was so infuriated by their apathy that I thought of using force – they are all little men, and I am rather large; moreover, I had an automatic and two rifles – but after a very little while I saw that it would be no earthly use; they would either kill me or run away, and I should be left worse off than before, and anyhow they had right overwhelmingly on their side. I had no claim on them at all, they did not want my money, and they were not in the least interested in Wetherill.

Then, a few days before the festival, an incident occurred that changed the face of things considerably. First you must know that I qualified as a medico, and that I had a fairly ample medicine chest with me; I never practiced, because I have quite enough money to live on without having to earn any, which is very delightful; nevertheless, I have always been much interested in surgery, and I was lucky enough to get my fellowship with quite a lot of gold medals attached, so when they brought in a chap who had been mauled in a very ugly way by a bear, I was able to patch him up in no time, which made a favourable impression. Then, the very next day after that, the little daughter of one of the more impor- tant men went down with what was obviously acute appendicitis. They had a man there who knew a good deal about illness gener- ally, and who was always called in to do what could be done in the way of massage – at which he was really very good indeed – and spells. He said, as well he might, that there was nothing left to do but mourn. I gave a spinal injection, and had the appendix out in time to save her. This made a really remarkable sensation; the girl had felt nothing more than the prick of the needle, and yet the appendix had been cut out and the wound sewn up. They gave me an entire herd of reindeer and some of the finest furs that I have ever seen. It would have taken a day to have counted the rein- deer, so I offered all but five of them to any six men who would come with me for six months into the north. Even that did not tempt them very much, but some of them said that they would think about it after the festival. They also gave me a superb feast, with every single delicacy that could be obtained. One surprising thing was a quantity of very fine strawberries, small, but extraordinarily sweet and full-flavoured. They had been brought up for the festival from far south in Finland, where there are acres upon acres of them growing wild. I should have mentioned that it was summer at this time, and the sun never set at all up there in the Arctic Circle, but just went round and round the horizon; at first one tended to lose all count of the time, but after a short while I found that life regulated itself by the amount of sleep that one needed – it is really remarkably little.

The festival came, and with it an incredible quantity of reindeer, driven by tribes of people, some going south to new pastures, and some going east or west. The largest tribe came in what would have been the afternoon if there had been any noon, and I stood among the people gathered to welcome them; to my intense surprise I saw at their head a man dressed as a priest of the Holy Russian Church; he stood a head and shoulders above the Lapps. I ran forward and greeted him in Russian, speaking as one did in the days before the Revolution had abolished all distinctions. He answered most joyfully, and embraced me, as the custom was, and we talked together for hours and hours. For long years he had spoken nothing but the Lapp tongue, and it was like coming out of prison, he said, to talk Russian again. His name was Father Sergei, and he had been a missionary to the Lapps at the time of the Revolution. He had heard about it, and about the horrible fate of his Church, and so he had escaped by staying out in the desolate north. He had very great influence over the Lapps, and he told them off terrifically for not having helped me to find Wetherill before; I do not know what he said to them, but he made them crawl about like smacked puppies. I believe he threatened to forbid the festival and only relented when they promised to do everything that was humanly possible for me as soon as it was over.

After he had done this we sat down together over a brew of the coffee that I had with me – it was the first he had had for a long time – and we talked. Father Sergei asked me innumerable questions about the outside world; I told him, to his great surprise, that Finland was not under the U.S.S.R., and that he could leave his wilderness as soon as he wanted to by going south to Helsinki, and taking a boat from there to anywhere in the world except Russia; he could obtain plenty of money to live on from the superb furs that he could have for the asking. He was extremely interested to hear about Finland, but the thought of leaving his Lapps never entered his mind; all he wanted from the world, he said, was books, medicines, and the chance of writing to such of his friends as were still living.

I conceived a very great admiration for him, not only because of his fine attitude towards his self-imposed task, with all its dreadful loneliness, but also because of his extreme goodness. It sounds most unpleasant, but he was easily the best man I have ever known, and I have met archbishops and cardinals: there was nothing obviously religious about him, he never asked any one whether he was saved, or anything remotely resembling it, and he had been known to knock the heads of two impudent Lapps together and kick them each nearly four feet out of his tent, but he also had a way of doing very decent things, and expecting no thanks for them. When I got to understand something of the Lapps' language, they told me of some of the great journeys he had made to help one or another of them when they had any trouble. Comparison of the Lapps whom he had made Christian with the rest showed that in religious matters too he was a very great man. I think he must have been the nearest approach to the more robust kind of medieval saint that one could find.

As we spoke together, he asked me why I had not taken an aeroplane to look for Wetherill – it had certainly seemed at first the most obvious way of finding him, but, as I told him, after I had taken a good deal of advice from men who had been in the far north, I had decided to come on foot, because it had been ascertained almost certainly that he had not passed beyond the extreme northern limit of the land, as he had been in radio communication with some scientists who were studying something odd among the floes of the ice cap surrounding the Pole; if he had come down in the tundra, the only way of finding him was to go among the only people who might possibly have seen him pass, because one would never see him in the dwarf brush that springs up in the Arctic summer. After the festival was over, and my expedition was formed and thoroughly victualled, Father Sergei said that if I did not mind he was coming with me. When I protested he said that he wanted to go as far north as men existed, not only in his everlasting fight against the heathen gods, but also because it was from the direction of my road that he had heard strange legends of the most remote tribes, which he wished to investigate. So he came, and I was very thankful indeed to have him with me.

We travelled slowly but steadily, and eventually we came to a part of the world that even Father Sergei had never touched upon. The speech of the few people we encountered became more and more different from that of the Christian Lapps, but still Father Sergei, with his marvelous knowledge of their dialects, was able to find, here and there, the tale of some one who had seen Wetherill pass over. One day we chanced upon a hunter who had seen the aeroplane himself; from his account it had been flying quite low. The journey was long and arduous, and it would be too tedious to recount day after day of slow marches, but at length we met a small party of men going north also; we had crossed their trail nearly three days before we caught up with them. They were more like pure Esquimaux than Lapps, though there is not very much difference, and they were shamans, witch-doctors, who were going to a certain place to join others of their craft for some purpose of which they would not tell us.

They could not understand more than about half of what our Lapps said to them, and they were distinctly hostile because we did not show them the reverence due to a shaman and a priest of the northern gods. They were dressed in a most peculiar way, with skulls of foxes hung round them, and pieces of scratched bone tied on here and there. One of them had a bison's horn that must have been prehistoric, or it might have come from the land of the North American Esquimaux, who worship in the same strange way, though I do not know how it could have got there, unless the tribes wandered right round the top of the world, which might be possible.

We went with these people, although they did not like it very much, and we travelled together for about a week. When we rested, the shamans used to sing together in a way that made the Lapps horribly frightened until Father Sergei went among them and cheered them up with a little sound theology, which sometimes took the form of a kick in the pants, and sometimes of a blessing or perhaps a joke at the expense of the shamans; nothing infuriated them more than when Father Sergei laughed at some of their spells, there was so little they could do about it when the man they cursed only laughed. I must confess, though, that they really frightened me sometimes when they squatted round, singing their dirges, and howling like wolves between each one.

At length we came to where the meeting of the shamans was to take place; it was the dwelling-place of a tribe who are, perhaps, the most northerly in the world – they are certainly exceedingly primitive. There was a remarkable crowd for so very desolate a country, and in the middle of them I saw the tail of an aeroplane sticking up in the air. Our shamans ran forward ahead of us, and when we arrived there was a most unholy hubbub. They surrounded us as we stood in a compact group. The Lapps were clearly frightened, and so was I – my first desire was to shoot the first half dozen – but Father Sergei beamed on them, and began talking in a very friendly sort of way. This rather nonplussed most of them, but two or three of the more cantankerous shamans howled him down, and began what was probably a kind of ritual dance; the others joined in, and they hopped round and round in a circle, with us in the middle, howling in a beastly way. Then Father Sergei came out on the top of his form; he laughed and laughed, holding his sides, and staggering to and fro with tears running down his cheeks – I really believe he thought that it was funny, but there was a prickly feeling all over my scalp, and I have seen some remarkably horrible things without being very much affected by them. They went on against the laughter for some time, until I was dizzy, trying to keep my eyes on them, but they could not prevail against it, so the three who began the dance flew at Father Sergei, snapping their teeth like wolves in rage; he laid them out, one, two, three, as cleanly as a champion heavyweight: they were perfect blows; his fists just went out and in three times like well-oiled pistons, and the shamans lay flat in front of him. There was a dead silence; Father Sergei spoke loud and sharply, obviously giving an order. After a moment's hesitation they all squatted down, and he began to speak in quite a low, persuasive tone. They seemed to understand most of what he said, and they listened closely. He went on and on. I kept looking round for a sign of Wetherill, but I could see nothing except the smashed plane. The three men who had been knocked out came to, and our Lapps led them firmly to the group squatting in front of Father Sergei, who went on talking and talking for what must have been close on two hours. Now and then they questioned him when he paused, and when he had finished we all sat down to a vast meal. As soon as I could I asked him about Wetherill and he said that he had not come to that yet, but that he was almost sure he was alive.

When every one had eaten as much as he could, Father Sergei began again; I went to sleep after a little while, but when I woke up he was still at it, and they were all listening with extreme attention. Here and there I could pick out a word, and sometimes a sentence, for I had picked up enough of the language for that, then I dozed off again. I was woken by some one shaking me by the shoulder. I opened my eyes, and there was Wetherill. Father Sergei was talking with about half a dozen of the shamans in the most friendly way; his great personality and his invincible sincerity had obviously established him with them.

Wetherill was looking very ill indeed, and immediately after our greetings were done I looked him over; three of his ribs had been staved in, and his left arm was irretrievably lacerated – it would have to be amputated right away. The operation took place a few hours later, with all the shamans looking on at a healthy distance; with good fortune I was able to make a clean job of it, and I also operated on a whitlow for one of the shamans and an ingrowing toe-nail for another. This helped the great prestige that Father Sergei had already won for us, and we stayed with the shamans, who behaved extremely well in the way of hospitality, until Wetherill was fit to travel. While he was convalescing he told Father Sergei and me how he had crashed while he was trying to land near the village, and how they had not been sure whether to take him for a god or a devil – they had compromised by tying him up until the shamans could decide – and that was why they were all coming together when we arrived on the scene, for the messages going out had taken nearly as long as I had in my journey from the south. It was only the very healthy freezing air that had kept Wetherill from dying, and his iron constitution pulled him round remarkably quickly, but if we had been even a few days later, he would have been dead.

He was ready to travel just in time for us to go south and to escape the long Arctic night, when the sun disappears for six months and the only day-time is when the moon is shining. While we were waiting, Father Sergei talked as I have never heard a man talk before. He lectured the shamans every day, and talked to each one with quite inexhaustible energy whenever he had a moment free, and he impressed them as they had never been impressed in their lives before. When we were ready to go, and our Lapps seemed really happy for the first time since they had set out, he told me, quite casually, that he was going to stay up there right through the winter because he liked the shamans, although they were certainly as unattractive a crowd as I have ever seen, or smelt for that matter. He felt, he said, that he could not leave them with nothing better than a few scratched bones to believe in and to rely upon. 'They'll be good Christians or I'll be a shaman when next we see the sun,' he said as we parted.

We came down south by the same route, and we reached the sea just as the first ice-floes were forming in the Baltic, and in

Helsinki, where my money was of some use, I made a collection of every single thing that would be of service to Father Sergei and left enough money to equip a party of Finns to take them up to him. Then we took ship, and so we came home.

Publishing History

by Terry Zobeck

The Return
First published in *The Last Pool and Other Stories* (1950); rewritten version of 'The Mayfly Rise', which was first published as 'by Patrick Russ' in *John O'London's Weekly* (10 May 1940)

The Last Pool
First published in *The Last Pool and Other Stories* (1950), and later revised in *The Chian Wine and Other Stories* (1974)

The Green Creature
First published in *The Last Pool and Other Stories* (1950)

The Happy Despatch
First published in *The Last Pool and Other Stories* (1950)

The Virtuous Peleg
First published in *The Last Pool and Other Stories* (1950) and later revised in *The Walker and Other Stories* (1955) and then again in *The Chian Wine and Other Stories* (1974)

The Curranwood Badgers
First published in *The Last Pool and Other Stories* (1950) as 'The Drawing of the Curranwood Badgers', and later rewritten in *The Chian Wine and Other Stories* (1974)

It Must Have Been a Branch, They Said
First published in *The Last Pool and Other Stories* (1950)

The Slope of the High Mountains
First published in *The Last Pool and Other Stories* (1950) as 'The Steep Slope of Gallt y Wenallt'; revised and first published in *Harper's Bazaar* (January 1954) and collected in *The Walker and Other Stories* (1955)

The Long Day Running
First published in *The Last Pool and Other Stories* (1950), and later revised in *The Chian Wine and Other Stories* (1974)

Naming Calls
First published in *The Last Pool and Other Stories* (1950)

The Dawn Flighting
First published in *The Last Pool and Other Stories* (1950)

The Trap
First published in *The Last Pool and Other Stories* (1950)

The Little Death
First published in *The Last Pool and Other Stories* (1950)

Samphire
First published in *Harper's Bazaar* (March 1953) and collected in *The Walker and Other Stories* (1955)

The Clockmender
First published in *The Walker and Other Stories* (1955), and later revised in *The Chian Wine and Other Short Stories* (1974)

Not Liking to Pass the Road Again
First published in *Irish Writing* (March 1952) and collected in *The Walker and Other Stories* (1955)

The Voluntary Patient
First published in *The Walker and Other Stories* (1955), and later revised in *The Chian Wine and Other Short Stories* (1974)

Billabillian
First published in *The Walker and Other Stories* (1955)

The Soul
First published in *The Walker and Other Stories* (1955)

On the Bog
First published in *The Walker and Other Stories* (1955); rewritten and first published in *Irish Press* (10 November 1973); collected in *The Chian Wine and Other Stories* (1974)

The Passeur
First published in *The Walker and Other Stories* (1955)

Nicolas
First published in *The Walker and Other Stories* (1955)

Hans Brueckner on the Edge of the Sea
First published in *The Walker and Other Stories* (1955)

The Lemon
First published in *The Walker and Other Stories* (1955), and later revised in *The Chian Wine and Other Short Stories* (1974)

A Journey to Cannes
First published in *The Walker and Other Stories* (1955)

The Tunnel at the Frontier
First published in *The Walker and Other Stories* (1955)

Lying in the Sun
First published in *Harper's Bazaar* (August 1955) and collected in
The Walker and Other Stories (1955)

The Path
First published in *The Walker and Other Stories* (1955)

A Minor Operation
First published in *The Walker and Other Stories* (1955)

The Walker
First published in *Harper's Bazaar* (October 1953) and collected
in *The Walker and Other Stories* (1955), and later rewritten as 'The
Valise' for *The Chian Wine and Other Stories* (1974). Republished
in its original form in the *Collected Short Stories* (1994)

The Flower Pot
First published in *Lying in the Sun and Other Stories* (1956)

The Party in the Cave
First published in *Lying in the Sun and Other Stories* (1956)

The Overcoat
First published in *Lying in the Sun and Other Stories* (1956)

The Stag at Bay
First published in *Lying in the Sun and Other Stories* (1956), and
later revised in *The Chian Wine and Other Stories* (1974)

The Falling Star
First published in *Lying in the Sun and Other Stories* (1956)

The Handmaiden
First published in *Lying in the Sun and Other Stories* (1956), and
later revised in *The Chian Wine and Other Stories* (1974)

The Thermometer
First published in *Lying in the Sun and Other Stories* (1956), and later revised in *The Chian Wine and Other Stories* (1974)

The Centurion's Gig
First published in M. R. Hodgkin (ed). *Winter's Tales for Children 4* (1968); not previously collected

The Rendezvous
First published in *The Chian Wine and Other Stories* (1974)

The Chian Wine
First published in *The Chian Wine and Other Stories* (1974)

A Passage of the Frontier
First published in *The Cornhill* (Spring 1974) and collected in *The Chian Wine and Other Stories* (1974)

On the Wolfsberg
First published in *The Chian Wine and Other Stories* (1974)

Simon
First published in the *Daily Telegraph* (22 January 1994) and collected in *Patrick O'Brian: Critical Appreciations and a Bibliography*, ed. A. E. Cunningham (1994)

As Patrick Russ

Skogula – the Sperm Whale
First published as 'Skogula' in *Chums Weekly* (20 October 1931) and collected in *Beasts Royal* (1934)

A Peregrine Falcon
First published as 'A Tale About a Great Peregrine Falcon' in *Great Heart: The Church of Scotland Magazine – for Boys and Girls* (March 1933) and later revised in *Beasts Royal* (1934)

Wang Khan of the Elephants
First published by Oxford University Press in *The Oxford Annual for Scouts, 15th Year* (1933) and collected in *Beasts Royal* (1934)

The White Cobra
First published by Oxford University Press in *The Oxford Annual for Scouts, 16th Year* (1934) and collected in *Beasts Royal* (1934)

Shark No. 206
First published in *Beasts Royal* (1934)

Python
First published in *Beasts Royal* (1934)

The Condor of Quetzalcoatl
First published in *Beasts Royal* (1934)

Old Cronk
First published in *Beasts Royal* (1934)

Gorilla
First published in *Beasts Royal* (1934)

Rhino
First published in *Beasts Royal* (1934)

Jehangir Bahadur
First published in *Beasts Royal* (1934)

Jellaludin
First published in *Beasts Royal* (1934)

The Salmon
First published in *Britannia and Eve* (September 1935); not previously collected

Cheetah
First published in *The Oxford Annual for Boys, 28th Year* (1935); the original version not previously collected

The Snow Leopard
First published by Oxford University Press in *The Oxford Annual for Scouts, 17th Year* (1935); not previously collected

Giant Panda
First published in *Zoo* (July 1936); not previously collected

Noughts and Crosses
First published by Oxford University Press in *The Oxford Annual for Boys, 29th Year* (1936). Republished in *The Road to Samarcand* (2007)

Two's Company
First published by Oxford University Press in *The Oxford Annual for Boys, 30th Year* (1937). Republished in *The Road to Samarcand* (2007)

No Pirates Nowadays
First published by Oxford University Press in *The Oxford Annual for Boys, 33rd Year* (1940). Republished in *The Road to Samarcand* (2007)

One Arctic Summer
First published by Oxford University Press in *The Oxford Annual for Boys, 31st Year* (1938); not previously collected